Physiological Psychology

SECOND EDITION

SECOND EDITION

Physiological Psychology

MARK R. ROSENZWEIG
University of California, Berkeley

ARNOLD L. LEIMAN
University of California, Berkeley

 RANDOM HOUSE   NEW YORK

We dedicate this book affectionately to our wives, children, and grandchildren. We appreciate their support and patience over the years of this project.

	Janine			Lannon	
Anne	Suzanne	Philip		Jessica	Timothy
Jim	Kent				
	Lauren				
	David				
	Gregory				

Second Edition

98765432

Library of Congress Cataloging-in-Publication Data

Rosenzweig, Mark R.
  Physiological psychology.

  Bibliography: p.
  Includes index.
  1. Psychophysiology. I. Leiman, Arnold L.
II. Title. [DNLM: 1. Psychophysiology. W1 103 R819p]
QP360.R66 1989   152   88-31795
ISBN: 0-394-37237-9

Manufactured in the United States of America

Cover photograph: Cross-sectional positron emission computed tomography images of glucose metabolism in the brain of a normal human subject during a state of thinking (left) and during perception of a pattern (right). Lighter and warmer colors correspond to higher metabolic rates. (Courtesy of Drs. Michael E. Phelps and John C. Mazziotta, UCLA School of Medicine)

Text illustrations: Nelson W. Hee and Vantage Art

Preface to Second Edition

The pace of progress in physiological psychology and related disciplines has been impressive in the years since we prepared the first edition of this book. Clearly a new edition is needed to incorporate the advances in both findings and theoretical interpretations. In addition, preparing this second edition of *Physiological Psychology* has allowed us to make several improvements over the first edition:

- This edition benefits from the comments of many instructors and students who used the first edition so that the present edition is even more readable, better organized, and easier to use.
- The excellent program of two-color illustrations has been augmented with additional illustrations. The same medical illustrator who collaborated with us to produce most of the illustrations for our first edition, Nelson Hee, has worked with us again to produce new illustrations and to modify some of the original ones.
- Drawing upon the impressive advances in research and theory that have been made over the past few years makes many aspects of this account both more integrated and more understandable.
- New clinical applications have been added throughout the text, such as applications to eating disorders, pain, Alzheimer's disease, and anxiety and stress.

The second edition of *Physiological Psychology* continues the features that students and instructors found helpful in the first edition, and it adds new features that users requested. Two rather long chapters in the first edition are now divided into two chapters each; this makes for easier assignments and more specific focus. New sections have been added. For example, Chapter 3 discusses differences among animals and the evolution of the human brain. Chapter 6 contains a new section on psychopharmacology. The request for more information on certain topics has led to the inclusion of special Reference Sections at the ends of Chapters 2, 6, and 7. There is a Reference Section in Chapter 2 on brain anatomy, in Chapter 6 on synaptic chemistry, and Chapter 7 includes a table of body hormones. These Reference Sections provide additional information that is readily accessible but that does not interrupt the flow of the chapters.

Daily newspapers and popular magazines take up topics in physiological psychology and related fields even more frequently than when the first edition of this text appeared, so it is more important than ever to have a good background of knowledge against which to evaluate exciting and sometimes sensational claims. Research in physiological psychology explores the bodily bases of our experience and behavior: the ways in which bodily states and processes produce and control behavior and cognition, and the ways in which behavior and cognition influence bodily systems. Many scientific disciplines contribute to this theme, so we draw upon the research of psychologists, anatomists, biochemists, endocrinologists, engineers, geneticists, immunologists, neurologists, physiologists, and zoologists. In order to gain a panoramic view of physiological psychology, we try to rise above the limits of any single specialty.

We have tried to make this material accessible to students from a variety of interests and backgrounds. Both the behavioral and biological foundations are provided for each main topic. Well-prepared students can skip or skim some of the background material, but students who need it should study it carefully before proceeding.

Chapter 1 introduces a fourfold approach to studying physiological psychology—descriptive, comparative/evolutionary, developmental, and biological mechanism (Table 3-1, page 13). These perspectives are further developed in Chapters 2–6 and each of the following Chapters (2–18) examine the subject matter from all four perspectives so students can see the various themes carried out across chapters linking concepts together.

We present *Physiological Psychology* in a logical, progressive order in five main parts:

Part One: Bodily Systems Basic to Behavior. *Chapters 2–4.*

This part takes up the basic structure of the human brain in Chapter 2. Chapter 3 discusses the nervous system, and differences among animals, since these perspectives will be used in many subsequent chapters. Chapter 4 takes up the development of the brain and behavior over the life span, and developmental considerations will also be important in some later chapters.

Part Two: Communication and Information Processing within the Body. *Chapters 5–7.*

Communication and processing of electrical signals in the nervous system is the theme of Chapter 5. Chemical signalling at junctions between nerve cells and the application of neurochemistry to behavior (psychopharmacology) are the topics of Chapter 6. Chapter 7 is devoted to hormones as a chemical communication system.

Part Three: Information Processing in Perceptual and Motor Systems. *Chapters 8–10.*

Information processing in sensory and perceptual systems is taken up in Chapters 8 and 9. Sensory inputs to the brain do not merely provide ''pictures in the head''; they often incite the individual to act. Most classes of movement are not directly triggered by sensory and perceptual events but may involve intrinsic patterns of action. How information processing occurs in the motor system is the subject of Chapter 10.

Part Four: Control of Behavioral States: Motivation. *Chapters 11–15.*

How bodily systems function so that all the basic needs are satisfied, often in succession, is the overall question of motivation that we take up in Part Four. The chapters treat sex, temperature regulation, thirst and drinking, eating and regulation of energy, sleeping and waking, and emotions and mental disorders.

Part Five: Learning, Memory, and Cognition. *Chapters 16–18.*

The capacities to learn and remember make it possible to deal with a complex and changing world and thus increase adaptive success. How experience can change the properties of the nervous system is the major mystery of the biological sciences. Chapters 16 and 17 report many aspects of research dedicated to solving this mystery. Chapter 18 discusses that most elaborate products of brain function, the biology of language and cognitive states that are distinctively human.

Experience has shown that this order of presentation is a practical and effective one. We realize, however, that some instructors may prefer a different order of topics or may want to omit some areas of study, so we have written each chapter as a relatively self-contained unit. Recognizing that courses also vary in length from a single quarter or semester to two semesters, we should point out that most of this text can be covered in a single quarter; in that case the instructor may decide to omit a few chapters depending upon his or her emphasis. Specific suggestions for courses with various orientations are made in the Instructor's Manual. On the other hand, the text provides most of the basic material for a two-semester course; in this case the instructor can assign some supplementary reading to fill out particular areas.

Many features of the text are designed to enhance students' mastery of the material:

- We have put together what we feel is the finest two-color illustration program in a physiological psychology text available today. A medical illustrator collaborated with us to produce hundreds of meaningful illustrations specifically designed to clarify important concepts. Graphs and data from many sources have been reorganized and redrawn for student comprehension.
- To aid student understanding, each chapter (1) is preceded by an outline that functions as an organizational framework for the chapter, (2) contains an ''orientation'' that lays the groundwork for the discussion, (3) concludes with summary/main points to highlight and review important concepts, and (4) lists recommended readings.
- Concepts and data have been carefully chosen and presented at a level appropriate for students with widely varying backgrounds.
- Key terms are written in boldface and defined at their first main use; they are also included in the glossary.
- Brief boxed articles feature contemporary applications and historical information, providing relevant examples from real life and a broad perspective on specific topics.
- A study guide offers a complete chapter outline, a review of general concepts, a list of study objectives, illustrations from the text with study questions, chapter tests, self-evaluation exercises, concept applications, and answers to all questions and exercises.
- The authors will provide a semiannual newsletter, which will present exciting recent research.

In preparing this second edition, we have benefitted from the skilled help of the staff of Random House, including especially Elaine Rosenberg, Barry Fetterolf, and Susan Badger.

Mark R. Rosenzweig
Arnold L. Leiman

Contents

PART FOUR

CONTROL OF BEHAVIORAL
STATES: MOTIVATION 395

11 Sex 397

12 Heating/Cooling,
Drinking 447

15 Emotions and Mental
√   Disorders 567

DON JUAN: . . . Will you not agree with me
. . . that it is inconceivable that Life,
having once produced [birds],
should, if love and beauty were her
object, start off on another line
and labor at the clumsy elephant
and hideous ape, whose grandchildren
we are?

THE DEVIL: You conclude then, that Life
was driving at clumsiness and
ugliness?

DON JUAN: No, perverse devil that you
are, a thousand times no. Life was
driving at brains—at its darling
object: an organ by which it can
attain not only self-consciousness
but self-understanding.

George Bernard Shaw
Man and Superman, Act III

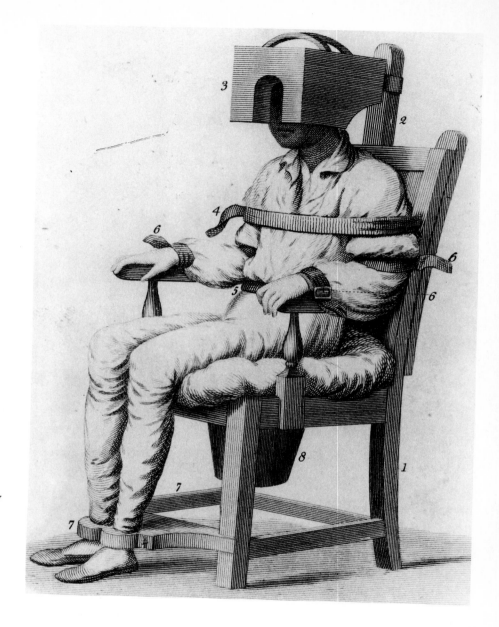

1 Physiological Psychology

WHAT IS PHYSIOLOGICAL PSYCHOLOGY?

A legend from India (retold by Thomas Mann in his book *The Transposed Heads*) illustrates how both head and body contribute to identity and personality. In this story the beautiful Sita marries a slender, intellectual young merchant. She is also attracted to his strong, brawny best friend, a blacksmith. One day each young man beheads himself in a temple of the goddess Kali. Sita enters the temple, looking for them, and finds them lying in pools of blood in front of the statue of Kali. Horrified, Sita prays to Kali, begging her to restore the men to life. Kali grants the wish and instructs Sita to place the heads carefully on the bodies. Sita undertakes the task with feverish energy and soon sees the men come back to life. Only then does she realize that she has placed each head on the wrong body! Now the three young people are faced with a baffling problem: Which young man is Sita's spouse? The one with the merchant's head and the smith's body? Or the smith's head on the merchant's body? While the legend explores the complexities of this puzzle, it also considers how each head affects the body which it now controls and also how the body exerts reciprocal influences on the head.

Fortunately we need not solve Sita's dilemma. We recognize that individual identity, personality, and talents are mainly functions of the brain; nevertheless, we also acknowledge the influences on the brain of other bodily systems, such as endocrine glands.

This book explores the ways in which bodily states and processes produce and control behavior and the ways in which behavior influences bodily systems. This theme has great scope and breadth; it spans many scientific disciplines. Thus we will draw on the research of psychologists, anatomists, chemists, endocrinologists, engineers, geneticists, neurologists, physiologists, and zoologists. In order to gain a panoramic view of the rapidly developing field of physiological psychology, we will try to rise above the limits of any single specialty.

The frequent coverage in the press of topics in physiological psychology reflects growing popular interest in this field. Articles illustrate the rapid pace of research and indicate the relevance of brain research to pressing human problems. Newspapers and magazines herald new findings that improve our understanding of why we do what we do and why we are what we are. Research in physiological psychology and related fields is throwing light on many aspects of normal behavior, including sex, learning and memory, language and communication, the behavioral roles of sleep and daily rhythms, and the sensitivity and selectivity of our perceptual processes.

Basic Questions About Capacities of the Human Brain

The accelerated pace of advance in physiological psychology, neuroscience, and related fields has provided answers to some fundamental questions and offers prospects of new productive approaches (e.g., Hillyard, 1982; Gerstein, Luce, Smelser & Sperlich, 1988). Sophisticated measures of behavior coupled with new techniques for stimulating and recording bodily processes are increasing enormously the power and scope of research. Here are some of the exciting current areas of research.

Brain Growth & repair ontologically

1. *How does the brain grow, maintain, and repair itself over the life span, and how are these capacities related to behavior?*

   Within a few months after conception, and well before birth, the developing human is equipped with a brain that contains billions of nerve cells organized in precise arrays with specific interconnections. The plan for development of the human brain resembles in many ways those of other mammals, and even those of all other vertebrates, but with important species-specific adaptations. Each species has to be prepared to carry out many behaviors at birth and to acquire others soon after birth. The developmental blueprint not only specifies the arrangement of most nerve cells long before birth, but it also provides for and depends upon environmental influences to help shape neural development after birth.

Processing info

2. *How does the brain acquire, process, and use information about the environment?*

   Investigators have learned much about how the world about us is represented in circuits and activities of the brain. Sensory stimuli—from simple touches to complex sounds and elaborate displays of color and form—are processed by many specialized brain regions. This sensory-perceptual processing helps to activate and control coordinated bodily responses, from fine eye movements to the graceful leap of a dancer.

regulate behavior

3. *How does the brain monitor and regulate motivated behaviors, such as reproduction, eating and energy balance, sleeping and waking, and emotions?*

   The organization of many regions of the nervous system is influenced by neurochemicals, including hormones, and many neural circuits are activated or inhibited by chemical messages. For example, investigators are now studying both similarities in and differences between the sexes in details of brain structure and chemistry as clues to understanding both commonalities and differences in behavior.

4. *How does the brain acquire and store information and later make it available for use?*

learning
& memory

Learning and memory are among the most extraordinary abilities of living beings. Breakthrough research in this area is exploring how the brain accomplishes these feats.

Each of the foregoing questions will be taken up in the later parts of this book. Some of the examples that we will consider may seem almost as fantastic as the legend of the transposed heads. Certainly some of the accomplishments of research on brain-behavior relationships would have been hailed as miracles only a generation ago. These findings have led to curing psychoses, abolishing pain, restoring partial sight to some blind people, and stimulating the growth of the brain and thereby improving the capacity to learn. These and other achievements that are now becoming familiar to us would have seemed unbelievable a few decades ago. As science fiction writer Arthur C. Clarke has stated, ''The science of one generation was the magic of the preceding one.'' Meanwhile, one specific example is presented in the next paragraphs.

The Body Can Kill Pain

An example of a productive realm of research that has provided new insights into brain mechanisms of behavior is the study of perception and control of pain. Humans have always sought remedies to relieve pain. In China, for more than 3000 years, **acupuncture,** the insertion and rotation of needles in various parts of the body, has been used for blunting pain. Seeking freedom from pain through the use of opiates has almost as long a history. In fact, trying to understand how opiates control our perception of pain is advancing our understanding of normal body mechanisms for suppressing it.

Studies of heroin addiction during the 1970s resulted in the discovery that opiates accumulate in particular sites in the brain and that these regions are especially important in controlling pain. Opiates accumulate in these areas because they attach to particular cells that seem to ''recognize'' them. This attraction suggested that perhaps the brain manufactures and uses opiatelike substances, since it did not seem likely that evolution could have anticipated the availability of addictive drugs. Rather, it seemed that opiates mimic a natural process: the body's ability to produce opiatelike substances that control pain.

In just a few years, a great deal has been learned about this built-in mechanism for inhibiting pain. Various regions of the brain do indeed contain naturally produced chemicals that are called endogenous **opioids.** Such compounds can relieve pain, and in some cases they are more effective than morphine. Stimulation by electrodes implanted in regions of the brain containing opioids produces dramatic relief of pain, relief that outlasts the period of stimulation.

The discovery of the opioids has also increased our understanding of other pain remedies. For example, people who suffer from pain frequently get relief from inert pills, such as sugar tablets. This result, called the **placebo effect,** usually takes place when the pills are given in a medical environment, accompanied by the confident reassurances of a physician. The psychological factors that underlie the placebo effect have long been a mystery. Now some researchers suggest that the placebo gives relief because the clinical setting promotes the release of opioids. Acupuncture too may work by causing the release of opioids, since chemicals that block the action of opioids also inhibit the pain relief produced by acupuncture. Perhaps some of the magic that banished suffering in ages past was simply the workings of natural brain chemicals that evolved to enable us to cope with pain.

The Malfunctioning Human Brain

Like any complex mechanism, the brain is subject to a variety of malfunctions and breakdowns. By a conservative estimate, at least one person in five around the world suffers from neurological and/or psychiatric disorders. Table 1-1 shows the estimated numbers of U.S. residents afflicted by some of the main neurological disorders. Table 1-2 gives estimates of the numbers of U.S. adults who suffer from certain major psychiatric disorders in a six-month period. The division of disorders between Tables 1-1 and 1-2 reflects the traditional distinctions between neurology and psychiatry, but much of psychiatry is becoming more oriented toward neuroscience.

The toll of these disorders is enormous, both in terms of individual suffering and in social costs. This has impelled research that is leading to understanding of the mechanisms involved and in some cases to alleviation and even to prevention of these disorders. Here are some examples of research that is providing relief from some of these grave disorders—examples that will be discussed in later chapters.

1. The introduction of effective antipsychotic drugs in the 1950s has enabled many mental patients to lead fuller lives in the community. Studies of the effects of these drugs have also produced profound insights into the nature of some psychiatric disorders.
2. Experts now believe that by the year 2000 the incidence of mental retardation in the United States can be cut to half of that in 1975 through the application of principles learned in basic research. Contributions to this improvement are

Table 1-1 Some Major Neurological Disorders and Estimated Numbers Affected in the United States

Alzheimer's disease	3,000,000
Epilepsy	2,000,000
Stroke	1,800,000
Head and spinal cord trauma	1,000,000
Early developmental disorders (mental retardation, cerebral palsy, perinatal injuries)	750,000
Parkinson's disease and Huntington's disease	500,000

Table 1-2 Major Psychiatric Disorders: U.S. Adults Showing Disorders in a Six-Month Period

Alcohol and drug abuse	15,000,000
Severe anxiety	16,000,000
Severe depression	10,000,000
Schizophrenia	1,500,000

U.S. Population

19%

coming from genetic counseling, early diagnosis of certain metabolic disorders, better nutrition, genetic engineering, and adequately stimulating environments.

3. Discoveries that reveal the modes of action of habit-forming drugs and their effects on the nervous system give hope of effective cures of people addicted to drugs and prevention of lasting damage to infants born to mothers who take drugs.

4. Anxiety is a common feeling, as is depression. Pharmacological and other treatments are helping many who suffer from these problems, and current research is pinpointing the neural circuits that underlie anxiety.

5. The fastest growing affliction in advanced societies is Alzheimer's disease, a profound loss of cognitive abilities that strikes especially people over 65. Current research is exploring some of the causes and brain mechanisms of this grave condition.

A Neurochemical Revolution in Psychiatry

Throughout the world—whether in rural societies in remote areas or in industrial centers—some people spend each day in deep anxiety, plagued by hallucinations, delusions of persecution, and irrational thoughts and sentiments. Psychotic disorders have played a tragic part in world history.

For many years there was little hope of relief for this suffering. All sorts of nostrums derived from plants and animals were tried in an effort to reverse the course of these disorders. A variety of physical treatments was also explored; Figure 1-1 gives an example. But for centuries the main method of treatment of severely disturbed people was prolonged confinement, often in the squalor of overcrowded mental hospitals. A turning point came in the 1940s as a result of research on drugs. By now this research has led to a revolutionary new perspective in the treatment of psychiatric patients.

While searching in the 1940s for a chemical to relax muscles during surgery, Henri Laborit and other French investigators came across a substance

Figure 1-1 The Tranquilizer, a device used for psychiatric therapy by Benjamin Rush in 1811. (National Library of Medicine, Bethesda, MD)

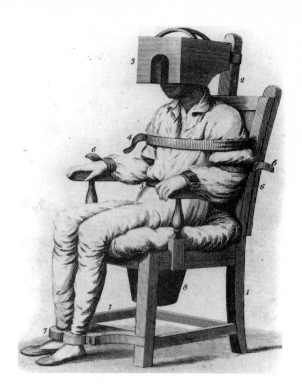

that did that and more. This substance—**chlorpromazine**—seemed to produce a tranquilizing effect without putting people to sleep. The tranquilizing effect seen in surgical patients inspired psychiatrists in the 1950s to test this drug as a treatment for psychosis. Early research with compounds of this type was hampered by their rather weak effects and undesirable side effects. Therefore an important advance was the introduction of tests with experimental animals to screen compounds for their sedative effects (Swazey, 1974). Many studies indicated that these chemicals have remarkable antipsychotic properties. Today so many people can lead useful, rewarding lives while controlling psychosis with these drugs that some psychiatrists even believe that the main role of psychotherapy is to encourage patients to accept medication. Research on the mechanisms of antipsychotic drugs has also led to productive hypotheses about the nature of schizophrenia.

As is true of many areas of research, the successes have not been without costs. The drugs that alleviate many psychoses have come into such widespread use that they pose social problems. Drug taking has become for many people an accepted way of dealing with daily problems. It can rule the lives of some people. Have the advances of psychiatry that have aided the few led to impairment of the lives of the many? Knowledge of the responses of the brain to chemical treatments is essential in this continuing assessment.

Integrating Laboratory and Clinical Approaches

Basic research and clinical practice now influence each other reciprocally; that is, basic research is providing both concepts and techniques that are being applied to understanding and helping people with malfunctioning brains. At the same time, observation of these patients provides both data and challenges that stimulate further understanding of brain mechanisms of behavior. This exchange is mutually beneficial, and the boundaries between laboratory and clinic are disappearing. Research on the functions of the two cerebral hemispheres discussed in the next paragraphs illustrates the productive interplay between laboratory and clinic.

Two Brains in One Head?

Suppose that each time a right-handed person buttoned a shirt, the person's left hand sought to unbutton it! Two separate controllers would seem to be in charge. Most of us are saved from such frustration because information from the right and left sides of the body is integrated by pathways that connect the two sides of the brain. But what happens when these connections are severed? Can we then observe two different types of consciousness? To consider this prospect, we should know that the structures of the two sides of the brain are very much alike, although some anatomical differences are present.

Functional differences between the cerebral hemispheres of human brains become especially evident after brain damage such as that resulting from a stroke. For instance, injury to certain parts of the left cerebral hemisphere can produce striking changes in speech and language, whereas injury to the right hemisphere rarely affects speech. Damage to these parts of the left hemisphere causes speech impairment in virtually all right-handed individuals and in about 50% of left-handers. This situation used to be described as ''cerebral dominance,'' implying that a talkative left cerebral hemisphere dominated a mute right hemisphere.

New information about hemispheric specialization of function has come from studies of patients in whom the connections between the right and left cerebral hemispheres have been severed surgically: **split-brain** individuals. Work with such patients in the 1930s had not revealed clear differences between the functions of the two hemispheres, but that was because of lack of appropriate methods of behavioral assessment. Coming from a background of animal research, Roger Sperry (1974) and his collaborators understood how to test separately the functioning of the two hemispheres and they found remarkable differences. These results prompted Sperry to speak of separate forms of consciousness in the two hemispheres of the brain. Indeed, one of his patients *was* seen to button a shirt with one hand and try to unbutton it with the other. For his research with split-brain subjects and other contributions, Sperry was awarded the Nobel Prize in 1981.

Tests have indicated differences in cognitive style between the two hemispheres. The left is said to be analytic and verbal, whereas the right has been characterized as spatial and holistic. The differences in the ways the cerebral hemispheres process information have prompted some researchers to suggest that the educational needs and capabilities of the cerebral hemispheres differ.

Those who urge attention to the creative potential of the right hemisphere have alleged that the educational system has "left-sided" prejudices. This is surely an exaggeration. We suggest that you hold off before you choose favorite cerebral sides. Chapter 18 offers some moderating ideas.

Ways of Looking at Behavior

[handwritten: 4 Perspectives for understand + study behavior]

[handwritten: 1) describe of behavior 2) evolution of " 3) ontology 4) biology (immediate time span)]

To study and understand behavior, we can employ four main perspectives. Each one yields different information, and the combination of perspectives is especially powerful. The four perspectives are (1) describing the behavior, (2) studying the evolution of the behavior, (3) observing the development of the behavior over the life span, and (4) finding the biological mechanisms of the behavior. Putting it another way, once we have described a behavior, we can seek to account for it on three different time scales. Over the time scale of evolution, we can ask how the behavior and its mechanisms evolved and what is their survival value. Over the scale of the life span, we can ask how the behavior and its mechanisms develop. And in the immediate present, we can ask how the mechanisms operate to produce the behavior that we see.

I. Describing Behavior

[handwritten: Structural vs. Functional (How vs. why]

Until we describe what it is we want to study, we cannot get very far. Depending on the goals of our investigation, we may describe behavior in terms of detailed acts and processes or in terms of results or functions. Thus an *analytical* description of limb movements might record the successive positions of the limb and its parts or the contraction of the different muscles. A *functional* behavioral description would state whether the limb was being used in walking, running, hopping, swimming, or shooting dice.

To be useful for scientific study, a description must be precise and analytical; that is, it must help reveal the essential features of the behavior. It must employ accurately defined terms and units. The methods and operations used by researchers must be specified so that other investigators can repeat and verify them.

II. Studying the Evolution of Behavior

[handwritten: 1) continuity across species 2) species specific adaptation]

Darwin's theory of **evolution through natural selection,** as updated and elaborated, is central to all modern biology and psychology. This perspective provides rich insights into many kinds of behavior and behavioral mechanisms, so we will use it in most of the chapters to come. From this perspective emerge two rather different emphases: (1) the *continuity* of behavior and biological processes among species and (2) the *species-specific adaptations* in behavior and biology that have evolved in different environmental niches. At some points in this book we will concentrate on continuity, that is, on features of behavior and its biological mechanisms that are common to many species. At other points we will look at species-specific behaviors.

[handwritten margin note: Over the course of evolution— Continuity & Species specific Adaptation]

Continuity

Nature is conservative. Bodily or behavioral inventions once arrived at may be maintained over millions of years and may be seen in animals that otherwise appear to be very different. The nerve impulse, for example, is essentially the same in a jellyfish, a cockroach, and a human being. Some of the chemical compounds that transmit messages through the bloodstream (hormones) are also the same in diverse animals (although the same hormone may affect different metabolic processes in different species). Similar—but not identical—sex hormones occur in all mammalian species. Male and female mammals produce the same sex hormones, although in different relative amounts and during different time cycles.

[handwritten margin note: Similar adaptions may have evolved from diff ancestors]

But similarity of a feature between species does not guarantee that the feature can be traced back to a common ancestor. Similar but not identical solutions to a problem may have evolved independently in different classes of animals. For example, color vision has emerged independently in insects, fish, reptiles, birds, and mammals. Much current research on neural mechanisms of learning and memory is being done with relatively simple invertebrates. The assumption here is that there is an evolutionary continuity of mechanisms among a very wide range of species. Some findings suggest, however, that more complex invertebrate and vertebrate animals may have evolved additional mechanisms of learning beyond those that they share with simpler organisms.

Species-Specific Behaviors

Different species have evolved specific ways of dealing with their environments. An earthworm's sensory endowments, for example, are quite different from those of a robin. Certain species of bat rely almost exclusively on hearing to navigate and to find their prey. The vision of these species has degenerated until it has become unusable. But other species of bat are visually oriented and depend on their eyes to find their way around and to secure their food. Human beings use both vision and audition. However, we are not sensitive to electrical fields in the environment, whereas certain kinds of fish are highly sensitive to them. These fish emit electrical pulses and use the resulting electrical fields to guide their locomotion.

Communicative behavior differs greatly among species. Some species rely chiefly on visual signals, some on auditory signals, and some on olfactory signals. In many species the production of signals does not require learning but simply follows an inherited species-specific pattern. In other species (including some songbirds), the young bird must learn the song. And although there are many varieties of song, they all conform rather closely to the pattern of the species.

Human beings can produce a wide variety of vocal sounds, but any language uses only a fraction of them. Moreover, the functional significance of sounds is rather arbitrary in human languages, since the same sequence of sounds may have different meanings in different languages.

[handwritten margin note: III.]

Observing Development of Behavior over the Life Span

Observing the way a particular behavior changes during the life span of an individual may give us clues to its functions and mechanisms. For example, we know from observation that learning ability in monkeys increases over several years of development. Therefore we can speculate that prolonged maturation of neural circuits is required for complex learning tasks. In rodents the ability to form long-term memories lags somewhat behind the maturation of learning ability. Young rodents learn well but forget more quickly than older ones. This difference provides one of several kinds of evidence that learning and memory involve different processes. We can study the development of reproductive capacity and of differences in behavior between the sexes along with changes in bodily structures and processes. This enables us to throw light on bodily mechanisms of sex behaviors.

Determining the Biological Mechanisms of Behavior

The history of a species tells us the evolutionary determinants of its behavior, and the history of an individual tells us the developmental determinants. To learn about the actual mechanisms of an individual's behavior, we study his or her present bodily endowments and states. Our major aim in physiological psychology is to examine those bodily mechanisms that make particular behaviors possible. For example, in the case of learning and memory, we would like to know the sequence of electrophysiological and biochemical processes that must occur between the initial capture of an item of information and its eventual retrieval from memory. We would also like to know what parts of the nervous system are particularly involved in learning and memory. In the case of reproductive behavior, we would like to know the developmental processes in the body that produce the capacity for reproductive behavior. We also want to understand the neuronal and hormonal processes that underlie reproductive behavior.

We have defined four ways of looking at behavior, and Table 1-3 shows how each of them can be applied to three kinds of behavior. We will take up each of the entries in the table in later chapters. In fact, we will use these four perspectives to examine all the categories of behavior that we consider in the later parts of this book: sensation, perception, and motor coordination (Part Three); motivation (Part Four); and learning, memory, and cognition (Part Five).

Levels of Analysis in Studying Brain and Behavior

Finding explanations for behavior often involves dealing with several levels of biological analysis. Each level of analysis deals with units that are simpler in structure and organization than the level above. Table 1-4 shows how we can analyze the brain into successively less complex units until we get down to single nerve cells and their still simpler constituents.

Scientific explanations usually involve analyzing something on a simpler or more basic level of organization than that of the structure or function to be explained. In principle it is possible to reduce each explanatory series down to the molecular or atomic level, though for practical reasons this is rarely done. For example, the organic chemist or the neurochemist usually deals with large complex molecules and the laws that govern them and seldom seeks explanations in terms of atoms.

Naturally in all fields different problems are carried to different levels of analysis, and fruitful work is often being done simultaneously by different workers at several levels. Thus in their research on visual perception, behavioral psychologists advance analytical descriptions of behavior. They try to determine how the eyes

Table 1-3 Four Research Perspectives Applied to Three Kinds of Behavior

	Kinds of Behavior		
Research Perspectives	**Sexual Behavior**	**Learning and Memory**	**Language and Communication**
1. Descriptive			
(a) Structural description	What are the main patterns of reproductive behavior and sex differences in behavior?	In what main ways does behavior change as a consequence of experience, for example, conditioning?	How are the sounds of speech patterned?
(b) Functional description	How do specialized patterns of behavior contribute to mating and to care of young?	How do certain behaviors lead to rewards or avoidance of punishment?	What behavior is involved in making statements or asking questions?
2. Evolutionary	How does mating depend on hormones in different species?	How do different species compare in kinds and speed of learning?	How did the human speech apparatus evolve?
3. Developmental	How do reproductive and secondary sex characteristics develop over the life span?	How do learning and memory change over the life span?	How do language and communication develop over the life span?
4. Mechanisms	What neural circuits and what hormones are involved in reproductive behavior?	What anatomical and chemical changes in the brain hold memories?	What brain regions are particularly involved in language?

move while looking at a visual pattern, or how the contrast among parts of the pattern determines its visibility. Meanwhile, other psychologists and biologists are studying the differences in visual endowments among species and trying to determine the adaptive significance of these differences. For example, how is the presence (or absence) of color vision related to the life of a species? At the same time, other investigators are tracing out the brain's structures and networks that are involved in different kinds of visual discrimination. Still other neuroscientists are trying to ascertain the electrical and chemical events that occur at synapses in the brain during visual learning.

Table 1-4 Levels of Analysis of Nervous System

Level	Examples
Organ	Brain, spinal cord
Major region	Cerebral cortex, cerebellum
Subregion	Motor cortex, visual cortex
Basic processing unit	Circuits of nerve cells
Nerve cell	Two hundred or more varieties of nerve cells (e.g., pyramidal cell, Purkinje cell)
Functional contacts between nerve cells	Chemical synapse
Functional regions of nerve cell membranes	Synaptic receptor region

Useful applications can be found at many levels of analysis of a system. For a given problem, one level of analysis is often more appropriate than another. For example, common problems of visual acuity are caused by variations in the shape of the eyeball. These problems can be solved by prescribing corrective lenses without having to analyze the brain processes involved in pattern vision. On the other hand, a partial loss of sight in certain parts of the visual field suggests pressure on the two optic nerves where they run together. This may be an early sign of a tumor whose removal restores full vision.

Other restrictions of the visual field are caused by localized damage to the visual area of the cerebral cortex. Recent research shows that training can help to enlarge the field in some of these cases. If epileptic attacks of a person are regularly preceded by a peculiar visual image, it is possible that the person may have a scar or an injury to the visual cortex. Understanding how color vision works has been advanced by studying how information from different kinds of retinal cells converges on nerve cells and how the nerve cells process this information. Investigators are also studying the way visual patterns are analyzed by the brain at the level of nerve cells and their connections.

As we consider explanations of many kinds of behavior in terms of bodily events, we will point out the main levels of analysis that are currently being used to study each problem. We will also indicate some of the applications of each level of research.

Comparing Species and Individuals

How do similarities and differences among people and animals fit into physiological psychology? The anthropologist Clyde Kluckhohn observed that each person is in some ways like all other people, in some ways like some other people, and in some ways like no other person (Kluckhohn, 1949). As indicated in Figure 1-2, we can extend this observation to the much broader range of animal life. In some ways each

Each person shares some characteristics with . . .

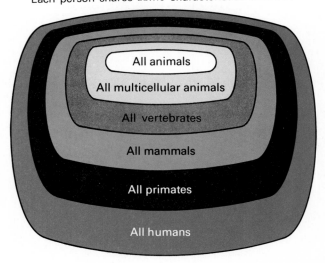

Figure 1-2 Similarities and differences among species.

person is like all animals (for example, in needing to ingest complex organic nutrients). In some ways each person is like all multicellular animals, in some ways like all vertebrates (for example, in having a spinal column). In some ways human beings are like all mammals (for example, in suckling the young), and in some ways like all other primates (for example, in having a hand with an opposable thumb and a relatively large and complex brain).

Areas of similarity define regions within which findings about one kind of animal can be properly applied to other kinds. Thus much of the fundamental research on the mechanisms of inheritance has been done with the bacterium *Escherichia coli*. The findings proved to be so widely applicable that some molecular biologists proclaimed, "What is the true of *E. coli* is true of the elephant." More recently it has been found that—although more complex animals do share many basic processes and chemistry of genetics with *E. coli*—there are also some important differences in their genetic mechanisms. With respect to each biological property, researchers must find which animals are identical and where differences arise. When we seek model animal systems with which to study human behavior or biological processes, we must ask this question: Does the proposed model really share the same sphere of identity with human beings with respect to the aspect to be studied?

Findings made with animal subjects have been successfully applied to biological mechanisms of many kinds of behavior in people. You will see examples in every chapter of this book. For example, in all animals that have nervous systems, there are both excitatory and inhibitory influences of one nerve cell on another. Study of these processes in one species can be successfully applied to other species. Again, in the case of hormones, some mechanisms of hormone action are the same in invertebrates, birds, and mammals. Some hormones are very similar among widely different orders of animals. Research with animals has helped to illumine relations between body and behavior in people in many areas, among them (1) perception of color and form, (2) mechanisms of pain and relief from pain, (3) drug addiction, (4) muscular coordination, (5) roles of hormones in sex behavior, (6) control of hunger and thirst, and (7) causes of impairments of memory.

But even within the same species, individuals differ from one another: cat from cat, blue jay from blue jay, and person from person (Figure 1-3). Physiological psychology seeks to understand individual differences as well as similarities. This interest in the individual is one of the most important differences between psychology and other approaches to behavior. The lottery of heredity ensures that each individual draws a unique genetic makeup (the only exception being identical twins). The way the individual's unique genetic composition is translated into bodily form and behavioral capacities is part of our story. Furthermore, each individual has a unique set of personal experiences. Therefore the way each person is able to process information and store the memories of these experiences is another part of our story. Our focus on physiological approaches to behavior will not ignore the individuality of people but will help to show how this individuality comes about.

We will be drawing on animal research throughout this book. Therefore we should comment on some of the ethical issues of experimentation on animals. Human beings' involvement and concern with other species goes back into prehistory. Early humans had to study animal behavior and physiology in order to escape

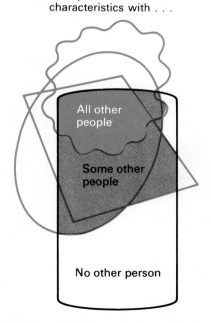

Each person shares some characteristics with . . .

All other people

Some other people

No other person

Figure 1-3 Similarities and differences within a species. The different forms represent different individuals with partially overlapping traits.

some species and to hunt others. When humans domesticated some species about ten thousand years ago, closer observation and interaction became possible. Formal studies of animal physiology and behavior began only in the nineteenth century.

Without experimentation on animal subjects in the last hundred years, there would not have been the enormous progress we have seen in medicine, physiology, and psychology. Today animals—or animal tissues—are used in a wide variety of medical tests and in the development of new medical treatments. The fact that these tests work testifies to the basic resemblance of our physiology to that of other species.

In view of these resemblances, people have also become increasingly concerned about humane use of animal subjects. Many scientific associations have prescribed ethical standards for experiments on animals, codes derived from scientists' own concerns with their subjects. An example is the detailed guideline adopted by the American Psychological Association; governments also set standards for the care and housing of animal subjects (Figure 1-4). In many cases experimenters today are trying to use simpler and more abundant species rather than complex, rare ones. These precautions are important because learning about human behavior and its

Figure 1-4 Guidelines for animal research of the American Psychological Association and U.S. Department of Health and Human Services.

biological bases inevitably requires research on animals of other species as well as on human beings. Further improvements in human health and well-being and reduction of the disorders listed in Tables 1-1 and 1-2 depend upon ongoing research, much of which requires animal subjects.

Finding Relationships Between Brain and Behavior

Experiments and theories in many disciplines have contributed to our understanding of the working of the body in relation to behavior. Since the focuses of different disciplines vary, they provide insights that complement each other. The anatomist portrays the structure of nervous systems, the components and the pathways of the brain. The physiologist examines how these components work, often studying the electrical signals of the nervous system. The chemist identifies the chemicals found in the brain and charts the metabolic pathways that generate different substances. The engineer seeks to determine whether quantitative concepts derived from inanimate systems can be applied to brain functions. Physiological psychologists are a bit more eclectic, but generally start with an interest in the mechanisms of behavior. Their investigations include both (1) observing and measuring behavior and (2) observing and measuring bodily structures and processes.

Figures 1-5, 1-6, and 1-7 illustrate three approaches to relating bodily and behavioral variables. Figure 1-5 shows the most commonly employed approach, **somatic intervention,** which involves altering some structure or function of the brain or body and seeing how this alters behavior. Here somatic intervention is the independent variable, and the behavioral effect is the dependent variable. We will describe many kinds of somatic interventions with both humans and other animals in different chapters of this text. A few examples are:

1. A hormone is administered to some animals but not to others. The two groups are later compared on various behavioral measures.
2. A part of the brain is stimulated electrically, and behavioral effects are observed.
3. A connection between two parts of the nervous system is cut, and changes in behavior are measured.

The opposite approach, illustrated in Figure 1-6, is **behavioral intervention,** which involves intervening in the behavior of an organism and looking for resultant changes in bodily structure or function. Here behavior is the independent variable, and bodily measures are the dependent variables. Among the examples that we will consider in later chapters are the following:

Figure 1-5 Somatic interventions and behavioral effects.

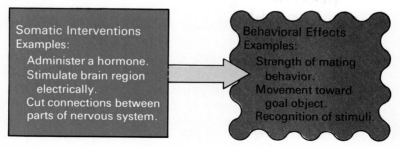

Somatic Interventions
Examples:
   Administer a hormone.
   Stimulate brain region
      electrically.
   Cut connections between
parts of nervous system.

Behavioral Effects
Examples:
   Strength of mating
      behavior.
   Movement toward
      goal object.
   Recognition of stimuli.

Figure 1-6 Behavioral interventions and somatic effects.

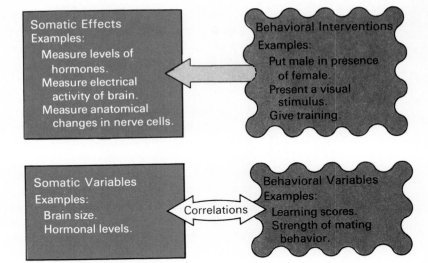

Figure 1-7 The correlational approach.

1. Putting two adults of opposite sex in the presence of each other may lead to increased secretion of certain hormones.
2. Exposing a person or animal to a visual stimulus provokes changes in both electrical activity and blood flow in parts of the brain.
3. Giving animals training is accompanied by electrophysiological, biochemical, and anatomical changes in parts of their brains.

The **correlational approach** to brain-behavior relations, shown in Figure 1-7, consists of finding the extent to which a given bodily measure covaries with a given behavioral measure. Some questions examined in later chapters are:

1. Is there a significant correlation between brain size and intelligence?
2. Are individual differences in reproductive activity correlated with levels of certain hormones in the individuals?

Finding such correlations should not be taken as proof of causal relationship, however. For one thing, even if a causal relation does exist, the correlation does not reveal its direction, that is, which variable is independent and which is dependent. For another, two terms might be correlated only because a third factor determines the values of the two factors measured. The existence of a correlation does indicate, however, that there is some link—direct or indirect—between the two variables. This often stimulates investigators to formulate hypotheses and to test them by interventive techniques.

Putting these three approaches together yields the circle diagram of Figure 1-8. This diagram incorporates the basic approaches to studying relationships between bodily processes and behavior. It can also serve to emphasize the theme (brought out in the myth of the transposed heads) that the relations between brain and body are reciprocal; each affects the other in an ongoing cycle of bodily and behavioral

Figure 1-8 The three main approaches to studying relations between bodily processes and behavior.

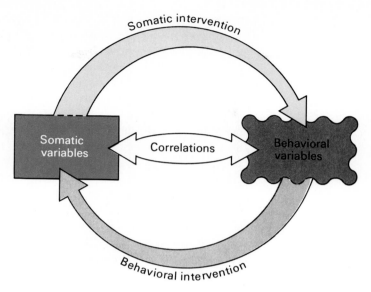

interactions. We will see such reciprocal relationships in each of the main sections of the book.

The Many Names and Uses of Physiological Psychology

Over the years the field that relates behavior to bodily processes has acquired a variety of names and an increasing number of applications. Let us note some of both in order to show the scope of the field. The vigor of this field is evidenced by the number of different academic departments that offer courses relevant to this area.

Names for This Field

Since the last century, the study of relations among mental processes, behavior, and bodily processes has been known as physiological psychology. We have chosen to keep this term even though many alternatives have been suggested in recent years. Some instructors and investigators prefer to denote the field by the broader term *biological psychology*. Others who come to this area through physiology or the neurosciences use such terms as *physiology of behavior* or *behavioral neuroscience*. Other designations stress relations of physiological psychology to clinical neurology; such terms include *neuropsychology* and *behavioral neurology*. Our text is being used in courses that go by each of these designations, plus a number of others. If the scope of the field is made clear, the exact title is not important.

Uses of Physiological Psychology

Physiological psychology is now included in many programs of study. Among the main subject fields that draw upon physiological psychology are general psychology, behavioral sciences, neurosciences, and health sciences. Almost every textbook in introductory psychology has a section devoted to physiological psychology, and fuller knowledge of physiological psychology is important for deeper understanding of psychology in general.

In the health sciences, there is growing recognition of the important of reciprocal interactions between behavior and bodily structure and function. For example, an area called behavioral medicine is emerging (Miller, 1983). The American Psychological Association, in its criteria for accreditation of graduate programs in professional psychology (including clinical, guidance, and school psychology), requires that each student demonstrate competence in four substantive areas. The first area listed is ''biological bases of behavior (e.g., physiological psychology, comparative psychology, neuropsychology, sensation, psychopharmacology)'' (American Psychological Association, 1980). A professional specialty that draws largely upon physiological psychology is neuropsychology, a field that focuses on impairments related to neural dysfunction.

Investigators who conduct research and who teach in the neurosciences find a home in many departments and disciplines. Some are in psychology departments, and many others are members of university departments such as physiology, neuroscience, and pharmacology. It is clear that there is much need for people whose training involves both behavioral and physiological sciences.

Many readers of this book will take only a single course in physiological psychology, while others will go on to careers in this field or related fields. Whatever your own case, this book is meant to help you toward a fuller understanding of behavior and its biological bases.

Our goal in writing this book has been to provide an interesting and coherent account of the main ideas and research in physiological psychology. Because there are so many pieces to tie together, we have introduced a given piece of information when it makes a difference to the understanding of a subject rather than withholding it until we arrive at the precise pigeonhole in which it belongs. We have sought to communicate our own sense of interest and excitement about the mysteries of mind and body. We hope you will join us in seeking knowledge of this fascinating field.

Recommended Reading

Adelman, G. (1987). *Encyclopedia of the neurosciences*. Boston: Birkhausen.

To keep in touch with progress in this field, you can find reviews and evaluations of research in the following publications:

Annual review of neuroscience. Palo Alto: Annual Reviews. (Founded in 1978; Vol. 11 published in 1988.)

Annual review of psychology. Palo Alto: Annual Reviews. (Founded in 1950; Vol. 39 published in 1988.)

Trends in neuroscience. Amsterdam: Elsevier. (Founded in 1978; Vol. 11 published in 1988.)

PART ONE

Bodily Systems Basic to Behavior

Within your head is an information processing system that contains at least 100 billion nerve cells. The architecture of the nervous system includes elaborate patterns of connection among these cells. In many instances thousands of connections can be found on a single nerve cell! A ubiquitous web of nerve fibers connects the brain to every part of the body, monitoring, regulating, and modulating the functions of every bodily structure and system. The workings of this vast assembly make possible our perceptions, thoughts, movements, motives, and feelings. The essence of our identity is locked up in the character of our brain.

Our first objective in this section is to provide a description of the basic structures of the adult human brain; this is the goal of Chapter 2. Our next aim, in Chapter 3, is to consider nonhuman nervous systems from the perspective of evolution and the role of the nervous system in species-typical adaptation. For every animal another time frame is significant: the life history of the individual. In Chapter 4 we will describe changes that occur in the nervous system over the course of the life span and the interplay of developmental controls such as genes and experience.

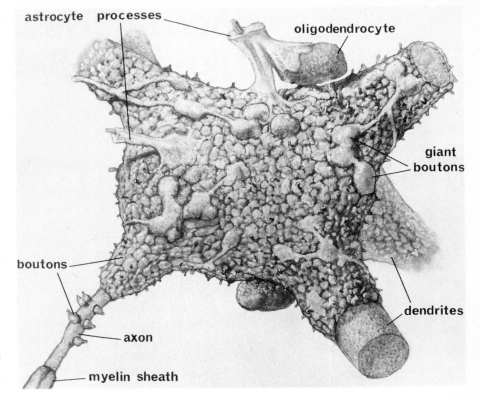

2 Neuroanatomical Bases of Behavior

ORIENTATION

Thoughts, feelings, perceptions, and acts—all are products of the workings of the human brain. These accomplishments depend on the architecture of the brain and the ways it works. The architecture of the brain is the topic of this chapter. The basic ways in which the brain works will be taken up in Chapters 5 and 6.

The architecture of the brain includes its structural components and the extensive network of linkages among brain regions. The paths and circuits of the human brain form the anatomical substrate for the many facets of human information processing. This structural substrate is a highly precise arrangement of its components; our efforts to achieve a biological understanding of behavior must start with an appreciation of elements, their connections, and their arrangements into networks that process information. Our objective in this chapter is to provide some of the essentials about the architecture of the nervous system that are especially important for subsequent chapters. Within the body of this chapter we provide the main points; additional details are provided in a reference section (pages 54–73) at the end of the chapter. At some points in later chapters, we will refer back to the discussions and information in the reference section.

Some Historical Views of the Brain

It is only recently that the central role of the brain has been recognized. In this section we will note some of the main ways in which the brain has been viewed throughout history.

The Central Importance of the Brain: Ancient History

The knowledge that the brain mediates and controls behavior emerged rather recently in human history. When Tutankhamen was mummified (around 3300 years ago), four important organs were preserved in alabaster jars in his tomb: the liver, the lungs, the stomach, and the intestines. The heart was preserved in its place within the body. All these organs were considered necessary to ensure the pharaoh's continued existence in the afterlife. The brain, however, was removed from the skull and discarded. Obviously it was not considered important for the afterlife.

Neither the Old Testament (written from the twelfth to the second century B.C.) nor the New Testament mentions the brain. However, the Old Testament mentions the heart hundreds of times and makes several references each to the liver, the stomach, and the bowels as the seats of passion, courage, and pity. "Get thee a heart of wisdom," said the prophet.

The heart is where Aristotle, the most prominent scientist of ancient Greece, located mental capacities. He considered the brain to be only a cooling unit to lower the temperature of the hot blood from the heart. Other Greek thinkers, however, did consider the brain to be the seat of intellect and the organ that controls behavior. Thus Hippocrates, the great physician of Greek antiquity, wrote as follows:

> Not only our pleasure, our joy and our laughter but also our sorrow, pain, grief and tears rise from the brain, and the brain alone. With it we think and understand, see and hear, and we discriminate between the ugly and the beautiful, between what is pleasant and what is unpleasant and between good and evil.

The dispute between those who located intellect in the heart and those who located it in the brain still raged 2000 years later, in Shakespeare's time: "Tell me, where is fancy bred, / Or in the heart or in the head?" (*Merchant of Venice,* Act III, Scene 2). We still reflect this ancient notion when we call people "kindhearted," "openhearted," "hardhearted," "fainthearted," or "heartless." Only in the nineteenth and twentieth centuries, with gradually increasing knowledge of the nervous system, did educated people in the Western world finally accept the brain as the mechanism that coordinates and controls behavior.

Around 350 B.C. the Greek physician Herophilus (called the Father of Anatomy) advanced the knowledge of the nervous system by dissecting bodies of both people and animals. Among other investigations he traced spinal nerves from muscles and skin into the spinal cord. He also noted that each region of the body was connected to separate nerves. A second-century Greco-Roman physician, Galen (frequently described as the Father of Medicine), treated the injuries of gladiators and dissected some animals. He advanced the idea that animal spirits—a mysterious fluid— passed along nerves to all regions of the body. Although this concept did not advance the understanding of the nervous system, Galen provided interesting drawings of the organization of the brain. His assessment of the behavioral changes produced by injuries to gladiators also drew attention to the nervous system as the controller of behavior.

Renaissance Studies of Brain Anatomy

The eminent Renaissance painter Leonardo da Vinci studied the workings of the human body and laid the foundations of anatomical drawing of the human body. He especially pioneered in providing views from different angles and cross-sectional representations. His artistic renditions of the body included portraits of the nerves in the arm and a portrait of the ventricles of the brain. But it remained for the anatomist Andreas Vesalius to provide the first elegant description of the shape and appearance of the brain and the course of nerves throughout the body (Figure 2-1). Detailed descriptions of the surface anatomy of the brain, based on examination of the brains of criminals, were rendered by artists employed by Vesalius.

Descriptions of the brain by Renaissance anatomists emphasized the shape and appearance of the external surfaces of the brain, since these were the parts that were easiest to see when the skull was removed. It was immediately apparent to anyone who looked that the brain has an extraordinarily strange shape. The complexity of its gross form led to the use of an elaborate, precise vocabulary to label different regions. Many of these labels are still in use. Most of them are Latin or Greek names of common shapes, forms, objects, and animals. The origin of some of these anatomical terms is illustrated in Figure 2-2.

Figure 2-1 Renaissance illustration of brain and nervous system; composite of two figures by Vesalius drawn in the sixteenth century.

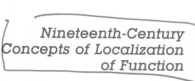

Nineteenth-Century Concepts of Localization of Function

A popular notion of the nineteenth century, called **phrenology,** is a background for contemporary interest in brain localization. Phrenology is the study of the shape of a person's skull, which is thought to reflect greater or smaller development of parts of the brain; each region is considered responsible for a behavioral faculty such as "love of family," "ambition," "intellect," or "curiosity" (Figure 2-3). The assignment of functions to brain regions was rather arbitrary in phrenology, but soon a more rational system of localization was discovered. The clues came from observations of effects of damage to the brain.

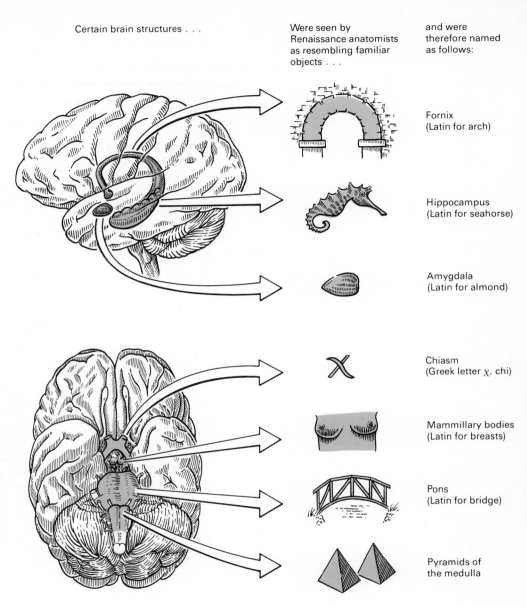

Certain brain structures . . .

Were seen by Renaissance anatomists as resembling familiar objects . . .

and were therefore named as follows:

Fornix
(Latin for arch)

Hippocampus
(Latin for seahorse)

Amygdala
(Latin for almond)

Chiasm
(Greek letter χ, chi)

Mammillary bodies
(Latin for breasts)

Pons
(Latin for bridge)

Pyramids of
the medulla

Figure 2-2 How some brain structures got their names.

Injuries to the head have long provided evidence about the brain's functions and about location of function. In the nineteenth century the French surgeon Paul Broca engaged in heated discussions about the relation between language and the brain. He argued against formidable critics that language ability was not a property of the entire brain but rather was localized in a restricted brain region. The theme that psychological functions could be localized in specific brain regions was strongly advanced when Broca presented a postmortem analysis of a patient who had been

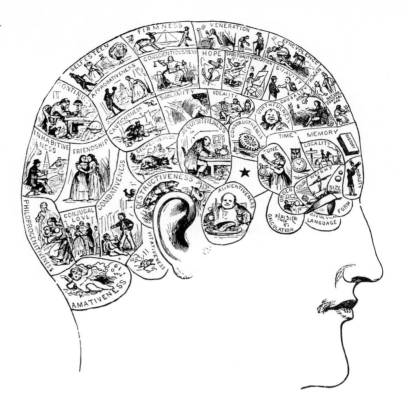

Figure 2-3 A phrenological head, illustrating concepts of brain localization that were popular in the early nineteenth century. (The Bettmann Archive)

unable to talk for many years. The findings of the autopsy of the brain conducted by Broca revealed destruction of a region within the frontal portions of the brain on the left side—a region now known as ''Broca's area.'' The study of additional patients further convinced Broca that language expression was mediated by a specific brain region rather than being a reflection of the activities of the entire brain. These nineteenth-century observations form the background for a continuing theme of research in biological psychology, notably the search for distinguishing differences among brain regions based on their structural attributes and the effort to relate different features of behavior to different brain regions. A major part of research in biological psychology is directed toward uncovering the behavioral specializations of different brain regions.

Large-Scale Views of the Human Nervous System

We start our description of the human nervous system with large-scale views and later in the chapter we move to the scale of microscopic views. Anatomists have some conventions for describing various viewpoints of the body and the brain. These conventions facilitate communication, and they are described in Box 2-1.

Central and Peripheral Divisions of the Nervous System

One major subdivision of the nervous system is the separation into the **central nervous system,** which refers to the brain and spinal cord, and the **peripheral nervous system,** which includes all nervous system parts that are outside the bony

BOX 2-1 | Orientation in the Nervous System

Because the nervous system is a three-dimensional structure, two-dimensional illustrations and diagrams cannot represent it completely.

There are three main planes in which the brain is usually cut in order to get a two-dimensional section from the three-dimensional object. The brain sections that appear at many places throughout this book are for the most part made in one of these planes. Thus you will find it useful to know the terminology and conventions that apply to them. See Box Figures 2-1 and 2-2.

The plane that bisects the body into right and left halves is called the **sagittal plane** (from the Latin for "arrow"). The plane that divides the body into a front (anterior) and back (posterior) part is called by several names: **coronal** (from the Latin for "crown") or frontal or transverse. By convention such a section is usually viewed from behind so that the right side of the figure represents the right side of the brain. The third main plane is the one that divides the brain into upper and lower parts. This is called the **horizontal plane** and is usually viewed from above.

The same main planes are used to describe the whole body. In addition, several directional terms are used, as also shown in Box Figure 2-1. **Medial** means "toward the middle" and is contrasted with **lateral**, "toward the side." The head end is referred to by any of several terms: anterior, **cephalic** (from the Greek for "head"), or **rostral** (from the Latin for "prow of a ship"). The tail end is called posterior or **caudal** (from the Latin for "tail"). **Proximal** (from the Latin for "nearest") means near the trunk or center, and **distal** means "toward the periphery" or "toward the end of a limb" (distant from the origin or point of attachment).

One pair of terms must be used carefully because their meanings are somewhat different depending on whether you are discussing four-legged or two-legged animals. These are **dorsal**, meaning "toward or at the back," and **ventral**, meaning "toward or at the belly or front." In four-legged animals, such as the cat or the rat, dorsal refers to both the back of the body and the top of the head. For consistency in comparing brains among species, dorsal is also used to refer to the top of the brain of a human or of a chimpanzee, even though in primates the top of the brain is not at the back of the body. Similarly ventral is used to designate the bottom of the brain of a primate as well as that of a quadruped.

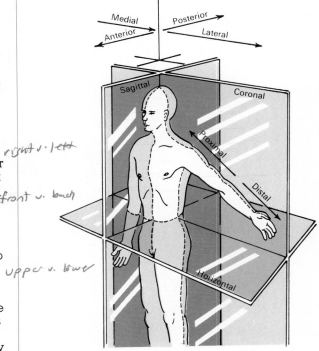

Box Figure 2-1 The main planes used in making anatomical sections, shown here in relation to the human body.

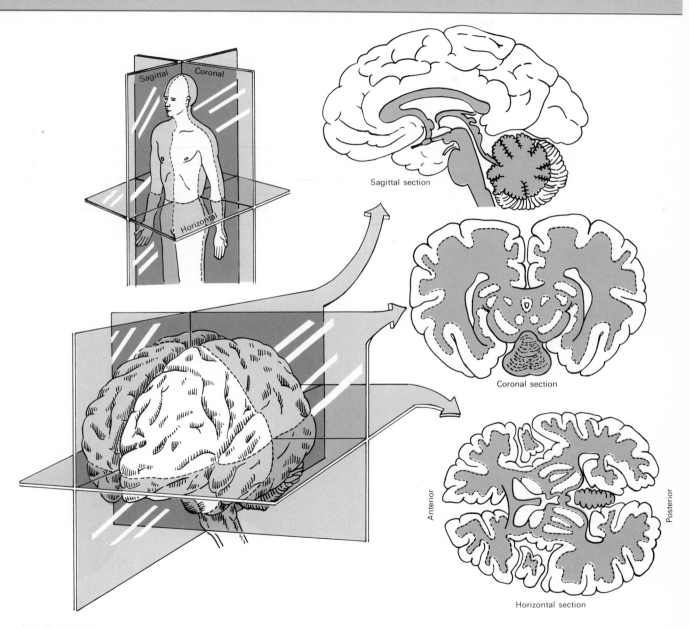

Box Figure 2-2   The main planes used in making anatomical sections of the brain.

skull and spinal column. The peripheral nervous system includes nerve branches throughout the body that transmit information to muscles (motor pathways) or arise from sensory surfaces (sensory pathways); it also includes pathways that lead from the central nervous system to various internal bodily organs, such as the heart. The peripheral nervous system also includes two parallel chains of clusters of nerve cells—called autonomic ganglia—that lie just outside the spinal column to its left and right.

Autonomiz ganglia

Coverings of the Nervous System

Both the brain and spinal cord are embraced by three sheets of tissue called **meninges.** The outmost sheet is a tough envelope called the **dura mater** (from the Latin for ''hard mother''), and the innermost layer, called the **pia mater** (from the Latin for ''tender mother''), is adherent to the surface of the brain and follows all its contours. The delicate membrane between the dura and pia is called the **arachnoid.** Spaces below the arachnoid are filled with cerebrospinal fluid, which is a clear, colorless liquid that can support and cushion the brain. Fluid compartments of the brain also include a series of chambers called **cerebral ventricles,** which are found within the brain (Figure 2-4). Cerebrospinal fluid is continually formed and circulates through the ventricles and subarachnoid spaces. It is formed at specific sites within the ventricles.

The Brain Seen from Three Orientations

Given the importance of the human brain, it is surprising that it weighs a mere 1400 grams, 2% of the average adult body weight. However, gross inspection of the brain reveals that what it lacks in weight it surely makes up for in intricacy. This gelatinous mass enclosed within the skull and spinal column and covered by connective

Figure 2-4 The cerebral ventricles in an adult human brain. The ventricles are filled with clear, colorless cerebrospinal fluid.

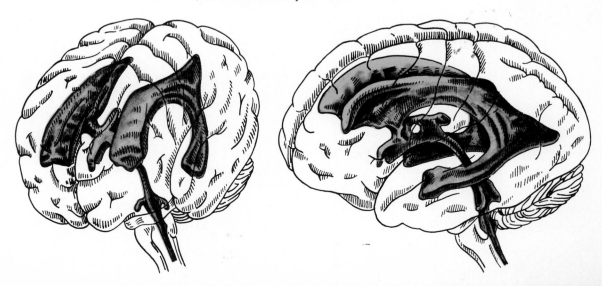

tissue membranes is an elaborately folded and contorted form. Viewed from the side (lateral view, Figure 2-5a) or from the top, the human brain is dominated by the paired cerebral hemispheres. The pattern of folding consists of ridges of tissue, called **gyri,** separated from each other by depths called **sulci.** Such folding enormously increases the cerebral surface area. Indeed, about two-thirds of the cerebral surface is hidden in the depths of these folds. The pattern of folding has many constant features in all humans, and this permits the labeling of major divisions of the cerebral hemispheres. Some larger folds separate major functional zones and thus provide a system for dividing the brain that is important in functional assessments. The major sectors of the cerebral hemispheres include the frontal, parietal, temporal, and occipital regions (Figure 2-5a). The boundaries defined by folds are not precise; some borders are clearly marked (e.g., lateral or sylvian sulcus), while others fade into adjacent areas. Details of the organization of the cerebral cortex and related systems are provided in the neuroanatomical atlas at the end of this chapter (Reference Figures 2-15, 16, and 17).

A view from a midline position (medial sagittal view, Figure 2-5b) shows a large bundle of axons called the corpus callosum, which connects the cerebral hemispheres to each other. This bundle connects corresponding points of the right and left hemispheres. The medial view also reveals a large portion of the temporal lobe. Deep within this lobe are some of the components of the limbic system, which is intimately involved in mechanisms of emotion and learning. This medial view also reveals other deeper lying structures, especially the thalamus, which includes regions that are part of the sensory and motor traffic to and from the cerebral hemispheres.

The lateral, midline, and basal views in Figure 2-5 show the cerebellum. The cerebellum, like the cerebral hemispheres, includes an elaborately folded surface sheet; in this case the folds are very closely opposed, almost like thin pancake layers. A major aspect of contemporary neurosciences is focused on understanding the neural machinery of the cerebellum with a primary focus on its role in the control of movements. Immediately below the cerebellum at the front of the brain stem is the pons, seen in the midline view of the brain. The pons includes regions involved in motor control and sensory analysis. Pathways linking the spinal cord and higher brain centers run through the brain stem.

A view of the human brain from a basal perspective (Figure 2-5c) shows many of the cranial nerves that bring information to the brain from various sensory surfaces or send information from the brain to the muscles of the body. This perspective also reveals the large extent of the temporal lobes, which is not readily seen from other perspectives.

If the human brain is cut in either a horizontal or transverse manner (see Box 2-1), two distinct shades of color are evident (Figure 2-6, page 34). The whitish areas of brain tissue contain tracts or large bundles of axons that appear relatively white because of the lipid content of myelin covering the axons. Darker gray areas are more dominated by cell bodies, which are devoid of myelin. A cross-sectional view also reveals outlines of distinct groupings of cells. Thus the term **white matter** refers to bundles of nerve fibers, and the term **gray matter** refers to areas that are rich in nerve cell bodies. Detailed identification of the structures and regions seen in these cross sections is provided in the neuroanatomical reference section (Reference Figures 2-10c and d).

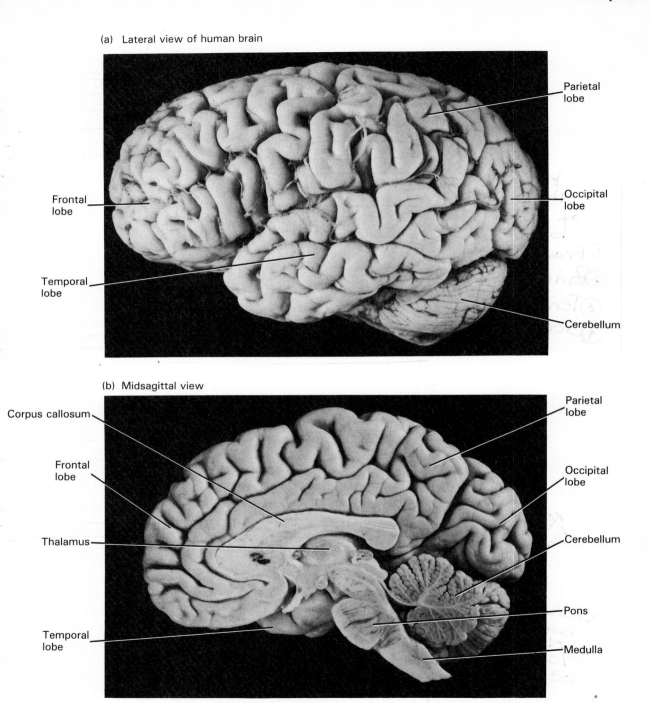

(a) Lateral view of human brain

Parietal lobe

Occipital lobe

Cerebellum

Frontal lobe

Temporal lobe

(b) Midsagittal view

Corpus callosum

Frontal lobe

Thalamus

Temporal lobe

Parietal lobe

Occipital lobe

Cerebellum

Pons

Medulla

Figure 2-5 Photographs of the human brain: (a) lateral view, (b) midsagittal view, (c) basal view. More detailed labeling is provided in Reference Figures 2-15, 2-16, and 2-17 at the end of the chapter. (Photos from Rijksuniversiteit Utrecht, Onderwijs Media Instituut. Illustrations reprinted with permission from Gluhbegovic and Williams, 1980.)

(c) Basal view

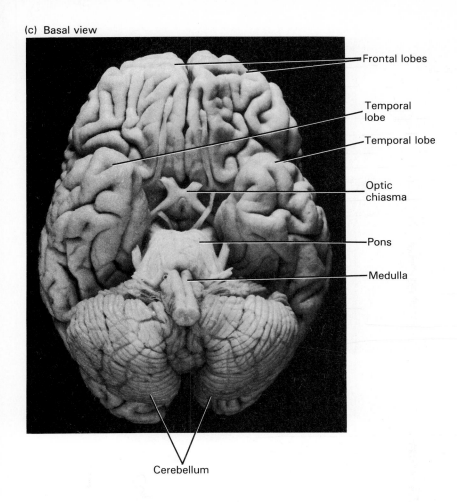

Frontal lobes

Temporal lobe

Temporal lobe

Optic chiasma

Pons

Medulla

Cerebellum

Subdividing the Brain: Clues from Development

The complex form of the adult human brain makes it hard to understand why anatomists use such terms as *forebrain* and *hindbrain* the way they do. For example, the part of your brain closest to the *back* of your head is labeled as part of the forebrain. How can we make sense of this?

The clue to subdividing the brain according to its structure lies in the way the brain develops early in life. In Chapter 4 we will consider brain development as a subject in its own right. But for now we will use brain development simply to help us describe the structures of the brain.

In a very young embryo of any vertebrate, the central nervous system looks like a tube (Figure 2-7). The walls of this tube are made of nerve cells, and the interior is filled with fluid. A few weeks after conception, the human neural tube begins to show three divisions at the head end (Figure 2-7a): the **forebrain** (or **prosencephalon**), the **midbrain** (or **mesencephalon**), and the **hindbrain** (or **rhombencephalon**). (The term *encephalon,* meaning "brain," comes from the Greek roots *en* meaning "in" and *kephalon* meaning "head.")

(a) Transverse or coronal section

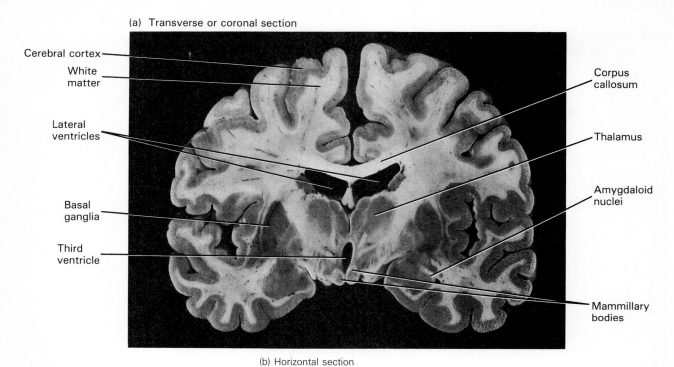

Cerebral cortex

White matter

Lateral ventricles

Basal ganglia

Third ventricle

Corpus callosum

Thalamus

Amygdaloid nuclei

Mammillary bodies

Figure 2-6 Photographs of sections of the human brain: (a) coronal section, (b) horizontal section. (Photos from Rijksuniversiteit Utrecht, Onderwijs Media Instituut.)

(b) Horizontal section

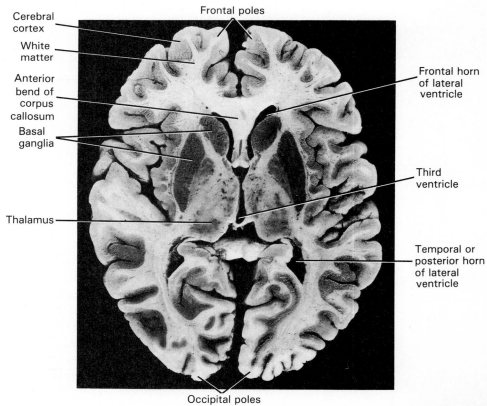

Cerebral cortex

White matter

Anterior bend of corpus callosum

Basal ganglia

Thalamus

Frontal poles

Frontal horn of lateral ventricle

Third ventricle

Temporal or posterior horn of lateral ventricle

Occipital poles

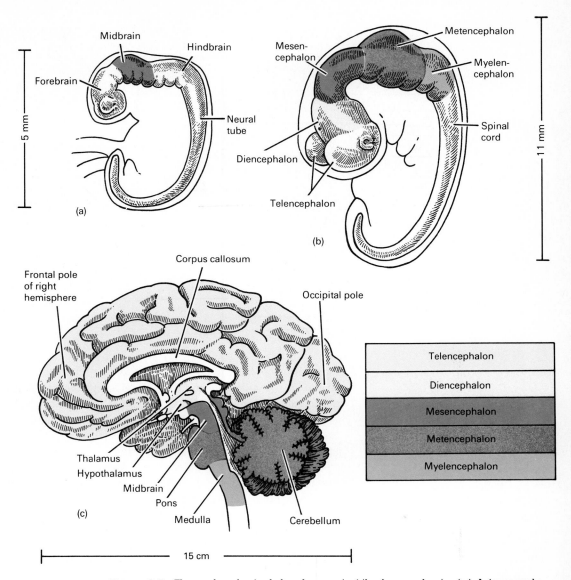

Figure 2-7 The embryological development of the human brain. (a) A few weeks after conception the head end of the neural tube shows three main divisions. (b) Six weeks after conception the five main divisions of the brain are visible. (c) The positions of these divisions are shown in the adult brain.

Six weeks after conception, the forebrain and hindbrain have already developed clear subdivisions (Figure 2-7b). At the fore end of the developing brain is the **telencephalon,** which will become the cerebral hemispheres. The other part of the forebrain is the **diencephalon** (or "between brain"), which will include the thalamus and the **hypothalamus.** The mesencephalon ("midbrain") comes next. Behind it the hindbrain has two divisions: the **metencephalon,** which will develop into the cerebellum and the pons, and the **myelencephalon or medulla.** Figure 2-7c shows

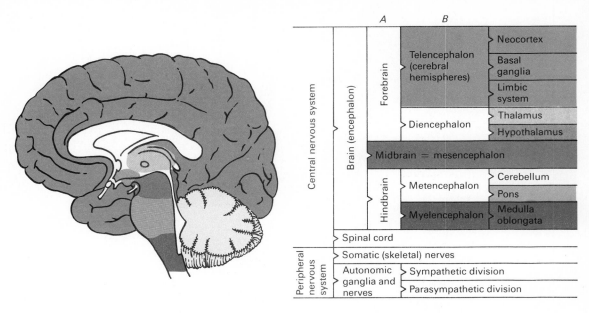

Figure 2-8   The major subdivisions of the central nervous system.

the positions of these main structures and their relative sizes in the human brain; the shading is the same as in part (b). The telencephalon has expanded so greatly that in a side view it would hide most of the other parts. That is why we present a medial view in part (c). Even when the brain achieves its adult form, it still remains a fluid-filled tube, but one of very complicated shape. All the cerebral cortex from front to back is part of the telencephalon, a division of the forebrain.

Using the top-down approach, let us go over major subdivisions of the brain. Looking at Figure 2-8, we will work our way from the largest, most general divisions at the left of the figure to more specific ones at the right. The variety of terms may be confusing at the beginning, but all these structures will appear again and again in later chapters, and you will have the chance to grow familiar with them.

Each of the five main sections of the brain shown in Figure 2-7 can be subdivided in turn. This is shown at the right in Figure 2-8.

Major Brain Regions: Some Functional Indications

Now that we have pointed out the main regions of the brain, let us note some functional characteristics of each (Table 2-1). Simple, capsule functional statements are given, and many of them will be expanded in later chapters. The brain regions described in Table 2-1 are taken up in the order in which they were presented in the right column of Figure 2-8.

Looking into the Living Human Brain

Major technical developments that have occurred since the mid-1970s have provided detailed portraits of the living human brain. These techniques involve elaborate computer analysis of such measures as x-rays, the distribution of radioactive

Table 2-1 Major Brain Regions: Some Functional Indications

Regions	For More Detailed Information, See Chapter
Cerebral cortex: Highest level of cognitive and perceptual analysis	8, 9
Basal ganglia: Coordination of complex motor functions	10
Limbic system: Integration of emotional experience and responses	15
Thalamus: Integrative region for sensory information directed to cerebral cortex	8, 9
Hypothalamus: Integrative region for motivational functions and regulation	11–13
Midbrain: Basic mechanisms of arousal. Fiber tracts between brain and rest of the body	14
Cerebellum: Involved in sensory-motor integrations; also involved in motor learning	10, 17
Medulla: Basic automatic control of essential body functions, such as respiration and circulation; modulated by higher neural centers	10

substances in the brain, or changes in the electromagnetic properties of molecules in the brain. All these tools yield intimate views of the living human brain that greatly facilitate clinical assessment of brain impairments and contribute to basic research.

A brief mention of some earlier techniques provides some perspective for newer developments. An ordinary x-ray of the head, a technique that has been used since early in the twentieth century, reveals an outline of the skull with little or no definition of brain tissue. Since the x-ray density of virtually all parts of the brain is the same, there is very little contrast between regions of the brain. To provide contrast between brain tissue and blood vessels, investigators inject substances into blood vessels. The resultant x-ray pictures are called **angiograms.** To visualize the ventricles, they inject gases into the ventricles of the brain, giving pictures that are called **pneumoencephalograms.** A recent development makes use of computerized enhancement of contrast among brain tissues.

Angiograms are x-rays taken after special dyes are injected into blood vessels in the head. Such pictures provide possible evidence of vascular disease. They also form the basis for inferences about adjacent tissue. It is possible to make these inferences because the outline of the principal blood vessels is rather constant from one human being to another. Therefore deformations in the shape of blood vessels provide a basis for concluding that adjacent neural tissue is abnormal. For example, an expanding brain tumor may be revealed by an angiogram.

Recent developments in computers enable us to generate portraits of the brain that resemble actual cross sections of the brain (Figure 2-9). Computer techniques achieve virtually direct views of the brain rather than the inferential view afforded by angiograms or pneumoencephalograms. These portraits are referred to as tomograms (from *tomus,* ''a crosscut'' or ''section,'' and *gram,* ''a record'' or ''picture'').

Computerized axial tomograms (CAT scans) involve moving an x-ray source in an arc around the head. To obtain the picture, a patient is placed on a table and the patient's head is inserted in the middle of a doughnut-shaped ring (Figure 2-9c). An x-ray source is moved in a circular path around the head; it delivers a small amount of x-radiation that passes through the head. Absorption of this radiation within the head depends on the density of the tissue. A ring of detectors opposite the x-ray source analyzes the amount of x-radiation that has passed through the head. The x-ray tube and detectors are moved to a new position, and the same analysis is performed, so a composite picture is built up based on the x-ray views at different angles around the head. Figure 2-9 shows a typical CAT scan of one level of the brain. Each picture element (called a pixel) in the final portrait is the result of a complex mathematical analysis of this small brain region viewed from many different angles. The spatial resolution of this technique has now been improved to the point where small changes, like shrinkage of a gyrus, can be visualized.

Figure 2-9   (opposite) Looking into the living human brain. Until recently, detailed anatomical observations of the human brain could be made only after death by cutting sections (a, b). New, noninvasive techniques make it possible to see and highlight detailed sections of the living human brain. These techniques include computerized axial tomography (CAT; c, d), positron emission tomography (PET; e, f), and magnetic resonance imaging (MRI; g, h). The left column indicates the techniques, and the right column shows pictures obtained with them. All are horizontal sections. ((b) Rijksuniversiteit Utrecht, Onderwijs Media Instituut; (h) from Edelsman, 1984.)

Techniques

Images

(a) Gross–anatomical dissection

(b) Anterior

Posterior

(c) CAT

3

2

1

1

Detectors

2

3

Moving
X–ray
source

(d)

(e) PET

(f)

(g) MRI

Coil

Magnet
rings

(h)

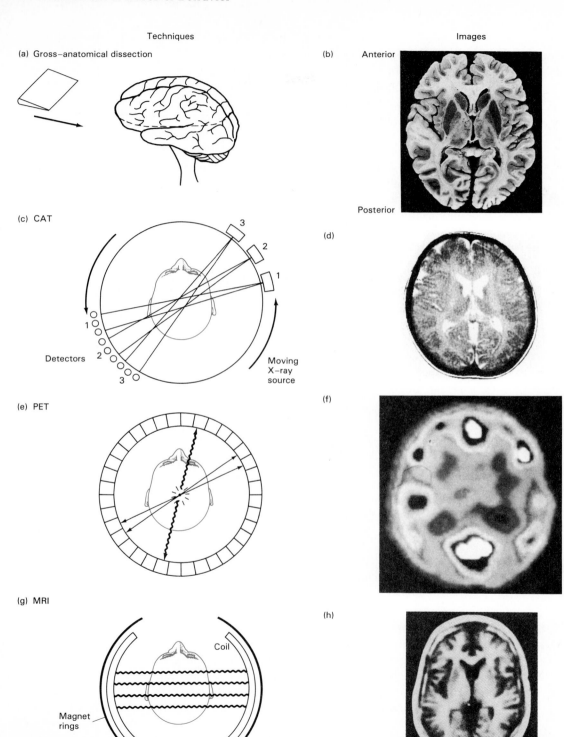

Recent elaboration of this technique provides a dynamic view of the brain—a picture of the physiological functioning of the brain that offers a very different perspective from the more static representation provided by CAT scans. A CAT scan cannot distinguish a living brain from a dead one, but new techniques actually picture brain activity. One of these new techniques, called positron emission tomography (PET), involves the injection of radioactive chemicals whose emission can be assessed by detectors outside the body (Figure 2-9e). Computerized analysis of these data yields a startling picture of the differential uptake and use of the chemicals in different brain regions. The most commonly used substance is a type of radioactive glucose that is taken up into different brain regions according to the level of each area's metabolic activity (Figure 2-9f). A color transform of this information yields a vivid picture which readily highlights areas of intense metabolic response. By using this technique, it is possible to note regions that are abnormal in metabolic responses even if they are structurally intact.

Some brain structural changes elude the grasp of both CAT and PET techniques. Another development, magnetic resonance imaging (MRI), generates pictures that provide some of these details without the use of potentially harmful radioactivity. MRI involves the use of radio waves and other magnetic energy and is a way to register the basic orientation of molecules. Patients lie within a large magnet (Figure 2-9g), and the molecular effect of applied magnetic fields is registered by a coil detector whose successive outputs are computer analyzed. The resultant image (Figure 2-9h) can highlight extremely small changes in the brain, such as the loss of myelin around groups of axons, which characterizes demyelinating diseases.

Microscopic Views of the Human Nervous System

In this chapter and in many other places in this book, we will be considering structures that vary greatly in size—from the intact human brain (which measures about 15 centimeters [cm] from front to back) to the walls or membranes of neurons (which are about 7 nanometers [nm] thick, that is, seven-billionths of a meter). If we compare these two measures—the size of the brain (15 cm, or 15×10^{-2} meter [m]) and the thickness of a cell wall (7 nm, or 7×10^{-9} m)—the first is 20 million times as large as the second. Table 2-2 lists aspects of the brain that can be studied at different degrees of magnification. It also lists some of the main organizational levels of the brain, from large to small. (See Reference Section at the end of this chapter, pp. 54–73, on neuroanatomical methods.)

The Fine Structure of the Nervous System

In the late nineteenth century, anatomists sought to understand the bases of differences among brains by making microscopic studies of the finer elements. Their studies showed that brains were composed of a large assembly of oddly shaped cells. Some anatomists thought that these cells were continuous with one another, a kind of nearly endless series of interconnected tubes. In this view information in the nervous system was carried through continuous channels. However, a brilliant Spanish anatomist, Santiago Ramón y Cajal, offered a forceful rejoinder. His elegant anatomical observations, which were begun at the end of the nineteenth century, are cited to this day. From his studies, Ramón y Cajal offered a perspective that is called the **neuron doctrine.** The neuron doctrine says that the brain is com-

Table 2-2   Size of Brain Structures, Levels of Magnification, and Units of Measure

Magnification	Structures Seen at This Magnification	Sizes of Structures	Units of Measurement
1 (life size)	Whole brain	Adult human brain measures about 15 cm from front to back	1 centimeter (cm) = 10^{-2} meter (m)*
×10	Cerebral cortex; large tracts of fibers	Cortex of human brain is about 3 mm thick	1 millimeter (mm) = 10^{-3} m
×100 (10^2)	Layers of cortical cells	Large neuron cell bodies are about 100 μm in diameter (0.1 mm)	0.1 mm = 10^{-4} m = 100 micrometers (μm, microns)
×1,000 (10^3)	Parts of individual neurons	Large axons and dendrites are about 10 μm in diameter (0.01 mm)	0.01 mm = 10^{-5} m = 10 μm
×10,000 (10^4)	Synapse (end bouton and dendritic spine)	An end bouton is about 1 μm in diameter	1 micrometer (μm) = 10^{-6} m
×100,000 (10^5)	Detailed structure of synapse	The gap or cleft between neurons at a synapse is about 20 nm across	0.1 μm = 100 nanometers (nm) = 10^{-7} m

*The meter, the unit of length in the metric system, equals 39.37 inches. A centimeter is one-hundredth of a meter (10^{-2} m); a millimeter is one-thousandth of a meter (10^{-3} m); a micrometer is one-millionth of a meter (10^{-6} m); and a nanometer is one-billionth of a meter (10^{-9} m).

posed of separate cells that are distinct units; that is, the cells are separate structurally, metabolically, and functionally. These nerve cells (also called **neurons**) are the basic units of the nervous system. According to this doctrine, information is transmitted from cell to cell across a space at specialized junctions called **synapses.** The advent of electron microscopic studies of the nervous system in the early 1950s reinforced the neuron doctrine. The high resolution abilities of the electron microscope showed that Ramón y Cajal was clearly correct: Nerve cells are indeed separated from each other by small spaces.

A look through a light microscope at a section of a brain reveals an incredible range of cell sizes and shapes woven together in very elaborate networks whose designs vary in different brain regions. Our focus in this section is on the structural properties of these elements, particularly those properties most directly related to the fundamental tasks of a nervous system: to transmit, integrate, and discriminate information. The main constituents of brains related to these functions are:

1. Individual nerve cells linked at specialized regions called synapses.
2. A second class of cells called **glial cells** (or glia or neuroglia).
3. The space between these cells, called the **extracellular space,** which constitutes 10–15% of the volume of the brain. It contains many ions and large molecules in the extracellular fluid.
4. Fluid compartments, including blood vessels and compartments containing cerebrospinal fluid.
5. Cells of connective tissue origin that form coverings of the brain; these compartmentalize major parts of the brain and provide some attachments to the skull.

Types of Nerve Cells

The variety of cell types in the brain is far greater than in any other organ. At least 200 geometrically distinguishable types of nerve cells are found in the brains of mammals (for examples, see Figure 2-10). Distinctions among these cells are made in terms of size and shape. These differences in size and shape reflect the ways neurons process information. It must be kept in mind that nerve cells are not simple

200 Different Cells in brain

Figure 2-10   Some kinds of nerve cells. (a) Pyramidal cell from cerebral cortex. (From Sholl, 1956) (b) Purkinje cell, cerebellar cortex. (From Zecevic and Rakic, 1976) (c) Basket cell, cerebellar cortex. (From Palay and Chan-Palay, 1974) (d) Multipolar cell from pons. (From Mihailoff, McArdle, and Adams, 1981) (e)–(f) Four of the 21 identified kinds of cells in the hilar region of the hippocampus. (From Amaral, 1978) The beginning of the axon of each cell is indicated by an arrow.

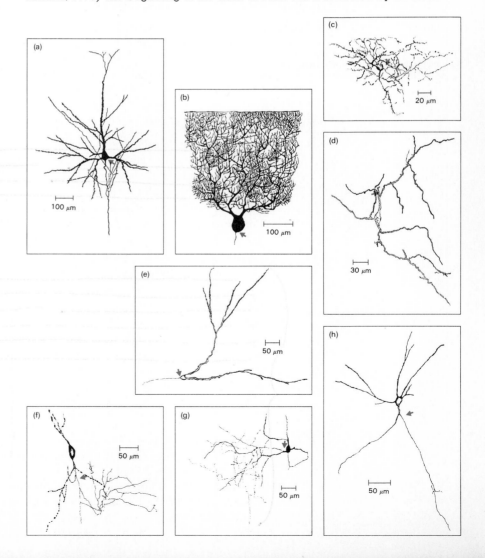

relays that transmit the information they receive. Rather, the typical neuron collects signals from several sources, integrates the information, transforms it, encodes it into complex output signals, and distributes these signals to a large number of other cells. The ways in which information is represented and processed in the nervous system are determined by the transactions of nerve cells and their intrinsic properties as distinctive cells. (We will discuss these processes in detail in Chapters 5 and 6.)

Although this structural diversity vastly complicates our task, there are some simplifications we can use to understand the fundamental structural properties of nerve cells. Many kinds of neurons have three distinct structural zones or parts that are directly related to the functional properties of the cell. These are (1) a **cell body** region, which is defined by the presence of the nucleus, (2) extensions or processes of the cell body called **dendrites** (from the Greek *dendron,* ''tree''), which increase the receptive surface of the neuron, and (3) a single extension, the **axon.** In many neurons the axon is only millimeters in length, but in spinal sensory and motor neurons, it can reach a meter or more. In order for you to wiggle your toes, long axons must carry the instructions from the spinal cord to muscles in your foot. Long fibers of sensory neurons then carry messages back to the spinal cord.

Anatomists use the shapes of cell bodies, dendrites, and axons to classify the many varieties of nerve cells into three principal types: multipolar, bipolar, and monopolar neurons. **Multipolar neurons** are nerve cells with many dendrites and a single axon. Most of the neurons of the vertebrate brain are multipolar (for example, the cell in Figure 2-11d). **Bipolar neurons** are nerve cells with a single dendrite at one end of the cell and a single axon at the other end (Figure 2-11b). This type of nerve cell is found in some vertebrate sensory systems, including the retina and olfactory system. **Monopolar neurons** are nerve cells with a single branch leaving a cell body, which then extends in two directions. One end is the receptive pole, the other the output zone (Figure 2-11c). This is the dominant type of neuron in invertebrate nervous systems. It is also found in the mammalian nervous system.

Another common way of classifying nerve cells is by size. Examples of small nerve cells are the types called **granule** (''grains''), **spindle,** and **stellate** (''star-shaped''). Large cells include the types called **pyramidal, Golgi type I,** and **Purkinje.** Each region in the brain is a collection of both large and small neurons. Vertebrate nerve cell bodies range from as small as 10 μm to as large as 100 μm.

Related to classification by size is the division of neurons into two classes: **projection neurons** and **local-circuit neurons.** We have been discussing mainly neurons that carry messages to widely separated parts of the brain or body; these are called projection neurons, and they tend to be large. Most neurons, however, make all their contacts only with other neurons that are located close by and are within the same function unit; these are local-circuit neurons, and they tend to be small. Within the human retina, for example, there are hundreds of millions of tiny neurons that form local circuits, but only one million retinal ganglion cells carry messages to the brain. Local-circuit neurons are relatively more abundant in more complex animals. For example, in the frog, whose movements are relatively simple and stereotyped, the ratio of local-circuit neurons to projection neurons in the cerebellum is about 20 to 1. In the mouse, which has more complex and elaborate motor patterns, the corresponding ratio is 140 local-circuit neurons for each cerebellar projection cell. In human beings this ratio is 1600 to 1!

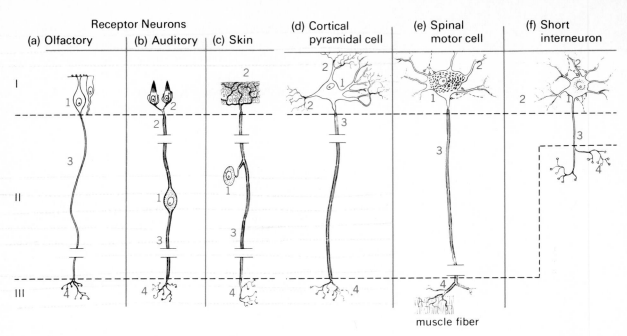

Figure 2-11 Structural and functional parts of neurons.

	Functional	Anatomical
I	Input zone	Dendrites, and sometimes also cell body
II	Conducting zone	Axon, and sometimes also dendrites
III	Output zone	Axon terminals

1	cell body
2	dendrites
3	axon
4	axon terminals

The Cell Body

The nerve cell body contains the nucleus, which includes the genetic instructions and also the plans and controls for all the metabolic activities of the cell. We can get some idea of the complexity of the chemical processes within a nerve cell by knowing that a typical nerve cell contains, among other constituents: millions of protein molecules, billions of lipid molecules, hundreds of billions of RNA molecules, and trillions of potassium ions! The cell body is the synthetic and metabolic center of the nerve cell. Moreover, many of the molecules are metabolized and broken down at a rapid rate, so new molecules must be produced at a rapid rate. The membrane of the cell body has many tiny specialized subregions. Some of these are receptors for hormones; others pass food or waste materials into or out of the cell.

From a functional viewpoint, the cell body and the dendrites are specialized for receiving and integrating information. The axon is specialized for the conduction of information toward other cells.

The Axon

A typical axon has several regions that are structurally and functionally distinguishable (Figure 2-12). In multipolar neurons the axon originates out of the cell body from a cone-shaped region called the **axon hillock.** (Chapter 5 will describe the functional features that distinguish the axon hillock from the main portion of the axon.) The axon beyond this region is tubular in form with a diameter ranging from 0.5 μm to 20 μm in mammals and as large as 500 μm in the "giant" axons of some invertebrates. The length of an axon also varies appreciably, ranging from a few micrometers to a meter or more. With very few exceptions, nerve cells have only one axon. But axons often divide into many branches called collaterals. Because of this extensive branching, a single nerve cell can exert influence over a wide array of other cells. Toward its ending, an axon or collateral typically divides into numerous branches of fine diameter. At the end of the branches, there are some specialized structures forming the synapse, the connection to the next nerve cell. We will discuss the structural properties of the synapse shortly.

Wrapped around most axons are sheaths formed by nonneural accessory cells that lie close to the axon. For many axons, mainly larger diameter ones, these accessory cells come close to the axon and form a regular wrapping around it. This coating around the axon is called **myelin,** and the process of the formation of this wrapping is called **myelinization** (Figure 2-13). This sheathing improves the speed of conduction of neural impulses. Anything that interferes with the myelin sheath can have catastrophic consequences for the individual. This is seen in various demyelinating diseases, such as multiple sclerosis.

Within the brain and spinal cord, the myelin sheath is formed by a kind of glial cell (of which we will be seeing more soon). For axons outside the brain and spinal cord (that is, in peripheral nerves), the accessory cell that forms myelin is called the **Schwann cell.** A single Schwann cell produces the myelin coat for a very limited

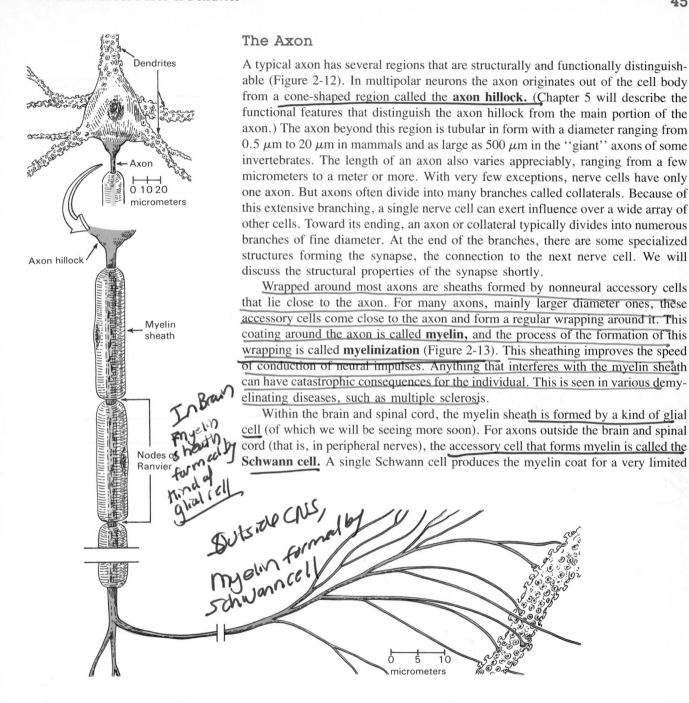

Figure 2-12 A typical myelinated axon. At the upper left, the axon starts at the axon hillock of a cell body. Note that the diameter of the axon is much smaller than the diameter of the dendrites. A short distance after it emerges from the hillock, the axon acquires a myelin sheath. The segments of myelin, shown at the left, are about 1 mm long, and they are interrupted by nodes of Ranvier where the axon is uncovered. Near its termination the axon loses its sheath and divides into many fine branches.

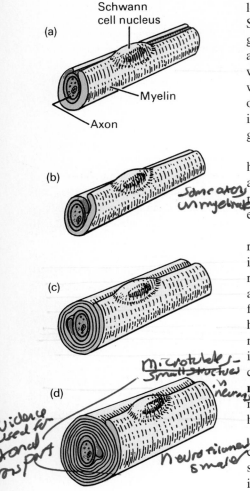

(a)

Schwann
cell nucleus

Myelin

Axon

(b)

*Some axon
unmyelinated*

(c)

*Microtubules —
Small structure
is neuron*

(d)

*Evidence
used for
axonal
transport*

*Neurofilaments —
smaller*

Figure 2-13 Sequence of formation of myelin sheath in the peripheral nervous system by a Schwann cell. The flat Schwann cell surrounds a length of the axon in (a) and then wraps itself several times around the axon (b)–(d). Figure 2-14 is an electron microscopic picture of the final stage.

length of the axon, seldom extending for more than 200 μm. Hence numerous Schwann cells are needed to myelinate the length of a single axon. There are small gaps in the coating provided by successive Schwann cells. Such a gap, where the axon membrane is exposed, is called a **node of Ranvier.** The regularity of the wrapping process is nicely illustrated in cross sections of the axon (cuts across the width) as shown in Figure 2-14. A subsequent section will describe the development of myelin in the brain. Its importance is demonstrated by the fact that myelinization increases over very extended periods of time in human beings, in some brain regions up to 10–15 years.

Many axons do not have a close wrapping of myelin. These axons generally have very fine diameter; they are commonly referred to as **unmyelinated** fibers or axons. Although these fibers do not have an elaborate coating, they do have a relationship with an accessory cell. What happens is that several axons become embedded in troughs of the Schwann cell and no regular wrapping is elaborated.

Many of the materials synthesized in the cell body are transported to distant regions in the dendrites and axons. This transportation of materials within the axon is referred to as **axonal transport** or protoplasmic streaming. Measurements of the rate of flow of substances in axons range from a ''slow'' system (1–3 mm/day) to a ''fast'' system (400 mm/day). Many constituents of the cell have been shown to flow within axons and dendrites. How does anything move in these structures? This has been studied mainly in axons whose length and uniformity (in some types of neurons) facilitate such investigation. Some investigators have observed structures in axons referred to as **microtubules** (20–26 nm in diameter) that look like hollow cylinders (Figure 2-15). There are also systems of smaller diameter (10 nm) called **neurofilaments;** these look like rods. Considerable evidence suggests that these microtubules and neurofilaments are involved in axonal transport, but several other hypotheses are also being investigated (Ochs, 1982; Weiss, 1982).

Experiments using drugs that selectively interfere with the structure of the microtubules give a hint as to how substances flow down an axon. One such substance, colchicine, seems to have the effect of blocking the flow of some materials in the axon while not interfering with its electrical excitability. This kind of evidence suggests that the microtubule system is important for the phenomenon of axoplasmic streaming. Some of the most exciting aspects of contemporary neurobiological research have been concerned with deciphering the molecular machinery of this phenomenon and many other aspects of the molecular properties of individual nerve cells.

Dendrites and Synapses

The diversity of shape of nerve cells arises primarily from the variation in the shape of **dendrites,** the extensions of nerve cells that arise from the cell body and branch out in highly complex ways. The shape of the **dendritic tree**—the full arrangement of a single cell's dendrites—provides clues about a particular cell's information processing. All along the surface of the dendrite there are many contacts, the synapses. In cortical pyramidal cells, dendrites have been found to account for 95% of the cell volume.

Figure 2-14 Electron micrograph of myelinated and unmyelinated axons. In the center of the figure is a cross section of a myelinated axon with highly regular concentric layers of myelin. At lower right are four unmyelinated axons embedded in troughs in a Schwann cell. (From Peters, Palay, and Webster, 1976)

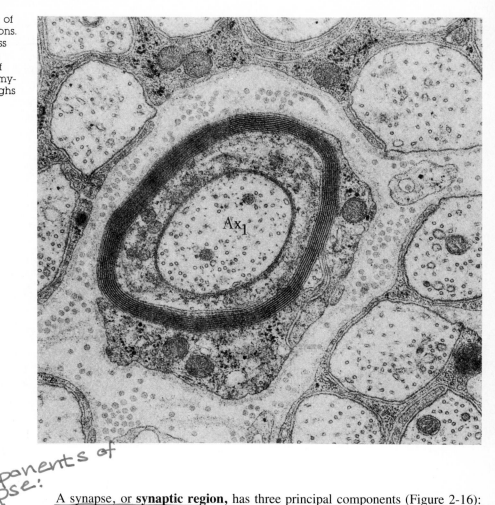

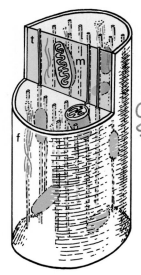

10 micrometers

Figure 2-15 Diagram of an axon to illustrate tubule systems that may be involved in axonal transport: microtubules (t) and neurofilaments (f). A mitochondrion (m) is also shown.

A synapse, or **synaptic region,** has three principal components (Figure 2-16): (1) the presynaptic specialization, in many instances a swelling of the axon terminal called the **synaptic bouton** (button), (2) a specialized postsynaptic membrane in the surface of the dendrite or cell body, and (3) a **synaptic cleft,** that is, a space between the presynaptic and postsynaptic elements. This gap measures about 20–40 nm.

Detailed electron microscopic examination of the presynaptic terminal reveals the presence of many small spherical components called **synaptic vesicles.** They range in size from 30 to 140 nm. There is strong evidence that these vesicles contain a chemical substance that can be released into the synaptic cleft. This release is triggered by electrical activity in the axon. The released substance flows across the cleft and produces changes in the postsynaptic membrane. Such a chemical is called a **synaptic transmitter.** Many different transmitters have been identified in the brain, and other substances are being tested to determine whether they too are synaptic transmitters. The changes in the postsynaptic membrane are the basis of the transmission of excitation or inhibition from one cell to another. The synaptic cleft is filled with a dense material that is different from nonsynaptic extracellular regions. Similarly, the surface of the postsynaptic membrane is different from adjacent regions of the membrane. It contains special receptors that capture and react to molecules of the transmitter agent.

Numerous synapses cover the surfaces of dendrites and of the cell body. Some

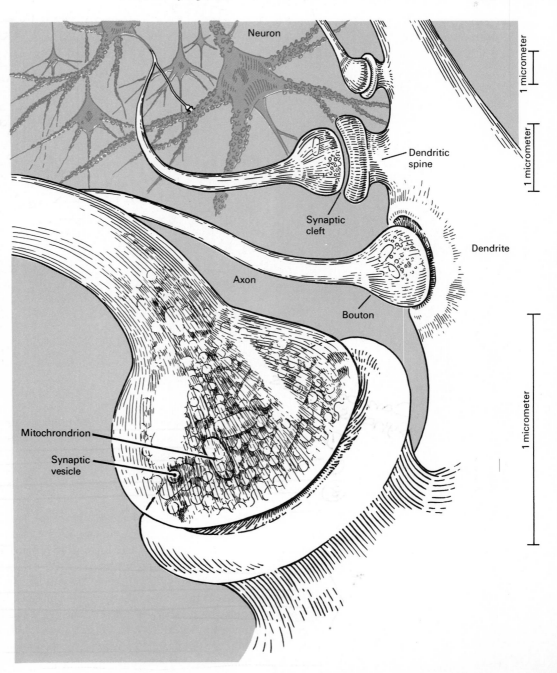

Figure 2-16 Synapses terminating on dendritic spines or on the surface of a dendrite. Note that the scale of magnification changes from near to far.

Figure 2-17 This shows how densely synaptic endings cover the surface of a nerve cell body and the dendrites. A few endings even occur on the initial segment of the axon. (From Poritsky, 1969)

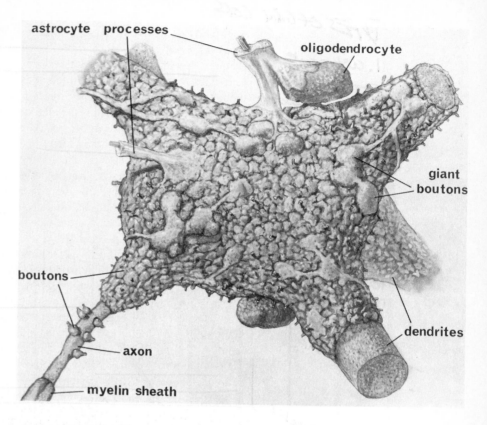

(handwritten note: Commons 5000 - 10,000 synapses. Motoneurons = Contraction of motor neuron)

individual cells of the brain have as many as 100,000 synapses, although the more common number for larger cells is around 5000 to 10,000. Figure 2-17 illustrates the density of the synaptic contacts on the surface of a nerve cell in the spinal cord whose axon goes to muscles. (Such a cell is called a **motoneuron,** a contraction of motor neuron.) Synaptic contacts are particularly numerous in nerve cells with elaborate dendrites.

Along the dendrites on many nerve cells of the brain there are outgrowths called **dendritic spines** or thorns (Figure 2-16). These spines give some dendrites a rough or corrugated surface. They have become the focus of considerable attention, since they seem to be quite variable elements, which may be modified by experience (Chapter 17). Both the size and number of dendritic spines are affected by various treatments of the animal, such as training or exposure to sensory stimuli.

Glial Cells

(handwritten note: most numerous)

In some regions of the primate brain, the cells that are most abundant are not neurons but **glia** or **neuroglia.** Their name is derived from the original conception of their function—that these cells serve as something like glue (in Greek, *glia* means "glue"). Unlike nerve cells, neuroglia can increase in number throughout the life of an animal. Although many aspects of the functional roles of neuroglia remain a puzzle, there are some facts—and many interesting ideas—about their function.

Microscopic observation of glial cells enables us to distinguish several different types (Figure 2-18). One type, called an **astrocyte** (Latin *astra,* "star"), is a star-shaped cell with numerous processes or extensions that run in all directions. Some astrocytes form end feet on the blood vessels of the brain. These end feet look as though they are attached to the vessels by suckerlike processes.

Another type of glial cell is the **oligodendrocyte.** This cell is much smaller than an astrocyte and has fewer processes (Greek *oligo,* "few"). Oligodendrocytes are commonly associated with nerve cell bodies, especially the bodies of larger neurons. Because of this association, they are frequently regarded as satellite cells of neurons (hence their designation as perineuronal satellite cells).

There is a third type of glial cell: the **microglia.** As their name suggests, they are extremely small. Microglia migrate in large numbers to sites of injury in the nervous system. They are apparently activated by disease states to remove cellular debris from injured or dead cells.

The functions of glial cells differ with their appearances (Figure 2-18). Initially glia were presumed to provide structural support for the neural elements within the central nervous system. It was suggested that they occupied spaces among the neurons and their extensions. Clearly structural support—or some aspects of it—is one biological role of glial cells. Extensions of astrocytes form the tough sheets that wrap around the outer surface of the brain, the dura mater. It also appears that bundles of extensions of astrocytes interweave among nerve fibers, as though acting as a structural support. Glial cells may also serve a nutritive role, providing a pathway from the vascular system to the nerve cells, delivering raw materials that nerve cells use to synthesize complex compounds.

The manner in which glial cells surround neurons, especially the synaptic surfaces of neurons, also suggests that one of their roles is to isolate receptive surfaces to prevent interactions among axons in the vicinity of synapses. This indicates that part of the action of glial machinery may be directed toward segregating inputs to nerve cells.

Oligodendroglia produce myelinization of axons in the central nervous system. This process differs from myelinization involving Schwann cells in the periphery as follows: A single oligodendroglial cell may myelinate several segments of the same axon or several different axons, whereas a single Schwann cell myelinates only a single segment of one cell.

Glial cells are of clinical interest because they are the cells that form the principal tumors of the brain and spinal cord. Furthermore, some classes of glia, especially astrocytes, respond to brain injury by changing in size, that is, by swelling. This process is referred to as **edema.** The swelling interferes with the function of neurons and is responsible for many symptoms of brain injuries.

The Evolution of Nerve Cells

Nerve cells share many attributes with other cells in the body but are distinctly different in at least one regard: *Nerve cells have developed the special ability to generate and transmit electrical signals over relatively long distances.* In the evolution of cells, it is the emergence of this property that is of primary significance in understanding the biological origins of the nervous system.

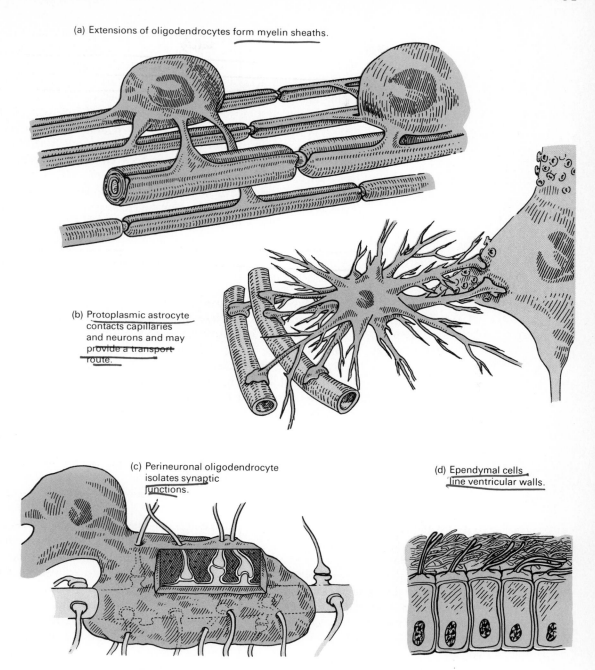

(a) Extensions of oligodendrocytes form myelin sheaths.

(b) Protoplasmic astrocyte contacts capillaries and neurons and may provide a transport route.

(c) Perineuronal oligodendrocyte isolates synaptic junctions.

(d) Ependymal cells line ventricular walls.

Figure 2-18 Some types of glial cells and some of their functions.

One view of the evolutionary development of this attribute suggests that there is a relationship between the appearance of the electrical capabilities of nerve cells and increases in body size of primitive creatures. Originally, cells that made up external, skinlike surfaces of these creatures were quite close to the muscles that moved them. In such primordial creatures, composed of only a few compact groups of cells, communication was readily achieved by the passage of substances across closely abutted membranes. When body size gradually increased over the eons, in response to various evolutionary pressures, nerve cells became an interesting solution to the problem of communication between sensory surfaces and muscles. The emergence of the electrical responsiveness of nerve cells made possible the communication of messages over longer distances. Some support for this picture of the evolution of nerve cells is offered by the fact that skin surfaces and neurons develop from the same layer of embryonic tissue. This view of evolution implies that the shape of a nerve cell is a critical feature, which predicts the functional attributes of a given nerve cell. This is a theme we will return to in several sections of this book.

Levels of Analysis in Anatomical Studies of the Brain

Up to now we have discussed brain architecture at different levels of complexity, ranging from gross structure to single cells. There are many different levels of structural analysis in neuroscience research, some of which we will discuss in subsequent chapters. Figure 2-19 presents portraits of different levels of anatomical analysis of the brain. Each of these levels views brain structure from a different level of detail, somewhat akin to zooming from a wide-angle picture down to an extremely narrow telephoto view. Different levels of structural analysis are appropriate for different physiological and behavioral correlations, as we will see in later discussions.

Summary · Main Points

1. The nervous system reaches all parts of the body because it monitors, regulates, and modulates the activities of all parts and organs of the body.

2. The main divisions of the brain can be seen most clearly in the embryo. These divisions are the forebrain, composed of the telencephalon and diencephalon; the midbrain, or mesencephalon; and the hindbrain, composed of the metencephalon and myelencephalon.

3. New techniques are making it possible to visualize the anatomy of the living human brain and regional metabolic differences using external monitoring devices. These techniques include computerized axial tomographic x-rays (CAT scans), positron emission tomography (PET scans), and magnetic resonance imaging (MRI scans).

4. The typical neuron of most vertebrate species has three main parts: (1) the cell body, which contains the nucleus, (2) dendrites, which extend the receptive surface of the cell body, and (3) an axon, which carries impulses from the neuron. Because of the varieties of functions they serve, nerve cells (or neurons) are extremely varied in size, shape, and chemical activity.

5. Neurons make functional contacts with other neurons, or with muscles or glands, at specialized junctions called synapses. At most synapses a chemical transmitter liberated by the presynaptic terminal diffuses across the synaptic cleft and binds to special receptor molecules in the postsynaptic membrane.

6. The brain is made up of glial cells as well as neurons. There is a variety of glial cells, which serve many functions: they produce myelin sheaths around axons, exchange nutrients and other materials with neurons, and remove cellular debris.

Figure 2-19 The main levels of organization of the brain, ranging from the whole brain at the upper left to synaptic contacts at the lower right. In several cases, a specific example is identified.

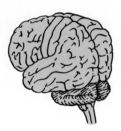

Whole brain

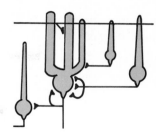

Local circuit (e.g., basic cerebellar circuit)

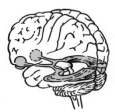

Brain system (e.g., the visual system is shown in brown)

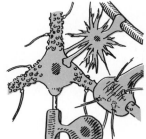

Basic neuroglial compartment

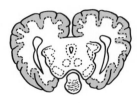

Brain region (e.g., the cerebral cortex is shown in brown)

Nerve cell (e.g., a pyramidal cell)

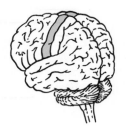

Brain subregion (e.g., the primary motor cortex is shown in brown)

Synaptic assembly

Basic processing unit (e.g., a cerebral cortical column)

Synapse

7. The structure of the brain can be studied at many anatomical levels, from the whole brain to parts of the cells. Each level of analysis can reveal different features of nervous system functioning.

Recommended Reading

Angevine, J., & Cotman, C. W. (1981). *Principles of neuroanatomy*. New York: Oxford University Press.

Gluhbegovic, N., & Williams, T. H. (1980). *The human brain*. New York: Harper & Row.

Nauta, W. J. H., & Feirtag, M. (1986). *Fundamental neuroanatomy*. New York: W. H. Freeman.

Netter, F. (1983). *Nervous system*. (Vol. 1) in the Ciba Collection of Medical Illustrations.

Noback, C. R. (1981). *The human nervous system*. New York: McGraw-Hill.

Peters, A., Palay, S. L., & Webster, H. de F. (1976). *The fine structure of the nervous system*. Philadelphia: Saunders.

Neuroanatomical Reference Section

In this section we present some detailed anatomical information which extends the coverage of this chapter and can serve as a reference for later chapters.

Neuroanatomical Methods

The ability to see and measure nerve cells and trace their connections is vital to solving many problems in physiological psychology and neuroscience. A few of these problems are: How do neurons grow and make connections during individual development? In what ways do the nervous systems of men and women differ? What differences in nerve cells and their connections characterize Alzheimer's disease? What changes occur in nerve cells as a consequence of learning? What changes serve to store memories? What changes in neurons and their connections permit recovery of function after damage to parts of the nervous system?

Improved methods of visualizing nerve cells and tracing their tangled and intricate connections are enabling researchers to make progress on these and many other questions about neural bases of behavior. Why have these neuroanatomical questions posed difficult problems for investigators? If you cut a thin slice of brain tissue and look at it under a microscope, it is hard to see any brain cells; they have very low contrast with surrounding areas such as extracellular space. In order to see details of cells using a light microscope, you have to use special chemical agents to make cells or parts of cells stand out from the background. Tracing pathways in the nervous system is difficult because axons from different sources look alike, and fibers with different destinations often travel together over parts of their routes; thus it is hard to disentangle one set from the rest. Investigators have had to devise ways of marking one set of fibers so that they stand out visually from the rest. In this section we will describe first some of the methods devised to visualize cells in the nervous system and then some methods used to trace pathways in the nervous system.

Visualizing the Fine Structures of the Brain

In order to see the details of cells using the light microscope, you have to use chemical agents to make cells or parts of cells stand out. In the middle of the nineteenth century, dyes used to color fabrics provided the breakthrough. Dead, preserved nerve cells treated with these stains suddenly become vivid, and hidden parts become evident. Dyes produce this effect because different dyes have special affinities for parts of the cell, such as membranes, the nucleus, or the myelin sheath. Optical filters attached to the microscope can increase the clarity.

Some staining methods outline the full cell, including details like dendritic spines. The Golgi method, which is the most common (Reference Figure 2-1a), is often used to characterize the variety of cell types in any region. For reasons that remain a mystery, this technique stains only a small number of cells. As a result, they stand out in dramatic contrast to adjacent unstained cells.

Dyes can also be injected directly into living cells. Another method uses stains to outline the cell body. This Nissl method can be used in such measurements as size of cell body and density of cells in particular regions (Reference Figure 2-1b). Stains of myelin sheaths outline axons. Recent innovations also include techniques that cause certain nerve cells to light up when exposed to ultraviolet light (Reference Figure 2-1c). This happens because nerve cells have particular ingredients that become fluorescent when treated in certain ways. Some antibodies, when attached to membranes of nerve cells, provide a fluorescent surface. Such

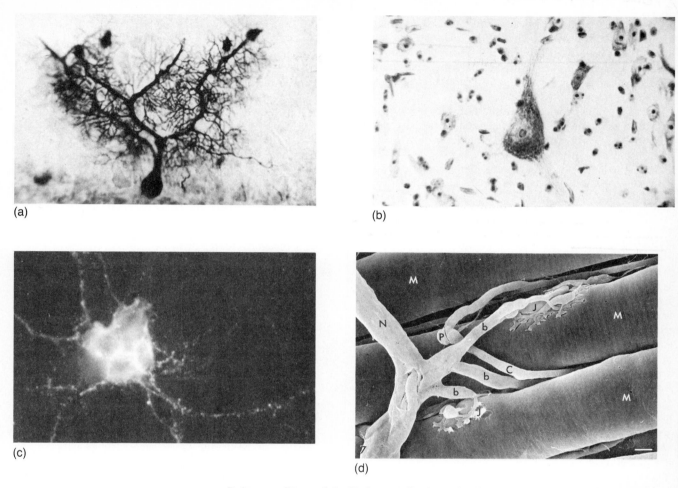

(a)

(b)

(c)

(d)

Reference Figure 2-1   Various methods of visualizing nerve cells. (a) Golgi stain of Purkinje cell (Leiman). (b) Nissl stain of hippocampal neurons (Leiman). (c) Fluorescence picture of sympathetic neurons. (From Marchisio et al., *Journal of Neurocytology*, vol. 10, no. 1: 49 (Figure 3). Reprinted by permission of Chapman and Hall.) (d) Scanning electron micrograph of neuromuscular junction. N is the axon of a neuron, M is muscle, and J neuromuscular junction. (From Desaki and Uehara, *Journal of Neurocytology*, vol. 10, no. 1: 103 (Figure 7).)

techniques from immunology are increasingly being applied to studies of the brain's structure.

Some histological techniques can reveal aspects of the dynamic neurochemistry of nerve cells, particularly the cell's metabolic processes. One of these procedures, **autoradiography,** involves administering a radioactive substance that nerve cells use, such as glucose or amino acids. Experimenters give such a substance to a living animal, then present the animal with a stimulus condition that results in neural activity. This activity produces a need for the radioactive nutrient, which the animal's active brain

cells take up. The experimenters then sacrifice the animal, cut thin sections of brain tissue, and place them on slides, which they then cover with photographic emulsion. Radioactivity emitted by the compounds in the cell causes deposition of silver, just like the effect of light on film. This produces fine dark grains in cell bodies that have taken up the radioactive substance.

Improved methods of viewing tissue have also broadened our understanding of the fine structure of cells. For years light microscopy was all that was available. Observations with light microscopes provide good detailed resolution down to about 2 μm. The

electron microscope

advent of electron microscopy, however, extended the range of resolvable structures a hundredfold. It became possible to see some of the smallest details within cells. Scanning electron microscopy adds a dimension of depth. The synaptic endings and other structures take on a startlingly intimate appearance (Reference Figure 2-1d).

All these forms of microscopic study are now being coupled with computers, providing rapid, automatic, quantitative assessment of aspects of nerve cells, such as dendrite length. In the years ahead, these techniques will increasingly supplement the heretofore intuitive judgments of anatomists.

Another approach to the marking of cells of the brain comes from the application of immunological techniques. These techniques allow neuroanatomists to mark groups of cells that share some common attribute; it is a way of looking simultaneously at a large group of relatives. In the nervous system, a common attribute that groups cells might be similar membrane components or chemicals within a cell. Immunological techniques arise from the fact that highly specific antibodies can be developed that will react to one of the components of the brain. We know that production of an antibody follows exposure to particular substances called **antigens.** Some parts of the brain can be made to act as antigens. For example, researchers can now break down nerve cells into particular fractions that are relatively homogeneous, such as small portions of postsynaptic membranes. When these fractions are injected into host animals, they are responded to as antigens, and the host animal forms new antibodies to the injected material. If these antibodies are removed and injected into another animal, they will react with specific membranes or parts of nerve cells. The places where they react can be seen when the antibody is joined with another marker molecule—usually a substance that becomes fluorescent when exposed to ultraviolet light (Reference Figure 2-2).

Highly purified and specialized antibodies can now be developed using some newer techniques of molecular biology. These substances, called **monoclonal antibodies,** are developed from cell fusion techniques that enable investigators to generate cell lines that produce specialized antibodies. Using this approach, antibodies have been developed that recognize particular nerve cell proteins and can readily separate different classes of cells.

monoclonal antibody

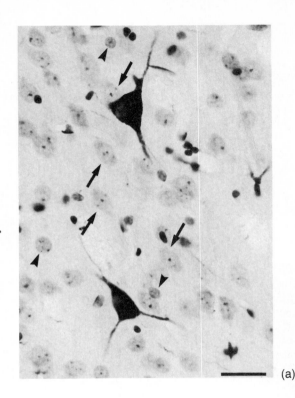

(a)

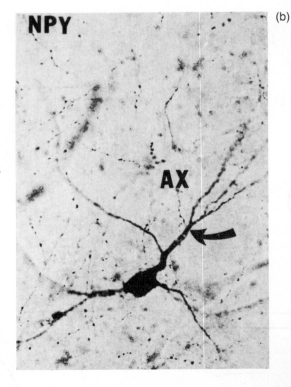

(b)

Reference Figure 2-2 Photomicrographs of nerve cells highlighted by immunocytochemical techniques. These nerve cells became more evident because their surfaces responded to antibodies to choline acetyltransferase. In (a) arrowheads point to dendritic branching. In (b) arrows point to nonsensitive nerve cells and arrowhead points to nonsensitive glial cells. (From (a) Phelps, Houser, and Vaughn, 1985; (b) Chan-Palay, 1985.)

Tracing Pathways in the Brain

The cells of the brain are interconnected through a complex web of pathways. To understand the circuits formed by these cells and their extensions, it was necessary to develop techniques that clearly outlined the terminals of particular cell groups or showed the cells of origin of particular axon tracts. Although at first glance this task seemed insurmountable—remember, our brain contains billions of neurons—anatomists were not daunted. Recently, classical anatomical techniques that rely on visualizing the products of degenerating axons have been coupled with newer microscopic procedures and ways of marking tracts with either radioactive or other chemicals that are taken up in axons and travel the length of an entire cell.

Classical anatomical techniques for tracing pathways usually involve the following procedures: First, the cell bodies of origin are surgically damaged with a restricted lesion—one confined to a small region. The axons of the cells begin to degenerate, and during this phase they are especially sensitive to various silver salts. When the dying axons are exposed to silver compounds, they acquire a dark brown-black color. By examining a series of sections for the presence of such marked axons, it becomes possible to trace a pathway over some distance. Newer procedures that accomplish the same goal involve the injection of radioactive amino acids into a collection of cell bodies. These radioactive molecules are taken up by the cell and transported distally to the tips of the axons. Brain sections are then coated with a sensitive emulsion like a film. After some time (which ranges from hours to weeks), the slides are developed and stained. If the pathway originates in the area of the injected cells, developed silver grains will be located in axons and their terminals.

Another recently devised technique to determine the cells of origin of a particular set of axons employs the substance **horseradish peroxidase** (HRP), an enzyme found in the roots of horseradish and many other plants. It is a type of protein that also contains carbohydrates, and its reaction products can be stained, revealing dark granules. This substance acts as a tracer of pathways because it is taken up into the axon at the terminals and transported back to the cell body. All along the way stainable reaction products are formed—akin to footprints along a pathway. This process is illustrated in Reference Figure 2-3.

Neural Systems

The machinery of the brain can be understood at several levels, ranging from the properties of single cells to the large-scale characteristics of the whole brain. In this section we will consider anatomical data at the level of aggregates of cells that can be described as neural regions or systems. Introducing some of the features of neural systems will be helpful for subsequent discussions of information processing in these regions.

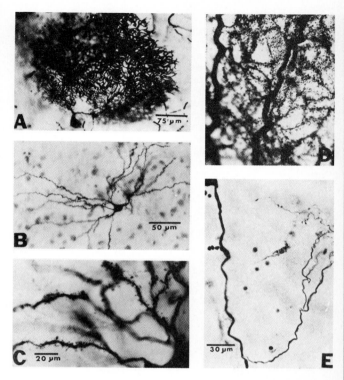

Reference Figure 2-3 Nerve cells stained with horseradish peroxidase (HRP). (Kitai and Bishop, 1981)

The Cerebral Cortex

Neuroscientists have long argued that the understanding of human cognition depends on unraveling the structure and fundamental functions of the cerebral cortex. In fact, we virtually define human life in terms of the workings of the cerebral cortex, since many governments now accept electrical silence of the cerebral cortex as a criterion for defining death. Within this folded sheet, there are about 50 billion to 100 billion neurons—the majority of the neurons in the human brain. If the cerebral cortex were flattened, it would occupy an area of about 2,000 cm^2, or a square about 18 inches on a side (Hubel & Wiesel, 1979). How are these cells arranged? How do the arrangements allow for particular feats of human information processing? In this section we will take an opening look at the architecture of the cerebral cortex. In many other sections of the book, we will be concerned with how cortical circuits are arranged and what goes on in these networks.

The earliest work on the structure of cerebral cortex sought to understand the nature of the cellular ingredients and the character of their arrangements. Are the cells of the cerebral cortex arranged

Reference Figure 2-4 The layers of the cerebral cortex, (a) and (b), and a cortical pyramidal cell (c). Part (a) is stained (Nissl stain) to show cell bodies. Part (b) shows shapes and positions of typical cells, using the Golgi stain. Parts (a) and (b) are enlarged about 60 times. Part (c) shows a pyramidal cell enlarged about 200 times. All of the cell is seen, except that the axon continues off the bottom of the figure. (Parts (a) and (b) from Rakic, 1979; part (c) from Sholl, 1956. Parts (a) and (b) reprinted by permission of MIT Press from *The Neurosciences: Fourth Study Program*, edited by Francis O. Schmitt and Frederic G. Worden, copyright © 1979 by The Massachusetts Institute of Technology.)

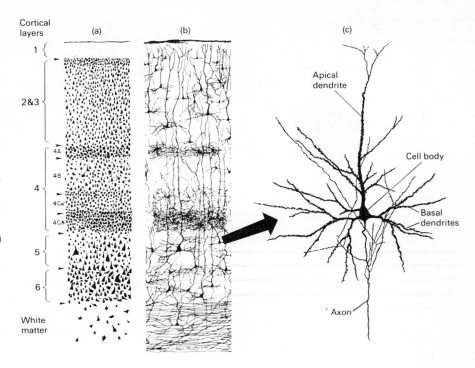

in distinctive geometric patterns? To answer this question anatomists have relied on some of the selective properties of dyes or stains. They used stains that outlined cell bodies and ignored cell extensions (especially axons), or they used stains that emphasized the appearance of axons. To show types of cells, anatomists use a stain developed by Golgi that outlines a few cells in their entirety. Armed with these techniques, they have been able to decipher many of the structural mysteries of the cerebral cortex.

The large number of neurons of the cerebral cortex are arranged in distinct layers; this is described as a laminar form of organization. Cell body and axon stains, such as those illustrated in Reference Figure 2-4, show that the cerebral cortex consists of six distinct layers. Each cortical layer is distinct because it consists of either groups of cells of particular sizes or patterns of dendrites or axons. For example, the outermost layer is distinct because it has few cell bodies, and a deeper layer stands out because of the grouping of neurons with large cell bodies. This laminar arrangement shows some variation across the cerebral cortex, suggesting a division of the cortex into subregions defined in terms of small differences in the aggregation of nerve cells. Reference Figure 2-5 is a map based on several criteria of cell spacing. Divisions based on these structural criteria also seem to define functional zones.

The most prominent kind of neuron in the cerebral cortex—the **pyramidal cell**—usually has its cell bodies in layers 3–5. At the right of Reference Figure 2-4 is an enlargement of a single pyra-

midal cell. One dendrite of each pyramidal cell (called the apical dendrite) usually extends to the outermost surface of the cortex. The pyramidal cell also has several dendrites (called basal dendrites) that spread out horizontally from the cell body. Frequently nerve cells of the cortex appear to be arranged in columns. Nerve cells in a single column tend to have similar functional properties, as we have learned from studies of cortical functions in the analysis of sensory inputs.

The variation in thickness of the different layers of cerebral cortex is related to differences in their functions. Incoming fibers from the thalamus terminate especially in layer 4, so this layer is particularly prominent in regions that represent sensory functions. In fact, in part of the visual cortex in the occipital lobe, layer 4 is so prominent that it appears to the naked eye as a stripe in sections cut through this area. This is why this part of the visual cortex is known as **striate** (striped) **cortex.** Fibers that leave the cerebral cortex arise especially from layer 3, which is particularly prominent in the main motor regions of the cortex. Layer 3 is also characterized by rather large pyramidal cells.

Some brain regions have distinctive geometrical arrangements of cells that can function as information-processing units. In the cortex one can see columns of nerve cells, which run the entire thickness of the cortex from the white matter to the surface (Reference Figure 2-6). In humans they are about 3 mm deep and about 400–1000 micrometers (μm) in diameter. Within such a column,

Reference Figure 2-5 Regions of the cortex as delineated in a classical cytoarchitectonic map by Brodmann (1909).

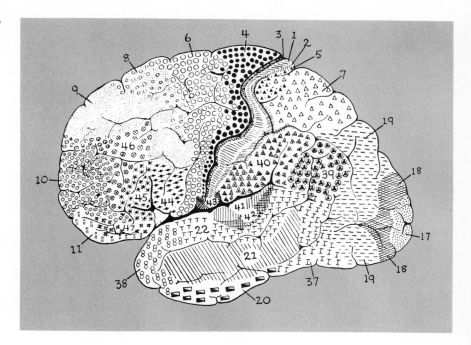

Reference Figure 2-6 Arrangement of neurons in cortical bands in primary visual cortex. (a) Cross section of visual cortex. (b) Surface view of cortical columns. (From Hubel and Wiesel, 1979)

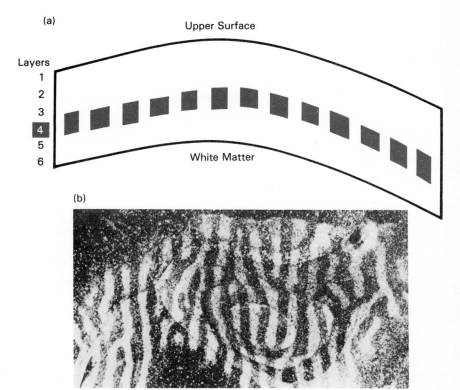

Striate visual cortex

the functional connections among cells (synaptic connections) are mainly in the vertical direction, but there are also some horizontal connections. Mountcastle (1979) calls these units macrocolumns and estimates their number in the human cerebral cortex to be about one million. Macrocolumns are thought to be the functional modules of cortical operations.

The macrocolumns are composed, in turn, of what Mountcastle has called minicolumns. These are vertical columns of neurons. On the average such columns are about 30 μm in diameter in the human cortex, and there are an estimated half billion of them. The number of cells per minicolumn has been counted in five species, from mouse to human, and in several cortical regions (Rockel et al., 1974). Regardless of species and of cortical region, a minicolumn contains about 110 neurons (with a standard deviation of about 10%).

Connections between cortical regions are mainly tracts of axons (Reference Figure 2-7). Some of these connections are short pathways that loop beneath the cortex to nearby cortical regions, while others travel longer distances through the cerebral hemispheres. The largest of these pathways is the corpus callosum, through which run connections between corresponding points on the two hemispheres. Longer links between cortical regions involve multisynaptic chains of neurons that loop through subcortical regions such as thalamus and basal ganglia.

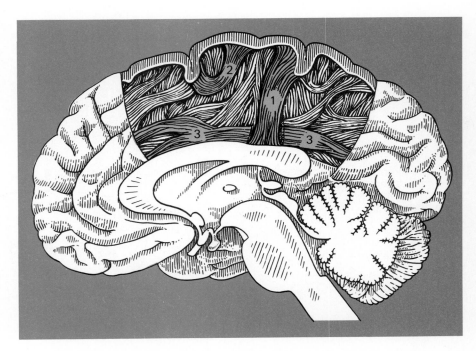

Reference Figure 2-7   Tracts shown in a dissection of a human brain. The right hemisphere is seen from the medial aspect. Part of this hemisphere has been dissected to reveal three kinds of tracts: (1) Long projection fibers running to and from the cerebral cortex. Some of these go through the corpus callosum. (2) Short tracts that arch between nearby parts of the cortex; these are called arcuate fibers. (3) Long tracts that run in an anterior-posterior direction. The long tract shown here is the cingulum (Latin for "belt") which lies just over the corpus callosum near the medial wall of each hemisphere. It has been cut to show the full length of the projection fibers.

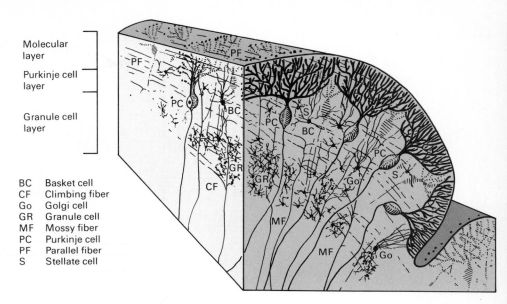

Molecular
layer

Purkinje cell
layer

Granule cell
layer

BC   Basket cell
CF   Climbing fiber
Go   Golgi cell
GR   Granule cell
MF   Mossy fiber
PC   Purkinje cell
PF   Parallel fiber
S   Stellate cell

Reference Figure 2-8   A cross section of a folium of cerebellar cortex showing the main types of neurons.

The Cerebellum

In the back of the head, lodged between the cerebral hemispheres and brain stem, there is another elaborately folded structure that is intimately involved in the control of body movements. It is called the **cerebellum,** the largest part of which is the cerebellar cortex (Reference Figure 2-8). It is so deeply folded that almost 85% is hidden from surface views. The arrangement of nerve cells within this sheet is considerably simpler than that in cerebral cortex. A middle layer is composed of a single file of very large cells called **Purkinje cells,** after the anatomist who first described their wondrously elaborate fan-shaped dendritic pattern. All along the surface of these dendrites are numerous dendritic spines. An outer molecular layer is composed of an orderly array of axons that runs parallel to the surface; hence they are called **parallel fibers.** In the

depths beneath the Purkinje cells is a huge collection of very small cells called **granule cells,** whose axons form the parallel fibers of the surface. The circuitry of this brain region is now known in detail, and its relationship to motor control is described in Chapter 12.

The Limbic System

Deep within the cerebral hemispheres there is a collection of interconnected areas including various subcortical regions that have become known as the **limbic system.** (The term *limbic* reflects the fact that these regions form a border around the core of the brain; the Latin word *limbus* means ''border.'') In early work the relations among these areas were dominated by their links to olfaction. However, much research since the late 1950s has focused on the

Reference Figure 2-9 The main structures of the limbic system.

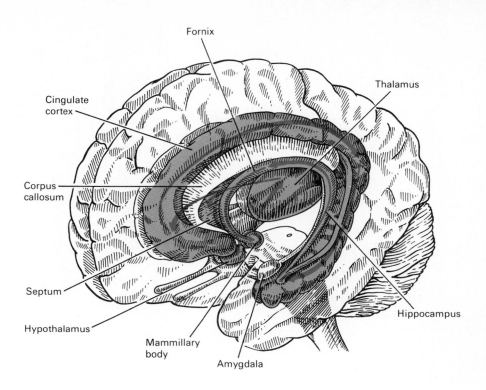

[Handwritten: limbic structure = cingulate cortex, amygdala, hippocampus]

[Handwritten: striate region]

role of these structures in motivation and emotion. Reference Figure 2-9 shows some of the limbic system, including **cingulate cortex, amygdala,** and **hippocampus.** Major tracts connecting these nuclei include the **fornix** and **mammillothalamic tract.** Relations between the limbic system and emotion will be taken up in Chapter 15. The hippocampus and amygdala have also been implicated in learning and memory formation, as will be discussed in Chapter 17.

Basal Ganglia *[Handwritten: Motor control]*

Within the forebrain there are several large nuclei that are involved in motor control. Collectively they are known as the **basal ganglia** (Reference Figure 2-10a and c), including the **caudate nucleus, globus pallidus,** and **putamen.** The **amygdala** is sometimes included among the basal ganglia. Brain stem structures related to the basal ganglia include the **red nucleus** (or nucleus ruber) and **substantia nigra.** (The latter is named for its dark pigmentation.) The fiber band called the **internal capsule** is seen as a light stripe running between the caudate nucleus on its medial side and the

globus pallidus and putamen on its lateral side. Lateral to the putamen is another light-colored band of fibers called the **external capsule.** Because of its striped appearance, this region of the brain is sometimes called the **striate region** (or striatum, or corpus striatum). Together the globus pallidus and putamen form a somewhat lens-shaped body, so anatomists called the combined structures the **lentiform nucleus** (or lenticular nucleus). The structures that make up the basal ganglia are summarized in Reference Table 2-1. Several motor impairments in humans arise from injuries or degenerative diseases in this system. Chapter 10 describes some of the functional properties of the basal ganglia in motor organization and accomplishments. Diseases in basal ganglia have also been connected to some unusual psychiatric disorders (Chapter 15).

Diencephalon

Reference Figures 2-10b and d show the position of the **diencephalon.** The largest portion of the diencephalon consists of the **thalamus**—paired egg-shaped arrangements of cells continuous with the brain stem. (The term *thalamus* comes from a Greek word

Reference Table 2-1

Structures of the Basal Ganglia

Basal ganglia
   Caudate nucleus
   Lenticular nucleus
      Putamen
      Globus pallidus
   Amygdala
   External and internal capsules
Related structures
   Red nucleus
   Substantia nigra

meaning ''room'' or ''bridal chamber'' and was assigned because the two halves of the thalamus surround the third ventricle.) It contains several distinct groupings of nerve cells that are especially important as the distributors of afferent inputs to the cerebral cortex. These cells are also significant relays in various motor control pathways. Just below the thalamus there is a small region with a powerful influence on behavior called the **hypothalamus.** The different nuclei in this structure play important roles in control of metabolic activity, endocrine glands, emotion, circadian rhythms, sleep, and temperature regulation, among other basic physiological regulatory systems.

Fluid Environments of the Brain

The brain is more than a large assembly of nerve cells arranged in clever networks! In fact, it is filled with fluids. Some of these, such as the elaborate network of vessels carrying blood, are obviously part of the metabolic support system. In addition, there are large compartments of fluid that give the brain buoyancy without which the movements of the head would send soft brain tissue careening against the skull.

The Ventricular System of the Brain

Inside the brain are cavities filled with a clear, colorless fluid (Figure 2-4). This fluid (formerly known as ''animal spirits'') is called **cerebrospinal fluid.** It has two main functions:

1. The fluid that fills the space between the brain and the inside of the skull acts mechanically as a shock absorber for the brain. The brain floats in cerebrospinal fluid as the head moves.
2. Cerebrospinal fluid also mediates between blood vessels and brain tissue in exchange of materials.

Each hemisphere of the brain contains a complexly shaped lateral ventricle. The third ventricle lies on the midline, surrounded by the two halves of the thalamus. The cerebrospinal fluid is formed in the lateral ventricles. It flows through the third ventricle and down a narrow passage to the fourth ventricle, which lies anterior to the cerebellum. A little below the cerebellum is a small aperture, through which cerebrospinal fluid leaves the ventricular system to circulate over the outer surface of the brain and spinal cord.

Circulation of Blood in the Brain

Because the brain works intensely, it has a strong metabolic demand for its fuels, oxygen and glucose. Since the brain has very little reserve of either, it depends critically on its blood supply to bring these fuels. Blood is delivered to the brain via two main channels, the carotid and the vertebral arteries (Reference Figure 2-11, page 66).

The **common carotid arteries** ascend the left and right sides of the neck. The **internal carotid artery** enters the skull and branches into anterior and middle cerebral arteries (Reference Figure 2-11), which supply blood to large regions of the cerebral hemispheres. The **vertebral arteries** ascend along the bony vertebrae and enter the base of the skull. They join together to form the **basilar artery,** which runs along the ventral surface of the brain stem. Branches of the basilar artery supply blood to the brain stem and to posterior portions of the cerebral hemispheres. At the base of the brain, the carotid and basilar arteries join to form a structure called the **circle of Willis.** This joining of vascular paths may provide some needed ''backup'' if any of the main arteries to the brain should be damaged or blocked by disease.

The actual delivery of nutrients and other substances to brain cells and the removal of waste products take place at very fine capillaries that branch off from small arteries. This exchange in the brain is quite different from exchanges between blood vessels and cells in other body organs. We speak of the **blood-brain barrier** because many substances move from the capillaries into the brain cells with greater difficulty than they move from capillaries into the cells of other organs. The brain is thus protected from exposure to some substances found in the blood. This barrier to passage occurs because the cells that make up the walls of capillaries in the brain (**endothelial cells**) fit together very tightly, so they do not readily let large molecules through. In the hypothalamus, however, the blood-brain barrier is relatively weak. This feature may be what enables the hypothalamus to sense and react to circulating substances.

(a) Basal Ganglia

Caudate nucleus

Lentiform nucleus:
(putamen and
globus pallidus)

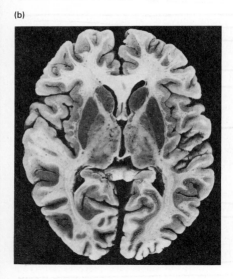

Reference Figure 2-10 The main structures of the basal ganglia and diencephalon shown in brain phantoms (a, d), horizontal sections (b, c), and coronal sections (e, f). ((Photos b & e) Rijksuniversiteit Utrecht, Onderwijs Media Instituut.)

(b)

(c)

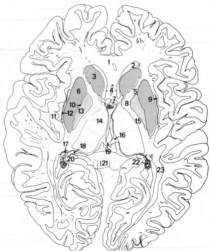

1. Genu of corpus callosum.
2. Frontal horn of lateral ventricle.
3. Head of caudate nucleus.
4. Septum pellucidum.
5. Anterior limb of internal capsule.
6. Putamen.
7. Column of fornix.
8. Genu of internal capsule.
9. External capsule.
10. Lateral medullary lamina.
11. Cortex of insula.
12. Claustrum.

13. Globus pallidus.
14. Thalamus.
15. Posterior limb of internal capsule.
16. Habenular nucleus.
17. Tail of caudate nucleus.
18. Fimbria of hippocampus.
19. Habenular commissure.
20. Hippocampus.
21. Splenium of corpus callosum.
22. Choroid plexus in temporal horn of lateral ventricle.
23. Retrolenticular part of internal capsule.

(d) Diencephalon

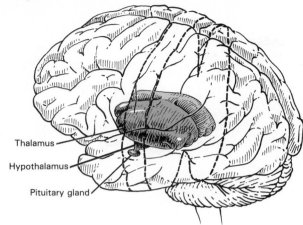

Thalamus

Hypothalamus

Pituitary gland

1. Body of corpus callosum.
2. Body of caudate nucleus.
3. Central part of lateral ventricle.
4. Septum pellucidum.
5. Choroid plexus of lateral ventricle.
6. Columns of fornix.
7. Anterior thalamic nuclear group.
8. External capsule.
9. Lateral thalamic nuclear group.
10. Medial thalamic nucleus.
11. Putamen.
12. Lateral medullary lamina.
13. Internal capsule.
14. Reticular thalamic nuclei.
15. Interthalamic adhesion.
16. Lateral part of globus pallidus.
17. Medial medullary lamina.
18. Mamillothalamic fascicle.
19. H_1 field of Forel.
20. Zona incerta.
21. H_2 field of Forel.
22. Claustrum.
23. Medial part of globus pallidus.
24. 3rd ventricle.
25. Hypothalamic nucleus.
26. Optic tract.
27. Amygdaloid nuclear complex.
28. Mamillary body.
29. Basis pedunculi.

(e)

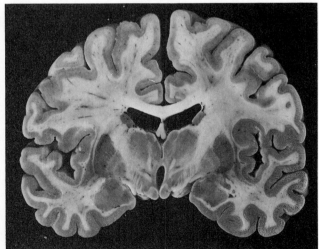

(f)

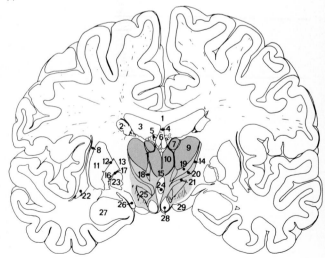

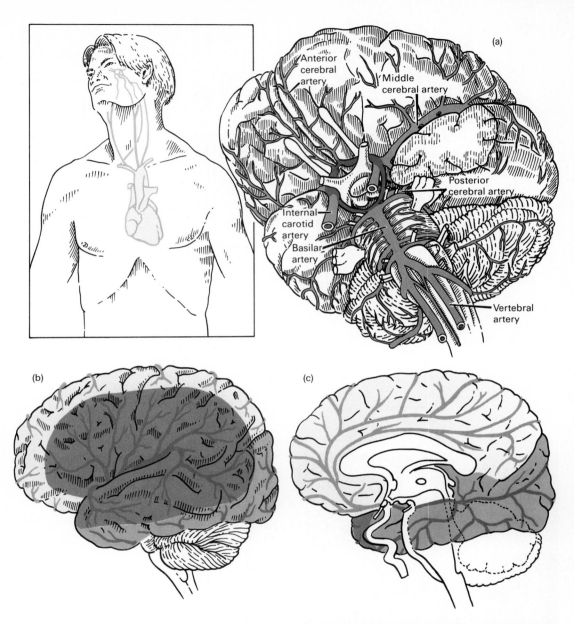

Reference Figure 2-11 The blood supply of the human brain. The orientation of the brain in (a) is shown by the figure at the upper left. Part (a) shows the principal arteries. The basilar and internal carotid arteries form a circle at the base of the brain known as the circle of Willis (shown in dark brown). Different regions of the cerebral cortex are supplied by the anterior, middle, and posterior cerebral arteries. This is shown in (b) for the lateral surface of the brain and in (c) for the medial surface. The field of the branches of the anterior artery is shown in light brown; the field of the branches of the middle cerebral artery is shown in dark brown, and the field of branches of the posterior cerebral arteries is shown in an intermediate shade of brown.

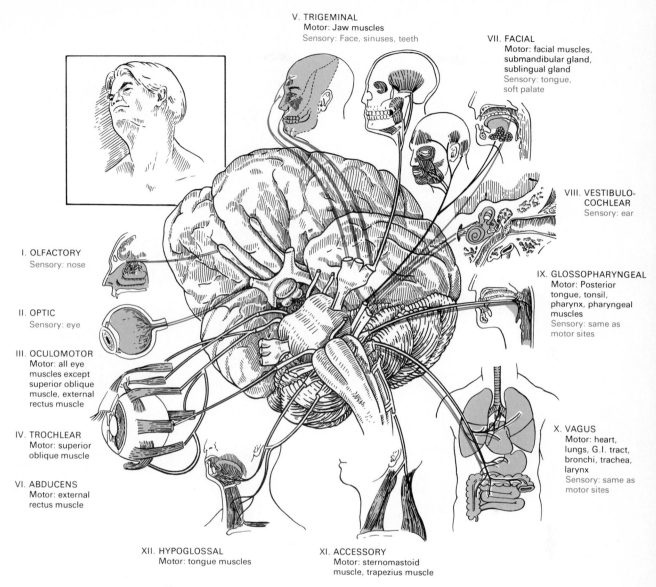

V. TRIGEMINAL
Motor: Jaw muscles
Sensory: Face, sinuses, teeth

VII. FACIAL
Motor: facial muscles,
submandibular gland,
sublingual gland
Sensory: tongue,
soft palate

VIII. VESTIBULO-
COCHLEAR
Sensory: ear

I. OLFACTORY
Sensory: nose

II. OPTIC
Sensory: eye

III. OCULOMOTOR
Motor: all eye
muscles except
superior oblique
muscle, external
rectus muscle

IV. TROCHLEAR
Motor: superior
oblique muscle

VI. ABDUCENS
Motor: external
rectus muscle

IX. GLOSSOPHARYNGEAL
Motor: Posterior
tongue, tonsil,
pharynx, pharyngeal
muscles
Sensory: same as
motor sites

X. VAGUS
Motor: heart,
lungs, G.I. tract,
bronchi, trachea,
larynx
Sensory: same as
motor sites

XII. HYPOGLOSSAL
Motor: tongue muscles

XI. ACCESSORY
Motor: sternomastoid
muscle, trapezius muscle

Reference Figure 2-12 The cranial nerves. The main functions of each of the 12 pairs of cranial nerves are shown.

Peripheral Nervous System

The brain and spinal cord are linked to sensory organs, muscles, and glands via the pathways that compose the **peripheral nervous system.** There are three main sets of pathways in this system: **cranial nerves** (connected directly to the brain), **spinal nerves** (connected at regular intervals to the spinal cord), and **autonomic ganglia** (including the two chains of sympathetic ganglia and the

more peripheral parasympathetic ganglia). Let us look in more detail at each of these three.

Cranial Nerves

The 12 pairs of cranial nerves in the human brain are mainly concerned with sensory and motor systems associated with the head (Reference Figure 2-12). Some cranial nerves are exclusively sensory pathways to the brain, for example, the olfactory, optic, and

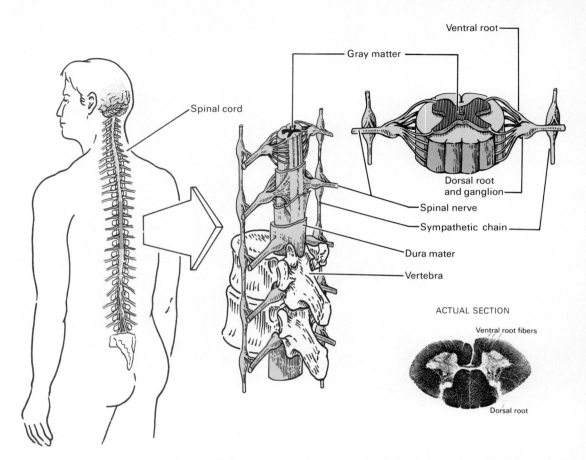

Reference Figure 2-13 The spinal cord and spinal nerves. The diagram to the left shows a general view of the spinal column with a pair of nerves emerging from each level. The diagram in the center shows how the spinal cord is surrounded by bony vertebrae and enclosed in a membrane, the dura mater. Each vertebra has an opening on each side through which the spinal nerves pass. The diagram at the upper right shows the location of spinal cord gray matter and the white matter that surrounds it. In the gray matter are interneurons and the motoneurons that send axons to the muscles. The white matter consists of myelinated axons that run up and down the spinal column. The photograph at the lower right shows an actual cross section of the cord; it comes from the cervical (neck) region. The stain used on this section turns the fatty sheaths of the axons dark, so the white matter looks dark in this presentation. (Photograph from *Structure of the Human Brain: A Photographic Atlas, Second Edition,* by Stephen DeArmond, Madeleine Fusco, and Maynard Dewey. Copyright © 1976 by Oxford University Press, Inc. Reprinted by permission.)

Functions
1) sensory 2) motor 3) mixed

auditory nerves. Others are exclusively motor pathways from the brain, for example, oculomotor nerves (to eye muscles) and facial nerves (to face muscles). The remaining cranial nerves have mixed sensory and motor functions. The trigeminal, for example, serves facial sensation and controls chewing movements. All these nerves pass through small openings in the skull to enter or leave the brain. The vagus nerve is one cranial nerve that extends far from the head. It runs to the heart and intestines. Its long and involved route is the reason for its name, which is Latin for "wandering."

Spinal Nerves

Along the length of the spinal cord there are 31 pairs of spinal nerves, with one member of each pair for each side of the body (Reference Figure 2-13). These nerves join the spinal cord at regu-

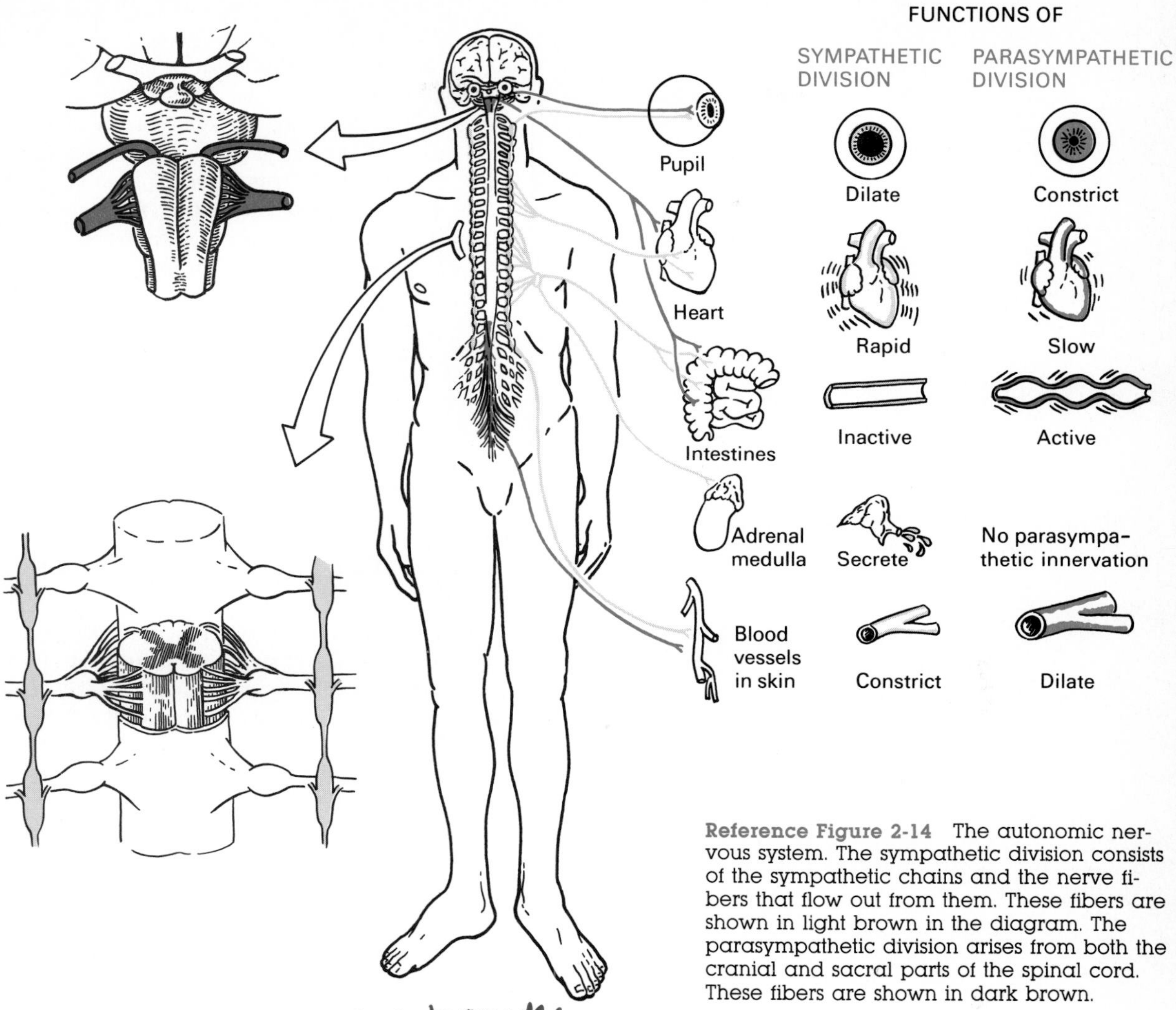

FUNCTIONS OF

SYMPATHETIC DIVISION	PARASYMPATHETIC DIVISION
Pupil	
Dilate	Constrict
Heart	
Rapid	Slow
Intestines	
Inactive	Active
Adrenal medulla	
Secrete	No parasympathetic innervation
Blood vessels in skin	
Constrict	Dilate

Reference Figure 2-14 The autonomic nervous system. The sympathetic division consists of the sympathetic chains and the nerve fibers that flow out from them. These fibers are shown in light brown in the diagram. The parasympathetic division arises from both the cranial and sacral parts of the spinal cord. These fibers are shown in dark brown.

[handwritten: Fusion of 2 distinct branches 2 roots]

larly spaced intervals through openings in the bony structures of the spinal column. Each spinal nerve consists of the fusion of two distinct branches, called **roots.** These are functionally different. The **dorsal** ("back") **root** of each spinal nerve consists of sensory pathways to the spinal cord. The **ventral** ("front") **root** consists of motor pathways from the spinal cord to the muscles.

The name of a spinal nerve is the same as the segment of spinal cord to which it is connected: **cervical** ("neck"), **thoracic** ("trunk"), **lumbar** ("small of the back"), or **sacral** ("bottom of the spinal column"). Thus the T12 spinal nerve is the spinal nerve that is connected to the twelfth segment of the thoracic portion of the spinal cord. Fibers from different spinal nerves join to form peripheral nerve segments, usually at some distance from the spinal cord.

Autonomic Nervous System

[handwritten: Sympathetic & parasympathetic]

The sympathetic chains form part of the **autonomic nervous system** (Reference Figure 2-14). This system controls smooth muscles in organs and in the walls of blood vessels. Therefore one of its vital functions is shifting blood from one part of the body to another to adjust for different activities.

Besides the sympathetic chains, the other main part of the autonomic system is the **parasympathetic division.** This gets its name (*para,* "around") because its outflow from the spinal cord occurs both above and below the sympathetic connections. As Reference Figure 2-14 shows, the parasympathetic division arises from both the cranial and the sacral parts of the spinal cord. For many bodily functions, the sympathetic and parasympathetic divisions act in opposite directions, and the result is very accurate control. For example, the rate of heartbeat is quickened by the activity of sympathetic nerves during exercise. The heartbeat is slowed by the vagus nerve (part of the parasympathetic system) during rest. In the case of the pupil of the eye, sympathetic nerves cause the muscles of the iris to contract in dim light so that the pupil enlarges, whereas in bright sunlight parasympathetic nerves relax the muscles and narrow the pupil.

Most of the time both divisions of the autonomic system are active, with a carefully modulated balance between the two. We can generalize by saying that the sympathetic division predominates during muscular activity and aids the expenditure of energy. On the other hand, the parasympathetic division predominates during building up of bodily resources and helps the body to conserve energy. The autonomic nervous system got its name during the last century, when people supposed that it acted independently of the rest of the nervous system. Now the autonomic system is known to be under the control of brain centers. Its activities have been found to be carefully monitored and closely integrated with ongoing bodily events.

Human Brain Photographs with Detailed Labeling

Figures 2-5a, b, and c are photographs of the human brain with a minimum of labeling of structures. In Reference Figures 2-15, 16, and 17, the same photographs are presented along with diagrams that permit detailed labeling of structures and regions.

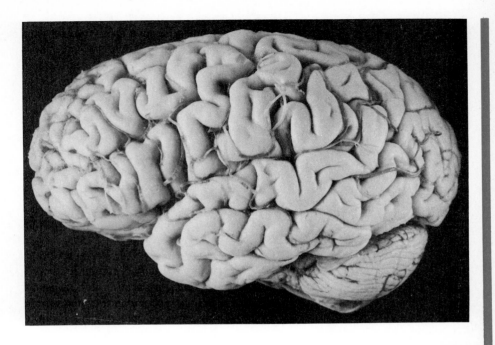

Reference Figure 2-15   Lateral view of the human brain showing the extent of each of the four lobes. (Photo from Rijksuniversiteit Utrecht, Onderwijs Media Instituut.)

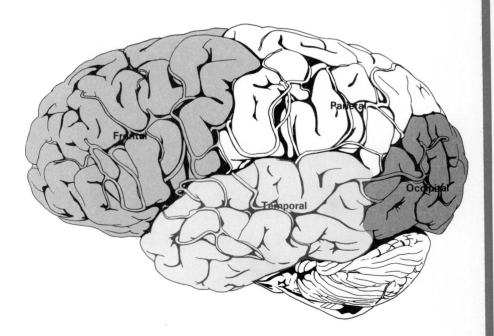

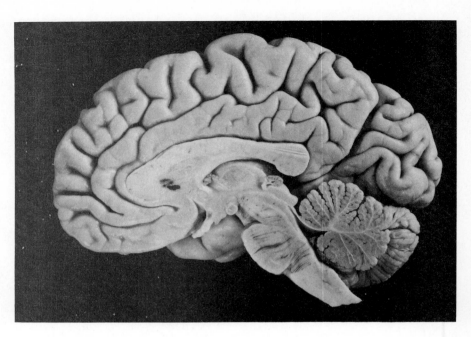

Reference Figure 2-16 Medial saggital view of the human brain. Regions and structures are identified in the figure. (Photo from Rijksuniversiteit Utrecht, Onderwijs Media Instituut.)

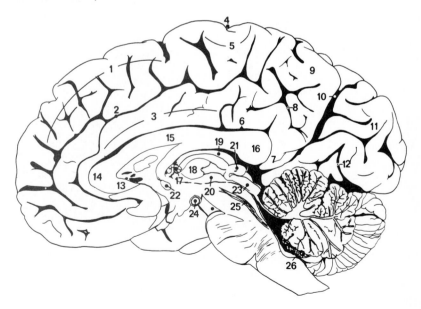

1. Medial frontal gyrus.
2. Cingulate sulcus.
3. Cingulate gyrus.
4. Central sulcus.
5. Paracentral lobule.
6. Callosal sulcus.
7. Isthmus of cingulate gyrus.
8. Subparietal sulcus.
9. Precuneus.
10. Parieto-occipital sulcus.
11. Cuneus.
12. Calcarine sulcus.
13. Rostrum of corpus callosum.
14. Genu of corpus callosum.
15. Trunk of corpus callosum.
16. Splenium of corpus callosum.
17. Choroid plexus in interventricular foramen.
18. Interthalamic adhesion.
19. Habenular trigone.
20. Hypothalamic sulcus.
21. Pineal body.
22. Anterior (rostral) commissure.
23. Tectum of midbrain.
24. Mammillary body.
25. Medial longitudinal fascicle.
26. Choroid plexus of 4th ventricle.

Reference Figure 2-17 Basal view of the human brain. Regions and structures are identified in the figure. (Photo from Rijksuniversiteit Utrecht, Onderwijs Media Instituut.)

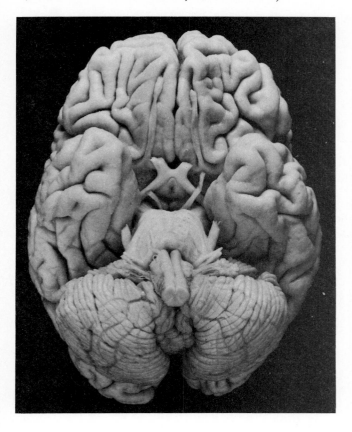

1. Frontal pole of left cerebral hemisphere.
2. Olfactory bulb.
3. Olfactory tract.
4. Orbital sulci and gyri.
5. Straight gyrus.
6. Temporal pole of left cerebral hemisphere.
7. Olfactory trigone.
8. Optic nerve.
9. Optic chiasma.
10. Anterior (rostral) perforated substance.
11. Optic tract.
12. Tuber cinereum with infundibulum.
13. Oculomotor nerve.
14. Mammillary body.
15. Uncus of parahippocampal gyrus.

16. Basis pedunculi.
17. Basilar sulcus of pons.
18. Trigeminal nerve.
19. Abducens nerve.
20. Pyramid of medulla oblongata.
21. Facial nerve.
22. Vestibulocochlear nerve.
23. Glossopharyngeal nerve.
24. Vagus nerve.
25. Cranial roots of accessory nerve.
26. Spinal roots of accessory nerve.
27. Rootlets of hypoglossal nerve.
28. Flocculus.
29. Ventral rootlets of 1st cervical spinal nerve.
30. Pyramidal decussation.

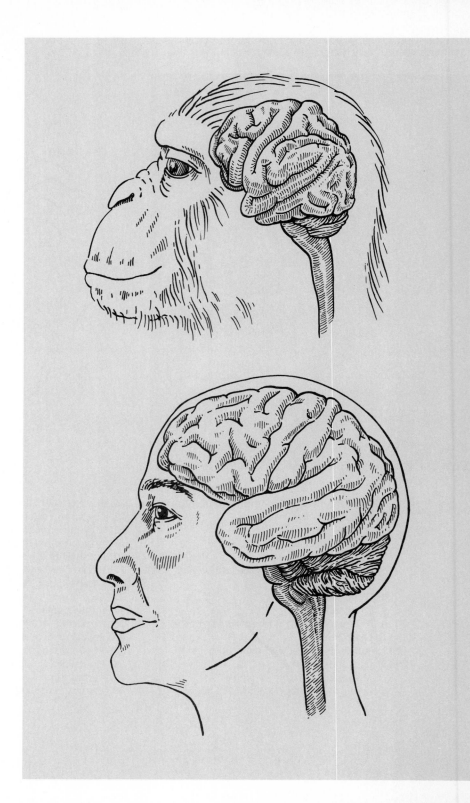

3 Comparative and Evolutionary Perspectives on the Nervous System

ORIENTATION

The efforts of people to understand themselves have invariably led to inquiries about other animals as well. After all, we share many biological and behavioral features with all animals, and so it is not surprising that the search for understanding ourselves leads us to apes, monkeys, carnivores, rodents, birds, and amphibia (Figure 3-1). Their brains are all built on the same basic plan as ours, although there are some ways in which theirs are simpler and some ways in which theirs differ distinctively from ours. The quest to understand the nervous system has also led to the study of animals that are quite different from us—invertebrates and even single-celled animals. But it would be a tall order to describe the nervous systems of all the different creatures in this world. By some estimates the insects alone—buzzing, crawling, and flying about us—account for over one million species. Obviously the task of describing, cataloging, and understanding the relationships between the nervous system and behavior in even a small fraction of earth's inhabitants would be awesome (and dull) unless we had some rationale beyond mere completeness.

One traditional reason for interest in such an undertaking is human centered, based on the question, "Why does the human being end up on top of the animal order?" This human-centered perspective has often been criticized because of the implicit picture of other animals as "little humans," a view that few modern scientists see as a valid basis for comparison. A more contemporary concern with human lineage considers comparative studies as part of a story of evolutionary history—the phylogeny of humans. Trends and comparisons among extant animals coupled with fragmentary but illuminating data from fossil remains yield some ideas about the millions of years of history of the human brain—the forces that shaped it.

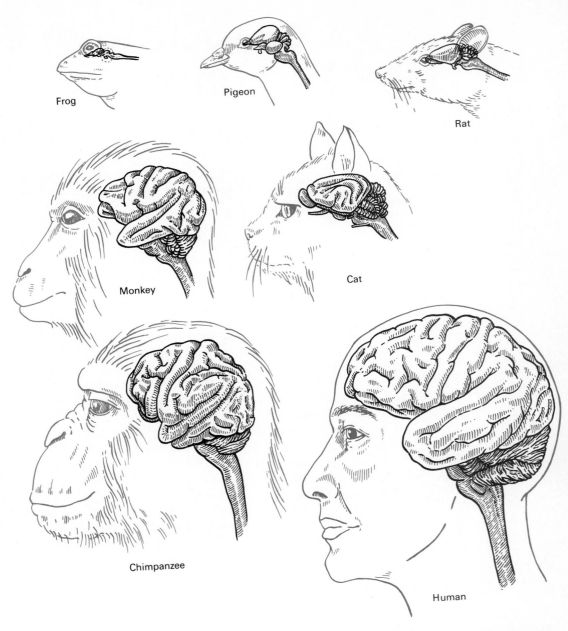

Figure 3-1 Comparison of the sizes and shapes of the brains of several representative vertebrates, all drawn approximately four-tenths life size. The figure shows both relatedness and diversity among extant vertebrates but is not meant to imply evolutionary development of the human brain.

Of course, no current animal is simply sitting around providing researchers with the details of human biological history; rather, each species is busily engaged in satisfying the requisites of survival, which must include an active interchange with its environment. Different animals with varying biological histories show different solutions to the dilemmas of adaptation. In many cases it can be shown that adaptations to particular ecological niches are related to differences in brain structure. Understanding the neural structures and mechanisms mediating specific behaviors in various animals can provide both a perspective and clues about the neural bases of human behavior. For example, some simple animals show changes in behavior that arise from experience. Understanding the changes in the nervous system of these simpler creatures that permit memory formation and storage is likely to provide insight into the workings of more complex animals, including human beings.

Animals Without Nervous Systems

Some creatures exist solely as single cells, enclosed by one continuous membrane. Of course, any single-celled animal has the machinery for elaborate biological processes, such as the transport of substances across its membrane. Membranes of such organisms also contain specialized receptive regions that recognize particular chemicals. Animals without nervous systems also include some multicellular creatures, sponges, for example, which are differentiated in form and function but do not have a rapid communication system, such as that provided by a nervous system. But even animals without nervous systems show distinctive behaviors, including orientation to particular stimuli, and some researchers have argued that these animals might be the simplest organisms to use in exploring such complex functions as information processing, memory, and movements. Some examples of this approach, using two types of unicellular organisms, bacteria and protozoa, are presented in the following section.

Bacteria

Swimming and tumbling describe not only the behavior of athletes but that of bacteria. Although many of us have come to regard bacteria with disdain and fear, over the years researchers developed many of the basic ideas of biochemical genetics using these cells. Now neuroscientists exploring molecular mechanisms of behavior have studied various responses in bacteria. Gravitational, chemical, and thermal stimuli elicit predictable response patterns in bacteria. For example, bacteria move into and around a capillary tube that contains an attractant sugar.

A leading researcher in this field, Daniel Koshland, wrote a book called *Bacterial Chemotaxis as a Behavioral System* (1980), which describes both bacterial response patterns and the nature of receptor processes that underlie these behaviors. His studies indicate that bacterial cells have specialized receptors that detect differences among a wide range of external conditions, such as chemical concentrations and temperature. Receptors sensitive to these stimuli are located within the membrane that encloses this organism. Through a series of chemical steps, these receptor mechanisms activate a simple motor apparatus that produces prolonged periods of swimming and tumbling. In any collection of bacteria, there are some cells that are more or less responsive to particular stimuli. Strains developed from subpopulations permit a closer scrutiny of genetic mechanisms that control receptor activities. Further, particularly interesting to biological psychologists is the finding that bacteria possess a memory system that stores information about prior chemical exposure for a brief period. The similarities and differences between information processing in nerve cells and in bacteria may provide a way to understand some of the basic features of membrane events in the nervous system.

Protozoa

Some of the simplest creatures to have inhabited the laboratories of neuroscientists are unicellular animals—Protozoa. Most of these creatures are but mere flecks a few hundredths or tenths of a millimeter in length. Actually, although Protozoa are described as single cells, their cytoplasm contains well-defined specialized structures. Unlike bacteria, these animals have distinct cellular structures such as a nucleus, a digestive system, and a motor apparatus. In fact, electrical responses recorded from these cells have properties very similar to those of nerve cells.

One type of Protozoan—*Paramecia*—has been studied in behavioral research. Paramecia move about by the coordinated beating of cilia. These threadlike extensions are quite versatile: Changes in direction of movement can be accomplished by shifts in cilia orientation. The form of locomotion and its direction can be observed as a paramecium responds to such environmental stimuli as specific chemicals. These animals are not all peas from the same pod. In fact, genetics studies show that it is possible to develop strains that are distinctive in their patterns of movement (Kung, 1979). Explorations of the molecular basis of these strain differences in locomotor behavior may provide valuable information about the ways genetic information controls the relevant cell structures and processes. Such knowledge might be useful in guiding studies on the genetic influences on nervous system organization and function in more complex animals.

Invertebrates

Most of the animals on earth are invertebrates, animals without backbones. In fact, this group far exceeds vertebrates in many ways, including number, diversity of appearance, and variety of habitat. Their abundance is clearly demonstrated by the following estimate: For each human on earth, there are at least one billion insects, just one type of invertebrate. Neuroscientists have especially focused on the use of invertebrates because of the relative simplicity of their nervous systems and the great varieties of behavioral adaptation they display. Simplicity of structure has not precluded some forms of behavior, such as forms of learning and memory, that are readily seen in more complex creatures. Furthermore, invertebrates possess elaborate sensory systems that permit detection of some stimuli with exquisite sensitivity. Every conceivable niche on land, sea, or air has been successfully exploited by one or more invertebrate species. A leading researcher in the area of comparative neurosciences, T. H. Bullock, recently asserted that "we cannot expect truly to comprehend either ourselves or how the nervous system works until we gain insight into this range of nervous systems, from nerve nets and simple ganglia in sea anemones and flatworms to the optic lobes of dragon flies, octopuses, and lizards to the cerebral cortex in primates" (Bullock, 1984, p. 473).

His message has been well heeded by investigators of the neural mechanisms of behavior. Faced with the enormous complexity of the vertebrate brain with its billions of nerve cells, researchers have explored the nervous systems of some invertebrates that have only hundreds or thousands of neurons. The dream of providing an exhaustive description of the ''wiring diagram'' of the nervous system and how it relates to behavior seems attainable with these creatures. Complex aspects of behavior, such as memory and species-typical appetitive or agonistic behaviors, have been explored in an exciting manner in several invertebrates that have become laboratory favorites. The structures of the nervous systems of some representative invertebrates will be discussed in this section.

Coelenterates: The Simplest Nervous Systems

Anyone who has walked along an ocean beach has seen ''blobs'' that look like floating saucers. These are jellyfish, a type of coelenterate. Other animals in this phylum become especially apparent at low tide, for example, the colorful sea anemones that seem to pose as flowers. Coelenterates are the simplest multicelled animals that possess a nervous system.

Within this group there is some diversity in the character of the nervous system. Sea anemones have a nervous system that consists of nerve cells scattered through the body tissue in a seemingly random and diffuse network. This kind of organization does not involve connections to a centrally placed structure such as a brain.

In contrast to this form of nervous system organization, some other coelenterates have an organization of nerve cells aggregated in clumps of cells that are considered to be primitive ganglia. In these animals, sensors and effectors are distributed in distinct, regular groups around the body surface. For example, jellyfish have four tentacles, and nerve cells related to these structures are concentrated in distinct bundles at the base of each tentacle; all are connected in a ring around the body of the animal (Mackie, 1980). Cells within this ring generate regularly repeated nerve cell activity that provides the basis for swimming rhythms. It is clear that even with the simplest of nervous systems it is possible to observe complex forms of information processing.

Flatworms: Planaria

Planaria are traditional inhabitants of many biological laboratories, and they also were briefly popular in experimental studies of learning in the 1960s. Some researchers found that this animal could acquire classically conditioned responses and some forms of discrimination learning. *Planaria* added a special twist to studies of learning because they could regenerate an entire body from fragments of the original organism. More intrigue was added to the story by the demonstration that the animal that regenerates a head end from a tail section could display some memory established in the whole animal. Sensational claims then emerged that a naive planarian could acquire specific knowledge by eating a trained planarian. This gave rise to the hope that memory-encoding molecules could be isolated and studied. Although a few investigators reported reliable transfer of information by cannibalism, most were unable to replicate the alleged effects, so the topic dropped out of consideration.

Even without this claim to fame, planaria are especially important in comparative neuroanatomy because they appear to be the first animals in evolutionary history to have a nervous system that consists of a distinct brain at the head end. Present-day flatworms thus seem to be the most primitive extant animals that have a brain. The structure of this brain is different from those of other invertebrates described later. The nerve cells are multipolar and scattered thoughout the brain (Koopowitz & Keenan, 1982). A ladderlike chain of axons connects the brain to other body parts along the length of the animal. Small collections of nerve cells in the periphery control local reflexes. The role of the brain in peripheral control is shown in studies of Koopowitz and Keenan (1982). In a marine planarian, they showed that an animal that had not eaten recently will grasp food and pass it to the region of the mouth. However, if the brain is disconnected from the rest of the body, the animal will continue to bring food to the mouth although the gut is completely filled with food.

Annelids: Leeches and Earthworms

The common earthworm and leeches, especially medicinal leeches, bring a particular sophistication to the structure of wormlike creatures. The bodies of these animals are arranged in distinct segments, each controlled by local collections of nerve cells arranged in elaborate ganglia. For example, the central nervous system of the medicinal leech includes a chain of 21 ganglia linked at one end to a head ganglion and connected at the other end to a tail ganglion (Figure 3-2). Each ganglion innervates the adjacent part of the body via two bundles of axons. Ganglia along the length of the leech are connected by bundles of axons. In each ganglion, nerve cells are arranged around the outer surface, and the core of the ganglion, called the neuropil, consists of a dense intermixing of the extensions of these monopolar nerve cells.

A major innovation seen in the annelid nervous system has attracted the attention of neuroscientists. In some types of annelids, a large-diameter nerve fiber extends along virtually its entire length—a giant fiber that seems quite important in the mediation of escape behaviors. In addition, the medicinal leech has two very large nerve cells (called the colossal cells of Retzius) with cell bodies large enough to be readily seen with low-power magnification. These cells are identified by such inspection and are members of a class of nerve cells in invertebrates that have become known as identifiable cells—those that are similar in form and position in all members of a species.

Molluscs: Aplysia

Slugs, snails, clams, and octopuses are a few of the almost 100,000 species of mollusc. These are soft-bodied animals that display an enormous range of both bodily and behavioral complexity. Some molluscs, such as the octopus, show extraordinary problem-solving capabilities, while still other molluscs exist in a near parasitic form. The head end of molluscs usually consists of a mouth, tentacles, and eyes. The typical structure also includes a footlike appendage and a visceral section that is frequently covered by a protective envelope called the mantle. A very simple marine mollusc, *Aplysia,* has gained considerable notoriety because of its successful use in cellular studies of learning, which we describe in some detail in Chapters 16 and 17. In this section we will briefly review the principal structures of the nervous system of *Aplysia*.

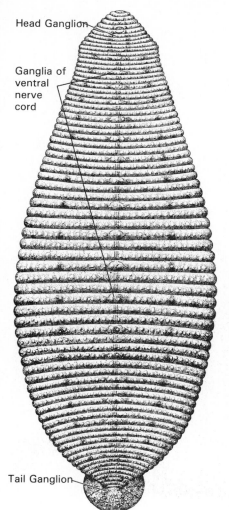

Head Ganglion

Ganglia of
ventral
nerve
cord

Tail Ganglion

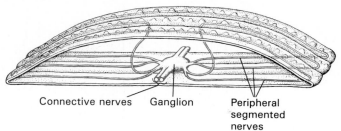

Connective nerves   Ganglion   Peripheral
segmented
nerves

Figure 3-2   The nervous system of the leech. This figure shows a chain of ganglia linked at one end to a head ganglion and at the other end to a tail ganglion. (Adapted from Steut and Weisblat, 1982)

The nervous system of *Aplysia* consists of a set of four paired ganglia at the head end that forms a ring around the esophagus (Figure 3-3a). Below these ganglia there is a single abdominal ganglion. The various ganglia are interconnected by tracts. One of the head ganglia—the cerebral—innervates the eyes and the tentacles; a second head ganglion—the buccal—innervates mouth musculature. The other two paired ganglia innervate the foot. The abdominal ganglion controls such major visceral functions as circulation, respiration, and reproduction. Comprehensive research by Kandel and his collaborators over the past twenty years has led to detailed maps of identifiable cells in these ganglia, especially the abdominal ganglion. Since the nervous system of *Aplysia* includes many identifiable cells (Figure 3-3b), it has become possible to trace definitive circuits mediating various behaviors in this animal (Kandel, 1976). Work with *Aplysia* has also provided some of the most detailed understanding of the molecular basis of learning that is currently available (Kandel et al., 1986). It has given strong support for the view that simpler invertebrate nervous systems can provide good models for examining complex features of nervous system operations, such as information storage.

Arthropods: Insects

Insects, with over one million species, have no rival in the animal kingdom for color, architecture, and variety of habitats. The life cycle of many insects provides an example of striking morphological changes that not only affect the skeleton of the animal but also involve a resculpturing of the nervous system. The sense organs of insects also display great variety and sensitivity. Success in the battle for survival has left many distinctive marks in this group of animals, and it is easy to appreciate why neuroscientists have focused much research on the neural mechanisms of the behavior of insects.

The gross outline of the adult insect nervous system consists of a brain in the head end and ganglia in each body segment behind the head. Bundles of axons interconnect ganglia and the brain. The number of ganglia varies; in some insects all of the ganglia of the chest and abdomen fuse into one major collection of cells. In other insects there are as many as eight ganglia in a chain. The brain itself contains three major compartments: the protocerebrum, deutocerebrum, and tritocerebrum

Figure 3-3 Identified nerve cells in a ganglion of an invertebrate, the sea hare *Aplysia*. (a) Dorsal view of *Aplysia* with the positions of the ganglia indicated in brown. (b) Dorsal view of the abdominal ganglion with several identified neurons labeled. Neurons included in the circuit for habituation are labeled in brown. (c) Ventral view of abdominal ganglion with several identified neurons labeled. ((a) Adapted from *Cellular basis of behavior: An introduction to behavioral neurobiology* by Eric R. Kandel. W. H. Freeman and Company. Copyright © 1976. (b) and (c) from Frazier et al., 1967, and Koester and Kandel, unpublished.)

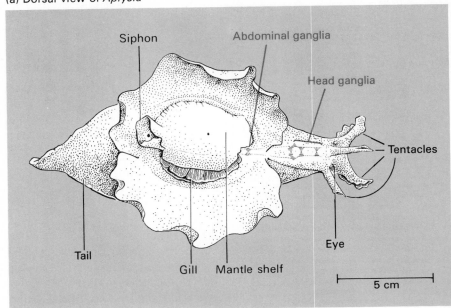

(a) Dorsal view of *Aplysia*

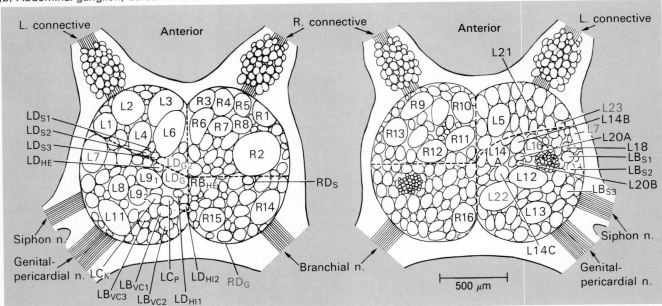

(b) Abdominal ganglion, dorsal surface

(c) Abdominal ganglion, ventral surface

(Figure 3-4). The most complex part of the insect brain is the protocerebrum, which consists of a right and left lobe, each continuous with a large optic lobe, an extension of the compound eye. Within the optic lobe there are distinct masses of cells that receive input from the eye as well as from the brain. Electrical stimulation of various sites within the protocerebrum of various insects elicits complex behaviors.

Figure 3-4 The nervous system of a typical insect. The brain, with subdivisions called protocerebrum, deutocerebrum, and tritocerebrum, is linked via bundles of axons (connectives) to a group of ganglia in the thorax and abdomen.

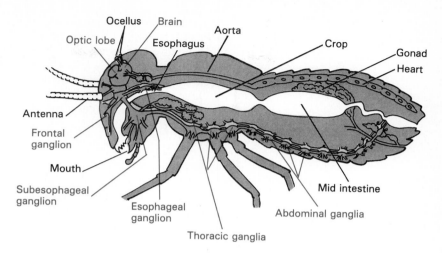

The relative sizes of different components of the protocerebrum differ among insects, and some of these variations may be particularly relevant to behavioral variations. For example, a portion of the protocerebrum called the corpus pedunculatum is especially well developed in social insects; the behavior of these animals tends to be more elaborate than that displayed by solitary insects. The deutocerebrum contains the nerves leading from the antennae, and the tritocerebrum is a small part of the insect brain beneath the deutocerebrum from which run the connectives to the nerve cord.

One prominent feature of the nerve cord of insects is giant fibers—axons that are much bigger than the majority. The properties of these giant fibers have been explored in some interesting studies using cockroaches. In these insects, receptive cells in the tail that can be excited by wind connect with giant interneurons with very large axons that ascend the nerve cord to the head. Along the way they excite some motoneurons. Studies by Camhi (1984) have shown that these giant fibers are very important in the mediation of rapid escape movements.

Some Main Features of Invertebrate Nervous Systems

Although there are more than one million species of invertebrates and biologists have studied but a small fraction of this collection, it is possible to present some tentative generalizations about the main features of invertebrate nervous systems. Except for the first two points, these features are not true of the vertebrate nervous system.

1. The overwhelming number of invertebrates have a basic plan that consists of a central nervous system and a peripheral nervous system.
2. More complex invertebrates have a ''brain,'' and comparisons of species at different levels of evolutionary development reveal that more highly evolved invertebrates show increasing brain control over ganglia at lower levels.
3. In the simpler invertebrates, the most common type of nerve cell is the monopolar neuron.
4. Wherever ganglia are formed in the invertebrate nervous system, they have a characteristic structure: an outer rind that consists of monopolar cell bodies

and an inner core that consists of the extensions of the cell bodies forming a dense neuropil.

5. Many invertebrate ganglia typically include some large identifiable neurons.
6. Large axons in many invertebrate nervous systems are commonly found as elements in rapid escape circuitry.
7. Large-scale changes in the structures of the nervous system frequently occur among invertebrates during metamorphosis.
8. In many invertebrates the nervous system is built around the gastric tract.

Vertebrate Brains

The animal world includes 10,000 to 20,000 vertebrate species. Anatomists have examined the brains of many classes of these animals, and it is apparent that vertebrates with larger bodies tend to possess larger brains. No matter what the size of the brain, however, all vertebrates have brains with the same major subdivisions. The main differences among vertebrates occur in terms of both the absolute and the relative sizes of different regions.

A comparison of the human and rat brains illustrates basic similarities and differences (Figure 3-5). You can see that each of the labeled structures in the human brain has its counterpart in the rat brain. This comparison could be extended to much greater detail, down to nuclei and fiber tracts. Even small structures in the brains of one species are found to have their exact correspondences in the brains of other species. The types of neurons are also similar throughout the mammals. So is the organization of the cerebellar cortex and the cerebral cortex.

The differences between the brains of humans and of other mammals are mainly quantitative; that is, they concern both actual and relative sizes of the whole brain, brain regions, and brain cells. The brain of an adult human being weighs about 1400 grams (g), whereas that of an adult rat weighs a little less than 2 g. In each case the brain represents about 2% of total body weight. The cerebral hemispheres occupy a much greater proportion of the brain in the human than in the rat. Because the human cerebral cortex is so large, it develops gyri and fissures so that a great deal of cortical surface can surround the rest of the brain. The rat cerebral cortex, on the other hand, is smooth and unfissured. The rat has, relatively, much larger olfactory bulbs than the human. This difference is probably related to the rat's much greater use of the sense of smell. The size of neurons also differs significantly between human and rat. In the case of large neurons in the motor cortex, the difference in volume between human and rat is about 30 to 1. With respect to the large Purkinje cells in the cerebellar cortex, the difference is about 4 to 1. In addition, there are great differences in the extents of dendritic trees in humans and in rats. A recent study by Purves and Lichtman (1985) showed that the dendritic arbors of the neurons of a sympathetic nervous system ganglion vary according to body size in comparisons of different species. Smaller animals have cells with less extensive dendrites, perhaps as a result of innervation by fewer neurons than those of large animals.

Behavioral adaptations of species have been related in some cases to differences in relative sizes of brain structures. To give one example, some species of bat find their way and locate prey by audition; other species of bat rely almost entirely on vision. In the midbrain the auditory center (the inferior colliculus) is much larger in bats that depend on hearing, whereas bats that depend on sight have a larger visual center (the superior colliculus).

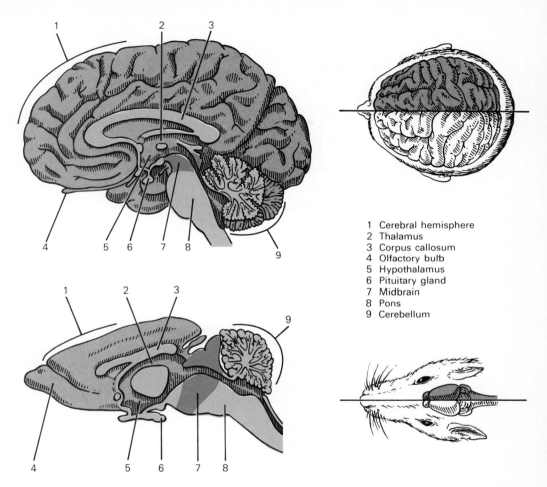

Figure 3-5 Comparisons of human and rat brain structures in mid-sagittal views of the right hemisphere. The rat brain has been enlarged about six times in linear dimensions in relation to the human brain. Note that the cerebral hemispheres are relatively much larger in the human brain, whereas the rat has the relatively larger midbrain and olfactory bulbs.

1 Cerebral hemisphere
2 Thalamus
3 Corpus callosum
4 Olfactory bulb
5 Hypothalamus
6 Pituitary gland
7 Midbrain
8 Pons
9 Cerebellum

Findings from comparative research provide important perspectives for understanding the relationships between brain and behavior in humans. We will discuss these findings at several points in later chapters, for example, in connection with sensory processes and perception, with motivation, and with learning and memory.

Most comparative biological research today is concerned with differences in the animal world, which reflect the long evolutionary struggles for adaptation. Different animals with varying biological histories show different solutions to the dilemmas of adaptation. Instead of worrying about the alleged evolutionary supremacy of our species, those who are studying comparative anatomy and behavior are trying to figure out how behavioral differences or specializations are related to bodily differences. Figure 3-6 provides examples. It shows that adaptations to particular ecological niches are related to differences in brain structure. As a general rule, the relative

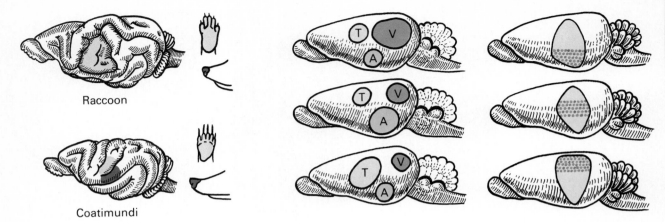

Raccoon

Coatimundi

Figure 3-6 Diversity of organization of cerebral cortex in relation to differences in behavioral functions. The left column shows the brains of the North American raccoon and its Central American relative, the coatimundi. The coatimundi uses olfaction as much as touch. The raccoon cortex contains a large area representing the forepaw but a tiny olfactory area, whereas in the coatimundi cortex, olfaction has as large a representation as does the forepaw. The middle column shows schematically the differential sizes of cortical representations in animals that emphasize vision (top), audition (middle), and touch (bottom). Note also that in the midbrain the superior colliculus (midbrain visual center) is large in the visual animal, while the inferior colliculus (midbrain audition center) is large in the animal that relies on hearing; such a difference is observed in bats that use mainly vision versus bats that use mainly audition. The right column illustrates the different expansion of the tactile area according to whether an animal feels chiefly with its mouth and snout (top), its hands (middle), or its tail (bottom).

size of a region is a good guide to the importance of the function of that region for the adaptations of the species. In this sense "more is better," but even small brain size is compatible with some complex behavior (Mann, Towe & Glickman, 1988). Our understanding of how these differences in size and structure of the brain promote behavioral specializations should help us understand the neural basis of human behavior. For example, the size of some regions in the human temporal lobes seems to be related to language function, as Chapter 18 will show.

Evolution of Vertebrate Brains

During the course of evolution, the characteristics of the nervous system have changed progressively. One especially prominent feature during the last hundred million years has been a general tendency for the brain size of vertebrates to increase, and the brains of our human ancestors have shown a particularly striking increase in size over the last 2 million years. How, then, has the evolution of the brain been related to changes in behavioral capacity?

It would help us learn about the evolution of the brain if we could study the brains of fossil animals. But brains themselves do not fossilize, unfortunately. Two methods of analysis have proved helpful. One is to use the cranial cavity of a fossil skull to make a cast of the brain that once occupied that space. These casts (called **endocasts**) give a good indication of the size and shape of the brain.

The other method is to study present-day animals, choosing species that show

Figure 3-7 Broad outlines of the historical record of the vertebrates. For each vertebrate class, the width of the pathway is proportional to the known number of species in each of the geological periods. (Adapted from G. G. Simpson, *The meaning of evolution, second edition* (New Haven: Yale University Press, 1967).)

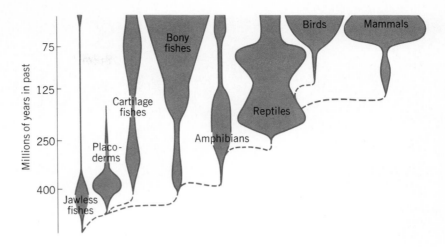

various degrees of similarity to (or difference from) ancestral forms. Although no modern animal is an ancestor of any other living form, it is clear that some present species resemble ancestral forms more closely than others do. For example, present-day frogs are much more similar to vertebrates of 300 million years ago than are any mammals (see the historical record of the vertebrates in Figure 3-7). Among the mammals some species, such as the opossum, resemble fossil mammals of 50 million years ago more than do other species, such as the dog. Anatomists who study the brains of living species can obtain far more detailed information from them than from endocasts, because they can investigate the internal structure of the brain: its nuclei, fiber tracts, and the circuitry formed by connections of its neurons.

But care must be taken not to interpret the evolutionary record as if it were a linear sequence. Note that the main classes of vertebrates in Figure 3-7 represent different lines or radiations of evolution that have been proceeding separately for at least 100 million years. Thus a particular evolutionary development may not have been available to mammals even if it occurred before the first mammals appeared. For example, among the sharks (which belong to the cartilage fishes in Figure 3-7), some advanced forms long ago evolved much larger brains than primitive sharks. But this cannot account for the large brains of mammals. The line of descent that eventually led to mammals had separated from that of the sharks before the large shark brains evolved.

Different evolutionary lines have independently discovered many tricks for survival. To establish the fact that a characteristic was probably inherited from a common ancestor, one must show that it is held in common by most members of the classes that derived from that ancestor. Few species of each class have yet been studied in detail, so conclusions must still be regarded as tentative, although some are worth considering. (Northcutt, 1981).

Changes in Vertebrate Brains Through Evolution

Recent research shows that even the most primitive living vertebrate, the lamprey (a kind of jawless fish), has a more complex brain than it used to be given credit for. The lamprey not only has the basic neural chassis of spinal cord, hindbrain, and

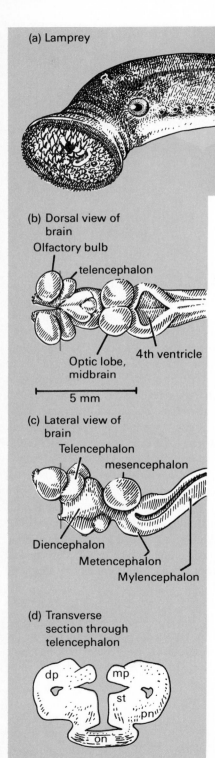

(a) Lamprey

10 cm

(b) Dorsal view of brain

Olfactory bulb

telencephalon

4th ventricle

Optic lobe, midbrain

5 mm

(c) Lateral view of brain

Telencephalon

mesencephalon

Diencephalon

Metencephalon

Mylencephalon

(d) Transverse section through telencephalon

dp

mp

st

pn

on

midbrain, but it also has a diencephalon and telencephalon (Figure 3-8). Its telencephalon has cerebral hemispheres and other subdivisions that are also found in the mammalian brain. All the brain regions mentioned here occur in the brains of all vertebrates.

The differences among the brains of vertebrate species lie not in the existence of basic subdivisions but in their relative size and elaboration. At what stages of vertebrate evolution do various regions of the brain first became important? The lamprey has large paired optic lobes in the midbrain, which probably represent the lamprey's highest level of visual integration. In the frog, too, the relatively large optic tectum in the midbrain is the main center for vision in the brain. In birds and mammals complex visual perception requires an enlarged telencephalon.

Reptiles were the first vertebrates to exhibit relatively large cerebral hemispheres. Reptiles were also the first vertebrates to have a cerebral cortex, but their cortex does not show layers, as the cortex of mammals does. Part of the cortex in reptiles appears to be homologous to the hippocampus in mammals. The hippocampus in mammals is called **paleocortex** (from the Greek root *paleo,* meaning "old") because this cortex is old in an evolutionary sense.

Primitive mammals, such as the opossum, have a relatively large amount of paleocortex and of related structures grouped under the name of the **limbic system.** This system is named after a Greek term for "border" or "periphery" because the limbic system forms a border around the underlying brain structures. (We will take up the limbic system in Chapter 15 in connection with emotion and motivation, and in Chapters 16 and 17 in connection with learning and memory.)

All mammals have a six-layered **neocortex.** In more advanced mammals the neocortex accounts for more than half the volume of the brain. In many primates,

Figure 3-8   (a) A lamprey, the most primitive living vertebrate. The lampreys belong to the order of jawless fish. The location of the brain and spinal cord are shown in blue. (b) Dorsal view of lamprey brain. The brain shows all of the main divisions found in brains of more advanced vertebrates. (c) Lateral view of lamprey brain. (d) Transverse section through lamprey telencephalon. The main part of the telencephalon, the pallium, is not separated into cortex and white matter, and the hemispheres are not joined by a corpus callosum. (dp = dorsal pallium, mp = medial pallium, on = optic nerve, pn = preoptic nucleus, and st = striatum)

such as the great apes and humans, the neocortex is deeply fissured, so that a large cortical surface covers the brain. In the more advanced mammals, the cortex is what is mainly responsible for many complex functions, such as perception of objects. Regions of the brain that were responsible for perceptual functions in less highly evolved animals—such as the midbrain optic lobes (in the lamprey) or the midbrain optic center (in the frog)—have in the modern mammal become visual reflex centers or way stations in the projection pathway to the cortex. (We will take up the neocortex in several chapters in connection with not only perception but also complex cognitive functions.)

Evolution of Brain Size

It is often said that the brain increased in size with the appearance of each succeeding vertebrate class shown in Figure 3-7. But this is a questionable generalization. For one thing, there are exceptions among the present-day representatives of the various classes—birds appeared later than mammals but do not have larger brains. For another thing, the generalization arose from the old way of viewing vertebrate evolution as being one linear series of increasing complexity rather than as a series of successive radiations.

Actually there is considerable variation in brain size within each line of evolution if we compare animals of similar body size. For example, within the ancient class of jawless fish, the hagfish, considered to be the advanced members of that class, possess forebrains four times as large as those of lampreys of comparable body size. The increase of brain size in relation to behavioral capacity has been studied most thoroughly in the mammalian line.

Study of brain size is complicated, however, by the wide range of body sizes. You would not expect animals that differed in body size to have the same brain size. But exactly what relation holds between the size of the body and that of the brain? A general relationship was found first for present-day species and then applied successfully to fossil species as well. This function turns out to be useful in finding relationships between brain and behavioral capacities, as we shall see.

Relating Brain Size to Body Size

We humans long believed our own brains to be the largest of all brains, but this belief was upset in the seventeenth century when it was found that the elephant brain weighs three times as much as our own! Later whale brains were found to be even larger. (Table 3-1 shows brain weights and body weights of certain adult mammals.) These findings puzzled thinkers who took it for granted that human beings are the most intelligent of animals and therefore must have the largest brains. As a way of overcoming this difficulty, they proposed that brain weight should be expressed as a fraction of body weight (see column 3 of Table 3-1). On this basis humans outrank elephants, whales, and all other animals of large or moderate body size. But a mouse has about the same ratio of brain weight to body weight as a man, and the tiny shrew outranks a human on this measure. So we wonder how much brain is needed to control and serve a body of a given size. Let us examine this question.

Look at the brain and body weights in Table 3-1. Do you see any pattern? When we consider a larger sample of animals and the values plotted in Figure 3-9, then

Table 3-1   Brain Weights and Body Weights of Certain Adult Mammals

Living Mammals	Approximate Brain Weight (g)	Approximate Body Weight (g)	Brain Weight as a Percentage of Body Weight	Encephalization Factor k
Shrew	0.25	7.5	3.33	0.06
Mouse	0.5	24	2.08	0.06
Sheep	100	40,000	0.25	0.08
Leopard	135	48,000	0.28	0.10
Malay bear	400	45,000	0.89	0.32
Chimpanzee	400	42,000	0.95	0.30
Human	1,400	60,000	2.33	0.95
Indian elephant	5,000	2,550,000	0.20	0.27
Fossil hominids (estimates)				
Australopithecus (about 4–6 million years ago)	450	50,000	0.90	0.33
Homo habilis (about 1.75 million years ago)	550	50,000	1.10	0.41
Homo erectus (about 0.7 million years ago)	950	50,000	1.90	0.70

Source: Most animal data from Crile and Quiring (1940); data on fossil hominids from Jerison (1973).

some generality appears. All the brain weight–body weight points fall within one of two diagonal areas (one for higher and one for lower vertebrates). Since both scales are logarithmic, the graph encompasses a great variety of animal sizes, and departures from the general rule tend to be minimized. Each diagonal area in Figure 3-9 has a slope of two-thirds. This slope reflects the fact that the weight of the brain is roughly proportional to the two-thirds power of body weight. More formally stated, $E = kP^{2/3}$ where E = brain weight, P = body weight, and k is a constant for a species but varies among classes and species of animals. The constant k is greater

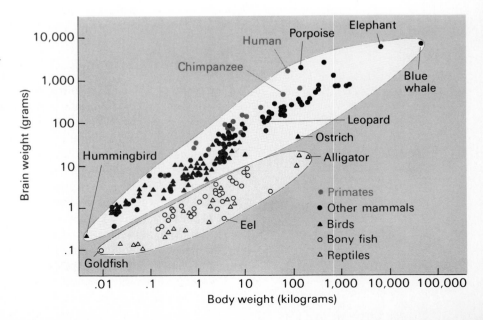

Figure 3-9   Brain size plotted against body size for some 200 species of living vertebrates. Data for mammals and birds fall within the upper brown area, and data for reptiles and fish fall within the lighter brown area. (Adapted from Jerison, 1973; based largely on data of Crile and Quiring, 1940)

for animals that evolved more recently than it is for those closer to ancient forms. In other words, complex vertebrates typically have a brain size that is about ten times larger for a given size of body than the brain size of simpler vertebrates.

Note that the brain weight–body weight points for complex vertebrates do not fall exactly on a diagonal line running through the middle of the oval. Some are located above the diagonal (such as those for human, porpoise, and crow). Others are below it (such as ostrich and opossum). The value of the constant k for a given species is related to the vertical distance of its position from the diagonal on the graph. So, although 0.07 is the mean value of k for complex vertebrates, we can find the particular value of k for each species. In these terms human beings rate higher than any other species. You can see that on the graph the point for humans is located farther above the diagonal than the point for any other species. Values of k for the species in Table 3-1 are given in column 4.

Brain size has been studied in many species of mammal, both living and fossil. These studies have yielded clues about the selection pressures that have led to larger brains. We will first see how brain size has evolved with regard to ecological niche, and especially the methods of obtaining food. Then we will take up the brain size among the relatively direct ancestors of modern humans.

Brain Size and Diet

Within several families of mammals, species that eat leaves or grass have brains that are relatively smaller than those of species that feed on food sources that are distributed less densely and less uniformly, such as fruit or insects. This relationship has been found among families of rodents, insectivores (such as shrews and moles), and lagomorphs (such as rabbits and pica) (Clutton-Brock & Harvey, 1980). It is also true of primates (Mace, Harvey, & Clutton-Brock, 1981). Within the order of bats, which includes several hundred species, relatively large brains have evolved several times. When body size is held constant, species of bats that eat mainly fruit or nectar or live mainly on blood have brain weights that are about 70% greater than those of species that live mainly on insects captured in flight. Finding fruit and assessing its quality requires integrating information from several senses, whereas the species that capture insects in flight rely entirely on hearing. Eisenberg and Wilson (1978, p. 750) argue that larger brains are found among those bat species whose foraging strategies are ''based on locating relatively large packets of energy-rich food that are unpredictable in temporal and spatial distribution.''

Hominid Brains

Another approach to evolutionary relationships between brain and behavior comes from the study of **hominids,** that is, primates of the family Hominidae, of which humans *(Homo sapiens)* are the only living species. This approach is intriguing for the light it sheds on our distant ancestors, and it helps us understand how the body adapts to the environment through natural selection.

The structural and behavioral features that we consider characteristic of humans did not develop simultaneously. Our large brain is a relatively late development. According to one estimate the trunk and arms of hominids reached their present form about 10 million years ago. (Note that the time span of human evolution and the dates of various fossils have been altered by recent methods of dating. All authorities do not agree on these dates; they should be considered only approximate.) Hominids began walking on two feet at least 3 million years ago. The oldest stone tools date back at least 2.5 million years. The tool users were bipedal ape-men called Australopithecines, creatures with a brain volume of about 450 cubic centimeters (cc), about the size of the modern chimpanzee brain. They made crude stone tools, which chimpanzees do not, and used them in hunting and in breaking animal bones to eat. With use of tools their jaws and teeth became smaller than the ape's and more like those of modern human beings. But the brain did not grow. A brain volume of about 450 cc sufficed for the life of Australopithecine. Moreover, this was a successful animal, lasting relatively unchanged for about 2 million years.

Campsites suggest that these early hominids lived in small nomadic groups of 20 to 50 individuals. The males hunted, and the females gathered plant foods. This life of hunting and gathering was a new life style that was continued by later hominids. In Chapter 11 we will see some implications of this life style combined with the increase in brain size for human sexuality.

About three-quarters of a million years ago, the Australopithecines were replaced by *Homo erectus*. This creature, which had a much larger brain—almost 1000 cc—made elaborate stone tools, used fire, and killed large animals. *Homo erectus* had not only a larger brain than his predecessor but also a smaller face. These trends continued in the development of the modern human, *Homo sapiens*. Fossils and tools of *Homo erectus* are found throughout three continents, whereas those of the Australopithecines are found only in Africa. It may be that *H. erectus* represented a level of capacity and of cultural adaptation that allowed the hominids to expand into new environmental niches and to overcome barriers that kept earlier hominids in a narrower range.

Evolution of the brain and increased behavioral capacity advanced rapidly from the Australopithecines to modern humans (Figure 3-10). By the time *Homo sapiens* appeared, about 200,000 years ago, brain volume had reached the modern level, about 1400 cc. Thus, after remaining virtually unchanged in size during about 2 million years of tool use by the Australopithecines, the brain almost tripled in volume during the next 1.5 million years.

The human brain now appears to be at a plateau of size. The recent changes in human life style—such as the appearance of language (perhaps only about 40,000 years ago), the introduction of agriculture and animal husbandry (about 10,000 years ago), and urban living (the last few thousand years)—have all been accomplished and assimilated by a brain that does not seem to have altered in size since *Homo sapiens* appeared.

A change in any organ during evolution indicates that there was pressure from the environment for modification and that the change conferred advantages with respect to the survival of the species. A rapid change, as in the size of the hominid brain, suggests that it brought strong advantages for survival. Can we than tell in what ways the evolution of the human brain accompanied and made possible certain changes in human behavior?

As we mentioned before, in size and general shape the Australopithecine brain resembled that of a modern chimpanzee. It is clear, however, that the chimpanzee is a more distant relative of humans than the Australopithecine is. Some investigators

Figure 3-10 Aspects of hominid evolution. (Adapted from Tobias, 1980)

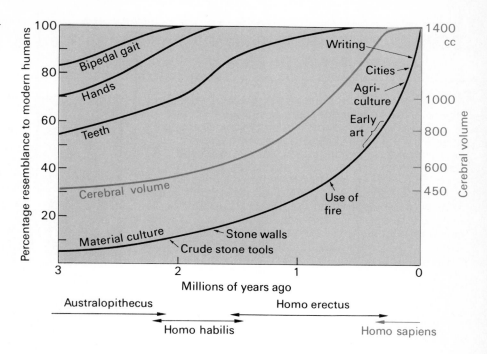

(Kohne et al., 1972) have compared DNA sequences and interpreted them as showing that our ancestors diverged from those of the chimpanzee about 30 million years ago. Another investigator (Sarich, 1971) interprets the data on DNA and also on albumin and hemoglobin as indicating that the human and chimpanzee lines diverged only 4 million to 5 million years ago. Even if we take the more recent estimate as valid, the chimpanzees have still had 4 million to 5 million years to evolve in their direction while we humans evolved in ours. All species that have survived to the present have been busy over the eons leading their own lives and adapting to their own environmental circumstances. We cannot think of them as sitting around to provide a picture gallery of our ancestors!

The fact that hominids made stone tools at least 2.5 million years ago and used them in hunting also distinguishes the Australopithecine from the chimpanzee, even though their brain sizes were similar. Field observations have shown chimpanzees to use some tools—twigs, branches, leaves—but they have never been seen to fashion a stone, even crudely. They catch small game occasionally, but not in the frequent manner that is suggested by the collections of bones of prey found in association with Australopithecine tools and fossils. So the Australopithecine was clearly our closer relative, further advanced toward human culture than the chimpanzee. Its brain organization probably also differed somewhat from that of the chimpanzee. With these reservations, let us see how the modern human brain differs from that of the chimpanzee.

Prominent differences between the organization of the brain of *Homo sapiens* and of chimpanzee include the following:

1. The human brain shows a larger expansion of the motor and sensory cortical areas devoted to the hands.

BOX 3-1 | Brain Structural Asymmetry: The Right Side of the Brain Is Not Built Like the Left Side

A quick glance in the mirror and an equally fleeting view of other vertebrates seem to suggest that bilateral symmetry of the body is commonplace among animals. But a closer look at some more exotic creatures supplies an initial caution. For example, the aquatic world includes some strange examples of exceptions to the plan of body symmetry. Some crabs, such as the fiddler crab, have a left claw that is consistently much larger than the right. Among flatfish, such as flounder, there are some startling examples of bodily asymmetry that also includes the brain (Rao & Finger, 1984). Some adult flatfish have both eyes on the same side of the head! This structural oddity emerges during the course of development. At first, when the fish hatches from an egg, it has an ordinary fishlike symmetrical form. But slowly, as it develops, one eye migrates across the top of the head. Some flatfish are right-eyed, with both eyes on the right side of the head, while others are left-eyed. Although both eyes are on one side of the head in these animals, there is symmetry in the brain visual regions. However, the olfactory system reveals a striking brain anatomical asymmetry (Box Figure 3-1). The right olfactory receptor (ROR) and pathways, including the brain, are distinctly larger than their counterparts on the left.

Structural asymmetry in the brain of other non-

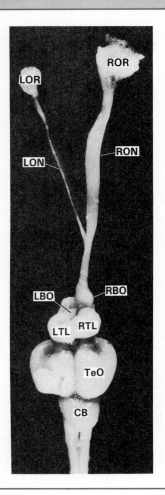

Box Figure 3-1 Dorsal view of the brain and olfactory organs of the winter flounder showing gross asymmetry in the olfactory system. The olfactory organ, nerve, bulb, and telencephalon of right side are larger than their contralateral counterparts. (From P. D. P. Rao and T. E. Finger. 1984. *J. Comp. Neurol.* 63:492–510.)

2. The human brain is like the chimpanzee brain in having a limbic system that is involved in vocalization. However, the human brain shows, in addition, large cortical regions devoted to the production and perception of speech.
3. When it comes to speech, manual dexterity, and other functions, the human brain shows striking hemispheric specialization of functions. In the chimpanzee the two hemispheres are more equivalent in function. (Interesting examples of asymmetry of the nervous system are not restricted to primates; see Box 3-1.)
4. The primary sensory regions of the cortex are somewhat greater in the human than in the chimpanzee. But the main expansion in the human cortex lies outside these sensory regions; that is, in the human a larger proportion of the brain is devoted to more varied and more elaborate processing of information.

human vertebrates has also been described, though to a somewhat limited extent. In some lower vertebrates, such as Amphibia, there is marked asymmetry within the diencephalon in a region called the habenular nucleus. The thickness of the cerebral cortex of the rat brain shows some asymmetries: It is greater on the right side than the left but only in posterior cortical regions of male animals (Diamond, Dowling, & Johnson, 1980). Studies with nonhuman primates show anatomical asymmetries in the region of the temporal lobe analogous to similar findings in humans. Functional studies in nonhuman vertebrates reveal many examples of lateralization. Included in these are observations of the effects of lesions of the brain. In later sections we note that a surgical cut of the left hypoglossal cranial nerve of adult male chaffinch results in the loss of the bird's song. Right-sided damage has little impact on the chaffinch's vocal behavior (Nottebohm, 1981).

Laterality in human behavior is commonplace. Most of us all over the world are right-handed in tasks involving finely coordinated activities, such as handwriting or tool use. Small differences in external appearance are also evident in humans. Look in the mirror and smile. During such expressive gestures a slight facial asymmetry is observed, and some investigators believe this is important for emotional expression (Chapter 18). But what about the human brain? Although anatomical differences between the human cerebral hemispheres went unnoticed by anatomists for a long time, recent research on functional differences between the cerebral hemispheres has refocused research on human brain anatomical specializations, including asymmetry of structure.

Asymmetries in the morphology of the human brain are now well documented in several parts of the brain. Some regions of the temporal lobe relevant to verbal behavior are distinctly larger on the left side of the human brain (Galaburda et al., 1978). There is a gross asymmetry of the overall length and breadth of the right and left cerebral hemispheres. The frontal pole is larger on the right, while some parietal and occipital regions are wider on the left side of the brain (Chui & Damasio, 1980). Many other findings also add to the conclusion that brain asymmetry is characteristic of humans. Relations between these anatomical findings and lateralized performance remain important research questions.

Thus the expansion of cortical areas and hemispheric specialization appear to have made possible human beings' social cooperation in gathering plants and in hunting and their ability to make increasingly complex tools and weapons. These behaviors, which increased humans' chances for survival, could be developed further only as the brain increased further in size and complexity. So selection for advantageous behavior also entailed selection for more powerful brains. Charles Darwin realized this when he wrote:

> In many cases, the continued development of a part, for instance the beak of a bird or the teeth of a mammal, would not aid the species in gaining its food, or for any other object; but with man we can see no definite limit to the continual development of the brain and mental faculties, as far as advantage is concerned.

The survival advantage that accrues to those with larger brains does not hold only for human beings, or primates, or mammalian predators and prey. It would even be too limited to maintain, as George Bernard Shaw did in the dialogue cited at the beginning of this book, that large brains are the specialty of the mammalian line. Within each of the lines of vertebrate evolution there is variation in relative brain size, with the more recently evolved species usually having the larger encephalization quotients. Furthermore, in each vertebrate line it is the dorsal part of the telencephalon that has expanded and differentiated in the more advanced species. As we find more such common responses to selection pressures, they may reveal the ''rules'' of how the nervous system adapts and evolves (Northcutt, 1981).

Evolution of Chemical Messengers

It is probable that long before nerve cells evolved, organisms were regulating and coordinating their functions and activities by using chemical molecules as messengers. The advent of neural signaling did not replace chemical messengers but instead extended the possibilities of chemical communication; that is, chemical stimulation at one end of a neuron leads to output of chemical messenger molecules at distant terminals of the neuron, as we will see in Chapter 6. Furthermore, chemical signaling still exists in organisms with complex nervous systems; they have endocrine systems whose hormonal messengers are closely coordinated with neural signals.

Although we cannot directly measure chemical messengers in fossils of early organisms, simple present-day organisms that resemble early forms of life employ many chemical messengers, some of which are similar to those of complex organisms. For example, yeast cells manufacture steroid molecules that closely resemble mammalian sex hormones. The hypothesis that chemical messengers are very old in evolution is supported by the fact that they are so widespread. For example, some peptide molecules that mammals use as neurotransmitters are also found not only in unicellular animals, such as protozoa and amoebas, but also in other unicellular organisms, such as yeast, and even in higher plants (Le Roith, Shiloach, & Roth, 1982).

Because human beings and other vertebrates employ many of the same chemical messengers as do invertebrates, many studies of invertebrate neurochemistry and behavior have turned out to be relevant for the understanding of vertebrate nervous systems.

Summary · Main Points

1. Comparative studies of the nervous system provide some understanding of the evolution of the human brain. They also provide a perspective for understanding species-typical behavioral adaptations.

2. The nervous system of invertebrate animals ranges in complexity from the nerve net organization of coelenterates to the quite complex structures of octopus. The nervous system of simpler invertebrates may provide a simplified

model for understanding the nervous system of complex vertebrates.

3. Some of the distinctive features of invertebrate nervous systems include large, identifiable monopolar neurons and large axons that are frequently components of circuits mediating rapid escape behaviors.

4. The main divisions of the brain are the same in all vertebrates. Differences among these animals are largely

quantitative, as reflected in differences in the relative sizes of nerve cells and various brain regions.

5. Size differences in brain regions among various mammals are frequently related to distinctive forms of behavioral adaptation.

6. Evolutionary changes in brain size are apparent when one compares fossils and contemporary animals. The brain size of a species must be interpreted in terms of body size. The overall rule for vertebrates is that brain weight is proportional to the two-thirds power of body weight.

7. Some animals have larger brains than predicted by the general relation between brain and body weights. Humans, in particular, have larger brains than would be predicted from their body size.

8. Within each of the lines of vertebrate evolution, there is variation in relative brain size, with the more recently evolved species usually having the larger encephalization quotients.

9. Chemical molecules were probably used as messengers before the advent of the nervous system. Such chemicals are evident in many forms of life and continue as an important part of the signals of nervous systems.

Recommended Reading

Bullock, T. H., & Horridge, G. A. (1965). *Structure and function in the nervous system of invertebrates*. San Francisco: W. H. Freeman.

Masterton, R. B., Hodos, W., & Jerison, H. (Eds). (1976). *Evolution, brain and behavior: Persistent problems*. Hillsdale, N.J. Lawrence Erlbaum.

Sarnat, H. B., & Netsky, M. G. (1981). *Evolution of the nervous system* (2nd ed.). New York: Oxford University Press.

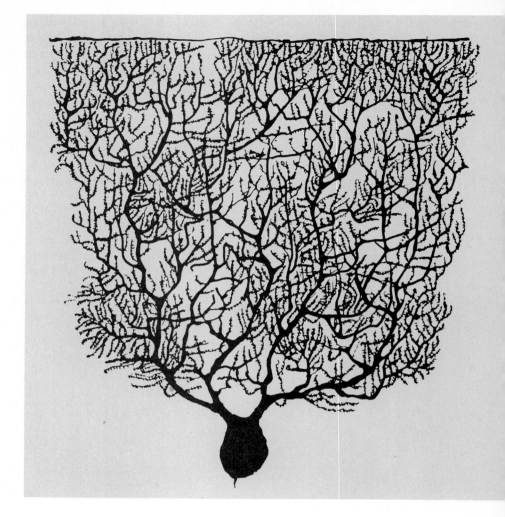

4 Development of the Nervous System over the Life Span

ORIENTATION

Age puts its stamp on our behavior and that of all animals. The pace, progression, and orderliness of changes are especially prominent early in life. However, the life sciences now emphasize change as a feature of the entire span of life. Change is a relentless property of biological states. Shakespeare put it well in *As You Like It* when he said:

> . . . from hour to hour, we ripe and ripe,
> And then, from hour to hour, we rot and rot.

Two calendars have provided the time frames for brain development. In the previous chapter we used the time frame of evolution—the course of brain development over millions of years. In the first part of this chapter, the focus is on the structural flux of the brain during the typical course of an individual's life. Later chapters will give examples of behavioral and physiological changes in the brain that accompany development.

Features of adult brains, described in Chapters 2 and 3, will now be seen as they progress during life from the womb to the tomb. For example, the fertilization of an egg leads to a body with a brain that contains billions of neurons with an incredible number of connections. The pace of this process is extraordinary. During the height of prenatal growth of the human brain, neurons are added at the rate of 500,000 per minute!

There are many problems to consider, including the way nerve cells form and what controls the formation of connections among various regions of the brain. Does the brain develop by an intrinsically guided process that obligingly follows blueprints "written in genes"? How does experience help to guide the emerging brain?

The growth and development of a nervous system is an intriguing process, especially in its relation to the ontogeny of behavior. Many psychological theories emphasize development and try to assign relative weights to the roles of nature and nurture. How important is early life to later cognitive and emotional behavior? Studies of the structural and functional developments of the brain can provide insights into these issues.

In the Beginning

The journey from fertilized egg to mature organism is exceedingly complicated. Picture, if you can, the number of neurons in the mature human brain. Recent estimates have ranged from 100 billion to a trillion, the latter figure offered by Kandel and Schwartz (1985). Yet these billions of cells show highly ordered species-characteristic patterns of organization—an awesome achievement of developmental and evolutionary processes! Many aspects of the brain are being investigated, ranging from chemical influences to the ways in which experience affects the "wiring" of the brain.

Brain Weight from Birth to Old Age

One index to brain development is afforded by measurements of the weight of the brain at different stages of life. Weight can be considered as a kind of summary of many developmental processes. A study by Dekaban and Sadowsky (1978) gives a definitive portrait of the weight of the human brain over the life span. This study was based on measurements of the brains of 5826 people, selected from more than 25,000 cases from several cities. Researchers weighed the brains of individuals who died from causes that do not exert major influences on the brain. Figure 4-1 shows the changes with age in the weights of brains in males and females. Note the rapid increase over the first five years. Brain weight is at its peak from about age 18 to about age 30, after which there is a gradual decline. Now let us see how the brain starts its developmental journey.

The Emergence of Brain Form

Another kind of summary of brain development is provided by examining changes in the gross form of the brain. A new human being begins when a sperm about 60 micrometers (μm) long penetrates the wall of an egg cell 100–150 μm in diameter. This event begins a program of development that leads to a new individual. The

Figure 4-1 Human brain weight as a function of age. Note that the age scale has been expanded for the first five years in order to show data more clearly during this period of rapid growth. (Adapted from Dekaban and Sadowsky, 1978)

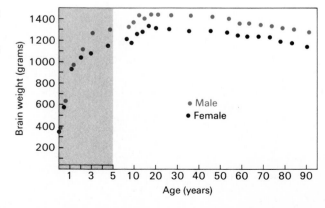

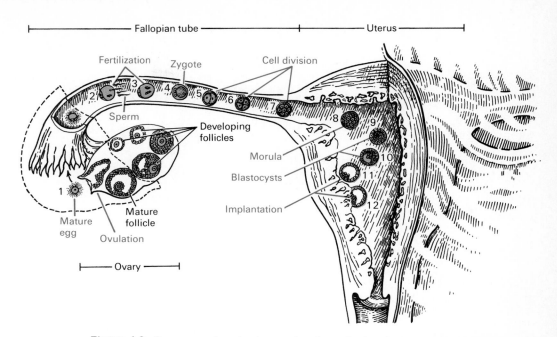

Figure 4-2 Summary of early stages of embryonic development. The sequence begins on the left with release of a mature egg (1) and fertilization by sperm in the Fallopian tube (2)–(3). The fertilized egg or zygote (4) begins to divide (5)–(7) in the Fallopian tube. When a cluster of homogeneous cells—the morula (8)—has formed, separation of cell layers forms the blastocyst stage (9)–(10), and the process of implantation in the uterus begins (11)–(12). The duration of these processes is about one week for the human being.

start of this program takes place in the Fallopian tube, the duct leading from the ovary (Figure 4-2). This union results in a cell with 46 chromosomes, the normal number for humans. These chromosomes contain the complete genetic blueprint for the new individual. Rapid cell division is the beginning of the developmental program. Within 12 hours the single cell has divided into two cells, and after three days these have become a small cluster of homogeneous cells, like a cluster of grapes, about 200 μm in diameter.

During this period the ball of cells has been moving toward the uterus. After several days it arrives there. Fluid from the uterine cavity then enters the ball of cells and separates them into two groups: (1) an outer cell group that later becomes the placenta and (2) an inner cell mass that becomes the embryo itself. A cavity forms within the ball of cells. At this stage our organism is called a **blastocyst** (this term comes from the Greek *blastos,* ''sprout'' or ''bud,'' and from the Greek word for bladder, to denote a budding hollow organism). At the end of the first week the blastocyst is implanted in the uterine wall, as the placental cells extend into this wall.

During the second week the emerging human embryo shows three distinct cell layers. These layers are the beginnings of all the tissues of the embryo (Figure 4-3). The nervous system will develop from the outer layer, called the **ectoderm** (from

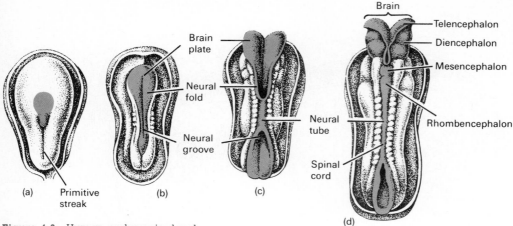

Figure 4-3 Human embryonic development during weeks 2 through 4. (a) The embryo has begun to implant in the uterine wall and consists of two cell layers. (b) Formation of three layers of cells and thickening of one of these layers—the ectoderm—leads to the development of the neural plate. (c) Beginning of neural groove. (d) Neural groove has closed along the length of the embryo; the closing of the groove at the anterior end of the anterior neuropore results in the rudimentary beginning of the brain.

the Greek words for "outer" and "skin"). As the cell layers thicken, they grow into a flat oval plate. In the ectodermal level of this plate, a middle or median position is marked by a groove—the primitive groove. At the head end of the groove is a thickened collection of cells. This stage occurs two weeks after fertilization. Ridges of ectoderm then form on both sides of the middle position. These are the neural folds. The groove between them is then known as the neural groove.

The pace of events now becomes faster. The neural folds come together and convert the groove into the **neural tube.** At the anterior part of the neural tube, three subdivisions become apparent. These subdivisions correspond to the future forebrain (**prosencephalon**), midbrain (**mesencephalon**), and hindbrain (**rhombencephalon**). (Recall these regions from Chapter 2, Figure 2-7.) The cavity of the neural tube ends up as the cerebral ventricles and the passages that connect them. (The morphology of the ventricular system was depicted in Figure 2-4.)

By the end of the eighth week, the human embryo shows the rudimentary beginnings of most body organs. The rapid pace of development of the brain during this period is reflected in the fact that at the end of eight weeks the head is one-half the total size of the embryo. (Note that the developing human is called an embryo during the first ten weeks after fertilization; thereafter it is called a fetus.) Figure 4-4 presents a sequence of views of the prenatal development of the human brain from weeks 10 through 41.

Cellular Aspects of Nervous System Development

Four delicately controlled cellular processes underlie the gross anatomical changes in the nervous system during embryonic and fetal life: (1) cell proliferation, (2) cell migration, (3) cell differentiation, and (4) cell death. These events occur at different rates and times in different parts of the neural tube. (Our focus here is on the nervous system; however, similar events are, of course, involved in the formation of other organs.)

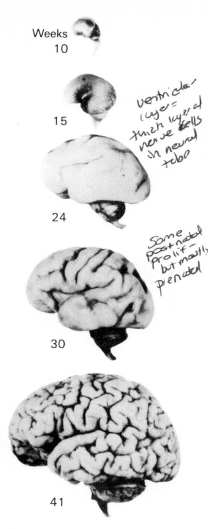

Weeks
10

*ventricular
layer =
thick layer of
nerve cells
in neural
tube*

15

24

*some
postnatal
prolif-
but mostly
prenatal*

30

41

Figure 4-4 Lateral views of the human brain during fetal development. Note the gradual process of development of gyri and sulci. The numbers show gestational ages in weeks. Brains are shown at one-third actual size. (From J.-C. Larroche, Chapter 11, Part II, "The development of the central nervous system during intrauterine life," Figure 1 (p. 258) and Figure 2 (p. 259). In F. Falkner (Ed.), *Human development* (Philadelphia, Pa.: W. B. Saunders, 1966).)

*radial glia –
act as guide
wires*

Cell Proliferation *– production of nerve cells*

The production of nerve cells is called **cell proliferation.** Nerve cells have their beginnings as a single layer of cells along the inner surface of the neural tube. Initially the walls of the neural tube are composed of a population of like cells. These cells gradually form a closely packed layer, the **ventricular layer** of cells (ventricular cells) which keep on dividing (Figure 4-5). (The ventricular layer is also called the ependymal layer.) Each cell divides, giving rise to "daughter" cells which, in turn, divide. All neurons and glia are derived from cells that originate in the ventricular layer. Recent evidence suggests that some cells of the ependymal layer give rise to glia and others to neurons. The separation between these two types of cells takes place quite early in the organization of the ependymal layer. In most mammals the process of forming neural cells in the ventricular layer continues until birth, but very few are added after birth (Rakic, 1974). Postnatal addition of nerve cells does occur in some brain regions. For example, within the human cerebellum cells are added for months after birth.

There is a species-characteristic "birthdate" for each part of an animal's brain. This means that there is an orderly chronological program for brain development, and it is possible to state the approximate days during development on which particular neuron groups are formed. Of course, given the complexity of vertebrate brains, it is quite difficult to trace the path of cell development from the initial small population of ependymal cells. Descendants disappear in the crowd. However, in some simpler invertebrate nervous systems with very few neurons, cell lineages can be traced more easily and completely.

Cell Migration

at this stage, nerve cells = neuroblasts –   *migration almost usually complete at birth*

Neurons of the developing nervous system are always on the move! At some stage the nerve cells that form in the ventricular layer through mitotic division begin to move away. This process is known as **cell migration.** Nerve cells at this stage are known as **neuroblasts.** They acquire short extensions at the "head" and "tail" ends. Some descriptions of the migrating cells compare them to a trail of active ants (Figure 4-6)! In primates the migration of nerve cells in most regions of the brain is virtually complete by birth. But in rat brains, nerve cells continue to migrate in some regions for several weeks following birth.

Cells during this phase of brain development do not move in an aimless, haphazard manner. Clues to the process of cell migration come from studies using radioactive substances that become incorporated into the cell before migration. These substances "tag" the cell so that it can be followed and its migratory paths clearly outlined. Many elegant studies of this process by Rakic (1985) show that some cells in the developing brain move along the surface of an unusual type of glial cell that appears quite early. These glial cells extend from the inner to outer surfaces of the emerging nervous system (Figure 4-7). The glial path acts as a series of guide wires, with each newly formed nerve cell creeping along its length. **Radial glia** is the name given to this collection of guide wires. Some later forming nerve cells migrate in a different manner. These cells are attracted to the surfaces of neurons. Rakic

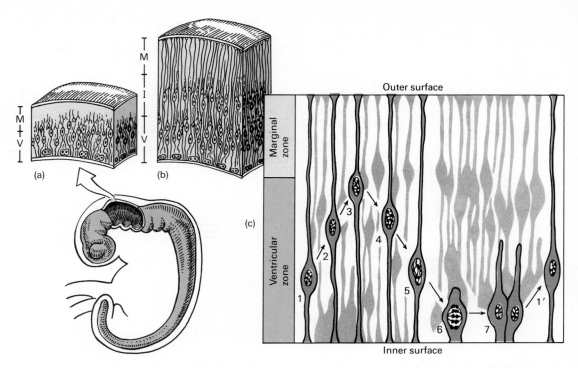

Figure 4-5 Proliferation of cellular precursors of neurons and glia. Part (a) shows a small section of the wall of the neural tube at an early stage of embryonic development when only ventricular (V) and marginal (M) layers are seen. Later, as shown in (b), an intermediate (I) layer develops as the wall thickens. Part (c) shows the migration of nuclei of neurons from the ventricular layer to the outer layers. Some cells, however, return to the ventricular layer and undergo division, and then the daughter cells migrate to the outer layers.

Figure 4-6 Migration of the precursors of the Purkinje cells of the chick cerebellum. At 8 days, these cells appear as a large group of "ants" streaming away from the region of the initial formation. At 11 days, they have begun to form a distinct layer. This layer becomes more spread out by 14 days, and at 19 days it is a single cell layer over an extended surface of tissue that has begun to form folds. (From Levi-Montalcini, 1963)

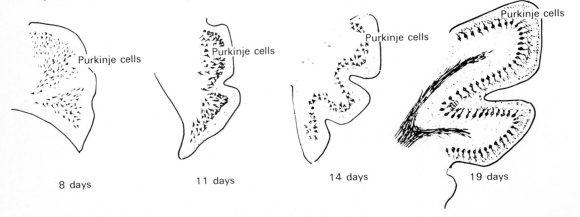

Figure 4-7 Early in development, radial glial cells span the width of the emerging cerebral hemispheres as shown at the top. They act as guide wires for migration of neurons, as shown in the enlargement at lower left. A further enlargement at the right shows a neuron migrating along a single radial glial fiber. (From Cowan, 1979, after Rakic)

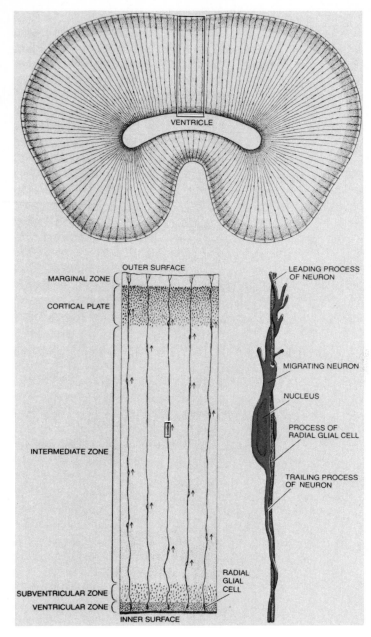

(1985) has described examples of this migratory mechanism in the cerebellum in which newly formed nerve cells migrate along the axons of earlier formed nerve cells. In fact, some neurons creep laterally along horizontal axons and then follow glia downward into the cerebellar cortex. Some disorders of brain development involve failures in the mechanism of cell migration, which result in either a vastly reduced population of cells or a disordered arrangement.

Migration of cells and the outgrowth of nerve cell extensions, such as dendrites and axons, also involve various chemicals. Adhesion of parts is important to this process; molecules that promote the adhesion of developing elements of the nervous system have been described by some researchers, who call them CAM—cell adhesion molecules (Edelman, 1984).

CAM

Cell Differentiation

At first, new nerve cells bear no more resemblance to mature nerve cells than they do to the cells of other organs. Once cells reach their destinations, however, they begin to acquire the distinctive appearance of neurons characteristic of their particular region. This process is **cell differentiation.** Figure 4-8 shows the progressive unfolding of Purkinje cells of the cerebellar cortex. Outgrowths from dendrites of these cells appear after the beginnings of their alignment into a single row. Slowly more and more branches form, progressively expanding the receptive surface of the Purkinje cell. What starts this process of dendrite expansion remains a mystery. Some influences are known. For example, intrinsic self-organization is certainly an important factor; nerve cells in tissue culture grow in a typical manner although they are deprived of some usual connections (e.g., Seil, Kelley, & Leiman, 1974). However, many contemporary research studies also show that the neural environment influences nerve cell differentiation. Any given region in the mature nervous system contains a collection of nerve cells that may include two or more types. For example, in the cerebellar cortex there are Purkinje cells and granule cells. However, all the cells that migrate to a region are neuroblasts that at first look just alike. Thus a given neuroblast has the potential to be transformed into one of several different types of nerve cells.

neuroblasts differentiate to one of many types of cells

The multiple potentialities of the growing neuroblast in any region seem to be programmed in an orderly fashion. One general rule that reflects this order is: In a region that becomes organized into layers (for example, the cerebral cortex or cerebellar cortex), large cells are produced first, followed by small cells. Thus in the cerebellum the large Purkinje cells form first. When they are aligned in a row, the neuroblasts that will become the smaller granule cells begin to migrate.

The formation of the typical shape of a neuron depends in part on determinants within the individual cell and in part on influences from neighboring cells. Some parts of a given cell grow in a typical manner no matter what the environment. Other components seem to respond to features of the environment in the brain, such as the presence of other cells.

Cell Death

crucial stage

As strange as it may seem, **cell death** is a crucial phase of brain development, especially during embryonic stages. In fact, in some regions of the brain and spinal cord, most of the nerve cells die during prenatal development. An example of this kind of developmental phenomenon is shown in Figure 4-9. Several factors influence this process. Among these is the size of the field on the body surface that will ultimately be connected to a region of the central nervous system. For example, in tadpoles, if an investigator removes a leg before connections from the spinal cord

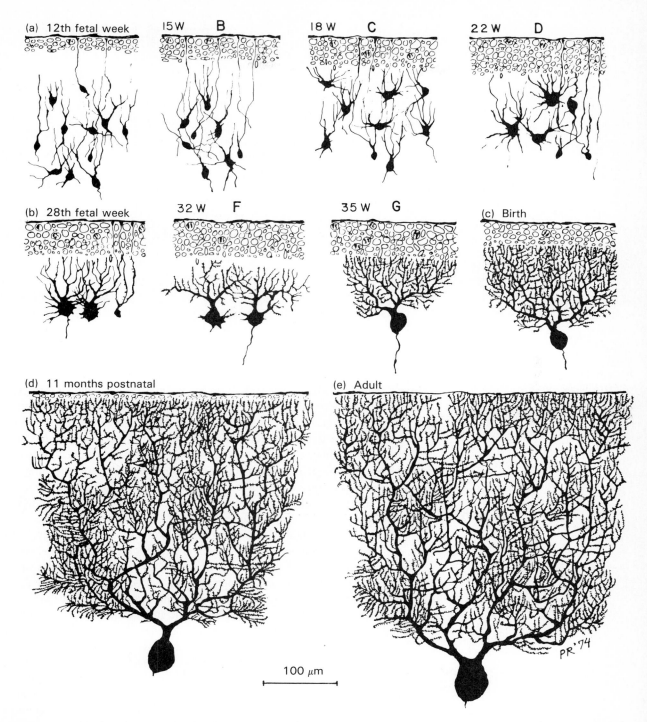

Figure 4-8 Development of Purkinje cells in the human cerebellum at various fetal and postnatal ages, showing differentiation of form. (From Zecevic and Rakic, 1976)

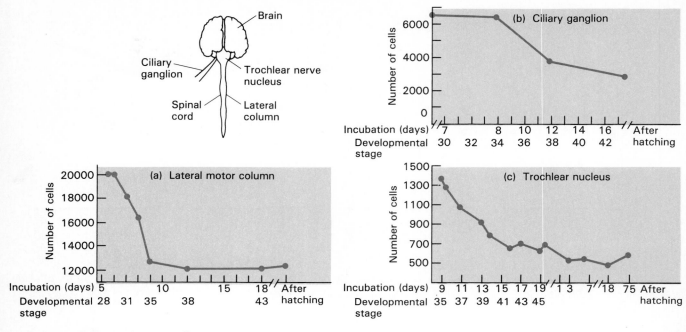

Figure 4-9 Patterns of nerve cell death during early development of the nervous system of the chick. (a) Lateral motor column. (Adapted from Hamburger, 1975), (b) Ciliary ganglion. (Adapted from Landmesser & Pilar, 1974), (c) Trochlear nucleus in brain stem. (Adapted from Cowan & Wenger, 1967)

have formed, many more developing spinal motoneurons die than if the leg had remained in position. Conversely, grafting on an extra leg—which is possible with amphibians—appreciably reduces the usual loss of cells, so that the mature spinal cord in this instance has more than the usual number of neurons. These observations suggest that the target of a developing population of nerve cells—the place they connect to—influences the survival of these cells. Some researchers have suggested that during development there is competition among cells for connections to target structures that include other nerve cells and end organs, such as muscle. According to this view, those cells that readily make connections remain; those without a place to form synaptic connections die.

Another determinant of the pace and extent of cell death is the level of certain natural chemicals. For example, in some invertebrate nervous systems, cell death is induced by the action of particular hormones. This type of nerve cell death is seen during insect metamorphosis. Truman (1983) has described nerve cell death in moth nervous systems triggered by the hormones that produce the transformation from caterpillar to moth. The Mauthner cell of some amphibians changes as a result of the secretion of thyroid hormones. The cell degenerates as the animal's life style changes from aquatic to terrestrial.

Nerve cell death may also effect a numerical matching between developing cell populations. For example, to consider a hypothetical case, nerve cell population A contains 100 cells. Its axons extend toward nerve cell population B, which consists of 50 cells. The excess number in nerve cell population A assures connection to nerve cell population B, but there will probably be a group of cells that will not be needed after effective links are forged. The result: A group of cells in nerve cell population A dies. The mediating mechanism might be the ability to take up a "survivor" factor from the environment of the target population. Some investigators have also suggested that cell death might remove "incorrect connections." Critical tests of this interesting suggestion fail to confirm it, however (Lance-Jones, 1984). It certainly seems that nerve cell death during development is a mechanism for "sculpturing" the developing nervous system.

remove, "incorrect connections (failed to confirm this)

Later Developmental Processes

Between birth and maturity the human brain increases fourfold in weight and size. Similar changes from infancy to adulthood are also evident in cats, rabbits, rats, and other animals (Table 4-1). What kinds of postnatal changes in structure account for such growth in weight and size of the brain? Let us consider four types of structural changes at a cellular level that characterize brain development during early postnatal periods.

Myelinization

The development of the sheath around axons—a process called **myelinization**—greatly changes the rate at which axons conduct messages. This should have a strong impact on behavior, since it profoundly affects the temporal order of events in the nervous system. Unfortunately there are few studies using both modern biological and behavioral techniques to relate biological attributes of the nervous system to changes in behavior. So the job of relating changes in behavior to myelinization is still open and in need of recruits.

In humans the most intense phase of myelinization occurs shortly after birth. (However, some investigators believe that myelin can be added to axons over the entire course of life.) The first nerve tracts in the human nervous system to become myelinated are found in the spinal cord. Myelinization then spreads successively into the hindbrain, midbrain, and forebrain. The earliest myelinization in the peripheral nervous system is evident in cranial and spinal nerves about 24 weeks after conception. Within the cerebral cortex, sensory zones myelinate before motor zones; correspondingly, sensory functions mature before motor functions.

Sensory before Motor

Formation of Synapses and Dendrites

The biggest changes in brain cells from birth to maturity take place in the branches and connections among neurons. Figure 4-8 has already shown the huge increase in

---

Table 4-1   Increments in Brain Weight from Birth to Maturity in Some Mammalian Species

Species	Newborn (g)	Adult (g)	Increment (%)
Guinea pig	2.5	4	60
Human	335	1300	290
Cat	5	25	400
Rabbit	2	10.5	425
Rat	0.3	1.9	530

Source: From Altman (1967).

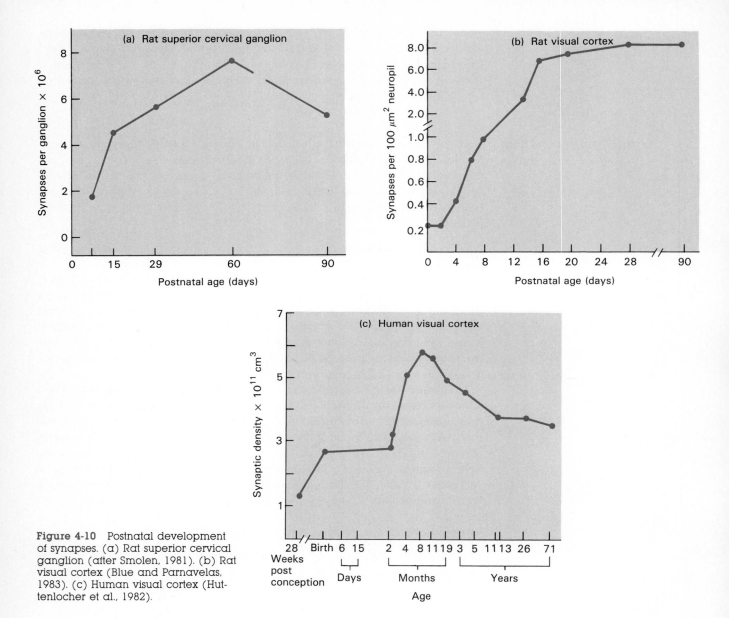

Figure 4-10 Postnatal development of synapses. (a) Rat superior cervical ganglion (after Smolen, 1981). (b) Rat visual cortex (Blue and Parnavelas, 1983). (c) Human visual cortex (Huttenlocher et al., 1982).

the length of dendrites, which seems to involve processes akin to those involved in the growth of axons. At the tips of dendrites there are growth cones, which are swollen ends from which extensions emerge. Some investigators have even found dendrite growth cones in adult animals. This can be related to the exciting finding that elongation of dendrites may continue throughout life in response to functional demands.

Synapses increase at a rapid rate, particularly on dendrites (Figure 4-10). In many nerve cells, synapses are formed at dendritic spines. The spines themselves proliferate rapidly after birth. These connections can be affected by postnatal experience, as we will see in Chapter 17. In order to support the metabolic needs of the expanded dendritic tree, the nerve cell body greatly increases in volume.

Production of Neurons after Birth

Traditionally many investigators of nervous system ontogeny have believed that most mammals at birth have all the nerve cells they will ever have. They have explained the postnatal growth in the brain entirely in terms of growth in the size of neurons and the addition of nonneural (glial) cells. Within recent years, however, they have modified this belief, primarily because it now appears that small neurons are added for some period following birth. Some investigators have even argued that birth may trigger an acceleration in the rate of production of these small cells. This view has not gained wide support, however. Other investigators have argued that it is the maturity of the brain that determines the time of birth.

The most widely accepted current view is that all the larger neurons the brain will ever contain are there at birth. However, there are a few regions around the brain ventricles, called the subventricular zones, in which mitotic division of the precursors of nerve cells remains evident after birth. Several regions of the brain of rats, including the olfactory bulb and the hippocampus, appear to add small neurons derived from this region. In fact, it has been claimed (Graziadei & Monti-Graziadei, 1978) that nerve cells of the olfactory end organ are replaced throughout life.

The dogma that no new neurons are added to the adult nervous system is strongly challenged by some exciting new research by Nottebohm (1987) on the neurology of bird song (discussed in Chapters 11 and 18). Briefly, it is known that bird song development in males of some species is under hormonal control, dependent on the male hormone testosterone. In earlier work Nottebohm determined the parts of the bird brain that are responsible for song learning and performance. During the course of this work, he noted that at least one part of the relevant brain circuit for bird song is large in spring and shrinks to half that size in the fall. This seasonal change in the size of the brain region is related to male hormone levels and singing behavior. Some of this seasonal variation in the size of the brain region is accounted for by seasonal variations in dendritic length and branching. However, Nottebohm has presented evidence that the increase in the spring is also related to the addition of new neurons. Apparently, new neurons are formed in the subventricular zone and then migrate to the nearby brain stem vocal control region. Substantial gains and loses in the number of neurons are evident during the course of a year. These observations suggest the need to reexamine the belief that the adult brain does not add new neurons. At the very least such renewed research could supply a better understanding of the conditions that lead to the usual cessation of neuron addition in adulthood.

Formation of Glial Cells

Glial cells develop from the same populations of immature cells as neurons. The influences that determine whether the cell develops into a neuron or a glial cell

[margin note: where neurons, glial cells added through out life]

remain a mystery. Unlike neurons, glial cells continue to be added throughout life. At times that process can become aberrant, resulting in glial tumors (gliomas) of the brain. The production of glia continues longer than the production of neurons and shows its greatest change later. In fact, the most intense phase of glial proliferation in many animals occurs after birth, when glial cells are added from immature cells located in the subventricular zones.

Examples of the Formation of Neural Regions

Any brain region is characterized by a distinctive arrangement of nerve cells and their processes. In some brain regions, such as the cerebellar cortex and cerebral cortex, nerve cells are arrayed in distinct layers. A discussion of the developmental factors that are involved in the acquisition of the characteristic form of a region provides a focus on the complexity of brain ontogeny. The developmental assembly of each region of the brain follows a precise timetable; some parts of the schedule appear to rely on mutual interactions of cells in the developing region. To show how a particular region acquires its characteristic orderly form, let us take the cerebellar cortex and the cerebral cortex as examples.

Formation of the Cerebellar Cortex

As we saw in Chapter 2, the adult cerebellar cortex consists of a structure with numerous folds (called folia) and a laminar (layered) arrangement, as follows:

[margin note: folia e laminar (folds e layered]

1. An outer molecular layer with small cells and a band of fibers (axons)
2. A middle layer of large cells (the Purkinje cell layer)
3. A deep, thick layer of very small cells—the granule cell layer

We saw this laminar arrangement of the adult cerebellum in Reference Figure 2-8. The initial migration of cells that form the cerebellum involves the Purkinje cells, which at first are small and scattered but which later become a single, uniform row of large cells (Figure 4-11).

In human beings, Purkinje cells grow most rapidly between late pregnancy and about a year after birth. In the rat, they grow most rapidly just after birth, from day 2 to day 30. After the Purkinje cells arrive on the scene, the smaller cells of the cerebellum form. Initially their migratory pattern takes them to the external granular surface. They then descend around and past the Purkinje cells to form the deeper cell populations. The fact that in the rat most of the development of the cerebellum occurs after birth has made these developmental processes relatively easy to study. Any of a number of treatments, including mild exposure to x-rays, interferes with newly developing neuroblasts but does not harm cells that are already differentiated or that are relatively mature.

[margin note: After Purkinje cells smaller cerebellar cells form]

Three different populations of small cells develop in sequence: basket cells, stellate cells, and granule cells. Altman (1976) exposed young rats to x-rays over the course of a few days, which prevented the development of one or more kinds of these small cells in the rats' brains. This had disastrous consequences for the development of the large dendritic fan of the Purkinje cells.

Giving a burst of irradiation on each of days 4 through 7 prevents the formation

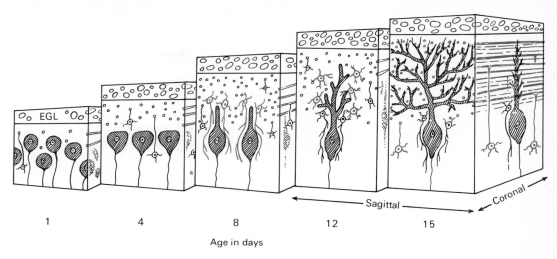

Age in days

Figure 4-11 Schematic drawings of the development of cells in the cerebellum of the rat, emphasizing the maturation of Purkinje cells. EGL stands for the external granule layer to which cells migrate during early cerebellar development. By post-natal day 4, the Purkinje cells are arranged in a single layer. From day 4 through day 7, basket cells develop (shown in brown at day 8), and the main dendrite of the Purkinje cell grows toward the surface of the cerebellum. From day 8 through day 11, stellate cells form (shown in brown at day 12), and the main branches of the Purkinje cell dendrites grow. From day 12 on, a large number of granule cells form (shown in brown in the day-15 block); the granule bodies migrate down below the Purkinje cells, but their axons form the parallel fibers that synapse with the small spiny branches of the Purkinje dendritic tree. (Adapted from Altman, 1976)

of basket cells. This in turn prevents the regular upward growth of the main dendrite of the Purkinje cells; the main dendrites may grow in any direction and become twisted. Irradiation on days 8 through 11 prevents formation of the stellate cells and thereby interferes with growth of the main branches of the Purkinje cell dendrites. Finally, irradiation on days 12 through 15 reduces the number of granule cells and diminishes the complex branching of the dendritic tree of the Purkinje cells (Altman, 1976). The irradiation also produces behavioral effects; it interferes with posture, and impairment of maze learning has also been reported (Pellegrino & Atlman, 1977).

Formation of the Cerebral Cortex

The 50 billion neurons of the human cerebral cortex are arranged in layers, the cells of each layer differing in form and size. This arrangement of layers shows variations in different parts of the brain. These variations have been used to define the borders of different cortical regions. Here we will look at the way the cerebral neocortex grows and achieves this distinctive layered organization.

Examining the closed neural tube of a human embryo at the end of the third week after fertilization reveals a zone of cells all around the inner surfaces. This early proliferation of cells at the rostral end results in the formation of the cortical plate, the beginnings of the cerebral cortex. Intense cell division at this end continues to produce cells that will in time become the neurons of the cerebral cortex. This rapid proliferation continues until the sixth month of fetal life, by which time the cerebral cortex has its full complement of neurons. They are now aligned in layers, although they scarcely resemble the cortical layers in the adult brain.

The formation of cell layers in the cerebral cortex follows a regular process, although the guiding mechanisms remain controversial. Cells that are formed along the ventricular (ependymal) surface migrate away from it. Each new cell migrates beyond those born earlier (Figure 4-12). This new cells move closer to the cortical surface. The oldest cells are found at the deepest layer. The generation time—the mitotic cycle for the production of a cortical cell—is about 11 hours and remains constant throughout the development of the cortex. However, migration time—the interval between cell birth and arrival at its final position—becomes progressively longer, taking about five days for the last group of new cortical cells. The most intense phase of dendritic growth and synapse formation in the cerebral cortex occurs after birth. The elaborateness of human postnatal cortical development is illustrated in Figure 4-13.

Why Neural Connections Go Where They Go

All members of a species generate similar types of nerve cells. Furthermore, these cells have a characteristic arrangement. This order is evident in the ways in which the cells are grouped together in different brain regions. The structural feature that is of particular interest for behavior is the orderliness and specificity of connections among individual cells and among regions. Clearly the adaptive behavior of any animal depends on how the brain is ''wired''—that is, on the ways in which connections are formed. Is the process of the formation of connections an unvarying one, specified by mechanisms controlled by the genetic machinery? Three current answers to this question can be summarized as follows:

1. The main connections that form during development are closely specified by innate mechanisms.
2. Detailed aspects of central connections can be modified by training or experience.
3. There is intense competition among individual neurons and among groups of neurons to form connections, so that if some units are inhibited or removed, their connections are taken over by adjacent neurons.

Let us examine some of the research that has given rise to these conclusions.

Billions of nerve cells, all growing at once, somehow manage to make appropriate connections with each other and to form the intricate circuits that mediate complex behavior. One neuron sends out an axon that is less than a millimeter long. Another neuron sends its axon along a particular tract for more than a meter. At the end of its path, each axon forms connections at specific sites within a specific brain region. Indeed, some axons terminate on particular *portions* of the dendrites of specific nerve cells. When you think about this formation of pathways and connections in the nervous system, it seems as though each nerve cell has instructions about a particular address, a site at which it must establish connections. How can we

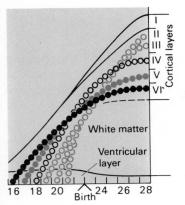

Figure 4-12 Migration of cells into cerebral cortex in the rat. Cortical cells of the rat originate and start their migration before birth. The earliest cells to originate migrate to the lowest layers of the cortex; the cells produced in the few days before birth form the upper cell layers (II and III). Migration of cells to the upper layers continues for several days after birth. (Adapted from Berry, Rogers, and Eayrs, 1964)

Figure 4-13 (a) Development of the thickness of the cerebral cortex of humans. (From Rabinowicz, 1986) (b) Histological view of cerebral cortex in early development of humans. Left panel—one month, middle panel—six months, right panel—24 months. (From Conel, 1939, 1941, and 1959)

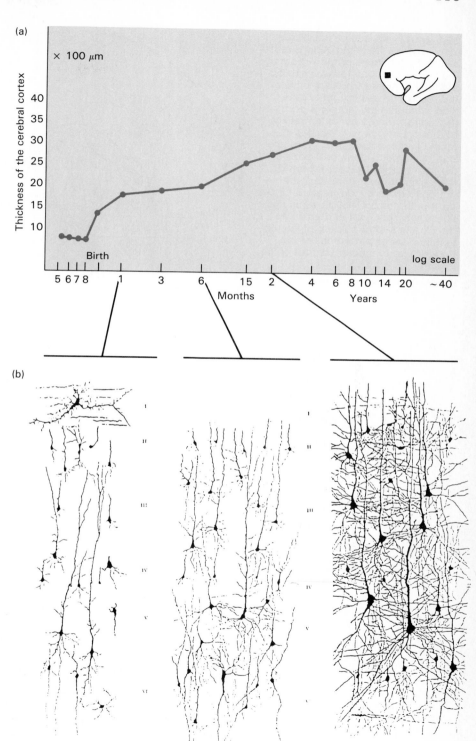

Figure 4-14 An outline of the frog's visual system. The visual field is represented by the large arrow in front of the frog's head. The lateral parts of the field stimulate the nasal parts of the retinas; the central part of the field stimulates the temporal parts of the retinas. The output of the retina (the axons of ganglion cells) is directed to the tectum on the opposite side of the head. Temporal parts of the retina project to rostral parts of the tectum and nasal parts of the retina go to more caudal regions. Upper parts of the retina (not shown in this illustration), also called dorsal, are directed to lateral portions of the tectum, and lower parts of the retina (ventral) go to medial portions of the tectum.

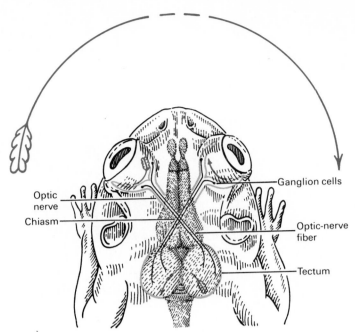

Optic nerve

Chiasm

Ganglion cells

Optic-nerve fiber

Tectum

[handwritten margin note: account for highly ordered connections that are formed during brain development]

account for the highly ordered connections that are formed during the development of the brain?

Pioneering research on this complex problem was done by Roger Sperry, an American neuropsychologist and neuroembryologist who was awarded a Nobel Prize in 1981. In the 1940s he started a series of experimental observations of the visual systems of amphibia and fish. These studies capitalized on the remarkable abilities of these animals to regenerate tissue, including neural tissue. As we will see, many studies of neural development concern the visual system, partly because vision plays such an important role in behavior, and partly because of the orderly spatial projection of the visual field, from the retina up through the visual centers of the brain (Figure 4-14). Later we will see that development of the visual system in mammals is clearly influenced by early experience with visual stimuli.

Layout of the Amphibian Visual System

To understand some of Sperry's main experimental observations, let us briefly consider the layout of the visual system in amphibia and fish. The **retina** is a population of photosensitive elements that provides a map of the visual world (Figure 4-14). The axons of the output nerve cells in the retina form the **optic nerve.** In amphibia these fibers cross to the opposite side of the brain and terminate in an orderly way in a structure called the **optic tectum.** This is the chief neural center for vision in these animals. The surface of the tectum provides, in a sense, a map of the retina. Thus an object at a given place in the outside world excites a particular place in the retina, which in turn activates a specific locus in the optic tectum. It almost seems as if each point in the retina "knows," or becomes aware in the course of development, which place to connect to in the optic tectum. One could imagine that there is some sort of a label in each growing axon that tells the axon where to go.

The initial studies of Sperry (and others) did not require any fancy anatomical or physiological tools. Instead, experimenters let the visual behavior of amphibia tell them about connections in the brain that are related to perceptions of visual space. Many amphibians show highly stereotyped responses to visual stimuli. They correctly orient toward and attack small moving objects with the flick of a tongue, especially when the objects resemble small insects, such as flies. Therefore their responses can be used to reveal the representation of the visual field in the brain.

Specificity of Retinal-Tectal Connections

[handwritten: regeneration of cells in reptilian optic tectum]

In initial experiments Sperry cut the optic nerve and watched the way visually guided behavior reappeared. After the nerve fibers grew back to the optic tectum (a period of months), the animals were able to perform just as accurately as before! What does the restoration of this behavioral response imply about the reestablishment of connections between the retina and the optic tectum? Two alternative possibilities must be considered:

[handwritten: 1. Experience shapes new cells]
[handwritten: or]
[handwritten: 2. fibers in nerve grow back]

1. The regrowing axons enter the tectum in a tangle of random connections, and experience (success or failure in locating food) determines the survival of connections for reporting locations in space; that is, the networks are reeducated about location of objects.

2. Fibers in the nerve grow back to their original positions on the optic tectum and simply reestablish the original map of the visual world

[handwritten: no reeducation]

Several now classic experiments enabled Sperry to choose between these alternatives. What he did was to rotate the eyes of a newt 180 degrees. This inverted the newt's visual field completely. Both up and down and right and left were reversed. After the visual connections regenerated, the animal's behavior was found to be reversed: When a small lure was presented in the upper half of the visual field, the tongue flicked down. When the lure was presented near the nasal portion of the horizontal axis, the animal aimed to the side. These reversals of behavior persisted for years! Despite the fact that these responses were markedly maladaptive, there was no apparent "reeducation" of location behavior.

[handwritten: Sperry chose #2]
[handwritten: ✗ doctrine of neurospecificity]

These observations led Sperry to conclude that the regenerating optic axons reconnect to their original positions in the tectum. They re-create a pattern of orderly connections. Sperry's explanation has come to be known as the **doctrine of neurospecificity.** He argued that during the differentiation of the cells of the retina, each cell acquires a unique identity. It becomes specified, as though it had a label relating it to a certain position in the animal's visual field (Figure 4-15a). Axons emerging from such cells, according to Sperry, are unique biochemically. When they reach the tectum, they seek cells that have a similar chemical identity. There is thus a matching of cells according to a chemical label.

Limits to Neurospecificity

Suppose that we were to extend the concept of neurospecificity to cover the genesis of all nervous system connections; that is, suppose that we maintained that there was virtually total, rigid, genetic specification of neural connections. We would run into many problems. An obvious one is that the limited information capacity of genes makes the notion of different chemical labels for each neuron implausible.

[handwritten: ① too much info for genes]

BOX 4-1 | Degeneration and Regeneration of Nervous Tissue

When a mature nerve cell is injured, several forms of regrowth can occur. However, complete replacement of injured nerve cells is rare in mammalian nervous systems. Box Figure 4-1 illustrates several characteristic forms of degeneration and regeneration in the peripheral and central nervous system. Injury close to the cell body of the neuron produces a series of changes that result in the eventual destruction of the cell. This process is called **retrograde degeneration.**

Transecting the axon at some distance from the cell body produces loss of the distal part of the axon (the part separated from continuity with the cell body). This process is called Wallerian or **antero-grade degeneration.** The part of the axon that remains connected to the cell body may regrow. Severed axons in the peripheral nervous system regrow readily. Sprouts emerge from the part of the axon that is still connected to the nerve cell body and advance slowly toward the periphery. Some animals have an enviable advantage. After an injury to the brain, several fish and amphibians appear to be able to regenerate large parts of the brain itself.

From an experimental point of view, our interest in regeneration of the nervous system lies principally in the fact that regeneration involves processes that seem similar to original development. Studying regeneration may thus increase our understanding of the original processes of growth of the nervous system. From a therapeutic viewpoint, these studies may help scientists learn how to induce repair and regrowth of damaged neural tissue in humans.

Box Figure 4-1   Types of degeneration of nerve cells. (a) Prior to injury. (b) and (c) Anterograde degeneration; injury causes loss of the distal section of the axon. (d) and (e) Retrograde degeneration. Injury also causes degeneration of the cell body, resulting in some cases in complete atrophy. (f) Transneuronal degeneration. Loss of input may produce changes in other cells in the pathway. (g) Recovery. Injured axons may sprout new endings.

Furthermore, some genetic capacity must also be allotted to the planning of such mundane organs as arms, legs, and heart. Alternatives to total individual specification have been suggested, employing chemical gradients determined by very few substances. Figure 4-15b presents one such view.

Several experiments have also cast doubt on the likelihood that there is complete predetermined specification of all neural connections. These experiments have shown that there is some plasticity in retinal tectal connections. Such plasticity or

Figure 4-15 (a) Neurospecificity hypothesis of determinations of neural connections. Specific sites on the receptor surface are represented by different letters. Connections to the brain are made only to like sites (a to A, b to B, and so forth). Each position is coded by some unique state or chemical. (b) Chemical gradients as determinants of neural connections. Here connections are not defined by a specific unique chemical but by gradients of two dimensions (shown here by black and brown gradients). Every locus can be identified by a position on the two gradients.

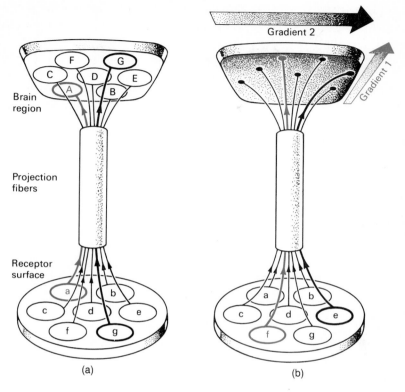

(a)　　　　(b)

adaptability suggests that, at the very least, it is possible that tectal neurons might be able to respecify their properties during the regrowth period. Good examples are the so-called size disparity experiments. In one such experiment, Yoon (1979) showed that when half the tectum is removed, the entire retina will then map onto the remaining half tectum. This suggests that connections within the tectum are capable of modification.

Experiments on retinal-tectal specificity also reveal that there is a kind of recognition process that may involve specific chemical agents. Attempts to ascertain the details of this process have directed attention to the molecular features of chemical recognition.

Determinants of Brain Growth and Development

Many states, both internal and external, influence the emergence of the form, arrangements, and connections of the developing brain. In the case of development, as in the cases of some other topics that we will consider in later chapters, it is useful to think of both direct determinants and modulatory influences. A direct determinant (or intrinsic factor) is one that is involved in the basic processes that produce or control a phenomenon. In the development of the nervous system, certain genes and the processes they control are direct determinants. For example, some kinds of neurons receive genetic instructions to form dendritic spines, whereas other kinds of neurons in the same organism never form spines. A modulatory influence (or extrinsic factor) is one that can either facilitate or inhibit basic processes but that does not directly control them. In the development of the nervous system, modulators such as nutrition and experience can influence the rate or extent of development. For example, in neurons that form dendritic spines, modulating factors determine how many spines are formed.

The effectiveness of modulating influences is often critically dependent on the stage of development at which they are present. A particular biochemical state present in the early life of an embryo may exert vastly different influences than the same state present during fetal development or early postnatal stages. In this section we will discuss some examples of intrinsic and extrinsic factors that can exert significant influence in the development of brain structure. We will not give an exhaustive list but only describe a few well-investigated phenomena.

Genetic Determinants

For a long time psychologists have shown the role of genetics in a variety of behaviors in many species of animal. More recently, research has begun to explore genetic control of brain anatomy and physiology as part of the program of understanding the ways in which genes influence and control behavior (Hall, Greenspan, & Hams, 1982; Wimer & Wimer, 1985). Of course, genes do not work in isolation. Most of this work should be viewed as the interaction of genetic instructions with other developmental influences.

Selective breeding procedures have been used for years by scientists and farmers to produce distinctive animals. These techniques have also been used by researchers in behavioral genetics, who have charted changes of behavior through generations. Use of these techniques with simpler animals has begun to connect genetic effects on the nervous system with effects on behavior. Bentley (1976) has shown that the calling songs of crickets have intricate patterns that can be manipulated by selective breeding. These song patterns change in distinctive ways as genes of a particular type are introduced by controlled mating through several generations. Recordings made from neurons in the crickets' nervous system reveal that the genetically controlled variability in songs is directly related to the impact of genes in changing the arrangements of neural networks.

An unusual breeding technique is one that produces genetically identical animals called **clones,** which used to be known mainly in science fiction and horror films. But life imitates fiction! Studies of the genetics of the development of the nervous system are using carbon copy creatures. Researchers develop these animals by means of asexual reproduction, and all offspring have the same genes. Using clones of grasshoppers, Goodman (1979) compared the uniformity and variability in the growth and development of different neurons. Although the basic shape of larger cells showed considerable uniformity, many neurons of cloned grasshoppers showed differences in neural connections between "identical" individuals.

If heredity is identical, does that mean that neural connections are identical? In order to study this question, human identical twins or twins of any other mammals are not very useful subjects because their nervous systems are too complex and one cannot find the same cell to compare in two individuals. Some investigators therefore took up this question with a tiny crustacean, daphnia, well known to many aquarium owners (Macagno, Lopresti, & Levinthal, 1973). Female daphnia can reproduce without fertilization by males, and they produce lines of genetically identical female offspring (or clones). Furthermore, daphnia have a fixed number of neurons that can be identified under the microscope. The eye contains exactly 176 sensory neurons, and these make synaptic contacts with exactly 110 neurons of the optic ganglion. Furthermore, a particular sensory neuron makes contact with only a few specific neurons in the ganglion. But the exact number of synapses established between a particular sensory neuron and a specific neuron in the ganglion can vary by more than 3 to 1 from one individual daphnia to another within a clone. Even between the right and left sides of the eye of an individual, where there are symmetrically placed "twin" neurons, one twin neuron may form more synapses than the other. Thus both within and between individual daphnia, neurons with exactly the same heredity differ in the numbers of their synaptic connections. Similarly, the form of the axonal branches differs both within and between cloned daphnia, as shown in Figure 4-16.

Among vertebrates, it is harder to find identical neurons in order to compare synaptic connections. The investigators who had studied this question in daphnia moved on to a fish that reproduces parthenogenically, like daphnia, producing

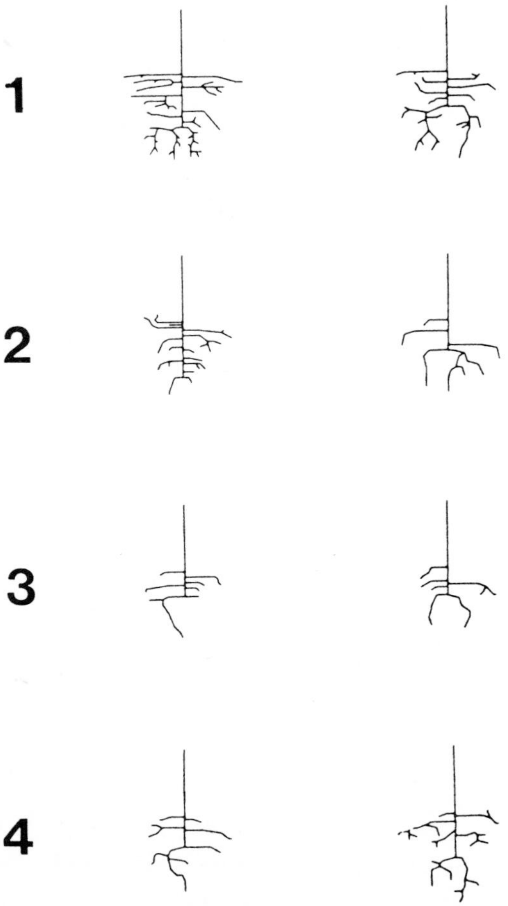

Figure 4-16 The same neuron in four identical twins in a clone of insects. The two examples of the branching pattern are shown in the two columns. The variability pattern is greater from one genetically identical animal to another than between left and right side in the same individual. (Macagno et al., 1973)

daughters that are genetically identical to each other and to their mother. In these fish the nervous system is complex, but each animal has a single giant Mauthner cell in each side of the brain. Microscopic examination showed that, although the pattern of dendritic branching of the Mauthner cell is similar from individual to individual among a clone, there are individual differences in the detail of branching and of synapses. Thus the finding in daphnia could be extended to at least the Mauthner cell in the fish brain (Levinthal, Macagno, & Levinthal, 1976).

Among genetically identical mammals, the differences in the nervous system are even greater. Thus in highly inbred strains of mice where all individuals of the same sex are essentially identical genetically, a specific region of the brain (such as a part of the hippocampus) shows a difference in the number of neurons that amounts to a small percentage among individuals (Wimer et al., 1976).

No direct observations of this sort have been made for human identical twins, although such twins often differ in size at birth, and presumably their brains differ at least as much as do those of inbred mice. Some indirect evidence indicates that for human identical twins the branching pattern of nerve endings in the skin must differ. The evidence is that even identical twins show some differences in their fingerprints, although their prints are more similar than are those of fraternal twins. The skin of the fingertips is richly innervated, so differences in the pattern of the ridges of the skin must mean differences in distribution of nerve endings. Furthermore, the tiny sweat glands of the fingertips have their openings along the ridges of skin. The sweat glands are supplied with nerve endings that control the secretion of sweat, so again the differences in the pattern of ridges must mean differences in the locations of the nerve endings that run to the sweat glands. This example indicates that among human beings, as among other animals, identity of heredity does not mean identity in every detail of the nervous system. We should note that the pattern of fingerprints forms during the fourth month of pregnancy, so these individual differences are determined well before birth. Further differences between the nervous systems of identical twins may be caused by responses to differential experiences, as we will see in Chapters 16 and 17 when we consider effects of experience and learning on the anatomy of the nervous system.

Genetic Mutants

Sometimes nature, with the help of researchers, produces unusual animals that show a sudden change in genetic structure, a mutation that is related to marked anatomical or physiological change. These effects may appear in the course of selective breeding, especially in highly inbred strains, or may result from exposure to toxic substances that produce genetic changes.

Mutants—animals that display these changes—are interesting to study because their suddenly changed genetic characteristics may be quite specific and striking. This gives evidence of genetic controls in their development that are more subtle in other animals. For example, Greenspan and Quinn (1984) described mutants of the fruit fly *Drosophila* that had memory problems. These mutants—affectionately labeled "Dunce," "Amnesiac," and "Turnip"—either failed to learn or *could* learn but forgot rapidly. Recent evidence points to biochemical deficits in these mutants that might account for failures of memory (Dudai, 1988). We will discuss these studies in Chapter 17 when we take up neural mechanisms of learning and memory.

Many mutants of *Drosophila* have highly specialized defects in some part of the nervous system (Hall & Greenspan, 1979). The strength of research on *Drosophila* mutants derives from the wealth of specific mutations, each one involving a distinct impaired development process. For example, a lethal *Drosophila* mutant, "Notch," has an enlarged nervous system because too many precursor cells are produced. Studies of this mutant may enable researchers to attain a better understanding of processes that control the number of cells produced during early embryological development.

Over 150 mutations in mice involve the nervous system (Sidman, Green, & Appel, 1965). In these animals special defects appear during the development of the nervous system. Some mice fail to grow in particular brain regions. Others show specific anatomical derangements, such as a failure to myelinate or to arrange cells in their characteristic alignments. The mutants of one group, especially intriguing to researchers, all have impairments due to single genes that affect the postnatal development of the cerebellum. The names of these animals—"Reeler," "Staggerer," and "Weaver"—reflect the locomotor impairment that characterizes them. The impact of these genes on the size and arrangement of the cerebellum is illustrated in Figure 4-17. The cerebellum of Reeler shows an abnormal positioning of cells. There are no characteristic layers in the cerebellum, hippocampus, and cerebral cortex. Strangely, although cells of these regions are in abnormal positions, many connections to these cells are appropriate (Caviness, 1980). The cerebellum of Weaver has far fewer granule cells than a normal cerebellum, which might arise from a failure of these cells to migrate or form appropriate connections. Atrophy of the cerebellum is also evident in Staggerer, according to Sotelo (1980), who has shown that this animal fails to form synaptic connections between granule cells and Purkinje cells. The axon of the granule cell—the parallel fiber—comes close to the dendritic surface of the Purkinje cell, but postsynaptic specializations simply do not develop. Each of these mouse mutants shows impairment due to a single gene, related to the development of a specific kind of cell. Studies of these animals are bringing deeper understanding of the processes of neural development and their behavioral consequences.

Biochemical Influences

The brain consists of many different cell groups that develop at different times. The rules that orchestrate the emergence of this complex structure are undoubtedly elaborate. But one notion that all investigators share is that various bodily substances regulate the process.

This section give examples of two kinds of biochemical conditions that regulate neural growth. An example of intrinsic control is **nerve growth factor (NGF),** a substance that seems to control development of a particular class of nerve cells. An example of extrinsic biochemical influence is the role of nutrition in brain growth.

Intrinsic control Nerve Growth Factor

More than twenty years ago, investigators discovered a substance that markedly affects the growth of neurons of spinal ganglia and of the ganglia of the sympathetic nervous system (Levi-Montalcini, 1982). This substance is nerve growth factor. Its

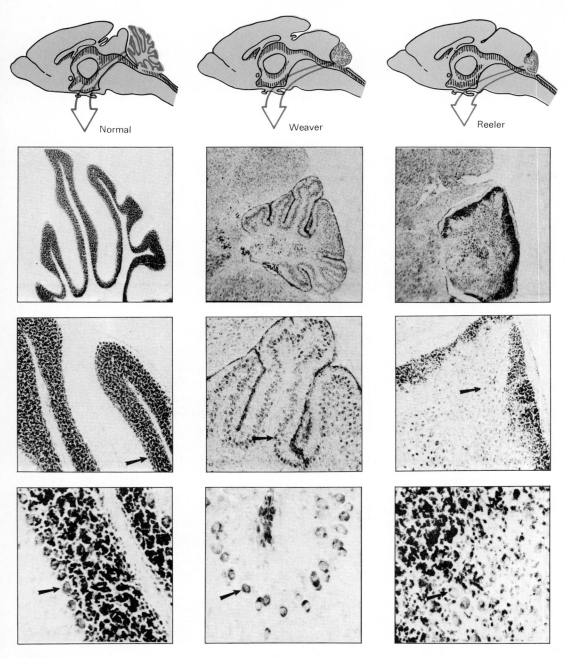

Figure 4-17 Cerebellar mutants of the mouse. The left column shows sections of the cerebellum in a normal mouse at three levels of magnification (25×, 66×, and 250×). The middle column shows comparable views in the mutant Weaver. Note the almost complete absence of granule cells while the alignment of Purkinje cells (arrows) is normal. The right column shows sections from the cerebellar mutant Reeler. Marked derangement of customary layering of cells is evident. Both mutants show overall shrinkage of cerebellum. (Leiman)

discovery earned Levi-Montalcini and Cohen a Nobel Prize in 1986. Originally, NGF was found in a variety of unusual places, including the salivary glands of mice, certain skin tumors, and the venom of a snake. More recently precise biochemical techniques have revealed its presence in the nervous system. Researchers found that if they administered NGF to an animal fetus, it resulted in the formation of sympathetic ganglia with many more cells than usual. These cells were also larger and had many extensive processes (Figure 4-18). If they administered it postnatally, NGF produced enlarged sympathetic nervous system cells. More recently it has been shown that nerve growth factor can reverse the degenerative effects of a drug that selectively destroys brain cells containing particular synaptic transmitters.

Part of the interest in NGF arises from the possibility that it is an example of control mechanisms in the development of the nervous system. There may be many such substances, each one controlling a particular cell type at a specific developmental period.

Nutrition and Brain Growth and Development

The good fortune of having adequate nutrition is not uniformly shared by people throughout the world. Periodic starvation confronts many, and this problem grows more urgent as population growth threatens to overwhelm the food resources of many nations. For many years people believed that the brain was less susceptible to the effects of diet than other parts of the body. It is certainly true that the adult brain is much less affected by dieting or overeating than are most other organs. But there is now evidence that malnutrition is detrimental to the brain, especially during early development. In fact, various forms of malnutrition that occur during critical growth periods of the brain in humans and other animals can produce irreversible changes in brain structure (Winick, 1976). Relating these cerebral changes to behavior is a complicated issue. It is hard to disentangle the effects of social disadvantage from the effects of dietary deficiencies, since most of these studies involve mothers and infants living in impoverished circumstances (Balderston et al., 1981).

We have learned something about the effects of early malnutrition from studies that compared undernourished children with matched controls who had no early nutritional deficiency. Studies in Mexico, Chile, Yugoslavia, and South Africa have shown that early malnourishment reduces later performance on many kinds of tests of mental capacity (Tizard, 1974). Malnourishment occurs more commonly in families that live in the kind of poverty that also poses other potent barriers to children's development. However, many of these studies show that later behavioral impairment depends on the time of life at which the child underwent a period of malnutrition. Children have a greater chance of behavioral recovery if the malnutrition occurred later rather than earlier in life.

The effects of severe early malnutrition can be counteracted to a large extent by nutritional and behavioral rehabilitation, especially if it begins by the age of 2 and is maintained into adolescence (Nguyen, Meyer, & Winick, 1977; Winick, Meyer, & Harris, 1975). This research was done with Korean orphans who were adopted by middle-class American families. All the children came from orphanages and were less than 5 years old when they were adopted. The study was done retrospectively;

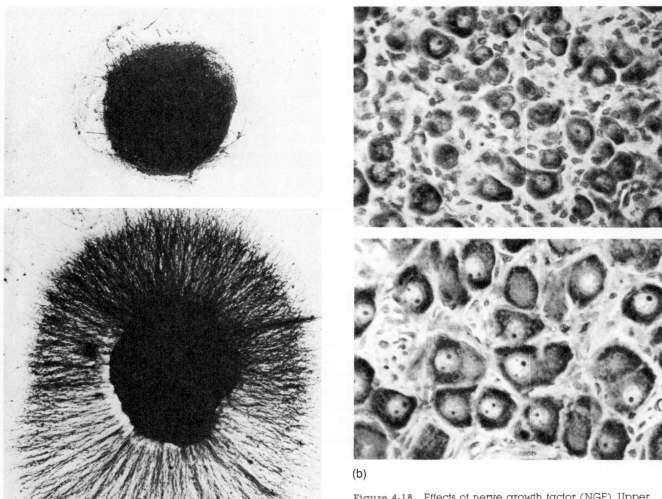

(a)

(b)

Figure 4-18 Effects of nerve growth factor (NGF). Upper figure shows a spinal ganglion grown in isolation outside the body (in vitro) without the presence of NGF. Lower photograph is a spinal ganglion grown under similar circumstances but with NGF added to the bathing solution. This figure shows marked proliferation of axonal processes radiating in all directions. (From R. Levi-Montalcini, *Science*, vol. 143 (January 1964): 105–110, Figures 1, 2, and 10. Copyright 1964 by the American Association for the Advancement of Science.)

that is, it was based on records available when the children were adolescent. The children were divided into three groups according to their height at the time of admission to the agency:

1. Severely malnourished, below the 3rd percentile (according to Korean norms)
2. Moderately malnourished, from the 3rd through the 24th percentiles
3. Well-nourished, at or above the 25th percentile

Figure 4-19 Effects of early and late adoption of malnourished infants on growth, intelligence, and achievement. Nutrition groups: 1, severely malnourished upon admission to adoption agency; 2, moderately malnourished; and 3, well-nourished. (Early adoption results from Winick, Meyer, and Harris, 1975; late adoption results from Nguyen, Meyer, and Winick, 1977)

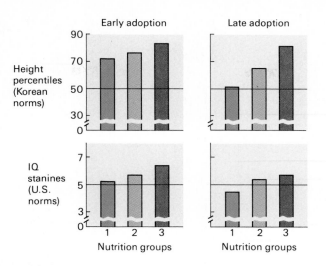

The malnourished groups developed well in their adoptive families, and they all came to exceed Korean norms of height and weight, although not reaching American norms. In IQ and school achievement tests, the means for all three groups adopted by the age of 2 later exceeded American means (Figure 4-19). Among those adopted after the age of 2, the children in group 1 (who suffered from severe early malnutrition) did not quite reach American norms, but children in the other two groups did. Although some differences related to their early malnutrition persisted, these differences were rather small. This is an important study because it demonstrates that the effects of severe early malnutrition can largely be overcome if rehabilitation starts early and is kept up.

The critical importance of early malnutrition with respect to later impairment of mental capacities has been emphasized in neuroanatomical and neurochemical studies. Dobbing (1976) stresses the fact that the brain is most vulnerable to malnutrition during the period of rapid brain growth. These periods vary for different animals (Figure 4-20). In humans the period of fastest brain growth and, according to Dobbing, maximum vulnerability to malnutrition occurs in late pregnancy and the first months of postnatal life. Similar malnutrition in the adult produces negligible effects.

Some permanent effects of malnutrition during early periods of rapid brain growth have been shown in experiments with animals. Body size and weight as well as brain structure and behavior are affected (Dobbing, 1974). For example, the size of the cerebellum in rats is especially sensitive to postnatal malnutrition, since this structure forms mainly just after birth in the rat.

Experience and Brain Development

The young of many species are born in a highly immature state, both anatomically and behaviorally. For example, in humans the weight of the brain at birth is only one-fourth of its adult weight. Behaviorally, the infants of many species are totally dependent on the parents. In these species developments in brain and in behavior

Figure 4-20 Rate of development of the brain in relation to birth. The time scale is different for various animals, ranging from days to months. This figure shows that the peak periods for brain development are quite different for various animals. The rat, for example, shows mainly postnatal increments of brain weight. In contrast, the main development of the guinea pig brain occurs before birth. (Adapted from Dobbing, 1972)

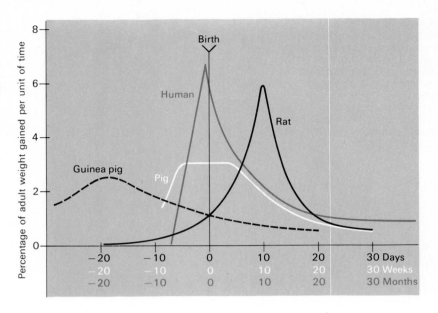

[handwritten margin notes:]
brain & behavior development vary together

induce, modular or maintain development

— induction

— modulating more evident

seem to vary together. According to recent studies, the successes and failures of early experience can affect the growth and development of brain circuits.

Varying experience during an individual's early development has been found to alter many aspects of behavior, brain anatomy, and brain chemistry (Gottlieb, 1976; Rosenzweig & Bennett, 1977, 1978). Interpretation of these findings suggests that experience can play three different roles in development and that it is important to distinguish among them: It can *induce* development, it can *modulate* development, and it can *maintain* ongoing development or results (Figure 4-21).

Induction of development is the most impressive possible role of experience. Some experimental treatments, such as early administration of sex hormones, can channel development into the male or the female body type (as we will see in Chapter 11). But can experience have an equally striking role? Evidence is scant, but **imprinting** may be an example of experiential induction of a behavior pattern. For example, male mallard ducklings were raised for their first 8 to 10 weeks with other duck species. As mature drakes, they were given the choice of mating with mallard ducks or with ducks of the species with which they had been raised. Whereas normally reared mallards all choose mallards, about two-thirds of the experimental animals chose the other species (Schutz, 1965).

When it comes to experience modulating development, we have more evidence. There can be negative as well as positive effects. For instance, "Exposure to certain sounds can either accelerate or decelerate hatching time in quail embryos. . . . Prior exposure to light facilitates the young chick's behavioral approach to a flickering light, whereas prior exposure to sound delays the approach to a source of visual flicker" (Gottlieb, 1976, p. 32). Early recognition of species and parental vocalizations depend upon the embryo being exposed to specific kinds of auditory stimulation before hatching (Hall & Oppenheim, 1987).

The role of experience in maintaining development has been shown in experi-

Figure 4-21 Schematic illustration of different kinds of effects of experience on brain development. (a) versus (b) Experience can *induce* changes—here the growth of a set of axon terminals. (c) versus (d) Experience can *modulate* development—here causing growth to reach a plateau earlier. (e) versus (f) Experience can maintain growth—here the endings decline unless experience occurs.

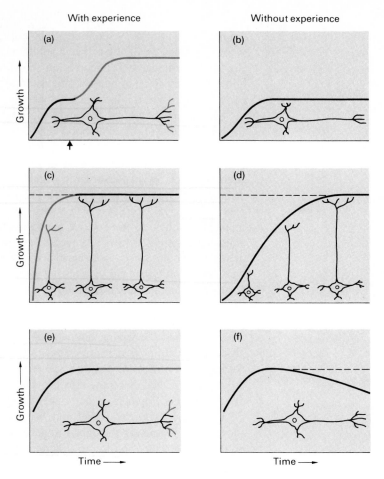

With experience

Without experience

ments with the visual system, as we will see. Sensory deprivation that begins shortly after birth and continues for several weeks can cause some of the developing cells to atrophy: "If you don't use it, you'll lose it."

Visual Deprivation and Disuse

Some people do not see forms clearly with one eye, even though it is intact and a sharp image is focused on the retina. Such impairments of vision are known as **amblyopia** (from Greek words for "dull" or "blunt" and for "vision"). An example of this disorder is seen in people with a "lazy eye": one that is turned inward (cross-eyed) or outward. Some children are born with this kind of misalignment of eyes. They "see double" rather than seeing a single fused image. If the deviated eye is not surgically realigned by the time the person reaches late childhood, vision becomes impaired. By the time the person reaches adulthood, there is virtually total suppression of pattern vision in the deviated eye. Realignment of the eyes in adulthood does not restore acute vision to the turned eye. This is quite striking, since throughout the person's development light enters this eye in a normal manner and the nerve cells of the eye continue to be excited. Similar misalignment of the eyes, when it appears for the first time in adulthood, produces double vision; the eye sees two separate images. This condition shows no change with further aging. These clinical observations of humans suggest that unusual positioning of the eyes during early development might change connections or circuits in the brain.

Other forms of amblyopia can be more subtle. Partial deprivation of form vision for long periods during childhood can result in deficits that persist even when the optical problems are corrected by eyeglasses in adulthood. This is especially likely to occur when defects are partial or subtle and not easily assessed in young children. Astigmatism is a visual disorder in which lines at some orientations do not appear as clear as lines at other orientations. This happens when the shape of the eyeball is not exactly spherical. Children with such a disability are partially deprived of visual input, since they do not receive clear stimuli in certain directions. Later in life, when their astigmatism is discovered, eyeglasses cannot provide completely adequate correction. Since this abnormal visual input started early in life, brain circuits were apparently changed in a lasting way.

Understanding the cause of amblyopia in people has been greatly advanced by visual-deprivation experiments with animals. These experiments have revealed some startling changes that are related to disuse of the visual system during early critical periods. Depriving animals of light to both eyes (binocular deprivation) produces structural changes in visual cortical neurons. Animals reared without visual input show a loss of dendritic spines and a reduction in synaptic density. Cragg (1975) emphasized that these effects occur most extensively during the early period of synaptic development in the visual cortex (Figure 4-22).

Pioneering work by Hubel and Wiesel, who shared a Nobel Prize in 1981, showed that restricting the deprivation of light to one eye (monocular deprivation) produces much more profound structural and functional changes in the visual cortex. Depriving an infant cat or monkey of vision in one eye leads to an absence of response by the deprived eye when the animal reaches adulthood. This is illustrated by a graph, usually called an **ocular-dominance histogram,** that portrays the strength of a neuron's response to stimuli presented to either the left or the right eye. Most cortical neurons are excited equally by input to either eye (Figure 4-23).

Figure 4-22 Brain development in the visual cortex of the cat. Synaptic development occurs most intensely from 8 to 37 days after birth, a period during which use can have profound influence. Note also that brain weight and cell volume rise in a parallel fashion and precede synaptic development. (Adapted from Cragg, 1975)

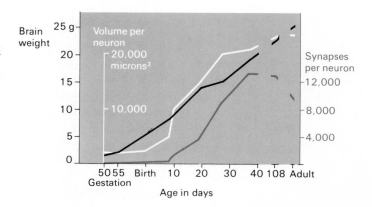

Figure 4-23 (a) Ocular dominance histogram of cells recorded from visual cortex of normal adult cats. (b) Ocular dominance histogram after early eye misalignment, that is, squint. (c) Ocular dominance histogram following monocular visual deprivation through the early critical period. (d) Ocular dominance histogram following binocular deprivation. (Adapted from Hubel and Wiesel, 1965; Wiesel and Hubel, 1965)

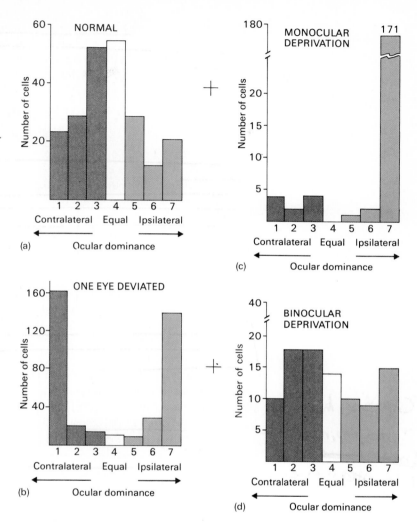

Fewer neurons are activated solely by inputs to one eye. When there has been monocular deprivation during an animal's early development, there is a striking shift in this graph. Most cortical nerve cells respond only to input to the nondeprived eye. In cats the susceptible period for this effect occurs during the initial 4 months of life. In nonhuman primates the sensitive period is extended to age 6 months. The mechanisms proposed for this effect bring us to a possible understanding of the forms of amblyopia described at the beginning of this section. It has been suggested that during a person's early development, axons representing input from each eye "compete" for synaptic places. Active, used synapses become effective connections and predominate over inactive, disused synapses.

Researchers also offer an explanation like this to account for amblyopia produced by misalignment of the eyes. An animal replica of this human condition was produced by cutting muscles on one side of the eye in young cats (Hubel & Wiesel, 1965). The ocular-dominance histogram of these animals reveals that cells of the visual cortex show binocular sensitivity that is greatly reduced. A much larger proportion are excited by stimulation of either right or left eye than can be seen in control animals. This effect occurs because after surgery the cells of the visual cortex do not receive synchronous input from both eyes.

Early Exposure to Visual Patterns

At birth the visual cortex is quite immature, and most synapses have yet to form. This raises the question of whether early experience affects the development of the visual cortex. Evidence cited in the previous section shows that profound disuse results in changes in both structure and response of visual pathways. The modifiability of the developing brain is also evidenced when animals are exposed to certain visual patterns during early development.

Experiments in which visual patterns are manipulated early in an animal's life have used patterns such as horizontal or vertical lines (Blakemore, 1976), a field of such stripes seen through goggles (Hirsch & Spinelli, 1971), or small spots of light (Pettigrew & Freeman, 1973). This is a very controversial field. Some research groups report results that differ from those reported by others. Nevertheless, the weight of current results suggests that these various visual experiences during the critical early periods of life modify the responses of nerve cells in the visual cortex. The sensitive period for these effects is the same as that for producing the effects of monocular deprivation.

According to a detailed survey (Movshon & van Sluyters, 1981), the variety of experiments and results in this area fail to provide any simple or uniform conclusions. Various results support the hypotheses that sensory stimulation is required to induce development of the visual system, to modulate ongoing development, or to maintain development that is programmed genetically. It appears therefore that experience *can* play each of the three hypothesized roles in neural development.

Nonvisual Experiences

Effects of early experiences on the brain can also be produced by manipulating nonvisual sensory inputs—a rat's whiskers, for example. Thomas Woolsey and collaborators (1976, 1981) found a unique clustering of nerve cells in a region of the cerebral cortex of the rat that receives input from the vibrissae (whiskers). The arrangement of these hairs on the skin is distinctive. The hairs are aligned similarly for all animals of the same species (See Figure 4-24). In the region of the cortex in which the vibrissae are represented, Woolsey noted clusters of cells that he called barrels, because the way they were arrayed made them look like the walls of a barrel. Figure 4-24 also shows that the layout of these cortical barrels corresponds to the map of the vibrissae. If some vibrissae are cut one to four days after birth, their cortical barrels do not develop. However, the barrels that represent adjacent intact vibrissae tend to be enlarged.

Manipulating an animal's capacity to smell also affects its brain during developmental stages. Studies by Meisami (1978) showed that the two nostrils of rats are relatively independent, with cross connections evident only at the pharynx. When one nostril is occluded early in life, the rat can breathe, but the olfactory mucosa—the sensory surface in the nose—is not stimulated on the occluded side. After

Figure 4-24 Locations of whiskers and cortical barrels in young mice. Arrangement of barrels in the somatosensory cortex is shown on the right. (a) Each barrel receives its input from a single whisker on the opposite side of the mouse's snout. (b), (c) If one row of whiskers is destroyed shortly after birth (as indicated by the brown dots), the corresponding row of barrels in the cerebral cortex later will be found to be missing and the adjoining barrels to be enlarged. (d) If all whiskers are destroyed, the entire group of barrels will have disappeared. The illustration is based on work of Thomas A. Woolsey of Washington University School of Medicine. (From W. M. Cowan, *The Development of the Brain.* Copyright © 1979 by Scientific American, Inc. All rights reserved.)

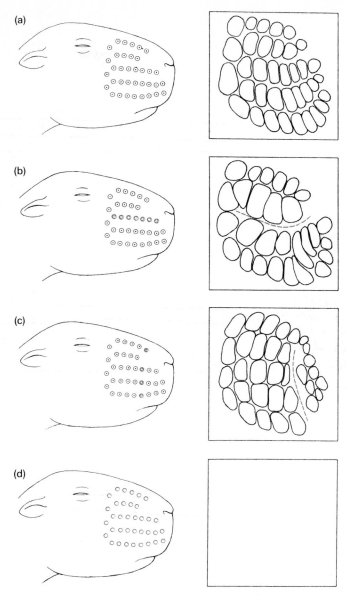

causing rats to experience this occlusion for some weeks, Meisami compared the growth of the rats' olfactory bulbs—the region of the brain that receives inputs from sensory receptors in the nose. There was a marked difference in size between the bulbs receiving inputs from the occluded and the normal nostrils. The olfactory bulb connected to the blocked nostril exhibited atrophy.

We have given only a few examples of the many experiments showing that sensory stimuli influence the development of the brain with respect to both structure and function. The effects differ depending on variables such as age of the subject, duration of the experience, and the stimulation given.

Aging of the Brain

The passage of time brings us an accumulation of joys and sorrows—perhaps riches and fame—and a progressive decline in many of our abilities. Changes with age seem to be inevitable in biological systems. Let us first survey some of the characteristics of normal aging. Then we will look on some of the pathological exaggerations of the aging process, notably Alzheimer's disease.

Normal Aging

Many aspects of structure and function change through the span of a human life. Though responding more slowly seems inevitable with aging, many of our cognitive abilities show little change throughout the adult years until we reach an advanced age. What happens to brain structure from adolescence to that day when we all get a little forgetful and walk more hesitantly? Does the structure of the brain change continuously throughout the life span of any animal? Data from autopsies on humans give us a few clues about how the brain changes progressively during adulthood.

Changes in the structure of the brain that accompany aging can be viewed at different levels, from subcellular structures to overall brain morphology. Differences in brain weight have often been examined in relation to aging. For years people have questioned the relevance of aging to these weight changes, since it was hard to distinguish changes due to aging from changes that arise from disease states that shortly lead to death. An excellent recent study eliminated such confounding factors (recall Figure 4-1). Changes are very small up to the age of 45, after which time the weight of the brain begins to decline significantly. Brain weight of elderly humans is 7–8% less than that of the peak of adult weight (Creasy & Rapaport, 1985). The course of these changes is the same for men and women, even though women generally live seven to ten years longer than men. Data also emphasize that aging is a variable state. Declines are evident in all people, but the declines are exaggerated in some. To some investigators this serves to emphasize the genetic contribution to aging and reinforces the idea that if you want to live long, choose parents and grandparents who have lived long.

In the brains of aged persons, one frequently finds that the folds of cerebral cortex have atrophied and that the lateral ventricles have enlarged. These changes are marked, however, only in cases of severe Alzheimer's disease, which we will discuss shortly.

A common measurement of structure used in studies of brain aging is the number of neural and glial cells in particular volumes of tissue. Investigators map specific regions and count the number of cells in various areas, using tissue taken from people who have died at different ages. These studies suggest that cell changes begin as early as the third decade and are specific to particular regions. Even more noticeable than the decrease in the number of cells is the loss of synaptic connections, which is especially prominent in the frontal regions. PET scans of elderly people add a new perspective to aging changes. Studies of normal oldsters reveal that cerebral metabolism remains almost constant. This is in marked contrast to the decline of cerebral metabolism in Alzheimer's disease.

Two regions of the motor system can be used to show how different aging functions can be. In the motor cortex a type of large neuron—the Betz cell—starts to change by about age 50, and by the time the person reaches about age 80, many of these cells have virtually shriveled away (Scheibel, Tomiyasu, & Scheibel,

1977). In contrast, other cells involved in motor circuitry—those in an area of the brain stem called the inferior olive—remain about the same in number over at least eight decades of life.

[margin note: Others completely intact.]

In young nervous systems, lesions in many parts of the brain and spinal cord induce the regrowth of axons and the formation of new connections (Chapter 16). But in adults, though axonal sprouting is also seen, it is much less vigorous. Furthermore, several investigators (for example, Scheff, Bernardo, & Cotman, 1978) have shown that the brains of aged rats are much less able to grow axon collaterals after lesions of a brain tract. Thus it appears that the brains of aged animals are less able than the brains of young ones to compensate anatomically for progressive reduction in cells and synapses.

[margin note: Older brain less adaptive to loss of cells & synapse]

Alzheimer's Disease: A Pathological Exaggeration of Aging

Since the beginning of this century, the population of people over the age of 65 in the United States has increased eightfold. By the year 2000 at least 30 million people will be in this age group. Most people reaching this age lead happy, productive lives, although at a slower pace than that which characterized their earlier years. However, it has become strikingly clear that there is a growing number of elderly people for whom age has brought a particular agony—the disorder called **Alzheimer's disease,** named after the neurologist who first described a type of dementia appearing before the age of 65. This disorder is now considered to be the same as the form of dementia that appears later in life, senile dementia. At the present almost 2 million Americans over the age of 65 suffer from Alzheimer's disease, and the progressive aging of our population means that a swelling of these ranks will occur in the next 20 to 40 years.

Alzheimer's disease is characterized by a progressive decline in intellectual functioning. It begins as a loss of memory of recent events. Eventually this memory impairment becomes all-encompassing, so extensive that Alzheimer's patients cannot maintain any form of conversation since both the context and prior information are rapidly lost. Simple questions—''What year is it?'' ''Who is the president of the United States?'' or ''Where are you now?''—become impossible to answer. Cognitive decline is progressive and relentless. In time, patients become disoriented and easily lose themselves in familiar surroundings. A recent manual—''The Thirty-Six Hour Day''—is a comment on the enormity of the nursing problems that families of Alzheimer's patients face.

Observations of the whole brain of patients reveal striking cortical atrophy especially evident in frontal, temporal, and parietal areas. Studies on brain metabolism of patients are especially revealing. PET scans following administration of a radioactive form of glucose show marked reduction of oxidative metabolism in posterior parietal cortex and some portions of the temporal lobe. A substantial decline in glucose utilization precedes the emergence of more severe cognitive impairments (Foster et al., 1984).

Microscopic studies of the brains of Alzheimer's patients reveal a set of characteristic cellular changes. Some cells show abnormalities of the neurofilaments of the cell, referred to as **neurofibrillary tangles.** These are abnormal whorls of filaments which formed a tangled array in the cell (Figure 4-25b). Histological studies also show strange patches of degenerating axon terminal, termed **senile plaques** (Figure

Figure 4-25 (a) Location of basal forebrain nuclei in the brain and distribution of cholinergic axons. (b) Neurofibrillary tangles seen in a cross section of the cerebral cortex of an aged person. One example is pointed out by the arrows. (c) Senile plaques in the cerebral cortex of an aged patient. (Photographs courtesy of F. J. Seil)

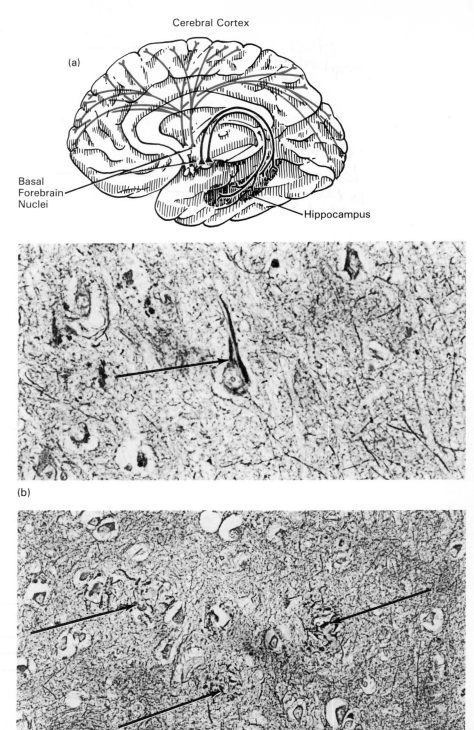

Cerebral Cortex

(a)

Basal Forebrain Nuclei

Hippocampus

(b)

(c)

4-25c). Contained within each plaque is a substance called amyloid, which is composed of unusual protein. The number of senile plaques is directly related to the magnitude of cognitive impairment. Investigators have also noted both of these cellular changes, typical of Alzheimer's disease, in the brains of Down's patients. Recently, researchers have especially focused on changes in a group of forebrain cells that may hold a key to the fundamental understanding of Alzheimer's disease. A striking loss of neurons in a subcortical region called the nucleus basalis of Meynert (Figure 4-25a) has been described in several anatomical studies. The axons of these cells extend to many cortical regions and the cells contain acetylcholine, a substance used for transmitting neural activity to other cells (discussed in Chapter 6). Deficiencies of the acetylcholine system are characteristic of the brains of Alzheimer's disease patients, and other chemical neurotransmitters may also be involved. Cases reported by Coyle, Price, and Delong (1983) showed a consistent and marked decline in the number of cells in this region, which was not seen in immediately adjacent brain areas. This is not simply an exaggeration of change seen routinely with aging, since normal aged individuals show little loss of neurons in this area as they grow older (Chui et al., 1984).

The causes of Alzheimer's disease remain shrouded in mystery. A familial factor is evident in some patients, especially those who show an early onset of dementia (starting between 40 and 60 years of age). One recent report documented the presence of Alzheimer's disease in 52 members of a family charted for several generations. A study of the family suggested a dominant form of inheritance of Alzheimer's disease (Nee et al., 1983). However, hereditary factors are not so evident in the vast majority of cases. Some investigators have focused on the possibility that the disorder involves a transmissible agent, such as a virus or subviral particle (Price, Whitehouse, & Struble, 1985). This notion is especially buoyed by research data that show the role of unusual viruses in degenerative brain diseases such as kuru. Since the salts of aluminum placed directly on the cerebral cortex produce neurofibrillary tangles in experimental animals, some investigators have suggested that toxic amounts of the metal might be responsible for Alzheimer's disease. A focus on aluminum is also inspired by the finding of relatively large amounts of aluminum in the brains of Alzheimer's patients. However, this change might arise as a consequence of the disorder rather than as a cause of it. Another hypothesis about the origins of Alzheimer's disease emphasizes autoimmune phenomena. According to this view, antibodies would selectively attack neurons that contain acetylcholine might arise within the patient's body. An exciting recent suggestion emphasizes that nerve growth factor is essential for the survival of cells containing acetylcholine. Deficiencies in NGF might be the primary cause of Alzheimer's disease, according to Hefti and Weiner (1986). Intensive research is now focused on the causes and treatment of Alzheimer's. The aging of our population suggests there is not much time left before we face an enormous public health problem. Replacement of lost brain cells by transplant has been suggested as therapy for this and other degenerative brain diseases; see Box 4-2.

BOX 4-2 | Brain Transplants or Grafts: Help for the Future?

Research on surgery of the nervous system sometimes makes the present look like the future. We have grown accustomed to heart transplants, kidney exchanges, corneal gifts, and so forth. But what about brain transplants? Journalists once asked Christiaan Barnard, the first surgeon to transplant a human heart (in 1967), what he thought about a brain transplant. He noted all the awesome technical difficulties: connecting axons, blood vessels, nerves, and all else. Then he seemed to recoil from the very idea by noting that such surgery should really be called a *body* transplant. (Shades of the transposed heads in Chapter 1!)

A short while ago brain or body transplants were unreal, the stuff of science fiction. The boundaries of the real have been extended a bit further, however, with demonstrations of the successful isolation of the entire brain of a chimpanzee by White (1976). He was able to maintain an isolated brain for at least one to two days by connecting it to machines that supplied oxygen and nutrients in the circulation.

More immediate, less quixotic hopes for humans come from work on a less grand scale, transplanting small portions of the brain as grafts. Can a piece of the brain be removed from one animal and donated to a second? This prospect is particularly important for possible compensation in brain disorders that involve deficiencies of specific chemicals generated in certain brain regions.

This field has developed very rapidly. Experimental work of the 1980s clearly shows that brain transplants are feasible and that added tissue does become part of the host's brain circuitry (Sladek & Gash, 1984). In fact, we are close to systematic efforts to replace degenerated brain areas of humans using brain grafting techniques, as some examples from the current animal research literature illustrate. These studies not only show that new cells become part of the "wiring diagram" of the host's brain; brain transplants in various animal studies can also correct impaired function produced by brain lesions. Research

shows that in some ways brain tissue is much easier to transplant than many other body tissues because brain tissue is less likely to be rejected by the actions of the immune system.

Most brain transplant studies have involved the insertion of a small piece of tissue into a brain cavity, such as the ventricle, or on the surface of the brain. Donor tissue is derived from embryonic or fetal animal brains. Some more recent transplant techniques have included the injection of dissociated embryonic nerve cells into deeper brain regions. This injection technique involves a suspension of cells floating in a solution after their connections have been disrupted by either mechanical or chemical means (Bjorklund & Stenevi, 1984). Box Figure 4-2 shows the sequence of steps involved in the cell suspension technique.

Functional recovery produced by brain transplants has been seen in a number of remarkable experiments. One such experiment with rats examined the impact of a brain transplant on performance of a T-maze task that involved spatial alternation. Following frontal cortical brain lesions, rats do poorly on this task. However, their performance is restored when frontal cortical tissue from fetal animals is transplanted to their frontal region (Labbe, Firl, Mufson, & Stein, 1983). Compensation for motor deficits has been a common type of test used to assess the functional advantages of brain transplants. Some of these tests attempt to model Parkinson's disease, a disabling brain disorder that involves destruction of cells in a brain stem area (the substantia nigra). These cells contain a chemical—dopamine—that is important to the proper functioning of brain circuits controlling movements. As an initial step in producing a rodent model of Parkinson's disease, the substantia nigra on one side of the brain stem is destroyed. This operation leads to a drop in the level of dopamine similar to that observed in the brains of patients with Parkinson's disease. Motor impairments produced by this surgery include body rotation and postural asymmetries. Injection of grafts of substantia nigra obtained from

Maldevelopment of the Brain and Behavior Impairments

The fact that the processes that guide development of the human brain are so multiple, intricate, and complex also means, unfortunately, that there are many ways in which they can go wrong. The many factors that control brain development—those that govern cellular proliferation, migration, differentiation, and formation of synapses—are subject to failures that can have catastrophic consequences for adaptive

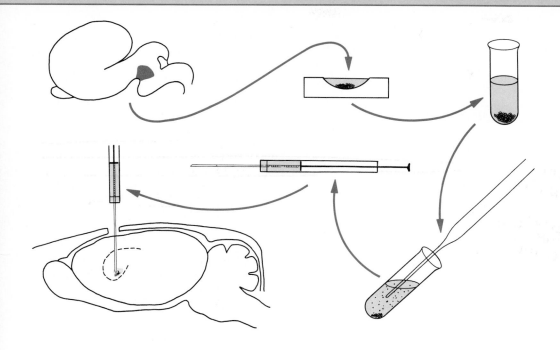

Box Figure 4-2 An example of a type of transplant procedure. Pieces of the brain are removed and cells are separated and then directly injected as a suspension into the brain. (Adapted from Björklund et al, 1983)

fetal animals led to recovery from the motor deficits and an increase in the brain level of dopamine (Bjorklund et al., 1981; Gage & Bjorklund, 1984; Perlow et al., 1979). Similar types of transplants of substantia nigra have also aided recovery of motor impairments seen in aged rats (Gage et al., 1983). This has raised the prospect that brain transplants might be useful in treating some of the brain degeneration associated with Alzheimer's disease. Transplanting cells and tissue into the brain is now seen as offering promise as therapy. A new window has been opened on the treatment of some of the most anguishing of human afflictions—those that arise from the death of brain cells.

behavior. The magnitude of this problem is reflected in the incidence of disorders that produce marked cognitive impairment. In the United States approximately 3.6 children per 1000 between the ages of 5 and 17 have IQ levels below 50.

In this section we will discuss some examples related to genetically controlled states and prenatal maternal conditions.

Genetically Controlled
States

Examples of genetically controlled states that cause developmental disorders focus on the actions of mutant genes and chromosomal anomalies.

Actions of Mutant Genes

Many metabolic disorders profoundly affect the developing brain. Some, which are associated with recessive inheritance, generally appear very early in life. In this category are about a hundred different disorders involving disturbances in the metabolism of proteins or carbohydrates or lipids. Characteristically the genetic defect is the absence of a particular enzyme that controls some critical biochemical step in the synthesis or breakdown of a vital body product. Two main results of enzymatic deficits can affect metabolic and structural states of the brain: (1) certain compounds build up to toxic levels; and (2) compounds needed for either function or structure fail to be synthesized.

[handwritten margin note: 1) enzyme builds to toxic level 2) or components are deficient necessary]

An example of the first kind will be given here; it is **phenylketonuria (PKU),** a recessive hereditary disorder of protein metabolism that at one time commonly resulted in mental retardation. One out of 50 persons is a heterozygous carrier; one in 10,000 births is an affected homozygous victim. The basic defect is the absence of an enzyme necessary to metabolize phenylalanine, an amino acid present in many foods. The brain damage caused by phenylketonuria probably comes about because there is an enormous build-up of phenylalanine. High concentrations of phenylalanine in the blood of newborns can have diverse origins and consequences. PKU is one example of this class of disorders, and newer views have suggested a more complex genetic origin than has been considered in the past (Rowley, 1984; Scriver & Clow, 1980).

The discovery of PKU marked the first time that an inborn error of metabolism was associated with mental retardation. Nowadays there are screening methods, required by law throughout the United States and in many other countries, that assess the level of phenylalanine in children a few days after birth. This is important because brain impairment can be prevented by administering diets that are low in phenylalanine. Recent evidence suggests that such dietary control of phenylketonuria is critical during early years, especially before age 2, and that the diet can be relaxed during adulthood. However, recent studies show that behaviorally normal mothers with PKU have a high percentage of mentally retarded offspring. This may be related to the mother's phenylalanine levels, although dietary treatment during pregnancy does not seem to reduce these fetal effects (Kolodny & Cable, 1981).

Success in treating phenylketonuria kindled enthusiasm for research on the analysis and possible treatment of many other forms of mental retardation controlled by genes that influence metabolic processes. Chromosomal analysis, biochemical techniques, and forms of fetal visualization are powerful tools that are providing better prediction and treatment for this class of disorders.

A dominantly inherited striking neurological disorder—Huntington's disease—is described in Box 4-3.

Chromosomal Anomalies

One in every 200 live births exhibits some kind of chromosomal anomaly: either an abnormal number of chromosomes (usually 45 or 47 instead of 46) or modifications

BOX 4-3	Huntington's Disease: A Genetic Detective Story

Sometime during the early 1800s, a woman living on the shores of Lake Maracaibo in Venezuela became afflicted with a disease that has ravaged many of her more than 3000 descendants. This community has become an important part of a genetic detective story that is unfolding through the use of international observations coupled with contemporary neurological and genetic techniques.

To begin this story it is important to note that the genetic blueprint that guides the growth and development of the brain can be lethal for many humans, since it strongly determines the occurrence of particular diseases. Hundreds of diseases have been traced to genetic flaws. In some cases these disorders appear early in life; in other cases early development of the brain proceeds normally, but suddenly, during adulthood, a profound brain disorder appears with little or no warning. In the latter instance descendants of an afflicted person are haunted by the prospect of eventually succumbing to a disorder they see unfolding in a parent or other older relative. One of the cruelest of these genetically controlled disorders is **Huntington's disease.**

George Huntington was a young physician whose only publication (in 1884) was a description of a strange motor afflication of a nearby family. He correctly saw that this was an inherited neurological disorder passed from generation to generation. We now know that this disease is transmitted by a single dominant gene so that each child of a victim has a 50% chance of developing the disease. It usually first makes its appearance between the ages of 30 and 45, so that most victims have children before knowing whether they will ultimately succumb to this disorder. Sadly, this assures continuing generations of ravaged individuals unless some technique could be developed that would inform descendants of patients about their genetic susceptibility to the disorder.

Huntington's disease can first be noticed in very subtle behavioral changes: little twitches of the face and some clumsiness. Subtlety is rapidly lost as a continuing stream of involuntary jerks engulf the entire body. Aimless movements of the eyes, jerky leg motions, and writhing of the body make breathing and eating complicated. Quite frequently profound dementia becomes evident; in a small percentage of patients, cognitive changes are the earliest signs of emerging disorder.

The neuroanatomical hallmark of Huntington's disease is the destruction of the caudate nucleus, a main component of the brain systems that control movement. A very sad picture, the understanding of which eluded investigators for many years.

The first prospects of identifying individuals at risk for Huntington's disease emerged when researchers started to study the fishing village in Venezuela where so many patients were found. Patterns of intermarriage in this isolated village assured that the single case that initially appeared 150 years ago had multiplied many times and now includes at least 100 current cases and several thousand at risk for the disease. Researchers have compiled elaborate pedigree histories of virtually all individuals in this town and obtained skin and blood samples. Data from this group combined with those obtained from Huntington's disease victims in the United States have led to some remarkable genetic findings. Scientists working with the most modern analytic tools of biochemical genetics have now come up with a genetic marker of this disease in the DNA molecule (Gusella et al., 1983; Folstein et al., 1985). The identification of this marker is leading to studies that will enable identification of the locus of the defective gene and the pathways that lead to brain destruction. The test for the marker now allows susceptible individuals to be identified before they become ill. Clearly, such genetic identification holds personal risks, but it also raises the prospect of aiding people to plan their futures better. Ultimately perhaps genetic engineering techniques will enable appropriate intervention to prevent the spread of this gruesome disease.

in the structure of the chromosome. Generally disorders involving nonsex chromosomes have a more profound impact on behavior than those involving sex chromosomes.

The most common form of cognitive disorder due to a chromosomal anomaly is **Down's syndrome.** The disorder associated with 95% of these cases is an extra chromosome, number 21 (hence the designation trisomy 21). This disorder is strikingly related to the age of the mother at the time of conception (Table 4-2). The behavioral dysfunctions are quite varied. Most cases of Down's syndrome have

Table 4-2   Risk of Babies with Down's Syndrome Related to
            Maternal Age

Mother's Age at Birth of Child	Risk of Down's Syndrome
Under 30	1:1500
30–34	1:1000
35–39	1:300
40–44	1:100
45 and over	1:40

Source: Karp (1976).

very low IQs, but some rare individuals attain an IQ of 80. Brain anomalies in Down's syndrome are also varied. Recent biopsies of the cerebral cortex of Down's sufferers show abnormal formation of dendritic spines.

A recently discovered mouse model that involves an extra chromosome results in structural and behavioral changes analogous to Down's syndrome in humans (Epstein, 1986). Investigation of this model is providing valuable insights into how the extra chromosome causes the structural and behavioral abnormalities.

Prenatal Maternal Conditions

Even in the protected environment of the womb, the embryo and fetus are not immune to what is taking place in the bodily state of the mother. Maternal conditions, such as virus infection, exposure to drugs, and malnutrition, are especially likely to result in developmental disorders in the unborn child. Let us consider examples of disorders resulting from two of these conditions.

Exposure to Drugs During Pregnancy

Concern with the maternal environment as a determinant of brain development has recently spawned a new field: **behavioral teratology.** (Teratology is the study of malformations, from the Greek *teras,* "monster.") Those who work in this field are especially concerned with the pathological behavioral effects of drugs ingested during pregnancy. The heavy use of behaviorally active drugs in recent years has focused attention on their connection with several developmental disorders.

Fetal Alcohol Syndrome

Although recent research has demonstrated alcohol's potential to affect fetal growth and development, there is a long history of concern about alcohol and pregnancy, dating back to classical Greek and Roman times. Aristotle warned that "foolish, drunken . . . women . . . bring forth children like unto themselves, morose and languid" (cited in Abel, 1982). By now, the wisdom of this observation is well supported by abundant research studies. Children born to alcoholic mothers show a distinctive profile of anatomical, physiological, and behavioral impairments that is now known as the "fetal alcohol syndrome" (Abel, 1984; Colangelo & Jones, 1982). Prominent anatomical effects of fetal exposure to alcohol include distinctive changes in facial features (e.g., sunken nasal bridge, altered shape of the nose) and features of the eyelids. Intrauterine growth deficiencies are particularly evident because children born to alcoholic mothers are deficient in both height and weight at birth. Few of these children catch up in the years following birth (Colangelo & Jones, 1982). The most common problem associated with fetal alcohol syndrome is mental retardation, which can vary in severity although it is a persistent characteristic. No alcohol threshold has yet been established for this syndrome, but it is clear that it can occur with relatively moderate intake during the course of pregnancy. In addition to mental retardation, fetal alcohol syndrome children show other neurological signs. Hyperactivity, irritability, tremulousness, and other signs of motor instability are commonly seen. Researchers have yet to establish whether these effects are mainly mediated by alcohol, its toxic metabolites, or the effects of alcohol on the metabolic health and nutrition of the mother. Another possibility is an effect on the circulatory links between the parent and child. This syndrome may not be distinctive to alcohol; heavy use of marijuana seems to exert a similar effect on fetal growth and development (Hingson et al., 1982).

Two Calendars for Brain Development

Let us now try to bring together research on brain development along the two vastly different time scales: the weeks and months of growth of an individual and the millions of years of evolution. We might use the analogy of the different but equally essential contributions of an architect and a carpenter in building a house. The architect, in preparing the plans, calls on a long history of human knowledge about structures that meet the basic human needs: rest, work, recreation, eating, child care, and so on. The structure must be comfortable, safe, and affordable, and must conform to the tastes of the community. The carpenter has to use these plans to construct the house, translating the two-dimensional information given on the blueprints into a three-dimensional structure. At a number of points during the building process, the carpenter's judgment and interpretation are called for. So two houses built by different carpenters from the same blueprints will not be identical. Another reason for differences in houses is that the materials available for their construction may not be exactly the same. The architect tries to foresee some of the problems of construction and to build safety factors into the plans, so that small deviations or errors will not seriously impair the safety or utility of the completed building.

We are not the first to use such an analogy. An anonymous wit pointed out that a baby is the most complicated object to be made by unskilled labor. And psychologist-information scientist J. C. R. Licklider characterized God as a great architect but a sloppy workman.

The plans for construction of the brain have certain characteristics that we should note and comment on:

1. New plans are never started from scratch. Instead, older plans are reused and modified to adjust to specific situations.
2. Not every detail is specified. Part of the program is implicit in the list of materials and methods of construction. The plans would be hopelessly complex and voluminous if every detail had to be specified.
3. Allowances are made for interaction between the materials and the environ-

ment. An architect knows how certain shingles will weather in a given climate to produce a desired appearance and how landscape planting will stabilize the soil and beautify the home's setting. So, too, the genetic plans for the brain take advantage of information provided by the environment. These plans allow for interaction between the developing organism and its environment.

The reuse and successive modification of genetic plans mean that the early embryological stages of development of all vertebrates are similar. The early neural tubes look very much the same in the embryos of a frog, a rat, or a person. Furthermore, the basic divisions of the brain are the same in all these forms. However, the whole structure has been scaled up in the mammals, and especially in the primates, and some parts have been enlarged relative to others.

The genetic code does not seem to have room for all the information necessary to specify the complete wiring diagram for each part of the nervous system. It achieves some economy by using the same information to apply to many different parts of the structure. Thus the same gene may specify aspects of neural circuitry in different areas of the brain. Any mutation of the gene may therefore cause an abnormal arrangement of neurons in both the cerebellar and cerebral cortex. Also, certain hormones stimulate the growth of neural connections throughout the nervous system, as we will see in Chapter 7. And some fine details of the wiring do not seem to be specified but are simply worked out locally.

Both economy of genetic instructions and adaptation to individual circumstances are achieved by counting on the environment to furnish certain information necessary for development. Each species has evolved in relation to a particular ecological niche, and its program of development utilizes the environment as a source of information and stimulation. Thus, for example, most vertebrates are exposed to patterned visual stimulation soon after birth. By the time of exposure, the basic plan of the visual system has been laid down. But formation of detailed connections and maintenance of the visual circuitry require input from the environment. Precise coordination of input from both eyes requires fine tuning of the system. There are so many variables in the structure of the eyes that it would be extraordinarily costly for genetic specification to bring about perfect alignment of the two retinal images. The program of the genes has come down to us after millions of years of trial-and-error improvements, but it has its limits. So certain adjustments are required after the individual goes into operation, so to speak. Small misalignments of the two retinal images can be compensated for by minor "rewiring" of the central visual connections. But if the misalignment between the two eyes is too great, as when the eyes are crossed, then the input of one eye is usually suppressed. Double vision is thereby avoided. The ability to learn from our environment and experience enables us to adjust to particular environments and life styles. (Chapters 16 and 17 will consider the biological mechanisms of learning and memory.)

You can now see that the short-range and long-range calendars provide complementary perspectives on the development of the nervous system and behavior. We will call on both perspectives to illuminate brain-behavior relations in many areas of physiological psychology.

Summary · Main Points

1. Early embryological events in the formation of the nervous system include an intrinsically programmed sequence of cellular processes: (a) the production of nerve cells (cell proliferation), (b) the movement of cells away from regions of mitotic division (cell migration), (c) the acquisition, by nerve cells, of distinctive forms (cell differentiation), and (d) the loss of some cells (cell death).

2. Fetal and postnatal changes in the brain include myelinization of the axons and development of dendrites and synapses. Although most neurons are present at birth, most synapse development in humans occurs after birth.

3. Neurospecificity is the doctrine that the formation of neural pathways and synapses follows an innate plan that specifies the precise relations between growing axons and particular target cells. The extent to which specific connections are determined genetically is a matter of current controversy.

4. Among many determinants of brain development are (a) genetic information, (b) growth factors, such as nerve growth factors, and (c) nutrition.

5. Experience affects the growth and development of the nervous system. This is shown by experiments in which animals undergo sensory deprivation during critical early periods of their development. Results indicate that experience may induce and modulate formation of synapses and may also maintain them.

6. The brain continues to change throughout life. Old age brings loss of neurons and synaptic connections in some regions of the brain. In some people the changes are more severe than in others, and pathological changes occur in the condition known as Alzheimer's disease or senile dementia.

7. Various kinds of maldevelopment of the brain can occur as a result of genetically controlled disorders. Some are metabolic disorders, such as phenylketonuria (PKU), and involve the body's inability to manufacture a particular enzyme. Other hereditary disorders, such as Huntington's disease, appear only in adulthood. Each defect is probably governed by a single gene.

8. Some forms of mental retardation, such as Down's syndrome, are related to disorders of chromosomes, particularly an excess number of chromosomes.

9. Impairments of fetal development that lead to mental retardation can be caused by drugs, such as alcohol or marijuana, that are used during pregnancy.

Recommended Reading

Greenough, W. T., & Juraska, J. M. (Eds.) (1986). *Developmental neuropsychobiology*. Orlando, Fla.: Academic Press.

Hopkins, W. G., & Brown, M. C. (1984). *Development of nerve cells and their connections*. Cambridge, England: Cambridge University Press.

Jacobson, M. (1978). *Developmental neurobiology*. New York: Plenum.

Lund, R. D. (1978). *Development and plasticity of the brain*. New York: Oxford University Press.

Purves, D., & Lichtman, J. W. (1985). *Principles of neural development*. Sunderland, Mass.: Sinauer.

Spreen, O., Tupper, D., Risser, A., Tuoko, H., & Edgell, D. (1984). *Human developmental neuropsychology*. New York: Oxford University Press.

TWO

Communication and Information Processing in the Body

Underlying all behavior—seeing, mating, eating, learning—is the processing of information. The sources of information include sensory receptors, ongoing neural activity, and endocrine events. The integrated behavior of an individual depends on the signals that communicate information within the nervous system and from one part of the body to another. In these chapters we will take up basic questions about the nature of information processing in the body, the ways scientists have investigated the underlying activities, and some applications of their research. We will discuss neural communication and information processing in Chapters 5 and 6; we will take up hormonal communication in Chapter 7. The neural and endocrine systems work together in many kinds of behavior.

For ease of discussion, we can separate the signals that control and integrate behavior into two categories: neural and hormonal. Neural signals take two main forms: (1) Neurons produce changes in electrical potentials across their membranes and conduct these changes along their membranes. These electrochemical signals are the topic of Chapter 5. The usual way of investigating these signals is to put electrodes into (or close to) nerve cells and record their electrical activity. (2) In most cases one neuron communicates with another by releasing a specific chemical substance into the synapse—the functional region between the neurons. Many drugs and chemical agents influence behavior by affecting neural transmission at synapses. Chapter 6 takes up synaptic chemistry and psychopharmacology.

Hormonal signals are biochemical compounds secreted into the blood by endocrine organs (such as the pituitary gland or the thyroid gland). Unlike neural messages, which are confined to nerve cells, hormonal messages spread throughout the body, but they are taken up only by cells or organs that are prepared to receive them. We can think of endocrine organs as broadcasting their messages to be picked up by any receivers that are tuned in. Hormonal communication is the subject of Chapter 7.

The chapters in Part Two not only sketch the basic processes of communication and information processing in the body, but they also relate these mechanisms to the behavior of daily life and to some major dilemmas of human behavior. Thus they take up aspects of cognition and personality, and they deal with problems such as epilepsy, drug addiction, and psychosocial dwarfism.

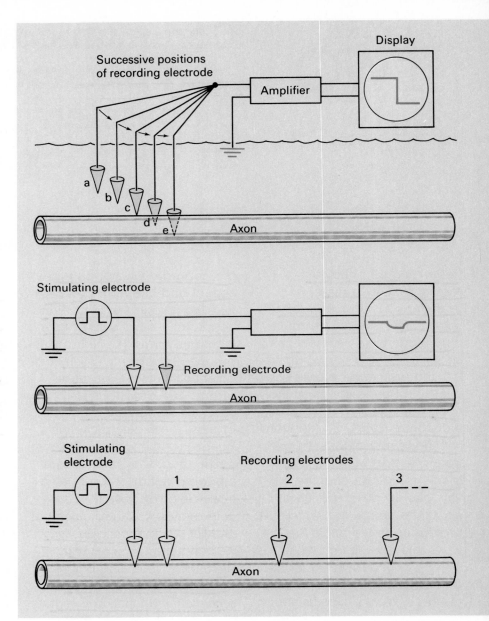

5 Information Processing in the Nervous System

ORIENTATION

To this point we have emphasized architectural features of the nervous system. We have seen that nerve cells come in a variety of sizes and shapes; further, they are arranged in all sorts of circuits and larger assemblies of neurons. Now our focus shifts to considering the character of the business of nerve cells and their arrangements into circuits. What are the elementary signals of these cells, and how is information integrated and transmitted in the nervous system? We will first describe the basic electrical signals of nervous systems and then describe how these basic responses of nerve cells operate in information-processing networks. We will then discuss the physicochemical basis of these electrical events. In humans it is possible to record some indications of brain electrical activity using small electrodes placed on the scalp. These electrical events summarize the activities of many brain cells and can provide some interesting windows to the human brain. Attention, personality, and intelligence are all being related to electrical activity of the human brain. These electrical events also provide a way to describe the condition of electrical activity gone awry—the state of seizure disorders.

Electrical Signals in the Nervous System

One of the most powerful "inventions" in animal evolution was the electrical signaling of neurons. This invention appears in animals as diverse as human beings, insects, and jellyfish—in fact, in almost all multicellular animals. These neural signals underlie the whole range of thought and action, from composing a symphony or solving a mathematical problem to feeling an irritation on the skin and swatting a mosquito.

To understand how the nervous system works, investigators measure three different kinds of electrical events in studying the activity of single neurons:

1. The **resting potential,** or **membrane potential,** that neurons show when they are inactive. This small difference in potential between the inner and

outer surfaces of the membrane results from the separation of electrically charged particles: ions. Many other kinds of cells, such as muscle cells and blood corpuscles, also have membrane potentials. The uniqueness of nerve cells is that they use changes in the resting potential as signals that can be transmitted to other cells and integrated in complex ways.

2. **Nerve impulses,** or **action potentials,** brief propagated changes that travel rapidly along the axon in some kinds of neurons. These changes are conducted in chain-reaction fashion, maintaining a uniform size as they advance, and they enable axons to serve as channels for rapid communication.

3. **Local potential changes** that are initiated at postsynaptic sites. These local or **graded potentials** vary in size and duration. They are not propagated, but spread passively, so that the amplitude of such a potential decreases progressively with distance from its site of origin. These are also called **postsynaptic potentials.** Interaction among graded postsynaptic potentials is the basic mechanism by which the nervous system processes information.

Let us consider each of these three kinds of potentials in order to see the characteristic states of the neuron at rest and during activity. These potentials can be thought of as the basic vocabulary of the nervous system. Knowing the vocabulary, we can understand much about how information is communicated and processed in the nervous system. Some neurophysiologists have pushed the analysis of these potentials to another level and have investigated the ionic mechanisms of neural activity. We will review the ionic mechanisms later in the chapter.

Resting Membrane Potential

A few simple experiments will display the characteristics of electrical potentials in nerve cells. Our initial experimental setup is shown in Figure 5-1. It includes an axon placed in a bathing fluid that resembles extracellular fluids, a pair of electrodes—the one with a very fine tip is called a microelectrode—and devices to amplify, record, and display electrical potentials. As we advance the microelectrode toward the axon, we see that as long as the microelectrode remains outside the axon, there is zero potential difference between the microelectrode tip and a large electrode placed at some distance from the axon in the bath. There are no potential differences between any two electrodes placed in the extracellular medium, since the distribution of ions in the extracellular fluid is uniform or homogeneous.

When the electrode suddenly penetrates the membrane of the axon (point d in Figure 5-1), we note an abrupt drop in potential to a level of −70 to −80 millivolts (mV). That is, the inside of the axon is electrically negative with respect to the outside. This difference, called the **membrane potential,** demonstrates that the axonal membrane separates charges. It shows that the fluid environment of the intracellular compartment is different in composition from that of the extracellular fluid. We will discuss the manner in which that difference is created in the section on ionic mechanisms.

Our hypothetical experiment would be hard to perform with just any axon. Most axons of mammals are less than 20 micrometers (μm) in diameter and quite difficult to pierce in this manner. Nature provided neurophysiologists with an extraordinary solution to this problem: **giant axons,** especially those of the squid. Squid axons can attain a diameter of 1 millimeter (mm), so fat and apparent to the unaided eye

Figure 5-1 Recording the resting potential of the neural membrane. When the tip of the recording electrode is in the extracellular fluid or even touching the surface of the neuron, no potential is recorded between it and the reference electrode in the fluid. But as soon as the electrode penetrates the axon, a resting potential of approximately −70 mV is recorded.

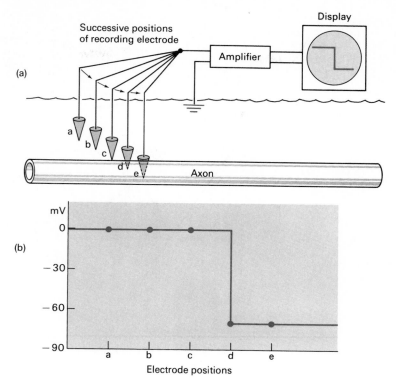

that observers originally thought that the axons must be part of the circulatory or urinary system (Figure 5-2). The zoologist J. Z. Young inaugurated the use of the squid giant axon for neurophysiology in 1938. Electrodes in the form of capillary tubes 0.2 mm in diameter can be inserted into a giant axon without altering its properties or activity. The membrane seems to seal around the inserted electrode tip. Experiments with giant axons soon led to fundamental advances in the understanding of neural membrane structure and function. We owe a nod of gratitude to the squid!

Nerve Impulses

The next experiments require a source of electrical stimulation. We must also add two terms to our vocabulary: **hyperpolarization** refers to increases in membrane potential (a greater negativity inside the membrane), and **depolarization** refers to reductions of the membrane potential (decreased negativity). The stimulator will provide hyperpolarizing or depolarizing electrical pulses, and our objective is to describe the effects such stimuli have on the membrane potential.

Figure 5-3 displays the changes in membrane potential that occur in response to successively stronger stimulus pulses. The application of hyperpolarizing stimuli to the axonal membrane results in responses that are almost mirrors of the "shape" of the stimulus pulse. These responses are passive reflections of the stimulus, with distortions at the leading and trailing edges due to an electrical property of the membrane: its capacitance, the ability to store electrical charges.

Figure 5-2 Drawing of a squid with the mantle nerve emerging from its ganglion. The giant fiber is embedded in the mantle nerve. Contraction of the mantle is produced by activity in these nerves. This results in ejection of water and powerful reverse movement. The giant axon (b) is about 400 μm in diameter. (From J. C. Eccles, 1973)

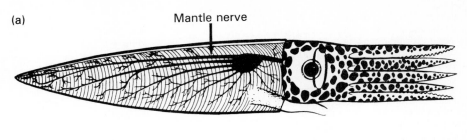

(a) Mantle nerve

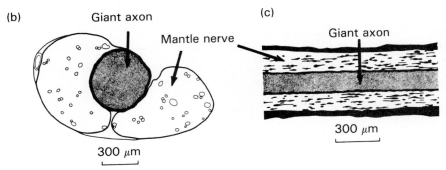

(b) Giant axon — Mantle nerve — 300 μm

(c) Giant axon — 300 μm

If we placed several fine electrodes at successive positions along the axon, but all within 1 mm of the site of stimulation, we would see another important attribute of biological potentials in a conducting medium. If we applied a hyperpolarizing pulse, we would note progressively smaller responses at greater and greater distances from the stimulus site. In fact, there is a simple law that describes this relationship: In a conducting medium, the size of a potential decays as a function of the square of the distance. Since the amplitudes of these responses decline with distance, they are examples of local or graded potentials.

Now let us present a series of depolarizing pulses (Figure 5-3). The membrane response to the initial few stimuli is a series of depolarizing changes, with some distortions. These again are local, graded responses. However, things change suddenly when the depolarizing stimulus reaches a level of 10–15 mV. At this level a rapid, brief (0.5–2.0 msec) response is provoked: the action potential or nerve impulse. This is a brief transmembrane change in potential that momentarily makes the inside of the membrane positive with respect to the outside. Our experiment has now illustrated the notion of the **threshold** of the nerve impulse, that is, the stimulus intensity just sufficient to elicit a nerve impulse.

What happens when we increase the level of depolarizing stimuli in successive pulses until they get well above threshold? This experiment displays a significant property of axonal membranes: With further increases in depolarizing stimulation, the amplitude of the nerve impulse does not change (Figure 5-4). Thus the size of the nerve impulse is independent of stimulus magnitude. This is referred to as the **all-or-none** property of the nerve impulse. Increases in stimulus strength are represented in the axon by changes in the frequency of nerve impulses. With stronger stimuli, the interval between successive nerve impulses gets shorter.

If we continue our experiment on this axon and now employ either very strong

Figure 5-3 Effects of hyperpolarizing and depolarizing stimuli on the axon. The upper section of the figure shows a setup for stimulation (to the left) and for recording (to the right). When a series of hyperpolarizing stimuli of increasing amplitude is delivered, the axon shows hyperpolarized responses that are graded in amplitude. With depolarizing stimuli, graded responses occur to weak stimuli, but when depolarization of 10–15 mV occurs, the axon gives a large response called an action potential, or nerve impulse.

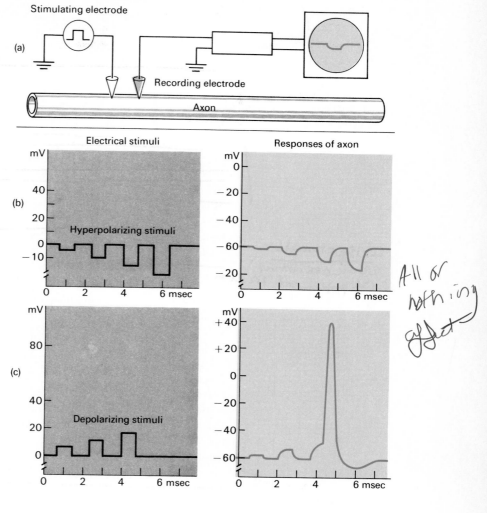

All or nothing effect

Figure 5-4 When one presents depolarizing stimuli (a) that are stronger than threshold (suprathreshold stimuli), the amplitude of the nerve impulses (b) remains fixed and is not influenced by the strength of the stimulus. This fixity of amplitude is referred to as the all-or-none property of action potentials.

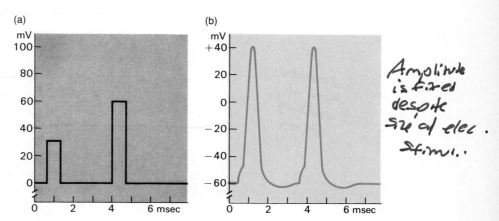

Amplitude is fixed despite size of elec. stimu..

stimuli or stimulating pulses that are closely spaced in time, we observe another important property of axonal membranes. As we offer our beleaguered axon more and more intense stimuli, we note that there seems to be an upper limit to the frequency for nerve impulse activity: about 1200 impulses per second. The same underlying property is also shown in experiments in which we compare the effects of varying the interval between two successive stimuli; that is, we space our stimuli closer and closer together until, at some brief interval, only the initial pulse will elicit a nerve impulse. In this case the axon membrane is said to be **refractory** to the second stimulus. There is a period following the initiation of a nerve impulse in which the membrane is totally insensitive to applied stimuli. This is called the **absolute refractory phase** and is followed by a period of reduced sensitivity, the **relative refractory phase.**

A closer look at the form of the nerve impulse shows that the return to baseline is not simple. Rather, many axons show oscillations of potential following the nerve impulse. These changes are called **afterpotentials,** and they are related to changes in excitability following an impulse.

Propagation of Nerve Impulses

The axon is specialized to communicate nerve impulses over its entire length. How is the nerve impulse conducted along the axon? To explore this process we will add to our experimental setup by placing recording electrodes at several points along the axon (Figure 5-5). The nerve impulse is initiated at one end of the axon, and records are obtained from electrodes along the length of the axon.

These records show that the nerve impulse appears with increasing delays at the successive positions along the length of the axon. The nerve impulse initiated at one location on the axon spreads in a sort of chain reaction along the length, traveling at speeds that range from less than 1 m/sec in some fibers to more than 100 m/sec in others.

How does the nerve impulse travel? Basically the nerve impulse is a change in membrane potential that is regenerated at successive axon locations. It spreads from one region to another because the flow of current associated with this small and rapid potential change stimulates adjacent axon segments. The segment of axon that is just beyond the activated area is supplied with depolarizing current because an electrical circuit is formed along the length of the axon, linking successive regions. The nerve impulse established at one place on the axon is then regenerated at successive points along it.

If we record the conduction speed of impulses in axons that differ in diameter, we see that the rate of conduction varies with the diameter of the axon. Relatively large, heavily myelinated fibers are found in mammalian sensory and motor nerves. In these neurons conduction speed ranges from about 5 m/sec in axons 2 μm in diameter to 120 m/sec in axons 20 μm in diameter. The highest speed of neural conduction is only about one-third the speed of sound in air, whereas it was once thought to be as great as the speed of light! (See Box 5-1.) These relatively high rates of conduction aid the speed of sensory and motor processes. Small unmyelinated mammalian nerves have diameters of 1 μm or less, and their conduction speeds range downward from 2 m/sec.

The myelin sheathing on the larger mammalian nerve fibers speeds conduction.

Figure 5-5 Propagation of the nerve impulse along an axon. When a stimulus is delivered at 1 msec on the trace, an action potential appears promptly at recording electrode 1 as shown in recording 1. Electrodes 2 and 3 record potential changes of exactly the same form and amplitude but delayed successively in time (as shown in records 2 and 3) as the impulse propagates along the axon.

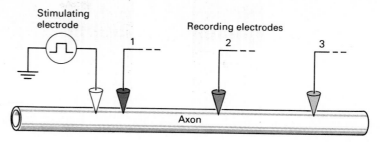

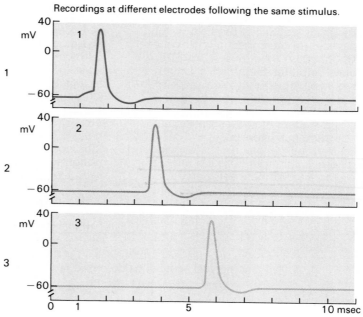

The myelin is interrupted by small gaps, called **nodes of Ranvier,** that are spaced about every 1 mm along the axon (recall Figure 2-12). Since the myelin insulation offers considerable resistance to the flow of ionic currents, the impulse jumps from node to node. This is called **saltatory conduction,** from the Latin *saltus* meaning a "leap" or "jump." (The more familiar word *somersault* comes from the Latin *supra* meaning "over" and *saltus*). The evolution of rapid saltatory conduction in vertebrates has given them a major behavioral advantage over nonvertebrates.

Invertebrate axons are unmyelinated, and most are small in diameter and slow in conduction. An exception to this rule is that many invertebrates have a few giant axons that mediate critical motor responses, such as escape movements. In the invertebrate as in the vertebrate, the speed of conduction increases with axon diameter. The giant axon of the squid has an unusually high rate of conduction for an invertebrate, but the rate still is only about 20 m/sec, considerably slower than that of many mammalian fibers.

The importance of myelin sheathing in promoting rapid conduction of neural impulses helps explain why myelinization is an important index of maturation of the

BOX 5-1 | Do Nerve Impulses Travel at the Speed of Light?

How rapid is neural activity? This problem concerned physiologists even before they knew the nature of the nerve impulse. Late in the eighteenth century, the pioneer physiologist Albrecht von Haller estimated 50 m/sec for neural activity in the human being. His estimate was based on the rapidity of reading aloud, although the method by which he reached his estimate was not described very clearly. Early in the nineteenth century, the great teacher of physiology Johannes Müller said that neural messages must travel exceedingly rapidly—because thought is so fast! He supposed that neural impulses might travel at the speed of light, or at least too rapidly ever to be measured in the short stretches of nerve available.

Hermann von Helmholtz, an outstanding physiologist and physicist and student of Müller, proved his professor wrong. In a famous experiment in 1848, Helmholtz made a frog muscle contract by shocking its nerve at two different distances from the muscle. He measured the time interval between nerve shock and onset of muscle contraction in each case. When Helmholtz applied the shock 5 cm from the muscle, the contraction started 0.0013 sec later than when he shocked the nerve 1 cm from the muscle. From these data he calculated that the speed of the nerve impulse is about 30 m/sec (about 65 mi/hr). The result amazed Helmholtz's contemporaries. It demonstrated that the nerve impulse—a concept that up to then had seemed insubstantial—could be measured quantitatively.

The discovery that nerve impulses travel at moderate speeds encouraged further investigations in both physiology and behavior. Helmholtz's colleague Emil Heinrich duBois-Reymond measured the electrical action potential of the nerve. And duBois-Reymond's student Julius Bernstein measured the rate of conduction of the electrical action current. He showed that it was the same as that of the functional signal measured by Helmholtz. This series of physical measurements accomplished a major advance: It related behavior to bodily processes. The discovery of the moderate speed of the nerve impulse also encouraged the study of reaction times, and this research helped found the science of psychology. More sophisticated research into reaction time continues today.

nervous system, as described in Chapter 3. It also helps to explain the gravity of diseases that attack myelin.

Postsynaptic Potentials

Postsynaptic potentials are electrical events elicited at postsynaptic sites by the activity of presynaptic axons. They vary in amplitude and can be either positive or negative potential changes. Interaction between these potentials, in the form of summation and subtraction, is the basis of information processing in the neuron, as we will see. Although observations of these electrochemical changes are commonplace today, this is a relatively recent scientific breakthrough. Before the early 1950s, the nature of communication across synapses was a topic of vigorous argument (Eccles, 1982).

The problem of how messages get from one neuron to another has a curious history of changes and controversies. At first it was a nonproblem. Communication among parts of the nervous system seemed to be so swift and complete that scientists in the last century concluded that nerve cells merged into each other, so that impulses flowed with no interruption. But other evidence suggested that nerve cells are separate, even though they make intimate functional contacts. One indication of independence was that when a nerve cell body is destroyed, either in an experiment or by disease, all the branches of the neuron die, but the other neurons with which it is in contact usually remain functional. In 1892 the "neuron doctrine" proclaimed that nerve cells are independent units (as noted in Chapter 2). This doctrine was

neurons
independent
Neuron → from each
Doctrine → other

based largely on extensive anatomical evidence gathered and formulated by the great Spanish neuroanatomist Santiago Ramón y Cajal. One person who remained unconvinced was the eminent Italian neuroanatomist Camillo Golgi. (In Reference Figure 2-1a, we saw the use of a staining technique developed by Golgi.) These two anatomists were jointly awarded the Nobel Prize in 1906, and in their lectures of acceptance, they continued to take opposite stands on the neuron doctrine. Since the 1950s definitive evidence has come from electron microscopy. Electron micrographs have shown that even where neurons make their closest functional contacts with each other, each cell is surrounded by its own complete membrane.

Once you realize that neurons are separate entities, you have to account for their ability to communicate with each other. As early as the mid-nineteenth century, duBois-Reymond proposed two possible mechanisms by which one neuron could excite another or could excite a muscle fiber: Either the electrical nerve impulse stimulates the adjacent cell, or the neuron secretes a substance that excites the adjacent cell. Attempts to prove variants of the electrical or the chemical hypothesis provoked lively controversies for a century. Eventually it was found that the nervous system employs both mechanisms—but at different kinds of junctions.

Experimentation on postsynaptic potentials was done with a setup like that shown schematically in Figure 5-6. When a microelectrode is inserted delicately into the cell body of a neuron, the membrane seals around the electrode, and the neuron continues to function normally. During the 1950s and 1960s, experiments on synaptic transmission in mammals involved spinal motor neurons because they are large and many characteristics of their inputs were known. The receptive surface

Figure 5-6 Synaptic potentials recorded when a neuron is stimulated by an inhibitory presynaptic neuron (b) or by an excitatory presynaptic neuron (c). Note that the presynaptic recordings are similar in the two cases, but the postsynaptic response to the inhibitory neuron is hyperpolarizing, whereas the postsynaptic response to the excitatory neuron is depolarizing.

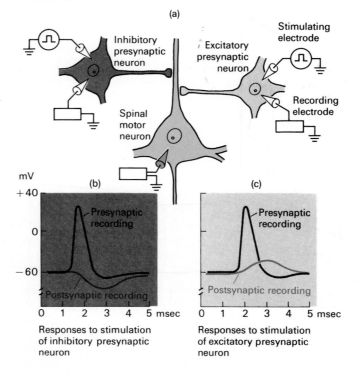

of each spinal motor neuron has many synaptic connections, some of which were known on the basis of their behavioral effects to be excitatory and some to be inhibitory. By selecting the presynaptic cell to stimulate, investigators can see how the motor neuron responds to signals from either excitatory or inhibitory connections. The responses of the presynaptic and postsynaptic cells are shown on the same records so that their time relations can be compared readily.

Stimulation of an excitatory presynaptic neuron leads to an all-or-none action potential in the presynaptic cell. In the postsynaptic cell, a small local depolarization is seen. Generally it takes the combined effect of several excitatory synapses to elicit an all-or-none potential from a postsynaptic neuron. If **excitatory postsynaptic potentials (EPSPs)** are elicited almost simultaneously by several neurons that converge on the motor cell, these potentials can summate and produce a depolarization that reaches the threshold and triggers an action potential. Note that there is a delay: The postsynaptic depolarization begins about half a millisecond after the presynaptic impulse. This delay was important evidence that the postsynaptic effect was not just an attenuated reflection of the presynaptic action current.

Further evidence that the synapse makes a special contribution came from analysis of the results of presynaptic inhibitory stimulation. This is shown in the bottom records of Figure 5-6. The action potential of an inhibitory presynaptic neuron looks exactly like that of the excitatory presynaptic fiber. Neurons have only one kind of propagated signal. But the postsynaptic local potentials show opposite polarities. When the inhibitory neuron is stimulated, the postsynaptic signal is an *increase* of the resting potential. This hyperpolarization is inhibitory for the motor neuron—it decreases the probability that the neuron will fire an impulse—so it is called an **inhibitory postsynaptic potential (IPSP).**

If a chemical step is required in synaptic transmission, a number of phenomena could be explained, for instance, the delay of about 0.5 msec in synaptic transmission. Time is required for the transmitter agent to be released, diffuse across the synaptic gap, and react with receptor molecules in the postsynaptic membrane. The chemical hypothesis also explains why the synapse acts as a sort of one-way valve; that is, transmission proceeds from presynaptic terminals to postsynaptic cells but not in the reverse direction. When we stimulate the axon of the postsynaptic cell, we do not see any changes in the presynaptic terminals. The reason is that the presynaptic terminal can liberate a chemical transmitter, but the synaptic membrane of the postsynaptic cell cannot. The axon also normally conducts impulses in only one direction because the action potential starts at the **axon hillock,** the place where the axon emerges from the cell body. As the action potential progresses along the axon, it leaves in its wake a stretch of refractory membrane. Propagated activity does not spread from the hillock back over the cell body and dendrites because the membrane of the cell body and dendrites, although chemically sensitive, is not electrically excitable and will not produce a regenerated impulse. By the early 1950s, a combination of chemical transmission and ionic mechanisms appeared to offer a complete account of transmission at synapses.

Shortly after the chemical hypothesis seemed to have won out for good, an excitatory synapse in the crayfish central nervous system was found to operate by purely electrical means (Furshpan & Potter, 1957). Then an inhibitory electrical synapse was found in the goldfish. Even more surprisingly, Martin and Pilar (1963) found synapses in the chick that employ both chemical and electrical transmission. Subsequent research has revealed electrical as well as chemical synapses in many mammals—in fact, in all species that have been investigated in this regard. However, chemical transmission occurs much more frequently.

Electrical Synapses

[handwritten annotation: 2nd kind of Synapse-less common — pre + post close]

At **electrical synapses** the presynaptic membrane comes even closer to the postsynaptic membrane than it does at chemical synapses; the cleft measures only 2–4 nm, as shown in Figure 5-7. This is in contrast to the separation of 20–30 nm at chemical synapses. The narrowness of the gap at electrical junctions means a very low electrical resistance between the presynaptic and postsynaptic surfaces. As a consequence, current flow associated with nerve impulses in the presynaptic axon terminal can travel across the narrow cleft to the postsynaptic membrane. Transmission at these synapses is then quite similar to conduction along the axon. The principal contrast with axonal transmission is that most of these connections are directional or polarized, which means that the connection works in only one direction. This is demonstrated by experiments that involve electrical stimulation of the postsynaptic cell with the intention of seeing whether it is possible to produce a nerve impulse that goes back across the gap to the presynaptic terminal. Depolarization of the presynaptic axon terminal cannot be produced in this manner. The mechanism of one-way transmission at electrical synapses is not as well understood as that at chemical synapses. Electrical synapses work with little time delay. They are frequently found as part of neural circuits that mediate escape behaviors in simpler invertebrates. They are also found where many fibers must be activated synchronously, as in the vertebrate oculomotor system for control of rapid eye movements. In contrast with chemical synapses, electrical synapses show little evidence of modifiability with use.

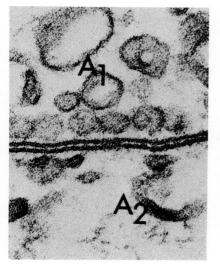

Figure 5-7 Electrical synapse in crayfish. A_1 indicates the presynaptic axon and A_2 is the postsynaptic axon. A few vesicles are seen on both sides, but their function is not known. (magnification × 130,000) (From G. D. Pappas and D. P. Purpura, *Structure and function of synapses* (New York: Raven Press, 1972), p. 26.)

Information Processing by Small Neural Circuits

Synaptic transmission and impulse conduction not only achieve the communication of signals but also transform messages in ways that make complex behavior possible. A few examples will show some of the capabilities of neurons for processing information.

The nerve cell, with its synaptic inputs, is able to perform both summation and subtraction of input signals. These operations are possible because of the characteristics of synaptic inputs, the way in which the neuron integrates the postsynaptic potentials, and the trigger mechanism that determines whether a neuron will fire off an impulse. As we have seen, the postsynaptic potentials that are caused by the action of transmitter chemicals can be either depolarizing (excitatory) or hyperpolarizing (inhibitory). These potentials spread passively over the neuron from their points of origin on dendrites and on the cell body. The trigger mechanism for mammalian neurons is located at the initial segment of the axon, which, in mammalian multipolar neurons, is the axon hillock. Thus what determines whether the neuron will fire off an action potential is whether depolarization reaches the critical threshold at the axon hillock.

A Model for Nerve Cell Information Processing

For an analogy to nerve cell information processing, look at the physical model shown in Figure 5-8. Here the cell body is represented by a metal disc. For simplicity, no dendrites are shown, and all input endings are on the cell body. The presyn-

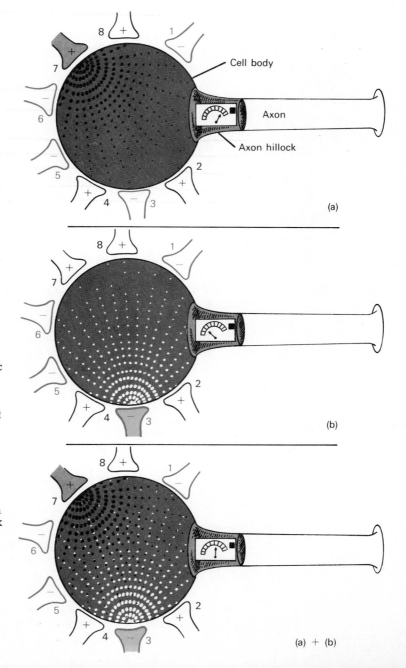

Figure 5-8 Physical model of summation of synaptic influences on activity of postsynaptic neuron. Tubes representing presynaptic endings (1–8) can each deliver a blast of hot (+) or cold (−) air to the metal disc that represents the cell body. Each arrival of an impulse at a presynaptic ending leads to a blast of air. In (a) a pulse of hot air at 7 causes local heating of the cell body. This heat spreads over the disc, dissipating as it goes; only a small proportion of the heat reaches the axon hillock. In (b) a pulse of cool air at 3 leads to local cooling of the cell body, and this effect also spreads passively, the temperature change diminishing as it travels. Since 3 is relatively close to the axon hillock, a greater proportion of the change at 3 reaches the hillock than was true of the change at 7. In (c) since 3 cools and 7 warms, these effects partially cancel each other. The hillock contains a thermostatic device that triggers activity in the axon only where the temperature reaches a certain level. The disc integrates all the temperature changes, and the axon hillock senses the algebraic sum.

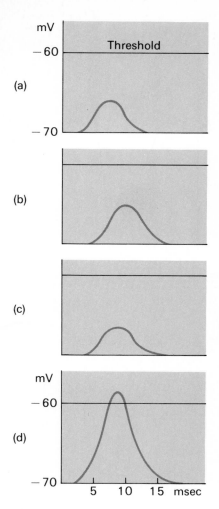

Figure 5-9 Summation of excitatory synaptic potentials. Graphs (a), (b), and (c) represent inputs that differ in amplitude and time. Graph (d) represents their algebraic summation.

aptic terminals are represented by tubes through which blasts of hot or cold air can be delivered; hot air represents excitatory synaptic action and cold air, inhibitory synaptic action. The axon hillock contains a thermostat. If the temperature rises above the resting level of 30 degrees to a critical level of 45 degrees (the threshold), the thermostat closes a circuit and triggers a propagated impulse.

Suppose an impulse arrives at ending number 7, as shown at (a) in Figure 5-8. A pulse of hot air is delivered, causing local heating of the cell body. This heat spreads out over the disc, dissipating as it spreads so that only a small proportion of the heat reaches the axon hillock. Part (b) of Figure 5-8 shows what happens when a blast of cold air is delivered at ending 3. The resultant local cooling spreads passively, so that the change of temperature diminishes as it travels. Since 3 is relatively close to the axon hillock, a greater proportion of the change reaches the hillock than was true of the change that originated at 7. If 3 and 7 are activated simultaneously, since one cools and the other warms, these effects partially cancel each other. Thus the net effect is the difference between the two: The neuron *subtracts* the inhibitory postsynaptic potential from the excitatory postsynaptic potential. If two excitatory terminals are activated simultaneously, their effects sum at the hillock: The neuron *adds* postsynaptic potentials that have the same sign. The summation of potentials across the cell body is called **spatial summation.** Only if the overall resultant of all the potentials is sufficient to raise the hillock temperature to the threshold level is an impulse triggered off. Usually it requires the convergence of excitatory messages from several presynaptic fibers to fire off a neuron. Figure 5-9 illustrates how potentials add algebraically.

Summation can also take place between postsynaptic effects that are not absolutely simultaneous, since the effects last for a few milliseconds. The closer they are in time, the greater the overlap and the more complete the summation. This is called **temporal summation.** But even successive impulses arriving at the same terminal can produce postsynaptic effects that summate. Thus, although the impulses are all-or-none, the postsynaptic effect can be graded in size: A rapid barrage of impulses produces a larger postsynaptic potential than a single impulse does.

Dendrites were omitted from Figure 5-8 for simplicity, but let us see how they add to the story. Dendrites augment the receptive surface of the neuron and increase the amount of input information the neuron can handle. The farther out on a dendrite a potential is produced, the less effect it will have on the axon hillock. When the potential arises at a dendritic spine, its effect is further reduced because it has to spread down the shaft of the spine. Thus information arriving at various parts of the neuron is weighted in terms of the distance and path resistance to the axon hillock.

Examples of Processing in Local Circuits

Circuits of just a few neurons can accomplish powerful feats because of the ability of the neuron to add and subtract and to show temporal and spatial summation of postsynaptic potentials. Thus local circuits can select one type of stimulus out of a welter of stimuli; they can enhance the difference between two stimuli; they can classify stimuli into groups; they can generate motor patterns; and they can correlate inputs, provide an internal clock, and synchronize activities with it. Let us briefly consider an example from visual perception.

This example of information processing in a local circuit is seen in a circuit that produces contrast effects at boundaries between two kinds or levels of stimulation.

Figure 5-10 A retinal neural circuit that sharpens contours by lateral inhibition. Lateral inhibitory connections depress neural activity, especially among cells receiving a high level of illumination. A contrast effect occurs at the boundary between cells receiving high and low levels of illumination.

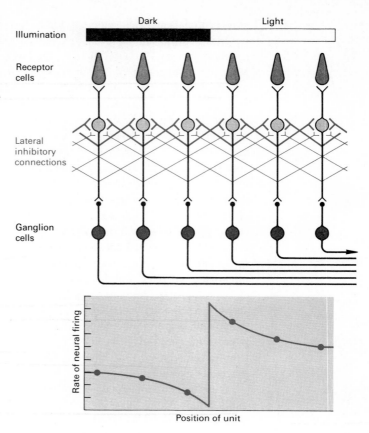

Thus red appears more saturated when it borders green, and white appears brighter next to black. Most animals with vision show such contrast effects, which are based on neural circuitry. The neurons that are connected to adjacent visual receptors make inhibitory connections with each other. Here there is **divergence** of messages from each neuron to many adjacent ones. When one patch of neurons is strongly stimulated by light and a neighboring patch is only weakly stimulated by it (Figure 5-10), the inhibitory signals cause a contrast effect at the boundary. Within the strongly stimulated group of neurons, there is mutual inhibition, which reduces the level of excitation. But the units just inside the boundary of the strongly light-stimulated patch are only slightly inhibited by their neighbors on the dark side, so the greatest level of excitation occurs on the light side of the boundary. These units strongly inhibit their neighbors on the dark side, so the lowest level of excitation is found just on the dark side of the boundary. Thus the inhibitory interconnections within the spatial array of units produce contrast, or sharpening of the perception of various patterns of light.

[handwritten margin notes:] Divergence— One neuron spreads info to many adjacent ones

Contrast

Ionic Mechanisms of Excitation and Conduction

Now that we have seen some of the main characteristics and functions of electrical signals in neurons, let us examine the mechanisms that produce these potentials. This section will provide a nontechnical explanation; more complete accounts can be found in many sources (for example, Kandel & Schwartz, 1985; Kuffler & Nichols, 1985).

Mechanisms of the Resting Potential

Consider the distribution of ions across the simplified and idealized neural membrane in Figure 5-11. Inside the cell there is a high concentration of potassium ions, each of which has a positive electrical charge (K^+). There is also a high internal concentration of large protein ions, each with a negative charge. Finally, the axon has low internal concentrations of sodium (Na^+) and chloride (Cl^-) ions. Because of their negative charges, the protein and chloride ions are called **anions.** Positively charged ions, such as K^+ and Na^+, are called **cations.** The cell membrane contains many small pores through which the potassium ions can flow in or out relatively easily but which are not permeable to the other ions.

What happens when the neuron is placed in a solution that contains the same concentrations of ions as exist inside the cell? Some potassium ions may flow in or out, but there will be no net change, and no charge will develop across the membrane. What happens when the neuron is placed in a solution, such as blood plasma or seawater, that has a low concentration of potassium and high concentrations of sodium and chloride? (The concentrations inside and outside the squid axon are

Figure 5-11 Distribution of ions inside a neuron and outside the neuron in the extracellular space. Note that most K^+ ions are found in the intracellular space, whereas most Na^+ and Cl^- ions are in the extracellular space. Some exchange between the intracellular and extracellular spaces occurs through channels in the cell membrane.

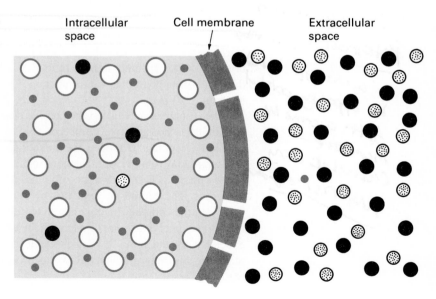

Intracellular space   Cell membrane   Extracellular space

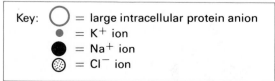

Key: ◯ = large intracellular protein anion
  • = K^+ ion
  ● = Na^+ ion
  ⊗ = Cl^- ion

Table 5-1   Concentrations of Ions Inside and Outside Squid
             Axons (millimoles)

Ion	Inside Neuron	In Blood	In Seawater
Potassium (K^+)	400	20	10
Sodium (Na^+)	50	440	460
Chloride (Cl^-)	40–150	560	540

shown in Table 5-1.) Certain laws of physical chemistry govern the movements of
ions in solutions. For example, substances in solution move from regions of high
concentration to regions of low concentration, unless there is some impeding force
like a membrane. In the absence of other forces, potassium ions tend to move out of
the cell, since their concentration is 20 times greater inside than outside. This
creates a potential difference across the membrane, since positive charges (potassium ions) leave the inside and accumulate outside. If the membrane were permeable to anions, one anion would accompany each positive ion out and no potential
difference would occur, but the membrane of the axon is impermeable to large
anions. When the potential difference across the membrane becomes large enough,
it stops the net outflow of positive ions. This occurs because the positive ions
outside repel each other but are attracted to the negative ions inside.

   At this point in the process, the tendency of the ions to flow from the regions of
high concentration is exactly balanced by the opposing potential difference across
the membrane. This potential is called the **potassium equilibrium potential** and is
so predictable according to the laws of physical chemistry that it is possible to
calculate the equilibrium potential by an equation, called the **Nernst equation.** The
Nernst equation represents the voltage that develops when a semipermeable membrane separates different concentrations of ions. It predicts that the potential across
the squid axon membrane will be about −75 mV, inside to outside. The actual value
is about −70 mV.

   The discrepancy between the predicted and observed values occurs because the
membrane is not absolutely impermeable to sodium ions. Small numbers leak in
gradually, tending to reduce the membrane potential. This in turn causes more
potassium ions to move out. Eventually the leakage would cause the concentrations
inside and outside the cell to become the same, and the membrane potential would
disappear. The neuron prevents this by pumping sodium out of the cell and potassium into the cell just rapidly enough to counter the leakage. Thus maintaining the
membrane potential demands metabolic work by the cell. In fact, most of the energy
expended by the brain—whether waking or sleeping—is thought to be used to
maintain the ionic gradients across neuronal membranes so that neurons will be
ready to conduct impulses.

The Action Potential

It used to be thought that the action potential resulted from a momentary increase in
membrane permeability to all ions, so that the membrane potential dropped to zero.
But research with the squid axon revealed a more interesting story. The action
potential is actually larger than the resting potential. There is an "overshoot" that
briefly makes the inside of the neuron positive with respect to the outside. The

change of potential was shown in Figure 5-3. The amplitude of this overshoot is determined by the concentration of sodium ions (Hodgkin & Katz, 1949), even though sodium does not affect the resting potential. At the peak of the nerve impulse, the potential across the membrane approaches that predicted by the Nernst equation with respect to the concentration of sodium ions: about $+40$ mV.

Thus in its resting stage the neural membrane can be thought of as essentially a "potassium membrane," since it is permeable only to K^+, and the potential is about that of the potassium equilibrium potential. But the active membrane is a "sodium membrane," since it is mainly permeable to Na^+ and the membrane potential tends toward the **sodium equilibrium potential.** Thus the action current occurs during a sudden shift in membrane properties, and these revert quickly to the resting state.

What causes the changes from K^+ permeability to Na^+ permeability and back again? A reduction in the resting potential of the membrane (depolarization) increases Na^+ permeability. This can be thought of as "opening gates" at the ends of some pores, or **ion channels,** in the membrane. These gates admit Na^+ but no other ions. As some sodium ions enter the neuron, the resting potential is further reduced, opening still more Na^+ channels. Thus the process accelerates until all barriers to the entry of Na^+ are removed, and sodium ions rush in. This increased permeability to Na^+ lasts less than a millisecond; then a process of inactivation blocks the Na^+ channels. By this time the membrane potential has reached the sodium equilibrium potential of around $+40$ mV. Now positive charges inside the nerve cell tend to push potassium ions out, and the permeability to K^+ also increases somewhat, so that the resting potential is soon regained.

Earlier in this chapter we stated that the sequence of electrical events observed during conduction of a nerve impulse could be explained in terms of ionic mechanisms. Now we see that they can be accounted for in detail by the sequence of Na^+ and K^+ currents (Hodgkin & Huxley, 1952).

The absolute and relative refractory phases also can be related to these changes in permeability. When the Na^+ channels have opened completely during the rise of the nerve impulse, further stimulation does not affect the course of events. Also, during inactivation of the Na^+ channels, when stimulation cannot reopen them, the action current falls off. So, during the rising and falling phases of an action potential, the neuron is absolutely refractory to elicitation of a second impulse. While K^+ ions are flowing out and the resting potential is being restored, the neuron is relatively refractory.

Gating Ion Channels

Because changes in the permeability of the nerve membrane to Na^+ and K^+ ions during the course of the nerve impulse are so important, many investigators are studying the mechanisms that control these events. Most recent volumes of the *Annual Review of Neuroscience* have one or more chapters on this topic. One problem under study is finding the molecular bases of the voltage sensors that indicate when the changes are initiated and also the "gates" in the ionic channels. Gating is thought to involve rearrangements in the shape or positions of charged molecules that line the channel. Making such changes requires the expenditure of energy. Several research groups have reported the measurement of tiny electrical currents that seem to be related to molecular rearrangements that open or shut gates in ion channels; these have been called gating currents.

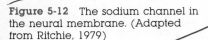

Figure 5-12 The sodium channel in the neural membrane. (Adapted from Ritchie, 1979)

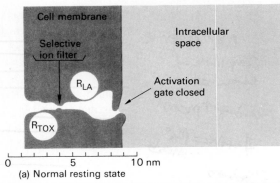

Extracellular space

Cell membrane

Selective ion filter

Intracellular space

R_{LA}

Activation gate closed

R_{TOX}

0   5   10 nm

(a) Normal resting state

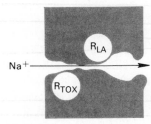

R_{LA}

Na$^+$

R_{TOX}

(b) Sodium channel open during rising phase of action potential

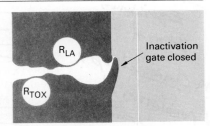

R_{LA}

Inactivation gate closed

R_{TOX}

(c) Sodium channel closed by inactivation gate during falling phase of action potential

Since the ion channels in axon membranes are too tiny to be seen even with the electron microscope, how can investigators determine their structures and modes of operation? The solution has been to test pharmacological substances that affect one or another aspect of the functioning of the channels. Important clues emerge from knowing the sizes and shapes of such molecules and knowing whether they are effective at only one or the other side of the membrane. The sodium channel has been an object of special study, and detailed understanding of its structure and mechanisms is beginning to emerge (Ritchie, 1979).

Figure 5-12 is a schematic picture of a sodium channel in the membrane at a node of Ranvier in a myelinated axon. Let us look at some of the features of this model and some of the main evidence on which they are based. Certain toxins of animal origin, when applied to the outer surface of the membrane, block the sodium channel (but no others). These are tetrodotoxin (TTX) and saxitoxin (STX). The size and structures of TTX and STX, together with those of other molecules that do or do not alter Na$^+$ permeability, suggest the following dimensions of the sodium channel. The outer part is an antechamber that measures 0.9 nm by 1.0 nm. Deeper in the membrane, the channel narrows to a pore 0.3 nm by 0.5 nm. In this narrow ionic selectivity filter, there is a binding site to which metal cations bind, as well as TTX and STX. This receptor for toxins is labeled R_{TOX} in Figure 5-12. A narrow part of the structure of the TTX and STX molecules enters the pore and sticks there because the rest of the molecule is too wide to pass. Thus the channel is blocked to Na$^+$ ions.

Tetrodotoxin is found in the ovaries of the pufferfish, which is esteemed as a delicacy in Japan. Fish markets in Japan display dried pufferfish, blown up like globes. If the pufferfish ovaries are not removed properly and if the fish is not cleaned with great care, people who eat it may be poisoned because their neurons cannot function. People die from this cause each year, and now neuroscientists know why.

In contrast to toxins that act at a site near the outer surface of the membrane, certain local anesthetics act at a different site that is accessible only from inside the membrane. This receptor for local anesthetics is labeled R_{LA} in Figure 5-12.

Whereas the action of local anesthetics is temporary and wears off, a permanent change is caused if the enzyme pronase is introduced within the axon. Pronase destroys the inactivation gate that normally shuts the Na^+ channel. Two kinds of scorpions have evolved venoms that block processes basic to neural conduction. The venom of the *Leiurus* scorpion impairs the inactivation gate, but the venom of the *Centruroides* scorpion specifically impairs the activation gate. Thus it is clear that different molecular processes control the two kinds of gating of the sodium channel. A snake that we will mention in Chapter 6 has evolved a toxin that blocks chemical transmission at synapses that use acetylcholine. Blocking either conduction of impulses or synaptic transmission is an effective way for an animal to kill its prey.

Signal Variability in Nerve Cells

The picture of nerve cell signals we have presented to this point is a portrait of a typical cell operating under baseline conditions. Additional information-processing flexibility in the nervous system comes from exceptions to these modal properties. There are many such exceptions, but a brief mention of a few provides a sense of the diversity of neuron ''life styles.''

- Some nerve cells have very short axons or no axons at all, and in these cells communication with other cells does not involve nerve impulses.
- Nerve cells differ in impulse threshold, that is, the amount of depolarization necessary for initiating a nerve impulse.
- Nerve cells vary in the relationship between magnitude of depolarization and rate of nerve impulse firing. This means that for some neurons small increments in depolarization produce large changes in nerve impulse firing, while in other cells the slope of the relation is shallower.
- Neurons also differ in the property of pacemakerlike activity, that is, some cells are autorhythmic, regularly generating nerve impulses independent of synaptic inputs. These cells might be especially important in controlling rhythmic behaviors.
- Neurons differ in responses of synapses to successive nerve impulses. At some synapses facilitating effects are seen, which means that the size of successive synaptic potentials grows. In contrast, at other synapses decremental effects are evident successive responses. Both these effects show that the history of recent use affects what happens at a synapse. This provides some memorylike devices that may be related to broader behavioral states such as learning and memory.
- Temperature affects the rate of firing of some neurons, allowing them to act as internal temperature sensors.

- Neurons are influenced by hormones and neuromodulators that circulate in the brain. These agents are called modulators because by themselves they do not produce significant neural effects.

Comparing Nerve Cell Signals

In this chapter we have discussed several different attributes of electrical events in nerve cells. In Table 5-2 we present in tabular form a summary of the principal similarities and differences in these potentials. The table emphasizes the distinctive characteristics of each kind of signal.

Gross Electrical Potentials of the Brain

In 1929 the German psychiatrist Hans Berger published a paper that illustrated the electrical activity of his son's brain. This was more than family pride. Berger had used his son as a subject in studies in which he recorded the electrical activity of the brain by using electrodes (discs about the size of a dime) placed on the scalp. He had placed one such electrode at the front of the skull and the other at the back. Potential differences between these two electrodes measured a mere 5 μV. The record revealed regular oscillations with a frequency of about 10 hertz (Hz), which Berger called the **alpha rhythm** (Figure 5-13). At that time electronics was in its infancy, and the recording of such low-voltage biological signals was difficult and not readily accepted. Berger's accomplishment of scalp recordings of brain electri-

Q. If A.P. acts on EPSP, when does ↑PSP EPSP in turn become A.P for next neuron

Table 5-2   Characteristics of Electrical Signals of Nerve Cells

Type of Signal	Signaling Role	Typical Duration (msec)	Amplitude	Character	Mode of Propagation	Ion Channel Opening	Channel Sensitive to
Action potential	Conduction along a neuron	1–2	About 100 mV overshooting	All-or-nothing, digital	Actively propagated, regenerative	First Na^+ then K^+, in different channels	Voltage (depolarization)
Excitatory postsynaptic potential (EPSP)	Transmission between neurons	10–100	From less than 1 to more than 20 msec	Graded, analog	Local, passive spread	Na^+/K^+	Chemical (neuro-transmitter)
Inhibitory postsynaptic potential (IPSP)	Transmission between neurons	10–100	Depolarizing or hyperpolarizing, from less than 1 to about 15 mV	Graded, analog	Local passive spread	K^+ or Cl^- or K^+/Cl^-	Chemical (neuro-transmitter)

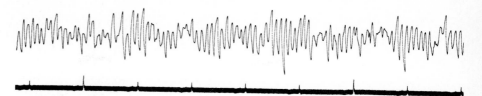

Figure 5-13 Alpha rhythm recorded from scalp in the occipital region of awake relaxed human subject with eyes closed. Time markers show 1-second periods. (Leiman)

cal activity was greeted with skepticism until other researchers confirmed his observations and established that the potentials really do orginate in the brain. This psychiatrist in search of a physical record of the mental activity of the brain had begun the field of **electroencephalography (EEG)**: the study of the electrical activity of the brain, observed with large electrodes. This is referred to as measuring gross potentials, in contrast to measuring potentials recorded from single cells, because the EEG represents the activity of many cells and is recorded at some distance from them. In some ways it is akin to the electrocardiogram, which records the activity of the heart from electrodes on the skin. Techniques for studying the intact human nervous system are few, and scalp recording of human brain activity, via electrodes, offers a way of examining the functioning of the human brain.

Another rationale for this electrophysiological approach stresses clinical aspects. Brain potentials provide significant diagnostic data, for example, in distinguishing forms of seizure disorders. They also provide prognostic data, for example, predictions of the functional effects of brain injury. Indeed, in most states of the United States, brain potential data are used in the legal definition of death. In the control of seizures, brain potentials may even form part of a treatment program using **biofeedback** of brain potentials. New developments in computer technology designed to offer detailed quantitative analysis of brain potentials have buoyed hopes for an even greater clinical contribution, especially in psychiatric areas.

A rationale for basic research into the gross potentials of the brain has been offered be several investigators (Freeman, 1978; John, 1977). Let us consider an analogy. At college football games, a section of students often entertains the crowd with card stunts, spelling out messages and forming pictures. Each participant holds a single piece of cardboard, one side of which is white and the other colored. By lifting one or the other side according to a plan paced by a leader, these rooters present a coherent message: ''Go Bears.'' No single individual can convey that message with a card, no matter how well intended or feverish the pace of moving the card. The message is a product of the entire ensemble of card-carrying fans. Furthermore, the display arises only from a plan that spells out the joint activity. A random presentation of cards would give spectators across the stadium no message— simple confusion. The brain is a large collection of separate elements, and even the most trivial behavior involves thousands of cells. Recordings of brain electrical activity with large electrodes can present a glimpse at the simultaneous workings of populations of neurons.

Spontaneous Electrical Rhythms of the Brain

Investigators divide brain potentials into two principal classes: those that appear spontaneously without specific stimulation and those that are evoked by particular stimuli. We will consider the two classes in succession.

Electrical activity of the brain recorded from the scalp reveals several distinctive properties. The most prominent property is that, even in the absence of stimulation, there are oscillations of brain potentials. A pattern of incessant electrical activity characterizes the human brain. Trains of rhythmical variations of electrical activity are the hallmark of gross potentials, such as those in Figure 5-13. These potentials can be categorized according to their principal frequency components. Broad psychological categories, such as arousal or attention, are related to the principal frequency components of the gross potentials of the brain.

Scientists over the years have tried to discover the functional properties of the alpha rhythm. Ranging from 8 to 12 Hz, alpha rhythm is especially noticeable in recordings from posterior regions of the skull. Many individuals readily show alpha activity when they close their eyes and relax. Easing tension is so much a part of the alpha state that in recent years we have seen the application of alpha recording to the pursuit of pleasure. Commercially available gadgets can provide a person with a record of alpha activity, usually in the form of a tone that comes on either when alpha occurs or when it reaches some desired amplitude. This is used by some people as a clue to their state of relaxation. It can also be used in a form of biofeedback training. The connection between relaxation and prominent alpha activity evident in biofeedback experiments has reinforced the view that alpha rhythms represent an "idling" state of the brain.

Clinical neurologists use alterations in spontaneous brain activity in the diagnosis of many disorders. Disordered biochemical, anatomical, and neurophysiological states of the brain can markedly change certain properties of spontaneous brain potentials. That is what happens in cases of epilepsy and other seizures.

Table 5-3 shows that the frequency of spontaneous or ongoing brain potentials varies directly with level of arousal. More rapid oscillations—beta waves of 18–30 Hz—are common in vigilant states, while quite slow oscillations—delta waves of 0.5–5 Hz—occur in a state of deep sleep in normal humans (see Chapter 14).

Table 5-3   Characteristics of Human EEG Waves

Type of Wave or Rhythm	Frequency Range (Hz)	Amplitude or Voltage (μV)	Region of Prominence or Maximum	Condition When Present
Alpha	8–12	5–10	Occipital and parietal	Awake, relaxed, eyes closed
Beta	18–30	2–20	Precentral and frontal	Awake, no movement
Gamma	30–50	2–10	Precentral and frontal	Awake, excited
Delta	0.5–5	20–200	Variable	Deeply asleep
Theta	5–7	5–100	Frontal and temporal	Awake, reduced vigilance

Figure 5-14 An averaged event-related potential recorded from the scalp of a human observer in response to auditory clicks. See text for description of the components of the response. (Adapted from Kutas and Hillyard, 1984)

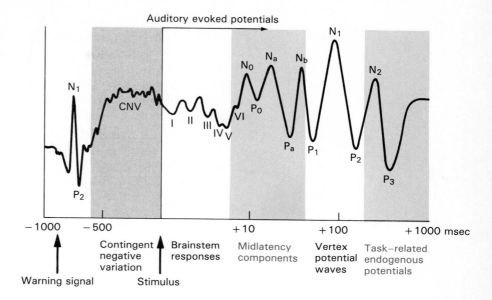

Event-Related Potentials

Gross potential changes provoked by discrete stimuli—usually sensory stimuli, such as light flashes or clicks—are called **event-related potentials** (Figure 5-14). In the usual experiment, a series of event-related potentials is averaged to obtain a reliable estimate of stimulus-elicited brain activity. Sensory-evoked potentials have distinctive characteristics of wave shape and latency that reflect the type of stimulus, the state of the subject, and the site of recording. More subtle psychological processes, such as expectancy, appear to influence some characteristics of evoked potentials, as we will see.

Auditory-Evoked Brain Stem Potentials

Computer techniques enable researchers to record brain potentials at some distance from the sites at which they are actually generated. This is akin to the ability of a sensitive heat detector to pick up minute sources of heat that are located at a distance. An example of this that has attracted considerable research and clinical attention is known as "auditory-evoked brain stem potentials." To record this response, subjects are fitted with headphones through which they hear a long series of clicks. The brain potentials elicited by these stimuli are recorded from an electrode on the scalp and summed using a computer. Figure 5-14 shows an example of the summed response. The warning signal that precedes the stimulus evokes a response called the Contingent Negative Variation, shown on the gray background in Figure 5-14. Different components of the response to the stimulus range in latency from short (up to 10 msec) though medium (10–100 msec), to relatively long (over 100 msec). First to appear is a series of short latency waves that are commonly designated by Roman numerals. The neural generators of these waves are located far from the site of recording; these generators are located in the auditory nerve and successive levels of the auditory brain stem pathways. These responses then provide a way to assess the neural responsiveness of the brain stem and especially its auditory pathways. For example, reduction in amplitude of certain waves or increases in their latency have been valuable in detecting hearing impairments in very young children and noncommunicative persons. Hidden hearing deficits in children initially diagnosed as autistic have been revealed in this manner. Another use of these brain stem–evoked potentials is in the assessment of brain stem injury or damage, such as that produced by tumors or stroke. Components that originate above the brain stem are identified in the figure as negative (N) and positive (P) potentials.

Cortical Event-Related Potentials: Mid- and Long-Latency Components

Long-latency components of scalp-recorded potentials tend to reflect the impact of information-processing variables, such as attention, decision making, and other complex psychological dimensions. Another way of contrasting these events with early latency events, such as the brain stem potentials, is to compare the sorts of factors that affect them. The later potentials are influenced more by endogenous factors, such as attention. In contrast early latency responses are more determined by exogenous factors; they are more stimulus-determined so that dimensions like stimulus intensity have a far more profound effect on early components of event-related potentials than on longer latency components. Note that stimulus intensity certainly affects longer latency components but in a far more individual manner. In the following discussion, we will provide examples of the use of these longer latency event-related potentials in explorations of personality and cognitive states.

1. Event-Related Potentials in Augmenters-Reducers.   A particular mid-latency component of a cortical event-related potential (measured from the peak of P_1 to the peak of N_1 in Figure 5-14) shows a regular increase in its amplitude with increments in stimulus intensity in many individuals, as you might expect. In contrast, however, there are some people who show a vastly different pattern. With increases in stimulus intensity, especially when intensity is already rather high, they display reductions in the amplitude of the event-related potential. These people are referred to as ''reducers,'' while those who show increases are called ''augmenters.'' There are many complicating variables argued about in the research literature associated with this distinction. Some of these relations are seen only with visual stimuli, and in some cases the phenomenon of augmenting-reducing is seen only at some scalp locations. However, many studies suggest tantalizing relations between this event-related potential distinction and some personality traits. In a very speculative review of some biological aspects of personality, Zuckerman (1984) argues that this neurobiological distinction is related to a dimension he calls ''sensation seeking,'' that is, seeking thrills and adventure and engaging in risky activities. From his review of a number of studies, Zuckerman argues that high-sensation seekers tend to be augmenters, and low-sensation seekers tend to be reducers. Augmenting-reducing also shows some relation to the personality dimension ''extraversion-introversion.'' Extraverts are alleged to be more reducers in frontal cortical-evoked responses than are introverts (Bruneau, Roux, Perse, & LeLord, 1984). There are many studies concerned with this phenomenon, some of which we will pursue further in Chapter 15.

2. Attention and Event-Related Potentials. We are clearly able to respond selectively to some events and completely ignore others; indeed, at times the nonattended event seems almost not to have occurred at all! By now many behavioral studies have explored various kinds of attentional factors, and some behavioral studies have proposed hypothetical neural models to account for various perceptual phenomena involving attention. Some have argued that the unattended information simply is blocked at the periphery—a kind of peripheral gating. For the most part, however, researchers have argued that attention involves some sort of cortical mechanism. A typical experiment showing the impact of attentional instructions is reported by Hillyard, Simpson, Woods, VanVoorhis, and Münte (1983). Subjects were presented with two tones delivered to the right and left ears, respectively. The subject's task was to pay attention selectively to one of the tones in one ear at a time. Tones in the attended ear (or channel) evoked a larger negativity in one of the mid-latency components of the event-related potential. Switching attention to the other ear reversed the relative size of responses to the two stimuli. These investigators argue that this reflects the neural action of a channel-selection mechanism in the brain that selectively augments particular stimuli. Data from this study are displayed in Figure 5-15.

3. Event-Related Potentials and Intelligence. Do the minute potentials recorded from the scalp tell us anything about very complex dimensions of cognition, such as intelligence? Some investigators have advanced the proposal that evoked potentials from the scalp can provide clues about the efficiency of brain information processing, a characteristic that seems to be a feature of intelligence. Different characteristics of the evoked potential have been examined for relations to intelligence defined

Figure 5-15 Effects of attention on auditory event-related potentials. Attending to the left or the right ear alters the potentials, as described in the text. The colored regions show these differences. (Adapted from Hillyard et al., 1984)

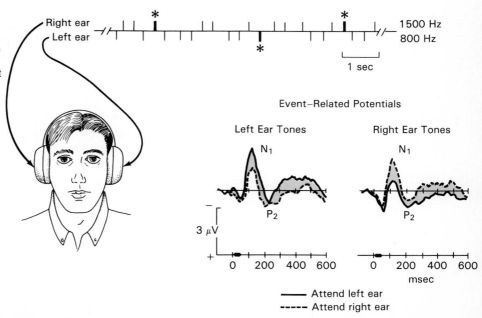

by various standardized psychological tests. Some researchers have used measures of evoked potential complexity; others have examined either latency or amplitude of the responses elicited by simple auditory or visual stimuli. In one study researchers administered the Raven's Advanced Progressive Matrices Test, which, it is alleged, is a relatively culture-free intelligence test (Blinkhorn & Hendrickson, 1982). They then measured event-related potentials elicited by a series of tone bursts. The correlation between the psychological test score and a measure of auditory-evoked potential magnitude was +0.54, a highly significant correlation. In contrast, tests emphasizing verbal abilities, probably related to academic achievement, were uncorrelated with this EEG measure. Perhaps somewhere hidden in these potentials are some reflections of the cognitive strategies that are fundamental to intelligence, and several investigators are trying to discover them. Some questions relevant to neural activity and cognition are pursued at greater length in Chapter 18.

Epilepsy

Epilepsy has provoked wonder and worry since the dawn of civilization. (The name comes from a Greek word meaning ''to seize or attack.'') To some ancient Greeks, epilepsy was a sacred disease—possession by a god. In the Middle Ages, afflicted humans were regarded as being possessed instead by a devil, and they were subject to many forms of cruelty. In the history of medicine, proposed cures include bloodletting, trephining (producing a hole in the skull), application to the head of high-voltage electric fish, and ingestion of various plants, particularly peony and mistletoe. Views about the origin and cure of epilepsy have varied over the years. This is not surprising, since many people display seizures at some point in their life. O'Leary and Goldring (1976) estimated that 30 million people worldwide suffer from epilepsy.

Types of Seizure Disorder

What is epilepsy? Most investigators now agree that it is a disorder marked by major sudden changes in the electrophysiological state of the brain. These changes and their behavioral accompaniments are referred to as seizures. The metaphor of an electrical storm has frequently been used to characterize the electrical state of the brain during seizures, and the term is apt.

Several types of seizure disorders can be distinguished both behaviorally and neurophysiologically. **Generalized seizures** involve loss of consciousness and symmetrical involvement of body musculature. Grand mal and petit mal are two common types of generalized seizure and account for the largest number of patients.

Grand mal seizures involve an EEG pattern evident at many places in the brain (Figure 5-16) with individual nerve cells firing in high-frequency bursts. The behavior connected with this state is dramatic. The person loses consciousness, and the muscles of the entire body suddenly contract, producing stiff limbs and body. This ''tonic'' phase of the seizure is followed one to two minutes later by a ''clonic'' phase that consists of sudden alternating jerks and relaxation of the body. An interval of confusion and sleep follows this phase. When most nonprofessionals refer to epilepsy, they generally mean grand mal seizures.

Petit mal epilepsy is a more subtle varient of generalized seizures. It is revealed by a distinctive electrical pattern in EEG recordings called the spike-and-wave

Figure 5-16 Electrical activity of the brain (EEG) characteristic of a grand mal convulsion. Each line is a recording from a different cortical position: before (1), during (2, 3), and after a seizure (4). (From *Neurological Pathophysiology* by Sven G. Eliasson, Arthur L. Prensky, and William B. Hardin, Jr. Copyright © 1974, 1978 by Oxford University Press, Inc. Reprinted by permission.)

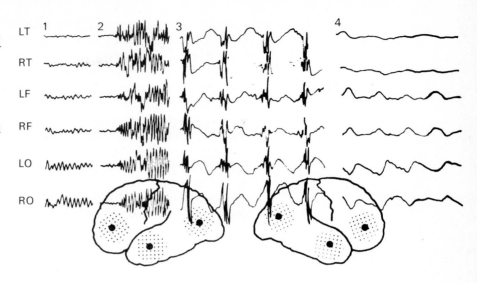

pattern (Figure 5-17). Periods of such unusual electrical activity can occur many times a day. During these periods the person is unaware of the environment and later cannot recall events that occurred during these periods. Behaviorally the person does not show unusual muscle activity, except for a cessation of ongoing activity and sustained staring; that is, the person's eyes do not move from a particular position for a long period. The term *absences* has been used to describe this state.

Both grand mal and petit mal are generalized seizures because they arise from pathology at brain sites that project to widespread regions of the brain. In contrast, there are **partial seizures** that arise from pathological foci that have less extensive

Figure 5-17 EEG from a patient with petit mal epilepsy. The illustration shows the abrupt onset and termination of a 3-Hz high-amplitude discharge with a pattern called "spike and wave." (From *Neurological Pathophysiology* by Sven G. Eliasson, Arthur L. Prensky, and William B. Hardin, Jr. Copyright © 1974, 1978 by Oxford University Press, Inc. Reprinted by permission.)

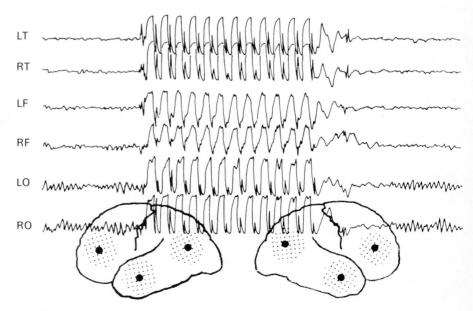

anatomical distribution. Some partial seizures involve no impairment of consciousness. For example, focal motor seizures involve repetitive motor spasms that frequently start in the periphery of a limb and move to adjacent muscles; such a spasm may start in the fingers and move to the forearm. Partial seizures that orginate in the temporal lobe may involve strange sensory impressions, sudden feelings of anxiety, and elaborate acts performed automatically, such as complicated gestures.

Seizures arise from pathological electrical activity of brain cells that can be caused in many different ways. Frequent causes are mechanical events, such as head injury; various chemicals, including some environmental toxins; and metabolic faults, some of which are genetically determined. The basic cellular event is the abnormal synchronous discharge of large groups of neurons. Seizure potentials can reach 5 to 20 times the amplitude of normal EEG waves. The complete sequence of events leading to this state remains an unsolved problem.

Epilepsy and Personality

Those frequent storms of electrical activity that invade the brains of epileptics may leave many marks, including some personality changes. For years clinical neurologists have suggested a connection between at least one type of seizure disorder—temporal lobe epilepsy—and certain personality attributes. Work in this area is not all in the hands of brain researchers. On occasion lawyers have advanced the claim on behalf of their clients that an aggressive act was the product of either a seizure of temporal lobe origin or the consequence of a long history of epilepsy. Although many of the data and speculations in this area are shrouded in controversy (Hermann & Whitman, 1984), some threads of consistency are seen across several studies.

Infrahuman studies have demonstrated changes in emotionality that occur with brain damage in temporal lobe structures involved in some forms of seizure disorder. These data are described in Chapter 15. Other investigators have also noted that temporal lobe epilepsy is associated with various psychiatric disorders. An interesting profile of personality characteristics of temporal lobe seizure patients has been provided by Bear and Fedio (1977). They examined the clinical literature for personality traits of temporal lobe epileptics that were commonly noted by neurologists in their informal observations of patients. Two questionnaires were developed using the description of these traits—one filled out by the patient and the other completed by a physician. Epilepsy patients' responses were compared with a control group that included patients with other neurological disorders. Epilepsy patients more frequently than control-group respondents described themselves as humorless, deeply involved with weighty issues of personal destiny, and concerned with broad religious themes. Other data show that some of these attributes are coupled with a striking decline in sexual interests and, in a few patients, a flash anger that is occasionally associated with a sudden violent attack. The intensity of these characteristics is associated with the frequency of seizures and the history of the disorder over the life span.

What accounts for this syndrome? It is important to note that these attributes are not characteristic of all people who suffer from seizures or even all temporal lobe patients. However, Geschwind (1983) argues that it is an important phenomenon that displays some behaviorally significant features of seizures. He suggests that these personality characteristics do not arise from psychological stress associated with seizures, nor does the syndrome arise from a brain lesion. Instead Geschwind offers the intriguing speculation that it arises from the transient abnormal electrical activity that occurs between seizures. This electrical event is called a "spike" because of its rapid, high-amplitude character on EEG recordings. Geschwind believes that it produces periodic unusual excitation of the limbic system that can produce changes in emotional responses. As a consequence, routine environmental events acquire excessive emotional significance because they occur during a period of heightened limbic system activation, the condition that supplies emotional tone to experience. Thus some patients come to attribute deep significance to otherwise routine events.

Every now and then newspapers supply us with reports of some hideous aggressive act of a person who claims to have no recollection of the event. In some of these instances, temporal lobe epilepsy is invoked as the culprit in arguments of diminished legal responsibility. There are at least two different aspects to this argument. On one hand, it is argued that rage and aggression may be actual automatic components of a seizure. On the other hand, there is the argument that intense aggression associated with criminal assaults might arise from a life history of temporal lobe or other types of seizure disorders. Some important research data are now available that address these issues. In 1981 a large group of investigators concerned with seizure disorders (Delgado-Escueta et al., 1981) sat as a panel and evaluated the aggressive acts of 13 patients selected from a group of 5400 patients with epilepsy. These patients were selected because they were thought to have aggressive behavior associated with their seizures. Seizures were recorded on videotape so that their possible aggressive character could be assessed. Some of these people had a history of assaulting others. Spontaneous nondirected aggressive acts were observed in some patients during the height of epileptic paroxysms, and there was amnesia for all such acts. The panel emphasized that if a legal defense argues that aggression is a component of the seizures of the defendant, it should have to provide evidence that aggression or violence is a part of a typical seizure of the defendant.

Another link to human violence is seen in controversial data showing unusually high percentages of abnormal EEGs in populations of criminal offenders, especially those involved in violent acts. Although there are many such reports, the causal links to violence are difficult to determine. In addition, in some such studies abnormal electrical activity is linked to other neurological impairments, which may be more significant determiners of aggressive behavior. The importance of this topic for both patients and society makes it an intriguing one, whose last chapter has yet to be written.

Animal Models and Mechanisms of Seizure

Electrical storms can occur in the brains of many nonhuman creatures, and this provides researchers with opportunities to explore detailed neural mechanisms of seizure. Spontaneous seizures appear in many breeds of dog, especially beagles. Several unusual forms of epilepsy, including an inherited form, are seen in rodents. For example, in one strain of mouse, a mutation involving a particular chromosome produces a spontaneous seizure pattern that bears considerable resemblance to petit mal seizures in humans. These animals show spike-and-wave complexes such as those seen in the human EEG records of Figure 5-17. The trait is inherited in a recessive mode, and studies of metabolic activity show striking increases in this activity in thalamic sites and some frontal cortical regions. The dramatic resemblance of this seizure pattern to some types of human disorder suggests that further research with this animal model will aid in understanding the genetic mechanism that leads to seizure disorders in some humans (Noebels & Sidman, 1979).

Other animal models of seizure use some kind of treatment to induce seizure activity. In some cases application to the brain of "epileptogenic" substances provides a model of focal epilepsy. Substances that have this property include the antibiotic penicillin and aluminum hydroxide, an ingredient found in some common antacids. One interesting model of seizure disorders uses repeated direct electrical stimulation of brain regions as the epileptogenic stimulus; the process of establishing seizures in this way has been described as "kindling." The reason for the term is evident in the procedure that is used to produce a seizure focus (McNamara, 1984). To establish seizure activity in this model, an animal is presented with an initially subconvulsive electrical stimulus delivered directly through implanted electrodes to a particular brain site. Over a period of days, this stimulus comes to produce both behavioral and electrophysiological signs of seizure activity. Eventually seizures appear spontaneously. Kindled seizures can be produced by stimulation of many brain sites but the most effective seems to be the amygdala. Seizure activity kindled by stimulation of the amygdala requires very few stimulus repetitions. Studies of the anatomical network necessary for the establishment of kindling have shown the importance of structures within the brain stem, especially the substantia nigra. Microinjections into this region of substances that promote the actions of an inhibitory synaptic transmitter (GABA) block the kindling effect.

These various experimental models of human seizure disorders coupled with limited studies on human epileptogenic tissue (Schwartzkroin, 1984) suggest several different kinds of mechanisms of seizure. One broad class of seizure mechanisms involves interference with the effectiveness of inhibitory synaptic mechanisms. Such interference can leave unchecked the powerful excitatory synaptic activation of some regions and, as a result, massively synchronized paroxysms of neural activity can occur. Many animal models show such change in the integrity of inhibitory pathways. A second class of seizure mechanisms involves modification of the principal control mechanisms of neural membranes. If the basic properties of membrane gates are altered, then control of depolarization states can change and result in more powerful and sustained excitatory states. Support for this mechanism is seen in studies that have described membrane derangements that produce "paroxysmal depolarizing potentials" (Prince, 1984). A third class of mechanism involves the possible regrowth of brain connections following injury. It is well known that traumatic injury of the brain leads in many cases to seizure disorders in humans. Some researchers have suggested that connections formed after brain injury might involve excessive excitatory synaptic activity. There are many other suggestions that have been offered to account for seizure disorders. This is a fascinating area that involves many afflicted individuals. Clearly the benefits of an excitable and richly interconnected brain come at a great price for some people. A wealth of contemporary research is aimed at lessening this cost.

Summary · Main Points

1. Nerve cells are specialized for receiving, processing, and transmitting signals.

2. Neural signals are changes in the resting potential, which is the normal small difference in voltage between the inside and outside of the cell membrane.

3. A propagated impulse (also called an action potential) travels down the length of the axon without diminishing in amplitude; the impulse is regenerated by successive segments of the axon.

4. Postsynaptic potentials are not propagated. They diminish in amplitude as they spread passively along dendrites and the cell body. Excitatory postsynaptic potentials are depolarizing (they decrease the resting potential.) Inhibitory postsynaptic potentials are hyperpolarizing (they increase the resting potential.)

5. Cell bodies process information by integrating (adding algebraically) postsynaptic potentials across their surfaces.

6. A propagated impulse is initiated at the initial segment of the axon when excitatory postsynaptic potentials summate to reach the threshold.

7. The potentials of a neuron can be explained by differences in the concentration and ease of movement of ions. The resting potential occurs because the neuron contains a relatively high concentration of potassium ions and the extracellular fluid contains a relatively high concentration of sodium ions. When the membrane is depolarized, sodium channels open, Na^+ rushes in, and the membrane potential reverses. Within a millisecond, the sodium channels are inactivated and the resting potential is restored.

8. During the action potential, the neuron cannot be excited by a second stimulus; it is absolutely refractory.

9. Some synapses use electrical transmisson and do not require a chemical transmitter. At these electrical synapses, the cleft between presynaptic and postsynaptic cells is extremely narrow.

10. The electrical activity of the brain can be recorded outside the skull by an electroencephalogram (EEG). Both spontaneous electrical activity and event-related potentials are being related to cognitive and emotional states and to personality variables.

11. Epileptic seizures are correlated with abnormally large EEG waves. Most cases of epilepsy can be controlled by the use of drugs.

Recommended Reading

Junge, D. (1981). *Nerve and muscle excitation* (2nd ed.). Sunderland, Mass.: Sinauer.

Kandel. E. R., & Schwartz, J. H. (Eds.). (1985). *Principles of neural science* (2nd ed.). New York: Elsevier/North-Holland.

Kuffler, S. W., & Nicholls, J. G. (1985). *From neuron to brain* (2nd ed.). Sunderland, Mass: Sinauer.

Schwartzkroin, P. A., & Wheal, H. V. (Eds.). (1984). *Electrophysiology of epilepsy*. New York: Academic Press.

Shepherd, G. M. (1988). *Neurobiology*. (2nd ed.). New York: Oxford University Press.

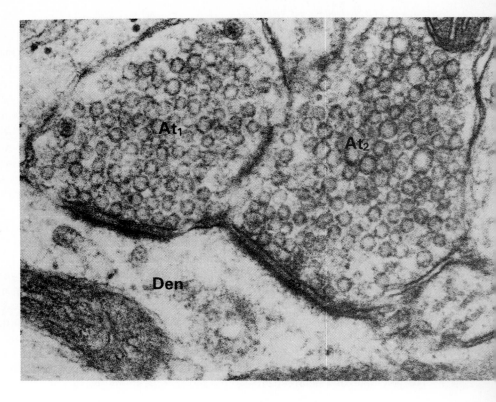

6 Synaptic Chemistry and Psycho-pharmacology

ORIENTATION

Much biological communication of information is conveyed by naturally occurring chemical compounds. To take one example, a substance diffuses across a synaptic gap and excites the neuron on the other side. For an example on a different scale, a dog leaves a chemical signal that informs other dogs about its presence. The principal focus of this chapter is on chemical transmission at synapses, a topic that was introduced in Chapter 5. Many drugs that modify behavior do so by acting on synaptic events, so we will also take up drugs that affect synapses. This leads naturally into the section on psychopharmacology, where we will consider further classes of substances that affect behavior, such as synaptic poisons, stimulants, psychedelic drugs and hallucinogens, antidepressants, anti-anxiety drugs and antischizophrenic drugs. Drug abuse and addiction will also be treated.

Chemical signals

Chemical signals are amazingly varied and ubiquitous: They are vital throughout the plant and animal kingdoms. They range from small and simple molecules to highly complex ones. Different chemical signals affect almost all the structures and processes in organisms. Because of this enormous variety, there are many different ways in which chemical signals can be classified. For example, they can be classified in terms of their chemical structures, their distributions in the body, the processes they regulate or influence, and the drugs that affect them. Box 6-1 presents an initial overview of the subject, classifying chemical signals according to the relationship between the ''sender'' and the ''receiver'' of the signal. This classification also corresponds fairly well with the distances over which the signals convey information, from tiny distances inside single cells to fairly long distances between organisms.

BOX 6-1 | Main Classes of Chemical Signals Within and Between Organisms

Eight categories are used in referring to natural chemical signals that convey information within and between organisms. We cover all eight categories with one or two examples given for each.

In the case of **intracellular signals**, the same cell does the sending and the receiving within its own boundaries. An example is the so-called **second messenger** (brown arrow) released within the cell when certain specific external signal molecules (black arrow) react with receptor molecules at the cell surface. A particular second messenger that we will refer to in this and later chapters is cyclic adenosine monophosphate (cAMP).

Intracellular signals:

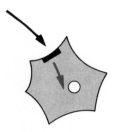

In **autocrine** function the signal secreted by a cell into its environment feeds back to the same cell, as indicated by the brown arrow, and affects its own activity. An example is that some presynaptic terminals have autoreceptors to take up released synaptic transmitter molecules and thus monitor their activity. In this case the signal molecules serve both an autocrine and a synaptic transmitter function. (Autocrine signals, like many chemical signals, are secreted by the cells that produce them. This is the reason why the names of several kinds of chemical signals include the root *crine* from the Greek *krinein*, meaning "to secrete.")

Autocrine function:

In **paracrine** function, the released chemical signal (brown arrows) diffuses to nearby target cells (light color) through the intermediate extracellular space. The strongest impact is felt in the nearest cells. Insulin has both paracrine and endocrine functions, as we will see in Chapter 7.

Paracrine function:

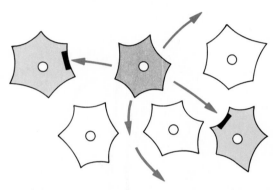

In **synaptic transmitter** function (sometimes called *neurocrine* function), the released chemical signal diffuses across the synaptic cleft, as indicated by the colored arrows, and causes a change in the polarization of the postsynaptic membrane. Typically synaptic transmitter function is more highly localized than paracrine function. A number of synaptic transmitters will be discussed later in the chapter; several are listed in Table 6-1.

Synaptic transmitter:

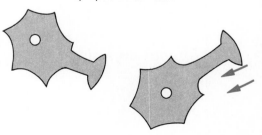

In **neuromodulator** function the chemical signal influences the activity or "gain" of neurons, often at synaptic junctions. This may occur in either of two ways. (1) It may occur through a modulatory ending (indicated in brown) on a presynaptic end button, as shown in the upper part of the accompanying figure. This is a special case of transmitter function. (2) Modulation may occur through a more diffuse action on several adjacent synapses, a sort of sprinkler function; this is shown in the lower part of the figure and can be considered as a special case of paracrine function. The neurotransmitters norepinephrine and serotonin appear to act as neuromodulators in several locations in the brain.

Neuromodulator function:

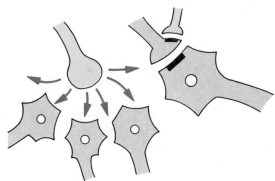

In **endocrine** function the chemical signal is released into the bloodstream and is taken up selectively by target organs. The endocrine system is the subject of Chapter 7. Some nerve cells release **neuroendocrines** in this way. For example, hypothalamic-releasing hormones are secreted by cells in the hypothalamus and carried by special capillaries to the anterior pituitary gland where they affect the activity of local cells.

Endocrine function:

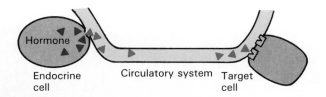

Hormone

Endocrine cell   Circulatory system   Target cell

The term **pheromone** is used to designate a chemical signal that is released outside the body of an animal and that affects other members of the same species. The name comes from the Greek root *pherein*, "to carry," and the ending of the word *hormone*. Examples of pheromones are the odors that many mammals put down in their urine or in secretions of glands to mark their territories or convey information about their reproductive status. Pheromones also mark trails for some species, such as ants.

Pheromones:

Finally, many chemical signals that are released by one species affect the behavior of other species. Such signals that convey information from one species to another can be called **allomones** (W. L. Brown, 1968), from the Greek root *allo* meaning "other" and the ending of the word *hormone*. Allomones can carry messages between animal species or from plants to animals. The illustration indicates in brown the scent by which flowers attract insects and birds to pollinate them and also the agents that some plants produce which interfere with insect growth hormones, thus preventing potential predators from maturing.

Allomones:

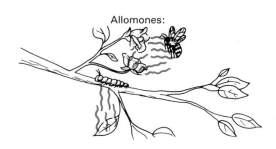

Chemical Transmission at Synapses

The major form of chemical communication in the nervous system occurs at synapses. The sequence of events during chemical transmission at a synapse includes the following steps:

1. Propagation of the nerve impulse into the axon terminal.
2. A set of processes triggered by the impulse that align some vesicles onto the presynaptic membrane.
3. Release of transmitter molecules from vesicles into the synaptic cleft.
4. Entry of transmitter molecules into special receptor molecules in the postsynaptic membrane.
5. This leads to opening of ion channels in the postsynaptic membrane, and the resulting flow of ions alters the polarization of the postsynaptic neuron.

Figure 6-1 shows the main structures involved in chemical synaptic transmission: synaptic vesicles, the synaptic cleft, and the postsynaptic membrane in which the receptors are located. We will note some of the main characteristics of these structures and then take up the main processes of chemical transmission.

Synaptic vesicles are located within the axon terminal of the presynaptic neuron. These vesicles are small globules that, in a given synapse, are usually the same size and show the same staining properties but vary in size and appearance among different synapses. The size ranges from 40 nanometers (nm) to 200 nm. From the time that they were discovered in electron micrographs in the 1950s, synaptic vesicles were linked with chemical transmission, and they have since been demonstrated to store packets of the chemical transmitter used at the particular synapse. As is true of chocolates in a box, the size and shape of the vesicles provide clues to the identities of the transmitters they contain. It used to be believed that any given neuron uses only a single transmitter, but some end boutons have been found to contain two or more kinds of vesicles and transmitters.

[handwritten margin notes: Synaptic vesicles — vary in size, appearance only at different synapses]

Figure 6-1 Electron micrograph of two synapses in the cerebral cortex of a rat. S_1 and S_2 show the synaptic junctions with prominent postsynaptic thickenings on the membrane of the dendrite (Den). The axon terminals (At_1 and At_2) are filled with synaptic vesicles. (magnification × 100,000) (From Peters, Palay, and Webster, 1976)

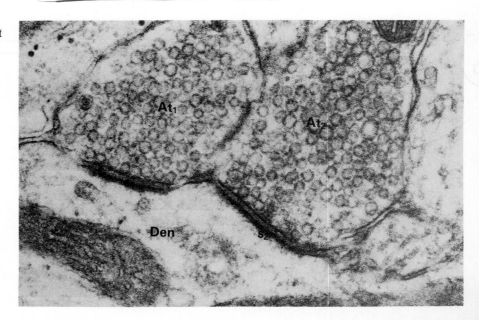

Chemical transmitters are substances liberated at presynaptic terminals that produce changes in electrical potentials in the postsynaptic membrane. There are many different transmitter substances. Even if a given neuron may produce only one transmitter substance at all its terminals, some terminals of the same cell may be excitatory and others inhibitory, depending on the receptor molecules. The transmitter is manufactured at the terminal and stored in vesicles for release into the synaptic cleft. Several substances—such as acetylcholine (ACh) and norepinephrine (NE)—have been demonstrated to be synaptic transmitters, and many more substances are presumed to be. Some of these substances are listed in Table 6-1. Since transmitters are often referred to in terms of chemical families (such as the "catecholamines"—norepinephrine, dopamine, and epinephrine), the chemical classifications are shown in the table to provide a convenient reference.

The **synaptic cleft** is the space between the presynaptic and postsynaptic neurons. Only about 20–30 nm separates the facing membranes of the two neurons. This is not an empty space; it contains complex molecules organized in distinctive patterns that may guide transmitters to their postsynaptic sites.

Receptor sites, located on the postsynaptic side of the cleft, are regions of specialized membrane that receive and react with the chemical transmitter. These sites contain specialized **receptor proteins,** which have an affinity for certain transmitters. The transmitter-receptor reaction causes a change in membrane potential in the direction of depolarization (at an excitatory synapse) or hyperpolarization (at an inhibitory synapse). The receptor membrane has different staining properties from the rest of the membrane.

Storage and Release of Transmitters

receptor proteins — affinity for certain transmitters

Delay btw the 2 parts

When a nerve impulse reaches a presynaptic terminal, vesicles in contact with the presynaptic membrane discharge their contents into the synaptic cleft, where the molecules quickly diffuse to the receptor on the other side (Figure 6-2). Actually there is a delay of at least 0.5 msec between the arrival of the impulse at the presynaptic ending and the first sign of a potential change at the postsynaptic membrane because chemical steps are required to release the synaptic transmitter. The

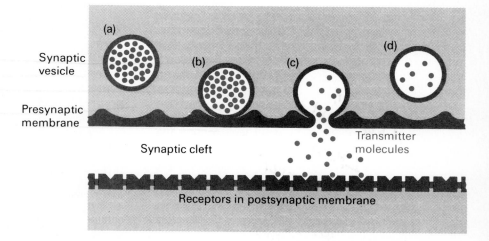

Figure 6-2 Discharge of transmitter molecules from synaptic vesicles into the synaptic cleft. At (b) a synaptic vesicle fuses with a discharge site in the presynaptic membrane, and at (c) it ruptures, liberating transmitter molecules into the cleft. The molecules diffuse across the cleft and are taken up by special receptors in the postsynaptic membrane. Meanwhile, the emptied vesicle is recycled (d) and supplied again with molecules of transmitter.

arrival of the nerve impulse at the presynaptic terminal causes calcium ions (Ca^{2+}) to enter the terminal. Recent work has shown that the entry of Ca^{2+} is controlled by a substance called calmodulin (Means & O'Malley, 1983). The greater the influx of Ca^{2+}, the greater the number of vesicles released by the impulse. If the concentration of Ca^{2+} in the extracellular fluid is reduced, fewer vesicles are released. (Calcium is also important in the liberation of hormones from endocrine glands.) Most synaptic delay is caused by the processes related to the entrance of calcium ions (Ca^{2+}) into the terminal. Small delays are caused by diffusion of the transmitter across the cleft and reaction of the transmitter with the receptor.

The vesicles for a given transmitter in a synapse all appear to contain the same number of molecules of transmitter chemical. The release of each vesicle causes the same change in potential in the postsynaptic membrane. Normally a nerve impulse causes release of the contents of several hundred vesicles at a time. But if the concentration of calcium is lowered at a synapse, only a few vesicles are released per impulse, and the size of unit depolarizations can then be measured. The number of molecules of transmitter per vesicle is not yet known accurately, but it is probably in the tens of thousands. The presynaptic terminal normally produces and stores enough transmitter substance to ensure that the neuron is ready for activity. Intense stimulation of the neuron reduces the number of vesicles, but after a time, more vesicles are produced to replace those that were discharged. Neurons differ in their ability to keep pace with a rapid rate of incoming signals. The production of the transmitter chemical is governed by enzymes that are manufactured in the neuron cell body close to the nucleus. These enzymes are transported actively down the axons to the terminals. If they were not, synaptic function could not continue.

The Nature and Role of Receptor Proteins

How does the joining of the chemical transmitter with the receptor protein in the postsynaptic membrane cause changes in the polarity of that membrane? How can the same chemical transmitter cause depolarization at some synapses but hyperpolarization at others? **Acetylcholine (ACh),** for example, is an excitatory transmitter at synapses between motor nerves and skeletal muscles, but an inhibitory one between the vagus nerve and heart muscle. It is a positively charged ion, but far too little of it is released to account directly for the positive synaptic potentials at excitatory junctions, and direct transfer of charges could not produce the negative effect at inhibitory junctions.

The action of a key in a lock is analogous to the action of a transmitter on the receptor protein (Figure 6-3). Just as a particular key can open different doors, a particular chemical transmitter can lead to the opening of different channels in the neural membrane. At excitatory synapses where it is the transmitter, ACh opens channels for both sodium and potassium ions, as Jenkinson and Nicholls (1961) demonstrated by following the movement of radioactive Na^+ and K^+ ions. Increasing the permeability to both cations drives the membrane voltage down toward zero. At inhibitory synapses, ACh opens a different door. It increases the permeability of the membrane to chloride ions (Cl^-), which increases the potential across the membrane (hyperpolarizes it). Thus the receptor protein itself must be different at different kinds of synapses. Not only must ACh react with proteins that provide different channels for Na^+, K^+, and Cl^-, but other transmitter chemicals (such as norepi-

Figure 6-3 Lock-and-key model of transmitter-receptor function. Each synaptic transmitter has a particular shape that fits only one kind of receptor molecule. Two kinds of transmitters and their receptors are diagrammed here.

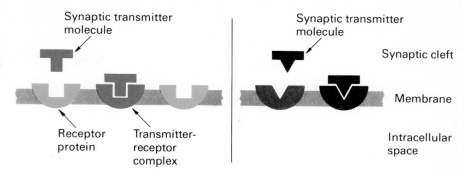

nephrine, gamma aminobutyric acid [GABA], and probably a host of others) must fit like keys into their specific locks.

The key-and-lock analogy is strengthened by the observation that various chemicals can fit onto receptor proteins and block the entrance of the key. Some of the preparations being used in this research resemble the ingredients of a witch's brew. Large quantities of ACh receptor are obtained from the electric organs of eels and rays. Two blocking agents for ACh are poisons: curare and bungarotoxin. Curare is famous as the arrowhead poison used by South American Indians. Extracted from a plant, it greatly increased the efficiency of hunting: If the hunter managed to hit any part of his prey, the poison soon paralyzed the animal. Bungarotoxin is a lethal poison produced by the bungarus snake of Taiwan. This toxin has proved very useful in studying acetylcholine receptors because a radioactive label can be attached to it without altering its action. With such labeling it is possible to investigate the number and distribution of receptor molecules at various kinds of synapses, as well as details of transmitter-receptor binding.

Just as there are master keys that fit many different locks, submasters that fit a certain group, and keys that fit only a single lock, so there are chemical transmitters that fit several different receptor molecules, and others that fit only one. As one example out of many, acetylcholine acts on at least four kinds of receptors. Two main kinds of cholinergic receptors are called **nicotinic** and **muscarinic,** named after the compounds nicotine and muscarine. Nicotine mimics chiefly the excitatory activities of ACh, and muscarine mimics chiefly the inhibitory actions. Cholinergic receptors (those responding to ACh) at neuromuscular synapses on skeletal muscles and in autonomic ganglia are nicotinic. Cholinergic receptors on organs innervated by the parasympathetic division of the autonomic system are muscarinic; this is true of such effectors as heart muscle, the intestines, and the salivary gland. Most ACh receptors in the brain are muscarinic. They were thought to be exclusively so, but now small numbers of nicotinic receptors have been found in the brain, and some brain cells show the curious property of responding to both nicotine and muscarine. Most nicotinic sites are excitatory, but there are also inhibitory nicotinic synapses, and there are both excitatory and inhibitory muscarinic synapses. Not only acetylcholine but also the transmitters norepinephrine and dopamine have been found to produce different effects by acting upon different receptor molecules. A multiplicity of types of receptor for each transmitter agent appears to be a device to produce specificity of action in the nervous system.

The three-dimensional structure of the nicotinic acetylcholine receptor molecule is becoming known in considerable detail from recent research (Miller, 1984). It resembles a lopsided dumbbell with a tube running down its axis. The handle of the dumbbell spans the cell membrane (which is about 7 nm thick); the larger sphere extends about 5 nm above the surface of the membrane, and the smaller sphere extends about 2 nm inside the cell. The sides of the ion channel (the tube that runs through the handle) consist of five subunits arranged like staves in a barrel. Two units are alike and the other three are different. The genes for each of the four types of subunits have recently been isolated (Mishina et al., 1984), and neuroscientists have been able to assemble complete or incomplete receptors to study how they work.

Typically receptors for synaptic transmitters are located in the postsynaptic membrane, but receptors for serotonin and dopamine also occur on the presynaptic side (Usdin & Bunney, 1975). It is thought that these so-called **autoreceptors** provide a negative feedback mechanism. Through them the transmitter can inform the axon terminal, "I am doing my job, no more release is needed."

The number of receptors for a given transmitter in a region of the brain varies widely according to a number of factors; quantifying these changes has provided valuable insights for several areas of neuroscience. For example, this method has shown when various transmitter systems become active in fetal life and how the number changes over the life span. The number of receptors remains plastic in adults: There are not only seasonal variations, but many kinds of receptor show a regular daily variation of 50% or more in number, as we will see when we take up circadian rhythms in Chapter 14. The numbers of some receptors have been found to vary with the use of antidepressants and other psychoactive drugs, as is discussed in Chapter 15. And Chapter 17 describes how some receptors have been found to increase with training.

The Second Messenger: Boosting the Effect of Transmitters

At many synapses chemical transmission involves a further step. The action of the transmitter on the receptor alters the concentration of another substance in the postsynaptic cell (Figure 6-4). If we think of the transmitter as the first signal or messenger at the synapse, then the substance within the cell is a **second messenger.** The second messenger amplifies the effect of the first and can initiate processes that lead

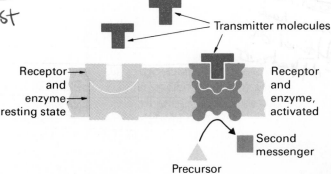

Figure 6-4 Arrival of a synaptic transmitter (or a hormone) at a receptor in a neural membrane can lead to formation of a second messenger inside the cell. The transmitter activates the receptor and the associated enzyme; the enzyme then converts some of the precursor within the cell into the second messenger.

Transmitter molecules

Receptor and enzyme, resting state

Receptor and enzyme, activated

Second messenger

Precursor

to changes in electrical potential at the membrane. In many cases second messengers also lead to biochemical changes within the neuron. As we will see in Chapter 7, many hormones also act by causing the release of a second messenger within their target cells. In 1971 Earl W. Sutherland was awarded the Nobel Prize for research on second messengers that he began in the 1950s. He showed that in many cases the second messenger is the small molecule **cyclic adenosine monophosphate (cyclic AMP or cAMP).**

The second messenger system works relatively slowly, so it seems to be involved in longer lasting actions, such as motivational states or formation of long-term memories, rather than in relaying sensory information or motor commands. Cyclic AMP has been implicated in synaptic activities of the transmitters dopamine, norepinephrine, and serotonin. ACh acts directly, without intervention of a second messenger, at neuromuscular synapses. But many cholinergic synapses in the brain appear to use another second messenger, cyclic guanosine monophosphate (cyclic GMP). After the second messenger has carried out its activity, it is inactivated by an enzyme, phosphodiesterase. Drugs such as caffeine, which inhibit this enzyme, allow the second messenger to act more strongly and for a longer period. Thus they intensify the effects of the transmitter.

Cessation of Action of Synaptic Transmitters

When a chemical transmitter is released, its postsynaptic action is not only prompt, but usually very brief as well. This brevity ensures that, in many places in the nervous system, postsynaptic neural signals closely resemble presynaptic signals in their timing, that is, the message is repeated faithfully. Such accuracy of timing is necessary in many neural systems, for example, to ensure rapid changes of contraction and relaxation of muscles in coordinated behavior. The prompt cessation of transmitter effects is achieved in one of two ways. In the case of some transmitters, the synapse is soon cleared of the transmitter by **re-uptake** by the presynaptic terminal. This not only cuts off the synaptic activity promptly, but also spares the terminal the necessity of manufacturing some of the needed transmitter.

Cessation of the effects of neurotransmitters can also be achieved by enzymes that break down the transmitter. For example, ACh, as well as some other transmitters, has a special enzyme that acts with amazing speed to split up and thus inactivate the transmitter. The enzyme that inactivates ACh is called **acetylcholinesterase (AChE).** It hydrolyzes ACh into choline and acetic acid, and then these products are recycled (at least in part) to make more ACh in the end bouton. AChE is found especially at synapses, but it is also found elsewhere in the nervous system. Thus if any ACh escapes from a synapse where it is released, it is unlikely to survive and get to other synapses where it could start false messages.

Synaptic Events: A Recapitulation

Now we recommend that you use Figure 6-5 to review the stages in the transmission of nerve impulses at chemical synapses. This will also emphasize sources of variability in synaptic activity, since each step is subject to variation in the amounts of necessary substances and the rates of reactions. The review will also set the stage for the next section, in which we consider the vulnerability of synaptic events to chemical agents and drugs that can either facilitate or impair synaptic transmission. If you are uncertain about any point, the section headings and index will tell you where to find the original discussion.

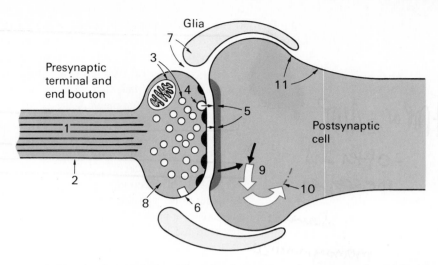

Figure 6-5 Summary of events and steps related to transmission at chemical synapses. 1. Axonal transport of enzymes and precursors needed for synthesis of transmitter agents, vesicle wall, and so forth. 2. Propagation of action potential over presynaptic membrane. 3. Synthesis of transmitter and its storage in vesicles. 4. Depolarization of presynaptic terminal causes influx of Ca^{2+}, which leads vesicles to fuse with release sites and to liberate transmitter into synaptic cleft. 5. Binding of transmitter to receptor molecules in postsynaptic membrane, initiating postsynaptic potential. 6. Binding of transmitter to an autoreceptor in the bouton membrane. 7. Enzyme present in extracellular space and in glia splits excess transmitter and prevents it from passing beyond the synaptic cleft. 8. Re-uptake of transmitter stops synaptic action and provides transmitter for subsequent transmission. 9. Second messenger is released into postsynaptic neuron by certain transmitter-receptor combinations. 10. Inactivation of second messenger by enzyme. 11. Postsynaptic potentials spread passively over dendrites and cell body to the axon hillock.

Chemical Transmitters: Confirmed and Candidates

No one knows how many different synaptic transmitter agents there are, but the number of probable transmitters grew from a few to several dozen during the 1980s, and the list is surely not yet complete. For many of these substances, the evidence that they actually function as transmitters and the evidence about their physiological roles are still rudimentary. Substances definitely proved to be transmitters include acetylcholine (ACh), norepinephrine (NE), dopamine (DA), serotonin (5HT), gamma-aminobutyric acid (GABA), and glutamic acid (see Table 6-1). There is considerable positive evidence for several other substances, but most investigators want to see more before they are convinced. Even if a substance is known to be a transmitter in one location, it may be hard to prove that it acts as a transmitter at some other location where it is found. For example, acetylcholine was long accepted as the transmitter agent at vertebrate neuromuscular junctions, but it was harder to prove that it serves as a transmitter in the central nervous system (CNS) as well. And investigators are still finding important information about the distribution and roles of ACh in the CNS. For example, there is much current work on its role in Alzheimer's disease, as reported in Chapter 4. The number of suspected peptide transmitters is increasing especially rapidly. About thirty small peptides have been identified within sensory and autonomic neurons and in several CNS pathways.

Table 6-1   Some Synaptic Transmitters and Transmitter Candidates: Classification, Location, and Functions

Transmitters and Transmitter Candidates	Locations in Nervous System	Some Behaviorial Functions or Relevance (E = Excitatory; I = Inhibitory)
Amines		
Quaternary amine		
Acetylcholine (ACh)	Neuromuscular synapses and autonomic ganglia have nicotinic cholinergic receptors; widely distributed in CNS where most cholinergic receptors are muscarinic	E at neuromuscular synapses and most central synapses; I at heart and some other autonomic junctions
Monoamines		
Catecholamines		
Norepinephrine (NE)	CNS (see Figure 6-6), especially in neurons from locus coeruleus; also a hormone of adrenal medulla	E and I; involved in arousal and wakefulness; control of eating; learning and memory
Dopamine (DA)	CNS (see Figure 6-7), especially in neurons from substantia nigra	I; in circuits involved in control of voluntary movement; emotional arousal; learning and memory
Epinephrine	Similar to NE but less extensively distributed in CNS	Similar to NE, but less thoroughly studied in CNS
Indolamines		
Serotonin (5-hydroxytriptamine, 5HT)	CNS (see Figure 6-8)	E and I; in circuits involved in mechanisms of sleep and emotional arousal
Melatonin	CNS, especially in pineal gland	I; effects on reproductive cycles and status
Amino acids		
Gamma-aminobutyric acid (GABA)	Widely distributed in CNS	I; the main inhibitory transmitter
Glutamic acid	Widely distributed in CNS	E; perhaps the main excitatory transmitter
Glycine	CNS, especially spinal cord	I; strychnine causes convulsions by competing with glycine at spinal receptors
Histamine	Widely distributed in CNS, especially in hypothalamus	Neural functions still under investigation. Also acts nonneurally in allergic reactions and on gastric secretions
Neuropeptides		
Opioid peptides*		
Enkephalins		
[Met]enkephalin	Widely distributed in nervous system, especially diencephalon and brain stem	Mostly I, for example, in pain circuits, but E in hippocampus
[Leu]enkephalin		
Endorphins		
Beta-endorphin	Intermediate lobe of pituitary; hypothalamus	Mostly I, but E in hippocampus

(Continued on page 192)

Table 6-1 *Continued*

Transmitters and Transmitter Candidates	Locations in Nervous System	Some Behaviorial Functions or Relevance (E = Excitatory; I = Inhibitory)
Dynorphins		
Dynorphin A	Hippocampus; spinal cord	
Peptide hormones†		
Vasopressin	Hypothalamus	I; may modulate memory formation; may interact with other transmitters.

* Most opioid peptides are derived from three parent molecules: proenkephalin, pro-opiomelanocortin, and prodynorphin.
† Other neuroactive peptide hormones include oxytocin, cholecystokinin (CKK), substance P, angiotensin II, somatostatin, hypothalamic-releasing hormones, and many more. For further information on these, see J. R. Cooper, F. E. Bloom, and R. H. Roth, *The Biochemical Basis of Neuropharmacology,* 5th ed. New York: Oxford University Press, 1986.

Considering the rate at which these substances are being discovered and characterized, it would not be surprising if there turned out to be several hundred different peptides serving to convey information at synapses in different subsets of neurons.

What does it take to place a substance on the select list of proved transmitters? The criteria come from the anatomical and functional characteristics that we have discussed. To prove that a particular substance is the chemical transmitter at a particular synapse, we must demonstrate the following facts:

1. The chemical exists in the presynaptic terminals.
2. The enzymes for synthesizing the transmitter exist in the presynaptic terminals.
3. The transmitter is released when nerve impulses reach the terminals.
4. It is released in sufficient quantities to produce normal changes in postsynaptic potentials.
5. Experimental application of appropriate amounts of the chemical at the synapse produces changes in postsynaptic potentials.
6. Blocking the release of the substance prevents presynaptic nerve impulses from altering the activity of the postsynaptic cell.

Investigators have been able to study the transmitters acetylcholine and norepinephrine more thoroughly than other transmitters because each of the two occurs alone at certain peripheral sites in the nervous system. ACh is the transmitter at skeletal neuromuscular junctions in vertebrates, and it is also the transmitter in the ganglia of the autonomic nervous system. NE is the transmitter from neurons of the sympathetic division of the autonomic nervous system to most of the visceral effector organs, such as the heart and the stomach. For example, release of NE in the heart causes the heartbeat to accelerate. Within the central nervous system it was difficult until recently to trace noradrenergic fibers because they intertwine in a complex way with nerve fibers from other systems. Now, however, techniques of histofluorescence and immunohistochemistry have made it possible to map the distribution of noradrenergic pathways in the brain.

Distribution and Localization of Some Transmitters

Some synaptic transmitters are widely distributed through the mammalian nervous system and others are not. The two major inhibitory transmitters, GABA and glycine, are widely used at synapses throughout the brain. Some well-known transmitters—acetylcholine, norepinephrine, serotonin, and dopamine—account for a small proportion of the excitatory synapses in the brain, but the major excitatory transmitters have not yet been identified with certainty. Among the best candidates are the amino acids glutamate and aspartate (Feldman & Quenzer, 1984).

Finding whether and where a particular transmitter system is used in the brain is often difficult; several methods have been tried. For instance, specific stains may make a transmitter visible in histological sections, thus permitting detailed localization. With certain staining techniques, neurons containing a given transmitter fluoresce in ultraviolet light. A method of identifying the specific receptor molecules for a particular transmitter is to bind to them radioactively tagged forms of the neurotransmitter itself, or of compounds that are agonists or antagonists of the transmitter. This not only shows where the transmitter is used, but it also permits quantification of receptor molecules, and it has revealed new facts about synaptic mechanisms.

Figures 6-6 through 6-8 show the brain locations of a few transmitter systems that we will consider later with respect to behavior. To abbreviate long-winded phrases like "those synapses at which acetylcholine is the transmitter," investigators have devised shorter labels, using the Greek root *ergon,* meaning "work"; for instance, "cholinergic synapses." When we write about the transmitters norepinephrine (or noradrenaline), dopamine, and GABA, we will use the terms *noradrenergic, dopaminergic,* and *GABAergic.*

Norepinephrine (NE) is a synaptic transmitter, a neuromodulator, and a hormone. (Norepinephrine is also known as noradrenaline and got its name because, as a hormone, it is secreted by the adrenal gland. The adrenal gland is situated just above the kidney and is named from the Latin words *ad* meaning "at" and *renes* meaning "kidney"; the Greek equivalents are *epi* meaning "above" and *nephros* meaning "kidney." Although the preferred name for the hormone and neurotransmitter is norepinephrine, the synapses where it is used are called noradrenergic. *Nor* is short for *normal,* because this is the parent compound from which epinephrine, or adrenaline, is derived.)

At many synapses where it occurs, NE acts in classical fashion as a neurotransmitter, stimulating the postsynaptic neuron. This is especially the case in peripheral parts of the nervous system. But at many synapses in the brain, NE acts as a **neuromodulator;** that is, it does not stimulate certain neurons itself, but it alters the response of these neurons to other transmitters. For example, NE has been shown to prolong the response of some neurons to the synaptic transmitter glutamate; instead of giving only a few spike potentials to stimulation by glutamate, in the presence of NE the cell gives a barrage of impulses (Nicoll, 1982). Furthermore, whereas the action of NE as a neurotransmitter is brief—on the order of a millisecond—its action as a neuromodulator lasts longer—on the order of seconds. The neuromodulator action of NE also tends to be much more widespread and diffuse than its transmitter action. In the brain NE is produced mainly in a relatively small number of neurons whose cell bodies lie in midbrain and brain stem nuclei, particularly the **locus coeruleus.** Although these cells are rather few in number, their axons branch

Figure 6-6 Diagrammatic representations of noradrenergic pathways
and cell bodies in the brain of the
rat. (a) Dorsal view of brain. In
(b) these pathways and cell clusters
are projected onto a sagittal view of
the brain. The cell clusters are designated A1, A2, and so forth. (DB =
dorsal bundle, VB = ventral bundle of
noradrenergic fibers) (Adapted from
Ungerstedt, 1971)

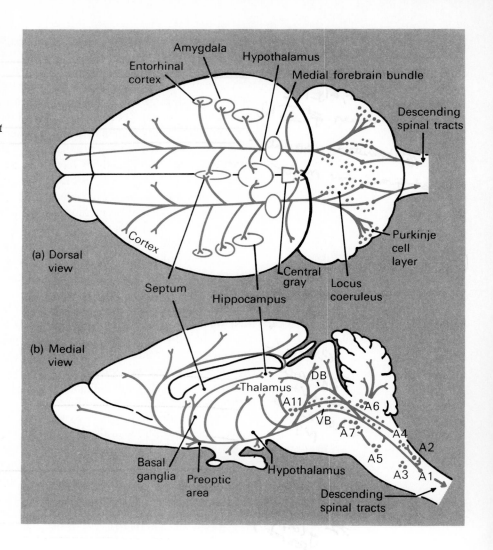

extensively and project to wide regions of the brain (Figure 6-6). Thus the cerebral
noradrenergic system is highly divergent: a few cells influence many cells in large
regions of the brain. NE as a neuromodulator can act, in a sense, to "turn up the
gain" for much of the brain. It has been implicated in wakefulness and arousal
behavior (Chapter 14), in intracranial self-stimulation (Chapter 15), and learning
and memory (Chapter 17). For a review of the anatomy and physiology of the
norepinephrine system, see Feldman and Quenzer (1984).

Dopamine (DA) is produced mainly by neurons whose bodies lie in the basal
forebrain and brain stem; the axons project to the basal ganglia, the olfactory system, and a limited part of the cerebral cortex (Figure 6-7). Later in this chapter, we
will consider dopaminergic transmission in relation to schizophrenia, to psychotic-
like behavior caused by LSD, and to brain mechanisms of reward and drug addiction. We will also take up dopamine neurons with respect to control of voluntary

Figure 6-7 Representation of dopaminergic pathways and cell bodies in rat brain. As in Figure 6-6, these pathways lie on either side of the sagittal plane, but for simplicity they are projected onto this diagram of the sagittal plane. (Adapted from Ungerstedt, 1971)

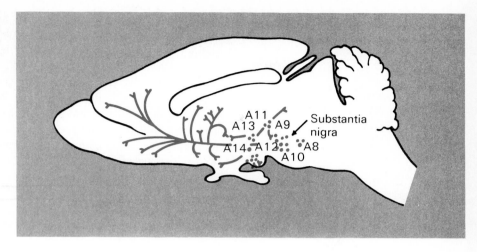

movements (Chapter 10) and emotional arousal (Chapter 15). For a review of the anatomy and physiology of the dopamine system, see Feldman and Quenzer (1984).

Serotonin (5HT) is produced in the central nervous system, mainly by cells in the midline of the brain stem (Figure 6-8). Like some other neurotransmitters, serotonin was first discovered outside the nervous system. It was identified in the blood and was found to constrict blood vessels—hence its name, a serum factor that affects tonus, or muscle tone of blood vessels. The neurons that produce serotonin form the **raphe nuclei,** which lie along the midline in the brain stem. (The Greek word *raphe,* meaning "seam" or "suture," is used in anatomy to refer to a seamlike union between two parts of an organ.) These neurons send long axons to structures throughout the cerebral hemispheres. We will refer to serotonergic activ-

Figure 6-8 Schematic representation of the major organizational features of the ascending serotonergic (5-HT) systems of adult rat brain. The mapping was accomplished by light-microscope radioautography after intraventricular administration of radioactively labeled 5-HT. (Adapted from Parent, Descarries, and Baudet, 1981)

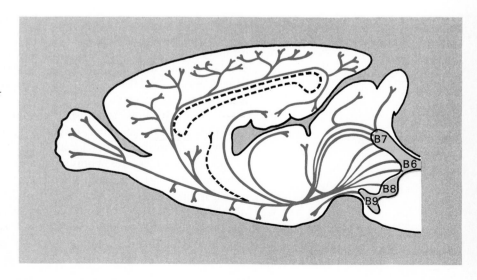

ity in connection with research on the mechanisms of sleep (Chapter 14). It is estimated that serotonin is the transmitter at fewer than 0.1% of brain synapses, so a transmitter can play important although highly circumscribed roles.

The **endogenous opioids** are a family of peptide transmitters, the first members of which were discovered in 1975. (Endogenous refers to the fact that they are produced within the body, and opioid to the fact that some of their actions resemble those of opiate drugs such as morphine.) The opioids have been called the body's own narcotics. Some of them have been named endorphins, a contraction of ''endogenous morphine'' (that is, morphine formed within the body). The discovery of these transmitters occurred in a way very different from the way the other transmitters were discovered. For those we have already discussed, the transmitter chemical was known before its receptors were found, but the reverse was true of the endogenous opioids.

Investigators had long suspected that narcotics might act on postsynaptic receptors in the brain. Some narcotics are effective in such small doses that they could not be acting chemically in a widespread way, but they could be affecting neural messages at specific sites. Animal studies showed that localized application of narcotics to some brain sites caused relief from pain, whereas application to other regions had no effect. One way to see whether a narcotic acts on certain receptors is to label the narcotic or a narcotic antagonist with a radioactive marker and see whether it binds to sites in neural tissue. This was first done with **naloxone,** a potent antagonist of several narcotics that is often administered to people who have taken drug overdoses. The results showed that naloxone binds to synaptic regions of cells taken from rat brains and that the narcotic receptors are concentrated in specific regions of the brain that process the perception of pain. This receptor location seems to be related to the ability of narcotics to relieve pain.

There is no reason why the body should have evolved receptors that bind external narcotics unless it also produced some substance of its own that acts on these receptors. In 1975 experimenters began to look for the key or keys that would fit the receptor locks. Success was announced by the pharmacologists John Hughes and Hans Kosterlitz (1975), who isolated from pig brain two highly similar peptides that bind to the narcotic receptors. Since these substances occur in brain, they were named **enkephalins** (from the Greek roots *en* meaning ''within'' and *kephalon* meaning ''head''). Soon afterward the same enkephalins were found in the brains of other mammals. Research with animal subjects showed that the enkephalins relieve pain. It also showed that they are addictive. We will consider these substances later in regard to pain perception (Chapter 9).

Some investigators have associated certain transmitters with particular behaviors, as if a given transmitter served in only one brain circuit. For example, Substance P (a transmitter in the dorsal horn of the spinal cord) was linked with transmission of pain messages, both in the cord and centrally. But research has shown Substance P to exist in many other locations in the brain, most of which do not appear to have any connection with pain. Another example is the opioids, which, like morphine, were thought of largely in regard to inhibition of pain. But the opioids have been found to influence a variety of behavioral and physiological processes in addition to pain: temperature regulation, respiration, cardiovascular responses, even epileptic seizures. (Morphine also affects many of these processes;

respiratory depression is one of the dangerous effects of overdoses of morphine.) The opioids have also been implicated in reinforcement or reward, memory consolidation, attention, and male copulatory performance.

The fact that a transmitter may play a role in many different brain circuits means that a variety of different effects will occur if the activity of that transmitter is increased or diminished throughout the brain. Normally, however, different brain circuits act relatively independently, and transmitters play only a local role.

Families of Synaptic Transmitters

Some synaptic transmitters are closely related to each other in their chemical structures, and this has practical consequences that we will take up shortly. One example is the catecholamine group: dopamine, norepinephrine, and epinephrine. Another example is the two enkephalins, which differ only in a single amino acid. In this section we will first examine some relationships among transmitters a little more closely, and then we will consider some of their implications.

A great deal of current research involves the catecholamine transmitters **dopamine, norepinephrine,** and **epinephrine.** The catecholamines are synthesized from tyrosine, which is a plentiful amino acid. Tyrosine is obtained from foods, and it is also derived from another dietary amino acid, phenylalanine; furthermore, tyrosine can be synthesized by mammalian cells, so it is not an "essential" dietary amino acid. Through a series of steps, each regulated by specific enzymes, the sequence of products shown in Table 6-2 is synthesized. (A fuller version of this material, including structural diagrams of the catecholamines and their precursor amino acids, appears in the reference section at the end of this chapter, in Reference Table 6-1, page 217.)

In a cell that uses dopamine as its transmitter, the sequence of transformations in Table 6-2 proceeds only as far as the synthesis of dopamine. A cell that uses norepinephrine must first produce dopamine, so any systemic treatment that affects the synthesis of dopamine will also affect the production of norepinephrine. The catecholamines are relatively abundant in the brain; it is estimated that they serve as transmitters at about 15% of synapses in the striatum and at about 5% of those in the hypothalamus.

The catecholamine transmitters are also known as **monoamines** because they contain a single amine group, NH_2. Another monoamine, but one that contains the indole group rather than the catechol group, is the transmitter serotonin. **Serotonin** (also known as 5-hydroxytryptamine or 5HT) is synthesized from the essential amino acid tryptophan. Tryptophan is one of the least plentiful amino acids, and diets low in tryptophan cause low levels of serotonin in the nervous system. Serotonin can be converted to another transmitter, melatonin.

Added discussion of some families of neurotransmitters will be found in the reference section at the end of this chapter (pp. 216–217).

The fact that several transmitters are related chemically poses problems both for research and for therapeutic treatments that affect synaptic activity. One problem for research is that similar transmitters are often difficult to distinguish when one attempts to trace pathways in the CNS or to determine which of two related transmitters is employed at a given site. These problems are yielding to investigation as more precise techniques are devised. Another problem is that an experimental at-

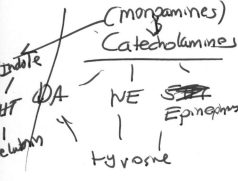

Table 6-2   Synthesis of the Catecholamine Transmitters

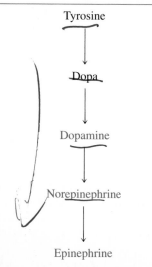

Tyrosine

↓

Dopa

↓

Dopamine

↓

Norepinephrine

↓

Epinephrine

tempt to affect one transmitter system may also influence other synapses that use related transmitters; this complicates attempts to determine precisely what processes and neural circuits are involved. For example, drugs that inhibit the enzyme monoamine oxidase were found to be antidepressants. Attempts to relate this to dopaminergic circuits were complicated by the fact that monoamine oxidase acts on all the catecholamines—and also the indolamines such as serotonin. Another problem in attempts to devise therapeutic treatments is the fact that interventions that affect one kind of synapse may also affect others that use a related transmitter. For example, patients with the neurological disorder called Parkinson's disease suffer from a deficiency of dopamine. Administering the precursor L-dopa alleviates the symptoms of Parkinson's disease by increasing the production of dopamine, but it also causes increased production of norepinephrine and epinephrine, leading to overactivity of the sympathetic nervous system.

Psychopharmacology

From time immemorial people have sipped, swallowed, or chewed liquids, plants, and animals. They have also learned to shun toxic liquids, plants, and animals. Social customs and dietary codes evolved to protect people from harmful foods. This long history of seeking, testing, and using different substances came not only from the need for nourishment but also from the need for relief of pain, and control of anxiety, and from the desire for pleasure. In many cases the basis of an effect lies in the nervous system, especially in its synapses, which are particularly sensitive to drugs and poisons. The blood-brain barrier shelters the central nervous system from some of the drugs that enter the body, but many other drugs can penetrate the brain, and most of these can affect behavior by altering synaptic processes.

The subject of psychopharmacology is vast and is changing at a rapid pace: Researchers are steadily discovering new compounds and learning about the physiological and biochemical mechanisms of drugs that affect behavior. Legal and illegal manufacturers are pouring new drugs onto the market. As drugs are used over a period of time, many show more serious disadvantages than were realized at the start. For example, many drugs that were approved for treatment of anxiety or depression have since been withdrawn, are used with greater caution, or have been replaced by agents considered to be more effective or safer. Some illegal drugs have also been reevaluated in terms of their capacity for abuse and their social costs. Cocaine is an example. Whereas a 1973 report of the National Commission on Marihuana and Drug Abuse stated that cocaine had shown little harm in the United States, a report issued in late 1984 by the National Institute on Drug Abuse called cocaine abuse "an epidemic of serious adverse consequences" (Adams & Durrell, 1984, p. 9). The 1984 report cited several indices to show that there is a cocaine epidemic: a rising tide of emergency room admissions and deaths; admission to drug treatment centers, often with multiple drug problems; dependency; and a great volume of calls to a toll-free cocaine hotline, sometimes as many as 1000 per day. Thus the greater availability of cocaine and a decade's experience with it have forced a radical reevaluation of the drug that has resulted in media and public attention.

Our coverage of psychopharmacology will necessarily be brief and incomplete; readers who wish to pursue this topic further can use the references in the text and some recommended books listed at the end of the chapter. New findings will undoubtedly make some of our discussion out of date over the next few years, but much of the basic material on synaptic effects of drugs will continue to form part of the growing picture of knowledge. Our discussion will also point out relations between this subject and topics taken up in other chapters.

Effects of Drugs on Synapses

The synapse is such a strategic site in neural functioning that many plant and animal substances have evolved to influence it. In the few centuries that people have been able to create new chemical compounds, there has been an increasing flood of new substances that affect synapses, with both good and bad effects. We will consider here several classes of drugs: poisons, stimulants, psychedelic or hallucinogenic drugs, anxiolytics (drugs that decrease anxiety), antidepressants, and antipsychotics. Research in this area has both practical and theoretical aspects, and each aids the other; attempts to protect and improve health have increased knowledge about synaptic functions of drugs, and increased knowledge about effects of drugs at synapses has yielded important new ways to safeguard and improve health.

Observation of effects of substances on animals goes far back into human history, and the initial human use of many substances is said to have been prompted by seeing their effects on animals (R. K. Siegel, 1979). For example, an Ethiopian tradition claims that the human use of coffee originated around the ninth century when a herder noticed that his goats became unusually frisky after eating the small bright red fruits of the wild coffee tree. Different groups of Indians in Mexico attribute the use of tobacco to observations of insects or birds that ate it. Some groups are said to have noticed that several species of insects ate tobacco leaves with a speed that suggested the presence of stimulants. More poetic is the tradition of the Huichol Indians of Mexico: Their ancestors noticed that certain birds favored tobacco flowers and that tobacco enabled these birds to fly high and strong and to see great visions. Thus the Indians consumed tobacco in an attempt to communicate with the gods and to see visions. The human use of coca leaves is said to have started when pack animals in Peru, short of food, ate coca leaves and were able to continue their work. The common names of many plants reflect either harmful or beneficial effects on particular species. Names that reflect disturbed behavior or toxicity include locoweed, henbane, sheep's bane, and flea bane. Attractiveness to certain species has inspired names such as catnip, hare's lettuce, dog grass, swine grass, and pigeon candy.

Some native groups used plant substances medicinally because of their effects on animals. Thus people in tropical Asia observed that birds fell down after flying in and around certain trees, leading to the discovery of *Rauwolfia serpentina* (reserpine) and its use in folk medicine. Reserpine inhibits the storage of catecholamine transmitters in synaptic vesicles. It was used extensively in the West in the 1950s to treat mania and excited schizophrenic states. Although reserpine is no longer used for these purposes, it was important in devising hypotheses about the synaptic bases of depression. Many such folk remedies are being investigated throughout the world, and this has given rise to a field called ethnopharmacology.

Poisons   Chemical warfare is carried out by many plant and animal species, and natural chemical weapons for both defense and offense probably stretch far back into the history of life forms. There is evidence that by the beginning of the Mesozoic Era, some 225 million years ago, flowering plants were producing two kinds of defensive chemicals. One is the tannins, which inhibit growth of fungi and also taste bitter. The bitter taste undoubtedly deterred some animals from eating tannin-producing plants, but the plants also evolved an even more effective chemical defense against animal predators: alkaloid compounds, which include many psychoactive agents, such as curare, the opium alkaloids (morphine and codeine), and lysergic acid. Other psychoactive plant substances also evolved, and we will mention some of them in the next paragraphs. Animals evolved both defensive and offensive chemical weapons as well, as we shall see after we have surveyed the plants.

One plant that protects itself against predators by producing neurotoxic alkaloids is the locoweed of the Western Plains. This plant received its common name because if sheep or cattle eat it, they seem to "go crazy" or "loco." Another neurotoxic plant alkaloid is curare, which, as we noted earlier, paralyzes animals by blocking acetylcholine receptors. The common potato produces alkaloids that inhibit the enzyme acetylcholinesterase, which in turn inactivates acetylcholine after its release; inhibiting the enzyme impairs synaptic functioning. When potatoes are diseased, bruised, or exposed to light, these and other alkaloids increase to levels that can be lethal to humans (Ames, 1983). These alkaloids are major determinants in resistance of potatoes to insects and diseases. In trying to obtain higher insect resistance, breeders have increased the levels of these alkaloids; one cultivated variety of potato had to be withdrawn because of its toxicity to humans.

Caffeine may have evolved to protect plants against insect predators (Nathanson, 1984). It has been found to cause uncoordinated behavior in insects and to inhibit their growth and reproduction. The direct action of caffeine is to inhibit certain enzymes (phosphodiesterases) that metabolize cyclic AMP; thus caffeine prolongs the action of cAMP in the postsynaptic neuron, which accounts for its stimulant action. The insecticidal power of caffeine may not be seem so surprising when we note that nicotine is also a natural insecticide. It is interesting to reflect that the substances for which people cultivate the coffee bush and the tobacco plant evolved as a means of protecting these plants against predators.

Many animals have also evolved substances for defense or offense that act by altering synaptic activity of predators or prey. In the last chapter, we mentioned the poison of the pufferfish (tetrodotoxin [TTX]) and the venoms of certain scorpions that affect ion channels in the neuron. The venom of the bungarus snake (bungarotoxin) is lethal because it binds firmly to the acetylcholine (ACh) receptor in the postsynaptic membrane and does not allow ACh to act, thus causing paralysis. The venom of the black widow spider attacks the synapse in another way: It stimulates cholinergic axon terminals strongly, causing a high rate of release of ACh. The result is a burst of uncoordinated activity followed by depletion of the transmitter so that no further impulses can be transmitted and paralysis results.

Scientists have isolated or produced many compounds that block the inactivation of ACh by acetylcholinesterase (AChE). One of these is a compound called physostigmine, which has been used in research and for limited medical purposes. Recently there have been indications that this drug may be effective in helping some patients with Alzheimer's disease by enhancing the activity of deficient amounts of cerebral ACh. The same drug was used by some West African peoples for trials by ordeal. A person suspected of being guilty of an offense was made to swallow some beans that contain physostigmine. A confident person would swallow them quickly, and reaction in the stomach would cause the beans to be thrown up rapidly. But an anxious, doubtful person would chew and swallow the beans slowly, allowing the physostigmine to be absorbed in the blood and to poison the suspect. Thus, depending upon dose and circumstance, the same drug may be helpful or harmful.

Stimulants   Many naturally occurring and artificial stimulants are widely used. Caffeine, whose synaptic action was just mentioned, occurs in both coffee and tea, and it is added to other beverages. A related compound, theophylline, also occurs in tea, and it also inhibits the phosphodiesterases that metabolize cAMP. Nicotine, as mentioned earlier, mimics the action of one class of ACh receptors, and therefore these receptors are called nicotinic receptors. Most nicotinic receptors are found in neuromuscular junctions and in autonomic ganglia. When nicotine is absorbed by smoking or chewing tobacco, it increases the heart rate, both directly, by stimulating sympathetic ganglia, and also indirectly, by stimulating the adrenal gland to release epinephrine. Among the other actions of nicotine are increasing blood pressure, increasing secretion of hydrochloric acid in the stomach, and increasing motor activity of the bowel. These neural effects, quite apart from the effects of tobacco tar on the lungs, contribute to the unhealthful consequences of heavy and prolonged use of tobacco products.

The **amphetamine** molecule resembles the structure of the catecholamine transmitters (norepinephrine, epinephrine, and dopamine) (see Reference Table 6-1). Amphetamine causes the release of these transmitters from the presynaptic terminals, and it also potentiates their transmitter activity in two ways: (1) blocking the re-uptake of catecholamines, and (2) competing with the catecholamines for the enzyme that inactivates them (monoamine oxidase [MAO]). These effects of amphetamine prolong the presence of the catecholamine transmitters in the synaptic cleft, thus enhancing their activity.

Because amphetamine stimulates and enhances the activity of the catecholamine transmitters, it has a variety of behavioral effects. On a short-term basis, it has been used to produce heightened alertness and even euphoria, and to ward off boredom. Its short-term use can promote sustained effort without rest or sleep and with lowered fatigue. Although a person may be able to accomplish more work and feel more confident by using amphetamine, most studies show that the quality of work is not improved by the drug; it appears to increase motivation but not cognitive ability. There may also be annoying side effects caused by activity of amphetamine at synapses of the autonomic nervous system; such symptoms include high blood pressure, tremor, dizziness, sweating, increased rate of respiration, and nausea.

If the use of amphetamine is prolonged, the user exhibits "tolerance," which means that the intake of the drug has to be increased in order to sustain the desired effects. Continued intake at higher doses often leads to sleeplessness, severe weight loss, and general deterioration of mental and physical condition. Prolonged use may lead to symptoms that are virtually identical to those of paranoid schizophrenia: compulsive, agitated behavior and irrational suspiciousness. In fact, some users of amphetamine have been diagnosed as schizophrenic by doctors who did not know their history of use of the drug. Study of this syndrome has led to hypotheses about schizophrenia and possible therapy for it, as we will see later in this chapter and in Chapter 15. Addiction to amphetamine and other drugs will be discussed later in this chapter.

Psychedelic or Hallucinogenic Drugs

Some users of amphetamine experience hallucinations, but other agents, such as **LSD (lysergic acid diethylamide),** mescaline, and psilocybin, are even more likely to alter sensory perception and produce peculiar experiences. These drugs have been termed **hallucinogens,** but their effects are rather different from the hallucinations that psychotic patients experience. Hallucinations not induced by drugs are usually auditory and threatening, and people who experience hallucinations tend to believe that the voices they hear are real. The effects of LSD and related substances are reported to be predominantly visual and interesting, although they can become frightening. Users often see fantastic pictures with intense colors. Subjects are often aware that these strange perceptions are not real events in the environment. Another term applied to such drugs is **psychedelic** agent.

Psychedelic agents are quite diverse chemically; most but not all of them have been found to affect one or another of the amine synaptic transmitter systems. For example, mescaline affects the norepinephrine system; LSD and psilocybin act on the serotonergic synapses; the drug muscarine, one of several psychoactive agents found in certain mushrooms, acts on cholinergic synapses.

LSD was synthesized in 1938 by Albert Hofmann, a Swiss pharmacologist, who was looking for new therapeutic agents. Tests with animals did not appear to show effects, so the compound was put aside. Then one day in 1943, Dr. Hofmann experienced a peculiar dreamlike, almost drunken, state. When he closed his eyes, fantastic pictures of intense color and extraordinary plasticity seemed to surge toward him. The state lasted about two hours. Correctly suspecting that he had accidentally ingested a small amount of LSD, Hofmann began to investigate the compound. LSD proved to be amazingly potent; a fraction of a milligram was enough to induce psychedelic effects. In the 1950s many investigators worked on LSD, mainly with the idea that it might provide a useful model psychosis that would suggest clues about the biochemical processes in mental illnesses. The structure of LSD resembles that of serotonin, and LSD was soon found to act on serotonergic synapses, but the mechanism by which it exerts its psychedelic action is still unknown.

A recent experiment to study the mechanism of LSD effects on freely moving cats was accomplished by recording the electrical activity of single neurons in a brain stem nucleus (the raphe nucleus) while making television records of the cats' behavior (Trulson & Jacobs, 1979). It is impossible to tell whether cats are experiencing abnormal perceptions, but under the influence of LSD, they show characteristic bizarre behavior: limb flicking, head shaking, staring, and appearing to investi-

Figure 6-9 Cats show abnormal behavior under the influence of LSD. They flick their limbs and appear to investigate objects that the experimenter cannot see. Recordings of electrical activity of single neurons in the raphe nucleus of the brain stem in these animals show that LSD inhibits these cells. (Drawings made from television recordings, courtesy of Barry L. Jacobs.)

gate objects that the experimenter cannot see (Figure 6-9). LSD was found to inhibit the firing of cells in the raphe nucleus, and the behavioral changes increased in proportion to the decrease in neural firing. But the behavior was not completely associated with firing rate. For one thing, although the observed neural changes were over within six hours, the behavioral changes lasted considerably longer. Also, the raphe cells responded fully to subsequent doses of LSD, whereas the behavioral effects showed tolerance. These discrepancies may indicate that while the effects of LSD on serotonergic raphe cells initiate the peculiar behavior, cells further along in the circuits account for some of the other characteristics. Research continues in the attempt to trace out the circuits that underlie these behaviors. Many users of LSD have reported ''flashbacks,'' that is, experiences as if a dose of drug had been taken although the person is drug-free. These episodes suggest that even brief use of LSD may cause some permanent neural changes.

Phencyclidine is a special type of anesthetic agent that makes many people feel dissociated from themselves and their environment; subjects also report such effects as agitation, excitement, hostility, and hallucinations. Known popularly as PCP, phencyclidine is often sold illegally as some other psychedelic drug. Toxic reactions include the ''four Cs.'' At lower doses these are (1) combativeness and (2) catatonia; some users become aggressive and violent. Large overdoses of phencyclidine results in (3) convulsions or coma that may last for days and (4) confusion that may last for weeks. Users sometimes develop a psychotic condition that resembles schizophrenia. Several cities report that phencyclidine is commonly found in emergency room overdose cases and in psychiatric admissions (Julien, 1981). Phencyclidine has some effect on several synaptic transmitters, but it does not seem to be specific to any one, so it presents a puzzle for research.

Anti-Anxiety Drugs (Anxiolytics)

Severe anxiety is estimated to afflict about 8% of adult Americans. Anxiety in this sense does not include vague feelings of unease or mild apprehension but only severe states that prevent people from carrying on normal daily activities. These clinical states of anxiety include phobias, such as those that prevent some people from taking an airplane or even from leaving their houses, and also frank attacks of panic. Freud called attempts to deal with anxiety the most difficult task that confronts clinicians.

Many substances have been used to combat anxiety. Such substances are called **anxiolytics** (named from anxiety and the Greek term *lytic* meaning ''to loosen or dissolve''). One substance that has long been used as an anxiolytic in many cultures is alcohol. Alcohol does decrease anxiety in some people, but it also has many harmful effects, some of which will be disucssed later in this chapter. Opiates and barbiturates have also been used to relieve anxiety, but they seem to be sedatives or, in higher doses, to produce stupor rather than being true anxiolytics. In the early 1960s, a rather effective new family of anxiolytics was found, the **benzodiazepines.** The benzodiazepines include some of the most frequently prescribed drugs, especially diazepam (trade name, Valium). The benzodiazepines bind with high affinity to receptors that appear to be found exclusively within the central nervous

Figure 6-10 Schematic representation of the GABA receptor-ionophore complex and its component parts. The portion labeled G indicates the GABA receptor, BZ indicates the benzodiazepine receptor, P-B indicates the picrotoxin—barbiturate receptor, and Cl the chloride ion channel. Each component of the three-receptor complex (a) can exist as an individual entity (e), (f), and (g) or in combinations of two (b), (c), and (d). (Adapted from Olsen, 1982)

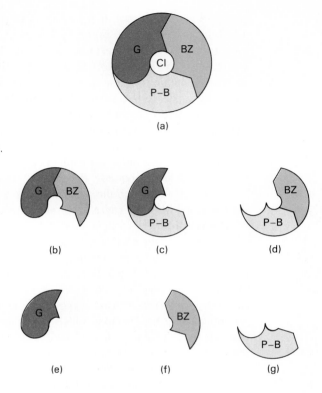

system. These receptors are associated with and appear to enhance the activity of a subset of receptors for the inhibitory transmitter GABA, thus producing larger inhibitory postsynaptic potentials than would be caused by GABA working alone. In fact, there appear to be several different receptor complexes that include GABA receptors, some facilitating and some inhibiting the effect of GABA, and this probably provides for specificity of action (see Figure 6-10).

Why should the brain have receptors for the benzodiazepine drugs? Just as in the case of the opioid narcotics, neuroscientists do not suppose that such receptors evolved in anticipation of the drugs. They have therefore been searching for a natural substance in the nervous system that binds to the so-called benzodiazepine receptor, but the quest has taken much longer than the search for the enkephalins and endorphins. A recent announcement (Ferraro et al., 1984; Marx, 1985) suggests that the substance is a novel peptide and that it acts to produce anxiety, counteracting the inhibitory effects of GABA. Anxiety is, under some circumstances, an appropriate response. The subject of anxiety and anxiolytic drugs will be taken up more fully in Chapter 15.

Antischizophrenic Drugs (Antipsychotics)

Although the psychoses include not only schizophrenia but also the major affective disorders (depression and manic episodes), the term *antipsychotic drug* is used for agents that are employed to alleviate schizophrenia or to prevent its recurrence. These drugs are also called neuroleptics.

In Chapter 1 we noted that the introduction of the drug chlorpromazine in the 1950s produced a revolution in the treatment of schizophrenia and in psychiatric thinking. Investigators promptly began trying to find even more effective drugs and also to determine how chlorpromazine and other antischizophrenic drugs produce their effects. It was found that these drugs block transmission at synapses where dopamine (DA) is the transmitter agent; moreover, almost all drugs that block dopaminergic transmission have therapeutic effects in schizophrenia. Therefore the hypothesis was formulated that an increase in activity of dopamine is involved in the development of schizophrenia. Further research has led to a more precise hypothesis that only one of several classes of DA receptors is involved in schizophrenia and its cure. Now research is focused on studying these specific DA receptors and learning about their functional roles. The dopamine hypothesis of schizophrenia will be discussed further in Chapter 15.

Antidepressants

Since millions of people are afflicted by depression (as reported in Table 1-2), many drugs have been tested for antidepressant effects, and many new drugs have been synthesized to treat depression. Two main classes of antidepressant drugs are the monoamine oxidase (MAO) inhibitors and the tricyclic antidepressants. Further novel antidepressants are coming into use.

The **MAO inhibitors** were developed for another therapeutic purpose and were found by accident to be antidepressants. These drugs were developed in the 1950s for the treatment of tuberculosis. They are toxic to the tubercle bacillus, although the mechanism of this toxicity is not completely known. It was soon observed that the MAO inhibitor iproniazid had a euphoric effect on tuberculosis patients. It was not clear at first whether the drug made patients happy because it reduced the symptoms of tuberculosis or whether it had a specific euphoric effect. Clinical tests on depressed patients showed that iproniazid benefited many of them, and animal research showed that it inhibited MAO and thus prolonged the action of catecholamine transmitters. Although the MAO inhibitors were widely used for a time as antidepressants, they had some drawbacks: They caused annoying side effects in some people, and they reduce the ability to metabolize many other drugs and certain foods. Because of these effects, some of the MAO inhibitors have been withdrawn, but others are still being prescribed.

A class of drugs commonly used as antidepressants are the compounds known as **tricyclic antidepressants.** The structure of these compounds resembles that of chlorpromazine and related antipsychotic drugs. For this reason the tricyclic drug imipramine was originally tested for antipsychotic activity. Although it did not help schizophrenic patients, imipramine appeared to elevate the mood of some depressed patients, and further tests with other depressed patients confirmed the antidepressant action. The mechanism of the antidepressant action of the tricyclics is still a matter of debate. Originally the therapeutic effect was attributed to the fact that these drugs inhibit the re-uptake of catecholamines in the presynaptic terminals. But whereas this inhibition occurs after a single administration, relief from depression occurs only after two to three weeks of daily administration. There are indications that sustained administration causes a reduction in the number of catecholamine receptors in the postsynaptic membranes and also a reduced level of concentration of the transmitters, Thus, although the tricyclic antidepressants are widely used, it is not yet clear whether depression is caused by too much or too little activitation of the catecholaminergic synapses. Also, it is probable that only a specific subset of these synapses is involved in depression. The more that is learned about the neural mechanisms of depression, the more investigators will be helped to discover specific and reliable treatments for it.

Lithium in Control of Mania

The most effective pharmacological agent to treat and prevent manic episodes is lithium. Although it has no effect on mood in normal individuals, lithium alleviates manic episodes and helps to prevent the recurrence of both mania and depression. Trials with psychiatric patients occurred after a scientist noticed that lithium calmed the behavior of guinea pigs, and the results with manic patients were spectacular. Such patients may jump from idea to idea and talk incessantly, often grandiosely; their behavior may be dangerous to themselves and to others. Lithium promptly restored normal behavior to most of these patients. Why it does so is still a mystery. Lithium is much simpler chemically than the other substances we have been considering—it is a chemical element—but the reason for its therapeutic effectiveness is still not known. Lithium interacts with neural processes in many ways, and a number of hypotheses have been proposed and tested (Feldman & Quenzer, 1984). In spite of the effectiveness of lithium in combating mania in many patients, it is not universally effective. The search to understand its mechanisms continues in the hope of finding a still more effective treatment.

Drugs Affect Each Stage of Synaptic Transmission

Almost all of the behavioral effects that we have seen in the last few pages are caused by activities of drugs on synaptic events and processes. In Figure 6-5 we reviewed ten steps that occur in the transmission of information from one neuron to the next at a chemical synapse. Now let us review in Table 6-3 how certain drugs affect these ten steps. We will concentrate on synapses that use either the transmitter acetylcholine or one of the catecholamine transmitters. Those actions that are specific to catecholaminergic synapses are shown in color in the table. The effects listed in the table are keyed to the numerical points listed in Figure 6-5. Let us comment on some of these agents and their effects.

If axonal transport is inhibited by drugs such as colchicine, then enzymes that are manufactured in the cell body are not replaced in the presynaptic terminals. Since enzymes are needed to direct the manufacture of transmitter chemicals and vesicle walls, colchicine prevents the replenishment of the transmitter agent as it is used up. Thus synaptic transmission fails. The tranquilizing drug reserpine does not interfere with synthesis of transmitters, but it inhibits storage of catecholamine transmitters (dopamine, epinephrine, and norepinephrine) in vesicles.

Even if a terminal has an adequate supply of transmitter stored in vesicles, various agents or conditions can prevent the release of transmitter when a nerve impulse reaches the terminal. Low concentration of calcium in the extracellular fluid is such a condition: the impulse leads to release of transmitter by causing an influx of Ca^{2+}, which guides vesicles to release sites. Also, specific toxins prevent

Table 6-3   Synaptic Events and Drugs (Numbers of Events Are Keyed to Figure 6-5)

Synaptic Events	Drugs
Presynaptic events	
1. Block axonal transport	Colchicine
2. Block propagated nerve impulse	TTX and STX prevent increased permeability to Na^+
3. Interfere with synthesis or storage of transmitter	Hemicholinium blocks uptake of choline
	Reserpine inhibits vesicular storage of catecholamines
4a. Interfere with mobilization of vesicles by Ca^{2+} influx	Low concentrations of Ca^{2+} Calcium ion binding agents
4b. Block release of transmitter	Botulinum toxin blocks release of ACh Tetanus toxin blocks release of GABA
4c. Facilitate release of transmitter	Amphetamine facilitates release of catecholamines
	Black widow spider venom causes prompt release and thus depletion of ACh
Postsynaptic events	
5a. Block receptor molecules	Curare, bungarotoxin block nicotinic ACh receptors
	Atropine, scopolamine block muscarinic ACh receptors
	Phenothiazines (for example, chlorpromazine) block dopamine receptors
5b. Reduce number of receptor molecules	Tricyclic antidepressants reduce number of catecholamine receptors
6. Mimic transmitter at autoreceptor molecules	LSD mimics serotonin at autoreceptors and thus slows transmission at serotonergic synapses
7. Inhibit enzyme that inactivates transmitter	Physostigmine, eserine, DFP inhibit AChE
8. Prevent re-uptake of transmitter, depleting stores available for subsequent transmission	Cocaine, amphetamine, imipramine inhibit re-uptake of NE
9. Inhibit release of second messenger or inhibit its activity	Nicotine and certain heavy metals (for example, lead and lanthanum) block activation by NE of the synthesis of cAMP
10. Inhibit inactivation of second messenger and so enhance its activity	This is done by the methyl xanthines: caffeine (in coffee and tea) and theophylline (in tea)

the release of specific kinds of transmitter. (Table 6-3 gives examples.) For instance, botulinum toxin, which is formed by microorganisms that multiply in improperly canned food, poisons many people each year by blocking release of acetylcholine (ACh).

Other agents act in the opposite way, by stimulating or facilitating the release of certain transmitters. The venom of the black widow spider causes the release of ACh, as we already noted. Amphetamine facilitates the release of the catecholamine transmitters, and it also inhibits their re-uptake, which further potentiates their synaptic action.

The postsynaptic receptor molecules can be blocked by various drugs. For example, curare blocks nicotinic ACh receptors. Since the synapses between nerves and skeletal muscles are nicotinic, curare results in paralysis of all skeletal muscles, including those used in breathing. Behavior can be disrupted not only by blocking transmitter-receptor action, but also by prolonging it. Agents that inhibit the enzyme AChE allow ACh to remain active at the synapse and alter the timing of synaptic transmission. Effects can range from mild to severe, depending on the anti-AChE agent and its dosage. The drug eserine has temporary and reversible anti-AChE effects. Mild doses of it are used in certain medical conditions when ACh action at neuromusculer junctions is weak and inadequate. On the other hand, some organic phosphorus compounds like DFP are potent and persistent inhibitors of AChE. DFP is the active ingredient in certain insecticides which must be used with caution because they are also highly toxic to human beings.

Drug Abuse and Addiction

Drug abuse and addiction have become a social problem that afflicts millions of individuals and also disrupts the lives of their families, friends, and associates. The whole community is affected because of crimes, traffic accidents, fires, and other social disorders caused by drug users; because of the costs associated with helping drug users control their abuse; and because of costs associated with the control of drug trafficking. An estimate of the large number of people who abuse drugs in the United States was shown in Table 1-2. For over a century, scientists have been investigating drug addiction, and much has been learned, even though fully effective means to combat addiction have yet to be discovered. Both physiological and behavioral mechanisms for drug addiction have been discovered; some investigators put more emphasis on the physiological mechanisms and some on the behavioral mechanisms. We will consider both kinds of mechanisms, taking examples mainly from abuse of cocaine, the opiate drugs (such as morphine and heroin), and alcohol, because these have been studied most fully. Some terms related to drug abuse and addiction are defined in Table 6-4.

Although our main concern is with drug abuse by humans, it is worth noting that many cases have been reported in which animals in the wild administer drugs to themselves and even become addicted (R. K. Siegel, 1979). For example, there are reports of elephants repeatedly becoming intoxicated on fermented fruits. When confined to game preserves, elephants accept alcohol, and when their space is restricted, which presumably is stressful, they increase their drinking. In other examples baboons have been observed to consume tobacco in the wild, and intoxicating mushrooms are eaten by cattle, reindeer, and rabbits. These observations

---

Table 6-4 Drug Abuse—Some Terms Defined

Some of the main terms having to do with drug abuse are listed and defined below.

Drug abuse The self-administered use of any drug in a manner that deviates from the approved medical or social patterns within a given culture (Jaffe, 1980). Such misuse can include agents such as morphine and tranquilizers but also tobacco, coffee, laxatives, or vitamins.

Drug addiction A state in which compulsive use of a drug is characterized by "overwhelming involvement with the use of the drug, the securing of its supply, and a high tendency to relapse" into using the drug after stopping (Jaffe, 1980).

Drug dependence A condition in which an individual requires a drug to function normally. A distinction is often made between **physical** dependence and **psychological** dependence.

    Physical dependence An adaptive state produced by repeated use of a drug, which manifests itself by intense physiological disturbances (**withdrawal syndrome**) when use of the drug is halted.

    Psychological dependence A condition characterized by intense drive or craving for a drug whose effects the user feels are necessary for a sense of well-being.

Tolerance Diminished response to administration of a drug after repeated exposure to it.

Withdrawal syndrome (abstinence syndrome) A constellation of symptoms that occur when an individual stops use of a drug to which dependence has developed. Prominent among the symptoms are autonomic system disturbances and psychological distress: hot and cold flashes, goose flesh, elevated body temperature, aching bones and muscles, rapid heart rate, perspiration, diarrhea, nausea, pupillary dilation, insomnia, anxiety, fear, panic, and craving for the drug.

---

suggest that the propensity for addiction is rather widespread among animals. In fact, numerous laboratory investigations with animal subjects have revealed important facts about the bases of addiction.

Addictive drugs are no exception to the generalization that most drugs produce multiple effects, and this has made it difficult to determine which mechanisms are most important in producing addiction. For example, cocaine has these major characteristics: (1) it is a local anesthetic; (2) it is a psychomotor stimulant, speeding the heart rate and certain responses; and (3) its administration promptly leads to pleasurable feelings so that it is a rewarding or reinforcing agent. Opiate drugs, such as morphine, also have a variety of effects, including but not limited to the following: (1) they lead to predominance of parasympathetic activity and depression of the activity of the heart and respiratory system; (2) a prompt result of administration is pleasurable and reinforcing; (3) their use leads to development of tolerance so that dosages must be increased to maintain effects; and (4) they lead to development of strong physical dependence, that is, after repeated use, abstinence from the drug causes a severe withdrawal syndrome. The withdrawal syndrome is so striking that some investigators have proposed that development of dependence is the basic characteristic of addiction. Others insist that the one property that is shared by all habit-forming drugs is the strong rewarding property (e.g., Wise, 1984). Still others argue that addiction is an attempt to adapt to chronic distress of any sort through habitual use of a drug (e.g., Alexander & Hadaway, 1982). This is an area of current controversy and we cannot survey it thoroughly here, let alone present a simple conclusion, but we will indicate some of the main findings and positions.

Reward phenomena may provide valuable clues to the brain mechanisms underlying addiction because the brain mechanisms of reward have been a productive field of research since the 1950s. In 1954 two young psychologists, James Olds and Peter Milner, made a discovery that started a whole new field of research. They found that electrical stimulation of some regions of the brain produces a rewarding effect: Animals will learn to press a lever or perform other behaviors in order to obtain stimulation of brain regions through implanted electrodes. The general topic of reinforcement will be taken up in Chapter 15. For our present discussion, it suffices to note that a core part of the reward circuits is made up of dopaminergic neurons whose cell bodies are located in the midbrain; they send their axons forward to some sites in the limbic system and to the cerebral cortex, as Figure 6-7 shows. Discoveries involving effects of drugs on reward circuits are beginning to be used to aid cocaine abusers, both as primary therapy and as adjuncts to psychotherapy (Kleber & Gawin, 1984).

The reward circuits of the brain are normally stimulated by behaviors that have survival value: eating food, drinking water, maintaining appropriate body temperature, sexual activity, and social and parental interactions. Evolution of brain circuits that provided prompt reinforcement for adaptive behaviors clearly promoted survival. But addictive drugs can stimulate these circuits powerfully and directly, without requiring behaviors that are essential for life and health. They procure pleasure without cost in the short run, although longer-term effects are disastrous. Such drugs, as one investigator warns, ''are unlikely to serve the further evolution of man so long as they provide shortcuts to the pleasures of reward and bypass the adaptive activities that have led to these pleasures over most of our evolutionary history'' (Wise, 1984, p. 28).

Since tolerance and dependence develop for many habit-forming drugs on prolonged use, the mechanisms of these effects have also been studied intensively. For some drugs at least, the desire to avoid the severe discomfort of withdrawal may be as important in maintaining drug use as is the pleasure obtained by consuming the drug. A variety of mechanisms have been suggested and investigated; we will note some of the more prominent ones.

Changes in amounts of several synaptic transmitters are caused by use of opiate drugs. The brain levels of ACh increase and those of NE decline, and this appears to account for some of the features of tolerance to morphine and of morphine withdrawal (Redmond & Krystal, 1984). Thus during use of opiates there is predominance of activity of the parasympathetic system (reflected in such symptoms as constriction of the pupils and slowed heart and respiratory rates). Withdrawal leads to a sudden increase in release of NE, and withdrawal is characterized by a predominance of activity of the sympathetic system (reflected in such symptoms as pupillary dilation, increased heart and respiratory rates, and perspiration). Some aspects of withdrawal are intensified by giving cholinergic agonists, whereas both muscarinic and nicotinic blockers reduce some aspects of the syndrome. Inhibitors of NE synthesis substantially block the morphine withdrawal syndrome in animals that have developed tolerance to the drug. Changes in numbers or conformation of receptors for opiates have also been claimed in some studies of morphine tolerance, but findings on this topic are contradictory (Redmond & Krystal, 1984).

Many of the effects of physical dependence can be seen in newborn infants born to mothers who took drugs during pregnancy. Pregnant women are now cautioned not only against use of opiate drugs but also against substances such as alcohol and tobacco because of deleterious effects on the fetus.

Role of Learning in Tolerance and Withdrawal

The effects of opiates can be conditioned to the environmental or behavioral circumstances in which the drug is administered. In fact, Pavlov (1927, pp. 35 ff.) showed that the salivation induced by administration of morphine could be conditioned to a previously neutral stimulus. Such results indicate why various rituals and procedures of drug procurement and use may come to elicit reinforcing effects similar to the drug itself. An example of this phenomenon is the "needle freak," who by the act of injection alone or by the injection of inert substances obtains significant reinforcement. But the effects are somewhat complex because there is also conditioning of adaptive countereffects to the drug. This has been studied in relation to effects of morphine on body temperature. Administration of morphine leads to a rise in body temperature (hyperthermia). If a rat is injected with morphine once a day for several days in a particular experimental room, then just placing the animal in that room will elicit a rise in body temperature. But the animal also responds to morphine-induced hyperthermia by mobilizing heat-dissipating responses that tend to return its temperature toward normal. In fact, conditioning of both hyperthermic and hypothermic responses occurs, but the conditioning takes place to different stimuli: Hyperthermia becomes associated with environmental stimuli, such as visual or auditory stimuli, but it does not become conditioned to the time of day at which the drug is administered. In contrast, the countereffect of hypothermia becomes conditioned to temporal cues but not to environmental cues (Eikelboom & Stewart, 1981).

The act of obtaining the drug can also add to the reinforcing effects of the drug. Reports of this by drug users are supported by results of an animal experiment: Rats were put on a schedule in which on alternating days either they ran down an alley to a compartment where they received an injection of amphetamine, or they received a "free" injection in another compartment without having to run for it. When the rats were subsequently given their choice of compartments, they consistently chose the one to which they had run for injection (La Cerra & Ettenberg, 1984). Thus the stimuli associated with active drug seeking had acquired reward value.

The fact that tolerance is partly learned may help to explain some cases of death from drug overdoses: Tolerance develops in the environment in which an individual frequently takes the drug, and high doses are taken, but if the drug is then taken in a different environment, the high dose may not be tolerated, and a serious reaction or even death may occur. This explanation has been tested in an animal experiment (S. Siegel, Hinson, Krank, & McCully, 1982). Rats were given an injection of heroin solution every other day, starting with a dose of 1 milligram per kilogram of body weight and gradually working up to 8 mg/kg. On alternate days they received an injection of inactive material. Some rats received heroin in the animal colony room and the inactive material in a distinctive room; for other rats the rooms were reversed. Finally, on the test day, each of these experimental rats, plus control rats that had always received injections of the neutral material, were given an injection of 15 mg/kg heroin. Half of the experimental animals received the high dose of heroin in the same room in which they had previously received heroin; half received it in the other environment. Of the rats that received 15 mg/kg in the room where they had come to tolerate heroin, the high dose caused 32% mortality. The rats that received the high dose in the environment where they had experienced only a neutral substance showed 64% mortality. And the control rats that had never previously had heroin suffered even higher mortality. Thus both heroin groups had developed tolerance in comparison with the control group, but tolerance was significantly greater in the environment in which the drug had habitually been taken.

The Adaptive Hypothesis of Addiction

The adaptive hypothesis views drug addiction as a continuing attempt by the user to reduce distress that existed before drug use began (Alexander & Hadaway, 1982). The investigators who espouse this position criticize the view that addiction is a condition brought about by use of the drug; neither learning nor physiological effects of drug use seem to them important in the development of addiction. In support of their position, they point out that many people who try opiate drugs do not become addicted, and that under some circumstances prolonged use can be stopped without re-addiction. For example, medical patients who have been given regular doses of opiates to relieve pain during treatment show very low rates of re-addiction after release. Of Vietnam veterans who had become addicted to heroin overseas, only 12% relapsed to addiction within three years after their return. Alexander and Hadaway suggest that three conditions must be met if drug addiction is to develop: (1) the drug is used to adapt to distress; (2) the user perceives no better means of adaptation; (3) use of the drug ultimately leads to an *increase* in the original distress.

Further support for this adaptive orientation comes from recent reports that the majority of opiate addicts who seek treatment have other psychiatric disorders, the most common of these being major depressive disorders, antisocial personality, and alcoholism (Hubbard et el., 1984; Rounsaville et al., 1982). Furthermore, the more severe a person's psychological problems, the less likely is the drug treatment program to be successful for that person.

In spite of the growing attention to personality factors and psychological difficulties in addiction, many investigators are unwilling to limit themselves to the adaptive approach. As we have seen, there are also observations and experiments that indicate the importance of other factors in the development of drug addiction: learning, access to brain reward mechanisms, and development of physical dependency. Yet another factor is genetic predisposition, as discussed in Box 6-2. A recent review of etiology and treatment of addictive behaviors calls attention to an emerging integration of biological, psychological, and sociological approaches in a biopsychosocial model (Marlatt et al., 1988). So severe are the personal and social problems related to substance abuse and drug addiction that this is a pressing area of research in which we can hope to see important new findings during the next years.

When Does the "Same" Drug Treatment Have Different Effects?

What might appear to be the same drug treatment may have widely different effects, depending upon a variety of factors. Let us examine some of the reasons for such differences.

Species differences are major factors that account for differences in drug effects. Some species are more susceptible than others to a particular substance. Thus, for example, insecticides are chosen so that they are lethal to insects but relatively harmless to people and to domestic and farm animals.

Within a species, subgroups and individuals differ in susceptibility. Some ethnic differences are known. For example, many Asians lack one of the enzymes that metabolize alcohol; for such people, consuming alcohol promptly produces unpleasant symptoms including nausea, dizziness, blurred vision, and confusion (Reed, 1985). The systematic exploration of ethnic differences in responses to drugs—pharmacoanthropology—is only in its infancy (Kalow, 1984). Among individuals, much of the variation in responses to medicines results from inherited variations in responsiveness (Weinshilboum, 1984). For this reason a person may find that a substance or an amount may be habit-forming or toxic even if his or her friends appear to handle it without difficulty.

In the same individual, a drug may vary in effectiveness depending upon the time of day at which it is taken (Scheving, Vedral, & Pauly, 1968). This variation occurs because there are daily rhythms in many aspects of physiology, including body temperature, metabolic rate, synthesis of enzymes, and secretion of hormones. (Such circadian rhythms will be discussed in Chapter 15.)

Dosage of many substances can change markedly the kind of effect obtained. The sixteenth-century alchemist Paracelsus declared, ''The dose makes the poison,'' and this statement has recently been taken as the title of a book on drug toxicology by Ottoboni (1984). Many substances that have favorable or innocuous effects if taken occasionally and in low amounts become habit-forming and/or toxic if taken frequently or in high doses: These include substances such as caffeine, alcohol, anti-anxiety drugs, and many others.

The same dosage of a drug given to the same individual may vary in effectiveness depending upon how often the individual has taken the drug previously. For some drugs ''tolerance'' develops readily; that is, the dosage must be increased rapidly in order to maintain the same effect. Toxicity and addiction can also build up over time. Many cocaine users who come for medical treatment have been using the drug for four to five years before being overwhelmed by their addiction.

The effectiveness of some drugs varies according to what other drugs are taken at the same time: Some drugs taken in combination potentiate or synergize each other's effectiveness. Thus, for example, doses of alcohol and of barbiturates that a person could withstand separately may prove lethal if consumed together. On the other hand, some drugs are antagonists; for example, naloxone opposes many of the effects of morphine and so is used as an antidote for overdoses of morphine.

Some combinations of substances produce an effect that neither one alone causes. For example, the drug Antabuse is used in attempts to cure alcoholism; taken by itself, Antabuse has no effect, but it blocks an enzyme needed for one stage in the metabolism of alcohol. (This is the same enzyme that is missing in many Asian people, as already mentioned.) If a person who has taken Antabuse ingests alcohol at any time during the next few days, a toxic product of alcohol builds up in the blood producing disagreeable symptoms, including nausea, dizziness, blurred vision, and confusion.

Because drugs taken in combination may either synergize or counteract each other's effects, a person should exercise precautions whenever two drugs are taken together:

BOX 6-2 | Genetics of Alcoholism

Alcohol is a substance that has been so widely used over such a long period of time that studies of genetic influences on alcoholism are possible. Such studies are not only of scientific interest but they are also socially relevant because excessive consumption of alcohol is a major cause of disease and death as well as of violent crimes, traffic accidents, fires, and lost production (Institute of Medicine, 1980). Alcoholism is one of a number of conditions included in a series of studies in Denmark on hereditary and social factors involved in various diseases and mental disorders. Denmark was chosen for these studies because of its excellent records of adoption and other family information. The investigations in Denmark were some of the first to demonstrate conclusively that alcoholism does run in families (Schulsinger, 1980). More specifically, the best predictor of whether a boy would become alcoholic was whether his biological father was alcoholic. This was just as true if the boy had been adopted as an infant into a family without alcoholic members as if he had stayed in his own family. It should be noted that these findings concerned only alcoholism and were unrelated to heavy drinking or problem drinking. Genetic tendencies of the same sort were found in females, but the rate of alcoholism is so low among Danish females that there were too few cases for findings to be conclusive.

More recent studies have indicated that there are at least two kinds of alcoholism, and genetic studies are clearer when these kinds are considered separately (Cloninger, 1987; Loehlin, Willerman, & Horn, 1988). Distinguishing characteristics of the two types are shown in Box Table 6-1. Women alcoholics are

mainly of Type 1; both types of alcoholism are common in men, but most men hospitalized for treatment of alcoholism are of Type 2. Type 1 alcoholism has been described as "milieu-limited" because it is likely to appear only if genetic predisposition is coupled with environmental exposure to heavy drinking or other environmental provocation. Type 2 tends to appear regardless of environmental background; the risk of alcohol abuse in adopted-away sons of Type 2 alcoholic fathers was nine times as great as in sons of all other fathers.

Brain wave patterns differ between the two types and may reveal a predisposition to alcoholism: In a decision-making test, both abstinent Type 2 men and their male children show a reduced P_3 component of the event-related potential (Begleiter et al., 1984). This pattern of response suggests that individuals at risk for Type 2 alcoholism are deficient in their ability to attribute significance to targeted stimuli. The possibility of detecting who is predisposed to alcoholism may be an important aid to prevention. In addition to these two types of alcoholics, many individuals with antisocial personality may abuse alcohol, but the genetic tendency for antisocial personality is distinct from heredity for alcoholism (Cloninger & Reich, 1983).

In order to study the mechanisms of genetic factors in alcoholism, animal models have been developed (Wimer & Wimer, 1985). If mice are habituated to alcohol, some show severe symptoms upon withdrawal, even including seizures, whereas others show only mild reactions. Genetic selection experiments have produced inbred lines of mice that show either severe or mild withdrawal symptoms, and further

1. A person considering the possibility of using a medication should take into account all medications and substances currently being taken. This includes over-the-counter drugs, substances such as coffee, tea, tobacco, alcohol, stimulants, depressants, and other psychoactive agents.

2. A person taking any psychoactive agent (including but not limited to alcohol, excitants, depressants, or anxiolytics) should be aware of the possibility of synergies. For example, doses of depressants and of alcohol that do not separately pose an immediate threat to life may be lethal if taken together.

Effects of combinations may differ greatly according to dosages. An example is the interaction between caffeine and alcohol. Many believe that caffeine can counteract the effects of alcohol, but any helpful effects occur only when the consumption of alcohol has been small to moderate. Recent studies in both England and the United States found that volunteers who drank alcohol to the point of intoxication were further impaired by drinking coffee! Those who drank two cups of coffee

Box Table 6-1   Distinguishing Characteristics of Two Types of Alcoholism

Characteristic Features	Type 1	Type 2
Alcohol-Related Problems		
Usual age of onset (years)	After 25	Before 25
Spontaneous alcohol-seeking	Infrequent	Frequent
Fighting and arrests when drinking	Infrequent	Frequent
Psychological dependence (loss of control; prolonged binges)	Frequent	Infrequent
Guilt and fear about alcoholism	Frequent	Infrequent
Personality Traits		
Novelty seeking (impulsive, exploratory, distractible)	Low	High
Harm avoidance (cautious, shy, apprehensive, inhibited)	High	Low
Reward dependence (eager to help others, sympathetic, sentimental)	High	Low

Adapted from Table 1, C. R. Cloninger (1987). Neurogenetic adaptive mechanisms in alcoholism. *Science, 236,* 410–416, by permission of the American Association for the Advancement of Science.

experiments are being conducted to learn how these lines differ physiologically.

Genetic factors are suspected in other sorts of addiction besides alcoholism, but there has not been much study of these conditions. As in other cases of genetic predisposition, having the predisposition does not imply the inevitability of the disorder. On the contrary, such information can be used to help avoid the situations in which a susceptible person may become addicted, and it should also help research efforts to find effective cures for addiction.

committed nearly twice as many errors in tests of coordination as the drunk volunteers who did not drink the coffee (Goulart, 1984).

Two batches of the ''same'' drug may not actually be the same, especially if they are obtained from an illegal source. Many illegal drugs are adulterated or are entirely different from what they are claimed to be. Some ''designer drugs,'' synthesized to resemble heroin, have proved lethal, and others have crippled users. For example, a contaminant in synthesized heroin has caused symptoms of Parkinson's disease in young people and provided new clues to the cause of this disease—at great personal expense to the users (Shafer, 1985). (Parkinson's disease is a motor disorder that we will discuss in Chapter 10.)

The examples in this section demonstrate that in order to predict the effects of a particular drug treatment, you have to have information about the drug, the individual who takes it, the time of administration, previous usage, and many of the surrounding circumstances.

Summary · Main Points

1. Chemical signals are vital throughout the plant and animal kingdoms. The signal molecules vary greatly in size and complexity and in the distances over which they travel, from intracellular signals to those that travel between organisms.

2. At most synapses the transmission of information from one neuron to another requires a chemical that diffuses across the synaptic cleft and binds to receptor molecules in the postsynaptic membrane.

3. Many substances have been identified as synaptic transmitters and others are being tested. There are some ''families'' of transmitters that are similar to each other chemically.

4. At many synapses, chemical transmission causes the release of a ''second messenger,'' which amplifies and prolongs the transmitter's effect.

5. Many drugs exert their principal effects on chemical synapses, and all the steps in chemical transmission are affected by various drugs.

6. Drugs that affect synapses cause a variety of behavioral effects; these effects include stimulating, paralyzing, relieving or preventing anxiety (anxiolytics), alleviating or preventing the recurrence of schizophrenia (antipsychotics), combating depression, and controlling mania.

7. Drug abuse and addiction are being studied intensively. Some investigators put greater stress on physiological mechanisms of addiction whereas others stress behavioral mechanisms. Currently prominent hypotheses relate addiction to such mechanisms as effects of drug tolerance and dependence, the role of learning in tolerance and withdrawal, and attempts to reduce preexisting distress.

8. A hereditary predisposition to alcoholism has been demonstrated, and genetic factors are suspected in other sorts of addiction.

9. The ''same'' drug treatment may have widely different effects, depending upon a number of factors; these include species and individual differences, circadian rhythms, dosage, previous usage, combinations with other drugs, and interactions of combinations with dosages.

Recommended Reading

Cooper, J. R., Bloom, F. E., & Roth, R. H. (1986). *The biochemical basis of neuropharmacology* (5th ed.). New York: Oxford University Press.

Feldman, R. S., & Quenzer, L. F. (1984). *Fundamentals of neuropsychopharmacology*. Sunderland, Mass.: Sinauer.

Julien, R. M. (1981). *A primer of drug action* (3rd ed.). San Francisco: W. H. Freeman.

Kandel, E. R., & Schwartz, J. H. (1985). *Principles of neural science* (2nd ed.). New York: Elsevier/North Holland.

Meltzer, H. Y. (Ed.). (1987). *Psychopharmacology: The third generation of progress*. New York: Raven.

Reference Section

Families of Synaptic Transmitters and Evolution of Transmitters

This section gives information about some families of synaptic transmitters to supplement the material about the catecholamines presented on page 197. First we present somewhat fuller material about the catecholamines, and then we take up the following groups: (1) amino acid transmitters, (2) the enkephalins and endorphins, and larger molecules from which they and related compounds are derived.

The Catecholamine Synaptic Transmitters

We have already mentioned that the catecholamine transmitters are synthesized from the amino acid tyrosine and that these transmitters have rather similar structures (page 197 and Table 6-1).

The similarity of their structures can be seen in Reference Table 6-1, which presents structural diagrams of the precursor amino acids and of the catecholamine transmitters. The site of change at each step is indicated by a colored circle. Reference Table 6-1 also shows the basic catechol nucleus, which is common to all of this family of synaptic transmitters. And it shows at the right the rather similar structure of amphetamine, which stimulates the release of the catecholamines and binds to the re-uptake receptors for these transmitters.

Amino Acid Synaptic Transmitters

Not only do amino acids serve the building blocks of these and other synaptic transmitters, but certain amino acids are also employed as transmitters by some neurons. Other synaptic transmit-

Reference Table 6-1 **Synthesis and Structures of the Catecholamine Transmitters**

Phenylalanine

Tyrosine

Tyrosine hydroxylase

Dopa

Dopamine

Catechol nucleus

Dopamine–β–hydroxylase

Amphetamine

Norepinephrine

Epinephrine

systems and is probably the major inhibitory transmitter in the mammalian nervous system.

The Endogenous Opioid Peptides and Their Precursor Molecules

The opioid peptides are not synthesized directly but are split out of larger precursor molecules (Khachaturian et al., 1985). Thus [Met]enkephalin and [Leu]enkephalin, each of which consists of only five amino acid units, are contained within the parent molecule, proenkephalin, which consists of over 250 amino acid units. Actually, each molecule of proenkephalin contains six molecules of [Met]enkephalin and one molecule of [Leu]enkephalin as well as other opioids. Proenkephalin is manufactured by many neurons in the central and peripheral nervous system and in the adrenal medulla. Typically the enkephalins occur in neurons whose axons are short to medium in length.

Another opioid precursor, pro-opiomelanocortin, is the source of a potent opioid, beta-endorphin, and some less active opioids. As its name indicates, pro-opiomelanocortin also contains other

molecules including melanocyte-stimulating hormone and adrenocorticotropic hormone (ACTH). Pro-opiomelanocortin is synthesized mainly in a few locations where it is processed to yield different end products: In the anterior pituitary gland it is processed to yield mainly ACTH; in the intermediate lobe of the pituitary gland and in a nucleus of the hypothalamus it is processed to yield mainly melanocyte-stimulating hormone and beta-endorphin. Neurons that contain beta-endorphin are chiefly long-projection neurons that run through the medial hypothalamus, diencephalon, and pons.

Finally, pro-dynorphin yields several opioids including dynorphin A, dynorphin B, and two neoendorphins. Each of these opioids contains the [Leu]enkephalin molecule plus additional amino acid units, so there is structural similarity between the enkephalins and the dynorphins. The dynorphins are distributed widely throughout the CNS, from regions of the cerebral cortex to the dorsal horn of the spinal cord.

ters are derived from amino acids with only a single intervening chemical step. In fact, it is estimated that amino acids and closely related compounds are the transmitters at most of the synapses in the nervous system. **Glutamic acid** and the closely similar **aspartic acid** are thought by many investigators to be two major excitatory synaptic transmitters in the CNS. At first investigators doubted that they serve this specific transmitter function because they are so widely distributed in the nervous system and they play so general a role in metabolism. Nevertheless, a specific synaptic role for glutamic acid was found in invertebrates, where it is the neuromuscular transmitter, just as ACh is in vertebrates. Then evidence of a dual role for glutamatic acid—metabolic and synaptic—was found in vertebrates (Snyder, 1975). **Gamma-aminobutyric acid** (GABA) is synthesized directly from glutamic acid. It is widely distributed in both invertebrate and vertebrate nervous

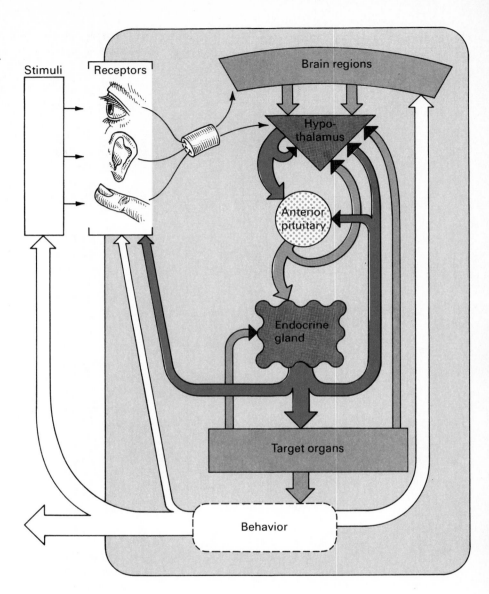

7 Hormones: A Chemical Communication System

ORIENTATION

Without regular supplies of some hormones, our capacity to behave would be seriously impaired; without others we would soon die. Tiny amounts of some hormones can modify our moods and our actions, our inclination to eat or drink, our aggressiveness or submissiveness, and our reproductive and parental behavior. And hormones do more than influence adult behavior; early in life they help to determine the development of bodily form and may even determine an individual's behavioral capacities. Later in life the changing outputs of some endocrine glands and the body's changing sensitivity to some hormones are essential aspects of the phenomena of aging. Endocrine glands come in a variety of sizes and shapes, and they are located in many parts of the body. Figure 7-1 gives the names and locations of the main endocrine glands.

Communication within the body and the consequent integration of behavior were considered the exclusive province of the nervous system up to the beginning of the present century. Only then did some investigators become aware that the endocrine system participates importantly in these functions.

Of course, the importance of certain glands for behavior had long been known. For instance, Aristotle accurately described the effects of castration in birds, and he compared the behavioral and bodily effects with those seen in castrated men. Although he did not know what mechanism was involved, it was clear that the testes were important for the reproductive capacity and sexual characteristics of the male. This question was approached experimentally in 1849 by A. A. Berthold, a professor at Göttingen. He castrated young roosters and observed declines in both reproductive behavior and secondary sexual

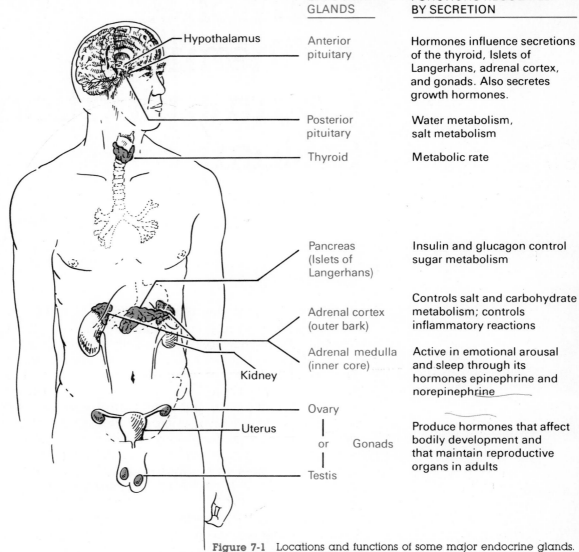

ENDOCRINE GLANDS	FUNCTIONS REGULATED BY SECRETION
Anterior pituitary	Hormones influence secretions of the thyroid, Islets of Langerhans, adrenal cortex, and gonads. Also secretes growth hormones.
Posterior pituitary	Water metabolism, salt metabolism
Thyroid	Metabolic rate
Pancreas (Islets of Langerhans)	Insulin and glucagon control sugar metabolism
Adrenal cortex (outer bark)	Controls salt and carbohydrate metabolism; controls inflammatory reactions
Adrenal medulla (inner core)	Active in emotional arousal and sleep through its hormones epinephrine and norepinephrine
Gonads	Produce hormones that affect bodily development and that maintain reproductive organs in adults

Figure 7-1 Locations and functions of some major endocrine glands.

characteristics, such as the rooster's comb. Then in some birds he replaced one testicle, devoid of its neural connections, into the body cavity. This restored both the normal behavior of these roosters and their combs. Berthold concluded that the testes release some substance into the blood that is necessary for both male behavior and male structures. Berthold's observation did not seem very important to his contemporaries because it could not be related to the concepts of that time. Only in retrospect is it considered important—as the first experiment in endocrinology.

The creative French physiologist Claude Bernard also helped to set the stage in the nineteenth century for the emergence of endocrinology. Bernard stressed the importance of the "internal environment" in which cells exist and the fact that this environment must be regulated. As he put it, a constant internal bodily environment is a necessary condition for independent activity in the external environment. Then late in the nineteenth century, clinical and experimental observations showed the importance of several glands—including the thyroids, the adrenal cortex, and the pituitary—for maintaining a constant internal environment and thus for normal health and behavior.

The emergence of endocrinology as a separate discipline can probably be traced to the experiments of Sir William Maddock Bayliss and Ernest Henry Starling, around 1905, on the hormone **secretin.** This substance is secreted from cells in the intestinal walls when food enters the stomach; it travels through the bloodstream and stimulates the pancreas to liberate pancreatic juice, which aids in digestion. By showing that special cells secrete chemical agents that are conveyed by the bloodstream and regulate distant target organs or tissues, Bayliss and Starling demonstrated that chemical integration can occur without participation of the nervous system.

The term **hormone** was first used with reference to secretin. Starling (1905) derived the term from the Greek *hormon,* meaning "to excite or set in motion." The term **endocrine** (from the Greek roots *endo,* meaning "within," and *krinein,* meaning "to secrete") was introduced shortly thereafter. *Endocrine* is used to refer to glands that secrete products into the bloodstream. The term *endocrine* contrasts with **exocrine,** which is applied to glands that secrete their products through ducts to the site of action. Examples of exocrine glands are the tear glands, the sweat glands, and the pancreas, which secretes pancreatic juice through a duct into the intestine. Exocrine glands are also called duct glands, while endocrine glands are called ductless.

We should note here that there is a possible source of confusion: Some glands may have separate functions that lead to different classifications. Thus the pancreas is a duct gland insofar as the secretion of pancreatic juice is concerned. But other cells in the pancreas—the islets of Langerhans—do not make contact with the pancreatic ducts; instead they secrete the hormones insulin and glucagon into the bloodstream.

In the following sections of this chapter we will consider the mechanisms by which hormones accomplish their functions, the main endocrine glands and their hormones, and examples of hormonal influences on physiology and on behavior. Then we will compare the endocrine and nervous systems as mechanisms of communication and coordination, and we will show how the activities of the two systems are integrated in the control of behavior.

The widespread reliance of life forms on hormonal messengers should be recalled here. As we saw in Chapter 4, hormones are found throughout the animal kingdom, and there are hormones and hormonelike substances in plants. It is only in the vertebrates that there are special endocrine glands to secrete and store hormones, such as the thyroid gland and the adrenal glands, but hormonal functions evolved long before there were endocrine glands. In fact, many human hormones do not come from endocrine glands but are secreted from such sources as neurons in the hypothalamus or cells in the lining of the digestive tract. Recently the heart has been found to produce a hormone that helps to regulate blood pressure and sodium balance in the body. The fact that the heart is not only a pump but, like many other organs, also secretes a hormone, complicates heart transplant operations. In many cases hormones are the same or closely similar over a wide variety of animal species.

Mechanisms of Hormone Action

We will soon be considering the effects of specific hormones on behavior. In preparation for this material, let us look briefly at three aspects of hormonal activity: the effects of hormones, the mechanisms by which they exercise these effects, and the ways in which their secretions are regulated.

How Do Hormones Affect the Body?

Hormones affect many everyday behaviors in people and other animals, and they do so by influencing organs. Hormones exert these far-reaching effects by (1) promoting the proliferation, growth, and differentiation of cells and (2) modulating cell activity. These early developmental processes are promoted by various hormones such as thyroxine, a hormone of the thyroid gland. Without it mental development is stunted. Although neural proliferation and differentiation occur mainly during early development, cells in some organs divide and grow at later stages of life, too. For example, male and female hormones cause secondary sexual characteristics to appear during adolescence—breasts and broadening of the hips in women and facial hair and enlargement of the Adam's apple in men, for instance.

In cells that are already differentiated, hormones can modulate the rate of function. For example, thyroxine and insulin promote the metabolic activity of most of the cells in the body. Other hormones modulate activity primarily in certain types of cells. For example, a hormone from the anterior pituitary gland—called luteinizing hormone (LH)—promotes the secretion of sex hormones by the testes and by the ovaries.

How Do Hormones Act?

Hormones exert their varied influences on target organs in two main ways:

1. The peptides and amine hormones (see Table 7-1) usually bind to specific receptors on the surface of target cell membranes and cause the release of a **second messenger** in the cell. (As we saw in Chapter 6, the release of a second messenger can also be caused by some synaptic transmitters.)
2. The steroid hormones pass through the membrane and bind to specific receptor proteins in the cytoplasm. The steroid-protein complex then enters the

Table 7-1 Some Hormones Classified by Type of Chemical Compound

Amines	Polypeptides	Steroids
Epinephrine	Adrenocorticotropic hormone (ACTH)	Sex hormones
Norepinephrine	Follicle-stimulating hormone (FSH)	Estrogens
Thyroxine	Luteinizing hormone (LH)	Progestins
	Thyroid-stimulating hormone (TSH)	Androgens
	Insulin	Adrenal cortex
	Glucagon	hormones
	Oxytocin	Glucocorticoids
	Antidiuretic hormone (vasopressin)	Mineralocorticoids
	Polypeptides that are releasing hormones	
	Growth hormone-releasing hormone (GrHRH)	
	Thyrotropin releasing hormone (TRH)	
	Luteinizing hormone-releasing hormone (LHRH)	

nucleus. There it interacts with the genome and initiates the transcription of specific genes, leading to the production of specific proteins.

We will now consider these two main modes of action in a little more detail, and we will examine some other ways in which hormones affect cellular function.

The same second-messenger compound transmits the messages of most, if not all, of the peptide and amine hormones. This compound is **cyclic adenosine monophosphate (cAMP).** It may seem surprising that the same second messenger can mediate the effects of many different hormones, but recall from Chapter 5 that the same kind of neural impulses can convey all sorts of neural messages. The situation here is similar.

The specificity of hormonal effects is determined by the selectivity of receptors in cell membranes and in the specific genes that are affected in the cell. For example, adrenocorticotropic hormone (ACTH) is taken up selectively by receptors on the membranes of cells in the adrenal cortex, and in these cells cAMP leads to the synthesis and release of adrenal cortex hormones.

The peptide hormones usually act relatively rapidly, within seconds to minutes. While this is rapid for hormonal action, it is, of course, much slower than neural activity. There can also be prolonged effects. For example, ACTH also promotes the proliferation and growth of adrenal cortical cells and thereby increases the long-term capacity to sustain production of their hormones. The surfaces of many kinds of cells are studded with receptors for peptide and amine hormones, just as the membranes of neurons are riddled with special channels for different kinds of ions.

The steroid hormones typically act more slowly, requiring hours for their effects to occur. The specificity of action of steroid hormones is determined by the intracellular receptors. The steroid hormones pass in and out of many cells in which they have no effect. However, if there are appropriate receptor molecules in the cytoplasm, these receptors bind the hormone so that it becomes concentrated in its target cells. Thus one can study where a hormone is active by observing where radioactively tagged molecules of the hormone are concentrated. For example, when tagged estrogen is administered systemically, it accumulates in several specific tissues, including the reproductive tract, and in some groups of cells in the hypothalamus.

As mentioned earlier, there are also other ways that hormones can affect cells. For example, there is evidence that estrogen, as well as its slow, long-lasting action, just mentioned, has a rapid, brief effect on some neurons. This may involve receptors at the membrane of these neurons (Moss & Dudley, 1984). This membrane mechanism probably mediates the negative feedback action of estrogen on gonadotropin secretion, and it may also be a way of modulating neural excitability in reproductive behavior. Such multiple mechanisms of hormonal activity are now a subject of intense study.

What Regulates Secretion of Hormones?

negative feedback
— basic control

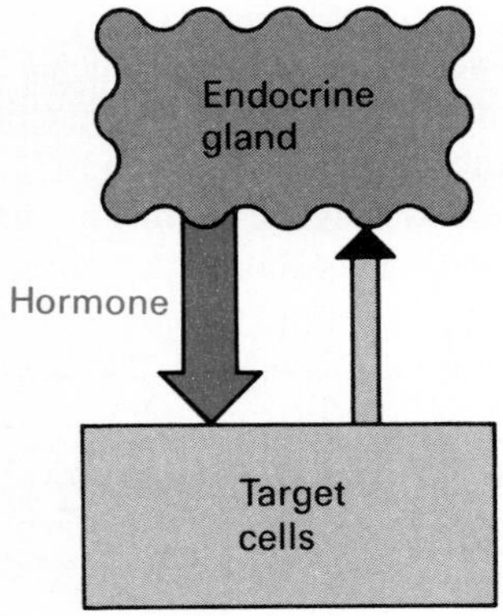

Figure 7-2 Negative-feedback control of hormonal secretion. A black arrowhead indicates inhibition in this figure and in Figures 7-3 and 7-4.

Neural link or hormonal link

Some endocrine glands secrete hormones at a fairly stable rate over long periods of time, whereas others vary with stimulation. In either case secretion is usually monitored and regulated so that the rate is appropriate to ongoing bodily activities and needs. The basic control used is a **negative-feedback system.** We will begin our study with simple negative-feedback systems; then we will move on to systems with larger numbers of links.

The simplest kind of system that regulates hormones is diagramed in Figure 7-2. The hormone acts on target cells, changing the amount of a substance in the extracellular fluid; this, in turn, regulates the output of the endocrine gland. Thus, for example, the hormone insulin helps to control the level of glucose circulating in the blood in the following way: Ingesting glucose leads to release of insulin. The insulin causes extracellular glucose to enter muscle and fat and stimulates increased use of glucose. As the level of glucose in the blood falls, the pancreas responds by secreting less insulin, so a balance tends to be maintained. The negative-feedback action of a hormone is like that of a thermostat: In a heating system, when the temperature falls below a set level, the thermostat switches the furnace on. When the temperature rises a few degrees, the thermostat turns the furnace off, so the temperature is held rather constant. And just as the thermostat can be set to different temperatures at different times, the set points of endocrine feedback systems can also be changed to meet varying circumstances.

The next order of complexity in endocrine systems is illustrated in Figure 7-3. Here the hypothalamus controls the endocrine gland. This control may occur through a neural link, as in control of the adrenal medulla, or through a hormonal link, as in control of release of growth hormone by the anterior pituitary. The secretion of the endocrine gland affects target cells, and the negative feedback goes to the hypothalamus, bypassing the endocrine gland.

One further degree of complexity is exemplified by control of thyroid secretion, illustrated in Figure 7-4. This secretion is regulated by the anterior pituitary hormone called thyroid-stimulating hormone (TSH). This hormone is one of several anterior pituitary hormones that affect the secretion of another endocrine gland, and these are all called **tropic hormones.** (Tropic, pronounced with a long *o* as in *toe*, means "directed toward.") Release of TSH is controlled in turn by the hypothalamic hormone called thyrotropin-releasing factor (TRF). Feedback in this case is from the endocrine gland hormone to the hypothalamus and to the anterior pituitary.

Thus the regulation of these chemical messages can be analyzed in terms of concepts borrowed from systems analysis or servomechanisms. In Chapter 10 we will see similar concepts employed in the analysis of control of motor functions.

Main Endocrine Glands and Their Hormones

We will restrict our account in this chapter to some of the main endocrine glands, their hormones, and some of their principal effects. Our treatment must be simplified because a thorough treatment would require a complete volume. A more complete listing of hormones and their functions appears in the reference table at the end of the chapter (pages 245–246). For more details see such texts as Gorbman (1983) and Hadley (1984). As you read the chapter, keep in mind that most hormones have more varied functions than are mentioned here and that several hormones may act together in producing effects.

Pituitary Hormones

Resting in a depression in the base of the skull is the **pituitary gland,** about 1 cc in volume and weighing about 1 g. The term *pituitary* comes from a Latin word meaning "mucus"; it received this name from an outmoded belief that it removed waste products from the brain and secreted them into the nose! A true "mighty mite," the pituitary used to be referred to as the master gland, a reference to its

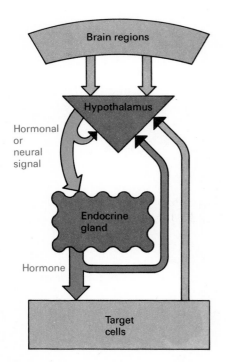

Figure 7-3 A more complex endocrine control circuit that includes the hypothalamus and other brain regions.

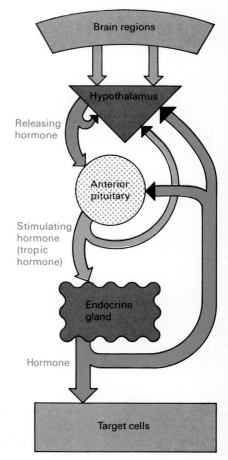

Figure 7-4 Complex control of endocrine secretion, involving the hypothalamus and the anterior pituitary gland.

Pituitary (2 parts - separate!)
Orig. from 1. anterior
glandular tissue (ant. adenohypophysis)
orig = neurale 2. posterior
tissue (neurohypophysis)

regulatory role in regard to several other endocrine glands. As Figure 7-5 shows, the pituitary gland consists of two main parts. These are completely separate in function and are derived from different embryological sources. The two parts are the **anterior pituitary,** or **adenohypophysis,** and the **posterior pituitary,** or **neurohypophysis.** The term *hypophysis* comes from Greek roots meaning "an outgrowth

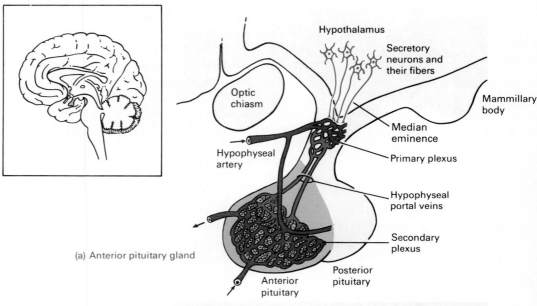

(a) Anterior pituitary gland

Figure 7-5 The pituitary gland. (a) Anterior pituitary gland. (b) Posterior pituitary gland.

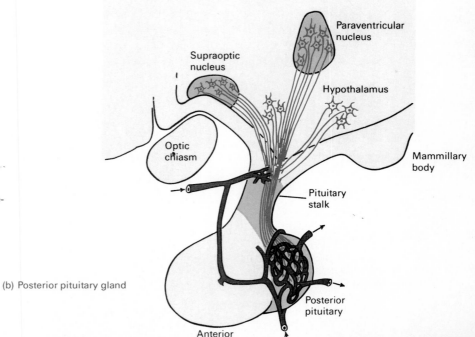

(b) Posterior pituitary gland

from the underside of the brain.'' The root *adeno-* comes from a Greek word meaning ''gland,'' because the anterior pituitary originates from glandular tissue. The neurohypophysis derives from neural tissue.

The stalk of the pituitary, called the **infundibulum** in the belief that it was a funnel into the gland, is also shown in Figure 7-5. It consists of axons and is richly supplied with blood vessels. All these axons go to the posterior pituitary; the anterior pituitary does not receive any neural input.

Anterior Pituitary Hormones

The cells of the anterior lobe of the pituitary secrete a variety of substances. Most of these secretions are called tropic hormones, because their principal role is the control of endocrine glands situated elsewhere in the body. Figure 7-6 shows activities of several tropic hormones.

most secretions = tropic hormones b/c primarily control endocrine glands elsewhere in body

Growth hormone (also known as somatotropin or somatotropic hormone, STH) acts on many tissues of the body to influence the growth of cells and tissues. It exerts this action by an impact on protein metabolism. The daily production and release of growth hormone is especially prominent during the early stages of sleep. In fact, some sleep stages are needed for growth hormone release. Several other factors influence growth hormone release, such as a fall in blood sugar, starvation, exercise, and stress (see Box 7-1).

Many other hormones of the anterior pituitary control the production and release of the products of other endocrine glands. Let us note briefly four of these tropic hormones.

Adrenocorticotropic hormone (ACTH) controls the production and release of hormones of the adrenal cortex. Measurements of the level of this hormone in blood show a marked circadian rhythm. **Thyroid-stimulating hormone (TSH)** increases the release of thyroxine from the thyroid gland and markedly affects thyroid gland size by increasing iodide uptake.

Two tropic hormones of the anterior pituitary influence the hormone activities of the gonads. One of these is known as **luteinizing hormone (LH)** in females and as **interstitial cell-stimulating hormone (ICSH)** in males. LH stimulates the release of the developed eggs in the ovary and affects the uterine lining by producing changes that prepare for the implantation of a fertilized egg. In males this hormone stimulates production of testosterone by the testes. The other tropic hormone that influences gonadal hormone activities is the **follicle-stimulating hormone (FSH).** This hormone stimulates the secretion of estrogen in females and of testosterone in males; it also influences both egg and sperm production.

release of tropic hormones partly due to releasing hormones from hypothalamus

Secretion of the tropic hormones is partly determined by ''releasing hormones'' that are produced in the hypothalamus and are transported to the anterior pituitary by blood vessels that run along the infundibulum. The releasing hormones will be taken up soon when we turn to the hypothalamus.

The Posterior Pituitary

The posterior pituitary gland contains two principal hormones, the **antidiuretic hormone** (also called **vasopressin**) and **oxytocin.** At one time it was thought that these substances were produced and stored in cells of the posterior pituitary, to be

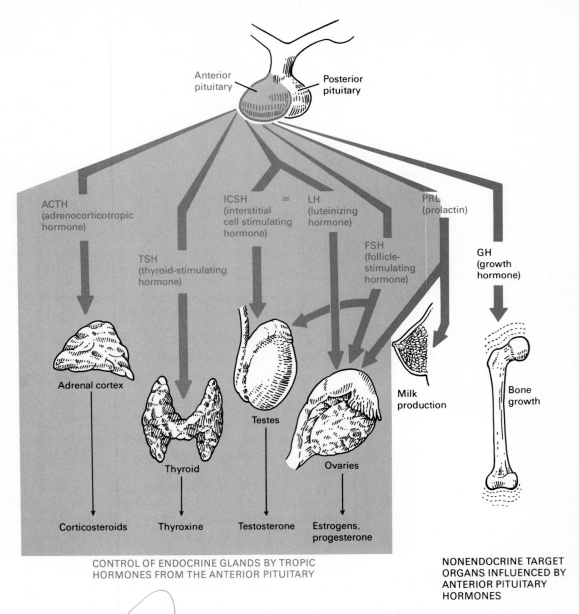

Anterior pituitary

Posterior pituitary

ACTH
(adrenocorticotropic hormone)

TSH
(thyroid-stimulating hormone)

ICSH
(interstitial cell stimulating hormone)

LH
(luteinizing hormone)

FSH
(follicle-stimulating hormone)

PRL
(prolactin)

GH
(growth hormone)

Adrenal cortex

Thyroid

Testes

Ovaries

Milk production

Bone growth

Corticosteroids

Thyroxine

Testosterone

Estrogens, progesterone

CONTROL OF ENDOCRINE GLANDS BY TROPIC HORMONES FROM THE ANTERIOR PITUITARY

NONENDOCRINE TARGET ORGANS INFLUENCED BY ANTERIOR PITUITARY HORMONES

Figure 7-6 Secretions of the anterior pituitary gland include both tropic secretions (shown in the brown area to the left) and hormones that affect nonendocrine target organs.

released upon arrival of appropriate neural signals from hypothalamic centers. Justification for this viewpoint came from the clear presence of an extensive system of nerve fiber endings in this region of the pituitary. Recently, though, the view of the neural role in posterior regions of the pituitary gland has undergone a major change.

BOX 7-1	Stress and Growth: Psychosocial Dwarfism

Genie had an extremely deprived childhood. From the age of 20 months until the age of 13 years, she was isolated in a small closed room, and much of the time she was tied to a chair. Her disturbed parents provided food, but nobody held Genie or spoke to her. When released from her confinement and observed by researchers at the age of 13 years 9 months, she looked as if she were only 6 to 7 years old (Curtis, 1977).

Other less horrendous forms of family deprivation have also been shown to result in failure of growth. This syndrome has been referred to as psychosocial dwarfism to emphasize that the growth failure arises from psychological and social factors mediated through the central nervous system and its control over endocrine functions (Green, Campbell, & David, 1984). When these children are removed from stressful environmental circumstances, many begin to grow rapidly. The growth rates of three such "psychosocial dwarfs," both before and after periods of emotional deprivation, are shown in Box Figure 7-1. These children seem to recover much of the growth deficit that occurred during prolonged stress periods.

How do stress and emotional deprivation produce impairments of growth? These effects appear to be mediated by changed outputs of several hormones, including growth hormone (somatotropin), somatomedin, and cortisol. The first two of these hormones promote cell growth, but high levels of cortisol inhibit growth. Assays in some children with psychosocial dwarfism show virtually no release of growth hormone, and this may be caused by absence of growth hormone-releasing factor from the hypothalamus (Brasel & Blizzard, 1974). Disturbed sleep has been cited as a cause of this failure (Gardner, 1972). Growth hormone is typically released during certain stages of sleep, as we will see in Chapter 15, and children under stress show disturbed sleep patterns. Other children with psychosocial dwarfism show normal levels of growth hormone but low levels of somatomedin, and this hormone along with growth hormone appears to be necessary for normal growth. Still other psychosocial dwarfs show elevated levels of cortisol, probably as a result of stress, and this hor-

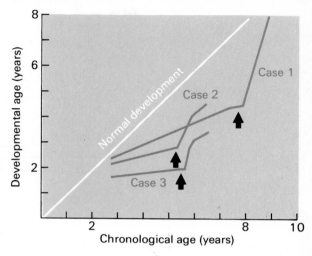

Box Figure 7-1 Growth rates of three cases of psychosocial dwarfism. Removal from environment causing psychological stress is indicated by an arrow for each case. (Adapted from Brasel and Blizzard, 1974)

mone inhibits growth. Some affected children show none of these hormonal disturbances. Possibly there are still other routes through which emotional factors influence growth. Another possibility is that the hormonal measurements may not have been taken promptly enough. Resumption of growth often begins rapidly when the child is removed from the stressful environment, so that delaying even a day or two may miss the hormonal dysfunction.

Growth is an example of a process that involves a large number of factors—hormonal, metabolic, and dietary—and which can therefore malfunction in a variety of ways. Cases of psychosocial dwarfism are turning out to be more common than previously supposed, and investigators who study this syndrome are calling for further awareness of and attention to it (Green, Campbell, & David, 1984).

Contemporary data clearly show that cells in various hypothalamic nuclei, especially the **supraoptic nucleus** and the **paraventricular nucleus,** synthesize hormones that are transported along their axons (where they appear as dense granules) to the axon terminals. Nerve impulses in these cells result in release of this neurosecretory material into the rich vascular capillary bed of the neurohypophysis. Actually the axon terminals of these nerve cells abut capillaries; Figure 7-5b shows the relations of these secretory nerve cells and capillaries.

Signals that activate the nerve cells of the supraoptic and paraventricular nuclei appear to be related to osmotic pressure of blood. (Aspects of this problem are related to thirst and water regulation, which will be discussed in Chapter 12.) Secretion of antidiuretic hormone (ADH) leads to conservation of water, because ADH inhibits the formation of urine—hence the designation antidiuretic. The two quite different names for this hormone reflect the sequence of research on it. The first effect to be identified was its increase of vascular pressure—hence its designation as vasopressin. But later it became clear that the major physiological role of this hormone is its potent antidiuretic activity; it exerts this effect with less than one-thousandth of the dose needed to alter blood pressure. Therefore, antidiuretic hormone is clearly a more suitable term, although many investigators still use the older term.

Oxytocin, another hormone stored in axon terminals of the posterior pituitary, is involved in milk "letdown," the contraction of cells of mammary glands. The mechanism mediating this phenomenon provides a good example of the interaction of behavior and hormone release. When an infant or young animal begins to suckle, there is a delay of 30 to 60 seconds before milk is obtained. This delay results from a sequence of events that consists of several steps. The stimulation of the nipple activates receptors of the skin, which transmit this information through a chain of several neurons and synapses to hypothalamic cells that contain oxytocin. This hormone is released from the posterior pituitary and travels via the vascular system to the mammary glands, where it produces contraction of cells surrounding storage sites for milk and thus results in the availability of milk at the nipple (see Figure 7-7). For human mothers this reflex response to suckling frequently becomes conditioned to baby cries, so milk appears promptly at the start of nursing.

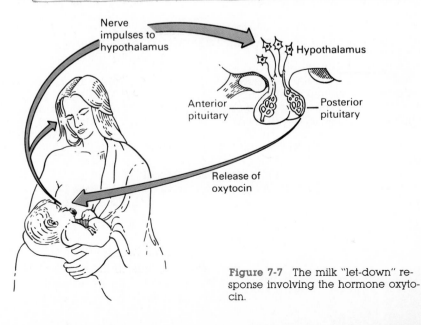

Figure 7-7 The milk "let-down" response involving the hormone oxytocin.

[margin handwritten note: the signals reg. those nuclei: prob. due to osmotic pressure?)]

Oxytocin also produces powerful internal contractions of the uterus and may facilitate delivery once labor has begun. Injections of oxytocin are frequently used to accelerate delivery in instances of prolonged labor that can threaten the viability of the fetus.

Hypothalamic Hormones

[handwritten margin note: ant. pit. secretion controlled by releasing hormone]

The secretions of the anterior pituitary are controlled by releasing hormones produced in neurons of the hypothalamus. These neurons are found in various parts of the hypothalamus, including the median eminence (see Figure 7-5). The median eminence is surrounded by an elaborate profusion of capillaries (the hypophysial-portal capillaries and veins). Endings of neurons of the median eminence lie close to these capillaries. These axons convey large granules that contain hormones. The contents of the granules are released into the surrounding capillaries, through which blood flows into the anterior pituitary. The blood supply of the anterior pituitary thus contains many hormones that have been transported via the portal circulation from the median eminence. The list of these hormones now includes growth hormone-releasing hormone, thyrotropic-releasing hormone, and luteinizing hormone-releasing hormone.

The hypothalamic hormones are a further control element in the regulation of endocrine secretions. The neurons that synthesize these regulatory hormones are subject to two kinds of influences:

1. They receive neural influences from other brain regions via the synaptic contacts of these cells. In this manner the endocrine system is influenced by *[handwritten margin note: neural influence]* a wide range of neural signals originating from both internal and external events. Thus the outputs of endocrine glands can be regulated in accordance with ongoing events. Also, endocrine secretion can be subjected to learned controls.

2. The cells that synthesize the releasing hormones are directly affected by *[handwritten margin note: circulating messages]* circulating messages, such as hormones and blood sugar, because they are not shielded by a blood-brain barrier.

Adrenal Hormones

[handwritten margin note: adrenal gland - next to each kidney — 1 outer = cortex 2. inner = medulla 1. glucocortoids]

Adjacent to each kidney is an **adrenal gland,** which secretes a large variety of hormones. There are two major portions of the adrenal structure in mammals. The outer bark of the gland, the **adrenal cortex,** is composed of three distinct layers of cells, each producing different hormones. The core of the gland is the **adrenal medulla,** really a portion of the autonomic nervous system, which is richly supplied with nerves from autonomic ganglia. In many nonmammalian vertebrates, these are two separate glands.

The adrenal cortex produces and secretes a variety of steroid hormones. One group is called **glucocorticoids** because of their effects on carbohydrate metabolism. Hormones of this type, such as **cortisol,** produce marked changes in glucose metabolism, increasing the level of blood glucose. They also accelerate the breakdown of proteins. In high concentrations they have a marked anti-inflammatory effect, which results in the decrease of bodily responses to tissue injury. More extensive biological actions of these substances are evident in their effects on appetite and muscular activity.

A second group of adrenal cortical hormones is called **mineralocorticoids** because of their effects on ion concentrations in some body tissues, especially the kidney. **Aldosterone** is one such hormone, and its secretion results in conservation of sodium and release of potassium into urine. As a consequence a homeostatic equilibrium in the distribution of ions in blood and extracellular fluids is maintained.

The adrenal cortex also produces sex hormones; the steroid structure of these hormones is closely related to the molecular structure of the glucocorticoids and mineralocorticoids. The chief sex hormone secreted by the human adrenal cortex is called **androstenedione;** it is responsible for the adult pattern of body hair in men and women. In some females the adrenal cortex produces more than the usual amounts of sex hormones, and this can virilize the appearance of girls and women.

Regulation of the level of circulating adrenal cortical hormones involves several steps, as shown in Figure 7-8. The importance of the pituitary hormone adrenocorticotropic hormone (ACTH) can be demonstrated simply: Removal of the pituitary results in shrinkage of the adrenal cortex. ACTH promotes steroid synthesis in the adrenal; indeed, cortisol is secreted by the adrenal cortex only when ACTH is present.

Figure 7-8 Regulation of endocrine secretions of the adrenal cortex.

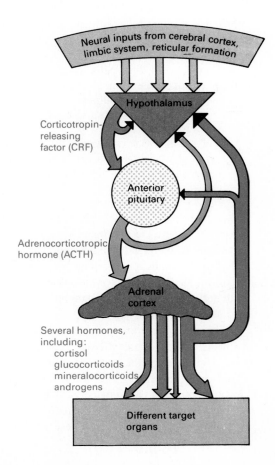

A negative-feedback effect on ACTH release is produced by adrenal steroids, especially cortisol. As the level of adrenal cortex hormones increases, ACTH secretion is suppressed, so the output of hormones from the adrenal cortex then diminishes. When the levels of adrenal steroids fall, the pituitary ACTH-secreting cells are released from suppression, and the concentration of ACTH in the blood rises. This occurrence, in turn, leads to increased output of adrenal cortex hormones. ACTH secretion is also controlled by hypothalamic mechanisms and the appropriate releasing hormone, **corticotropin-releasing hormone (CRH)** or **factor (CRF).** CRH provides the signal that produces the daily rhythm of ACTH release. A prominent influence on ACTH secretion is also exerted by stress, both physiological and psychological. (Further discussion of stress and ACTH appears in Chapter 15.)

The hormones of the adrenal medulla are two amine compounds, **epinephrine** and **norepinephrine.** We have already discussed these compounds in Chapter 6, where we saw that they are also synaptic transmitters at certain sites in the nervous system.

[handwritten margin notes: adrenal medulla - epinephrine + norepinephrine]

Pancreatic Hormones

[handwritten margin notes: islets of Langerhans secrete into bloodstream; insulin, glucagon]

Throughout the **pancreas** (located near the posterior wall of the abdominal cavity) are clusters of cells called **islets of Langerhans,** which secrete hormones directly into the bloodstream. These collections of cells are intermingled among other cells that perform an exocrine function, secreting digestive enzymes into ducts leading to the gastrointestinal tract.

Hormones secreted by the islets of Langerhans include **insulin** and **glucagon,** both of which have potent and frequently reciprocal actions dealing with glucose utilization. Insulin is produced in one type of cell within the islets (beta cells), and glucagon is secreted by another type (alpha cells).

Both nonneural and neural factors regulate the release of insulin. The level of glucose in the bloodstream, which is monitored by cells of the islets of Langerhans, is a critical determinant of insulin release. As the level of blood sugar rises above a norm of concentration, insulin is released. Among the actions of insulin are increased glucose uptake in some tissues, such as muscle, and reduced liver output of glucose. These effects produce a lowering of blood glucose. Note that this reaction is a direct-feedback effect that does not involve a tropic hormone.

[handwritten margin notes: insulin released from crit. amount of blood sugar => increased glucose uptake in some tissues => lowering of blood glucose]

[handwritten margin notes: No tropic hormone]

The effects of insulin directly antagonize those of glucagon. In contrast with the actions of insulin, the actions of glucagon increase blood glucose levels. The hormonal regulation of secretion of both insulin and glucagon is summarized in Figure 7-9. In addition, there is paracrine action between adjacent alpha and beta cells of the islets of Langerhans; that is, insulin and glucagon can oppose each other locally within the pancreas as well as using the endocrine route. The reciprocal action of insulin and glucagon helps to keep blood glucose within the range that is necessary for proper functioning of the brain and of other organs.

[handwritten margin notes: local + endocrine opposition maintains glucose balance for proper functioning]

The release of insulin is also controlled by neural impulses that arrive at the pancreas via the vagus nerve. When a person eats, insulin is released even before any glucose reaches the bloodstream. This early release occurs in response to taste stimulation in the mouth. Cutting the vagus nerve in experimental animals prevents the rapid release of insulin in response to eating, but it does not interfere with the response to glucose in the bloodstream. Furthermore, even stimuli that are normally

Figure 7-9 Regulation of blood glucose levels by (a) glucagon, (b) insulin, and (c) both glucagon and insulin.

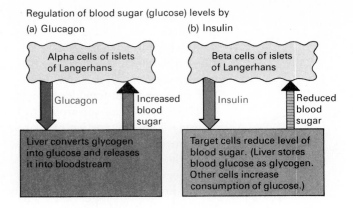

Regulation of blood sugar (glucose) levels by

(a) Glucagon

Alpha cells of islets
of Langerhans

Glucagon | Increased blood sugar

Liver converts glycogen
into glucose and releases
it into bloodstream

(b) Insulin

Beta cells of islets
of Langerhans

Insulin | Reduced blood sugar

Target cells reduce level of
blood sugar. (Liver stores
blood glucose as glycogen.
Other cells increase
consumption of glucose.)

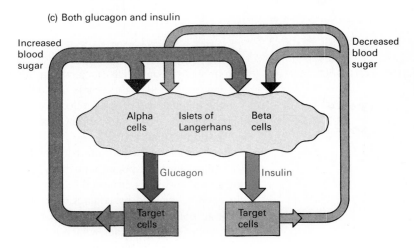

(c) Both glucagon and insulin

Increased
blood
sugar

Decreased
blood
sugar

Alpha
cells   Islets of
Langerhans   Beta
cells

Glucagon   Insulin

Target
cells   Target
cells

associated with eating can cause the release of insulin. This response is a conditioned one, and it also operates via the nervous system, since it is eliminated by
cutting the vagus nerve.

Thyroid Hormones

Situated just below the vocal apparatus in the throat is the **thyroid gland;** this gland
produces and secretes several hormones, including **thyroxine** and **calcitonin.** Certain cells of the thyroid produce the hormones, and a saclike collection of cells
called the thyroid colloid stores them. The thyroid is unique among endocrine
glands because it stores large amounts of hormone and releases it slowly; normally
the thyroid has at least 100 days' supply of hormones.

The control network for regulating thyroxine levels in blood is shown in
Figure 7-10. The major control is exerted by **thyroid-stimulating hormone (TSH)**
from the anterior pituitary gland. The secretion of TSH is controlled by two factors.
The dominant one is a negative-feedback relation with the level of thyroid hormone
circulating in the blood; the second and less important factor is a hypothalamic
neurohumor, **thyrotropin-releasing hormone (TRH).** When the level of circulat-

1. TSH regulates
thyroxine
2. TRH - less import

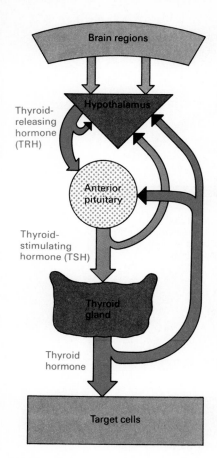

Brain regions

Hypothalamus

Thyroid-releasing hormone (TRH)

Anterior pituitary

Thyroid-stimulating hormone (TSH)

Thyroid gland

Thyroid hormone

Target cells

Figure 7-10 Regulation of secretion of thyroxine.

ing thyroid hormone falls, this leads to secretion of both TRH and TSH; when TSH reaches the thyroid gland, it causes release of thyroid hormone.

Knowledge of the feedback controls of thyroid output is often used in diagnosing undersecretion (hypothyroidism) or oversecretion (hyperthyroidism) of the thyroid gland. Both are relatively common disorders. The TSH level in the blood is almost invariably raised in people with hypothyroidism. As hypothyroidism develops, the TSH level rises before the person shows low circulating levels of thyroid hormone, because increased TSH keeps up the level of thyroid hormone as long as possible.

Thyroid hormone is the only substance produced by the body that contains iodine, and the manufacture of thyroxine is critically dependent on the supply of iodine. In parts of the world where iodine is in short supply in foods, many people may suffer from hypothyroidism. In such cases the thyroid gland may enlarge in the attempt to produce more hormone, a condition known as goiter. Iodized salt is now widely used to prevent this condition.

The major role of the thyroid is the regulation of metabolic processes, especially carbohydrate utilization. It also has an influence on growth, which is especially evident when profound thyroid deficiency starts early in life. Besides stunted bodily growth and characteristic facial malformation, thyroid deficiency produces a marked reduction in brain size and cellular structure. This state is called **cretinism** and is accompanied by mental retardation; we will discuss it further when we talk about the effects of hormones on learning and memory.

Both hyperthyroidism and hypothyroidism lead to many behavioral disorders. Hyperthyroid individuals often seek help because of symptoms that include nervousness, irritability, and insomnia. A contrasting picture is seen in hypothyroidism with apathy, retarded speech, and a hoarse voice.

Gonadal Hormones

Virtually all aspects of reproductive behavior, including mating and parental behavior, depend on hormones. Since Chapter 11 is devoted to reproductive behavior and physiology, at this point we will only briefly note relevant hormones and some pertinent aspects of anatomy and physiology. The gonads of male and female vertebrates produce hormones and also gametes (sperm and eggs). Hormone production is critical both for reproductive behavior and for the production of sperm or eggs.

The Testes

Within the testes are several cell types. Interspersed among the sperm-producing cells are the Leydig cells, which produce and secrete the hormone **testosterone.** (The name testosterone comes from the roots for ''testes'' and ''sterone.'' Testosterone and other male hormones are called **androgens** from the Greek roots *andr* meaning ''man'' and *gen* meaning ''to produce or create.'') Production and release of testosterone is regulated by a hormone of the anterior pituitary; this anterior pituitary hormone is sometimes called **interstitial cell-stimulating hormone (ICSH),** and sometimes it is called **luteinizing hormone (LH).** The pituitary hor-

[handwritten margin notes: Leydig cells produce & secrete testosterone; LH regulates production & release]

Figure 7-11 Regulation of function of the testes, including secretion of testosterone.

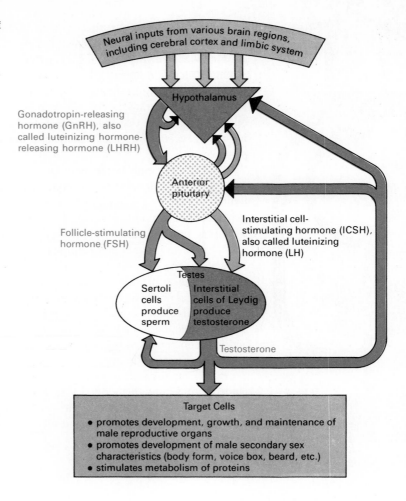

Handwritten margin notes: GnRH (or LNRH) regulates LH release

mone in turn is controlled by a hypothalamic releasing factor, **gonadotropin-releasing hormone (GnRH),** also called **luteinizing hormone-releasing hormone (LHRH).** Testosterone controls a wide range of bodily changes that become visible at puberty, including changes in voice, hair growth, and genital size. Levels of testosterone vary during the day in adult males, although the connection between daily rhythms in this hormone and behavior remains a mystery. In species that breed only in certain seasons of the year, testosterone has especially marked effects on behavior and appearance. Regulation of secretion of testosterone is summarized in Figure 7-11.

The Ovaries

The paired female gonads, the ovaries, also produce both the mature gametes (ova) and hormones. However, hormonal activities of the ovary are more complicated than those of the testes. Production of ovarian hormones occurs in cycles whose

Ovaries→2 classes
of hormones

↓ NRH
↓↓
↓H ↓ FSH
↓ ↓
Est, Progesteron

duration varies with species—in human beings they last about four weeks, whereas in the rat the cycles last only four days. The ovary produces two major classes of hormones: the **estrogens** and the **progestins.** (The term *estrogen* comes from the Greek roots *estrus* meaning "female sexual receptivity" and *gen* meaning "to produce or create." *Progestin* comes from *pro* meaning "favoring" and *gest* meaning "gestation.") Ovarian production of these hormones is under the control of two anterior pituitary hormones, **follicle-stimulating hormone (FSH)** and **luteinizing hormone (LH).** (LH is identical to ICSH found in males.) The release of the anterior pituitary hormones is controlled by a hormone from the hypothalamus, **gonadotropin-releasing hormone (GnRH),** also called **luteinizing hormone-releasing hormone (LHRH).** Figure 7-12 presents a model of the regulation of ovarian hormones.

Figure 7-12 Regulation of function of the ovaries, including secretion of ovarian hormones.

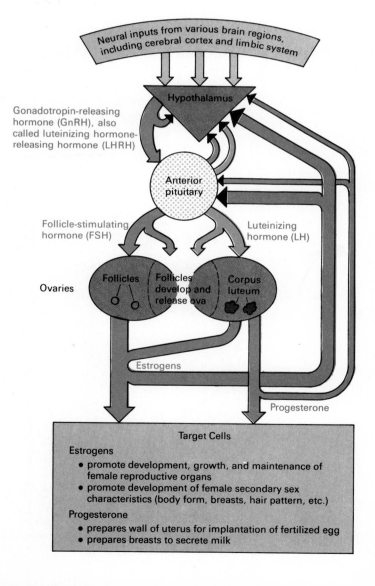

Target Cells

Estrogens
- promote development, growth, and maintenance of female reproductive organs
- promote development of female secondary sex characteristics (body form, breasts, hair pattern, etc.)

Progesterone
- prepares wall of uterus for implantation of fertilized egg
- prepares breasts to secrete milk

Relations Among Gonadal Hormones

Interestingly, all three classes of sex hormones—the androgens, the estrogens, and the progestins—have closely related chemical structures. They and the adrenal cortical steroids are all derived from cholesterol, and all have the basic structure of four interconnected carbon rings. Furthermore, estrogens are synthesized from androgens, and androgens are synthesized from progestins, as Table 7-2 shows. Different organs differ in the relative amounts of these hormones they produce. For example, the testis converts only a relatively small proportion of testosterone into estradiol, whereas the ovary converts most of the testosterone it makes into estradiol. The adrenal cortex secretes significant amounts of androstenedione without metabolizing it further. Much of the testosterone that enters brain cells is converted within those cells to estradiol. We will consider the functions of these sex hormones in Chapter 11.

Some Hormonal Effects

As we mentioned earlier, endocrine influences on structural or functional states frequently involve the interaction of several different hormones. In this section we will consider briefly some hormonal effects on homeostasis and on learning and memory; these are effects that have multiple endocrine determinants. (Hormonal effects on growth were considered in Box 7-1.)

Table 7-2 Basic Pathways in the Synthesis of Sex Hormones

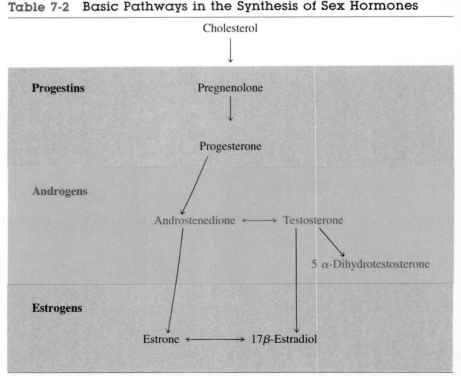

An arrow may represent more than a single metabolic step. Single-headed arrows indicate irreversible reactions; double-headed arrows indicate reversible reactions.

Hormones and Homeostatic Mechanisms

Many bodily mechanisms have evolved to ensure the relative constancy of the internal environment. American physiologist Walter Cannon called these mechanisms **homeostatic** (from the Latin roots *homeo*, meaning "same," and *stasis*, meaning "standing or remaining"). Hormones play major roles in regulating many basic processes that are significant for homeostasis, such as those that govern the distribution of ions and fluids and those that control the concentration of glucose in blood and brain. We will consider the regulation of glucose in the blood as an example of the hormonal role in glucose homeostasis.

Glucose in blood is usually found in a concentration that varies between 80 and 130 mg/100 milliliters. Some hormones lead to an increase in glucose concentration in the blood; these include glucagon, growth hormone, and cortisol. Decrease in glucose concentration in blood is produced by insulin. The balance among these hormones maintains the glucose concentration of blood within a range that provides for maximal production of energy in a variety of circumstances. The level of blood sugar itself also inhibits the secretion of some hormones.

Failure in these controls has major consequences for bodily organs. High blood levels of glucose (hyperglycemia) can produce pathological changes in body tissues, such as diabetic blindness. Such destruction of tissue may arise from the use of metabolic pathways that produce unusual metabolites. This is evident in diabetes mellitus, a disorder characterized by insulin deficiency.

Homeostatic mechanisms dealing with glucose regulation are particularly prominent during periods of stress or strong exercise. Hormonal changes accompanying these states enhance the release of glucose from the liver. But if insufficient glucose is released, the central nervous system is unable to produce its full response. A normal rate of release is part of the alarm reaction, the prompt "fight or flight" response of the body to any stressor. If the stressful situation continues, then long-term reactions occur that involve several other hormones.

Hormonal mechanisms in other homeostatic systems will be taken up in later chapters: water balance in Chapter 11 and hormonal mechanisms in energy balance and body weight in Chapter 12.

Effects of Hormones on Learning and Memory

Thyroid hormone imp for early NS development

Hormones affect both the early development of capacities to learn and remember and the efficient utilization of these capacities after they have been formed. Thyroid hormone, as already indicated, is important in the early development of the nervous system. Insufficient thyroid secretion results in fewer synaptic connections than usual, and this condition is linked to cretinism. Experimental studies have given us more information about this condition: If a drug that inhibits thyroid function is administered to infant rats, the results are a demonstrable decrease in the formation of cortical synapses and significantly impaired learning ability. Giving such "experimental cretin" rats enriched experience as they grow has been reported to ameliorate their behavioral deficiencies to a large extent (Davenport, 1976). (The effects of enriched experience on the brain will be discussed in Chapter 17).

After the developmental period, the ability of juvenile or adult animals to learn and remember has been shown to be affected by the hypothalamic hormones ACTH, vasopressin (antidiuretic hormone, ADH), oxytocin, and also by particular fractions or analogs of these hormones, and by the catecholaminergic hormones of the adrenal medulla, norepinephrine and epinephrine (McGaugh, 1983; Martinez, 1985). Some of these studies will be taken up in Chapter 17. One hypothesis being tested in this research is that the emotional aspects of a learning situation affect the release of hormones, and the hormones present during the posttraining period modulate the formation of memory; that is, the pleasure or pain or stress involved in an episode of learning will, through their hormonal aftereffects, help to determine how well the situation is remembered. Such hormonal effects may be important in reinforcing learning.

Comparisons of Neural and Hormonal Communication

Now that we have surveyed hormonal communication in this chapter and neurochemical communication in Chapter 6, we can compare the two systems and note their differences and similarities.

Neural communication works somewhat like a telephone system: Messages travel over fixed channels to precise destinations. In contrast, hormonal communication works somewhat like a broadcasting system: Many endocrine messages spread throughout the body and can be picked up by any cells that have receptors for them. (Some hormonal messages, however, have a less broad distribution; for instance, the hypothalamus sends releasing factors only a few millimeters through the portal vessels to the anterior pituitary gland.) Neural messages are rapid and are measured in milliseconds. Hormonal messages are slower and are measured in seconds and minutes. Most neural messages are "digitized," all-or-none impulses, whereas hormonal messages are "analog," that is, graded in strength.

Another difference between neural and hormonal communication involves voluntary control. You cannot, at a command, increase or decrease the output of a hormone or a response mediated by the endocrine system, whereas you can voluntarily lift your arm or blink your eyelids or perform many other acts under neuromuscular control. This distinction between neural and hormonal systems, however, is not absolute. Many muscular responses cannot be performed at will, even though they are under neural control. An example is heart rate, which is regulated by the vagus nerve to meet changing demands during exercise or stress but which very few people can change promptly and directly. Sometimes it is said that we do not have voluntary control over responses mediated by the autonomic nervous system; these involve smooth muscles and glands rather than skeletal muscles. But that conclusion is too sweeping: Children are toilet trained to achieve voluntary control of the smooth sphincter muscles used to hold back urination and defecation. Biofeedback techniques may enable people to overcome health problems by altering their heart rate and blood pressure (Miller, 1978). Training can also produce control over hormonally mediated behavior. For example, rats whose skeletal musculature is paralyzed can be trained to alter the rate of secretion of urine into the bladder (Miller & Dworkin, 1978); this response presumably involves antidiuretic hormone. We have seen examples of the conditioning of other responses that involve hormones— the milk letdown response mediated by oxytocin and the prompt release of insulin during eating. So there is a general distinction between the involuntary endocrine system and the skeletal muscular system that is accessible to voluntary control, but it should not be taken as an absolute distinction.

In spite of differences, the neural and hormonal systems show important similar-

[Handwritten margin notes:]

Neuron — hormone
1. fixed destinations — : general release to cells w/ receptors (some localization)
2. rapid. — 2. slow
3. all or none (digitized) — 3. analog (graded)
4. Some voluntary control (exceptions) — heart rate — 4. No vol. control (exception training → hormonal control?)

Figure 7-13 Comparison of (a) hormonal communication and (b) neural communication at a synapse.

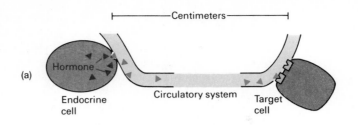

(a)

Hormone

Endocrine cell

Circulatory system

Target cell

Centimeters

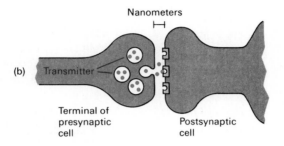

(b)

Transmitter

Nanometers

Terminal of presynaptic cell

Postsynaptic cell

ities. The nervous system uses specialized biochemical substances to communicate across synaptic junctions in much the same way that the endocrine system uses hormones (see Figure 7-13). Of course, the distance traveled by the chemical messengers differs enormously in the two cases—the synaptic cleft is only about 30 nm wide (30×10^{-9} m), whereas hormones may travel a meter or so from the site of secretion to the target organ. Nevertheless, the analogy between chemical transmission at synapses and hormonal communication holds up in several specific respects:

1. The presynaptic ending of a neuron produces its particular transmitter chemical and stores it for later release, just as an endocrine gland stores its hormone for secretion.
2. When an electrical nerve impulse reaches the presynaptic terminal, it releases the transmitter agent into the synaptic cleft between neurons. Similarly, endocrine glands are stimulated to secrete hormones into the bloodstream, some glands responding to neural messages and others to chemical messages.
3. There are many different synaptic transmitter chemicals, and there are many different hormones, and more and more biochemical compounds are being found to serve as both. Examples are norepinephrine and epinephrine, which act as transmitters at many brain synapses and which are also secreted as hormones by the adrenal medulla. Other substances that serve as a hormone at some locations and as a synaptic transmitter at other locations include ACTH, vasopressin, and melanin-stimulating hormone.
4. The synaptic transmitter reacts with specific receptor molecules at the surface of the postsynaptic membrane. Similarly, many hormones react with specific receptor molecules at the membrane of their target cells; most organs do not have receptors for a given hormone and therefore do not respond to it.
5. In many cases when hormones act on receptor molecules, a second messenger is released within the target cells to bring about changes within the cell.

This process has been studied extensively in the endocrine system, and more recently it has been discovered that some neural effects also involve the release of second messengers in the postsynaptic neuron. Moreover, the same compound—cyclic AMP—acts as a second messenger in many places in both the nervous and the endocrine systems.

Some neurons in the hypothalamus actually synthesize hormones, as we saw earlier. These so-called neurosecretions make it hard to draw a firm line between neurons and endocrine cells. In fact, it has been suggested that the endocrine glands may have evolved from **neurosecretory cells** (Turner & Bagnara, 1976). A different hypothesis stems from recent findings that both hormonal peptides and neuropeptides are native to unicellular organisms, that is, that both the nervous system and the endocrine system are derived from chemical communication systems in our remote unicellular ancestors (Le Roith, Shiloach, & Roth, 1982). Much current research is devoted to determining the functions of the peptide compounds in the brain (Krieger, 1983). Some may be used as neurotransmitters. On the other hand, the peptides typically have a slower onset of effect and a longer duration of action than do transmitters, so it has been suggested that they act as **neuromodulators,** substances that alter reactivity of cells to the specific transmitters (Barchas, 1977).

[handwritten margin note: Suggest peptides act as neuromodulator]

Integrated Activities of Hormonal and Neural Systems

Although we have focused on the endocrine system in this chapter, the endocrine system participates in interactions with many other organs, including, of course, the nervous system. Figure 7-14 incorporates the endocrine system into a larger schema of reciprocal relations between body and behavior. Let us examine some of the relations indicated by the figure.

Incoming sensory stimuli elicit nerve impulses that go to several brain regions, including the cerebral cortex, cerebellum, and hypothalamus. Behavioral responses bring further changes in stimulation. For example, the person may approach or go away from the original source of stimulation, and this action will alter the size of the visual image, the loudness of sound, and so forth. Meanwhile the endocrine system is altering the response characteristics of the person. If the evaluation of the stimulus situation calls for action, energy is mobilized through hormonal routes. The state of some sensory receptor organs may also be altered, thus modifying further processing of stimuli.

Many behaviors require neural and hormonal coordination. For example, when a stressful situation is perceived through neural sensory channels, hormonal secretions prepare the individual to make energetic responses. The muscular responses for "fight or flight" are controlled neurally, but energy is mobilized for them through hormonal routes. Another example of neural and hormonal coordination is the milk letdown response.

[handwritten margin note: Coordination; Fight or Flight (muscles (neural) / energy (hormone)]

Four kinds of signals from one cell to another are possible in a system with both nerve cells and endocrine cells: neural to neural, neural to endocrine, endocrine to endocrine, and endocrine to neural. All four kinds can be found in the courtship behavior of the ring dove. Friedman (1977) observed this by placing a male dove in a position where he could see a female through a window. The visual stimulation and perception involve neural-neural transmission. The particular visual stimulus

[handwritten margin note: neural to endocrine; N to N; E to E; E to N]

Figure 7-14 The endocrine system incorporated into the overall schema of reciprocal relations between body and behavior.

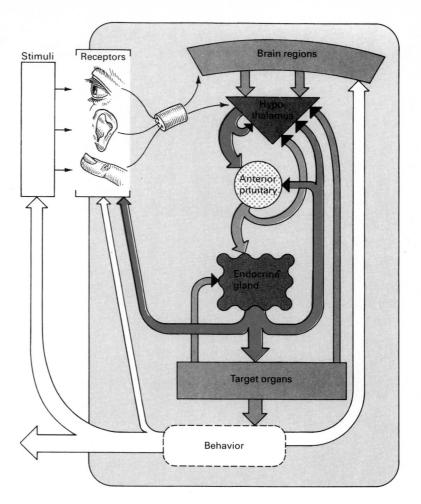

activates a neural-endocrine link, which causes some neurosecretory cells in the hypothalamus to secrete interstitial cell-stimulating hormone. Then there is a series of endocrine-endocrine signals that causes increased production and release of the hormone testosterone. Testosterone, in turn, alters the excitability of some neurons through an endocrine-neural link and thus causes the display of courtship behavior. The female dove responds to this display, thus providing new visual stimulation and further neural-neural signals. (We will discuss the complex interactions of male and female doves further in Chapter 11, where we will see other examples of coordination of neural and endocrine activities.)

Our circle schema in Figure 7-15 can be used to consider how relations are being found between endocrine activity and behavior. Here are a few examples: The level of circulating hormones can be altered by chemical intervention, and this can affect behavior. For example, there is an uncommon disease (Cushing's syndrome) in which the level of adrenal glucocorticoid hormone is elevated, causing obesity, hypertension, and mental disorders. Since cortisone was introduced as a drug in

Figure 7-15 Circle schema representation of reciprocal relations between
endocrine activity and behavior.

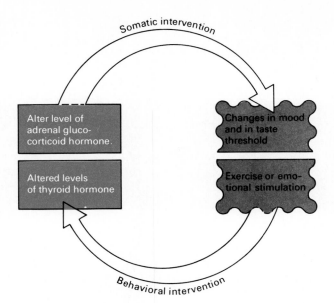

1949, cases of Cushing's syndrome have shown up in occasional patients who have
been treated with cortisone in doses that caused an oversupply of the hormone. In
experimental animals removal of the adrenals causes excretion of salts, which
greatly increases the animals' preference for salty water. In fact, adrenalectomized
rats show an amazing sensitivity for very weak salt solutions.

Experiential interventions also cause rapid changes in the output of many endocrine glands. For example, the output of thyroid hormone responds to many environmental influences. Starting to exercise increases the level of thyroxine in the
circulation. Putting animals in a cold temperature also increases thyroid activity,
and keeping them there increases the size of the thyroid gland. On the other hand,
physical stresses, pain, and unpleasant emotional situations decrease thyroid output,
probably as a consequence of diminished release of thyroid-stimulating hormone
from the anterior pituitary gland. Sensory stimulation and emotional experience
influence the thyroid system by modulating the secretion of thyrotropin-releasing
hormone from the hypothalamus.

Summary · Main Points

1. Hormones are chemical compounds that act as signals in the body. They are secreted by endocrine glands or
specialized cells into the bloodstream and are taken up by
receptor molecules in target cells.

2. Some hormones, such as thyroxine, have receptors
in a wide variety of cells and can therefore influence the
activity of most cells in the body. Others, like gonadal hormones, find receptors in only certain special cells or organs.

3. Hormones act by promoting the proliferation and
differentiation of cells and by modulating the activity of
cells that have already differentiated.

4. Peptide and amine hormones bind to specific receptor molecules at the surface of the target cell membrane and
cause the release of molecules of a "second messenger"
inside the cell. Steroid hormones pass through the membrane and bind to receptor molecules in the cell.

5. A negative-feedback system monitors and controls the rate of secretion of each hormone. In the simplest case, the hormone acts upon target cells, leading them to change the amount of a substance in the extracellular fluid; this in turn regulates the output of the endocrine gland.

6. Several hormones are controlled by a more complex feedback system; a tropic hormone from the hypothalamus regulates the release of an anterior pituitary hormone, which in turn controls secretion by an endocrine gland. In this case feedback of the endocrine hormone acts mainly at the hypothalamus and anterior pituitary.

7. Endocrine influences on various structures and functions often involve more than one hormone, as in the cases of growth, metabolism, and learning and memory.

8. Neural communication differs from hormonal communication in that neural signals travel rapidly over fixed pathways, whereas hormonal signals spread more slowly and throughout the body.

9. The neural and hormonal communication systems have several characteristics in common: Both utilize chemical messages; the same substance that acts as a hormone in some locations is a synaptic transmitter in others. Both manufacture, store, and release chemical messengers. Both use specific receptors and may employ second messengers.

10. Many behaviors involve the coordination of neural and hormonal components. The transmission of messages in the body may involve neural-neural, neural-endocrine, endocrine-endocrine, or endocrine-neural links.

Recommended Reading

Gorbman, A. (1983). *Comparative endocrinology*. New York: Wiley.

Hadley, M. E. (1984). *Endocrinology*. Englewood Cliffs, N.J.: Prentice-Hall.

Leshner, A. (1978). *An introduction to behavioral endocrinology*. New York: Oxford University Press.

Reference Table

Table 7-3 Main Endocrine Glands or Sources in the Human Body, Their Hormones, and Principal Effects

Glands	Hormones	Principal Effects
Anterior pituitary	Growth hormone	Stimulates growth
	Thyrotropic hormone	Stimulates the thyroid
	Adrenocorticotropic hormone	Stimulates the adrenal cortex
	Follicle-stimulating hormone	Stimulates growth of ovarian follicles and of seminiferous tubules of the testes
	Luteinizing hormone	Stimulates conversion of follicles into corpora lutea; stimulates secretion of sex hormones by ovaries and testes
	Prolactin	Stimulates milk secretion by mammary glands
	Melanocyte-stimulating hormone	Controls cutaneous pigmentation in lower vertebrates
Posterior pituitary (storage organ for certain hormones produced by hypothalamus)	Oxytocin	Stimulates contraction of uterine muscles; stimulates release of milk by mammary glands
	Vasopressin (antidiuretic hormone)	Stimulates increased water reabsorption by kidneys; stimulates constriction of blood vessels (and other smooth muscle)

(Continued on page 246)

Table 7-3 (Continued)

Glands	Hormones	Principal Effects
Hypothalamus	Releasing hormones	Regulate hormone secretion by anterior pituitary
	Oxytocin, vasopressin	*See under* Posterior pituitary
Adrenal cortex	Glucocorticoids (corticosterone, cortisone, hydrocortisone, etc.)	Inhibit incorporation of amino acids into protein in muscle; stimulate formation (largely from noncarbohydrate sources) and storage of glycogen; help maintain normal blood sugar level
	Mineralocorticoids (aldosterone, deoxycorticosterone, etc.)	Regulate sodium and potassium metabolism
	Sex hormones (especially androstenedione)	Regulate facial and bodily hair
Testes	Androgens (testosterone, dihydrotestosterone, etc.)	Stimulate development and maintenance of male primary and secondary sexual characteristics and behavior
Ovaries	Estrogens (estradiol, estrone, etc.)	Stimulate development and maintenance of female secondary sexual characteristics and behavior
	Progestins (especially progesterone)	Stimulate female secondary sexual characteristics and behavior, and maintain pregnancy
Thyroid	Thyroxine, triiodothyronine	Stimulate oxidative metabolism
	Calcitonin	Prevents excessive rise in blood calcium
Pancreas	Insulin	Stimulates glycogen formation and storage; stimulates carbohydrate oxidation; inhibits formation of new glucose
	Glucagon	Stimulates conversion of glycogen into glucose
Mucosa of duodenum	Secretin	Stimulates secretion of pancreatic juice
	Cholecystokinin	Stimulates release of bile by gallbladder; may be signal of satiety for food
	Enterogastrone	Inhibits secretion of gastric juice
Pyloric mucosa of stomach	Gastrin	Stimulates secretion of gastric juice
Parathyroids	Parathormone	Regulates calcium phosphate metabolism
Pineal	Melatonin	May help regulate pituitary, perhaps by regulating hypothalamic releasing centers
Thymus	Thymosin	Stimulates immunologic competence in lymphoid tissues
Adrenal medulla	Epinephrine (adrenaline)	Stimulates syndrome of reactions commonly termed "fight or flight"
	Norepinephrine (noradrenaline)	Stimulates reactions similar to those produced by adrenaline but causes more vasoconstriction and is less effective in converting glycogen into glucose.

PART THREE

Information Processing in Perceptual and Motor Systems

Light from the sun warms our skin and stimulates our eyes. A chorus of sounds, ranging from the songs of insects to the hearty performances of opera singers, stimulates our ears. Winds bend the hairs on the skin and carry substances that lead to a sense of pleasant or unpleasant odors. The food we eat affects receptors in the mouth, the stomach, and the brain. All about us there is a wide range of energies and substances that excite our senses and supply our brains with a vast array of information about many external and internal happenings. The success of any animal—including humans—in dealing with the tasks of survival depends on its ability to construct reliable representations of some of the physical characteristics of its environment, both internal and external. In most cases, however, sensory systems are not slavish, passive copiers and reflectors of impinging stimuli— quite the contrary. Evolutionary success calls for far more selec-tive action. For any species sensory systems construct only partial and selective portraits of the world.

Sensory inputs to the brain do not merely provide "pictures in the head"; they often incite the individual to act. Different inputs lead to distinct adjustments of the body. Picture the simple case when a sound occurs suddenly: Our eyes almost automatically turn toward the source of the sound. Movements elicited by sensory events range in complexity from slight eye motions to elaborate sequences of movements, such as species-characteristic escape behavior. Of course, many acts are coupled to sensory information in a different way. These classes of movements are not directly driven or triggered by sensory events but reflect intrinsic programs of action, which may involve sensory inputs only as modulators. How information processing occurs in both perceptual and motor systems is our theme in Part Three.

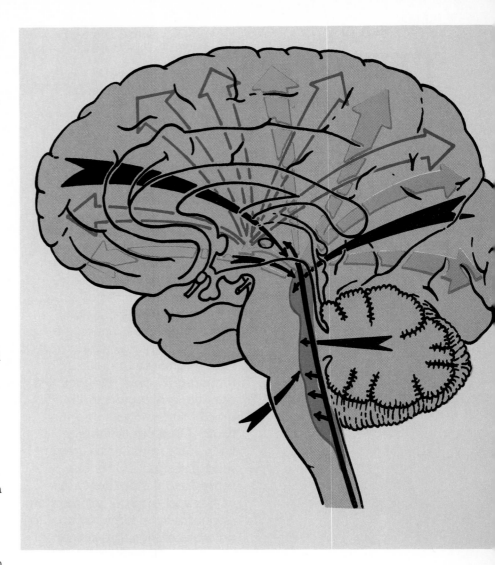

8 Principles of Sensory Processing and Experience: Touch and Pain

ORIENTATION

Sensory systems enable us and other animals to recognize, appreciate, and assess aspects of the world that are necessary for survival. For each species certain features of its surroundings have become especially significant for adaptive success. Although each species in some ways has distinctive windows for viewing the world, the basic processes mediating perceptual accomplishments are much alike in many species. We will consider some of these basic principles of sensory processing and then examine how particular sensory systems work.

All animals have specialized parts of the body that are particularly sensitive to some forms of energy. These body parts—collections of receptors—act as filters: They respond to some stimuli and exclude others. Furthermore, they convert energy into the language of the nervous system—electrical signals. In any animal, processing sensory information involves codes that are rules that relate attributes of stimulus energy, such as intensity, to activity of nerve cells. Knowing these rules, the experimenter should be able to look at a pattern of nerve impulses and distinguish between a beautiful sunset and a tasty bit of food. Of course, we are only slowly gaining understanding of these rules, and up to now our knowledge of coding has been mainly restricted to rather simple stimulus dimensions, such as color and spatial location. Part of the complexity of the problem comes from the fact that processing of sensory neural activity involves many different brain regions, and each may use different transformations of signals. Moreover, the way an event is represented in the nervous system can be different at various brain regions, because each region does not merely passively reflect the barrage of neural inputs. Rather, active processing takes place. These processes can be described as filtering, abstracting, and integrating; all of these affect the way events are represented in the brain.

All this information processing requires extensive neural circuitry, and the evolution of specialized sensory receptors has led to the development of related regions of the brain. In fact, by examining the relative sizes of sensory regions of the nervous system in a given species, one can tell the degree to which different senses contribute to the adaptation of that species to its environment. This is just one of the many ways in which the theme of localization of function comes into the study of sensory and perceptual processes.

In recent years the pace of advances in sensory research has quickened. Within a textbook of physiological psychology, it is impossible to convey the progress in each sensory system. Our solution is to start this chapter with some general principles and then to focus on touch and pain. The next chapter will be devoted to seeing and hearing.

Design of Sensory Systems

Before we discuss the actual properties of sensory mechanisms, it is helpful to consider some ideal properties from both biological and engineering perspectives. Suppose that you had the opportunity to take part in the original design of a sensory system. (Emperor Charles V of the Holy Roman Empire once remarked, ''If I had been present at the Creation, I could have offered some useful advice.'') As a participant in the planning sessions, you can suggest criteria for ideal features. You can ask for the best! Remember, however, that the best probably costs more in terms of number and precision of components. Some compromises may therefore become necessary. Also, different design criteria may come into conflict, and this may require further compromises.

What attributes would you suggest for our model? As it turns out, evolution has provided close-to-optimal sensory systems, taking into account the needs of animals in particular environmental niches and the costs and benefits of various sensory mechanisms. Let us consider some of the ideal features and also some realistic compromises.

Discriminating Among Forms of Energy

The kinds of energies and the range of substances in the world are quite broad. Different kinds of energy, such as light and sound, need different receptors to convert them into neural activity, just as you need a camera and not a tape recorder to take a picture. The different sensory systems (or modalities) must be separate in the brain, too, rather than converging on a common sensory system, as ancient hypotheses held.

We gain information by distinguishing among forms or kinds of stimulus energy. The poet may write ''The dawn came up like thunder,'' but most of the time we want to know whether a sudden dramatic sensory event was auditory or visual, tactile or olfactory. Furthermore, different senses furnish us with quite different information: We see a car hurtling toward us, hear the thin whine of a mosquito circling us, or smell gas escaping; but we might not *hear* the car until it is too late, and we would not *smell* the mosquito or *see* the gas. So our model sensory system should provide for detecting and distinguishing among different forms of energy.

This requirement was considered by the pioneer physiologist Johannes Müller early in the nineteenth century. He proposed the doctrine of ''specific nerve energies,'' which states that the receptors and neural channels for the different senses are independent and operate in their own special ways. For example, no matter how the eye is stimulated—by light or mechanical pressure or electrical shock—the sensation that occurs is always visual. Müller formulated his hypothesis before the nature of nervous transmission was known, so he could suppose that the different sensory systems of the brain used different kinds of energy to carry their messages. Now we know that the messages for the different senses—such as seeing, hearing, touch, pain, and temperature—are kept separate and distinct not by the way systems carry their messages but by keeping their neural tracts separate.

It would be quite costly, however, for each animal species to be sensitive to all the kinds of energy in its environment. Each species therefore evolved the sensory detectors needed to respond to certain forms of stimulation, but for other forms of stimulation, it is only poorly equipped or not equipped at all.

Responding to Different Intensities

Many forms of energy occur over a broad range of intensities. For example, a sonic boom brings to the ear millions of times more energy than the tick of a watch; from the wan light of the first quarter moon to sunlight at noon there is a difference of 1 to 10 million in energy. Our ideal system should be able to represent stimulus values over these broad ranges so that the viewer can discriminate accurately, neither groping in the dark nor being dazzled by too much light. Of course, sensitivity to very feeble stimuli may require highly specialized, and therefore costly, sensory detectors, so we will have to settle for some realistic lower limit.

If the system is to respond to a wide range of intensities, it should be sensitive to differences in intensity; that is, it should be able to provide large responses for small changes in the strength of a stimulus. Actually there are few circumstances in which the absolute value of a stimulus is of major adaptive significance. In most instances sensitivity to change in the stimulus is the important signal for adaptive success. Thus we respond mainly to changes, whether these are changes in intensity or quality or location of the stimulus.

Responding Reliably

Reliability in a sensory system means that there should be a consistent relation between any signal in the external or internal environment and the sensory system's response. Imagine your confusion if a cold stimulus randomly elicited the responses cold, warm, painful, and slippery. To establish useful representations of the world, our ideal system must work reliably.

Responding Rapidly

Optimal adjustment to the world requires that sensory information be processed rapidly. As a driver, you have to perceive the motion of other cars swiftly and correctly if you are going to avoid collisions. Similarly, it does not do a predator much good to recognize prey unless it can do so both rapidly and accurately. Alas, we have come up against a conflict between optimal properties.

A customary way to provide reliability is to increase the number of components. Using several different circuits to process the same stimulus (**parallel processing**) is a conventional way to ensure reliability. Indeed, the "backup" plans ensuring reliability in engineering designs generally provide such "fail-safe" options. However, increasing the number of components in our biological systems requires greater metabolic expense and may compromise speed.

Suppressing Extraneous Information

Did you ever try to hold a conversation on a disco floor? If so, could you hear anything besides the overwhelming input of the music? This example illustrates a paradox. Previously we called for the design of a sensory analyzer with exquisite sensitivity and reliability. But now we are arguing that this extraordinary device should include a provision for ignoring some of the world! From moment to moment, particular stimuli loom especially important, whereas other stimuli fade into insignificance. The fragrance of perfume may be quite compelling in the presence of a loved one but a bit too much when reading a road map. As we will see, sensory devices of different sorts accomplish suppression in a variety of ways. These include varying thresholds, adaptation, and different forms of direct and indirect controls.

How are the ideal properties we have just discussed realized in the actual sensory systems of human beings and of other species? This chapter and Chapter 9 explore the answers to this question.

Diversity of Sensory Worlds

Different species detect different aspects of the world. From the physicist's point of view, the stimuli that animals detect are forms of physical energy or chemical substances that can be defined and described by using the scales or measures of physics and chemistry. But as we have said, not all the forms of physical energy that the physicist or chemist can describe are necessarily potential stimuli for any animal. Indeed, some forms of energy cannot be detected by the sensory systems of *any* existing animal. Table 8-1 classifies sensory systems and the kinds of stimuli related to each system. The term **adequate stimulus** refers to the type of stimulus for which a given sensory organ is particularly adapted. Thus the adequate stimulus for the eye is photic energy; although mechanical pressure on the eye or an electrical shock can stimulate the retina and produce sensations of light, these are not adequate stimuli for the eye.

Even within a given sensory modality, the receptor organs of different species show great diversity, as the eyes in Figure 8-1 indicate. This topic is taken up further in the next chapter in a section on evolution of eyes.

Range of Responsiveness

For any single form of physical energy, the sensory systems of a particular animal are quite selective. For example, humans do not hear sounds in the frequency range above 20,000 hertz (Hz), a range we call ultrasonic. But to a bat, air vibrations of 50,000 Hz would be sound waves, just as would vibrations of 10,000 Hz. Primates in general are deficient in the ability to hear sounds between 20,000 and 80,000 Hz, although many small mammals have good sensory abilities in this range.

In the visual realm, too, some animals can detect stimuli that we cannot. Bees

Table 8-1 Sensory Systems and Adequate Stimuli

Type of Sensory System	Modality	Adequate Stimuli
Mechanical	Touch	Contact with or deformation of body surface
	Hearing	Sound vibrations in air or water
	Vestibular	Head movement and orientation
	Joint	Position and movement
	Muscle	Tension
Photic	Seeing	Visible radiant energy
Thermal	Cold	Decrement of skin temperature
	Warm	Increase of skin temperature
Electrical	(No common name because humans do not have this sense)	Differences in density of electrical currents
Chemical	Smell	Odorous substances dissolved in air or water in the nasal cavity
	Taste	Taste stimuli; in mammals the categories of taste experience are sweet, sour, salty, bitter
	Common chemical	Changes in CO_2, pH, osmotic pressure

Figure 8-1 *Variety of eyes. (a) Squid. (b) Turtle. (c) Snake. (d) Tarsier. (e) Eagle. (Photographs by (a) Jen and Des Bartlett/Photo Researchers. (b) Karl H. Maslowski/Photo Researchers. (c) Tom McHugh/Photo Researchers. (d) A. W. Ambler/National Audubon Society/Photo Researchers. (e) Gordon S. Smith/Photo Researchers.)*

see in the ultraviolet range. Some snakes perceive the wavelengths beyond the other end of our visual spectrum, infrared wavelengths that we can only feel as heat. Species differences in sensory abilities are related to characteristics of sensory receptors, our next topic.

Kinds of Receptors

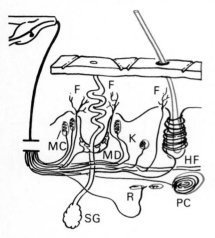

F	Free nerve ending
HF	Hair follicle
K	Krause's end bulb
MC	Meissner's corpuscle
MD	Merkel's disc
PC	Pacinian corpuscle
R	Ruffini's ending
SG	Sweat gland

Figure 8-2 Cross section of the skin showing various kinds of receptors.

Detection of energy starts with the properties of **receptors,** the biological devices that initiate the body's responses to particular energies or substances in the environment. They do so either by converting energies into biological signals or by converting contact with substances into signals. Devices that convert energy from one form to another are known as **transducers,** and the process is called **transduction.** Receptors are therefore the starting points for the neural activity that leads to sensory-perceptual experiences.

The receptor itself may consist of the termination of a nerve fiber, such as free nerve endings in the skin (Figure 8-2). But in most kinds of receptors, the nerve fiber ending is associated with a nonneural cell, which is the actual site of energy conversion. For example, various kinds of corpuscles are associated with nerve endings in the skin. The eye has specialized receptor cells that convert photic energy into electrical charges that stimulate the fibers of the optic nerve. The inner ear has specialized hair cells that transduce mechanical energy into electrical signals that stimulate the fibers of the auditory nerve.

Across the animal kingdom, receptors offer enormous diversity. A wide array of sizes, shapes, and forms reflects the varying survival needs of different animals. For some animals, such as some snakes, detectors of infrared radiation are essential, while several species of fish employ receptors of electrical energy. Evolutionary processes have led to the emergence of specialized sensors attuned to the inputs or signals characteristic of particular environmental niches. So we can look at receptors as embodying strategies for success in particular worlds. Indeed, quite often there is a close fit between optimal receptor characteristics from an evolutionary viewpoint and criteria for optimal performance derived from engineering.

Events at Sensory Surfaces

The structure of a receptor determines the forms of energy to which it will respond. In all cases the steps between the impact of energy at some receptor and the initiation of nerve impulses in a nerve fiber leading away from the receptor involve local changes of membrane potential, which are referred to as **generator potentials.** (In most of its properties, the generator potential resembles the excitatory postsynaptic potentials discussed in Chapter 5.) These electrical charges are the necessary and sufficient conditions for generating nerve impulses. They are part of the causal link between stimulus and nerve impulse.

The details of the generator potential process have been explored by Loewenstein (1971) in elegant studies on a receptor called the **Pacinian corpuscle.** This receptor is found throughout the body—in skin and muscle—but is especially prominent in tissue overlying the abdominal cavity. In consists of a neural fiber that enters a structure resembling a tiny onion that consists of concentric layers of tissue separated by fluid (Figure 8-3).

Mechanical stimuli delivered to the corpuscle produce a graded electrical potential whose amplitude is directly proportional to the strength of the stimulus. When

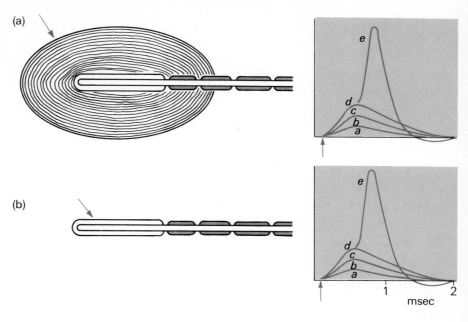

this electrical event reaches sufficient amplitude, the nerve impulse is generated (Figure 8-3). Careful dissection of the corpuscle, leaving the bared axon terminal intact, shows that this graded potential—the generator potential—is initiated in the nerve terminal. Pressing the corpuscle bends this terminal, which leads to the generator event. The sequence of excitatory events is as follows:

1. Mechanical stimulation deforms the corpuscle.
2. This deformation leads to mechanical excitation of the tip of the axon.
3. This leads to the generator potential, which, when it reaches threshold amplitude, can elicit nerve impulses.

In some receptor systems, the generator events are more complicated. This is true, for example, of hair cells in the inner ear. Some researchers have suggested the following sequence of events:

1. Mechanical stimulation bends hairs.
2. Receptor potential is elicited in the hair cell by membrane deformation.
3. A chemical is released at the base of the hair cell.
4. A transmitter flows across the cleft and stimulates the nerve terminal.
5. The generator potential is produced in the nerve cell.

Let us now examine the sensory events that stimuli elicit at sensory receptors.

Principles of Sensory Information Processing

Thinkers in ancient Greece believed that the nerves were tubes through which tiny bits of stimulus objects traveled to the brain, there to be analyzed and recognized. And even when accurate knowledge of neural conduction was gained in this century, many investigators still thought that the sensory nerves simply transmitted accurate information about stimulation to the neural centers. Now, however, it is clear that the sense organs and peripheral sensory pathways convey only limited— even distorted—information to the centers. The brain is an active processor of information, not a copier. In fact, a good deal of selection and analysis takes place in the peripheral sensory pathways. Here we will examine some basic aspects of the processing of sensory information—coding, sensory adaptation, lateral inhibition, suppression, receptive fields, and attention.

Coding

Information about the world is represented in the circuits of the nervous system by electrical potentials in single nerve cells or groups of cells. We have just considered the first step in this process—the transformation of energy at receptors (that is, transduction). Now we must ask: How are these events represented in the neural pathways? In some manner electrical events in nerve cells "stand for" or represent stimuli impinging on an organism. This process is often referred to as coding. (A code is a set of rules for translating information from one form to another. Thus a message in English can be put into a code for transmission, such as the dot-dash Morse code of telegraphy.) Sensory information can be encoded into all-or-none action potentials in several ways: the frequency with which the impulses occur, the rhythm at which they occur (for instance, one impulse every second), the clustering of impulses, and so forth. We will examine possible neural representations of the intensity, quality, position, and pattern of stimuli.

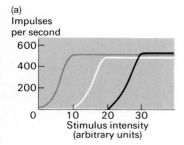

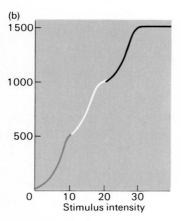

How Intense Is the Stimulus?

We respond to sensory stimuli over a wide range of intensities. Furthermore, within this range we can detect small differences of intensity. How are different intensities of the same stimulus represented in the nervous system?

Within a single nerve cell the frequency of nerve impulses can represent stimulus intensity, as the graph in Figure 8-4a shows. However, only a limited range of different sensory intensities can be represented in this manner. The maximal rate of firing for a single nerve cell, obtained under highly artificial conditions, is about 1200/sec. Most sensory fibers do not fire more than a few hundred impulses per second. The number of differences in intensity that can be detected in vision and audition is much greater than this code could offer. Therefore variations in the firing rate of a single cell simply cannot account for the full range of intensity perception.

Multiple nerve cells acting in parallel provide a broader opportunity for the coding of the intensity of a stimulus. As the strength of a stimulus increases, new nerve cells are "recruited," and thus intensity can be represented by the number of active cells. A variant of this idea is the principle of intensity coding called **range fractionation** (Figure 8-4b). According to this hypothesis, a wide range of intensity values can be accurately noted in the nervous system by cells that are "specialists" in particular segments or fractions of an intensity scale. This mode of stimulus coding requires an array of receptors and nerve cells with a wide distribution of thresholds, some with very high sensitivity (a low-threshold group) and others with much less sensitivity (and higher thresholds).

Figure 8-4 Range fractionation in sensory coding. (a) Rate of firing in three nerve cells, each with different thresholds. Each varies its response over a fraction of the range of stimulus intensities. (b) Combination of firing rates of the three cells. Although none of the nerve cells shown in (a) can respond more frequently than 500/sec, the sum of all three can vary in response rate from 0 to 1500/sec.

What Type of Stimulus Is It?

Within any sensory modality, we can readily discriminate qualitative differences among stimuli. For example, we can discriminate among wavelengths of light, frequencies of sound, and a variety of skin sensations such as touch, warmth, cold, and pain. What kind of coding underlies these qualitative differences?

An important part of the answer is the concept of **labeled lines.** This view states that particular nerve cells are intrinsically labeled for distinctive sensory experiences (Figure 8-5). Neural activity in the ''line'' provides the basis for our detection of the experience. Its qualities are predetermined. Clearly major separation of sensory experiences into modalities involves labeled lines; stimulation of the optic nerve, for instance, always yields vision and never gives us sounds or touches. But there is controversy surrounding coding for submodalities. Limitations to the idea are particularly evident in vision. For example, there does not seem to be a separate labeled line for each discriminable color, although there do appear to be separate lines for a few main colors. The wealth of different colors appears to result from spatial and temporal activities of only a few different kinds of cells, as we will see in Chapter 9.

Where Is the Stimulus?

The position of an object or event, either outside or inside the body, is an important feature of the information that a person or animal gains by sensory analysis. Some sensory systems reveal this information by the position of excited receptors on the sensory surface. This feature is most evident in the visual and somatosensory system. Seeing the position of an event or object and feeling the site of a stimulus on the skin both depend on which receptors are excited. Each receptor in either system activates pathways that convey unique position information. In these systems the

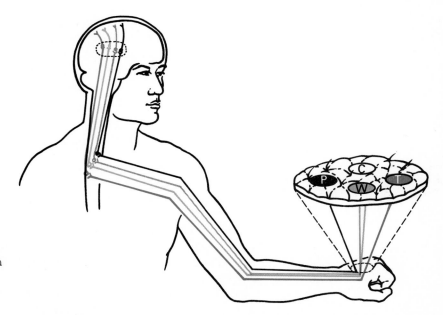

Figure 8-5 The concept of labeled lines. Each receptor (C, P, T, and W) has a distinct pathway linking the receptor surface to the brain. Thus in this example, different qualities of skin stimulation are represented by distinct places in the nervous system from the periphery to the brain.

spatial properties of a stimulus are represented by labeled lines that uniquely convey spatial information. In both the visual and the tactile system, cells at all levels of the nervous system—from the surface sheet of receptors to the cerebral cortex—are arranged in an orderly, maplike manner. The map at each level is not exact but reflects both position and receptor density. Thus more cells are allocated to the spatial representation of sensitive, densely innervated sites like the fovea of the eye or skin surfaces like the lips than to less sensitive sites like the periphery of the eye or the skin of the back.

Information about location is not restricted to sensory systems laid out like a map. We all know that we can detect quite accurately the source of a sound or an odor. In neither system are the peripheral receptors excited in a manner that corresponds directly to the position or location of the relevant stimulus. Locating a stimulus in these systems can involve unilateral or bilateral receptors—that is, one ear or nostril or both ears or nostrils. The mechanism for detecting position differs markedly, depending on whether bilateral or unilateral activation has occurred.

Can you tell the direction from which a sound comes if you use only one ear? Research shows that sound position can be determined with considerable accuracy with one ear if the sound lasts for several seconds, but not if it is sudden and brief. Monaural (one-ear) detection of sound location depends on head movements; it is a sampling, in successive instants, of sound intensity—like radar scanning. Some animals with movable external ears (like the cat) can replace head movements with movements of the external ear. Monaural detection of stimulus location also depends on short-term memory, since successive stimuli are compared for intensity.

Bilateral receptor systems—the two ears or the two nostrils—provide a different solution to determining the location of sounds or odors. In both cases the relative time of arrival of the stimulus at the two receptors, or the relative intensity, is directly related to the location of the stimulus. For example, the only condition in which both ears are excited identically is when the sound source is equidistant from the ears, in the median plane of the body. As the stimulus moves to the left or right, asymmetrical excitation of receptors of the left and right sides occurs. Our auditory localization circuits allow us to judge accurately whether a sound source is slightly to the right or left of center when the difference in time of arrival at the two ears is only a few millionths of a second. Specialized nerve cells that receive inputs from both left and right ears and measure stimulus disparities between left and right are discussed in Chapter 9.

What Is the Identity of the Stimulus?

Being able to recognize objects requires the ability both to perceive patterns of stimulation and to recall patterns that have been learned previously. Usually these abilities go together, but in some cases of brain damage, they can become divorced. (We will consider in Chapter 18 some rare cases of people who can see and describe faces but who can no longer recognize familiar faces.)

Perceiving patterns requires information about different parts or aspects of the stimulus display, and often this information is obtained by movements of the receptor organ. For example, we scan a scene with our eyes. We turn our heads while listening; other animals turn their ears. To identify an object by touch, we move our fingers to obtain information not only about its shape but also about its firmness, elasticity, and so on. Both skin receptors and receptors in the joints are involved in this exploration. When we taste food, we move it over our tongue, since receptors for different taste qualities are located on different parts of the tongue. Even in the case of odors, we sniff to bring new whiffs of odorous air to the receptors in our nose. So different bits of information are captured during our inspection of the stimulus pattern. How these are integrated neurally into a unified perception is a question for which we have only partial answers so far.

Sensory Adaptation

Processing of sensory information also makes use of *adaptation* of receptors; adaptation is the progressive loss of sensitivity that many receptors show as stimulation is maintained. Adaptation can be demonstrated by recording nerve impulses in a fiber leading from a receptor (Figure 8-6); observations of the time course of nerve impulses show a progressive decline in the rate of discharges as the stimulus is continued.

1. **Tonic receptors** are those in which the frequency of nerve impulse discharge declines slowly or not at all as stimulation is maintained. In other words, these receptors show relatively little adaptation.
2. **Phasic receptors** are those that show quite a rapid fall in the frequency of nerve impulses.

Adaptation means that there is a progressive shift in perception and neural activity away from accurate portrayal of the physical event. Thus the nervous system may fail to register neural activity even though the stimulus continues. Such a striking discrepancy does not imply a weakness in the integrity of receptors; rather it

Figure 8-6 Adaptation in receptor pathways. This illustration shows adaptation of a receptor whose receptive field is located on the fifth finger. Three different levels of stimulus intensity are shown. The decrease in rate of firing is more rapid with the least intense stimulus (A). (From Knibestöl and Valbo, 1970)

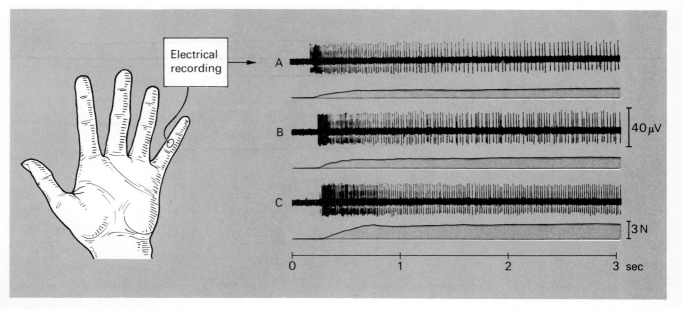

emphasizes the significance of changes of state, or stimulus transients, as the effective properties of stimuli.

The eminent sensory researcher Georg von Békésy, who received the Nobel Prize in 1961, emphasized that adaptation is a form of information suppression that prevents the nervous system from becoming overwhelmed by stimuli that offer very little ''news'' about the world. For example, the pressing of a hair on the leg by pants may be continuous, and we are saved from a constant neural barrage repeating this fact by several suppression mechanisms, including adaptation.

The bases of adaptation include both neural and nonneural events. For example, in some mechanical receptors, adaptation develops from the elasticity of the receptor cell itself. This situation is especially evident in the Pacinian corpuscle, which detects mechanical pressure. Maintained pressure on a corpuscle results in an initial burst of neural activity and a rapid fall to a virtual zero level. The size of this receptor enables experimenters to remove the corpuscle (the accessory cell) and apply the same constant stimulus to the terminal region of the sensory nerve fiber, that is, to bend the tip of the neuron. In this instance maintained mechanical stimulation produces a continuing discharge of nerve impulses. This result suggests that for this receptor adaptation is a property of the nonneural component, the corpuscle. In some receptors adaptation reflects a change in the generator potential of the cell. Changes in this electrical property of a receptor are probably produced by ionic changes that result in hyperpolarization.

Lateral Inhibition

In many cases when a stimulus impinges uniformly on an array of receptors, we perceive the stimulation as being strongest at the edges. For example, Figure 8-7 shows a series of bars, each one a uniform gray. But each bar *appears* to be lighter at its left side, where it touches a darker strip. Contrast also occurs in tactile sensation: If you press the end of a ruler against the skin of your forearm, you will probably feel the pressure of the corners of the ruler more strongly than the pressure all along the line of contact.

This sharpening of perception is based on a neural process called **lateral inhibition;** that is, the neurons in a region are interconnected, either through their own axons or by means of intermediary neurons (interneurons), and each neuron tends to inhibit its neighbors. We saw an example of this in Chapter 5 when we discussed information processing by simple neural circuits (refer to Figure 5-10). Many of these lateral inhibitory connections occur at the periphery or at lower levels of sensory systems, but they can also occur in the brain.

Information Suppression

We have noted that successful adaptation and survival do not depend on exact copying of external and internal stimuli. Rather, our success as a species demands that our sensory systems accentuate, from among the many things happening about us, the important changes of stimuli. Without selectivity we would suffer from an overload of information and would end up with a confusing picture of the world. Suppression of some sensory inputs may also reduce the metabolic expense of nervous system activities. So it appears that, at the least, it would be extravagant to

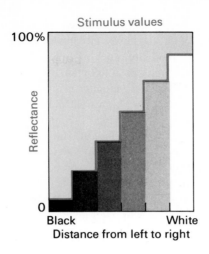

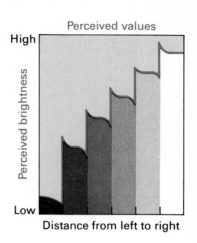

Figure 8-7 Perceptual consequences of lateral inhibition. The series of bars at the left goes from black to white. The values of stimulus intensity are plotted in the center graph; each bar is uniform across its width. The right-hand graph plots perceived brightness; each bar appears brightest at its left edge and darkest at its right.

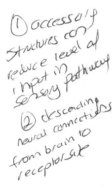

stand unsheltered from excessive sensory inputs (even if we could) and that, at worst, unselected representation of the world would be overwhelmingly confusing.

Information in sensory systems is constrained or suppressed in at least two ways. In many sensory systems, accessory structures can reduce the level of input in the sensory pathway. For example, the closure of the eyelid reduces the level of illumination that reaches the retina. In the auditory system, contraction of the middle ear muscles reduces the intensity of sounds that reach the cochlea. Note that in this form of sensory control the relevant mechanisms change the intensity of the stimulus before it reaches the actual receptors.

A second form of information control probably involves descending neural connections from the brain to the receptor surface. For example, in the auditory system, a small group of cells located in the brain stem have axons that exit from the brain along the pathway of the auditory nerve and connect with the base of the receptor cells. Electrical stimulation of this pathway can attenuate the effects of sounds, although in a more selective manner than the action of middle ear muscles. For years auditory physiologists have sought a connection between the activities of this efferent pathway to hair cells and selective attention. Might receptors for specific frequencies be inhibited by impulses from neural centers? Establishing this connection has proved elusive, but it continues to be a possible functional role for these fibers.

Processing of Sensory Information by Successive Levels of the Central Nervous System

Sensory stimulation leads to responses and perceptions. How do these products come about? In brief, they occur because different levels and regions of the brain process information from receptor surfaces in distinctive ways. These sites of information processing are located along pathways that lead from the sensory surface to the highest levels of the brain, and each sensory system has its own distinctive pathways. Specifically, pathways from receptors lead into the spinal cord or brain stem where connections are made to distinct clusters of nerve cells. These cells in turn have axons that connect to other nerve cell groups, and the eventual terminations of this pathway are sets of neurons in regions of the cerebral cortex. Each sensory modality, such as touch, vision, or audition, has a distinct collection of tracts and stations in the brain that are collectively known as the sensory or afferent pathway for that modality.

Each station in any pathway is thought to accomplish some basic aspect of information processing. For example, there is important information processing at the spinal level. Painful stimulation of the finger will lead to reflex withdrawal of the hand, mediated by spinal circuits. At the brain stem level, other circuits can turn the head toward the source of stimulation. Presumably the most complex aspects of sensory representations occur at the level of the cerebral cortex. A major goal of contemporary studies of sensory processing is to understand the transformations of signals at each level in afferent pathways within the brain.

As sensory information enters the brain, it travels in divergent pathways so that there is more than one representation of that modality at each level of the nervous system. This is illustrated for the somatosensory system in Figure 8-8. This figure shows six different somatosensory regions in the monkey cortex. Each of them is a full orderly representation of either the body surface or deep body tissues. Similar collections of maps are found at different levels of the auditory and visual pathways (C. N. Woolsey, 1981a, b, c). A main way of studying these brain maps is to record the **receptive fields** of the cells that comprise them, so let us see what receptive fields are and how they are measured.

Receptive Fields

The receptive field of a sensory neuron is the stimulus region and the features that cause the cell to alter its firing rate. To determine the receptive field of a neuron,

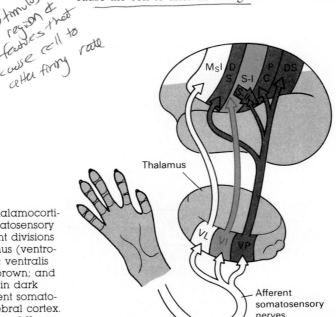

Figure 8-8 Some of the thalamocortical connections of the somatosensory system in monkeys. Different divisions of the ventrolateral thalamus (ventrolateral, VL, shown in white; ventralis intermedius, VI, shown in brown; and ventroposterior, VP, shown in dark gray) send axons to different somatosensory regions of the cerebral cortex. (Adapted from Merzenich and Kaas, 1980)

Figure 8-9 Determining receptive fields in the somatosensory system. This illustration shows the procedures used to determine the receptive field characteristics of somatosensory neurons of the cerebral cortex. Changes in the position of the stimulus are related to the record of response of neural spikes.

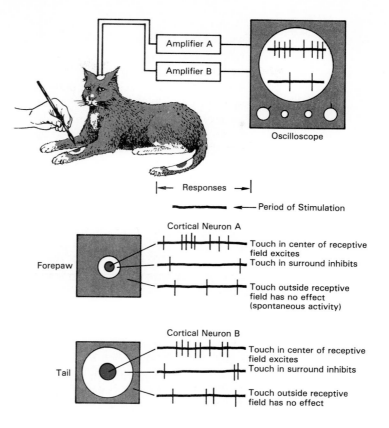

investigators record its electrical responses while they use a variety of stimuli to find what makes the activity of the cell change from its resting rate. Figure 8-9 represents such determination. Neuron A responds to touch on a region of the forepaw. Light touch in the center of the region causes the rate of firing to increase markedly above the resting rate. Light touch in a band that surrounds this central region produces a decrease in firing rate below the resting level. Thus this receptive field includes an excitatory center and an inhibitory surround. Other receptive fields have the reverse organization, with inhibitory centers and excitatory surrounds. Neuron B, a few millimeters away on the somatosensory cortex, responds to stimulation on part of the tail. Receptive fields differ also in their sizes and shapes. They also differ in the quality of stimulation that activates them; for example, some cells respond preferentially to light touch and others to painful stimuli. Although we have taken these examples from neurons in the cortex, receptive fields are studied for cells at all levels, and we will see examples in other brain regions later in this chapter and the next chapter.

Different Cortical Fields Process Different Aspects of Perception

Several lines of evidence indicate that the different cortical areas that represent the same receptive surface actually receive somewhat different inputs, process the information differently, and make different contributions to perceptual experiences and behavioral responses. Different inputs are shown both by the fact that they receive fibers from different divisions of the thalamus (Figure 8-8) and also by the fact that the maps, although orderly, differ in their internal arrangements. Some geographic maps exaggerate a particular aspect; for example, the "New Yorker's map of the United States" magnifies New York while shrinking the rest of the country. Similarly, cortical representations of the body surface enlarge the representation of the hand, but some do so more than others.

In somatosensory cortical regions, area I (S-I in Figure 8-8) maps the contralateral side of the body. Area S-II maps both sides of the body in registered overlay, that is, the left-arm and right-arm representations occupy the same part of the map, and so forth. Some of the somatosensory maps are more sensitive to the skin surface, others to muscles and joints; some of the representations are more sensitive to stationary stimuli, others to movement (Mountcastle, 1984).

It seems likely that different cortical regions are simultaneously processing different aspects of perceptual experience, but the details of this processing are not yet known. In spite of this specialization, it would certainly be incorrect to suppose that a given cortical sensory region receives a packet of information and processes it completely without further communication with other brain regions. For one thing, there are back-and-forth exchanges between cortical and thalamic regions. For another, the different cortical regions for a given modality are interrelated by fibers that make subcortical loops.

Even though each modality is represented by several topographically organized fields that all have direct thalamic input, there are still reasons for referring to one field as primary for each sense: The primary area is the main source of input to the other fields for the same modality, even though they also have direct thalamic inputs. Developmentally the primary area is the first to myelinate. The cytoarchitectural structure of the primary area has the clearest sensory characteristics; these are the small size of neurons and a thick fourth layer. But being first in these ways does not mean that the primary sensory cortex is necessarily simpler or more basic in perceptual functions than the other cortical fields for the same modality.

Discovering the separate and joint contributions of different sensory regions to perception remains a challenge. It appears that recent findings cannot be encompassed by a strict hierarchical model with its schema of primary, secondary, and association areas.

Qualifications About Cortical Maps

Our description of cortical representation of sensory fields may make them seem to be too separate from each other, too fixed and static, so let us qualify this description in some major ways.

There is considerable overlap among representation of different sensory modalities. For example, some cells in a "visual" area respond also to auditory stimuli, and others respond to tactile or vestibular stimuli. This will be taken up in the next section on intermodal or intersensory effects.

There are significant individual differences in cortical maps. Lashley and Clark (1946) plotted the location and extent of striate cortex by anatomical techniques in several spider monkeys and called attention to large individual differences. Van Essen (1981) has used electrophysiological recording to map several visual cortical regions in macaques and has noted individual differences as large as two to one in the size of striate cortex. So when we describe general features of cortical representation, it should not be forgotten that there are individual differences in anatomy that may well determine differences in behavior.

Sensory maps in the brain appear to change with the current state of the individual, including both the motivational state (such as hunger, as we will see in Chapter 13) and the degree of arousal.

Change in response to motivational state

The maps may not be fixed permanently but may change somewhat over time, even in adults. In cases of increased or decreased use of a part of the body, such as certain fingers, the cortical representation has been reported to expand or contract and may show reorganization (Kaas, Merzenich, & Killackey, 1983). The extent to which the cortical representations are dynamic is currently a matter of controversy, and we do not want to anticipate the final resolution of this question. But since the use of the term *map* may have suggested a fixed representation, we want to mention the real possibility that the representation may actually change over time.

not Afp

Intermodal or Intersensory Effects

Many sensory areas in the brain do not exclusively represent a single modality but show a mixture of inputs from different modalities. Individual sensory cells may also respond to stimuli of more than one modality. Thus some ''visual'' cells also respond to auditory or tactile stimuli. There is intersensory convergence at such **polymodal** cells, and they provide a mechanism for intersensory interactions. An example of such intersensory effects is the fact that cats often do not attend to birds unless they can both see and hear them; neither sense alone is sufficient to elicit a response (Meredith & Stein, 1983). Recently investigators have found that many brain cells show very different responses to stimulation of two or more modalities than to stimulation of only one modality. This interaction can take any of several forms. For example, some cells respond only weakly or not at all to a sound or a light but respond strongly when both stimuli are presented at once. Some cells that respond to lights show a weaker response when a sound is also presented. Some cells that respond well to a light respond even more strongly when a sound is also present, although they show no response to the sound alone. To study such effects is much more demanding than to use single stimuli because it requires repeated testing with different combinations of stimuli of different intensities. But such investigation is important to understand several perceptual effects.

For example, some perceptions require combinations of different modalities; thus flavors represent integrations of both tastes and odors. Much of what we ordinarily think of as ''taste'' has a large component of odor. For example, if you block your nose, it is hard to discriminate the flavor of a raw potato from a raw apple. This is why food may lose its flavor when you have a bad cold.

When you have your eyes open, perception of the position of the body is usually determined jointly by visual and vestibular inputs. If you are looking at a target and your head moves, your eyes move within their sockets to compensate and keep your gaze on target. In the absence of gravity, as in space flight, the usual correspondence between vision and the pull of gravity on the body is upset, and the lack of this concordance is probably a major factor in the nausea that many astronauts feel during their first days in space.

In some cases the input from one sensory modality may dominate the input from another. For example, in a movie theater you perceive the sound as coming from the person whom you see speaking on the screen, but if you close your eyes you may realize that the sound is actually coming from a speaker located to one side of the screen. In this case your auditory localization has been overruled by sight.

Visual perception of spatial position, as well as auditory localization, can be strongly influenced by perceived bodily position, as recent experiments reveal (Lackner & Shenker, 1985). In these experiments subjects sat in the dark and estimated the position of the index finger in space. Actually the arm was restrained in a padded support that fixed the elbow in a bent position with the index finger in the midline of the body, about 50 cm ahead of the subject's face. The head was also fixed in position, because the subject clamped his or her jaw on a bite board. Stimulation of the biceps muscle with a mechanical vibrator caused subjects to feel that the arm extended, even though it did not actually move. If a small light was attached to the index finger, in 85% of all trials the subjects reported that the light began to move shortly after the arm started to extend. The light was seen to move in the same direction as subjects felt their arms moving, although on the average the light was not perceived as moving quite as far. The subjects also reported that their eyes moved to follow the light, even though neither the light nor the eyes actually moved. Similarly, if a small loudspeaker emitting clicks was attached to the finger, then subjects reported that the sound began to move shortly after they felt the arm move. And if both a light and a speaker were attached to the finger, both were perceived to move when vibratory stimulation caused illusory movement of the arm. The light and sound had some effect on perception of movement of the arm, too; when the other stimuli were present, the reported movements of the arm were slightly smaller than when light and sound were absent. Thus there were reciprocal effects between these senses.

It appears that some brain maps have characteristics that favor such intersensory integration. Thus in the superior colliculus, which is usually referred to as the midbrain visual center, many cells in the deeper layers respond to tactile or auditory as well as visual stimuli. Furthermore, the organization of the maps for these different modalities is similar; that is, cells that respond to stimulation at a particular position with regard to the animal are in register for the visual and somatic representations. This has been found in reptiles as well as in mammals (Gaither & Stein, 1979). It is not yet clear whether this similarity of organization between reptiles and mammals represents only convergent evolution, or whether it may indicate an ancient plan of brain representation of sensory modalities that was retained in the transition from reptilian to mammalian forms over 180 million years ago. However this correspondence of sensory maps arose, it probably favors intersensory effects and the consistency of spatial perception, whichever senses one is using. Furthermore, the maps for the different senses in the colliculus are also in register with a map of motor responses. This supports quick reflex responses in space, like quickly swatting a mosquito on the back of your hand whether you see it alight or hear its whine or feel it displace a hair.

Attention   The concept of attention is laden with many meanings that are not easy to disentangle. One view emphasizes the state of alertness or vigilance that enables animals to detect signals. In this view attention is a generalized activation that attunes us to inputs. Another view is that attention is the process that allows selection of some sensory inputs from among many competing ones. Some investigators view attention in a more introspective manner, arguing that attention is a state of mental concentration or effort that makes it possible to focus on a particular task. As you see, a notion that may seem self-evident has considerable complexity. The treatment of this state in physiological studies has included measurements ranging from assessments of cerebral blood flow during states of alertness to firing rates of single cells during selective responding to particular stimuli. The role of the brain stem reticular formation in attention has also been the subject of intensive research. Studies of impairment of attention have helped to illuminate the mechanisms of attention.

Cerebral Correlates of Attention

Several kinds of brain measures show correlations with attention and changes in awareness. Measures of cerebral blood flow show shifts to the cortical region involved in attention. Thus there is increased blood flow in the upper parts of the temporal lobe when a subject listens to spoken words. The EEG shows an activation pattern of rapid, small-amplitude waves over the whole skull during attention. When a subject is alertly waiting for a signal to perform an action, a particular scalp potential appears—the contingent negative variation (Figure 8-10). Evoked potentials—those elicited in the EEG by stimuli—are significantly larger when the subject attends to the stimuli than when he or she ignores them.

Recordings from individual brain cells are also being used to find details of attentional mechanisms. In this work monkeys are trained to fixate a spot of light and then to release a lever for reward as soon as the spot dims. Responses are recorded from cortical cells whose receptive fields include the fixation spot; some cells are in the frontal cortex and some in the posterior parietal cortex. Then the situation is complicated by presenting a second spot of light, which falls within the receptive field of the cell whose activity is being recorded. In some cases monkeys are trained to shift their gaze promptly to the second light as soon as the fixation light goes off. About half the visually responsive cells in both the frontal and parietal regions show vigorous responses while the animal is preparing to shift its gaze. In other cases monkeys are trained to keep fixating on the first spot but to release the lever for reward as soon as the second light turns off. Now many of the parietal cells show enhanced responses while the monkey attends to the off-center spot, but the responses of the frontal cells are not enhanced. The investigators concluded that enhancement of the frontal response may reflect transfer of visual information to the oculomotor system, whereas enhancement in the parietal area ''seems to function as a general attention system when the stimulus is important to the animal regardless of the motor strategy the animal uses to handle the stimulus'' (Bushnell, Robinson, & Goldberg, 1978).

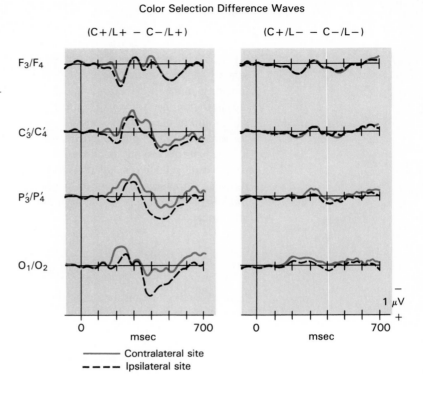

Figure 8-10 Difference ERPs associated with stimuli of attended versus unattended color. Left column shows difference waves reflecting selection for color at the attended location, and right column shows difference waves associated with color selection at the unattended location. The differences are clearly greater at the attended location (left column). This is true for all brain regions from frontal (F) to occipital (O). (Adapted from Hillyard and Munte, 1984)

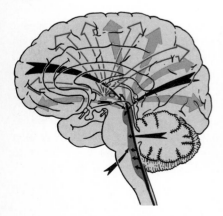

Figure 8-11 Brain stem reticular arousal system. This system, shown in brown, receives input from sensory fibers and from the cerebral cortex (black arrows). It projects widely to the cortex as shown by the open arrows.

Brain Stem Reticular Formation and Attention

As sensory neurons run toward the midbrain and diencephalon, they also send side branches to a special part of the brain stem. This region is the **brain stem reticular formation,** and it plays a major role in attention. (The word *reticular* comes from a Latin term meaning "network," and the name was chosen because this region contains small, densely branching neurons.) The diffuse pathways of the reticular formation allow messages in one sensory channel to arouse wide regions of the brain (Figure 8-11). Electrical stimulation of the reticular formation results in prompt and widespread activation of the EEG. Conversely, damage to the reticular formation or inhibition of its activity by drugs results in a depressed or even comatose individual. The many synaptic interruptions in reticular pathways make this region especially susceptible to influence by neuromodulators and by drugs.

Cortical Regions and Attention

Certain regions of the cerebral cortex have been particularly implicated in attention. The evidence for this comes both from impairment of attention in people and animals with localized cortical damage and from recording electrical activity of cells in different cortical regions while animals attend to stimuli or await stimuli in order to obtain rewards. One cortical region that appears to play a special role in attention is the inferoparietal lobule in the posterior parietal lobe (Figure 8-12). Many cells here

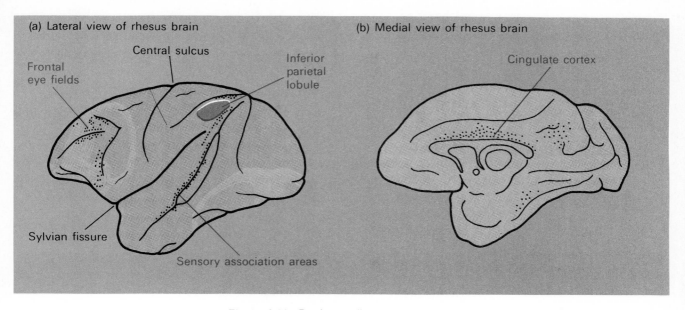

Figure 8-12 Regions of the cortex that are implicated in attention, shown on lateral (a) and medial (b) views of the monkey brain. The inferior parietal lobule (brown) in the posterior parietal lobe seems to play a special role. It has strong connections with the three cortical regions that are shown by stippling. (Adapted from Mesulam et al., 1977)

are polymodal. Some of them are especially responsive when a trained monkey is expecting the appearance of a stimulus (Mountcastle et al., 1981). Lesions of this area in monkeys result in inattention or neglect of stimuli on the contralateral side. (In Chapter 18 we will see that this symptom is especially severe in people with lesions of the right parietal lobe.) The frontal eye fields (see Figure 8-12) seem to be involved in attentive visual exploration of space. The posterior part of the cingulate cortex (around the posterior part of the corpus callosum) has been implicated in motivational aspects of attention. These three cortical areas have especially prominent anatomical connections with each other, and each receives strong input from the reticular formation as well as from sensory fibers (Mesulam, 1981).

Touch and Pain

Touch

Skin surrounds our bodies and provides a boundary with our surroundings. It is a delicate boundary, which harbors an array of sensors that enable us to detect and discriminate among many types of impinging stimuli. All forms of touch from the most delicate movement of a single hair to the most forceful pressing of the flesh are recorded by skin sensors. Among primates a very important aspect of skin sensations is the active manipulation of objects by the hands, which enables identification and manipulation of various forms. The ability to detect heat and cold readily adds to the versatility of the skin. More complex aspects of skin sensations are evident in the worlds of pain that we are all too aware of. In this section we will examine how skin senses work, and later in this chapter we will discuss pain.

Skin Sensations over the Body

Touch is not just "touch"! Careful studies of skin sensations using a variety of stimuli reveal that qualitatively different sensory experiences can be provoked by skin excitation. These include pressure, vibration, tickle, "pins and needles," and more complex dimensions, such as smoothness or wetness. Skin sensations vary not only qualitatively but also spatially across the extent of the body surface. Studies on the "two-point" threshold reveal spatial discrimination differences on the body surface. This measure is readily obtained by determining how far apart two points, such as the tips of two pencils, must be in order to perceive them as separate points. As the two points of the pencils are brought closer together on the body surface, they are perceived as one point. Some parts of the body, such as the lips and fingers, have very low two-point thresholds, whereas other parts, such as the back or leg, have very high two-point thresholds.

What Is in Skin?

The average person has about 10 to 20 square feet of skin. Skin is not a simple structure but is made up of three separate layers, with the relative thickness of each layer varying over the body surface. The outermost layer—the epidermis—is the thinnest and varies most widely, ranging from a very flexible relatively thick layer on the surface of the hands and feet to the delicate outer layer of the eyelid. Each day millions of new cells are added to the outermost layer. The middle layer—the dermis—contains the rich network of nerve fibers and blood vessels in addition to the network of connective tissue called collagen, which gives skin its strength. The character of skin is further complicated by other specialized outgrowths, such as hair or feathers, claws, hooves, and horns. The deepest layer—subcutaneous tissue—contains fat cells, which act as thermal insulators and cushion internal organs from mechanical shocks.

Within the skin there are several receptors with distinctive shapes (Iggo, 1982). One type we have already mentioned—the Pacinian corpuscles. These are found deep within the dermis and are the largest receptors found in some skin areas, around muscles and joints, and within the gut. These are fast-responding receptors whose excitation is delivered to fast-conducting nerve fibers. The Pacinian corpuscles respond accurately to vibration of the skin over a wide range of stimulus frequencies, but they show little evidence of discrimination of spatial stimuli. Another type of receptor, called Meissner's corpuscle, is especially densely distributed in skin regions where quite sensitive spatial discriminations are possible, but these receptors respond poorly to vibrating stimuli. The regions where Meissner's corpuscles predominate include the fingertips, tongue, and lips. Also found in these regions are oval-shaped receptors called Merkel's discs, which are sometimes found in bundles where they are especially sensitive to touch. Detection of heat and cold at the skin has been associated with activation of two other receptor types—Ruffini endings and Krause end bulbs. Some investigators, however, have cautioned us about too readily equating sensory categories and distinct structural classes of receptors (Melzack & Wall, 1962). The psychological categories of skin sensations have been developed independently of structural categories or receptor types, and it is not yet clear whether these two can be related to each other in a simple way.

A new technique for recording from human peripheral nerve—called microneuronography—has allowed researchers new insights into mechanisms of touch perception in humans. Now it is possible to relate measures of tactile sensitivity in alert subjects to nerve impulse activity in their peripheral nerves. Some findings about the mechanism of perception of the human hand show how this technique is used. Within the smooth skin of the hand, it has been estimated that there are 17,000 tactile units comprised of four main types that are distinguished by the size and shape of their receptive fields and various functional properties, such as the response to maintained stimulation (adaptation) (Valbo & Johansson, 1984). Two of these groups of peripheral nerve fibers have small receptive fields that are especially dense at the fingertips. One of these two groups shows rapid adaptation to maintained skin indentation, while the other group continues to respond as mechanical stimulation is maintained. It is believed that each of these groups involves a different end-organ receptor in the skin. The other two main groups of fibers show very large receptive fields—in some cases they may encompass an entire finger. The fibers with large receptive fields also include a fast-adapting and a slow-adapting subgroup. The slow-adapting, large receptive field group of nerve fibers also shows special responsiveness to mechanical stimuli that move across the skin in particular directions. A summary of these data is presented in Figure 8-13.

Microneuronographic studies have revealed some striking insights about tactile sensitivity. Fast-adapting fibers have very low thresholds to mechanical stimuli. In fact, a single nerve impulse in some of these fibers can lead to touch perception. A single electrical stimulus can also be detected.

Information Transmission from Skin to Brain

Inputs from skin surfaces are directed to the spinal cord. Within the cord, as shown in Figure 8-14, somesthetic fibers ascend to the brain in at least two major pathways: (1) the dorsal column system shown to the right in Figure 8-14 and (2) the anterolateral system (also referred to as spinothalamic). Inputs to the dorsal column system enter the spinal cord and ascend to the medulla, where they synapse at the gracile and cuneate nuclei. The axons of postsynaptic cells form a fiber bundle that crosses in the brain stem to the contralateral side and ascends to a group of nuclei of the thalamus. Outputs of the thalamus are directed to postcentral cortical regions referred to as the somatosensory cortex. The anterolateral or spinothalamic system has a different arrangement. Inputs from the skin to this system synapse on cells in the spinal cord, whose axons cross to the contralateral side of the spinal cord and ascend in the anterolateral columns of the spinal cord. At least some of the input to this system is related to pain and temperature sensations.

The skin surface can be divided into bands, or **dermatomes,** according to which spinal nerve carries most axons from each region (Figure 8-15). (A dermatome is a strip of skin innervated by a particular spinal root.) The pattern of dermatomes is

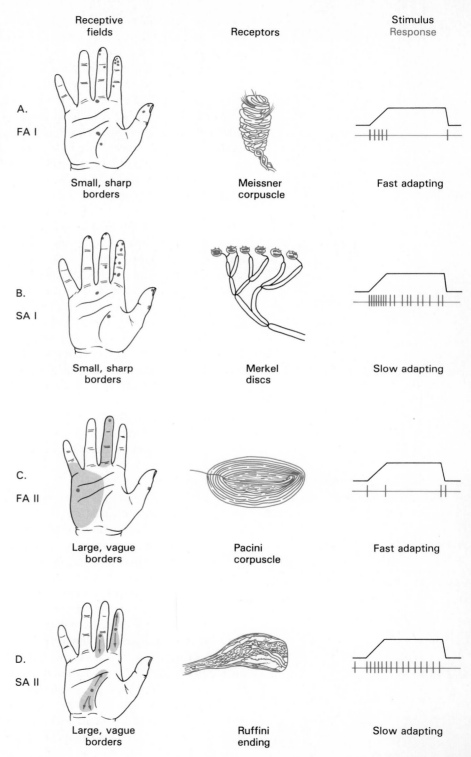

Figure 8-13 Properties of skin mechanoreceptors in the human hand related to touch. Left column shows receptive field size. Middle column shows type of skin receptor. Right column shows stimulus marker and electrophysiological response. Each row shows characteristics of types of tactile units. (A) Fast-adapting type 1 fibers (FA I). (B) Slow-adapting type 1 fibers (SA I). (C) Fast-adapting type 2 fibers (FA II). (D) Slow-adapting type 2 fibers (SA II). (Adapted from Valbo and Johansson, 1984)

Receptive fields

Receptors

Stimulus
Response

A.
FA I

Small, sharp borders

Meissner corpuscle

Fast adapting

B.
SA I

Small, sharp borders

Merkel discs

Slow adapting

C.
FA II

Large, vague borders

Pacini corpuscle

Fast adapting

D.
SA II

Large, vague borders

Ruffini ending

Slow adapting

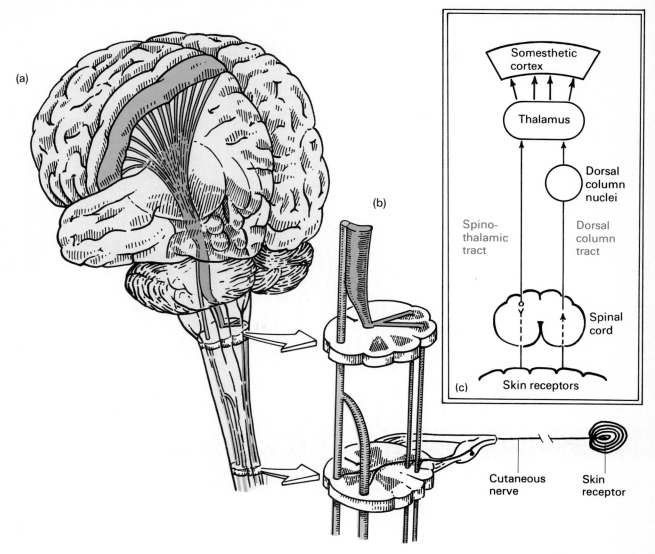

Figure 8-14 The somesthetic system. (a) General view of the system including ascending spinal tracts, thalamic relay, and primary cortical representation. The spinal tracts are seen in greater detail in (b), including crossed and uncrossed spinal pathways. All afferent messages cross before reaching the thalamus. The main pathways are diagrammed in (c).

hard to understand when seen for a standing person, but the pattern becomes comprehensible when depicted on a person in a quadrupedal posture, as shown at the middle of Figure 8-15.

All brain regions concerned with somatic sensation have their cells arranged according to the plan of the body surface. Thus each region is a map of the body in which the relative areas devoted to bodily regions reflect the density of body inner-

Figure 8-15 Bands of skin or dermatomes. Each dermatome is served by
a different spinal nerve. The main
regions of the spinal cord (a) serve
the main groups of dermatomes (b).

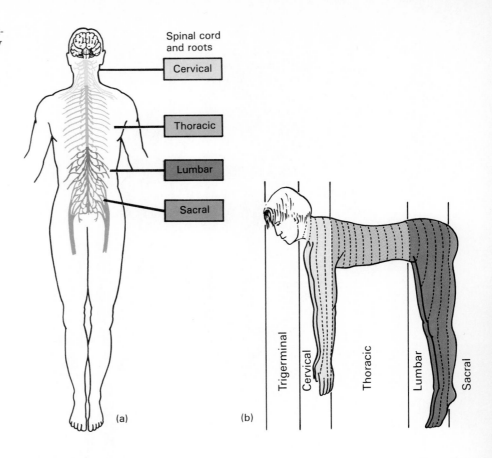

vations. Since many fibers are involved with the sensory surface of the head, especially the lips, there is a particularly large number of cells concerned with the head;
in contrast, far fewer fibers innervate the trunk, and the number of cells involved in
representing the trunk are far fewer. The relative sizes of the cortical representations
are shown in the grotesque sensory homunculus in Figure 8-16.

Cortical Columns:
Specificity for Modality
and Location

We saw in Chapter 2 that the cerebral cortex is organized into vertical columns of
neurons, and now we find more about the functional significance of these **cortical
columns.** It had long been known that the cortex contains large functional regions,
such as the somatosensory areas and the visual areas, and that each of these regions
is a sort of map of the sensory world. Then, in pioneering work beginning in the
1950s, Mountcastle (1984) mapped the receptive fields of individual neurons in
somatosensory cortex using microelectrodes. This work revealed that each cortical
cell not only has a precise receptive field, but that it responds to only one submodal-
ity. For example, a particular cell responds only to a given kind of stimulation, such
as light touch, and another cell responds only to deep pressure. Furthermore,
Mountcastle found to his surprise that within a given column of neurons, all the

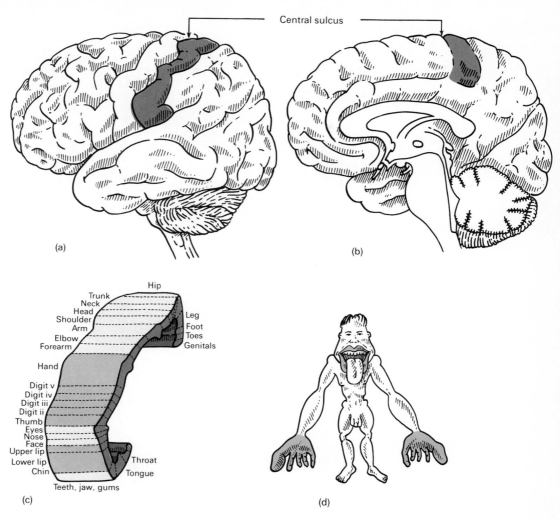

Figure 8-16   Representation of the body surface in the primary somatosensory cortex. Location of the primary somatosensory cortex on the lateral surface (a) and on the medial surface (b) of the human brain. The order and size of representations of different regions of skin are shown in (c). The homunculus (d) depicts the body surface with each area drawn in proportion to the size of its representation in the primary somatosensory cortex.

cells respond to the same location and quality of stimulation. All the columns in a band of adjacent columns respond to the same quality of stimulation, and then another band is devoted to another kind of stimulation. This columnar organization is diagramed in Figure 8-17, which depicts some of the columns in the somatosensory cortex that represent the fingers of the left hand.

Each column extends from the surface of the cortex (Layer I) down to the base of the cortex (Layer VI). Area 3b of the cortex receives input from receptors near

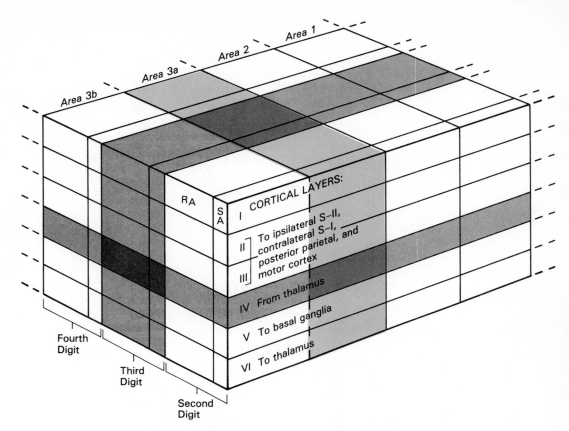

Figure 8-17 Columnar organization of somatosensory cortex, illustrated diagram-matically for a region of cortex that represents some of the fingers of the left hand. The different regions of somatosensory cortex—Brodmann's areas 3b, 3a, 2, and 1— receive their main inputs from different kinds of receptors. Thus 3b receives most of its projections from the superficial skin, including both rapidly adapting (RA) and slowly adapting (SA) receptors, and these can be seen to be represented in sepa-rate cortical columns or slabs. Area 3a receives input from receptors in the muscle spindles; it is shown in light brown in the diagram. The cortex is seen to be orga-nized vertically in columns and horizontally in layers. Layer IV, where input from the thalamus arrives to the cortex, is shaded in gray. (Adapted from Kaas et al., 1979)

the surface of the skin, including both rapidly adapting (RA) and slowly adapting (SA) receptors. Each of these types of receptors feeds information to different cortical columns. Moving the stimulation to a slightly different region on the skin shifts the excitation to a different cortical column. Area 3a of cortex contains cells that respond to stimulation of the stretch receptors in the muscles, and within area 3a each change in location means stimulation of a different column. Thus the col-umns code for both location and quality of stimulation. In Chapter 9 we will see that the same kind of columnar organization also holds for the visual and auditory areas of the cerebral cortex. The discovery of the columnar organization of sensory cortex has been called ''perhaps the most important single advance in cortical physiology in the past several decades'' (Kandel, 1985).

Localization on the Body Surface

The surface of the body is represented at each level of the somatosensory nervous system by an organization of nerve cells that provides a spatial map of the body surface. The first stage of this map of body position is seen in the organization of individual dermatomes at a spinal level. Although individual dermatomes overlap to some extent, there is an orderly arrangement along the length of the spinal cord. At various levels of the brain, the surface of the body is again represented by an orderly map of nerve cells. Thus the sensory topography of relevant thalamic cells and cortical areas preserves body topography.

The extreme detail of somatosensory system mapping of certain body surfaces is shown in work on ''cortical barrels'' in rodents (T. Woolsey et al., 1983). Sections of rat somatosensory cortex obtained by slicing the cortex in a plane tangential to the surface reveal some unusual groupings of cells in circular patterns. Successive sections of tissue in this plane suggested an analogy to the sides of a barrel, so these groupings were named cortical barrels. The wall of the barrel consists of tightly packed cell bodies surrounding a less dense area.

Electrical recordings of cells in a barrel revealed the startling fact that each barrel is activated by one whisker on the opposite side of the head. Further, the layout of whiskers on the face of the animal (Figure 4-24) corresponds to the layout of barrels in the cortex. (Whiskers are important to rodents in finding their way through narrow passages in the dark. In Chapter 4 we noted the importance of intact facial whiskers for the development or maintenance of cortical barrels. Rats whose whiskers were removed early in life did not form cortical barrels.)

Somatosensory Perception of Form

The functions of the somatosensory cortex in discriminating forms have been studied in monkeys both by observing effects of lesions in this region and by recording from individual neurons while the monkeys' hands were stimulated. Lesions impaired the ability of the animal to discriminate the form, size, and roughness/smoothness of tactile objects (Norrsell, 1980). Each of these impairments could be localized to a subregion of somatosensory cortex: Lesions in one area affected mainly the discrimination of texture; lesions in a second area impaired mainly the discrimination of angles; and lesions in a third area affected all forms of tactile discrimination (Randolf & Semmes, 1974).

Temporal/spatial aspects of touch have been studied using complex stimuli (Darian-Smith et al., 1980). In this research metal strips of varied widths and spacing were moved at different rates of speed under the fingertips of monkeys while recordings were made from sensory nerves. No single fiber could give an accurate record of each ridge and depression in the stimulus. But the ensemble of fibers provided an accurate representation, especially at optimal spacings and speed of presentation of the stimulus. Spatial discrimination of more complex stimuli is being studied in a similar way, using stimuli such as Braille dots or other small forms.

Cells in the somatosensory cortex can be classified into several categories according to the characteristics of their receptive fields (Iwamura & Tanaka, 1978). About one-quarter of the cells responded to simple pressure stimulation of points on the skin. Another quarter responded best to specialized stimulation of the skin (for example, by a moving probe or by a narrow band or rod). Another quarter of the cells could be activated either by stimulation of the skin or by movement of one or more finger joints. About one-eighth of the cells responded specifically to manipulation of joints. The remainder of the cells could not be activated when the experimenter stimulated either skin or joints, but some of these cells responded strongly when the animal grasped an object and manipulated it.

Some of these "active touch" cells had highly specific response characteristics. For example, one unit responded actively when the monkey felt a straight-edged ruler or a small rectangular block, but it did not respond when the monkey grasped a ball or bottle; the presence of two parallel edges appeared to be crucial for effective activation of this cell. In the same electrode penetration, another cell was found that responded best when the monkey grasped a ball, responded well to a bottle, but did not respond at all when the monkey manipulated a rectangular block. Grasping objects causes complex patterns of stimulation of skin receptors and joint receptors. This information about cutaneous and joint stimulation must reach many cortical units. Apparently different cells require particular combinations of input if they are to respond. These units with complex receptive fields in the somatosensory cortex are somewhat like units with complex visual or auditory receptive fields. These complex somatosensory units may be involved in discrimination and recognition of objects by touch, but more research will be required to learn how they function in somatosensory perception.

In human observers the posterior part of the parietal cortex is activated during exploration of objects by touch (Roland & Larsen, 1976). This was found by recording blood flow in the cortex under three conditions:

1. The experimenter moved the passive hand of the observer over the stimulus object.
2. The person moved his hand energetically but did not touch an object.
3. The person explored an object by touch.

Only in the last of these conditions was there specific activation of the posterior parietal cortex, so this region may be particularly involved in active touch.

Pain

Pain is an unpleasant experience that can cause great suffering. It then seems hard to imagine that it has a "biological role." Is it some perverse revenge of evolutionary gnomes?

Clues to the adaptive significance of pain can be gleaned from the study of rare individuals who never experience pain. Such people have a congenital insensitivity or indifference to pain. In some cases they can discriminate between the touch of the point and head of a pin, but a pinprick is painless. Case descriptions note that their bodies show extensive scarring from numerous injuries (e.g., Manfredi et al., 1981). Deformation of fingers, hands, and legs is common. Most of these people die young, frequently from extreme trauma to the body. These cases suggest that pain guides adaptive behavior by providing indications of harm. Such experiences are so commonplace for most of us that we easily forget the guiding role of pain: The experience of pain leads to behavior that removes the body from a source of injury.

Psychological Aspects of Pain

In some parts of the world, people endure with stoic indifference rituals, including body mutilation, that would cause most other humans to cry in pain. Incisions of the face, hands, arms, legs, or chest, walking on hot coals, and other treatments clearly harmful to the body can be part of the ritual. Comparable experiences are common in more ordinary circumstances, such as the highly ''charged'' athlete who continues to play a game with a broken arm or leg. War experiences also highlight the complexity of the pain experience. Beecher (1959) has indicated that soldiers injured in battle ask for drugs to control pain at a rate far less than that of civilians sustaining comparable injuries. His explanation for the difference is that the meaning of the experience is very different to each group. To the soldier a severe injury can signal relief from combat, if only for a while. In contrast, similar injuries to a civilian can signal economic loss and personal inconvenience. Learning, experience, emotion, and touch and culture all seem to affect pain in striking ways.

Detailed psychological studies of the experience of pain further emphasize its complexity. The mere description of pain as mild or intense is inadequate to describe the pain that is distinctive to particular disease or injury conditions. Further, in order to assess pain-relief intervention, some kind of quantitative measurement is necessary. Several approaches to pain measurement in humans and other animals appear in contemporary research (Chapman et al., 1985). One example is evident in the work of Melzack (1984), who has provided a detailed quantitative rating scale that examines the language of pain. This rating scale—called the McGill Pain Questionnaire—consists of a list of words arranged into classes that describe three different aspects of the pain experience: (1) the sensory quality, (2) the affective quality, and (3) an overall evaluative quality. Patients are asked to select the set of words that best describes their pain, and within the selected sets, to identify the word that is relevant to their condition. Quantitative treatment of this scale includes adding up the number of selected words and the rank value. One of the interesting aspects of the scale is that it can distinguish among pain syndromes, meaning that patients use a distinctive constellation of words to describe a particular pain experience. For example, data obtained from different patient groups show that the pain of toothache is described differently from the pain of arthritis, which in turn is described differently from menstrual pain. It is a distinctive grouping of descriptors that distinguishes different syndromes rather than a simple dimension of intensity. In fact, descriptors chosen by patients permit a diagnostic differentiation among a group of eight pain syndromes (Melzack, 1984). Changes in patients' descriptor patterns also permit physicians to assess the effectiveness of pain control treatments. The simply query by a physician, ''Is the pain still there?'' may soon be replaced by a more detailed analysis that will provide better clues about the effectiveness of procedures used to control the suffering of pain. Pain is a complex perception, and our measurement of it needs to recognize the complexity.

Laboratory research studies with pain stimulation of normal volunteers has employed other methods and measures. Early research work emphasized measurement of "pain threshold," which is that point on a range of stimuli where pain is first sensed. Other measures in studies where a continuum of pain stimuli is presented include "pain tolerance" level; this is the most intense stimulus the subject is willing to sustain. Both these measures are strongly influenced by psychological states such as anxiety, expectancy, and the subtle aspects of instructions from experimenters. Further, some researchers believe that these measures are not very sensitive to pain-relief interventions that are very effective in clinical situations. Recently, laboratory research methods have relied more on the type of assessments and measures that are found in clinical research. A simple situation commonly used in this type of laboratory research includes asking the subject to rate a pain stimulus on a scale of pain intensity. In some situations the subject indicates the extent of pain by moving a lever over a range which on one side signifies "no pain" and at the opposite side indicates "severe pain." The subject moves the lever whenever he or she feels a change, and this provides an assessment of the temporal course of pain and the changes produced by pain-relief efforts. More elaborate psychophysical techniques have also been employed in laboratory studies of pain, including signal detection methods.

Advances in pain research, including the development of effective drug intervention, depend to a great extent on basic research using animals. In addition, understanding pain in animals offers a distinctive insight into their adaptive behaviors. Comparative observations of pain behavior in humans and other animals led Dennis and Melzack (1983) to raise several interesting speculations about pain expression. They argue that pain involves two different dimensions—actual tissue trauma and threat. Pain associated with body injury or trauma leads to a maintained neural input from the injured region. The role of this signal is to foster behavior that aids the restorative and healing process, which includes a wide array of behavioral changes including sleep, locomotor activity, grooming, feeding, and drinking. Dennis and Melzack suggest that the appropriate behavioral response to trauma may be relative inactivity. In contrast with actual injury or trauma, the pain associated with threat of tissue damage may activate quite a different behavioral system. In the case of threat, pain develops at the initial contact with the noxious stimulus which, if maintained, would produce tissue damage. Pain perception in this case can minimize the effect of the offending stimulus by evoking vigorous activity that moves the organism from the noxious condition. These two different behavioral dimensions of pain perception may be related to the multiple pain pathways ascending in the spinal cord and brain stem, an issue that is discussed later in this section.

Dennis and Melzack (1983) note another interesting aspect to pain expression, notably, the value of certain aspects of pain expression that seem to serve as a social signal to other animals. For example, what would seem to be the adaptive value of screeching after a painful stimulus? They argue that such expression probably is significant for both species and individual survival. It signals the potential of harm to other nearby members of the same species; further, it might release care-giving behaviors of conspecifics, such as grooming, defense, and feeding, that enhance the survival of the victim.

Pathways and Pain

Contemporary studies of pain mechanisms have described the characteristics of receptors in the skin that transmit pain information and the relevant pathways of the central nervous system. There remain many unknowns in our understanding of pain pathways, and research continues to elaborate on the complexity of the distribution of neural activity initiated by pain stimuli. In this section we will discuss some features of peripheral and central nervous system pathways that mediate pain.

Peripheral Mechanisms of Pain

In most cases the initial stimulus for pain is the partial destruction of or injury to tissue adjacent to certain nerve fibers. This tissue change results in the release of a chemical substance or substances that most likely activate pain fibers in the skin. Various substances have been suggested as the chemical mediators of pain. They include histamine, various proteolytic enzymes, and prostaglandins—a group of unusual hormones. Some researchers have isolated other substances that are associated with the inflammation that accompanies pain (Granstrom, 1983). This is a very important area that may lead to the development of new pain-relieving drugs that act at the periphery.

Are there peripheral receptors and nerve fibers that are specialized for the signaling of noxious stimulation? Over the years this issue has generated considerable controversy. Some researchers have argued that there are no specialized receptors or fibers that respond to noxious stimulation but rather that pain is initiated by some pattern of stimulation of a broad class of peripheral afferent fibers. Other researchers have argued that pain involves a specialized class of slower conducting afferent fibers. Contemporary research reported by Perl (1984) has clarified this issue. He has shown that there are several populations of peripheral afferent fibers that respond to noxious stimulation. One class includes myelinated, high-threshold mechanoreceptors. However, the most common pain receptors of the skin are the terminals of a group of thin, unmyelinated fibers (C-fibers). These respond to strong mechanical stimulation and other noxious stimuli such as heat (Figure 8-18). Repetitive activation of these fibers by noxious stimulation can lower thresholds considerably, a kind of sensitization to noxious stimuli. Thus contemporary research has clearly established that there are specific groups of nociceptors—receptors that respond selectively to noxious stimulation. Information about pain is then transmitted in specialized pain fibers.

Central Nervous System Pathways and Pain

Afferent fibers from the periphery that carry nociceptive information terminate within the superficial layers of the dorsal horn of the spinal cord. Some of these nociceptive cells of the spinal cord are strongly modulated by systems of fibers that originate in various brain regions, providing a basis for the relief of pain. This is discussed in the sections immediately following. There are several distinct tracts in the spinal cord that ascend to the brain carrying pain information (see Figure 8-19). Especially prominent among these is the spinothalamic tract. Pain fibers entering the spinal cord synapse on dorsal horn neurons whose axons cross the spinal cord

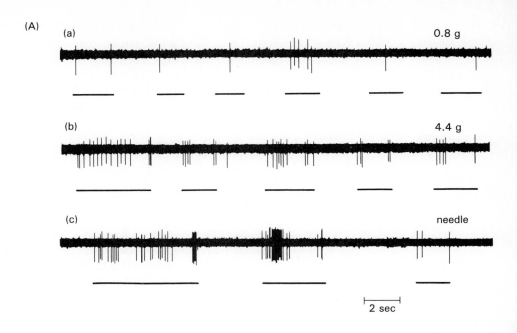

(A)

(a)   0.8 g

(b)   4.4 g

(c)   needle

2 sec

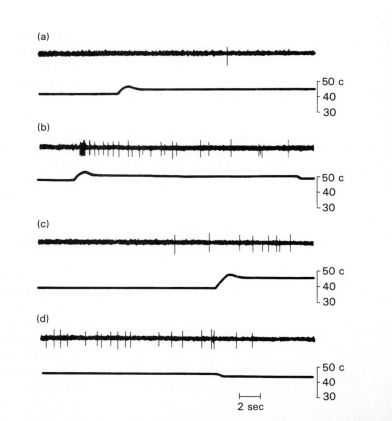

Figure 8-18 (A) Responses of a C-fiber polymodal receptor to mechanical stimulation of the skin. *Bars* indicate approximate time of skin contact at one spot of receptive field. (a) Von Frey stimulator bending at 0.8 g. (b) Von Frey stimulator bending at 4.4 g. (c) Needle pressed hard enough to penetrate skin. (From Bessou and Perl, with permission) (B) Responses of a C-fiber polymodal nociceptor to cutaneous heating (same unit as in Figure A). *Upper traces:* Recording from afferent fiber. *Lower traces:* Temperature of the thermode (2 mm^2 contact) on the receptive field. (a) Initial heating. (b) Begins 10 s after (a). (c, d) Continuous record after thermode had passively cooled from heating in (b). (From Bessou and Perl, 1969, with permission)

(B)

(a)

50 c
40
30

(b)

50 c
40
30

(c)

50 c
40
30

(d)

50 c
40
30

2 sec

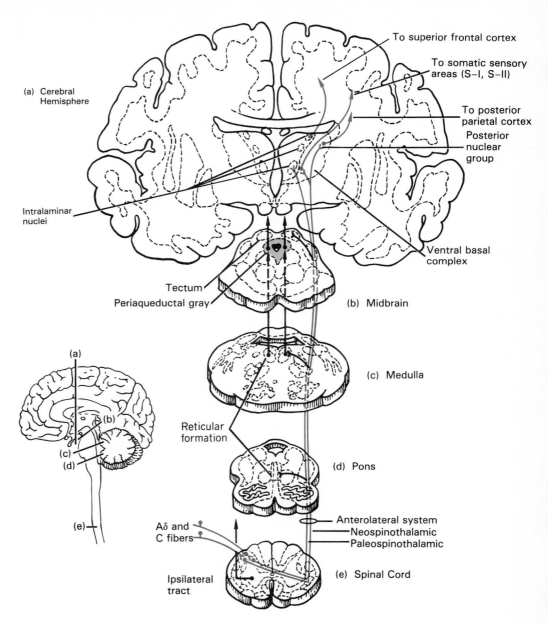

Figure 8-19 Pain pathways in the central nervous system.

and terminate in several nuclei of the thalamus. Several other pain pathways have been identified within the spinal cord. The pain response properties of various parts of these pathways have been clearly established; much like peripheral fibers, there are many cells at different levels of the central nervous system that respond preferentially to intense mechanical stimuli and other sources of pain. One interesting and persistently puzzling aspect of pain pathways is that their interruption reduces pain perception only in a transient manner. After a pathway in the spinal cord is cut, pain is diminished only to return after an interval of weeks or months. The usual way of interpreting these data is that pain perception is strengthened in the remaining intact pathways. However, there is more to the story of pathways of pain, as we will see next.

A further complexity in the properties of central nervous system pain pathways is related to the complexity of the pain experience itself. Some researchers have suggested that the pain experience has a dual character. One aspect is the "sensory-discriminative" feature—the perception that a painful event has occurred and the detection of the place(s) where it was initiated and the character of the event that produced the noxious experience. Another aspect of the perception of noxious events has been referred to as the "motivational-affective" component of pain—the emotional feature that leads to species-typical defense and escape behaviors (Casey, 1980). Some separateness of brain pathways mediating these different aspects of pain has been demonstrated, using the combined techniques of brain stimulation and nerve cell recordings. Some researchers have shown that within the brain stem there are sites where electrical stimulation elicits escape behavior much like that provoked by pain stimuli. Further, nerve cells in this region are preferentially sensitive to noxious stimulation. Finally, the depiction of brain pathways for pain is also complicated by an array of brain sites that modulate pain in a profound manner. The description of pain control systems has led to new hope that we may eventually be able to control pain. The following sections explore this theme.

Control of Pain: Mechanisms and Pathways

Relief from the suffering of pain has long been a dominant concern of humans. Throughout history different remedies have been offered. Renewed attention to pain relief arose following an insightful paper presented by Wall and Melzack (1965), who suggested that pain was subject to many modulating influences including some that acted as "gates" controlling the transmission of pain information from the spinal cord to the brain. In addition, research activities in this area intensified as we became more aware of the limited repertoire available to control pain. Developments within the past twenty years arising from both the study of human pain syndromes and basic animal research have led to some fascinating ideas about pain and its relief. In this section we will describe some of the main thrusts of contemporary efforts in this area.

Opiates and Pain Relief

Over the centuries opium has been admired for its pain-relieving effects. Opium, derived from the seed pod of a poppy plant, is the source of morphine, which is the most potent form of pharmacological control of pain that is available. For years researchers attempted to determine how pain control is achieved by opiate drugs, and success was finally achieved when scientists showed that the brain contained natural opiatelike substances. This finding inspired the view that the brain possesses intrinsic mechanisms that control the transmission of pain information. In effect the brain might modulate pain in a manner akin to that produced by exogenous opiates such as morphine. Several classes of endogenous opioids have now been discovered, as was discussed in Chapter 6, and various ideas about how these substances fit in the circuitry of pain information have been presented (Basbaum & Fields, 1984). In this section we describe some of the newer observations on brain controls of pain.

As we noted in Chapter 6, there are three distinct families of endogenous opioid-like substances: the enkephalins, the dynorphins, and β-endorphin. These substances are differently distributed in the brain, although their concentrations in the brain stem have especially drawn interest because these regions were the first to be implicated in pain control. Early observations by several investigators showed that stimulation of the periaqueductal gray area of the brain stem produced potent analgesia in rats. The anatomy of this region is shown in Figure 8-20. Injection of opiates into this area accomplished the same result, suggesting that the region contained synaptic receptors for opiatelike substances. Inputs to the periaqueductal gray area are quite diverse and include axons arising from some cerebral cortical sites,

Figure 8-20 Circuit of pain inhibition. The right-hand side shows details of synaptic interactions at each level. (Adapted from Basbaum and Fields, 1984)

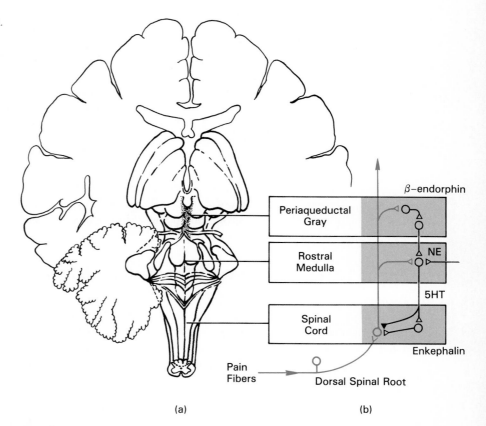

(a)   (b)

amygdala, and hypothalamus. Most important, there is a strong input from the spinal cord, which presumably delivers nociceptive information. A model of brain stem control of pain transmission in the spinal cord has been presented by Basbaum and Fields (1978, 1984). Their proposed circuitry is shown in Figure 8-20b. According to this model, excitation of periaqueductal gray neurons leads via endorphin-containing neurons to neurons in the medulla. In the rostral medulla, these descending influences activate serotonin-containing neurons that descend into the spinal cord and inhibit neurons that transmit information from the periphery. In this way, pain information is blocked by a direct gating action in the spinal cord. Electrical stimulation of the descending tract elicits inhibition of the response of spinal cord sensory relay cells to noxious stimulation of the skin. They offer considerable supporting evidence for this model, including the anatomical and physiological demonstration of pathways that descend from the brain stem to various levels of the spinal cord. The neuropharmacology of this proposed circuit is complex, and additional research is needed to elaborate on many of the details of descending inhibitory mechanisms.

Pain Relief from Electrical Stimulation of the Skin

Human history is filled with examples of the use of strange techniques to achieve relief from pain. Certainly one of the more unusual procedures involves the administration of electrical currents to the body. Centuries ago this included the application of electric fish or eels to sites of pain. More recently, a new procedure called transcutaneous electrical nerve stimulation (TENS) has gained prominence as a way to suppress certain types of pain that have proven difficult to control. TENS involves the delivery of electrical pulses through electrodes attached to the skin, which excite nerves that supply the region to which pain is referred. The stimulation itself does not produce pain but rather a sense of tingling. In some cases dramatic relief of pain can outlast the duration of stimulation by a factor of hours! The best pain relief is produced when the electrical stimulation is delivered close to the source of pain. Especially successful pain suppression has been achieved with this procedure when it is used with patients whose pain is derived from peripheral nerve injuries. The analgesic action of this technique is at least partially mediated by endogenous opioids since naloxone administration partially blocks the analgesic action of TENS.

Pain Relief from Mechanical Stimulation

Painful accidental injuries to the body are a common feature of our existence; picture the last time you stubbed your toe on a piece of furniture. In addition to a string of expletives, these situations lead to the self-administration of skin stimulation produced by vigorous rubbing of the injured area. Of course, there are many physiological aspects to such ''first aid,'' but is it possible that skin stimulation following an injury produces an analgesic response? Some recent research shows that a special type of tactile stimulus—vibratory stimulation—can alleviate some types of clinical and experimental pain in humans.

A large-scale study by Lundeberg (1983) using patients with either chronic or acute pain systematically explored pain alleviation by vibratory stimulation applied to the skin. In this study acute-pain patients were defined as those suffering from pain for less than 14 days, while chronic-pain patients were those who had been experiencing pain for 6 months to 22 years. Pain was assessed in several ways. The McGill Pain Assessment Questionnaire was filled out by patients in addition to a simple seven-point scale (0 = no pain, 6 = excruciating pain). Subjective assessment of pain was also measured by a rating system that consisted of a simple lever that patients could move from a neutral position to one side when pain was reduced or to the other side when pain was increased. The treatment in these studies consisted of the application of an electromechanical vibrator to different body sites depending on the apparent origin of the pain. The study included a wide array of disorders. Comparisons of pain relief were made with the effectiveness of electrical stimulation of the skin (TENS), aspirin, and a kind of placebo vibrator in which the sounds of vibration were apparent but actual vibration was not produced. Usually vibratory stimulation was applied for prolonged periods; a 45-minute stimulus period was commonly used. In a large percentage of both chronic- and acute-pain patients, pain reduction was noted; the duration of pain relief ranged from 3 to 12 hours. The best results were obtained with 100- to 200-Hz stimuli applied with moderate pressure to the skin surface (see Figure 8-21). This method of pain relief was as effective as the TENS procedure.

A detailed psychophysical study of the method using normal subjects has been presented in further research (Bini et al., 1984). In this study pain was induced in volunteer subjects by electrical stimulation through an electrode placed directly into the median nerve at the wrist. Pain induced by this method usually was referred to the finger. Vibratory stimuli were applied to the region of the finger where pain was perceived. Subjects reported their estimates of the magnitude of the pain by moving a lever along a scale that ranged from 0 to 5. Nerve stimulation was administered at an intensity that the subject indicated was the highest "bearable." Vibratory skin stimulation was then applied, and subjects indicated any change in pain by movements of their rating lever. Striking analgesia was evident when vibratory stimuli were applied in the region of the skin area of projected pain. Analgesic effects were not evident when vibratory stimulation took place outside the area of projected pain. Other skin treatments, such as brushing, pressure, or cooling, had much less of an analgesic effect, leading to the conclusion that vibratory stimulation is extremely effective in alleviating pain.

Figure 8-21 (Left) Experimental setup for application of vibratory stimuli to a facial pain area. Subject moves lever to indicate pain change. (Right) The effect of vibratory stimulation on pain in the upper left jaw. Vibratory stimuli are applied for 1, 5, 10, 15, or 30 minutes, respectively. Pain reduction is indicated by downward deflection (100 percent indicates complete relief of pain) and upward deflection indicates increase in subjective pain intensity. Horizontal bars within figure indicate duration of vibratory stimulation. (Adapted from Lundeberg, 1983)

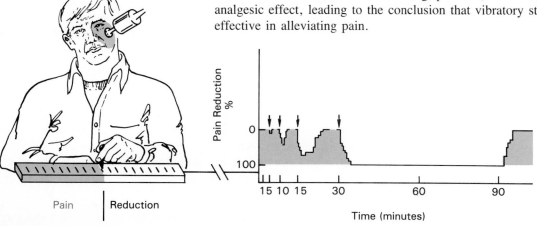

Placebos

Scientists are skeptical souls who are inclined to regard miraculous cures with a
critical eye. Over the years one of the realms that has particularly elicited skepticism
is the action of placebos in controlling pain. The word *placebo* is derived from a
Latin word that means ''I shall please,'' and it came to be used to describe something given to a patient to please rather than to cure. It has always been viewed as
a kind of hocus-pocus cure: Included historically in this group of substances are
such unusual concoctions as crocodile dung, moss scraped from the head of a
hanged criminal, crystallized tear from the eye of a deer bitten by a snake, and many
more mundane items, such as chemically inert pills.

Hard-headed contemporary scientists have used the inert pill—a placebo—as
the control substance in experiments that evaluate the effects of chemically active
substances. But clinical lore has always been filled with reports of the potency of
placebos. Now some striking observations by researchers have provided clues about
why placebos seem to relieve pain in some patients. Studies by Levine et al. (1978)
used volunteer subjects who had just had their wisdom teeth extracted—an especially painful procedure that one could expect to produce some miserable people!
These patients were told that they were being given an analgesic but were not told
what kind. Some of these patients received morphine-based drugs, and some were
given saline solutions—the placebo. Pain relief was produced in one out of three
patients given the placebo. To explore the mechanisms of the placebo effect, these
researchers gave naloxone to other patients who were also administered the placebo.
Recall that naloxone blocks the effects of both exogenous opiates and endogenous
opioids or opiatelike substances. Patients given the placebo and naloxone did not
obtain pain relief, which implies that placebo relief of pain is mediated by an
endogenous opioid system. This effect was seen primarily with high doses of naloxone in placebo responders (those who reported relief of dental pain following administration of the inert pill).

A critical analysis of studies of the mechanisms of placebo effects by Grevert
and Goldstein (1985) has pointed to a number of deficiencies in these studies.
Factors such as suitable control groups and dose level of naloxone have proved
critical in placebo research. Further, we now know that there are several types of
opioid receptors in the brain, and the affinity of naloxone for these various receptors
is quite different. Thus a negative effect of naloxone administration is not definitive
in excluding the possible mediation of endogenous opioids. In a study designed to
deal with criticisms of previous placebo research, Grevert, Albert, and Goldstein
(1983) showed that naloxone did not completely prevent placebo-induced analgesia
but rather reduced the effectiveness of a placebo. This was established in experiments involving normal subjects in whom pain was induced by the inflation of a
pressure cuff on their arm. This suggests that both opioid and nonopioid mechanisms contribute to placebo analgesia; the same conclusion comes from studies of
stress-induced analgesia discussed below. Future studies dealing with this phenomenon will help in our understanding of the multifaceted character of pain relief.

Acupuncture

Several visitors to China during the past decade have described in glowing terms the
relief from pain produced by acupuncture. Some greeted acupuncture procedures

with skepticism, while others pointed to the fact that this method of pain therapy was developed by ancient Chinese and has stood the test of hundreds of years of use. The earliest description of acupuncture is at least 3000 years old. The acupuncture procedure has been described in many different ways but basically consists of the insertion of needles at designated points on the skin. In some cases the needles are manipulated once in position, and in other instances electrical or heat stimulation is delivered through the inserted needles. The points at which needles are inserted are related to the locus of pain and some of the characteristics of the pain condition.

Acupuncture has gained popularity as another procedure to employ in many different types of acute and chronic pain. Many have extolled its virtues in the popular press, and it has been heralded as a way to control pain of diverse origins. Detailed clinical assessments have tended to be more reserved and emphasize that only a small number of people achieve continued relief in chronic pain conditions. At least part of the pain-blocking character of acupuncture appears to be mediated by the release of endorphins (Pomeranz, 1983). Application of opioid antagonists prior to acupuncture also blocks its pain-control effects. More research is needed in clinical settings to delimit the character of this type of pain control. Animal models of the procedures used with human patients are also promoting an understanding of this ancient but enduring remedy.

Stress-Induced Analgesia

Inhibition of pain has been shown in many laboratory situations that involve unusual treatments, such as brain electrical stimulation. Such studies demonstrate the existence of pain-control circuitry, but they do not provide information about the customary ways inhibitory systems are activated. What are the conditions that cause endorphin-mediated pain control to become activated? To answer this question, researchers have examined pain inhibition that might arise in stressful circumstances. Some researchers have suggested that stress-provoked activation of the brain systems that produce analgesia might come about when pain threatens to overwhelm effective coping strategies. Studies concerned with how pain might control pain itself have revealed some new perspectives on mechanisms mediating these effects.

Several years ago researchers showed that exposure of rats to mild foot shock produced analgesia. Some other forms of stress, such as cold water swimming, also produced inhibition of pain responses. Other observations suggested that such stress-induced analgesia was mediated by brain endogenous opioids. In fact, the analgesia produced by stress was similar in several respects to that produced by opiates (Bodnar et al., 1980). Like opiates, repeated exposure to stress resulted in declining analgesic effectiveness. In addition, cross-tolerance is observed between opiates and stressors, which means that diminished analgesia to repeated stress also results in reduced pain inhibition by opiates. However, anatagonists to opiates, such as naloxone, have had variable effects on stress-induced analgesia, which has raised the prospect that perhaps some part of stress-produced analgesia is not mediated by endogenous opioids. Newer research has explored this theme more completely.

Studies reported from the laboratory of John Liebeskind—a leading researcher in the area of pain—have employed rats in stress situations that consisted of inescapable foot shock (Terman, Shavit, Lewis, Cannon, & Liebeskind, 1984). Different groups of rats were exposed to different regimens of foot shock, and changes in pain threshold were assessed using a common technique called the tail-flick test. This assessment is a measure of the level of radiant heat that produces a quick flick of the tail of the rat. In these studies the role of endorphins was assessed by the administration of an opiate antagonist—naltrexone. In this experimental situation, the stress of inescapable shock produces an increase in tail-flick latency, which shows that the shock stress produces an analgesic effect. Administration of naltrexone produces a curious complication. When analgesia is produced by short periods of foot shock, naltrexone reverses the analgesic response, which demonstrates that it is produced by an opioid system in the brain. However, anatagonists to opiates have little effect on stress-produced analgesia if it is produced by prolonged periods of foot shock. This finding demonstrates that stress activates both an opioid-sensitive analgesic system and a pain-control system that does not involve opioid circuitry. Relatively precise parameters of the stress-inducing stimuli seem to determine which system is activated. Similar elements are probably involved in both pain-control circuits since spinal lesions disrupt both forms of stress-induced analgesia. Some separateness in the pathways is shown by the demonstration that some brain stem lesions can affect the opiate-mediated analgesia without affecting the nonopiate (Terman et al., 1984). These findings are very important in determining clinical strategies for intervention in humans. Further research may help to clarify whether there are additional forms of pain relief that are controlled by other circuits.

Summary · Main Points

1. A sensory system furnishes selected information to the brain about internal and external events and conditions. It captures and processes only information that is significant for the particular organism.

2. Ideal sensory systems discriminate among some of the available forms of energy, respond over a wide range of intensities, are highly sensitive to a change of stimuli, respond reliably and rapidly, and suppress unwanted information.

3. Stimuli that some species detect readily are completely unavailable to other species that lack the necessary receptors.

4. Some receptors are simple free nerve endings, but most include cells that are specialized to transduce particular kinds of energy.

5. Transduction of energy at sensory receptors involves production of a generator potential that stimulates the sensory neurons.

6. Coding is the translation of receptor information into patterns of neural activity.

7. Adaptation refers to the progressive decrease in the rate of impulses as the same stimulation is maintained. This decline is slow in the case of tonic receptors but rapid for phasic receptors. Adaptation protects the nervous system from redundant stimulation.

8. Mechanisms of information suppression include accessory structures, descending pathways from neural centers to the receptor, and central circuits.

9. The receptive field of a cell is the stimulus region that changes the response of the cell.

10. The succession of nuclei in a sensory pathway is thought to allow for different and perhaps successively more elaborate kinds of processing.

11. Attention refers to the temporary enhancement of certain sensory messages during particular states of the individual. Attention is thought to involve the reticular activating system in the brain stem reticular formation.

12. The skin contains several distinct types of receptors that have specific sensitivities. Inputs from the skin course through several distinct spinal pathways including the dorsal column system and the spinothalamic tract.

13. The surface of the body is represented at each level

of the somatosensory system, and at the level of the cerebral cortex there are multiple maps of the body surface.

14. Pain guides adaptive behavior by providing indications of harmful stimuli. Pain is a complex state that is strongly influenced by cultural factors and many aspects of individual experience.

15. Pain sensation is subject to many controlling or modulating conditions. These include circuitry within the brain and spinal cord that employs endorphin synapses. One component in the modulation of pain is descending pathways arising in the brain stem that inhibit incoming neural activity at synapses within the spinal cord.

16. Pain control has been achieved using drugs (including placebos), electrical stimulation and mechanical stimulation of the skin, and acupuncture, among other methods.

Recommended Reading

Autrum, H., Jung, R., Lowenstein, W. R., MacKay, D. M., & Teuber, H. L. (Eds.). (1971–1981). *Handbook of sensory physiology* (9 vols.). Berlin and New York: Springer-Verlag.

Fields, H. L. (1988). *Pain*. New York: McGraw-Hill.

Goodwin, A. W., & Darian-Smith, I. (Eds.). (1985). *Hand function and the neocortex*. Berlin: Springer-Verlag.

Kitchell, R. L., & Erickson, H. H. (Eds.). (1983). *Animal pain*. Bethesda, Md.: American Physiological Society.

Masterton, R. B. (Ed.). (1978). *Handbook of behavioral neurobiology: Vol. 1. Sensory integration*. New York: Plenum.

Rowe, M., & Willis, W. D. (Eds.). (1985). *Development, organization and processing in somatosensory pathways*. New York: Alan R. Liss.

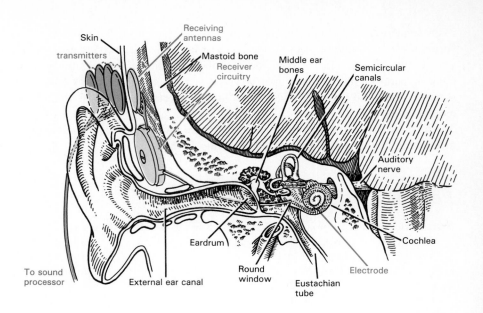

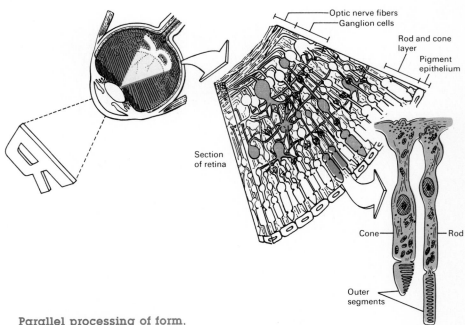

9 Hearing and Seeing

ORIENTATION

Sounds and sights are the main avenues of information about the world that guide human behavior. Indeed, for most vertebrates audition and vision are the principal links to the world. These are the distance senses that define the aspects of the outside world that are most important for any particular animal. Across various species the differences that are seen in the operation of these sensory systems are more quantitative in character than qualitative; each species seems to have a particular range of visual or auditory stimuli that it is especially tuned to process. For humans the sounds of speech are especially important; for the bat very high frequencies, imperceptible to us, guide the rapid flight that results in a meal.

In this chapter we will review some of the main attributes of the auditory and visual systems. Work in these areas has progressed at a very rapid pace, and our intent here is both to communicate some basic information and to highlight the realms of exciting newer developments. We will begin with a discussion of audition since hearing evolved from special mechanical receptors akin to the class of somatosensory elements we discussed in the previous chapter.

Hearing

Sounds are an important part of the adaptive behavior of many animals. For humans sounds produced by speech organs form the basic elements of the thousands of human languages. The melodic song of a male bird attracts a female; the grunts, screeches, and burbly sounds of primates signal danger or the need for comfort or satisfaction. Whales, owls, and bats exploit the directional property of sound to locate prey and avoid obstacles. The use of sounds by all these different animals emphasizes a distinctive feature of auditory information processing—the fact that temporal features of acoustic signals can be discriminated with great accuracy. Your auditory system can detect rapid changes of sound intensity and frequency. In fact, the speed of auditory information processing is so good that the frequency analysis of the ear rivals that of modern electronic gadgets.

The Beginnings of Auditory Perception

The detection of airborne vibrations is the particular specialty of human hearing and that of many other mammals. How do vibrations of air particles become the speech, music, and other sounds we hear? The beginnings of auditory perception are determined by the character of all the peripheral components of the auditory system which shape the forces that act on the auditory nerve fibers. In this section we will discuss these initial stages in auditory excitation. For some basic aspects of the auditory stimulus, see Box 9-1.

BOX 9-1 | Technical Background: The Auditory Stimulus

Most animals produce sound, and hearing lets us detect energies that we and other animals produce, either for communication or incidentally to other activities. Sound is a repetitive change in the pressure of some medium, commonly air or water. In air the change arises because air particles are moved by a vibrating mechanical system, such as the glottis of the larynx in speech, a tuning fork, or the cone of a loudspeaker. As the tuning fork moves away from a resting position, it compresses air particles, which increases air pressure above atmospheric pressure. As the tuning fork swings to the other side of its rest position, air particle density is briefly reduced with respect to atmospheric pressure. An alternation of compression and expansion of air is called one cycle. Box Figure 9-1 presents an illustration of the changes in the spacing of air particles produced by a vibrating tuning fork. The sound produced by a tuning fork has only one frequency of vibration, so it is called a pure tone and can be represented by a sine wave.

A pure tone is described physically in terms of two measures:

1. Frequency, or the number of cycles per second, measured in hertz (Hz) (for example, middle A has a frequency of 440 Hz).
2. Amplitude or intensity, the distance of particle movement in some period of time, usually measured as pressure, or force per unit area, measured in dynes per square centimeter (dynes/cm^2).

Most sounds are more complicated than a pure tone. For example, a sound made by a musical instrument contains a "fundamental" frequency and "harmonics." The fundamental is the basic frequency, and the

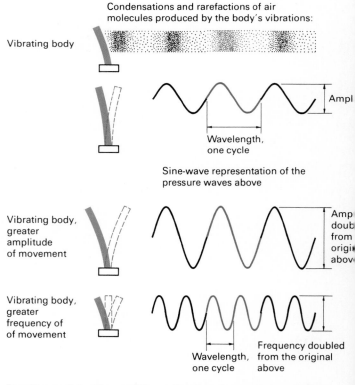

Box Figure 9-1 **The auditory stimulus. A pure tone or sine wave vibration can vary in both amplitude and frequency.**

harmonics are multiples of the fundamental. For example, if the fundamental is 440 Hz, then the harmonics are 880, 1320, 1760, and so on. When

External Ear Sound waves are collected by the external ear (Figure 9-1), which consists of the part we readily see, called the **pinna,** and a canal that leads to the eardrum. The external ear is a distinctly mammalian character and, within this group, there is a wide array of ear shapes and sizes. In part the size of the external ear reflects evolutionary factors related to heat dissipation. Note, for example, in Chapter 12, the small size of the ear of an arctic-dwelling fox contrasted to the large ears of a fox living in a warm climate. The acoustic properties of the external ear are quite important since the shape is a significant determinant of the physical transformation of sound energies. Not only does the external ear serve to funnel sounds, but the "hills and valleys" of the external ear modify the character of sound that reaches the middle and inner ear. Some frequencies of sound are amplified and others are

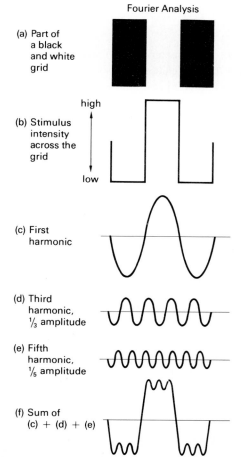

Fourier Analysis

(a) Part of a black and white grid

(b) Stimulus intensity across the grid — high / low

(c) First harmonic

(d) Third harmonic, ⅓ amplitude

(e) Fifth harmonic, ⅕ amplitude

(f) Sum of (c) + (d) + (e)

different instruments play the same note, they differ in the relative intensities of the various harmonics, and this difference is what gives each instrument its characteristic quality, or timbre. Any complex pattern can be analyzed into a sum of sine waves, a process called **Fourier analysis** after the French mathematician who discovered it. (We will see later that Fourier analysis can also be applied to visual patterns.) Box Figure 9-2 shows how a complex wave form can be analyzed into sine waves of different frequencies.

Since the ear is sensitive to a huge range of pressures, sound intensity is generally expressed in **decibels (dB),** a logarithmic scale. The definition of a decibel is as follows:

$$N\,(\mathrm{dB}) = 20 \log P_1/P_2$$

where N is the number of decibels and P_1 and P_2 are the two pressures to be compared.

The common reference level in hearing studies (P_2 in the above notation) is 0.0002 dyne/cm^2; this is the least pressure necessary for an average human observer to hear a 1000-Hz tone. In this scale a whisper is about 10 times as intense as 0.0002 dyne/cm^2, and a jet airliner 500 ft overhead is about a million times as intense as the reference level; in decibel notation the whisper is about 20 dB above threshold and the jetliner is about 120 dB above threshold. Normal conversation is about 60 dB above the reference level.

Box Figure 9-2 Illustration of Fourier analysis. A complex repeating pattern, such as this square wave, can be analyzed into component sine waves.

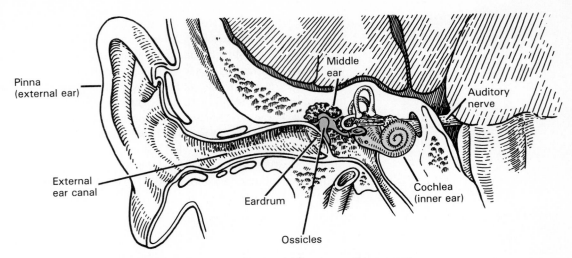

Figure 9-1 The external ear, middle ear, and inner ear.

dimmed. For this reason the shape of the external ear is particularly important in sound localization. Some animals have an elaborate set of muscles associated with the external ear, which enables the animal to point the external ear to the source of sound. Animals with acute auditory localization abilities, like bats, have especially mobile ears.

Middle Ear   Between the acoustic gathering of the external ear and the receptor cells of the inner ear, there is a group of structures, including bones and muscles, that constitute the structures of the **middle ear** (Figure 9-1). A chain of three tiny bones called the **ossicles** connects the eardrum (**tympanic membrane**) at the end of the external ear canal to an opening to the inner ear called the **oval window.** The ossicles are the smallest bones in the body. Small displacemenets of the tympanic membrane move the ossicular chain. What is the role of these bones in transmitting sound? They are necessary because it is extremely difficult for the minute mechanical forces of air particles to compress fluid. The mechanical linkages of the middle ear focus the pressures on the large tympanic membrane onto the small oval window; this arrangement produces a vast amplification of sound pressure that is capable of stimulating the fluid-filled inner ear.

The effects of intense sound are attenuated in transmission through the middle ear bones by muscles associated with two of these bones, the malleus, connected to the tympanic membrane, and the stapes, connected to the oval window. These muscles, when activated, prevent easy movement of the middle ear bones and limit the effectiveness of sounds. Very intense sounds activate these muscles, preventing injury to cochlear hair cells from prolonged, intense stimulation. These muscles also become active during body movement and swallowing; they are the reason we hear few of the sounds produced by the workings of our own bodies.

Inner Ear The mechanical character of sound is converted into neural activity within the complex structures of the inner ear. A detailed look at the inner ear is necessary for an understanding of sound transduction. In mammals the auditory portion of the inner ear is a coiled structure called the **cochlea** (from the Greek *kochlos,* meaning "snail"; see Figure 9-2). This structure is located within the temporal bone. In an adult person, this complex organ measures only about 4 mm in diameter—about the size of a pea. Unrolled, the cochlea would measure about 35 to 40 mm in length. The region nearest the oval window membrane is the base of the spiral, and the end or top is the apex. Along the length of the cochlea are three principal canals: (1) the **tympanic canal,** (2) the **vestibular canal,** and (3) the **cochlear duct.** A cross section of the cochlea illustrating this division is shown in Figure 9-2c. The entire structure is filled with noncompressible fluid. Hence if anything is to occur within this structure when the oval window is pushed, there must be a movable outlet membrane. This membrane is the **round window,** which separates the cochlear duct from the middle ear cavity.

The principal elements for auditory transduction are found on the **basilar membrane.** The basilar membrane of the cochlea is about five times wider at the apex than at the base, although the cochlea itself narrows toward the apex. Within the cochlear duct and riding on the basilar membrane is the **organ of Corti.** The organ of Corti sits on top of the basilar membrane and contains the sensory cells **(hair cells),** an elaborate framework of supporting cells, and the terminations of the auditory nerve fibers. There are two sets of sensory cells, a single row of **inner hair cells** and three rows of **outer hair cells** (see Figure 9-2d). The hair cells are cylindrically shaped with a diameter of approximately 5 micrometers (μm) and a length of 20 to 50 μm. From the upper end of the hair cell protrude hairs, or cilia (Figure 9-2e). Each cell may have as many as 100 to 200 of the hairs. The length of the cilia is about 2–6 μm, and the cilia of the outer hair cells extend into indentations in the bottom of the **tectorial membrane.** (Inner hair cells do not seem to make direct contact with the tectorial membrane.)

Auditory nerve fibers synapse at the base of the hair cells. Whereas each inner hair cell receives its own auditory nerve fiber, several outer hair cells share a single fiber. On each side of the human head, about 50,000 auditory fibers from the cochlea enter the brain stem and synapse in a complex of cells called the dorsal and ventral **cochlear nuclei.** In addition, both the afferent fibers (running from sense organs to the central nervous system) and the efferent fibers (carrying impulses outward from the brain) make contact in the vicinity of the hair cells. The activity in the efferent fibers may modulate the excitability of the terminals of the nerve fibers and hair cells (Teas, 1989).

Box 9-2, page 300, reviews the evolution of the complex organ of hearing.

Auditory Transduction at the Hair Cells

The processes that link the elaborate mechanical events within the cochlea to auditory nerve fiber excitation remain something of a puzzle even after years of intense investigation. For many years researchers have known that large electrodes placed in and around the cochlea record two types of sound-provoked electrical responses.

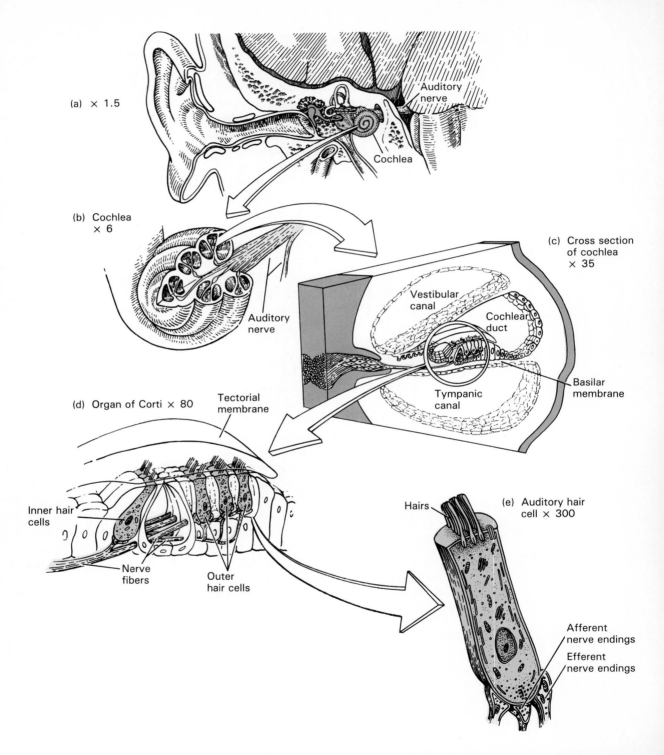

(a) × 1.5

Auditory nerve

Cochlea

(b) Cochlea
× 6

Auditory nerve

(c) Cross section
of cochlea
× 35

Vestibular canal

Cochlear duct

Tympanic canal

Basilar membrane

(d) Organ of Corti × 80

Tectorial membrane

Inner hair cells

Nerve fibers

Outer hair cells

Hairs

(e) Auditory hair cell × 300

Afferent nerve endings

Efferent nerve endings

Figure 9-2 Structure of the inner ear at successively higher levels of magnification. (a) Section through head, magnification × 1.5. (b) Cochlea, × 6. (c) Cross section of cochlea, × 35. (d) Organ of Corti, × 80. (e) Auditory hair cell, × 300.

One type, called the cochlear microphonic, is a virtual mirror of the acoustic wave form (that is, almost as though it were the output of a microphone). The other type of potential, called the summating potential, is the envelope of the cochlear microphonic potential. For a long time investigators thought that these potentials were related to the reception process and might actually be the generator of events. Evidence pertinent to this notion included the fact that when hair cells were destroyed by drugs, such as some antibiotics, or acoustic trauma, the potentials disappeared. New evidence has clarified this issue.

Recent techniques have enabled a closer examination of the intimate details of the principal elements in the transduction process—the hair cells (Hudspeth, 1983). The fluid movements of the cochlea, excited by sounds, produce vibrations of the basilar membrane. This results in the bending of the ends of hair cells that are inserted into a membrane that is roughly parallel with the basilar membrane (called the tectorial membrane). The upward deflection of the basilar membrane causes the hair cells placed between these two membranes to bend. Recordings by Hudspeth (1983) from isolated individual hair cells suggest that each hair cell may have a direction of maximum sensitivity.

For years the small size of hair cells and their inaccessibility limited our understanding of the details of the transduction process. Recent technical achievements have begun to provide a closer look at the events linking sound to the excitation of hair cells. Hudspeth (1983) has shown that very small displacements of hair bundles cause rapid changes in ionic channels of the hair cell membrane. The drop in potential of the hair cell membrane produced by these ionic changes affects calcium ion movements at the base of the hair cell. The inward movement of calcium in this region causes vesicles within the base of the hair cell to fuse with the membrane and to release their chemical contents. These transmitterlike molecules cross the gap separating the hair cell from the terminals of the auditory nerve and combine with receptors on the nerve ending. This in turn results in depolarization—a type of generator potential that then leads to the activation of the nerve impulse. Some movements of the hair bundle produce the opposite effect—a hyperpolarization that closes down calcium channels and reduces the amount of released transmitter. These events are illustrated in Figure 9-3, page 302, from the work of Hudspeth.

Intracellular recordings of the responses of outer hair cells in mammals, made by Dallos (1985), showed that two types of electrical response can be recorded from these cells: (1) a rapidly changing event like the cochlear microphonic and (2) a more slowly changing baseline change analagous to the summating potential.

Brain Pathways of the Auditory System

Input to the brain from the auditory nerve is distributed in a complex manner to both sides of the brain (Figure 9-4, page 303). Each auditory nerve fiber divides into two main branches as it enters the brain stem. Each branch goes to a separate segment of a group of cells called the **cochlear nuclei,** consisting of a dorsal and ventral segment (Figure 9-4). The output of the cochlear nuclei is somewhat complicated and involves multiple paths. One set of paths goes to the **superior olivary complex,** which receives inputs from both right and left cochlear nuclei. The bilateral input to this set of cells is the first level for binaural interaction in the auditory system and is therefore of primary importance for mechanisms of auditory localization. Several other parallel paths all converge on the **inferior colliculus,** which is the auditory

| BOX 9-2 | **Evolution of Hairs That Hear Distant Objects** |

The evolutionary history of the auditory-vestibular system is better known than that of other sensory systems because the receptors are encased in bone, which leaves fossil remains. Combined studies of fossils and of many living animals have yielded a detailed story of the origins of hearing (van Bergeijk, 1967; Wever, 1974). We will summarize some of the most important points here.

It is generally accepted that the auditory end organ evolved from the vestibular system, which detects movement and position. In turn, the vestibular system evolved from the **lateral-line system**, a sensory system found in many kinds of fish and some amphibians. The lateral-line system is an array of receptors along the side of the body; tiny hairs emerge from sensory cells in the skin. These hairs are embedded in small gelatinlike columns called **cupulae**. Movements of water in relation to the body surface stimulate these receptors so that the animal can detect currents of water and movements of other animals, prey, or predators. Information from the lateral line also helps schools of fish stay in formation, since each fish feels the currents made by the others. A specialized form of lateral-line organ is the lateral-line canal, a groove that partially encloses the cupulae. It is speculated that the first semicircular canals developed from a stretch of lateral-line canal that migrated into the body. Having a stretch of canal away from the surface of the body gave the animal a sensor for turns to the right or left, and this receptor was free of effects of stimulation of the skin. Sensitivity to change of direction was optimized when the canal developed into a roughly circular form.

The lamprey has lateral-line receptors; some of them are shown in Figure 3-8 as the row of circles extending back from the eye. Different species of lamprey have one or two semicircular canals on each side, and these detect turning movements of the head. The lamprey also have larger chambers in the vestibular apparatus, the saccule and the utricle, which detect position and linear movements of the head. The saccule and utricle are also specialized developments from the lateral-line system. The sensitivity of these organs to position and to movements is increased by tiny bits of bone that weight the cupulae. These crystals are called otoliths (from the Latin roots for "ear" and "stone"). The sea lamprey has otoliths, as do mammals, including humans (see Figure 9-12). The lamprey does not, however, possess an end organ for hearing. That first emerged in fish with jaws.

The development of the inner ear came about in fish through the evolution of an organ, the swim bladder, that served an entirely different function, aiding balance. Many species of fish have this gas-filled cavity in the abdomen. Vibrations in water cause the air bladder to contract and expand, which increases sensitivity to such vibrations. In some families of fish the sac extended and made contact with the vestibular labyrinth; in others a series of bones connected the swim bladder with the labyrinth. In both cases the animals acquired increased sensitivity to vibrations in the environment, and a new part of the labyrinth evolved in conjunction with this vibratory sense. This duct, the lagena (from the Latin for "flask"), is found in bony fishes, amphibians, reptiles, and birds. It corresponds to the cochlea found in mammals.

So the auditory system evolved out of the vestibular system, which in turn arose from the lateral-line system. More recently evolved animals show longer auditory ducts with greater numbers of hair cells and auditory nerve fibers (Box Figure 9-3). Presumably this larger system is the basis for the excellent discrimination of frequencies and auditory patterns in the

---

center of the midbrain. Outputs of the inferior colliculus go to the **medial geniculate nucleus** of the thalamus. Axons of postsynaptic cells of the medial geniculate in turn extend to the **auditory cortex** of the temporal lobe. The auditory cortex consists of several adjacent regions, most of which represent the positions on the basilar membrane in an orderly map.

Many sensory systems include both ascending and descending pathways. Thus in addition to afferent pathways reaching to higher levels of the brain, there are efferent pathways that lead back to the periphery. The auditory system provides a striking example. At lower levels of the brain stem, there is a group of cells whose

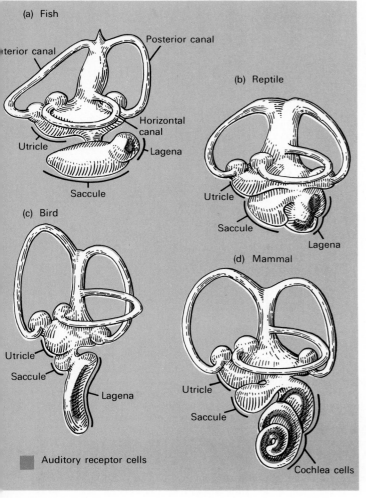

(a) Fish

Posterior canal

terior canal

Horizontal canal

Utricle

Lagena

Saccule

(b) Reptile

Utricle

Saccule

Lagena

(c) Bird

Utricle

Saccule

Lagena

(d) Mammal

Utricle

Saccule

Cochlea cells

Auditory receptor cells

higher animals.

Although we can look at these evolutionary developments as steps toward our own vestibular and auditory organs, there is no need to think of them as having occurred for that purpose. Each adaptation was retained in natural selection because it served a function. Variability of sensitivity among animals allowed evolution of increased sensitivity and of new modes of sensation.

Box Figure 9-3 Evolution of the inner ear and the vestibular apparatus. During evolution the auditory end organ (shown in brown) has become progressively larger and more complex, allowing finer discrimination. (Adapted from Retzius, 1881, 1884)

axons form a bundle and travel out the auditory nerve to the cochlea. These efferent fibers branch profusely in the cochlea and synapse at the base of virtually every hair cell. Many studies have sought to determine the functional role of this group of fibers. Their action is predominantly inhibitory, as shown by the fact that electrical excitation of this bundle reduces the frequency of sound-provoked nerve impulses in the afferents of the auditory nerve. Some investigators have suggested that this efferent pathway can be used to suppress noise and to enhance auditory signals (Dewson, 1968; Teas, 1989). This efferent pathway may also be used to protect the hair cells from damage due to intense sounds (Wiederholt, 1988).

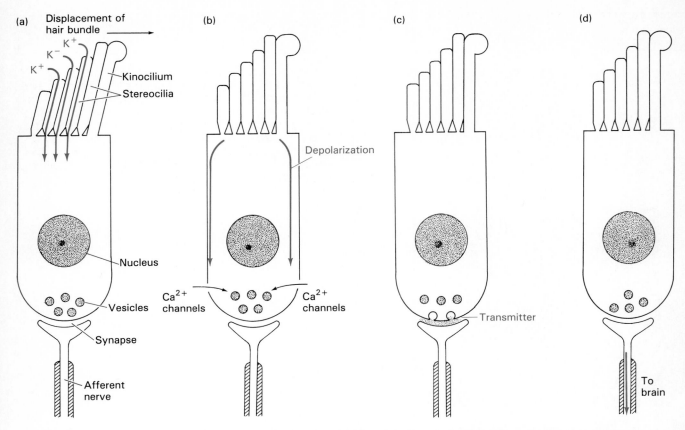

Figure 9-3 Response of a hair cell culminates in the transmission of an electrical signal to the brain along the afferent nerve fiber at the base that contacts the cell. The response is shown schematically in the panels of this illustration. When the hair bundle is displaced, the transduction channels open (a). Potassium ions (shown in color) flow into the cell, and the potential difference between the cell and the surrounding fluid falls. The reduction in potential difference, which is called a depolarization and is shown in color, spreads almost instantaneously through the cell (b). In the lower part of the cell are channels that selectively admit calcium ions. The depolarization causes these channels to open, whereupon calcium flows in. Near the base of the cell are vesicles containing a neurotransmitter. The calcium ions cause the vesicles to fuse with the basal part of the hair cell's surface membrane (c). In fusing, the vesicles release the neutrotransmitter they contain. The transmitter, whose chemical nature is not known, diffuses across the synaptic space between the hair cell and the neuron: it then excites the neuron, which sends a message to the brain along a fiber of the eighth cranial nerve (d).

How We Discriminate Pitch

Most of us can discriminate very small differences in frequency of sound over the entire audible range from 20 Hz up to 15,000–20,000 Hz. The ability to detect a change in frequency is usually expressed as the minimal discriminable frequency difference between two tones. The detectable difference is about 2 Hz up to 2000 Hz, at which point it grows larger. Note that pitch and frequency are not

Figure 9-4 (a) Auditory pathways of the human brain. (b) Schematic diagram of human auditory pathways.

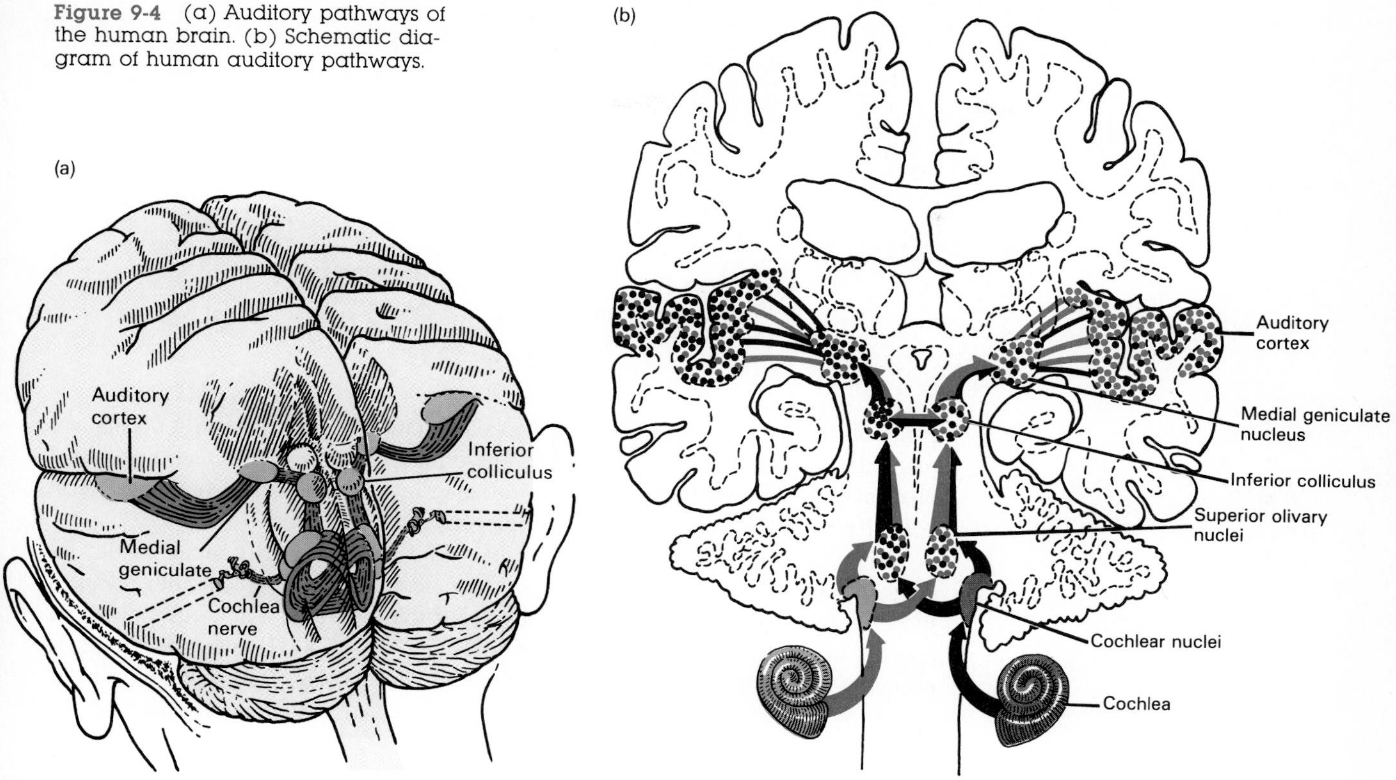

synonymous terms. **Pitch** relates solely to sensory experience, that is, to the responses of subjects to sounds, whereas **frequency** describes a physical property of sounds. The reasons for emphasizing this distinction are many, including the fact that frequency is not the sole determinant of pitch experience, and changes in pitch do not precisely parallel changes in frequency.

How do we account for the ability to discriminate frequencies? Two theories have most commonly been offered. One, described as **place theory,** argues that pitch perception depends on the place of maximal displacement of the basilar membrane. "Place," according to this view, also includes which neurons are stimulated in the central auditory pathways—that is, particular nerve cells respond to particular stimulus frequencies. The alternative theory, now most commonly known as **volley theory,** emphasizes the relations between stimulus frequency of sounds and the pattern or timing of neural discharges. According to this perspective, the firing pattern of a single nerve cell reveals the stimulus frequency of the input, because each time the stimulus changes frequency, the pattern of discharge is altered. The crudest representation of this idea would suggest, for example, that a 500-Hz tone is represented by 500 nerve impulses per second, whereas this same neuron represents a 1000-Hz tone by a frequency of 1000 nerve impulses per second. In both cases the

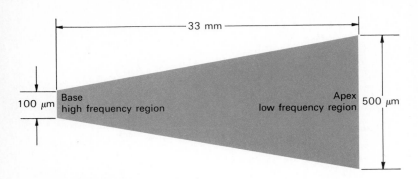

Figure 9-5 The basilar membrane and stimulus frequency. In this diagram the basilar membrane is represented as being uncoiled. The top diagram shows the dimensions of the basilar membrane. Note that different scales are used for length and width. In the marginal column, note that as the frequency of stimulation increases, the position of the peak of movement of the membrane is displaced progressively toward the base.

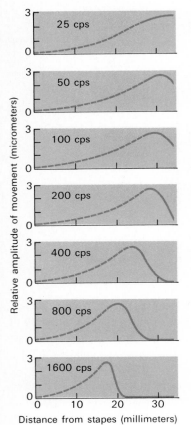

firing of the nerve impulse is "phase locked" to the stimulus; that is, it occurs at a particular portion of the cycle. Such a phase locked representation can be accomplished more accurately by several fibers than by a single fiber—hence the term *volley*, which denotes simultaneous flight of several missiles.

These views—place and volley theory—are not necessarily antagonistic; indeed, the best contemporary view of pitch perception incorporates both perspectives. This combined view is referred to as **duplex theory.** The volley principle appears to operate for sounds from about 20 to 1000–1500 Hz, whereas the place principle holds especially for sounds above about 1000 Hz. Let us examine some physiological results that support the place theory and some data that support the volley theory.

As already noted, the region of maximal vibration along the basilar membrane is related to stimulus frequency. With a change of frequency, there is a change in the region of maximal disturbance (Figure 9-5). Georg von Békésy devised an ingenious way to observe directly the location of the maximal amplitude of traveling waves in animal cochleas, and he reported fairly sharp frequency tuning. More recent studies employing vastly different techniques for the observation of basilar membrane movement show that the relations between basilar membrane locus and stimulus frequency are even sharper than Békésy had observed (Rhode, 1984). For complex sounds with several frequency components, the cochlea accomplishes a sort of Fourier analysis; the different frequencies are represented by peaks of vibration at different places along the basilar membrane. The accuracy of place representation of auditory frequency has improved over the course of evolution with the lengthening of the basilar membrane and an increase in the number of hair cells and auditory nerve fibers.

Place along the basilar membrane is preserved in brain representations of stimulus frequency. This arrangement was found by examining the responses of single nerve cells when an animal is presented with stimuli of varying frequency and intensity. Data obtained in these experiments are plotted as tuning curves, which describe the frequency sensitivity of nerve cells at different intensity levels. Figure 9-6 shows tuning curves obtained from single neurons in the auditory nerve. Sharply tuned neurons are evident at all levels of the auditory system, ranging from the auditory nerve to the cortex. These findings suggest that cells at successive levels are not in a hierarchical relationship with respect to frequency assessment.

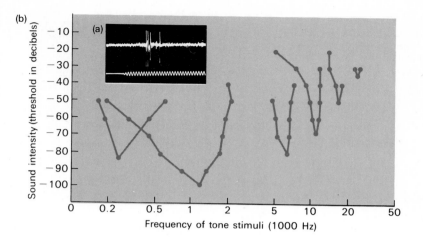

Figure 9-6 Example of tuning curves of auditory system nerve cells and how they are obtained. The curves are obtained by measuring neural responses (shown in inset, Leiman) to sounds of different intensities and frequencies. These curves are threshold measurements. The graph illustrates six neural units recorded from the auditory nerve. (From Kiang, 1965)

In recent years an abundance of neurophysiological data has suggested that pitch sensation may also involve coding that uses the temporal patterns of discharge in nerve cells as the information signifying the sound frequency. In this way single neurons may be able to convey frequency information over a broad range. In these experiments the measurement of temporal pattern is usually the distribution of the intervals between the nerve impulses elicited by a stimulus. A neuron can be said to code the frequency of the sound if this distribution is either the same as the interval between successive cycles of the sound or some integral multiple of it. This kind of coding is quite prominent at frequencies below about 1500 Hz, although it has also been noted up to 4000 Hz. It would seem, then, that the frequency properties of a sound can be coded in the auditory pathway in terms of both (1) the distribution of excitation among cells—that is, place coding or tonotopic representation—and (2) the temporal pattern of discharge in cells extending from the auditory nerve to the auditory cortex. Each level of the auditory system—the cochlear nuclei, inferior colliculi, lateral geniculate bodies, and auditory regions of the cerebral cortex— maps frequencies in an orderly arrangement of sites. An example of this tonotopic mapping in the inferior colliculus is shown in Figure 9-7.

Complex sounds, such as speech, contain mixtures of frequencies. The auditory system makes a useful although incomplete Fourier analysis, so that we respond to the presence of different frequencies in a complex sound. For example, we discriminate vowel sounds because each vowel sound has its own characteristic frequency bands, and we identify musical instruments by the relative intensities of different harmonic frequencies.

How We Localize Sounds

Under the best of conditions, a person can locate the position of a sound source with an accuracy of about one degree. This ability depends on the interaction between the two ears, although under some circumstances monaural detection of acoustic sources is almost as good as binaural. (Monaural localization is possible when sounds are of long duration and the head is free to move.) What stimulus features are important for binaural analysis of auditory localization?

Figure 9-7 Map of auditory frequencies in the inferior colliculus of the cat. (a) Lateral view of cat brain, showing plane of section through inferior colliculi. (b) Transverse section through inferior colliculi. (c) Location of the 2-DG labeled cells with 2000-Hz stimulation. (d) Location of labeled cells with 20,000-Hz stimulation. (e) Tonotopic mapping of inferior colliculus of cat from 2-DG studies of Servière, Webster, and Calford (1984).

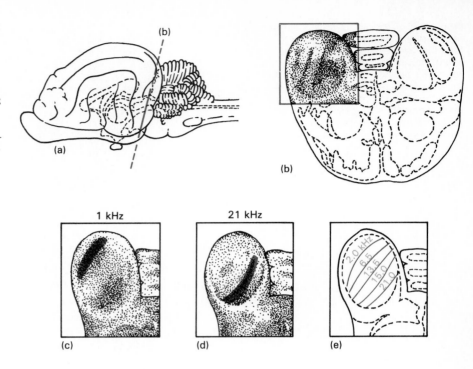

The cues for auditory localization used by a binaural processing system are the differences between the two ears in (1) sound intensity and (2) time of arrival. More complex differences also count, such as the frequency spectrum. Which of these interaural cues is most important in any circumstance depends on the properties of the sound and the acoustic environment (for example, sound reflection). Interaural intensity differences arise for some sounds when they are not in the median plane of the body, since the head casts a sound shadow. The sound frequencies that are effectively blocked depend on the size of the head, since long waves of low-frequency sounds get around the head. These effects are illustrated in Figure 9-8. At low frequencies, no matter where sounds are presented in the horizontal plane, there are virtually no intensity differences between the ears. For these frequencies time differences are the principal cues for sound position. At higher frequencies the sound shadow cast by the head produces significant interaural intensity differences. Human listeners cannot tell by monitoring their own performance that they are using one cue to localize high-frequency sounds and another cue to localize low-frequency sounds. In general we are aware of the results of neural processing but not of the processing itself.

How are the binaural features of an acoustic environment analyzed by the nervous system? There are many opportunities for binaural interaction at various levels of the brain stem. Thus single nerve cells can receive inputs derived from both ears. The lowest level at which interaural effects occur is the superior olivary complex; below this level of the auditory system, interaural effects cannot occur. Several investigators have shown that cells within the superior olivary region are particularly sensitive to interaural differences of time or intensity. The inferior colliculus

Figure 9-8 Cues for binaural hearing. The two ears receive somewhat different information from sound sources located to one side or the other of the observer's midline. The head blocks some frequencies (greater than 1000 Hz), producing binaural differences in sound intensity. Also, sounds take longer to reach the more distant ear, resulting in binaural differences in time of arrival.

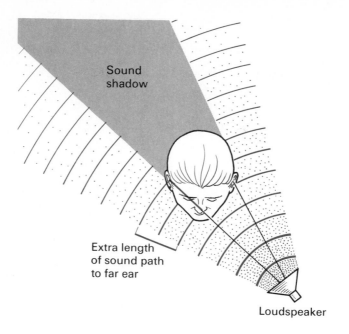

receives inputs from several brain stem nuclei with binaural inputs, so investigators have closely examined the binaural properties of neurons in this region. Are there neurons at the inferior colliculus that respond to some sound positions but not others? Different answers have been obtained for different species.

For mammals there is little evidence for precise feature detectors abstracting little pieces of acoustic space (Masterton & Imig, 1984). One might conclude either that the detection of acoustic position is the product of the summation of many cells active in particular spatial and temporal patterns or that feature detection relevant to auditory localization is processed at some higher level. Middlebrooks and Pettigrew (1981) tested for spatial selectivity in cortical neurons of the cat, using a setup like that shown in Figure 9-9a in which sounds could be produced anywhere in a sphere around the cat's head while responses of individual neurons were recorded. About half the neurons showed some spatial selectivity. Some of these neurons responded to a sound that originated anywhere in the contralateral hemifield. An example of such a receptive field is shown by the large gray zone in Figure 9-9b. Other location-sensitive neurons had relatively small receptive fields that responded to sounds in line with the axis of the contralateral ear. An example of the receptive field of such an axial unit is shown by the colored patch in Figure 9-9b. The axial units were located in the part of the primary auditory cortex where units are tuned to the higher frequencies; this is consistent with the fact that higher frequencies have sharper "sound shadows" and are called quasi-optical. There was no indication of a systematic map of sound space, such as occurs in the brain of the owl.

In the owl—whose livelihood depends on accurate auditory localization—detailed and elaborate neural representations of auditory space have been found. In the avian equivalent to the inferior colliculus, some of the cells are arranged rather like a spherical representation of space; that is, each space-specific cell has a recep-

(a)

(b)

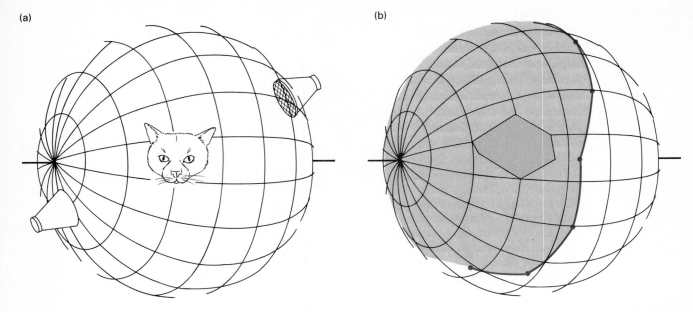

Figure 9-9 Auditory neurons in cat cortex which are sensitive to the spatial location of the sound source. A loudspeaker was moved on the surface of an imaginary sphere, 1 meter in radius. About one-quarter of all neurons in primary auditory cortex had hemifield receptive fields, such as the one shown in gray in (b). Another quarter had axial receptive fields, aligned with the axis of the ear contralateral to the neuron. (After Middlebrooks and Pettigrew, 1981)

tive field that includes sounds coming from a small cone of space centering on the owl's head. Successive cells in the nucleus represent neighboring regions of auditory space (Knudsen, 1984b; Knudsen & Konishi, 1979).

In the optic tectum of the owl, auditory and visual space are both represented, and the maps for the two senses correspond closely (Knudsen, 1981). Most cells in this region respond to both auditory and visual stimuli, and all of the auditory cells respond specifically to spatial direction. In most cases the visual receptive field of a cell is enclosed within the auditory receptive field of the same cell. Perhaps this close alignment of auditory and visual maps of space provides signals for motor responses with regard to the position of the stimulus.

The next section describes how early experience affects auditory experience and its mechanisms.

How Experience Affects Auditory Perception

At birth the human infant has diverse hearing abilities. In fact, there is good evidence that the fetus responds to sounds. Postnatal developments involve elaborate structural changes throughout the auditory pathways. Accompanying these changes are progressive improvements in perception of complex sounds such as speech. Since the world after birth is filled with a complex array of sounds, it is reasonable to ask whether the infant's experiences with sound have any impact on the progressive structural and physiological development of the auditory system. Does experience in some way shape or modulate connection formation in the auditory system? One aspect of auditory experience that is especially interesting in this regard is auditory localization. At birth many animals show a coarse ability to localize sounds. Human infants often show eye movements to the side where a sound stimulus occurs. However, changes in the size of the ears and head change the character of information used for auditory localization, and various studies have shown that animals improve their localization abilities as they mature.

The role of auditory experience in the development of sound localization is implied by some observations in bilaterally deaf children fitted with different types of hearing aids (Beggs & Foreman, 1980). One group of children was given a hearing aid that delivered the same sound to both ears. A second group of children was fitted with a separate hearing aid for each ear so that they, in contrast with the first group, experienced somewhat different cues at the two ears (dichotic stimuli). Of course, both groups experienced impoverished auditory environments. When examined years later, the group that had been fitted with binaural aids was significantly more accurate in auditory localization than the group that experienced comparable overall levels of sounds but were deprived of dichotic clues for localization.

Some of the most elegant studies in this area have been performed by Knudsen (1984) using an especially acute binaural perceiver—the owl. To assess the impact of early deprivation of binaural inputs, he placed a plug in one ear of the owl, which reduced sound intensity by 20–40 dB. Different groups of owls experienced this treatment at various ages. When the plug was placed in the ear, the animal made large localization errors to the side of the open ear. Owls that were younger than eight weeks at the time of plugging slowly began to compensate for the binaural disparity produced by the ear occlusion. However, with removal of the ear plugs, these animals made large localization errors to the opposite side. Older animals are less likely to show adjustment during this postplug period in which the animal is experiencing new relations between auditory cues and locations in space. Recently, Knudsen and Knudsen (1985) showed the critical role of vision in this process of adjustment of auditory localization. They noted that barn owls with one ear plugged did not correct their auditory localization errors if they were deprived of vision. Furthermore, if these animals are fitted with prisms that deviate vision by 10 degrees, the adjustment of auditory localization is matched to this visual error.

Neurophysiological studies of these owls reveal some features of the underlying mechanisms (Knudsen, 1985). Within the optic tectum of barn owls, there are nerve cells that are bimodal—they respond to both visual and auditory stimuli. Knudsen found that these neurons are selective for sound source locations and visual spatial information. Both the auditory and visual spatial sensitivities are similarly aligned; that is, they correspond to approximately the same positions. When the correspondence between auditory localization cues and visual position is changed by the use of an ear occluder, an interesting finding is noted. Despite the fact that correspondence was altered by the ear plug, when tested months later, the auditory receptive fields aligned well with the visual receptive fields. But removal of the ear plug caused the cells' most sensitive auditory receptive areas to shift away from the alignment with the visual fields of a nerve cell. These changes in auditory spatial tuning did not occur in an adult animal that had been similarly treated, which suggests that this experience-dependent process involves a critical period during early development. Thus these neurophysiological data correspond with the data obtained in the behavioral studies of sound localization already noted. Changes noted in these studies might arise from either structural modifications of growing neural circuits or modulations of synaptic efficacy.

Deafness and Its Rehabilitation

Health surveys have indicated that at least 5 million to 10 million people in the United States have some form of disabling hearing impairment. These disabilities range in severity from occasional difficulties in speech perception (41- to 55-dB drop in sensitivity between 500 and 2000 Hz) to a complete inability to hear anything (91-dB drop between 500 and 2000 Hz). Many of these hearing impairments arise early in life, and current estimates indicate that there are about 100,000 children in the United States with a major hearing handicap.

Types of Hearing Disorder

Hearing disorders are generally classified on the basis of the site of pathological changes. The principal classes are:

1. **Conductive deafness,** which refers to hearing impairments associated with pathology of the external or middle ear cavities.
2. **Sensorineural deafness,** which refers to hearing impairments originating from cochlear or auditory nerve lesions.
3. **Central deafness,** which refers to hearing impairments related to lesions in auditory pathways or centers, including sites in the brain stem, thalamus, or cortex.

We will discuss each of these types briefly in turn.

Conductive Deafness

Conductive deafness refers to hearing loss based on a failure to deliver mechanical excitation to the cochlea. It can result from as simple a cause as an ear wax obstruction or from more complex conditions that affect easy movement of the middle ear bones. Middle ear infections can also affect transmission of mechanical energies. Since the middle ear is connected (through the Eustachian tube) to the upper respiratory tract, throat infections can, under some conditions, gain access to the middle ear. This is especially a problem with young children since the length of the tube connecting the middle ear with the pharynx is short early in life. The loss of sensitivity characteristic of conductive deafness extends across all sensitivities, although there is a tendency for a greater involvement of higher frequencies.

Sensorineural Deafness

Hearing impairments that involve destruction of cochlear mechanisms, especially the integrity of hair cells, include the largest class of deafened individuals. The conditions that generate cochlear impairment are quite varied and include hereditary disorders, metabolic dysfunctions, exposure to toxic substances, trauma, and loud sounds. The end result is the same: Auditory nerve fibers do not deliver acoustic information to the brain in a normal manner. We will discuss some examples that have especially attracted attention.

Drug-induced deafness comes particularly from the toxic properties of a group of antibiotics that includes Streptomycin, Kanomycin, and Gentamicin. The ototoxic (ear-damaging) properties of these substances were first discovered in the treatment of tuberculosis by using Streptomycin. Although this antibiotic was remarkably effective in the treatment of the disease, it became evident soon after its introduction that there was a tremendous price to pay for the cure—many patients showed severe cochlear and/or vestibular damage. In some patients Streptomycin produced total, irreversible loss of hearing. This antibiotic and several related ones caused the virtually complete destruction of hair cells in the cochlea. Generally the highest frequencies are first affected. This result conforms to the histological observations of the progression of destruction; that is, the first signs of change are noted in the basal cochlear region. The endings of the auditory nerve near the hair cells remain viable, permitting new types of prostheses (described below).

Noise-induced hearing impairments primarily involve inner ear mechanisms. Interest in environmental issues of noise pollution and the advent of rock music have made this problem prominent and have also furnished much business to audiologists and otologists. Acoustic damage to the cochlea can be produced by exposure to either intense sudden sounds or chronic high-level sounds. The initial histological changes seen in the inner ear primarily involve hair cells, the outer hair cells being more susceptible to sound trauma than are inner cells. The progression of changes with continued sound exposure can in some individuals lead to destruction of the organ of Corti and the nerve fibers that innervate it. Figure 9-10 shows such destruction in a region of the cochlea. In time the initial locus of involvement in the cochlea spreads, even without additional acoustic trauma. It should be emphasized that such pathology is most often caused by intense acoustic trauma resulting from exposure to sounds greater than 120 dB, such as occurs close to a jet engine or a rock band.

Recent research suggests that loud sounds coupled with the use of some over-

Figure 9-10 Right cochlea of a person who died at age 71 after long-term exposure to intense noise. The cochlea shows marked degeneration of auditory nerve fibers. This view is obtained after removal of overlying temporal bone. (From Bredberg, 1968)

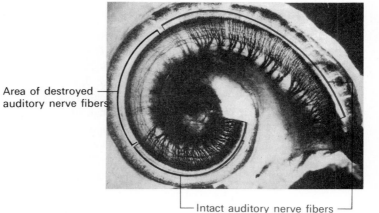

Area of destroyed auditory nerve fibers

Intact auditory nerve fibers

the-counter drugs can have profound effects on hearing. One example of this is seen in research using aspirin. Aspirin has been widely used for almost a century, and it has become common clinical knowledge that it can affect hearing. This has been especially seen in arthritis patients who customarily take large doses of aspirin to combat both pain and joint inflammation. In these patients the hearing loss caused by aspirin can be impressive—a reduction of up to 40 dB for high tones coupled with the development of a sensation of noises or ringing in the ears (called tinnitus). Another aspect of hearing loss related to aspirin is seen at much lower doses. Studies by McFadden and Plattsmier (1983) have shown that the temporary hearing loss produced by exposure to intense sound is greatly magnified when the subject has been taking a relatively small dose of aspirin for two days. The doses were one to three regular adult-size aspirins per day, a dosage commonly used by people during colds, flu, or headaches. At this level aspirin-alone effects are minimal. However, doses this low vastly accentuate the hearing threshold shift produced by an exposure to loud sounds. In addition, aspirin prolongs the duration of the recovery period following exposure to loud sound.

Central Deafness

Hearing loss that is caused by brain lesions or impairments is seldom a simple loss of sensitivity (Bauer & Rubens, 1985). An example of the complexity of changes in auditory perception following cerebral cortical damage is evident in word deafness, a disorder in which people show normal speech and hearing for simple sounds but cannot recognize spoken words. Some researchers have suggested that the basis of word deafness is an abnormally slow temporal analysis of auditory inputs. Some other examples of central deafness are seen in the syndrome of ''cortical deafness'' in which patients have difficulty recognizing both verbal and nonverbal auditory stimuli. This is a rare syndrome that arises from a bilateral destruction of inputs to the auditory cortex. Fortunately cortical deafness is usually transitory, which may reflect the diversity of central auditory pathways—the existence of parallel processing in the auditory system.

Electrical Stimulation of the Auditory Nerve in Deaf Humans

In recent years researchers have tried to restore hearing in profoundly deaf individuals by directly stimulating the auditory nerve with electrical currents (Loeb, 1985; Schindler, 1986). Progress in this endeavor has been rapid, and researchers' initial ''dreams of glory'' have produced an electronic device that has received the approval of the U.S. Food and Drug Administration for widespread clinical use. Who will gain by the use of this device? In several types of sensorineural hearing loss, the damage that produces deafness involves mechanisms that affect the hair cells. Research has established that, although patients may have experienced total destruction of the hair cell population, the electrical excitability of the auditory nerve remains unchanged. This type of clinical problem is seen with the damage produced by ototoxic drugs, such as some antibiotics. What kinds of sensory responses are provoked by electrical stimulation of the auditory nerve? The usual technique employed in these studies involves insertion of a small group of wires through the cochlea to the endings of the auditory nerve (Figure 9-11). In these patients electri-

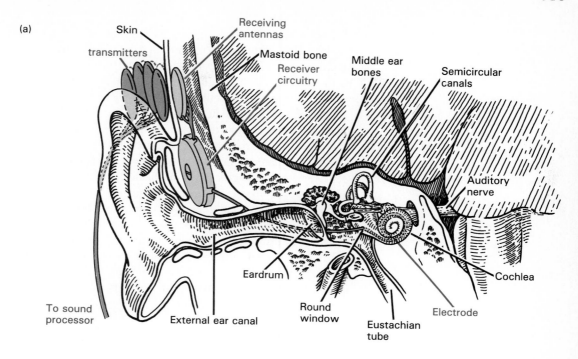

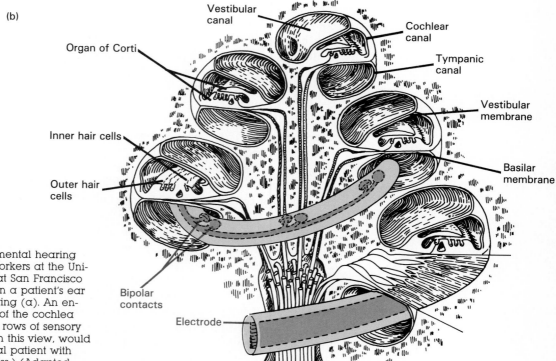

Figure 9-11 Experimental hearing aid developed by workers at the University of California at San Francisco is shown implanted in a patient's ear in the cutaway drawing (a). An enlarged interior view of the cochlea appears in (b). (The rows of sensory hair cells, included in this view, would be absent in a typical patient with sensorineural deafness.) (Adapted from Loeb, 1985)

cal stimulation produces pitch sensations that are partially related to the tonotopic organization of the cochlea. Unfortunately the effective number of chanels is limited by many technical factors, so that although an array of electrodes can be inserted, the range of frequencies that can be excited is limited. The amount of information conveyed in this manner is very limited in comparison with the range of frequencies we appreciate in normal hearing. Nevertheless, many observations in deafened humans show that when stimulation is controlled by the sounds picked up by a microphone, the resulting pattern of electrical stimulation of the auditory nerve greatly facilitates some acoustically mediated behaviors. For example, this partial replacement for the process of mechanical-to-neural transduction enables deaf people to detect some environmental sources of sounds, such as an automobile or the approach of another individual—all simple but critical aspects of acoustically mediated behavior that are taken for granted by hearing individuals but that constrain the behavior of deaf people. A more exciting prospect for this form of sensory prosthesis is its potential usefulness in aiding perception of speech and thus facilitating communication. Researchers are exploring this question, which is intimately tied to a more complete understanding of the "speech code" (Moore, 1984).

Vestibular Perception

When you go up in an elevator, you feel the acceleration clearly. When you turn your head or when you ride in a car going around a tight curve, you feel the change of direction. If you are not used to these kinds of stimulation, sensitivity to motion can make you "seasick." It is the receptors of the **vestibular system** that inform the brain about mechanical forces, such as gravity and acceleration, that act on the body.

The receptors of the vestibular system lie in portions of the inner ear that are continuous with the cochlea. (The term *vestibular* comes from the Latin word for "entrance hall"; the term is used because the system lies in hollow spaces in the temporal bone.) In mammals one portion of the vestibular system consists of three **semicircular canals,** fluid-filled tubes, each oriented in a different plane (Figure 9-12a and b). Connected to the end of each canal is a saclike structure called the **utricle** (a little uterus). Lying below this is another small fluid-filled sac, the **saccule** (a little sac).

Receptors in these structures, like those of the auditory system, are groups of hair cells whose bending leads to excitation of nerve fibers. In each semicircular canal, the hair cells (Figure 9-12d) are in an enlarged region, the **ampulla** (Figure 9-12c). Here the cilia of the hair cells are embedded in a gelatinous mass (Figure 9-12e). The orientation of the hairs is quite precise and determines the kind of mechanical force to which they are especially sensitive. The three semicircular canals are at right angles to each other; thus one or another detects angular acceleration in any direction. The receptors in the saccule and utricle respond to static positions of the head. The sensitivity of these receptors to movement is increased by the presence of little bony crystals (otoliths) on the gelatinous membrane (Figure 9-12e and f). At the base of the hair cells in these receptors are nerve fibers whose connections to the hair cells are much like the connections in the auditory portions of the inner ear. The evolution of the vestibular end organs is described in Box 9-2.

The structural arrangements of brain pathways dealing with vestibular excitation

Figure 9-12 Peripheral structure of the vestibular system. (a) Position of vestibular apparatus in temporal bone. (b) Orientation of semicircular canals, utricle, and saccule. (c) An ampulla, or end, of semicircular canal and hair cells, enlarged in (d). (e) Receptor surface of saccule and utricle showing otolith crystals, enlarged in (f).

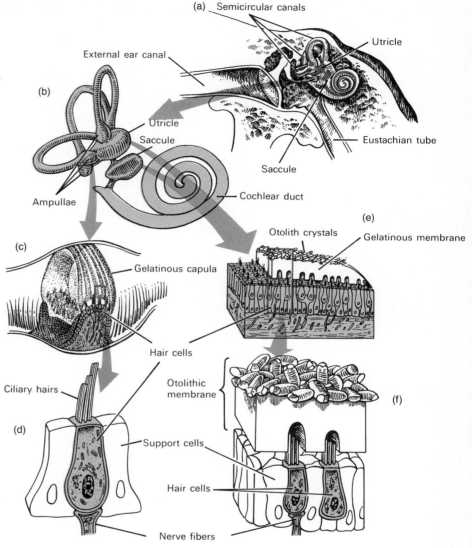

reflect its close connection to various muscle adjustments in the body. Nerve fibers from the vestibular receptors of the inner ear enter lower levels of the brain stem and synapse in a group of nuclei, the vestibular nuclei (Figure 9-13). Some of the fibers bypass this structure and go directly to the cerebellum, a center for motor control. The outputs of the vestibular nuclei are quite complex, as is appropriate to their influences on the motor system.

There is one aspect of vestibular activation that many of us would prefer did not exist. Certain types of body acceleration—such as those we experience as a passenger in an ocean-going boat, an airplane, a car, or an amusement park ride—can produce distress known as motion sickness. This same effect can be produced by

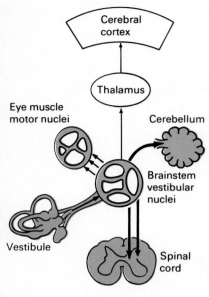

Figure 9-13 Main pathways of the vestibular system.

"caloric stimulation," which consists of pouring warm water in one ear canal; this sets up movements of inner ear fluids, simulating mechanical stimulation. Motion sickness is produced especially by low-frequency movements that an individual cannot control. For example, passengers in a car suffer from motion sickness, but the driver does not. One major theory of motion sickness—sensory conflict theory—says that the malady arises from contradictory sensory messages, especially a discrepancy between vestibular and visual information. To illustrate, as an airplane suddenly moves up, the vestibular system is excited but the eyes see the constancy of the plane's interior; the resulting disorientation is distressing. Some investigators have pointed out that there can also be conflicts of information within the vestibular system. For example, going sharply around a curve can produce conflicts between information about acceleration and forces related to gravity (Benson, 1982). Why do we get motion sickness at all? An experimental psychologist, Michel Treisman (1977), has theorized that the sensory conflict of some conditions of motion sets off responses that evolved to rid the body of swallowed poison. In this case, various sensory inputs from the eyes, nose, and taste buds signal danger—leading to dizziness and vomiting up the potential toxin. Such a response has obvious significance for preservation of life, although it is not helpful in response to movements of vehicles. A person whose vestibular system has been destroyed by toxic drugs or by side effects of antibiotics does not experience motion sickness.

Seeing

Vision plays a preeminent role in the adaptation of many animals, especially diurnal species. Even animals that inhabit relatively dark ecological niches, such as owls, bats, and deep-sea fish, need information from light receptors. Some nocturnal animals have huge eyeballs in comparison to their body size, presumably to help them capture the small amounts of light available at night. Some invertebrates are so greedy for light that they have multiple light receptors scattered about the body, and some amphibia have photoreceptors directly in their brain! The visual perceptions of each species depend upon how the brain processes the basic information it receives from the eye about the spatial distribution of various wavelengths of light. Different kinds of processing of the same input information allow us to make decisions about the color, position, depth, and form of visual stimuli. Research on visual information processing is a very active contemporary field. We will review some of the highlights, proceeding from the eye into the nervous system.

The Beginnings of Visual Perception

The eye is an elaborate structure that enables us not only to capture light but to form detailed spatial images that allow us to perceive objects and scenes. Its functions require both internal and external muscles under delicate neural control. We will briefly examine the eye and then consider how such an elaborate organ evolved. The transduction of light into neural activity involves a series of steps in receptor cells of the retina starting with photochemical transformations.

The Vertebrate Eye as an Optical Instrument

Our ability to discriminate visual objects and scenes depends upon a whole series of structures and processes. First among these are the structures and processes of the eye that enable it to form relatively accurate optical images upon the light-sensitive cells of the retina. The eye has many of the features of a camera, starting with lenses to focus light (Figure 9-14). Light travels in a straight line until it encounters a change in the density of the medium, which causes light rays to bend. (Box 9-3 describes some of the features of the optical stimulus.) The cornea of the eye, whose curvature is fixed, causes a marked bending of light rays, and the lens, whose shape is controlled by the ciliary muscles inside the eye, makes further adjustments. As the viewer controls the degree of contraction of the ciliary muscles, the lens can be made to focus images of nearer or farther objects on the retina; this process of focusing is called accommodation. In many people the shape of the eyeball is such that the lens cannot bring images into sharp focus on the retina. Eyeglasses or contact lens can correct such conditions, and operations to change the curvature of the cornea are also being used for this purpose. As people get older, the lenses become less elastic and therefore less able to change their curvature. Bifocal or trifocal eyeglasses then permit accurate viewing at different distances.

The amount of light that enters the eye is controlled by the size of the pupil, just as the aperture controls the light that enters a camera. We mentioned in Chapter 2 that pupillary dilation is controlled by the sympathetic division of the autonomic system, and constriction by the parasympathetic division. Usually both divisions are active, so pupil size reflects a balance of the influences of the two divisions. When you have an eye examination, a drug may be used to block acetylcholine transmission in the parasympathetic synapses of the iris; this relaxes the sphincter muscle fibers and permits the pupil to open widely. Some drugs, such as morphine, stimulate the sympathetic division, and intensely constricted pupils are a symptom of overdose of such drugs.

The lens and the fluid inside the eyeball absorb specific wavelengths of light. Thus before light energy strikes the retina, the visual stimulus has already been filtered, and its wavelength distribution has been substantially modified.

Muscles attached to the outside of the eyeball control the direction of gaze

Figure 9-14 Structures of the human eye.

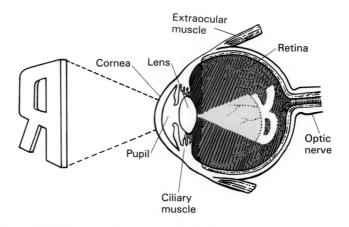

BOX 9-3 | Technical Background: The Visual Stimulus

The physical energy to which our visual system responds is a band of electromagnetic radiation. This radiation comes in very small packets of energy called **quanta**. Each quantum can be described by a single number, its wavelength (the distance between two adjacent crests of vibratory activity). The human visual system responds only to quanta whose wavelengths lie within a very narrow range, from about 400 to 700 nanometers (nm) (see Box Figure 9-4). Such quanta of light energy are called **photons** (from the Greek word meaning "light"). The band of radiant energy in which animals can see may be narrow, but it is well suited for accurate reflection from the surface of objects in the size range that we

deal with in most of our behavior. Radio waves are good for imaging objects of astronomical size, while X-rays penetrate below the surfaces of objects.

Each photon is a very small amount of energy; the exact amount depends on its wavelength. A single photon of wavelength 560 nm contains only 3.55×10^{-19} joule of energy. A 100-watt (W) light bulb gives off only about 3 W of visible light—the rest is heat. But even the 3 W of light amounts to 8 quintillion (8×10^{18}) photons per second! When quanta enter the eye, they can evoke visual sensations. The exact nature of such sensations depends both on the wavelengths of the quanta and on the number of quanta per second.

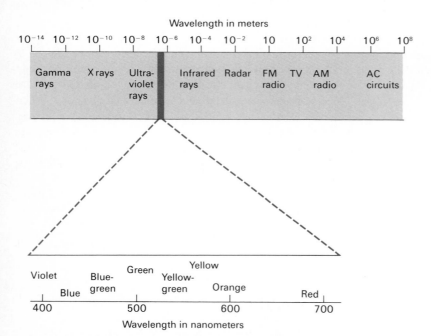

Box Figure 9-4 **The electromagnetic spectrum of which visible light, enlarged below, is only a small fraction.**

(Figure 9-15), just as the photographer aims the camera. Fixating still or moving targets requires delicate control of these muscles. When we view distant objects, the two eyes move in parallel, but when we view a nearby object, the two eyes converge upon the target. In this respect the visual system resembles a three-dimensional camera with a pair of lenses. In such a system, both convergence and accommodation are involved in focusing.

This brief survey shows that at the level of the visual receptor organ, delicate and elaborate control of both intraocular and extraocular muscles is important in finding, focusing, and following visual stimuli. Some of these processes are controlled largely through reflexes, such as control of pupillary size by the level of ambient illumination. Others depend upon feedback involving the perceptions that result from processing visual information. In any case they all depend upon stimulation of the light-sensitive cells of the retina, and we turn now to that next step in the visual processes. In this respect the eye resembles a television camera, where an array of many small light-sensitive elements transmit electrical signals depending upon the intensity of the illumination they receive.

Evolution of Eyes

When we look at a complex organ like the eye of a mammal, an octopus, or a fly, it is hard to imagine how it could have evolved. But inspection of different species of living animals reveals an unbroken gradation from very simple light-sensitive cells to increasingly more complex organs with focusing devices. Some of the steps along the way to eyes like those of a mammal or an octopus are the following:

1. Concentrating light-sensitive cells into localized groups that serve as photoreceptor organs. This is an improvement over scattered receptor cells because it facilitates responding differently to stimuli that strike different parts of the body surface.
2. Clustering light receptors at the bottom of pitlike or cuplike depressions in the skin. This improves discrimination among stimuli that come from different directions, and it increases the contrast of a stimulus against a background of ambient light.
3. Narrowing the top of the cup into a small aperture, so the eye can focus well, like a pinhole camera.
4. Closing over the opening with transparent skin or filling the cup with a transparent substance. This protects the eye against the entrance of foreign substances that might injure the receptor cells or block vision.
5. Forming a lens by thickening the transparent skin. This improves the focusing of the eye while allowing the aperture to be relatively large; thus vision can be acute even when light is not intense.

Inspection of different species reveals that photoreceptor organs have evolved independently in at least 40 different phyletic lines (Salvini-Plawen & Mayr, 1977), so the evolution of an organ of vision is clearly not unusual in the history of animal forms. Among the living representatives of at least 20 of these phyletic lines, it is possible to see a regular series of increasingly efficient eyes, including 15 different lines that have each evolved eyes with lenses to focus light.

Apparently all that is needed as the starting point for development of eyes is the existence of light-sensitive cells. Natural selection will then favor the development of auxiliary mechanisms needed to improve vision. Many kinds of cells show some light sensitivity, and different phyletic lines have used different starting points. The most common start has been cells of epidermal (skin) origin, but several lines (including the chordate-vertebrate ancestry) derived their visual receptors from cells of neural origin.

(a) Muscles of the right eye seen from right side

(b) Up-down movement

Superior rectus

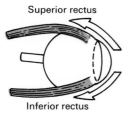

Inferior rectus

(c) Rotation

Superior oblique

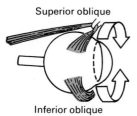

Inferior oblique

(d) Right-left movement

Medial rectus

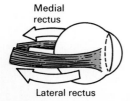

Lateral rectus

Figure 9-15 Muscles of the eye and the kinds of movements produced by different muscles.

Three basic ways of forming a visual image are to use a lens (a camera eye), a pinhole aperture, or a compound eye formed of narrow tube receptors (ommatidia) that fan out to point in different directions. Animals that use lenses include not only vertebrates and some cephalopods (like the octopus) but also some insects and some bivalves. Animals with pinhole eyes include the abalone and the nautilus. Animals with compound eyes formed of ommatidia include the insects and most crustacea (such as crabs). The three main methods of forming visual images do not exhaust the mechanisms that have evolved: Some animals use mirrors to form images (for example, scallops), and in a microscopic marine animal (*Copilia*), the few light receptors sweep back and forth and scan the image formed by the lens (Land, 1984).

The fact that the cephalopods (such as squid and octopus) evolved a visual system that in many ways resembles that of vertebrates (from fish to humans) suggests that there are major constraints on the development of a visual system for a large, rapidly moving animal. Let us note some of the major similarities and differences between the visual systems of cephalopods and vertebrates. In both the eyes are relatively large, allowing for many receptors and for ability to gather large amounts of light. The incoming light is regulated by a pupil and focused by a lens. An important difference in eye structure is seen in the organization of the retina. In the vertebrate eye, the light must travel through neurons and blood vessels to get to the receptors, and the area where the neural axons and blood vessels enter and leave the retina is a blind spot. In the cephalopods, in contrast, the organization is more efficient: The light reaches the receptors directly; the neurons and blood vessels lie behind the receptors and there is no blind spot. The detailed structure of the receptor cells is quite different in cephalopods and vertebrates. Also, the visual stimulus causes depolarization of cephalopod (and most invertebrate) retinal receptor cells, but it causes hyperpolarization of fish and mammalian retinal receptors. In octopus and in fish, the eyes move in the head, and each eye is moved by six pairs of muscles. Such eye movements may seem obvious, but most mammals, except for primates, do not move their eyes in their heads but mainly direct their gaze by moving the entire head. The major similarities between cephalopod and vertebrate eyes provide examples of convergent evolution. The differences provide examples of ways in which similar functions can be achieved with somewhat different structures and processes, starting from different origins.

The Retina

The first stage of visual information processing occurs in the **retina,** the receptive surface inside the eye (Figure 9-16). Several types of cells form distinct layers within the retina (Figure 9-16b). The receptive elements proper—the **rods** and **cones**—synapse with **bipolar cells,** which in turn connect with **ganglion cells;** the axons of the ganglion cells form the **optic nerve.** From the receptive elements to the ganglion cells there is an enormous compression of input; the human eye contains about 125 million rods and cones but only one million ganglion cells. **Horizontal cells** and **amacrine cells** in the retina (Figure 9-17) complete the nerve cell population; these cells are especially significant in inhibitory interactions within the retina. The large number of retinal cells permits a great deal of information processing to occur at this level of the visual system. The resultant signals converge on the ganglion cells.

Studies of human sensitivity to light reveal the existence of two different func-

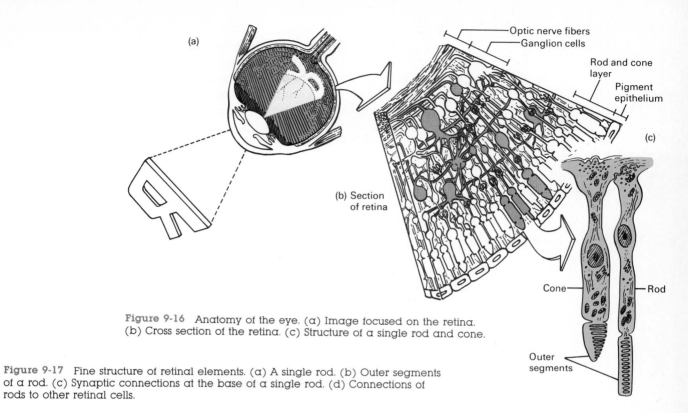

Figure 9-16 Anatomy of the eye. (a) Image focused on the retina. (b) Cross section of the retina. (c) Structure of a single rod and cone.

Figure 9-17 Fine structure of retinal elements. (a) A single rod. (b) Outer segments of a rod. (c) Synaptic connections at the base of a single rod. (d) Connections of rods to other retinal cells.

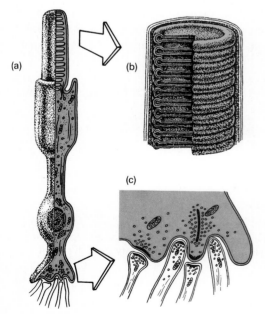

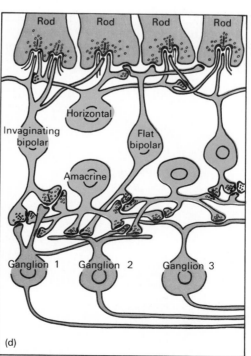

tional systems corresponding to two different populations of receptors in the retina. One system works at low levels of light intensity and involves the rods; this system is called the **scotopic system** (from the Greek word for ''darkness''). The other system operates at higher levels of light and shows sensitivity to color; this system involves the cones and is called the **photopic system** (from the Greek word for ''light''). The workings of these two systems, with their somewhat different sensitivities, enable our eyes to operate over a wide range of intensities. Characteristics of the photopic and scotopic systems are summarized in Table 9-1.

The extraordinary sensitivy of both kinds of visual receptors is determined by their unusual structure and biochemistry. A portion of the structure of both rods and cones, when magnified, looks like a large stack of pancakes (Figure 9-17b). Each layer within the pile is called a disc. The stacking of discs increases the probability of capturing quanta of light. This feature is especially important since light is reflected in many directions by the surface of the eyeball, the lens, and the fluid media of the eye. Because of the dispersion of light, only small amounts actually reach the retinal surface.

The quanta of light that strike the discs are captured by special photopigments. The pigment in the rods is called **rhodopsin.** The pioneering studies of George Wald (1964) established the chemical structure of this and other visual pigments. He showed that this protein molecule changes shape when exposed to light. Recent research has shown that the light-altered form of rhodopsin possesses enzymatic activity and initiates a cascade of events: Capture of each quantum of light leads to the closing of hundreds of sodium channels in the photoreceptor membrane and blocks the entry of a million sodium ions (Schnapf & Baylor, 1987). Closing the channels creates a generator potential that represents the initial electrical signal of activation of the visual pathway. The size of the receptor potential is related to stimulus intensity. Sensitivity of the rod is partly determined by prior exposure to light; thus a given intensity of stimulation will cause a larger receptor potential if

Table 9-1 Summary of Properties of the Photopic and Scotopic Visual Systems

Property	Photopic System	Scotopic System
Receptors*	Cones	Rods
Number of receptors per eye (approx.)	6 million	120 million
Photopigments†	Three cone opsins: the basis of color vision	Rhodopsin
Sensitivity	Low: needs relatively strong stimulation; used for day vision	High: can be stimulated by weak light intensity; used for night vision
Location in retina‡	In and near fovea	Outside fovea
Receptive field size	Small, so acuity is high	Large, so acuity is low

*See forms of cones and rods in Figure 9-16c.
†See Figure 9-22 for spectral sensitivities of photopigments.
‡See Figure 9-25 for distribution of cones and rods across the retina.

preceded by smaller rather than by larger stimuli. There are three different cone pigments, as will be discussed later in relation to color vision.

Brain Pathways of the Visual System

from optic nerve
segregated at
optic chiasm

after cross
= optic tract
— most
terminate in
lateral geniculate
nucleus
Part of Thalamus

— some end in
Superior colliculus

axons of post synaptic
cells in the LGT
= optic radiations
on. nucleus
which end in
occipital cortex
— area 17

The results of visual processing in the retina converge on the ganglion cells; their axons form the optic nerve, which conveys visual information to the brain. In any vertebrate animal, some or all of the axons of the optic nerve cross to the opposite cerebral hemisphere (Figure 9-18). A larger proportion of axons cross over in those animals with laterally placed eyes who have little binocular overlap. In humans axons of the optic nerve are segregated into two groups at the **optic chiasm.** At this point axons from the half of the retina toward the nose (nasal retina) cross over to the opposite side of the brain. The half of the retina toward the side of the head, the temporal retina, projects its axons to its own side of the head. The degree of optic tract crossing varies greatly among species; it amounts to 90% crossing for the rat and about 50% for primates.

The **optic tract** is the term applied to the axons of the retinal ganglion cells after they cross the optic chiasm. Most optic tract axons terminate in the **lateral geniculate nucleus,** which is part of the thalamus. Some axons leave the optic tract to end in the **superior colliculus** in the midbrain. Relatively small bundles of axons go to nuclei in the diencephalon; they are involved in the control of daily cycles of behavior (circadian rhythms), which we will discuss in Chapter 14.

Synaptic interactions in the lateral geniculate may involve influences derived from other brain regions (for instance, the reticular formation). The axons of postsynaptic cells in the lateral geniculate form the **optic radiations,** which terminate in the primary visual areas in the **occipital cortex.** In addition to the **primary visual cortex** shown in Figure 9-18, surrounding regions of the cortex are also largely visual in function. It is at the cortical level that inputs from the two eyes converge, making possible binocular effects.

Multiple Cortical Visual Areas

preserves order
but not size
many visual
areas

Recent studies have revealed several cortical areas for each sensory modality, and most of these areas are laid out in an orderly topographic map of the receptor surface (C. N. Woolsey, 1981a,b,c). (By "topographic" we mean a systematic representation but one that does not necessarily preserve size relations; this is like a rubber-sheet map that preserves order but not size.) For example, recent examination of the cortex of the owl monkey (a New World monkey) reveals at least six visual areas, each of which is a topographic representation of the retina (Figure 9-19a). No other species has yet been mapped as completely, but in the macaque (an Old World monkey) it also appears that most of the cortical visual regions consist of orderly maps of the retina. Evidence is accumulating that different cortical regions participate in parallel in processing different aspects of visual perception, such as color, location, depth, pattern, and form. Much of the basic work on visual neurophysiology has been done with cats, but study of color vision requires primates because, among mammals, only primates have good color vision.

Functionally Distinct Parallel Pathways from Thalamus to Cortex

Each sensory region of the cortex receives input from one or more regions of the thalamus. Some divisions of the thalamus project to a single cortical region, and some project to more than one. There is further divergence of sensory information.

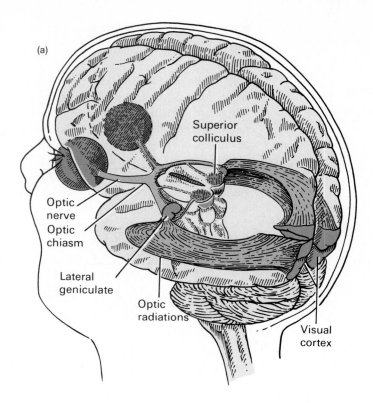

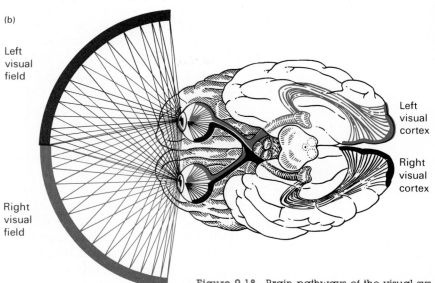

Figure 9-18 Brain pathways of the visual system. (a) Visual pathways in the human brain. (b) Representation of the visual fields on the retinas and their projections to the cerebral hemispheres. The right visual field, shown in color, projects to the left cerebral hemisphere, and the left visual field projects to the right hemisphere.

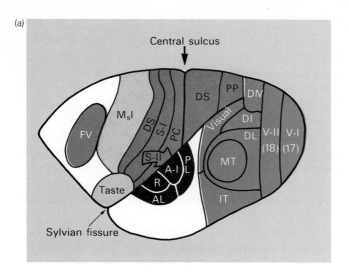

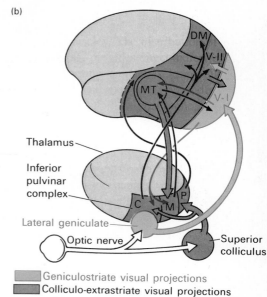

Geniculostriate visual projections
Colliculo-extrastriate visual projections

Figure 9-19 (a) Subdivisions of neocortex with sensory functions in a New World monkey. Most of the occipital and parietal cortex shows systematic representations of sensory surfaces, as do parts of the temporal and frontal regions. *Visual subdivisions:* V-I, primary visual area (corresponding to Brodmann's Area 17); V-II, second visual area (or Area 18); DI, dorsointermediate; DL, dorsolateral; DM, dorsomedial; IT, inferotemporal; MT, middle temporal; and FV, frontal visual. There may also be visual functions in PP, posterior parietal. *Auditory subdivisions:* A-I, primary auditory area; AL, anterior lateral; PL, posterior lateral; and R, rostral auditory field. *Somatosensory subdivisions:* S-I, primary somatosensory area; S-II, second somatosensory area (hidden in the Sylvian fissure); DS, deep sensory representation (muscles and joints); PC, posterior cutaneous area; PP, posterior parietal; and M_sI, motor sensory area I. (b) Some of the thalamocortical connections of the visual system in monkeys. The optic nerve sends axons to both the lateral geniculate nucleus and the superior colliculus. The lateral geniculate projects to the striate cortex (V-I). The superior colliculus projects to the inferior pulvinar complex of the thalamus. The central (C) and posterior (P) divisions of the inferior pulvinar project to the visual cortical regions outside of V-1, and the middle (M) inferior pulvinar receives a large projection from the extrastriate cortex. Some corticocortical connections are also shown. (Adapted from Merzenich and Kaas, 1980)

The sensory regions of the cortex send axons back to the thalamus, usually to their own sources of input but sometimes to other thalamic divisions as well. Some of the thalamocortical projections of the visual system of the monkey are shown in Figure 9-19b.

Columnar Organization of the Primary Visual Cortex

The organization of the primary visual cortex into columns has a richness undreamed of only a few years ago. It is even more complicated than the organization of the somatosensory cortex that we discussed in Chapter 8 because the primary visual cortex has separate representations for at least four dimensions of the visual stimulus. Overall the primary visual cortex represents locations in the visual field and has larger, finer mapping of the central region than of the periphery. But within a particular area that represents a certain part of the visual field, there are separate bands or stripes of cells that represent the ipsilateral and contralateral eyes. Within these bands are columns in which all the neuron-receptive fields are selective for stimuli with the same angular orientation within the visual field. That is, in one column all the cells are "tuned" to upright stimuli (at 0-degree orientation); in an adjacent column, all cells respond best to stimuli at 10 degrees from the vertical; in another column, at 20 degrees, and so forth. Furthermore, it has been found rather recently that, in primate brains, within the ipsilateral and contralateral bands of columns for each area, there are "blobs" or "pegs" that may be related to color vision (Hendrickson, 1985; Livingstone & Hubel, 1984). Figure 9-20 gives a diagrammatic representation of the organization of the primate visual cortex. (Compare with Figure 8-16 for somatosensory cortex.)

Let us see a little more of this complex organization and the methods that are being used to study it (Gouras, 1985; Hendrickson, 1985; Kandel, 1985). The first aspect to be discovered (by electrophysiological recording of the receptive fields of individual neurons) was the existence of elongated bands of cells responding preferentially to stimulation of one eye. Each band was 350–500 micrometers (μm) wide. Although these bands consist of thousands of individual cortical columns, they were given the name **ocular dominance columns** (ODCs), and this term continues to be used. The ocular dominance is especially clear in the broad layer IV of the primary visual cortex where any cell responds to only one eye; above and below layer IV, most cells respond to stimulation of both eyes.

New anatomical tracing techniques that proliferated beginning in the 1970s confirmed the existence of ODCs and furnished further information about them. For example, when a small dose of radioactive amino acid is injected into one eye, some of it is transported along neurons, crossing synapses and reaching the visual cortex. Autoradiographic examination of the cortex then reveals parallel bands of radioactivity in layer IV, and these corresponded to the ODCs. Then activation of neurons outside layer IV was demonstrated by use of the 2-deoxyglucose autoradiographic technique that we described in Chapter 2. When a monkey had one eye covered while radioactive 2-deoxyglucose was administered, subsequent autoradiography showed not only bands about 350 μm wide in layer IV but also dots of radioactivity about 150 μm wide in the other layers; these dots ran along the centers of the ocular dominance bands. The presence of these dots shows that some of the neurons in other layers of the bands are also mainly monocular.

Within the ocular dominance bands are individual columns 30–100 μm in diameter. Microelectrode recording has shown that all the cells within each column share the same preference for stimuli at a given orientation or azimuth within the visual field. As the recording electrode is moved from one column to the next, the preferred axis of orientation shifts by about 10 degrees. In Figure 9-20 the preferred axis of orientation is shown diagrammatically at the top of each column along the right face of the figure, but this orientation is characteristic of all the cells through the depth of the column.

Peg-shaped regions of cortex interrupt the progression of orientation columns. Cells in these pegs or "blobs" do not respond preferentially to orientation, but they show color preferences. These cells are double-opponent cells (for example, re-

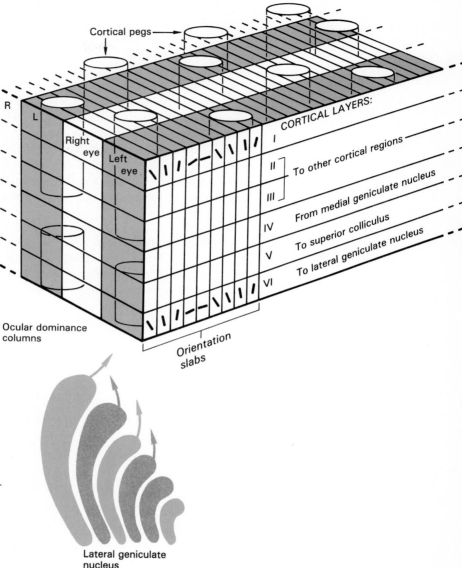

Figure 9-20 Organization of primary visual cortex of primates into cortical bands and columns. Cells in the lateral geniculate nucleus (lower left) send segregated projections to the cortex. Cells from the right eye are represented in layers 1, 3, and 6 of the geniculate (shown in color), and these project to right ocular dominance columns in the cortex. Left ocular dominance columns alternate with right columns. Finer subdivisions are columns in which all cells are tuned to stimili at a particular visual angle. Cortical "pegs" or "blobs" are seen at the upper and lower cortical layers; cells in these regions mediate color vision and receive their inputs from the four upper layers of the geniculate. (Adapted from Kandel and Schwartz, 1985)

sponding with excitation to red and with inhibition to green—a red plus-green minus neuron), and their receptive fields are round with no axis of orientation. The cortical pegs are about 150–200 μm in diameter and run along the centers of ocular dominance columns; they are more plentiful and larger in regions of cortex that map the center of the visual field, and they are smaller and spaced further apart in regions that represent the periphery. Chemical techniques suggest that neurons in the pegs are prepared for a higher rate of activity than the interpeg cells. For example, the pegs can be revealed anatomically by using a stain for an enzyme (cytochrome oxidase) that is characteristic of mitochondria and whose activity varies with the level of the cellular activity of neurons. Also, enzymes of both the acetylcholine and GABA transmitter systems are found preferentially in the pegs.

Although recordings in macaque monkeys indicate that neurons in the pegs are associated with color perception, it is not yet clear how general the association is. Appearing to support such a relationship is the observation that the pegs are found in most primates but not in carnivores or rodents, but further scrutiny raises questions. The pegs occur even in nocturnal primates whose retinas are poor in cones, but they do not occur in cone-rich rodents, such as ground squirrels; such a distribution does not seem to be consistent with color function. The differential inputs and outputs of the pegs and the interpeg regions also provide questions for further research. Working out the detailed organization, connections, and functions of visual cortex provides enough problems to keep many scientists occupied for decades to come.

How We See Color

For most of us, the visible world has several distinguishable hues: blue, green, yellow, red, and their intermediates. For about 8% of human males and about 0.5% of females, some of these color distinctions are either absent or at least less striking. Although the term *color blindness* is commonly used to describe impairments in color perception, even people with impaired color vision do distinguish some hues; complete color blindness in humans is extremely rare.

The appearance of a patch of light has other aspects besides its hue. The color solid (Figure 9-21) is used to illustrate three basic dimensions of our perception of light:

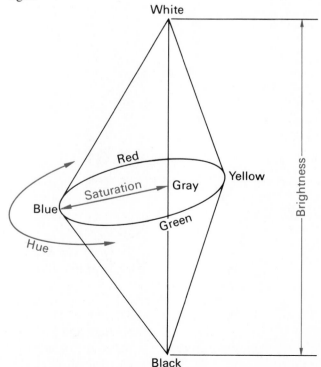

Figure 9-21 The color solid illustrating three basic dimensions of perception of light.

1. **Brightness,** which varies from dark to light and is the vertical dimension in the figure.
2. **Hue,** which varies around the color circle through blue, green, yellow, orange, and red.
3. **Saturation,** which varies from rich full colors at the periphery of the circle to gray at the center. For example, starting with red at the periphery, the colors become paler toward the center, going through pink to gray.

Color perception in mammals depends both on the existence of receptor cells that are specialized for bands of certain wavelengths of light and on the processing of this information by neurons in the local circuits of the retina.

Receptor Cells for Color

Cones are the receptors for color vision. Animals that have all-rod retinas, such as the rat, are color blind. Early in the nineteenth century, it was hypothesized that three separate kinds of cones provide the basis for color vision. This **trichromatic hypothesis** was endorsed in 1852 by the great physiologist-physicist Hermann von Helmholtz and became the dominant position. Helmholtz believed that blue-sensitive, green-sensitive, and red-sensitive cones would be found, and that each type would have a separate path to the brain. The color of an object would be recognized, then, on the basis of which color receptor was activated. This would be like discriminating among touch, cold, and warmth on the basis of which skin receptors are activated. A different explanation was proposed by the physiologist Ewald Hering. He argued on the basis of visual experience that there are three opposed pairs of colors—blue-yellow, green-red, and black-white—and that three physiological processes with opposed positive and negative values must therefore be the basis of color vision. As we will see, both this **opponent-process hypothesis** and the trichromatic hypothesis are encompassed in current color theory, but neither of the old hypotheses is sufficient by itself.

Are there three classes of cones with different color properties? Measurements of cone photopigments in the last few years have borne out the trichromatic hypothesis in part. Each cone of the human retina does have one of three pigments. These pigments do not, however, have the narrow spectral distributions that Helmholtz had predicted. The color system that Helmholtz postulated would have given rather poor color vision and poor visual acuity. Color vision would be poor because only a few different hues could be discriminated; within the long-wavelength region of the spectrum there would be only red and not all the range of hues that we see. Acuity would be poor because the grain of the retinal mosaic would be coarse; a red stimulus could affect only one-third of the receptors. Actually acuity is as good in red light as in white light.

In fact, the human visual system does not have color receptors, each sensitive only to a restricted part of the visible spectrum. Two of the three retinal cone pigments respond to lights of almost any wavelength. The pigments do have somewhat different peaks of sensitivity, but these are not as far apart as Helmholtz predicted. As Figure 9-22 shows, one peak occurs at about 419 nanometers (in the blue part of the spectrum), another at about 531 nm (green), and the third at about 559 nm (yellow green). Note that none of the curves peaks in the red part of the spectrum.

Figure 9-22 Spectral sensitivity of human photopigments. The most up-to-date information on the spectral absorbance of human retinal photopigments comes from microdensitometer analyses of the outer segments of individual cones and rods. The data in this figure are based on receptors from seven eyes (3 female, 4 male). The brown curve with a maximum at 419 nm is based on 5 short-wave sensitive cones; the brown curve that peaks at 531 nm, on 45 medium-wave sensitive cones; and the brown curve with a maximum at 559 nm, on 53 long-wave sensitive cones. The black curve is the mean for 39 rods. (From Mollon, 1982)

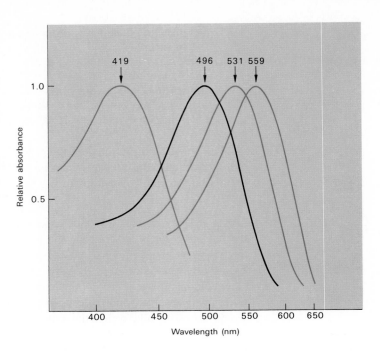

Under ordinary conditions almost any visual object stimulates cones of at least two kinds, thus providing for high visual acuity and good perception of form. The spectral sensitivities of the three cone types are somewhat different from each other, and neural processing detects and magnifies these differences to extract the color information. Certain ganglion cells and certain cells at higher stations in the visual system are color-specific, but the receptor cells are not. Similarly, the receptors are not form-specific, but form is detected later in the visual centers by comparing the outputs of different receptors. Since the cones are not color detectors, the most appropriate brief names for them can be taken from their peak areas of wavelength sensitivity: short (S) for the receptor with peak sensitivity at 419 nm, middle (M) at 531, and long (L) at 559.

The genes for retinal color pigments have recently been located on human chromosomes, and the amino acid sequences for the cone pigments have been determined (Nathans, 1987). The similarities in structure of the three genes suggests that they are all derived from a common ancestral gene. In particular, the genes for the middle and long wavelength pigments occupy adjacent positions on the X chromosome and are much more similar to each other than either is to the gene for the short wavelength pigment on chromosome 6. The fact that humans and Old World monkeys have both M and L pigments whereas New World monkeys have only a single longer wave pigment had already suggested that differentiation of the M and L pigments was rather recent, in evolutionary terms. Furthermore, the genes for the M and L pigments are variable among individuals, and particular variants among these pigment genes correspond to variants in color vision (so-called color blindness).

That is, detailed examination of a person's photopigment genes can now show whether the person has normal color vision or has one of the recognized deficiencies of color discrimination.

Retinal Color Circuits

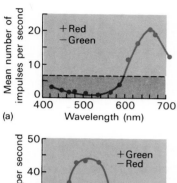

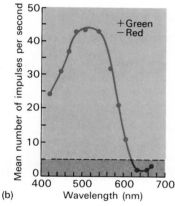

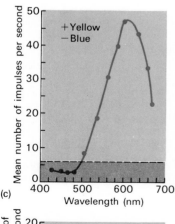

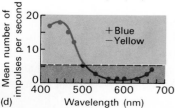

The neural circuits that extract color information and that contrast the brightness of adjacent parts of the visual field are located in the retina. Thus a great deal of neural processing takes place in the retina, where there are hundreds of millions of nerve cells. The results of this processing are carried to the higher centers by the one million axons of each optic nerve. The complexities of retinal anatomy are indicated in Figures 9-17 and 9-18. The retinal ganglion cells are thus projection neurons, and the other retinal cells are local-circuit neurons, according to the distinction between projection and local-circuit neurons made in Chapter 2.

Recordings have been made from ganglion cells in Old World monkeys, which show color discrimination just like that of human beings with normal color vision. It was found that most ganglion cells and cells in the dorsal layers of the lateral geniculate nucleus are spectrally sensitive; they fire to some wavelengths and are inhibited by other wavelengths. Lateral geniculate cells show the same response characteristics as retinal ganglion cells but are more convenient to record from, so most of the work has been done with them. A leader in this research is Russell L. De Valois, and much of the information in this section comes from his reports. Figure 9-23a shows the response of such a cell as a spot of light in the center of the cell's receptive field is changed from one wavelength to another. The firing is inhibited from about 420 to 600 nm, then it is stimulated from about 600 nm on. Such a cell is called plus red, minus green ($+R - G$). Since two regions of the spectrum have opposite effects on the cell's rate of firing, it is an example of what is called a **spectrally opponent cell.** Figure 9-23 shows examples of responses of the four main kinds of spectrally opponent cells.

Each spectrally opponent ganglion cell presumably receives input from two different kinds of cones through bipolar cells. The connections from one kind of cone are excitatory, and those from the other kind are inhibitory. The patterns of connections are shown in Figure 9-24. The ganglion cells thus record the difference in stimulation of different populations of cones. For example, a $+G-R$ cell responds to the difference in excitation of M minus L cones; a $+R-G$ cell responds to L minus M. (We noted in Chapter 6 that a neuron can process information by subtracting one input from another; this is an example of such information processing.) Although the peaks of the sensitivity curves of the M and L cones are not very different, the M minus L difference curve shows a clear peak around 500 nm (in the green or blue-green part of the spectrum). The L minus M difference function shows a peak around 650 nm (in the orange part of the spectrum). So subtracting one cone function from the other yields two distinctly different neural response curves. The spectrally sensitive neurons can properly be called color cells, whereas the cones are

Figure 9-23 Responses of four main types of spectrally opponent lateral geniculate cells in macaque monkeys. These cells are called spectrally opponent because each is inhibited by light in one part of the spectrum and is excited by light in another part. (From De Valois and De Valois, 1975)

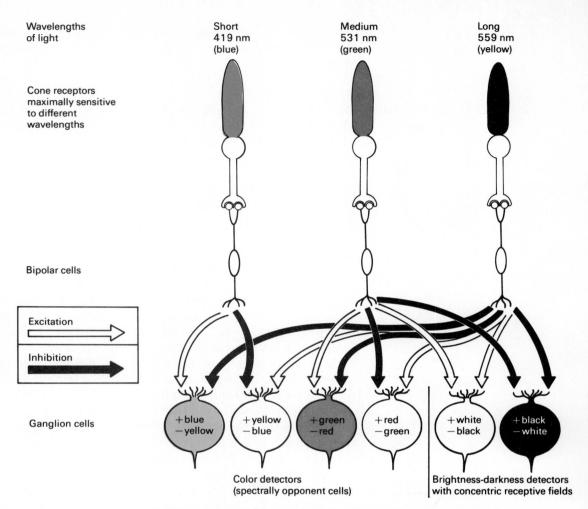

Wavelengths of light

Short 419 nm (blue)

Medium 531 nm (green)

Long 559 nm (yellow)

Cone receptors maximally sensitive to different wavelengths

Bipolar cells

Excitation

Inhibition

Ganglion cells

+blue −yellow

+yellow −blue

+green −red

+red −green

+white −black

+black −white

Color detectors (spectrally opponent cells)

Brightness-darkness detectors with concentric receptive fields

Figure 9-24 A model of the connections of the color vision systems in the retina. (Adapted from De Valois and De Valois, 1975)

best considered as light receptors that feed into many circuits—for detection of form, depth, and movement as well as of hue.

In the monkey lateral geniculate nucleus 70 to 80% of the cells are spectrally opponent, whereas in the cat very few spectrally opponent cells are found, about 1%. This difference corresponds to the ease with which monkeys can discriminate wavelengths and the extreme difficulty of training cats to discriminate even large differences of wavelength.

Cortical Color Circuits

In the cortex color information appears to be used for different kinds of information processing. Some cortical cells are spectrally opponent and may even sharpen or enhance differences of hue. These cells may contribute to perception of color. It has been reported that some cortical visual regions, especially V4, are particularly rich in color-sensitive cells and even show perceptual effects of chromatic context (Zeki, 1983). Perception of color appears to require the cortex in humans, because some cortical lesions destroy perception of color. But Boynton (1988) points out that we are still far from understanding how the activity of the different cortical regions combines to produce our perception of color.

The color vision that we enjoy is rare among mammals. It is very poorly developed in rodents (such as rats) and in carnivores (such as dogs and cats). It is moderately well developed in prosimians (such as *Tupaia*) and is highly developed in monkeys and apes. Perhaps human color vision goes back to our tree-living, fruit-eating ancestors. Color vision is not confined to certain mammalian species, though. Apparently it has evolved independently in several lines, including some molluscs, some insects, some fish, and some reptiles.

How We Locate Visual Stimuli

The ability to locate visual stimuli in space depends on our ability to answer two questions: In what direction does the stimulus object lie? (This is a question about the visual field.) And how far away is it? (This is a question of depth perception.)

Visual Field

Each successive level of the visual system is a detailed map of the visible world. First the retina receives an accurate image, projected on it by the optics of the eye, especially the cornea and lens. Next the retina sends signals along axons to the visual areas of the diencephalon and midbrain, and these preserve the spatial array. Finally other axons then convey the visual information to several visual areas in the cerebral cortex, and again these show detailed maps of the visible world.

Although the neural maps preserve the order of the visual field, each emphasizes some regions at the expense of others; that is, each map is topographic and does not provide exact copies of spatial relations in the external world. One reason that the maps are topographic is that some portions of the retinal surface have a denser concentration of receptors than others. The region called the **fovea** (from the Latin word for a "small depression" or "pit") has a dense concentration of cones and provides a central region of maximal acuity (Figure 9-25a). The data on cone concentration in Figure 9-25a come from a classic study by Østerberg (1935), but they are based on only one retina. Now Curcio et al. (1987) have measured four other retinas. Østerberg's data fall in the range, but the four retinas showed a 3:1 spread in the number of cones per square millimeter in the fovea. Could this be related to individual differences in visual acuity?

The rods show a different distribution; they are absent in the fovea but are more numerous than cones in the periphery of the retina. A gap in the retinal surface, which is not noticeable under ordinary viewing conditions, is produced by the entrance of blood vessels to the retina. There are no receptors at this small region of the retina and light that strikes it cannot be seen, so this region is called the **blind spot.**

The fact that projection of visual space onto brain regions is topographic does not mean that our spatial perception is distorted. Rather it reflects the acuity of spatial discrimination, which is greatest in the central part of the field. It is for this

Figure 9-25 Visual acuity and retinal position. Cones are concentrated in the fovea and their concentration falls off rapidly on either side. Rods are lacking in the fovea and show their greatest concentration about 20 degrees from the fovea. About 16 degrees to the nasal side of the retina is a disc where the ganglion cell axons leave the retina and through which the retinal arteries and veins pass. There are no receptors in this region, and small objects whose images fall on it cannot be seen, so it is called the blind spot. (From data of Østerberg, 1935.) Acuity is maximum at the fovea, as shown in the lower graph. It declines with distance from the fovea rather similarly to the reduction in concentration of cores in the upper graph.

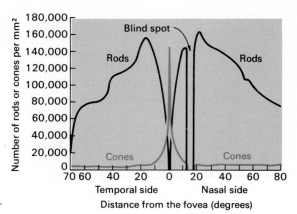

(a) Frequencies of rods and cones across the retina

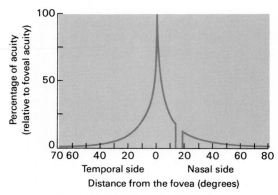

(b) Variation of visual acuity across the retina

reason that reading is done with the fovea and that the eye jumps from spot to spot along a line of printing or along any scene that is inspected.

The extreme orderliness of the mapping of the visual field is demonstrated by the study of regions of blindness brought about by injuries. The location of such a perceptual gap, or **scotoma,** in the visual field is accurately predicted by the locus of injury in the visual pathway. Although the word *scotoma* comes from the Latin word for "darkness," a scotoma is not a dark patch in the visual field; rather it is a spot where nothing can be perceived. Although a person cannot perceive, in the usual sense, within a scotoma, in some cases a person can nevertheless perform some visual discriminations; see Box 9-4 on "blindsight."

Scotoma-spot where nothing can be perceived

Depth Perception

Many people believe that the basis of depth perception was discovered by Renaissance artists who accurately analyzed scenes into lines and angles. But recent research has shown that depth can be perceived in the absence of lines and angles and that depth perception in certain targets can precede the perception of form. Also, the way in which the visual system accomplishes the perception of depth has continued to afford controversy and novel observations, even during the last decade.

BOX 9-4   "Blindsight"?

Until recently it was confidently believed that human beings needed the occipital cortex for spatial vision—or for any vision at all. Even if the lower levels of the visual system were operating normally, damage to the cortex could result in blindness. Then it was found that a monkey with its occipital cortex removed could be trained to point accurately at spots of light in order to earn rewards. The apparent discrepancy in visual capacity of humans and monkeys after damage to the visual cortex could be taken in different ways. It could be interpreted as revealing a fundamental difference in brain-behavior relations in human beings and nonhuman primates. Or it could serve as a challenge to investigate the visual capacities of brain-injured patients by employing behavioral techniques similar to those used with nonverbal animals. A few investigators have taken up this challenge.

Patients who have had only the visual cortex destroyed are rare, but a few of them have been studied in some detail. A patient studied by Weiskrantz and his colleagues in England is a good example (Weiskrantz, 1985). This patient had a small tumor removed from the visual cortex of his right hemisphere, and on subsequent routine testing he appeared to be completely blind in the left-half fields of both eyes, even to intense lights. In the first experimental tests, the subject was asked to reach out and touch the position on a screen at which a visual stimulus was projected briefly in the blind field. (This is the same sort of task that monkeys were trained to perform in order to obtain rewards.) It seems like an odd task to ask of a person who says he cannot see, but the subject was asked to "guess" where the stimulus might be on each trial, and he cooperated. It soon became apparent that he could locate stimuli quite accurately. When the results of these trials were shown to the subject after several hours of testing, he was astonished. Later he described "feelings" that something might be present, but he consistently refused to call this the "seeing" that he had in his right-half fields. Later this subject was asked to guess if the stimulus was a horizontal or a vertical line, or X versus O. He showed about 75% accuracy with stimuli 12

degrees in size and even greater accuracy with larger stimuli. His acuity threshold in the "blind" half field was less than 2 min of arc. The investigators termed this capacity "blindsight." The patient does not perceive, yet he performs visual discriminations. This distinction raises important questions for both application and theory. *does perceive but does discrimnat*

Could patients develop both the acuity and the confidence in blindsight so that they could use it in daily life? In monkeys with lesions in part of the striate cortex, the ability to detect a spot of light in the "blind" area increased with training. Moreover, the training was specific, since the areas of the visual field that received practice recovered more rapidly than those that did not receive practice (Mohler & Wurtz, 1977). Humphrey (1970) reported that a monkey with a completely destroyed striate cortex not only learned to discriminate targets but also used vision to avoid obstacles. Active training, rather than imposing stimuli on a passive animal, appears to be necessary for improving visual discrimination after lesions of the striate cortex (Cowey, 1967). At the outset of such training, the animal seems to discover that it possesses a viable visual space; after this discovery is made, performance can improve rapidly.

Observations on blindsight have suggested that vision can come to be mediated by noncortical pathways, especially visual circuits involving the superior colliculus. However, some investigators have questioned the existence of the phenomenon of blindsight. For example, Campion, Latto, and Smith (1983) suggest the possibility that light scatter to regions of the retina that stimulate intact visual cortex can mediate this effect. Additionally, they proposed that blindsight might reflect the residual vision of damaged but not destroyed visual cortical areas. Studies on blindsight have provoked a lively debate because these observations have particular relevance to rehabilitative efforts for humans with cortical blindness. People can perform in many ways on the basis of barely detectable or even subliminal stimuli. But further research is needed to determine whether training of blindsight can be used in practical situations by blind people.

New knowledge about depth perception came from work on random-dot patterns (Julesz, 1971; Julesz and Spivack, 1967). In such stimuli the left and right random-dot targets are identical except that a central region (a square or some other form) in one of the targets is shifted horizontally by a small distance. Each of the targets appears to have the same random texture, and no form is seen in either of

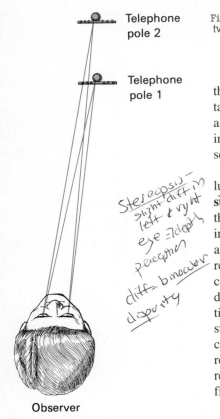

Telephone pole 2

Telephone pole 1

(handwritten margin notes) Stereopsis – slight diff in left & right eye = depth perception diff binocular disparity

Observer

Left eye   Right eye

them. When the targets are viewed stereoscopically (the left eye viewing the left target and the right eye, the right target), the horizontally shifted region is perceived as being displaced in depth. Depending on the direction of the shift, it is seen either in front of or behind the surrounding area. Only when the depth is perceived stereoscopically does the form of the shifted region appear.

The slightly different views that the two eyes have of a scene provide the stimulus basis for perceiving depth (see Figure 9-26). This phenomenon is also called **stereopsis** (from Greek roots for ''depth'' and ''vision''). The difference between the views of the two eyes is called **binocular disparity.** Recent work has now indicated the mechanism of stereopsis (Poggio & Poggio, 1984; von der Heydt et al., 1978). Many cortical cells have narrowly tuned receptive fields with little or no retinal disparity; that is, they are tuned to the fixation plane or very close to it. Other cells do show retinal disparity, but different cells are not tuned to a wide range of different depths. Rather there are only two types of cells with broad retinal disparities: One set is excited by stimuli in front of the fixation plane and inhibited by stimuli behind the fixation plane, and the other set has the opposite responses. The cells in both the striate and the peristriate areas thus fall into three categories with regard to retinal disparity: those tuned to the fixation plane, those tuned to the region beyond the fixation plane, and those tuned to the region in front of the fixation plane.

At about the same time that this research was being conducted, psychophysical results with human observers gave independent evidence of the existence of only a few pathways or channels for depth. Investigators found that some ''normal'' viewers are actually partially stereo-blind; that is, some subjects are specifically unable to localize, by means of stereoscopic clues alone, the depth of an object beyond the fixation plane; other subjects are unable to use such clues to locate the depth of an object in front of the fixation plane (Jones, 1978; Richards, 1977). These results point to the existence of two broadly tuned depth channels. One channel is for objects anywhere beyond the fixation plane and another is for those in front. Either channel may be missing or may function poorly in occasional individuals.

Figure 9-26   The visual scene as viewed by each eye. The difference between the two views is called binocular disparity.

How We Perceive Pattern and Form

We recognize individuals and classify stimuli according to their sizes, shapes, and locations in the visual field. How these aspects of spatial vision are accomplished by neural circuits has been and continues to be the object of intensive research. Much of this work involves the study of the electrical activity of neurons at various levels of the visual system and attempts to relate it to visual perception. Most investigators assume that recognition of visual scenes first requires the analysis of complex patterns into some kind of subunits, with each individual cell in the visual pathway responding only to certain aspects of the part of the pattern that occurs within the receptive field of the cell. Then these subunits must be synthesized into a complex

(handwritten margin notes) Subunits Synthesized into complex pattern

pattern. But so far the problem of determining the initial analysis has not been solved.

The two main current models of pattern analysis are the **feature detector model** and the **spatial frequency filter model.** Let us examine each of these in turn and consider their strengths and weaknesses in accounting for the facts of form perception.

Feature Detector Model

The receptive fields of cells in the visual system differ from one level of the system to another. The receptive fields of retinal ganglion cells are concentric and of two basic types: either with an excitatory center and an inhibitory surrounding ring ("on" center and an "off" surround) or the opposite organization with an "off" center and an "on" surround. The center and its surround are always antagonistic and tend to cancel each other's activity. This feature explains the finding that uniform illumination of the visual field is less effective in arousing a ganglion cell than is a well-placed small spot or a line or an edge passing through the center of the cell's receptive field. Ganglion cells also differ in the temporal characteristics of their receptive fields. In the cat, there are three main types of ganglion cells (Sherman, 1985): about three-quarters of the ganglion cells show sustained activity as long as the stimulation is maintained; these tonic receptors have been called **X cells.** For about 5% of the cells the activity is transient, starting strongly but then waning rapidly; these phasic receptors are called **Y cells.** (There are also **W cells** with sluggish and somewhat variable responses.) We will see later that the W, X, and Y cells project separately from the retina to the higher visual centers and serve different functions. Cells in the lateral geniculate body have concentric receptive fields with properties much like those shown at the retina; see the thalamic cell (A) in Figure 9-27.

The next station, the visual cortex, provided a puzzle, however. The spots of light that were effective stimuli for ganglion or lateral geniculate cells did not prove to be very effective at the cortical level. Success in stimulating cortical visual cells was announced in 1959 when Hubel and Wiesel reported that visual cortical cells require more specific stimuli—elongated stimuli, lines or bars in a particular position and at a particular orientation in the visual field (Figure 9-27, cell B). Some cortical cells also required movement of the stimulus before they would respond actively. For some of these cells, just the fact of movement was sufficient, while others were even more demanding, requiring motion in a specific direction (Figure 9-27, cell C).

The ability of special stimuli to produce vigorous responses in visual cortical cells was soon verified by others, and it led to a great amount of productive research. The success of this research also led to general acceptance of the theoretical model proposed by Hubel and Wiesel, but challenges to this model have emerged in recent years. Let us first note a few more findings of Hubel and Wiesel and then take up their theoretical model.

Cortical cells were categorized into four classes according to the types of stimuli required to produce maximum responses. So-called **simple cortical cells** responded best to an edge or a bar of a particular width and with a particular direction and location in the visual field. These cells were therefore sometimes called bar detec-

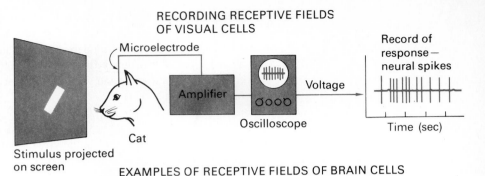

Figure 9-27 Responses of brain cells to specific stimuli. Microelectrode recording reveals that cells in the brain vary greatly in their receptive fields. Visual cells in the thalamus have concentric receptive fields like those of retinal ganglion cells. But cortical cells may show orientation specificity (B) or respond only to motion in a particular direction (C) or even be sensitive to only a particular shape.

RECORDING RECEPTIVE FIELDS
OF VISUAL CELLS

Microelectrode

Amplifier

Oscilloscope

Voltage

Record of response— neural spikes

Time (sec)

Cat

Stimulus projected on screen

EXAMPLES OF RECEPTIVE FIELDS OF BRAIN CELLS

A. Thalamic cell with concentric field; "on" center.
　1. Response to light in center of cell's field
　2. Response to light in periphery of cell's field

Stimulus

Response

Period of stimulation

B. Orientation-sensitive cortical cell. This cell responds strongly only when the stimulus is a vertical stripe.

C. Cortical cell sensitive to the direction of motion. This cell responds strongly only when the stimulus moves down. It responds weakly to upward motion, and does not respond at all to sideways motion.

tors or edge detectors. **Complex cortical cells** had receptive fields like the simple cells, but they also showed some latitutde for location; that is, they would respond to a bar of a particular size and orientation anywhere within a particular area of the visual field. Cells called **hypercomplex 1** had clear inhibitory areas at the two ends; that is, the best response was shown if the bar was of limited length, and extending the length beyond this limit reduced the response. Later work showed that even simple and complex cortical cells possess this property, at least to some extent. Finally some cells were called **hypercomplex 2;** these cells responded best to two line segments meeting at a particular angle. Hubel and Wiesel mentioned this type only briefly, but it gave rise to a great amount of theorizing.

The theoretical model of Hubel and Wiesel can be described as a hierarchical

2. complex cortical cells -
sim. to simple but w/
latitude for locat'n
3. hypercomplex 1
inhibitory at either end
i.e. bar optimal if particular
length
4. hypercomplex 2
2 line segments meeting
at same angle

one; that is, more complex events are built up from inputs of simpler ones. For example, a simple cortical cell could be conceived as receiving input from a row of lateral geniculate cells. A complex cortical cell could be thought of as receiving its input from a row of simple cortical cells. Other theorists extrapolated from this model of Hubel and Wiesel, cascading circuits of cells to detect any possible form. Thus it was suggested that with enough successive levels of analysis, a unit could be constructed that would enable a person to recognize his or her grandmother, and there was frequent mention in the literature of such hypothetical **"grandmother cells."**

A hierarchical model of this sort might work, but critics pointed out various problems with it, some of a theoretical nature and others arising from empirical observations. For one thing, a "grandmother-recognizing" circuit would require vast numbers of cells, probably even more than the number available in the cerebral cortex. Each successive stage in the hierarchy is obviously built on the preceding one, but Hoffman and Stone (1971) found practically no difference in latency of response between simple and complex cortical cells. If anything, the complex cells had slightly faster responses, although the hierarchical theory requires the simple cells to respond earlier. Further work showed that the projection from retina to cortex was by parallel systems rather than by successive hierarchical systems. The X ganglion cells project mainly to simple cortical cells, while the Y ganglion cells project mainly to complex cortical cells (Wilson & Sherman, 1976). Also, cortical projections of the X cells are almost entirely to the primary visual cortex (also called striate cortex), whereas Y cell projections are found outside the striate area as well as within it. At the same time that difficulties with this model were being recognized, an alternative model was emerging.

Spatial Frequency Filter Model

To discuss this model, we must become familiar with a way of regarding spatial vision that is quite different from the familiar viewpoint (Westheimer, 1984; DeValois & DeValois, 1988). By the spatial frequency of a visual stimulus, we mean the number of light-dark cycles it shows per degree of visual space. For example, the parts of Figure 9-28 differ in the spacing of the bars and therefore in their spatial frequencies.

The spatial frequency technique applies Fourier analysis or linear systems theory rather than an analysis of visual patterns into bars and angles. When we discussed the auditory stimulus in Box 9-1, we saw that any complex, repeating auditory stimulus can be analyzed into the sum of sine waves. The same principle of Fourier analysis can be applied to visual patterns. If the dimension from dark to light is made to vary according to a sine wave pattern, we get a visual pattern like the one shown in Figure 9-29. A series of black and white stripes, like that shown in Figure 9-28, can be analyzed into the sum of a visual sine wave and its odd harmonics. A complex visual pattern or scene can also be analyzed by the Fourier technique; in this case frequency components at different angles of orientation are also used. To reproduce or perceive the complex pattern or scene accurately, the system has to handle all the spatial frequencies that are present in it. If the high frequencies are filtered out, the small details and sharp contrasts are lost; if the low frequencies are filtered out, the large uniform areas and gradual transitions are lost. Figure 9-30 shows how filtering spatial frequencies affects a photograph.

[handwritten: visual systems tuned to diff spatial frequencies]

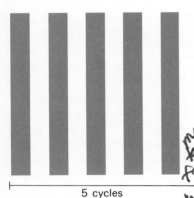

10 cycles

5 cycles

Figure 9-28 Spatial frequencies. The upper grating has twice the spatial frequency of the lower grating, since twice as many bars occur in the same space.

In 1968 Campbell and Robson suggested that the visual system includes several channels that are tuned to different spatial frequencies, just as the auditory system has channels for different acoustic frequencies. This suggestion was soon supported by results of an experiment on selective adaptation to frequency (Blakemore & Campbell, 1969). In this experiment a person spent a minute or more inspecting a visual grating with a given spacing, such as the upper or lower half of Figure 9-28, and then sensitivity to gratings of different spacings was determined. The results showed that the sensitivity was depressed at the frequency to which the subject adapted. The suggestion of multiple spatial frequency channels

had revolutionary impact because it led to entirely different conceptions of the way in which the visual system might function in dealing with spatial stimuli. It suggests that rather than specifically detecting such seminaturalistic features as bars and edges, the system is breaking down complex stimuli into their individual spatial frequency components in a kind of crude Fourier analysis. . . . Irrespective of the eventual judgment of the correctness of this particular model, Campbell and Robson's conjecture will remain pivotal in having opened the eyes of vision researchers to the many ways in which the visual system could analyze the world using elements not akin to our verbal descriptions of scenes. (De Valois and De Valois, 1980, p. 320)

The responses of cortical cells to spatial frequency stimuli were then measured (De Valois, Albrecht, & Thorell, 1977; Hochstein & Shapley, 1976; Maffei & Fiorentini, 1973). Cortical cells were found to be tuned more accurately to the dimensions of spatial frequency grids than to the width of bars.

Among retinal ganglion cells, the X cells were found to be tuned to higher spatial frequencies than neighboring Y cells. The X cells showed an optimal tuning for frequencies about three times higher than for Y cells, so Sherman (1985) suggested that X cells discriminate fine features of visual patterns while Y cells respond to coarser aspects of patterns.

[handwritten: more tuned to spatial freq than to bars]

[handwritten: X cells - optimal tuning 3X y cells = ∴ x cells discriminate fine features / y cells = coarser]

Figure 9-29 Visual grids with sinusoidal modulation of light intensity. If the light intensity is strongly modulated as in the black sine wave in (a), the grid has high contrast (b). If the intensity is less strongly modulated as in the brown curve, the grid has lower contrast (c). The light bands in (b) and (c) appear broader than the dark bands because of nonlinearity of the visual receptors.

(a) Spatial distribution of stimulus intensity

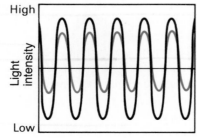

High

Light intensity

Low

(b) High–contrast spatial grid

(c) Low–contrast spatial grid

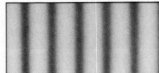

(a)

(b)

(c)

Figure 9-30 Groucho Marx subjected to spatial filtering. (a) Normal photograph. (b) Blurred or low pass spatial frequency filtered. (c) Reproduced in outline or high pass spatial frequency filtered. (Vision Consultants, Dr. John W. Mayhew and Dr. John P. Frisby)

Evaluating the Spatial Frequency Model

The spatial frequency model continues to inspire a great deal of research (Shapley & Lennie, 1985), although the concept of multiple spatial frequency channels does not require a thoroughgoing Fourier analysis of the optical image (Westheimer, 1984). In fact, rather than an infinite or even a large number of sinusoidal components in a Fourier analysis, the receptive field of a cortical cell typically shows only an excitatory axis and one clear band of surround inhibition on each side.

The spatial frequency approach has proved useful in analyzing various aspects of human pattern vision, including perception of patterns of bars and plaids (De Valois, De Valois, & Yund, 1979), analysis of optical illusions (Ginsburg, 1971, 1975), and interactions of different parts of a pattern on perceptual responses (Palmer, in press). For example, the Müller-Lyer arrowhead illusion (Figure 9-31) can be interpreted in terms of spatial filtering. The arrow with the outward arms is actually longer than the inward-arm arrow if only the low-frequency information is considered. While the higher frequency channels of the visual system give accurate information about the positions and lengths of lines in this figure, the low-frequency channels also contribute information about size, and they indicate that the outward-arm arrow is longer. Various patterns used as examples by Gestalt psychologists can also be interpreted from this approach. Thus Wertheimer's array of dots that can be seen either as individual dots or as larger objects (columns) in fact do have these different characteristics depending upon whether they are seen through high spatial frequency or low spatial frequency channels; when a low-pass filter is used, this classic figure consists of solid columns.

Figure 9-31 The Müller-Lyer arrowhead illusion.

Parallel Processing of Form, Movement, and Color

Parallel Retinal Projection Systems

Evidence for parallel processing of different aspects of visual perception is accumulating from several directions of research. These include investigating the functions of the different systems that project from the retina into the brain and studying effects of brain damage on perception.

Investigators studying the responses of retinal ganglion cells in the cat first observed differences among them in terms of temporal characteristics of their responses, as we noted earlier. Then tracing the axons of these ganglion cells revealed that the different types have different destinations. Findings made with primates are somewhat different from those obtained with the cat, so we will review both sets of findings.

In the cat, the W cells, about 10% of all the retinal ganglion cells, are small cells most of which project to the superior colliculus. The X cells, about 80% of the total, have medium-sized cell bodies and project to the lateral geniculate nucleus. The Y cells, about 5–10% of the total, have large cell bodies with extensive dendritic trees that collect input information from relatively large receptive fields; their axons are of large diameter and conduct rapidly, mainly to the lateral geniculate but also to the superior colliculus. Within the lateral geniculate nucleus, the endings of the X and Y cells are segregated anatomically.

The role of these systems in cortical functioning is not yet known with certainty (Sherman, 1985), but some investigators suggest the following functions and pathways: The information from the W cells is processed to control head and eye movements in response to visual stimulation. The X cells have small receptive fields, and their information is processed for detailed, high-resolution analysis of visual form. In contrast, the Y cells have large receptive fields, and their information is used for basic analysis of form and movement; they probably help the cat to locomote through visual space and direct its eyes and attention to objects moving through the visual field. Although there are relatively few Y cells in the retina, each Y cell makes contact with many geniculate cells, so the Y pathway includes one-third of the cells in the cat's lateral geniculate. From the geniculate, the Y-cell pathway proceeds not only to Area 17 but also to visual Areas 18 and 19 and to other areas of the cortex. Further information about these projective systems can be found in the review by Sherman (1985).

The differences in spatial function of the X and Y systems can be related to effects of stimulus deprivation during the critical period of visual development. Keeping one eye of a kitten closed during its first few months causes impairment of development, especially of the Y cells. The poor spatial discrimination that these kittens show is probably due chiefly to the lack of development of their Y-cell pathways.

Primates also show retinal ganglion cells with a variety of properties, but the classification of ganglion cells worked out for the cat cannot be applied directly to primate ganglion cells. Investigators who study primate visual systems take the organization of the lateral geniculate nucleus as their key, and the anatomy of the lateral geniculate is rather different from that in the cat. As Figure 9-20 shows, the primate geniculate has six layers. The four dorsal layers are called parvocellular because the cells are small (from the Latin *parvus,* meaning "small"). The two ventral layers are called magnocellular because their cells are large. The magnocellcular layers contain cells whose properties resemble those of the cat's Y cells (with large receptive fields and phasic activity), and they also contain some cells with more X-like properties. Importantly, the cells of the magnocellular layers do not show spectrally opponent wavelength responses, that is, they do not discriminate color. The cells of the parvocellular layers are similar to feline X cells in having small receptive fields and tonic responses, but they discriminate colors. Some investigators suggest that the magnocellular system is equivalent to the entire feline thalamocortical visual system and that the parvocellular system is a new system that evolved in the primates.

Investigators in this field now use the names of the principal divisions of the lateral geniculate to designate two main subdivisions in primate visual pathways: the **parvocellular system** appears to be mainly responsible for analysis of color and form and for recognition of objects; the **magnocellular system** appears to be mainly responsible for perception of depth and movement (Livingstone & Hubel, 1988). From the geniculate, the different divisions project to different layers and areas of the cerebral cortex. In the primary visual area, the parvocellular and magnocellular projections are segregated but intermixed. For example, the cortical "blobs" or "pegs" in Figure 9-20, collection of cells that are thought to mediate color vision, are part of the parvocellular system. Beyond visual area 2, the two systems appear to segregate more completely. The projections of the magnocellular and parvocellular systems and the discriminations they are believed to mediate are summarized in Table 9-2.

Clinical Evidence for Parallel Processing

We have seen that the anatomical layout of the visual system supports the concept of parallel processing of visual information, that is, the idea that different aspects of a visual scene are processed by different neural circuits at the same time. Such aspects include the form, the color, and the movement of the stimulation. Clinical evidence

---

Table 9-2 Parallel Projection Systems in the Primate Visual System

Characteristics	Magnocellular System	Parvocellular System
Projection in lateral geniculate nucleus	Two ventral layers	Four dorsal layers
Projections in cerebral cortex	Interdigitated in visual areas 1 and 2 but more separate thereafter.	
	Middle temporal (MT), parietal-occipital region	Area 4, temporal-occipital region
Discriminations mediated:	"Where"	"What"
	Spatial depth	Form, shape
	Movement	Color

supports the same concept, because either genetic anomalies or injury to the brain may prevent some aspects of visual perception from occurring while leaving other aspects intact. We have already mentioned, for example, that some people whose vision is otherwise normal are partially blind for stereoscopic vision. Observations with such subjects point to the existence of two broadly tuned channels for visual depth, one for locations anywhere beyond the fixation point and the other for locations anywhere closer to the viewer than the fixation point. Either channel can work without the other. In some cases damage to the brain results in the inability to distinguish hues, although other aspects of vision seem unimpaired; such cases are likely to result from damage in cortical areas 18 and 37 (Kolb & Whishaw, 1985). In other cases there is inability to discern movement of objects; these cases are likely to involve damage at the junction of the temporal and occipital regions. Some unfortunate individuals, after localized damage to the brain from stroke, can no longer recognize certain classes of objects even though they can describe them in terms of form and color. Such a disability is called an **agnosia** (from the Greek roots *a* meaning ''not'' and *gnosis* meaning ''knowledge''). A rare but particularly striking kind of agnosia is the inability to recognize faces (called prosopagnosia); it is apt to involve damage to cortical areas 20 and 21 in the right hemisphere. One such case gave the name to a recent book, *The Man Who Mistook His Wife for a Hat* (Sacks, 1985). (We will further discuss agnosias resulting from brain damage in the last chapter of this book.)

(handwritten margin note:) Clinical — some areas damaged, others intact ∴ not all hierarchical

Summary · Main Points

Hearing

1. The beginnings of auditory perception involve a sequence of steps in the ear in which sound waves are modified by the structural and functional properties of the external and middle compartments.

2. The transduction of mechanical energy into excitation of the auditory nerve takes place within the inner ear (cochlea). A key step in this process is the bending of the hair cells as rapid movements of the cochlear fluids vibrate the basilar membrane.

3. Changes in ion channels of the membrane of hair cells produce generator currents that lead to the release of substances at the base of the hair cells. These released molecules combine with receptors on the terminals of the auditory nerve leading to excitation of auditory nerves.

4. Discrimination of pitch involves two different types of neural coding: For low frequencies nerve impulses are phase locked to the stimulus (volley theory), whereas higher frequencies are represented by the place of maximal stimulation along the basilar membrane (place theory).

5. Sound frequencies are mapped in an orderly manner throughout the auditory pathways of the brain. This is the principle of tonotopic mapping.

6. Auditory localization depends mainly on differences in time of arrival (for low-frequency sounds) and intensity (for high-frequency sounds). Many nerve cells in the auditory system are excited by inputs from either ear; some of these cells are particularly sensitive to a narrow range of difference in time or intensity cues of the auditory stimulus.

7. Sound exposure early in life can influence auditory localization behavior and the response of neurons in auditory pathways.

8. Deafness can be caused by pathological changes at any level of the auditory system. Conductive deafness refers to impairments in the transmission of sound to the cochlea produced by changes in the external or middle ears. Sensorineural deafness refers to hearing impairments that arise from damage to the cochlea or auditory nerve. Central deafness refers to hearing impairments that arise from lesions in the brain pathways of the auditory system.

9. Some forms of deafness can now be aided by direct electrical stimulation of the auditory nerve; this electrical stimulation is controlled by devices that record and transform acoustic stimuli.

Seeing

10. The vertebrate eye is an elaborate structure that forms detailed and accurate optical images on the receptive cells of the retina.

11. Many different phyletic lines have independently evolved photoreceptor organs; several have evolved eyes with lenses to focus light.

12. The first stage of visual information processing occurs in the retina where cells that contain photopigments can be excited by photic energy. Two kinds of retinal receptor cells, rods and cones, are the initial stages of two systems—the scotopic (dim light) and photopic (bright light) systems.

13. Brain pathways of the visual system include the lateral geniculate nucleus in the thalamus, the primary visual cortex, and further cortical regions. Some ganglion cell axons run to the superior colliculus in the midbrain.

14. There are several visual areas in the cortex, each presenting a topographic map of the visual field, but each processing a different aspect of visual information, such as form, color, and movement.

15. The primary visual cortex is organized in columns, as is true of somatosensory and auditory cortices. Columns and groups of columns provide separate representations of the two eyes, angular orientation of stimuli, position in the visual field, and color.

16. Discrimination of hue in Old World primates and humans depends both on the existence of three different cone photopigments and the fact that retinal connections yield four different kinds of color ganglion cells (or spectrally opponent cells).

17. Location of visual stimuli in space is aided by detailed spatial maps that are present at every level of the visual system. Binocular perception of depth (stereognosis) depends upon cortical cells tuned for stimulation at the plane of fixation, or in front of or behind that plane.

18. For perception of visual patterns and forms, there are two main current models: the feature detector model and the spatial frequency filter model.

19. In both cats and primates, parallel projective systems from the retina to the brain mediate different aspects of visual projection.

20. Clinical evidence also supports the concept of parallel processing, because either genetic anomalies or injury to the brain may impair some aspects of visual perception while leaving others intact.

Recommended Reading

Barlow, H. B., & Mollon, J. D. (Eds.). (1982). *The senses*. Cambridge, England: Cambridge University Press.

DeValois, R. L., & DeValois, K. K. (1988). *Spatial vision*. New York: Oxford University Press.

Fein, A., & Levine, J. (Eds.). (1985). *The visual system*. New York: Alan R. Liss.

Jacobs, G. (1982). *Comparative color vision*. New York: Academic Press.

Pickles, J. D. (1982). *An introduction to the physiology of hearing*. New York: Academic Press.

Romand, R. (Ed.). (1983). *Development of auditory and vestibular systems*. New York: Academic Press.

Rose, D., & Dobson, V. G. (Eds.). (1985). *Models of the visual cortex*. New York: Wiley.

Yost, W. A., & Nielsen, D. W. (1985). *Fundamentals of hearing*. New York: Holt, Rinehart and Winston.

10 Movements and Actions

ORIENTATION

Our behavior and that of other animals includes a wide range of acts that extend in complexity from finger movements to elaborate athletic feats. Elegance, grace, and complexity describe the leaps of ballet dancers as well as the flight pattern of an insect (Figure 10-1). But even ordinary everyday movements involve an intricate sequence of muscle activity. Think, for example, of all the muscles involved when you say a single word. The tongue, larynx, throat, lips, chest, and diaphragm must work in a highly coordinated manner to produce even the simplest speech sound. And there is little room for error if what you say is to be understood. The difference between saying "time" and "dime," for example, depends mainly on whether your vocal cords are relaxed or tensed during the start of the word.

Any coordinated movement implies that there are underlying neural mechanisms that can choose the appropriate muscles. Further, for coordinated movements to occur, neural mechanisms in the brain and spinal cord must precisely determine appropriate amounts of excitation and/or inhibition at relevant synapses. Finally, and most importantly, motoneurons must be activated in the proper order. How are these tasks accomplished? The answers to this question extend from a consideration of specific muscles to a consideration of the complex control systems of the brain. As we will see, research into these control systems is yielding new methods of neurochemical treatment and physical therapy for people who suffer from faulty motor behavior.

In the next three sections we will consider movements and their coordination from different points of view—the behavioral view, the control systems view, and especially the neurobiological view.

Behavioral View

Crawling, walking, flying, and swimming are some of the many ways to move from one place to another. Close analysis of the movements and acts of different animals offers some notions about the underlying mechanisms. For example, observation of the vigorous beating of insect wings suggests that the nervous system of this animal contains a rhythm generator, an oscillator. The varied gaits of four-legged animals

(a)

(b)

Figure 10-1   Complex acts. (a) Graceful leap of ballet dancers. (Martha Swope) (b) An insect in flight. (Stephen Dalton FIIP FRPS)

suggests that different oscillators are coupled in precise but flexible ways. The great versatility of learned movements in people shows the range of complex adjustments possible in the motor system. To start our discussion, we need ways of classifying movements and action patterns.

Classifying Movements and Action Patterns

Efforts to classify movements began quite early in the study of the biology of movements when a distinction was drawn between the "machinelike" actions of nonhuman animals and the "voluntary" behavior of humans. In the seventeenth century the philosopher Descartes particularly emphasized this distinction, and in the eighteenth and nineteenth centuries it was advanced by discoveries of the basic properties of the spinal cord. During this time scientists noted that the dorsal roots of the spinal cord serve sensory functions and that the ventral roots contain motor fibers; sensorimotor connections seemed to provide the basis for simple movements. In the same period experiments with so-called **spinal animals** (animals whose spinal cord has been disconnected from the brain) demonstrated that stimulating the skin could elicit simple, stereotyped limb movements, such as withdrawal from painful stimulation.

In the late nineteenth and early twentieth centuries the British physiologist Charles Sherrington reported an extensive series of studies using spinal animals. He showed that skin stimulation in these animals, such as pinching, provoked simple acts. Many such observations led him to argue that the basic units of movement are

reflexes, which he defined as simple, highly stereotyped, and unlearned responses to external stimuli. The size or magnitude of a reflex was, he showed, directly related to the intensity of the stimulus. His work ushered in an era of intensive attempts to identify the varieties of reflexes and to chart their pathways in the nervous system, particularly in the spinal cord. Some reflexes involve only pathways in the spinal cord linking dorsal and ventral roots, while others involve longer loops connecting spinal cord segments or even brain regions.

Many stereotyped responses can be elicited by stimulating skin surfaces, muscles, or joints. We owe many of our basic survival capabilities to the rapid and automatic nature of these responses. But are reflexes the basic units of more complex movements and acts? Unfortunately, a successful explanation of any concept often breeds presumption. And so it has been in this area. The reflex perspective has appropriately invited criticism when it has tried in a rather simple fashion to explain complex behaviors. For instance, Sherrington thought that complex acts were simply combinations of simpler reflexes strung out in some temporal order. The strongest criticism of this perspective has been directed toward attempts to analyze complex sequences of behavior, such as speech, in reflex terms. For example, reflex explanations of speech emphasize that the movements and sounds associated with each element of speech provide the stimuli that instigate the next element. If this were true, speech would be a series of stimulus-response units chained together, each response triggering off the next unit.

But, on the contrary, it appears that the speaker has a plan in which several units (speech sounds) are placed in a larger pattern. Sometimes the units get misplaced, although the pattern is preserved: ''Our queer old dean,'' said English clergyman William Spooner, when he meant, ''Our dear old Queen.'' In fact, Spooner was so prone to mix up the order of words or sounds in his sentences that this type of error is called a spoonerism.

Recent investigators have shown that many complex sequences of behavior are determined by an internal plan, rather than being generated by a ''chain'' of reflexes. These acts may also occur without exact guidance or control by sensory feedback. Examples of this kind of internal plan for action range from skilled movements, such as piano playing, to a wide repertoire of escape behaviors of simpler animals like crayfish.

Animals can perform a bewildering array of acts. An important step in developing an understanding of acts and their neural mechanisms is to classify these behaviors. A movement classification scheme generated from an ethological perspective is shown in Table 10-1. This scheme focuses on the functional properties of acts rather than on their exact muscle relations. A major characteristic of many movements is that they are rhythmic—there is an orderly repetition of movements and of muscle contractions. This feature is true in locomotion, breathing, chewing, scratching, the beating of the heart, and the peristaltic movements of the intestines. How patterns of rhythmic movements are programmed and modulated will be taken up in a later section.

Table 10-1 can also be used to make a distinction between movements and acts. The upper part of the table, simple reflexes, includes brief, unitary activities of muscle that we commonly call movements. These events are discrete, in many cases limited to a single part of the body, such as a limb. The lower parts of the table list

Table 10-1   A Classification of Movements and Examples of Each

I. **Simple Reflex**	
Stretch	Knee jerk
Sneezing	Startle
Eye blink	Pupillary contraction

II. **Posture and Postural Changes**	
Standing	Rearing
Lying	Balancing
Sitting	Urination posture

III. **Locomotion**	
Walking	Creeping
Running	Crawling
Swimming	Stalking
Flying	Hopping

IV. **Sensory Orientation**	
Head turning	Touching
Eye fixation	Sniffing
Ear movement	Tasting

V. **Species-Typical Action Patterns**
Ingestion: tasting, chewing, biting, sipping, drinking
Courtship: display, sniffing, chasing, retreating
Escape and defense: hissing, spitting, submission posture, cowering
Grooming: washing, preening, licking
Gestures: grimacing, tail erection, squinting, tooth baring, smiling

VI. **Acquired Skills**			
Speech	Dressing	Sculpting	Sports
Tool using	Painting	Auto driving	Dancing

complex, sequential behaviors, frequently oriented toward a goal. Different movements of several bodily parts might be included in such behavior. This more complex event we distinguish as an act or action pattern.

Ethologists have called the complex species-specific responses **fixed-action patterns.** Actually there is considerable variation in the timing and form of these response sequences, both between two individuals and within the same individual at different times. For this reason Barlow (1977) has suggested that the term **modal-action pattern** is preferable; this term implies that a typical pattern of behavior is being described, but it allows for individual variation.

Techniques of Analyzing Movements and Acts

Bewildering variety and complexity confront the researcher who seeks to define, describe, and quantify movements and acts. Global descriptions are readily available with motion pictures, though, and high-speed photography provides an intimate portrait of even the most rapid events.

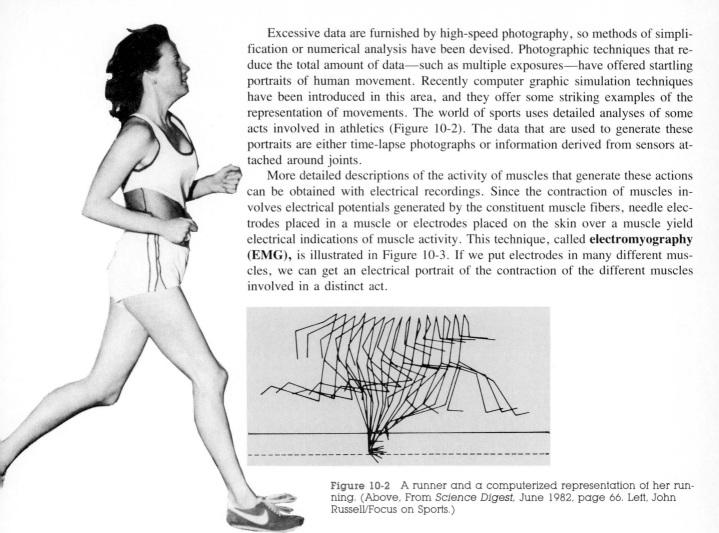

Excessive data are furnished by high-speed photography, so methods of simplification or numerical analysis have been devised. Photographic techniques that reduce the total amount of data—such as multiple exposures—have offered startling portraits of human movement. Recently computer graphic simulation techniques have been introduced in this area, and they offer some striking examples of the representation of movements. The world of sports uses detailed analyses of some acts involved in athletics (Figure 10-2). The data that are used to generate these portraits are either time-lapse photographs or information derived from sensors attached around joints.

More detailed descriptions of the activity of muscles that generate these actions can be obtained with electrical recordings. Since the contraction of muscles involves electrical potentials generated by the constituent muscle fibers, needle electrodes placed in a muscle or electrodes placed on the skin over a muscle yield electrical indications of muscle activity. This technique, called **electromyography (EMG),** is illustrated in Figure 10-3. If we put electrodes in many different muscles, we can get an electrical portrait of the contraction of the different muscles involved in a distinct act.

Figure 10-2 A runner and a computerized representation of her running. (Above, From *Science Digest,* June 1982, page 66. Left, John Russell/Focus on Sports.)

Acquiring Motor Skills

We do not have to learn how to withdraw a hand from a hot stove, or how to breathe, or how to swallow. These and many other acts are highly stereotyped reflexes; no aspect of a person's attention changes their essential character. ''Involuntary'' is the word commonly used to characterize these responses. In contrast, we need explicit training to know how to generate speech and handwriting, to play tennis, to use a keyboard, and to perform numerous other acts, ranging from trivial to extraordinary, that are in the general experience of humans. The characteristics of these acts are highly variable, frequently idiosyncratic, and show considerable variability among individuals. These acts are commonly referred to as ''voluntary'' motor skills. How are these skills acquired?

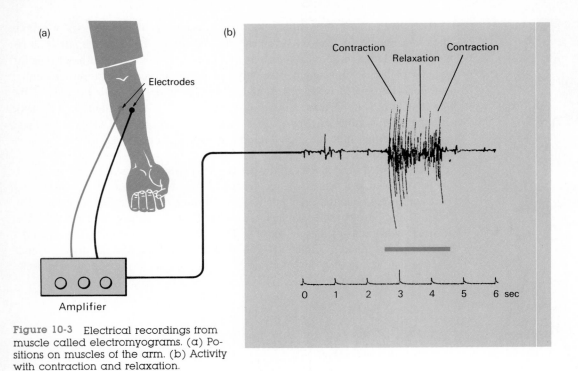

Figure 10-3 Electrical recordings from muscle called electromyograms. (a) Positions on muscles of the arm. (b) Activity with contraction and relaxation.

The performance of any skilled movement shows that several types of information are essential to acquiring a motor skill. A model of skill learning is shown in Figure 10-4 (Keele & Summers, 1976). This model posits that input to muscles is provided by a hypothetical movement program in the brain that directs the timing and force of neural outputs to muscles (the motor outflow). Feedback from receptors in joints and other modes of information about movements—visual or auditory—are matched to a model of skilled performance. Feedback information thus provides input about errors, which are gradually reduced; in some cases the need for monitoring the movement may be eliminated. Welford (1974) notes that at this stage of skilled movement learning there is a loss of conscious awareness of the act—there is a feeling of automatic execution. He believes that faster performance becomes possible because feedback control loops exert less impact.

Control Systems View

Engineering descriptions of the regulation and control of machines have provided a useful way of looking at the mechanisms that regulate and control the movements of animals. In designing and building machines, engineers commonly encounter two problems: (1) how to prevent or minimize error and (2) how to accomplish a task quickly and efficiently. These are the considerations of accuracy and speed. Two forms of control mechanisms are commonly employed to optimize performance according to these criteria; they are referred to as **closed-loop** and **open-loop control mechanisms.**

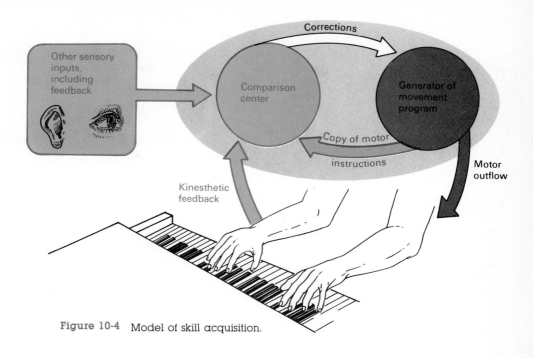

Figure 10-4   Model of skill acquisition.

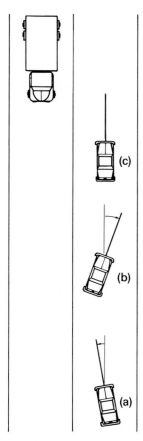

Figure 10-5 Example of feedback control in auto driving. (a) Auto veers to the left. (b) Overcorrection turns the car to the right. (c) Target is achieved.

The essence of closed-loop control mechanisms is that they provide for the flow of information from whatever is being controlled to the device that controls it. We have already considered closed-loop mechanisms when we discussed control of endocrine secretion in Chapter 7 (Figures 7-2 through 7-4). We used the example of a thermostat controlling room temperature to point out some of the characteristics of a negative-feedback system. Now we can consider a more complex example in which a human being—an automobile driver, for example—plays a major role. In this case the variable being controlled is the position of an automobile on the road (see Figure 10-5). Continuous information in this instance is provided by the driver's visual system, which can demand correcting movement.

Let us consider this example in terms of the formal sort of diagram customarily used for studying feedback control mechanisms (Figure 10-6). This diagram is a formal description of closed-loop (that is, feedback) systems. In terms of our analogy, the controlled system is the automobile. The input is the position of the steering wheel, and the output is the position on the road. The transducer is an element that measures output, and the error detector measures differences between actual output and desired output (control signal). In this example the transducer, error detector, and controller all refer to properties of the person driving the car. Specifically, the transducer refers to the driver's visual system, the error detector to some properties of the perceptual system, and the controller to the muscle apparatus used in steering. The actual position of the car is compared with its desired position on the road, and corrections are supplied to the controlled system to minimize the

Figure 10-6 Diagram of feedback control mechanism.

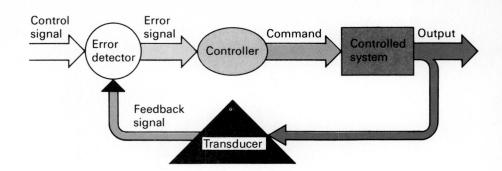

discrepancy (assuming the desire to stay on the road). The only way the car could stay on the road without feedback control (as, for example, driving with your eyes closed) would be with the aid of accurate memory of all the turns and bends in the road. (In terms of our next discussion, such a memory system could be considered a form of open-loop control.)

Some nonliving systems employ closed-loop controls; others employ open-loop mechanisms. Open-loop controls are those that do not involve external forms of feedback; output is measured by a sensor but the activity is programmed. Open-loop controls are needed in mechanical systems that must respond so rapidly that no time is available for the delay of a feedback pathway. The way elevators work furnishes a familiar example of open-loop control: Their rates of acceleration and deceleration are preset. Pressing the button for a given floor sets off the whole predetermined program.

In addition to offering speed of response, open-loop systems have the benefit of freedom from error and variability. To achieve this freedom, they employ devices that supply a control signal known to be effective or to *anticipate* potential error. In living systems such accurate anticipation may arise from prior learning. For instance, in all the acts involved in learning to play a piano, some neural elements may acquire the properties of open-loop control because some features of the brain motor system may provide anticipatory controls based on the errors initially involving closed-loop or feedback instructions. This form of open-loop control is also known as "input feed forward." Obviously it must involve a mechanism that can make educated guesses about the kind of correction that might be needed.

Neurobiological View

Adaptive acts are produced by instructions generated by neural processing in the brain and spinal cord; these in turn lead to neural activity in motoneurons connecting to muscles. There are many different components in this neural machinery arranged in different levels of complexity. Some researchers have distinguished four different levels of hierarchically organized motor control systems in the central nervous system. The first level is the spinal cord, which deals with reflex responses. Processing at this level is relatively rigid and involves many automatic mechanisms. The next level is the brain stem, which deals with integrating motor commands from higher levels of the brain and transmits inputs from the spinal cord. The next highest level is the primary motor cortex, where some of the main commands for action are

Figure 10-7 Diagram of the main components of the neural system for control of movement.

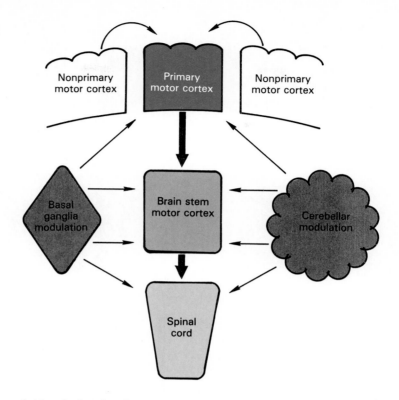

initiated. Another level of cortical processing is evident in the activities of areas adjacent to motor cortex that are called nonprimary motor cortex. We will examine the properties of each level of neural control after we have considered some of the characteristics of muscles and bones that determine the properties of movements. Other brain regions also modulate the activities of these hierarchically organized control systems. The cerebellum and basal ganglia have potent influences on motor systems. Input from the body surfaces, muscles, joints, and exteroceptors is directed to all levels of motor control and modulating systems. The basic plan of the organization of motor control is sketched in Figure 10-7. Our discussion will follow the organizational scheme of this figure.

What Is Controlled: Skeletomuscular Activity

Any act owes its character both to the mechanical properties of the body and to neural signals to muscles. Let us consider briefly the ways in which these mechanical properties determine and limit movement.

Mechanics of the Skeletal System

Some properties of acts arise from characteristics of the skeleton and muscle themselves. For example, the length, shape, and weight of the limbs determine characteristics of an animal's stride. Muscles have some springlike properties that influence the timing of behavior, and the rate and force of muscular contractions set limits on some responses.

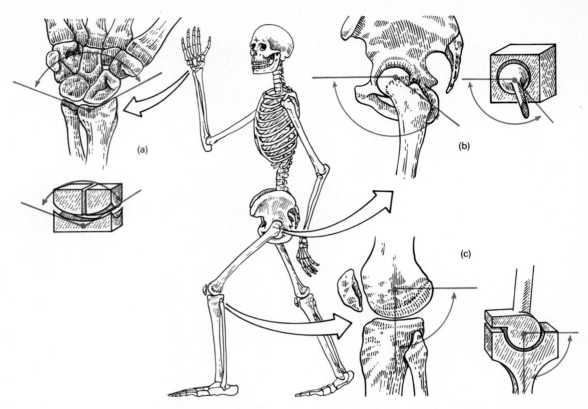

Figure 10-8   The human skeleton showing examples of joints and movements. Next to each enlarged joint is a mechanical model that shows the kinds of movements the joint can perform. (a) Wrist joint, which moves in two principal planes, lateral and vertical. (b) Hip joint, a "universal joint." (c) Knee joint, which has a single plane of motion.

The skeletal system of any vertebrate consists of many separate bones of different shape, weight, and length. Through painful experience we know that bones themselves do not bend. The primary sites for bending occur at the joints, where bones meet. The exact appearance of different joints varies, and these differences determine how a particular body part can be used. Figure 10-8, which illustrates the human skeleton, shows examples of some joints and their movement possibilities. Note that some, like the hip, are virtually "universal" joints, permitting movement in many planes. Others, like the elbow or knee, are more limited and tolerate little deviation from the principal axis of rotation.

Both the weight and shape of any bone are also significant in the operation of a joint, since they are important properties of the leverlike actions at joints. Many features of movement differences between species can be directly predicted from comparisons of the size and shape of relevant bones. For example, a comparison of the hands of humans with those of other primates shows why humans alone are capable of the precision grip of objects between the thumb and forefinger.

Mechanics of the Muscular System

Our bare skeleton must now be clothed with muscles. The distribution of muscles on the body—their size and attachment to bones—provides direct indications of the forms of movement that they mediate. By contracting, some muscles produce forces that sustain body weight, and others produce actual movement around a joint. In contrast, other muscles do not act on the skeleton at all—for example, the muscles that move the eyes, lips, and tongue and those that contract the abdomen. The molecular mechanisms of contraction of **muscle fibers** have been revealed in recent research (see Box 10-1).

The contraction of muscle fibers leads to movements or to maintenance of posture according to the ways in which any muscle is mechanically attached to a bone or bones. The arrangement around a typical joint is illustrated in Figure 10-9. Muscles are connected to bone by tendons. Around a joint different muscles are arranged in a reciprocal fashion. Thus when one muscle group contracts (shortens), the other is extended; that is, the relation of the muscles is antagonistic. Coordinated action around a joint may then require that one set of motoneurons be excited while the antagonistic set is inhibited. It is also possible to lock the limb in position by graded contraction of the opposed muscles.

Speed, precision, strength, and endurance are all desirable qualities in muscular movements, but behavioral acts differ in their requirements for these qualities. Matched to these requirements are at least two main types of muscle fibers, "fast" and "slow." Eye movements, for example, must be quick and accurate so that we can follow moving objects and shift our gaze from one target to another. But fibers in the extraocular muscles do not have to maintain tension for long periods of time because the neural program uses them in rotation; that is, it allows some fibers to relax while others contract. The extraocular muscles are therefore made up of "fast" muscle fibers. In contrast, in the leg muscle, "fast" fibers react promptly and strongly but fatigue rapidly; they are used mainly for activities in which muscle

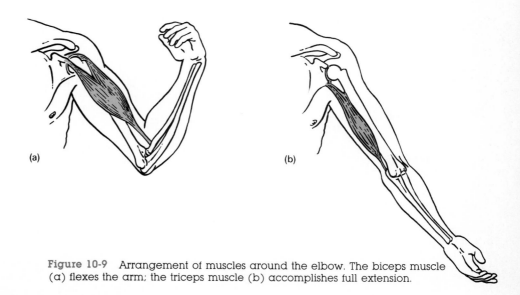

(a)　　　(b)

Figure 10-9 Arrangement of muscles around the elbow. The biceps muscle (a) flexes the arm; the triceps muscle (b) accomplishes full extension.

BOX 10-1 | How Muscles Contract

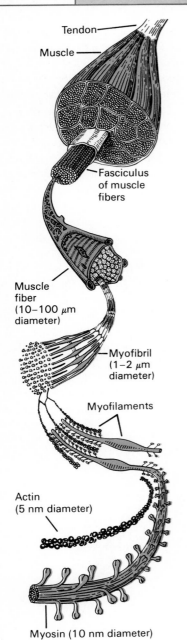

Tendon

Muscle

Fasciculus
of muscle
fibers

Muscle
fiber
(10–100 μm
diameter)

Myofibril
(1–2 μm
diameter)

Myofilaments

Actin
(5 nm diameter)

Myosin (10 nm diameter)

The basis of most of our movements is the contraction of muscle fibers. How muscles contract has been the object of intensive investigation; in these studies the components of the fibers have been identified and their physiology analyzed (Hoyle, 1970; Murray & Weber, 1974).

Each muscle fiber is made up of many filaments of two kinds arranged in a very regular manner (Box Figure 10-1). There are bands of relatively thick filaments and bands of thinner filaments, giving the fibers a striped appearance. The two kinds of filaments always overlap somewhat, as Box Figure 10-1 shows. Contraction of the muscle increases the overlap—the filaments slide past each other, shortening the overall length of the muscle fiber.

What causes the fibers to move past each other? Under higher magnification the thick filaments are seen to have paddle-shaped extensions or cross-bridges that make contact with the thin filaments (Box Figure 10-2). During contraction these cross-bridges rotate, pushing the thin filaments. Actually a cross-bridge moves through a certain distance and then breaks contact; it moves back, makes a new contact, and pushes again. Note this action of the cross-bridge shown in dark brown as it moves through a cycle in diagrams (a)–(e) of Box Figure 10-2. A single muscular contraction involves several cycles of such paddling actions. The movements of the cross-bridges are initiated when calcium ions come into contact with parts of the muscle filament proteins. And the release of calcium ions is controlled by muscle action potentials that are triggered by nerve impulses. Thus the motor nerves control a series of electrophysiological, chemical, and mechanical events that accomplish mechanical contraction of the muscle fibers.

Box Figure 10-1 The composition of muscles. Note that successive parts of the diagram show progressively greater magnification, from lifesize at the top to 2 million times at the bottom.

Box Figure 10-2 **The movement mechanism of muscle fibers.**

tension changes frequently, as in walking or running. Mixed in with them are "slow" fibers that are not as strong but have greater resistance to fatigue; they are used chiefly to maintain posture.

Because of their differential needs for rapid energy, fast and slow muscle fibers use different enzymes for metabolism. Consequently investigators have been able to stain the two types of fibers differently and to count the proportion of each type in various muscles. The proportions of fast and slow fibers are found to vary among muscles, and this variation provides a way of classifying muscles.

Differences in precision of control of various movements are also achieved by differences in the density of motor axons to muscle groups. Fine neural control is achieved when a single axon connects to only a few muscle fibers. An understanding of this concept is aided by the definition of a **motor unit;** this is a single motor axon and all the muscle fibers it innervates. The term **innervation ratio** refers to the ratio of motor axon to the number of fibers. Low innervation ratios characterize muscles involved in fine movements, like those of the eye (1:3 ratio). In contrast, muscles of the leg have innervation ratios of one to several hundred; thus the same call for contraction goes to hundreds of leg fibers at the same time.

Monitoring Movements: Sensory Feedback from Muscles and Joints

To produce rapid coordinated movements of the body, the integrative mechanisms of the brain and spinal cord must have information about the state of the muscles, the positions of the limbs, and the instructions being issued by the motor centers. This kind of information about bodily movements and positions is called **proprioceptive** (from the Latin roots for *self* and *reception*). A recent review of proprioception in control of movements is given by Hasan and Stuart (1988).

The sequence and intensity of muscle activation are monitored by sensory receptors, which provide information about the state of muscles and joints, and this information is used by the circuits that initiate and guide movements. There are several kinds of sensory receptors that can provide information about the state of muscle length or contraction. Two major kinds of receptors are shown in Figure 10-10: **muscle spindles,** which lie in parallel with the muscle fibers, and **Golgi**

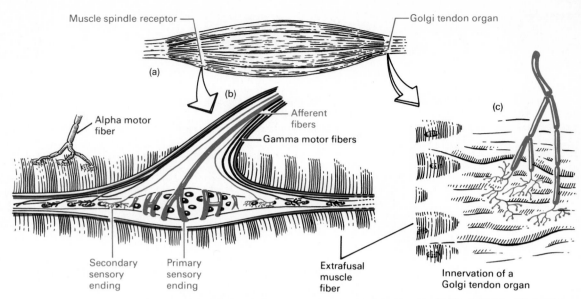

Figure 10-10 Muscle receptors. (a) Location of muscle spindles in body of muscle and Golgi organs in tendons. (b) Typical structure of muscle spindle. Two types of receptor endings are shown: primary and secondary. Gamma motor fibers control a contractile portion of the spindle. (c) Typical sensory ending of Golgi tendon organ.

tendon organs, which lie in series with muscles, one end attached to tendon, the other to muscle. The mechanical sensitivities of the spindles and tendon organs differ. Stretching a muscle, which occurs in many kinds of movements, activates especially the spindles and transiently the tendon organs. Shortening a muscle during contraction activates the tendon organs because they lie in series with the muscle. So together these two kinds of receptors transmit to the central nervous system a range of information about muscle activities (Figure 10-11).

Classical studies in physiology, especially those of Sherrington, emphasized the importance of these receptors for movement. Mott and Sherrington (1895) showed that after they cut the afferent fibers from muscles, monkeys failed to use the deafferented limb, even if the efferent connections from motor neurons to muscles were preserved. The deafferented limb is not paralyzed, since it can be activated, but lack of information from the muscle leads to relative disuse. This picture has been qualified by Teodoru and Berman (1980); they have shown that a monkey can flex a deafferented limb in a purposive manner in response to a visual signal that is used as a conditioned stimulus for shock avoidance. Simple forearm flexion to avoid shock occurred in these animals, although during free behavior the arm looked paralyzed.

Although deafferenting one forearm leads to apparent paralysis of that limb, the result is quite different if both forearms are deafferented. In the latter case the monkey recovers coordinated use of its forearms over a few months (Taub, 1976). When one limb is deafferented, the monkey makes do with the other. But when both are deafferented, the monkey has to learn to use them and is able to do so. The results show that the monkey becomes capable of fairly well-coordinated movements even though it lacks feedback from its arms.

Even if only one arm is deafferented, forced use of it can lead to return of coordinated use of the two arms. This result was shown in experiments in which the hand of the intact limb was placed inside a ball, which prevented the monkey from grasping objects with it but allowed finger movements and thus prevented atrophy. Slowly the deafferented limb gained dexterity, and over the course of several weeks fine movements like those needed for feeding were achieved. After several months the ball on the intact hand was removed, and the monkey made coordinated movements of both limbs. However, if the forced usage lasted for less than four months, movements of the deafferented limb regressed rapidly.

The portrait of deafferentation in humans provides some striking insight into the significance of sensory feedback. A recent report has described a patient with a loss of sensory input from muscles, joints, and skin but whose motor functions were spared (Marsden, Rothwell, & Day, 1984). This patient engaged in a wide range of manual activities including repetitive alternating hand movements and some grasping movements. A striking example of preserved motor abilities was reflected in his ability to drive his manual shift car! On the other hand, the disabilities of this patient should not be slighted. Fine movements of the fingers, such as writing or fastening buttons, were drastically impaired. In addition, it was quite difficult to acquire new movements of the hand. For example, after buying a new car, this patient found that he was unable to acquire the arm movements necessary to drive it, and he had to continue to use his old car. These researchers have suggested that sensory feedback is especially important in movements that require sustained motor contraction or those that are relatively new movement patterns. Thus sensory feedback is an important ingredient in skilled performance and in motor learning.

The Muscle Spindle

The muscle spindle of vertebrates is a complicated structure consisting of both afferent and efferent elements. Figure 10-10 illustrates the principal components of the spindle. The spindle gets its name from its shape—a sort of cylinder that is

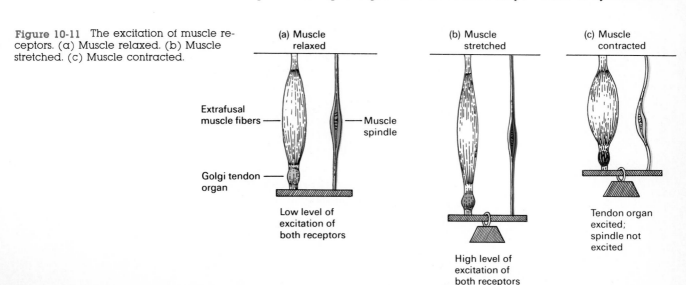

Figure 10-11 The excitation of muscle receptors. (a) Muscle relaxed. (b) Muscle stretched. (c) Muscle contracted.

(a) Muscle relaxed

Extrafusal muscle fibers

Muscle spindle

Golgi tendon organ

Low level of excitation of both receptors

(b) Muscle stretched

High level of excitation of both receptors

(c) Muscle contracted

Tendon organ excited; spindle not excited

thicker in the middle and tapers at its two ends. The Latin term for spindle, *fusus,* is used to form adjectives referring to the muscle spindle; thus the small muscle fibers that are found within each spindle are called intrafusal fibers, and the ordinary muscle fibers that lie outside the spindles are referred to as extrafusal fibers.

There are two kinds of receptors in the muscle spindle: (1) the primary or central sensory ending (also called annulo-spiral endings) and (2) the secondary or distal sensory ending (also called flower spray endings). As shown in Figure 10-10, these endings are related to different parts of the spindle. The primary ending wraps in a spiral fashion around a region called the nuclear bag (the central region of the intrafusal fiber). The secondary fibers terminate toward the thin end of the spindle.

How does excitation of these elements occur? Suppose a muscle is stretched, as occurs when a load is placed on it. For example, if you were trying to hold your arm straight out in front of you, palm up, and someone put an object in your hand, that would put an additional load on your biceps. The muscle spindle is also stretched, and the resulting deformation of the endings on the spindle sets up nerve impulses in the afferent fibers. When a muscle is stretched, there are two factors to consider. One is the rate of change of muscle length. In our example the rate of change is jointly a function of the weight of the load and the rate at which it is applied. The second factor is the force that must be continually exerted by the muscle to prevent dropping of the load. In our example this force is a function only of the weight of the load.

The different receptor elements of the muscle spindle are differentially sensitive to these two features of muscle length changes. The primary (central) endings show a maximum discharge early in stretch and then adapt to a lower discharge rate. In contrast, the secondary (distal) endings are maximally sensitive to maintained length and are slow to change their rate during the early phase of stretch. Because of this differential sensitivity, primary endings are called dynamic and secondary endings are called static indicators of muscle length. This distinction probably arises from the difference in the way in which these receptors are embedded in the spindle rather than from a difference in the nerve fibers themselves.

Efferent Control of the Muscle Spindle

Muscle spindles serve not only to help maintain postures but also to coordinate movements. Spindles are informed of planned and ongoing actions through innervation by special motor neurons that alter the tension within the spindle and thus control the sensitivity of its receptors. These motor neurons are called **gamma efferents** (to distinguish them from the faster conducting **alpha motoneurons,** which go to skeletal muscle fibers, as shown in Figure 10-10). The gamma efferents are connected to a contractile region of the spindle (called the myotube region). The cell bodies of these fibers are found in the ventral horns of the spinal cord. The activity in the gamma fibers causes a change in the length and tension of the spindle, which modifies its sensitivity to changes in the length of adjacent extrafusal muscle fibers. Hence the number of impulses elicited in the primary and secondary afferents is a function of two factors: (1) muscle stretch and (2) the resting tension in the muscle spindle.

Corresponding to the dual nature of the afferent parts of the spindle, there are two classes of gamma efferent control. The dynamic gamma efferent fiber makes the primary sensory endings in the spindle more responsive to changes in muscle length. The static gamma efferents modulate the sensitivity of both primary and secondary fibers, resulting in an increased response to maintained stretch, while attenuating the response to varying stretch. One reflection of the importance of the gamma efferent system is the fact that about 30% of all efferent fibers are gamma efferents.

Now let us see how the gamma efferents are involved in coordinating movements. Suppose that instead of continuing to hold your arm out straight ahead, you move your forearm up and down. If the muscle spindle had only one fixed degree of internal tension, it could not help to monitor and coordinate this movement. As the forearm moves up, the extrafusal and intrafusal fibers both shorten. Shortening the spindle, as we have noted, removes the tension, so the sensory endings should no longer respond. But the real situation is more complicated and more effective. As the muscle shortens, the gamma efferents correspondingly increase the tension on the intrafusal fibers. We have pointed out that feedback devices can have their set points changed; for example, you can alter the desired temperature on a thermostat. In this case the muscle spindles are informed of the desired changes in muscle length, so they help to monitor any departure from the program being carried out.

While the muscle spindles are primarily responsive to stretch, the Golgi tendon organs are especially sensitive to muscle contraction or shortening. They are rather insensitive to passive muscle stretch because they are connected in series with an elastic component. They function to detect overload that could threaten damage to muscles and tendons. Stimulation of these receptors inhibits the muscles that pull on the tendon and thus, by relaxing the tension, prevents mechanical damage.

Neural Control of Movements at the Spinal Level

The nerve cells directly responsible for excitation of muscle are those found in the ventral region of the spinal cord—spinal motoneurons—and in the brain stem nuclei of several cranial nerves. (See Reference Figures 2-12 and 2-13 for the anatomy of the spinal cord and cranial nerves.) This is the simplest level in the neural control of motor neurons. Firing patterns of these cells determine the timing of onset, coordination, and termination of muscle activity. Understanding the physiology of movement means acquiring knowledge of the source of the inputs to motoneurons, their origins, and their workings. This is a difficult task since a variety of influences converge on the motoneurons. Some arise solely at a spinal level from muscle afferents and the intrinsic circuitry of the spinal cord. Other influences are directed to motor cells from several brain pathways. For this reason, spinal and cranial motoneurons are called the final common pathway.

Motoneurons innervating the muscles of the head region are found in motor nuclei of the cranial nerves (for example, the facial nerve nucleus and the trigeminal motor nucleus); those innervating the musculature of the rest of the body are found in the spinal cord. The motoneurons differ from each other in certain important properties. These differences contribute to graded muscle activity—coordinated contraction over time as opposed to sudden intense twitches. The principal difference among motor cells is in size, which leads to important physiological differences. In general small motoneurons innervate slow muscles and are more easily excited by synaptic currents; therefore they are activated before large motoneurons are. Large motoneurons innervate fast muscles and tend to respond after small cells because they are also less readily excited by synaptic currents. Their discharge characteristics are more phasic or abrupt. Many spinal levels contain both large and small motoneurons.

Spinal Reflexes

One way to study spinal mechanisms is to transect the connections between the brain and spinal cord (producing what is termed a spinal animal) and then observe the forms of behavior that can be elicited below the level of the section. (All voluntary movements that depend on brain mechanisms are lost, of course, as is sensation from the regions below the section.) Immediately after the cord is transected, a condition referred to as **spinal shock** occurs. This condition is an interval of decreased synaptic excitability in the neuron population of the spinal cord after it is isolated from brain communication. The period may last for months in humans, although for nonprimates like cats and dogs, it may last only a few hours. During this period no reflexes mediated by the spinal cord can be elicited by either skin stimulation or excitation of muscle afferents.

Following this interval various kinds of reflexes can be elicited, and the properties of these movements in spinal animals have enabled us to gain some understanding of the basic organization of spinal nerve cells with respect to movement control. These include various stretch reflexes that may function well enough to support the weight of a standing animal for rather brief periods. Stimulation of the skin of a spinal animal can also elicit reflex effects, which can be readily demonstrated in a spinal cat or dog with intense stimulation of the toe pad. This stimulation results in abrupt withdrawal of the stimulated limb, a response called the **flexion reflex.** Unlike the stretch reflex, which involves a monosynaptic pathway, the flexion reflex involves a multisynaptic pathway within the spinal cord. Other behaviors evident in the spinal animal include bladder emptying and penile erection. Thus some very basic properties of movement are ''wired in'' to the organization of the spinal cord itself and do not require the brain. Some of these responses are illustrated in Figure 10-12.

The behavior of the spinal animal also reveals the presence of pattern generator circuits in the spinal cord. For example, mechanical stimulation of the feet or electrical stimulation of the spinal cord can elicit rhythmic movements of the legs. If a high spinal transection is performed, as diagramed in Figure 10-12c, the alternating movements of the limbs are coordinated as in walking; this indicates that the pattern generators for the different limbs are linked (Grillner, 1985). Further discussion of pattern generation in locomotion is presented in a subsequent section of this chapter.

Stretch Reflex

A good example of automatic control at the spinal level is the stretch reflex. Stretch of a muscle results in its contraction, a reaction known as the **stretch reflex.** The physiological condition for muscle stretch can be readily understood under condi-

STIMULATION **RESPONSE**

(a) Stretch reflex

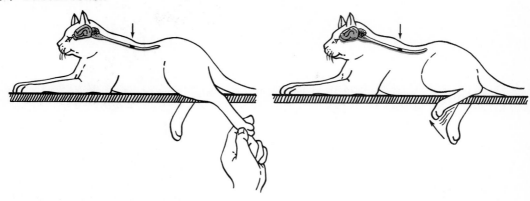

(b) Flexion reflex and crossed extension

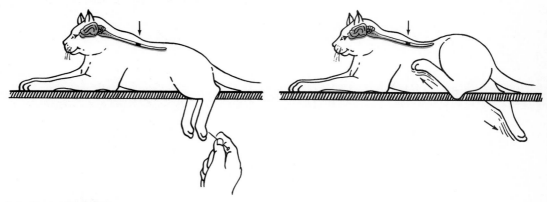

(c) Scratch reflex

Figure 10-12 Spinal reflexes in the spinal cat. The site of transection of the spinal cord is shown in brown. (a) Stretching the hind limb evokes muscle contraction opposing stretch. (b) Painful stimulation of the pad elicits hind limb flexion on the same side of the stimulation and extension of the contralateral hind limb. (c) Scratching the flank below the level of section elicits accurate, rhythmic scratching movements.

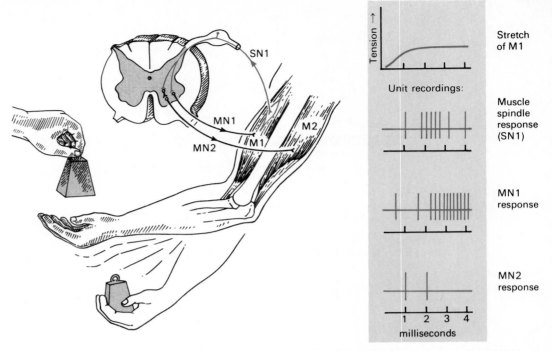

Figure 10-13 The stretch reflex circuit. MN1 is the motor nerve to muscle 1 (M1) and MN2 is the motor nerve to muscle 2 (M2). Characteristic responses at different stages in the circuit are shown on the right.

tions of an imposed weight or load. For example, in Figure 10-13 a weight (disturbance) is added to the hand, which imposes sudden stretch on muscle 1 (M1). A similar condition can be imposed on many joints simply by gravitational forces (that is, the weight of the body). The circuit that precludes dropping the load, or simply falling from the weight of our body, is one that links muscle spindles and the relevant muscles. The simplest depiction of the events portrayed in Figure 10-13 is the following sequence:

1. Disturbance imposed.
2. Muscle stretched.
3. Muscle spindle afferent elements excited.
4. Excitatory synaptic potentials produced by muscle spindle afferents at the synaptic junctions. (These afferents connect directly—that is, monosynaptically—to the motoneurons, whose fibers go to the stretched muscle.)
5. Motoneuron output received by muscle, producing contraction and thereby opposing muscle stretch.

This sequence describes a simple negative-feedback system that tends to restore the limb in our illustration to its "desired" position. Additional influences exerted by the activation of the muscle spindle system include the inhibition of the motoneurons supplying the antagonistic muscle (M2). These effects are exerted disynaptically ("two synapses"). Thus in the illustration of Figure 10-13, spindle information terminates on the interneuron whose output goes to the motoneuron supplying M2. At this junction inhibitory postsynaptic activity is produced. This combined action then involves spindle-produced excitation of the stretched muscle (and its synergists—that is, muscles working the same way) and inhibition of the antagonistic muscle system.

Of course, spinal reflexes do not usually function in isolation. They are integrated and modulated by the activity of brain circuits, to which we now turn.

Selective Potentiation of Spinal Neural Circuits

Control of movements involves **selective potentiation** of neural circuits; that is, activity of certain circuits is enhanced, whereas activity of other circuits in inhibited. For an example of the operation of the principle of selective potentiation in locomotion consider how an animal is able to walk over rough, uneven terrain. Walking involves two phases of movement of each leg: (1) the swing phase when the limb is off the ground and advancing (this is initiated by the flexion reflex) and (2) the stance phase, providing support and propulsion, involving the extension reflex. During locomotion these two phases are evoked in regular alternation by a spinal pattern generator. When an animal is walking on a level surface the alternating phases accomplish smooth locomotion, but what happens when obstacles are encountered? For example, what happens if during movement a tap is delivered to the front or top of the paw? This is the part of the foot that is most likely to encounter something that might trip the animal or that could push its foot out from under it.

Experiments have shown that the same stimulus to the front of the foot in a spinal cat can evoke either a flexion response or an extension response, depending on the phase of leg movement when the tap is delivered (Forssberg, Grillner, & Rossignol, 1975). As the leg swings forward in the cycle, a tap to the front of the foot elicits flexion at all joints in the leg—the toes, the ankle, the knee, and the hip. This lifts the leg and may allow it to clear an obstacle that might otherwise block the swing and trip the cat. If the same tap is delivered as the cat is starting the stance phase, the stimulation elicits or strengthens the extension reflex. This hastens the completion of the stance phase and strengthens it, so that a moving object that might have swept the cat's foot out from under it is less likely to do so.

Thus, depending on the phase of the leg movement, there is selective potentiation of one kind of reflex and inhibition of the other kind. Identical stimuli thus evoke opposite reflexes of flexion or extension, depending upon the immediate state of the animal. When we turn soon to motivation, in the next main part of this book, we will also see the force of this principle of selective potentiation.

Brain Control of Movements

Pathways from the brain to cranial and spinal motoneurons are many and exceedingly complex, especially from a functional viewpoint. A block diagram of the relations of major brain regions associated with movement control was presented in Figure 10-7. Complex movements clearly involve programs of the brain, and uncovering these programs is a major focus of work in this area. Some of the pathways deliver quite discrete information, which can be established by looking at the characteristic conditions that produce activity in a path. For example, the vestibulospinal pathway provides important information about head position, and this information produces an impact on postural muscles to effect body adjustments.

The variety of pathways from the brain to the spinal motoneurons is illustrated in Figure 10-7. Ideas about the differential role(s) of each of these systems in the integration and control of movement have relied heavily on observations of changes in posture and locomotion produced by natural or experimental interferences in these regions. Clinical data derived from people with brain damage have generated useful anatomical and functional distinctions between two major divisions of the motor system, called the pyramidal and extrapyramidal motor systems.

The **pyramidal system** (or **corticospinal system**) refers to neuron cell bodies within the cerebral cortex and their axons, which pass through the brain stem, forming the pyramidal tract (Figure 10-14). The pyramidal tract is most clearly

2 Divisions of motor System
1. Pyramidal System (Corticospinal System
1. Extra Pyramidal System

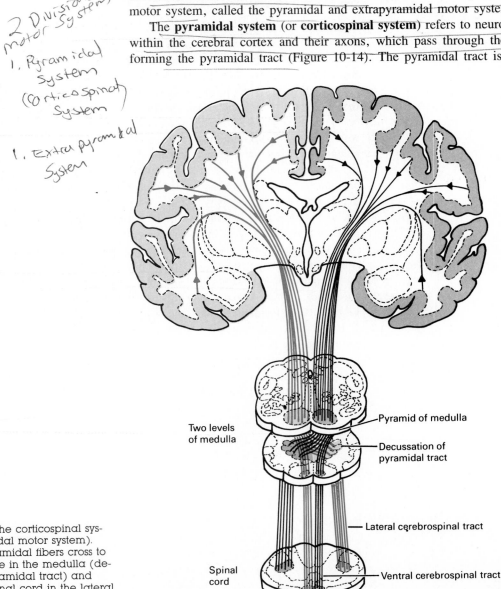

Two levels of medulla

Pyramid of medulla

Decussation of pyramidal tract

Lateral cerebrospinal tract

Spinal cord

Ventral cerebrospinal tract

Figure 10-14 The corticospinal system (or pyramidal motor system). Most of the pyramidal fibers cross to the opposite side in the medulla (decussation of pyramidal tract) and descend the spinal cord in the lateral cerebrospinal tract.

distinguished from other motor tracts where it passes through the anterior aspect of the medulla. In a cross section of the medulla, the tract is seen as a somewhat wedge-shaped anterior protuberance (pyramid) on each side of the midline. For many animals the motor cortical sector partially overlaps the somatosensory cortex.

In addition to the corticospinal outflow through the pyramidal tract, there are many other motor tracts that run from the brain to the brain stem and spinal cord. Since these tracts run outside the pyramids of the medulla, they and their connections are sometimes called the extrapyramidal system.

Brain Stem Level

The brain stem contains several components that are critical for control of movements. First, scattered throughout this region are cranial motor nuclei whose axons innervate muscles of the head and neck (Figure 10-15). Second, pathways originating at higher levels course through the brain stem and, in some cases, they connect to various brain stem regions. Finally, within the brain stem there is an extensive pool of interconnected neurons called the reticular formation, which modulates various aspects of movements. Some zones of the reticular formation facilitate movements whereas other zones are inhibitory. These effects are transmitted in descending tracts that arise from various sites in the reticular formation and connect to spinal interneurons where they influence the excitability of spinal motor circuitry. Neurons of the reticular formation are also involved in the control of basic regulatory mechanisms concerned with breathing.

Primary Motor Cortex

In humans brain lesions involving the pyramidal pathway commonly produce a partial paralysis of movements on the side of the body opposite the brain lesion. This disturbance is greatest in distal muscles, such as those of the hand, and it particularly involves flexor muscles. Humans with these lesions are generally described as ''disinclined'' to use the affected limb.

Because human lesions arise from accidental injury or disease, they are usually not limited to a single neural system. The symptoms of corticospinal system injury and some of the complexity of the observed changes may arise in part from involvement of other motor control systems. In other primates experimental lesions restricted to the pyramidal tracts appear to produce some similar changes, although the overall picture is less severe. Six weeks following the bilateral interruption of the pyramidal tracts, monkeys can run, climb, and reach accurately for food. The persistent deficits they display are the limited ability in individual finger movements and the overall tendency of slower-than-normal movements, which rapidly ''fatigue.'' Although they have difficulty in releasing food from the hand, they can readily release their grip while climbing. In mammals other than primates, the impairments following pyramidal lesions are less severe.

What do these deficits mean in terms of the overall functional role of the corticospinal system? This problem has plagued many investigators, and definitive answers have not yet been found. Attempts to provide answers have involved recording from pyramidal cells during various movements and closer examination of the anatomical relations between the motor cortex and other levels of movement control systems. We will consider briefly some of the ideas emerging from these studies.

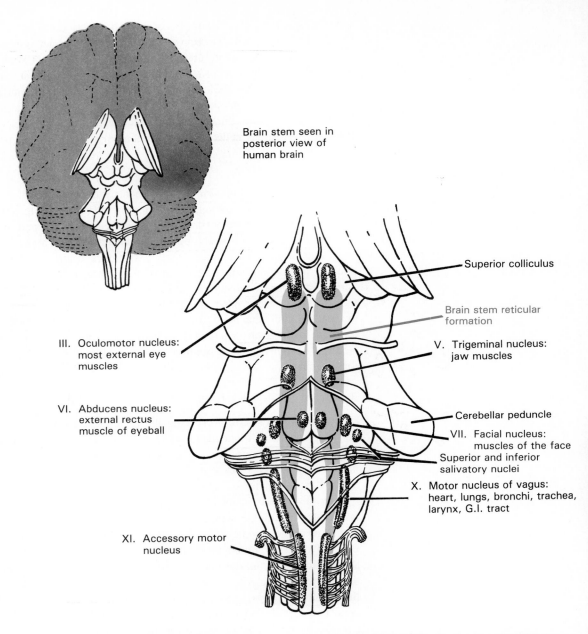

Brain stem seen in posterior view of human brain

Superior colliculus

Brain stem reticular formation

III. Oculomotor nucleus: most external eye muscles

V. Trigeminal nucleus: jaw muscles

VI. Abducens nucleus: external rectus muscle of eyeball

Cerebellar peduncle

VII. Facial nucleus: muscles of the face

Superior and inferior salivatory nuclei

X. Motor nucleus of vagus: heart, lungs, bronchi, trachea, larynx, G.I. tract

XI. Accessory motor nucleus

Figure 10-15 Brain stem nuclei of cranial nerves and the brain stem reticular formation. The brain stem is seen from the rear. The corresponding cranial nerves are shown in Reference Figure 2-12.

In the late nineteenth century, several experimenters showed that electrical stimulation of some regions of the cerebral cortex could elicit body movements, particularly flexion of the limbs. These early findings—and many similar experiments continuing to the present—have led to maps of movements elicited by cortical stimulation, particularly those elicited by a region of the cortex just anterior to the somatosensory cortex, which has come to be known as the **motor cortex.** A map of

Motor cortex

the human motor cortex is shown in Figure 10-16. The largest motor regions in these maps are devoted to the most elaborate and complex movements in any species. For example, humans and other primates have extremely large cortical fields concerned with hand movements. More recent studies have shown that "colonies" of cells are related to particular muscle groups, and their cortical structural representation may be in vertical columns (Ghez, 1985), an organizational principle similar to that noted in cortical sensory systems. Although a large fraction of the pyramidal tract fibers originate in the so-called motor area of the cortex, this fraction accounts for only about one-third of the total number of pyramidal fibers. Another large component comes from the postcentral gyrus (somatosensory cortex)—about one-

[handwritten: Post central gyrus (Somatosensory cortex)]

Figure 10-16 Map of human primary motor cortex on the lateral (a) and medial (b) surfaces of the brain. (c) The sequence and sizes of motor representations of different parts of the body. (d) The proportions of the homunculus show the relative sizes of motor representations of parts of the body.

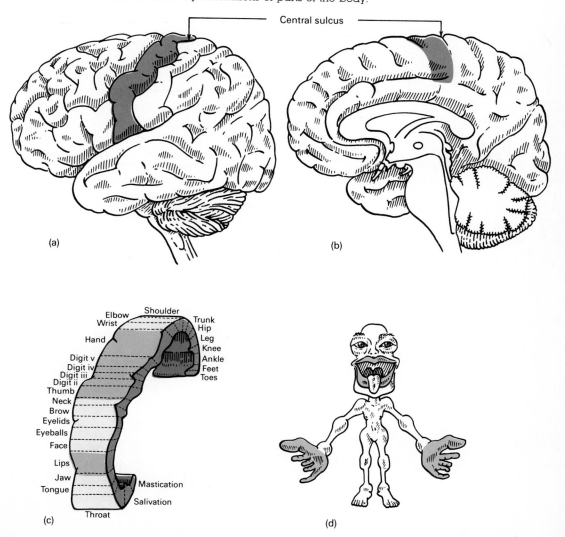

fifth. Still other pyramidal fibers arise from many other cortical regions. Thus control of motor function is dispersed among cortical areas.

Data like those derived from clinical observation and studies involving motor cortex stimulation have suggested to many that the motor cortex–pyramidal tract system provides the executive mechanism for voluntary movements. According to this view, the motor cortex represents particular kinds of movement, and the activation of these cells is the command for the excitation of relevant spinal and cranial motoneurons. Anatomical studies that define the relations between the motor cortex and the spinal motoneurons provide only ambiguous support for this view, however. In primates the pyramidal tract has some monosynaptic connections with spinal motoneurons, particularly those relevant to the control of distal segments of the upper limbs (that is, hands, wrist, and fingers). However, most pyramidal tract neurons influence spinal motoneurons through polysynaptic routes and share control of these motor cells with other descending influences. Comparisons of the number of pyramidal tract fibers in a variety of mammals indicate that the size of the pyramidal tract is principally related both to body size and to the complexity of species-typical motor behavior. It seems doubtful that the pyramidal tract is required for initiation and execution of motion, since many active mammals have very small pyramidal tracts.

A more direct examination of pyramidal tract function has involved recording from these cells during movements. This experiment seeks to determine the relations between measures of neural firing (for instance, velocity or force) and degree of limb displacement. Evarts et al. (1984) recorded from brain cells in monkeys trained to make particular limb movements (Figure 10-17). They found that pyramidal tract neurons discharged prior to a movement, and the firing rate of some cells

Figure 10-17 Graph of latencies of motor cortex cells in response to visually triggered movements. (a) Experimental setup. (b) Type of hand movement. (c) Graph that shows that most motor units in the precentral cortex fire before the start of a response (R), whereas most units in the postcentral cortex fire after the response starts.

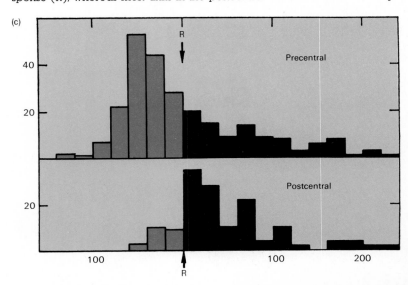

was related to the force generated by the movement. The final position of a limb—its displacement—was less obviously related to individual motor cortex cell-firing patterns.

Although most views about the motor cortex–pyramidal tract function emphasize voluntary movement and executive control as the principal functional features of this system, some investigators have posed alternatives. The neurophysiologist Arnold Towe (1971) has emphasized that this system is a rather late evolutionary development. For example, among existing vertebrates only mammals have a corticospinal system. Many nonmammalian vertebrates without a pyramidal tract, such as birds and fish, display a vast range of elaborate movement patterns. Towe further notes, as we described earlier, that transection of this tract does not preclude movements of the limb. He believes that this system is not the executive mechanism of voluntary movement per se but rather a mechanism for controlling the excitability of networks organized elsewhere (for example, in the brain stem). The corticospinal system is more directly involved in the monitoring of many external environmental inputs and in guiding but not initiating movement on the basis of sensory assessments. This novel perspective may provide a valuable insight for future research.

Nonprimary Motor Cortex

Large portions of the frontal lobe between primary motor cortex and the prefrontal area are called **nonprimary motor cortex.** Two regions are distinguished within this area—the supplementary motor cortex, which lies mainly on the medial aspect of the hemisphere, and premotor cortex, which is anterior to primary motor cortex (Figure 10-18). The supplementary motor cortex receives input from the basal gan-

Figure 10-18 Map of human motor cortical areas. Primary motor cortex (shown in dark brown) lies just anterior to the central sulcus. Anterior to the primary motor area are premotor cortex (light brown) and supplementary motor cortex (gray).

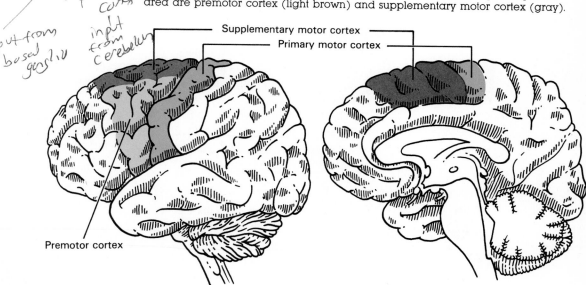

Supplementary motor cortex
Primary motor cortex
Premotor cortex

(a) Lateral view

(b) Medial view

glia, and the premotor cortex receives input from the cerebellum. We will soon discuss the roles of the basal ganglia and the cerebellum in modulating movements. These nonprimary motor cortical regions have long been suspected of being involved in the control of skilled movements, and this emphasis has been supported by recent studies of brain responses during voluntary movements. First we will consider some nonhuman primate studies and then examine some intriguing observations in alert human subjects.

Controled skilled movements

Single unit recordings in awake monkeys have shown that many nerve cells in nonprimary motor cortex change their discharge rate just before the onset of operantly conditioned movements, such as key press following the onset of a sensory stimulus. Some nerve cells in these regions also respond to the onset of a sensory stimulus without evidence of elicited movement (Wise & Strick, 1984). Such data have raised the prospect that these regions are involved in the sensory guidance of movements. Additionally, single unit recording studies also reveal that the nonprimary motor cortical areas are especially active during the preparation of skilled movements.

Anatomical studies in humans have shown some interesting comparative findings. Premotor cortex is much larger in relative size in humans than in other primates (Freund, 1984). Patients with bilateral damage of the supplementary motor cortex are unable to move or speak voluntarily, although some automatic and reflex movements remain. These are long-lasting effects that suggest that this region is involved in the conception and initiation of movement (Freund, 1984). Patients with unilateral lesions of premotor cortex retain fine motor control of the fingers but are impaired in the stability of stance and gait. A gross impairment of coordination of the two hands is also evident.

Blood flow and metabolic studies by Roland (1980, 1984) offer interesting observations. He noted that in simple tasks, such as keeping a spring compressed between two fingers of one hand, the blood flow is markedly raised in the hand area of the contralateral primary motor cortex and in the adjacent somatosensory area. Increasing the complexity of this and other motor tasks extends the area of blood flow increase to the supplementary motor cortex. Finally, a dramatic finding is evident when the subjects are asked to rehearse mentally the complex movement sequence: In this state the enhanced blood flow is restricted to the supplementary motor cortex.

These research data clearly point to the prominence of nonprimary motor cortex in the control and governance of complex motor activities. Presumably the activities of these areas are integrated with those of the motor cortex to produce coordinated behavior.

Modulation of Motor Control

many other regions involved

Disorders of human movements that arise from brain injuries or disease have suggested that in addition to the brain regions already discussed, there are many other brain regions involved in some aspects of motor control. The exact role of these brain regions remains to be specified, but at the least they can be said to modulate the functioning of regions that are more directly involved in motor controls. These modulatory systems include the basal ganglia and cerebellum, which will be discussed in this section.

Basal Ganglia

The **basal ganglia** include a group of forebrain nuclei (for example, the caudate, putamen, and globus pallidus) and some closely related major brain stem structures (substantia nigra and red nucleus). The locations and major connections of these structures are shown in Figure 10-19. Lesions of these regions in humans produce movement impairments that seem quite different from those following interruption of the pyramidal system. These impairments will be discussed in a later section.

Studies show that inputs to the basal ganglia come from an extensive region of the cerebral cortex, as well as from thalamic nuclei and substantia nigra. Within each structure of the basal ganglia there is a topographic representation of body

Figure 10-19 The basal ganglia, cerebellum, and their motor connections.

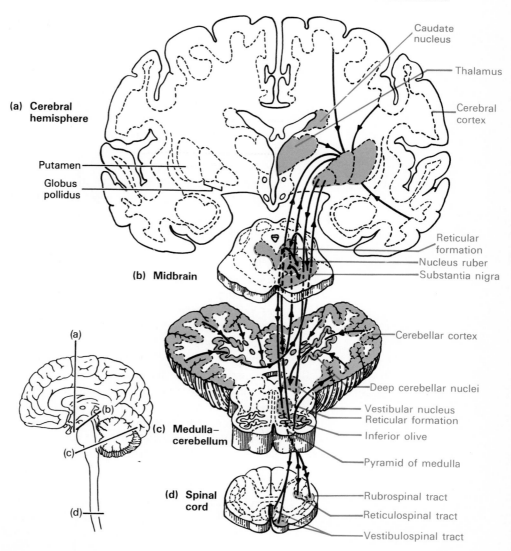

musculature. These data also suggest a subdivision of the basal ganglia into two major systems. One is focused on the caudate nucleus, whose inputs are especially derived from frontal association cortex. The other system is focused on the putamen; these inputs are derived from sensorimotor cortical zones. In keeping with these differences of connection, lesions within these subdivisions produce characteristic functional differences (DeLong et al., 1984). Lesions of the caudate result in impairments of relatively complex behavior, seen, for example, in dealing with spatial aspects of behavior—where to respond. In contrast, the effects of lesions in the putamen are more exclusively motor in character, affecting the strength and rate of responses.

Animal studies of basal ganglia have involved both lesions and recording of single-unit activity during motor responses (DeLong et al., 1984). Results of these studies have suggested that the basal ganglia may play a role in determining the amplitude and direction of movement rather than affecting the initiation of actions. The activities of basal ganglia networks thus seem to modulate the patterns of activity initiated in other brain circuits that control movements, such as motor and premotor cortical systems. An additional aspect of basal ganglia functions has been suggested by Evarts et al. (1984). Their experiments indicate that basal ganglia are especially important in the generation of movements influenced by memories in contrast to those guided by sensory control.

Cerebellum

The cerebellum in higher vertebrates consists of a many-folded sheet (whose appearance and location in the human brain was shown in Reference Figure 2-28). This structure is found in virtually all vertebrates, and its size in some vertebrate groups varies according to the range and complexity of movements. For example, the cerebellum is much larger in fish with extensive locomotor behavior than it is in less active fish, and it is also large in flying birds, as compared with species that do not fly.

The cell types and basic circuitry of the cerebellum are shown in Figure 10-20. All the output of the cerebellar cortex travels via the axons of Purkinje cells, all of which synapse with the deep cerebellar nuclei. At this synapse they produce only postsynaptic inhibitory potentials. Hence all the circuitry of the extensive cortical portion of this system, which includes 10 to 20 billion granule cells in humans, acts to produce patterns of inhibition on motor cells.

Inputs to the cerebellar cortex are derived from both sensory sources and other brain motor systems. Sensory inputs include the vestibular system, muscle and joint receptors, and somatosensory, visual, and auditory sources. Both pyramidal and nonpyramidal pathways contribute inputs to the cerebellum and in turn receive outputs from the deep nuclei of the cerebellum. Thus the cerebellum could be characterized as receiving elaborate information both from systems that monitor movements and from systems that execute movements. For this reason the cerebellum has long been considered to play a role in the feedback control of movements. It has also been suggested that the cerebellum elaborates neural "programs" for the control of skilled movements, particularly when these are repeated and become automatic. Recently the cerebellum has been demonstrated to be involved in acquisition and retention of motor responses, as we will discuss in Chapter 17.

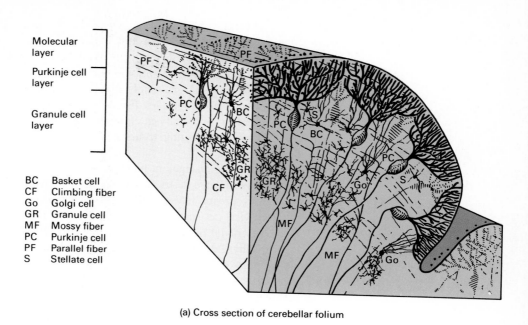

Molecular
layer

Purkinje cell
layer

Granule cell
layer

BC	Basket cell
CF	Climbing fiber
Go	Golgi cell
GR	Granule cell
MF	Mossy fiber
PC	Purkinje cell
PF	Parallel fiber
S	Stellate cell

(a) Cross section of cerebellar folium

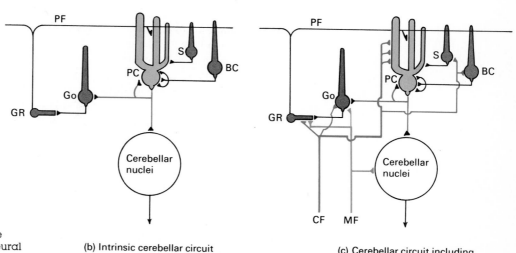

Figure 10-20 A folium of the cerebellum and the basic neural circuits of the cerebellum.

(b) Intrinsic cerebellar circuit

(c) Cerebellar circuit including input connections

Human Movement Disorders

Much of the machinery of the body is involved in movement, so the behavioral characteristics of impaired movements and acts provide clues about the locus and characteristics of pathology in the motor system. In this section we will present examples of impaired movement and the bodily conditions that underlie them, starting with the skeletomuscular system and proceeding to disorders related to successive levels of central neural control.

Peripheral Motor
Impairments

Many metabolic conditions can affect the chemistry and structure of muscle. In Chapter 7 we noted that several hormones—especially thyroid—affect muscle chemistry and function. Chronically low levels of thyroid hormone produce muscle weakness and slowness of muscle contraction. Several muscle diseases are more mysterious in origin, seemingly involving biochemical abnormalities that lead to structural changes in muscle, disorders referred to as muscular dystrophy. Many of these disorders, especially in children, are due to hereditary metabolic abnormalities. Genetic engineering techniques may offer ways of diagnosing and treating these disorders.

Pathological changes in motor neurons produce movement paralysis or weakness. Virus-induced destruction of motor neurons, in the form of polio, was once a frightening prospect, especially in the United States and Western Europe. Polio involved viral destruction of motor neurons of the spinal cord and, in more severe types, of cranial motor neurons of the brain stem.

Movement disorders involving the neuromuscular synaptic junction include a variety of reversible poison states. For example, in tropical areas of the world snake bites cause neuromuscular blocks by releasing toxic substances. Venom of some highly poisonous snakes contains a substance that blocks postsynaptic receptor sites for acetylcholine. Studies on the mechanisms of action of this venom have led directly to an understanding of one of the more debilitating neuromuscular disorders—**myasthenia gravis,** a disorder characterized by a profound weakness of skeletal muscles. (The word **myasthenia** comes from Greek roots *myo* meaning ''muscle'' and *asthenia* meaning ''weakness''; *gravis* means ''grave or serious.'') Symptoms often begin in the muscles of the head, producing drooping of the eyelids, double vision, and slowing of speech. In later stages paralysis of the muscles involved in swallowing and respiration can become life threatening.

Physiological studies of myasthenia gravis have shown abnormalities in synaptic transmission (Rowland, 1986). The main defect observed in these studies is a reduction in synaptic potentials recorded at the neuromuscular junction. Studies by Drachman (1983) showed that the neuromuscular junctions of myasthenic patients had a markedly reduced number of acetylcholine receptor sites. In addition, the morphology of these junctions in patients is flattened and simplified in comparison to normal synaptic junctions (Figure 10-21). As a result of these changes at the neuromuscular synapse, transmission is much less effective, and presynaptic action potentials are frequently unable to trigger postsynaptic muscle action potentials. Basic research studies in animals and continuing studies in patients have established that antibodies directed against acetylcholine receptors on muscle cause these changes. Apparently myasthenic patients spontaneously develop these antibodies, which attack their own postsynaptic membranes. Serum taken from patients and injected into animals can produce the same effect. Many studies implicate the thymus gland in the generation of this autoimmune disease (Engel, 1984). Cells in the thymus may actually generate the anti-acetylcholine receptor antibody, and there is clinical evidence that removal of the thymus helps patients. Temporary depletion of antibodies by removing the plasma from blood of patients—a procedure called plasmapheresis—is another type of successful clinical intervention.

Figure 10-21 Diagrams of normal and myasthenic neuromuscular junctions. The myasthenia gravis junction shows reduced numbers of acetylcholine receptors (stippling); sparse, shallow postsynaptic folds; a widened synaptic space; and a normal presynaptic nerve terminal. (Adapted from Drachman, 1983)

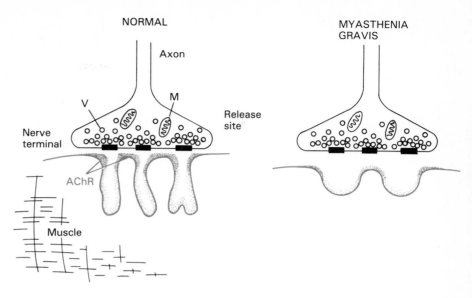

Spinal Motor Impairments

War, sports, and accidents cause many forms of human spinal injuries that result in motor impairment. Injuries to the human spinal cord commonly develop from forces to the neck or back that break bone and cause compression of nervous tissue of the spinal cord. Sudden acceleration of the head with respect to the back, such as occurs in car accidents, can also produce spinal injury.

Complete transection of the spinal cord produces immediate paralysis with a loss of reflexes below the level of injury, a condition known as flaccid paralysis. It occurs chiefly when a considerable stretch of the spinal cord has been destroyed. In contrast, some forms of spinal cord injury produce a transection without widespread destruction of tissue. In this case reflexes below the level of injury are frequently excessive, since the intact tissue lacks the dampening influence of brain inhibitory pathways.

In many of these injuries, the spinal cord is not severed but is bruised or compressed. Physiological changes in the spinal cord after injury vastly amplify the direct effects of an accident. Swelling, hemorrhaging, and a sharp drop in blood flow accentuate the injury. Drugs are now being used to limit the spreading effects of injury. For example, endorphins probably released at the time of injury contribute to the intensity of acute trauma, and endorphin blockers administered at the time of injury in experimental animals limit the long-term effects of spinal trauma. Reconnecting the injured spinal cord remains a dream that no longer seems as farfetched as it did only a few years ago. Investigators working on the spinal cord of lampreys have shown that months after the spinal cord was severed, these animals could swim again (Cohen, 1982). Anatomical studies on lampreys using marker dyes demonstrated that axons had grown across the surgical gap in the spinal cord. In rats and cats, axon sprouting is seen at the site of spinal trauma and may mediate some aspects of spinal reflex recovery (Goldberger & Murray, 1985). These observations buoy the hope that regeneration is possible in the injured human spinal cord. Perhaps the accuracy of the regenerative process in humans with spinal injury can be controlled by using grafts of nerve tissue that act as "guide wires" (Aguayo, 1985). The use of enzymes to prevent scar formation might also remove an obstacle to adaptive forms of reconnection in the injured human spinal cord. Putting the spinal cord back together after injury may render obsolete the wheelchairs that today signal a tragic limitation in rehabilitation.

The Brain Stem and Motor Impairment

Strokes, injuries, and diseases affecting the brain stem have profound effects on movement since the main pathways connecting the forebrain and spinal cord course through this region. In addition, there are several densely packed collections of nerve cells, including cranial nerve motor nuclei, which control and modulate various aspects of movement and actions. Some of the syndromes involving the brain stem are quite dramatic in character. One disease characterized by extensive cell loss in the brain stem produces an unusual combination of symptoms, including loss of voluntary control of vertical eye movements, slowed and garbled speech, body- and neck-muscle rigidity, and dementia. This disorder is called progressive supranuclear palsy. (Palsy means "paralysis," and supranuclear refers to the fact that the lesions lie above the brain stem nuclei for eye movements). Recently detailed postmortem studies of patients have revealed characteristic neurotransmitter losses in the basal ganglia that communicate with the brain stem motor nuclei (Kish et al., 1985; Ruberg et al., 1986). Researchers have noted a marked reduction in dopamine in the caudate nucleus and putamen but not in dopaminergic pathways to the limbic system. Furthermore, cholinergic cells in the basal ganglia that are the targets for the dopamine-containing axons also degenerate. Cholinergic losses in this disorder may account for the intellectual decline in patients.

In the late 1930s the brilliant baseball career of a player for the New York Yankees—Lou Gehrig—brought public awareness to an unusual degenerative disorder that involves destruction of the motoneurons of the brain stem and spinal cord. This syndrome is formally known as amyotrophic lateral sclerosis, although journalists more commonly refer to it as Lou Gehrig's disease. Recently renewed awareness was focused on this disorder by the late Senator Jacob Javits, who pointed out the personal struggles involved in a disease that progressively paralyzes a person while leaving intellectual prowess intact. Characteristic symptoms at the start of the disorder depend on the level of the nervous system at which motor neuron destruction begins (Tandan & Bradley, 1985). The origins of the disease remain a mystery. A wide range of causal factors is under investigation, including genetic susceptibility, premature aging, toxic minerals, viruses, immune responses, and endocrine dysfunction.

Motor Impairments and Cerebral Cortex

Motor impairments that follow strokes or injury to the human cerebral cortex are a familiar part of the clinical investigation of the brain. The most common change is a paralysis or partial paralysis (paresis) of voluntary movements, usually the result of injury to the contralateral cerebral cortex. In addition, some degree of spasticity is seen, especially in the form of increased rigidity in response to forced movement of the limbs. The spasticity reflects the exaggeration of stretch reflexes. Abnormal reflexes, such as the flaring and extension of the toes elicited by stroking the sole of the foot (Babinski reflex), also become evident. In the months following cerebral cortical injury, there is some change in the clinical picture. The initial paralysis is slowly modified with some return of voluntary movements of the proximal portion of limbs, although fine motor control of fingers is seldom regained. This picture in humans is quite different from that observed in many other mammals. For example, in rodents deficits caused by ablation of motor cortex are far more fleeting, while in other primates they are largely restricted to fine movements of the limbs.

Damage to nonmotor zones of the cerebral cortex, such as some regions of parietal or frontal association cortex, produce more complicated changes in motor control. Injury to these regions can produce apraxia, which is defined as the inability to follow simple commands for learned movements. For example, common tests for apraxia include such commands as "Wave goodbye," "Stick out your tongue," "Smile," or more complex commands such as "Fold a letter and place it in an envelope." Subjects with apraxic disorders may be unable to follow these commands even though they show no paralysis, intellectual impairment, or motivational deficit. Curiously, the patient can perform the very same acts during routine spontaneous behavior (Heilman & Rothi, 1985).

Motor Impairments Involving Modulatory Systems

The modulatory roles of the basal ganglia and cerebellum are particularly evident in a wide array of motor disorders in humans that arise from damage to these systems. Impoverished movements, wild explosive flinging of limbs, and unusual writhing are some of the many indicants of a failure of modulation by basal ganglia and cerebellum. In this section we will provide some examples of human motor disorders that arise from damage to these two main modulatory systems.

Basal Ganglia

Diseases of the basal ganglia produce slowness of movement, marked changes in muscle tone, and many distinctive abnormal movements whose character is specifically related to the anatomical sites of damage within this system. Many of the signs of basal ganglia damage reflect the release from the constraints that the basal ganglia usually impose on motor control. In the absence of these constraints, the activity initiated by other regions appears unchecked. In some instances these changes in movement arise from loss of inhibitory synaptic activity. Three forms of tremor arise from a failure of modulatory systems:

1. **Tremor-at-rest,** which is movement that occurs when the affected region, such as a limb, is fully supported; it is even seen when no movement is being attempted.
2. **Postural tremor,** which is manifested when the person attempts to maintain a posture such as holding an arm or leg extended.
3. **Intention tremor,** which is provoked only during voluntary movement—for example, when the person reaches out to grasp an object.

Tremor-at-rest (usually with a frequency of 5–6 cycles/sec) is particularly characteristic of **Parkinson's disease,** the most common human disease involving the basal ganglia. Tremor-at-rest in this disease (which is also characterized by other movement dysfunctions) involves the extremities and can also affect the eyelids and tongue. It is a degenerative disease arising primarily between the ages of 40 and 60. Initially it involves a loss of cells in the brain region called the substantia nigra. Great advances have been made in recent years in the treatment of this disorder because of fundamental advances in knowledge of the anatomical relations between the substantia nigra and the caudate nucleus and because of the discovery of the synaptic transmitter in this pathway. Output from the substantia nigra goes to the caudate nucleus and involves dopamine as a synaptic transmitter. Patients show a deficit of dopamine in the caudate nucleus; when they are given replacement therapy with a precursor of dopamine (L-dopa), there is a decrease in tremor, in addition to a relief of additional symptoms. A Parkinson-like syndrome may also follow the use of certain tranquilizers, particularly a class called phenothiazines, the best known of which is the drug chlorpromazine. This syndrome occurs because these drugs either interfere with the storage of dopamine or block the postsynaptic receptor membrane at sites where dopamine is a transmitter. Clues to the origins of this disease also come from cases caused by an illegal drug (Box 10-2).

Postural tremor can be caused by disease processes in the basal ganglia or cerebellum. There are also some forms of congenital postural tremor.

Intention tremor appears most commonly at the end of a movement and can result from any of a large number of pathological conditions that involve either the basal ganglia or the cerebellum.

The most extreme examples of increased movements involving basal ganglia dysfunctions are choreic movements and ballism. **Choreic movements** are uncontrollable, brief, and forceful; they look like strange exaggerations of normal movements. They may include a jerking movement of fingers, a facial grimace, or a dancelike movement of the feet. **Huntington's chorea** is a genetic disorder characterized by these unusual movements in addition to profound changes in mental functioning. In some patients a marked loss of cells in the caudate nucleus has been found. (Chorea comes from a Greek term for ''dancing.'' Chorus comes from the same root, since originally a chorus danced as well as sang.) The genetic and neuroanatomical aspects of Huntington's chorea were described in Box 4-3.

Ballism refers to an uncontrollable, violent tossing of the limbs. The movement is sudden and may involve one side of the body. Lesions in a region called the subthalamic nucleus can produce this syndrome in humans and monkeys.

The preceding examples of increased movements involving extrapyramidal system diseases are hyperkinetic disorders (*hyper* means ''above normal''; *kinetic* refers to movement). They demonstrate the major role that inhibition plays in normal motor control; without adequate inhibition a person is compelled to perform a variety of unwanted movements. There is also a major class of hyperkinetic effects involving motor stiffness (akinesia) and rigidity (increase of muscle tone). These deficits are also part of Parkinson's syndrome.

Cerebellum

Since the cerebellum modulates many aspects of motor performance, it is not surprising that its impairment leads to many abnormalities of behavior. Observation of

BOX 10-2 | The Frozen Addicts

Parkinson's disease has been very difficult to study because until quite recently it was not possible to find or produce a similar disorder in laboratory animals. Recently mistakes in the synthesis of drugs for illegal sale have led to the first valuable model of Parkinson's disease. This saga began when several drug addicts were admitted to a hospital in California with an unusual array of symptoms. Especially puzzling was the fact that they were in their twenties yet presented an unmistakable portrait of Parkinson's disease, which almost always occurs in people 50 or older. The movements of these young patients were slow, they had tremors of the hands, and their faces were frozen without expression. All of these drug addicts had recently used a "home-brewed" synthetic form of heroin. That fact, coupled with the recollection of a report of an unusual disorder that arose from a laboratory accident published several years earlier led to the conclusion that the synthetic heroin contained a neurotoxin that produced brain damage typical of Parkinson's disease (Kopin & Markey, 1988; Langston, 1985). In addition, the diagnosis of Parkinsonism in these cases was confirmed by the therapeutic response to L-dopa.

Moving step by step in a trail that resembles a detective story, various researchers pieced together a scenario of what had happened. Chemical studies led to the identification of a contaminant in the synthetic heroin, now known as MPTP (an abbreviation of the much longer chemical name). Many addicts have been exposed to this substance, but relatively few have come down with this Parkinson-like disorder. However, recent studies have shown that those who are currently without symptoms show a decline in brain dopamine concentrations as revealed by PET scans (Calne et al., 1985). This exposure may make them more vulnerable to Parkinson's disease with further aging.

An important step was achieved when MPTP was injected into research animals. Although rats and rabbits showed only minimal and transient motor impairments, the effects seen in monkeys were startling. Monkeys were as sensitive to the toxin as humans and developed a permanent set of motor changes that are virtually identical to those seen in humans with Parkinson's disease. Furthermore, the sites of damage in the brain are identical to those seen in Parkinson's patients. The substance MPTP is found in high concentrations in areas such as the substantia nigra and caudate nucleus. High concentrations occur in these areas because MPTP binds selectively to a form of the enzyme monoamine oxidase, in which these regions are rich. As a result of interaction with this enzyme, a highly toxic metabolite—MPP^+—is formed. Recently researchers have suggested that the natural pigment neuromelanin found in substantia nigra might account for the selectivity of damage produced by MPTP (Snyder & D'Amato, 1985). They have shown that MPP^+ binds with a special affinity to this pigment. Thus cells with neuromelanin accumulate MPP^+ to toxic levels, and since cells of substantia nigra contain large amounts of the pigment, they are particularly vulnerable to the destructive impact of MPP^+. In other parts of the brain, MPP^+ levels decline following exposure; in contrast, MPP^+ levels in substantia nigra cells may actually continue to increase for some time following exposure. In view of this binding mechanism, differences among species become more comprehensible. Monkeys and humans have pigment within nigral cells, while those of rodents are unpigmented. Animals can be protected against the toxic impact of MPTP by the administration of monoamine oxidase inhibitors and certain other drugs (D'Amato et al., 1987). Conceivably such drugs could retard the progression of Parkinson's disease in human patients.

Discovering a primate model of this disease has opened an exciting set of research opportunities that may yet remove the shroud of mystery that has always enveloped Parkinson's disease. Some researchers have speculated that Parkinson's disease in humans may arise from an unknown toxic exposure. In two cases involving laboratory workers, MPTP-induced disease has arisen from either inhalation or skin contact with MPTP. This suggests that a brief and almost trivial contact with MPTP may be sufficient to begin the disease. Some environmental toxins, such as certain herbicides, might provide exposure to MPP^+ (Snyder & D'Amato, 1986). At the very least, this drug model should illuminate aspects of the mechanism of cell death in Parkinson's patients. In addition, the MPTP model has already resulted in new suggestions for drug treatments that hold considerable promise for human sufferers.

symptoms permits an examiner to tell with considerable accuracy what part of the cerebellum is involved (Dichgans, 1984).

A relatively common lesion involving the cerebellum is a tumor that usually occurs in childhood. The tumor damages a part of the cerebellum with close connections to the vestibular system and therefore causes disturbances of balance. The patient walks ''like a drunken sailor'' and has difficulty even standing erect. Often the feet are placed widely apart in an attempt to maintain balance. The abnormalities usually involve the legs and trunk but not the arms. Normally the world seems to hold still as we walk or move our heads because movements of the eyes compensate for movements of the head. Some patients with lesions of the cerebellum, however, see the world around them move whenever they move their heads. If normal subjects are given prismatic lenses, they learn to compensate for the new relationship between movement of the eyes and perceived change of direction. Patients with lesions of the vestibular part of the cerebellum cannot do this, suggesting that this part of the cerebellum is important for such learning.

In some alcoholic patients there is degeneration of the cortex of the anterior lobe of the cerebellum. When it is damaged, abnormalities of gait and posture are often seen. The legs show ataxia (loss of coordination), but the arms do not. Loss of coordination and swaying indicate that the patient is not compensating normally for the usual deviations of position and posture. Several investigators have proposed that the cerebellum works like a comparator in a negative-feedback circuit, comparing ongoing movements with target levels and sending corrective instructions to overcome any departures from planned values. (Such a feedback system was diagramed in Figure 10-6.) The fact that the cerebellar cortex has motor and sensory maps of the body that are in register (that is, that are perfectly superimposed) may favor the comparison of ongoing acts with planned positions and rates of motion of parts of the body.

Some diseases of the cerebellum may cause difficulties in speaking; this is mainly a motor problem rather than a cognitive difficulty. Present evidence indicates that a posterior region just to the left of the midline is most often involved in cerebellar speech disorders, and other regions of the cerebellum may also be involved (Gilman, Bloedel, & Lechtenberg, 1981). Difficulties of motor coordination are common with damage to the lateral aspects of the cerebellum. One such problem is called decomposition of movement because gestures are broken up into individual segments instead of being executed smoothly. A patient who showed this problem after damage to his right cerebellar hemisphere described it this way: ''The movements of my left hand are done subconsciously, but I have to think out each movement of my right arm. I come to a dead stop in turning and have to think it out before I start again.'' Thus the cerebellum is not needed to initiate acts or to plan the sequence of movements but to facilitate activation and to ''package'' movements economically (Brooks, 1984).

New Developments in Treatment of Movement Disorders

From ancient times people have sought to replace parts of the body lost by accident or disease. Artificial limbs and artificial teeth are two familiar examples of what are called **prosthetic devices** or prostheses (from the Greek term for ''an addition''). With advances in knowledge of the mechanisms of movement and its neural controls, prosthetic devices are constantly being improved and are able to replace the missing member more completely than ever before. The use of the term *prosthesis* has been expanded to include an artificial addition that does not replace a part of the body but that aids functioning. An example is the electronic pacemaker, which ensures regularity of functioning of the heart when the heart's own electrical pacing has become irregular.

An Artificial Arm Controlled by Thought

Although artificial arms and hands have an ancient history, their usefulness was limited until recently. In some cases mechanical hands have had movable parts to which tendons of forearm muscles could be attached so that the amputee could have a certain amount of movement. Some people learn to grasp and manipulate to a certain extent with these devices, but prolonged training is required. More recently, improved artificial hands and arms have been devised that an amputee can use readily with very little training. The artificial arm seems to do whatever the user intends. Small motors are installed in the arm to power the movements; the operation of the motors is controlled by a minicomputer in the arm. The computer receives information about the activity of intact muscles in the person's shoulder, chest, and neck. Whenever a person moves an arm, simultaneously there are coordinated and compensatory contractions of muscles in the nearby parts of the body, and the pattern of these contractions varies according to the particular movement of the arm. The computer can thus tell what arm movement is intended by analyzing the pattern of activation in the associated parts of the body. The different motors in the artificial arm are then operated with more or less force, depending on the pattern of activation. Feedback occurs through the pull of the arm on the rest of the body.

Researchers are now attempting to provide more complete feedback of the movements and stresses within the artificial arm. To do this they are placing various detectors within the arm that produce stimulation in the form of touches or vibrations on adjacent patches of skin. This technique gives more adequate feedback, but the amputee has to learn how to interpret and use it.

Biofeedback and Movement Disorders

The acquisition of complex motor skills necessary for athletic feats or playing a musical instrument shows that learning can change brain control of movement. Learned control of movement initiation, organization, and termination is evident in many of the skills we acquire during our lives, as we saw earlier. Is it possible that we can, through training, reduce or eliminate abnormal movements? Many studies have now shown that operant conditioning techniques, developed in animal research, can be employed for therapeutic purposes in a range of movement disorders that arise from brain impairments. This therapeutic technique is also known as **biofeedback,** because the signals used for operant modification are derived from the actual movements of an individual. Let us consider the procedures used in these clinical studies.

All biofeedback procedures are similar even though the applications are diverse. Some movement or postural deviation or level of muscle tension is detected by a special recording device. In some cases these motor states are observed by electromyography, which can provide accurate information about the activity of very small motor units. Information about these motor events or states is conveyed to the patient in the form of light or sound displays. More specifically, the motor events detected by the recording device are made to control the turning on and off of light or sound. The patient is thus informed about the movement, posture, or tension of some body part by exteroceptive information in addition to the usual array of muscle and joint receptor information. The subjects are instructed to try to keep the signal off (or on) for as long a period as possible, using any means, including thought, imagery, or just plain relaxation.

Major successes in using this procedure in motor disorder treatment have been reported, especially in reducing muscle tension and the strength of abnormal movements. Reduction in tension headaches produced by excessive tension of forehead muscles can result when biofeedback signals from these muscles are provided to patients. A remarkably effective use of biofeedback has been described by Brudny (1976) in the treatment of torticollis, a neuromuscular disorder characterized by extreme contraction of neck muscles producing a deviation of the head. This reaction is frequently spasmodic, producing an intermittent, marked neck muscle contraction on one side. Brudny (1982) has shown that biofeedback techniques can be used to inhibit spastic activity of neck muscles and to increase the tension of neck muscles on the opposite side of the neck in order to oppose the force that produces neck deviation. The role of biofeedback in rehabilitation following cerebral trauma is seen in a case treated by Bernard Brucker (described by Miller, 1985). After being hit by an auto at the age of three, a boy was left with very rigid, spastic movements. He could not bend his right elbow or open his right hand. At the age of nine he received two weeks of biofeedback sessions, which emphasized the attainment of strength and coordination. The treatment enabled him to use his hand in many daily activities, such as dressing and eating. The relevant feedback signal was electromyographic information from involved muscles.

Development of Motor Functions

Understanding of motor functions is aided by seeing how they begin early in the life span, how they develop during childhood and maturity, and how they decline in the latter part of the life span.

Fetal Development and Activity

Developmental views of movements must start with the womb, since the life of the fetus is not passive and quiet. Indeed, some pregnant mothers have been almost thrown out of bed by a surprising and vigorous kick of a fetal child.

The development of human fetal movements is being studied by ultrasonic echograms (Birnholtz, 1981; Birnholtz & Farrell, 1984). This technique permits even small movements, such as isolated eye movements, to be seen in early fetal life. Localized reflexes begin to develop around 11–12 weeks after conception. These reflexes are selective motor changes that do not involve the entire body. Mouth opening and swallowing are evident at this stage. Tongue movements appear at 14 weeks.

The functional role of the vast range of fetal reflexes has been debated for many years. A thoughtful discussion by Hall and Oppenheim (1987) distinguishes among three different potential functional roles of fetal movements:

1. Early behavior may simply reflect the fact that a neural circuit is being formed that will be functionally significant at a later developmental stage.
2. Early fetal behavior is a necessary ingredient in the shaping of subsequent, more elaborate responses. For example, the ''spontaneous'' movements of a fetal human may be necessary for the subsequent orderly development of walking.
3. Fetal behavior may serve an immediate adaptive function.

As we noted earlier, decisive evidence is lacking for the influence of fetal rehearsal on later motor performance. Hall and Oppenheim (1987) cite several studies that show that the administration to amphibian embryos of drugs that block neural activity does not affect the later emerging swimming ability of a tadpole. However, they note several studies which show that fetal behavior responses are important adaptations to fetal development itself, especially musculoskeletal development. Skeletal muscles of fetal animals do not develop normally when fetal movements are impaired.

Child Motor Development

Motor abilities of human infants have been the focus of many studies in child psychology. A common way of describing the development of motor skills early in life is to specify the ages at which infants and children reach typical motor accomplishments, such as standing, running, and object handling. The lengthening of bones and the acquisition of muscle mass along with other biomechanical changes account for many early skills. For example, the neural program for walking is available at birth, as you can see by holding a newborn infant erect (supporting its weight) and bringing its feet in contact with a solid surface. Under this condition the infant will make stepping movements of the feet. However, walking does not appear until 12–18 months, because neither the skeletal system nor muscle organization are sufficiently developed until this time—human bones harden slowly.

The timetable for the emergence of various reflexes has been determined for several animals. Reflex development in the cat and the dog has been studied by Fox (1970), who examined these animals every day from birth to 2–4 months by observing a set of reflex behaviors. Responses he employed included reflex withdrawal from painful stimuli, usually elicited by pinching a toe pad; the righting reflex, a response elicited by placing an animal on its back, which is followed by the animal attempting to turn over and position itself on its feet; the forelimb-placing reflex, which consists of extension of the forelimb when contact is made with a hard surface like a tabletop; and the auditory startle reflex. The time of onset of adultlike reflex responses is typical for each species and is related to the sequence in which different behaviors are required by the species.

Motor Changes with Aging

As we get older, we grow weaker and slower. This common observation may dismay us, but it is amply supported by experimental observations. Debate occurs only about estimates of the magnitude of these changes. Although speed and strength decline, is it possible that there is a bonus of aging in accuracy of skilled motor performance?

Strength in humans reaches its peak in the age range 20–29 and shows accelerating decline for each subsequent decade. Changes in strength occur in virtually all motor outputs, and this decline seems to arise from changes in properties of muscles and joints. Human performance studies in work settings indicate that this decline is less evident in people who engage in strenuous work.

Speed clearly falls prey to the ravages of the years. Both simple and complex motor tasks take longer after the peak period of 20–29. Over the life span and across many tasks this decline is from 20% to 40%. It arises from changes both in the muscle system and in information-processing networks that command movements. Some relatively simple tasks seem to show major changes. Speed of writing decreases between the age groups 20–29 and 60–69. The slowdown in writing and many similar tasks that involve small muscle movements does not arise from muscular limitations but rather from changes in central processing involving decisions that provide movement guidance. This result is demonstrated in studies showing that effects of aging are reduced when special warning signals are given that prepare the subject for the intended movement. Some benefit from slowing is evident in the form of increased accuracy of movement, provided tasks do not involve complex perceptual information.

The physiological substrates of these motor declines are evident at many levels of the neuromotor system. In the brain both neurochemical and neuroanatomical changes have been shown. For example, in normal adults the levels of enzymes that synthesize dopamine decline with age, and the amount of dopamine in the basal ganglia decreases by about 13% per decade of life (Stahl et al., 1986).

In Chapter 4 we explored some of the neuroanatomical changes that occur with aging. Scheibel et al. (1977) have drawn particular attention to the loss of Betz cells, a class of large nerve cells in the human motor cortex. Progressive loss in this cell population, Scheibel believes, reduces the number of fibers in a fast-conducting pathway from the brain to motoneurons in the spinal cord involved in locomotion.

Aged rats show movement disorders that are particularly evident during swimming. A similar impairment can be seen in young rats after injury to dopamine cells. Movement disorders of aged rats can be markedly reduced by administration of L-dopa, a precursor of dopamine, and apomorphine, a drug that stimulates dopamine receptors (Marshall & Berrios, 1979). These findings are consistent with findings in postmortem studies of human brains. Thus it appears that declining activities of dopamine-containing cells and their postsynaptic receptors participate importantly in movement impairments of the aged.

Comparative Views of Movements and Acts

Comparisons of the similarities and differences in various animals in the accomplishment of particular acts can provide a useful perspective for understanding the anatomy and physiology of movement. Some differences depend on anatomical specializations in bones, like long hind-limb bones that aid in jumping. Other differences emphasize neural specializations like the fineness of forelimb innervation, which allows the dexterous use of forelimbs in primates. In this section we will consider comparative perspectives on locomotion, escape behavior, and vocalization.

Locomotion   In the animal world the task of moving about is fulfilled in many different ways. For some animals locomotion is accomplished by changes in body shape. Picture the sweeping curves of the body of a snake moving through the grass or the oscillations of the tail of a fish in water. More dramatic examples of changes in body shape as the basis for locomotion are the sudden jet propulsion of squid and the backward, darting escape movement of crayfish produced by sudden tail flexion. Locomotion in many other animals, like humans, is accomplished by specialized limb structures that provide the force for movements. A cross-species comparison of maximal speed of locomotion is provided in Figure 10-22. Some animals, like the cheetah, maintain their maximum speeds for only very short distances.

However locomotion is accomplished, there is a common basic characteristic—rhythm. For all animals, moving about consists of repetitive cycles of the same act, be it the endless beating of wings or the repetition of particular sequences of leg movements. In contemporary research in the neurosciences, considerable attention has been given to the possible neural basis of the repetitive cycles of locomotion. Do these repetitive cycles develop from the sensory impact of movement itself, or do they reflect endogenous oscillators that provide the basic locomotor programs that motoneurons obligingly obey? In addition to the repetitive, cyclical character of locomotion, there are other features that demand a neural understanding. For example, any single cycle of a locomotor act involves the coordinative sequential activation of many muscles whose excitation is carefully graded. Comparisons in many animals, from insects to humans, indicate that the repetitive cycles of locomotor acts are generated by intrinsic oscillators.

Rhythmic movements appear to be generated by mechanisms within the spinal cord. These rhythms can be independent of brain influences and afferent inflow. Such central generation of locomotor rhythms has recently been shown by Grillner and his associates (Grillner, 1985; Grillner & Zangger, 1979). In their study electromyographic records of hind-limb muscles of cats with spinal cord section and dorsal root cuts reveal a ''walking'' pattern that lasts for seconds when a single dorsal root is briefly stimulated with electrical pulses (Figure 10-23, page 392). Outputs from spinal motoneurons or muscles also show different types of coordination that are variants of typical locomotor patterns, like galloping. The activity of the relevant muscles shows phase relations quite similar to characteristic muscle time differences found in the observation of actual movements in intact animals. Three intact adjacent spinal segments provide the minimal amount of spinal processing necessary for generation of part of the locomotor rhythm. Spinal pattern generators investigated in this and other studies provide the neural patterns necessary for various locomotor acts. Thus pathways to the spinal cord from the brain do not generate the essential rhythm but may control onset and provide corrections arising from other influences registered by the brain. Generation of locomotor rhythms has been demonstrated especially clearly in invertebrate preparations (Selverston, 1985).

Escape and Avoidance   The array of responses that provide animals with defense against predation includes
Behavior   escape and avoidance responses. These acts appropriately involve great speed and agility. The rapid darting backward of crayfish, the scurrying away of cockroaches,

| mph | 0 | 10 | 20 | 30 | 40 | 5(|
| kph | 0 | 16 | 32 | 48 | 64 | 8(|

Figure 10-22 Comparisons of maximal speed of locomotion of several common vertebrate species. The fastest flier shows about twice the speed of the most rapid runner, which is twice as fast as the fastest swimmer.

and the elegant evasive behavior of the moth pursued by a bat are all examples of successful escape responses. These behaviors in simpler invertebrates have been studied in depth at both behavioral and neural circuit levels because they have a highly stereotyped character. The escape system of cockroaches provides an interesting example of this type of investigation. Camhi (1983) has described the characteristics of the eliciting stimuli and the mediating neural circuits. As a predator approaches, a cockroach turns away and rapidly runs. Cockroaches detect potential predators with very sensitive wind detectors found on antennalike appendages called cerci on the rear end of the body. Each cercus holds about 200 hairs. After

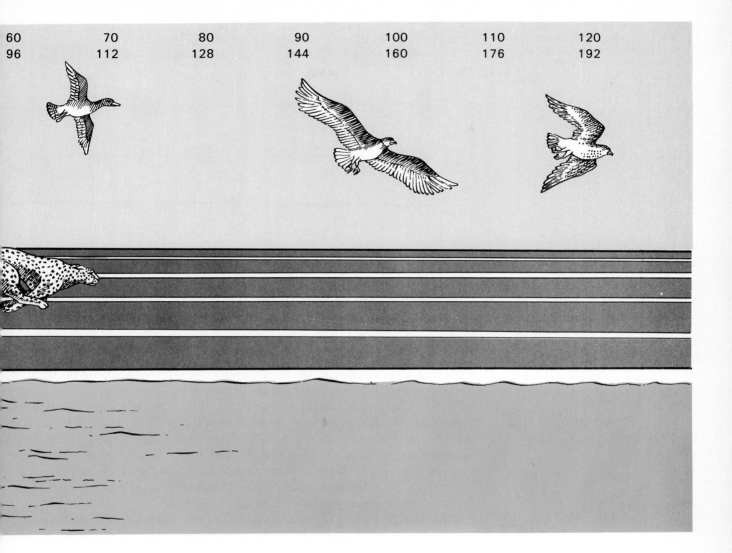

removal of the hairs on the cerci, cockroaches are unable to escape from potential predators. These receptors are quite sensitive and seem to be the only cues for escape behavior. In addition, they do not respond to wind acceleration produced by movements of the animal itself. The acceleration of self-produced movements is much lower than that produced by an approaching predator.

The neural network that leads to the activation of evasive movements in the cockroach includes two giant neurons, one on each side of the body, that connect to the hair cells. These giant neurons ascend through the body of the animal and connect to neurons controlling leg muscles. Persistence of neural activity seems to

Figure 10-23 Pattern of walking shown in electromyograms of hind-limb muscles in an acute spinal and deafferented cat. (Grillner and Zangger, 1979)

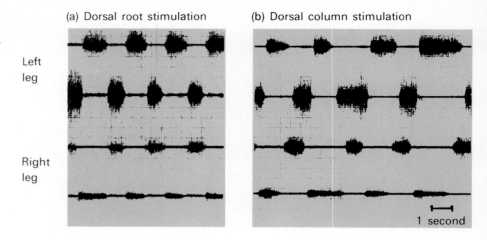

(a) Dorsal root stimulation

(b) Dorsal column stimulation

Left leg

Right leg

1 second

be a feature of this circuit since the cockroach normally runs a considerable distance following a single puff of air. Other motor neurons that mediate escape reactions are the giant neurons of the squid, mentioned in Chapter 5.

Speech, Vocalization, and Crying

Human speech involves the delicate coordination of many muscles, including those of the respiratory mechanism, the vocal folds (or cords) of the throat, and the vocal cavity extending from the throat through the mouth.

Muscles involved in expiration of air include those of the diaphragm and chest. These control both absolute levels of air pressure and the changes of air pressure that mark the pauses of speech. Some of the fibers of the human pyramidal tract end in the thoracic region of the spinal cord. We have noted that this tract is especially involved in control of skilled movements such as those of the fingers. In this case the thoracic connections are probably not for the control of respiration but rather for the complex use of the respiratory muscles in speech.

The detailed shaping of sounds involves muscles controlling the vocal folds (vocal cords) and the shape of the vocal cavities in the mouth and throat. Many of the relevant muscles like those of the lips involve a low innervation ratio, since delicate control is a major requirement for sounds to become intelligible signals. For example, note the very small differences in tongue position in the production of the consonants "d" and "t" or effects of equally subtle lip and tongue positions in production of "b" and "p."

Feedback control in speech is particularly interesting because it is multimodal—that is, it involves muscle receptors, tactile receptors, and sounds. The neural organization of speech—the representation in the brain of programs of movements—is presented in Chapter 18.

In many animals, including humans, structures used for breathing are also used to produce species-typical sounds. In most cases these sounds are produced by forcing air out of either lungs or a pouch so that it flows across a structure that can vibrate when stretched in particular ways. Coordination of muscle activity is essential at several steps. Human speech production has already been discussed. In other mammals, too, these steps include control of expiration from the lung, which determines airflow across the vocal folds, pressure on the vocal folds, and changes in the shape of the vocal cavities, such as the throat and mouth. Many of the vocalizations of animals are quite complicated and demand highly precise movement control lest they become acoustic gibberish.

Vocal behavior in nonhuman primates involves some startling and elaborate facial movements. Many investigators have recorded the sound repertoire of primates, and some have mapped the locus of brain regions involved in sound production. For instance, Detlev Ploog (1981) has examined the vocal behavior of the squirrel monkey, a small South American primate that lives in a dense jungle habitat. Auditory signals are particularly valuable for communication in this environment. Types of vocalizations and the social value or setting of these sounds were charted, and studies were then performed to see whether characteristic vocalizations could be elicited by localized brain stimulation. Maps of the distribution of brain sites that yield vocal responses that mimic naturally produced sounds show a concentration of subcortical regions especially dense in areas that relate to control of emotional responses. Stimulation of motor pathways did not produce a characteristic sound, thus suggesting that the program for vocal behavior is not directly accessible in the motor system itself. In this case it seems to be organized in other subcortical areas. Lesions of a restricted brain stem region cause loss of vocal behavior in the monkey. (In contrast to the emphasis on subcortical control of vocalization in nonhuman primates, human speech is largely organized at the cerebral cortex.)

The vocal repertoire of many young animals includes the sounds of crying. As a motor activity, crying is a complex sequence of acts that are relatively stereotyped (Newman, 1985). In human infants each "unit" of crying ranges from 1/2 to 1 second repeated 50–70 times per minute. This basic oscillatory pattern is evident at birth and remains the same until later infancy when there is greater interindividual variability. The sound pattern of human crying at birth provides an indication of the developmental integrity of the central nervous system (Lester, 1985). For example, infants who have experienced various types of birth trauma have cries that include an increase in the basic sound frequency and variability in this fundamental frequency. Pitch that varies widely may signal that brain activity is disordered in character, perhaps lacking fine inhibitory controls. Sound spectrographic analysis of infant cries is opening the door to a new approach to diagnostic assessment of human infants.

Summary · Main Points

1. All behavior that we see consists of either the secretion of glands or muscle contractions. Muscle contractions are regulated by neural impulses that arrive at the muscles over motor nerve fibers.

2. Reflexes are patterns of relatively simple and stereotyped movements that are elicited by stimulation of sensory receptors; their amplitude is proportional to the intensity of the stimulation.

3. The control of many reflexes occurs through closed-loop, negative-feedback circuits. Some behaviors are so rapid, however, that they are open-loop; that is, the pattern is preset and determined intrinsically without feedback control.

4. Many learned, skilled acts also have open-loop control and are not influenced by stimulus intensity, so long as the intensity exceeds the threshold.

5. When a muscle is stretched, a reflex circuit causes contraction, which works to restore the muscle to its original length; this response is the stretch reflex. The stretch of the muscle is detected by special receptors, called muscle spindles, that are built into the muscle.

6. The sensitivity of the muscle spindle can be adjusted by efferent impulses that call for different degrees of contraction of the muscle. This adjustment allows flexible control of posture and movement.

7. The final common pathway for impulses to skeletal muscles consists of motoneurons, whose cell bodies in vertebrates are located in the ventral horn of the spinal cord and within the brain stem. The motoneurons receive impulses from a variety of sources, including sensory input from the dorsal spinal roots, other spinal cord neurons, and descending fibers from the brain.

8. Circuits within the spinal cord underlie the spinal reflexes, which can occur even when the cord is transected, severing connections to the brain.

9. The corticospinal tract is especially well developed in primates and is mainly involved in controlling fine movements of the extremities. Its fibers originate mainly in the primary motor cortex, and they run directly to spinal motoneurons or to internuncial cells in the spinal cord.

10. Brain regions that modulate movement include the basal ganglia (caudate, putamen, globus pallidus), some major brain stem nuclei (substantia nigra and red nucleus), and the cerebellum.

11. Movement disorders can arise because of impairment at any of several levels of the motor system: the muscles, the motor neurons and neuromuscular junctions, the spinal cord, brain stem, cerebral cortex, basal ganglia, and cerebellum. The characteristics of the movement disorders depend upon and permit diagnosis of the locus of the impairment.

12. Some movement disorders can be alleviated by the use of prosthetic devices; others can be alleviated by directly stimulating a particular region of the brain. Biofeedback has proved effective in overcoming several kinds of movement disorders.

13. Many locomotor acts depend on oscillatory pattern generators in the nervous system.

14. Some acts like speech involve very delicate coordination of many muscles.

Recommended Reading

Brooks, V. B. (1986). *The neural basis of motor control*. New York: Oxford University Press.

Smyth, M. M., & Wing, A. M. (Eds.). (1984). *The psychology of human movement*. New York: Academic Press.

Talbot, R. E., & Humphrey, D. R. (Eds.). (1979). *Posture and locomotion*. New York: Raven.

Towe, A., & Luschei, E. (Eds.). (1981). *Handbook of behavioral neurobiology: Vol. 5. Motor coordination*. New York: Plenum.

PART FOUR

Control of Behavioral States: Motivation

So far we have considered the basic equipment and capacities of an organism: the integrative functions of the nervous and endocrine systems, the capabilities of sensory and perceptual systems, and the ways in which motor responses are formed and coordinated. But we have not yet paid much attention to how the organism selects among the many options that these systems provide. The behavioral repertoire of most mammals includes obtaining food and eating, finding water and drinking, experiencing vivid dreams, grooming, engaging in sexual behavior, communicating with others, shifting position to a somewhat warmer or cooler spot, withdrawing from painful or threatening situations, and experiencing more and less pleasant feelings. Most of these behaviors are clearly necessary to maintain the health of the individual or to perpetuate the species. But these different kinds of activities cannot all be accomplished at the same time. Some require motor acts that are incompatible with others—an animal can't flee danger and feed at the same time. Some require different times of day or places—a time and a place suitable for sleeping aren't likely to afford water to drink. So responding to one motive often precludes satisfying another at the same time, and different motives may have to be satisfied in succession. How bodily systems function so that all the basic needs are satisfied is the overall question of motivation that we will take up in Part Four.

11 Sex

ORIENTATION

A tourist at a restaurant in France noticed a fly in his soup. Calling over the waiter, the tourist summoned up his best French and said, "Garçon, observez le mouche dans ma soupe." The waiter corrected, "LA mouche." To which the tourist replied, "What sharp eyes you have!"

In some species males and females do look a great deal alike. Species differ greatly, however, in how similar or different the two sexes appear to be. Those in which the two sexes are clearly different are said to be "sexually dimorphic" (dimorphic means different in form); see Figure 11-1. In some familiar dimorphic species, the adult male is usually larger than the female (for example, humans, dogs, or turkeys), and in some the male is more highly visible either because of coloration (for example, red-winged blackbird or mandrill baboon) or because of some appendage (for example, antlers of a male moose or the mane of a male lion). But in other species the female is larger (for example, hyena, hamster, or marsh hawk) or more brightly colored (for example, kingfisher or phalarope).

Sex brings variety to life—in more ways than are usually realized. There are, of course, the differences in appearance and behavior between women and men and the specific behaviors involved in mating, childbirth, and parental care. There are also the marked differences that occur during development and that are related to changes in reproductive status and assumption of gender identity. The great variety among people—the differences even within a family—also is due to sexual reproduction. Sexual reproduction provides genetic permutations that are not available in nonsexual reproduction, such as occurs in many plants and some animals. In sexual reproduction each parent provides half the genetic heritage of the new individual; the precise contribution of the parent to a particular new individual is a random assortment of alternative genes. There are so many possibilities that—except for identical twins—no two human beings have exactly the same heredity.

The genetic variability due to sexual reproduction has resulted in a relatively rapid evolution. With many varied individuals alive at a given time, those better suited to current environmental challenges have a reproductive advantage. Thus life has penetrated new ecological niches, and new species have evolved.

Which is the female in each pair?

(a) Mandrill baboons

(b) Peacock and peahen

(c) Ring doves

(d) Praying mantises

(e) Jacanas

Figure 11-1 Which is the female in each pair? In mandrill baboons (a), the male is larger and has bright blue areas on the face. In peafowl (b), the cock is larger and more brightly colored than the hen. In ring doves (c), the external appearance of the two sexes is identical, but they behave differently during courtship. Among praying mantises (d) and jacanas (e), the female is larger than the male.

Sexual reproduction requires a division of labor, but this can be accomplished in rather different ways, as some examples will illustrate. In many species members of the two sexes live apart for much of their lives. Reproduction requires that this separation be overcome sufficiently to permit egg and sperm to unite. When and how the two sexes unite vary enormously among species. In some species of mammals, for example, a female copulates only one day each year; in others the female copulates during a mating season that lasts a few months; and in still others the female can mate all during the year. In some species of animals, courtship is initiated by the female, in some by the male, and in some species both sexes engage in reciprocal activity from the start. Further differences are seen in care of the young. The young of some species are on their own from the moment of birth or hatching, while the young of other species need parental care for days, months, or even years. The female parent is the main care giver in most species, the male in others, and in some species both share parental responsibilities.

In the face of all the variety of sexual behavior and anatomy, are there some general conclusions that we can draw about reproductive and parental behaviors and their bodily mechanisms? Can we understand the diversity of behavior and appearance in terms of some general principles? The wide scope and extensive volume of research on sexual behavior help us to consider this topic from the four main viewpoints described in Chapter 1. We will start our investigation by describing some main aspects of reproductive and other sex-linked behaviors. We will then take up the evolution of these behaviors and their development during the lifetime of the individual. Finally, we will survey what is known and what is hypothesized about the neural and hormonal mechanisms that mediate sex behaviors.

Descriptive Studies of Reproductive Behavior

We will start our examination by noting the successive stages of reproductive behavior and the types of interactions that occur between the partners. Then we will see what descriptive studies have shown about the reproductive behavior of three kinds of animals that are used for many experiments in this field—the ring dove, the rat and other rodents, and the fruit fly. Descriptive studies of human sex behavior will also be mentioned. In later sections we will relate many aspects of these behaviors to hormonal and neural processes and events.

Phases and Reciprocal Relations in Mating

The mating behavior of many animals shows four successive stages (Figure 11-2), and each stage demands interaction between two individuals. Successful completion of the pattern requires exchange of stimulation between the partners. Many descriptions of mating behavior have focused on the male as initiating and showing greater variety in copulatory behavior; the female's contribution has often been described

Figure 11-2 Stages in reproductive behavior, showing interaction between male and female partners. The postcopulatory phase includes a temporary decrease in the sexual attractiveness of the partner and inhibition of appetitive (proceptive) behavior. Inhibition is represented by arrows with black arrowheads. (Adapted from Beach, 1977)

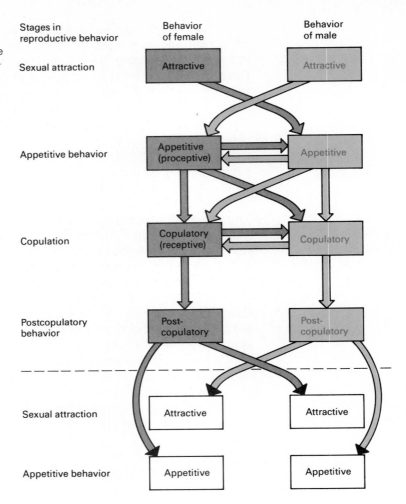

chiefly in terms of her receptivity and cooperation. But some recent treatments have emphasized a more balanced approach (Beach, 1976, p. 105):

> At each stage both sexes are equally involved; which is to say that sexual attraction is mutual, sexual initiative is assumed and appetitive behavior is engaged in by both sexes, and mating involves consummatory and postconsummatory phases in females as well as males.

The first stage, **sexual attraction,** is needed to bring the male and female together, and in many species this meeting occurs only when both are in a reproductive state. Attractiveness of female animals can be scored by measuring the males' responses to them under standardized conditions; typical measures include strength or rapidity of approach and occurrence of seminal ejaculation during mating. For example, in some species of monkeys and apes the males respond to the sight of the "sex skin" of the female when this swells under the influence of estrogen. But attraction is not a one-way process in which females attract males. When female monkeys are in **estrus** (the state of female sexual receptivity), they are likely to approach males; and they prefer to approach normal males rather than castrated ones. In the case of dogs, males are strongly attracted to the odor of vaginal secretions of a bitch in heat (estrus). The attractiveness can be reduced either by bringing the female out of heat or by castrating the male. Female dogs in heat prefer the odor of normal male dogs to castrates, but when the female goes out of heat this preference disappears.

Attractiveness of females has been found to be related to the level of estrogen; this result has been found in several species—rat, dog, monkey, baboon, and chimpanzee. Females of these species have regular cycles in which high concentrations of estrogen occur around the time of ovulation. Thus attractivity maximizes the probability of copulation when the female is fertile and susceptible to impregnation. But levels of estrogen are not the only determinants of attractivity, as has been shown in two ways:

1. In some experiments the ovaries were removed from female dogs and later they were administered equal amounts of estrogen. In spite of their having the same level of hormone, some females evoked more responses from males than did others.
2. Among dogs and monkeys, not all males prefer the same females; thus attractivity resides in part in the eye (or the nose) of the beholder.

Animals do not just emit stimuli that attract members of the opposite sex. They often engage in a second stage, **appetitive behavior;** with regard to mating, this is defined as behavior that helps to establish, maintain, or promote sexual interaction. For example, the male may pursue the female and attempt to copulate. The female may approach the male and adopt the copulatory posture. Beach (1977) has proposed the term **proceptive behavior** for female appetitive sexual behavior. The term *proceptive* means actively seeking and promoting mating behavior. Types of proceptive behavior include approaching males and remaining close to them, making specific responses that invite or solicit copulation, and showing alternating approach and retreat behavior. Moving away appears to orient the male to the mounting posture necessary for copulation of quadrupeds. Female rats usually run away from the male with a special kind of hopping and darting movement that excites the male and increases the probability of copulation. Proceptivity, like attractivity, is greatest during that part of the estrous cycle when the concentration of estrogen is highest. If the ovaries are removed, eliminating the main source of estrogen, proceptivity wanes, but it can be restored by administering estrogens. Administration of androgens has also been reported to increase proceptivity of both monkeys and rats.

The third stage, **copulatory behavior,** comprises a species-specific pattern that is highly stereotyped in most species. The principal acts of the male mammal are mounting the female, thrusting with the hindquarters, inserting the erect penis **(intromission),** and expelling semen forcefully **(ejaculation).** The essential female acts are assuming the posture that facilitates intromission and maintaining it until ejaculation within the vagina has occurred. Readiness to show these female responses that are necessary and sufficient for the male to achieve intravaginal ejaculation is often referred to as **receptivity,** or receptive behavior. In some species (for example, the cat), estrogen is the only hormone necessary for receptivity, whereas in others (for example, the dog) receptivity occurs when estrogen is high and progesterone is beginning to rise. In the latter case, progesterone acts synergistically with estrogen. The neural mechanisms appear to be simpler for receptivity than for proceptivity, and receptivity shows fewer individual differences than does proceptivity. For instance, removing the cerebral cortex of a female rat does not impair receptivity, but it disorganizes proceptive responses. In a female rat whose cerebral cortex has been removed, her hopping, darting, and crouching responses are not oriented toward the male or synchronized with his responses. Consequently the attractivity of such females is reduced; males consistently choose to mate with intact females even though decorticated females are equally receptive.

Some species show a fourth stage, specific **postcopulatory behavior.** This behavior may involve responses such as the after-reaction of rolling (in the cat) and grooming (in the rat). There are also changes in willingness to engage in further

Figure 11-3 Reproductive behavior of ring doves. The cycle begins soon after a male and female are placed in a cage containing nesting material and an empty glass bowl (1). Courtship activity is characterized initially by the "bowing coo" of the male (2). The male and then the female utter a distinctive "nest call" to indicate their selection of a nesting site (3). There follows a week or more of cooperative nest building (4), culminating in the laying of two eggs (5). The adults take turns incubating the eggs (6), which hatch after about 14 days (7). The squabs are fed "crop milk" (8). As the young birds learn to peck grain, the parents continue to feed them, but with increasing reluctance (9). When the squabs are between 2 and 3 weeks old, the adults ignore them and may start a new cycle of reproductive behavior (10). (From D. S. Lehrman, "The reproductive behavior of ring doves." Copyright © 1964 by Scientific American, Inc. All rights reserved.)

mating. After completion of a copulatory sequence, many animals do not mate again for a period of time, even if a receptive partner is available. This refractory period may last for minutes, hours, or days, depending on the species and the circumstances. In many species an animal will show a shorter refractory period to mate with a new partner than with the partner with which it has mated most recently.

Reproductive Behavior of the Ring Dove

The ring dove is a small relative of the domestic pigeon; it is named for the black semicircle around the back of its neck (see Figure 11-3). The male and female are identical in appearance and can be distinguished only by examining the internal reproductive organs through a surgical procedure. In the laboratory the ring dove breeds for most of the year if the length of day and the temperature are suitable. The birds mature sexually at about five months of age. When a female and a male ring dove with previous breeding experience are placed in a cage containing an empty glass bowl and a supply of nesting material, the birds enter their normal behavioral cycle, which psychologists have described in detail (Cheng, 1979; Lehrman, 1965).

The male is the first to show sexual attraction; he promptly begins courtship: strutting around, bowing and cooing at the female, and chasing her. Only the male exhibits the bow-coo behavior. A day or two after the male begins to court the female, she may start to show characteristic responses, flipping her wings in a special way and approaching the male. The sight of the male's courtship behavior and the sound of his cooing are clearly attractive to the female. Even if the birds are separated by a glass partition, these stimuli evoke clear neuroendocrine responses

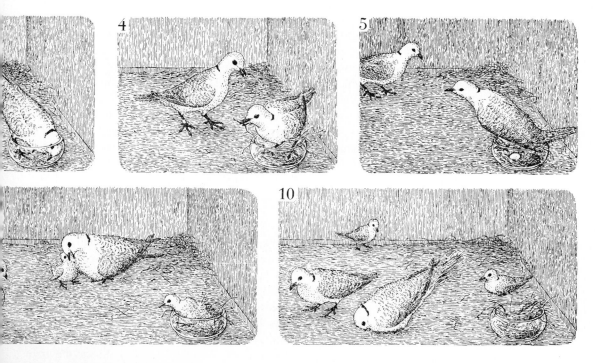

(Friedman, 1977). After a few days together, the birds usually show that they have selected a nest site by crouching on it and uttering a distinctive nest-coo. In the laboratory cage the nest site is the glass bowl; in nature it would be a concave place on the ground. If the male is paired with a female that is not easily aroused, he will continue to bow-coo and nest-coo at an undiminished frequency for weeks if the female fails to nest-coo. As soon as the female begins to nest-coo, the male's nest-coo behavior tapers off. Her behavior signals when the male should stop cooing and move on to the next behavior in the sequence, nest building. The two sexes show different and complementary activities in this phase, with the male gathering and carrying nest material to the female, who does most of the nest construction. Nest building normally occupies a week or more. Having a complete nest is an essential signal that ends nest-building activities.

When the nest is finished, or nearly complete, the birds begin the stage of copulation. For copulation the female squats low; the male mounts on her back, flapping his wings to keep his balance, and his **cloaca** contacts that of the female. (Doves, like many birds, do not have a penis or a vagina. Sperm are discharged and eggs are laid through the cloaca, the same passage through which the bird eliminates wastes.)

Once the female becomes noticeably more attached to the nest, indicating that she is about to lay her eggs, copulation ceases. About a week after the beginning of nest building, she produces the first egg; the second egg appears two days later. Thereafter the male and female birds alternate in sitting on the eggs, the male for about six hours in the middle of each day and the female for the rest of the time.

The eggs hatch after about 14 days, and the parents feed the young ''crop-milk,'' a thick liquid secreted at this stage of the cycle from the adult's crop (a pouch in its gullet). The squabs (young doves) leave the nest when they are about 10–12 days old, but they continue to beg for food and to receive it from their parents. Over the next few days, the parents feed the young birds less and less, and the squabs develop the ability to peck for grain on the floor of the cage. The male parent often continues supplying crop-milk to the young for several days after the female has stopped. When the young are about 15–25 days old, the adult male may start courtship again. The entire cycle lasts about six or seven weeks. In nature only a single cycle usually occurs each year, unless the first eggs were infertile; in that case the birds may go through the reproductive cycle again (Cheng, 1977).

Each phase of the reproductive cycle is influenced by particular hormonal states, as we will see later. The level(s) of one or more hormones affects the behavior, and in turn the behavior stimulates neuroendocrine links that alter the secretion of hormones.

Reproductive Behavior of Rodents

Rodents are diverse and notoriously successful at reproduction—virtually regardless of habitat. Unlike birds, rodents do not engage in lengthy courtship, nor do the partners tend to remain together for prolonged periods. Attraction occurs largely through odor. Species of rodents differ a great deal in some aspects of their reproductive behavior, and a few examples of this diversity will be mentioned in the course of this description. Appetitive behavior of the female rat was already described—darting, hopping, and withdrawing. Females of some other rodent species show similar behavior, while those of other species do not. In copulation the male

Figure 11-4 Copulation of rats. The raised rump of the female (the lordosis posture) and her deflected tail make intromission possible. (From Barnett, 1975)

mounts the female from the rear and grasps her flanks with his forelegs. If the female is receptive, she stands still and assumes a posture that aids intromission; in this female posture (called **lordosis**), the hindquarters are raised and the tail is turned to one side (Figure 11-4). When the penis has been inserted into the vagina, some species, such as the house mouse, show repetitive intravaginal thrusts, whereas other species, such as the Norway rat, have but a single pelvic thrust per intromission.

Some species can ejaculate the first time the penis is inserted into the vagina. In other species the male dismounts and then mounts again, requiring several intromissions before ejaculation. Most rodents ejaculate more than once during a single episode of mating; the Northern pygmy mouse is an exception. After ejaculation the male in most rodent species withdraws the penis and dismounts, but in some species the penis remains swollen in the vagina for many minutes, a response called a ''lock.'' Locking was thought to be characteristic of carnivores, but it has also been found in several species of rodent.

The conclusion of a sequence is demonstrated when the animal does not engage in further copulatory behavior even if a receptive partner is available. The duration of the postejaculatory refractory period may last from a few minutes to 24 hours or more, depending on the species.

In the rat only the mother cares for the young. Toward the end of the 21-day period of pregnancy, the female builds a nest. Rats are born in a rather undeveloped state (and are therefore said to be **altricial**)—they have no hair and cannot regulate their body temperature, and their eyes and ears do not open until about 13 days after birth. The mother keeps the rat pups warm, nurses them, and retrieves them if they wiggle out of the nest. Some other rodents, such as the guinea pig, are born in a much more fully developed state (they are **precocial**). Precocial young do not stay long with their mother, and if necessary they can get along without maternal care soon after birth.

Reproductive Behavior of the Fruit Fly

Study of the fruit fly, genus *Drosophila*, has been extremely important to the advancement of genetics; the inheritance of both anatomical features and behavioral characteristics has been studied extensively, and we know a great deal about the

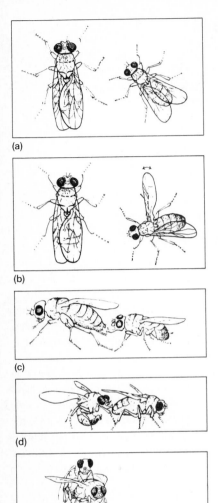

Figure 11-5 Reproductive behavior of *Drosophila*. The male (a) orients to the female, (b) vibrates the near wing and lowers the other wing, (c) licks the genital region of the female, and (d) assumes the copulation posture. If the female is receptive, the pair then copulates (e). (From Manning, 1965)

courtship and copulatory behavior of several subgenera and species of *Drosophila*. Besides providing us with genetic information about mating patterns, descriptions of this behavior in *Drosophila* provide us with an example of complex, relatively stereotyped behavior in a "simple" animal and show mating behavior mediated in part by chemoreceptors.

In brief, here are the main steps: The male taps the female with a foreleg. Receptors on the foreleg pick up chemical and tactile information necessary to species identification. If the female is of his species, the male then stands close to her side and follows her if she moves (See Figure 11-5a). He extends the wing closest to her head and vibrates it. This response may aid stimulation of chemical receptors on her antennae by emphasizing his odor, but it is also an auditory stimulus; different species vibrate their wings at different rates, and this action provides a distinctive "courtship song." The duration of the wing-vibrating phase differs among species. Although *Drosophila* can mate successfully in the dark, vision aids the male to orient to the female, and the sight of her movement stimulates his courtship (Tompkins et al., 1982). If the male is successful, the female does not attempt to move away and shows receptivity. The male circles behind the female, extends his proboscis, and licks her genital region. The male then attempts to copulate, and the cooperating female spreads her wings and opens her genital plates to permit intromission.

Although this pattern shows an invarient sequence of behaviors, recent evidence demonstrates that it is not a **fixed-action pattern,** that is, a behavior that, once started, necessarily continues through the full cycle. For one thing the progression from one stage to the next depends upon a continuous exchange of cues between the male and the female. The female may break off the pattern at the early stage. Also, the effect of the male's courtship song lasts for several minutes in the female, and this change in responsiveness is controlled by genes that are involved in learning and memory (Quinn & Greenspan, 1984).

The elaborate courtship behavior of *Drosophila* probably serves more than one function. For one thing it probably helps to keep different species of *Drosophila* reproductively separate. Different species show characteristic differences in frequency of wing beat in courtship, and a female responds only to the frequency of her own species. The courtship behavior may also play a part in sexual selection. The female is unreceptive at first and responds to a male that courts vigorously and that is more likely to be more fertile than a less active suitor.

Various kinds of mutant *Drosophila* are unable to perform one or another part of the mating sequence. Such mutants would be unable to reproduce in nature, but they can be studied in the laboratory. By use of genetic techniques, investigators have been able to learn about some of the neural controls of mating in *Drosophila*, as we will see later.

Neither *Drosophila* parent cares for the young, and this is true of most insects and even of many species of vertebrates. The female *Drosophila* does, however, tend to lay her eggs where they are likely to survive and where the young are likely to find food when they hatch.

Human Reproductive Behavior

There was little objective information about human sexual behavior in the 1940s, as biology professor Alfred Kinsey found when he started to look into the subject. To fill the gap, Kinsey began to ask friends and colleagues for detailed information about their sexual histories. Kinsey then constructed a standardized set of questions and procedures. He attempted to obtain information for representative samples of the U.S. population categorized by sex, age, religion, and education. Eventually he and collaborators obtained detailed information from tens of thousands of men, and they published an extensive survey of sexual behavior of the American male (1948). An equally detailed survey of the sexual behavior of the American female followed a few years later (1953).

A further step was to make behavioral and physiological observations of people while they engaged in sexual intercourse or masturbation. Perhaps the first person to undertake such studies was John B. Watson, the founder of behaviorism. But his research on intercourse in the early 1920s led to a scandal and the loss of his professorship. The largest and best-known project of this kind began in the middle 1950s and is headed by physician William Masters and psychologist Virginia Johnson (1965, 1966, 1970). These studies have provided greatly increased knowledge about the physiological responses that occur in various parts of the body during intercourse, their time courses, and their relations to what is experienced.

Among most species of mammals, including nonhuman primates, the male mounts the female from the rear, but among humans face-to-face postures are most common. A great variety of coital postures has been described, particularly from the Orient. Many couples vary their postures from session to session or even within a session. The variety of reproductive behavior, both within and among individuals, is a characteristic that differentiates humans from other species.

Typical response patterns of men and women have been summarized by Masters and Johnson (1965); see Figures 11-6a and b. Both sexes show four phases: increasing excitement, plateau, **orgasm** (the climax of sexual experience marked by extremely pleasurable sensations), and resolution. In spite of this basic similarity of male and female responses, there are also some typical differences. One important difference is the greater variety of commonly observed sequences in women. Whereas men have only one basic male pattern, women have three typical patterns, as shown in Figure 11-6b. The second main difference between the sexes is that most men, but not women, have an absolute refractory phase following an orgasm. Most men cannot achieve full erection and another orgasm until some time has elapsed; the length of time may vary from minutes to hours, depending on individual differences and on other factors. Many women can have multiple orgasms in rapid succession.

In the male pattern, excitement mounts in response to stimulation, which may be mental or physical or both. The rate of rise of excitement varies with many factors. If stimulation continues, the level of excitement reaches a high plateau. At some point during this stage, the reflexive orgasmic responses are triggered. Then there is a gradual dissipation of excitement during the resolution phase. Usually the rising phase and the resolution phase are the longest parts of the cycle. The plateau phase typically lasts only a few minutes, and orgasm usually lasts a minute or less.

The most common pattern in women (A in Figure 11-6b) is similar in form to the male pattern. The first two phases in both sexes are marked by congestion of the blood vessels of the genitalia. This response produces penile erection in the man and vaginal lubrication and swelling in the woman. Orgasm is marked by rhythmic muscular contractions in both sexes; in the woman these occur in the muscles around the vagina. There are also typical sex differences in the temporal patterns of

Figure 11-6 Sexual response cycles of (a) men and (b) women. These are schematic diagrams and do not represent any particular physiological measure, although heart rate varies in this manner. (a) A typical male pattern with an absolute refractory phase after orgasm. (b) Three patterns often observed in women. There is much individual variation around both the male and female modal patterns. (Adapted from Masters and Johnson, 1965)

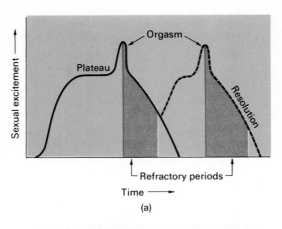

(a)

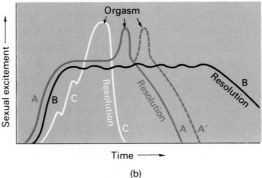

(b)

response. Women are usually somewhat slower than men to reach orgasm during intercourse and, as noted, they have no refractory phase.

Two other patterns are also observed frequently in women. In pattern B the high level of excitement in the plateau phase does not quite trigger orgasmic release; after a prolonged plateau period, sexual excitement dissipates gradually. Pattern C, on the other hand, is rapid and explosive. The orgasmic response is reached without a plateau, and resolution is also rapid. Orgasm in this pattern tends to be both longer and more intense than the other forms.

The similarities and differences in sexual responses exemplify the generalization of Chapter 1 that in some ways each person is like all other people, in some ways like some other people, and in some ways like no other person. The existence of differences among groups and individuals does not contradict or lessen the value of research into biological determinants of behavior. Some of the behavioral differences are related to differences in genetic makeup; some are related to differences in levels of hormones. And some of the behavioral differences can be explained by experience and learning; these, too, have biological bases, and we will consider biological mechanisms of learning in Chapters 16 and 17.

The fact that the orgasmic response is reflexive and cannot be withheld once a certain level of excitement has been reached does not mean that it is not subject to learning and other psychological influences. It is now known that many autonomic responses can be altered in their thresholds and time courses through appropriate training. Current forms of sex therapy based on studies of physiological responses are claimed to help many individuals experience sexual stimulation more fully and to help many couples coordinate their behavior more adequately (Kaplan, 1974; Masters & Johnson, 1970).

Development: Becoming a Man or a Woman

The developmental perspective is especially useful in the study of sex and behavior. It helps to answer the question: "How does a person assume the **gender identity** of a man or a woman?" That is, how does one identify one's self, and become identified by others, as a male or a female? The striking changes in sexual anatomy and in reproductive status over the life span are obviously important. So too are the several stages of sexual development that occur prenatally in humans and that lead to progressive divergence between the sexes. But achieving one's gender identity involves major social and cultural influences that can be just as important as the development of the anatomical-physiological endowment. The main steps toward adult gender identity, the prenatal and postnatal ages at which they occur, and the main factors involved are presented diagrammatically in Figure 11-7.

The role that hormones play in the development and differentiation of body structures is called their **organizational role.** Later in life some hormones also play an **activational role** in that they evoke or modulate reproductive behavior. In some cases activation cannot take place unless specific organization has already occurred, but in other cases activation does not require prior hormonal organization. Typically, organizational effects occur early in life and are permanent, whereas activational effects occur later and are reversible. Not all hormonal effects can be classified by this dichotomy (Arnold & Breedlove, 1985). For example, structural changes are classified as organizational, but in some cases large changes in levels of sex hormones can cause changes in the size of neurons in the brains of adult animals. Nevertheless, organization and activation are useful concepts to keep in mind as we examine the roles that hormones and other factors play in the development of a man or a woman.

"It's a girl!" Prenatal Differentiation of Reproductive Structures

The sequence of events that leads to development of a baby girl or baby boy can be likened to a relay race with different runners who cover different parts of the course (Money, 1977). First in line is the X or Y chromosome contributed by the male parent to pair with the X chromosome from the female parent. The XX or XY chromosomal pattern determines whether the undifferentiated embryological gonad will develop as ovary or testis.

Differentiation of the gonad into testes begins at about the seventh week after conception in humans; if the gonad is to differentiate into an ovary, it begins to do so later, at about the twelfth week. The testes must develop early because the androgens they produce are required for the next stages of development of males. At this stage (7 to 12 weeks after conception) two systems of primitive ducts exist in each embryo. One is the **Müllerian duct system,** which can develop into female reproductive structures—the oviducts, uterus, and upper vagina. The other is the **Wolffian duct system,** which can develop into male structures—the epididymides, the vas deferens, and the seminal vesicles (see Figure 11-8). The presence or absence of the testes determines which of these duct systems develops.

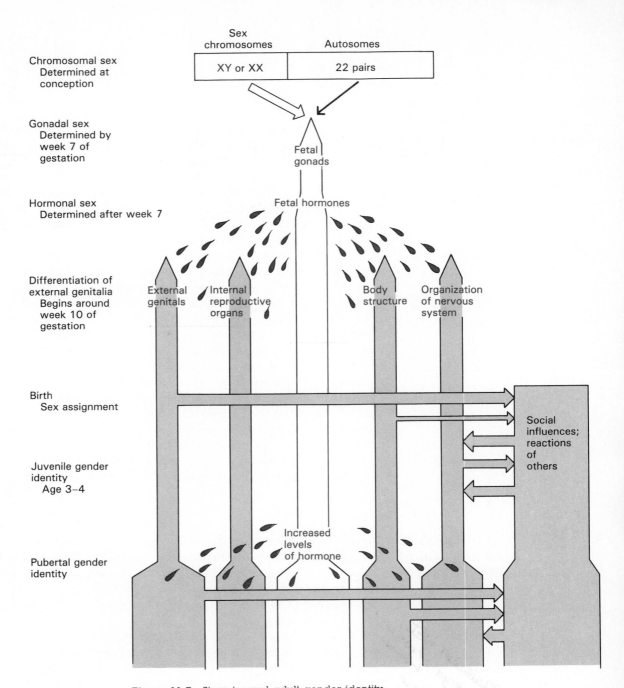

Chromosomal sex
Determined at
conception

Gonadal sex
Determined by
week 7 of
gestation

Hormonal sex
Determined after week 7

Differentiation of
external genitalia
Begins around
week 10 of
gestation

Birth
Sex assignment

Juvenile gender
identity
Age 3-4

Pubertal gender
identity

Figure 11-7 Steps toward adult gender identity.

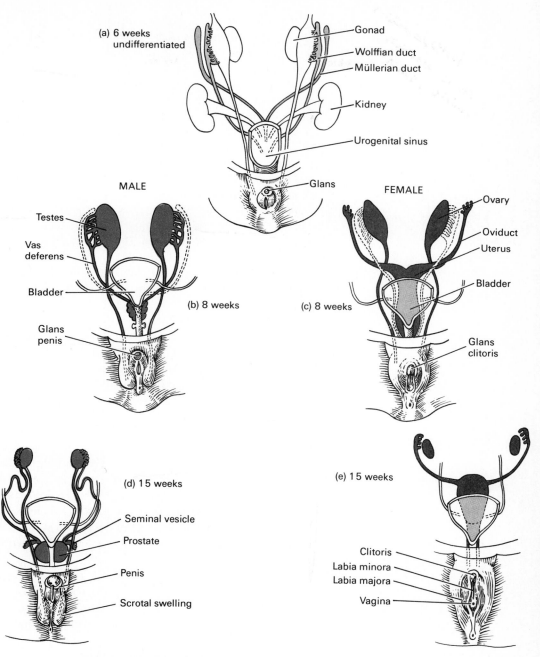

Figure 11-8 Fetal differentiation of human male and female reproductive structures from a common undifferentiated state in the six-week-old embryo.

*testes secretion
stims wolffian
inhibits Mullerian*

The testes secrete a substance that acts as the next runner in the race; it induces development of the Wolffian system and inhibits development of the Müllerian system. Although the biochemical structure of the Müllerian regression factor is not yet completely known, it appears to be a peptide hormone. It used to be thought that the ovaries secreted a substance that promoted development of the female duct system, but it has been found that the absence of testes ensures female development, which occurs even if *no* gonads are present.

Next the testes, if they are present, promote the differentiation of the external genitalia into the masculine form by secretion of the androgen dihydrotestosterone. Until the end of the twelfth week after conception, the external genitalia remain undifferentiated. If androgens do not act upon these tissues, they then differentiate as female genitalia. Thus the glans of the undifferentiated genitalia becomes the glans penis under the influence of androgens; in the absence of androgens it develops into the glans clitoris (Figure 11-8). The fetal labioscrotal swelling develops, under the influence of androgens, into the scrotum, and the testes descend into the scrotum from their original position near the kidneys. In the absence of androgens, the fetal labioscrotal swelling develops into the labia majora of the vulva. The typical male or female form of the genitalia is recognizable by the twelfth week after conception.

Even if the fetus is female and therefore does not possess testes, its genitalia may nevertheless assume masculine form under the influence of androgens in certain clinical conditions. The adrenal cortex normally produces small amounts of androgens, but an overactive fetal or maternal adrenal gland may produce enough androgens at the critical period of fetal development to cause the genitals to assume masculine forms. Another cause of masculine appearance of the infant genitalia is the administration of androgenic drugs to pregnant women.

Despite what we have just said, the presence of circulating androgens does not, by itself, guarantee masculinization of the genitalia. The tissues must receive the hormonal message and respond to it. There are rare individuals with XY chromosomes whose tissues do not respond to androgens, so the person develops the external appearance of a female (see Box 11-1). Thus a person with XY chromosomes can have a female appearance, and a person with the XX pattern can, if stimulated by androgens at the critical stage of development, have an external masculine appearance. The form of the external genitals usually determines how a child is classified and brought up.

Social Influences on Gender Identity

The last runner in the relay race that determines gender identity is social experience. The relative importance of experience and of biological factors (such as sex hormones) in determining gender identity is a question of considerable current interest and investigation. This can be studied in people whose upbringing and biology (that is, chromosomal pattern) do not reinforce each other. In some cases the appearance of the genitals at birth is neither completely masculine nor completely feminine, and the parents or physician may err in identifying the baby's sex. For example, when an overactive adrenal cortex during the fetal period causes a girl's genitals to develop a masculine appearance, at birth this genetic female may be recognized as a girl or may be classified as a boy. In the latter case, the child raised as a boy usually acts like a boy and wants to develop into a man. At the age of puberty, masculiniza-

BOX 11-1 A Genetic Male with a Female Body Form

The person shown in Box Figure 11-1 has the male XY genetic pattern but a woman's form. This is one of the rare people who are deficient in androgen receptors, so androgens have no effect on brain or body. What are some of the results of this condition for anatomy and for personality? The individual has testes, since differentiation of the testes does not depend on androgens, but the testes remain within the body cavity although they produce gonadal hormones normally. Since the body cells are insensitive to androgens, the external genitalia develop in the female form, and at birth the baby is considered to be a girl. At puberty the testes increase their production of both androgens and estrogens. The normal male level of estrogens is sufficient to produce the complete feminization of the bony structure and outer contours of the body, including feminine growth of the breasts, if the androgens do not inhibit this. The androgen-insensitive person does not, however, have reproductive capacity, and this sometimes leads to recognition of the condition. The vagina is short and requires surgical lengthening. The uterus is undeveloped because the testes released the Müllerian regression factor during the fetal period. There are no ovaries, and at puberty there is no menstruation. These individuals tend to have no body hair or only small amounts of it because growth of body and facial hair is stimulated by an androgenic hormone, androstenedione, which is secreted principally by the adrenal cortex; there is reduced sensitivity to this hormone as well as to other androgens.

A study of 14 androgen-insensitive women and girls past puberty (chromosomal males but social females) showed that they did not differ in personality from the common patterns of American women (Money & Ehrhardt, 1972). Most were interested in children, although most had resigned themselves to the impossibility of pregnancy. Most were active heterosexually, and none reported adult homosexual experience. Some had married, and "two of the married women each had adopted two children, and they proved to be good mothers with a good sense of motherhood" (p. 111). Almost all of the androgen-insensitive women rated themselves as being fully content with the female role. In such individuals the

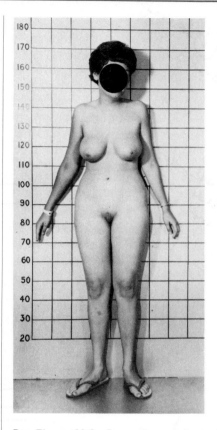

Box Figure 11-1 An androgen-insensitive genetic male. Although this person's chromosomes have the male XY pattern, insensitivity to male hormones caused body development to follow the female pattern. (From J. Money and A. A. Ehrhardt, *Man and Woman*, *Boy and Girl*, copyright 1972 by the Johns Hopkins University Press, Baltimore MD. By permission.)

male chromosomal pattern is irrelevant; the factors of hormonal organization of the brain, sex assignment at birth, rearing, and body form all are consistent with female gender identity.

---

tion of the body can be induced by means of androgen therapy; this biological treatment is necessary to provide a body form that corresponds to the learned gender identity. Such a person is a man in gender identity and gender role, although his chromosomal pattern is XX. Research on effects of the congenital adrenal condition on personality will be considered later in the chapter (page 422).

In some cases a later, more accurate identification of sex causes a reversal of sex assignment; that is, the parents decide to shift and rear the child as a girl rather than a boy, or vice versa. When such a change is made before age 3 or 4, it proceeds easily (Hampson, 1965). Beyond this age personality problems may arise, because the child's gender identity seems to be established by about age 3. Sometimes, however, adults have apparently been able to switch successfully from one sex role to the opposite one. Hampson (1965) claims that in all such cases of successful sex reversal he has studied, the persons had had longstanding reservations about their ''true sex'' and had viewed themselves as a kind of role ''imposter'' prior to the change. Although it is widely held that sociocultural experience can predominate over biological factors in determining gender identity (for example, see Money & Ehrhardt, 1972), some recently studied cases indicate the need to reevaluate this conclusion. These cases, to be taken up shortly, suggest that exposure to normal levels of male hormones from fetal development through puberty may be able to override the effects of being reared as a girl to the age of puberty.

Do Sex Hormones Organize Brain Circuits?

Much research and controversy have been stimulated by the finding that the presence or absence of androgens around the time of birth appears to determine the nature of adult sexual behavior in rats and other rodents. Nor are sex differences in behavior confined to reproductive activities; there are also sex differences in many other behaviors, such as aggression and exploratory behavior. Since behavior is mediated by neural circuits, one effect androgens might have on development is to organize brain circuits as well as peripheral bodily structures. This concept originated from studies begun in the 1930s in which administration of androgens to newborn female rats was found to masculinize their behavior. The treated female rats failed to ovulate as adults, and they showed increased tendency to exhibit masculine copulatory behavior (mounting) and decreased tendency to show feminine copulatory behavior (such as lordosis).

A new stage in research on hormonal influences on organization of the brain began in the early 1970s with the discovery of anatomical differences between the brains of males and females of several species (Arnold & Gorski, 1984; Feder, 1984). In several cases such differences have been eliminated or even reversed in animal experiments involving early hormonal treatments. For example, rats of the two sexes were found to differ in the number of one kind of synapse in the preoptic region of the brain; this difference was abolished by administering androgen to newborn females or by castrating newborn males (Raisman & Field, 1973). A nucleus in the medial preoptic area of the rat was found to be six times as large in males as in females, and the size of this nucleus could be altered by treating newborn rats with hormones (Gorski et al., 1977, 1978). And discovery of a similar anatomical difference between the brains of human males and females (de Vries, de Bruin, Uylings & Corner, 1981) supports the concept that hormones influence the organization of the human brain. In some species of songbirds, the volume of brain regions that control vocal behavior was found to be several times larger in males than in females (Nottebohm & Arnold, 1976), and these differences could be altered by early hormonal treatments. A sexually dimorphic nucleus in the spinal cord of rodents (Breedlove & Arnold, 1981) has proved to be an excellent model for experimental work. We will examine some of these dimorphisms and their dependence on gonadal hormones shortly, but first we need to see a little more about how these hormones work in the nervous system.

Estrogens Mediate Some Effects of Androgens

A puzzling fact emerged from experiments in which gonadal hormones were given to rats and other rodents around the time of birth: Not only testosterone but also estradiol and other estrogens had the effect of masculinizing behavior and preventing ovulation. Later it was found that testosterone can be metabolized to estradiol and dihydrotestosterone, among other products, as we saw in Table 7-2. These conversions can take place either in the gonads or within neurons. The fact that estrogens play a primary role in masculine differentiation in the rat is supported by the following findings: (1) Drugs that block the conversion of testosterone to estradiol inhibit masculine development; even though testosterone reaches the cells, it needs to be converted there to estradiol in order to have a masculinizing effect. (2) Rats that are genetically insensitive to androgens are behaviorally masculinized even though their genitals appear feminine; thus the androgens act directly on genital development but require transformation to estrogens in order to work on some neural structures.

Finding that estrogens as well as androgens lead to masculinization of brain and behavior gave rise to a further question: How is it that any animals show female behavior? Why are normal neonatal female rats not masculinized by the estradiol secreted by their ovaries? Two different answers have been proposed. The more widely accepted position is based on the discovery of an estrogen-binding protein (alpha fetoprotein, AFT) present in the blood plasma of fetal rodents (Nunez et al., 1971). Many investigators believe that whereas estrogens are bound by AFT and thus prevented from entering into the brain during the fetal and early postnatal period, androgens are free to enter the brain. Some testosterone is then converted in neurons to estradiol, which masculinizes some neural cells; other neural cells are affected directly by testosterone itself. Estrogens administered experimentally can accomplish masculinization because they are given in amounts sufficient to saturate the binding system. An alternative answer has been proposed by Döhler et al. (1984): They doubt that AFT prevents estrogens from reaching neurons, because AFT has been found inside neurons; AFT may even be a transport agent for estrogens. Rather than accepting the binding hypothesis, Döhler and colleagues suggest that sexual brain differentiation is governed quantitatively, a moderate amount of estrogen being necessary for the female pattern of functioning whereas a high level of estrogen is required for male differentiation of neural circuits. This would then be a case where a quantitative difference in level of estrogen in neural cells leads to qualitative differences in neural organization and behavior. Further work will be required to decide between these alternative hypotheses.

As we consider various sexual dimorphisms in the nervous system, it will be important to find what roles different gonadal hormones play. We will also want to see the extent to which the concept of sexual organization of the brain, largely developed through research with rodents, can be applied to primates, including human beings.

Until recently it appeared that estrogens played no role in the organization of brain circuits. This conclusion had come from experiments showing that removal of the sources of estrogen—the ovaries and the adrenal glands—in newborn rats did not prevent female organization of the brain: As adults, if primed with estrogen, these rats ovulated and showed female sexual receptivity in mating tests. Later it was realized that immature rats store estrogen for several days, so elimination of the sources of estrogen does not remove the hormone from the body during the period that is critical for sexual organization of the brain. Since the hormone could not be removed from the body, another approach was then devised: Newborn rats were treated with a compound that binds to estrogen receptors within cells and thus prevents estrogen from acting. When these rats were tested as adults, it was found that the early antiestrogen treatment prevented them from ovulating, and it reduced markedly the number who showed sexual receptivity in mating tests (Döhler et al., 1984). Thus these tests of reproductive behavior indicate that early estrogen is necessary for normal female organization of the nervous system in the rat. Furthermore, there are indications that estrogens affect, in subtle but measurable ways, both early brain development (e.g., Diamond, 1980) and development of exploratory behavior (Stewart & Cygan, 1980).

A clear example of the hormonal effects on the brain circuits controlling sexually dimorphic behavior has been found in certain birds. This behavior is the singing that male birds use both to court females and to keep other males out of their territory. The brain circuits that control song behavior have been traced for the canary (Nottebohm, 1980) and the zebra finch (Arnold, 1980). Several of the brain nuclei in these circuits are significantly larger in the male than in the female, and one large nucleus in the male brain cannot be seen at all in the female brain (Figure 11-9). Many of the cells in these nuclei accumulate androgens. In the case of the canary, a female that has already bred and produced eggs can be transformed, by treatment with androgens, to show male behavior, including singing (Nottebohm, 1979). When this treatment is effective, the sizes of the brain nuclei that control song are found to have enlarged toward the sizes seen in males. In the case of the zebra finch, hormonal treatment of the adult female does not cause her to sing, but hormonal treatment of a newly hatched female can cause her to acquire song and to show enlarged brain nuclei for song production.

Experimenters have found that even within the same brain nucleus, different aspects of dimorphism can be controlled by different sex hormones. Gurney (1981) implanted pellets of hormone in female zebra finches on the day after they hatched, and when they became adult he measured three aspects of vocal control nucleus RA (shown in Figure 11-9). The measures were (1) the number of neurons in the nucleus, (2) the mean diameter of cell bodies of neurons in the nucleus, and (3) the mean spacing between neurons. This last measure gives an indication of the density of connections between neurons: The more connections there are, the further the neuron cell bodies are forced apart. The effects, measured in comparison with control birds that received no hormonal treatment, depended on which of three hormones the experimental birds received: testosterone, estradiol, or dihydrotestosterone (DHT). Testosterone masculinized all three aspects of the female nucleus, doubling both cell number and cell size and increasing neuronal spacing almost fivefold. Estradiol, in contrast, had little effect on cell number, but it was practically as effective as testosterone in masculinizing both cell size and spacing. DHT

Figure 11-9 Schematic drawings of the brains of male and female songbirds. The circles represent brain regions involved in song production. The area of each circle is proportional to the volume of the brain region, and these regions have been magnified so that their relative sizes can be seen clearly. Dots mark the regions that pick up testosterone, and the numbers indicate the percentages of cells labeled when radioactive testosterone was injected. (HV, hyperstriatum ventrale; IC, intercollicular nucleus; MAN, magnocellular nucleus of anterior neostriatum; RA, nucleus robustus of the archistriatum; X, area X of the locus parolfactorium; XII, nucleus of the XIIth cranial nerve.) (Adapted from Arnold, 1980)

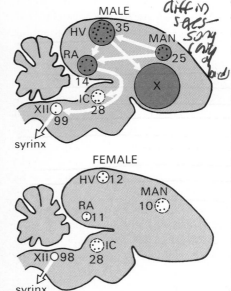

Figure 11-10 Sexually dimorphic nucleus of the preoptic area of rat. (a) On a lateral view of the rat brain, the brown line shows the plane of a frontal section through this area. (b) A frontal section at this level. The brown rectangle in (b) shows the region enlarged in the actual brain sections below. (ac, anterior commissure; cc, corpus callosum; oc, optic chiasm; scn, suprachiasmatic nucleus; v, third ventricle.) The enlarged sections show the striking difference in size of the sexually dimorphic nuclei of the preoptic area (SDN/POA) in normal adult male and female rats. (Sections courtesy of Roger A. Gorski)

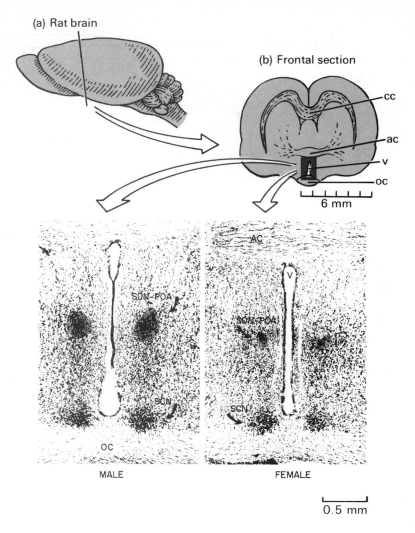

showed a different pattern, doubling cell number, causing a slight increase in cell size, and having no effect on cell spacing. Thus it appears that testosterone achieves its effects on cell number by being transformed to DHT within the neurons; it affects neuronal size and spacing by being transformed to estradiol. So cell number appears to be regulated independently of cell size and spacing.

The first sexually dimorphic nucleus to be found in a mammalian brain is in the medial preoptic area of the rat (Gorski et al., 1977, 1978). The size of this sexually dimorphic nucleus of the preoptic area (SDN-POA) is six times as large in adult male rats as in females (Figure 11-10), and the size can be altered by treating newborn females with either testosterone or estradiol (Gorski et al., 1981). Thus testosterone normally affects this nucleus through the estradiol route. Confirmation of this conclusion was obtained by using rats with a mutation (*tfm*) that reduces the number of androgen receptors to 10–15% of the normal number but does not affect estrogen receptors. (This defect is like that of the androgen-insensitive humans

Est. masc.
this region for
brain

described in Box 11-1.) In rats with the *tfm* mutation, the SDN-POA was found to be masculine in size, demonstrating that estradiol masculinizes this region of the brain. Although this nucleus is useful for studying effects of hormones on development, its usefulness is limited by the fact that the functional significance of the SDN-POA has not yet been defined. The general region is known to be important for regulation of masculine sexual behavior, but the preoptic area is involved in many integrative processes, and the details remain to be worked out.

A sexual dimorphism of the nervous system with known function is the spinal nucleus of the bulbocavernosus muscle (SNB) in rodents. In rats and other rodents, the female has no bulbocavernosus—a muscle that in the male attaches to the penis. This may seem obvious, but in most mammals, including carnivores and primates, both females and males possess bulbocavernosus muscles, although they differ in form. The SNB in male rats was found by injecting horseradish peroxidase (HRP) into the bulbocavernosus muscle and locating cells in the spinal cord that contained HRP. The SNB in adult male rats has about three times as many neurons as in the female, and the cells present in the female SNB are only about half as large as those in the male; the dimorphism can be seen in Figure 11-11 (Breedlove & Arnold,

SNB - imp
in that it is
sexually differentiated

Figure 11-11 Transverse sections of the spinal cord of young adult rats showing a sexually dimorphic nucleus. Within the colored rectangle in the right half are several large densely stained neurons of the spinal nucleus of the bulbocavernosus (SNB); this section comes from a male rat. For comparison the left half is a comparable section from a female rat, but there are few large dark neurons in the region of the SNB. (From Breedlove and Arnold, 1981)

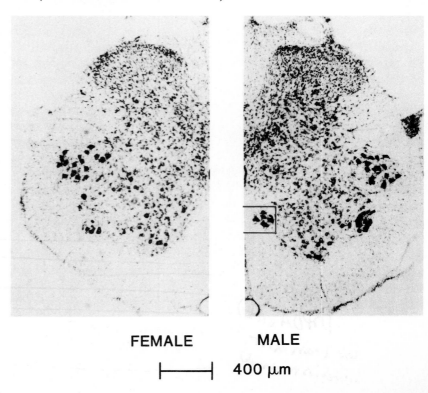

FEMALE   **MALE**

├─────┤ 400 µm

1980). (What function the smaller number of cells in the female SNB serves is not known.)

This dimorphic nucleus has been used as a further model system to investigate the roles of hormones in both the development and the adult status of the nervous system. The sex differences in the spinal nucleus were found to be due to early exposure to androgens, with estrogens playing little or no role. Furthermore, cell number and cell size could be regulated independently of each other in terms of developmental timing. If testosterone was administered to female rats, it masculinized the number of SNB cells if given before postnatal day 5 but not if given thereafter; the effect was greatest with prenatal administration of testosterone. The critical period for increasing the size of SNB cells extended beyond postnatal day 11. DHT was ineffective if given prenatally but was about as effective as testosterone when administered postnatally. Male rats with the androgen-insensitive mutation (*tfm*) produce normal levels of androgens, but the bulbocavernosus muscle does not develop, and their SNB is similar to that in females (Breedlove, 1984). Thus hormonal influences on the development of this spinal nucleus are quite different from those that regulate development of the sexually dimorphic nucleus of the preoptic area.

What is the mechanism by which testosterone causes a greater number of neurons to be present in the SNB of adult males than in females? Recent research has shown that in the fetal stage the SNB of female rats resembles that of males; the presence of testosterone in the late prenatal and early postnatal periods protects SNB neurons from the extensive cell death that would otherwise occur in this nucleus (Breedlove, 1984).

Following the lead of this research with the rat, a similar spinal nucleus in dogs and human beings (Onuf's nucleus) has now been investigated and found to be sexually dimorphic (Forger & Breedlove, 1986).

Sex Differences in the Human Brain?

Claims and counterclaims about possible anatomical sex differences in the human brain have been advanced for over a century (McGlone, 1980; Swaab & Hofman, 1984). In the early 1980s, some investigators reported that the corpus callosum is dimorphic in shape and is relatively larger in females (Baack, Lacoste-Utamsing, & Woodward, 1982; Lacoste-Utamsing & Holloway, 1981). But earlier detailed studies of the corpus callosum had not found such a difference, nor was it confirmed in some subsequent research (e.g., Witelson, 1985). Although it seems doubtful that sexual dimorphism will be found in any aspect of the gross anatomy of the human brain, dimorphism has been reported in some brain nuclei. Thus Dutch investigators found a sex difference in the shape of a hypothalamic nucleus that is related to circadian rhythms—the suprachiasmatic nucleus (de Vries, de Bruin, Uylings, & Corner, 1984). Then, following the reports of the sexually dimorphic nucleus in the preoptic area of the rat brain shown in Figure 11-10, other Dutch anatomists found that an analogous nucleus exists in the human brain; furthermore, this nucleus is 2.5 times as large in men as in women and contains over twice as many neurons in men (Swaab & Fliers, 1985). This appears to be the first report of a sex difference in cell numbers for a region of the human brain. In both sexes the volume and cell number of the nucleus decreases sharply with age, but the 2:1 male to female ratio persists.

Does Hormonal Organization of Brain Circuits Apply to Primates?

Most of the research on organizational effects of sex hormones has been done with rodents, although we have also seen examples with birds and human beings. Some critics have suggested that the concept of organizational effects of sex hormones not only began with rodent research but cannot properly be extrapolated beyond rodents (Bleier, 1983). This appears to be too restrictive a position. It is true that some findings are not the same for rodents and primates, but the overall pictures are similar. Let us note both some differences and some similarities.

First, there are two ways in which early androgens do not affect monkeys in ways that rats are affected: (1) The hypothalamus of the male monkey can support ovulation if an ovary is implanted in its body; thus early androgen does not prevent ovulatory competence of the monkey hypothalamus as it does in the rat hypothalamus (Knobil, 1974). (2) Although researchers have investigated whether early androgen would diminish receptivity in female monkeys, as it does in female rats, they have found no such evidence in monkeys (Goy & Resko, 1972).

There are two ways in which early androgens *do* affect behavior of primates, suggesting altered organization of the brain: (1) Early androgens do reduce proceptive behavior in female monkeys although, as we just saw, they do not diminish receptivity (Thornton & Goy, 1983). Since proceptive behavior normally precedes receptive behavior, a female that is not proceptive will normally not get to show whether it is receptive, so careful procedures are needed to test this. (2) Giving androgens prenatally to female monkeys masculinizes their play behavior (Goy & Phoenix, 1971). Thus although early androgens do not have all the effects on primate brains that they have on rodent brains, there is clear evidence of organizational effects on primate brains.

The finding of sex differences in the human brain, even before birth, is further evidence that sex hormones affect brain organization. Now let us consider evidence about possible organizational effects of sex hormones on human personality.

Does Prenatal Sexual Development Influence Personality?

Does the normal course of differential sexual development have any influences on personality differences between males and females? Is abnormal exposure to hormones during fetal development reflected in personality? These are difficult questions to answer for several reasons: personality traits are variable and rather hard to measure; personality development is influenced by many factors, so teasing out one variable is hard to do; the question of sex differences may be difficult to consider dispassionately since it is related to political and social rights of the two sexes. We will note some important findings while remaining aware of the incomplete and in many cases inconclusive nature of research in this area.

Sex Differences in Personality

What sex differences in personality are clearly established? Psychologists Eleanor Maccoby and Carol Jacklin (1974) gathered and evaluated thousands of studies that attempted to measure purported differences between boys and girls, men and women. They concluded that many alleged sex differences disappear when attempts are made to measure them objectively, and only four main sex differences were regarded as being fairly well established. In a critical review of the Maccoby and

Jacklin book, Jeanne Block (1976) pointed out several methodological difficulties in the attempt to evaluate studies of sex differences. For one thing, most of the studies considered by Maccoby and Jacklin were of children below the age of five, when some sex differences may not yet have become established. In fact, Block showed that when she classified the studies according to age of the subjects, the older the subjects were (up to young adulthood), the larger was the proportion of studies that showed significant sex differences in personality. Block concluded that there are more sex differences in personality than Maccoby and Jacklin accepted.

Since the time that Maccoby and Jacklin conducted their survey, more rigorous and conclusive ways of reviewing research have developed. Although incomplete surveys and informal ways of combining data from different studies are still the norm, there are now quantitative methods to summarize and analyze research literature, as described by Green and Hall (1984). In one such quantitative assessment of studies on social influence, for example, Eagley and Carli (1981) found that men were less affected by social influence than were women in several kinds of social situations. These differences were not large, but they were statistically significant.

Although we have reservations about the review of Maccoby and Jacklin, it is still the largest such attempt to date, and the sex differences it found are sure to be accepted, even if there are also others. The four main sex differences that Maccoby and Jacklin regard as established are the following:

1. Girls have greater verbal ability than boys. The magnitude of the mean difference varies among studies, commonly being about one-quarter of a standard deviation.
2. Boys score higher in visual-spatial ability. The male advantage on spatial tests increases through the high school years and reaches about 0.4 standard deviation.
3. Boys have higher scores in mathematical ability.
4. Boys and men are more aggressive than girls and women.

Even though these differences are statistically significant, they are not large in practical terms, and they are not very useful in predicting differences between any two people. For example, it is clear that although girls have the higher mean score in verbal abilities, many boys score higher than the average girl. Similarly, many girls score higher on spatial abilities than the average boy. The general similarities in performance of the two sexes are more striking than the differences. Nevertheless, since such group differences do show up consistently, it is useful to ask to what extent any of them can be attributed to biological determinants. Maccoby and Jacklin conclude that biological factors are implicated most clearly in measures of aggression and visual-spatial ability. Evidence for a biological component in the greater aggressiveness of males rests on the following bases:

1. It is universal in all cultures that have been studied.
2. A similar sex difference is found among nonhuman primates (Figure 11-12).
3. Levels of aggression are increased by androgens and decreased by estrogens; for example, prenatal treatment of female monkeys with androgens significantly increases their aggressiveness and the amount of rough-and-tumble play.

Figure 11-12 Sex differences in aggressive behavior of young rhesus monkeys. Males wrestle frequently, like those in the foreground. Females are more sedate, like those in the background. (Photograph courtesy of H. F. Harlow)

The case for biological determination of visual-spatial ability comes primarily from genetic studies. These indicate the existence of a recessive sex-linked gene that contributes to high scores on tests of spatial ability. About half the men and a quarter of the women show this factor phenotypically. Other genetic factors that also affect spatial ability do not seem to be sex-linked. Of course, training and practice also influence visual-spatial skills, so the sex-linked tendency may be reinforced in some sociocultural circumstances and not in others.

Fetal Endocrine Abnormalities and Personality

To study effects of unusual prenatal endocrine influences on human personality, investigators depend on spontaneous endocrine abnormalities or on medically prescribed hormonal treatments of pregnant women (Ehrhardt & Meyer-Bahlburg, 1981; Rubin, Reinisch, & Haskett, 1981). Prenatal hormonal effects have been reported in some sexually dimorphic behaviors, such as energy expenditure and childhood rehearsal of parental roles, but the effects are rather subtle. Here are a few examples.

In a genetic condition of congenital overgrowth of the adrenal gland (congenital adrenal hyperplasia, or CAH), the adrenal cortex does not secrete cortisol but from fetal life onward secretes an excess of androgens. As a result, if the fetus is female, the external genitalia are masculinized; the appearance of genetic males is not changed because their testes normally produce androgens. Postnatally the condition can be corrected by replacement therapy with corticosteroids that hold adrenal androgen production to a normal level. In girls the external genitalia can be surgically feminized in the first weeks of life. With proper regulation of hormones, pubertal development occurs normally, and sexual functioning and fertility are normal.

Personality studies have indicated some differences between such prenatally androgenized children and their siblings or matched normal controls. CAH girls showed a long-term childhood pattern of high energy expenditure (intense outdoor activity, identification as a tomboy) and decreased rehearsal of female parenting (low interest in doll play and baby care). While statistically significant, these trends were not extreme, they fell toward one end of the spectrum of accepted female behavior in our culture. Furthermore, the observed differences in personality may have been caused in part at least by social influences. Because the parents of the CAH girls were aware of the ambiguous genitalia at birth, it is possible that these girls were raised somewhat differently from the control girls. CAH boys differed from controls only in showing higher levels of energy expenditure in play and sports.

A group of 38 genetic males in a rural community in the Dominican Republic was found to have an enzyme deficiency that prevented conversion of testosterone to dihydrotestosterone and thus severely retarded development of masculine external genitalia (Imperato-McGinley et al., 1974, 1979, 1981). The internal reproductive structures were male, but the external genitalia were ambiguous in form, and 18 of these children were raised as girls. At the age of puberty, not only did the genitalia develop masculine form but, despite their upbringing, in 17 of 18 cases gender identity changed, and the boys directed their sexual interest toward females. This report is surprising in view of findings noted above that gender identity is usually difficult to change after age three or four. But it should be noted that in most of the cases studied in the United States where sex of rearing was contrary to chromosomal and gonadal sex, further methods were used to reinforce the effects of rearing. These included removal of the gonads and therapy with hormones of the assigned sex. In the case of the subjects in the Dominican Republic, there were social pressures against changing gender identity and gender role, but these were not supplemented by surgical or hormonal treatments. When the presumptive girls did not grow breasts and instead developed a male bodily form at puberty, they changed over to male gender identity. The rather permissive atmosphere of the rural Dominican community did not pose an insurmountable barrier to this change. In fact, it is clear that the people of this community are aware of this disorder and accept it as unusual but not alarming. Thus we see that more research will be needed to define clearly how sociocultural factors and biological factors interact in forming gender identity.

The studies reported in this section suggest that prenatal presence of hormones can have some effects on personality and behavior as well as on bodily structure. Perhaps some subtle differences in personality reflect differences of prenatal exposure that are completely within the normal range of hormone levels, but this result has not been demonstrated. The question of possible hormonal effects on personality is a complicated one, and more research is needed before we can decide the extent to which prenatal hormones may determine individual differences in personality.

Evolution of Sex

Evolution through natural selection depends on differences in individual animals' reproduction and survival. The success of individuals from an evolutionary point of view means reproduction of their genes. Thus an evolutionary approach to reproductive behavior is particularly appropriate, since it deals with the behavior that makes evolution possible.

Sexual reproduction promotes a richness of genetic combinations, as we mentioned earlier. The result is that offspring of a sexual union can more readily occupy a large range of environments than can offspring of asexual reproduction. "Sex, then, is an adaptation for survival; it is probably the master adaptation" (Adler, 1978, p. 658). Sex means both separateness of male and female and union of sperm and egg. The incredibly varied ways in which this union can occur account for much of the variety of animal form and behavior. In this section we will consider some of the criteria that must be met for successful reproductive behavior and then take up some implications of evolution and of cultural development for human sexuality.

Adaptations for Sexual Reproduction

Here are some major tests that must be met for successful reproductive behavior in complex animals:

1. Male and female must remain together or come together. This criterion requires mechanisms for attraction, such as those we saw in the ring dove, and for recognition of species, sex, and sexual maturity.

2. Where several potential mates of the right species and reproductive status are available, the individual must select a mate. The selection affects the probability that her or his genes will survive. In many species the female undertakes a larger burden of reproduction than the male in the nutritional and mechanical burdens of pregnancy. So the female may be more careful in selecting a mate, and the male may exhibit elaborate courtship behavior to demonstrate his fitness. In many species both males and females show preferences for particular members of the opposite sex in displaying appetitive behavior. (In this and other points we are not implying that "reproductive strategies" are conscious or intentional. They are bodily and behavioral adaptations that have evolved because they achieve certain consequences, but they do not require any awareness on the part of the actors.)

3. Reproduction is more likely to be successful if it occurs at a favorable time and place. In many parts of the world, food supplies are best only in a short season. Animals that live there may mate at a time that ensures that the young will be born when food supplies are likely to be optimal. Other species may migrate long distances to reproduce in favorable locales.

4. Once the time, place, and partner have been chosen, specific copulatory behavior is required to unite sperm and egg. Copulation involves a complex set of reciprocal behavioral adjustments. Particular neural circuits mediate these behaviors, and in many species these circuits are facilitated by altered levels of hormones. When we described the copulatory patterns of rodents, we noted that there is much variety among species. Dewsbury (1975) attempted to relate these differences to the ecologies in which the various species have evolved. Thus whether ejaculation of semen occurs during a single brief insertion of the penis or requires multiple insertions appears to be related to whether the environment is exposed to predators or protected from them. We do not yet know enough about the behavior of many species of rodents under field conditions to be able to test some hypotheses about the possible significance of their reproductive patterns. Dewsbury has not found any linear pattern in the evolutionary history of reproductive behavior among rodents. Instead certain patterns seem to have evolved repeatedly in response to the particular selection pressures that have acted on particular species.

5. In some species reproduction requires a postcopulatory physiological response in the female. For example, female cats and rabbits ovulate only after they copulate, a condition called reflex ovulation or coitus-induced ovulation. In such species successful mating is not restricted to a regular ovulatory period of the female's cycle. In species where ovulation spontaneously occurs cyclically, copulation stimulates the secretion of luteinizing hormone and progesterone, which promotes implantation of the fertilized ovum into the wall of the uterus. In some species receptivity is turned off after copulation, which prevents disruption of pregnancy.

6. The behavior of parents can increase the likelihood that their young will survive. A few examples will illustrate the range and variety of this behavior. In some species both parents participate, as in the case of the ring dove. When both parents care for the young, they are usually similar in appearance. In other species only one parent cares for the young. In mammalian species, when only one parent is the care giver, it is always the mother; in other species it may be the father. Among species of birds, if only one parent is the care giver, it usually has the duller, plainer plumage, which probably helps to protect parent and young against predators. Usually this plainer parent is the female, but there are exceptions, such as the phalarope. The female phalarope is larger and more colorful than the male; she displays during courtship, chooses the nesting site, and defends it against other females. Once she lays eggs, she departs; the male phalarope incubates the eggs and cares for the young.

The class of animals called mammals is characterized by the presence of female mammary glands used to nourish the young. Some theorists have stated that one cannot explain the origin of mammary glands on the basis of selection for fitness of the individual because the glands contribute to the nutrition of another individual. But these glands are clearly important for survival of the mother's genes in her offspring, and it is reproductive survival that is the basis of evolution.

In some vertebrate species, neither parent cares for the young. This is true, for example, of turtles, frogs, and some birds. But in these cases the female often helps to favor development of her young by placing the eggs in a location that is likely to foster successful hatching and subsequent growth. The cuckoo often escapes parental duties by laying its eggs in the nest of another species, which then cares for the young cuckoo. (This habit of the cuckoo is the origin of the word cuckold, applied to the husband of an unfaithful wife.)

Sexual Selection

Trying to understand differences between the sexes has proved to be difficult for everyone, including scientists. Charles Darwin observed the striking anatomical and behavioral differences between males and females of many species, but he was unable to explain these differences by natural selection; so he introduced the concept of **sexual selection** (Darwin, 1871). Darwin conceived of natural selection as depending on the success of both sexes of a species with respect to general conditions such as obtaining food and avoiding being injured or killed. He used sexual selection to explain why certain individuals have a reproductive advantage over others of their sex and species. For example, among elephant seals certain adult males mate with numerous females, while other males are not allowed to mate at all

(a) (b)

Figure 11-13 Reproductive behavior in elephant seals. (a) Dominant male seal and his harem. The small seals with black pelts are pups. Peripheral adult males are seen beyond the harem. (b) Dominant male prepares to copulate with a member of his harem. Note the large dimorphism of size between male and females. (Photographs by M. R. Rosenzweig)

(Figure 11-13). Certain female elephant seals have been found, season after season, to mate with more vigorous or able males than do other females.

From the start some scientists thought it was incorrect to make a distinction between natural selection and sexual selection, and this is still a matter of debate (Le Boeuf, 1978). The separation is less sharp today than in Darwin's day because geneticists have redefined fitness in terms of the contribution to the gene pool of the next generation rather than in Darwin's general sense of improved chances for survival. Much current research is devoted to the study of the "reproductive strategies" used by males and females in many species to ensure that their genes continue in the next generation. Some of it involves field studies of natural populations whose members are studied over successive generations. As a consequence of these studies, sexual selection and reproductive strategies are no longer considered to be limited to the time of mating; they now include all characteristics that facilitate mating and fertilization and those involved in parental care.

The basis of sexual selection is thought to be the unequal investment that the two sexes make in a single offspring. A current formulation of this hypothesis goes along the following lines: Originally the sex cells (gametes) of both sexes were probably the same size. Organisms simply liberated sex cells into the water where they lived, the way many fish now spawn, and those cells that united formed offspring. These gametes were too large for the organism to produce in great quantities but too small to contain enough food to support extensive development of the embryo. Specialization to produce either tiny gametes or large gametes would yield greater fitness, and both kinds of change occurred (Figure 11-14). Eventually one sex, which we now call males, began to produce smaller sex cells and more of

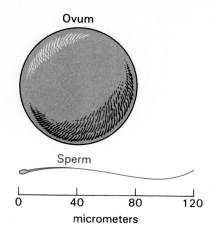

Ovum

Sperm

0   40   80   120
micrometers

Figure 11-14 Relative sizes of human ovum and sperm; both are magnified about 450 times.

them. Since the small sperm had little food supply, they could not live long and had to make contact with the ova as soon as possible. Mobile sperm therefore evolved. A further development was selection of males that placed sperm closer to females, and this development culminated in internal fertilization. Females specialized in the other direction, producing large gametes with adequate food supplies to permit extensive growth of the embryo. The larger size of the egg relative to that of the sperm meant that the female made a larger investment of energy and metabolism in the individual offspring than did the male. Once she made this greater initial investment, it became advantageous for the female to protect it by additional investments including, in many species, parental care. An indication of the differential investments of female and male ring doves in their offspring is given in Figure 11-15. In many species there is an even greater difference between the investments of the two sexes.

Mating Systems

The differential investments by males and females of many species in their offspring have been related to different mating systems among classes and species of animals. There are many possible mating systems; the categories that are most com-

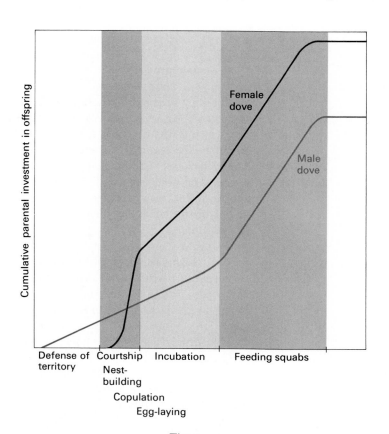

Figure 11-15 Hypothetical curves of cumulative investments of a female and a male ring dove in their offspring through the reproductive cycle. (Adapted from Erickson, 1978, and Trivers, 1972)

Figure 11-16 Distributions of mating systems among birds and mammals. The graphs show percentages of species that fall into four main classifications. Estimates for birds (from Lack, 1968) are rather precise, so percentage figures are shown. Estimates for mammals are not very precise, so their graph is shown as a broad band and percentages are not given. (Data for birds from Lack, 1969; estimates for mammals after Daly and Wilson, 1978)

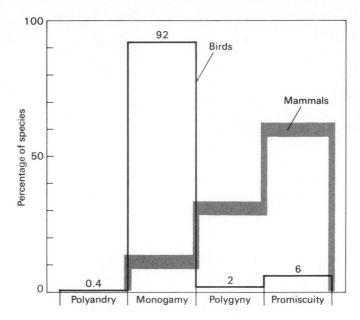

monly observed are monogamy, polygyny, polyandry, and promiscuity (see Figure 11-16).

In **monogamy** (from the Greek roots *mono,* meaning "one," and *gamos,* meaning "spouse") one female and one male form a breeding pair. The pair may last for one breeding season or for a lifetime. Lifelong monogamy has been found in many species of birds, such as doves. The constancy of doves has been known for centuries, which is why they have been used as a symbol of love. Monogamy is also seen in certain species of small antelopes, in some primates (gibbons), and in many human societies. (It does not mean that remating will not occur if the pair are separated or if one member dies.) The term **pair bond** is used to describe this rather durable and exclusive relation between a female and a male. Much current research is studying the conditions under which such relations occur and the mechanisms of pair bonding.

Polygamy (from the Greek roots *poly,* meaning "many," and *gamos,* meaning "spouse") can take either of two forms. **Polygyny** (from *poly* and *gyny,* meaning "woman" or "wife") is the mating of one male with more than one female. Polygyny occurs in some birds (such as the ostrich), in many mammals (such as the elephant seal, deer, and macaque monkeys), and in many human societies. **Polyandry** (from *poly* and *andros,* meaning "man") is the mating of one female with more than one male. This system is rather rare. It occurs in a few species of birds (such as the jacana in Figure 11-1e) and in a few human societies.

Promiscuity refers to instances where animals mate with several members of the opposite sex and do not establish durable associations with sex partners. In many species of rodents there is intense promiscuous competition of males for females.

Mammals differ from birds in the relative frequencies of these different mating systems, as Figure 11-16 indicates. The distribution for birds is based on estimates by Lack (1968); he estimates that among the approximately 8600 species of birds, 92% are monogamous, 2% polygamous, less than 0.5% polyandrous, and 6% show promiscuous male competition for females. Only crude estimates are available for mammals because the mating systems of most of the approximately 4000 species of mammals have not yet been studied. Almost 1700 of the mammalian species are rodents, and in this order polygyny and promiscuous competition of males for females predominate. The same appears to hold true for the other better known mammalian orders—insectivores (for instance, moles and shrews), pinnipeds (such as seals), ungulates (such as cattle and deer), and primates. Among the carnivores (for example, dogs) monogamy may be more common.

Among both bird and mammalian species, the mating system is related to sexual dimorphism in body size. Darwin observed that in birds the two sexes are of closely similar size in monogamous species, whereas in polygynous species the male tends to be larger than the females. The same relation between degree of sexual dimorphism in size and the degree of polygyny (the number of females that mate with a single male) has been documented for several orders of mammals including primates (Alexander et al., 1979). Polygyny for these mammalian species has been quantified from field reports of the sizes of harems. The relationship between polygyny and dimorphism seems to be weaker in primates than in seals or ungulates, but even here it is highly significant statistically. Furthermore, this apparent weakness may be due, in part at least, to the less accurate estimates for the primates under field conditions.

Evolutionary Implications for Human Sexuality

Human beings share the major adaptations of all mammals for reproductive behavior, but they are also molded by the family history of the hominid line and by the cultural developments of our own species, *Homo sapiens*. If we were investigators from another planet and knew that human beings were moderately large mammals with a mild degree of sexual dimorphism of size (the mean ratio of male stature to female stature is 1.08), we might expect to find a slightly polygynous mating system (Alexander et al., 1979). Anthropologists have studied marriage practices in hundreds of human societies (Bourguignon & Greenbaum, 1973) and have found much variety. When the findings are grouped into large categories (Figure 11-17), polygyny is seen to exist in most societies, but in many of them it is practiced by only a small minority. Polyandry exists but is exceedingly rare. Monogamy is the only accepted form in many societies, and it is actually far more prevalent than this statement suggests: Even in societies that accept polygamy, most marriages are monogamous.

Of course, we know much more about our human heritage than just that it is part of the mammalian story. Human evolution involved a large increase in brain size and the development of life styles with divisions of labor between the sexes. Sex roles became specialized not only with respect to reproductive functions, as in all other mammals, but also in connection with the economy of the group. The sex differences in economic roles were not absolute; there was sharing, and different cultures assigned tasks differently. However, all the distinctively human activities required more ability to learn than had simpler ways of life, and as human cultures became steadily more complex, the emphasis on learned behavior increased.

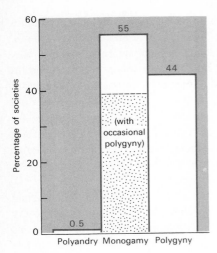

Figure 11-17 Distribution of marriage norms in human societies. The data are based on 854 societies representing all regions of the world and for which rather full information is available in the human relations area files. Monogamy is the most frequent form of marriage, although in 39% of societies the predominant monogamy is accompanied by occasional polygynous marriages. (Based on data from Bourguignon and Greenbaum, 1973)

This evolutionary history may help to account both for the wide range of sexual behaviors and sexually differentiated behaviors that exist among groups within our own culture and for the much wider range that has been seen among human cultures. Some anthropologists and psychologists also see in this history a possible basis for those tendencies toward differences in temperament and ability that we have already described. Let us consider briefly this approach to sex differences and then turn to the kaleidoscopic picture of sexuality among human cultures.

From the results of research on human prehistory and studies of anthropology, Beach (1977) has proposed the following explanation of the evolution of behavioral characteristics of human males and females (pp. 18–19):

It is conceivable that, as human evolution proceeded, natural selection operated to produce or widen genetic differences between males and females, which slowly but progressively improved the capacities of the two sexes to perform their separate roles, and thus increased the effectiveness of the social group as a survival mechanism. Potentially adaptive sex differences could have involved both emotional and intellectual traits, but the most significant variables might well have been sex-related differences in certain motivational characteristics and special types of learning ability. . . . Sex differences in such ''potentials'' or ''propensities'' would be relative rather than absolute. They would be manifest in more rapid and efficient learning of masculine patterns by males and feminine patterns by females.

The power and flexibility of human learning, made possible by the large human brain, have permitted an amazing variety of sexual patterns among human societies and subcultures. It is not that ultimate biological constraints for reproduction can be ignored but rather that human biological capacities can be used with great flexibility and can be incorporated into cultural systems that interpret sexuality in vastly different ways. When Kinsey published his descriptions of sexual behavior in the United States in the 1940s and 1950s, many people were surprised at the differences among American subcultures, which were defined by region, education, and religion. But much more extreme differences have been described by anthropologists (see, for example, Davenport, 1977). Almost opposite attitudes toward sexuality can be found: In some cultures sexuality is evaluated negatively—shunned and even feared—and sexual intercourse is largely restricted to procreation. In other cultures the expression of sexuality is highly valued and encouraged; it is celebrated in art and song, and beauty of all kinds is associated with sex.

Neural and Hormonal Mechanisms of Reproductive Behavior

With sexual behaviors showing such variety and complexity, many investigators are seeking to find and understand the bodily mechanisms that mediate them. What are the neural and hormonal mechanisms of female and male reproductive behaviors? If hormones help to organize brain circuits, what are the basic features of these circuits? Are some of the organizational effects of hormones due to their effects on peripheral bodily structures rather than on the nervous system?

Although our understanding of the bodily mechanisms that mediate sex behaviors is still far from complete, many parts of the picture are being filled in by animal experiments and clinical studies with people. We will consider first the attempts to trace the neural pathways and brain regions involved in reproductive behavior, and then we will turn to hormonal modulation of these circuits. Since interactions between the nervous system and the endocrine system are so prominent in reproductive behavior, we cannot present completely separate accounts of them; instead we will go back and forth between neural mechanisms and hormonal influences.

Sexual Reflexes

Some neurally based

erection & ejaculation in humans at spinal level

Some motor responses are based on neural circuits within the spinal cord, as we saw in Chapter 10, and this basis has also been found in the case of sexual reflexes. If the spinal cord is transected or severely injured so that no nerve impulses pass between the brain and the part of the spinal cord below the injury, some reflexes can still be elicited in the lower trunk and legs. These reflexes are mediated entirely by spinal circuits. Both erection and ejaculation in males are mediated at the spinal level, in humans as well as other mammals. A paraplegic patient (a person whose spinal cord has been transected or severely injured by an accident or disease) cannot exercise voluntary control over the musculature below the level of the transection, nor is there any sensation from below this level. But by using spinal reflexes, some paraplegic men have been able to impregnate their wives.

Sexual Reflexes in Spinal Male Animals

In male dogs, stimulation of different parts of the penis can evoke three different reproductive reflexes (Hart, 1978):

1. Shallow pelvic thrusting with partial erection of the penis. In normal copulation this response precedes achievement of intromission.
2. The intense ejaculatory reaction. Expulsion of seminal fluid is accompanied by strong pelvic movements and alternate stepping of the hind legs. This reflex is the only reproductive reflex with a short duration and an abrupt end. Continued stimulation does not prolong the response.
3. Maintenance of erection and emission of seminal fluid. This response lasts about 10–30 minutes, decreasing in intensity. This reflex probably occurs in the intact male during the copulatory lock.

These reflexes are differentially affected by the hormone testosterone, as we will see.

Coordinate autonomic & skeletal nerves

Note that these spinal reflex patterns include not only responses mediated by autonomic nerves (such as erection and ejaculation) but also responses mediated by skeletal nerves (for instance, movements of the legs). This is a good example of the coordination of autonomic and skeletal responses.

Sexual Reflexes in Spinal Female Animals

Spinal female dogs and cats show several reflexive mating responses to stimulation of the genital region. For example, the hindquarters curve toward the side of stimulation, and the tail is raised or arched to the side. In the intact animal, these receptive responses would aid intromission. Elevation of the pelvis (the lordosis response) is not seen in animals whose spinal cord is cut in the midthoracic region, because this reflex requires back muscles above as well as below the level of transection. In animals with spinal transections in the upper thoracic region, elevation of the pelvis can be elicited.

In the rat the lordosis response is so stereotyped that it has been assumed to be a spinal reflex, but so far this assumption has not been proved. This observation has led to the suggestion that the lordosis response is organized in the brain in the rat (Pfaff et al., 1972). But it is hard to believe that a response that is mediated at the spinal cord in the dog and cat requires brain circuits in the rat (Hart, 1978), and study of this issue is continuing.

Hormonal Influences on Spinal Reflexes

Spinal reflexes are not fixed and unchangeable; rather they can be modulated in several ways. Normally nerve impulses from the brain facilitate some spinal circuits and inhibit others. For example, a female cat or dog may be stimulated to assume the full receptive posture just by the presence of the male without any tactile contact between the two; a sow may show lordosis when stimulated by the mating call of the boar. This stimulation occurs through distance receptors and pattern analysis in the brain. In addition, spinal reflexes show some changes that can be classified as learning—they show habituation, sensitization, and conditioning (such changes will be considered in Chapter 16). Another main source of modulation of spinal reflexes is the action of hormones, which we will take up here.

Studies of dogs with intact nervous systems have shown that surgical removal of the gonads (castration) causes reduced motivation to copulate in some males; even in those dogs that continue to mount and achieve intromission, there is a pronounced decline in duration of the copulatory lock, and the intense ejaculatory response may be less strong than in intact animals. Experiments were therefore undertaken with spinal dogs to see whether testosterone would affect these reflexes.

In the experiments the dogs were castrated, and each animal was given injections of testosterone during one period of testing and no hormone during another period (Hart, 1968). The most obvious effect of lack of testosterone was on the duration of stimulated lock response. Dogs that were first tested with testosterone injections had a mean lock duration of 12 minutes; after hormonal treatment was stopped, the duration declined progressively and fell to 4 minutes after 60 days. Dogs that were first tested without testosterone treatment showed a lock duration of 2 minutes; when treatment started, this time increased progressively, reaching 10 minutes after 60 days. While these autonomic aspects of the responses were clearly affected by presence or absence of testosterone, the skeletal responses of the leg and the back muscles did not reveal any effects of hormonal treatment.

The results just reviewed clearly demonstrate effects of hormone on reflexes that are mediated by spinal circuits, but do they prove that the hormone is acting directly on spinal neurons? Not necessarily. It has been pointed out that both sensory and motor components of the response mechanism are affected by sex hormones. Sensory receptors in the skin of the rat's penis atrophy in the absence of androgens and regenerate when androgens are restored (Beach & Levinson, 1950). Also, the size of the penile muscles that play a role in erection and ejaculation is affected by androgens (Hayes, 1965). Can effects of hormones on such peripheral structures account for all the hormonal influences without any necessary involvement of the nervous system? One way to differentiate between effects of a hormone on the penis and effects on the nervous system is to use the hormone dihydrotestosterone (DHT). At low levels (25 micrograms, μg) DHT maintains the size and sensitivity of the penis, but it does not maintain sexual behavior in castrated rats (Feder, 1971; Hart, 1973). Thus these findings go against an exclusively peripheral interpretation. Higher doses of this hormone (200 μg or more) do restore sexual responses, and with these doses the hormone was found to accumulate in ventral horn cells in the spinal cord (Sar & Stumpf, 1977). Thus it appears that at least part of the influence of testosterone must be exerted directly on spinal neurons if sexual behavior is to occur.

[handwritten margin note: at least in part direct affect on spinal reflex (neurons)]

Brain Regions and Reproductive Behavior

While many aspects of copulatory reflexes are integrated at the spinal level, sexual attraction and appetitive behavior in vertebrates require the involvement of brain regions. Furthermore, brain regions modulate the activity of the spinal circuits, either facilitating or inhibiting them. The preoptic area has been demonstrated to be important for male reproductive behavior in a wide range of vertebrate classes—mammals, birds, frogs, and fish. For female reproductive behavior, the important brain regions lie in the anterior or lateral hypothalamus, posterior to the preoptic area. Let us survey briefly some of the main evidence that has led to these conclusions about preoptic and hypothalamic sites. Figure 11-18 shows these regions in the rat, a species used in much of this research.

[handwritten margin note: – preoptic area for men – anterior hypothalamus for females]

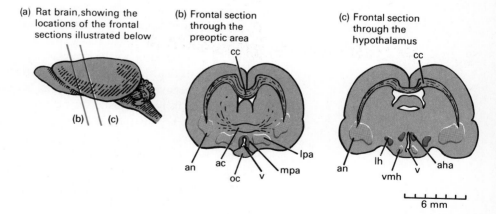

Figure 11-18 Areas of the rat brain important to reproductive behavior. The lateral view of the rat brain in (a) shows where the sections in (b) and (c) were made. (ac, anterior commissure; aha, anterior hypothalamic area; an, amygdaloid nuclei; cc, corpus callosum; lh, lateral hypothalamus; lpa, lateral preoptic area; mpa, medial preoptic area; oc, optic chiasm; v, third ventricle; vmh, ventromedial hypothalamus.) Experiments described in the text show the medial preoptic area (in b) to be important for male reproductive behavior of several species. A lesser amount of work indicates that for female reproductive behavior, one or another hypothalamic site (in c) is important.

The Preoptic Area and Male Reproductive Behavior

[handwritten: larger nucleus in male preoptic area]

Several experimental techniques provide convergent evidence elucidating involvement of the preoptic area (POA) in male reproductive behavior. Recall that a nucleus in the medial preoptic area is much larger in the male rat than in the female, as we saw in Figure 11-10. Bilateral destruction of this area abolishes copulatory behavior in male rats (Larsson & Heimer, 1964), cats (Hart et al., 1973), dogs (Hart, 1974), and monkeys (Sling et al., 1978). Although the spinal circuits are intact in these animals, they lack facilitation from brain circuits, and only occasional mounting without intromission is seen in the brain-lesioned males. In intact rats, facilitating the POA by stimulating it with implanted electrodes increases or even elicits male sex behavior (for example, Perachio et al., 1973; van Dis & Larsson, 1971). Cells in the POA pick up androgens from the blood. Male sex behavior can be restored in castrates by implanting small quantities of testosterone directly into the brain; in the rat, at least, the POA is the most sensitive region for producing this effect (Johnston & Davidson, 1972).

The preoptic area also is involved in the male copulatory behavior shown by female rats. Female rats often mount other females and sometimes show pelvic thrusts. These behaviors were abolished in females after lesions of the POA, but typical female sex behavior was not affected (Singer, 1968). Implants of testosterone in the POA of females facilitated mounting behavior; estradiol also facilitated mounting, but only if implanted posterior to the POA (Dörner et al., 1968a, b).

Hypothalamic Areas and Female Reproductive Behavior

The hypothalamic foci where lesions effectively abolish female sex behavior vary somewhat from species to species. In the rat, lesions of the anterior hypothalamus were most effective in abolishing typical female reproductive behavior, whereas in the female hamster, lesions of the ventromedial nucleus were more effective than those in the anterior hypothalamus (Kow et al., 1974). But lesions in some hypothalamic regions posterior to the preoptic area have been found to be effective in several mammalian species. (Studies of nonmammalian species have focused more on male sex behavior than on female sex behavior.) Implants of estradiol into the hypothalamus facilitate female sex behavior in several species of rodents; usually these sites are slightly anterior to the sites of effective lesions. Thus in the rat, hormone implants into the medial preoptic area increase lordosis responses, whereas lesions in the anterior hypothalamus abolish these responses (Singer, 1968). It is chiefly the lesion experiments that differentiate between the neural substrates that underlie male and female sex behavior and that point to the importance of one or another hypothalamic route for female reproductive behavior.

Hormonal Influences on Reproductive Behavior

[handwritten: 1. form structure; 2. facilitate behavior; 3. modulatory role]

Hormones are involved in at least three different ways in reproductive behavior:

1. As we have already seen, a fetal testicular hormone plays an organizational role in forming the reproductive structures and shaping certain brain circuits.
2. Hormones also play an activational role in eliciting or facilitating reproductive behavior that is based on already organized neural circuits and effector structures.
3. Beyond these two generally acknowledged roles, it now appears that hormones play a further **modulatory role** (or maintenance role) in maintaining

the sensitivity of neural circuits and other structures to hormonal influences; that is, the presence of hormones over prolonged periods affects the susceptibility of tissues to respond to short-term changes in hormonal level.

As we hinted earlier, the successive phases of the ring dove's reproductive behavior can be related to the activational and modulatory roles of hormones. In this section we will first look at these hormonal influences on the behavior of the dove. Then we will consider hormonal influences on reproductive behavior in nonhuman mammals, and finally we will examine hormonal influences on human sexual behavior.

Hormonal Influences on Reproductive Behavior of the Dove

Investigators are trying to cross-check hypotheses that specific hormones elicit or modulate certain behaviors by performing three kinds of experiments:

1. Remove the hormone or the source of the hormone and see if the behavior disappears or at least declines substantially.
2. Replace the hormone and see if the behavior then reappears.
3. Determine, under normal conditions, whether the concentration of the hormone increases in the system when the behavior appears and decreases when it disappears.

Research with the ring dove illustrates the use of these methods.

The roles of hormones in the complementary sequences of reproductive behaviors of the female and the male dove have been the subject of intensive research since the 1950s. Although the full story is still not known, this work demonstrates several major relations between hormones and behavior.

The initiation of courtship behavior by the male dove requires both a normal adult level of testosterone and also the presence of an adult female. An adult male that has been castrated for several weeks will not show much courtship even in the presence of a female. (Circulating testosterone is metabolized by the body in a few hours, but androgens set up effects in the nervous system that last for days or weeks.) Replacement of testosterone by injection then leads to courtship of the female. Even a normal adult male will not court unless a female is present, so the stimulus situation is just as important as the hormonal and neural factors. When a male that has been isolated is placed in the presence of a female, the concentration of testosterone begins to rise. An increase can be detected within a few hours, and the level continues to rise during the first few days of courtship (see Figure 11-19). This rise is not necessary for initiation of courtship, however, because it occurs after courtship has begun. In free-living birds of several species, the males show elevated levels of testosterone during the season when they attempt to establish territories and to attract mates, competing aggressively with other males (Wingfield et al., 1987).

The behavior of the female dove during courtship shows a clearer relation to levels of sex hormone than does that of the male. The sight of a male directing courting responses toward her causes a rise in the female's level of estrogen; this rise begins a day or two after the pair is caged together and continues until about the start of nest building (Figure 11-19a). The different responses of the female during

Figure 11-19 Hormonal changes in male and female ring doves during the reproductive cycle. Levels of estradiol, progesterone, and testosterone were measured in blood plasma. The weight of the crop gives an index of the level of the hormone prolactin, which cannot yet be measured directly in the dove. Note the rapid rise of estradiol in the female and of testosterone in the male early in courtship (prelaying days). (Adapted from Silver, 1978)

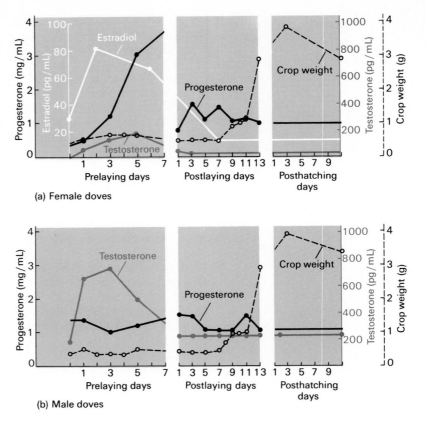

(a) Female doves

(b) Male doves

successive stages of courtship correlate closely with the rise in the level of estrogen (Cheng, 1974). Removal of the ovaries abolishes the female's attractive and proceptive responses. Administration of estrogen restores these responses, and they return to the normal order of stages, from wing flipping to proceptive crouching. Estrogen alone does not restore nest-orientated behaviors, however; these require the addition of progesterone. Normally progesterone also rises during courtship, but it lags behind estrogen (Figure 11-19a). The combination of these two hormones leads to nest-cooing, nest building, egg laying, and incubation.

Normally birds that have not gone through courtship and nest building will not incubate eggs that are presented to them. But if an isolated female is given estrogen and progesterone injections for a few days before the eggs are offered, then she will incubate. Similarly, an isolated male will incubate if he has been prepared by injections of testosterone and progesterone.

The suppression of mating behavior during incubation has been attributed to secretion of prolactin from the anterior pituitary. Although prolactin certainly causes production of crop milk by both parents, the effect on willingness to mate seems to be exerted chiefly on the female. Tests of willingness to mate are made by taking birds at various stages of the reproductive cycle and placing them in another cage with a new partner. A female will accept a new partner at certain parts of the cycle but not while prolactin secretion is high. When prolactin has declined in the female and she has stopped feeding the squabs, the female is ready to breed again. The male, even though his prolactin level remains substantial, is willing to recommence mating with his partner, so prolactin does not inhibit mating in the male.

Thus the progress from one behavioral stage to the next in the reproductive cycle is guided in the female by changing amounts of estrogen, progesterone, and prolactin. The changes in the ovarian hormones, estrogen and progesterone, are elicited by perception of the courtship of the male, and the increase in prolactin is elicited by tactile and visual stimulation from the eggs. The synchrony between the behavior of the two parents that is necessary for successful reproduction is mainly achieved by the male's adjusting his behavior to that of the female; it does not appear to be influenced by changing levels of hormones. Except for the effect of prolactin on secretion of crop milk, the only hormonal requirement of the male is a steady supply of testosterone. This hormone, plus stimulation by the behavior of the female, allows him to play his successive roles during the reproductive cycle.

It is worth stressing the bidirectionality of the behavioral interactions. In terms of our circle schema, interventions into the hormonal system affect behavior, and behavioral interventions (such as allowing a female to see a courting male) affect levels of hormones. Some of these interventions and effects are summarized in Figure 11-20.

Figure 11-20 Summary of behavioral and hormonal changes during the reproductive cycle of ring doves. The figure shows the reciprocal relations between male and female and between behavioral and somatic variables.

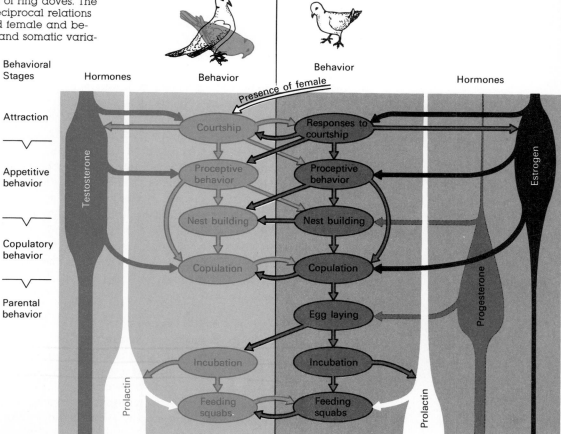

Hormonal Influences on Reproductive Behavior in Nonhuman Mammals

How do hormones influence the reproductive behaviors of mammals? To what extent is the story similar or different for different species of mammals? To what extent is it the same or different for the two sexes? We will pursue these questions next.

In some species of mammals, the nonpregnant adult female goes through a regular cycle of production of estrogen and progesterone. In the rat this cycle lasts 4–5 days, and in women the cycle lasts about 28 days (whence the term *menstrual cycle,* from the Latin word *mens,* meaning ''month''). Reproductive males of these species maintain a rather steady day-to-day average level of androgens (although there are marked short-term fluctuations). The cyclical production of hormones in females is necessary for regular production of ova and associated changes in the reproductive tract. Do these hormonal changes also govern attractive, proceptive, and receptive behavior? In the case of males, do individual differences in levels of androgens account for individual differences in strength and amount of reproductive behavior? We will consider these questions in the following paragraphs.

Hormonal Effects in Nonprimate Females

In rats, and in practically all nonprimates, the levels of ovarian hormones are a major determinant of female reproductive behavior. Removing the ovaries results in virtually complete disappearance of sexual receptivity. Over two thousand years ago, Aristotle reported a fact already well known to animal husbandmen: ''The ovaries of sows are excised with a view to quenching their sexual appetites.'' Modern knowledge of hormones has enabled investigators to perform replacement experiments in order to find the respective roles of estrogen and progesterone and to determine relations between levels of hormones and various behaviors. In some species estrogen alone will restore receptive behavior (for example, in cats, dogs, rabbits, goats, rats, and monkeys), whereas in others the two hormones appear to be necessary (such as in mice, guinea pigs, and cows). In rats repeated low doses of estrogen restore the lordosis response. Receptivity can be quantified by the ''lordosis quotient,'' the number of times a female shows lordosis divided by the number of times she is mounted by a male. The lordosis quotient was found to be monotonic function of the dose level of replacement estrogen (Davidson et al., 1968). Estrogen does not produce its behavioral effects promptly; it must be present at least one or two days before any behavioral effect is seen. Progesterone than takes a few hours to produce its effects. The complete series of events that intervene between the rise of ovarian hormones in the circulation and the facilitation of neural circuits is still only incompletely known.

Hormonal Effects in Primate Females

Among primates the dependence of female reproductive behavior on hormones is less clear, and there is much individual variability. Some female monkeys remain receptive after removal of the ovaries, although males are less attracted to them. Attempts to correlate female proceptivity with the stage of the menstrual cycle have not produced completely consistent results. Furthermore, testosterone as well as estrogen and progesterone seem to play a role in behavioral changes during the cycle. It is important to note that animal studies show larger interindividual differ-

Figure 11-21 Fluctuations in hormone levels of female monkeys during the menstrual cycle. (picogram = 10^{-12} gram; nanogram = 10^{-9} gram) (Adapted from Herbert, 1978)

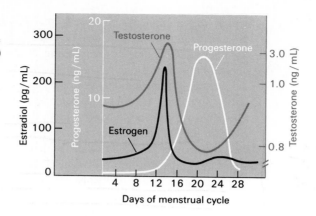

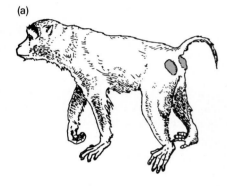

(a)

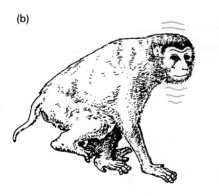

(b)

Figure 11-22 Proceptive behavior of female rhesus monkeys. (a) The "presentation" posture in which the female turns her genitalia toward the male, the tail deviated aside. The "sex skin," indicated in brown, is actually pink. (b) The "head duck" in which the female bobs her head up and down and raises her genitalia from the ground. (Herbert, 1978)

ences in initiative (proceptivity) than in receptivity. In the face of these complexities, we can only sketch some of the better established findings and some current conclusions.

The attractiveness of female monkeys to males is increased by the surge of estrogen that occurs slightly before the middle of the menstrual cycle (Figure 11-21). The estrogen causes changes in secretions of the vagina and causes swelling of the "sexual skin" on the buttocks (Figure 11-22). Some males respond to both the olfactory and the visual stimulation. In an ovariectomized female, replacement therapy with estrogen restores attractiveness, as measured by responses of males. This effect holds whether the estrogen is put into the general circulation or whether it is placed directly into the vagina, so the nervous system need not be involved. Adding progesterone, which normally increases after ovulation (Figure 11-21), decreases attractiveness.

Some investigators think that proceptive behavior—attempts by the female to get the male to copulate—is affected especially by the androgens that are secreted by the female's ovaries and adrenal glands. Note in Figure 11-21 that female monkeys actually have higher blood concentrations of testosterone than of estradiol (the most common estrogen), but estradiol is a far more potent hormone on a per-weight basis. Note also that the level of testosterone fluctuates more or less in parallel with the level of estrogen during the menstrual cycle. If both the ovaries and the adrenal glands are removed, then no more testosterone is secreted. Replacement therapy with cortisol makes up for basic adrenal functions, and replacement with estrogen restores attractiveness, but the otherwise normal, healthy female makes few attempts to gain access to the male (Everitt & Herbert, 1972). Thus estrogen, which makes female primates attractive and receptive, does not cause proceptive behavior. Injections of testosterone restore proceptive behavior, and so does implantation of a small amount of testosterone into the hypothalamus (Everitt & Herbert, 1975), so this effect is mediated by the nervous system. Whether proceptivity varies with the changes in testosterone levels during the menstrual cycle is not entirely clear. Irregular variations in secretion and in cycle length complicate such research. Using statistical procedures to allow for such variability, Bonsall et al. (1978) conclude that there is a statistically significant peak in proceptivity of female rhesus monkeys in midcycle, and seven of nine females showed such an effect. On the other hand, Johnson and Phoenix (1978) were unable to find a significant relation between proceptive behavior and hormonal fluctuations during the menstrual cycles of ten female rhesus monkeys. If there is indeed a cycle of proceptivity in female monkeys, it is largely overshadowed by interindividual and intraindividual variability.

The need for care in interpreting observations in this field is shown by the apparent effects of progesterone on proceptivity. Injection of this hormone increases the attempt of female monkeys to gain access to males. Does this mean that progesterone stimulates brain regions for proceptive behavior, just as testosterone does? Further work showed that very small doses of progesterone placed in the vagina counteracted the local effects of estrogen but did not alter blood levels. In this case, too, the females increased their sexual invitations to males. The experimenters suggest that the progesterone made the females less attractive to males, who were therefore responding sluggishly. So the females had to increase their attempts to invite copulation in order to obtain responses from the males (Baum et al., 1977).

Female primates show some receptivity even though they are ovariectomized and adrenalectomized. Replacement of estrogen causes a major increase in receptivity, and adding androgen brings receptivity to fully normal levels. Progesterone seems to have little or no effect on receptivity. Thus the different aspects of reproductive behavior of female primates are all affected by hormonal levels, and the sex hormones—estrogens, progesterones, and androgens—play clearly different roles in this behavior.

Hormonal Effects in Male Mammals

Male mammals show less prompt effects of gonadal hormones on reproductive behavior than do females. In the rat, for example, some males show the full copulatory pattern for weeks after castration, even though androgens disappear from the body within a few hours; the behavior does decline, but not nearly as rapidly as the levels of androgens (Davidson, 1966b). Among cats, males with mating experience continue to mate for weeks after castration, but few males without prior experience copulate in tests that follow castration (Rosenblatt & Aronson, 1958). Thus neural circuits that have been altered by experience may not require hormonal facilitation.

Differences among males in reproductive behavior seem to depend less on levels of androgens in the circulation than on differences in sensitivity of brain cells to the hormones. The first clue to individual differences in sensitivity came from surprising results on the measurement of reproductive behavior in male guinea pigs before and after castration (Figure 11-23; Grunt & Young, 1953). The animals were divided into three groups—high, medium, and low—according to their preoperative performance on mating tests. Under replacement therapy (days 27–36) the groups showed the same ranking (Figure 11-23), and doubling the dose of testosterone did not alter this ranking. In male ring doves, individual differences in male courtship behavior are also restored after castration by androgen replacement therapy (Hutchison, 1971). Results such as these have led workers to consider the possibility of individual differences in sensitivity of neurons to hormones.

In our discussion of the development of the reproductive structures, we noted that occasional genetic males are insensitive to androgens and therefore develop an external female appearance. Less complete differences in sensitivity are also possible. Sensitivity to hormones can also vary over time. It has often been observed that the longer the number of weeks after castration before replacement therapy has begun, the larger are the doses needed to restore reproductive behavior. The same effect has been shown for replacement by brain implants of testosterone in the dove

Figure 11-23 Hormone level does not completely determine amount of sex behavior. After castration of male guinea pigs reduced their sex activity, the same amount of testosterone was given to each animal, beginning at week 26. The group that had shown high sex activity before castration became high again; the animals that were originally the lowest remained lowest. Doubling the amount of hormone did not increase the ratings. (Adapted from Grunt and Young, 1953)

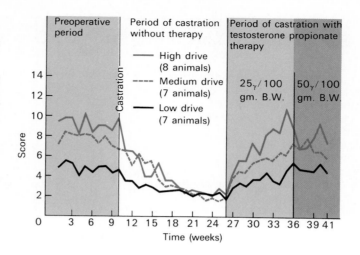

(Hutchison, 1976). This result demonstrates that the decline in sensitivity is a cerebral effect and is not caused by peripheral (sensory or muscular) changes. Moreover, brain circuits may normally be more sensitive to androgens than are peripheral structures. Thus to keep rats mating normally requires only half the level of testosterone needed to keep their seminal vesicles at normal weight (Davidson, 1972). Thus variations of androgen levels within or above the normal range do not affect sexual performance. Somewhat higher levels of secretion provide a safety factor, ensuring that performance will not be adversely affected by fluctuations in the rate of secretion (Damassa et al., 1977), but they do not cause superior performance.

Hormonal Influences on the Sexual Behavior of Women

Attempts to relate hormonal levels to sexual behavior in women are based on several sorts of evidence—the variations in hormonal levels that occur normally during the menstrual cycle, departures from the normal cycle because of some deficiency in the neuroendocrine system, and effects of administered hormones, usually for purposes of birth control. Many studies, reviewed by Bancroft (1978), have investigated the relative frequency of sexual intercourse during the menstrual cycle, but the results are not clear-cut. Most studies report a peak following menstruation, although some report a peak before menstruation and some report a peak around midcycle at the time of ovulation. A peak at midcycle would be understandable in that it would increase the possibility of fertilization, but the evidence for such a peak is mixed and inconclusive. Rather the picture is one of individual variability.

The use of oral contraceptives does not seem to have major effects on the timing of intercourse during the cycle. This observation indicates that the exact timing of the ovarian hormones is not of major behavioral importance; neither is the timing of the hypothalamic and pituitary hormones, since they are inhibited by the oral contraceptives (see Box 11-2).

Cessation of menstruation in women before the age of menopause may be traced to any of three levels in the neuroendocrine system. The most common cause is at the hypothalamic level. The surge of luteinizing hormone (LH) that is required for ovulation does not occur, although there is a steady level of secretion of LH and

BOX 11-2 | Hormones in Reproduction and Contraception

Investigation of the female endocrine cycle is making it possible to control reproduction both to aid people in having the children they want and in avoiding having unwanted children. The human menstrual cycle will be discussed here in relation to reproduction. Whether this cycle can be related to changes in behavior is considered in this chapter.

During a 28-day menstrual cycle, follicle-stimulating hormone (FSH) from the anterior pituitary begins to rise a few days before the menses and stimulates development of an ovarian follicle with its egg (Box Figure 11-2). FSH also stimulates the ovary to secrete estrogens, principally estradiol, which act on the uterus to build up its inner lining. The estrogens reach their peak around day 12, which triggers a surge in production of luteinizing hormone (LH) that occurs the next day; ovulation follows within 24 hours. The follicle that released the ovum now becomes a corpus luteum, which secretes the hormone progesterone. Progesterone causes further development of the uterine wall that prepares it for implantation of a fertilized egg. If an egg is fertilized, after undergoing several cell divisions, it secretes a hormone that keeps the corpus luteum producing progesterone. Later the placenta secretes progesterone. If fertilization does not occur, the secretion of progesterone declines after about day 24, which leads to the sloughing off of the lining of the uterine wall in menstruation.

For women in whom ovulation does not occur regularly, the regularity can often be improved by hormonal treatment. Sometimes such treatment causes several eggs to be released at the same time, so that births of quintuplets or sextuplets are more common than they were before the advent of induced ovulation.

Prevention of ovulation can also be accomplished by hormonal treatments, which is the basis of the birth control pills that have been developed since the 1950s. These pills combine a synthetic estrogen with progestin, a progesteronelike compound. These synthetic hormones perform two functions:

1. They suppress the pituitary gonadotropic hormones through negative feedback, so there is no stimulation of a follicle to develop an ovum; that is,

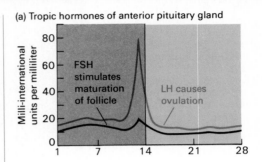

(a) Tropic hormones of anterior pituitary gland

FSH stimulates maturation of follicle

LH causes ovulation

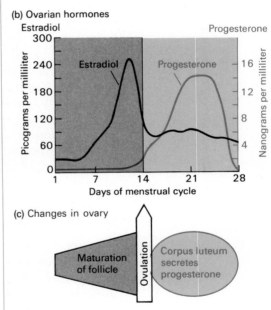

(b) Ovarian hormones

Estradiol   Progesterone

Estradiol   Progesterone

Days of menstrual cycle

(c) Changes in ovary

Maturation of follicle | Ovulation | Corpus luteum secretes progesterone

Box Figure 11-2 Cycles of changes during the human menstrual cycle: (a) tropic hormones of the adrenal pituitary gland, (b) ovarian hormones, and (c) the ovary.

the brain detects the elevated level of steroid hormones in the blood and therefore does not send gonadotropic-releasing factor to the pituitary.
2. They act to stimulate the uterine wall and thus cause a menstrual cycle.

follicle-stimulating hormone (FSH). This surge appears to be the most vulnerable stage in the female reproductive sequence (Federman, 1979). It is inhibited in many conditions, including nutritional deficiency, pathological refusal to eat (anorexia nervosa), and many kinds of psychological distress or anxiety. This condition, often called hypothalamic amenorrhea or psychic amenorrhea, demonstrates the importance of neural control of the ovarian hormones. A rarer cause of amenorrhea is a pituitary defect; in this case the levels of both LH and FSH are low, unlike the condition in hypothalamic amenorrhea. Amenorrhea may also be caused by ovarian failure, but this condition is rare in young women.

At the average age of 48 in the United States, a woman stops producing ripe follicles in the ovaries, and menopause occurs. There is a sharp increase in FSH at this time, showing that the failure is not in the central command but in the ability of the ovaries to respond. Because of the feedback relations in control of the ovarian hormones, a decline in their level causes a rise in FSH (Figure 7-12). The failure of production of ripe ova, of course, makes conception impossible. Lack of development of follicles also prevents the secretion of estrogen and progesterone by the ovaries, although some estrogen may still be secreted by the adrenal cortex. The decline in the level of estrogen may produce a variety of symptoms, but it does not cause cessation of sexual behavior.

Thus while the endocrine system is vital for reproduction, individual differences in hormonal levels have not been shown to influence strongly the frequency or quality of sexual behavior. Bancroft concludes: "There has been a widespread need to find a simple hormonal key to the understanding of human sexual behavior. There is no reason why we should expect to find simple relationships" (1978, p. 514).

Hormonal Influences on the Sexual Behavior of Men

In healthy men from ages 18 to 60, the values of testosterone show a rather wide normal range from about 350 to 1000 nanograms per 100 milliliters of blood. Individual differences within this range appear to have no significance for sexual behavior. Beyond the age of 60 or so, the mean value of testosterone tends to fall progressively, although about half the healthy men over 80 still have values that are within the normal range for younger men.

A man who complains of lack of potency or fertility often also shows a testosterone value below 400 and/or a low sperm count. Current methods often permit diagnosis of the level of the neuroendocrine system that is deficient, and appropriate therapies then aid many cases. A disorder can occur at any of three levels:

1. The hypothalamus may not furnish normal amounts of the gonadotropin-releasing hormone (GnRH).
2. The pituitary may not release sufficient amounts of luteinizing hormone (LH) and follicle-stimulating hormone (FSH). The pituitary gonadotropins are not released steadily but in pulses, so more than one sample is required for an adequate test. If the values are low, GnRH can be administered to see whether the pituitary will respond with normal release of LH and FSH.
3. The failure may be in the testes, which, although they are being stimulated by adequate amounts of pituitary gonadotropin, are not producing enough testosterone. In this case the level of LH is found to be above normal, since the hypothalamus and pituitary are not receiving enough negative feedback from testosterone.

Thus in men 60 and over, the fall in testosterone is accompanied by a rise in LH, which indicates a primary decline in gonadal function.

For men in whom the level of testosterone is below the threshold level and who complain of lack of sexual responsiveness, administration of testosterone every few weeks has been shown to be helpful in restoring sexual activity. Thus in one double-blind study, six hypogonadal men were given either a long-lasting form of testosterone or an inactive control substance once every four weeks, and they kept daily records of their sexual activity and experience. In five of the six subjects, stimulatory effects of testosterone on sexual activity were rapid and reliable, and they were not due to a placebo effect (Davidson et al., 1979).

Several studies have asked whether homosexuals differ from heterosexuals in gonadotropins or in gonadal hormones. The results, reviewed by Bancroft (1978) and Meyer-Bahlburg (1984), have varied widely. Among studies that appear to have been done carefully, some have found male homosexuals to have lower testosterone levels than heterosexuals, some have reported no significant difference, and some have found higher values for the homosexuals. It appears highly unlikely that differences in hormonal production among men can be held responsible for sexual orientation in general, although hormonal differences may be a contributing factor in some homosexual men. Fewer investigations have been made so far of possible endocrine factors in female homosexuality. The majority of women homosexuals appear to have estrogen and androgen levels within the normal range for adult females. There are indications that perhaps a third of those studied have elevated testosterone levels, but it has been suggested that problems of sampling may account for this apparent difference. Bancroft doubts that any simple answer about homosexuality will emerge from endocrine studies, but research in this area continues.

Thus in the man as in the woman, most individual differences in sexual behavior cannot be explained by individual differences in hormonal levels. Hormones are certainly important in early development of reproductive structures and in later development of secondary sexual characteristics. They also play an activational role in facilitating the initiation of sexual behaviors and in maintaining them. But wide variations in hormonal levels do not have clear effects on the amount or quality of human sexual activities. Once the neural circuits for these behaviors have been established, other sources of stimulation can suffice even in the absence of endocrine facilitation.

Summary · Main Points

1. Sex brings variety to life in many ways, including sex differences in appearance and behavior, sex-related changes in appearance and behavior over the life span, and genetic permutations that have made rapid evolution possible.

2. Mating behavior shows four stages: sexual attraction, appetitive or proceptive behavior, copulatory behavior, and postcopulatory behavior. Each stage demands interaction between the female and the male.

3. In mammals the XY or XX chromosomal pattern determines whether the gonads of the embryo will develop into testes or ovaries.

4. Two systems of primitive ducts exist in each embryo; they allow for the possible development of either masculine or feminine internal reproductive structures. The female system will develop unless a fetal testicular substance is secreted. Similarly, the external genitals assume the feminine form unless androgens transform them to the masculine appearance.

5. Sex differentiation of brain structures has been found in rats and songbirds and now in humans. The two sexes differ in the sizes and connections of some brain structures, and these differences can be altered by hormonal treatments.

6. Prenatal sexual development appears to exert some influences on human personality and behavior. Although many alleged sex differences in personality have not been substantiated, there is good evidence that, on the average, girls exceed boys in verbal ability, boys exceed girls in visual-spatial ability and in mathematics, and males of all ages are more aggressive than females. More research must be done before we can decide the extent to which these sex differences are biologically determined.

7. Successful sexual reproduction requires that the sexes come together and select suitable partners, that the time and place for reproduction be suitable, and that specific copulatory (and sometimes postcopulatory) behavior occurs. Furthermore, parental care can increase the probability that offspring will survive.

8. Sexual selection has been used to explain the reproductive advantage of certain individuals over others of their sex and species. The basis of sexual selection is the unequal investment that the two sexes make in a single offspring.

9. Evolutionary implications for human sexuality are found both in adaptations shared with other mammals and in the specific history of human evolution. The tripling of brain size in the hominid line has promoted variety and flexibility of human behavior, including reproductive behavior. During human evolution there may also have been selection for somewhat different sex roles.

10. Many of the motor responses involved in copulation are integrated by spinal circuits. Testosterone directly affects these responses in males. These spinal responses are normally modulated by the activity of brain regions.

11. Sexual attraction and appetitive behavior in vertebrates require brain activity. The preoptic area is especially involved in male reproductive behavior; hypothalamic areas posterior to the preoptic area are especially involved in female behaviors.

12. Hormones play an organizational role in developing reproductive organs and neural circuits; later they play an activational role in eliciting or facilitating reproductive behavior. They also help to maintain and modulate the sensitivity of neural circuits to hormones.

13. In the ring dove, the complementary sequences of behaviors in female and male are beautifully integrated. The female's transition from one stage to the next is marked by changes in the levels of estrogen, progesterone, and prolactin. The male can ensure his role at most stages with an adequate and steady supply of androgens and a tendency to follow the behavioral lead of the female as she moves from one stage to the next.

14. In mammals, reproductive females of some species go through a regular cycle in which levels of estrogen and progesterone rise and fall. In the rat, proceptivity and receptivity depend on the hormonal cycle. In primates the dependence on hormonal changes is less complete.

15. Estrogen is the main determinant of attractiveness of the female primate to the male. Progesterone decreases attractiveness by acting on peripheral structures such as the sexual skin on the buttocks. Proceptive behavior is determined largely by the androgens secreted by the ovaries and adrenal glands. Both estrogens and androgens enhance receptivity, although some receptivity remains even in the absence of either hormone.

16. Male mammals show less clear-cut effects of hormones on reproductive behavior than do females. Males will continue to copulate for weeks after castration or even indefinitely, especially if they were experienced. Differences among males seem to depend less on their levels of androgens than on sensitivity of brain cells to androgens.

17. In human females and males, hormones are important in early development of reproductive structures, in later development of secondary sexual characteristics, in activating and initiating sexual behaviors, and in maintaining these behaviors. But wide variations in hormonal levels do not seem to affect the quality or quantity of sexual activities.

18. Once neural circuits for reproductive behaviors have been established, other sources of stimulation can suffice in the absence of hormonal facilitation.

Recommended Reading

Adler, N. T. (Ed.). (1981). *Neuroendocrinology of reproduction*. New York: Plenum.

Beach, F. A. (Ed.). (1977). *Human sexuality in four perspectives*. Baltimore: Johns Hopkins University Press.

Crews, D. (Ed.). (1986). *Psychobiology of reproductive behavior: An evolutionary perspective*. New York: Prentice Hall.

Daly, M., & Wilson, M. (Eds.). (1983). *Sex, evolution and behavior* (2nd ed.). North Scituate, Mass.: Duxbury Press.

DeVries, G. J., DeBruin, J. P. C., Uylings, H. B. M., & Corner, M. A. (Eds.). (1984). *Progress in brain research: Vol. 61. Sex differences in the brain*. Amsterdam: Elsevier.

Rosen, R., & Rosen, L. R. (1981). *Human sexuality*. New York: Knopf.

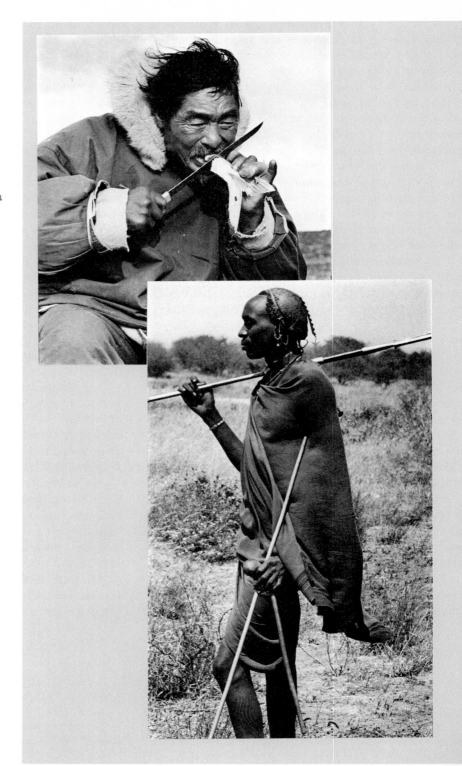

12 Heating/Cooling, Drinking

ORIENTATION

Naked inhabitants of central Australia sleep comfortably without shelter through a winter night when the temperature falls to 4°C. An American anthropologist visiting this semi-arid desert region shivers miserably under a light blanket, but after a few weeks the American adapts to the stress of the nighttime cold. Throughout this time the anthropologist and the aborigines have maintained core body temperatures close to 37°C (98.6°F). By adapting to local conditions, people have been able to live on almost all the earth's surface, except in regions of extreme cold or extreme altitude (Figure 12-1). Now human beings are even learning how to live for extended periods beneath the seas and in outer space.

Our bodies, and those of other animals, are complex life-support systems that have evolved over millions of years. Within the body the cells are kept within a narrow range of temperatures that ensures optimal functioning, even though the external temperature may be much colder or warmer. The cells are immersed in a fluid medium with nearly constant characteristics and are supplied with nutriments. These internal constancies are characteristic of mammals and birds (although we will consider certain exceptions later). As we noted in Chapter 7, Claude Bernard stressed the importance of constancy of the internal environment, and Walter Cannon coined the term **homeostasis** to describe it.

In this chapter we will consider processes that regulate body temperature and thirst (fluid content); Chapter 13 takes up the related topic of hunger (food stocks and metabolism). In many cases the regulation keeps conditions relatively constant, but in some cases there is a controlled change, such as a small drop of body temperature during sleep or a large drop during hibernation. Each of these three systems is vital in itself, and all are interrelated. For instance, maintaining body heat requires metabolic expenditure, which draws on the body's stocks of food; cooling the body involves evaporation of moisture from the lungs or body surface and thus entails loss of water. We will see other interactions among these systems later on.

(a)

Figure 12-1 Adaptation to extreme climates involves changes in behavior, physiology, and anatomy. Examples are seen in comparing (a) an Eskimo from arctic Alaska with (b) a Nilotic inhabitant of tropical Africa. ((a) © Karl H. Maslowski, 1977/Photo Researchers, Inc. (b) © Lynn McLaren/Photo Researchers, Inc.)

(b)

Properties of Homeostatic Mechanisms

The homeostatic mechanisms that regulate temperature, body fluids, and metabolism are all **negative-feedback systems.** That is, in each case a desired value or zone is established; this desired value is called the **set point,** or set zone, by analogy with the setting of a thermostat (Figure 12-2). (We first discussed negative-feedback systems in connection with regulation of hormonal secretion in Chapter 7.) When the heating system of a building is controlled by a thermostat, a drop in temperature below the set level will activate the thermostat, which turns on the heating system.

Figure 12-2 Thermostatically controlled heating and cooling systems.

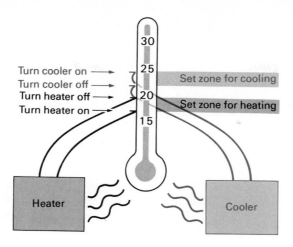

When the thermostat registers a small rise in temperature, it turns off the heating system. (Note that there is a small range of temperature between the ''turn on'' and ''turn off'' signals, otherwise the heating system would be going on and off very frequently. Thus there is really a ''set zone'' rather than a ''set point.'') The setting of the thermostat can be changed; for example, it can be turned down at night to save energy. The building may also have a cooling system that is thermostatically controlled with set temperatures that cause it to go on and off. Thus active systems prevent the internal temperature from getting either unpleasantly hot or uncomfortably cool.

The body temperature for most mammals and birds is usually held within a narrow range, about 36–38°C (97–100°F)—though the set zone can be altered depending on overall conditions and current goals of the organism. Temperatures in certain parts of the body are monitored closely by internal receptors, and deviations from the desired value are noted. If the deviation exceeds a threshold amount, then corrective action brings the temperature back within the set zone. Physiological adjustments are carried out automatically and internally whereas other corrective actions require behavioral interaction with the environment, including learned behaviors in some cases. This model appeals to many investigators because it is similar to an understood physical system and can encompass many behavioral observations. Nevertheless, a negative-feedback circuit with a built-in set zone is not the only kind of model being considered, as we will see.

Multiple Control Systems

For guaranteed performance of vital mechanical and electrical functions, space capsules are designed with multiple monitoring units and with parallel systems or backup devices. Thus the failure of one unit or system is not lethal, since other systems can guarantee the same objective. Evolution has similarly endowed our bodies with multiple systems. In fact, this endowment has complicated researchers' attempts to find the mechanisms that ensure the constancy of bodily conditions; interfering with one or another mechanism often produces little or no effect, since parallel or alternative mechanisms assume the burden. Nevertheless, we will seek to find the signals that initiate corrective action and the signals that terminate it for each homeostatic bodily system.

Regulation of Body Temperature

Our cells cannot remain alive outside certain limits of temperature, and much narrower limits mark the boundaries of effective functioning. Above about 45°C (113°F) most proteins become inactivated and begin to lose the precise three-dimensional structure they need for their bodily functions. Below 0°C (32°F) the water inside cells begins to form ice crystals that disturb the internal organization and the membranes of cells, killing them. The enzyme systems of mammals and birds are most efficient only within a narrow range around 37°C; a departure of a few degrees from this value seriously impairs their functioning. Even though cells can survive wider fluctuations, the integrated actions of bodily systems are impaired. Children, for example, may become delirious with a few degrees of fever. Other animals have a wider tolerance for changes of bodily temperature. Isolated nerves and muscles continue to function reasonably well in physiology laboratories even though their temperature is changed over 10°C or more, but the integrated behavior of mammals cannot survive such a change of internal temperature.

Types of Regulation

For centuries it has been recognized that mammals and birds differ from other animals in the way they regulate body temperatures. Our ways of characterizing the difference have become more accurate and meaningful over time, but popular terminology still reflects the old division into "warm-blooded" and "cold-blooded" species; warm-blooded included mammals and birds, while all other creatures were called cold-blooded. As more species were studied, it became evident that this classification was inadequate. A fence lizard or a desert iguana—both cold-blooded—usually has a body temperature only a degree or two below ours and so is *not* cold. Therefore the next distinction was made between animals that maintain a constant body temperature, called **homeotherms** (from the Greek *homeo,* meaning "same," and *therm,* meaning "heat"), and those whose body temperature varies with their environment, called **poikilotherms** (from the Greek root *poikilo,* meaning "varied"). But this classification also proved inadequate, because among mammals there are many that vary their body temperatures during hibernation. Furthermore, many invertebrates that live in the depths of the ocean never experience a change in the chill of the deep waters, and their body temperatures remain constant.

The current distinction is between animals whose body temperature is regulated chiefly by internal metabolic processes and those whose temperature is regulated by, and who get most of their heat from, the environment. The former are called **endotherms** (from the Greek root *endo,* meaning "internal"), and the latter are called **ectotherms** (from the Greek root *ecto,* meaning "exterior"). Most ectotherms do regulate their body temperature, and they do so mainly by behavioral means, such as locomoting to favorable sites or changing their exposure to external sources of heat. Endotherms (mainly mammals and birds) also regulate their temperature by choosing favorable environments, but primarily they regulate their temperatures by making a variety of internal adjustments.

Regulation by use of external heat sources was the first to evolve and uses rather simple mechanisms, so we will discuss ectothermy before endothermy.

External/Behavioral Thermoregulation

The marine iguana of the Galapagos Islands stays under water for an hour or more eating seaweed in water that is 10–15°C cooler than its preferred body temperature. Then it emerges and lies on a warm rock to restore its temperature. While warming up, it lies broadside to the sun to absorb as much heat as possible (Figure 12-3a). When its temperature has reached the desired level, 37°, the iguana turns to face the sun and thus absorb less heat, and it may extend its legs to keep its body away from warm surfaces (Figure 12-3b). Many ectotherms regulate their temperatures in similar ways. Some snakes, for example, adjust their coils to expose more or less surface to the sun and thus keep their internal temperature relatively constant during the day.

Bees regulate the temperature inside the hive by their behavior. When there are larvae or pupae, the bees keep the temperature in the brood area of the hive at 35–36°C. When the air temperature is low, the bees crowd into the brood area and shiver, thus generating heat. When the air temperature is high, the bees reduce the

Figure 12-3 Behavioral control of body temperature. (a) A Galapagos marine iguana, upon emerging from the cold sea, raises its body temperature by hugging a warm rock and lying broadside to the sun. (b) Once its temperature is sufficiently high, the iguana reduces its surface contact with the rock and faces the sun to minimize its exposure. These behaviors afford considerable control over body temperature. (Photographs by M. R. Rosenzweig)

(a) (b)

temperature in the brood area by fanning with their wings and by evaporative cooling (Heinrich, 1981).

Mammals and birds, which are endotherms, also control their exposure to the sun and to hot or cold surfaces in order to avoid making excessive demands on their internal regulatory mechanisms. For example, herring gulls stand oriented toward the sun or broadside to it, depending on the ambient temperature (Lustick, Battersby, & Kelty, 1978). In hot desert regions many small mammals, such as the kangaroo rat, remain in underground burrows during the day and appear aboveground only at night when the environment is relatively cool.

Human populations have devised many cultural practices to adapt to conditions of cold or heat. For example, Eskimos learned to design clothing that insulates well but permits dissipation of heat through vents. Other Eskimo cultural adaptations include the design of efficient shelters, sharing of body heat, choice of diet, and use of seal oil lamps (Moran, 1981).

Whether an animal is an ectotherm or an endotherm, if it is placed in a laboratory situation where there is a gradient of temperature from warm to cold, it will spend most of its time at its preferred environmental temperature. The choices show that the preferred temperature differs from species to species. Even animals as simple as bacteria converge on an optimal temperature zone. A nude sedentary person prefers an air temperature of about 28°C (82°F); a well-clothed sedentary person prefers an air temperature of about 22°C (72°F). If a person or animal is placed in an experimental situation that consists of two compartments, one heated above the subject's preferred temperature and the other cooled below the preferred temperature, then the subject alternates frequently between the two regions and thereby helps to keep its internal temperature within the desired range.

To summarize this topic, a leading researcher in the area, Bligh (1985), categorized thermoregulatory responses of ectotherms and endotherms into three behaviors: (1) changing exposure of the body surface, for example, huddling or extending the limb; (2) changing external insulation, for example, by using clothing or nests; and (3) selecting a place or surround that is less thermally stressful, for example, by moving to the shade or into a burrow. These classes of thermoregulatory behaviors are affected by a variety of factors, including homeostatic signals, hormones, biological rhythms, and experiential and cognitive factors, with the latter looming as especially important in the regulation of human thermoregulatory behavior. With respect to the latter point, humans seldom wait for their body to get cold before putting on a coat. Humans anticipate homeostatic signals because they are able to use representations of the world based on experience.

Internal Regulation

Our usually accurate regulation of body temperature results from a precise balancing of processes that increase and maintain heat against processes that lose heat. What are some of these processes of heat gain and heat loss? How and where is temperature monitored in the body? How are the processes that gain, conserve, and lose heat controlled? When an animal reduces the burden of regulating temperature by entering a state of torpor (as some species of bat do daily) or by hibernating for months (as ground squirrels do), is the animal's temperature still controlled, or does it simply fall to that of the environment? We will answer these questions in the following paragraphs.

Table 12-1 Influence of Activity on Heat Production of an Adult Person

Activity	Heat (kcal/hour)
Resting or sleeping	65
Awake, sitting quietly	100
Light exercise	170
Moderate exercise	290
Strenuous exercise	450
Very strenuous exercise	600

Mechanisms of Heat Gain

Metabolism—utilization of stored food in the body—releases heat, so all living tissues produce heat. Table 12-1 shows the amounts of heat produced per hour by an adult person engaging in different activities, from sleep to strenuous exercise. (The unit of heat is a kilocalorie, abbreviated kcal; 1 kcal is enough heat to raise the temperature of 1000 cubic centimeters of water 1°C.) When the body is at rest, a considerable proportion of the heat is produced by the brain (about 20 out of 65 kcal). As bodily activity increases, the heat production of the brain does not rise much, but that of the muscles can increase nearly tenfold. Muscles, like mechanical devices, produce a good deal of heat while they are accomplishing work. Muscles and gasoline engines have about the same efficiency; each produces about four or five times as much heat as mechanical work. Some of the main ways the human body gains, conserves, and dissipates heat are shown in Figure 12-4.

Heat production is closely related to the area of body surface, since heat exchanges with the environment occur largely at the surface of the body. A big animal like an elephant has relatively little skin surface compared to the volume of its body; a small animal like a canary or a rat has a large surface-to-volume ratio. The ratio of surface to volume decreases with increasing volume, as shown in Figure 12-5. Surface-to-volume relations are important for generating and dissipating body heat, because heat is produced by body tissue (volume) and dissipated at the body surface.

Table 12-2 shows the body sizes of several species in terms of weight, surface

Table 12-2 Body Size and Heat Production of Some Birds and Mammals

Species	Body Weight (kg)	Body Surface (m²)	Energy Output per Day		
			Total (kcal)	Per Unit of Body Weight (kcal/kg)	Per Unit of Body Surface (kcal/m²)
Canary	0.016	0.006	5	310	760
Rat	0.2	0.03	25	130	830
Pigeon	0.3	0.04	30	100	670
Cat	3.0	0.2	150	50	750
Human	60	1.7	1,500	25	850
Elephant	3,600	24	47,000	13	2,000

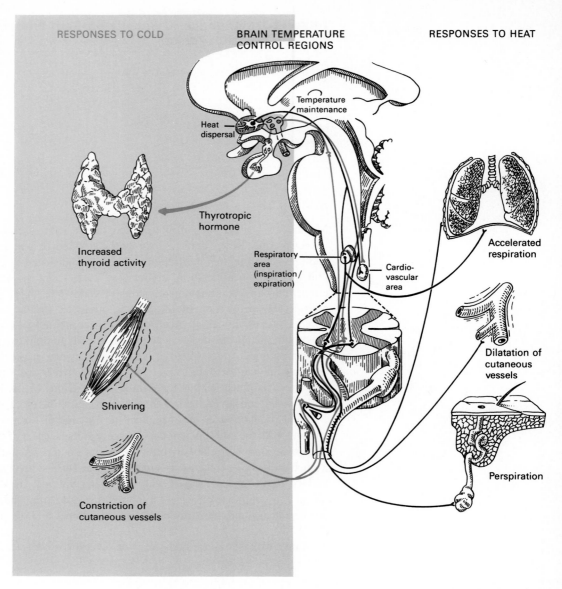

Figure 12-4 Some of the primary ways the human body gains, conserves, and loses heat, and their neural controls.

area, and heat production. Smaller animals, because of their larger surface-to-volume ratios, lose heat more rapidly to the environment, so they must produce more heat in relation to body size than do larger animals. For example, from the data of Table 12-2, we see that it takes 20 cats to equal the weight of a person, but the 20 cats produce twice the heat of the person of equal weight. (And that is why we have to buy so much cat food.) Per unit of body weight, small animals produce much more heat than large ones; from canary to elephant the ratio is more than 20 to 1.

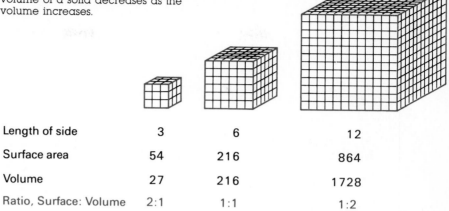

Figure 12-5 The ratio of surface to volume of a solid decreases as the volume increases.

Length of side	3	6	12
Surface area	54	216	864
Volume	27	216	1728
Ratio, Surface: Volume	2:1	1:1	1:2

The rate of heat production can be adjusted to suit conditions, particularly in certain organs. Deposits of brown fat are found especially around vital organs in the trunk and around the cervical and thoracic levels of the spinal cord. Under cold conditions the sympathetic nervous system stimulates increased metabolism of brown fat cells. The most conspicuous means by which heat is generated is muscular activity. At low temperatures nerve impulses cause muscle cells to contract out of synchrony, producing shivering rather than movements. In humans, shivering becomes evident when body temperature approaches 36.5°C. This response spreads from facial muscles to the arms and legs. The metabolic intensity of this response is reflected in the fivefold increase in oxygen uptake observed in extreme shivering. Shivering of small amplitude, not visible to casual observation, can be detected by fine intramuscular electrodes.

Mechanisms of Conserving Heat

In the face of an internal energy crunch, conservation in the body is important. When the environmental temperature is considerably lower than the preferred internal temperature, it requires great metabolic expense to keep body heat at the desired level. If animals did not have effective ways of conserving heat, they would die. With strong selection pressure for heat conservation, many different adaptations have evolved; a few of the principal ones concern body size, body shape, and skin adaptations.

Body size is an important means of conserving heat. Since the main need for warmth is at the core of the body, peripheral tissues can insulate the inner organs; the skin and the extremities are usually cooler than the core of the body. Because large animals do not need to make up as much heat loss as do smaller animals, the larger animals have lower metabolic rates, as we have already seen. Within a group of closely related mammals or birds, those living at lower temperatures will be larger than those living in warmer environments. And even in the temperate zone, a very small mammal like the shrew has to eat almost incessantly to meet its metabolic needs.

Figure 12-6 Two forms with the same volume but different surface areas.

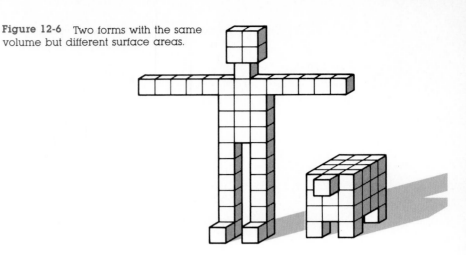

Figure 12-7 Variation in the size of the external ear in foxes from (a) arctic, (b) temperate, and (c) tropical climates.

(a)

(b)

(c)

Shape also affects heat conservation. The humanoid form in Figure 12-6 has exactly the same volume as the squat figure beside it, but the more slender form has almost twice as much surface area as the compact form. Because of its lower surface-to-volume ratio, the more compact body conserves heat better and therefore is better able to protect its internal temperature in a cold climate. Among human groups there has been a tendency for taller, more slender body forms to evolve in the tropics and for shorter, stockier physiques to evolve in the colder regions (Figure 12-1), but migrations and intermixture of human stocks have blurred this tendency. Among many animal groups, body appendages are smaller in arctic species than in related tropical species. Figure 12-7 illustrates this by showing variations in the size of the external ear in species of foxes from different climatic zones.

Fur of mammals and feathers of birds are special adaptations of the skin that serve as insulation from the environment. In cold environments large mammals usually have a thick coat of fur, but small mammals cannot grow thick fur without interfering with their locomotion. If fur or feathers are to serve their function of insulation properly, they must be kept in good condition, which is one reason why many mammals and birds spend a great deal of time grooming and preening. For an animal like the sea otter that spends its life in cold water, insulation is vital. A small area of matted fur that provides a channel for heat loss could be fatal to the otter. Most species of birds have a preen gland or oil gland near the base of the tail; the oil from this gland is used to dress the feathers and waterproof them.

Mechanisms of Heat Loss

Getting rid of heat can be important too. Even in a cold climate, energetic muscular activity produces heat that must be dissipated rapidly. In a hot climate, body temperature must be kept below that of the surrounding environment. Evaporation is an effective way to dissipate heat, and many ways of promoting evaporation have evolved. In people, horses, and cattle, sweating helps to prevent overheating. Many species, such as dogs, cats, and rats, have no sweat glands over most of their body surface, so they pant to evaporate moisture from the mouth, throat, and lungs. Rats have been observed to spread saliva over their fur to increase the area for evaporation. Honeybees have been found to prevent overheating of the head by using evaporation (Heinrich, 1979). At high air temperatures, they regurgitate droplets of nectar onto the tongue; evaporation reduces their temperature and at the same time concentrates the nectar.

Sending blood to the surface of the body helps to dissipate heat, as long as the environment is cooler than the body, and many animals lose heat in this way. The large ears of the elephant increase its surface appreciably; they are highly vascular, and blood is shunted there to dissipate heat. Rabbits also use their ears as major heat exchange surfaces. In some species the ears account for a quarter of the body surface. The amount of blood flow in the ear is controlled by the autonomic nervous system; when blood flow to the ear is constricted, body temperature rises. In human beings, too, the size of blood vessels in the skin strongly influences body temperature. Some areas are especially involved in this type of thermoregulatory response, including parts of the face, hands, and feet. Within these areas blood flow can vary 100-fold.

Camels adjust to heat in one of two ways, depending on the availability of water. When water is freely available, the camel uses evaporation through panting and respiration to keep its temperature between 36 and 38°C. When water is scarce, the camel lets its temperature drop to 34° in the cool of the night and allows it to rise as high as 41° in the afternoon. This process saves about 5 liters of water a day. By allowing its temperature to fall below normal during the night, the camel is capable of storing more heat during the day than if it started at 37°C (Schmidt-Nielsen, 1964).

On a hot day a dog can chase a rabbit until the rabbit dies from overheating of the brain. Why is this exertion lethal for the rabbit but not for the dog? Although running raises the body temperature of both animals, the dog's brain has a special cooling system that the rabbit's brain does not (Baker, 1979). This cooling system combines adaptations of the respiratory system for evaporation and of the circulatory system for a heat exchange network (see Figure 12-8). This network of blood vessels is located just below the base of the brain. In it, cooler venous blood coming from the periphery reduces the temperature of arterial blood before it enters the brain. The heat exchange occurs because the veins and arteries both subdivide into many fine vessels that come into close contact with each other. This intricate network of vessels was called the **rete mirabile,** or "wonderful net," by Galen, the great Roman anatomist of the second century. Galen observed this network in the brains of some domestic animals and supposed that it must be present in human beings. He thought that it was the site of transformation of the "animal spirit" (or animate fluid) from the arteries into the "psychic spirit" (or fluid) that he believed traveled through the hollow tubes of nerves. Actually there is no rete in human beings or in other primates, nor is there one in horses, rodents, marsupials, and many other species. Carnivores possess the rete, and so do sheep and cattle.

The venous blood that cools the rete comes mainly from the regions of the nose and mouth, and increased evaporative cooling occurs here during exercise. In the dog the extensive branching of the bones in the nasal passages provides a surface that is larger than all the rest of the body. The combined evaporative and heat exchange system is so effective that during the first 5–10 minutes of exercise, the dog's brain temperature actually falls below the resting level.

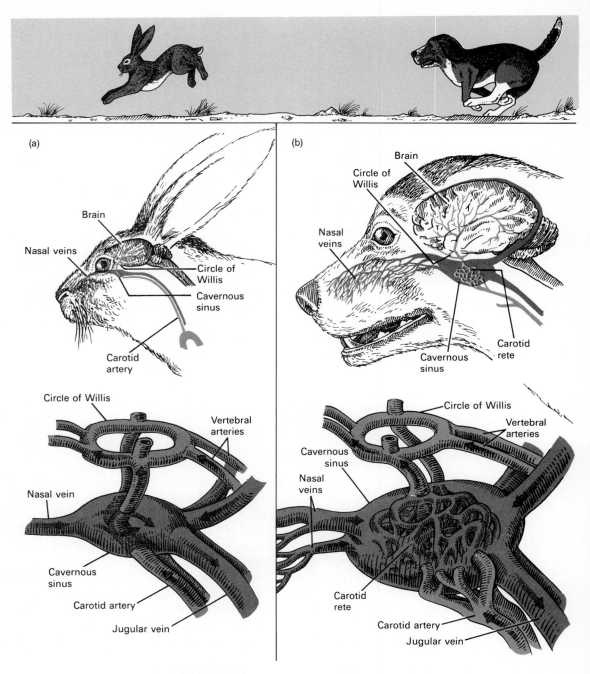

(a)

Brain

Nasal veins

Circle of Willis

Cavernous sinus

Carotid artery

Circle of Willis

Vertebral arteries

Nasal vein

Cavernous sinus

Carotid artery

Jugular vein

(b)

Brain

Circle of Willis

Nasal veins

Carotid rete

Cavernous sinus

Circle of Willis

Vertebral arteries

Cavernous sinus

Nasal veins

Carotid rete

Carotid artery

Jugular vein

Figure 12-8 Why exertion overheats some animals but not others. Exercise produces heat, but some species, such as the dog, have a special heat exchange cooling system. Other species, such as the rabbit, do not possess this special cooling system.

Monitoring and Regulating Body Temperature

The nervous system controls and regulates all the processes of heat production and heat loss that we have just reviewed, with assists in some cases from the endocrine system. What parts of the nervous system are active in these processes and what principles operate? Research, which has been conducted on these topics since the last century and at a rapid pace in recent years, has provided some answers.

In the 1880s physiologists observed that localized destruction of tissue in the hypothalamus of dogs elevated the body temperature. In classic experiments Barbour (1912) manipulated the temperature of the hypothalamus in dogs by implanting silver wires. When the wires were heated, body temperature fell; when the wires were cooled, body temperature rose. These results suggested that body temperature is monitored in the hypothalamus and that when temperature there departs in either direction from the desired level, compensatory actions are initiated. Later work involving electrical recording from single cells revealed cells that responded specifically to small increases or decreases of brain temperature; these cells are scattered throughout the preoptic area (POA) and the anterior hypothalamus.

Lesion experiments in mammals indicate that there are different sites for two kinds of regulation: (1) regulation by locomotor and other behaviors that mammals share with ectotherms and (2) physiological regulations that are characteristic of endotherms. Lesions in the lateral hypothalamus of rats abolished behavioral regulation of temperature but did not affect the autonomic thermoregulatory responses such as shivering and vasoconstriction (Satinoff & Shan, 1971; Van Zoeren & Stricker, 1977). On the other hand, lesions in the POA of rats impaired the autonomic responses but did not interfere with such behaviors as pressing levers to turn heating lamps or cooling fans on or off (Satinoff & Rutstein, 1970; Van Zoeren & Stricker, 1977). Here is a clear example of parallel circuits for two different ways of regulating the same variable.

Receptors at the surface of the body monitor temperature and provide information used in controlling thermoregulatory processes. If you enter a cold environment without protective clothing, you soon begin to shiver—long before there is a fall in your core temperature. If you enter a hot greenhouse or a sauna bath, you begin to sweat before there is any rise in your hypothalamic temperature. So the skin provides information to central circuits, which promptly initiate corrective action. The spinal cord has also been found to be a temperature-monitoring region; heating or cooling the cord in experimental animals causes compensatory responses. Information from different regions—hypothalamus, skin, and spinal cord—converges on the thermoregulatory circuits, a topic we will take up next.

Thermoregulatory Circuits

The neural circuits that regulate temperature are known only in part, and debate continues over which of a few possible basic designs is actually employed. Some possibilities that we will consider are these:

1. A feedback circuit with an endogenous (within the body) set point.
2. Multiple feedback systems, each controlling a different thermoregulatory response.

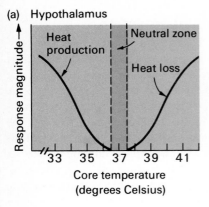

(a) Hypothalamus

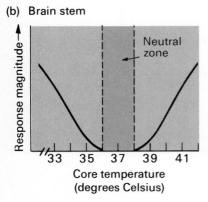

(b) Brain stem

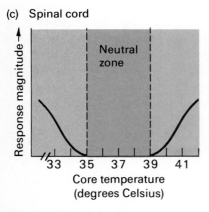

(c) Spinal cord

Figure 12-9 Thermal neutral zones of thermoregulatory systems at different levels of the nervous system. The neutral zones are narrower at the higher levels of the nervous system than at the lower levels. (Adapted from Satinoff, 1978)

3. Cross-linked reflex circuits for warmth sensors and cold sensors without an endogenous set point.

Many investigators employ the model of a negative-feedback circuit with an endogenous set point; this model is the thermostat model that we mentioned early in this chapter and showed in Figure 12-2. Later in this chapter we will see a feedback model for control of the body's stores of water, and Chapter 13 includes a feedback model for control of food.

A single "thermostat" seems inadequate, however, to account for all the facets of thermoregulation. For one thing, there appear to be different brain sites for behavioral and autonomic regulation of temperature, as already noted. But even two thermoregulatory circuits are not sufficient, as Satinoff (1983) emphasizes. For example, Roberts and Mooney (1974) warmed small sites in the diencephalon and mesencephalon of rats and measured three responses in the repertoire of heat loss behaviors. As a rat is exposed to increasing heat, it first grooms, then it moves about actively, and finally it lies quietly in a sprawled-out position. Local heating of brain did not produce this sequence; instead each of these behaviors tended to be elicited by heating points in a different region. The sprawled extension posture was elicited by heating points in the preoptic area, whereas grooming was elicited only from points in the posterior hypothalamus and ventral medulla. Locomotion was elicited by heating points that ranged from the septal area through the midbrain to the medulla, and it could occur in combination with sprawling or with grooming. These data indicate multiple independent channels from thermal detectors to motor effectors. There seems, in addition, to be a hierarchy of thermoregulatory circuits, some located at the spinal level, some centered in the midbrain, and others at the diencephalic level. Transections of the nervous system or ablations reveal some capacity for regulation at each of these levels. But spinal or decerebrate animals die in the cold or heat because they do not respond until body temperature deviates 2–3°C from normal values.

Satinoff (1983) interprets these findings in the following way: The thermal neutral zones are broader in lower regions of the nervous system (Figure 12-9). The thermoregulatory systems at the diencephalic level have the narrowest neutral zones, and they normally coordinate and adjust the activity of the other systems. This arrangement can give the impression of a single system, although in reality there are multiple interlinked systems.

While most investigators have conceived of a system with an established (although adjustable) set point, others have claimed that it is unnecessary to postulate a reference signal or set point (Bligh, 1985). These investigators suggest that the facts of temperature regulation can be accounted for in the following way: Stimulation of cold sensors activates heat production, and stimulation of warmth sensors activates heat loss. The apparent set point would then be the crossover point of the sensitivities of the two kinds of receptors (Figure 12-10). As body temperature deviated in either direction from this neutral point, heat production or heat loss would be elicited, thus tending to drive temperature back to the neutral point. In other words, the reciprocal antagonism of the two systems would accomplish homeostatic regulation of temperature. So that only one of the two processes would be active at a time, even though the distributions of sensitivities of the two kinds of receptors might

Figure 12-10 Apparent temperature set point at the crossover of response curves of cold sensors and warm sensors.

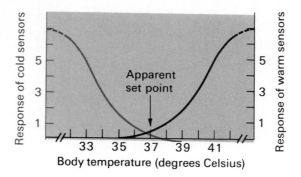

Figure 12-11 A thermoregulatory system involving reciprocally antagonistic components. No set point or internal reference signal is required. (Adapted from Bligh, 1979)

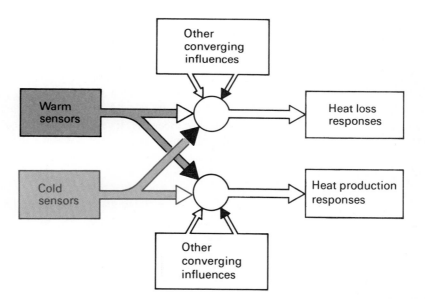

overlap, there would be crossed inhibitory influences between the two pathways; only the more strongly excited of the two would then lead to its response. Figure 12-11 shows the basic layout of such a circuit.

Could such a circuit without an explicit set point accommodate changes in the neutral or target temperature, such as those that occur with circadian rhythms, torpor, or hibernation? Such changes could be accomplished by modulating the activity of the receptor inputs of the two main circuits. Thermosensitive neurons in the mammalian hypothalamus are active over a range of temperatures, so there is scope for modulation. Although most of these neurons in a nonhibernator (guinea pig) became silent below 30°C, many in a hibernator (golden hamster) remained active to 15°C or below (Heller, 1985).

Temperature Control During Hibernation

Ground squirrels in the Sierra of California hibernate for about eight months of the year. During much of this time they conserve energy by allowing their temperature to fall to within a few degrees of their surroundings; core temperature may fall to 10°C or less. The hibernating ground squirrel curls up into a fur-covered ball, and its respiration and heart rates fall far below the waking values. At intervals during the long period underground, they awaken and warm up for a few hours, and then they hibernate again. Many species of small mammals show similar patterns.

The fall of body temperature as ground squirrels enter hibernation does not mean that they have abandoned endothermic regulation and returned to a more primitive ectothermic level. Unlike ectotherms, hibernators can rouse and return to a normal body temperature of 37° even when the surrounding temperature remains low. Recent laboratory studies have indicated that they lower their set point for temperature in a regular progressive manner. At any given hypothalamic temperature, if an implanted hypothalamic probe is cooled by only a few degrees, the squirrel responds by rewarming. Thus it appears that the animal's thermostat is turned down gradually as it enters into hibernation (Heller, Cranshaw, & Hammel, 1978). If the ambient temperature falls to dangerously low levels, the squirrel rouses; this "fail-safe" mechanism prevents it from freezing.

The alarm signal for rewarming and arousal is not located in the same place for all species. In the ground squirrel it is in the head; if the hypothalamus is slightly warmed while the rest of the body is chilled below the alarm level, the squirrel continues to hibernate. In contrast, the garden dormouse can be aroused by applying a cold stimulus to its feet. The dormouse hibernates on its back with its feet sticking up into the air, whereas the ground squirrel tucks its feet inside its ball-shaped hibernation posture.

It has been suggested that hibernation evolved as an adaptive extension of the decrease in temperature that occurs during the phase of sleep when EEG activity is slow (Heller, 1979). Electrophysiological studies have indicated similarities between hibernation and slow-wave sleep.

Learned Temperature Regulation

The Australian aborigines mentioned at the beginning of this chapter are able to withstand cold nights by exerting precise and localized vasomotor control over skin temperature. Unlike European or American subjects, they do not increase heat production during cold nights to compensate for loss. Rather they prevent loss by constricting their peripheral blood vessels, starting at temperatures higher than those at which Europeans first begin to show constriction. When the aborigines use fires, their vasomotor control shows precisely localized responses. The arterioles on the side of the body toward the fire are dilated, allowing heat to radiate in, while the arterioles on the other side are closed to prevent loss of heat (Hicks, 1964). This control is exerted through neural regulation of the constriction of blood vessels. A familiar and visible example of this control is seen when a person blushes. Since the nervous system regulates temperatures, people can learn to gain some control over it, as we will see next.

Learned Control of Skin Temperature

Probably all of us are capable of exerting precise localized control over peripheral circulation and skin temperature with suitable training. This notion has been studied not only out of curiosity but also to aid people who suffer from conditions such as

Raynaud's disease and migraine headaches. In Raynaud's disease the blood supply to the fingers may shut off upon exposure to the cold and sometimes in response to emotional states. Raynaud's disease can make it hard for a person to work in the cold and may subject its sufferers to frostbite.

Biofeedback training is effective in conferring self-regulation of skin temperature (Taub, 1977; Taub & School, 1978). Here are the basic procedures: The subject is seated comfortably in a dimly illuminated room with temperature-sensing devices attached to various points on one hand. The mean hand temperature is shown to the subject in terms of the intensity of a white feedback light. After a period of stabilization, the subject is instructed either to increase hand temperature (and the brightness of the light) or to decrease it. Subjects are told, "You will be able to change hand temperature without moving. In fact, it has been found that tensing the muscles interferes with this. Simply stay relaxed and think of your hand as being warmer [cooler]." Subjects are usually trained for a few successive days.

While many experimenters and laboratories have reported success with biofeedback training for temperature control, some have not, and the size of the effects varies considerably. Taub and School (1978) have reported experimental evidence that the "person factor" is extremely important in thermal biofeedback training—that is, the quality of interaction between the experimenter (or therapist) and the subject (or patient). With one group the experimenter maintained an impersonal attitude, using last names, discouraging extraneous conversation, and avoiding eye contact. With another group the same experimenter adopted a friendly attitude, using first names, making frequent eye contact, and encouraging development of a friendly relationship. Both groups showed significant learning, but at the end of the ten-day training period, the impersonally treated group showed a mean effect of only 0.7°C, whereas the group treated in a friendly manner achieved a mean change of 2.3°. This striking difference was the largest effect found for any of the numerous variables tested in these experiments. The investigators conclude: "It is almost impossible to overemphasize the importance of the experimenter-attitude variable for the success of thermal biofeedback training. It seems highly probable that the person factor is equally critical for the success of other types of biofeedback training" (p. 617). It is not yet known how the "person factor" translates into physiological mechanisms. Perhaps it involves no more than setting a level of muscular tension that favors learning.

Patients with Raynaud's disease were found to be as capable as normal subjects of learning to control skin temperature. Several studies have indicated that such training helps these patients to deal with cold and other stresses and to avoid disabling vasoconstriction. Positive results have also been reported for control of migraine headaches by biofeedback training of vascular responses. This subject appears to be a promising one for further research and application.

Learned Control of Core Temperature

Central or core temperature can also be affected by training. This has been studied in experiments in which animals are conditioned to the administration of morphine, which induces a rise in body temperature (hyperthermia). If the drug is given in conjunction with specific stimuli, those stimuli alone eventually elicit the rise in body temperature. Thus if a rat is injected with morphine once a day for several days in a particular experimental room, then just placing the animal in that room will elicit the rise in temperature. But the situation is more complex. The animal responds to the morphine-induced hyperthermia by mobilizing heat-dissipating responses and reducing its temperature. Therefore if a rat is given an injection of morphine at the same time every day for several days and then the drug is withheld, a hypothermic response will occur at about the time that the morphine had been given.

Understandably, reports have been somewhat varied and even contradictory, since both hyperthermia and hypothermia were being conditioned. In experimental conditions to test different hypotheses, it has recently been found that hyperthermia and hypothermia become associated with different kinds of stimuli. Hyperthermia becomes associated with environmental stimuli such as visual or auditory stimuli, but it does not become conditioned to the time of day at which the drug is administered. In contrast, hypothermia becomes conditioned to temporal cues but not to environmental cues (Eikelboom & Stewart, 1981). Thus both increases and decreases of body temperature can be learned, depending on the circumstances.

Development of Temperature Regulation

The young of many species cannot regulate their temperatures well and must be protected by their parents. Most birds must keep their eggs warm. For this purpose the parents of many species develop a specially vascularized area of skin (the brood patch), which transfers heat efficiently to the eggs. Rat pups, which are born without hair, cannot maintain body temperature if they are exposed individually to cold. The rat mother keeps her pups protected in a warm nest, and this response of the mother is related to her own thermoregulation (see Box 12-1). By the time their eyes open and they begin to stray from the nest at about 13 days of age, rat pups have developed physiological thermoregulatory reflexes and have grown a coat of fur. Other rodents, such as guinea pigs, are born in a more mature state. They show endothermic regulation from the start and do not need maternal protection.

Even though young rat pups are not capable of endothermic regulation, they do show ectothermic regulation, which evolved earlier. They accomplish ectothermic regulation by huddling together and varying their positions in the huddle in accordance with changes in temperature. Rectal temperatures and oxygen consumption were measured in pups of different ages placed in a cool chamber (23–24°C), either singly or in a group of four. In the 5-day-old rats, the temperature of the isolated pups fell below 30° in less than an hour, whereas those in the group maintained their temperatures above 30° for 4 hours (Alberts, 1978). Huddling also significantly reduced oxygen consumption. The form of the huddle changes according to ambient temperatures; it is loose in warm temperatures but tightly cohesive in the cold. The pups frequently change positions in the clump, sometimes being inside and at other times at the periphery. In effect, they share the costs and benefits of this group activity. Thus early in the rat's development its thermoregulation depends on social interaction, whereas later in its development the rat becomes capable of individual endothermic regulation.

Evolution of Temperature Regulation

Endotherms pay substantial costs for maintaining a high body temperature and keeping it within narrow limits. Much food must be obtained and metabolized, elaborate regulatory systems are required, and departures of body temperature of a

BOX 12-1 | The Warmth of Maternal Care

The rat mother's nesting with her young is determined largely by her own thermoregulation. That is, the mother receives thermal stimulation from the young, and this stimulation is a major determinant of how long she stays in contact with the young on successive visits to the nest (Leon, Croskerry, & Smith, 1978). The nursing mother has a somewhat elevated body temperature caused by increased levels of prolactin and ACTH. When she returns to the nest, contact with the pups helps to dissipate heat until they become warmed and no longer remove heat from the mother; at this point she leaves the nest. As the pups become larger and produce more heat, the mother progressively shortens her stays in the nest.

The role of maternal temperature in duration of mother-pup contact was tested in experiments in which the temperature of the mother was raised artificially (Woodside, Pelchat, & Leon, 1980). Different sites of warming were used—subcutaneous, body core, or brain. For the first two sites a fine coil of wire was inserted in a surgical operation; the wire was used to raise temperature by about 10°C over the existing

level. Such heating reduced mean nest stays to about half the normal duration. In tests of effects of heating the brain, warming electrodes were implanted surgically into the medial preoptic area in some rats and into the caudate-putamen in others. On trials in which heating was used, it began 15 minutes after a mother had started contact with her litter. On trials where no brain stimulation was delivered, contact lasted about 70 minutes. When the preoptic area was heated, the mother left the nest in about 3 minutes, that is, about 50 minutes earlier than she would have done without the brain stimulation. When the caudate-putamen was heated, the mother terminated contact about 25 minutes later; this slow response presumably occurred because the spread of heat from the caudate eventually warmed thermosensitive neurons elsewhere in the brain. So the contact in the nest that helps to keep the young rat pups warm is actually regulated not in terms of the temperature of the pups but in terms of that of the mother.

few degrees in either direction impair functioning. What benefits may have led to the evolution of such a complicated and costly system in comparison with that of the ectotherms who get along with somewhat lower mean body temperatures and who have a greater tolerance for changes in temperature?

Increasing the capacity to sustain a high level of muscular activity over prolonged periods may have been the principal gain in the evolution of endothermy (Bennett & Ruben, 1979). Table 12-1 showed that a person's metabolic rate (or heat production) can rise almost tenfold between resting and very strenuous exercise. A five- to tenfold increase above the resting level is the greatest that vertebrates can achieve, whether they are ectotherms or endotherms. It would probably be advantageous to have a higher differential between rest and maximal activity, but apparently about 1:10 is the best that vertebrate metabolic processes can handle. So to be able to engage in a high level of activity for a sustained period of time, an organism must maintain a relatively high basal level of metabolism.

Ectotherms are capable of bursts of high activity for a few minutes; in this case a major contribution is made by anaerobic metabolism. But a high level of anaerobic metabolism can be maintained for only a few minutes, and then the animal must rest and repay the oxygen debt. Thus reptiles and amphibians can perform as well as mammals and birds for short periods but not for long ones. Ectotherms can escape from and sometimes even pursue endotherms over short distances, but in a long-distance race the endotherm will win. It is likely that the capacity for internal thermoregulation evolved along with increasing capacity to sustain a high level of muscular activity through aerobic metabolism.

The thermoregulatory system, with its several mechanisms and different loci and levels of representation in the nervous system, has been cited by Satinoff (1983) as an illustration of the principle of evolutionary coadaptation; that is, a mechanism that evolved to serve one function turns out to have an adaptive value for a different system and evolves further to improve its value for the second system. The ectotherms already had a basic thermoregulatory system since they sensed internal and external temperatures and used this sensory ability to regulate locomotor behavior, moving into and out of different temperature zones in their environments. Then control of muscular activity, including shivering, was brought into the thermoregulatory system for internal heat production. A higher rate of heat production then made it advantageous to be able to dissipate heat quickly. Since animals at this stage already breathed and for that purpose had a good control of the vascular system, it was possible for thermal monitors to influence the rates of respiration and of peripheral blood flow. Thus different systems that already existed at the spinal and midbrain levels could be adapted to new requirements. There was no need to transfer these circuits to the forebrain. But to the extent that these functions were not handled perfectly well at the lower levels of the nervous system—if, for example, the narrower set zone of the hypothalamus conferred an advantage in natural selection— then an impetus toward a hierarchical organization evolved, with the higher centers tending to control the lower ones in thermoregulation. Another benefit of evolution of control of temperature is seen in the value of fever for fighting infection (Box 12-2).

Human evolution shows particular adaptations for thermoregulation. There has been much speculation on why human beings have hair on only part of the body surface, whereas other primates have full coats of hair. Perhaps humans evolved into "naked apes" to facilitate rapid dissipation of heat produced during prolonged pursuit of prey in their original tropical homelands. We may never be sure of the answer, but many studies have investigated differences among human groups that appear to be related to thermoregulation. Here are a few examples (So, 1980): Human body forms tend to be more linear in the tropics and more compact in arctic regions; these forms favor heat dissipation in the tropics and heat conservation in the arctic. Nostrils tend to be narrower in arctic regions, which aids conservation of heat. One worldwide survey of populations shows a correlation of 0.72 between breadth of the nose and an index that combines temperature and relative humidity (Roberts, 1973). The characteristic eyelid of Chinese people is believed to have evolved in the north to protect against loss of heat by evaporation from the eyes. Eskimos have fewer sweat glands on the limbs and trunk than do Europeans, but they have more sweat glands on the face. This distribution in the Eskimos is adaptive for the following reasons: Eskimos insulate the body from the cold by well-designed clothing, so sweat on the limbs or trunk would be uncomfortable and would defeat the insulation. When Eskimos are active, they need to dissipate heat, and the face is the only uncovered surface, so the face has to be richly supplied with sweat glands. Thus many differences in appearance among human groups appear to reflect adaptations to the thermal characteristics of the climatic zones in which they live.

BOX 12-2 | Too Hot!

During the course of a typical day, our body temperature varies less than one degree. This variation is quite regular, with the low points reached during early morning and the high points reached in late afternoon or early evening. Striking disturbances in the regularity of temperature control become evident during some illnesses and exposure to some environments. Fever is familiar to all of us as an accompaniment of disease caused by bacteria or viruses. In fact, we all view a rise in body temperature as a sign of pathology. What causes fever? Is fever biologically useful?

Fever begins with invasion of the body by microbes and the sequence of events that constitutes the mobilization of body defense mechanisms. Some microbes cause cells of the body defense systems, such as white cells in the blood, to release endogenous pyrogens—substances that elevate body temperature. These substances are the same ones that mediate inflammatory and immunological responses (Blatteis, 1984). They are carried to the brain, where they influence cells that are part of the temperature regulation system. Endogenous pyrogens act directly on nerve cells of the preoptic-anterior hypothalamus. However, fever can still be evoked after lesion of these cells. In fact, injection of endogenous pyrogens into several other brain regions can produce fever (Blatteis, 1984).

The impact of pyrogens is not to obliterate temperature control. Rather, many studies suggest that with fever, temperature becomes regulated at a higher level just as though the "thermostat" was suddenly raised. Observations of diseased persons suggest that there is an upper limit to fever of approximately 41.1°C. This upper level ensures that the body is not exposed to high temperatures at a level that might cause widespread cellular damage.

Is fever biologically advantageous or is it simply the "sting" of aggressive microbes? The adaptive value of body temperatures above normal has been shown in animal experiments using ectotherms such as reptiles. For example, Kluger (1979) described experiments in which desert iguanas were injected with bacterial pyrogens. These animals showed different survival rates depending on the temperature of the environment they were exposed to. Animals with higher body temperatures (as a consequence of exposure to heat) showed higher survival rates following microbe exposure than did those with lower body temperatures. This occurs over a range of 34–42°C, the usual body temperatures of endotherms. Enhanced survival with higher body temperatures comes about because elevated temperatures are harmful to survival of microbes in the body. Thus fever promotes recovery from illness following exposure to infectious agents by producing an environment that is lethal to viruses and bacteria. Injection of pyrogens also leads these animals to seek out a warmer environment. Ectotherms such as reptiles are valuable for this type of research because it is possible to prevent the rise in body temperature that follows pyrogen injection simply by maintaining the animal in a cool environment. (However, not all reptiles show responses to bacterial pyrogens (Cooker, 1987).) Research with animals that do respond clearly illustrates the adaptive value of fever. Kluger (1979) also noted some comparable work with mammals. For example, rabbits injected with a pathogen that produces fever show better survival rates if the magnitude of the increase in fever was about 2.25°C. Above or below that amount, there was increased mortality. The mechanism mediating this effect of fever may involve several of the body's defense mechanisms, including the production of interferon. This work has clear implication for therapeutic procedures used with humans, especially the use of drugs to combat fever. Antipyretic drugs, such as aspirin, may prolong illness by reducing fever. Moderate fever would, in view of this research, seem to be beneficial and is an "inexpensive" natural way of combating disease.

Drinking and Regulation of Body Fluids

Human beings are watery creatures. Water makes up more than half the weight of most adults. It is the main constituent of most of our tissues. Blood, which carries nutrients and oxygen to the tissues, is mainly water, and many ions are bound to

---

Table 12-3   Average Daily Water Balance of an Adult Person

Approximate Water Intake (mL)		Approximate Water Output (mL)	
Fluid water, including beverages	1200	Urine	1400
Water content of food	1000	Insensible water loss	900
Water from oxidation of food	300	Feces	200
	2500		2500

---

molecules of water as they pass through cell membranes. Water is also used to eliminate wastes from the body. Under average conditions in a mild climate, an adult human being turns over about 2500 milliliters (mL) of water per day, as shown in Table 12-3. We do not notice the evaporation of water from the lungs or from the surface of the skin when there is no visible sweating, so this process is called insensible water loss. Under very high heat, sweating may equal the other types of output, thus doubling the daily loss of water. Unless the output is balanced by input, a person's life is soon menaced.

Problems of regulating the intake and excretion of fluids have grown more complicated during the course of evolution. The first primitive organisms evolved in the ocean, and the composition of their internal fluids was very similar to the composition of the ocean in terms of ion content. But even these primitive organisms had to take in food and eliminate wastes and thus regulate exchanges with the environment. When marine animals invaded fresh water, with its lower osmotic pressure, the problems of fluid balance became more difficult. More elaborate systems of intake and excretion were required, and levels of various ions in the body fluids gradually changed. Then when animals left the water and emerged onto dry land, even more difficult problems had to be faced. The liquid internal environment of the cells had to be maintained in a nonliquid external environment. Internal regulation of different fluid compartments became more elaborate, and behavioral regulation was required to secure adequate amounts of fluid.

Different kinds of animals show very different patterns of fluid regulation, depending on their evolutionary histories and their ecological niches. Even among the mammals there are major differences. Some small desert mammals, such as the kangaroo rat, have no access to water and never drink. They live on seeds and other vegetation and obtain their water from food. On the other side of their fluid balance, they urinate very little and their urine is highly concentrated. Elephant seals get by without taking in fluids or food during the four or five months of each year when they are ashore during the mating season. They derive all the fluid they need by metabolizing stored food, and they excrete very little during this period. Elephant seals do not drink during the rest of the year, either. As mammals that have returned to the ocean, seals are no more able to live on salt water than are human beings, so they must obtain their water from the fish they eat.

Since the need for water is so vital, it is not surprising that animals have evolved effective mechanisms to regulate both the intake and the excretion of fluids. These mechanisms involve both internal physiological processes and behavior with regard to the environment. We will focus on the controls over the behavioral responses, but it is important to keep in mind that this is only one aspect of the regulation of the

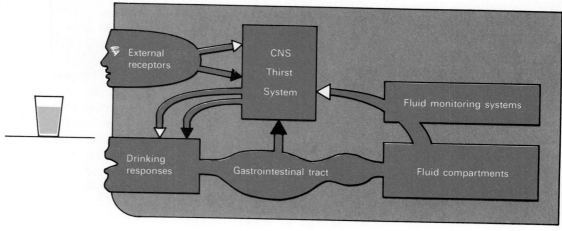

Figure 12-12 A simplified version of the basic systems that regulate fluid intake.

fluid balance of the body. A simplified version of the basic systems that regulate drinking is shown in Figure 12-12. (A more complete diagram will be shown later in Figure 12-15.)

Among the basic questions that investigators are studying are: How are fluid supplies in the body monitored? What factors cause a person or animal to start drinking? What factors cause drinking to stop? (In Chapter 13 we will take up similar questions about food supplies and eating, and we will see that eating and drinking are interdependent.) In the following sections, we will consider each of these questions in detail.

Monitoring the Body's Supplies of Water

About four-tenths of our body weight consists of water located inside the billions of cells of the body; another two-tenths is located outside the cells, either in the blood plasma or in the spaces between cells. It is usual to state that the water is divided between two compartments: **intracellular fluid** (or, simply, **cellular fluid**) and **extracellular fluid.** Extracellular fluid includes both fluid in the spaces between cells (interstitial fluid) and fluid in the vascular system. The body monitors the intracellular and extracellular compartments separately, as we will see. Usually the supplies of water in the two compartments vary in parallel, and water can move from one compartment to another. However, some disease conditions affect the two compartments separately, and investigators have found out how to manipulate and assess the two compartments separately. Depletion of intracellular fluid is normally more important in causing drinking than is depletion of extracellular fluid. Different mechanisms monitor intracellular and extracellular fluid, and we will consider them in succession.

Monitoring Intracellular Fluid

To see how intracellular fluid is monitored, we must first consider how water moves into and out of cells. Cell membranes are permeable to some substances and not to others. For instance, the membranes permit ions of potassium (K^+) to pass easily, as we saw for neurons in Chapter 4, but they are less permeable to sodium ions (Na^+); proteins are retained within cells and do not pass out through their membranes; molecules of water pass readily in and out through the membranes. The interstitial fluid and blood plasma contain about 0.9% salt (NaCl). A solution with a larger concentration of salt than 0.9% is called **hypertonic;** a solution with a lower concentration is **hypotonic.** If a person drinks a hypertonic solution or if salt is placed in a body cavity, the concentration of sodium ions in the blood and interstitial fluid soon increases. Sodium ions do not enter the cells readily, so there is a greater concentration of particles in the extracellular fluid than in the intracellular fluid. Whenever there is an unequal concentration of particles in the fluids on the two sides of a semipermeable membrane, fluid moves to the side with the greater concentration. This process is called **osmosis,** and the force involved is called **osmotic pressure.** Since the Na^+ ions cannot enter the cells, water leaves the cells in order to equalize the concentrations. As the volume of intracellular fluid decreases, the cells become smaller. If glucose is ingested or placed into the bloodstream, it enters cells easily and therefore does not cause a shift in water, but it does increase the **osmolality** (the number of particles per unit volume of solute) in both compartments.

Exactly what change in body fluids initiates drinking? Three competing hypotheses have been suggested. All are consistent with the observation that administering a hypertonic NaCl solution causes drinking. One hypothesis is that the concentration of sodium ions in the interstitial fluid is the effective stimulus (Andersson, 1978). A second hypothesis is that the concentration of particles of all sorts in the interstitial fluid (that is, the osmolality) is the effective stimulus. The third, and most generally accepted, hypothesis is that cellular dehydration is the effective stimulus (Gilman, 1937), and this hypothesis has been supported by recent experiments.

It had been shown in the 1950s that injecting small amounts of hypertonic NaCl solution into regions of the hypothalamus of experimental animals caused the animals to start drinking. This observation led to the suggestion that some of the cells in the hypothalamus are **osmoreceptors**—that is, they respond to changes in osmotic pressure. More recent experiments have applied other substances to these cells to characterize them better. Investigators tested responses to substances such as glucose (which readily crosses the cell membrane) and sucrose (which does not cross the membrane). Sucrose was found to stimulate the hypothalamic cells that responded to NaCl, but glucose did not. Thus these cells were not responding just to NaCl or to any increase in osmolality. Rather they responded to a change in osmotic pressure that caused an outflow of intracellular water; that is, the cells reported their own dehydration and decrease in volume. It might be appropriate to call these cells dehydration receptors, but it has become conventional to refer to them as osmoreceptors. Similarly, the response to a decrease of cellular fluid is often called **osmotic thirst.**

Electrical recording from single cells has shown that osmoreceptors are widely scattered throughout the preoptic area, the anterior hypothalamus, and the supraoptic nucleus. Research is still needed to define the connections of these cells to others and to trace the neural circuits by which drinking is initiated. We will see shortly that electrical stimulation of the preoptic area (POA) can lead to impressive increases in water intake.

Monitoring Extracellular Fluid

The response to a reduced volume of extracellular fluid is often called **hypovolemic thirst** (from the Greek root *hypo,* meaning "low," and the root *volemic,* which pertains to volume). The heart cannot function properly unless the amount of fluid in the vascular system is kept within fairly close limits. Loss of blood, as in hemorrhaging, reduces the fluids of the heart; reduced output of the heart lowers blood pressure, further reducing the supply to the heart. To prevent such an impairment of the circulatory system, a fall in blood volume must be reported and counteracted promptly. Neural reflexes accomplish this, and a chemical system may also be involved. Pressure receptors in the heart and in some arteries initiate neural signals in response to the fall of blood pressure; these signals help to elicit compensatory responses. One kind of response is to increase the muscular tension in the walls of the blood vessels. Another response is to release antidiuretic hormone (or vasopressin) from the posterior pituitary gland. This hormone acts to inhibit the removal of water by the kidneys and thus to hold water in the body.

Many investigators are convinced that yet another response to hypovolemia involves the kidneys and special chemicals in the blood. Other investigators are skeptical. Let us examine the hypothesis first and then come to the questions.

Diminished blood flow through the kidneys causes release of a substance called renin from the walls of the arterioles in the kidneys. Renin reacts with a substance in the blood to form angiotensin, which is then converted into **angiotensin II.** (The first demonstrated effect of angiotensin was to increase blood pressure, which is how it got its name: The Greek root *angeio* means "blood vessel," and *tensio* pertains to tension or pressure.) Very low doses of angiotensin II injected into the POA were found to be extremely effective in eliciting drinking, even in animals that were not deprived of water (Epstein et al., 1970). When administered to rats that had been deprived of food but not water, angiotensin II caused them to stop eating and start drinking; thus its effect is highly specific.

Exactly where in the brain angiotensin II has its effect is the subject of much current research. Although the original work on this question found the POA to be the most sensitive site, it was difficult to see how angiotensin II could reach receptors in this region since it does not penetrate the blood-brain barrier. Attention then focused on the **circumventricular organs.** As their name suggests, these organs lie in the walls of the cerebral ventricles (see Figure 12-13). They contain receptor sites that can be affected by substances in the cerebrospinal fluid, and information about

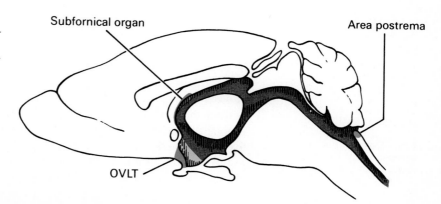

Figure 12-13 Mid-sagittal section of rat brain showing the circumventricular organs, which mediate between the brain and the cerebrospinal fluid. The circumventricular organs are shown in brown, and the ventricles and channels for cerebrospinal fluid are shown in gray. (OVLT, organum vasculosum of the lamina terminalis)

stimulation of these sites is carried by axons of the circumventricular cells into other parts of the nervous system.

Some researchers continue to maintain that cells in the POA respond to angiotensin II in experiments where leakage of the injected material into the ventricles could not have occurred. They suggest that angiotensin II may be generated in the brain as well as in the bloodstream. Determination of whether or not there are receptors for angiotensin II in the POA as well as in circumventricular organs and determination of the brain circuits that control the drinking responses stimulated by these receptors are topics of ongoing research.

A further problem related to the angiotensin story is whether the amount formed in the blood by reductions in blood volume is enough to stimulate thirst. Careful measurements indicate that not enough angiotensin is normally produced to evoke thirst (Abraham et al., 1975; Stricker, 1977). Therefore some investigators argue that many previous experiments involved responses to angiotensin II administered as a drug—pharmacological effects rather than normal physiological effects. Further research is needed to resolve this issue. Meanwhile there is no doubt that responses of pressure receptors in the heart and arteries cause neural signals of hypovolemia.

Initiation of Drinking

Withdrawal from jugular vein to sample concentration in cerebral circulation

Injection into carotid artery supply to brain

Withdrawal from leg vein to sample concentration in peripheral circulation

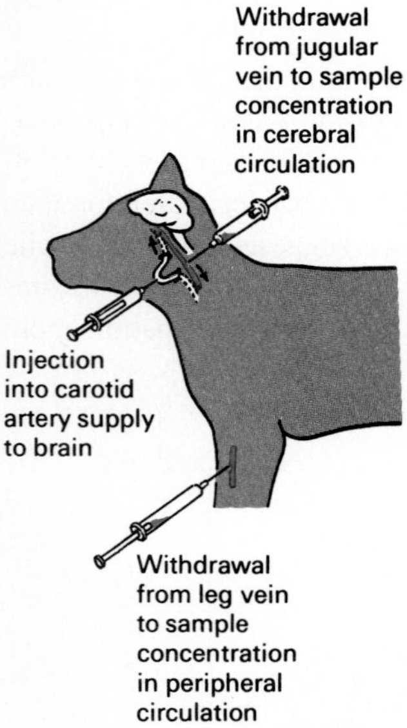

Figure 12-14 Method used to vary salt concentration separately in the cerebral circulation and the peripheral circulation.

Stimulating the preoptic area through implanted electrodes in unanesthetized, freely moving rats causes them to go promptly to a water spout and start to drink. As the POA stimulation continues, some animals may drink as much in 1 hour as they normally drink in 24 hours. During a 10-hour period of stimulation of the POA in a group of rats, the rats ingested almost their entire body weight in water. (Urination kept pace with intake, so the animals did not become waterlogged.) If instead of stimulating the POA, investigators destroy it, the animals totally refuse to drink, a condition called **adipsia** (from the Greek roots *a*, meaning "without," and *dipas*, meaning "thirst").

Normally a deprived individual lacks water to about the same degree in both the cellular and extracellular compartments. How can we find the relative importance of osmotic and hypovolemic deficits in initiating drinking? A telling method has been to vary salt concentration separately in either the cerebral circulation or the peripheral circulation of water-deprived dogs. Surgery was performed to bring a loop of the carotid artery to the surface of the skin on each side of the neck, and these loops were used for injections (Figure 12-14). Since the carotid arteries provide the main blood supply to the brain, injections into the loops can alter the concentration of the blood reaching the brain without significantly changing the blood in the rest of the body. The concentrations in the cerebral circulation were measured by withdrawing blood as it left the brain through the jugular vein; the concentrations in the peripheral circulation were measured in samples taken from a leg vein. Bilateral infusion of water into the carotid arteries at a rate that brought the tonicity of cerebral plasma down to the predeprivation level reduced water intake by three-quarters; infusion of isotonic saline had no effect on drinking. These results furnish further support for the conclusion that the body monitors cellular hydration in the brain and not in the rest of the body, since reducing saline in the brain but leaving it high in the body caused a marked reduction of drinking. The dogs drank only a small amount in a few minutes and then stopped, although the cells in the body were still dehydrated and the volume of extracellular fluid was still below normal (Ramsay, Rolls, & Wood, 1977).

The role of extracellular dehydration was tested in the dogs by infusing isotonic saline solution into the jugular vein. Restoring the plasma volume to predeprivation levels reduced drinking of water-deprived dogs by only one-quarter. Thus extracellular depletion is less important than is cellular depletion in controlling drinking. Tests with a small number of monkeys indicate that the same conclusion is true for them (Rolls, Wood, & Rolls, 1980).

Destruction of the lateral hypothalamus in rats causes them to refuse to drink or eat. This lateral hypothalamic syndrome has been investigated chiefly with regard to feeding behavior, so we will discuss it in detail in Chapter 13. Here we note, however, that even if the lesioned animals recover their ability to eat and to regulate their food consumption, they show a peculiar reluctance to initiate drinking. They confine their drinking to mealtimes, especially when dry food is being eaten. It seems as if water is used by these rats to lubricate the passage of food rather than being ingested for its own sake. It is not yet clear how the lateral hypothalamus enters into the system that controls consumption of water. It is probably not primarily concerned with monitoring water supplies. Perhaps it is important in facilitating the motor circuits that accomplish drinking.

Water-deprived animals or animals whose POA is stimulated will drink readily, but only if an appropriate liquid is available. This result shows that sensory input must combine with diencephalic activity in order to initiate drinking. How and where these two kinds of information are combined has apparently not been investigated, but there has been productive research into the comparable question of initiation of feeding, as we will see in Chapter 13.

Termination of Drinking

A dog deprived of water for 24 hours will drink avidly, consuming almost all it needs in only 2 to 3 minutes. A rat makes up its deficit more slowly, making up about half the deficit in 5 minutes and continuing to drink intermittently for about an hour. People fall in between these extremes, making up about two-thirds of their deficit in the first 2.5 minutes.

What mechanism operates to terminate drinking? One possibility is that the person or animal monitors the amount being ingested and that intake continues until an amount known to be equal to the deficit is reached. Another possibility is that the drinker continues until the deficits that initiated the behavior are completely overcome. But actually an animal's deficit is not in the stomach but in the tissues, and it takes some time for fluid to get from the stomach to the upper intestine and then into the cells. This time delay between drinking and rehydration of tissues makes even more striking the rapid termination of drinking in species like the dog. Clearly there are two phases in the controls for termination: First, there are signals that a sufficient amount of fluids has been ingested. Second, the fluid reaches the bodily compartments and thus eliminates the signals of deficit that helped to initiate drinking.

The factors that affect termination have been investigated by measuring the rate of change in bodily deficits after drinking and by stimulating one or another stage of the processes of ingestion and rehydration. Also, human subjects have made various ratings of their sensation of thirst and other feelings during rehydration. In the dog it is clear that drinking stops while the water is still in the gut and long before rehydration of either compartment has occurred. Although drinking stops in 2 to 3 minutes, it takes about 10 minutes before cellular or extracellular dehydration begins to fall. Thereafter they return to predeprivation levels in a period of 40 to 60 minutes (Rolls, Wood, & Rolls, 1980). Although people make up two-thirds of their deficit in the first 2.5 minutes, the beginning of dilution of plasma concentrations is first apparent only about 5 minutes later, and by another 10 to 15 minutes the changes in the cellular and extracellular compartments may become important in limiting further drinking.

How dogs can make up their water deficits so accurately and rapidly remains a mystery, in spite of much research. For instance, some investigators thought that monitoring intake through the mouth and throat was a possibility. This idea was investigated by attaching a tube surgically to the esophagus so that the water swallowed passed out through the tube and did not reach the stomach. In this case dogs drank far more water than their deficit, so monitoring oral intake by itself does not terminate drinking. The next factor studied was loading the stomach. But placing a balloon in the stomach and inflating it to distend the stomach had little effect on checking drinking. Water ingested reaches the small intestine of the dog in 2 to 3 minutes, and receptors there may play a role in terminating drinking. This theory has not been studied directly in the dog, but it has in the monkey, as we will see next.

In the monkey, as in the dog and the rat, stimulation of the mouth and throat is not sufficient to terminate drinking. But monitoring by the stomach seems to be more important in the monkey than in the dog, as shown by the following experiment: Monkeys were equipped with a tube to the stomach. They were allowed to drink until they stopped, and then the tube was used to drain the stomach; the monkeys resumed drinking almost immediately. In other monkeys surgically implanted tubes were used to place water directly in the small intestine (duodenum). Infusion of even a small amount of water into the small intestine would stop drinking, at least for a short period. Perhaps placing water directly into the intestine made the monkey uncomfortable, and it refused to drink not because its thirst was slaked but because it was under stress. The experimenters therefore performed two other tests. One was to see whether infusing water into the duodenum stopped eating as well as drinking. But the monkeys continued to eat, indicating both that the treatment did not make the animals uncomfortable and that it was specific to thirst. An even more telling test placed isotonic saline solution rather than plain water in the intestine. The saline did not stop drinking as the water did. This comparison showed that the monkeys responded to the tonicity of the water rather than simply to its bulk (Rolls, Wood, & Rolls, 1980). Thus the duodenum seems to contain osmoreceptors that monitor whether water has been ingested.

Taste and Drinking

How pleasant a liquid tastes helps to determine how much is consumed, and the state of hydration or dehydration helps to determine how good a fluid tastes. The influence of taste can easily be measured by seeing how much a person or animal drinks when offered a choice of fluids. When a fluid tastes sweet because sugar or saccharine has been added, people or rats or monkeys increase their intake significantly, but no such effect is seen in cats. Rats also prefer slightly salty water (0.7%) to plain water and will drink much more of the salt solution. Variety of flavors also increases consumption; both humans and rats drink significantly more when offered several palatable flavors in succession rather than having the same flavor repeatedly.

Figure 12-15 Basic systems that regulate fluid intake in a mammal.

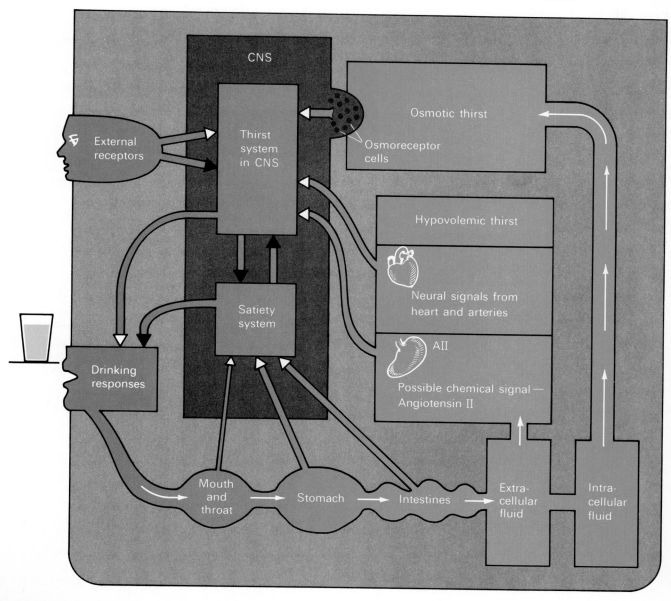

Perhaps less expected is the finding that people change their ratings of the palatability of water depending on their degree of deprivation or satiety (Cabanac, 1971). Subjects tasted a small amount of water and rated its pleasantness on a numerical scale. After being deprived of water overnight, subjects rated the taste of a sample as highly pleasant. Ratings of subsequent small samples taken at 5-minute intervals diminished slightly in pleasantness. But if subjects were allowed to drink to satiety, then the ratings of the next sample showed a large drop, to about 0.8 of the initial rating, and over the next few samples the palatability dropped to about 0.6 of the initial value. Some neurons in the hypothalamus of the monkey show similar changes in their firing rates. These neurons respond when the monkey drinks water. The rate of response goes up with deprivation or with intracarotid infusion of hypertonic saline solution but goes down as the monkey continues to drink water (Arnauld et al., 1975). Thus taste can contribute to drinking, and decrease of taste stimulation may play a role in termination of drinking.

The basic systems that regulate drinking are summarized in Figure 12-15. This diagram can help you to review the material on thirst and regulation of body fluids.

Summary · Main Points

1. Homeostatic mechanisms maintain relative constancy of internal bodily conditions such as temperature, water content, and food supplies. These mechanisms include both behavioral adjustments and internal physiological processes.

2. Ectotherms (such as amphibia and reptiles) regulate their body temperature chiefly by moving to favorable sites or by changing their exposure to external sources of heat. Endotherms (mainly mammals and birds) also use these behavioral methods and in addition make a variety of internal adjustments.

3. The lateral hypothalamus is involved in behavioral regulation of temperature; the preoptic area is involved in physiological regulation.

4. Temperature is monitored not only by regions in the basal forebrain but also by the spinal cord and receptors at the body surface. The higher levels of thermal regulation in the nervous system have narrow set zones, and the lower levels have wider ones.

5. Temperature regulation is usually thought to be accomplished by a negative-feedback system with a fixed set point (or set zone), but the data could also be explained by opposed heat gain and heat loss systems, perhaps with reciprocal inhibitory influences.

6. It is possible through training to gain some control over both skin temperature and core temperature.

7. Ectothermy evolved before endothermy, and some species (such as the rat) develop behavioral thermoregulation before they develop physiological thermoregulation. Endothermy may have evolved in order to increase the capacity for aerobic metabolism to sustain a high level of muscular activity over a prolonged period.

8. Water in our bodies is needed for blood circulation, temperature regulation, digestion, and elimination. About two-thirds of the human body is water, most of it within cells.

9. Intracellular fluid is monitored primarily by osmoreceptor neurons in the preoptic area. Extracellular fluid is monitored by pressure receptors in the heart and in certain arteries and possibly by angiotensin II, which may act on receptors in the circumventricular organs and on neurons in the preoptic area.

10. Depletion of intracellular fluid (called osmotic thirst) is a more potent stimulus to drinking than is depletion of extracellular fluid (hypovolemic thirst), but usually both effects work in parallel.

11. Stimulation of receptors in the mouth and throat does not terminate drinking. Rather, monitoring by the stomach and duodenum seems to provide the main signals that water has been ingested. As water moves into the fluid compartments, it eliminates the signals of deficit that initiated drinking.

12. Taste contributes to drinking, and water depletion causes fluids to be more palatable.

Recommended Reading

Hales, J. R. S. (Ed.). (1984). *Thermal physiology*. New York: Raven.

Heller, H. C., Cranshaw, L. I., & Hammel, H. T. (1978). The thermostat of vertebrate animals. *Scientific American, 239* (2): 102–113.

Rolls, B. J., Wood, R. J., & Rolls, E. T. (1980). Thirst: The initiation, maintenance, and termination of drinking. In J. M. Sprague & A. N. Epstein (Eds.), *Progress in psychobiology and physiology* (Vol. 9). New York: Academic Press.

Satinoff, E. (1983). A reevaluation of the concept of the homeostatic organization of temperature regulation. In E. Satinoff & P. Teitelbaum (Eds.), *Handbook of behavioral neurobiology: Vol. 6. Motivation*. New York: Plenum.

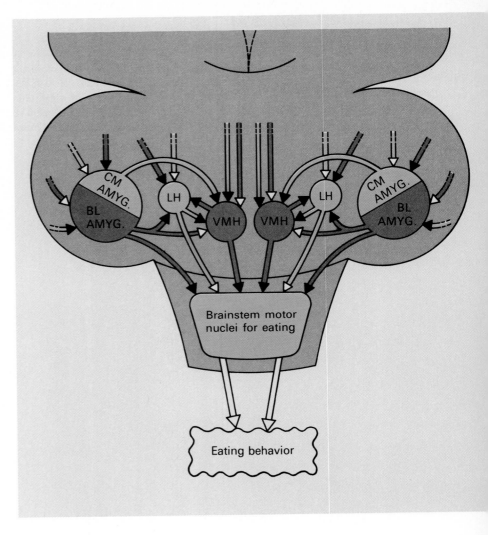

13 Eating and Regulation of Energy

Feast or famine—these are poles of human experience. So dependent are we on food for energy and to build and maintain our bodies that hunger is a compelling motive and flavors are powerful reinforcements. The structure of each species is closely related to the way in which it obtains and consumes food. For example, the mammalian class of vertebrates, to which we belong, is named for its distinctive way of nourishing the young. The need to eat shapes our daily schedules and molds our activities. Our newspapers are full of material that relates to food: news of successes or failures of food crops; famines and droughts; destruction of food by storms, floods, and swarms of locusts; laws and treaties governing import and export of foods; hunger strikes; recipes and articles about food; advertisements for restaurants and kitchen appliances; effects of diet and obesity on health; clinics to treat weight problems. A major part of the economy is devoted to the raising, processing and preparation, packaging, transporting and distributing, advertising, and selling of food. Much of our involvement with food has purely human cultural aspects, but our basic reliance on food for energy and nutrition is shared with all animals. In this chapter we take up general needs and physiological regulation of feeding and energy expenditure and also some species-specific aspects of food-related behavior and regulations.

Regulation of eating and of body energy are intimately related to the regulation of body temperature and water, which we considered in the last chapter, but our present topic is more complicated. One reason for the greater complexity is that food is needed not only to supply energy but also to supply **nutrients**. Nutrients, in the technical meaning of the term, are chemicals that are not used as sources of energy but that are required for effective functioning of the body; for example, they are needed for the growth, maintenance, and repair of bodily structures. Even for our own species not all nutritional requirements have yet been determined in detail. Of the twenty amino acids found in animal proteins, nine cannot easily be synthesized in the human body and must be obtained in food, so these nine are called essential amino acids. Similarly, a few fatty acids must be obtained from food. Other nutritional requirements include about fifteen vitamins and several minerals. We will take up specific hungers for some nutrients in the latter part of this chapter.

Simple Model Feeding Systems

The essentials of feeding systems are illustrated in relatively simple invertebrates such as the fly (Dethier, 1976) or the sea snail *Aplysia* (Kandel, 1976). When such animals are deprived of food, they become more active and start moving, more or less at random, until they encounter a smell or taste that signals food. Recognition of these stimuli is built into the animal's nervous system. The tendency of a fly to consume a sugar solution increases with the strength of the solution up to a certain level, but as the solution becomes even more concentrated, it repels the fly. The strength of the eating response also varies with sensory adaptation and with internal signals of fullness of the digestive tract. As the fly continues to taste the solution, its receptors adapt to the stimulus; this adaptation may proceed to the point at which the receptors stop firing, whereupon the fly ceases to consume that food. It will, however, be ready to ingest a food with a different flavor, a feature that promotes consumption of a variety of foods. When the digestive tract becomes full, mechanoreceptors in the gut send signals to the central nervous system, and the feeding reflexes are turned off. Feeding stops even if the sensory receptors are still signaling that tasty food is available. If the nerve from the gut to the neural centers is cut, the fly may continue to eat until it literally bursts.

Note that the basic tendency of the fly is to eat; feeding occurs whenever food is available unless the taste receptors are adapted or unless the gut receptors signal fullness. The basic components of the fly's feeding system are diagramed in Figure 13-1. Although the fly has a simple feeding system, it nevertheless competes rather successfully with us for food. Later, in Figure 13-12, we will see a diagram of the more complex feeding system of a mammal.

Figure 13-1 Diagram of the basic system that regulates feeding in the fly.

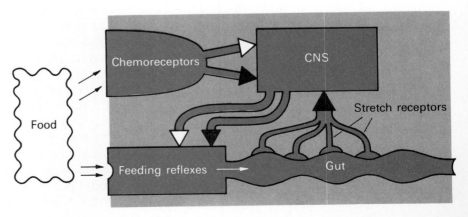

The pattern of intake of the fly is not absolutely constant. For instance, the female fly increases its intake of protein for a day or two every seven days or so, just after it lays eggs; in this way it secures the protein needed for the next clutch of eggs. The temporary increase in preference for protein is an example of a **specific hunger.**

The basic characteristics of the invertebrate feeding systems are also found in the feeding systems of mammals. In the mammal, however, these patterns are built into complex, multilevel nervous systems, and they allow feeding behavior to be integrated with a wide range and variety of behavioral patterns. Monitoring of food supplies is more elaborate than simply detecting the quantity of food in the gut. These complexities have made the task of identifying and describing the feeding systems much more difficult. We will see some of the aspects of mammalian feeding systems that have been well explored and others that are still open to investigation and controversy.

Comparative Feeding Behavior

Species differ greatly in respect to the way they get their food, the kinds of food they select, and the timing of their feeding. Some examples of these species differences will be noted here; the mechanisms will be discussed later.

Securing Food: Structural Adaptations

The initial step in dealing with hunger is securing food from the environment. For some marine animals, this step is relatively simple; they remain in place and extract food from the water that flows past them. Browsing animals eat plant food and in some cases migrate to follow available plants as the seasons change. Predators hunt other animals for their food. Each of these life styles requires many structural adaptations. Let us consider some that are specifically concerned with ingestion of food.

Devices animals use to obtain and direct food into the mouth exhibit a wide range of structural variations. Dramatic examples are seen among birds, which show extraordinary differences in beak size and shape (Figure 13-2). Major modes for obtaining food among birds include fishing, crushing seeds, catching insects in the air, extracting insects from bark, sipping nectar, and tearing flesh. Giant birds of prey like eagles tear up food and have powerful curved or hooked beaks; nectar feeders have long and slender bills that are effective in probing flowers. Some birds crack seeds and nuts to select particular parts, and these animals, such as finches and parrots, have short and stout beaks. Some birds, such as ducks and spoonbills, have special bills that allow them to strain small particles of food from the water. Of course, beak size and shape are only two of the many attributes related to bird feeding. Overall physical appearance, behavior, and habitat are certainly other significant determinants of feeding strategies and habits.

The food supply of mammals is extremely diverse, including other animals, seeds, grasses, roots, and the bark of trees. The teeth of mammals reflect their diversity of diet (Figure 13-3). Gnawing rodents have large incisors, and carnivorous animals usually have impressive canine teeth. Mammals that eat leaves and grasses have large teeth with flat grinding surfaces. An expert can identify a species, including fossil animals, by seeing a single tooth.

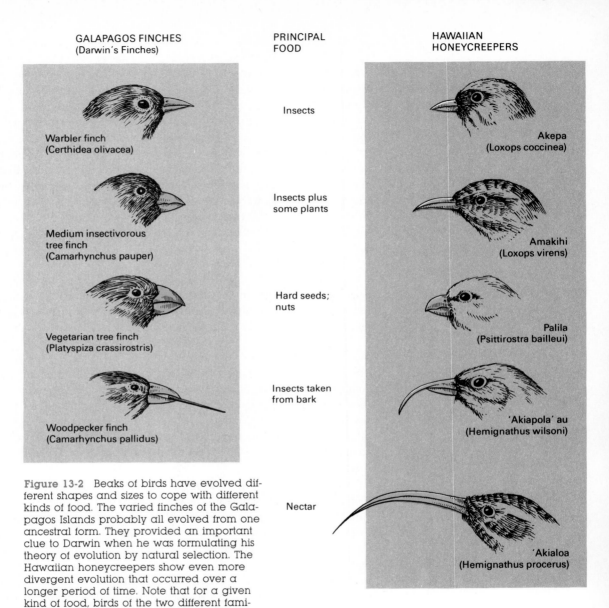

GALAPAGOS FINCHES
(Darwin's Finches)

PRINCIPAL
FOOD

HAWAIIAN
HONEYCREEPERS

Warbler finch
(Certhidea olivacea)

Insects

Akepa
(Loxops coccinea)

Medium insectivorous
tree finch
(Camarhynchus pauper)

Insects plus
some plants

Amakihi
(Loxops virens)

Vegetarian tree finch
(Platyspiza crassirostris)

Hard seeds;
nuts

Palila
(Psittirostra bailleui)

Woodpecker finch
(Camarhynchus pallidus)

Insects taken
from bark

'Akiapola' au
(Hemignathus wilsoni)

Nectar

'Akialoa
(Hemignathus procerus)

Figure 13-2 Beaks of birds have evolved different shapes and sizes to cope with different kinds of food. The varied finches of the Galapagos Islands probably all evolved from one ancestral form. They provided an important clue to Darwin when he was formulating his theory of evolution by natural selection. The Hawaiian honeycreepers show even more divergent evolution that occurred over a longer period of time. Note that for a given kind of food, birds of the two different families have evolved rather similar beaks.

Food Selection Among Animals

Although many environments offer a wide range of possible nutrients, most animals select particular diets. In fact, some animals have adapted to such a narrow range of foods that they starve if their food choice becomes unavailable. Zoologists make broad classifications of animals according to the foods usually eaten. Those that eat other animal material are carnivorous. Those that eat plant material are herbivorous. Insect-eating animals (such as many species of birds) are insectivorous. Nectar-eating animals (such as bees and hummingbirds) are nectivorous. Animals that eat a wide variety of foods—for example, human beings, rats, and cockroaches—are called omnivores.

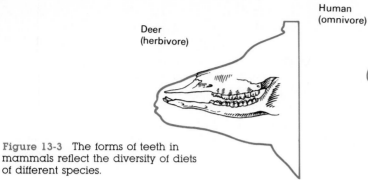
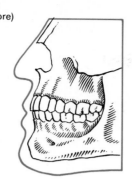
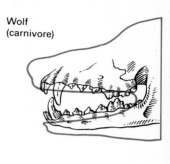

Deer
(herbivore)

Human
(omnivore)

Wolf
(carnivore)

Figure 13-3 The forms of teeth in mammals reflect the diversity of diets of different species.

Temporal Patterns of Feeding

Some species eat almost continuously, and others eat a few meals restricted to particular times during either the day or the night. Ecological factors, such as the availability of food sources, are particularly important in determining the frequency and timing of meals. Other determinants include the nutritive characteristics of food, pacing by internal clocks, and social learning, which is especially evident in humans. Some of these determinants will be discussed later in relation to the initiation and termination of feeding.

Many species go for weeks or even months without eating—for example, seals during breeding, whales during migration, penguins during incubation, and bears during hibernation. Apparently these long fasts occur when eating would be incompatible with some other more important activity. The mechanisms of long fasts will be considered later.

Mammalian Alimentary Tract and Digestion

For the cells of the body to receive and use vital nutrients, ingested food must be changed into simpler chemicals. These simpler substances are the products of digestion, a series of mechanical and chemical processes that take place in the digestive tract. A brief review of some of the main processes of digestion will set the stage for our consideration of control of feeding behavior.

The digestive tract begins at the mouth, where mechanical breakdown of food prepares for the chemical processes of digestion. Saliva provides a medium for dissolving food and also contains an enzyme that initiates the chemical breakdown of carbohydrates. Tasting and chewing food produce signals that start the secretion of digestive enzymes in the stomach.

Food passes to the stomach with the act of swallowing, a complex reflex involving an elaborate set of muscles of the mouth and throat. The esophagus is a tube that connects the mouth and stomach. Waves of movements in this tube propel food toward the stomach. The most intense digestive processes occur in the stomach. Structural characteristics of the stomach vary among animals; especially elaborate morphology is found among grazing animals (herbivores) because of their diet of varied grasses. Within the stomach, waves of movements keep food mixed while enzymes break down the substances. One enzyme breaks down protein into simpler constituents, amino acids. Another enzyme changes the proteins characteristically found in milk, while still another aids in the digestion of fats. Since the stomach also acts as a reservoir for food undergoing digestion, the presence and amount of food in the stomach could be expected to influence the timing of eating.

The contents of the stomach are directed in spurts to the small intestine. A muscular valve, the pyloric sphincter, separates the stomach from the small intestine. Within the small intestine, enzymatic action continues. Enzymes from the pancreas act on proteins, carbohydrates, and fat. Secretions from the liver and the small intestine further contribute to the digestive process. Rhythmic movements in the intestine contribute to mixing of the digestive process. Further along the length of the small intestine, absorption of the final simplified products of digestion takes place. These substances pass into capillaries and enter the bloodstream leading to the liver. Undigestible substances pass into the large intestine to form feces.

In addition to enzymes, hormones are secreted by cells of the stomach, and these regulate certain aspects of the digestive process. Some hormones regulate enzyme production. Some hormones may also act on brain cells to influence feeding behavior, as we will see later.

Energy Input and Expenditure

The body spends energy continuously, so there must be a continuous supply available. Energy intake, in contrast, is episodic, and many animals space their meals at wide intervals—hours, days, or even months apart. There must therefore be stores of readily mobilizable energy in the body to meet vital needs until a new supply is obtained. These stores should be independent of essential bodily organs, such as nervous tissue and muscles, so that those organs do not have to be consumed for energy. Body fat, the most concentrated form of energy storage, makes up the main reservoir in most animals.

Considering only energy balance and not food used for structural purposes, how are ingested calories utilized? Some energy is not converted to metabolizable form and is excreted. In a recent study of metabolism in the laboratory rat, about 75% of the ingested energy became available for use in various bodily functions (Corbett & Keesey, 1982). The available energy is used in one of three ways: (1) Some energy is used to process newly ingested food. Typically both metabolic rate and heat production rise just after a meal, and this has been interpreted as reflecting energy used to process food. The energy utilization for processing food amounted to about 8%. (2) The greatest part of the stored energy—about 55%—was used for basal metabolism, that is, for maintaining bodily heat and other resting functions, such as neural potentials. (3) Only about 12–13% was spent on active behavioral processes. In an environment more conducive to activity than a small metabolic chamber, the percentage of energy spent on active behavioral processes would probably have been somewhat larger.

To what extent are these different types of expenditure of energy adjusted when there is a deficit of energy stores in the body or an excess of energy stores? (These conditions could be caused by underconsumption or overconsumption of food.) It used to be supposed that only the expenditure of energy for active behavioral processes showed much elasticity—that basal metabolism and heat production caused by feeding are rather fixed. In fact, basal metabolism is known to follow a strict rule that relates energy expenditure to body weight (Kleiber, 1947): Energy expenditure in thousands of calories per day (kcal/day) is proportional to the 0.75 power of body weight in kilograms:

$$\text{kcal/day} = 70 \times \text{weight}^{0.75}$$

Kleiber proposed this rule originally on the basis of data for a sample of animals from mice to cattle, with body weights varying over a range of 3000 to 1 (a range of over 3 logarithmic units). It has since been shown to apply to an even greater range, from unicellular organisms to the largest mammals—a range of 18 logarithmic units (Hemmingsen, 1960)!

Although this relation holds for baseline conditions, if an animal or person is not at its "target" body weight, then basal metabolism departs from the value predicted by the Kleiber equation. For example, a large study of food deprivation in men showed a compensatory drop in basal metabolism that was disproportionately larger than the decrease in weight (Keys et al., 1950). In obese people, too, severe restriction of caloric intake affects metabolic rate much more than it affects body weight; see Figure 13-4. In this case restriction over 24 days caused basal metabolism to drop by 15%, whereas weight declined by only 6% (Bray, 1969). Animal studies show similar disproportions (e.g., Keesey & Corbett, 1984). Thus the resting rate of energy expenditure is really "basal" only for animals and people who are in energy balance. The expenditure of energy at rest drops substantially below "normal" (that is, the level predicted by the Kleiber formula) when body weight is reduced from the normally maintained level; such adjustments in the rate of energy expenditure play a significant role in maintaining energy balance and in keeping an individual's body weight relatively constant (Keesey & Powley, 1986).

The increase in metabolic activity that typically follows eating also shows a compensatory adjustment when weight has been lost. When rats are underfed, the usual heat increment following a meal is reduced so far that it is scarcely detectable (Boyle et al., 1981). Evidently, then, only a small fraction of the usual heat increment to a meal is actually required for processing the food. The remainder of the increment varies according to the organism's energy status or need.

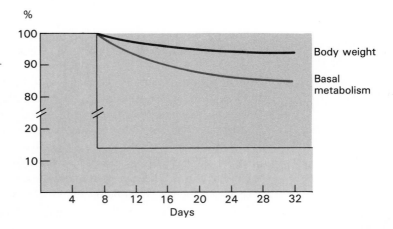

Figure 13-4 Weight loss and reduction of basal metabolism in six obese subjects during caloric restriction. After seven days on a 3500-calorie diet, intake was restricted to 450 calories and maintained for 24 days. The caloric intake is shown by the gray area of the graph, dropping to 13% at Day 7. Basal metabolism declined by 15%, whereas body weight declined by 6%. (Adapted from G. A. Bray. *Experientia 25* (1969): 1100–1101. By permission)

The rate of metabolism also adjusts to an excess of stored energy. It has long been known that both in animals and in humans overconsumption fails to produce as much increase of body weight as would be expected on the basis of the excess of calories. Animals who are given palatable diets rich in calories display elevated metabolic rates, and these rates go up disproportionately with the increases in body weight (Rothwell & Stock, 1982). Furthermore, the increase in metabolism is not mediated behaviorally; although metabolic expenditure goes up rapidly during diet-induced weight gain, bodily activity actually goes down.

Since people and animals adjust their energy expenditures in response to under- or overnutrition, they tend to resist either losing or gaining weight. This helps to explain how difficult it is for some people to lose weight and for others to gain. The relation between metabolic rate and body weight may also provide a way of finding when an individual is at his or her physiologically normal target weight (Keesey & Corbett, 1984). Only at this weight will the person's resting metabolism be at the level predicted by the Kleiber equation. A lower metabolic rate than predicted by the equation indicates that the person is below his or her physiologically normal weight. There are indications that people who hold their weight down by dieting may remain hypometabolic as long as their weight stays below the level that they used to maintain (Leibel & Hirsch, 1984).

Peripheral Sensory Control of Eating

Taste and somatosensory discrimination of food objects play important roles in control of eating. The role of taste was recognized early; then for a few decades it was neglected in favor of central events, but now taste is receiving renewed attention. Responses to taste are built into the nervous system. Newborn babies show characteristic responses when flavored solutions are put on the tongue. A sweet solution evokes relaxation often accompanied by a slight smile, which is frequently followed by eager licking and sucking. A sour solution causes pursing of the lips, often accompanied or followed by nose wrinkling and eye blinking. A bitter fluid causes an arched opening of the mouth with the upper lip elevated, the angles of the mouth depressed, and the tongue protruded; frequently this is followed by spitting or even vomiting. Two babies born with no functional brain above the level of the brain stem were also tested in this way and showed the same kinds of responses (Steiner, 1973). So there are inborn tendencies to accept or reject flavors without regard to need for food, and these are based on brain stem circuits. In adults, too, taste plays a major role in eating, and attractive tastes increase the consumption of both food and liquids beyond the amounts that would be expected based on need alone.

If peripheral sensory mechanisms of the face and mouth are impaired, disturbances in eating result. Cutting either the gustatory or trigeminal nerves causes animals to be unresponsive to food and to eat awkwardly. There is first a period of **aphagia,** or absence of eating, and then hypophagia, or reduction of eating, following which body weight is again regulated but at reduced levels. This may not be surprising in the case of the gustatory nerves, but why should the trigeminal nerves be important since they do not innervate taste receptors but serve tactile and kinesthetic receptors? Observation shows that when animals eat, food is explored by touching it with the tongue and lips, and somatosensory input is used to control grasping, handling, licking, and chewing the food. The trigeminal system has a large representation in the brain of the rat—much larger than does the gustatory system. Unilateral lesions of central trigeminal tracts cause neglect of stimuli from the contralateral side. A little later when we consider the role of the lateral hypothalamus in control of intake, we will see that some of the effects formerly attributed to this region are actually due to interruption of sensory tracts; that is, it has now been found that typical lesions of the lateral hypothalamus impinge on the pathways from the trigeminal and gustatory nerves to the thalamus and cortex. Therefore investigators are studying with renewed interest the role of sensory stimulation in initiating eating and in controlling ingestive behavior (Zeigler, 1983).

Feeding Control Systems in the Brain

Discoveries by the early 1950s had given rise to a "dual-center theory" of control of eating (Figure 13-5). According to this theory, the hypothalamus contains the primary control centers for hunger and satiety: A "hunger center" in the **lateral hypothalamus** (LH) facilitates eating, whereas a "satiety center" in the **ventromedial hypothalamus** (VMH) inhibits eating. All the other regions and factors that influence eating were presumed to act through these hypothalamic control centers. Further research aimed at filling in the details of this picture soon resulted in dethroning the hypothalamic regions from their exclusive status, and even the concept of a center or centers was challenged.

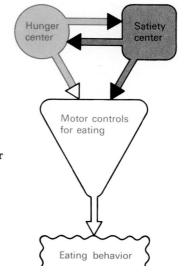

Figure 13-5 Diagram of dual-center theory of control of eating.

Many investigators are continuing to study the effects of hypothalamic lesions and cutting connections to these regions, as we will see. Others, however, assert that the syndromes caused by lesions of the medial and lateral hypothalamus do not provide neurological explanations for regulation of eating and of energy but rather provide only puzzles or challenges; these workers believe that other approaches will be more fruitful. We will review other methods as well, but research on brain circuits involved in eating and energy regulation is a major part of the story of attempts to understand this subject.

BOX 13-1 | Effects of a Hypothalamic Tumor on Human Behavior

A case involving a small, sharply localized tumor in a woman's brain demonstrates the multiple functions of the hypothalamus and shows how results of animal experiments can help in the interpretation of a person's motivated behavior (Reeves & Plum, 1969).

The patient was a 20-year-old bookkeeper. She first came to the hospital about a year after she had developed an abnormal appetite; she ate and drank large amounts and gained weight rapidly. She also had frequent headaches, and her menstrual periods had stopped. She was mentally alert, performed her work well, and showed no emotional abnormalities.

Another year passed, and her family brought her back to the hospital because of changes in her behavior. Now she was often uncooperative and at times attacked people around her. She was confused and sometimes could not remember correctly. She would no longer attempt arithmetic calculations. Tests showed reduced endocrine function involving the gonads, the thyroid gland, and the adrenal cortex. An operation revealed a tumor at the base of the brain, but it could not be removed. The young woman's outbursts of violent behavior became more frequent, especially if she was not fed frequently. Toward the end of her hospitalization, she had to be fed almost continuously in order to keep her reasonably tractable, and she was eating about 10,000 calories a day.

When she died, three years after the onset of her illness, the position of the tumor was determined precisely; it is shown in Box Figure 13-1. The tumor had destroyed the ventromedial nucleus of the hypothalamus. In animal studies destruction of the ventromedial nucleus has been found frequently to cause overeat-

ing and obesity. In some species, such as the cat, the same operation usually makes the animal display rage behavior more often and more readily than a normal animal does. Hypothalamic areas involved particularly in sexual receptivity and in mating behavior are also found nearby, but in the case of this patient the reduced gonadal function was probably caused by interruption of pathways by which the hypothalamus regulates the pituitary gland. This dysfunction would also explain the observed decreases in thyroid and adrenal cortex function, since these endocrine glands are also regulated by the anterior pituitary gland. The causes of the confusion and the malfunctioning of memory are not clear, although hypothalamic structures have been implicated in learning and memory.

In a similar case described by Beal et al. (1981), the patient also showed loss of memory. He slept most of the time, but when he was awake he ate almost continuously when food was available. At autopsy a tumor 2 cm in diameter was found in the third ventricle. The tumor had destroyed both the posterior hypothalamic nuclei, which probably caused the somnolence, and the ventromedial nuclei, which probably caused the hyperphagia.

These cases show how a small tumor—about the size of the last joint of the little finger—because of its location in a critical region of the brain, could affect a variety of motivated behaviors: eating, aggression, and sex. The neurologists who reported the first case concluded: "The findings provide a close functional correlation between the human and homologous lower mammalian ventromedial hypothalamic structures" (Reeves & Plum, 1969, p. 622).

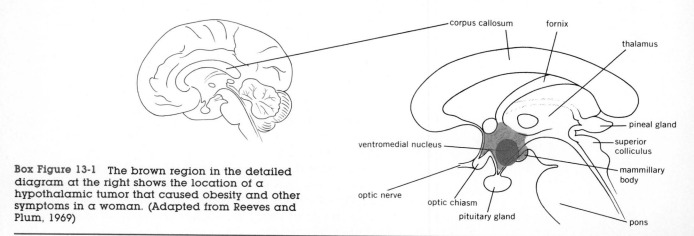

Box Figure 13-1 The brown region in the detailed diagram at the right shows the location of a hypothalamic tumor that caused obesity and other symptoms in a woman. (Adapted from Reeves and Plum, 1969)

Ventromedial Hypothalamus: The Satiety Center?

Occasionally a person develops a pathologically voracious appetite and soon becomes obese. Box 13-1 describes such a case. In the last century, physicians began to find that some of these patients had lesions or tumors at the base of the brain. In 1940, Hetherington and Ranson reported that bilateral lesions of the ventromedial hypothalamus (see Figure 13-6) caused rats to become obese. Further research by others showed that VMH lesions produce obesity in all the species that have been tested—monkeys, dogs and cats, several species of rodents, and some species of birds. Most of the studies have been done on rats, so our data come mainly from them, but we will show the relevance of these data to human behavior.

The VMH was promptly called a satiety center because destroying it seemed to prevent animals from ever being satiated with food, but this characterization was soon seen to be inadequate. Destruction of the VMH did not simply cause the rats to become mere feeding machines. Rather the eating habits of VMH-lesioned rats were still controlled by both the palatability of food and body weight, but these controls were no longer exerted in normal ways. If palatable food of high caloric content is available, VMH-lesioned rats typically show two phases of postoperative weight gain. At first they show an amazing increase in consumption, eating two or three times as much as normal; this condition is called **hyperphagia** (from the Greek roots *hyper,* meaning "over," and *phagia,* meaning "eating"). Body weight shoots up, a stage called the **dynamic phase of weight gain** (see Figure 13-7). But after a few weeks, weight stabilizes at an obese level, and food intake is not much above normal; this stage is called the **static phase of obesity.**

Some observations indicate that the obese VMH-lesioned rat regulates its weight at a new target value, considerably above the preoperative norm, but this regulation is not as complete as normal regulation. If an obese rat in the static phase is force-fed, its weight will rise above the plateau level; but when it is again allowed to eat on its own, body weight returns to the plateau level. Similarly, after an obese rat has been deprived of food and has lost weight, when given free access to food, it will regain its plateau level. This regulation is incomplete, however, because the plateau level depends on the availability of a palatable high-fat diet. If VMH-lesioned rats are kept on a diet of laboratory chow pellets, their weight does not rise much above that of control animals. If the food is adulterated with quinine to make it bitter, then body weight of the VMH-lesioned rats may fall below that of controls (Sclafani, Springer, & Kluge, 1976). VMH-lesioned rats tend to be finicky, not only in their exaggerated feeding reactions to the palatability but also in the amount of work they will perform to obtain food. The lesioned rats will not work as much as normals to obtain food.

Genes can result in a high target weight, as is seen in rats of the Zucker strain (Zucker & Zucker, 1961). Rats that are homozygous for the recessive fatty gene have fat cells that are more numerous and of larger size than those of their heterozygous littermates. These fat rats maintain their obesity even on diets strongly adulterated with quinine or when they are required to work hard to obtain food (Cruce et al., 1974). The Zucker fat rats provide a better example of the set-point interpretation of the control of feeding than do VMH-lesioned rats. Rats with lesions of the VMH and those with genetically caused obesity may provide models for two different kinds of human obesity.

(a) Rat brain, showing the locations of the frontal sections illustrated below

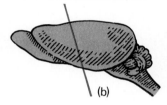

(b)

(b) Frontal section through the hypothalamus

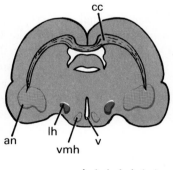

cc

an   lh   v   vmh

6 mm

Figure 13-6 Areas of the rat brain involved in control of eating. The lateral view of the brain in (a) shows the plane of the frontal section illustrated in (b). (an, amygdaloid nuclei; cc, corpus callosum; lh, lateral hypothalamus; v, third ventricle; and vmh, ventromedial hypothalamus)

Figure 13-7 Phases of weight gain after lesioning of the ventromedial hypothalamus.

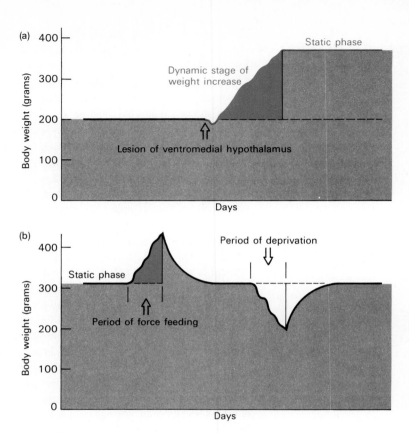

Lateral Hypothalamus: The Hunger Center?

The other part of the dual-center hypothesis was the hunger center. In 1951, Anand and Brobeck announced that bilateral destruction of the lateral aspect of the LH caused rats or cats to refuse to eat. This **aphagia** was so severe in some cases that animals died of starvation even in the presence of their usual food. The investigators proposed that the LH contains a ''feeding center'' and that the VMH normally acts as a brake on feeding by inhibiting the LH. Two important features about the effects of LH damage soon emerged (Teitelbaum & Stellar, 1954). First, the rats refused not only to eat but also to drink; they showed **adipsia** as well as aphagia. If the experimenters placed a bit of food or a drop of water on the lips or in the mouth of the rat, it spat out the food or water as if it were distasteful. Second, the aphagia and adipsia were not necessarily permanent. A few rats began to eat and drink spontaneously after about a week. Even those who did not recover in this way would eventually eat spontaneously if they were kept alive meanwhile by having food and water tubed into the stomach. So just as VMH destruction does not abolish all inhibition of eating, LH destruction does not permanently prevent eating and drinking.

An animal recovering from an LH lesion goes through four main stages (Wolgin, Cytawa, & Teitelbaum, 1976). In the first two stages, there is general neglect of sensory inputs and also a loss of behavioral activation. In stage 1 the animal is aphagic and adipsic; food or water seem aversive and are avoided, and body weight drops rapidly. In stage 2 the animal remains adipsic but becomes **anorexic** (showing lack of appetite) rather than refusing food. If a cat or rat in stage 2 is aroused by painful stimulation such as pinching the tail, it will eat, but when the painful stimulation ceases, the animal falls back into lethargy. At this stage amphetamine enhances eating. This is curious because many people use amphetamine or related drugs to suppress appetite. But amphetamine has both stimulating and appetite-suppressing effects, and at stage 2 the stimulating effect seems to be the more important one. In stages 3 and 4, specific deficits of the lesion on eating and drinking can be seen. In stage 3 the animal can regulate food intake but continues to refuse water. If water is the only liquid available, the animal does not drink and therefore soon stops eating. However, it can be trained gradually to accept water flavored with saccharine. Some rats with large lesions never recover beyond stage 3, but some get to stage 4, in which they can live on dry food and water. Even after recovery, LH-lesioned rats are deficient in their response to treatments that lower blood glucose, such as injections of insulin. Also, they tend to drink water only while they are eating; that is, they drink to aid ingestion of food rather than to regulate fluid.

Recovered LH-lesioned rats regulate their body weights with precision at a nearly constant percentage of the weights of control rats. The larger the size of the LH lesion, the lower is the target level of body weight. If food is restricted, the weights of LH-lesioned and control rats fall in parallel, and then the predeprivation level is regained when free access to food is restored (see Figure 13-8). Similarly, if eggnog is the only food available, both lesioned and control rats gain weight in parallel; and when the usual diet is restored, both groups then fall to their previous level. When food is adulterated with quinine, the LH-lesioned rats again show changes strictly in parallel with normal controls (Keesey & Boyle, 1973), whereas we saw that VMH-lesioned rats displayed an exaggerated reaction to quinine. Thus the LH-lesioned rats are said to defend a lowered weight target or set point (Keesey, 1980).

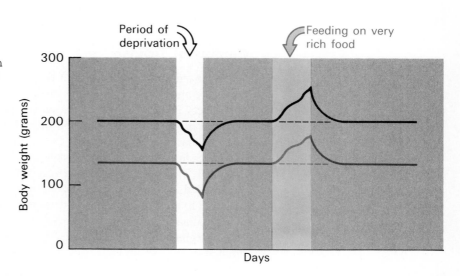

Figure 13-8 Regulation of body weight by normal rats (black line) and by rats that have recovered from lesioning of the lateral hypothalamus (brown line). The LH-lesioned rats regulate around a lowered target weight but in parallel with normal rats.

Human beings may become emaciated if they suffer from lesions or tumors in the lateral hypothalamus. Bilateral damage to the LH through accident or disease is, of course, rare, but even unilateral damage to the LH sometimes produces aphagia and adipsia in animals. Cases of LH anorexia in humans are about a quarter as frequent as cases of hypothalamic obesity (White & Hain, 1959).

Figure 13-5 summarizes some of the main aspects of the dual-center model:

- The two regions have opposite influences on both external behavior and internal adjustments. Activity of the LH enhances positive feeding stimuli, facilitates feeding responses, and promotes the mobilization and utilization of the body's food supplies. Activity of the VMH potentiates aversive feeding stimuli, facilitates withdrawal from food, and promotes storage and conservation of internal food supplies.
- Several kinds of evidence indicate that the VMH and the LH reciprocally inhibit each other (Hernandez & Hoebel, 1980). The effect of a partial lesion of one of these regions can be moderated by a partial lesion in the other. Thus a rat with small bilateral lesions in the LH is more likely to accept food if it also sustains damage in the VMH. Recording the electrical activity of single neurons in the VMH and the LH also demonstrates reciprocal innervation. Excitation of some of the cells in the one area causes decreases in the firing rate of certain cells in the other area. This result has been observed with electrical stimulation and also with injections of glucose or insulin, either systemically or to individual cells.

Dual-Center or Multifactor System?

The adequacy of the dual-center hypothesis was soon challenged by further observations. For one thing, controversies arose as to whether the lesions were effective because they destroyed integrative centers, as originally believed, or because they interrupted fiber tracts that passed through these regions. For another thing, it was found that many brain regions outside the hypothalamus are involved in regulation of feeding behavior, and they do not contribute solely by their connections to the hypothalamus. Among the regions whose destruction impairs the regulation of feeding are the amygdaloid nuclei, the frontal cortex, and the substantia nigra. In the next two sections, we present some examples of research on the question of centers versus tracts and the roles of amygdaloid nuclei.

Centers or Tracts?

When Anand and Brobeck (1951) first reported that LH lesions caused aphagia, they were aware that these lesions invaded the medial forebrain bundle and certain other tracts. Their analysis of the results convinced them, however, that no aphagia occurred in cases where the lesion missed the intended target in the LH and destroyed adjacent tissue, including the nearby tracts. More recently other investigators have studied this question in detail, cutting tracts anterior, posterior, or lateral to the LH. They have found clear effects on feeding behavior even when the LH was not invaded. Similar transection experiments have been conducted with tracts that run close to the VMH in order to determine whether the VMH actually plays a role in regulation of feeding. In complementary experiments investigators have employed techniques to destroy cells in a region without injuring fibers that pass through it.

Selective damage to the **nigrostriatal bundle** (NSB) causes many of the symptoms of LH destruction. The NSB is a dopaminergic tract that originates in the substantia nigra of the midbrain, passes through the LH and then through the globus pallidus, to terminate in the caudate-putamen. Cutting this tract or depleting its dopamine by using the drug 6-hydroxydopamine (6-OHDA) causes aphagia and adipsia (Marshall, Richardson, & Teitelbaum, 1974). Other effects are finickiness to quinine-adulterated food and failure to respond to lowered glucose.

Cutting the trigeminal nerves or their central tracts interferes seriously with ingestion of food or water, as was mentioned briefly. Initially rats with bilateral section of the trigeminal nerves will not eat hard, dry rat chow and would starve if they were not given soft, moist, palatable food. Gradually they progress through different diets until eventually they accept lab chow again. For prolonged periods, rats with trigeminal nerve section remain below their preoperative weight, and they are poor at increasing their intake when food is diluted calorically. Thus these rats resemble those with LH lesions.

Does destruction of tracts—the nigrostriatal bundle or the central trigeminal tracts—account for all the effects of lesioning the lateral hypothalamus?

A technique used to destroy cells of the LH without impairing the fiber tracts that pass through it employed kainic acid, a neurotoxin that overexcites and destroys some cell bodies close to its site of injection but that does not affect fibers that pass through the region. When a small amount of kainic acid was slowly infused into the LH over several minutes, rats became aphagic and adipsic. Histological examinations revealed a marked reduction of neurons in the LH but no signs of damage to axons of passage. Biochemical assays revealed no difference in dopamine levels in the brains of the experimental animals, confirming that NSB fibers were unaffected (Grossman et al., 1978; Stricker et al., 1978). Thus killing cell bodies in the LH, without affecting axons that pass through the region, impairs feeding and drinking behavior.

From the experiments in which either the LH neurons or the fiber bundles were impaired separately, we conclude that the hypothalamic cells play a more specific role in the resulting deficits of eating and drinking than do the fibers of passage, although impairing the fibers can also interfere with eating and drinking.

Amygdaloid Nuclei and Control of Feeding

Lesions of the amygdaloid complex can cause either aphagia or hyperphagia, depending on the parts of the amygdala destroyed (Figure 13-9). Bilateral lesions of the basolateral subdivisions of the amygdala cause hyperphagia, while bilateral lesions of the corticomedial subdivisions cause aphagia. These effects have been reported in cats, dogs, and monkeys, but they are most striking in rats (C. I. Thompson, 1980). With large lesions that destroy the amygdala and surrounding tissue, the basolateral effect predominates, and hyperphagia results.

The basolateral divisions send fibers to the LH, where they exert an inhibitory effect; that is, stimulation of the basolateral amygdala leads to inhibition of neurons in the LH. The same stimulation also excites cells in the VMH, probably across a synaptic relay. The corticomedial amygdala inhibits the same VMH cells that are excited by the basolateral amygdala.

Figure 13-9 Diagram of presumed connections from amygdaloid nuclei and hypothalamic nuclei to brain stem motor nuclei for eating behavior. The amygdaloid nuclei exert effects on the brain stem nuclei both directly and through the ventromedial and lateral nuclei of the hypothalamus. Note that the two main divisions of the amygdala have opposite effects on eating. (BL AMYG., basal lateral amygdala; CM AMYG., corticomedial amygdala) Activity of the basolateral amygdala suppresses eating, so ablation of this region causes hyperphagia.

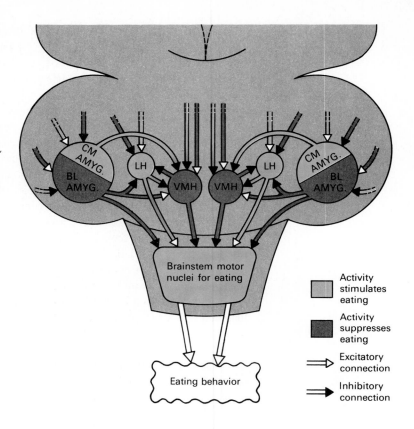

But the effects of the amygdala on feeding are not exerted entirely through the LH and the VMH. This result is shown by the finding that the hyperphagia caused by amygdaloid damage still persists after destruction of the VMH and the LH (Morgane & Kosman, 1960). Also, bilateral destruction of the amygdala leads to the peculiar symptom of indiscriminate eating, which is not found with hypothalamic lesions. For example, monkeys with bilateral temporal lobectomy were found to put anything into their mouths, including hardware, live mice, and snakes (which monkeys normally fear); later this symptom was attributed specifically to destruction of the amygdala. A human patient with extensive destruction of the temporal lobe was reported to exhibit an enormous and indiscriminate appetite, ingesting "virtually everything within reach, including the plastic wrapper from bread, cleaning pastes, dog food, and feces" (Marlowe, Mancall, & Thomas, 1975). So the amygdala affects eating both through the hypothalamus and independently of the hypothalamus.

Cycles of Change in Target Weight

We noted earlier that animals of several species show seasonal changes in body weight. One carefully studied case is that of golden mantled ground squirrels of the High Sierra. These ground squirrels gain weight in the summer and fall and lose weight in the winter during hibernation. Even if these animals are born and kept in a laboratory at a moderately warm temperature and do not hibernate, their weight continues to show regular circannual cycles, rising to a peak around July and August and falling to a trough around April and May. In order to study controls over the cycle, the experimenters surgically removed fat pads from several squirrels and studied them over the next months (Dark, Forger, & Zucker, 1984). In some animals the fat was removed during the annual phase of weight gain, and in others it was done during the phase of weight loss. Within two months each animal had compensated for the removal of fat and was back at about the body weight it would have been without the surgery. In the case of squirrels operated on during the phase of weight loss, the animals did not passively accept the total weight loss, but rather they first made up for most of the removal and then continued a regular controlled loss of fat. The recovery of fat did not involve a compensatory increase in consumption of food, so presumably it was accomplished by reduced expenditure of energy. This suggests that reduced expenditure of energy normally contributes to the seasonal development of obesity in this species. The accurate compensation in weight for loss of fat deposits indicates that there is a precise monitoring of the fat reserves, but we do not know how this is accomplished. Nor do we know how the cyclic changes in target weight are produced or communicated to the circuits that regulate energy expenditure and body weight.

Initiation of Feeding

How do the neural systems operate to initiate and terminate eating? In adult human beings, the time of starting to eat is largely a matter of custom and habit. Most of us eat on a rather regular schedule that is largely a matter of social convenience. In the United States the usual schedule consists of three meals a day, with the last meal at the end of the afternoon or early evening. In some parts of Europe, there are five regular meals—breakfast, second breakfast or coffee break, lunch, teatime, and a late supper. Among some African tribes, adults eat only one meal a day. This diversity of human meal patterns shows that learning and habit play major roles in initiation of eating.

Among different species of mammals, there is great diversity in spacing and duration of meals. Many animals must spend most of their waking hours eating. This phenomenon is true of most small mammals, because with their large surface-to-volume ratios they lose heat rapidly to the environment. It is also true of herbivores, since their food is low in caloric content and large amounts must be ingested in order to meet nutritional needs. Even these animals do not eat all the time, however, and research has studied the factors that initiate and terminate their feeding. Most intriguing is the case of large carnivores.

We are used to seeing large carnivores, such as African leopards, receive a single daily meal in a zoo. The timing of the meal is scheduled for the convenience of the viewing public, and the amount of food is planned to keep the leopard in good health. The leopard "wolfs" it down. In nature the timing and size of a carnivore's meals are much less regular. On one day the leopard may make several small kills and consume each promptly. On another day the leopard may kill a large antelope that proves too much to eat at a sitting. Rather than abandoning the rest of its prey to scavengers, the leopard may carry it up into a tree and stash it where the foliage hides it from the vultures above and where it is safe from jackals or hyenas. What factors determine when the leopard will stop one meal and when it will start another?

Future needs as well as present needs influence the feeding of many species. For example, animals that hibernate accumulate large stocks of fat, which enable them to survive the long period when they do not eat. Elephant seals also store fat in advance of the mating season, a period when they do not eat. Some species of birds accumulate fat resources before starting long migratory flights. Many species that do not undergo such extreme tests—like the leopard—nevertheless store some reserves so that they are not always on the edge of hunger. Thus the signals that initiate feeding are not the disappearance of bodily stores but rather indications that they are below some target level.

For many centuries the signal that initiated eating seemed obvious: A person eats when he or she feels hungry. Physiologists in the last century and the early part of the present century attributed feelings of hunger to some state of the stomach: Some claimed it was an increase in secretion of gastric juices, and others claimed it was a decrease; some claimed that feelings of hunger were induced by activity of the stomach, and others claimed that inactivity of the stomach was responsible. Then as investigators became capable of doing research on the brain—stimulating neurons, recording their electrical activity, and making localized brain lesions—interest in the control of feeding shifted from processes in the gut to neural processes. From the 1940s on, brain processes and brain circuits held center stage. Then in the 1970s and 1980s, an effort was made to bring peripheral processes back into the picture along with central processes. Now an account of the control of feeding includes taste and shifts in palatability, stomach activity and gastric secretions, monitoring of substances in the blood, and the interaction of excitation and inhibition in brain regions. In this section we will examine research that has supported this modern view. First we will take up studies that explore the effects of localized stimulation of the brain on eating. Then we review some investigations of how internal and external stimuli affect activity of brain sites that are related to eating.

Effects of Localized Stimulation of the Brain

Localized stimulation in different sites in the brain of an experimental animal can evoke different kinds of motivational behaviors—eating, drinking, copulation, aggressive attack, or fearful escape. This result was demonstrated by the Swiss physiologist Walter R. Hess in the 1940s, and his research brought him a Nobel Prize in 1949. Other investigators readily confirmed the occurrence of **stimulation-elicited behavior** (stimulation-induced feeding, stimulation-induced drinking, and the like). Nevertheless, the interpretation of these phenomena has stirred up much controversy and engendered a great deal of further research. One issue has been whether the stimulation really elicits a motivational state or whether it only forces the animal to perform consummatory acts as if it were a puppet whose strings were being pulled. Another issue has been whether stimulation at a particular site really elicits a specific motive; perhaps the brain stimulation only facilitates whatever motive is strongest at the time or most appropriate to the external circumstances (such as presence of food or water or a mate).

Tests have shown that electrical stimulation of the LH does not simply elicit stereotyped feeding movements. Quite different locomotor movements may be evoked on successive trials, depending on where the animal happens to be in relation to the food source when the brain stimulation starts. Also, the feeding responses are appropriate to the nature of the food, whether it is a liquid, a soft mash, or hard pellets. If the animal had previously learned when food deprived to press a lever to obtain food pellets, then it will readily begin to press the lever when the LH is stimulated. These results suggest that the stimulation produces a motivational state not unlike that caused by food deprivation.

Signals That Initiate
Feeding

Granted that feeding is initiated by activation of a neural system that includes the LH, what signals cause this activation? They could be either signals that act in an excitatory way on the feeding system (including the LH) or signals that inhibit the satiety system (including the VMH). Inhibiting the satiety system could initiate feeding, because the satiety system normally inhibits the feeding system.

Internal Monitoring

Many investigators have proposed that the body monitors its food stores. An indication that these supplies are falling below a set value could be the trigger that activates the feeding system. Many different indices of food stocks have been suggested. Among the most prominent are the rate of utilization of glucose and the supply of fat, which may be indicated by some by-product, such as free fatty acids. The signal (or signals) may well be material carried in the circulating blood. Evidence for this comes from experiments in which the peripheral circulation of two animals is joined surgically; this is called a **parabiotic** preparation. When one member of a pair of such parabiotic rats is fattened by being given highly palatable food or being force-fed, the partner shows a compensatory reduction of its fat stores (Harris & Martin, 1984; Pavamaswaren et al., 1977). Apparently a signal in the circulation indicates an oversupply of fat.

For a little background before considering the research on these hypotheses, let us note briefly some differences in the fuels used by the brain and the rest of the body and also shifts in these fuels as a function of time after eating. Note that the brain chiefly utilizes glucose and, unlike other organs, does not require insulin for this purpose. Under conditions of deficiency, the brain can also use ketone bodies, but these cannot completely replace glucose. The rest of the body has more flexible requirements, and when glucose is in short supply, the body shifts to other fuels, such as free fatty acids and ketone bodies, to spare glucose for the brain.

Since glucose is the primary fuel of the brain, it was logical to suppose that the brain might directly monitor the supplies of glucose. Evidence for this hypothesis has been accumulating since the 1950s. Some of the most convincing evidence has come from recordings of the activity of single neurons in the VMH and the LH (Oomura, 1976). Application of glucose to single neurons was found to stimulate about a third of the VMH neurons, whereas it had an inhibitory effect on about a third of the LH neurons. The generally opposite effects found in the two hypothalamic regions are shown diagrammatically in Figure 13-10. Insulin alone tended to hyperpolarize and inhibit VMH neurons, but it potentiated the response to glucose. The response of most brain cells to glucose is not facilitated by insulin; the fact that

Figure 13-10 Schematic representation of responses of cells of ventromedial hypothalamus (VMH) and lateral hypothalamus (LH) to glucose, insulin, and free fatty acids. Response frequencies are indicated as increases (up) or decreases (down) from the baseline frequency. (Adapted from Y. Oomura; Figure 2, in D. Novin et al. (Eds.), *Hunger: Basic Mechanisms and Clinical Implication* (New York: Raven Press, 1976), p. 149.)

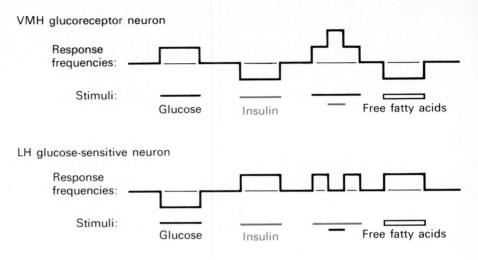

the VMH acts like body cells in this regard suggests that the VMH may be capable of monitoring the glucose utilization of tissues that depend on insulin for uptake of glucose. Note that glucose, especially in the presence of insulin, stimulates the VMH (a part of the satiety system) and inhibits the LH (a part of the feeding system). On the other hand, free fatty acids stimulate the LH and inhibit the VMH; their presence in the blood may indicate that lipid stores are being drawn upon. Thus initiation of the disposition to eat could be signaled by lack of glucose or by presence of free fatty acids or both.

Mayer (1953) proposed that it is not the absolute level of glucose but rather the rate of glucose utilization that is monitored by cells in the hypothalamus. Glucose utilization can be estimated by measuring the difference between concentrations of glucose in the arterial and venous blood (the A–V difference). A large A–V difference means that glucose is being taken up by the cells, and this uptake is correlated with satiety in human subjects. A small A–V difference reflects low uptake of glucose, a condition found to be associated with hunger. Diabetics feel hungry with high levels of glucose because without sufficient insulin most body organs cannot take up much glucose, so diabetics have a low A–V difference. Thus a low A–V difference of glucose may be one of the main signals leading to the state of readiness to eat.

Human beings usually report feeling hungry at mealtimes, even if they have eaten only a few hours previously and are in no significant state of depletion. Is this just habit or "imagination," or may there actually be a reduced A–V glucose difference at the usual mealtime? In rats that were put on a schedule of one meal per day at a fixed hour, a conditioned release of insulin and consequent lowering of blood glucose were observed in the few minutes before the expected meal (Wiley & Leveille, 1970; Woods et al., 1977). It seems likely that such conditioning occurs in people, since release of insulin has been measured when they look at food at mealtime (Rodin, 1976) or when they imagine food intake under hypnotic suggestion (Goldfine et al., 1970).

It is an old idea that contractions of the empty stomach cause hunger pangs and that it is these sensations that initiate eating. But hunger sensations and regulation of food intake have been found to persist in human beings in whom removal of vagus nerve connections to the stomach has eliminated stomach contractions. Human patients who have sustained total removal of the stomach report that they continue to experience hunger just as they did before the operation. Thus it is quite clear that it is monitoring in the central nervous system that provides the main signals that make mammals ready to eat.

External Stimuli and Initiation of Feeding

It is obvious that hungry people or animals do not eat unless there are edible objects available, but the importance of sensory information about such objects and other aspects of the environment is often overlooked in discussions of feeding behavior. Part of the initiation of feeding lies in perception of appropriate food objects. There is a two-way interaction: Perception of food objects can heighten the motivation to eat, and increased motivation can enhance the salience and palatability of food.

The importance of sensory stimulation for eating has been demonstrated both in LH-lesioned animals and in intact animals. Part of the difficulty with LH-lesioned animals is that they tend to ignore sensory stimuli. In stage 1 of recovery, sensory neglect and apathy can be counteracted by painful stimulation or by amphetamine. Later the stimuli from food objects can play this role. When cats make the transition from stage 1 (aphagia) to stage 2 (anorexia), visual stimuli are of primary importance (Wolgin, Cytawa, & Teitelbaum, 1976). If opaque occluders are placed over the eyes of cats in this stage, they will not approach food, and they will not eat even if food is placed right in front of their mouths. Needless to say, a normal cat that is blindfolded will find food placed anywhere in a room and will accept food presented to it. The transition to stage 3, when animals become able to maintain their weight on palatable food, coincides with the emergence of olfactory control over feeding. At this stage blindfolded cats will accept food and can find it in their cages. Smell also seems to activate the recovering animals both to search for food and to consume it.

Some hypothalamic cells respond specifically to the sight of food objects—but only when the animal is hungry! This result was found in recording the activity of single neurons with implanted electrodes in awake monkeys (Mora, Rolls, & Burton, 1976; Rolls, 1978). In a sample of several hundred neurons examined in the lateral hypothalamus, 13% had activity related to perception of food objects. In most of these neurons, the response occurred before the food was placed in the monkey's mouth, while the monkey looked at such objects as a peanut, a banana, or mash. These neurons did not respond to the presentation of nonfood objects, to muscular movements, or to emotional arousal. When the monkeys were fed until they were satiated, the neurons lost their responsiveness to food stimuli. When the monkeys were trained during a recording session to associate a neutral object with food, then the conditioned stimulus elicited responses from the "food" neurons.

The discovery of hypothalamic neurons that respond specifically to food does not, of course, show that such cells are unique to the hypothalmic areas; perhaps such neurons occur in other regions as well. Also, it does not prove that these cells play a role in initiation of feeding; perhaps they merely reflect responses to food objects, either muscular responses or glandular responses such as salivation. Experiments were therefore undertaken to test alternative interpretations. The route of visual information to the LH probably passes through the inferotemporal visual association cortex and the lateral amygdala. Ablation of either of these regions produces a syndrome in which monkeys do not recognize objects and tend to place all sorts of objects in their mouths. Recordings of single neurons in the inferotemporal cortex or the amygdala did not, however, reveal cells with specific responses to food objects.

To test whether the specific LH neurons might be participating in initiation of feeding responses, the investigators trained monkeys to respond in a special situation. The monkey, restrained in a chair for electrophysiological recording, faced a shutter that could open to reveal a stimulus object. When certain objects were shown, the monkey could obtain a small amount of fruit juice by licking a tube positioned just in front of its mouth. But when other objects were presented, a lick yielded aversive hypertonic saline solution. The monkey therefore learned to pay attention and to discriminate the food signals from the negative stimuli. Under these conditions the latency of response of hypothalamic neurons to food stimuli was 150–200 milliseconds (msec); the latency of response of the tongue muscles was about 300 msec; and the latency of contact with the tube was at least 400 msec. Thus the hypothalamic units clearly responded before the motor units. They may well participate in the initiation of feeding responses, but further research will be required to establish this definitively.

The research to date suggests the following conclusion: A disposition to eat, or a central motive state of hunger, is induced by internal signals that indicate either a lack of available food stores in the body or a level of stores that is below the current target value. Feeding behavior is initiated when the disposition to eat is accompanied by perception of appropriate food objects or of stimuli that have been conditioned to food. Feeding behavior can be terminated or weakened by activity of the satiety system, a subject we consider next.

Termination of Feeding

Fullness of the stomach has long been thought to be the signal to stop eating. This condition has been demonstrated to be the main signal that terminates feeding in the fly. Does the same simple arrangement work in mammals? Research has shown that the stomach also signals satiety in mammals, but chemoreceptors as well as mechanoreceptors in the stomach are probably involved, and the stomach may not be the only part of the gastrointestinal tract involved in satiety.

An animal's monitoring food intake through its mouth and throat does not produce satiation any more than oral monitoring terminates drinking. This result was found by feeding animals that had been equipped with esophageal fistulas (just as such tubes were used in the study of the control of thirst). These animals pass large amounts of food through the mouth, so it appears that the taste and kinesthetic sensations of food sustain feeding. But tasting food may play a role in satiation, in combination with other signals.

Neural signals from the stomach and especially hormonal signals from the stomach and duodenum are the major factors that produce satiety. There is good evidence that the stomach not only senses the bulk of food ingested but that it also assesses the caloric value of the food. The arrival of food into the duodenum causes the release of a hormone from the mucosal lining of the duodenum; several lines of evidence suggest that this hormone, **cholecystokinin** (CCK), is involved in satiety. (This hormone was originally found to cause contraction of the gallbladder, which aids in digestion; hence its name, from the Greek roots *cholo,* meaning ''gall'' or ''bile,'' *cysto,* meaning ''bladder,'' and *kinein,* meaning ''causing movement or contraction.'') Assessing the roles of the gastric and duodenal factors is important both in tracing out the specific processes involved in satiety and in developing therapies for dysfunctions such as obesity.

Evidence that CCK is important in satiety can be summarized briefly (Gibbs & Smith, 1984). Increased levels of CCK are measured in the blood within a few minutes after the start of eating; release is also elicited by placing emulsified fats, weak hydrochloric acid, or other materials into the duodenum of anesthetized cats or dogs. Eating can be suppressed in hungry rats, cats, or dogs by giving them intraperitoneal injections of CCK. The suppression of eating appears to be specific, because CCK does not reduce water intake in thirsty animals. If a rat equipped with an esophageal fistula is sham feeding, an intraperitoneal injection of CCK produces the normal sequence of behaviors that rats show when they have eaten their fill—a short period of grooming or exploration, then rest or sleep. The satiety does not appear to be produced by making the animal feel ill or nauseated. Gibbs and colleagues reached this conclusion because pairing CCK with saccharine does not cause the animal to develop an aversion to saccharine, whereas aversions are easily established by pairing flavors with substances known to produce illness, such as lithium chloride. When given to people, CCK shortened the duration of eating (Stacher et al., 1982) and elicited reports of satisfaction (Stacher et al., 1979).

Recent research has shown that CCK also exists in neurons of the cerebral cortex. (This is one case among many in which compounds that act as hormones in the digestive tract have also been found recently as probable neurotransmitters in the brain.) Furthermore, genetically obese mice have significantly lower amounts of this substance in their brains than do nonobese littermates (Straus & Yalow, 1979). A ten-peptide chain that is part of the larger CCK molecule has been found to bind selectively to the VMH and to suppress eating. Thus CCK may be a hormone or neurotransmitter at several levels of the feeding-digestive system—the gallbladder, the duodenum, and the cerebral cortex. A deficiency of CCK in the brain may be related to the unrestrained appetites of the obese mice.

How does CCK work to produce satiety and terminate eating? Circulating CCK does not act directly on the brain because it does not pass the blood-brain barrier. Moran and McHugh (1982) suggested that CCK has an indirect effect: It inhibits the passage of food from the stomach and therefore causes distention of the stomach. Thus CCK contributes to a feeling of fullness in the stomach, which has long been accepted as a signal for satiety. Consistent with this explanation is the finding that the ability of CCK to induce satiety is abolished or markedly reduced if the vagus nerve to the stomach is cut (Smith et al., 1981); it is the vagus nerve that conveys sensory impulses from the stomach to the central nervous system. This is probably not the whole story because CCK can also induce satiety if it is combined with sham feeding, that is, if food is passed through the mouth and throat but is not allowed to reach the stomach. Although the sensations of passage of food through the mouth and throat cannot by themselves produce satiety, nor can CCK by itself, the combination of these two kinds of stimulation is effective. More work is being done in several laboratories to close gaps in the story. Several other peptides released from the gastrointestinal tract during feeding are also being studied in connection with control and termination of feeding.

Recent research has been changing markedly the traditional pictures of the gut and of endocrine involvement in the control of food intake. The gut was seen as a simple reservoir where food is absorbed; now it is seen as an active neuroendocrine organ—a sensory sheet that reacts to the chemical and mechanical stimuli of ingested food. The important hormones were thought to be activated as a consequence of the absorption of food and to exert their effects slowly and indirectly by affecting metabolic and nutritional processes. Now some investigators are suggesting that different neuroendocrine mechanisms are stationed in succession along the inner surface of the gut and are activated by contact with food; furthermore, the neuroendocrine actions are held to be rapid, direct as well as indirect, afferent, and mutually reinforcing (Gibbs & Smith, 1984; Smith, 1983).

The role of brain neurotransmitter systems in satiety is also being studied, using several converging techniques. These techniques include stimulation of neural tracts that run to various hypothalamic sites, interruption of tracts, and localized administration of neurotransmitters into brain regions. Thus, for example, administration of norepinephrine into the medial hypothalamus inhibits a satiety mechanism; the result is to terminate bouts of feeding without affecting the initiation or frequency of meals. The animal thus treated eats longer meals. Administration of serotonin in the same region excites the satiety mechanism, so meals are shorter. There is also evidence that injection of dopamine into the lateral hypothalamus inhibits a feeding center. Research is being pursued to trace the neurotransmitter tracts that affect brain circuits for feeding and to integrate these influences with peripheral autonomic and hormonal influences (Hoebel & Leibowitz, 1981).

Now that we have considered the basic systems that regulate initiation and termination of eating in mammals, we summarize these systems in Figure 13-11.

Figure 13-11 Basic systems that regulate feeding in a mammal. The signals from the gastrointestinal tract to the satiety system are chemical as well as neural.

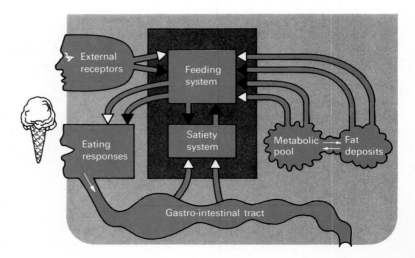

Specific Hungers and Learning

Food preferences change, partly because of shifting bodily needs and partly because of learning. People and animals learn (at least part of the time) to eat foods that improve their health and to avoid foods that poison them.

Some bodily needs seem to elicit unlearned specific hungers. We saw earlier that female flies increase their intake of protein in preparation for each clutch of eggs they produce. If the adrenal glands of a rat are removed so that it cannot retain much sodium chloride, it promptly begins to consume salt. A similar craving for salt was reported by Wilkins and Richter (1940) in a classic case. A 3½-year-old boy was brought to a hospital for examination because he showed marked development of secondary sexual characteristics. He refused most of the hospital diet and died suddenly one week after admission. Postmortem examination revealed an abnormality of the adrenal glands: The adrenal cells that produce gonadal hormones had overgrown and destroyed the cells that produce salt-regulating hormones. Inquiries then revealed that the boy had previously kept himself alive by eating great quantities of salt. He had refused foods that were not heavily salted, and ''salt'' was one of the first words he had learned. Many patients with Addison's disease, which involves destruction of the adrenal cortex, report a craving for salt; this craving can aid in early diagnosis of the disease.

Some substances that are important to health are not connected with specific hungers, but animals can learn to prefer foods that contain them. An example is thiamine (vitamin B). Rats made deficient in thiamine do not promptly recognize which of several available foods contains thiamine, but many of them will learn, over a number of days, to prefer that food. A flavor that has been associated with recovery from thiamine deficiency comes to be preferred over other flavors (Zahorik, Maier, & Pies, 1974). This effect has been called the medicine preference effect.

The opposite effect is called bait shyness, or taste aversion learning. If an animal eats a bit of a substance and then experiences a toxic effect, it will tend to avoid that substance in the future. Such learned aversions have been demonstrated in simple animals like slugs (Gelperin, 1975) and also in mammals, including people (Garb & Stunkard, 1976). It is not necessary that the ingested substance actually cause the toxic effect; if a harmless flavor is followed by injection of lithium chloride or by exposure to a high level of x-irradiation (both of which cause nausea), then a taste aversion is produced. For birds, visual cues (color or appearance of food) are more important than taste. Learning to avoid foods with negative consequences seems to occur very readily and strongly. It can occur in one trial and even if an interval of hours separates the experience of the flavor and the illness. It is reported to occur even if the toxic treatment is delivered while the animal is anesthetized, whereas other kinds of learning require wakefulness (Bureš & Burešová, 1981). Taste aversion learning in rats is impaired by damage to the gustatory region of the neocortex, the lateral hypothalamus, or the basolateral amygdala.

Obesity

Many people overeat and become obese, and some people abstain from food and become dangerously underweight. These facts test our knowledge of the processes of weight regulation and our capacity to use them effectively. We have seen that ventromedial hypothalamic brain lesions in people can give rise to hyperphagia and that lateral hypothalamic lesions can cause anorexia. So the animal lesion models help us to understand these cases. But we now know that many other lesions or transections in experimental animals can also cause disorders of weight control, and perhaps these have analogs in a variety of disease states in people. Beyond this, many obese or anorexic people do not show evidence of brain impairment, even on postmortem examinations. Perhaps the difficulties are more subtle, and some may require neurochemical rather than neuroanatomical analyses, as indicated by the findings of low CCK in the brains of obese mice. With control systems that are distributed at several levels of the nervous system and that include neurochemical and hormonal links, there are many possibilities for dysfunction.

These varied possibilities are borne out by a recent review in the *International Journal of Obesity* (Sclafani, 1984). It described 50 different animal models of obesity; that is, if you want to study a fat animal, there are 50 different ways you can go about obtaining or producing one. Several of these involve genetically obese strains of animals. Other methods involve use of special diets or force-feeding. Restricting activity can also be effective. Surgical lesions of certain brain regions or cutting certain neural tracts can also produce obesity, as we have seen. So can certain hormonal or pharmacological treatments. Sclafani states that attempts to classify kinds of human obesity have been less successful than animal studies, but he holds that study of animal obesities are providing important insights into the causes, consequences, and cures of human obesity.

Another approach is to consider obesity in relation to human evolution and history. Throughout human evolution, scarcity of food has been a recurring problem, and people have had to work long and hard to obtain enough to eat. Even today most nonindustrialized societies experience food shortages every few years—and some even more often. Thus human history has predisposed us to stock up our bodies for a famine, even though in advanced countries famine rarely arrives. History has also prepared us to exert effort in order to gain our livelihoods, but physical effort is less and less necessary in industrialized societies. The incidence of obesity has been increasing steadily in the United States over recent decades. Some investigators stress overconsumption of calorie-rich foods as the cause (e.g., Konner, 1982), whereas others emphasize the regulation of energy expenditure independent of food intake (e.g., J. K. Thompson et al., 1982). In support of the latter position, it has been observed that the populations of several countries (e.g., Argentina, Denmark, and Ireland) eat more but are less obese than the people of the United States. Certainly the restriction of activity has been demonstrated to lead to obesity in laboratory animals, and so have rich, palatable diets; the combination of inactivity and overeating may be especially effective. Obese patients have been characterized as having the behavioral repertoire of a clever, carnivorous tiger and the continual and easy access to food of a lucky, placid cow. Yet even under conditions of modern civilization many people manage to remain trim and fit. How do these individual differences occur?

One answer is that learning certainly plays a role. Fat parents are much more apt to have fat children than are thin parents. This is not mainly a matter of heredity because the effect of fat parents is just as great on adopted children—or even on pets! Furthermore, research with people and with animals shows that tendencies to eat a food and to stop eating it can be conditioned to particular states of the internal and external environments (Booth, 1981).

The problems of how regulation of energy and weight occur become especially urgent as the hazards of obesity become clearer. A National Institutes of Health panel recently declared obesity a disease and warned that even 5 or 10 pounds of overweight may be hazardous to health, increasing susceptibility to many diseases and reducing life expectancy (Kolata, 1985).

Fixing the Set-Point for Body Weight

A person or animal may regulate energy expenditure in such a way that body weight and fat stores are too high or too low for overall health and life expectancy. Sometimes such cases have been used to attack the idea that body weight or energy expenditure are being regulated. But rather than lack of regulation, such cases probably occur because the target or set-point is fixed at too high or too low a level. This is similar to a room being too hot or too cold for comfort, not because the heating or air-conditioning system is out of order, but because the thermostat has been set too high or too low. How are set-points fixed, and how can they be adjusted?

Earlier in this chapter we mentioned that many species typically go for weeks or months without eating and lose a great deal of weight. Could the same mechanisms be used by obese people? Do these animals become hungrier and hungrier as they abstain from eating, or do they show a progressive decrease in their set-point for body weight (Mrosovosky & Sherry, 1980)? As we saw earlier, weight of the golden mantled ground squirrel shows a regular annual cycle. Even ground squirrels that remain awake with food available during the winter lose weight, although not as much as squirrels that hibernate. When a squirrel emerges from hibernation and starts eating, it reaches the weight appropriate for the season rather than the higher weight at which it started hibernation. For another example, the female red junglefowl loses weight while it incubates its eggs. During this period it leaves the nest for less than 20 minutes per day. But even if food is made available at the nest, the junglefowl eats little and loses weight at the usual rate. If it is completely deprived of food for several days, however, the junglefowl then will eat more when food is restored and will regain the lower weight level that it was maintaining.

The neural mechanisms by which the set-points for body weight are modified are not yet known. An intriguing study has indicated hormonal control of weight regulation in the octopus (Wodinsky, 1977). The female octopus spawns only once in its life, eats less while caring for the eggs, and dies shortly after the eggs hatch. Removal of small endocrine glands in the optic lobes of the brain causes the octopus to stop caring for the eggs and to resume eating, and this operation greatly extends the lifespan. Mrosovosky and Sherry (1980) urge investigators to find natural physiological mechanisms for altering set-points. They hold out the possibility that such research might eventually make it possible for obese people to lose weight effortlessly even in the presence of palatable food.

A surprising example of adjustment of the set-point has come from surgical treatments for massively obese patients. In the 1960s, surgical operations were devised to bypass most of the intestine or most of the stomach in order to cut down the absorption of food in people whose weight could not be controlled in any other way. The operations have been successful, but not entirely for the expected reason: Decreased absorption accounts for only a quarter of the weight loss; three-quarters comes from decreased food intake, and this decrease seems to occur without any voluntary effort or any discomfort on the part of the patients (Stunkard, 1982). Many of the patients reported elation and increased self-confidence, in contrast to the depression that was common when they tried to diet. Attempts to understand the mechanism involved in reduction of the set-point in these patients has led to animal research. Recent experiments have been undertaken with genetically obese rats and also with rats made obese by hypothalamic lesions. In both cases intestinal bypass surgery resulted in decreased weight by resetting the level around which body weight is regulated (Stunkard, 1982). These experiments suggest that the main factor involved is persistent emptiness of the small bowel. If signals from this part of the gut are of importance in setting target weight, it may be possible to alter them by less drastic means than gastric or intestinal bypass operations.

Summary · Main Points

1. A relatively simple animal like the fly provides a model system for regulation of feeding. The fly is ready to eat whenever acceptable tastes or odors are encountered unless the relevant receptors are adapted or unless receptors in the gut signal fullness.

2. The ventromedial hypothalamus (VMH) used to be called the "satiety center" because its destruction can lead to overeating and obesity. But overeating occurs mainly during the dynamic phase of weight gain, and then weight stabilizes at a plateau. Also, weight gain occurs only if palatable food is available.

3. The lateral hypothalamus (LH) was called the eating center because its destruction causes aphagia and adipsia. However, if the animal is nursed through this stage, it may become able to regulate its food intake, although at a lowered target weight.

4. Some of the neural tracts that pass through the VMH or the LH account for some of the effects found when these regions are lesioned. But in general the functions of the tracts differ somewhat from the functions of the nuclei.

5. Other brain regions, such as the anterior neocortex and the amygdaloid nuclei, also contribute to control of feeding.

6. Stimulation-induced feeding occurs when electrical stimulation of the LH causes an animal promptly to begin eating available food even if it is satiated. The stimulated behavior is appropriate to the situation and is not simply forced motor movements.

7. Different brain sites have been found where stimulation elicits different motive states (hunger, thirst, copulation).

8. Regulation of weight is not necessarily around a fixed set-point. Some species show circannual cycles of body weight, related to such behaviors as migration, breeding, and hibernation.

9. The feeding system is activated by signals that the body's food stores are falling below a set value. One such signal may be a low rate of glucose consumption, reflected in a low arterial–venous glucose difference.

10. Sensory information about the availability of food is needed along with internal signals if feeding is to be initiated. Sensory signals may also heighten motivation. Some cells in the hypothalamus respond specifically to perception of the presence of food objects in the environment.

11. Termination of feeding is triggered by neural signals from the stomach and probably also by a hormonal signal—the release of the hormone cholecystokinin (CCK) when food reaches the duodenum.

12. Food preferences change, partly because of specific hungers and partly because of learning both to accept beneficial foods and to avoid foods that are accompanied by adverse consequences.

13. Adjustments in the rate of energy expenditure play a significant role in maintaining the energy balance and in keeping body weight relatively constant. Regulation is seen more clearly in energy expenditure than in intake of food.

Recommended Reading

Brownell, K. D., & Foreyt, J. P. (Eds.). (1985). *Physiology, psychology, and treatment of eating disorders*. New York: Basic Books.

Hoebel, B. G., & Novin, D. (Eds.). (1982). *Neural basis of feeding and reward*. Brunswick, ME.: Haer Institute.

Stunkard, A. J., & Stellar, E. (Eds.). (1984). *Eating and its disorders*. New York: Raven Press.

Thompson, C. I. (1980). *Controls of eating*. Jamaica, N.Y.: Spectrum.

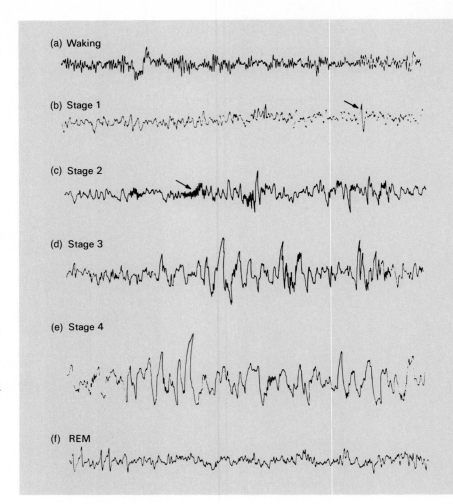

(a) Waking

(b) Stage 1

(c) Stage 2

(d) Stage 3

(e) Stage 4

(f) REM

14 Biological Rhythms and Sleeping/Waking

He made the moon for the seasons;
The sun knows the place of its setting.
Thou dost appoint darkness and it becomes night
In which all the beasts of the forest crawl about.
The young lions roar after their prey
And seek their food from God.
When the sun rises they withdraw
And lie down in their dens.
Man goes forth to his work
And to his labor until evening.

Psalm 104:19–23

ORIENTATION

All living systems from plants to humans show periodic changes. The frequency of these oscillations varies from the very rapid, such as brain potentials, to quite slow, such as annual changes like hibernation. Some of these periodic changes involve physiological systems whose character has begun to be discovered by researchers. Indeed, the regularity of some oscillations such as daily rhythms has a "clocklike" feature that is most intriguing. The attention of most researchers in this field is focused on daily rhythms—circadian processes. More recently attention has also been directed to both shorter and longer frequencies of rhythmical events—those that range from minutes to seconds and those that extend from a month to years. A daily rhythm that we are most familiar with is the sleep-waking cycle whose relevance to us is reflected in the fact that by the time we reach 60 years of age, most of us have spent 20 of those years asleep! Since sleep accounts for so large a slice of our lives and those of many other animals, it is quite surprising that the behavioral and biological features of sleep remained unstudied for so long. However, since the early 1960s sleep has been a major focus of investigation in physiological psychology. Attention has been directed to this issue for several reasons, and perhaps foremost among them is the recognition of the complexity of sleep; it is not simply nonwaking but rather the interlocking of elaborate cyclical processes, an alternation of different states. Further, the behavioral correlates of these different sleep states range from the suspension of thought to a galaxy of images and dreams. In this chapter we will discuss the characteristics of biological rhythms and patterns of sleep in human beings and other animals, the factors that influence sleep patterns, and the physiological events of sleep.

Biological Rhythms

Circadian Rhythms

Over the past 20 years, researchers have found that many of the functions of virtually any living system display an approximately 24-hour rhythm. Since these rhythms last about a day, they are called **circadian rhythms** (from the Latin *circa* meaning "about" and *dies* meaning "day"). By now circadian rhythms have been studied in a host of creatures at behavioral, physiological, and biochemical levels. One favorite way to study circadian rhythms in the laboratory takes advantage of the penchant of rodents to run in activity wheels when they are available. For the purposes of studying rhythmic behavior, a switch is attached to the wheel so that a computer registers each complete revolution. This revolution can be displayed on a recorder as a brief flick of a pen. The activity rhythm of a hamster in a cage where a running wheel is available is displayed in Figure 14-1. This behavior and many other responses show extraordinary precision—so much so that variation from one day to another in the beginning of activity may be only on the order of minutes. If the animal is placed in a continuously darkened environment or if input to the brain from the eye is blocked surgically, the onset of activity starts a little bit later each day because it lacks an environmental synchronizing stimulus such as light (Figure 14-1, lower portion). This means that the **free-running period** of the rhythm is a bit more than 24 hours. The free-running period, then, is the natural rhythm. (A period is the time between two similar points of successive cycles, such as sunset to sunset.)

The free-running period reflects the rhythmic character of the endogenous process that generates the circadian rhythm. This endogenous process at some level must involve an oscillatory circuit. If we now expose a nocturnal animal that is in a free-running condition to periodic light and dark, what is commonly seen is that the onset of activity becomes synchronized to the beginning of the dark period. The shift of activity produced by a synchronizing stimulus is referred to as a phase shift, and the process of shifting the rhythm is called **entrainment.** Very few environmental stimuli have the ability to entrain circadian rhythms. Light is the dominant one, although in human circadian rhythms it is highly likely that social stimuli can also serve as entrainment signals. The ability to entrain circadian rhythms by light stimuli implies that the endogenous oscillatory circuit has inputs from the visual system. This issue is discussed later.

Figure 14-1 Activity rhythms of a hamster in a running wheel. Each revolution of the wheel produces a brief pen deflection, which forms part of a dark horizontal line. Each line represents a single day. Normally, a hamster becomes active shortly before the start of the dark phase of the daily cycle and remains active during the dark period. Dark brown indicates the daily period of darkness. After several weeks, the optic tract was severed; this is indicated by the arrow. (From Zucker, 1976, based on Rusak, 1975)

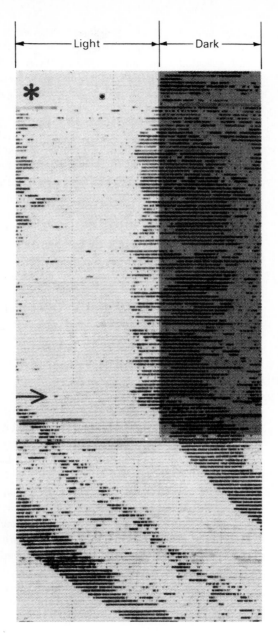

Biological Significance of Circadian Rhythms

Why are circadian rhythms valuable to an organism? The major significance of circadian rhythms is that they synchronize behavior and bodily states to changes in the environment. The inevitable fluctuations of light and dark during a single day have great significance for survival. For example, picture the small nocturnal rodent who can avoid many predators during the day by remaining hidden and who moves about hurriedly in the darkened night. An endogenous clocklike mechanism allows animals to anticipate periodic events, such as the appearance of daylight, and to engage in appropriate behavior before conditions change. It is common to speak of circadian rhythms as allowing for the temporal organization of an animal's behavior. Another important aspect of biological clocks is that they allow for resource partitioning—**diurnal** or daytime animals use daytime periods for obtaining food whereas nocturnal animals achieve adaptive success by satisfying the demands for an active life during dark periods.

Some Significant Properties of Circadian Clocks

Many experiments have explored the properties of circadian rhythms as seen in responses to many internal and external conditions. For example, are circadian clocks controlled by genetic factors? An interesting series of experiments on fruit flies has clearly established that clocks are inherited. In studies involving mutations, researchers were able to completely eliminate the circadian clock. Other mutations produced shortened or lengthened days (Konopka, cited in Kolata, 1985). Other experiments have also established that circadian clocks are relatively independent of temperature. This is a most important property since most metabolic processes are quite responsive to temperature; if the circadian mechanism had a similar sensitivity, animals simply would not be able to estimate time properly when external temperatures changed. Circadian clocks are also surprisingly resistant to many chemical substances that affect the nervous system.

Neural Pacemakers: Biological Clocks in the Brain

Where in the body are the clocks that drive circadian rhythms and how do they work? One way to establish the locus of circadian oscillators is to remove or damage different organs or sites and examine behavioral or physiological systems for any changes in circadian organization. The earliest use of this strategy by a pioneer in the field, Curt Richter, established that the brain was the site of the relevant oscillators. Richter had examined the effects of removal of various endocrine glands and showed that these operations had no effect in changing the free-running rhythm of blinded rats (Richter, 1967). Although Richter did show that hypothalamic lesions appeared to interfere with circadian rhythms, he did not pursue this work anatomically. In 1972, two groups of researchers clearly showed that a small region of the hypothalamus—the **suprachiasmatic nucleus (SCN)**—was the location of a circadian oscillator. (This nucleus gets its name from its location above the optic chiasm.) Stephan and Zucker (1972) showed that lesions in this region interfered with circadian rhythms of drinking and locomotor behavior, and Moore and Eichler (1972) showed that this same lesion interfered with daily rhythms of adrenal corticosteroid secretion. The impact of this lesion on activity rhythms of hamsters is shown in Figure 14-2.

The role of the suprachiasmatic nucleus is also nicely revealed in metabolic studies using autoradiographic techniques. Figure 14-3 shows the circadian variation in the metabolic activity of the suprachiasmatic nucleus. Clearly metabolic activity in this region is endogenously rhythmic, and this is evident in rats, cats, and monkeys. This metabolic tracing technique has also revealed some properties of fetal circadian clocks. In both rats and monkeys, the fetal suprachiasmatic nucleus shows a regular circadian rhythm of metabolic activity as revealed by the deoxyglucose technique. In these studies pregnant animals were injected with deoxyglucose,

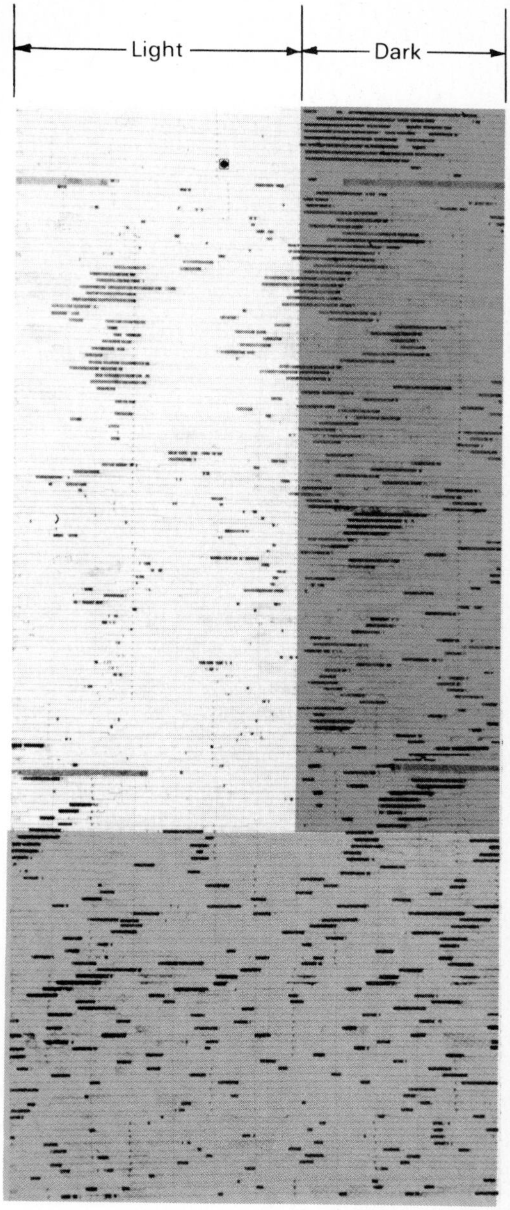

Figure 14-2 Lesions of suprachiasmatic nucleus eliminate circadian rhythms in hamster. Dark brown indicates the period of darkness and light brown indicates continuous light. (From Zucker, 1976, based on Rusak, 1975)

Figure 14-3 Daily variation in the metabolic activity of the suprachiasmatic nucleus (SCN), measured using 2-deoxyglucose. (a) Coronal section of the rat brain shows the darkly staining accumulation of 2-deoxyglucose in the SCN during the light phase. During the dark phase (b), the SCN does not stain darkly, indicating low metabolic activity. (From Schwartz, Smith, and Davidsen, 1979)

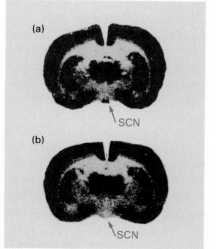

and measurements were made of the metabolic activity of the suprachiasmatic nucleus of both the parent and fetal animals. In rat fetuses a circadian rhythm in this brain region is evident shortly after this nucleus forms. The synchronizing of the fetal suprachiasmatic nucleus activity appears to be provided by as yet unknown signals from the mother (Reppert, 1985). Maternal control continues for a short time following birth. Researchers do know something about what to exclude as the maternal entrainment signal. The fetal rhythm survives removal from the mother of the pineal, adrenal, pituitary, thyroid, and ovaries. However, if the maternal suprachiasmatic nucleus is destroyed early in gestation, the suprachiasmatic metabolic activity of the litter is temporally scattered. Fetal clocks in this condition continue to function, but they are no longer in synchrony with each other. This reinforces the view that the fetal clock is driven by the mother.

[handwritten: Fetal clock driven by mom]

Recent developments in studying small pieces of brain tissue isolated from the body have revealed some fascinating properties of the suprachiasmatic nucleus. Slices of brain tissue are placed in a dish that is constantly bathed with fluids resembling the brain extracellular environment. These brain slices are also exposed to a mixture of oxygen and carbon dioxide gases that permits approximately normal metabolic activities. Studies of such isolated pieces of suprachiasmatic nucleus enable researchers to determine whether this area generates a circadian arrangement of neural activity completely isolated from other brain regions. Electrical recordings from these slices indicate that single cells of the suprachiasmatic nucleus show discharge rates that are synchronized to the light-dark cycle the animal had previously experienced. This is striking evidence for the endogenous character of the circadian oscillators in the suprachiasmatic nucleus. Another research finding that supports the same view comes from electrical recordings of the suprachiasmatic nucleus made in animals in which this region was partially isolated from other brain areas by large knife cuts. Again, striking circadian oscillations are evident in the temporal arrangement of neural activity (Inouye, cited in Turek, 1985).

What are the pathways that enable the entrainment of circadian rhythms by light-dark cycles? Across the animal kingdom there are some variations that are quite interesting (reviewed by Rusak & Zucker, 1979). Some invertebrates have photoreceptors not found in the eye that are part of the mechanism of light entrainment. For example, the pineal body of some amphibians is directly sensitive to light and is part of the mechanism of entrainment of circadian rhythms to light. In some birds whose eyes have been removed, it remains possible to entrain circadian rhythms by a light stimulus, which demonstrates that there are other photosensitive receptors that are involved in entrainment. However, in mammals, it is clear that retinal pathways mediate photoentrainment, since severing the optic nerve decisively ends the role of light in circadian rhythms of all varieties. Extensive research on the projections of the optic nerve to various brain regions laid the groundwork for systematic research that provided a clear identification of the entrainment pathway. Piece by piece the puzzle was assembled: lesions of the primary visual and accessory pathways did not alter entrainment to a light-dark cycle in rodents, although these animals appeared ''blind'' and showed no indication of visually guided orientation or discrimination behavior. Newer techniques of tracing pathways in the brain established the existence of a direct retinohypothalamic pathway in mammals (Moore, 1983), and lesions of this pathway interfere with photic entrainment. Researchers have also shown that a pathway from the lateral geniculate to the suprachiasmatic nuclei may also be pertinent to photic entrainment (Rusak et al., 1981). Figure 14-4 provides an outline of the circadian system including entrainment components.

[handwritten: mammals — retinal pathway mediate entrainment]

The work we have mentioned to this point shows that there is at least one major

Figure 14-4 A schematic model of the components of a circadian system.

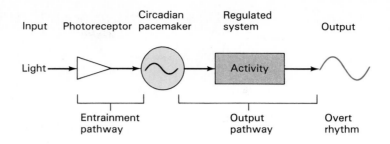

circadian oscillator in the brain that governs a number of circadian systems. Is this the only master oscillator? The answer is no: Some researchers have now shown that both free-running and entrained rhythms can be observed following suprachiasmatic lesions. One researcher, Moore-Ede (1983), has suggested that the circadian timing system of mammals consists of two master pacemakers that control many other secondary, passive oscillators. He suggests that there are two groups of circadian rhythms driven by two different master oscillators, one of which is found in the suprachiasmatic nucleus. He bases this suggestion on findings in humans of the desynchronization of various circadian rhythms seen when humans temporarily live in isolation chambers without timing cues, such as daily light-dark cycles (Figure 14-5). Under these conditions the core body temperature maintained its circadian rhythm, shortening a bit after day 35. After 35 days in isolation, the rhythm of rest and activity departed markedly from the 24-hour cycle and from body temperature. Researchers interpreted these results as the spontaneous uncoupling of two internal clocks. Moore-Ede's conception of the underlying mechanisms is presented in Figure 14-6. The issue of oscillators and what function each controls continues to be a major focus of current circadian rhythm research, and we can expect some resolution of this question with additional research results.

Figure 14-5 Desynchronization between the rest–activity and body temperature rhythms in a human subject in temporal isolation. Bed rest episodes (color) and body temperature (black) were entrained to a 24-hour day–night cycle on days 1–5, free-ran but maintained synchrony until day 35, then spontaneously desynchronized. After that point the period of the body temperature rhythm shortened and the rest–activity cycle increased its period. (Adapted from Czeisler et al., 1980)

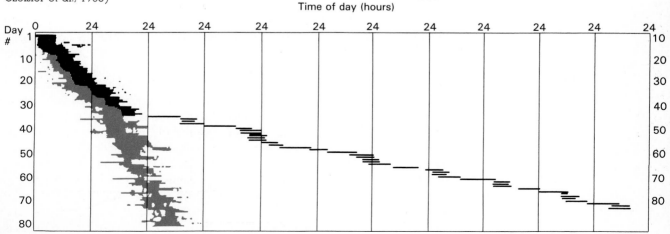

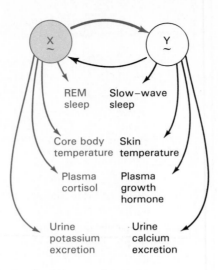

Figure 14-6 The two groups of rhythms appear to be driven by separate pacemakers. Pacemaker X drives the rhythms of REM sleep, core body temperature, plasma cortisol concentration, and urinary potassium excretion. Pacemaker Y drives the rest-activity cycle and the rhythms of slow-wave sleep, skin temperature, plasma growth hormone concentration, and urinary calcium excretion. The coupling force exerted by X on Y is approximately four times greater than that of Y on X. (Adapted from Moore-Ede, 1983)

Ultradian Rhythms

shorter than circadian

daydream

Among the many and diverse rhythmic biological events, there is a large group whose period is shorter than circadian rhythms. Such rhythms are referred to as **ultradian,** and their periods are usually from several minutes to several hours. The term *ultradian* is adopted for such phenomena because researchers in the field describe rhythms in terms of their frequency. A rhythm of less than 24 hours is a higher frequency event than a circadian event. Thus the "ultra" part of ultradian designates a greater frequency. Ultradian rhythms concern behaviors such as bouts of activity, feeding, sleep cycles, and release of hormones. Ultradian rhythms in humans have also been noted in more complex realms of behavior. In isolated human subjects who are without cues about time of day and in subjects in their normal environment, Kripke and Sonnenshein (1978) presented evidence showing a 90-minute cycle of daydreaming characterized by vivid sensory imagery. Ultradian rhythms in performance of various tasks may reflect fluctuations in alertness, a suggestion offered by Broughton (1985) to account for the presence of ultradian rhythms in the performance of poorly motivated subjects and their absence in highly motivated subjects. Support for this view is provided by the finding that there is an ultradian rhythm in frontal EEG frequencies.

The periods of ultradian rhythms seem to be correlated with such measures as brain and body size; more rapid cycles are typical of smaller animals (Gerkema & Daan, 1985). Several manipulations make these rhythms more apparent (and perhaps more regular); these include examining them early in development prior to the appearance of circadian rhythms, exposure to constant illumination (which dampens the circadian rhythm), and destruction of the suprachiasmatic nucleus. The functional advantage of nonrandom timing of such events within a single day is easy to see in some cases. For example, animals that flock together would be better served by synchronizing their foraging behavior so that individuals are not isolated and therefore subject to predation. Synchrony of grazing and rumination in herbivores is evident on any ranch. There are many other instances in the behavior of social animals where ultradian rhythmicity and synchrony of these rhythms among animals have advantages for survival.

Rhythmic fluctuations of hormone levels during the course of day have been noted by several researchers. For example, there is some evidence that the release of luteinizing hormone is pulsatile, once every 60 minutes (Knobil & Hotchkiss, 1985). These researchers have also shown that electrical activity in the hypothalamus (medial basal region) of monkeys shows a rhythmic form of bursts every hour. The work of Wilson et al. (1984) shows a strong positive relation between the electrical activity of the hypothalamus and levels of circulating luteinizing hormones.

What are the underlying mechanisms that generate ultradian rhythms? Two broad classes of generators have been suggested by Gerkema and Daan (1985). One type, they suggest, involves a renewal or homeostatic process, which means that the behavior is part of the generating mechanism controlling the timing of the behavior. For example, rhythms in foraging and feeding behavior may emerge from the regular and continuing interaction between hunger and feeding in species that eat frequently during the day. A second type of generator of ultradian rhythms consists of an underlying oscillator which drives regular physiological and behavioral events. Destruction of the suprachiasmatic nucleus, which destroys circadian timing of activity in voles, does not affect their ultradian feeding rhythms. However, lesions to other hypothalamic areas produce a breakup of ultradian rhythmicity. These lesions include parts of the rostral and basal hypothalamus. Work on the ultradian character of sleep cycles is presented in a subsequent section.

The area of ultradian events is a developing one with considerable import for the variability of behavior within a single day. Phenomena that fit ultradian rhythmicity are still relatively scarce, and the interrelations among various ultradian events remain to be determined. For example, do all ultradian rhythms reflect the operation of a single clock, which is a basic rest-activity clock, or are there many different oscillators that can separately control a variety of ultradian events?

Circannual Rhythms

The behavior of many animals is characterized by annual rhythms, some of which are driven in part by exogenous factors, such as food availability. A contribution of endogenous circannual oscillators to this process is shown in the persistence of annual rhythms under constant conditions. Obviously this is a realm of research that requires considerable patience, and the number of studies relevant to this topic is beginning to increase markedly. The pertinence to human behavior is also becoming more relevant in the form of seasonal disorders of human behavior (discussed in Chapter 15) that are quite striking. The types of problems that are relevant in this area are like those that have been explored in the analysis of circadian phenomena. Some examples of research are briefly presented.

The possibility that suprachiasmatic nuclei control circannual rhythms of ground squirrels maintained in constant conditions of photoperiod and temperature was assessed in studies by Zucker et al. (1983). These researchers measured activity rhythms, reproductive cycles, and body weight cycles. Zucker and his colleagues clearly established that suprachiasmatic lesions disrupted circadian activity cycles, but there were some animals in which these lesions did not affect seasonal changes

May also involve separate mechanism

in body weight and reproductive status. Circannual cycles, then, do not arise from a transformation of circadian rhythms and may involve a separate oscillatory mechanism.

Although seasonal rhythms do not arise from a transformation of the circadian oscillator, it is important to note that circannual changes in circadian rhythms can be demonstrated. This is nicely demonstrated in the work of Lee et al. (1986), who found annual changes in the daily pattern of wheel running behavior of golden mantled ground squirrels. It should be noted that golden mantled ground squirrels are ordinarily hibernators with a six-month period of relative inactivity. However, even animals kept in constant conditions of temperature and a light-dark cycle of 14 hours light and 10 hours dark maintained their activity cycles unvaryingly for several years. Every spring the onset of activity started earlier in the 24-hour period than during the fall.

Circanual Δ rhythm for circadian rhythm

Pronounced seasonal rhythms in gonadal hormones are evident in many animals. Is it possible that changes in these hormones, such as testosterone, account for annual cycles? Work reported by Zucker and Dark (1986) shows that annual cycles of body weight are not affected by gonadectomy in male ground squirrels. Annual cycles of hibernation and gonadal function in these animals survive early removal of the pineal gland.

Research in this area has clearly shown strong seasonal rhythms in many bodily functions. Such rhythms may mediate species-typical features of many behaviors such as reproduction and hibernation.

Sleeping and Waking

Defining and Describing Human Sleep

Sleep seems to be characterized by the absence of behavior; it is a period of inactivity with raised thresholds to arousal by external stimuli. For some animals we can add to this definition the feature of a distinctive reclining sleep posture, although this posture is less evident in hoofed mammals.

Sleep research gained momentum in the early 1960s when experimenters found that brain potentials recorded from electrodes on the human scalp (EEG) provided a way to define and describe levels of arousal and states of sleep. This measure of brain activity is usually supplemented with recordings of eye movement and muscle tension. The classification of sleep derived from these measures includes two main classes, **slow-wave sleep** and **rapid eye movement** or **REM sleep.** In humans it is possible to further divide the class of slow-wave sleep into four distinct stages.

What are the electrophysiological criteria or distinctions that define different sleep states? To begin, we note that the pattern of electrical activity in the fully awake, vigilant person appears as a desynchronized mixture of many frequencies dominated by waves of relatively fast frequencies (greater than 15–20 hertz [Hz]) and low amplitude. With relaxation and closing of the eyes, a distinctive rhythm

Figure 14-7 Characteristic EEG patterns for different stages of sleep. Scalp-recorded EEG of a person during relaxed waking, stages 1, 2, 3, and 4 of slow-wave sleep and REM. The arrow in the stage 1 tracing points to a sharp wave called a vertex spike that appears during this period. The arrow in the stage 2 tracing points to a brief period of sleep spindles characteristic of this stage. (Based on Rechtschaffen and Kales, 1968)

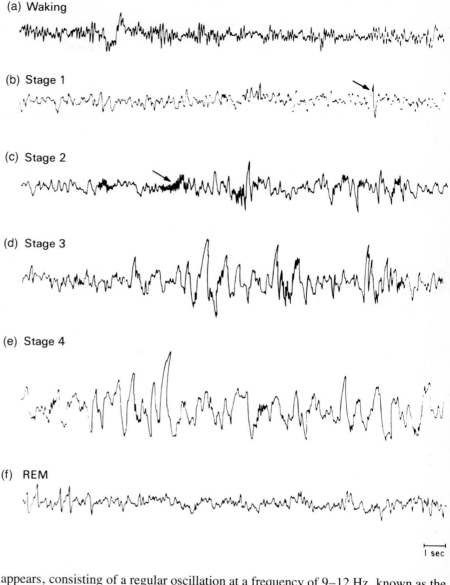

(a) Waking

(b) Stage 1

(c) Stage 2

(d) Stage 3

(e) Stage 4

(f) REM

1 sec

appears, consisting of a regular oscillation at a frequency of 9–12 Hz, known as the **alpha rhythm** (Figure 14-7a). It is particularly prominent in posterior scalp regions. As drowsiness sets in, the amplitude of the alpha rhythm decreases, and at some point it disappears and is replaced by much smaller amplitude events of irregular frequencies (Figure 14-7b). This stage is called **stage 1 slow-wave sleep;** during this period there is a slowing of heart rate and a reduction of muscle tension. Many subjects awakened during this stage would not acknowledge that they had been asleep, although they might have failed to respond to instructions or signals demanding action. This period usually lasts for several minutes and gives way to **stage 2 sleep,** which is defined by EEG events called spindles that occur in periodic bursts (Figure 14-7c). These are bursts of regular 14–18-Hz waves that progressively increase and then decrease in amplitude. About five spindles per minute occur in this stage. In addition, the EEG shows K complexes associated with spindles. These are large-amplitude negative-positive deflections that precede some spindles. Now our subject is quite unresponsive to the external environment, and under the closed eyelids the eyes begin to roll about in a slow, uncoordinated manner. In the early part of a night of sleep, this stage leads to **stage 3 sleep,** which is defined by the appearance of spindles mixed with quite large-amplitude slow waves (about one per second) (Figure 14-7d). During this period the muscles continue to relax, and heart rate and respiration rate fall lower. **Stage 4 sleep,** which follows, is defined by a continuous train of high-amplitude slow waves (Figure 14-7e). Stages 1 through 4 are all classified as **slow-wave sleep.**

After one hour a person has probably progressed through these stages in the first period of sleep. The human sleeper then returns quite briefly to stage 2, and a transition to something totally different occurs. Quite abruptly, scalp recordings display a pattern of small-amplitude, fast activity similar in many ways to that of the aroused vigilant person, but tension in postural neck muscles has disappeared (Figure 14-7f). (Because of this seeming contradiction—the brain waves look awake, but the musculature is deeply relaxed and unresponsive—one name for this state is **paradoxical sleep.**) Breathing and pulse rates become fast and irregular. The eyes now show rapid movements under the closed lids, so this stage is also referred to as **REM sleep, or rapid-eye-movement sleep.** These movements are much like the rapid movements characteristic of waking behavior. A host of distinctive physiological changes now occurs while our subject remains recumbent and, in terms of common behavioral descriptions, is decidedly asleep (see Table 14-1). Thus the EEG portrait shows that sleep consists of a sequence of states instead of just an ''inactive'' period.

Now let us consider the progression of these states through an ordinary night's sleep in humans, because the pattern changes somewhat during the course of the night.

A Night's Sleep   By now many subjects all around the world have displayed their sleep life to researchers in sleep laboratories. The bedroom the sleep subject walks into differs little from the usual sleep environment except for the presence of many wires. These lead to an adjacent room where machines record brain waves and experimenters stand by observing. The setting is aptly described by the title of a book by William C. Dement, a leading sleep researcher: *Some Must Sleep While Some Must Watch* (1974).

In this setting the subject goes to sleep in a usual way except that scalp electrodes are pasted in position on the scalp. In some studies cameras take pictures of changing body postures. Observations of major postural shifts during sleep reveal that most occur at phase transitions between slow-wave and REM sleep (Aaronson et al., 1982). Electrical recordings and behavior observation offer a portrait of a characteristic human sleep period. Although the onset, pattern, duration, and termination of sleep are affected by many variables, there is a regularity that allows a portrait to be drawn of the typical sleep state of adults.

Many different measures of the pattern of sleep can be obtained by scoring the

Table 14-1   Properties of Slow-Wave and REM Sleep

	Slow-Wave	**REM**
Autonomic activities		
Heart rate	Slow decline	Variable with high bursts
Respiration	Slow decline	Variable with high bursts
Thermoregulation	Maintained	Impaired
Brain temperature	Decreased	Increased
Cerebral blood flow	Reduced	High
Skeletal muscular system		
Postural tonus	Progressively reduced	Eliminated
Knee jerk reflex	Normal	Suppressed
Phasic twitches	Reduced	Increased
Eye movements	Infrequent, slow, nonconjugate	Rapid, conjugate
Cognitive state	Vague thoughts	Vivid dreams, well organized
Hormone secretion		
Growth hormone secretion	High	Low
Neural firing rates		
Cerebral cortex	Many cells reduced and more phasic	Increased firing rates; tonic activity
Event-related potentials		
Sensory-evoked	Large	Reduced
Drug effects		
Antidepressants	Increased	Decreased

several volumes of EEG records provided from a single night's observations. Incidentally, computer analysis techniques are permitting the development of automatic scoring and assessment of EEG records. Typical measures of a night's sleep include total sleep time, duration and frequency of different sleep states, and measures of the sequencing of sleep states.

The total sleep time of young adults usually ranges from 7 to 8 hours, and analysis of the distribution of sleep states shows that 45–50% of sleep is stage 2 sleep. REM sleep accounts for 25% of total sleep. An overall look at a graph of a typical night of adult human sleep (Figure 14-8) shows that repeating cycles of about 90–110 minutes duration recur four or five times in a typical night. The components of these cycles change in a regular manner through the sleep period. Cycles early in the night are shorter and are characterized by greater amounts of stages 3 and 4 slow-wave sleep. The latter half of a typical night's sleep is usually virtually bereft of stages 3 and 4 slow-wave sleep. In contrast, REM sleep is typically more prominent in the later cycles of sleep. The first REM period is the shortest, sometimes lasting only 5–10 minutes, while the last REM period just before awaking can last as long as 40 minutes in normal adults.

Regularities of sequence are also evident in examining human sleep cycles. REM sleep is invariably preceded by stage 2 slow-wave sleep. Exceptions to this pattern are seen only with infants and with some cases of disturbed nervous system

Figure 14-8 The course of a typical night's sleep in a young adult. (From Kales and Kales, 1970)

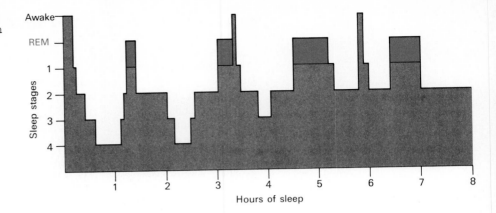

functioning. Brief arousals occasionally occur immediately after a REM period. Brief sleep periods called microsleeps occur during periods of wakefulness. These are bursts of stage 1 or 2 sleep, not longer than 10 seconds, with lapses of attention and responsiveness.

The sleep cycle of 90–110 minutes has been viewed by some researchers as the manifestation of a **basic rest-activity cycle** (Kleitman, 1969), and some have searched for cycles of similar duration during waking periods. For example, cycles of daydreaming during waking have an interval of approximately 100 minutes (Lavie & Kripke, 1981). Many other psychological and physiological properties show a 90–110 minute cycle; these include eating and drinking, play behavior of children, heart rate, and the relative dominance of one cerebral hemisphere over the other (Cohen, 1979).

Variations in the Human Pattern of Sleep

The portrait of human sleep shows many variations. Some differences can be clearly related to maturational status, functional states like stress, impact of drugs, and many other external and internal states. Changes over the life span will be considered shortly. We should note that some departures from this "normal" state of human sleep can be quite marked. Newspapers and scientific journals have made much of the unusual person who hardly sleeps at all. These cases are more than just folk tales. Dement (1974) reported that a Stanford University professor slept for only 3–4 hours a night for over 50 years and died at age 80. Reports of nonsleeping humans that can be verified by scientific observations are quite rare, however. After searching in vain for that exotic type of person and about to give up the quest, Meddis, a sleep researcher in England, found a cheerful 70-year-old retired nurse who said she had not slept since childhood. She was a busy person who easily filled up her virtually 23 hours of daily wakefulness. During the night she sat on her bed reading or writing, and about 2 A.M. she fell asleep for an hour or so, after which she readily awakened. She was persuaded to come to the sleep research laboratory for verification of her remarkable claim. For the initial two days in the laboratory she did not sleep at all since it was so interesting and there were people to talk with!

On the third night she slept a total of 99 minutes, and her sleep contained both slow-wave and REM sleep periods. At a later date, her sleep was recorded for five days and nights. On the first night she did not sleep at all, but on subsequent nights she slept an average of 67 minutes. She never offered complaints about not sleeping more and did not feel drowsy during either the day or the night. In his book *The Sleep Instinct* (1977), Meddis describes several other people who sleep either not at all or for about one hour per night. Some of these people report having parents who had a similar lack of sleep. The research literature also contains descriptions of people who fail to sleep because of brain injury or disease. Sleep patterns are malleable; they are influenced by many cultural variables, such as the characteristic daily schedule for a social group.

Some differences in sleep characteristics may be related to variations in human personality. Hartmann (1978) has offered some controversial work that compared and contrasted groups of short sleepers and long sleepers. Both groups consisted of normal volunteers who viewed themselves as sleeping for either a shorter or a longer time than most other people. Each subject slept several days in a laboratory and completed personality inventories and detailed interviews. Recording confirmed the subjects' reports of their characteristic duration of sleep and revealed interesting differences among them. The principal difference between short sleepers and long sleepers is in the time spent in REM sleep. Long sleepers spend an average of 121 minutes per night in this state, compared with 65 minutes for short sleepers. Slow-wave sleep differences between these groups are less marked, suggesting a fairly constant requirement for this phase. Psychological profile differences reveal that the short sleepers tend to show greater sociability, less nervousness, and can be described as efficient, energetic, sociable, adroit, and optimistic about life. Long sleepers include many more individuals who show greater personal stresses and appear mildly depressed. Generally they seem more indecisive than short sleepers and would be regarded as worriers. Hartmann (1978) suggests that certain life styles, especially those that generate worried concern about the world, may require more sleep and that the long REM periods of this group reflect the importance of this state in psychological recovery processes.

Evolutionary-Comparative Perspectives: Sleep in Different Animals

Behavioral and EEG descriptions of sleep states let us make precise comparisons of different sleep stages in a variety of animals. To date this technique has resulted in the description of sleep in a wide assortment of mammals and to a lesser extent in reptiles, birds, and amphibians (Campbell & Tobler, 1984). Since animals differ widely in various measures of sleep (for example, total sleep time per day or average length of REM sleep), it is hoped that such comparisons may enable researchers to determine what factors control the timing and periodic properties of sleep. How does the adaptive niche of an animal influence the properties of sleep? Do predators sleep differently from animals that are commonly preyed upon? What kind of ideas about the evolution of sleep can we develop from the study of contemporary animals? How is the evolution of sleep behavior related to evolutionary changes in nervous system structure?

The amount of daily life occupied by sleep and the percentage of sleep devoted to paradoxical sleep for a variety of animals are shown in Figure 14-9. Several

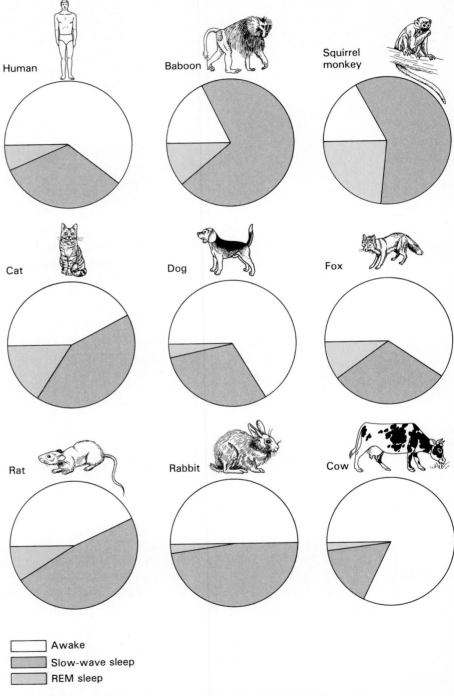

Figure 14-9 Comparisons of sleep states in various animals.

comparative generalizations can be drawn from these and many other observations in the experimental literature. Among mammals, all that have been investigated thus far, with the exception of the echidna (spiny anteater) and dolphin, display both REM and slow-wave sleep. The spiny anteater is an egg-laying mammal, a monotreme, that shows prolonged slow-wave sleep but no REM sleep. This creature is believed to have the oldest continuous history among current mammals. Its near rival for ancientness among existing mammals is the opossum, described by some sleep investigators as a "living fossil." The opossum (a marsupial—that is, an animal born at a very early developmental stage and spending a period of its development in a pouch) displays both slow-wave and REM sleep with EEG characteristics that are not distinguishably different from placental mammals. The comparisons between these two ancient mammals have suggested to some investigators that slow-wave sleep developed first (echidna date to about 130 million years ago). Comparisons of brain anatomy between these mammals or between echidna and all others may provide useful information about the structural developments during evolution that enable REM sleep to occur.

Although some researchers regard REM sleep as a more recent evolutionary development, Meddis (1979) has offered an interesting argument to the contrary. He notes that cycles of two main stages of sleep (REM and slow-wave or, as he describes them, active sleep and quiet sleep) are seen only in animals that regulate their temperature physiologically, that is, endotherms. Many data show that temperature regulation during REM sleep is poor, and this result leads him to suggest that REM sleep might be derived from ectotherms, animals that could survive with less accurate temperature regulation. It would be disastrous for endotherms to remain in a state in which they could not regulate their temperatures closely. Meddis offers a solution to the danger posed by REM sleep: slow-wave or quiet sleep, during which temperature regulation functions well. Thus slow-wave, quiet sleep may have evolved to rescue endotherms from markedly changing body temperature. According to Meddis, small animals have short periods of REM and short sleep cycles precisely because, given their limited body mass, they are more vulnerable to temperature changes produced by surrounding environmental variations.

Several other generalizations have been derived from comparative studies of sleep. In general, hoofed animals (donkey, cow, horse) sleep much less than other mammals, although the immature hoofed animals may display appreciable amounts of both slow-wave and REM sleep. Small animals have quite short epoch durations; an epoch is a period that consists of one episode of slow-wave sleep and a following episode of REM sleep. For example, for the laboratory rat, one sleep epoch lasts an average of 10–11 minutes, while for humans it lasts 90–110 minutes. This observation has contributed to the generalization that epoch duration is inversely related to metabolic rate (small animals tend to have high metabolic rates). But short epochs can also be caused by other demands. Some birds, such as the swift and the sooty tern, sleep briefly while gliding. The swift spends almost all its time in the air, except during the nesting season, and the sooty tern spends months flying or gliding above water, never alighting but catching fish at the surface.

Sleep in marine mammals, such as dolphins, whales, and seals, is especially intriguing because they must emerge at the surface of the water to breathe. One researcher who has explored the sleep of dolphins has shown that sleep in this animal is characterized by unihemispheric slow-wave sleep and the complete absence of REM sleep periods (Mukhametov, 1984). This means that one whole hemisphere is asleep while the other is awake! An example of EEG data that illustrate this unusual phenomenon is presented in Figure 14-10. During these periods of unilateral sleep, the animals continue to come up to the surface of the water to breathe; hence their sleep is not characterized by relative motor immobilization. This researcher also notes that sleep deprivation of one hemisphere does not increase the amount of sleep of the other hemisphere. Not all aquatic mammals are alike. Some seals show REM sleep and bilateral synchrony of slow-wave sleep. This usually occurs when they are out of the water.

Comparing the sleep of primates, we can see wide variations in temporal pattern, although the EEG waves look very similar and can be classified into the same stages of slow-wave and REM sleep. Stages 1 and 2 of slow-wave sleep predominate in the sleep of one primate, the baboon, which sleeps way out on the ends of smaller limbs of trees. Bert (1971) suggests that this location, which protects the baboon from predators, makes the total muscular relaxation of REM sleep more dangerous—the animal could fall out of the tree during REM sleep. Higher amounts of REM sleep are shown by the chimpanzee, which builds temporary nests on large branches.

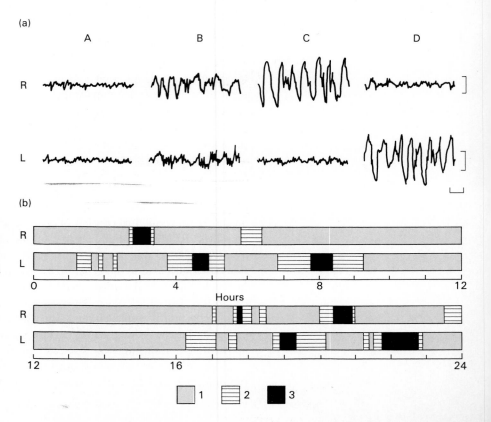

Figure 14-10 (a) EEG patterns in right (R) and left (L) brain hemispheres in a porpoise. A, bilateral desynchronization; B, bilateral intermediate synchronization; C, D, unilateral delta waves. Unipolar recording from roughly symmetrical areas of the parietal cortex. Time calibration 1 second, amplitude calibration 200 microvolts. (b) Diagrams of EEG stages 1 (desynchronization), 2 (intermediate synchronization), and 3 (delta synchronization) in right (R) and left (L) brain hemispheres of a bottlenose dolphin during a 24-hour session. Bipolar recording from roughly symmetrical areas of the parietal cortex. Time scale in hours. (From Mukhametov, 1984)

Most of the studies of sleep have been done with animals confined to the unusual environment of a laboratory, and some critics have suggested that the constraints of such a setting might tend to minimize the distinctive features of sleep for particular species. However, while this criticism might feel right intuitively, attempts to assess this possible limitation of laboratory studies do not offer much support. In a comparison of patterns of primates in the laboratory and in the field, several investigators have failed to note significant differences.

One way of organizing current comparative work has been offered by Meddis (1975). He suggests comparing animal groups according to these main features of sleep:

1. A circadian distribution of rest and activity.
2. At least one long period of inactivity per day.
3. Increased arousal thresholds to external inputs during the period(s) of inactivity.
4. Slow waves and associated inactivity.
5. REM sleep periods.
6. Species-typical sleep niches and a typical body position during sleep.

All vertebrates show a circadian distribution with a prolonged phase of inactivity, raised thresholds to external stimuli, and a characteristic posture during inactivity. In comparisons of various vertebrate classes, REM sleep is found in mammals, birds, and reptiles but not in monotremes, amphibia, or fish. Slow waves and associated sleep are evident only in mammals, birds, and monotremes.

Developmental Perspectives: Life Span Changes in Sleep

In any mammal the characteristics of sleep-waking cycles change during the course of life. These changes are most evident during early development, although the infant EEG in many species cannot be classified in precisely the same manner as that of an adult animal. In fact, the characteristic EEG picture of different stages of slow-wave sleep is not evident until age 5–6 in humans. At this age EEG data can be classified into stages just like adult EEG data. Infant behavior related to EEG findings enable researchers to distinguish between quiet sleep (similar to slow-wave sleep) and active sleep (similar to REM sleep). This distinction is drawn by differences in responses, such as muscle twitches, eye movements, respiration, and heart rate. Quiet sleep of infants is characterized by slower EEG, strong sucking, and irregular respiration. Active sleep is defined by the presence of phasic increases in respiration accompanying bursts of eye movements, very low amplitude EEG, facial grimacing, and occasional smiles. Let us look at the changing sleep patterns over the life span.

Sleep: Infancy Through Adulthood

Infants of virtually all mammalian species show larger amounts of total daily sleep than adults of the same species. They also show large percentages of REM or paradoxical sleep. For example, Figure 14-11 shows that in humans within the first two weeks of life, 50% of sleep is REM. REM sleep percentage is even greater in premature infants with about 80% REM sleep in infants born after 30 weeks gesta-

50% sleep
REM (infant)
80% (premature)

Figure 14-11 Changes in sleep with age in humans. (From Roffwarg, Muzio, and Dement, 1966)

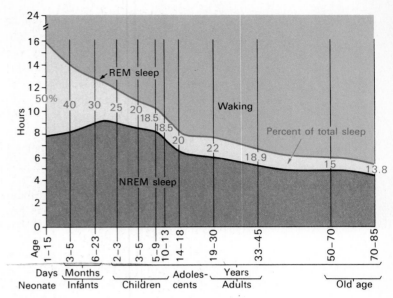

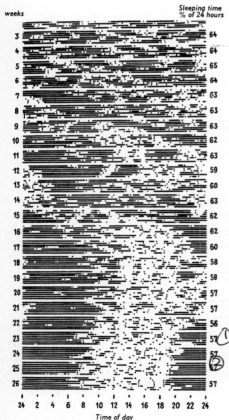

weeks

Sleeping time % of 24 hours

Figure 14-12 Development of circadian rhythm in the sleep-activity patterns during early infancy. The dark portions indicate time asleep and the blank portions, time awake. (From Kleitman and Engelmann, 1953)

Infants can directly go to REM

tion. Unlike normal adults, human infants can move directly from an awake state to REM sleep. By four months of age, REM sleep is entered through a period of slow-wave sleep. REM sleep of infants is quite active with muscle twitching, smiles, grimaces, and vocalizations. These behaviors during REM, especially smiles, are not related to any aspect of waking behavior; rather it has been suggested that they are endogenously generated (Challamel et al., 1985).

A clear cycle of sleeping and waking takes several weeks to become established in human infants. The establishment of a distinct 24-hour rhythm is illustrated for an infant in Figure 14-12. It is generally evident by 16 weeks of age. A further feature distinguishing infant from adult sleep is the number of changes of state and their average duration. Infant sleep is characterized by frequent state changes of shorter average duration than those seen in adulthood.

These features of the sleep of infants are attributable to the relative immaturity of the brain. This assertion can be demonstrated in several ways. First, premature human infants show even greater amounts of total sleep than full-term children. Second, some animals born in an advanced state of development (precocial animals), such as the guinea pig, show much less marked sleep pattern changes with aging.

The sleep patterns of mentally retarded children are different from those of normal children (Petre-Quadens, 1972). Examples of such differences include fewer eye movements during sleep and reduced amounts of REM sleep. Sleep EEG recordings at birth might be useful in identifying some suspected retarded children and facilitating early therapeutic intervention, especially in forms of mental retardation without biochemical or anatomical indicants.

A longitudinal study of normal infants has revealed an unusual REM event that is related to a measure of infant cognitive development (Becker & Thoman, 1981). In this study researchers noted an especially intense form of REM sleep in some infants. They showed eye and facial movements that were especially vigorous and almost seizurelike. This event was referred to as a REM ''storm'' and was particularly evident during the initial five weeks of life; then it usually abated. At the age of one year, two separate groups of infants were assessed using the Bayley Scale of Mental Development. The greater the number of REM storms at six months of age, the lower were the scores on the Bayley scale at the age of one year, although other measures, such as the amount of REM or slow-wave sleep, are not related to this measure of cognitive development.

Sleep in the Aged

In older age the parameters of sleep change more slowly than in early development. Figure 14-13 shows the pattern of a typical night's sleep in an elderly person. A decline in the total amount of sleep is evident, as is an increase in the number of arousals during a night's sleep. In the very elderly, insomnia (which may be partially confounded by daytime naps) is a common complaint (Miles & Dement, 1980). The most dramatic progressive decline is in stages 3 and 4 sleep—their amounts at age 60 are only 55% of what they are at age 20. The amplitude of slow waves during stages 3 and 4 also markedly declines with aging. The decline of amounts of stages 3 and 4 sleep in the aged is partly related to diminished cognitive capabilities at this age. This feature is emphasized by the marked reduction of stages 3 and 4 sleep in aged humans who show senile dementia. More recent data have raised a question whether the changes previously noted in the sleep patterns of the elderly are directly related to the aging process. A study by Reynolds et al. (1985) examining healthy seniors shows REM features comparable to features of young adults. Webb (1983) has emphasized the wide range of variability in sleep parameters of aged individuals, although he has also noted that a central difference between the young and the old is the older person's inability to maintain sleep; this is related to their sleep ''dissatisfaction.''

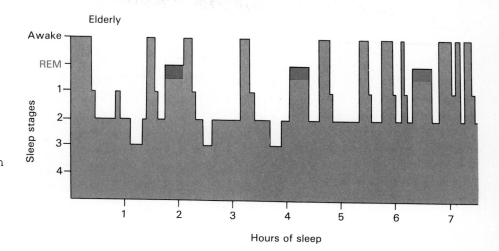

Figure 14-13 The customary pattern of sleep in an elderly person. This record is characterized by frequent awakenings, absence of stage 4 sleep, and a reduction of stage 3 sleep. (Adapted from Kales and Kales, 1974)

Functional Implications of
Life-Span Changes in
Sleep

What are the functional implications of these changes in sleep over the life span? The preponderance of REM sleep early in life led some investigators to suggest that this state provides some stimulation that is essential to the maturation of the nervous system. This hypothesis has not been developed in any detail and may confront some difficulties. Some support for the hypothesis comes from observations of the effects of REM deprivation in rats starting 11–12 days after birth. Elimination of this stage of sleep in rats is associated with reduced cerebral cortex size akin to that sustained by sensory deprivated animals (Mirmiran, 1986). It is also asserted that REM sleep deprivation in infancy interferes with the consequences of environmental enrichment for brain structures in rats. REM activity would appear to be rather random, and at an intuitive level an argument can be offered that patterned stimulation is an important developmental consideration. Another hypothesis is that REM sleep is important for consolidation of long-term memories. Since infancy is a time when much learning is taking place, this hypothesis may account for the large amount of REM sleep early in life. Other theoretical views suggest that the progressive changes in sleep states reflect comparable changes in the rate of development of information-processing capabilities. However, this assertion fails to establish close links of a causal nature between these parallel developments. The story of development and sleep is an intriguing but unfinished one.

Factors That Affect
Onset and Duration of
Sleep

Many studies have examined the impact of different environmental stimuli, social influences, and biological states on the pattern and temporal properties of sleep. From one viewpoint, sleep is an amazingly stable state. Major changes in the characteristics of waking behavior have only minor impact on subsequent sleep. For example, exercise before sleep seems to produce a shortening of the latency to the onset of the first sleep episode but has no impact on any other sleep parameter. Even social arrangements during sleep seem to have little impact. For example, Leiman and Aldrich in unpublished observations compared a sleeping-alone condition in cats with a condition of sleep with a more dominant or more submissive animal. During waking, dominance was strongly displayed by hissing and striking. However, continuous recording of waking and sleeping states revealed no significant impact on timing or pattern of sleep in either animal.

There are some conditions that can be manipulated by experimenters that do produce major shifts in sleep measures. These conditions are especially interesting because they reveal properties of sleep that give insight to its underlying mechanisms. We will examine some of these conditions in this section.

Sleep Deprivation

All of us at one time or another have been willing or not-so-willing participants in informal sleep deprivation experiments. Thus, we are all aware of some of the effects of partial or total sleep deprivation. Notably, it makes us sleepy! Why then do researchers examine the consequences of short- or long-term deprivation? A burst of sadism, perhaps? Or is sleep deprivation a way to explore some of the potential regulatory mechanisms of sleeping and waking? In general, the latter sentiment has guided the experimental investigation of deprivation as a factor affecting sleep-waking cycles. The majority of studies have been concerned with the phenomenon of sleep recovery. Does a sleep-deprived organism "keep track" of the amounts and type of lost sleep? And when the organism is given the opportunity to compensate, is recovery partial or complete? Can you pay off sleep debts? How many days of recovery sleep are necessary for any kind of compensation?

Disturbances During Sleep Deprivation

Another interest in sleep deprivation has drawn the attention of psychiatric researchers: Early reports in the sleep deprivation literature emphasized a similarity between instances of "bizarre" behavior provoked by sleep deprivation and features of psychosis, particularly schizophrenia. Partial or total sleep deprivation has been examined by these investigators in the hopes that it may illuminate some aspects of the genesis of psychotic behavior. A frequent emphasis in this work has been the functional role of dreams as a "guardian of sanity," partially inspired by early reports that REM deprivation can produce unusual emotional consequences that can be enduring. Tests of this hypothesis employing schizophrenic patients do not seem to confirm this view. For example, these patients can show sleep-waking cycles similar to nonpatients, and sleep deprivation does not exacerbate symptoms.

The behavioral effects of prolonged total sleep deprivation vary appreciably and may depend on some general personality factors and age. In several studies employing prolonged total deprivation—205 hours, or 8 to 9 days—some subjects showed occasional episodes of hallucinations. Only rarely is a psychotic state provoked by sleep deprivation in excess of 100 hours. The most common behavior changes noted in these experiments are increases in irritability, difficulty in concentrating, and episodes of disorientation. During each deprivation day, the effects are more prominent in the morning; by late afternoon and early evening, the subjects seem much less affected by the accumulating sleep loss. The subject's ability to perform tasks is best described in a quote from a review by L. C. Johnson (1969, p. 216): "His performance is like a motor that after much use misfires, runs normally for a while, then falters again." Tasks that elicit strong motivation and are brief in duration may show almost no impairment, even with prolonged sleep deprivation.

EEG effects during the course of sleep deprivation are particularly evident in measures of alpha rhythm—there is a progressive decline in the prominence of alpha rhythm. The EEG of these subjects takes on an appearance resembling stage 1 sleep, although the subjects move about. There is abundant evidence that sleep deprivation can provoke EEG and behavioral signs similar to those of people with seizure disorders.

Compensation for Lost Sleep

Many studies have been concerned with a possible compensation for sleep loss following total or partial sleep deprivation. To illustrate the recovery process in humans, Figure 14-14 provides data about 264 hours (11 days) of sleep deprivation in a young man. No evidence of a psychotic state was noted, and the incentive for this unusually long act was simply the young man's curiosity. This study was reported in scientific journals in 1966, and the self-appointed subject received considerable publicity at the time. Researchers got into the act only after the subject

Figure 14-14 Recovery of sleep after eleven days of total sleep deprivation. (Adapted from Gulevich, Dement, and Johnson, 1966)

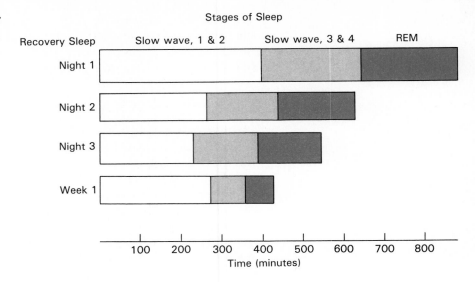

started his deprivation schedule, which is the reason for the absence of predeprivation sleep data. Nevertheless, these effects are comparable to many other data (although this subject appears to be the record holder for intentional sleep deprivation).

In the first recovery night, stage 4 sleep shows the greatest relative difference from normal. This increase in stage 4 sleep is usually at the expense of stage 2 sleep. However, the rise in stage 4 sleep during recovery does not completely make up for the deficit accumulated over the deprivation period. In fact, it is no more than reported for deprivation periods half as long. REM sleep with prolonged sleep deprivation shows its greatest recovery during the second postdeprivation night. The REM debt comes closer to being paid off, although it probably takes longer (that is, requires more recovery nights).

There have been many experiments with humans and other animals involving the "repayment of sleep debts." The experiments of the early 1970s dealing with this feature primarily involved rather short-term deprivation effects. The studies involved either total deprivation or, more usually, REM deprivation. The latter condition was achieved by forceful awakening of a subject whenever EEG signs of REM sleep appeared. These short-run, early-REM deprivation studies generally showed that in postdeprivation recovery sessions subjects made up for the loss of REM sleep in the form of longer duration REM episodes. With longer duration REM deprivation, the debt is paid off somewhat differently. In these instances recovery in terms of number of hours of REM sleep is not complete, but other forms of REM recovery become evident. For example, the loss of tension of postural muscles (for example, neck muscles), which is part of the signature of REM sleep, may appear in slow-wave sleep following prolonged deprivation. Thus the usual properties of REM sleep may be reallocated to other stages of sleep. This phenomenon has been observed in both humans and cats.

Recovery sessions may also involve another form of compensation. Several studies have noted that recovery night REM sleep is more "intense" than predeprivation REM episodes. Intensity in these experiments is evidenced by the number of rapid eye movements per period of time. Less consistent results have been obtained by using the arousal thresholds to either a sensory stimulus (such as a tone or buzzer) or direct stimulation of brain regions. Several investigators have noted that thresholds on REM recovery nights are higher than those of predeprivation REM sessions. These observations show that recovery REM sleep is somewhat dissimilar to usual REM sleep.

There is some evidence that the REM compensation phenomenon is particularly sensitive to the deprivation of the phasic events generally characteristic of this stage (for example, rapid eye movements). The pertinent data were derived from experiments with cats. One group of animals was totally deprived of REM sleep for two days, while another group was awakened for two days when phasic events occurred in either slow-wave sleep or REM sleep. The duration of these events in the slow-wave sleep of cats is rather trivial (1–2 minutes per sleep epoch). The rebound of REM sleep was greater in cats deprived of phasic events.

Many aspects of compensation following sleep deprivation remain to be explored. In recent years the confounding effects of stress induced by deprivation have limited research interest, although many important questions have not yet been resolved.

Sleep and Exercise

In many minds (especially parents') sleep restores whatever is used during a day's activities. From this perspective an especially active day should enhance the need for sleep and recuperative powers. One way to assess this notion is to examine the impact of daytime exercise on an evening's sleep. A simple task, but as Horne (1981) indicated in a review of the topic, it is characterized by many methodological difficulties. This is readily seen in data that show that the effects of exercise are different for trained athletes than they are for the more sedentary. Some of the effects of exercise on sleep may also be related to stress-induced changes mediated by adrenocortical hormones. Despite the methodological shortcomings of research in the area, there are some commonly agreed upon results. Marathon runners certainly constitute a group that would seem to be metabolically challenged. A study by Shapiro et al. (1981) showed effects on sleep of running 92 kilometers (km). This study involved a group of young adult males who were very fit and had experience in completing marathons. The intensity of the metabolic challenge was reflected in a marked increase in body temperature and a loss of weight during the race (despite the intake of considerable water). As a result of the potent exercise, total sleep time increased over control baseline values, and the most striking finding was the large increase in the percentage of slow-wave sleep stages 3 and 4. These effects persisted for several nights. This is a typical effect seen with trained and fit subjects—those accustomed to exercise. For others, the impact of exercise on sleep is more varied. A common finding is that exercise in such persons shortens the latency to the onset of sleep. This remains an interesting area whose data provide an important perspective on the presumed biological roles of sleep.

Effects of Drugs on Sleep Processes

Throughout recorded history humans have reached for substances that could enhance the prospects of sleep. Both sleep onset and maintenance have been aided by elixirs, potions, and, more recently, drugs. Early civilizations discovered substances in the plant world that induced sleep (Hartmann, 1978). Ancient Greeks used the juice of the poppy to obtain opium. Greek medicinals also included products of the mandrake tree, which we recognize today as scopolamine and atropine. Elixirs that combined the products of various plants provided sleep for many people until the birth of sleep pharmacology, which started with the synthesis of morphine from opium at the beginning of the nineteenth century. The preparation of barbituric acid in the mid-nineteenth century by the discoverer of aspirin, Adolph von Bayer, provided the basis for the development of an enormous number of substances—barbiturates that continue to be used for sleep dysfunctions.

Many chemicals that are not common sleeping pills can have consequences for sleep. Indeed, there are some suggestions in the clinical and experimental literature that drugs employed to control or ameliorate particular diseases may, through the roundabout route of modifying sleep, compromise their effectiveness. For example, the intense cardiovascular activation characteristic of REM sleep can be dangerous for heart disease patients. If drugs employed in the treatment of such diseases promote the likelihood of REM sleep, the vulnerability of the individual may, quite paradoxically, be increased.

The assessment of drug effects on sleep is beset with methodological difficulties. In the usual experiment, some substance is administered to a subject, and the sleep pattern is measured. Many studies clearly show that the effects of certain substances generally regarded as sleep inducers depend on both dosage and whether the assessment is made during a single night or over an extended period of time. The mode in which the drug is withdrawn also influences rebound or postdrug effects. As our knowledge of some of the underlying neurochemical events increases, some of the variability of results may become more understandable. One final critical note: Many assessments of the effects of drugs on sleep use normal young subjects who do not have apparent sleep disorders or complaints. Perhaps the use of such subjects limits the range of phenomena that could be examined. To provide an analogy: If you were interested in the antitubercular properties of some drugs, it is highly unlikely that you would assess this substance with subjects who show no signs of tuberculosis. There is simply no possibility of seeing a change in state since the tubercular state was not there in the first place.

One of mankind's oldest and simplest drugs is alcohol. Its effects on sleep seem to be typical of a larger class of "depressant" substances; that is, a relatively moderate dosage (comparable to two shots of whiskey within an hour) depresses REM sleep time. With continued consumption at this level over successive days, REM sleep recovers, and no effect is observable within three to five days. This result has suggested to some investigators that alcohol and similar drugs (such as barbiturates like those commonly used as sleeping pills) activate a REM compensation mechanism. Some data pertinent to this belief have been obtained from alcoholics during a withdrawal period. Following the cessation of alcohol intake, REM is markedly suppressed by the third day (which is also the period of maximum likelihood of delirium tremors in alcoholics). Then REM sleep becomes elevated for several days and again goes through a phase of suppression and recovery.

Marked suppression of REM sleep occurs with administration of antidepressant drugs (or "pep pills"). Amphetamine addicts may show a virtually complete absence of REM sleep during the period of drug use. Following cessation of drug use, rebound REM sleep in some cases may amount to 75% of the night's sleep and may occur as a rapid sleep onset phenomenon, unlike the normal case of a latency of 40 to 90 minutes. The preponderance of REM in the withdrawal sleep of amphetamine addicts may be related to the terrifying dreams they have during withdrawal. In a later section, we note that some other antidepressants inhibit REM sleep, but no subsequent rebound is evident.

A relation is evident between drug dependency and REM sleep. Substances that produce REM suppression and rebound are drugs that also cause dependency. In contrast, drugs that produce suppression without rebound do not lead to dependency. Some investigators (such as Hartmann, 1973) speculate that the physiological activities elicited by this second class of substances might replace the need for REM sleep. This class of drugs includes those used as antidepressants, such as monoamine oxidase inhibitors.

A 1979 report of a presidential commission has examined national reliance on and abuse of sleeping pills. They note that at least three-quarters of all prescriptions are written for sleep problems; very few of us have never taken medication to induce or maintain sleep. Viewed solely as a way to deal with sleep problems, current drugs fall far short of being a suitable remedy for several reasons. First, continual use of sleep medication results in a loss of the sleep-inducing property of these substances. Declining ability to induce sleep frequently leads to increased dosages that are self-prescribed and pose a health hazard. A second major drawback in the use of sleeping pills is that they produce marked changes in the pattern of sleep, both during the period of drug use and for a following period that may last for days. Most commonly during the initial phase of drug use a reduction of REM sleep occurs, especially during the first half of a night's sleep. A gradual adaptation to drug use is evident in the return of REM sleep with continued use of sleeping pills. Sudden withdrawal of many types of sleeping pill results in a period of REM rebound with an intensity that many people experience as unpleasant and may lead to a return to reliance on sleeping pills. A final major problem in the frequent use of sleeping pills is their impact on waking behavior. A persistent ''sleep drunkardness'' coupled with drowsiness, even with intense efforts at maintaining vigilance, impair productive activities during waking hours.

These problems have led to other biochemical approaches to sleep disorders. Primary among them is the attempt to promote increases in the concentration and release of neurotransmitters that may be involved in some aspect of sleep induction. Hartmann (1978) has emphasized serotonin as an important transmitter in this process. Serotonin levels in the brain can be strongly influenced by the administration of tryptophan, which is a precursor in the synthesis of serotonin. Human studies by Hartmann (1978) show that low doses of the precursor under double-blind conditions reduced sleep latency without changing the basic pattern of sleep. This observation in normal subjects has been confirmed in a population with mild insomnia. Further promise for tryptophan is shown by the absence of long-term tolerance effects and the absence of daytime effects on vigilance. More extensive clinical trials are urged by Hartmann. Meanwhile, grandmother's suggestion to take a glass of warm milk before sleep is not too far away from current neurobiological insights, since milk is a good source of tryptophan.

Circadian Rhythms and Sleep

Most of us are accustomed to a single period of sleep enjoyed over an interval starting late in the day and lasting until morning. The onset and termination of sleep seem synchronized to many external events, including light and dark periods determined by the earth's rotations. What happens to sleep when all the customary synchronizing or entrainment stimuli are removed, including changes of light or temperature? One way to get away from such stimuli is to find deep caves and to spend weeks there. Several experiments on sleep patterns in caves have been performed in which all cues to external time have been removed. Under such conditions a circadian rhythm of sleep-waking remains evident, although the biological clock slowly shifts away from 24 to 25 hours. Some individuals adopt much longer days, lasting up to 35 hours. In only one subject out of 147 did one researcher find a period shorter than 24 hours under isolation conditions (Wever, 1979). Why this shift away from 24 hours? One researcher offers the notion that this period derives from an endogenous circadian clock shaped by evolutionary forces to near our customary 24-hour rhythm but slowed by coupling to the mechanisms responsible for sleep onset. Some researchers have suggested that the relevant timer is the suprachiasmatic nucleus.

A systematic study of sleep rhythms in humans under isolated conditions has recently been offered by Weitzman and collaborators (1981). Their subjects, 10 adult men, spent 25–105 days individually in a small apartment totally free of time cues. A subject could go to sleep and awaken any time he desired; however, this sleep interval had to be the regular sleep period since naps were not allowed. Several physiological measurements were recorded, including body temperature and circulating hormone levels. EEGs were also recorded during the sleep periods. Unlike the subjects of cave experiments, these subjects had direct social contact with laboratory workers.

Under these conditions all subjects showed a sleep-waking rhythm that was longer than 24 hours (Figure 14-15). Three subjects adopted a "day" that ranged between 24.4 and 26.2 hours. However, three subjects had periods greater than 37 hours. These subjects demonstrated that some circadian rhythms can become uncoupled from each other, since the subjects continued to show a 24-hour temperature rhythm. This latter group of subjects had some sleep periods that were short (less than 10 hours) and others that lasted as long as 20 hours. Whether these episodes were long or short was related to the 24-hour temperature rhythm. Short sleep episodes began when body temperature was at its lowest level, while long sleep episodes began while body temperature was at its peak. Some changes in the distribution of sleep states were also seen in the experiment. For example, REM sleep occurred earlier during the sleep period, although its total percentage of sleep time remained the same. REM sleep also showed a specific time relation to body temperature, so the basic REM rhythm is not locked under these conditions to slow-wave sleep. These data show that sleep-waking rhythms are connected to oscillations in the brain that time other biological rhythms.

Research on circadian rhythms has begun to strongly influence work on sleep mechanisms especially dealing with the timing of the onset of sleep and the interaction between slow-wave and REM sleep (e.g., Daan et al., 1984; Kronauer et al., 1984; Winfree, 1982, 1983). In several of these hypothetical models, the temporal character of sleep is seen as the result of the interaction of two different oscillators

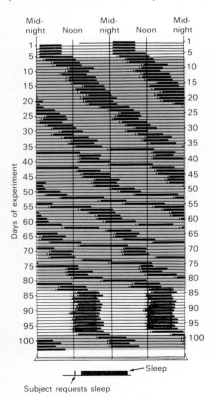

Figure 14-15 Sleep–waking pattern of a subject during periods of isolation from cues about the time of day. During these periods (indicated by brown shading) the subject drifts away from a 24-hour daily cycle. (From Weitzman et al., 1981)

that are weakly coupled to each other, as we discussed in relation to Figure 14-5. Other researchers have attempted to account for the properties of sleep and its relationship to other biological rhythms by emphasizing the control by a single suprachiasmatic pacemaker.

Psychological Aspects of Sleep States

By this point we can see that sleep is not analogous to switching off a motor. Rather it consists of different stages, and many brain cells continue to be active, although in different modes. Since the brain continues to be active, it is reasonable to inquire about the properties of mental activity during sleep. This work has focused on dreams, learning, and thresholds of arousal to external stimulation, subjects that we will consider next.

Mental Experiences During Sleep: The World of Dreams

One of the most exciting aspects of contemporary work in the psychobiology of sleep has been the active examination of the properties of thinking and imagery during various stages of sleep. In a typical experiment, the EEG is recorded and the subject is awakened at particular stages—1, 2, 3, 4, and REM—and questioned about thoughts or percepts immediately prior to awakening.

Until recent years the data strongly indicated that dreams were largely restricted to REM sleep. Studies during the early 1960s commonly showed that subjects reported dreams between 70 and 90% of the times that they were awakened in this stage—in contrast to an incidence of 10 to 15% for non-REM sleep periods. Indeed, at first it was thought that the rapid eye movements characteristic of this period were related to "viewing" dream scenes! In other words, if your dream was one of viewing a ping-pong match, your eyes would reveal that rapid to-and-fro movement of real-life observations of such a match. This scanning theory of eye movements during REM dreams now seems unlikely, particularly since there are many differences between the characteristics of eye movements during actual viewing of scenes and those of REM sleep.

Many studies have been concerned with dream reports after subjects were awakened from different states of sleep. Quite consistent across all these studies is a large percentage of dream reports on awakening from REM sleep. However, some investigators have increasingly questioned whether REM is the sole sleep state associated with dreams. Thus current studies have been directed at attempting to distinguish between the qualitative features of slow-wave and REM dreams. These data show that the dream reports of REM sleep are characterized by visual dream imagery, whereas the dream reports of slow-wave sleep are of a more "thinking" type. REM dreams are apt to include a story that involves odd perceptual experiences and the sense that "you are there" experiencing sights, sounds, smells, and acts. During such a dream, these events seem real. Slow-wave dreams, on the other hand, are characterized more as thoughts than sights. Subjects awakened from this state report thinking about problems rather than seeing themselves in a stage presentation. Cartwright (1978) has shown that the dreams of these two states are so different that judges can indicate the sleep state in which a dream occurred with 90% accuracy. Furthermore, awakenings from REM sleep result in more frequent reports of dreams than arousals from slow-wave sleep.

Studies of the content of dreams, especially during REM sleep, suggest that dreams during the first half of sleep are oriented toward reality. Details of these dreams show an incorporation of the day's experience, and the sequence of events is ordinary. In contrast, dreams during the second half of sleep become more unusual and less readily connected with the day's events. The sequence of events and the content of dreams become more emotionally intense and bizarre. The emotional quality of REM dreams may also reflect clinical variables, as indicated in sleep studies of depression. Dreams of depressed patients during the depths of this state are emotionally bland, with very reduced activity and mood. Terrifying dreams have become the subject of close scrutiny in studies presented in a book by Hartmann (1984) called *The Nightmare*. Nightmares are defined as long, frightening dreams that awaken the sleeper from REM sleep. They are occasionally confused with a "night terror," which is a sudden arousal from stage 3 or 4 slow-wave sleep marked by intense fear and autonomic activation. In night terror the sleepers do not recall a vivid dream but rather remember a sense of a crushing feeling on their chest as though being suffocated. Night terrors are frequently seen in children during the early part of an evening's sleep.

According to Hartmann, nightmares are quite prevalent, and some people are especially plagued by them. Among college students at least 25% report having one nightmare per month. During some illnesses people are more likely to experience nightmares. Some seizure victims have nightmares that precede seizures that occur at night. Medications that enhance the activity of dopamine systems, such as L-dopa, also make nightmares more frequent. The studies of Hartmann also suggest that individuals with frequent nightmares might be a more creative group, with "loose" personal boundaries. He suggests that these people are prone to either a greater or more rapid activation of dopamine systems.

Views about the functional role of dreams venture into a very ancient and persistent riddle that is not likely to be answered by currently available experimental approaches. In the history of humans, dreams have been viewed in many different lights. Van de Castle (1971) provides some interesting illustrations from primitive societies around the world. For example, Cuna Indians off the coast of Panama viewed dreams as predictors of imminent disaster, and their dream "analysts" had a variety of objects to ward off both dreams and their presumed consequences. For instance, a tomahawklike object was used to treat dreams of thunder and lightning. (These dreams were probably hypnagogic hallucinations—vivid sensory experiences reported by many normal humans that may occur at the start of sleep.) Primitive cultures placed great emphasis on the truthfulness of dreams. Perhaps this view continues in the arguments of some contemporary investigators who believe that dreams are important in resolving problems.

Perhaps "we dream in order to forget," speculate Crick and Mitchison (1983), who bring to the study of REM sleep some concepts of information theory and computer sciences. The essence of their argument is that REM sleep is a period of reverse learning, a state in which false or irrelevant memories that are routinely accumulated during the day are damped out—a kind of mental housecleaning. According to them, the cerebral cortex is a rich matrix of interconnected cells that supports elaborate cognitive abilities. Such an apparatus, they believe, might become overloaded with bizarre or unusual associations. The term *parasitic modes* is adopted by them from information scientists to refer to these potentially maladaptive associations. The events of REM sleep weaken the connections of the parasitic modes by "zapping" them! In a recent book, *Landscapes of the Night* (1984), Christopher Evans, a psychologist involved in computer analogies to human cognition, presents an idea akin to this notion. For him the events of dreaming are akin to the rummaging of a file clerk seeking to update the files, which are referred to as programs of the mind.

Neurobiologists have also enjoyed the prospect of speculating about the nature of dreams. Where do dreams come from? Throughout human history this issue has been debated, and quite often the origin of dreams was attributed to external stimulation or states of the body, especially the stomach (Hobson, 1988). By the nineteenth century, dreams came to be attributed to endogenous events in the brain that the dreamer cannot control. One such contemporary view is seen in the speculations of Hobson (1988), who named his notion the activation-synthesis hypothesis. This view states that within the pontile portion of the brain stem there is a set of cells that activates the dream state. This pontile generator goes on and off during sleep; one marker of its activation is rapid eye movements. Cerebral cortical sensory systems are activated by the dream state generator. Cerebral cortical systems are randomly bombarded by these bursts of pontile outputs, and cortical networks attempt to interpret the barrage of inputs. The absence of information from the outside world during this period makes reality testing impossible; hence the strange character of dreams. Thus the brain stem stimulus is elaborated by the perceptual, cognitive, and emotional structures of the forebrain—a synthetic process that attempts to put together a story from the minimal data provided by the bursts of random activation. According to this view, dreams are not disguised but rather an attempt to make the best from a limited set of data. Why do we have difficulty recalling these dreams? Hobson suggests that dream amnesia comes about because of a "change in the ratio of neurotransmitters affecting forebrain neurons." Testing of these ideas remains to be done.

For some, dreams are considered an innocent by-product of basic bodily restorative processes and have no significance by themselves. From this perspective there is no way to accomplish the biological role of sleep without the "accidental" provocation of dreams, since certain regions of the brain stem produce phasic activity of neurons that affects the visual cortex. This activity may excite visual cortical neurons to produce the perceptual elements of a dream. These random bursts are made more coherent by the cognitive activity of the dreamer. However, dreams per se, although reflecting personal attributes, may have little functional role.

At the other end of the spectrum is the perspective that emphasizes dimensions like "wish fulfillment" and the problem-solving role of these nightly adventures. For many individuals sleep without the ability to recollect their dreams is unsatisfactory sleep. Whether this response reflects acquired tastes for dreams or provides a hint about their functional role(s) is yet another problem for contemporary and future investigators.

Learning and Sleep

Every now and then we are confronted with newspaper reports and advertisements that herald some new technique or gadget that will enable us to learn something during sleep and remember it afterward. The appeal of such possibilities is over-whelming to some, including those who begrudgingly accept sleep as a necessary interference with the pursuit of knowledge and those who sport the fantasy that information can be transmitted by a deep embrace of a book. More seriously, sleep is obviously a living state in which many neurons are active; can we learn during this state? Also, do the learning experiences of a day influence the pattern of a night's sleep? Some researchers have suggested a relationship between REM sleep and the establishment of permanent memory. Others have suggested that REM sleep may serve as a kind of filter of the day's experiences.

Some things that happen during the course of a typical day are important for adaptive success, while others are trivial, repetitive events. Metabolic processes involved in establishing memory are "expensive" (as you will see in Chapter 16), and it might be that sleep serves to consolidate some of the day's events. Experiments in this area have examined whether sleep influences the effectiveness of subsequent learning. Further studies have looked at the effects of sleep deprivation—either selective or total—on learning. Additional questions in the study of sleep-learning connections are concerned with the effectiveness of retention when sleep occurs following learning. (Many students participating in the ritual of cramming for exams can provide personal data for this question.) Let us look at some of the experimental evidence.

Learning During Sleep

This controversial area has been beset with many conflicting claims (Aarons, 1976). About the only overall conclusion one can confidently draw from a large range of studies is that if you are relying on acquiring and retaining complex information during sleep, you had best find a backup system. Although several nonhuman experiments indicate that a simple conditioned response can be acquired during various sleep stages, evidence for people learning verbal materials is generally mixed.

One technique that might reveal the possibilities of learning during sleep would be to determine whether presleep learning could be reinforced by repetition trials presented during sleep. Such an experiment was reported by Tilley (1979), who presented subjects at bedtime with a series of pictures of common scenes or objects. Then during the initial part of sleep, they were presented with a series of taped words delivered over a speaker. The role of these stimuli was to habituate subjects to the presentation of sounds during sleep. Later that night they were presented with 10 words that were not previously presented; the words were titles of the pictures they saw prior to sleep onset. One group received these words during REM sleep and the other was presented with the list during slow-wave stage 2 sleep. They were awakened at 7 A.M. after a night's sleep and asked to (1) give a free recall of the names of the initial picture series they saw before going to sleep and (2) select the names of the pictures from a list of 60 words—a recognition task. Repetition of the names of pictures did not influence the free recall task, but the recognition task results showed the names of pictures were recognized better if they had been repeated during slow-wave stage 2 sleep. No significant effects were seen with repetitions during REM sleep. This researcher suggests that information presented during sleep can reinforce or reactivate memory storage processes and thus improve retention. Perhaps some type of sleep learning is possible.

Soviet investigators have developed an instructional program lasting several weeks in which the presentation of material during light sleep (toward the beginning and end of periods of sleep) is coordinated with presleep and postsleep instruction (Rubin, 1970). A committee of the U.S. National Research Council suggests that possible applications of learning during sleep deserve a second look by Western investigators (Druckman & Swets, 1988).

Some forms of learning less complicated than that of the previous example are possible in both humans and other animals, as shown by habituation experiments— experiments in which a stimulus is repeated without consequence over some period of time. For example, if a sudden loud sound is presented during slow-wave sleep, the subject—human or cat—will show EEG signs of arousal. Repetition of the stimulus becomes less likely to produce arousal. In some sense this response is not sleep learning since arousal is produced. However, this phenomenon indicates that the novelty of a stimulus can be detected in the sleeping state.

Another aspect of learning during sleep focuses on internally generated information. Common experience indicates that sleep includes episodes of cognitive and perceptual events that range from the mundane to the quite unusual. This is the stuff of dreams. Laboratory studies of dreams show that the mental life of sleep is quite active. These studies also show that memory for such events is fragmentary. No amount of therapy, drugs, cajolery, or whatever unearths much of the information generated by internal processes during sleep.

Formal studies of this phenomenon have involved waking subjects at varying intervals following the end of a REM episode. Many of those awakened within the first few minutes of the end of a REM episode report dreaming experiences. However, those subjects awakened 5 minutes after the end of a REM period have no recollection of the events during the period (Dement, 1974). It appears that no permanent memory traces are established for the cognitive and perceptual events of the REM episodes. An exception occurs if the dreamer awakens briefly just after the dream. (It is not always true, as psychoanalysts have hypothesized, that dreams protect us from awakening.) If waking occurs soon after a dream, then the dream may be recalled the next day.

It is probably beneficial that most dreams are never stored in long-term memory, since it would pose difficulties to store permanent traces of events that may not be accurate descriptions of a person's experience. Perhaps one of the roles of the slow-wave sleep that follows REM episodes is to provide the neural condition that precludes lasting storage of the events of REM periods.

Effects of Sleep on Long-Term Memory

In 1924, Jenkins and Dallenbach reported an experiment that continues to provoke research. They trained subjects in a verbal learning task at bedtime and tested them 8 hours later on arising; they also trained the subjects early in the day and tested them 8 hours later. The results showed better retention when a period of sleep occurred between a learning period and tests of recall.

What accounts for such an effect? Several differing psychological explanations have been offered. One suggests that during the waking period intervening between learning and recall, diverse experiences interfere with accurate recall. Sleep during this interval appreciably reduces the range of interfering stimulation. A second explanation notes that memory tends to decay and that this relentless process simply occurs more slowly during sleep. This is a passive process. A third explanation ties more directly to an emphasis on a positive functional contribution of sleep to learning. This view says that sleep includes processes that consolidate the learning of waking periods. Sleep is then seen as providing the conditions for a firm ''printing'' of enduring memory traces.

Experiments by Ekstrand and collaborators (1977) have added complexity to the original Jenkins and Dallenbach observations. In one experiment they compared the magnitude of memory loss in three groups, all of whom learned lists of paired associates. Group 1 learned a list in the evening and was tested for retention after an interval of 8 hours of no sleep; group 2 slept for half the night, was then awakened, learned the list, and had 4 hours of sleep before retention testing; group 3 learned the list of paired associates, slept 4 hours, and was then awakened and tested for retention. Group 2 showed the best recall. The experimenters' interpretation is that slow-wave sleep favors retention, but other interpretations are possible.

A recent experiment of this type by Idzikowski (1984) emphasizes the importance of sleep in consolidation. He showed that 8 hours sleep 16 hours after learning leads to better verbal retention than no sleep. A control experiment showed that this effect was not due to the stress of sleep deprivation. The special role of REM sleep in consolidation processes in human learning is emphasized in several recent reviews (Horne, 1985).

Many animal studies have explored the notion that sleep—especially REM sleep—is important for learning and retention. A recent review of this field by C. Smith (1985) explored several aspects of relevant research. One approach has been to examine the qualitative and quantitative character of sleep following training experiences as determined by electrical recording of brain activity. The most consistent finding in this type of study is that major increases in REM occur in sleep after learning. In several studies the increased REM was seen immediately at sleep onset following training. Such REM enhancement has been seen in avoidance learning situations, operant bar press, and enriched environment exposure. These increases in REM come about in some studies because REM episodes are longer and in other cases because the number of REM episodes is increased. In a few of the enriched environment exposure experiments, not only is REM increased but also slow-wave sleep amounts are enhanced. The functional significance of these REM increases following learning have been explored in some studies that included REM deprivation. In these studies REM deprivation was made to coincide with the period following learning during which REM increments were usually noted. The insertion of a ''window'' of REM deprivation retards the rate of learning in some studies. This deprivation window can be as short as three hours. The work of Bloch (1976) shows that if learning extends over several days, the increase in REM sleep is largest during the steepest part of the learning curve (Figure 14-16). These studies all show that the day's activities certainly affect the night's sleep.

Figure 14-16 Amounts of REM sleep and learning in rats: Sleep is recorded after learning sessions. (From Bloch, 1976)

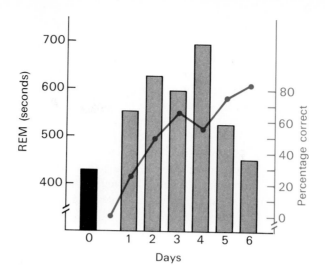

Other animal studies dealing with the role of REM sleep in learning and retention have approached this question in another way, by examining the effects of REM deprivation on learning acquisition and retention (C. Smith, 1985). In these studies animals were deprived of REM either following training or prior to acquisition. REM deprivation following learning has produced some equivocal results. Critics of this research literature have pointed out that some of the tasks employed in the studies may be too simple to require the REM mechanism. REM sleep deprivation prior to learning has resulted in more potent effects with some of these studies showing impairments of acquisition. Clearly the deprivation research accomplishments do not provide clear-cut support for a REM-learning connection. No doubt, this kind of study is difficult to perform because REM deprivation entails many physiological changes that might overwhelm more subtle effects that are pertinent to learning and associated phenomena. This remains an active area as researchers try to reconcile differences in results that appear in recording and deprivation experiments.

Sleep and Arousal Thresholds

The ease of waking an individual depends on many factors and especially on the stage of sleep. Variations in arousal thresholds suggest that sleep states differ in depth. A common way to assess the depth is to examine differences in stimulus intensity needed to awaken an individual in different sleep states. For example, stimuli are presented at different points in slow-wave or REM sleep, and the difference in the depth of these sleep states is measured by either the duration or the intensity of the stimulus needed to produce EEG signs of arousal.

Early studies with animal subjects seemed to show that arousal became more difficult during the progression from slow-wave to REM sleep. This result implied that REM periods are those of greatest depth of sleep. Further refinements in the studies (Wright & Leiman, 1971) showed that arousal thresholds during REM sleep are not homogeneous. Arousal thresholds are higher during REM periods of frequent eye movements (Price & Kreinen, 1980). A recent study used the procedure of training subjects to respond to a 1000-Hz tone during sleep by pressing a button (Bonnet, 1986). Thresholds for this response increased 38 dB at the beginning of stage 1 sleep and yet further (63 dB) by the end of stage 2. A continuous increase in threshold marks the progression through stages 1 and 2 sleep.

Arousal from sleep also depends on the relevance of the stimulus. In a classical demonstration, Oswald (1962) showed that the threshold of waking is lowest for the oral presentation of one's own name in contrast to other names. This stimulus preference is lost when the names are played backward from a tape recorder, so it is the meaning of the name and not just the acoustical stimulation that is important.

Neurobiological Aspects of Sleep States

During the course of sleep, many nervous and hormonal functions are dramatically modified. Some of these changes have strong implications for hypotheses about the presumed restorative role of sleep. In this section we will discuss some of the major physiological modifications that occur during sleep.

Autonomic and Skeletal Motor Changes During Sleep

During sleep physiological changes are evident in many systems. In the autonomic nervous system, such functions as heart rate, blood pressure, and respiration show progressive declines during slow-wave sleep but marked increases in REM sleep (Table 14-1). During REM sleep cerebral blood flow increases in some areas, which provides another example of the increased metabolic demands of REM.

For virtually all animals, sleep means the absence of activity of the skeletal musculature. How does the motor system become quiescent? This feature is especially puzzling since at the same time much of the brain is quite active. This contrast implies that motor pathways become reversibly uncoupled from the rest of the brain. Another motor system puzzle is the unusual episodic activity in nonpostural muscles during REM sleep—the rapid eye movements and sudden twitches of fingers, hands, and other muscle groups.

During the course of slow-wave sleep there is a reduction in monosynaptic and polysynaptic spinal reflexes. With REM sleep these reflexes are virtually abolished, resulting in profound loss of muscle tone. Some of this motor decrement depends on descending influences from the brain to the spinal cord, since reflex depression during sleep does not occur with spinal transection. Direct production of inhibitory postsynaptic potentials on spinal motoneurons during sleep has been recorded in cats. The usual loss of muscle tone during sleep can be abolished by lesions in the pons, suggesting a role for this region in producing motor uncoupling during sleep, especially REM sleep. Animals with this lesion actually move about clumsily, some looking as though they are orienting to something in the environment (Morrison, 1983). It is REM sleep without motor uncoupling.

A brain potential correlated with phasic motor events can be seen during REM sleep in recordings at the level of the pons, the lateral geniculate nucleus, and the occipital cortex; these potentials are called PGO spikes (pons, geniculate, occipi-

(a) NREM sleep

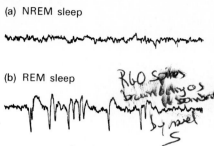

(b) REM sleep

2 seconds

Figure 14-17 PGO spikes recorded from the lateral geniculate of a sleeping cat during an REM episode. (A. L. Leiman)

tal). Their occurrence during a period of slow-wave and REM sleep is shown in Figure 14-17. In cats they appear 1–2 minutes before the onset of REM sleep and continue in bursts throughout the period of REM sleep. Studies of the origins of PGO spikes by Morrison (1983) reveal that they are controlled by distinct brain stem regions. He believes that PGO spikes are masked during slow-wave sleep but can be provoked during waking and REM sleep; he also believes that they represent the brain's response to novel or alerting stimulation. The role of the PGO spikes during REM sleep remains unknown, but Morrison suggests that the brain is functioning as though it were presented with intense barrages of novel stimulation.

Some views of the function of sleep emphasize that this state is important in providing a period of restoration following the demands of a prolonged waking period. From this viewpoint we would expect nerve cells of sensory and motor regions to show reduced firing rates during sleep. Studies of single nerve cells in the cerebral cortex reveal something different from this expectation, though. Some nerve cells actually increase their firing rates during sleep. This emphasizes that the brain does not stop working during sleep.

Hormones and Sleep

Hormonal relations to sleep have been explored from two different perspectives. First, some studies examined whether the release of particular hormones is especially prominent during sleep and related to particular sleep states. This work mainly involved the pituitary growth hormone. Second, a larger group of investigations looked at the effects of hormones on sleep states.

Daily rhythms are apparent in the secretion of hormones, including various pituitary hormones such as growth hormone, thyroid-stimulating hormone, and follicle-stimulating hormone. A specific link to sleep processes has been established for the pituitary growth hormone, which, in addition to being involved in growth processes, also participates in mechanisms governing the metabolism of proteins and carbohydrates. Several studies, which involved taking samples of human blood throughout the day, have shown that the highest concentrations of growth hormone in blood are evident at night. Blood plasma levels of growth hormone show a rise after the start of sleep. The trigger property of sleep with respect to growth hormone release is shown by observations that if sleep is advanced or delayed, the rise in blood plasma levels of growth hormone follows the onset of sleep, even if this involves a complete inversion of the day's schedule (Figure 14-18). More detailed examinations of the relation to sleep stages have shown that release is related to slow-wave sleep and particularly to stages 3 and 4. The exact nature of sleep control or regulation remains to be explored. For instance, is slow-wave sleep the exclusive causal condition for growth hormone release? How these events are synchronized also remains to be determined. Recent studies suggest that growth hormone may have direct effects on the brain and thus influence sleep. One group of researchers (Martin, Wyatt, & Mendelsohn, 1985) has shown that injections of growth hormone can reduce slow-wave sleep and increase REM sleep.

Hormones involved in pituitary-adrenal relations also seem related in a comparable manner to sleep, especially to REM sleep. Recall that the anterior pituitary is controlled by the hypothalamus and releases a hormone, adrenocorticotropin

Figure 14-18 Growth hormone secretion during a 24-hour period. Increases in the rate of secretion are seen during the early phase of sleep. (From Takahashi, 1979)

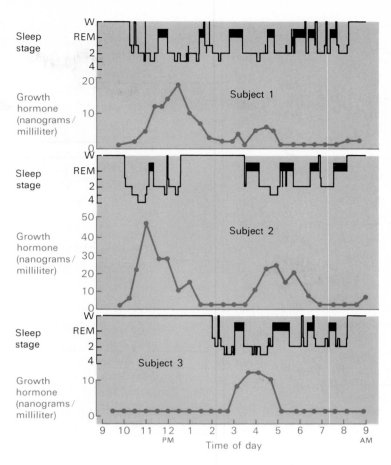

(ACTH), which stimulates the adrenal cortex to release glucocorticoids. The latter substances are referred to as stress hormones, partially because of the conditions for their release and their anti-inflammatory actions. One class of these substances released by the adrenal cortex, 17-hydroxycorticosteroids, reaches a peak level in the blood of humans during a late phase of sleep, 4 to 6 A.M. In one study peak level appeared in spurts, with rises occurring after REM onset. Many other observations point to the sleep dependency of this response, as opposed to a circadian effect; that is, there was evidence of a continued relation to REM sleep when days were made artificially long or short.

Levels of some sex hormones are also related to sleep. Starting around puberty, the level of testosterone shows a peak during sleep (Akerstedt, 1985). Further evidence of the relation to sleep is seen in the fact that the level of testosterone is reduced by sleep deprivation. An important hormone-sleep connection involves melatonin, the hormone made in the pineal gland, which is especially pertinent to the control of circadian rhythms in birds. Some researchers have begun to suggest a role for melatonin in the induction of sleep in mammals. One generalization that has been offered to account for the varied patterns of hormone activity during sleep is that sleep enhances the secretion and activity of anabolic hormones (those involved in the building of complex substances) and inhibits the release and activity of catabolic hormones (those involved in the breakdown of complex substances).

Neural Mechanisms of Sleep

Any complete theory of nervous system mechanisms that control sleep must explain the following basic questions:

1. Why and how does sleep start?
2. What accounts for the periodic properties of sleep, including the daily sleep-arousal cycle and the timing of successive episodes of slow-wave and REM?
3. What stops a prolonged period of sleep?

Various hypotheses, guesses, and conjectures have been offered by workers in the field, but there is still no comprehensive theory that successfully deals with these major questions. We will explore a variety of hypotheses. Some of them appear increasingly plausible; others, however tantalizing, still yearn for confirmation. Particular hypotheses treat only limited aspects of the broad phenomena of sleep. Some hypotheses are exclusively anatomical, dealing with neural circuits of sleep, whereas others are neurochemical.

Two alternative conditions that might govern the onset of sleep have been posited:

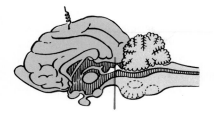

(a) cerveau isolé

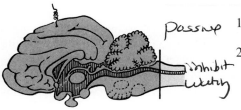

(b) encephale isolé

Figure 14-19 The levels of brain section in encéphale isolé and cerveau isolé preparations.

1. Sleep starts because the mechanisms promoting waking simply run down from a period of use. From this perspective sleep occurs as a passive process.
2. Sleep starts because the mechanisms promoting waking are actively inhibited. From this perspective sleep occurs as a result of the buildup of activity in an inhibitory center (or centers) whose output is directed to waking centers.

This distinction between active and passive processes has deeply influenced thinking in this area, with the passive view being dominant until quite recently. To develop some perspective on current views of active mechanisms, let us review briefly the progression of research and theories since the 1930s.

Sleep as a Passive Phenomenon

In the late 1930s, the Belgian neurophysiologist Frédéric Bremer performed some experiments that became the foundation of passive views of sleep onset and maintenance. In one group of cats, he examined cortical electrical activity after the brain stem was isolated from the spinal cord by a cut below the medulla. This physiological preparation he called an **encéphale isolé** (isolated brain); see Figure 14-19. These animals showed EEG signs of waking and sleeping. During EEG-defined wakeful periods, the pupils were dilated and the eyes followed moving objects. During EEG-defined sleep, the pupils were small, as is characteristic of normal sleep. (It should be noted that Bremer did not distinguish between slow-wave and REM sleep; this distinction was not discovered until the 1950s. By sleep Bremer meant slow-wave sleep.)

In another group of animals, Bremer examined cortical electrical activity following a cut at the upper level of the midbrain (between the inferior and superior colliculi). This preparation was called the **cerveau isolé** (isolated forebrain). These animals displayed persistent EEG sleep patterns with no instance of wakefulness either in terms of the EEG or pupil size and eye movements. These data were, at the time, interpreted to mean that sleep starts and is maintained by the loss of sensory input, a state of **deafferentation.** The cerveau isolé animals showed no signs of wakefulness, according to this interpretation, because transecting the upper brain stem reduced the normal flow of afferent input, which, according to this view, is a prerequisite for the waking condition.

Sleep as an Inhibition of Waking

In the late 1940s, Bremer's experiments were reinterpreted on the basis of experiments involving electrical stimulation of an extensive region of the brain stem known as the **reticular formation** (Figure 14-20). The reticular formation consists of a diffuse group of cells whose axons and dendrites course in many directions, extending from the medulla through the thalamus. Moruzzi and Magoun, two scientists prominent in the study of the role of the reticular formation, found that they could awaken sleeping animals by electrical stimulation of the reticular formation; the animals showed rapid arousal. Lesions of these regions produced persistent sleep in the animals, although this phenomenon was not observed if the lesions interrupted only the sensory pathways in the brain stem. This latter observation led to new views about the phenomena displayed in Bremer's experiments. The effects noted by Bremer were now interpreted as arising from interference from a waking or activating system within the brain stem. This mechanism remained intact in the encéphale isolé animal, but its output was precluded from reaching the cortex in the cerveau isolé animal. This "reticular formation" school argued that waking results from activity of brain stem reticular formation systems and that sleep results from the passive decline of activity in this system.

This conclusion started a long series of continuing experiments concerned with factors that control the excitability of the waking mechanisms of the reticular formation. Current views emphasize the importance of midbrain and pontine portions of the reticular formation in the maintenance of arousal, although there may be other processes involving more extensive regions that also mediate the maintenance of arousal.

Many influences seem to exert a dampening effect on the brain stem mechanisms of arousal. These include blood pressure, receptor afferent inputs, deactivation influences from the cerebral cortex, and influences from caudal regions of the brain stem. The existence of a caudal brain stem mechanism that can inhibit rostral activating mechanisms was shown in experiments in which sections were made between these two systems. Animals subjected to this treatment display persistent signs of wakefulness, suggesting that there is a dampening effect on the upper levels of the reticular formation from caudal regions. Stimulation of this caudal brain stem region also inhibits motor systems.

Defining the circuits for the inhibition of arousal mechanisms is complicated by experiments showing that several regions can exert similar controls over activating systems. M. Jouvet (1967), a long-time major sleep researcher, emphasized particularly a system of neurons coursing in the midline of the brain stem, called the **raphe nucleus** (Figure 14-21). These neurons contain the substance serotonin, which is

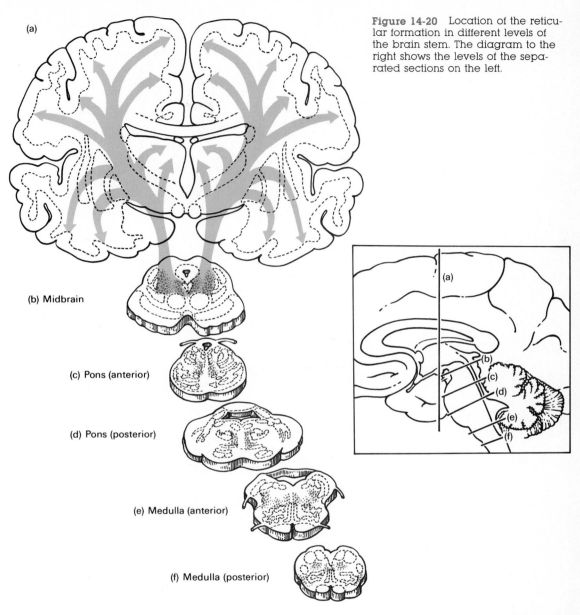

Figure 14-20 Location of the reticular formation in different levels of the brain stem. The diagram to the right shows the levels of the separated sections on the left.

(a)

(b) Midbrain

(c) Pons (anterior)

(d) Pons (posterior)

(e) Medulla (anterior)

(f) Medulla (posterior)

considered to be a synaptic transmitter. Other regions that have been implicated in the onset and maintenance of sleep, particularly slow-wave sleep, include portions of the medial thalamus, whose stimulation can produce sleep behavior in cats. Similar results have been produced by excitation of a group of forebrain regions, including the anterior hypothalamus. The integration of these various regions, in terms of a more defined circuit that depicts the forms of interaction in these diverse systems, has yet to be accomplished. For the moment it looks as though many regions of the brain are capable of controlling or modulating sleep induction. Perhaps all of them function by deactivating arousal mechanisms, although this has not been proved.

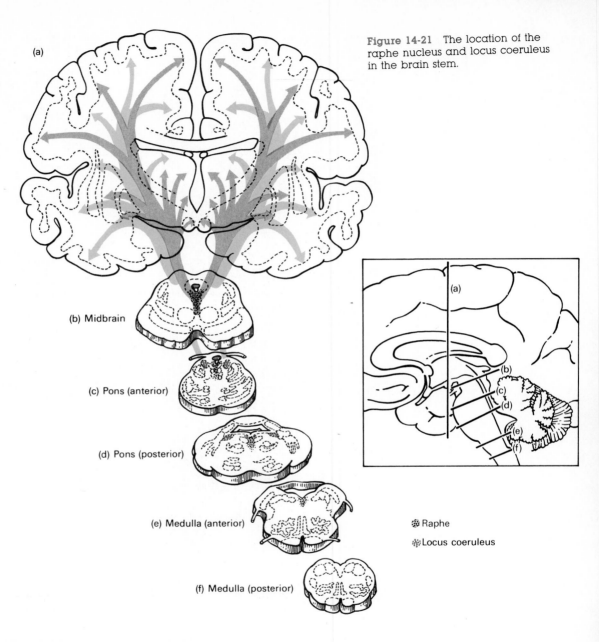

(a)

(b) Midbrain

(c) Pons (anterior)

(d) Pons (posterior)

(e) Medulla (anterior)

(f) Medulla (posterior)

Figure 14-21 The location of the raphe nucleus and locus coeruleus in the brain stem.

Raphe

Locus coeruleus

Chemical Controls of Sleeping and Waking: Sleep-Promoting Substances

Some of the apparent complexity of circuitry relevant to sleep-waking control has led in recent years to an approach that has emphasized a neurochemical perspective. One inspiration for this approach is derived from classical experiments and their contemporary relatives. Many years ago it was thought that sleep might result from the accumulation in the brain and body of a sleep-producing substance, a "hypnogen." The existence of such a substance was suggested by the experiments of Piéron in 1910. Piéron showed that the injection of cerebrospinal fluid from fatigued dogs into rested animals resulted in sleep in the rested animals. This basic kind of experiment has been done in many ways since that time, and some recent observations have renewed an interest in endogenous sleep factors, substances produced by the metabolic activities of the organism that can induce or promote sleep. These substances are searched for in blood, urine, cerebrospinal fluid, or extracts of the brain. Some of these proposed sleep factors are obtained following sleep deprivation, which presumably enhances their concentration. This procedure also corresponds to the notion that a sleep factor progressively builds up over the course of waking behavior. Other factors have been obtained from sleeping animals. In both cases their efficacy is determined by injection of the substances into other test animals to see whether they change the base level of sleeping behavior.

Factor S

Factor S is the name given to a sleep-inducing substance that Pappenheimer and collaborators (1975) extracted from the cerebrospinal fluid of sleep-deprived goats. When Factor S was injected into the cerebral ventricles of rats, it increased slow-wave sleep. Injections of the factor into the ventricles of cats also produced an increase in slow-wave sleep without effects on rapid eye movement sleep. Injections into the brain revealed some places in the basal forebrain region that are especially sensitive to sleep-inducing substances (Garcia-Arraras & Pappenheimer, 1983). A factor found in human urine closely resembles the properties of Factor S extracted from the cerebrospinal fluid of sleep-deprived animals. Some researchers critical of this work have asserted that the chemical composition of the sleep factor is like a product of bacterial membranes and have raised the prospect of contamination of the urine. Several lines of evidence argue against this prospect. An increase in slow-wave sleep of rats injected with a peptidelike factor derived from the human subjects was also noted.

Sleep-promoting substances can also be obtained from sleeping animals. This has been shown using a filtrate of blood obtained from animals in whom sleep has been induced by electrical stimulation of the thalamus. Low-frequency electrical stimulation in a rabbit of a thalamic region called the intralaminar nuclei induces slow-wave sleep. The chemical structure of the sleep-inducing substance has been determined, and it can be synthesized. The substance is called delta-sleep-inducing peptide. Preliminary studies have shown that it can produce increased sleep in humans suffering from chronic insomnia (Schneider-Helmert, 1985). There are many other proposed sleep factors that are presumed to be generated endogenously. This kind of work has raised the prospect that sleep onset is controlled by the accumulation of a "sleep factor" that might act as a neuromodulator.

Sleep onset may be controlled by accumulation of a sleep factor that may act as neuromodulator

Although the data we have just discussed seem promising in terms of the likelihood of there being sleep-promoting substances, there have been some observations with human conjoined twins that do not seem to support this view. Most of the so-called Siamese twins do not share vascular systems to any great extent, and so there are few opportunities for exchange of fluids. However, Webb (1978), in an interesting but seldom cited paper, described a set of conjoined twins joined along the chest and abdomen who shared a single heart. Two weeks after birth, behavioral observations were made on these children to assess the timing of sleep and waking. Minute-by-minute scoring was made of the following categories: quiet sleep, active sleep, crying, quiet awake, and active awake. Analysis of the data revealed a relative independence of these states in the twins. Some of the time, one twin was asleep while the other was awake. Even when both were asleep, there were considerable periods in which one twin was in a state of quiet sleep while the other was in a state of active sleep. These data seem to oppose a humoral theory of sleep onset or maintenance. Perhaps, however, the very young age at which these observations were made may have contributed to minimize the opportunity to adequately assess possible sleep factors.

Chemical Controls of Sleeping and Waking: Synaptic Transmitters

Many studies have shown that the level of several synaptic transmitters varies in a circadian manner. This raises the possibility that sleep onset and maintenance might be controlled by changes in the relative relations of different transmitter systems. Newer techniques have now opened a large-scale effort to map the changes in transmitters that might be related to sleep processes. We will examine some examples of current research concerned with several transmitters.

Serotonin

Research accomplishments since the mid-1960s clearly show that many dimensions of sleep are affected by serotonergic activity (Koella, 1985). Several different kinds of evidence have been obtained that support this view, including the effects on sleep of lesions of serotonin-containing neurons, behavioral effects of chemical enhancement or inhibition of these neurons, and electrical recordings relating sleep behavior to neural activity of brain stem serotonergic nerve cells. We will briefly consider examples of each of these types of evidence.

Destruction of the raphe nuclei (which are shown in Figure 14-21) leads to a profound drop in the forebrain concentrations of serotonin. In experimental animals this also produces an immediate profound drop in the amounts of slow-wave and REM sleep. Similarly, a neurotoxin, 5,6-dihydroxytryptamine, injected into the cerebral ventricles produces a selective impairment of serotonin-containing neurons and a marked drop in the level of slow-wave and REM sleep. These effects on sleep can be seen as late as ten days after a single treatment. Drug block of the synthesis of serotonin by a substance abbreviated PCPA produces a decrease in transmitter levels and a reduction in sleep, although repeated administration of PCPA becomes progressively less effective in reducing sleep levels. Pharmacological enhancement of serotonin activity frequently leads to prolongation of sleep; this can be accomplished by direct injection of the transmitter into the cerebral ventricles or by using drugs that enhance serotonin concentrations—for example, by the administration of the precursor for transmitter synthesis.

Measurements of serotonin levels in awake behaving animals is now possible using a technique called differential pulse voltametry—an electrical method of determining biochemical levels. Data obtained with this technique add some complexity to the story. In the laboratories of M. Jouvet some unusual data have been obtained relating serotonin levels to behavior (Cespuglio et al., 1984). Measuring at various brain sites that receive serotonergic nerve endings, these investigators showed that levels of serotonin are high in the waking state and become lower during slow-wave and REM sleep. This is consistent with neurophysiological observations of raphe nucleus cells, which show a cessation of discharge with the onset of slow-wave sleep. How can these data be reconciled with observations such as the effects of PCPA on insomnia? The explanation offered by Jouvet and his collaborators is that serotonin plays a role in the synthesis of a hypnogenic factor that is the direct agent responsible for sleep. Depletion of serotonin precludes the development of this factor. Supporting evidence summoned for this view is that the reversal of PCPA-induced insomnia takes about an hour—the time apparently necessary for the synthesis of the hypnogenic factor. It is clear that serotonin plays a role in some aspect of sleep regulation. However, the broad controlling role once attributed to serotonin in comprehensive neurochemical models of sleep must now be tempered by the recognition that many other transmitters also seem to be part of the sleep story.

Norepinephrine

In Chapter 6 we noted the complexity of the organization of brain stem norepinephrine cell groups and pathways. Given the complexity of the structural arrangement of these cell groups, it is not surprising that noradrenergic roles in sleep are also quite complex. One general theme in recent research findings is that norepinephrine is involved in the control of both waking and REM sleep. In addition, researchers believe that an increase in this transmitter accompanies or causes waking behavior. REM sleep appears only when norepinephrine activity decreases, suggesting that this transmitter is normally inhibitory to REM sleep (Gaillard, 1985).

A particular focus of sleep researchers is the noradrenergic cells in a cell group called locus coeruleus (Figure 14-21). Selective lesions of this area in cats produce some striking changes in the character of REM sleep, notably a persistent drop in PGO spikes and the loss of the drop in muscle tone that is so characteristic of REM sleep. These findings are interpreted to mean that noradrenergic neurons of the locus coeruleus are not needed for the initiation and maintenance of REM sleep but rather they control some of the phasic and tonic accompaniments of this state. Drug inhibition of brain norepinephrine synthesis (using alpha-methyl-para-tyrosine) produces a decrease in waking EEG activity in some animals, while drugs that enhance noradrenergic activity increase EEG signs of waking activity. Neurotoxins such as 6-hydroxydopamine, which damage norepinephrine terminals, produce some reduction of waking and REM sleep, although the effect is transitory. Observations using adrenergic receptor-modifying drugs lead to the conclusion that waking is increased by stimulation of alpha-adrenoceptors and by blockade of alpha-2-adrenoceptors, which also decrease REM sleep. The complexity of effects observed with treatments of noradrenergic systems has led to the view that this transmitter system is not part of the executive system controlling sleep but exerts an important neuromodulatory role (Monti, 1985).

Dopamine

A large research literature on the effects of dopamine agonists and antagonists indicates a role for this transmitter in regulation of sleep (Wauquier, 1985). Drugs that enhance the activity of dopamine systems, such as L-dopa, produce long-lasting behavioral arousal and decrements in slow-wave and REM sleep. Agonists and antagonists of dopamine produce complex biphasic effects on sleep which are dose dependent. For example, dopamine agonists at low doses decrease sleep latency while increasing the latency to sleep at high doses. These effects might be mediated by the fact that a reduction in motor activity is the prerequisite for the onset of sleep, although relevant pharmacological data are more complex than that.

Acetylcholine

A special role of cholinergic synapses in the mediation of some of the phenomena of REM sleep seems indicated by a variety of pharmacological data. In humans cholinergic antagonists, such as atropine and scopolamine (muscarinic antagonists), have such REM suppression effects as increasing REM latency (the time from sleep onset to the appearance of the first REM episode). Drugs that facilitate or enhance cholinergic synaptic activity, such as physostigmine (which blocks acetylcholinesterase), induce REM sleep in human volunteers (Gillin et al., 1985). This effect is produced if the drug is delivered during slow-wave sleep, although at higher doses it can produce wakefulness. These observations suggest that cholinergic mechanisms facilitate both wakefulness and REM sleep. The character of the REM induced by this treatment is described as entirely normal both in terms of its physiological and behavioral appearance (as judged by dream reports). The observation of decreased REM latency with cholinergic facilitation is especially pertinent to observations of possible cholinergic involvement in depression discussed later in this chapter. Toxicological data also support some of these findings. For example, farm workers accidentally exposed to anticholinesterase insecticides show increased amounts and early onset of REM sleep (Gillin et al., 1985).

Neurotransmitters and Sleep: An Integration

As the list of transmitters in the brain gets longer, so does the bibliography of papers dealing with transmitters and sleep. Earlier efforts to provide a comprehensive neurochemical model of sleep (for example, Jouvet, 1974), although elegant in their simplicity, now fly in the face of a brain that seems much more complicated than was envisaged not long ago. Is there a way to begin to put together the many facts so they tell a story? Recently Koella (1985) has bravely sought to provide the outlines of a systematic model of the neurochemical character of sleep. He has suggested that several transmitters act as vigilance-enhancing agents in different compartments of a vigilance control system. This especially characterizes the actions of adrenergic, cholinergic, and dopaminergic systems. According to this broad model, vigilance-suppression mechanisms involve serotonin along with several other neurotransmitters, which we did not include in this discussion. Sleep factors are viewed as feedback elements carrying information about the current state of both the body and the brain and affecting the central coordination of the vigilance control system. This model is still portrayed in broad strokes; perhaps further refinements will provide a more detailed integration of both neurochemical and other psychobiological data.

Biological Functions of Sleep

Why do most of us spend one-third of our lifetime asleep? However comforting that figure is to some of us, it magnifies the significance of questions about the biological role of sleep. The mystery is deepened by the existence of two dissimilar states of sleep with distinct physiological attributes. We have already touched upon some possible functions of sleep. Here we present a more comprehensive discussion of this topic.

Inquiries about the functions served by sleep are many, and our discussion emphasizes the major ideas. We should note that these proposed functions or biological roles of sleep are not mutually exclusive. There may be many roles served by sleep, and the list may include virtually all the suggestions offered in this section.

However profound the hypotheses and speculations about the functions of sleep, we must recognize that none is proved as yet. Furthermore, no theory has explained the phenomena of people who get along with little sleep or the occasional rare case of a patient who goes for months without sleep and nevertheless shows apparently normal intellect and personality.

Sleep Conserves Energy

Diminished energy expenditure is a property of an appreciable portion of sleep periods. For example, reduced muscular tension, lowered heart rate, reduced blood pressure, and slower respiration all occur during sleep. Reduced metabolic processes are also related to the characteristic lowered body temperature of sleep. These many indications of diminished metabolic activity during sleep suggest that one role of sleep might be to conserve energy. From this perspective sleep enforces the cessation of ongoing activities and thus ensures rest; it is a state of diminished metabolic requirements.

The importance of this function can be seen by looking at the world from the perspective of small animals. These animals have very high metabolic rates, and activity for them is metabolically expensive. It is very easy for demand to outstrip supply. Periods of reduced activity can be especially valuable if they occur when food is less likely to be located and secured. Some support for this view can be seen in comparative sleep data, which reveal a high correlation between total amount of sleep per day and waking metabolic rate. Some problems for this view become apparent, however, when we remember that at least part of sleep is characterized by intense metabolic expenditure, such as the phasic events of REM sleep.

Sleep Aids Predator Avoidance

The natural world has a large cast of characters who frequently interact in awkward ways. Notably some kinds of animals eat other kinds. Intense evolutionary pressures have generated a variety of tactics for avoiding predators. Some researchers have suggested that the stratagems of biological adaptation directly involve sleep. Meddis (1975) suggests that the immobility of sleep enhances survival. For some animals this immobility lessens the likelihood of encountering potential predators. In this manner, sleep can provide the device that leads to effective sharing of some ecological niche—survival without becoming a meal.

This possible functional role for sleep is underscored by some speculations about a distinct contribution of REM sleep. Snyder (1969) used the term *sentinel* hypothesis to explain a REM function as a periodic quasi-arousal that enabled the animal to assess possible danger. Recurrent REM sleep is then a protective device against predator dangers that might arise during sleep. From this view REM sleep complements the protection offered by a sleep habitat like a burrow or a tree. Support for this idea is scant, although it is true that small, frequently preyed upon animals have shorter sleep cycles.

Sleep Restores Weary Bodies

Why do we sleep? Obviously we sleep because we are tired, or so goes the most common refrain. Daily waking activities involve a vast expenditure of energy or body use, and some investigators view sleep as the state of restoration. The function of sleep is simply the rebuilding or restoration of materials used during waking, such as proteins. One prominent sleep researcher, Hartmann (1973), has suggested that there are two types of restorative needs that sleep deals with differently. One type is physical tiredness and the other is the tiredness associated with emotional activation.

Unfortunately the restorative perspective is weakly supported by research. In fact, what seems so simple at first glance becomes quite paradoxical. For example, a simple way to test this idea would be to look at the effects of changes in presleep activity on the duration or cycle of sleep. Can intense metabolic expenditure during the day influence sleep duration? The answers to this question deepen the mystery. In humans physical exercise before sleep shortens the latency of sleep onset. Some studies show a lengthening of early slow-wave sleep stages, but many do not provide unequivocal support for the notion of restoration. Growth hormone release during sleep seems to support a restorative hypothesis.

Some researchers have emphasized the special restorative needs of the brain in contrast to the rest of the body. They emphasize the complexity of the neurochemical machinery of the body and indicate that waking activities profoundly affect processes like the state of neurotransmitters. Morruzzi (1972), a famed researcher in this area, particularly argues that use affects the small neurons of the brain and that sleep is especially restorative to these cells. Larger nerve cells, according to this view, have a greater metabolic reserve.

Sleep Helps Information Processing

Many different events occur during the course of a single day, ranging from the casual inspection of a new face to a major reward honoring a distinct accomplishment. Moment by moment these events occur, some to be recalled years later, others to decay into oblivion with considerable ease. Previously we noted several connections between the phenomena of learning and the features of sleep. Many of these studies argue that sleep serves as a kind of information arbiter for the day. Accordingly, sleep is seen as a state that functions to sort the memories of the day, discarding some and helping others to consolidate. Thus persistence of memory appears to be affected in an operation controlled by sleep processes.

Sleep Disorders

The peace and comfort of regular, uninterrupted sleep each day may occasionally be disturbed by such occurrences as an inability to fall asleep, prolonged sleep, or unusual awakenings. What is unusual for some individuals may, however, be the customary and satisfactory sleep of others. Intensive work during the past decade concerned with unraveling sleep mechanisms in animals now offers some possibilities for understanding and treating human sleep dysfunctions. Sleep assessments have become a major focus of sleep disorder clinics that have become common in major medical centers. The Association for Sleep Disorder Clinics provides a forum for analysis of research needs and accomplishments. In turn the study of sleep disorders is also contributing to our basic knowledge regarding sleep processes. In this section we will examine examples of disordered sleep, ranging from the routine, commonplace experiences of many people to quite unusual states found in a few individuals.

The Association of Sleep Disorder Clinics has developed a diagnostic classification scheme for disorders of sleep and arousal (Weitzman, 1981). Table 14-2 lists the main diagnostic classes with examples. Our discussion follows that organization.

Table 14-2   A Classification of Sleep Disorders

1. Disorders of initiating and maintaining sleep (insomnia)
Ordinary, uncomplicated insomnia
   Transient
   Persistent
Drug-related
   Use of stimulants
   Withdrawal of depressants
   Chronic alcoholism
Associated with psychiatric disorders
Associated with sleep-induced respiratory impairment
   Sleep apnea

2. Disorders of excessive somnolence
Narcolepsy
Associated with psychiatric problems
Associated with psychiatric disorders
Drug-related
Associated with sleep-induced respiratory impairment

3. Disorders of sleep-waking schedule
Transient
   Time zone change by airplane flight
   Work shift, especially night work
Persistent
   Irregular rhythm

4. Dysfunctions associated with sleep, sleep stages, or partial arousals
Sleepwalking (somnambulism)
Sleep enuresis (bed-wetting)
Sleep terror
Nightmares
Sleep-related seizures
Teeth grinding
Sleep-related activation of cardiac and gastrointestinal symptoms

---

SOURCE: Adapted from Weitzman (1981).

Insomnias: Disorders of Initiating and Maintaining Sleep

All of us experience an occasional inability to fall asleep, perhaps fueled by the excitement of the day. But for some the inability to fall asleep and stay asleep is experienced as daily torture. Estimates of the prevalence of insomnia from surveys reported by Parkes (1985) range from 15% of the adult population of Scotland to one-third of the people surveyed in Los Angeles. Insomnia is commonly reported by people who are older, female, and users of drugs like tobacco, coffee, and alcohol. Actually insomnia seems to be the final common outcome for a number of situational, neurological, psychiatric, and medical conditions. It is not a trivial disorder; adults who regularly sleep for short periods show a higher mortality rate than those who regularly sleep 7–8 hours each night (Wingard & Berkman, 1983).

Some studies have found a discrepancy between the subject's reported failure to sleep and EEG indicants of sleep. Thus some insomniacs report that they did not sleep when actually they showed EEG signs of sleep and did not respond to stimuli during the EEG sleep state. In many studies, however, insomniacs show less REM sleep and more stage 2 sleep than normal sleepers. No differences are evident in the amounts of stage 3 and 4 sleep.

Situational factors that contribute to insomnia include shift work, time-zone changes, and environmental conditions such as "novelty" (that "hard" motel bed!). Usually these conditions produce transient sleep-onset insomnia—a difficulty in falling asleep. Drugs and neurological and psychiatric factors seem especially relevant to sleep-maintenance insomnia, which is a difficulty in remaining asleep. This type of sleep is punctuated by frequent nighttime arousals. It is a form of insomnia especially evident in disorders involving the respiratory system.

During sleep, respiration in some people becomes unreliable. In these cases respiration can cease or slow to dangerous levels; blood levels of oxygen show a marked drop. This syndrome, called **sleep apnea,** arises from either the progressive relaxation of muscles of the chest, diaphragm, and throat cavity or changes in the pacemaker respiratory neurons of the brain stem. In the former instance, relaxation of the throat obstructs the airway—a kind of self-choking. This feature is common in very obese people who sleep lying on their back. Frequent arousals are seen in these people so they are sleepy in the daytime. Insertion of a removable tube in the throat can restore a normal sleep pattern and eliminates excess daytime sleepiness.

Some investigators of sleep disorders have speculated that crib death (sudden infant death syndrome) arises from sleep apnea which develops from reduction in brain stem neural activity that paces respiration. Continuous monitoring of the sleep of infants at risk for crib death has helped to save the lives of some children.

Disorders of Excessive Somnolence

Although some of us might find it difficult to consider excessive sleeping as an affliction, there are many who are either drowsy all the time or suffer sudden attacks of sleep. In these cases sleep is not viewed as welcome rest but rather an encumbrance that endangers and compromises the quality of life. We will briefly note some of the more dramatic syndromes that fall into this category.

Narcolepsy

One of the largest group of patients found at sleep disorder clinics are people who suffer from narcolepsy. **Narcolepsy** is an unusual disorder that involves frequent, intense attacks of sleep, which last from 5 to 30 minutes and can occur any time during the usual waking hours. Narcoleptics frequently have associated problems like a sudden loss of muscle tone that can be provoked by abrupt or intense stimuli, including some that are generally considered ''nontraumatic,'' such as a burst of laughter. Individuals with this sleep disorder are distinguished from others by the appearance of REM at the onset of sleep. Indeed, the duration of a narcoleptic attack is similar to the usual period of a REM episode. Night sleep of narcoleptics is quite similar to normal sleep. Some investigators consider this disorder to involve a brain stem dysfunction that involves the failure of a waking mechanism to suppress the brain stem centers controlling REM sleep.

Many narcoleptics also show catalepsy, which is a sudden episode of muscle weakness leading to collapse of the body without loss of consciousness. These episodes, like narcoleptic attacks, are also triggered by sudden, intense emotional stimuli. In afflicted individuals this disorder continues throughout life and may show genetic transmission. No structural changes in the brain have been connected to this problem.

Recently the study of narcolepsy has been advanced by the discovery of a comparable disorder in dogs. In the sleep laboratories of William Dement, several strains of dog have been shown to exhibit several properties of narcolepsy. These animals show sudden motor inhibition (cataplexy) and very short latencies to sleep onset. Many instances of sleep-onset REM episodes are evident, just like those seen in human narcoleptics. Strong genetic control of this disorder is apparent in all strains of dog that have shown the phenomenon.

Sleep and Depression

The fact that sleep is disturbed in depression is not news, but the character of the change and the fact that induced changes in sleep might influence depression are new pieces in the puzzle of depression. Difficulty in falling asleep and inability to maintain sleep as evidenced by early morning awakening have been commonly noted in major depression. More recently, EEG sleep studies of depressed patients have shown certain abnormalities that go beyond difficulty in falling asleep. The sleep of patients with major depressive disorders is marked by a striking reduction in stages 3 and 4 of slow-wave sleep and a corresponding increase in stages 1 and 2 of slow-wave sleep. REM sleep changes include a shortened time from sleep onset to the first REM episode. Further, there is an altered temporal distribution of REM sleep as evidenced by an increased amount of REM during the first half of sleep, as though REM had been displaced toward an earlier period in the night (Gillin & Borbely, 1985). REM sleep in depressives is also more vigorous, as evidenced by very frequent rapid eye movements.

Are these sleep abnormalities specific to depression? This question remains steeped in controversy. Some of the abnormalities are seen in other psychiatric states and, most likely, some are rather nonspecific (Reynolds & Shipley, 1985). However, alterations of REM seem to have a special connection to depression; some studies have shown that shortened REM latency is correlated to a significant extent with the severity of depression. The role of REM in depression is also emphasized by some observations on the clinical effectiveness of various types of sleep therapies. The work of Vogel and colleagues (1980) focused on the fact that REM seems misplaced and extended in the sleep of depressives; according to them, depressives almost seem to start sleep where normals leave off. This analysis generated studies on the impact of selective REM deprivation on the symptoms of depression. A marked antidepressant effect of REM deprivation has been noted in several studies with patients suffering from major affective disorders. In these studies patients were awakened as they entered REM sleep, which reduced the overall amounts of REM sleep; the procedure was continued for two to three weeks. A control group of depressed patients was awakened from non-REM sleep, usually at the end of REM episodes. In these studies depression was evaluated using a common clinical rating scale. At the end of three weeks, the REM-deprived group showed a significantly lower depression score than the non-REM–deprived group. At the end of three weeks, the treatments were reversed, and at the end of another three weeks, the treatment effect also switched. It is of interest to note that several antidepressant drugs like monoamine oxidase inhibitors suppress REM sleep for extended periods. Vogel has asserted that REM deprivation improves severe depression to the extent that it modifies REM sleep abnormalities.

Another sleep therapy approach has emerged from the circadian analysis of sleep in depressed patients. Studies by Wehr and colleagues (1983) have found that depressed patients show abnormal phase relationships in some body rhythms in addition to alterations in REM cycles. Figure 14-22 shows the shift in phase relations between body temperature and sleep that seems to occur in depression. This analysis generated a type of circadian treatment for depression. Wehr and Goodwin (1982) had patients go to bed six hours before their usual time and reported that several patients showed a rapid amelioration of their depression.

Sleep studies of depression have generated several intriguing speculations about the biological nature of depression. Three major hypotheses derived from sleep studies have been assessed by Gillin and Borbely (1985). One major view, called the cholinergic-aminergic hypothesis, suggests that a change in the balance of cholinergic versus aminergic synaptic transmission may account for both depression and the accompanying changes in REM sleep. Basic to this hypothesized state is an increased sensitivity of cholinergic receptors. An interesting connection to sleep is seen in a pharmacological test that measures the time to induce REM sleep following the administration of a cholinergic agonist. Apparently, depressed individuals respond much faster than normals, and this rapid response is even evident in depressed patients following the remission of depressive symptoms; this suggests that cholinergic sensitivity is a trait marker for depressed patients. A second major idea that relates sleep and depression is called the phase advance hypothesis, the treatment implication of which was just discussed. Basically this idea proposes that depression is related to an impairment in the mutual interaction of oscillators that control REM, temperature, and other physiological rhythms. Consequences seem to be both the phase advance of REM sleep and the flattened circadian rhythms of depressives. Finally, the third major hypothesis relating sleep and depression— called the S-deficiency hypothesis—suggests that the propensity for sleep is governed by the build-up during wakefulness of a sleep factor (process S). The sleep process is held to be deficient in depressives, resulting in various REM changes. At the moment, disturbances in sleep characteristic of major affective disorders may

Figure 14-22 EEG sleep stages, wrist motor activity, and rectal temperature in an endogenously depressed woman (a) before and (b) after recovery. Temperature minimum occurs at the beginning of sleep during depression and at the end of sleep after recovery. (Adapted from Wehr, 1983)

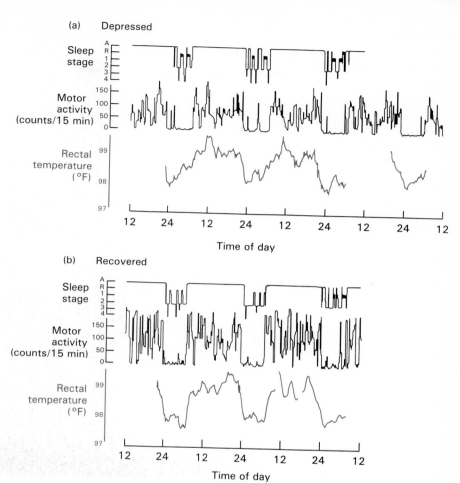

provide a way of examining some of the biological bases of depression. It remains unclear whether these deficits are reflections or components of the causal conditions or, at the least, the maintenance of depressed states. Intensive current research is seeking to clarify the connections and to use measures of sleep as a prognostic tool in depression treatments.

Disorders of the Sleep-Waking Schedule

Airplane travel across several time zones can wreak havoc on circadian sleep-waking cycles. This rapid shifting of time zones is matched by the circadian shifts seen in people who work at night. Irregular patterns characterize the sleep of such people, who also show shortened sleep.

More serious sleep pattern impairments are seen in people who show "delayed sleep phase syndrome" (Weitzman, 1981). These people have an exceptionally long latency to sleep onset and just seem out of synchrony with normal sleep sched-

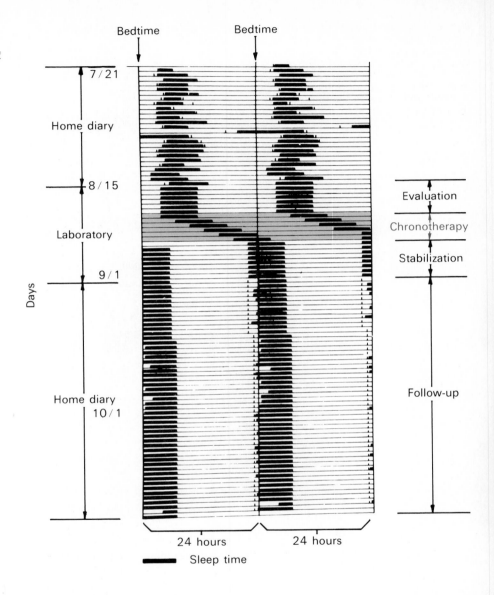

Figure 14-23 Impact of chronotherapy on a form of insomnia. Delay in the start of sleep resets the rhythm of sleep. (From Czeisler et al., 1981)

uling. Success in resetting the sleep rhythm is reported by Czeisler and collaborators (1981), who delay the time of sleep by 3 hours each day until the person is "in phase" again (Figure 14-23). This circadian therapy allows an effective new sleep onset rhythm to be established, sometimes after years of disorder.

Unusual Events Associated with Sleep Some people have sleep periods that include unusual events. These range from the embarrassing to the life threatening, such as bedwetting, sleepwalking, jerking legs, and paralysis.

One group of unusual behaviors provoked during sleep occurs most frequently in children. Sleepwalking (somnambulism) can consist of getting out of bed, walking around a room, and appearing awake. In most children these episodes last from a few seconds to minutes, and the child usually does not remember this experience. Studies in children show that such episodes arise out of slow-wave sleep, particularly stages 3 and 4. Sleepwalking disappears for most individuals as they get older. It has been suggested that the sleepwalker might be acting out a dream; this belief is without any evidence (Parkes, 1985). The main problem is attributed to the inability of sleepwalkers to awaken into full contact with their surroundings. Slow-wave sleep is also related to two other common sleep disorders in children, night terrors and bed-wetting. Night terrors occur after about an hour of sleep and are signaled by a sudden intense shriek. The adult equivalent of the nightmare results in awakening and a frequent report of a sense of pressure on the chest. In both children and adults, these experiences arise from stage 4 sleep and, in the absence of awakening, there is no recollection of the events. Bed-wetting episodes predominate in the first third of a night's sleep and also seem to be triggered during stages 3 and 4 sleep. Pharmacological approaches to these episodic interferences with sleep emphasize the use of drugs that reduce the amount of stages 3 and 4 sleep (and also decrease REM time) while elevating amounts of stage 2 sleep.

A common view of sleep (emphasized by parents) is its ability to heal and promote well-being. But there is another side to this story. REM sleep can aggravate some health problems, especially the class of ''stress diseases.'' Intense activation of autonomically innervated visceral organs can lead to an increase in the severity of tissue impairments in these systems. Gastric ulcers provide a good example of tissue pathology affected by REM sleep. Many ulcer patients report intense epigastric pain that awakens them from sleep. Although normal subjects show no elevation of gastric acids during REM episodes, gastric ulcer patients secrete three to twenty times more acid at night than do controls. Peaks of acid concentration are reached during REM episodes.

Similar attacks of illness occur among cardiovascular patients. A sad reminder is seen in hospital reports that show that cardiac patients are most likely to die during the hours of 4–6 A.M., the period of most intense and prolonged REM episodes. Further data are provided by the study of the time of occurrence of angina episodes. This chest pain syndrome is related to coronary artery disease. Kales (1971) showed that 32 of 39 such episodes in a hospitalized population occurred during REM episodes.

These examples indicate that REM states may involve significant physiological stresses in diseased people. Thus appropriate medical care for some patients might well include efforts to reduce the hazards of REM sleep.

Summary · Main Points

1. Many living systems show circadian rhythms that can be entrained by environmental stimuli, especially light. These rhythms synchronize behavior and bodily states to changes in the environment.

2. Neural pacemakers in the suprachiasmatic nucleus of the hypothalamus are the basis of many circadian rhythms. The basis of light entrainment in many cases is a pathway from the retina to the suprachiasmatic nucleus.

3. Rhythms shorter than 24 hours—ultradian rhythms—are evident in both behavior and biological processes. The underlying mechanism does not involve clocks in the suprachiasmatic nucleus.

4. During sleep almost all mammals alternate between two main states, slow-wave sleep and rapid-eye-movement (REM) sleep.

5. Slow-wave sleep in humans shows several stages defined by EEG criteria that include bursts of spindles and persistent trains of large, slow waves (1–4 Hz). During slow-wave sleep, there is a progressive decline in muscle tension, heart rate, respiratory rate, and temperature.

6. REM sleep is characterized by a rapid EEG of low amplitude, almost like the EEG during active waking behavior, but the postural muscles are profoundly relaxed.

7. In adult humans slow-wave sleep and REM sleep alternate every 90–110 minutes. Smaller animals have shorter sleep cycles and spend more time asleep per 24 hours.

8. The characteristics of sleep-waking cycles change during the course of life. Mature animals sleep less than the young, and REM sleep accounts for a smaller fraction of their sleep.

9. The prominence of REM sleep in infants suggests that REM sleep contributes to development of the brain and to learning.

10. Mental activity does not cease during sleep. Vivid perceptual experiences (active dreams) are frequently reported by subjects awakened from REM sleep; reports of "ideas" or "thinking" are often given by subjects awakened from slow-wave sleep.

11. Formation of memory is impaired when sleep deprivation—particularly REM sleep deprivation—follows learning sessions, so sleep may aid consolidation of memory.

12. Deprivation of sleep for a few nights in a row leads to impairment in performances that require sustained vigilance. During recovery nights following deprivation, the lost slow-wave sleep and REM sleep are partially restored over several nights.

13. Many drugs used to induce sleep inhibit REM sleep during the first few nights. When the drug is withdrawn, there is a rebound increase of REM sleep on the following nights.

14. Many brain structures are involved in the initiation and maintenance of sleep. Particular emphasis has been placed on brain stem structures, including the reticular formation, the raphe nucleus, and the locus coeruleus. The synaptic transmitters serotonin and norepinephrine are prominent in these structures and involved in control of sleep in addition to the modulating role of other transmitters. Sleep-promoting substances have been isolated from the blood and urine of mammals.

15. Researchers have suggested several biological roles for sleep, including conservation of energy, avoidance of predators, restoration of depleted resources, and consolidation of memory.

16. Sleep disorders fall into three major categories: (1) disorders of initiation and maintenance of sleep (e.g., insomnia); (2) disorders of excessive somnolence (e.g., narcolepsy); and (3) disorders of the sleep-waking schedule.

Recommended Reading

Borbely, A., & Valatx, J. L. (Eds.). (1984). *Sleep mechanisms*. Berlin: Springer-Verlag.

Hobson, J. A. (1988). *The dreaming brain*. New York: Basic Books.

Moore-Ede, M. C., Sulzman, F. M., & Fuller, C. A. (1982). *The clocks that time us*. Cambridge, Mass.: Harvard University Press.

Orem, J., & Barnes, C. D. (Eds.). (1980). *Physiology in sleep*. New York: Academic Press.

Parkes, J. D. (1985). *Sleep and its disorders*. Philadelphia: W. B. Saunders.

Schulz, H., & Lavie, P. (Eds.). (1985). *Ultradian rhythms in physiology and behavior*. Berlin: Springer-Verlag.

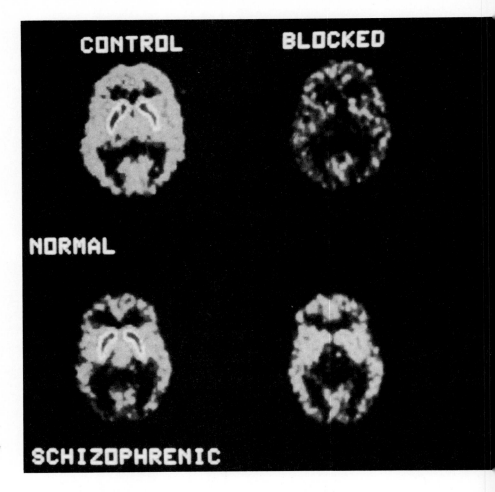

15 Emotions and Mental Disorders

ORIENTATION

The sound of unexpected footsteps in the eerie quiet of the night brings fear for many of us. But the sound of music we enjoy or the voice of someone we love can summon feelings of warmth. For some of us, feelings and emotions can become vastly exaggerated; for example, simple fears can become paralyzing attacks of anxiety and panic. Within any year 20% of us are afflicted with severe emotional disorders of one type or another. This startling figure is revealed in a recent survey of the state of mental health in the United States (Table 1-2). No story about our behavior is complete without consideration of the many events of a single day that involve feelings of one type or another.

The psychobiological study of emotions has progressed in several directions. One traditional area focuses on bodily responses during emotional states, especially facial expression and visceral responses such as heart rate changes. This area extends to maladaptive activation related to stress, such as that seen in some health impairments. The study of brain mechanisms related to emotional states has especially emphasized aggression, both because of its importance for human existence and because its lack of subtlety makes it relatively easy to examine experimentally. The topic of emotions also is closely identified with many aspects of mental disorders since marked emotional changes are among the more striking characteristics of many of these conditions. Our discussion in this chapter will focus on these major areas.

Emotions

What Are Emotions?

The world of emotions is quite complicated; it includes a wide range of observable behaviors, expressed feelings, and changes in body states. Indeed, the diversity of meanings of the word *emotion* has made the subject hard to study. After all, for many of us these are very personal states, difficult to define, describe, or identify except in the most obvious instances. Even simple emotional states seem much more complicated than states related to other conditions, such as hunger and thirst. Things become even more puzzling when we seek to describe emotions in non-human animals. Is the hissing cat frightened, angry, or perhaps enjoying the experience of tormenting another cat or its solicitous but apprehensive owner?

Three Different Aspects of Emotions

At least three aspects of the word *emotion* are evident in the psychobiological research literature:

1. Emotion as a private subjective feeling. Humans can report an extraordinary range of states, which they say they ''feel'' or experience. At times such reports are accompanied by obvious signs of enjoyment or distress. But frequently these reports of subjective experience are without overt indicators.
2. Emotion as an expression or display of distinctive somatic and autonomic responses—as a state of physiological arousal. This emphasis suggests that emotional states can be defined by particular constellations of bodily responses. Specifically these responses involve autonomically innervated visceral organs, like heart, stomach, and intestines. Presumably they are provoked by equally distinctive emotional stimuli, although the attributes that make a stimulus ''emotional'' are not precisely defined. Taking this second meaning, we can examine emotion in nonhuman animals as well as in human beings.
3. Emotion as a state of actions commonly deemed ''emotional,'' such as defending or attacking in response to a threat. This aspect of emotion is especially relevant to Darwin's view of the functional roles of emotion. He suggested that emotions had an important survival role because they aided in generating appropriate reactions to ''emergency'' events in the environment, such as the sudden appearance of a predator. In some instances emotions do not release a complete act such as attack or defense but signal possible future actions; this is especially evident in emotional gestures or displays.

Psychological Categories of Emotion

One continuing discussion relevant to the study of human emotions is whether there is a basic core set of emotions underlying the more varied and delicate nuances of our world of feelings. From a biological perspective, one of the reasons for interest in this question is the prospect that distinctly separate brain systems might be related to parts of this core set. Debate about the question has not been scarce. Wilhelm Wundt, the great nineteenth-century psychologist, offered the view that there were three basic dimensions—pleasant-unpleasant, tension-release, and excitement-relaxation. This listing has become more complex over time. Recently Plutchik (1985) speculated that there are eight basic emotions grouped in four pairs of opposites: (1) joy versus sadness, (2) acceptance versus disgust, (3) anger versus fear, and (4) surprise versus anticipation. He offers the view that all other emotions are derived from combinations of this basic array, which he believes is quite similar across all human societies. According to this view, emotional diversity also develops from the fact that both core emotions and combinations can occur at different intensity levels. Further research with humans dealing with the psychological structure of emotions is critical for developing a context for additional biological analysis.

Bodily Responses in Emotion: Theories of Emotion

In many emotional states, we can sense our heart beating fast, our hands and face feeling warm, our palms sweating, and a queasy feeling in the stomach. There seems to be an especially close tie between the subjective psychological phenomena we know as emotions and the activity of visceral organs controlled by the autonomic nervous system. Several theories have tried to explain the connections between emotions and visceral activity. These theories have raised the question of whether we can experience emotions without the activity of visceral organs.

Among the many theories of emotion, some focus on peripheral bodily events, some focus on central brain processes, and some seek to integrate both kinds of events. In this section we will discuss three prominent examples of such theories that especially emphasize peripheral events—the James-Lange theory, the Cannon-Bard theory, and Schachter's cognitive theory.

James-Lange Theory

Strong emotions and activation of the skeletal muscle and/or autonomic nervous systems are virtually inseparable. Expressions common in many languages capture this association—''trembling with rage,'' ''with all my heart,'' ''hair standing on end,'' ''a sinking feeling in the stomach.'' William James, the leading figure in American psychology around the turn of the twentieth century, suggested that emotions were the perception of bodily changes provoked by particular stimuli. From this perspective fear is evident because particular stimuli produce changes in bodily activity, which are then noted as an emotion. Thus our feeling of body changes *is* emotion.

About the same time, a Danish physician, Carl Lange, proposed a similar view, which he boldly stated in this quotation:

> We owe all the emotional side of our mental life, our joys and sorrows, our happy and unhappy hours, to our vasomotor system. If the impressions which fall upon our senses did not possess the power of stimulating it, we would wander through life, unsympathetic and passionless, all impressions of the outer world would only enrich our experience, increase our knowledge, but would give us neither care nor fear. (Lange, 1887)

The James-Lange theory thus emphasizes peripheral physiological events in emotion. It initiated many studies that attempted to link emotions with bodily responses, a direction that is a lasting interest in the field. Questions such as ''What are the responses of the heart in love, anger, fear?'' continue to form a prominent part of the biological study of emotions. Although the James-Lange theory initiated this research, it has not survived critical assessment.

Cannon-Bard Theory

If body states are emotions, then provoking changes in the body by various experimental treatments, such as surgical procedures or drugs, should change emotional responses. In addition, one would expect that different emotions should be characterized by different bodily responses. The simplicity of the James-Lange theory thus presented ready opportunity for experimental assessments.

Physiologist Walter Cannon studied relations between the autonomic nervous system and emotion. From these studies he offered strong criticism of the James-Lange theory. Humans with a spinal injury that prevents sensation from most of the body are ideal subjects on whom to study the role of visceral changes in emotion. Unfortunately a lack of consistency is evident in the few studies that have been reported. One investigator reported that paraplegics did not have a reduced level of emotions following spinal injury (McKilligott, 1959, cited in Toller, 1979). However, another researcher studying the same patients concluded that while emotions are not lost in patients with high spinal injuries, they do report a reduction in the intensity of their feelings (Hohmann, 1966).

Cannon further argued that visceral changes may be similar in different emotions and that some visceral changes may have very different emotional consequences, depending on the context. Indeed, there is a marked difference between tearfulness produced by sadness-inducing situations and that produced by an irritating stimulus like tear gas.

Cannon's own theory stressed cerebral integration of both emotional experience and emotional response. Noting that emotional states involved considerable energy expenditure, Cannon (1929) emphasized that some emotions are an emergency response of an organism to a sudden threatening condition. He said that the response produced maximal activation of the sympathetic component of the autonomic nervous system. Thus emotions produce bodily changes, such as increased heart rate, glucose mobilization, and other effects mediated by the sympathetic division of the autonomic nervous system. Activation of the viscera by the sympathetic system, according to his theory, comes about because emotional stimuli excite the cerebral cortex, which in turn releases inhibition of thalamic control mechanisms. Activation of the thalamus then produces cortical excitation, resulting in emotional experiences and autonomic nervous system activity. Cannon's theory focused on the brain and emotion, a focus that started many studies of the effects of brain lesions and electrical stimulation on emotion.

Cognitive Theory of Emotions

We have noted in our criticism of the James-Lange theory that activation of a physiological system by itself is not sufficient to provoke an emotion. For example, tears produced by a noxious gas do not ordinarily provoke sadness. Schachter

(1975) suggests that individuals interpret visceral activation in terms of the eliciting stimuli, the surrounding situations, and their cognitive states. An emotion is thus not relentlessly driven by physiological activation—especially that controlled by the sympathetic nervous system. Rather bodily states are interpreted in the context of cognitions and are molded by experience. According to Schachter, emotional labels—anger, fear, joy—depend on the interpretations of a situation, interpretations that are controlled by internal cognitive systems. Thus an emotional state is the result of an interaction between physiological activation and cognitive activities concerned with physiological arousal. According to this view, emotion not only depends on the interaction of arousal and cognitive appraisal but also the perception that a causal connection exists between physiological arousal and emotional cognition (Reisenzein, 1983).

Schachter's theory has not been without its critics (reviewed in Reisenzein, 1983; Leventhal & Tomarken, 1986). For example, the theory asserts that physiological arousal is "nonspecific," affecting only the intensity of a perceived emotion but not its quality. Yet recent data suggest that there is a specific pattern of autonomic arousal for each different emotion. In a study in which subjects were asked to pose facial expressions that were distinctive for particular emotions, autonomic patterns of the subjects were different for several emotions, such as fear and sadness (Ekman, Levenson, & Friesen, 1983). In addition, other data have shown that reduction or block of physiological arousal may not affect emotion. The latest version of these studies uses agents that block adrenergic beta receptors and thus reduce physiological arousal, such as the level of blood pressure or heart rate. These agents do not appear to reduce emotion in healthy individuals (Reisenzein, 1983). Reviewers also point out that many other predictions from the theory have failed to provide clear support for this view (Leventhal & Tomarken, 1986). The few positive data, like those cited at the beginning of this section, may be limited to novel contexts that elicit low to moderate autonomic arousal. Overall, peripheral feedback seems to have little impact on emotion.

The theories we have just discussed focus on relations between bodily events and emotion. Other types of theoretical views originate from observations of changes in emotional responsiveness that result from brain injury or disease.

Bodily Responses in Emotional States: Facial Expression

Our bodies reveal emotions in many ways. Overt expressions of emotion are evident in posture, gesture, and facial expression; all these dimensions are well cultivated by actors and actresses. Since the human face is hard to hide from view, it is a ready source of information for others. The prospect for communication is enhanced by the elaborate and finely controlled musculature of the face, which provides for an enormous range of facial expressions. In this section we will discuss the variety of facial expressions and the neural control of facial expressions.

Types of Facial Expression

An emphasis on facial expressions and emotion was noted quite early in a work of Charles Darwin, *The Expression of the Emotions in Man and Animals* (1872). In this book Darwin catalogued facial expressions of humans and other animals and

emphasized the universal nature of these expressions. He emphasized especially that facial expressions are connected to distinctive emotional states both in humans and nonhuman primates. Facial expressions were partly viewed as information communicated to other animals.

In recent times the work of Paul Ekman (1983) has provided rich insight into the properties of facial expressions. He and his collaborators have developed an array of analytic tools that enable objective description and measurement of facial expressions among humans of different cultures (Ekman, 1981). Analyses of facial information reveal that both static features of the face, such as structure of facial bones, and rapidly changing features of the face provided by facial muscles provide information. Figure 15-1 shows a variety of characteristic expressions in humans. How many different emotions can be detected in such expressions? Distinctive expressions are seen for anger, happiness, sadness, disgust, fear, and surprise, according to Ekman (1973). Facial expressions of emotions are similarly recognized or identified across many cultures. No explicit training is needed to interpret the expressions in any of these cultures. Cross-cultural similarity is also noted in the production of expressions specific to particular emotions. For example, people in a preliterate New Guinea society, when posing particular emotions, show facial expressions like those of advanced societies. Of course, universal expressions do not account for the full complement of human facial expressions (Ekman & Oster, 1979). Cultural differences may emerge in culture-specific display rules, which stipulate social contexts for facial expression. Thus some anthropologists have suggested that cultures that prescribe rules for facial expression and control and that enforce the rules by cultural conditioning might mask the universal property of facial expressions. The stimuli for expression may also differ among cultures.

Expressions that resemble particular adult expressions are evident in early infancy. For example, newborn humans show smiles during REM sleep periods. By 3–4 months, infants show differential responses to various facial expressions of adults. Much research indicates that by the ages of 4–5 years, children have acquired full knowledge of the appearance and meaning of many common facial expressions.

Facial expression in nonhuman primates has attracted the interest of researchers interested in cross-species emotional displays. Redican (1982) described distinctive primate expressions labeled as (1) grimace, perhaps analogous to human fear or surprise expressions, (2) tense-mouth display, akin to expressions of human anger, and (3) play face, similar in form to the human smile. In nonprimates the range of facial expressions is more limited since the character of facial muscles is quite different from that of primates. In nonprimates muscles of the face are more like a continuous sheet of more poorly differentiated muscles, which limits the range of facial expressions.

Most often facial displays are regarded as expressions or indicators of emotion. However, Fridlund et al. (1983) questioned whether many facial expressions reflect felt emotion. They point to the fact that a major role of facial expression is ''paralinguistic,'' which means that the face is accessory to verbal communication, perhaps providing emphasis and direction in conversation. These authors also note the display function of facial expressions, such as their social aspect. For example, they note the work of Gilbert et al. (1986) showing that subjects display few facial responses to odor when smelling alone but significantly more in a social setting. In support of the social display role of facial expression, they cite a study of Kraut and Johnston (1979), who noted that bowlers seldom smile when making a strike but smile frequently when they turn around to meet the faces of others watching them. Clearly the face is a final common pathway for many different functions.

Neurology of Facial Expression

How are facial expressions produced? Within the face there is an elaborate network of finely innervated muscles whose functional roles include production of speech, eating, respiration, and other roles in addition to facial expression. Most facial muscles attach to facial skin or an underlying tough tissue called fascia. In addition, there are some muscles that attach to skeletal structures of the head; these muscles enable movements such as chewing. The neural innervation of human facial muscles is derived from two cranial nerves: (1) the facial nerve, which innervates the muscles of facial expression, and (2) the trigeminal nerve, which innervates muscles that allow the jaw to move (See Reference Figure 2-12). Studies of the facial nerve reveal a complete independence of the right and left sides. The main peripheral branches of this nerve are illustrated in Figure 15-2, which shows that the main trunk divides into an upper and lower division shortly after entering the face. The origin of these nerve fibers is in the brain stem in a region called the nucleus of the

Figure 15-2 The neural innervation of muscles involved in facial expression. The main branches of the facial nerve are shown.

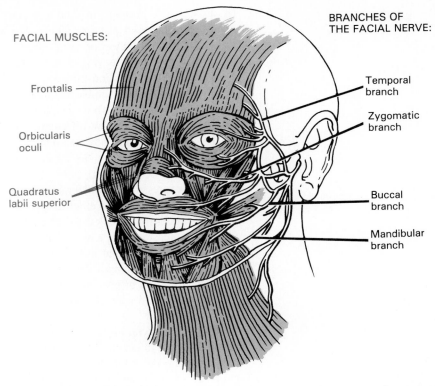

FACIAL MUSCLES:

Frontalis

Orbicularis oculi

Quadratus labii superior

BRANCHES OF THE FACIAL NERVE:

Temporal branch

Zygomatic branch

Buccal branch

Mandibular branch

facial nerve. Distinct subgroups of neurons within this nucleus form specific branches of the facial nerve, which, in turn, connect to distinct segments of the face. A clear separation within the facial nerve nucleus is seen between cells that control the muscles of the lower face and those that control muscles of the upper face.

Brain pathways that control facial expression are quite complex. Both direct and indirect inputs from the cerebral cortex activate the cells of the facial nucleus. In the human motor cortex, there is an extensive representation of the face (Figure 10-16). Innervation of the facial nucleus from cerebral cortex is both bilateral and unilateral, with the lower half of the face receiving contralateral inputs from cerebral cortex and the upper half receiving bilateral innervation. The functional correlate of this pattern of innervation is seen in our ability to readily produce one-sided movements of the lips, but unilateral movement of the eyebrows is a more exotic talent shared by few. A major difference in brain control of facial movements has been suggested for voluntary versus emotionally induced facial activity (Rinn, 1984). Voluntary activation of the facial nerve nucleus is achieved through the corticospinal system, whereas emotional activation of the face is presumed to involve subcortical systems. Support for this view comes from studies of patients who have sustained unilateral damage to the motor cortex. Such patients are unable to retract the corner of the mouth contralateral to the damaged hemisphere although both corners will retract during a period of spontaneous, happy laughter or amusement. An opposite syndrome is seen following damage to subcortical regions such as the basal ganglia, like that seen in Parkinson's disease. Patients in this instance are able to move the facial muscles voluntarily but lose spontaneous emotional expression of the face.

Bodily Responses in Emotion: Autonomic Responses

Although it is hard to hide the changing expressions of the face, the detection of visceral changes requires the scrutiny of electronic gadgets. When a subject is connected to devices that measure heart rate, blood pressure, stomach motility, dilation or constriction of blood vessels, skin resistance, or sweating of the palms or soles, we see a wealth of changes that are sensitive to emotional states. Devices that measure several of these bodily responses are called polygraphs, popularly known as "lie detectors." The use of polygraphs to detect lying in accused individuals is quite controversial; most psychophysiologists have argued against their use in these circumstances (Lykken, 1981).

Does the pattern of bodily response indicate the kind of emotion being experienced? This question, arising from the emphasis of the James-Lange theory, continues to intrigue investigators. Experimental studies explore whether people show patterns of reactions that are specific to particular events or stimuli. For example, if we recorded heart activity, stomach motility, skin temperature, respiration, and blood pressure during states of anger and fear, we would expect to see profiles distinctive for each state. Ax (1953) reported an oft-quoted experiment that shows such specificity in response to anger- and fear-provoking stimuli. In this study subjects had wires connected to them for recordings of several physiological measures. The states of anger and fear were induced by a confederate; he provoked anger by insulting behavior and fear by acting worrisome and incompetent in the presence of sparks deliberately contrived to elicit fear of electrocution. However hesitant one might now be about this kind of subject manipulation, it produced potent emotional states. Several differences in physiological patterns were seen, including greater increases in pulse rate and blood pressure in fear than in anger.

Individual Patterns of Autonomic Responses

Responses of various bodily systems reveal distinct patterns that are characteristic of the individual. This feature of visceral responses has been studied by Lacey and Lacey (1970), who refer to this characteristic as individual response stereotypy. Their work involved longitudinal studies of people extending over many years, from early childhood to adulthood. The stimulus situations they used to provoke autonomic responses included stress conditions such as immersing the hand in ice-cold water, performing rapidly paced arithmetic calculations, and presenting intense stimuli to the skin. They noted that across these conditions an individual profile of response can be seen, which is evident even in human neonates. For example, some neonates respond vigorously with heart rate changes, others with gastric motility changes, still others with blood pressure responses. Response patterns are remarkably consistent throughout life. This observation may provide the basis for understanding why the same intense stress might cause pathology of different organs in different individuals. It would seem that constitutional factors lead some of us to develop ulcers and others to develop high blood pressure in similar emotion-provoking situations. The concept of individual response stereotypy is therefore of considerable significance in the field of psychosomatic medicine.

Control of Autonomic Responses: Biofeedback

Heart rate, blood pressure, and respiration, among other autonomic responses, are influenced by many internal and external conditions. Yogis and others have dramatically demonstrated ways to control some internal conditions. Stories of their success in reducing heart rate and respiration to death-defying levels are part of the folklore surrounding mystics. Laboratory observations have documented unusual autonomic control in some of these individuals. Efforts of this sort powerfully demonstrate learned modulations of physiological systems that were at one time thought to be controlled by automatic mechanisms that could not be affected by experience.

Biofeedback procedures can increase as well as decrease the level of activity in autonomically controlled systems, a result shown in work on the blood pressure levels of people who have suffered spinal transections (Miller, 1980). Many of us have experienced a transient light-headedness that occurs when we rapidly stand up after a night's sleep. This fleeting response occurs because blood pressure transiently falls under the impact of gravitational forces. In the ordinary case, vascular reflexes rapidly adjust to normal. But paraplegic humans, especially those with high spinal lesions, may show a marked and maintained drop in blood pressure when moved to an upright posture. The absence of muscle tension over a large part of the body modifies the regulatory mechanisms of the vascular system, partly by changing the mechanical impact on blood vessels. This blood pressure failure forces some spinal-injured humans to maintain a horizontal position.

Miller (1980) has described biofeedback procedures that result in sustained elevation of blood pressure in such patients when they are moved to an upright position. Subjects are instructed to "try to increase" their blood pressure (Figure 15-3). Although they can make only tiny changes at the start, training that involves direct knowledge of results has been successful in many cases. Blood pressure information is continuously provided to the patient, and increases of systolic pressure cause a tone to sound. The patient is told to try to make the sound come on as frequently as possible. With success at one blood pressure level, the criterion is changed so that sound comes on only with yet higher blood pressure responses. Following such a regimen, spinal humans with this problem learn to increase their blood pressure when moved to an upright posture, enabling some to be fitted with braces and crutches and thus to become mobile. This learned increase in blood pressure becomes highly specific; that is, eventually it is not accompanied by heart rate changes. Biofeedback training to control skin temperature and thus alleviate such conditions as Raynaud's disease and migraine headaches was described in Chapter 12.

Bodily Responses in Emotion: Endocrine Changes

Humoral theories of emotion—those related to internal bodily secretions—have a long history and have involved many body organs including liver, spleen, and endocrine glands. This is reflected in common words used to express emotion, like "bilious" (derived from "bile"), meaning irritable, cranky, or unpleasant, and "phlegmatic" (from "phlegm"), meaning apathetic or sluggish. Current research explores the relations between hormones and emotions by:

1. Observing changes of hormone levels in the blood during experimentally or naturally produced emotional states. The technology of biochemical measurement of hormones has become quite precise and allows measurement of minute changes.

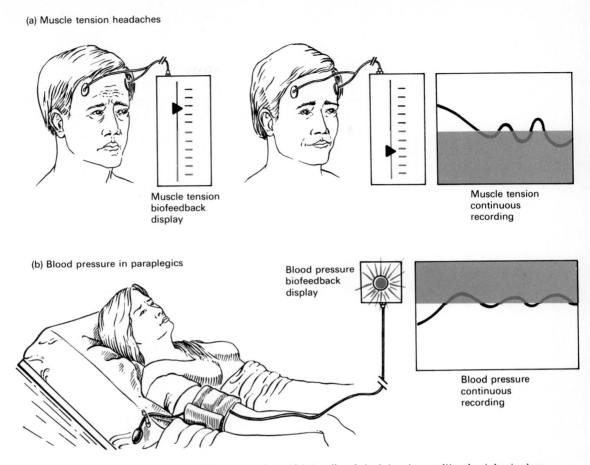

(a) Muscle tension headaches

Muscle tension biofeedback display

Muscle tension continuous recording

(b) Blood pressure in paraplegics

Blood pressure biofeedback display

Blood pressure continuous recording

Figure 15-3 Two examples of biofeedback training to modify physiological responses. (a) Biofeedback training to diminish frontal muscle tension that generates headaches. Signals to the subject in a display of muscle tension (electromyograms) show the current level and the optimal level (reduced tension). Muscle recording on the right shows progressive reduction of tension with training. (b) Biofeedback modification of blood pressure in a paraplegic. The display (light) shows when optimal level is reached, and the subject's task is to keep the light on for longer and longer periods as a progressively more upright posture is produced.

2. Observing changes in emotional states after administering hormones or after noting hormone deficiencies produced by endocrine disease. In the former case, a frequent interest has been mood changes produced by hormone treatments in women, generally from birth control pills.

We will consider some examples of research in each of these two directions.

Endocrine measurements accompanying emotional experiences have generally emphasized (1) assessment of epinephrine, released by the adrenal medulla and reflecting sympathetic activation of this gland, and (2) measurements of 17-hydroxycorticosteroids in blood or urine, which reflect the activities of the pituitary-adrenal cortical systems. Many studies clearly show that emotional stimuli or situations are accompanied by hormone secretions. Elevated urinary and blood levels of epinephrine or norepinephrine have been seen both prior to and during stressful and energetic activities like professional sport encounters, military maneuvers, and many other anxiety-provoking situations. Studies by Elmadjian and collaborators (1957, 1958) show that norepinephrine levels might be related to the intensity of the emotional encounter. Their data show elevated norepinephrine levels for individuals who react to an interview situation with intense emotional responses, including aggression, in contrast with those who respond more passively. However, norepinephrine levels may not distinguish the type of emotional display, since Levi (1965) has found similar epinephrine increases in women presented with film material that elicits pleasant and unpleasant responses. Adrenocortical responses also do not seem to differentiate the type of emotion. Brown and Heninger (1975) presented films that were either erotic or suspenseful and noted that both types of stimuli produced elevated cortisol levels in blood.

Various measures of fear and avoidance behavior of nonhuman primates and other animals have been investigated in many experiments. Figure 15-4 shows an extensive series of measures obtained in monkeys in the studies of Mason (1972). These animals engaged in an extended period of avoidance behavior in which they performed a lever-pressing response to avoid shock. The only cue controlling this behavior was time; responses had to be presented at some criterion rate (like once per minute) to avoid shock. In this situation hormone measures that show an

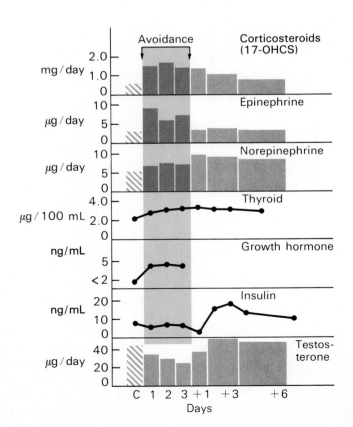

Figure 15-4 Pattern of hormonal responses to stress in a monkey. These graphs show control hormone levels and those during a three-day period of avoidance training and a six-day posttraining period. Note that some stress-induced hormone effects are quite persistent. (From Mason, 1972)

increase during avoidance periods include epinephrine, 17-hydroxycorticosteroids, thyroid activity, and growth hormone, while decreases are evident in insulin and testosterone.

Diminished hormone output produced by various disease states also influences emotional responses. Decreased thyroid output is frequently associated with depression. Depression is also seen in Addison's disease, an adrenal gland disorder that is accompanied by decreased glucocorticoid secretions.

Bodily Responses to Stress

Studies of stress have examined bodily responses both in laboratory situations and in real life circumstances. Let us see examples of research in both sorts of settings. Laboratory situations provide the precision of controlled stimulation but may lack the special emphasis of actual human circumstances.

Stress and the Stomach

The emphasis on stress, emotions, and human disease has generated many experimental inquiries concerned with autonomic reactivity during stress. A critical set of observations by Harold Wolff in the 1940s involved the case of a patient known as Tom. This patient had swallowed a caustic solution that had seared his esophagus, and thus he could not eat normally. To enable Tom to take in food, surgeons made a hole through the body wall into the stomach; a tube through this hole provided a route for nutrient fluids. The tube also let Wolff and his collaborators directly observe the surface lining of the stomach during the course of interviews that provoked emotional responses. During intensely emotionally laden phases of these interviews, Tom showed marked changes in the gastric mucosa, along with a dramatic buildup of stomach acid. Subsequent studies of humans with ulcers have shown marked elevation of hydrochloric acid in the stomach.

Laboratory studies of ulcer development in animals (for example, Ader, 1972) have involved stressful stimuli such as electric shock; these conditions can generate ulcers in some animals (Figure 15-5). Because the gastric erosions or ulcers produced in rats exposed to such conditions are believed to partially resemble the gastric ulcers seen in humans, it is of considerable interest to understand the psychobiological factors that lead to ulcer development in rats.

Various experimental conditions can be used to generate ulcers in rats. Preventing these animals from moving by using a body restraint is one of the oldest methods. The effect is especially evident in younger animals, particularly those that have sustained early separation from their mother. Section of the vagus nerve input to the stomach (which lowers stomach acid secretion) reduces the number of gastric lesions. Another determinant of ulcer formation in this experimental context is the level of the digestive substance pepsinogen secreted into the stomach. High levels in the stomach increase the probability of stomach lesions in rats.

Another experimental technique used to induce stomach lesions in experimental rats is the generation of strong emotional responses by employing electric shock. A variable that has been found to be especially important in this kind of experiment is the predictability of shock. Weiss (1977) has claimed that unpredictable electric shocks are more likely to contribute to gastric ulcer formation than predictable shocks. More recently Weiss (1984) has suggested that gastrointestinal pathology in rats is related to high levels of motor activity seen in response to stressful stimuli.

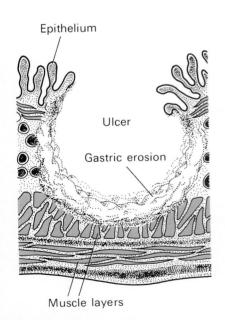

Epithelium

Ulcer

Gastric erosion

Muscle layers

Figure 15-5 Drawing of a cross-section of a gastric ulcer, showing erosion of outer layer of cells.

High activity either causes ulcers or is related to a mechanism common to disease susceptibility.

A classic experiment involving ulcer formation in monkeys by Brady (1958) came to be known as the "executive monkey" experiment. Pairs of monkeys in primate restraint chairs were placed next to each other. One animal, the "executive monkey," pressed a lever to avoid shock under conditions in which this response had to be repeated every 20 seconds to maintain continued shock avoidance. Whenever this monkey failed to press the lever within this interval, it received a shock. The second monkey received shocks at the same time, but it would not perform any response that could protect it from shocks. Executive monkeys in this experiment developed ulcers, whereas their adjacent partners failed to show gastric lesions. This experiment, in the years after its initial presentation, stimulated many research efforts, and most of them have failed to confirm Brady's finding. Indeed, in some rat experiments the responding animal is *less* likely to get ulcers, especially if shock is preceded by a warning signal. Experiments like these point to some of the psychological factors that contribute to gastric lesions. The links between these conditions and stomach pathology remain topics of continuing research efforts.

Stress Outside the Laboratory

Laboratory studies of human stress have used painful stimuli like exposure to electric shock or hand immersion in ice-cold water. Researchers of stress have frequently criticized the artificiality of such laboratory studies. Placing a hand in a bucket of ice cubes is certainly pale in comparison with dangerous situations that threaten life or produce psychological trauma. Some researchers have sought to use real-life situations as the arena in which to explore the biology of stress, but, of course, most human stress situations are not predictable, so baseline prestress assessments are not available. A few studies have avoided this difficulty and offered controlled observations of baseline conditions and prolonged observations through the course of a continuing potentially harmful situation. The most commonly used real-life situation is military training, especially aviator training and parachute training, where stress involves fear of bodily harm and fear of failure.

A monograph of Ursin, Baade, and Levine (1978) is the most recent example of the study of the psychobiology of stress in a parachute-training condition. The classical work in this area by Grinker and colleagues (1955) provided a comprehensive study of stress in this situation, involving both tower training and airplane jumps. However, this pioneering study took place long before the development of modern chemical assessments of circulating substances like hormones. The latest work by Ursin and his collaborators took advantage of contemporary analytic tools that allow the study of minute changes of hormone levels in blood. A group of young recruits in the Norwegian military were studied by using a variety of psychological and physiological measures before and during the early phase of parachute training. This training period involved a sliding ride along a long sloping wire suspended from a tower 12 meters high. Recruits were dressed in a suit equipped with a hook to a guide wire, and they slid along its course. This familiar situation in parachute training involves an experience somewhat like that of free fall. Initial apprehension is high, and at first the sense of danger is acute, although recruits know that they are not likely to lose their life in this part of the training. Physiological measures were obtained during a basal period prior to training and with successive jumps. On jump days two samples of blood were drawn to chart the time course of neuroendocrine events.

Autonomic activation in this situation is portrayed in Figure 15-6. Pituitary

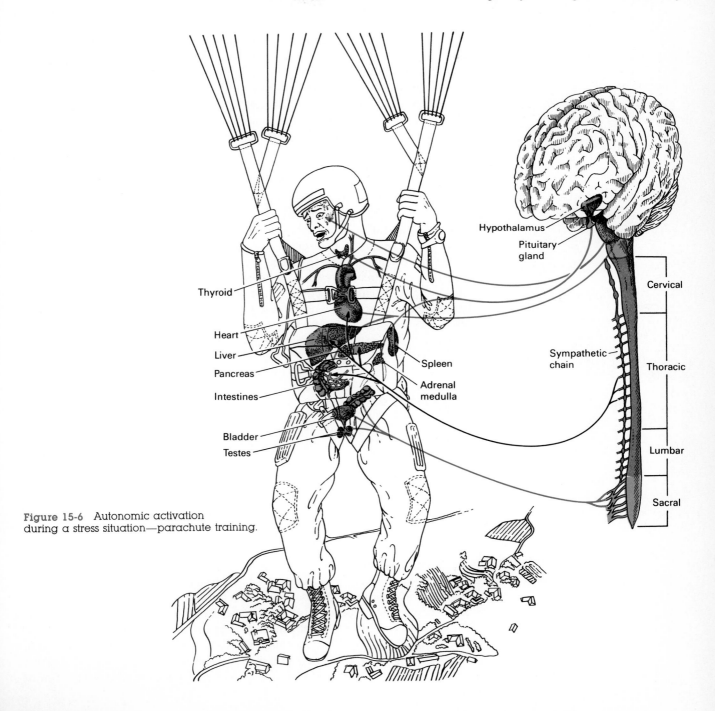

Figure 15-6 Autonomic activation during a stress situation—parachute training.

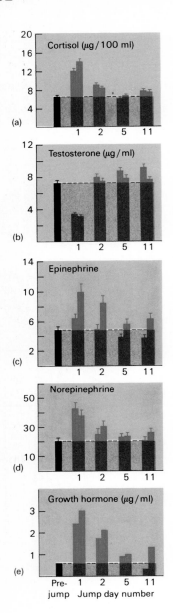

activation of the adrenal cortex during stress has been shown in many animal experiments, as noted in an earlier section. Figure 15-7a shows an elevation in cortisol in blood with initial exposure to the practice jump. Success in this task produces a rapid fall in the pituitary-adrenal response. Plasma testosterone levels fall below control levels on the first jump (Figure 15-7b), a finding that is also seen in rats and primates with exposure to noxious stimuli. In the parachute-training study, the effect is due to fear and disappears after initial exposure to the situation. Since this effect coincided with cortisol changes, the experimenters suggested that it might be mediated through the pituitary.

Urinary levels of epinephrine show a somewhat different pattern (Figure 15-7c). The initial jump day involved a marked elevation of urinary epinephrine, with a slow return to baseline with further parachute jumps. The pattern of norepinephrine secretion is somewhat different (Figure 15-7d), a finding evident in other studies, which emphasizes that elevated epinephrine might be related to active coping responses whereas norepinephrine might be related to less direct coping.

Clear-cut endocrine responses were also seen in changes of blood level of growth hormone (Figure 15-7e). In this experiment an evident elevation of growth hormone was seen during the day of the first jump.

Less dramatic real-life situations also evoke clear endocrine responses, as shown by research of Frankenhaeuser and her associates (1979). For example, riding in a commuter train was found to provoke release of epinephrine; the longer the ride and the more crowded the train, the greater was the hormonal response (Figure 15-8). Factory work also led to release of epinephrine; the shorter the work cycle—that is, the more frequently the person had to repeat the same operations—the higher were the levels of epinephrine. The stress of a Ph.D. oral exam led to a dramatic increase in both epinephrine and norepinephrine (Figure 15-8b, c).

Figure 15-7 Hormone changes during parachute training in military trainees. (From Ursin, Baade, and Levine, 1978)

Stress, Emotions, and Human Disease

The role of psychological factors in disease has been strongly emphasized by many psychiatrists and psychologists during the past fifty years. This field came to be known as psychosomatic medicine after an eminent psychoanalyst, Thomas French, suggested that particular diseases arise from distinctive sets of psychological characteristics. From this perspective ulcers were related to frustration of "oral" needs and the development of "oral dependency," hypertension was seen as arising from hostile competitive activities, and migraine headaches represented repressed hostile needs or impulses. Each disease state or illness was thought to be associated with a specific set of psychological characteristics—those that generated some form of unresolved conflict.

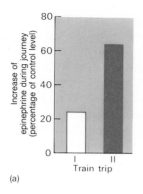

(a)

Figure 15-8 Hormone changes in humans arising from common social stresses. (a) Effects of small changes in crowding on a morning commuter train ride. Level I indicates percent increment of adrenaline secretion during a usual ride while II shows percent increment with a 10% increase in the number of passengers during a period of gasoline rationing. Levels of epinephrine (b) and norepinephrine (c) in a graduate student during a two-week period before thesis exams, during the exam, and following. (Adapted from "Psychoneuroendocrine Approaches to the Study of Emotion as Related to Stress and Coping" by M. Frankenhaeuser, *Nebraska Symposium on Motivation*, 1979, by permission of University of Nebraska Press.)

Although these ideas were prominent in the early development of psychosomatic medicine, current views make fewer claims for highly particular associations. Instead they emphasize that emotional responsiveness is only one factor among many that determine the onset, maintenance, and treatment of bodily disorders. Emotional stimuli activate a diversity of neural and hormonal changes that influence pathological processes of bodily organs. Studies in psychosomatic medicine have broadened in scope and now range from global evaluations of emotions, stress, and sickness to unraveling particular relations between emotions and bodily responses or conditions. A field called psychological medicine, or behavioral medicine, seems to be emerging in the wake of this developing interest (Stone, 1980). The interaction of the many factors that result in human disease is portrayed in Figure 15-9.

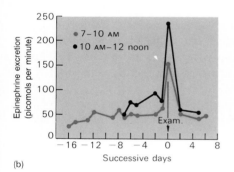

(b)

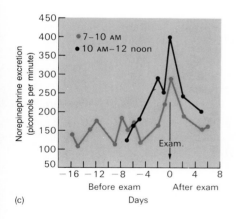

(c)

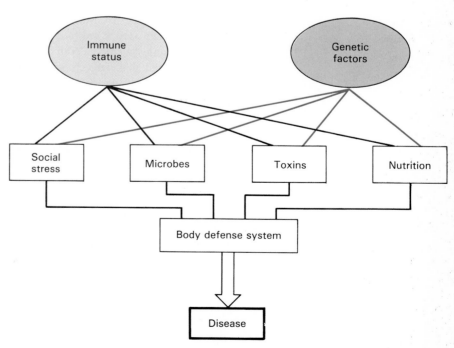

Figure 15-9 The interaction of factors involved in the development and progression of disease.

Connections between stress and human disease have been drawn in many different ways. Each new piece of evidence is tantalizing but generally several steps away from being conclusive. Perhaps the ambiguity is determined less by lack of ingenuity of experimenters than by the vast range of individual differences among people with regard to susceptibility to different diseases. Some of us are more constitutionally prone to failure in certain organs than others. Further, research on stress and human disease is bedeviled by the fact that stress is only a contributory condition to most disease states. Health habits, including nutritional variables, and patterns of coping with stress are probably of equal significance. This area is difficult to study, although it is of major importance to human life (Rodin and Salovey, 1989).

One global approach to linking stress and human disease is to study the covariation between precisely defined stressful life events and the incidence of particular diseases over a long period of time. Cancer and heart disease are leading causes of death and misery in human beings. The toll of these diseases in many countries has generated large-scale studies of the health habits, quality of life, and personal adjustment of large samples of people, including whole communities (Hurst et al., 1976). Most of these studies have been retrospective; that is, participants have been asked to report and rate experiences and emotional responses prior to the onset of an illness. In some instances relatives of deceased subjects provide this information. Behavior scales have been developed that allow a quantitative assessment of the frequency and number of stressful events that precede an illness. Although many methodological problems are evident in this approach, some consistent relations between stressful events and illness have been found.

Most research in this area seeks to show temporal relations between onset of illness and recent changes in the frequency of stressful events. A study of naval shipboard personnel by Rahe and his collaborators (1972) provides an example. Navy personnel were asked to report major life events associated with stress (such as death of family members or divorce) and a history of illness for a ten-year period. Results showed that subjects who reported few stressful events for a particular period had few episodes of illness in the following years. In contrast, subjects who experienced many stressful events reported a much higher level of illness for the following year. Many other studies seem to support this association between frequency of stressful life events and probability of illness in the future. However, cause and effect are intertwined in this research (Rabkin & Struening, 1976).

Mere frequency of stressful life events may be less related to serious illness than earlier studies emphasized. In a study of stressful events and heart attack, Byrne and White (1980) compared a group of coronary patients with a ''control'' group of people who were admitted to emergency rooms with suspected heart difficulties but who were rapidly diagnosed as not being heart attack cases. Questionnaires completed by the coronary patients gave researchers an estimate of the frequency and intensity of stressful life events for the year prior to hospitalization. Analysis of these data show that heart attack patients did not have a higher frequency of stressful events during the year prior to illness than did the controls. Nor was the intensity of stress events a factor that distinguished these groups. However, heart attack patients were significantly more distressed by stressful life events and tended to be more anxious. It would seem that the emotional impact of stress has greater significance for future serious illness than does the occurrence of stressful events.

Emotions, Stress, and the Immune System

For a long while, researchers viewed the immune system as an automatic mechanism—a pathogen, such as a virus, arrived on the scene, and soon the defense mechanisms of the immune system went to work, ultimately prevailing with their armory of antibodies and other immunological devices. Few thought of the nervous system as having an important role in the process, although the notion that the mind can influence well-being has been a persistent theme in human history. Times have changed dramatically! In the 1980s a new field has appeared called psychoneuroimmunology; its existence signals a new awareness that the immune system, with its collection of cells that recognize intruders, interacts with other organs, especially hormonal systems and the nervous system. Studies with both human and nonhuman subjects now clearly show psychological and neurological influences on the workings of the immune system. These interactions go in both directions; the brain influences responses of the immune system, and antibodies affect brain activities.

To understand this intriguing story we need to note some of the main features of the immune system. Basically there are two types of immunologic responses mediated by two different classes of cells called **lymphocytes.** One type, called B lymphocytes, mediates **humoral immunity,** which occurs when these cells produce antibodies (called immunoglobulins) that either directly destroy antigens like viruses or bacteria or enhance their destruction by other cells. A second type of immunologic response is called **cell-mediated immunity** and involves another class of cells known as T lymphocytes. These cells directly attack various antigens. They act as ''killer cells,'' forming a strong part of the body's attack against substances that can cause tumors. They are also the cells involved in the rejection of organ transplants. In addition, T cells interact with humoral reactions mediated by B cells. Some of these interactions involve enhancement of antibody reactions, and this response involves a kind of T lymphocyte called helper T cells. Other T lymphocytes suppress humoral reactions and are referred to as suppressor T cells. These basic components of the immune system also interact with other bodily substances and cells in producing a defense against disease and harmful substances. The organs of the body where these immune system cells are formed include the thymus, bone marrow, spleen, and lymph nodes. Figure 15-10 illustrates the main components of the immune system and their interactions.

The potentiality for interactions between the brain and immune system are revealed in many anatomical and physiological studies. Anatomical studies have noted the presence of nerve fibers from the autonomic nervous system in organs such as the spleen and thymus gland. Within these organs nerve endings are found among groups of lymphocytes, but the potential impact of their activity is still mysterious. It has been speculated that neural activity in these organs might directly affect the responsiveness of immune system cells by either enhancing or depressing various immune cell functions.

The bidirectional character of relations between the immune system and the brain is seen in other studies that show the effects of antibodies on the firing rates of brain neurons (Besedovsky et al., 1985). Other immune system products or regulators, such as interferon and interleukins, also affect brain activity. It thus seems that the brain is directly informed about the actions of the immune system. In fact one investigator has suggested that ''the immune system serves as a sensory organ for stimuli not recognized by the classical sensory system'' (Blalock, 1984).

Figure 15-10 The main components of the human immune system.

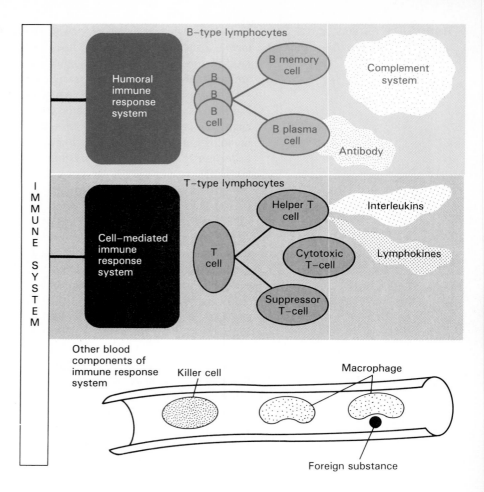

Another way in which researchers have shown the brain's role in immune system responsiveness has been to examine the effects of brain lesions on immune responses. Many studies show that lesions of the hypothalamus in experimental animals can influence immune processes such as antibody production (Stein et al., 1981). Some of these effects are quite specialized, involving responses to some antigens but not others. Furthermore, the specific hypothalamic site of the lesion also determines the character of immune effects. Some of the ways in which the hypothalamus influences immune system processes involve neuroendocrine mechanisms mediated through the pituitary gland. Under stressful conditions the hypothalamus produces corticotropin-releasing factor, which causes the release of adrenocorticotropic hormone (ACTH) from the pituitary. ACTH produces the release of corticosteroid hormones from the adrenal cortex, and one of the effects of these hormones is to suppress immunological responses.

The anatomical and physiological data described in the previous section suggest some bases for the role of psychological factors in immune system responses. How can we determine whether psychological factors such as emotions and stress affect either susceptibility or the type of response to infectious diseases? Several different research strategies have characterized studies in this area. One type of approach examines unusual immunological responses or disease history in emotionally disturbed populations. For example, do individuals with anxiety disorders have more frequent viral infections? Another approach has focused on searching for emotional factors in diseases that involve a failure or change in the immune system. For example, are there emotional differences between people with arthritis—which involves a failure of the immune system—and those with other diseases? The most common current approach to problems in this area studies the effects of stress on the immune system of humans and nonhuman populations. These various strategies are revealing the importance of emotions and stress in susceptibility to and outcome of disorders that involve the immune system. Here are some examples.

Psychological factors have been related to susceptibility to and progression of many infectious diseases. A large-scale review by Jemmott and Locke (1984) summarizes many of the studies in this area. For example, the relation between academic stress and immunologic functioning has been examined several times. Jemmott and others studied dental students during high-stress and low-stress periods and measured the level of a class of antibody found in saliva. They showed that during high-stress periods there was a diminished amount of this antibody group, indicating diminished immunocompetence. Most importantly, they noted that the student's perception of the stress of the academic program was a predictor of the level of circulating antibody; those who perceived the program as stressful showed the lowest levels. Critics of these kinds of data have argued that healthy subjects show considerable variability in the measures of immunological competence that are employed in this type of human study.

Studies using nonhumans allow for more precise interventions and yield intriguing data. For example, Ader (1985) has shown that it is possible to condition immunosuppression in rats. This was demonstrated in studies that involve the pairing of saccharin solution with the administration of a chemical immunosuppressive drug. Continued pairings of this type led to the ability of saccharin alone to reduce the response to pathogens. In similar experiments, Spector and colleagues (1985) have shown that it is possible to use classical conditioning techniques to enhance the activity of natural killer cells. Their research procedures involved exposure of mice to the odor of camphor for several hours. This treatment by itself had no impact on the immune system. Some mice were then injected with a chemical that increased the activity of natural killer cells. After the tenth session of pairings of odor and chemical, mice were presented with the odor of camphor alone and it was discovered that they showed a large increase in natural killer cell activity. This kind of Pavlovian conditioning of immune system responsiveness might be important as a treatment in some human disorders. It might substitute for injection of drugs that are used to enhance immune system responses and thus provide for fewer exposures to toxic treatments. Clearly a new era of observations of neural modulation and control of immune system responses has begun, and this may offer a new perspective on factors that control well-being.

An unusual association of handedness with immune system defects in humans has been discovered by researchers interested in cerebral hemisphere specialization of function. Left-handed people are more likely to suffer from immune system defects than right-handed people, according to the observations of Geschwind and Galaburda (1985). Some of these observations are considered in Chapter 18 where they are taken up in the context of the development of handedness and cerebral lateralization. Apparently some of the factors that influence the development of cerebral lateralization also influence the development of the immune system.

The immune system has also been implicated in cancer, our next topic.

Emotions and Cancer   Every now and then a newspaper or magazine article blares out a warning to readers about links between emotions and cancer. Mystery envelops many aspects of cancer, and its victims feel "chosen" by some evil forces, so it is not surprising that more subtle factors, such as emotions, have been singled out for scrutiny in trying to discover the cause of cancer. This realm of research is fraught with many contradictory claims. Two main directions of interest relating emotions and cancer are evident in current research efforts. One focus of work concerns the potential role of psychological factors as causes of cancer. A second direction of research has explored the impact of psychological influences on the course and outcome of cancer. A review of these problems by Greer (1983) offers a thoughtful assessment of the current state of affairs.

Do emotional states promote the onset of cancer? Most studies fail to reveal any direct relation between stressful experiences and the onset of cancer. Some personality studies, however, reveal relations between particular personality attributes and the likelihood of coming down with cancer. One of the oft-cited studies involved a large collection of students who entered Johns Hopkins School of Medicine between 1948 and 1964 (Thomas et al., 1979). Psychological tests and yearly questionnaires about health status were given to this population, and the data were related to disorders that appeared many years later. The group of 48 students who ultimately developed cancer were strikingly similar in personality attributes to those who committed suicide. They were described as "low-gear" people with little display of emotion and whose relation to their parents was characterized as cold and remote. In other studies, prior depression and feelings of hopelessness have been associated with cancers even after statistical adjustments for smoking habits. Some researchers have related breast cancer to a life-long suppression of anger (Greer, 1983).

The influence of psychological factors on the course of cancer has been explored in studies concerned with the reactivation of cancer after a long period of dormancy. Some researchers believe that reactivation in these instances can follow a period of severe emotional stress. Debate also surrounds another psychological aspect of outcome that has emerged from studies of survival time following the diagnosis of cancer. Several investigations have shown that long survivors had close personal relationships and coped better with illness-related problems; short-time survivors were characterized as responding with passivity, stoic acceptance, and attempts to forget (Weisman & Worden, 1977). The patient's response three months after mastectomy for breast cancer is also related to outcome five years after surgery according to Greer et al. (1979). They believe that survival without recurrence was associated with "fighting spirit or denial." Causal connections are difficult to draw in these efforts to relate psychological factors to the many aspects of cancer. Although methodological problems remain to be dealt with, current data clearly point to potentially important psychobiological interactions.

Clues to mechanisms that might account for the links between psychological factors and cancer are found in the animal research literature dealing with stress and the immune system. Research using nonhumans has shown that various types of stress produce increased amounts of circulating adrenal cortical hormones, especially corticosterone. Researchers have shown that corticosterone has potent effects on the immune system, including decreased circulating lymphocytes, shrinkage of the thymus gland, and some loss of tissue mass of lymph nodes. Thus the effectiveness of the immune system is reduced in stress states, and Riley (1981) has suggested that stress enhances vulnerability to cancer-causing agents such as viruses. Some experiments by this researcher lend support to the idea. In one study Riley stressed mice with implanted tumors by giving them a brief period of forced body rotation. Following this treatment the tumors grew to four times the size of those in control animals. A similar effect is produced by the direct administration of corticosterone without a stress experience, a finding that lends support to the view that stress-activated release of adrenal cortical hormones can increase cancer susceptibility or progression.

Emotions, Stress, and Cardiac Disease

Each day 3400 Americans suffer heart attacks, and many more suffer from other vascular disorders. About one-half of all cardiac-related deaths occur within a few minutes of the onset of symptoms. For many of these individuals, it appears that death is caused by the influence of the nervous system on mechanisms that control rhythms of the heart. One part of the story of the origins and progression of diseases involving the heart has focused on emotions and psychological stress. Common views of how heart attacks come about emphasize the role of emotions. Many an excited person has heard the admonition to "calm down before you blow a fuse!" In this section we will consider some psychological and physiological data that provide examples of the connections among emotions, stress, and heart disease.

Many psychological and sociological variables have been examined in studies of behavior patterns related to heart disease. A major theme instigated by the initial studies of Friedman and Rosenman (1959) has focused on differences between two behavior patterns—Type A and Type B—in the development and maintenance of heart disease. Type A behavior is characterized by excessive competitive drive, impatience, hostility, and accelerated speech and movements; in short, life is frantic, hectic, and demanding for such individuals. In contrast, Type B behavior patterns are characterized by a more relaxed style with little evidence of aggressive drive or an emphasis on getting things done fast. Of course, this is a crude dichotomy—many individuals have some of each pattern in their characteristic style. By now a large body of often-controversial research (summarized by Krantz & Glass, 1984) indicates that Type A individuals show a substantially higher incidence and prevalence of coronary heart disease than do Type B individuals. In the Western Collaborative Group study, following subjects for 8 1/2 years revealed that those who showed Type A behavior at the beginning of the study were twice as likely as Type B subjects to develop heart disease (Rosenman et al., 1975). This difference is also evident even after controlling for cigarette smoking, alcohol use, and nutritional differences. Clearly in many instances Type A behavior precedes heart disease. Physiological studies of Type A individuals reveal that the response of their sympathetic nervous system to stress is more intense than that shown by Type B individuals. A higher level of epinephrine and norepinephrine in blood during stress has also been noted in Type A people (Glass et al., 1980). Although the relationship between a behavior pattern and coronary heart disease seems strong, it is important to bear in mind that most Type A individuals do not show coronary heart disease even though the incidence is higher than in Type B persons. Some preliminary reports indicate that training to moderate Type A behavior can reduce the incidence of heart attacks (Siegal, 1984).

The phenomenon of sudden cardiac death, especially in younger people, highlights another aspect of the link between emotions and heart disease. Some actuarial data provide a poignant backdrop to this discussion. For example, the death of a wife leaves a widower with a probability of sudden death 40% higher than that of a married man the same age (cited in Syme, 1984). The role of the brain in the mediation of stress effects on the heart is seen in both animal and human studies. For example, cardiac disease is frequently seen in various brain disorders, especially those that involve destruction in the hypothalamus. Studies of people who have experienced life-threatening arrhythmias also reveal that a period of acute emotional distress preceded the attack in two-thirds of the patients. In addition, psychological stress produces unusual heartbeats in this population. An increased rate of sudden cardiac deaths is also seen following large-scale environmental disasters such as earthquakes.

Laboratory studies in guinea pigs show that stress can markedly reduce the threshold for heart arrhythmias that are elicited by the drug digitalis (Natelson, 1985). (This drug is often used to regulate heart rate, but at toxic levels it can prove fatal.) Comparing two different primate species, Mason (1984) has shown a possible relation between species-characteristic response patterns and disease. He notes that squirrel monkeys are excitable, restless, and frequently on the move. In contrast, titi monkeys are more low-keyed. At rest the squirrel monkey shows a much higher heart rate and higher levels of the hormone cortisol in blood. Long-term studies of these animals reveal that squirrel monkeys are susceptible to heart disease while in contrast titi monkeys are more prone to disorders of the immune system.

Brain Mechanisms and Emotion

Are there particular neural circuits for emotions localized in particular regions of the brain? This question has been explored in studies involving either localized brain lesions or electrical stimulation. Neuropharmacological studies have tried to determine the role of specific transmitters in particular emotions. Brain lesion studies involving clinical observations in humans or experimenter-produced lesions in nonhuman animals have focused on some dramatic syndromes of emotional change, such as the taming of monkeys following temporal lobe lesions. Brain stimulation studies have generated brain maps for various emotional responses, especially those involving aggression. In this section we will look at both types of studies and their results.

Brain Lesions and Emotion

Many studies have explored the brain mechanisms of emotion by investigating the effects of destruction of brain regions on behavior. These studies include both clinical investigations and surgical experiments with animal subjects.

Decorticate Rage

Ablation of the neocortex provided the oldest experimental demonstration of brain mechanisms and emotion. Early in this century, decorticate dogs were shown to respond to routine handling with sudden intense rage—sometimes referred to as "sham rage" because it lacked well-directed attack. Snarling, barking, and growling were provoked by ordinary handling, and this behavior also included strong visceral responses. Clearly, emotional behaviors of this type are organized at a subcortical level, and these observations suggested that the cerebral cortex provides inhibitory control of emotional responsiveness.

Klüver-Bucy Syndrome

Studies of brain mechanisms and emotion were advanced by the work of Klüver and Bucy (1938), who described a most unusual syndrome in primates following temporal lobe surgery. In the course of studies concerned with cortical mechanisms in perception, they removed large portions of the temporal lobe of monkeys. A dramatic portrait of behavior change was evident in these animals postoperatively. The syndrome was highlighted by an extraordinary taming effect. Animals who were wild and fearful of humans prior to surgery became tame and docile and showed neither fear nor aggression. In addition, they seemed to lose a sense of the meaning of many objects, as indicated by their ingestion of inedible objects. Frequent mounting behavior was seen and was described as hypersexuality. Lesions restricted to the cerebral neocortex did not produce these results, which implicated deeper lying regions of the temporal lobe, including sites within the limbic system. These observations formed a cornerstone in subsequent attempts to understand the role of subcortical structures in emotion.

Brain Models of Emotion

Studies of brain lesions and emotion have led to several anatomical models of brain circuits that mediate emotional behaviors. In this section, we will present two examples of models that seek to synthesize many empirical findings.

Papez Circuit of Emotion

Knowledge about brain anatomy and emotion has been derived from both experimental and clinical sources. In 1937, James W. Papez, a neuropathologist, proposed a neural circuit of emotions. Papez (pronounced Papes) derived his proposal from brain autopsies of humans with emotional disorders, including psychiatric patients. He also studied the brains of animal subjects, such as rabid dogs. He noted the sites of brain destruction in these cases and concluded that the necessary and sufficient destruction associated with impairment of emotional feelings involved a set of interconnected pathways in the limbic system. According to his circuit model, emotional expressions involved hypothalamic control of visceral organs, and feeling arose from connections to a circuit that includes the hypothalamus, the mammillary bodies, the anterior thalamus, and the cingulate cortex. The progression of activity in this circuit, as hypothesized by Papez, is shown by the arrows in Figure 15-11.

Papez's proposed circuit has been the source of much experimental work. Each region in the circuit has been lesioned or electrically stimulated to determine the relation to emotional processing. Aggression in particular has been a focus of many

Figure 15-11 Papez circuit of emotion.

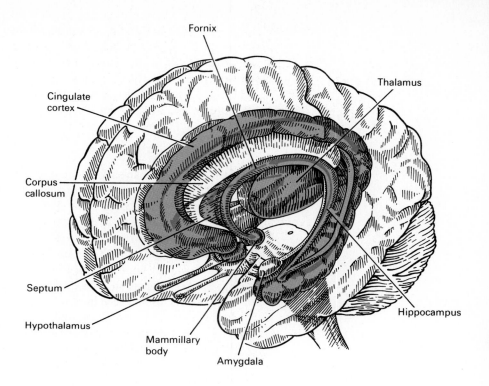

Figure 15-11 Papez circuit of emotion.

studies of the Papez circuit because of its importance in human affairs and the ease with which it can be observed in nonhumans. These studies have expanded the complexity of the circuitry, especially by adding roles for other structures in the limbic system, including the amygdala and the septal area.

The Triune Brain

A broad, speculative neural model of emotion has been presented by Paul MacLean (1970). His model arises from a diverse array of observations, including the study of limbic system seizures in humans, maps of behavior elicited by brain stimulation in monkeys, and an interpretation of the research literature on the evolution of the vertebrate brain.

According to MacLean, the human brain can be viewed as a three-layered system, with each layer marking a significant evolutionary development. The oldest and deepest layer represents our reptilian brain heritage and is seen in the current organization of the brain stem. It serves to mediate highly stereotyped acts that are part of a limited repertoire, including acts that creatures have to perform to survive, like breathing and eating. Routine maintenance is one way of describing these functions. In time another layer wrapped around the reptilian core; this two-layered system is seen in some lower mammals. This additional layer, MacLean argues, deals with species and individual preservation and includes the neural apparatus mediating emotions, feeding, pain escape and avoidance, fighting, and pleasure seeking. The set of relevant structures in this layer is the limbic system. With a further progression of evolution, a final, third layer developed; it consisted of the dramatic elaboration of the cerebral cortex and provided the substrate for rational thought, according to this speculative model.

MacLean has viewed his model as providing an understanding of the common features of emotional responses among many animals and an understanding of changes evident with progressively higher animals. From the standpoint of understanding the advantage of the development of the limbic system, he sees the elaboration of these structures as offering the reptilian brain freedom from stereotyped behavior and a flexibility that is driven by emotions. Many aspects of his speculation suggest interesting thoughts about neural aspects of emotions, although assessments of the broad scope of his model are not yet available.

Electrical Stimulation of the Brain and Emotion

Another productive approach to the neuroanatomy of emotion is to electrically stimulate sites in the brains of awake, freely moving animals and to note the effects on behavior. Such stimulation may produce either rewarding or aversive effects or may elicit sequences of emotional behavior.

Stimulation of the Brain and Positive Reinforcement

In 1954, psychologists James Olds and Peter Milner reported a remarkable experimental finding. They found that rats could learn to press a lever when the reward or reinforcement was a brief burst of electrical stimulation of the septal area within the limbic system. Another way to describe this phenomenon is brain "self-stimulation." Patients receiving electrical stimulation in this region are reported by Heath (1972) to feel a sense of pleasure or warmth, and in some instances stimulation in this region provoked sexual excitation.

The report of Olds and Milner (1954) is one of those rare scientific discoveries that starts a new field; many investigators following them have employed brain self-stimulation techniques. Some work has been concerned with mapping the distribution of brain sites that yield self-stimulation responses. Such studies can provide a portrait of the circuits of positive reinforcement (Figure 15-12). Other studies

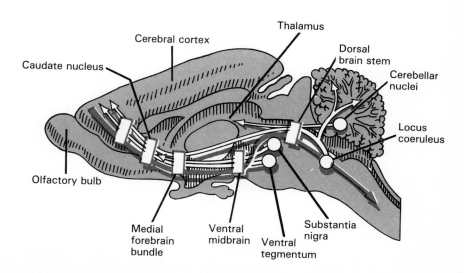

Figure 15-12 The distribution of reward sites in the rat brain.

have analyzed the similarities and differences between positive responses elicited by brain stimulation and those elicited by other rewarding situations, such as presentation of food to a hungry animal or water to a thirsty animal. Perhaps electrical stimulation taps in on the circuits mediating these more customary rewards. Quite recently research in this area has moved in a neurochemical direction with many efforts being made to identify the relevant transmitters in brain pathways that mediate self-stimulation behavior. Work in this area can be of particular importance in understanding the impact of many drugs on emotional responses of humans.

Self-stimulation is not a peculiar property of rat brains. It can be shown in diverse mammals including cats, dogs, monkeys, and humans. Nevertheless, it has been most extensively studied in rats. In these animals self-stimulation by lever pressing can go on for hours; response rates vary with both electrical current values and brain site. Early studies comparing self-stimulation with conditions that involve natural rewards—like food and water—seemed to reveal significant differences in reinforcement properties. For example, sudden extinction was seen with behavior reinforced by direct brain stimulation of self-stimulation regions; as soon as the electrical stimulation was interrupted, lever pressing ceased. However, more recent studies directly comparing responses for food, water, and electrical stimulation of the brain show similar features no matter which reinforcing condition is employed (reviewed in M. E. Olds & Fobes, 1981).

Self-stimulation is found with electrical stimulation of many different subcortical sites and a few frontal cortical regions. However, cerebral cortical stimulation in most regions does not have positive reinforcement properties. Concentration of positive brain sites is seen in the hypothalamus, although these sites also extend into the brain stem. A large tract that ascends from the midbrain to the hypothalamus—the medial forebrain bundle—contains many sites that yield strong self-stimulation behavior. This bundle of axons is characterized by widespread origins and an extensive set of brain regions where terminals of these axons can be found. The anatomical arrangements of self-stimulation sites seem similar in different animals, although positive sites are spread more extensively throughout the rat brain than in the cat brain. More recently the maps of self-stimulation sites have been compared to those of various neurotransmitters. A controversial idea that developed from observation of these maps is that dopamine is the transmitter for reward circuits (e.g., Wise, 1982). On the other hand, Gallistel et al. (1985) failed to find support for it, using a metabolic mapping technique with 2-deoxyglucose. They reported that a map of the self-stimulative circuitry aroused by stimulation of the medial forebrain bundle did not coincide with a more extensive map of the dopaminergic systems activated by stimulation of the substantia nigra. But this may mean only that some dopaminergic fibers and sites are engaged in other functions than reward. In a major review of the extensive research on brain mechanisms of reward, Wise and Rompre (1989) state the following two conclusions:

1. Dopamine plays an important role in the rewarding effects of stimulating many brain regions, but it is not involved in the rewarding effects of stimulating either the frontal cortex or the nucleus accumbens; the latter effects depend upon another transmitter (or transmitters).
2. Dopaminergic systems probably play a rather general role in motivation and

Figure 15-13 Distribution of sites in the hypothalamus from which electrical stimulation elicited defensive responses, flight, and attack and/or killing of prey (+, defense; ●, flight; ▼, prey-killing). Three different cross sections of the hypothalamus are shown. A is the most anterior. (FIL, nucleus filiformis; Fx, fornix; HA, anterior hypothalamus; HL, lateral hypothalamus; MFB, median forebrain bundle; SO, supraoptic nucleus; TO, optic tract; VM, ventromedial nucleus) (Adapted from Kaada, 1967)

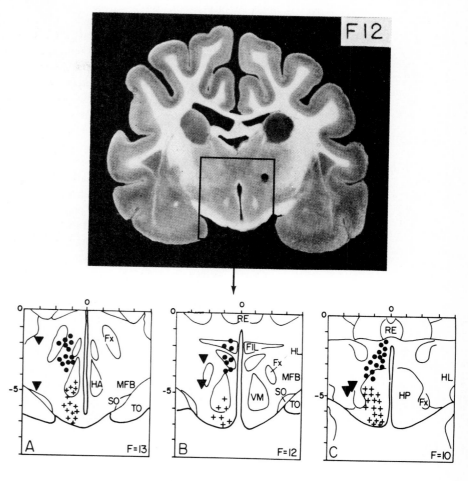

movement, a role that is essential to reward as well as to other aspects of motivation.

Maps of Elicited Emotional Responses

Electrical stimulation of the brains of alert, awake cats and monkeys implanted with electrodes has provided maps of the distribution of emotional responses. This work has especially emphasized limbic system sites and has focused particularly on aggression (described shortly). An example of the integration of behavioral and autonomic responses provoked by hypothalamic stimulation is shown in Figure 15-13, taken from the work of Kaada (1967). These maps show that very discrete components of both autonomic and behavioral responses are represented at selected loci in the limbic system and the hypothalamic regions. No instance of emotional response has been elicited by stimulation of the cerebral cortex.

**Psychobiology of
Aggression**

Violence, assaults, and homicide exact a high toll in many human societies; for example, homicide is the most prominent cause of death in young adults in the United States. Many different approaches to understanding aggression have investigated its psychological, anthropological, and biological dimensions. These concerted efforts have clarified many aspects of aggression along with its biological bases in hormonal and neurophysiological mechanisms. We will examine the results of these studies in this section.

What Is Aggression?

Surely we all know aggression! Alas, a more sustained consideration suggests that this all-too-familiar term is laden with many different meanings. In its ordinary, common usage, aggression defines an emotional state that many humans describe as consisting of feelings of hate and a desire to inflict harm. This perspective emphasizes aggression as a powerful inner feeling. However, when we view aggression as an overt response—overt behavior that involves actual or intended destruction of another organism—we see several different forms.

Attack behavior of an animal directed to a natural prey is seen by some as predatory aggression. However, Glickman (1977) has argued that this behavior is more appropriately designated as feeding behavior. Intermale aggression within the same species is found in virtually all vertebrates. Perhaps the relevance to humans is seen in the fact that the ratio of males to females arrested on charges of murder in the United States is 5:1, with a dominance in the age group 14–24. Further, aggressive behavior between boys, in contrast to that between girls, is seen quite early in the form of vigorous and destructive play behavior. Maternal aggression is seen in some animals and reaches an extreme form in the cannibalism of young by rodent mothers. Fear-induced aggression is seen in animals who are cornered and unable to escape. Some forms of aggression are seen as a component of sexual behavior. And, lastly, one form of aggression is referred to as irritable aggression; it can emerge from frustration or pain and frequently has the quality described as uncontrollable rage.

Hormones and Aggression

Male sex hormones play a major role in some forms of aggressive behavior, especially that seen in intermale social encounters. This association has been found in several types of experiments. One set of data relates levels of circulating androgens to different measures of aggressive behavior. Variation in hormones among a group of animals can arise from processes of development or seasonal circadian changes. With the advent of sexual maturity, intermale aggression markedly increases in many species. McKinney and Desjardins (1972) have shown aggressiveness changes in mice that start at puberty. Immature mice treated with androgen display increased aggression. Seasonal changes in testosterone are seen in many species, and increases in testicular size seem related to increased aggression in animals as diverse as birds and primates.

An additional line of evidence for the relation between hormones and aggression comes from observations of the behavioral effects of castration. Reductions in the level of circulating androgen produced in this manner are commonly associated with profound reduction in intermale aggressive behavior. Restoring testosterone by in-

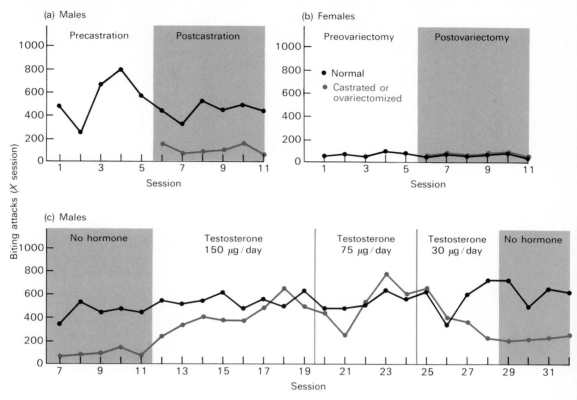

Figure 15-14 Effects of androgen on aggressive behavior of mice. During each session, the number of biting attacks on an inanimate object is counted. (a) Male behavior before and after castration. (b) Female behavior before and after the removal of the ovaries. (c) The effects of hormone replacement on the attack behavior of castrated males. Testosterone reinstates aggressive behavior in castrated males. (From Wagner, Beauving, and Hutchinson, 1980)

jection in castrated animals increases fighting behavior in mice in a dose-related manner (Figure 15-14).

The aggressive behavior of female mammals can also depend on reproductive hormones. Although the prevailing view among researchers is that males of most mammalian species are typically the more aggressive sex, there are examples of species where such dimorphism is not evident (Floody, 1983). For example, among spotted hyenas females are typically larger and rule a clan that can consist of up to 80 hyenas (Kruuk, 1972). Further, observations of aggression in intersexual encounters suggest that females might specialize in types of aggression that are dissimilar from males. For example, female aggressive behavior is particularly evident in territorial defense and mate selection, whereas male aggression is more likely to be seen in situations where males are pitted against each other in dominance situations. Observations of female aggressive behavior in rodents observed during different phases of the estrous cycle show covariation in some species but not others. For example, estrous hamsters are less aggressive than nonestrous females in response to conspecifics of either sex (Floody, 1983). Studies of changes in aggression during the menstrual cycle in various primates are steeped in controversy (Brain, 1984). At present there is no clear evidence linking hostility changes in women to the menstrual cycle, including the syndrome of premenstrual tension.

The idea of a relationship between hormones—especially androgens—and human aggression is laden with controversy. For example, arguments summoned in related legal briefs frequently cite the results of the literature on nonhuman animals. Some human studies have shown a positive correlation between testosterone levels and magnitude of hostility, as measured by behavior rating scales. But one study of prisoners (Kreuz & Rose, 1972) shows no relation between testosterone levels and several measures of aggressiveness; another study (Ehrenkrantz, Bliss, & Sheard, 1974) shows positive relations. Thus it is not clear that level of androgens in intact men is related to aggressiveness. Nevertheless, several attempts to modify the aggressive behavior of male criminals have involved sex hormone manipulation. Castration studies generally show that violence in sex offenders is reduced by this surgical procedure especially where ''excessive libido'' is considered as the instigator of sexual assaults (Brain, 1984). A reversible castration is achieved through the administration of antiandrogen drugs, such as cyproterone acetate, which exerts its impact by competing with testosterone for receptor sites. Several research studies using criminals who had engaged in sexual assault show that administration of these substances reduces sexual drive and interest (Brain, 1984). However, some researchers have suggested that the effects of antiandrogens on aggressive behavior are less predictable than their effects on sex behavior (Itil, 1981). There are many ethical issues involved in this approach to the rehabilitation of sex offenders, and the intricacies involved in such intervention have yet to be worked out. One important component of the discussions relevant to the use of hormone interventions in criminal populations is a more adequate appreciation of the links between aggression and sex behavior and the role played by hormones in this relationship.

Neural Mechanisms of Aggression

For many years researchers have electrically stimulated various brain regions in awake, behaving animals and thus sought to provide maps of the anatomy of aggressive acts. This work started with the pioneering experiments of Hess in the 1920s. The dramatic character of various components of feline aggressive behavior has made cats a favorite experimental animal. Figure 15-15 provides an example of the

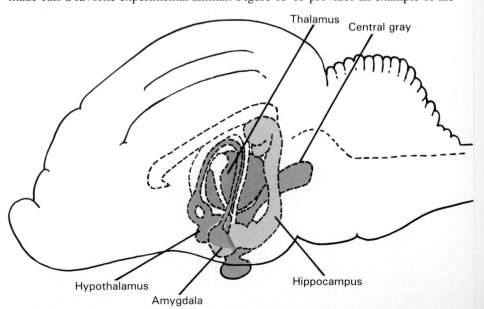

Figure 15-15 Distribution of brain sites in the cat that, during electrical stimulation, yield emotional responses. Stimulation of the inner zone of the hypothalamus (dark brown) and the central gray elicits hissing. Stimulation of the outer zone (light brown) produces flight. (From de Molina and Hunsperger, 1959)

mapping of various aggressive displays in cats. Most of the sites that elicit aggressive behavior are found within the limbic system and connected brain stem regions. Regions differ in the patterning of elicited behavior and the emphasis on particular components. For example, brain stem stimulation in the central gray area produces piloerection, hissing, claw retraction, and especially prominent, loud, characteristic vocalizations.

Controversies About the Neurology of Human Violence

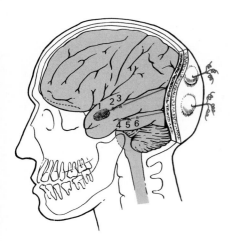

1. Pleasant; hopeful; relaxed; confident; complete opposite of seizure; creative; elated; floating; warm; peaceful; calm
2. Unpleasant; ''radio waves'' in chest
3. Feeling of ''looking on'' scene
4. Power gone; weak; weird
5. Odd; warm; floating; blurred vision
6. Breathless; difficult to communicate thoughts

Figure 15-16 Human aggression and temporal lobe stimulation. Responses of this patient to stimulation at different sites within the temporal lobe are shown. The amygdala is the oval body penetrated by the tip of the upper electrode. (Adapted from Mark and Ervin, 1970)

Some forms of human violence exhibited by individuals are characterized by sudden intense physical assaults. In a very controversial book, *Violence and the Brain*, Mark and Ervin (1970) suggested that some forms of intense human violence are derived from temporal lobe seizure disorders. They offer horrifying examples from newspaper accounts as preliminary evidence. For example, in 1966, Charles Whitman climbed a tower at the University of Texas and murdered by wanton shooting a number of passing individuals. Earlier he had killed family members, and letters he left behind revealed a portrait of a bewildered young man possessed by an intense need to commit violence. Postmortem analysis of his brain suggested the presence of a tumor deep in the temporal lobe. Other, more formal data cited by Mark and Ervin include the common occurrence of aggression in temporal lobe seizure patients and the long-controversial claim that a large percentage of habitually aggressive criminals display abnormal EEGs that indicate likely temporal lobe disease. They argue that temporal lobe disorders may underlie many forms of human violence and produce a disorder they label dyscontrol syndrome.

Mark and Ervin presented several detailed clinical reports of humans with possible temporal lobe seizure disorders. These patients had depth electrodes implanted within the temporal lobe. Electrical stimulation of various sites along the electrode tracts resulted in seizures typical of the patient. Characteristic data are shown in Figure 15-16. Intense assaultive behavior directly related to elicitation of temporal lobe seizure was seen. In some patients neurosurgical intervention—removal of some temporal lobe regions, especially the region of the amygdala—produced profound reduction in both seizure activity and reports of assaultive behavior.

Much of the controversy surrounding this monograph deals with the claim that a large proportion of human violence has this neuropathological origin (Valenstein, 1973). Vigorous controversy is also promoted by the implicit argument that neurosurgery can alleviate forms of violent behavior that many others feel are more readily understood as products of social distress and developmental impairment.

Violence and some forms of seizure disorders in humans have been linked in many other studies. Among both juveniles and adults arrested for violent crimes, there is a high percentage of people with abnormal EEG recordings (Lewis et al., 1979; Williams, 1969). A group of patients examined by Derinsky and Bear (1984) with seizures involving emotion-controlling structures of the limbic system showed aggressive behavior that occurred after the development of an epileptic focus localized within this system. None of these patients had a history that included traditional sociological factors linked to aggression, such as parental abuse, poverty, and use of drugs. In these patients aggression is seen as an event between seizures; directed aggression is seldom seen during an actual seizure involving the limbic system (Delgado-Escueta et al., 1981). Although the relation of violence and aggression to epilepsy remains controversial, there is a growing set of clinical observations that support this association in some individuals.

Discussions about the biology of human violence have also given considerable emphasis to certain abnormalities of human sex chromosomes. This interest was partially fostered by the observation that a murderer who had killed a group of nurses in their home had the rare XYY chromosome pattern. Some investigators noting the link to male hormones seen in infrahuman studies of hormones and aggression suggested a connection between an extra Y chromosome and violence. This chromosome disorder is a very rare occurrence, so testing of this relation proved difficult. A group of investigators who were aware of the very thorough birth and life history data in Denmark pursued a thorough analysis of the relation between human aggression and the XYY chromosome type (Mednick & Christiansen, 1977). To the surprise of some, they found that although XYY chromosome males were more likely to be in jail than normals, the crime that resulted in jailing was less likely to have been violent in nature. In fact, the cause for jailing was usually petty theft and similar offenses; diminished social intelligence of many of these men seemed to preclude the ability to hide their crimes. More recently Meyer-Bahlburg (1981) has expressed the view that there is no good evidence that XYY males have any gross abnormalities of androgen or gonadotropin production, although there is some evidence that they are more aggressive than normals prior to puberty.

Biology of Mental Disorders

The realm of mental disorders has become one of the most exciting challenges for biological approaches to human behavior. The size of the problem is formidable. Its magnitude is reflected in one of the most comprehensive surveys of mental disorder in the United States conducted by the National Institutes of Health (Myers et al., 1984; Robins et al., 1984; Burnham et al., 1987). The survey was conducted door-to-door and involved 18,000 adults in four major cities and one rural area. Overall, the report noted that within a six-month period almost 20% of adult Americans suffer from at least one type of disorder classified as psychiatric. At least 8% of us suffer from anxiety disorders, and another 6–7% are involved in drug dependency or abuse, especially involving alcohol consumption. Depression and related disorders affect 6% of the adult population, and at least 1 in 100 is schizophrenic. Rates for total mental disorders in men and women are comparable, although the types of disorders each sex develops are slightly different. Especially prominent sex differences are seen in depression, which is far more prevalent among females, and drug dependency and alcoholism, which are more evident in males. Certain psychiatric disorders tend to appear relatively early in life, for example, drug abuse and schizophrenia. The age range 25–44 shows peaks for depression and antisocial personality, whereas cognitive impairment occurs especially in people older than 65. Mental disorders exact an enormous toll on our lives, and efforts to understand them account for much research in realms ranging from cell biology to sociology. Although in the past many psychiatric dysfunctions have been approached from an exclusively psychological framework, current efforts have developed a distinct biological orientation. This orientation is leading to progressive refinements of the categories of mental disorders such as schizophrenia and anxiety. This accomplishment is aiding not only understanding but also therapeutic interventions.

Some seeds for a biological perspective in psychiatry were sown around the turn of the century. At that time, one widely prevalent psychosis accounted for 20–25% of the patient populations in mental hospitals. Descriptions of the patients emphasized these attributes: profound delusions, grandiosity and euphoria, poor judgment, impulsive and capricious behavior, and profound changes in thought structure.

This disorder was known in virtually all societies of the world and had been known for centuries. Many people regarded it as a functional psychosis derived from the stresses and strains of personal and social interactions. Then in 1911 the microbiologist Hideyo Noguchi discovered the cause of this profound psychosis. Examining the brains of patients during autopsy, he established that extensive brain changes were wrought by *treponema pallidum,* a bacterium of the class spirochete. This psychosis was produced by syphilis, a venereal infection that has journeyed through history with humans. Noguchi's discovery ushered in an era of biological psychiatry, which many believe is now reaching its golden age.

Schizophrenia

At one time one-half of all the mental hospital beds in the United States were occupied by patients diagnosed as schizophrenic. Many of these persons spent their entire lives incapacitated by hallucinations, delusions, and generalized abnormalities of feelings and thoughts. Advances in psychobiology and the neurosciences have brought a distinctly biological emphasis to work in schizophrenia, and many new findings have begun to lead to a hopeful view that major advances can be expected. Researchers continue to raise questions whether this disorder is a single entity or a family of related disorders, and biological research is helping to clarify the issue.

Schizophrenia is not distinctive to any particular modern society; rather it is a universal disorder found throughout the world. This conclusion is drawn from several sources. Long-term epidemiological studies of the World Health Organization present some relevant findings (Sartorius et al., 1986). Recently they compared the incidence of schizophrenia in specific cities in ten different countries. These included advanced, industrialized communities (Rochester, New York; Moscow, U.S.S.R.; Aarhus, Denmark) and impoverished cities in developing nations (Agra, India; Cali, Colombia; Ibadan, Nigeria). Data from the report show that the incidence of schizophrenia in all these cities was similar. Symptom pictures in all the varied cultures were also similar. However, major differences were seen in the mode of onset of the disorder. In developing nations onset of the disorder is acute for about 50% of patients, whereas acute onset characterizes only 26% of the patients in developed nations. Follow-up studies conducted over a two-year period also revealed that outcome is better in less industrialized countries, an intriguing finding that may relate to some of the social support networks available in developing nations.

Genetics of Schizophrenia

For many years genetic studies of schizophrenia were controversial, although the notion of inheritance of mental illness is quite old. Data and speculations in this research area sparked vigorous interchanges for several reasons. For one, early researchers in the area of psychiatric genetics seemed to couple presentation of data with urgings for eugenics measures, which were repugnant to many. In addition, early work failed to appreciate that environments are major modifiers of gene actions. For any genotype there will often be a large range of alternative outcomes that are determined by both developmental and environmental factors. A more contemporary view about genetic control of psychiatric disorders has resulted in major new perspectives on the genetics of schizophrenia.

The basic aim of studies in this area is to understand the role played by genetic factors in the causation and maintenance of schizophrenic states. If population studies of various types establish that there is a significant role for inheritance, then it becomes important to search for the mechanisms of such effects including the neurochemical, neurophysiological, and neuroanatomical processes that have gone awry. Genetic studies are also important in the development of preventive programs. For example, if a genetic contribution is established as a significant ingredient in the genesis of schizophrenia, then it would be important to generate programs to aid the at-risk population. A similar strategy for a type of mental retardation—phenylkatonuria—was described earlier in Chapter 4.

The world population of schizophrenics is estimated at about 10 million. Because of the large number of patients, scientists have been able to conduct a variety of genetic studies (Baron, 1986a, b). These include family or pedigree studies, twin studies, and adoption studies. We will take up each of these in turn.

Family Studies

If schizophrenia is an inherited disorder, then relatives of schizophrenic patients should show a higher incidence of schizophrenia than is found in the general population. In addition, the risk of schizophrenia among relatives should increase the closer the relationship, since close relatives share a greater number of genes. In general, parents and siblings of patients have a higher risk of being or becoming schizophrenic than do individuals in the general population. The risk is greater the closer the biological relatedness.

It is easy to find fault with family studies. For one thing they involve a thorough confusion of hereditary and experiential factors, since members of a family share both of these. In addition, the data usually depend on the recollections of relatives whose memories are likely to be clouded by zealous efforts to attribute ''blame'' in consideration of the origins of the disorder. ''Funny'' aunts and uncles now departed are easily designated as the responsible agents in the etiology of mental disorder. But better family studies restrict data to professionally diagnosed cases.

Twin Studies

In providing twins, nature gives researchers what would seem on casual glance to be the conditions for a perfect genetic experiment. Human twins can arise either from the same egg (identical twins) or from two different eggs (fraternal twins). Additionally, many twins have other siblings as well. Twin studies of schizophrenia are concerned with determining the occurrence of schizophrenia in twins, especially the difference in rate of occurrence between identical and fraternal twins. When both

Table 15-1 Concordance Rates of Schizophrenia for Monozygotic and Dizygotic Twins

Study	Concordance Rates (%)	
	Monozygotic	**Dizygotic**
A	61	10
B	82	15
C	75	14
D	42	9
E	38	10

individuals of a twin pair are schizophrenic, they are described as being concordant for this trait. If only one member of the pair is schizophrenic, the pair is described as discordant. Table 15-1 compares concordance rates in identical and fraternal twins as reported in several early studies. Concordance rates in these studies are much higher in identical twins. This fact is clear.

Contemporary studies continue to confirm this type of finding. One recent study using the twin method reported by Kendler and Robinette (1983) involved an unusual twin registry established many years ago. This extensive registry was developed from a search of birth certificates in 39 states for twins born during the years 1917 to 1927. The search yielded a list of 54,000 multiple births, which was then matched against an index of names maintained by the Veteran's Administration of people who had served in the armed forces. This identified the twins who were soldiers around World War II, and from the medical records it was possible to find 590 individuals of this twin group who had a recorded diagnosis of schizophrenia. An analysis of this population revealed that concordance for schizophrenia was greater in monozygotic (30.9%) than dizygotic twins (6.5%). This study provides additional evidence for the role of genetic factors in the etiology of schizophrenia.

But can we accept such data as reflecting the inheritability of schizophrenia? Twin studies of schizophrenia have been criticized on several grounds. Some data indicate that twins are unusual from a developmental perspective in that they usually show lighter birth weights and different developmental progress than nontwins. In addition, parental treatment of identical twins differs considerably from their interaction with fraternal twins, thus generating a compounding environmental variable.

Despite these weaknesses, twin studies do indicate the importance of genetic mechanisms in the development of psychotic disorders, particularly schizophrenia. They regularly show higher concordance rates for schizophrenia in identical twins than those observed in fraternal twins or ordinary siblings. However, it is important to note that even with identical twins concordance for schizophrenia is less than 100%. Although the genetic constitution is identical for both identical twins, one member of the identical twin pair may be schizophrenic and the other normal. However, Kendler (1983) notes that behavior similarity between identical twins is greater than in fraternal twins even when they were mistakenly treated as dizygotic by parents and themselves.

Studies of identical twins discordant for schizophrenia can provide useful information about the possible factors that lead to schizophrenia and those that protect against the emergence of it. Many studies emphasize the finding that the twin that developed schizophrenia tended to be the one who was more abnormal throughout life. The symptomatic twin frequently weighed less at birth and had an early developmental history that included more instances of physiological distress (Wahl, 1976). This developmental history is also connected with the parents' view of the symptomatic twin as more vulnerable. During development this twin was more submissive, fearful, and sensitive than the identical sibling. This type of study is in its infancy and may yet provide indications about how to protect against schizophrenia. We mention this aspect of genetic studies to show that genetic studies of schizophrenia are not ''fatalistic'' in design but rather can provide a positive view of prevention. The most striking case of schizophrenia in multiple births is presented in Box 15-1.

BOX 15-1 | Four Copies of Schizophrenia: The Genain Quads

The ultimate in the "twin method" is a study of an unusual multiple birth first described in a book entitled *The Genain Quadruplets* (Rosenthal, 1963). This book contained the sad tale of four identical quadruplets all of whom became schizophrenic by their early twenties. Based on current epidemiological data, this event is extraordinarily rare—only once in one and a half billion births is one likely to find a set of monozygotic quadruplets all of whom are schizophrenic. It is no surprise then that these quads were intensively studied, and 25 years after the initial review at the National Institute of Mental Health, they were reexamined. Recently several reports have been published that provide a longitudinal perspective on schizophrenia in what can be described as four copies of the same genes (Buchsbaum et al., 1984; DeLisi et al., 1984; Mirsky et al., 1984).

This story started in a small New England town where the quads were born. Although identical genetically, from the very earliest age they showed behavioral differences. The quad that seemed to lag in behavioral development and educational accomplishments would ultimately become the most severely ill of the group. As children they were described as sweet and well mannered, although their teachers noted that they did not display the investigative curiosity typical of young children. They seldom separated and seemed to lack distinctive individual personalities. An absence of fun and humor was noted in the home environment. Each became ill in her early twenties; the clinical description revealed withdrawal, hallucinatory experiences, delusional features, and other elements that were idiosyncratic to each quad. Thus, although the quads are concordant for the diagnosis of schizophrenia, it is important to note that they are not identical in the clinical manifestations of the disorder. The clinical picture since the initial diagnosis has changed very little. All four had psychotic periods during the 25 years between research evaluations, although they vary in the severity of recurrent episodes. One of the more severely ill quads remained for 10 years in a mental hospital.

The quads vary in their response to antipsychotic medication; when drugs are removed, two of the quads show obvious exacerbation of symptoms while one of them shows little change.

Technical developments over the last 25 years have allowed for a more specialized neurological assessment than was possible during their initial evaluation. For example, PET scan studies revealed relatively low glucose utilization in frontal cortical areas in comparison to normals. In contrast, the quads had higher posterior cerebral glucose use than normal controls. EEG data revealed reduced alpha rhythm amplitude, a finding that is similar to that observed with other schizophrenic patients. However, CAT scan studies, which show ventricular enlargement in many other schizophrenic patients, did not reveal any abnormalities in the quads. Sluggish response of the autonomic nervous system to arousing stimuli was also noted. Biochemical studies also revealed some unusual features. Dopamine beta hydroxylase, the enzyme that converts dopamine to norepinephrine, was lower in all quads than in controls. This finding has been seen in at least one study of chronic schizophrenics. An elevated concentration of phenylethylamine (PEA) was found in the urine of all four. PEA has been thought to be a potential endogenous hallucinogen. Several other biochemical measures that assess aspects of dopamine and norepinephrine metabolism did not differ from controls. The long years of intensive scrutiny of this exotic group did not reveal a single biological fault with any sort of striking or vivid clarity. The differences among the quads do serve to underscore the fact that genetic information is not the sole basis of schizophrenia. Rather, many environmental variables are undoubtedly a part of the picture of etiology and the maintenance of this state. Alas, the gains won in the quest for a biological understanding of schizophrenia come slowly. Perhaps tomorrow's new findings may offer a perspective on the Genain quads that is missing in today's efforts.

Adoption Studies

Criticisms of twin techniques led to adoption studies, which have produced substantial support for the significance of genetic factors in many psychiatric disorders. Most of the relevant data have come from Scandinavian countries, where quite complete data are available for follow-up studies of adoptees. In studies reported by Kety and his collaborators (1975), the biological and adopting parents of all children given up for adoption early in life in a particular time period were identified, and a determination was made of those who had been hospitalized for psychiatric difficulties. Psychiatric disorder was found to a higher degree among the offspring of schizophrenic parents than in a control group of children of nonschizophrenic parents who gave their children up for adoption. Further, if we change the point of reference and look at comparisons of the biological and foster parents of schizophrenic adoptees, striking evidence is displayed. The biological parents of schizophrenic adoptees are far more likely to have been schizophrenic than are the adopting parents. It should be emphasized that the rearing of these patients was almost entirely by adopting parents, and therefore social influences from a schizophrenic parent were virtually nil. Although the group of parents giving children up for adoption early in life is in general more likely to involve psychiatric problems than the general population, the differences between control and patient comparisons remain striking. The findings provide conclusive evidence for genetic factors that predispose to schizophrenia. A reexamination of these data using current diagnostic criteria continues to show a concentration of schizophrenia and related disorders among biological relatives of adoptees who developed schizophrenia (Kety, 1983).

Although the evidence for genetic transmission of predisposition to schizophrenia is clear, there is still controversy about alternative genetic models. Neither single gene models nor multifactor models fit all the data (Faraone & Tsuang, 1985). This poses a problem as to what advice to give in genetic counseling. More research is needed to clarify the mechanism of genetic transmission in schizophrenia. A new emphasis on relating schizophrenia to known genetic markers may prove useful in disentangling the nexus of causation (Baron, 1986b).

Brain Structural Changes and Schizophrenia

Since in many patients the symptoms of schizophrenia are so marked and persistent, is there a measurable structural change in their brains? Postmortem investigations of the brains of schizophrenics during the past 100 years have yielded occasional exciting findings that have been rapidly challenged by better controlled studies. Studies in this field usually involved aged patients or those who had been hospitalized for long periods. With the advent of computerized tomography (CAT scans), it has become possible to study brain anatomy in living patients at all stages of their illness. Data obtained from such cases have begun to show a consistent finding of changes in the size of the lateral ventricles in schizophrenic patients. Brain changes do occur in schizophrenia!

Weinberger and colleagues (1979) performed CAT scans on psychiatric patients and compared them with scans from a large control group of healthy individuals. Ventricular size was measured, and the results revealed a significant difference: The ventricles of chronic schizophrenics were larger than those of normals. Ventricular enlargement was not related to length of illness or to duration of hospitalization. In a follow-up study, Weinberger (1980) indicated that the degree of ventricular enlargement predicts the patient's response to antipsychotic drugs. Patients with the more enlarged ventricles show poorer response to these drugs in terms of reducing the psychotic symptoms. The ventricular enlargement found in schizophrenics implies atrophy of adjacent neural tissue. These studies could provide clues to the loci of changes in neural tissue that may account for the symptoms of schizophrenia.

These initial CAT scan studies have generated many new observations of structural changes in schizophrenia. The finding of enlarged lateral ventricles in schizophrenic patients has been confirmed in many studies, although an important qualifier has emerged: Patients with this anatomical characteristic form a distinct subgroup of schizophrenics. Attempts have been made to further characterize the patients with enlarged ventricles, and some controversies are apparent. Some researchers have shown that this group is characterized by a high degree of cognitive impairment and social maladjustment (Kemali et al., 1985). Some researchers have also suggested that patients with enlarged ventricles have more first-degree relatives with schizophrenia than do patients with normal ventricular size. CAT scans on patients have also revealed several other anatomical deficits whose character remains controversial. Several studies have noted marked shrinkage of the vermian region of the cerebellum in long-time patients, which is not related to prolonged drug use (Heath et al., 1979; Snider, 1982). Thicker regions in the corpus callosum of chronic schizophrenics whose disorder started early in life have also been noted both in anatomical preparations and some CAT scans (Bigelow et al., 1983).

The successes of CAT scan studies have renewed postmortem studies of schizophrenic brains. A detailed neuropathological study by Brown et al. (1986) included an elaborate set of controls for age and sex and excluded patients whose brain showed senile changes. Comparisons were made with patients who had been diagnosed as having affective disorders. Measurements of schizophrenic brains revealed enlarged lateral ventricles and parahippocampal cortical regions that were thinned. Thus enlarged ventricles seen in CAT scan studies might be the result of degenerative changes in the temporal lobe. Changes in the hippocampus of chronic schizophrenics were noted in studies by Kovelman and Scheibel (1984). These investigators compared the brains of chronic schizophrenics and age-matched medical patients without brain pathology. The region that was examined and a sample of the typical cellular differences is shown in Figure 15-17. They noted that the pyramidal cells of chronic schizophrenics were disoriented, a type of cellular disarray. Presumably the lack of normal cellular polarity is related to abnormal synaptic linkages including both inputs and outputs of these cells. The researchers assumed that these structural changes arise early in life and may reflect genetic or developmental problems.

A developmental anatomical focus is the main concern of several theoretical ideas that link brain anatomical plasticity to schizophrenia. One researcher has proposed that a fault in a programmed decrease in synapses during adolescence gives rise to a major rearrangement of brain structures that results in schizophrenia (Feinberg, 1982). Another researcher has suggested that genetic factors might predispose schizophrenic brains to show unusual plastic changes in response to the routine stresses of life (Haracz, 1984). This suggestion is derived from numerous observations showing that brain structures can be modified by experience (see Chapter 17).

Preliminary observations using PET scan techniques have revealed an unusual metabolic feature of schizophrenic brains: Schizophrenic patients show relatively less metabolic activity in frontal lobes as compared with their posterior lobes than do normal subjects (Buchsbaum et al., 1984). This observation, sometimes referred to as the hypofrontality hypothesis, has generated some controversy. Changes in frontal lobe structure and function are supported by EEG studies and recent MRI

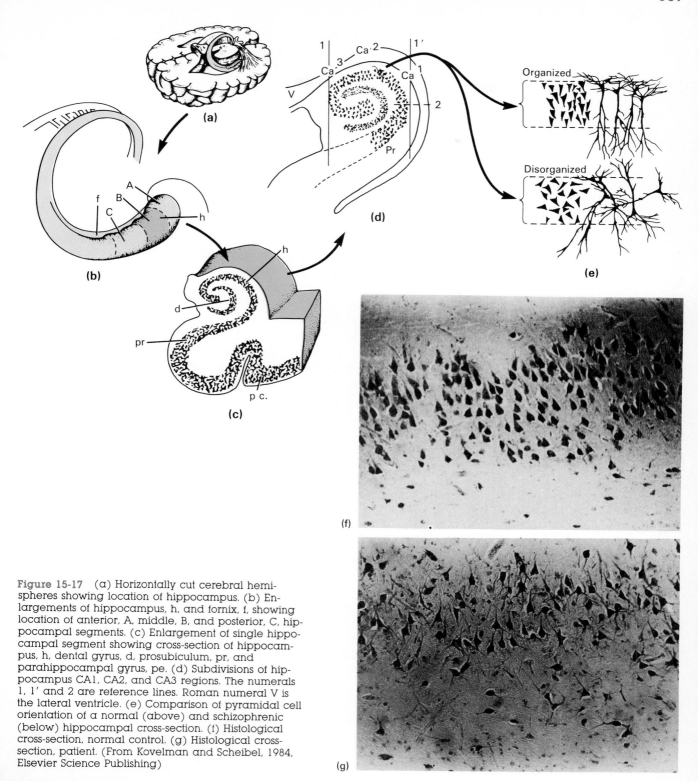

Figure 15-17 (a) Horizontally cut cerebral hemispheres showing location of hippocampus. (b) Enlargements of hippocampus, h, and fornix, f, showing location of anterior, A, middle, B, and posterior, C, hippocampal segments. (c) Enlargement of single hippocampal segment showing cross-section of hippocampus, h, dental gyrus, d, prosubiculum, pr, and parahippocampal gyrus, pe. (d) Subdivisions of hippocampus CA1, CA2, and CA3 regions. The numerals 1, 1′ and 2 are reference lines. Roman numeral V is the lateral ventricle. (e) Comparison of pyramidal cell orientation of a normal (above) and schizophrenic (below) hippocampal cross-section. (f) Histological cross-section, normal control. (g) Histological cross-section, patient. (From Kovelman and Scheibel, 1984, Elsevier Science Publishing)

observations of schizophrenic patients (Andreasen et al., 1986; Morihisa & McAnulty, 1985).

Clearly brain pathology in schizophrenia is being studied with renewed vigor. Many of the pathological changes that have been described are found in regions of the limbic system that have been involved in neural mechanisms of emotion. Some of these anatomical observations also seem to be generating a more useful classification system for schizophrenia since it is apparent that frank structural pathology is not a characteristic of all schizophrenic patients. Although methodological problems occur in this work and the reliability of some observations may prove weak, it is clear that these studies are opening an era of research that is quickening in its sense of success. There is light at the end of this tunnel!

Neurochemical Perspectives on Schizophrenia

Throughout history explanations of mental disorder have emphasized biological origins. Bodily factors assumed to be related to schizophrenia have included injury, infection, diet, and brain disease. As knowledge about the neurochemistry of the brain has grown, hypotheses about the basis of schizophrenia have become more precise. Several major views backed by large amounts of experimental data and clinical observation characterize contemporary orientations to the biological origins of schizophrenia. One view holds that schizophrenia arises from faulty metabolic processes in the brain that lead to excesses or insufficiencies of neurochemicals that are ordinarily found in the brain. In most cases these substances are neurotransmitters or neuromodulators. An example is provided by the most influential view in current work in schizophrenia, which focuses on the role of dopamine (described later). The functional effects of this type of change would be to produce under- or overactivity of some brain circuits. A second general perspective proposes that schizophrenia develops from faulty metabolic processes in the brain that produce abnormal substances that generate psychotic behavior. Such hypothetical substances, called **psychotogens** or **schizotoxins,** might be similar in some of their properties to hallucinogenic agents. The ''transmethylation'' hypothesis (also described later) is an example of this orientation.

Although exciting ideas and data are apparent in the research, several problems continue to frustrate major progress. First, it is very hard to separate biological events that are primary causes of psychiatric disorder from those that are secondary effects. Secondary effects are those that arise from the profound impairments of social behavior and may range from dietary limitations to prolonged stress. Treatment variables, especially long-term use of antipsychotic substances, also can mask or distort the search for primary causes, since they frequently produce marked changes in brain and body physiology and biochemistry. A second major problem in schizophrenia research is the definition of the term *schizophrenia.* Is it a single disorder or many disorders with very different origins and outcomes? Psychiatrists have wrestled with this problem for a long time, and many have suggested that schizophrenia is not a uniform label, since two major types of schizophrenia can be distinguished. One type, called process schizophrenia, shows an early history of social reclusiveness, and these patients become psychotic in later adolescence; very often they show a chronic lifelong course of intermittent or continuing psychotic episodes. No apparent situational factors appear to provoke the psychotic breakdown. The other type, called reactive schizophrenia, by contrast shows a more obvious connection to situational stress factors. These patients have a more acute psychotic period and have greater chances of making a satisfactory adjustment. More recently a somewhat similar distinction has been drawn between patients with "positive" symptoms, such as hallucinations and delusions, and those with "negative" symptoms, such as lack of emotional responding and movement retardation (Andreasen, 1985). These two patient groups differ in both psychological and biological attributes.

Dopamine Hypothesis

Many clinical and basic research findings have suggested that abnormal levels of dopamine form the basis of schizophrenia. Dopamine (as we saw in Chapter 6) is a synaptic transmitter in the brain, and its role in brain reward circuits was discussed earlier in this chapter. Early findings indicating the role of dopamine in schizophrenia came from several sources, including amphetamine psychosis, effects of tranquilizing agents, and Parkinson's disease.

Part of the dopamine story starts with the search for experimental models of schizophrenia. Basic scientific advances in the understanding of human disease frequently depend on the development of a controllable model of a disorder, usually an animal replica that can be turned on and off by experimenters. Some scientists involved in psychiatric research have suggested the effects of certain hallucinogenic agents as models of schizophrenia. There is no question that many drugs, such as LSD and mescaline, produce profound perceptual, cognitive, and emotional changes. And many aspects of psychoses are reproduced by these agents. However, several features of the behavioral effects of these drugs are quite dissimilar from those of schizophrenia. Most drug-induced psychoses are characterized by confusion, disorientation, and frank delirium; these are not typical symptoms of schizophrenia. Hallucinations produced by these drugs are usually visual, in contrast to the predominantly auditory hallucinations of schizophrenia. Schizophrenic patients given LSD report that the experience produced by the drug is very different from the experiences of their disorder, and psychiatrists can readily distinguish taped conversations of schizophrenics from those of subjects given hallucinogenic agents. One drug state, however, has come close to replicating the schizophrenic state— amphetamine psychosis.

Amphetamine abuse causes an unusual psychosis. Some individuals use amphetamine on an everyday basis as a stimulant. But if the same level of euphoria is to be maintained, the self-administered dose must be progressively increased and may reach as much as 3000 milligrams per day (mg/day). Contrast this level with the usual 5 mg taken to control appetite or prolong wakefulness. Many of these individuals develop paranoid symptoms, often involving delusions of persecution with auditory hallucinations. Suspiciousness and bizarre postures also are included in the portrait of this state. The similarity of amphetamine psychosis to schizophrenia is also suggested by the finding that amphetamine exacerbates symptoms in schizophrenia. The neurochemical effects of amphetamine are to promote release of catecholamines, particularly dopamine, and to prolong the action of the released transmitter by blocking re-uptake. Rapid relief of the amphetamine psychosis is provided by an injection of chlorpromazine—a substance that brings us to the second part of the story leading to the dopamine hypothesis.

Although excessive use of amphetamine can produce a state that mimics paranoid schizophrenia, current views emphasize that this effect is probably more related to amphetamine's effects on norepinephrine than dopamine (Carlton & Manowitz, 1984). Several other substances that increase dopamine activity may not produce symptoms that mimic schizophrenia.

In the early 1950s, the population of psychiatric hospitals in the United States was about half a million. This hospital population has dramatically decreased in size in the years since then. Several factors contributed to this reduction, the most significant being the introduction of a remarkable drug in the treatment of schizophrenia. In the search for a substance to produce muscle relaxation for surgery, French surgeon Henri Laborit discovered a compound that also reduced worry and preoperative tension. An insightful investigator, Laborit then collaborated with psychiatrists in using this substance on psychiatric patients; they found remarkable antipsychotic effects. This drug, **chlorpromazine,** was then introduced on a large scale in the psychiatric hospitals around the world and produced a profound impact on psychiatry. By now a massive number of well-controlled studies point to the fact that chlorpromazine and many other substances related to it (called phenothiazines) have a specific antipsychotic effect. Neurochemical studies show that this substance acts in the brain by blocking postsynaptic receptor sites for dopamine (Figure 15-18), specifically, the D_2 type of dopamine receptors. As noted in Chapter 6, there are several major dopamine-containing pathways. It is believed that a major action of antipsychotic drugs (also called neuroleptics) is on dopamine terminals in the limbic system. The origin of these cells is in the brain stem, near the substantia nigra. The clinical effectiveness of antipsychotic agents (also called tranquilizers) is directly related to the magnitude of postsynaptic receptor blockage of dopamine sites. This result suggests that schizophrenia may be produced either by abnormal levels of available and released dopamine or by excessive postsynaptic sensitivity to released dopamine, which might involve an excessively large population of postsynaptic dopamine receptor sites.

Another trail leading to the dopamine hypothesis of schizophrenia involves Parkinson's disease (discussed in Chapter 10). As we have noted, this disorder is caused by degeneration of nerve cells located in the brain stem (in a region called the substantia nigra). These cells contain dopamine, and some relief is produced by the administration of the substance L-dopa, which is a precursor for the synthesis of dopamine. L-dopa increases the amount of released dopamine. Two connections to schizophrenia and the dopamine hypothesis are apparent in the study of parkinsonian patients. First, some patients given L-dopa to relieve the symptoms of Parkinson's disease become psychotic. Second, some schizophrenic patients receiving chlorpromazine develop parkinsonian symptoms. In fact, movement disorders as a consequence of tranquilizer treatment may be permanent (see Box 15-2 on tardive dyskinesia). A link between schizophrenic brain atrophy and disturbed dopamine metabolism has been revealed in some studies. One group of researchers (van Kammen et al., 1983) reported that schizophrenic patients with enlarged ventricles show a marked reduction in spinal fluid levels of dopamine beta hydroxylase, which is an enzyme that is involved in the conversion of dopamine into norepinephrine.

Recently criticisms of a dopamine model of schizophrenia have been presented (Alpert & Friedhoff, 1980). Emphasized in these assessments is the fact that direct

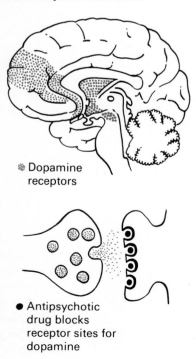

Figure 15-18 Distribution of dopamine receptors in the brain.

• Dopamine receptors

• Antipsychotic drug blocks receptor sites for dopamine

| BOX 15-2 | Tardive Dyskinesia and Supersensitivity Psychosis: Dilemmas in Drug Treatment of Schizophrenia |

Few would dispute the view that drugs like chlorpromazine have had a revolutionary impact in the treatment of schizophrenia. Many people who might otherwise have been in mental hospitals for the remainder of their lives can take care of themselves in nonhospital settings. Drugs of this class can justly be regarded as antipsychotic.

However, these drugs often have other effects that raise questions in psychiatry and pose novel research problems for the neurosciences. Soon after the introduction of these drugs, users were seen to develop various maladaptive motor symptoms (dyskinesia). Many of these symptoms were transient and were eliminated with a reduction in dose levels. But some drug-induced motor changes emerge only after prolonged drug treatment—after months and, in some cases, years—hence the term tardive, or late. Included in this set of motor effects are an array of involuntary movements, especially those involving the face, mouth, lips, and tongue. Elaborate uncontrollable movements of the tongue are particularly prominent, including incessant rolling movements and sucking or smacking movements of the lips. Twisting and sudden jerking movements of the arms or legs are seen occasionally in some patients. These effects of antipsychotic substances are seen in a large percentage of patients; estimates range as high as a third of all drug-treated patients. Female patients are usually more severely affected than males (Smith et al., 1979). The alarming aspect of this motor impairment is that it frequently continues as a permanent disability even when drug treatment is halted.

The underlying mechanism for tardive dyskinesia continues to be a puzzle. Some researchers claim that it arises from chronic blockade of dopamine receptors, which results in receptor site supersensitivity. However, critics of this view point out that tardive dykinesia takes a long time to develop and may be irreversible, a time course that is different from dopamine receptor supersensitivity. A GABA hypothesis of tardive dyskinesia has been offered by Fibiger and Lloyd (1984). They believe that tardive dyskinesia is the result of drug-induced destruction of GABA neurons in the corpus striatum. Neuroleptic-induced changes in enzymes related to GABA have been observed in experimental animals.

Another unusual effect of long-term drug treatment occurs in the nonmotor realm. Prolonged blockage of dopamine receptors with these drugs seems to increase the number of dopamine receptors and lead to receptor supersensitivity. In some patients discontinuation of the drugs or a lowering of dosage results in a sudden, marked increase in "positive" symptoms of schizophrenia, such as delusions or hallucinations. The effect is often reversible by increasing the dose level of dopamine-receptor blocking agents. However, there are some data suggesting that this "supersensitivity psychosis" might be enduring.

Both tardive dyskinesia and supersensitivity psychosis are pressing problems for future research, since they may limit the effectiveness of phenothiazines and related substances in the treatment of schizophrenia.

evidence of the level of functioning of dopamine receptors in patients is lacking or confusing. Although schizophrenic brains show an increase in dopamine receptors (Lee & Seeman, 1980), this result could develop from reduced dopamine turnover. Critics note that an increase in dopamine receptors is significant only in the presence of normal levels of dopamine. A further difficulty for this hypothesis is the lack of correspondence between the time at which drugs produce dopamine blockade (quite rapidly) and the behavior changes that signal the clinical effectiveness of the drug (usually on the order of weeks). Thus the relation of dopamine to schizophrenia may be more complex than that envisioned in the simple model of hyperactive dopamine synapses. Perhaps a type of dopamine impairment accounts for only some aspects of the schizophrenic syndrome (Carlton & Manowitz, 1984).

Schizotoxin Theories

Organic chemists have noticed a similarity in the chemical structure of manufactured hallucinogens and some substances found as normal ingredients in the brain. This structural similarity of natural and artificial substances raised the prospect that the brain might accidentally produce a psychotogen—a chemical substance that produces psychotic behavior. Metabolic faults in particular pathways might allow particular reactions to go on in the brain and convert an innocuous molecule into a behaviorally maladaptive substance capable of producing schizophrenic symptoms. A major hypothesis suggests that the addition of a methyl group (CH_3) to some naturally occurring brain compounds can convert some substances to known hallucinogenic agents. This hypothesis is known as the **transmethylation hypothesis;** it was initiated by the work of Osmond and Smythies in the 1950s and showed hallucinogenic properties for a substance called adrenochrome. This substance was viewed as a possible metabolic product of norepinephrine—now known to be a neurotransmitter in the brain as well as in the peripheral autonomic nervous system.

More recently many experiments have tested the idea that transmethylation could produce a compound that might act as a substance that produces schizophrenia—a schizotoxin. One way to test this idea is to administer substances (methyl donors) that provide a good supply of methyl groups. When administered to patients, some of these substances produce an exacerbation of symptoms, although the effect is not general to all such substances. This inconsistency, coupled with problems in understanding how the mechanism could account for the effects of tranquilizers, limits the current credibility of the proposal. A recent modification of the transmethylation hypothesis presented by Smythies (1984) has hypothesized that the fault in schizophrenia is an impairment in the transmethylation mechanism itself rather than the generation of an unusual schizophrenia-producing substance. To support this idea, Smythies presents some evidence that shows that the rate of transmethylation in some patients is slower than in normal subjects.

Can the body produce amphetaminelike substances by metabolizing norepinephrine? Recall from Chapter 6 that the amphetamine molecule resembles the molecules of catecholamine transmitters. Amphetamine psychosis resembles paranoid schizophrenia, and production of an amphetaminelike substance would be an extremely interesting finding. Recently several investigators have argued that phenylethylamine is produced in small quantities by the metabolism of norepinephrine. This substance has amphetaminelike properties. Current work seeks to assess levels of this metabolite in the bodies of schizophrenics. (Recall that it was elevated in the Genain quads, as mentioned in Box 15-1.)

Neurochemicals and Schizophrenia: A Commentary

The development of neurochemical tools since the mid-1970s has provided many opportunities to describe metabolic activities of the brain. Some of this work is limited by the fact that clues to brain events are primarily derived from analyzing metabolic products found in blood, urine, or cerebrospinal fluid. These fluids are remote from the sites at which significant changes may occur. Recent developments in PET scans using radiolabeled drugs may provide a more direct view of the neurochemical events of the schizophrenic brain. An example of the application of this technique to the portrayal of the distribution of dopamine receptors in the human brain is presented in Figure 15-19. Another issue in examining the neuro-

Figure 15-19   PET scans at the level of the caudate nucleus that indicate distribution of D_2 dopamine receptors in a normal subject (upper pair) and a schizophrenic patient (lower pair). Right upper and lower sections were obtained after the administration of haloperidol, a blocker of D_2 receptors. Light areas are regions of heavy concentration of dopamine. (Courtesy of D. F. Wong, Johns Hopkins Medical Center)

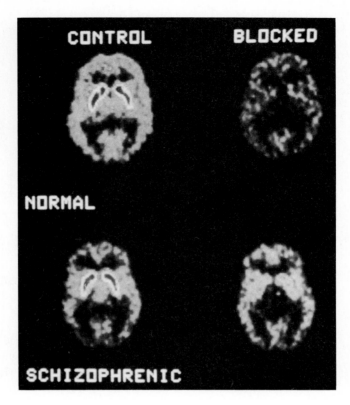

chemistry of schizophrenia is that our conceptions of the chemical machinery of the brain are rapidly changing, so a simplistic single transmitter view, such as the dopamine hypothesis, is difficult to reconcile with the elaborateness of interactive influences that modern research depicts.

An Integrative Psychobiological Model of Schizophrenia

Modern research strategies and techniques have produced a wealth of new data and hypotheses about various aspects of schizophrenia. At times it seems as though we have many pieces of a large puzzle whose overall appearance is yet to be evident. Some recent efforts at integration of the many psychological and biological findings in the field have resulted in important new views about the etiology of schizophrenia. One such model, presented by Mirsky and Duncan (1986), views schizophrenia as an outcome of the interaction of genetic, developmental, and stress factors. According to this model, at each life stage there are specific features that contribute to an enhanced vulnerability to schizophrenia. Genetic influences are seen expressed as ''brain abnormalities'' that provide the basic neurological substrate for schizophrenia. Intrauterine and birth complications—often evident in the life history reports of schizophrenic patients—may also contribute to schizophrenia-generating brain abnormalities. Mirsky and Duncan go on to suggest that through childhood and adolescence there are various neurological deficits that are manifested by behaviors such as impaired cognitive skills, attention deficits, irritability, and delayed gross motor development. A recent study has shown that similar neurological deficits are evident in the nonschizophrenic relatives of schizophrenic patients,

Figure 15-20 Model indicating how environmental stress and certain brain abnormalities can both contribute to producing a schizophrenic disorder. Disorders ranging from more mild to more severe are called, respectively, spectrum disorders, schizotypy, and schizophrenia. (Adapted from Mirsky and Duncan, 1986)

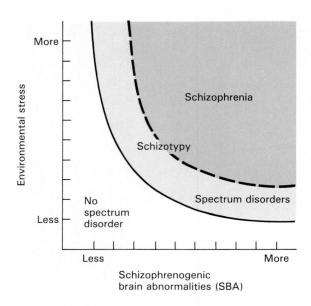

which lends further support for the existence of a genetic factor in the etiology of schizophrenia (Kinney, Woods, & Yurgelum-Todd, 1986).

According to the model presented by Mirsky and Duncan, the emergence of schizophrenia and related disorders depends on the interaction of a compromised biological substrate with environmental stressors. The proposed character of this interaction is portrayed in Figure 15-20. This shows that the magnitude of brain abnormalities in vulnerable individuals determines how much stress is needed to produce a schizophrenic disorder. Those people with many schizophrenic brain abnormalities may become symptomatic with relatively minor environmental stresses. Schizophrenia emerges, according to this model, when the combination of stress and brain abnormalities exceeds some threshold value. Sources of stress for the vulnerable individual include features such as some types of family interactions, the consequences of impaired attentional or cognitive skills, and the stress of "being different" during development, especially during adolescence. Models like this offer the opportunity to appreciate differences among patients. They also suggest that it may become possible to devise strategies for decreasing the likelihood of schizophrenia for the at-risk child. New biological aids, such as PET scans and genetic tools, might prove helpful in providing a more thorough identification and understanding of the at-risk child at a stage early in life when biological and environmental interventions might reduce the prospects of schizophrenia later in life.

Affective Disorders

Many of us go through periods of unhappiness that we commonly describe as **depression.** However, in some people a depressive state is more than a passing malaise and occurs over and over with a cyclical regularity. These people are usually over 40 years old, and women are two to three times as likely to suffer from depression as men. For such individuals depression is characterized by an unhappy mood, loss of interests, energy, and appetite, difficulty in concentration, and restless agitation. Pessimism seems to seep into every act. Periods of such **unipolar depressions** (that is, depressions that alternate with normal emotional states) can occur with no readily apparent stress. Without treatment the depression lasts for several months.

Some individuals have depressed periods that alternate with periods of excessively expansive moods that include sustained overactivity, talkativeness, increased energy, and strange grandiosity. This condition is called **bipolar illness** (also known as **manic-depressive psychosis**). Men and women are equally affected, and the age of onset is usually much younger than that in unipolar depression.

Genetic studies of unipolar and bipolar disorders reveal strong hereditary contributions. Concordance is much higher for monozygotic than for dizygotic twins. In monozygotic twins concordance rates are similar for twins reared apart and those reared together. Adoption studies show high rates of affective illness in the biological parents in comparison to foster parents.

Biological Theories of Depression

Work on the psychobiology of affective illness has been very much influenced since the 1960s by a theory offered by Joseph Schildkraut and Seymour Kety (1967) called the **monoamine hypothesis of depression.** According to this view, depressive illness is associated with a decrease in synaptic activity of connections that employ the synaptic transmitters norepinephrine and serotonin. This decrease is especially characteristic of hypothalamic and associated limbic system circuitry. Evidence offered for this hypothesis emphasizes the clinical effectiveness of two forms of treatment. Some antidepressant drugs inhibit monoamine oxidase and thus raise the level of available norepinephrine. Electroconvulsive treatment is especially valuable in many depressed patients, and these seizures have a strong impact on biogenic amines. In contrast, the drug reserpine, which depletes the norepinephrine and serotonin of the brain (by releasing intraneuronal monoamine oxidase, thereby breaking down these transmitters), results in a profound depression. This hypothesis continues to be summoned as a biological explanation of affective illness, although the clinical effectiveness of many drugs is not easily related to the monoamine system. An alternative hypothesis is that antidepressant drugs work by blocking neural receptors for histamine (Kanof & Greengard, 1978).

The treatment of manic episodes has advanced greatly in recent years with the use of lithium, a simple metallic ion. In the nervous system, lithium has an action similar to sodium: It can replace sodium in determining the resting and action potentials of nerves. It has diverse effects on various transmitters including decreased responses to norepinephrine. It is particularly potent in preventing manic excitement periods and some infrahuman studies show that lithium reduces aggressive behavior in rats and cats.

Simple increases or decreases in transmitter release may not account for the breadth of changes that encompass depression. Mood, sleep, eating and activity are but part of the changes. A simple monoamine hypothesis no longer seems tenable; in fact, some researchers have even argued the exact reverse state—increased catecholaminergic activity—as a factor in depression.

A very interesting broader view of changes in transmitters like norepinephrine

BOX 15-3 | Getting "Blue" in the Winter: Seasonal Affective Disorders

Seasonal rhythms characterize the behavior and physiology of many animals, including humans. Unfortunately for some people winter seems to inevitably bring a low period, which may become a profound depression. For many of these people, the winter depression alternates with summer mania. In wintertime affected people feel depressed, they slow down, generally sleep a great deal, and overeat. Come summer they are elated, energetic, active, and become thinner. This syndrome appears predominantly in women and generally starts to appear in early adulthood. In nonhuman animals it is clear that many such rhythms are controlled by the length of the day. For example, seasonal rhythms, such as migration or hibernation, may be triggered by changes in the duration of daylight. Some researchers have suggested that seasonal affective disorders in humans may show a similar dependence. To examine that prospect, several researchers have explored whether exposure to light can act as an antidepressant.

Studies by several researchers have examined the clinical effects of exposing patients to artificial light that simulates sunlight. In one investigation by Rosenthal et al. (1985), a group of patients was secured by a newspaper ad that described the typical features of seasonal affective disorder. The patients selected for the study had at least two winter season episodes of depression. A quantitative evaluation of the level of depression was achieved by the use of the Hamilton Rating Scale, which is a self-administered scale consisting of a number of items describing different features of depression. Experimental treatment consisted of two one-week exposures to additional light, separated by a one-week period of no additional light. Patients were exposed to bright light during two daily periods; one ran from 5:00 A.M. to 8:00 A.M., and the second lasted from 5:30 P.M. to 8:30 P.M. This distribution extended normal daylight and thus tended to simulate a long daylight period characteristic of summer. The effects of such light exposure as measured by the Hamilton Rating Scale showed that bright

lights have a significant antidepressant effect that is reversed upon withdrawal of the lights. No significant effects were noted following exposure to dim lights. The improvement in mood is seen after a few days and generally persists through the week of treatment. Removal of light readily produces relapse. Is the timing of the light exposure during a typical day an important factor? Studies by Wehr et al. (1986) compared the differences in two light exposure regimens in persons with seasonal affective disorder. One group received light in a distribution that simulated summer, and another group received the same amount of light distributed, however, in a winter manner. The results indicated that both light regimens were equally effective as antidepressants.

One important biological effect of light is the suppression of melatonin, a hormone found in the pineal gland that affects gonadotropins and may be of importance in controlling sleep. Exposure to darkness stimulates melatonin synthesis, whereas light suppresses it. People with seasonal affective disorder have been shown to have a high threshold for melatonin suppression. However, recent observations by Wehr and collaborators (1986) that involved exposure of patients with seasonal affective disorders to different light schedules (just cited) failed to demonstrate that phototherapy acts by suppressing melatonin secretion. They also noted that oral administration of melatonin did not influence this treatment. Other neurochemical mediators may be involved with this antidepressant effect of light. Serotonin may be of relevance since it has a marked seasonal rhythm in humans, with lower values in winter and spring than in summer or fall (Ergise et al., 1986). It is of particular interest that attention to this syndrome arose primarily because of animal research dealing with photoperiodic behavior and circadian control systems. This is yet another example of the significance of such basic research in ameliorating the distresses and diseases of humans.

---

has been presented by Siever and Davis (1985), who refer to their notion as a dysregulation hypothesis of depression. The essence of their view is that depression is not simply related to depletion of a transmitter but rather reflects a failure in a regulatory mechanism that governs transmitter operations. This dysregulation results in erratic transmitter activities so that they are no longer governed by external stimuli, time of day, or their own actions. There are several different levels in the pathway of noradrenergic system activity where such governance failure might emerge. For example, there is evidence that noradrenergic activity is governed by feedback-inhibitory activities that stabilize noradrenergic responses. Long-term stabilization of adrenergic synapses also occurs with maintained stress, which can enhance the basal activity of noradrenergic synapses. Dysregulation can emerge from these steps or others. In any case the consequence of impairment of the regulatory devices, according to Siever and Davis, is a transmitter system that is inappropriately responsive to external or internal needs. It becomes maladapted to environmental needs. This type of formulation can lead investigators to search for a quite different set of changes than those customarily sought in chemical assessments of patients. The clinical effects of some newer antidepressants seem to fit this formulation in that their mechanism of action appears more elaborate than simply affecting a single parameter of transmitter function or a single transmitter (Tyrer & Marsden, 1985).

Biological Approaches

Gender and Depression

Studies all over the world show that more women suffer from major depression than men. The most recent National Institutes of Health (NIH) epidemiological survey documents this for five areas in the United States—New Haven, Baltimore, St. Louis, Los Angeles, and Piedmont, North Carolina. All sites revealed a twofold difference for major depression. For example, New Haven had a rate of 2.2/100 for males and 4.8 for females. Similar recent findings have been noted in Sweden. What accounts for these sex differences? This question could be especially important in achieving an understanding of the causes of depression. Several hypotheses have been advanced. Some researchers argue that the sex differential arises from differences between males and females in help-seeking patterns, notably, greater female use of health facilities. However, the NIH survey cited above was a door-to-door survey, not an assessment of appearance at health centers; significant sex differences were still apparent.

Several psychosocial explanations have been advanced. One dominant theme emphasizes the view that depression in women arises from social discrimination that prevents them from achieving mastery by self-assertion. According to this view, inequities lead to dependency, low self-esteem, and depression. Another psychosocial focus leans on the learned helplessness model. According to this view, stereotypic images of men and women produce in women a cognitive set of classic femininity values, reinforced by societal expectations, in which helplessness is one dimension. But studies of depressed males and females do not seem to support this view.

A genetic interpretation of this gender difference in depression has also been advanced. According to this idea, depression is an X-linked inherited disorder. But relatives of male and female depressives show no differences in depression rates (which would be expected with X-linking). Thus, although there is a strong genetic determinant in depression, there does not seem to be a genetic basis for sex differences in depression.

Finally, some researchers have emphasized gender differences in endocrine physiology. Interest in this aspect is engendered by observation that clinical depressions often occur with events related to the female reproductive cycle, for example, before menstruation, while using contraceptive pills, following childbirth, and during menopause. Although several hormones have been linked to depression, there is little relation between circulating levels of hormones related to female reproductive physiology and measures of depression.

Another focus on the mystery of gender differences in depression is provided by recent epidemiological studies of the mental health of Amish communities (Egeland & Hostetter, 1983). An exhaustive survey of this religious community, which prohibits the use of alcohol and shuns modernity, reveals no sex differences in major depression. This suggests the possibility that in the general population heavy use of alcohol masks depression in many males and thus causes it to appear that fewer males than females suffer from depression. Examination of epidemiological data dealing with alcoholism shows another major gender difference, only this time males are mainly affected.

Biological Markers of Depression

For many years researchers have sought easily measurable biochemical, physiological, or anatomical indicators of various mental disorders. These indicators have been referred to as biological markers, and they may reflect factors relevant to the causes of a disorder or its current state. The development of such laboratory tests would be especially important because some behavioral assessments may not provide clues to genetic mechanisms or differential response to various drugs. Thus two patients might present a similar portrait of depression but respond differently to antidepressant drugs. The field of depression research has been especially productive in generating potential biological markers, in particular several that are linked to hormonal responses to stress that involve hypothalamic-pituitary systems.

Early work in this area focused on the hypothalamic-pituitary-adrenal system because observations showed elevated cortisol levels in hospitalized depressed patients. This suggested that ACTH was released in excessive amounts by the anterior pituitary. A method developed for the analysis of pituitary-adrenal function in Cushing's syndrome—an endocrine abnormality that includes high levels of circulating corticosteroids—included the administration of a substance called dexamethasone. This drug is a potent synthetic corticoid that ordinarily suppresses a typical early morning rise in ACTH. It is generally given late at night. Basically dexamethasone seems to "fool" the hypothalamus into believing that there is a high level of circulating cortisol. In normal individuals dexamethasone suppression is readily evident, but in many depressed individuals it fails to suppress circulating levels of cortisol. As depression is relieved, dexamethasone suppresses cortisol normally. It is claimed that the normalization occurs no matter what the cause of relief—lapse of time, psychotherapy, pharmacotherapy, or electroconvulsive shock therapy. One possibility that has been raised about the mediating mechanism is that in depressed people the cells of the hypothalamus are subject to abnormal excitatory drive from limbic system regions resulting in sustained release of ACTH. Many questions have been raised about the generality of this test of depression, its specificity, and its sensitivity to various clinical strategies that affect depression. It may be especially valuable in some subtypes of depression but not others (Schatzberg et al., 1983).

Other hormonal systems that have been explored in depression marker research include growth hormone and thyroid hormones. In some studies depressed patients have been shown to secrete twice as much growth hormone as controls over a 24-hour period (Kallin & Dawson, 1986). Some of this difference might be attributed to altered sleep patterns characteristic of depressed patients (Chapter 14). Both hypo- and hyperthyroid conditions have been associated with affective changes. Administration of thyroid hormone supplementation can enhance the responsiveness of patients to antidepressant drugs. However, additional studies are needed to determine whether any components of the hypothalamic-pituitary-thyroid axis are sensitive markers of depression.

Biology of Anxiety

At one time or another, all of us have had periods in which we feel apprehensive and fearful. For some this state takes on an intensity that is overwhelming and includes irrational fears, a sense of terror, unusual bodily feeling, such as dizziness, difficulty in breathing, trembling, shaking, and a feeling of loss of control. For some, anxiety comes in sudden attacks of panic that are unpredictable and last for minutes or hours. Anxiety can be lethal! A follow-up of patients with panic disorder reveals an increased mortality in men with this problem due to cardiovascular disease and suicide (Coryell et al., 1986). The American Psychiatric Association distinguishes two major groupings of anxiety disorders: phobic disorders and anxiety states. **Phobic disorders** are intense, irrational fears that become centered on a specific object, activity, or situation that the person feels he or she must avoid. **Anxiety states** include recurrent panic states, generalized anxiety disorders that are persistent in character, and posttraumatic stress disorders. There are several main areas in current anxiety studies that we will explore in this section.

Induction of Panic

In the study of anxiety and related disorders, a curious finding of a number of years ago has been reexamined and applied to current biological investigations of anxiety. Psychiatrists had observed that some patients experience intense anxiety attacks during or after vigorous physical exercise. It was thought that this effect might be derived from a buildup of blood lactate. This prospect stimulated two researchers—Pitts and McClure (1968)—to administer sodium lactate to anxiety patients. The infusions produced immediate panic attacks in patients that were like their naturally occurring episodes. This chemical treatment does not produce panic attacks in normals, and there is also a group of anxiety patients who are not vulnerable to the induced panic attacks. The study has recently been contested by Margraf et al. (1986) on the grounds that it fails to exclude confounding psychological factors. Their evidence is primarily the finding that patients also show a certain level of panic attack when infused with placebo. The reality of the lactate-induction effect is further supported by PET scan observations to be presented in the next section.

Several different notions have been presented to account for this phenomenon. Liebowitz and collaborators (1986) have reported on the possibilities of several mechanisms that include adrenergic systems. They note that the effect is not produced by calcium levels, changes in blood pH, or increases in plasma levels of epinephrine. The notion that lactate-induced panic is produced by an action on beta-adrenergic synapses is not supported by their observation that the block of these synapses with propranolol did not prevent lactate-induced panic. These researchers believe that the lactate-induced panic may involve central noradrenergic mechanisms of the locus coeruleus and its outputs. This suggestion is partially supported by the observation that another locus coeruleus stimulant—inspiration of 5% carbon dioxide—produces panic in clinically vulnerable individuals.

Anatomy of Anxiety

Very intriguing PET scan observations of patients with panic disorders have provided a portrait of the anatomy of anxiety. These studies by Reiman and collaborators (1986) revealed abnormalities in the resting, nonpanic state. This study compared patients whose panic disorder could be induced by injection of sodium lactate, patients who were not vulnerable to lactate-induced panic, and a group of normal controls. Those who were vulnerable to lactate-induced panic showed markedly abnormal parahippocampal blood flow. This abnormality consisted of left-right differences in blood flow, which appeared to reflect an abnormal increase in right parahippocampal blood flow. This region contains the major input and output pathways of the hippocampus. In addition to the regional effect, lactate-vulnerable panic patients also had abnormally high brain oxygen metabolism. Reiman and collaborators relate these findings to a theory of Gray (1982) that attaches importance to septohippocampal connections in the neurobiology of anxiety. They also cite observations by Gloor and colleagues (1982) that electrical stimulation of the region in awake patients commonly elicits sensations of strong fear and apprehension. Among other prospects the work of Reiman and collaborators raises the possibility that a biological indicant—PET scan data—can distinguish two major anxiety groups—those vulnerable to lactate-induced panic and those panic patients who are not vulnerable to this form of induced attack. The difference might reflect a fundamental difference in underlying biological mechanisms.

Anti-Anxiety Drugs: Clues to the Mechanism of Anxiety

Throughout history humans have imbibed all sorts of substances in the hopes of controlling anxiety. At various times the list included alcohol, bromides, scopolamine, opiates, and barbiturates. But it was not until 1960 that a drug was introduced that would forever change the treatment of anxiety. This drug was derived from a substance that had been developed as an antibacterial preparation. Some molecular changes in that substance produced the drug meprobamate, whose trade name, Miltown, became famous as a tranquilizing agent. Competition among drug companies led to the elaborate development of a class of substances called benzodiazepines, which have become the most common drugs used in the treatment of anxiety. Indeed, one type of benzodiazepine—diazepam (trade name Valium)—has been one of the most prescribed drugs in history. These drugs are commonly described as anxiolytic, although at higher doses they also have anticonvulsant and sleep-inducing properties.

Early behavioral and electrophysiological data established that benzodiazepines were associated in some way with the action of GABA synapses. (Recall that GABA is the most common inhibitory transmitter in the brain—Chapter 6.) In the late 1970s, many investigators showed that benzodiazepines exert their therapeutic

Figure 15-21 A PET scan that shows the distribution of benzodiazepine receptors in the human brain (light areas). The receptor is widely distributed, especially in cerebral cortical areas. (Dr. Goran Sedvall et al, 1986, Koralinsha Institute, Stockholm. Reprinted with permission from *Archives of General Psychiatry,* Vol. 43, No. 10, October 1986, p. 999.)

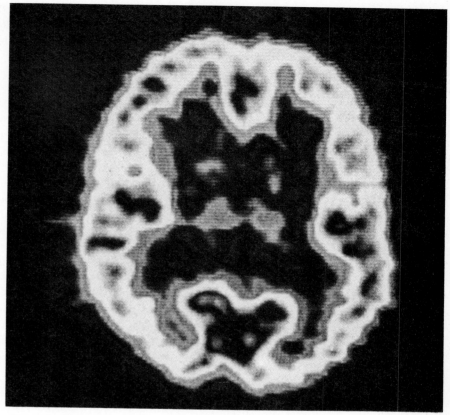

effects by interacting with special receptors in the brain. It was rapidly established that the benzodiazepine receptor interacts with receptors for GABA, which results in an enhancement of the action at inhibitory synapses in the brain that use GABA. Thus GABA-mediated postsynaptic inhibition is facilitated by benzodiazepines. The distribution of these receptors in the brain is shown in Figure 15-21. The benzodiazepine receptors are widely distributed throughout the brain and are especially dense in concentration in the cerebral cortex and some subcortical areas, such as the hippocampus and amygdala. The ultimate function of the benzodiazepine-GABA receptor complex is to regulate the permeability of neural membranes to chloride ions. When GABA activates its receptor upon release from a presynaptic terminal, chloride ions are allowed to move from the extracellular phase to the inside of the nerve cell. Benzodiazepine alone does little to chloride conductance. But in the presence of GABA, benzodiazepines markedly enhance GABA-provoked increases in chloride permeability. Recent research has also pointed to the existence of specific anxiety peptides that occur naturally in the brain and act in association with the benzodiazepine receptor (Marx, 1985). Early work indicated that a brain extract could decrease the binding of diazepam to its receptor; this implies that the brain extract works this way because it contains a material that also binds to this receptor. A compound derived from some of this work—beta-carboline—behaves like the natural anxiety-producing compound and can induce anxiety in experimental animals. When administered to human volunteers, a carboline compound produced motor tension, autonomic hyperactivity, and bodily effects that were de-scribed as severe anxiety (Dorrow et al., 1983). By now there is a vast array of information that implicates the GABA-benzodiazepine receptor complex as a key ingredient in the mechanism of anxiety.

Surgical Treatment in Psychiatry

Down through the ages, the mentally disabled have been treated by methods limited only by the human imagination. Some of the methods have been gruesome and were inspired by views that the mentally disordered were controlled by demonic forces. While twentieth-century psychiatry has been purged of such moralistic views, until recently treatment was on a trial-and-error basis, and inspiration for new efforts came from diverse sources. In the 1930s experiments on frontal lobe lesions in chimpanzees inspired Egas Moniz to attempt similar operations in patients. He was intrigued by the report of a calming influence in nonhuman primates, and at the time he tried frontal surgery little else was available. His observations led to the begin-ning of **psychosurgery,** defined as the use of surgically produced brain lesions to modify severe psychiatric disorders. Throughout its use there has been vigorous debate, which continues to the present (Valenstein, 1980; 1986).

During the 1940s frontal lobe surgery was forcefully advocated by several neu-rosurgeons and psychiatrists. A recent presidential commission on psychosurgery estimates that during this period 10,000–50,000 patients underwent this surgery. During the most intense period of enthusiasm, patients of all diagnostic types were operated on, and varieties of surgery were employed.

Interest in psychosurgery arose from the saddening sight of so many people in mental hospitals living empty, disturbed lives without hope of change. No drug to that point aided chronic schizophrenics, and the population of permanently hospital-ized continued to mount. Since psychiatric hospitals were becoming very crowded, many unusual remedies were tried. Today frontal surgery is limited to controlling emotional arousal accompanying intense pain. Its use in psychiatry has practically ended, although the commission on psychosurgery has urged further consideration of the role of surgery in psychiatry. (In an earlier section in this chapter we noted the related use of temporal lobe surgery for relief from violent behavior attributed to seizure activity.)

Assessments of the value of frontal lobe surgery in psychiatric treatment are steeped in controversy. Some researchers showed clinical improvements, and even recently William Sweet (1973) argued that more localized brain lesions might pro-vide significant aid in particular psychiatric disorders. Strong support for this view has been offered by Ballantine et al. (1987), who recently reported on the treatment of depression by stereotoxic cingulotomy—lesions that interrupt pathways in cingu-late cortex. Clinical evaluations revealed strikingly positive outcomes of this proce-dure in chronically depressed patients who were not aided by other treatments. However, the use of drugs has overshadowed psychosurgery, especially since surgi-cal results seem much less reversible than effects of drugs.

The development of techniques for accurate placement of depth electrodes in humans has led some surgeons to use subcortical lesions in psychiatric disorders. Some of these surgical targets were chosen on the basis of research results with nonhumans. For example, in Germany several surgeons have used hypothalamic lesions to "cure" sexual deviations (Roeder, Orthner, & Muller, 1972). But the ethical implications of such interventions are complex (Valenstein, 1980). This kind of work is partly inspired by lesion experiments in rats, but Beach (1979) has warned that this may reflect an inappropriate use of animal models.

Summary · Main Points

Emotions

1. The term *emotion* includes both private subjective feelings and expressions or displays of particular somatic and autonomic responses.

2. The James-Lange theory considered emotions as the perception of stimulus-induced bodily changes, whereas the Cannon-Bard theory emphasized brain integration of emotional experiences and responses. A cognitive theory of emotion argues that activity in a physiological system is not enough to provoke an emotion. Rather the key feature in emotion is the interpretation of visceral activities.

3. Facial expressions of particular emotions are similarly presented and recognized in many quite different human societies.

4. Biofeedback experiments involving visceral activity have shown learned modifications of heart rate and blood pressure that can be very specific.

5. The impact of emotions on human health can be seen in measures of illness following stress. Reports of illness tend to be higher in groups that sustain prolonged stress, although constitutional factors are also important.

6. The pathological toll of stress can be seen in experiments on ulcer formation in rats, especially when the animal cannot perform any adaptive response to the stressful stimulus.

7. Assessment of physiological effects of stress in real-life situations, in contrast to artificial laboratory situations, shows that stress produces elevations in several hormones, such as cortisol, growth hormone, and epinephrine. Successful completion of a stressful task reduces the level of hormone response on subsequent exposure to the same situation.

8. Brain regions involved in emotion include an array of interconnected sites within the limbic system.

9. Electrical stimulation of many sites within the limbic system is rewarding, as seen in self-stimulation experiments. Electrical stimulation of most sites in the cerebral cortex does not result in positive reinforcement. Dopamine plays an important role in many brain sites involved in reward.

10. Aggression has several hormonal relations, the most prominent being the association with the level of circulating androgens. In humans, however, the relation between the level of testosterone and criminal behavior is controversial. Argument also abounds about the role of temporal lobe epilepsy and the human "dyscontrol syndrome."

Mental Disorders

11. Biological approaches have enabled better distinctions to be made within large classes of mental disorders such as schizophrenia and anxiety.

12. There is strong evidence for a genetic factor in the etiology of schizophrenia. Consistent evidence comes from the study of the incidence of schizophrenia in families, twins, and foster-reared people.

13. Biological theories of schizophrenia include two general classes of ideas: (a) the view that schizophrenia comes about because of a failure at some level in the operation of neurotransmitters at synapses, and (b) the view that schizophrenia develops from a metabolic fault that results in the production of a toxic substance, a psychotogen with properties similar to known hallucinogenic agents.

14. The dopamine hypothesis attributes schizophrenia to excess release of or sensitivity to dopamine. Supporting evidence comes from studies on the effects of antipsychotic drugs, amphetamine psychosis, and Parkinson's disease.

15. Biological studies of affective disorders like unipolar depression reveal a strong genetic factor and also note the importance of levels of neurotransmitters.

Recommended Reading

Coles, M. G. H., Donchin, E., & Porges, S. W. (Eds.). (1986). *Psychophysiology: Systems, processes, and applications.* New York: Guilford.

Gentry, W. D. (Ed.). (1984). *Handbook of behavioral medicine.* New York: Guilford.

Moberg, G. P. (Ed.), (1985). *Animal stress.* Washington, D.C.: American Physiological Society

Pincus, J. H., & Tucker, G. J. (1985). *Behavioral neurology.* (3rd edition). New York: Oxford University Press.

Plutchik, R., & Kellerman, H. (Eds.). (1980). *Emotion: Theory, research, and experience: Vol. 1. Theories of emotion.* New York: Academic Press.

Snyder, S. H. (1980). *Biological aspects of mental disorder.* New York: Oxford University Press.

Valenstein, E. S. (1980). *The psychosurgery debate: Scientific, legal, and ethical perspectives.* San Francisco: W. H. Freeman.

PART FIVE

Learning, Memory, and Cognition

There is hardly a living creature that cannot change its behavior as a result of experience. The capacity to learn and remember makes it possible to deal with a complex and changing world and thus increases adaptive success. The language we speak, our skills in writing, driving, skiing, dressing these and many more human behaviors depend upon our learning and memory. Storing the lessons of experience implies that the properties of the nervous system can be enduringly changed. How this feat is accomplished is the major mystery of the biological sciences. By now investigators have developed many ideas and experimental strategies to try to find out how nervous systems accomplish the exploits of learning and memory. In this section we will consider many aspects of research in the biology of learning. Further, we will discuss the most elaborate products of brain function—the biology of language and cognitive states that are so distinctively human.

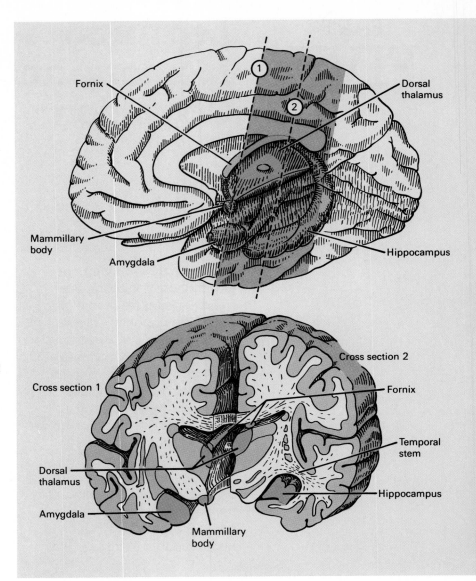

16 Learning and Memory: Biological Perspectives

ORIENTATION

Investigating the biology of learning and memory throws important light on almost all the topics that we have taken up so far because almost every aspect of behavior is affected by learning: how we perceive, the skilled motor acts we perform, our motivations, and the ways that we satisfy the goals. It has been said that all the distinctively human aspects of our behavior are learned: the language we speak, how we dress, the foods we eat, and how we eat them. It is true that as human beings we learn a great deal and are molded by what we learn, but nonhuman animals also depend upon learning. In fact investigators are becoming steadily more impressed by the amount and complexity of learning that even rather simple invertebrates can accomplish.

In order to make sense of learning and memory and of the research that is being devoted to them, we will use the four kinds of analysis that we defined in Chapter 1 and have used in subsequent chapters. First we will describe learning and memory, discussing the kinds and classifications that have proved useful. Second we will use a comparative and evolutionary approach, asking how abilities to learn and remember are distributed among animal species and how these abilities may have evolved. Third we will consider the development of abilities to learn and to remember over the life span. In the last part of this chapter we will take up the pathology of memory. Chapter 17 is devoted to the fourth kind of analysis, considering the biological mechanisms of learning and memory.

Forms of Learning and Memory

Almost all animals learn and remember, and learning takes many forms. We learn *how* to do things—to swim, to paint, to use chopsticks. We learn *what* things are—a dog, a chair, the Eiffel Tower—and who particular individuals are so that we can recognize a parent, a friend, or a neighbor by their visual appearance or by the sound of their voice. We learn the relations among different properties of objects—how a particular small oval greenish object (an olive) tastes, how a rose smells, how sand feels. We learn particular episodes—what happened last New Year's Eve, when we last saw a particular friend. We also learn not to respond to relatively constant events even though they still can be perceived; that is, we habituate to many visual, auditory, and olfactory stimuli around us.

The behavioral study of learning and memory has made important strides in recent years. This is reflected, for example, in the treatments of conditioning by Mackintosh (1984) and Rescorla (1988), who interpret conditioning as learning about relations and predictability among events rather than as formation of links between stimuli and responses. But this work is by no means complete. In fact, some investigators of the biology of learning and memory are concerned that, with the rapid rate of advances in neurosciences, progress in understanding the neurobiology of learning and memory may be limited mainly by the rate of development of appropriate behavioral analyses.

Associative Learning

Psychologists have categorized the main kinds of learning and memory as a step toward understanding these behaviors and their biological mechanisms. One kind is called **associative learning** because it involves learning relations among events—a stimulus and a response, a response and its consequence, or among two or more stimuli. For example, in **classical conditioning** (also called **Pavlovian conditioning**) an association is formed between an initially neutral stimulus and an event. At the end of the last century, Pavlov found that a dog would salivate when presented with an auditory or visual stimulus if the stimulus came to predict an event that already caused salivation. Thus if the experimenter rang a bell just before putting meat powder in the dog's mouth, repeating this sequence a few times would cause the ringing to elicit salivation.

In **instrumental conditioning** (or **operant conditioning**) an association is formed between behavior and its consequence(s). The first example of instrumental learning was Thorndike's report (1898) of cats learning to escape from a puzzle box (Figure 16-1). When placed in a small box with a latch inside, a cat would initially engage in a variety of behaviors and take quite a bit of time to free itself. But after several trial-and-error sequences, the cat learned to perform skillfully and economically the specific response (the conditioned response) that permitted escape (the reinforcement). A modern example of a situation for instrumental learning is an operant conditioning apparatus, often called a Skinner box.

Nonassociative Learning

Associative learning is contrasted with **nonassociative learning,** which involves experience with only a single stimulus or with two stimuli that do not have a necessary temporal relationship. Three kinds of nonassociative learning are **habituation, sensitization,** and **imprinting.** Most learning involves both associative and nonassociative components.

Figure 16-1 Puzzle box devised by Edward L. Thorndike in 1898 to study animal learning.

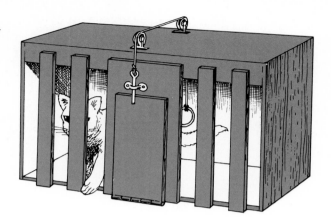

Habituation

Habituation refers to a decrement in responding to a stimulus as it is repeated (and when the decrement cannot be attributed to sensory adaptation or motor fatigue). Thus an animal responds less and less strongly to uniform gentle taps on its surface even though recording from sensory nerves shows that the taps are still eliciting afferent impulses and even though the muscles are not fatigued. An example of habituation in a human subject is shown in Figure 16-2. Behavioral studies of habituation show that it follows several rules, including the following:

1. The weaker the stimulus, the more rapidly the response declines in amplitude.
2. If the stimulus is no longer presented for a sufficiently long time, the response recovers spontaneously.
3. Habituation to one stimulus may cause at least partial habituation to a similar stimulus.

Habituation may also be accompanied by association. For example, the subject may learn that gentle taps have no consequence *in a particular situation*. That is, the habituated stimulus may also become associated with a specific environmental stimulus context. Associative learning may also be affected by habituation. If a stimulus has already been habituated, then it is harder to form a new association to it, within the same context. These are only a few of the ways in which associative and nonassociative learning may be bound together in natural and laboratory learning situations.

Dishabituation and Sensitization

When a response has become habituated, a strong stimulus (either of the same sort or even in another sensory modality) will often cause the response to succeeding presentations of the habituated stimulus to increase sharply in amplitude; it may become even larger than the original response before habituation (Figure 16-3). This increase in response amplitude to the baseline level is called **dishabituation,** the idea being that the habituation has been removed. Some investigators have

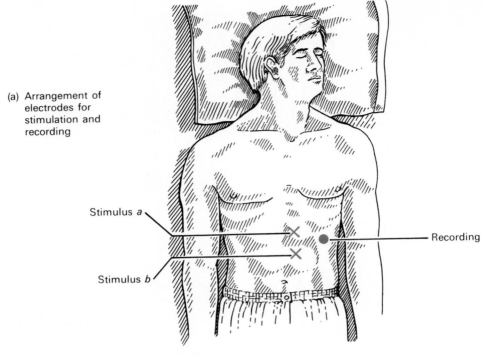

(a) Arrangement of electrodes for stimulation and recording

Stimulus *a*

Stimulus *b*

Recording

(b) Electrical responses of abdominal muscles

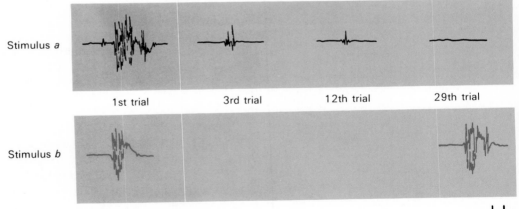

Stimulus *a*

1st trial   3rd trial   12th trial   29th trial

Stimulus *b*

20 msec

Figure 16-2 Habituation of the human abdominal reflex. While the subject reclines with eyes closed and wearing ear plugs, electrical stimulation of the skin elicits reflex responses of the abdominal muscles. When stimuli were applied at site *a* every 5–10 seconds, the amplitude of the muscular response diminished progressively, showing habituation. A single initial stimulus at site *b* elicited a large response. Then *b* was left unstimulated while site *a* received 29 successive stimuli and habituated. A single stimulus then applied again to *b* evoked a large response, so the habituation at *a* had not generalized to *b*. (Adapted from Hagbarth and Kugelberg, 1958)

Figure 16-3 Sensitization of the human abdominal reflex. (b) The reflex response of the abdominal muscles was first habituated to weak mechanical taps to the skin. A series of strong blows to the skin then sensitized the reflex. After a series of 3 sensitization stimuli, responses were elicited by the next 17 weak taps; after 10 sensitization stimuli, weak taps elicited responses for over 100 trials. (c) Sensitization by strong stimulation. After the habituation response in 1, a single electrical shock to the skin sensitized the response to the following tap, as shown in 2. (d) Sensitization by verbal stimuli. A weak electrical stimulus to the skin elicited no muscular response. The same weak stimulus became effective after the subject was told that the next shock would be painful. (Adapted from Hagbarth and Kugelberg, 1958)

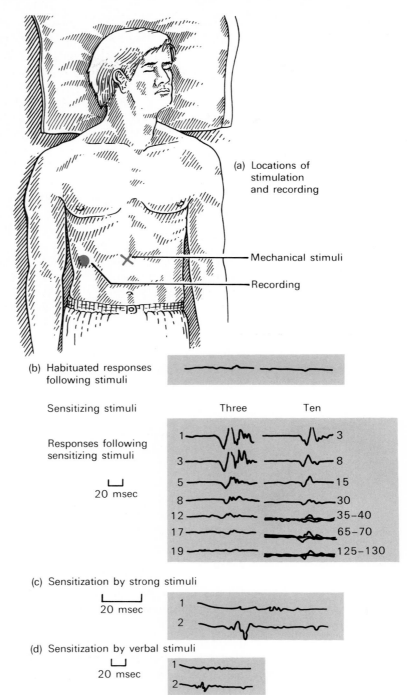

(a) Locations of stimulation and recording

Mechanical stimuli

Recording

(b) Habituated responses following stimuli

Sensitizing stimuli — Three — Ten

Responses following sensitizing stimuli

20 msec

(c) Sensitization by strong stimuli

20 msec

(d) Sensitization by verbal stimuli

20 msec

suggested that **sensitization** is a more accurate description of this phenomenon for several reasons. For one thing even a response that has not been habituated may increase in amplitude after a strong stimulus. For another thing a response that has been habituated may not simply regain its prehabituation amplitude after the strong stimulus but may reach a greater amplitude than before. Recent experiments with developing *Aplysia* have shown that dishabituation appears clearly earlier than sensitization, indicating that these are two separate phenomena (Carew, 1988).

Two special characteristics of sensitization are the following:

1. The stronger the stimulus, the more likely it is to produce sensitization.
2. With repeated presentations of the same sensitizing stimulus, it tends to lose its effect; that is, there is habituation of sensitization.

Imprinting

A striking kind of learning occurs early in the life of many precocial species: The young animal comes to follow the first relatively large moving object that it sees, and it appears to be content when close to that object and fearful or anxious if apart from it. Thus the chick normally follows and stays close to the hen, and the lamb becomes attached to the ewe. This kind of learning is called **filial imprinting.** Filial imprinting is a form of learning in which precocial animals in their first few days learn to approach and follow the first relatively large moving object they see. (Recall that precocial animals are born at a relatively advanced stage of development, whereas altricial animals are born at a relatively early stage.) It is clear that imprinting is a form of learning because the young animal will become imprinted on any large moving object, whether it is a hen or a toy truck or a person, and experience with that object is necessary for imprinting to occur. Furthermore, there is a critical period of only a few days during which filial imprinting can occur; if the young animal is not allowed to see any large moving object during that time, imprinting will not occur later. Once a young animal has imprinted on one object, it tends to avoid other large moving objects. Although imprinting normally aids the young in securing the protection of its mother and avoiding potentially dangerous animals, it occurs even if the object does not respond in any way to the young animal. Thus the learning is nonassociative. Filial imprinting occurs rather quickly and is lasting. Partly because of these characteristics, some investigators have chosen imprinting as a good situation in which to study mechanisms of learning. We will see in Chapter 17 that filial imprinting brings about measurable changes in the neurochemistry and anatomy of the brain (Horn, 1985).

Another kind of imprinting is also biologically important. This is **sexual imprinting** in which early experience influences choice of a mate later in life (Bateson, 1983a). Sexual imprinting occurs later than filial imprinting and is acquired over a longer span of time (Vidal, 1980). It is affected by the young animal's experiences with other animals, especially its siblings, as well as its mother. In some species the process of sexual imprinting occurs somewhat differently for males and females. Sexual imprinting occurs in altricial as well as precocial animals and is usually tested at sexual maturity. If a bird or a rodent is raised with members of another strain or species, the effects of sexual imprinting can be strong enough to lead it to attempt to mate with an animal of the other species (Bateson, 1983b; d'Udine & Alleva, 1983).

Sexual imprinting is not the only kind of learning that influences choice of mate. Animals have been found to select mates slightly different from those with which they grew up. Bateson (1983b) has suggested that the optimal difference an animal seeks in a mate is jointly determined by habituation, which makes highly familiar animals somewhat less attractive, and by sexual imprinting, which restricts the choice to members of the same species.

Representational Learning: Memories Versus Habits

Both in relation to behavior and in relation to neural mechanisms, several investigators of learning and memory have recently emphasized distinctions between memories that involve mental representations and those that do not. Recalling the face or the voice of a friend or what happened last New Year's Eve is an example of representational memory. Animals can form such memories, as careful tests show. Separate representations that are held in memory can later be integrated and used as bases for novel actions. In contrast to such representational learning, learning how to swim or even how to solve certain puzzles involves habits that some subjects describe as seeming to be "in the muscles," that is, almost automatic. They cannot tell how they are able to perform the skilled learned behavior and may even be surprised at their own performance. In the last century, psychologists like William James distinguished between **habits** and **memories.** Some psychologists are reviving this distinction according to which habits are stimulus-response bonds that are acquired automatically, and often gradually, through occurrences of stimulus-response-reinforcement contingencies. Memories, on the other hand, are cognitive representations; they are often acquired rapidly, and their acquisition does not require satisfaction of motives. Whereas habits are said to involve *knowing how*, memories are said to involve *knowing that*. Some other distinctions proposed recently overlap with the memory-habit distinction. One is that between **procedural knowledge** and **declarative knowledge:** A person shows procedural knowledge by being able to perform a task (which may include verbal tasks), whereas a person shows declarative knowledge by being able to state it. Another is the distinction between **semantic memory** and **episodic memory.** Semantic memory is generalized memory, like knowing the meaning of a word without knowing where or when you learned that word. A person shows episodic memory by recalling a particular incident or by relating a recollection to a particular time and place (such as remembering where and when you last saw a particular friend). Table 16-1 summarizes the distinctions between habits and memories and related pairs of terms.

A particular training procedure may result in either a habit or a memory or in both at once. For example, many investigators have held that classical conditioning results in reflexive, unconscious stimulus-response links. Others have held that conditioning rarely if ever occurs automatically and without conscious awareness in adult humans. Experimental evidence indicates that both sorts of learning can occur during conditioning. Wickens (1938, 1939, 1943a, b) performed a series of experiments in which he conditioned human subjects that a buzzer was followed by shock to the middle finger. (In the terminology of conditioning, the buzzer was the conditioned stimulus [CS] and the shock was the unconditioned stimulus [US].) In one

Table 16-1   Paired Terms Used to Distinguish Two Main Kinds of Memory

I	II	Author
Habit	Memory	James (1890); Mishkin and Petri (1984)
Semantic memory	Episodic memory	Bergson, 1911; Tulving (1972)
Knowing how	Knowing that	Ryle (1949)
Memory without record	Memory with record	Bruner (1969)
Procedural knowledge	Declarative knowledge	Squire (1984); Winograd (1975)
Stimulus-response	Representational	Ruggerio and Flagg (1976)*
Horizontal association	Vertical association	Wickelgren (1979)
Skill memory	Fact memory	Squire (1980)
Associative memory	Representational memory	Oakley (1981)*
Semantic memory	Cognitive mediation	Warrington and Weiskrantz (1982)
Skills	Conscious recollection	Moscovitch (1982)
Implicit memory	Explicit memory	Graf and Schacter (1985)
Nondeclarative knowledge (spared in amnesia)	Declarative knowledge (impaired in amnesia)	Shimamura (1988)

*Part of a three-part system.

series of experiments, the person's hand was placed palm down on a surface with the middle finger on an electrode. In a few trials, the person learned to extend the middle finger when the CS sounded, thus avoiding shock. Then the hand was turned palm up so that the back of the finger rested on the electrode. For most subjects as soon as the series of new trials began, the finger flexed at presentation of the CS, rather than continuing to extend, as in the training series. This was taken as evidence that the subjects had learned a representation of the situation and withdrew from the shock rather than being conditioned to a muscle response of extension. But in each of the four experiments, at least one subject during the test series initially gave a conditioned response with the same muscle group as in the training series and pressed the finger firmly onto the electrode when the CS sounded. One subject volunteered this comment after the experiment: "... a funny thing happened when the buzzer sounded the first few times [on the test trials]. First the finger went down as far as it would go ... and then it flew up ... the finger just acted that way of itself" (Wickens, 1939, p. 335). So it appears that in this situation the predominant form of learning was representational memory, but some unconscious, automatic habit formation also occurred.

There is evidence that the abilities to form habits and representational memories mature at different rates and that they make use of somewhat different brain circuits; we will consider this evidence in later sections. We will see that in some disorders of the nervous system representational memories and habits are affected differently.

Temporal Phases of Memory

The terms *learning* and *memory* are so often paired that it sometimes seems as if one of them necessarily implies the other. We cannot be sure that learning has occurred unless a memory can be elicited at some later time. (Here we are using "memory" in the common meaning of anything that shows that learning has occurred, and not in the more specialized sense of "representational memory.") But even if we can show that learning did occur, this observation does not guarantee that memory for the learned material can be retrieved again in the future. Even though short-term memory occurred, a long-lasting memory may never have been formed, or it may decay in time or be impaired by injuries to the brain, or the subject may be temporarily in a particular state in which a given memory cannot be retrieved.

The briefest memories are called **iconic** (from the Greek word for "image"). An example would be your impressions of a scene that is illuminated for only a moment. You may be able to grasp one part of the display, but the rest vanishes in seconds. (A very brief auditory memory is called "echoic," as if you could still hear it ringing in your ears.) These brief memories are thought to reflect the activity of sensory buffers, that is, continuation of sensory neural activity (see Figure 16-4).

Somewhat longer than iconic memories are **short-term memories.** For example, suppose that you want to call a person on the telephone using a number that you have never used before. You look up the number and, if nothing distracts or interrupts you, you dial the number successfully. You have used a short-term memory of the telephone number. If the line is busy, however, and you want to call back a minute or so later, you may have to look the number up again unless you have been repeating it to yourself in the meantime. If you rehearse or use the number, then it can remain in short-term memory until you turn to some other activity. Unfortunately there is no consistency in the use of the label short-term memory among investigators from different fields. Physiological psychologists and other biologists often use it to cover memories that are not permanent but that fade out over minutes or hours; some investigators have even used short-term memory to mean memories that last a few days. But researchers who study human verbal behavior usually restrict the term to memories that last for seconds up to a minute or so, if rehearsal is not permitted.

As an example of memory that lasts somewhat beyond the short term, suppose that you drive to school or work and park your car in a different place each day. If

Figure 16-4 Diagram of a multiple-trace hypothesis of memory storage. (Adapted from McGaugh, 1968)

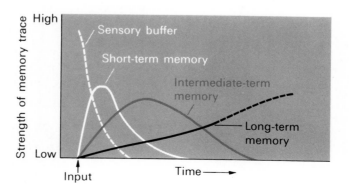

things go well, you remember each afternoon where you parked your car that morning, but you may very well not recall where you parked your car yesterday or a week ago. This is an example of what is sometimes called **intermediate-term memory,** that is, a memory that outlasts short-term memory but that is far from being permanent.

Beyond the memories that last for hours are memories that last for weeks, months, and years; these are called **long-term memories.** Many memories that do last for days or weeks nevertheless become weaker and may even fade out completely over time, so some investigators also use the term **permanent memory** to designate memories that appear to continue without decline for the rest of the life of an organism, or at least as long as the organism remains in good health.

The fact that some memories last only for seconds and others for months is not proof that short-term memories are based on different biological mechanisms from long-term memories. It is the scientist's task to find out whether these memories are based on the same or different processes. And as we will see, there are good reasons—both clinical and experimental—to conclude that different biological processes underlie short-term and long-term memory storage.

Memory Processes

Psychologists who study learning and memory suggest that several successive processes seem to be necessary to guarantee recall of a past event; these are **encoding, consolidation,** and **retrieval** (see Figure 16-5). The original information must enter sensory channels and then be encoded rapidly into a form that passes into short-term memory. Some of this information is then consolidated in long-term storage. Some cognitive psychologists hold that there is no essential difference between short-term and long-term storages; they claim that more deeply processed information is stored longer. Others claim that storage is accomplished by different neural processes in the short-term and long-term stores. Finally there are the processes of retrieval.

Figure 16-5   A scheme of memory processes that includes encoding, consolidation, and retrieval.

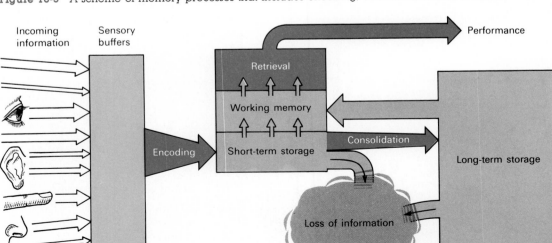

With these stages in mind, investigators have tried to find out whether particular examples of failure of recall in normal subjects involve failure of encoding or of consolidation or of retrieval, and whether pathological impairments of memory involve selectively one or another of these main processes.

Comparative and Evolutionary Approaches to Learning

There has been a good deal of speculation about the evolution of abilities to learn and remember, but it is not possible to do direct research on this subject, since we cannot measure the behavior of animals now extinct. We can, of course, compare the learning and memory capacities of existing species, some of which are more primitive than others in the sense that they resemble their ancient ancestors more closely, but this is not a direct route to the past. As we consider attempts at comparing learning ability among existing species in the following paragraphs, we will see that it is not a simple matter. Just as it is difficult and perhaps impossible to devise a ''culture-free'' intelligence test for human beings, so it has been difficult to devise tests for animals that do not favor the sensory and/or motor capacities of some species and work against others. The problem has become even more complicated now that recent research has shown that relatively simple animals are capable of a greater variety of learning than was suspected only a few years ago (Carew & Sahley, 1986). In part these findings have come from attempts to use ''simple systems'' to investigate the basic neural processes involved in learning and memory formation. Thus associative learning has now been found in the mollusc *Aplysia,* and complex conditioning has been found in the garden slug. On the other hand, the learning of many kinds of animals seems to be restricted to certain combinations of events and not to be able to encompass other relations. The wide distribution of learning throughout the animal kingdom has suggested implications for the evolution of abilities to learn and remember, and so do restrictions in these abilities. We will discuss these implications for evolution shortly.

Distribution of Learning Abilities Among Classes of Animals

Nonassociative learning appears to be very widely distributed throughout the animal kingdom. Rather simple animals with small nervous systems readily habituate to repeated mild stimuli, and they also show sensitization to strong stimuli. Furthermore, the time courses and other features of habituation and sensitization are similar whether studied in an earthworm, a mollusc, or a mammal. Some investigators have reported nonassociative learning even in paramecia, one-celled animals that, of course, do not have a nervous system. It appears that some kind of learning and memory are seen in all animals.

Until recently it was believed that associative learning probably had a more restricted distribution than nonassociative learning in the animal kingdom. For example, *Aplysia* had been used for many years to investigate neural mechanisms of habituation, and investigators had sought in vain for evidence of associative learning until it was discovered in 1980. Evidence for learning in the fruit fly, *Drosophila,* was long sought in order to try to relate learning to genetic factors which are very well known in *Drosophila,* but it was only in 1974 that investigators first announced successful training in these animals. Evidence of conditioning in the slug was first presented in 1975.

Part of the difficulty in assessing the capacity of a species to learn and remember is that these capacities may be highly specific. In recent years it has become evident that certain species can learn particular associations well even though they are very poor at other tasks that do not seem more difficult to us. Evidence for specificity has accumulated since the 1960s and has led to two successive and quite different concepts. First came the concept of **genetic constraints on learning,** which was prominent from the 1960s into the early 1980s. This formulation held that species-typical factors restrict the kinds of learning that a species can accomplish, or at least accomplish readily. For example, bees learn readily to come to a particular station to feed on a 24-hour schedule, which of course occurs in nature, but they cannot learn to come on an 8- or 12-hour schedule. Birds of some species do not learn the pattern of markings or even the color of their eggs even though they turn the eggs over frequently, yet they learn to recognize their young individually within three days after they hatch. This is just the time at which the chicks begin to wander about and pose a problem of confusing one nest's chicks with those of another. The interpretation of such observations changed in the 1980s. Rather than supposing that the genes of certain species constrain their general ability to learn and thus make them selectively stupid, some investigators hold it more likely that **specific abilities to learn and remember** evolve where these are needed (e.g., Gould, 1986; Jenkins, 1984).

The fact that learning and memory are so widespread among animal species provides support for attempts to study basic mechanisms of learning and memory in animals with relatively simple nervous systems. We will discuss this simple-system approach in the next chapter and see some of the findings that it has produced.

Comparisons of Learning Ability Among Species

A recent review of learning and intelligence among species led to the following conclusions (Rosenzweig & Glickman, 1985):

1. Nonassociative learning and certain kinds of associative learning (classical and instrumental conditioning) occur throughout the vertebrates and among invertebrates widely among arthropods and molluscs and perhaps some other phyla.
2. Cognitive learning (formation of ''memories'' in the sense of William James's use of the word) occurs in primates and some other, but perhaps not all, mammals. It also occurs in some large-brained species of other phyla, such as the cephalopods.
3. Not only qualitative differences in abilities to learn and remember but also quantitative differences can be important for individual behavior and therefore also for evolution.
4. Further investigation seems in order with regard to the hypotheses offered by some workers that particular complex cognitive abilities are found only within a few selected species.

These conclusions are based on the work of many psychologists who have attempted, since the beginning of this century, to compare the learning abilities of different species. They realized that if valid comparisons of learning ability could be found, they would contribute not only to knowledge of the distribution of abilities to learn and remember throughout the animal kingdom, but also to understanding of the evolution of these abilities and to relating intelligence to brain measures such as brain weight.

Formation of Learning Sets

In the attempt to compare the learning abilities of different species the study of formation of **learning sets** (Harlow, 1949) was an attempt to find a general-purpose intelligence test for animals. Essentially learning sets are formed when an animal— a monkey, for example—is given as many as 300 problems, one after the other, all based on the same principle. For example, the animal may be trained to choose one of a pair of objects (circle versus triangle) that the experimenter has arbitrarily designated as correct (Figure 16-6). This problem is called the object discrimination problem. On each trial that the monkey chooses the correct object, it is given a bit of food. After a number of trials, the monkey masters that problem, and then it is given another pair of objects and again has to learn which is correct. After hundreds of successive problems of this type, each with a different pair of objects, the monkey can solve a new problem very quickly. If its choice on the first trial is rewarded, it stays with that choice and makes no errors at all; if not rewarded, it switches to the other object and thereafter never errs. If one were to observe these monkeys after 300 prior problems, one might see their brilliant performance as insight, but we know that it is based on slow, cumulative learning.

Besides seeming to offer a general-purpose intelligence test for animals, formation of learning sets appeared to be a valid test for humans too: Improvement of performance of children over a similar set of problems was related to their intelligence as measured on an IQ test (Harter, 1965). Results of learning set formation for several species of mammals were compiled from a variety of sources. The results showed large interspecies differences, and the ranking of species conformed in general with ideas about phylogenetic status. Although these findings were widely reproduced, critics pointed out that the different original studies were not strictly comparable. The experimenters had used a variety of methods to train and test their subjects; for example, they gave different numbers of trials per problem, thus affecting the rapidity with which animals improve their performance on learning sets. Such criticisms cast doubt on the possibility of comparing abilities of different species.

Trying to obtain as much as possible from the learning set evidence, Passingham (1981) looked for the largest set of results available for different species in which exactly the same methods of training had been used. Reports of experiments using six trials per problem were found for rhesus monkey, squirrel monkey, marmoset, cat, gerbil, rat, and squirrel. The rhesus monkey had the fastest rate of improvement among these species. All three species of primates learned more rapidly than the cat, and the cat surpassed all three rodents. Thus the results seem to support the existence of differences in ''learning to learn'' and intelligence among mammals.

There does remain the concern that these experiments all used visual discrimination and may therefore have capitalized on the high visual acuity and color discrimination of primates. To take up this concern, we can ask (1) whether significant

Figure 16-6 Monkey making an object discrimination during an experiment on formation of learning sets. (Courtesy of H. F. Harlow)

differences in formation of learning sets occur among species of primates and also (2) whether they occur over a variety of species when the visual discrimination is well within the sensory capacities of all of them. Employing the first approach, Shell and Riopelle (1958) studied formation of learning sets in three species of platyrrhine monkeys, using the same experimental methodology for all three species. They obtained significant species differences: Spider monkeys improved more rapidly than did cebus monkeys, and cebus monkeys more rapidly than squirrel monkeys. Using simple spatial and brightness cues that are within the sensory capacity of all his subjects, Riddell (1979) obtained a measure of flexibility in reversal learning. He found successively better performance as he studied rats, shrews, squirrel monkeys, cebus monkeys, and people. From these and other findings, most investigators share a consensus that there are significant differences in learning ability among species.

Evolution of Learning and Intelligence

From our survey of comparative aspects of learning and intelligence, we can draw some tentative conclusions about how these capacities may have evolved. We have seen in earlier chapters that ''lower'' or simpler animals have specific sensory and motor abilities that are adapted to their particular environmental niches. Sometimes these abilities are keen and precise, such as the ability of bees to distinguish patterns of blossoms (although their form vision is not as acute as ours) and colors (including some in the ultraviolet part of the spectrum that we cannot see). Learning abilities of such animals may also be good in some ways but restricted in others, compared to the more general learning abilities of more complex animals. An example of such specificity has already been mentioned: the ability of bees to learn to come to a particular location for food on a 24-hour schedule but not on an 8- or 12-hour schedule. These shorter schedules do not occur in a bee's world.

It has been argued that learning and intelligence evolved because of the survival value in being able to predict events in the environment. An animal that can predict where it is likely to find food in its environment will have an advantage over one that wanders randomly in search of food; an animal that can predict that a particular response to a particular stimulus will be followed by pain is less likely to damage itself. Because of this, one theorist hypothesizes that the ability to form associations ''evolved very early and proved so powerful as a predictive mechanism that subsequent improvements in problem solving have arisen largely from the undoubted improvements in the quality of sensory processing and in the variability and skill of motor responses available'' (Macphail, 1985, p. 285). This assumes that both the neural circuitry and the detailed synaptic events that underlie learning and memory storage are the same for all animals with nervous systems, and neither of these assumptions is necessarily the case. Let us examine each in turn.

In order for an associative link to be formed, information of the different kinds to be associated must be available in the same neurons or at least in closely neighboring neurons, and that is not usually the case. Rather it has been suggested that simpler animals evolved specific circuits in which particular kinds of associations could be formed, and that during the course of further evolution these specific circuits came to be used in more general and plastic ways in higher animals (Rozin, 1976a). This is consistent with the hypothesis already mentioned from comparative studies of animal behavior that specific abilities to learn and remember have evolved where they had survival value.

Much of the evolution of learning and intelligence probably consisted first of the development of precise and elaborate systems to handle specific situations and then of the liberation of these systems from their restricted context. In other words, particular circuitry that evolved to handle particular problems (such as size constancy in perception or memory for food location) was initially accessible only to those input and output systems that it was designed to serve. With evolution some of these systems became connected to other systems; thus they became components in a hierarchy and could be used more widely. Also, circuits that were successful in a particular context probably served as models for circuits in related systems. Thus we see the modular structure of the cerebral cortex, where similar basic circuits are replicated many times to fit into different networks. This manifold replication of basic units in complex brains is one of the causes of the increase in brain size with evolution, a topic we considered in Chapter 3.

Developmental Approaches to Learning and Memory

Changes in the abilities to learn and remember over the life span are important both for understanding behavior at different ages and for providing clues about the neural mechanisms of learning and memory. Both infants and elderly people show characteristic problems of memory, and recently attempts have been made to show relations between these problems of the two extremes of age. Developmental studies of learning and memory are being conducted with a variety of species, ranging from humans and other mammals to molluscs.

Successive Appearance of Habituation, Dishabituation, and Sensitization in Aplysia

Since the 1960s the mollusc *Aplysia* has proved to be an excellent preparation in which to study the neural mechanisms of habituation and sensitization. Now psychologist Thomas Carew (1988) has shown that *Aplysia* is also well suited to investigate the emergence during development of different forms of learning and their neural mechanisms.

The youngest *Aplysia* that can be used for behavioral experiments are about 45 days posthatch (stage 9 of their development) but only about 1 mm in length. At this stage they already show habituation, but only if the stimuli are repeated at short time intervals of 1 second or less. As *Aplysia* mature, the stimuli can be spaced increasingly farther apart and still cause habituation. At stage 9, neither dishabituation nor sensitization can be evoked. A few days later, at developmental stage 10, *Aplysia* can be habituated to stimuli delivered at an interstimulus interval of 5 seconds, and a strong stimulus leads to dishabituation, but sensitization still does not occur. That is, a strong stimulus does not increase the size of subsequent responses unless the animal has already been habituated. Only in stage 12, when *Aplysia* are about 100 days posthatch, does sensitization first appear. At this age, stimuli presented 30 seconds apart can cause habituation. It has not yet been reported whether associative learning also appears at stage 12 or whether it requires additional maturity. Pinpointing when different kinds of learning emerge is an important technique: it allows investigators to differentiate among the kinds of learning and also to search for changes in the nervous system that occur at each of those times.

Infantile Amnesia   If you try to find your earliest memories, you probably cannot get back beyond the age of two or three, and you probably have few memories from before your fifth year. This amnesia is curious, because children are obviously learning a great deal and undergoing interesting experiences in their first few years. Why should these experiences not be retrievable in later years? Freud referred to this phenomenon as infantile amnesia. He speculated that memories for those years are repressed, but the amnesia applies to pleasant as well as unpleasant experiences. Some have suggested that the early memories were not coded effectively into linguistic terms and therefore cannot be recalled, but most children were already talking and describing events well at ages that they cannot remember as adults; also, adults can remember shapes and sounds that they cannot code effectively into language. Research with animal subjects has offered two other explanations for the ''amnesia of early childhood.''

The first of these biological explanations came from research with rats and mice, which showed that their ability to form long-term memories matures more slowly than does their ability to learn (Campbell & Coulter, 1976). Rat and mouse pups, like human babies, are altricial (born at a relatively early stage in their brain and behavioral development). On the other hand, the guinea pig is precocial, and experiments showed that infant guinea pigs can remember as well as can adults. In line with these findings, Campbell and Coulter suggested that human infants can remember words and faces that they have learned repeatedly but cannot retain memories for particular events (so-called episodic memories).

More recent research demonstrates that even for altricial animals—monkeys in this case—some kinds of material can be learned and remembered efficiently by infants whereas other kinds require greater maturation of the nervous system (Bachevalier & Mishkin, 1984). Such behavioral differences show up clearly during the early months and years while the nervous system continues to develop rapidly. The findings with regard to both age and brain circuits have been related to the distinction between habits and memories, so the experimental methods are worth careful examination here.

One problem involved concurrent learning of pairs of objects. A set of 20 different pairs of easily discriminable three-dimensional objects was presented once a day in a situation like the one shown in Figure 16-6. One object of each pair had arbitrarily been chosen to be correct; that is, if the monkey displaced it, it found a bit of food. Each pair was presented only once in the daily session. The next day the monkey was given the same set of 20 pairs of objects in the same order, but the right-left position within a pair was varied, so the monkey had to learn the identity of the correct object and not the spatial position. This problem is illustrated in Figure 16-7a, although the objects in the figure are less complicated than those used in the experiment. In order to improve its performance, the subject had to retain experiences from one day to the next.

The other problem was called ''delayed nonmatching to sample.'' In this problem each trial involved a pair of objects that the monkey had never seen before, and each pair was used only once. One of the pair was presented first, as the sample, in a central position on the tray; the monkey displaced it and obtained a bit of food. Then after a 10-second delay, both objects were presented in lateral positions on the tray, and the animal found a reward if it displaced the novel object. This problem is

Figure 16-7 Experimental designs for tests of (a) concurrent learning and (b) delayed nonmatching to sample. The actual test objects are three-dimensional and more complex than those illustrated here. Note that in (a) concurrent learning, the same pairs of objects are presented in the same order each day. In contrast, the delayed nonmatching to sample test in (b) uses new pairs of objects each day. The correct choice in each pair is designated by an asterisk

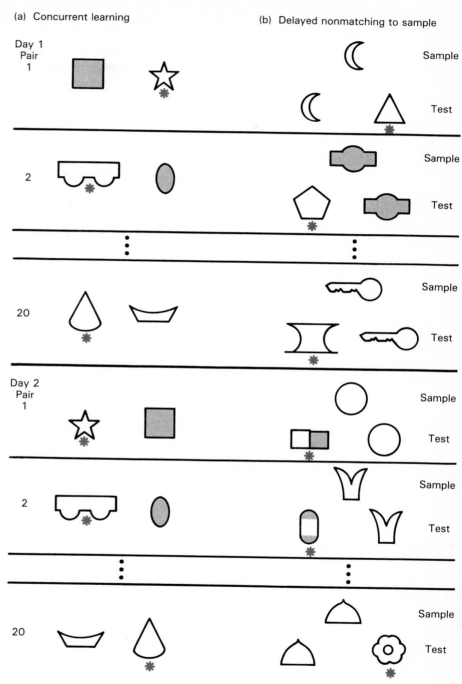

illustrated in Figure 16-7b. As in the other problem, the monkey was given 20 trials per day. In this problem the monkey had to remember the sample object for only 10 seconds, although the problem could later be made more difficult by extending the delay period between presentation of the sample and the pair.

Which one of these problems is easy for a 3-month-old monkey to learn, and which is not solved with full proficiency until the monkey is 2 years old? Before reading further, try to decide why one of the two problems should be easier for a young animal to solve.

Both tasks were employed with groups of monkeys that were 3 months, 6 months, 12 months, and 24 months of age. The concurrent object discrimination task was mastered easily by 3-month-old monkeys. They required an average of 10 daily sessions to reach 90% accuracy in choosing the correct object of each pair, and older animals were no faster in learning the objects. In contrast, whereas adult monkeys learn to perform delayed nonmatching to sample to 90% accuracy in less than 100 trials (5 days of experience with the task), 3-month-old monkeys could not master the principle of this task. A monkey had to reach 4 to 5 months of age before it could learn the nonmatching to sample task. Furthermore, adult monkeys can perform at better than 90% accuracy with delays of up to 2 minutes between the sample and the test; they can also perform well if given up to 10 sample objects before being given any of the day's tests. Monkeys 6 or 12 months of age do not equal 24-month-old monkeys on these more demanding versions of the task. We thus conclude delayed nonmatching to sample requires considerable maturation for good performance, whereas object discrimination learning does not.

How do the experimenters characterize the two tests in ways that account for the difference between the maturational demands they make? The discrimination learning task requires formation of associations between the appearance of an object and the occurrence of reward. These associations gain in strength through repetition, even though the repetitions occur 24 hours apart. Just as monkeys can form conditioned associations early in life, so can they acquire associations between appearance and reinforcement. In the case of delayed nonmatching to sample, the animal must form a ''memory''—a representation of the sample—and then use this memory at the time of the test, deciding which test object does not match it. The mature monkey forms this representation rapidly and uses it skillfully, but young monkeys appear to be incapable of the representational aspect of the task.

It is especially instructive that the failure of young animals to solve the delayed nonmatching task was accompanied by their success in learning object discriminations. If only the delayed nonmatching task had been used, the failure could have been attributed to any of a variety of factors. We might have wondered if the young animals could perceive the objects accurately or attend sufficiently to them or whether they were adequately motivated to perform. Since the object discrimination task used similar objects to those in delayed nonmatching, and since the spacing of trials, length of daily sessions, and food rewards were all the same for the two tasks, we can rule out such alternative interpretations and attribute the differences in success to differences in what the animals had to learn and remember. The strategy of comparing results of two or more carefully chosen tasks is called **dissociation.** Later in the chapter we will see an example of *double dissociation,* involving brain lesions in two locations and their differential effects on two behavioral tasks.

This investigation of what young animals can and cannot remember helps us to understand further "infantile amnesia." Adults clearly utilize the skills and meanings of words that they learned in their first three years. What they cannot recall are representational memories of those early years. It is not all recall that is lost from early childhood but only a specific kind.

Sex Differences in Development of Habit Formation

Developmental psychologists have found that young boys are slower to learn many habits than are young girls. This has also been found in young nonhuman primates, and it has been related to neonatal levels of testosterone (Hagger, Bachevalier, & Bercu, 1986). For example, in the study of concurrent object discrimination, it was female monkeys three months of age that were almost as quick to learn as were adults (means of 13 and 10 sessions, respectively). Three-month-old males were significantly slower (22-session mean). Lesions of inferotemporal cortex impair this learning in adults of both sexes and in infant females, but not in infant males; apparently this region is more mature in the three-month-old female than in the male.

To examine the possible roles of sex hormones in this kind of learning, levels of estradiol were measured in female infants just after they had acquired the object discrimination task; no correlation was found in the females. Similarly, levels of testosterone were measured in infant males after they completed the task. A significant correlation was found in the males (0.79, $p < 0.05$); the higher the level of hormone, the more days it took to learn the task. Three other infant males were then deprived of male hormones at birth and taught the task at three months. They learned just as rapidly as young females. Thus it appears that the high levels of testosterone found in male monkeys around the time of birth slow the development of one or more neural structures necessary for learning of this task. What the neural structures are and how broadly they influence learning are yet to be determined.

Effects of Aging on Learning and Memory

The capacity to learn and remember in older people has become a topic of heightened interest in recent years. This stems in part from the growing proportion of elderly people in the population of developed countries and in part from the recognition of forms of cognitive impairment that are more likely to affect older people, such as **senile dementia of the Alzheimer type** (SDAT). Most investigators agree that older people in normal health show some decrements in ability to learn and remember (Craik, 1986), and a review of both human and animal studies showed declines with age in both (Kubanis & Zornetzer, 1981). Nevertheless, there are some who do not concur. For example, a recent survey of research reported little indication of significant impairment of learning and memory among healthy older people as compared with younger subjects (Honzik, 1984). Trying to make accurate comparisons among people of different ages is fraught with difficulties that are related to both selection of subjects and selection of tasks: Apparent differences in learning ability may be caused by such factors as differences in educational levels, recency of formal learning, or motivation for the task. Even when such factors have been equated, however, differences related to age have usually been found on certain tasks although not on others. What kinds of tasks usually show decrements in performance with aging? Memory performance of normal elderly people tends to show some impairment on tasks of conscious recollection that require effort (Hasher & Zacks, 1979) and that rely primarily on internal generation of the memory rather than on external cues (Craik, 1985). In such cases giving the elderly subjects easily organized task structures or cues or both can often raise their performance to the level of the young. Thus the type of task helps to determine whether impairment will be seen. For many tasks the elderly perform as well or almost as well as the young.

With pathological forms of aging, such as that seen in Alzheimer's disease, the representational memory system deteriorates, and it has been suggested that what remains is the memory processes of infants (Moscovitch, 1985). In fact, testing the implication of this formulation led Moscovitch to discover a cognitive disability in amnesic patients like one that Piaget had described for 8–10-month old infants: After infants have searched successfully several times for an object that they have seen the experimenter hide in location A, when they see the object hidden at a new location, B, they continue to search for it at A. Most of the amnesic patients showed the same failure, even going by the object in plain sight in order to search for it at A; they appear to remember the search procedure and not the object being sought.

Studies of the effects of aging on memory are difficult to accomplish with human subjects, partly because of variability among people caused by both genetic and environmental factors. Therefore some investigators are using animal subjects in order to obtain an intimate and detailed understanding of the processes by which aging affects memory. Here again it is necessary to design experiments in such a way as to overcome effects of possibly confounding variables, such as differences in strength of motivation with age or differences in sensory acuity (Ingram, 1985). Evidence of slower learning with advanced age has been reported by some of these investigators (e.g., Bartus et al., 1985; Ingram, 1985; Sternberg et al., 1985). Furthermore, some indications have been found that dietary supplements (e.g., Bartus et al., 1985) or drug treatments (e.g., Sternberg et al., 1985) can prevent or decrease the occurrence of such deficits. Thus the animal research may also point to effective therapeutic measures.

Pathology of Human Memory

Enormous capacities to learn and remember are salient characteristics of humankind. We all know the meanings of thousands of words, and even vaster vocabularies are readily acquired by many people who live in border regions of the world or who have other reasons to master several languages. Most of us recognize hundreds or thousands of faces and countless visual scenes and objects, hundreds of voices and many other familiar sounds, and hundreds of different odors. In addition, depending on our interests and experiences, we may be able to recognize and sing or play a large number of tunes and identify and supply information about a great many athletes, musical performers, actors, or historical characters. Impairments of learning and memory occur through disease or accidents, and the types of impairment have long been scrutinized both to find clues to the mechanisms of memory and to find ways of treating its malfunctions. Characteristics that are common to most or all patients who suffer from **amnesia**—severe impairment of memory—include the following: (1) inability to form new memories beginning with the onset of the illness (**anterograde amnesia,** from the Latin for "moving forward"), (2) difficulty in retrieving memories formed before the onset of the illness (**retrograde amnesia,** from the Latin for "moving backward"), (3) relatively intact intellectual functions other than memory, as measured by standardized tests. (Of course in some cases amnesia may be combined with other cognitive or intellectual impairments.)

Some of the main questions about impairments of learning and memory are these: (1) Are there different types of impairment or is there only one basic type? (2) What aspects of learning and memory are spared when impairment occurs? (3) What brain regions are implicated in the impairments? Much progress is being made in answering these questions by studying "experiments of nature"—cases of damage to the brain that occur through diseases or accidents. Newer techniques of behavioral testing and of examination of the brain, both in living patients and postmortem, have provided valuable new data and findings. Neurologists and brain scientists have also studied learning and memory in disconnected parts of the nervous system, such as in one hemisphere of the brain when the corpus callosum has been transected for therapeutic reasons. Many of the clues that have been obtained from study of clinical cases have then been followed up and extended by research with animal subjects, where the intervention can be specified and controlled more accurately. Let us first examine some amnesic syndromes and then consider some research to follow up hypotheses derived from the clinical studies.

Amnesic Syndromes and Neuropathology

In the 1880s a Russian neurologist published a paper about a syndrome in which impaired memory was a major feature. This paper became a classic and caused the condition to be named after him—**Korsakoff's syndrome.** People suffering from Korsakoff's syndrome fail to recall many items or events of the past; if such an item is presented again or if it happens to be recalled, the patient does not show a feeling of familiarity with it. Korsakoff patients frequently deny that anything is wrong with them. They often show disorientation for time and place, and they may "confabulate," that is, fill a gap in memory with a falsification that they accept as correct.

The main cause of Korsakoff's syndrome is lack of the vitamin thiamine; this lack occurs in alcoholics who obtain most of their calories from alcohol and neglect their diet. Treating such a person with thiamine can prevent further deterioration; if the treatment is started before the person has become a full-blown Korsakoff case, the condition can be ameliorated. Over the years neurologists have examined brains of many patients who suffered from Korsakoff's syndrome in an attempt to locate the site(s) of damage. Unfortunately, very few patients have had both careful determination of their capacities and also detailed postmortem examination of the brain, so that one cannot have full confidence in the findings reported to date. Some of the cases may not actually have shown the specific memory deficits of Korsakoff's syndrome, since they were described as showing "mental confusion" or "clouding of consciousness" rather than being characterized in terms of performance on appropriate tests of memory. Also, some of the autopsy reports were sketchy and limited as to the brain regions considered. In these studies both the mammillary

Figure 16-8 Regions of the human brain that have been implicated in the formulation of long-term memories. (a) A lateral view of the brain shows the levels of the transverse sections shown in (b).

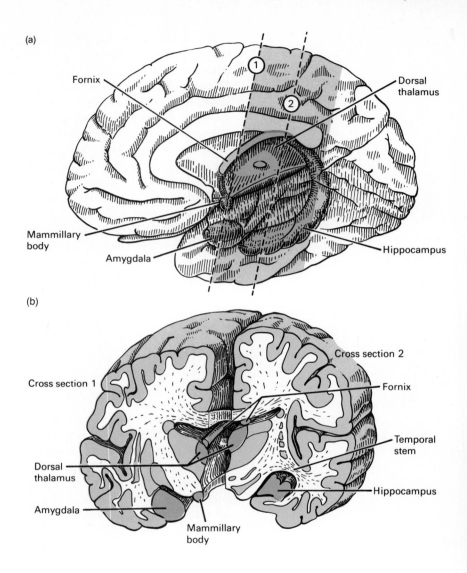

bodies and the dorsomedial nucleus of the thalamus have frequently, but not invariably, been found to be severely damaged (Figure 16-8).

In a thorough study, Mair and colleagues (1979) examined two patients over several years with a battery of behavioral tests; the brains of both were later examined in detail. Both brains showed shrunken, diseased mammillary bodies, and there was some damage in the dorsomedial thalamus. Temporal lobe structures, including the hippocampus and the temporal stem, were normal. Thus these cases confirm the less precise, earlier studies. Mair and co-workers characterize the mammillary bodies as "a narrow funnel through which connections from the midbrain as well as the temporal lobe neocortex and limbic system gain access to the frontal lobes" (p. 778).

In other patients, impairment of the hippocampus seemed to produce a striking deficit of memory formation, and this report has engendered both research and controversy ever since it appeared (Scoville & Milner, 1957). One of these patients became famous through a series of studies made of his case because he showed unusual symptoms after a brain operation in 1953; he is known by his initials, H. M. This man had suffered from epilepsy since childhood. His condition became progressively worse and was uncontrollable by medication; he had to stop work at the age of 27. The symptoms indicated that the neurological origins of the seizures were in the medial basal regions of both temporal lobes, so the neurologist removed such tissue bilaterally, including much of the hippocampus (see Figure 16-9). Similar operations had been performed before without harmful effects, although less tissue had been removed than in this case. Upon recovery from the operation, H. M. was

Figure 16-9 Brain tissue removed in the operation on patient H. M. The operation was performed bilaterally, but the diagram shows only unilateral removal on the left side so that the forms of the structures can be seen on the right. (a) The base of the brain, showing the extent of the operation and the levels of the transverse sections (b–e). (From Scoville and Milner, 1957)

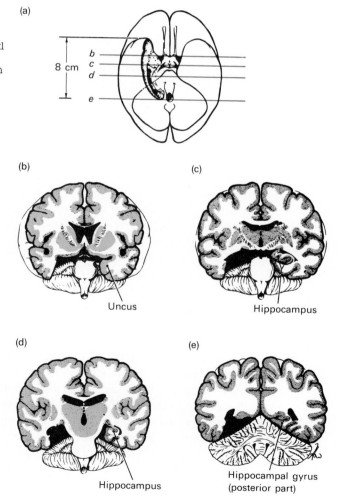

unable to retain new material for more than brief periods. Most of his old memories were intact, although there was amnesia for most events during the three years before the operation. Here is one example of his inability to learn new information: Six months after the operation H. M.'s family moved to another house on the same street; when H. M. went out, he could not remember the new address and kept returning to the old house. Also, H. M. could no longer learn the names of people he met, although he recognized the people he knew before the operation. He still retains a new fact only briefly; as soon as a distraction occurs, the newly acquired information vanishes. But H. M. does converse easily, and his IQ remains above average—118 when tested in 1962 and in 1977 but declining to 108 in 1983 (Corkin, 1983). Short-term memory is normal, but very few long-term memories are formed.

H. M. recognizes that something is wrong with him because he has no memories of the past several years or even of what he did earlier in the same day. His description of this strange state of isolation from his own past is poignant (Milner, 1970, p. 37):

> Every day is alone in itself, whatever enjoyment I've had, and whatever sorrow I've had. . . . Right now, I'm wondering, have I done or said anything amiss? You see, at this moment everything looks clear to me, but what happened just before? That's what worries me. It's like waking from a dream. I just don't remember.

After publication of the case of H. M., similar cases were reported that resulted not from brain surgery but from disease. Occasionally herpes simplex virus attacks the brain and destroys tissue in the medial temporal lobe, and this destruction can produce a severe failure to form new long-term memories, although acquisition of short-term memories is normal (for example, see Damasio et al., 1985a; Starr & Phillips, 1970). Rupture of the anterior cerebral arteries can also damage basal forebrain regions, including the hippocampus, and cause amnesia (Damasio et al., 1985b). An episode of reduced blood supply to the brain (ischemia) can also result in damage to the hippocampus and in deficits in memory formation. The temporal lobe patients, unlike patients with Korsakoff's syndrome, are not disoriented, and they do not confabulate, although they too are cut off from their recent past.

Research Inspired by "Hippocampal Amnesia"

H. M.'s memory deficit was ascribed to bilateral destruction of much of the hippocampus. This conclusion was reached because earlier surgical cases that had not shown memory impairment had involved less damage to the hippocampus, although they shared with H. M. damage to more anterior structures, including the amygdala. Soon after description of this case, investigators began to remove the hippocampus in experimental animals in order to try to reproduce the deficit and then study the mechanisms of formation of long-term memories. But after years of research, brain scientists had to confess failure: Neither in rats nor in monkeys did it appear possible to demonstrate failure of memory consolidation after bilateral destruction of the hippocampus (Isaacson, 1972). Different investigators have attempted to account for this puzzling discrepancy in different ways, and the widening research on this problem has led to considerable gains in knowledge—about the amnesic syndrome in people, about functions of the hippocampus, and about brain mechanisms of memory.

The main hypotheses proposed to account for the discrepancy between results of human cases and animal experiments focused either on the *kind of memory test* employed or on the *particular brain structure(s)* involved. Another possibility, which most investigators are reluctant to accept, is that the formation of memory involves different brain structures in human beings and in other mammals. Now let us examine some of the main findings of research conducted to resolve the enigmas of "hippocampal amnesia."

Importance of the Kind of Memory Test: What Is Lost and What Is Spared?

An early specific hypothesis was that the human impairment involves chiefly verbal material and that animals, of course, could not be tested for such deficits. An interesting finding with H. M. suggested that his memory deficit might be mainly restricted to verbal material and might not hold for motor learning. Milner (1965) presented a mirror-tracing test to H. M. In this test (see Figure 16-10) the subject

Figure 16-10 Mirror-tracing test, and learning by H. M. (a) The subject attempts to trace the outline of a form, keeping his pencil within the double boundary, while observing the form and his hand through a mirror. A barrier prevents direct observation of hand and form. (b) Performance of H. M. over three successive days. The record shows improvement within days (short-term memory) and retention from one day to another (long-term memory). (Data from Milner, 1965)

(a) Mirror-tracing task

(b) Performance of H. M. on mirror-tracing task

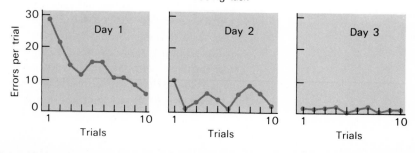

| BOX 16-1 | How Do You Live When You Can't Form New Memories? |

What is life like for a person who is suddenly severely impaired in the ability to form memories? Such a disaster has befallen some people as a consequence of disease, brain operations, or injury to the brain. A few of these cases have been investigated carefully, and they have furnished valuable information about memory and its mechanisms. The daily life of one of these people has been studied (Kaushall, Zetin, & Squire, 1981), and the description is illuminating.

N. A. had done well in school both scholastically and athletically, and he graduated in 1958. After a year of junior college, he joined the Air Force. One day in 1960 while N. A. was assembling a model airplane, a roommate took a miniature fencing foil from the wall, tapped N. A. from behind, and thrust forward as N. A. turned around. The blade entered the right nostril and penetrated the left hemisphere of N. A.'s brain. N. A. reports memories of the accident and of the minute or two afterward until he lost consciousness. During hospitalization several not uncommon neurological symptoms were noted, and they cleared up. But there was one unusual symptom and it persisted: N. A. was practically unable to form new long-term memories, especially for verbal material.

After several months N. A. was returned to the care of his parents. During the several years after the accident, psychologist H. L. Teuber and colleagues followed this case (Teuber, Milner, & Vaughan, 1968). Since 1975 a psychological-medical team has tested N. A. frequently and has also visited his home often (Kaushall et al., 1981).

Upon first meeting N. A., visitors are impressed with his normality. He has a relaxed and amiable manner and is polite and hospitable. He invites you to inspect his collection of guns and model airplanes and hundreds of souvenirs that he has acquired on trips with his parents. He describes the objects lucidly and intelligently, although he is sometimes unsure where he obtained a particular object. He does not exhibit confusion, and during a visit he does not show the same object twice.

But when you return for repeated visits, N. A. apologizes each time for not remembering your name and asks each time whether he has shown you his collections. By the third or fourth visit, these repetitions and other aspects of N. A.'s behavior "come to reveal a devastated life and an isolated mental world" (Kaushall et al., 1981, p. 384).

Although N. A. has an IQ of 124, he can neither hold a job nor form close personal relationships. N. A. has attended an outpatient treatment center for many years and is popular among staff and patients, but he cannot remember their names or their histories. He is alert and enjoys humor, but his socializing is limited

looks at both a printed star and his hand in a mirror and tries to stay inside the double boundaries while tracing the contour with a pencil. H. M. showed considerable improvement over several trials. The next day the test was presented again. When asked if he remembered it, H. M. said no, but his performance was better than at the start of the first day (Figure 16-10b). Over three successive days, H. M. never reported recognizing the problem, but his tracings showed memory. If an animal subject showed similar proof of memory, we would have no doubts, because we do not ask our animal subjects whether they recognize the test. Korsakoff patients have also been tested with mirror tracing, and they too retain improvements of performance while failing to show recognition of the task.

Two kinds of findings indicate that the memory problems of H. M. and other patients cannot be attributed solely to difficulties with verbal materials as such. First, such patients also have difficulty in reproducing or recognizing pictures and spatial designs that are not recalled in verbal terms. Second, although the patients have difficulty with the specific content of verbal material, they can learn procedural or rule-based information about verbal material (N. J. Cohen & Squire, 1980). A brief look at this research will make the distinction clear.

by his inability to keep a topic of conversation in mind, especially if there are interruptions. Also, his failure to acquire knowledge about current events or people prevents him from contributing much to conversations. Although N. A. was sexually active before his accident, he has had virtually no sexual contact since. He once made a date with a young woman he met at a picnic, but he failed to remember the appointment until two weeks later, and did not pursue the acquaintanceship further. His relationship with his mother is the dominant feature of his emotional life. He has said that he would have had a wife and family if he had not been injured but now believes that he will not be able to do so.

The only routines that N. A. can perform reliably are ones that he has learned through years of practice. Cooking or other activities that require correct sequencing of steps are very difficult for him. Even watching television is a problem because a commercial interruption may cause him to forget the subject. He spends much of his time tidying around the house, doing small woodworking projects, and assembling models. He constantly arranges objects and shows obsessive concern that everything be in its right place; he is irritated if he finds that anything has been moved. N. A.'s mother says that his obsessiveness and irritability developed since the accident.

Probably he strives for a rigorously stable environment to compensate for his deficient memory.

Despite his handicap, N. A. maintains a generally optimistic view of his life. In part this may reflect the fact that he remembers mainly experiences prior to 1960 when he was successful socially, athletically, and scholastically. Although he has had many frustrating experiences since his accident, these are not remembered in detail, and apparently they do not lead to depression. N. A.'s inability to form memories is as severe as that of patients with Korsakoff's syndrome, but he does not show the apathy, blandness, and loss of initiative that characterize them.

N. A. has formed some verbal memories after the accident, but they are spotty. Thus he knows that "Watergate" signifies some political scandal that took place in "Washington or Florida" but he cannot give any details or tell who was involved. Only occasionally does he write notes or instructions to himself as memory aids, and he tends to lose track of such notes. At one recent session when N. A.'s memory was being tested, he repeatedly tried to recall a question that he wanted to ask the investigator. Finally he searched his pockets and found a note that he had written to himself: "Ask Dr. Squire if my memory is getting better."

Subjects were asked to read successive sets of three moderately long words printed mirror-reversed, like this:

bedraggled   capricious   grandiose

The task is difficult, but subjects improve markedly with practice. No motor skill is involved but rather the ability to deal with abstract rules or procedures. If some words are used repeatedly, normal subjects come to recognize them and to read them easily. Brain-lesioned patient N. A. (see Box 16-1), Korsakoff subjects, and patients who had recently received electroconvulsive shock learned the skill of mirror reading well but showed impaired learning of the specific words and did not recognize the task on successive occasions. Thus the important distinction is probably not between motor and verbal performances but between procedural or rule-based information on the one hand and specific item content or data-based information on the other hand. The patients learned *how* but they did not learn *what*. So it is probably not animals' inability to speak that accounts for their immunity to effects of hippocampal lesions on storing memories.

Even with verbal material, some investigators found that amnesic patients showed fairly good recall with special methods of testing (Warrington & Weiskrantz, 1968). Although confirming that the patients seemed to be unable to learn even simple lists of words after several repetitions, these investigators noticed a curious fact: As the patients were given one list after another, the experimenters began to recognize as familiar many of the wrong responses that their patients produced. Analysis showed that many of the wrong responses were actually words from earlier lists in the experiment. Thus the words were being stored by the patients but were emerging at the wrong time. Further experiments showed that providing cues at the time of recall could substantially improve the performance of amnesic patients (Weiskrantz & Warrington, 1975). This result was taken as evidence that the defect was more in the retrieval than in the storage of memories. This finding may be of value in helping patients with partial destruction of medial temporal structures whose deficits are less severe than those of H. M. Amnesic patients and others who suffer from problems of memory can be aided both by using strategies of encoding and by cuing at retrieval (Poon, 1980; Signoret & Lhermitte, 1976).

A further development of this research was the study of **priming,** that is, aiding recall by presenting a fragment of a previously presented stimulus. A person who has examined a word or a drawing is aided in later recall of that stimulus if a fragment is presented. For example, if a person is shown the word *motor* and is later asked to fill in the blank in ''mo___'' with the first word that comes to mind, the response ''motor'' is more likely than ''motel,'' or ''mother,'' or other possibilities. Such completion performance of amnesic patients is influenced by prior presentation of a word just as much as is the performance of normal subjects. But in spite of showing a normal priming effect, amnesic patients are very poor on a yes/no recognition test for the same stimulus words, that is, they show little or no conscious recognition or representational memory for the words. Furthermore, the performance of normal subjects can be enhanced if they are instructed to use the word fragments as cues to recall the words they had previously examined, but this instruction does not change the performance of the amnesic patients (Graf, Squire, & Mandler, 1984). This and other kinds of evidence have led some investigators to conclude that the priming effect is qualitatively different from other kinds of memory and that priming is spared in amnesia (Schacter, 1985). The existence of a strong priming effect in amnesic patients suggested to some that amnesic patients possess good memories in general but suffer chiefly from difficulties in retrieving memories. Other evidence, however, demonstrates clearly that they are incapable of forming long-term representational memories.

Impairment of Memory in Animals with Hippocampal Lesions

Some investigators have attempted to narrow the gap between human and animal results by finding evidence of impairment of memory storage in animals with hippocampal lesions. Experiments with hippocampectomized animals revealed that they had greater difficulty than normals in abandoning earlier learning or strategies; they showed greater interference of earlier learning on later tasks (for example, see

Douglas, 1967; Kimble, 1968). The persistence of response in the animal subjects agreed with the observation of Warrington and Weiskrantz (1968) concerning persistence of responses from earlier lists of words. The animal subjects also showed difficulty in remembering spatial problems, but most of the results probably reflect difficulty with spatial discrimination of the operated animals rather than impairment of memory.

Recent evidence demonstrates that animals with lesions of the limbic structures do show a dissociation, with specific impairment of memory formation for certain kinds of tasks although not for others. One example is the task of delayed non-matching to sample which we described earlier in the section on developmental approaches. Monkeys with lesions in the amygdala and hippocampus cannot solve the delayed nonmatching problem, just as three-month-old monkeys are unable to solve it. In spite of being incapable of learning this task, the monkeys with limbic lesions performed normally on the concurrent recognition learning task, just as the young monkeys could (Malamut, Saunders, & Mishkin, 1980). Thus the limbic lesions appear to impair the ability to form representational memories. Nor is such research confined to primates. In rats, a T-maze task in which the correct arm in the second run is determined by the response on the first run requires a representational memory of the first run; performance on this task is impaired by limbic lesions (Thomas, 1984).

Thus the results of more discriminating tests of amnesic patients and animal subjects are converging (Zola-Morgan & Squire, 1985). In both amnesic patients and animals with limbic lesions, formation of some kinds of memory is severely impaired while formation of other kinds remains essentially normal. The kind of memory whose formation is impaired in these subjects is called representational or declarative. The kind of memory formation that is spared is called habit or procedural memory. Further findings that bear on human amnesia and proposed animal models for amnesia come from investigation of the sites of brain damage that impair memory, so we turn now to that subject.

Brain Sites in Amnesia

At the same time that some investigators were trying to resolve the apparent discrepancy between results of human and animal research by finding what abilities are lost and what are spared in amnesia, others were taking a different tack; they were examining critically whether the site of the lesion responsible for memory deficits is in fact the hippocampus or some other structure in the limbic system. Some were asking whether all cases of amnesia involve the same brain site(s); for example, is the amnesia of Korsakoff syndrome patients due to damage in the same site(s) as in temporal lobe patients?

Examination of the records of several cases suggested that the crucial site of damage that causes amnesia might be the temporal stem, the fibers that carry the afferent and efferent connections of the temporal cortex and amygdala but not of the hippocampus (Horel, 1978). (For the location of the temporal stem, see Figure 16-8b.) The temporal stem is vulnerable in the surgical approach that was used in the human operations on the medial temporal lobe, like that of H. M. Furthermore, Horel found that when he sectioned the temporal stem in monkeys, without damaging the hippocampus, it caused severe deficits in visual discrimination learning and

(a)

Anterior

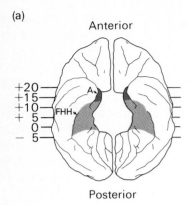

Posterior

(b)

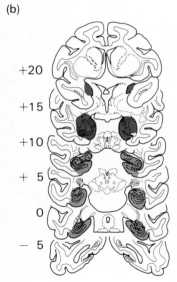

0 10 20 mm

Figure 16-11 Sites of experimental lesions of the amygdala and hippocampus in rhesus monkey brain. (a) The lesions are projected on a ventral view of the brain. The amygdalar lesion (A) is shown in dark brown and the hippocampal lesion (FHH) in light brown. The levels indicated at the left of diagram (a) show where the series of transverse sections in (b) were taken. (Courtesy of Dr. Mortimer Mishkin, Laboratory of Neuropsychology, National Institute of Mental Health)

retention (Horel & Misantone, 1974, 1976). Among the connections of the temporal lobe whose damage might be responsible for the memory defect are those to the medial magnocellular part of the medial dorsal nucleus of the thalamus. Pathology in this nucleus has been strongly implicated in the memory defects that occur in Korsakoff's syndrome (Victor, Adams, & Collins, 1971) and in patient N. A.

An independent indication that damage to the dorsomedial thalamus can impair memory formation comes from the case of the patient N. A. (Squire & Moore, 1979; Teuber, Milner, & Vaughan, 1968). N. A. became amnesic as a result of an accident in which a miniature fending foil entered his brain through the nostril. N. A. is markedly amnesic, primarily for verbal material, and he can give little information about events since his accident in 1960, but he shows almost normal recall for events of the 1940s and 1950s. Computerized tomography scans were made of N. A. in 1978, when the available techniques lacked high resolution. The only indication of damage was in the left dorsal thalamus. There may be damage elsewhere, but damage in the dorsomedial thalamus alone may be sufficient to impair gravely the formation of long-term memories. (The effects of this deficit on N. A.'s daily life are shown in Box 16-1.)

Mishkin (1978) also asked whether temporal lobe damage that impairs memory might involve a structure other than the hippocampus, but he reached a conclusion different from Horel's. Mishkin tested the effects of destroying either the hippocampus or the amygdala or both (Figure 16-11). The subjects were monkeys and the task was the delayed nonmatching to sample task that we saw in Figure 16-7b; in each test trial, one previously seen object was paired with a novel object. The results showed that neither the hippocampus nor the amygdala is essential for acquisition of this task, although destruction of either structure caused somewhat poorer performance than that of normal control animals (see Table 16-2). But monkeys deprived of both structures required far more trials to reacquire this task postoperatively than they had needed to learn it originally. In addition to this failure of recognition memory, animals with the combined ablation were unable to recall on the basis of a single trial whether or not an object had been rewarded. The amygdala and hippocampus share many input and output connections, so it is not surprising that they may be able to serve as alternative pathways between cortical association areas and subcortical targets. This does not mean that the amygdala and the hippocampus are identical in function but only that the functions of the two structures may overlap in an important way in regard to formation of memory.

Table 16-2   Effects of Removal of the Amygdala and the Hippocampus on Memory in Monkeys

Subject	Preoperative		Postoperative	
	Trials	Errors	Trials	Errors
Normal controls	73	24	0	0
Amygdala removed	100	33	140	39
Hippocampus removed	93	25	73	19
Combined removal of amygdala and hippocampus	130	32	987	270

Note: Data are numbers of trials and errors to criterion of 90% correct.
Source: From Mishkin (1978).

In a further study to test the hypotheses of Horel and of Mishkin, two kinds of intervention and two tasks were employed: The temporal stem was transected bilaterally in some monkeys whereas both the amygdala and the hippocampus were ablated bilaterally in others. The animals were tested both on a visual discrimination task and on delayed nonmatching to sample. The results demonstrated a **double dissociation:** Transection of the temporal stem impaired visual discrimination but did not affect ability on the memory task. On the contrary, combined ablation of the amygdala and hippocampus left visual discrimination intact but severely impaired formation of memory. Results of this study favor the hypothesis that destruction of either the amygdala or the hippocampus has only moderate effects on ability to form memories, but that combined lesions of these structures are devastating for memory (Zola-Morgan, Squire, & Mishkin, 1982).

Horel and Mishkin both remind us that the temporal lobe includes several important structures and that investigators showed tunnel vision in concentrating almost exclusively on the hippocampus for 20 years in attempting to explain the temporal lobe amnesic syndrome. Now we should be cautious about concluding that the amygdala and/or hippocampus are involved in all kinds of learning. In fact, a study by Pigareva (1982) reported that in learning to switch the significance of conditioned stimuli, intact rats do more poorly than rats in which both the amygdala and the hippocampus have been largely destroyed!

By now three different laboratories have studied the effects of hippocampal ablation on the delayed nonmatching to sample test. The results are consistent in showing significant impairment compared to control animals, especially as the delay period is extended to over one minute (Squire & Zola-Morgan, 1985). Thus a deficit caused by ablation of the hippocampus alone can be demonstrated in monkeys, even though coupling ablation of the amygdala makes the deficit much more severe.

Postmortem examinations of the brains of some amnesic patients indicate that lesions confined to the hippocampus may cause severe deficits in the ability to form long-term memories. A convincing case of this type has recently been reported (Zola-Morgan, Squire, & Amaral, 1986). The patient was a man who suffered an episode of insufficient blood supply to the brain (ischemia) that followed cardiac bypass surgery. He survived for five years after the operation, and thorough psychological testing showed a severe deficit of memory formation but no signs of dementia or of significant cognitive impairment other than memory. He was very poor on tests such as paired-associate learning and story recall, but he showed intact capacity for priming. When he died at age 57, a thorough examination of the brain was undertaken, using hundreds of serial sections. The examination disclosed a bilateral lesion of the CA1 subfield of the hippocampus; it extended through the entire anterior-posterior length of the hippocampus. Although damage appeared elsewhere, most other brain regions appeared normal, including ones that have been implicated in memory function in other cases: the mammillary bodies, the dorsomedial nucleus of the thalamus, and the amygdala. The investigators conclude that a circumscribed lesion limited to a subfield of the hippocampus can produce a clinically significant impairment of memory. Experimental studies with rats are showing that neurons in the CA1 zone of the hippocampus are especially vulnerable to ischemia of the forebrain and that rats that sustain such damage are severely impaired in memory formation (Volpe, Pulsinelli, & Davis, 1985).

When we first described Korsakoff's syndrome, we mentioned that the dorsomedial thalamus and the mammillary bodies have been implicated in its memory deficit. It has therefore been suggested by some workers that damage to these diencephalic sites causes Korsakoff's amnesia, whereas damage to quite different sites causes temporal lobe amnesia. Research with animals shows clear deficits in memory following lesions confined to the dorsomedial nucleus of the thalamus (Aggleton & Mishkin, 1983; Zola-Morgan & Squire, 1985a). With regard to involvement of the mammillary bodies, the picture to date is less clear (Zola-Morgan & Squire, 1985b).

Other workers, however, claim that the specific sites are linked into a single brain system required for memory formation and that there is neither anatomical nor behavioral evidence for different kinds of amnesia. Weiskrantz (1985) argues for this unitary position. Among other evidence to support it, he cites a recent study by von Cramon et al. (1985) on the location of thalamic damage due to strokes, which is associated with well-studied amnesic conditions. The location of the damage, established by computerized tomograms, is shown in Figure 16-12. The area of damage common to all seven patients (shown by the colored area in the figure) is almost entirely outside of the dorsomedial nucleus of the thalamus but includes the entry of the mammillothalamic tract and another fiber tract (ILA) that carries projections from the temporal lobe cortex and amygdala to the dorsomedial thalamus. Thus these patients suffered damage both to midline connections (the fornix-fimbria system, connecting to the hippocampus and to the mammillothalamic tract) and to temporal lobe structures (among which amygdalar connections relay to and from the frontal cortex through thalamic nuclei). There may thus be a single large system required for formation of long-term representational memories and subject to disconnection by damage at various points. This is a topic of much current research and controversy and to which study of both amnesic patients and animal subjects is steadily contributing.

Are There Different Types of Amnesia?

Just as there is controversy about whether there is only one brain system required for formation of memories, so there continues to be dispute as to whether there is one basic kind of amnesia, as Weiskrantz (1985) and others maintain, or more than one, as Zola-Morgan and Squire (1985) and others claim. Attempting to solve this problem is complicated by the fact that human cases of amnesia are usually mixed with other symptoms and that the pattern may change with the severity of the deficits.

No one doubts that a person with Korsakoff's syndrome can be distinguished from a person who suffers from a temporal lobe memory deficit, but the distinctive differences may not involve memory formation. For example, Korsakoff patients are unable to solve certain problems that temporal lobe patients perform readily (Lhermitte & Signoret, 1976), but this may reflect the fact that frontal lobe cortex is also impaired in Korsakoff patients; that is, different disorders may frequently occur together in certain kinds of patients, but this does not prove that these symptoms have the same cause or that they are obligatorily related. For this reason investigators have been attempting to find whether there are different kinds of memory disorders when memory is clearly separated from other functions.

Figure 16-12 Regions of the thalamus related to memory loss in human patients; the upper illustrations (a) show horizontal sections through the inferior thalamus, and the lower illustrations (b) show sections through the middle thalamic region. The colored areas are the areas of damage shared by all seven amnesic patients in the study; damage was defined by CAT scans. The dark gray area is the region served by the polar and paramedian thalamic arteries; obstructions of these arteries caused the damage to these patients.

The following structures are shown for orientation: AC, position of the anterior commissure, which is also shown as Ca; PC, position of the posterior commissure, which is also shown as Cp; F, fornix; GP, globus pallidus; Put, putamen. The distance between AC and PC is 25 mm. Sites within the thalamus are: Co, commissural nuclei; M, dorsomedial nucleus; IML, internal medullary lamina. The sites crucial for amnesia appear to be the fiber tracts of IML and the mammillothalamic tract which lies just lateral to IML in the colored area in the anterior part of (a). Two patients with large lesions in M but with these tracts intact did not show memory dysfunction. (Adapted from von Cramon, Hebel, and Schuri, 1985)

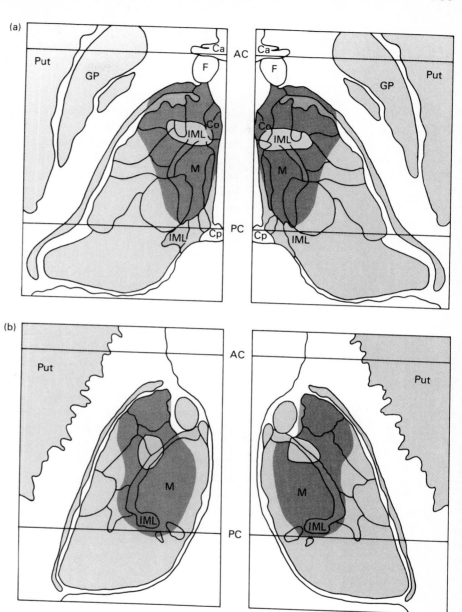

A problem in these studies is that the capacities and inabilities of a class of patients may change with the severity of the condition. For example, Alzheimer's disease patients show changes in their capacities to form memories as the disease progresses. A frequently used test involves learning and later recalling a list of 20 pairs of words. Normal subjects learn most easily the pairs at the start of the list (the ''primacy effect'') and at the end of the list (the ''recency effect''); learning and recall of the middle are poorer because of interference effects. Early in Alzheimer's disease, patients do not show the normal primacy effect but still benefit from the recency effect. As the disease progresses, even the recency effect is lost, and eventually the patient becomes unable to learn any of the list.

One clear example of a distinction between disorders of memory has to do with deficits of short-term versus long-term memory formation. Most of the research on memory deficits has dealt with problems of formation of long-term memories, but a few patients have been found whose main difficulties are with short-term memory (Warrington, 1982); that is, they have difficulty forming short-term memories, but once these are formed, long-term retention is normal. These patients are thus quite different from temporal lobe patients, such as H. M., who have no difficulty with short-term memory but who fail to form long-term memories. Little is known so far about the neurological involvement of the patients with deficits of short-term memory.

Patients also differ in the extent to which their difficulties involve memories that were formed before the brain damage that caused amnesia. Korsakoff syndrome patients show extensive retrograde as well as anterograde amnesia. On the other hand, patients with temporal lobe involvement, such as H. M., usually show only a moderate period of retrograde amnesia, although their anterograde amnesia is severe. For example, H. M., who became amnesic in 1953, is very poor at recognizing photographs of faces that appeared in the newspapers in the 1950s and 1960s, but he made normal scores on photographs from the 1940s and 1930s. In contrast, patients who were afflicted with Korsakoff's syndrome in the 1950s are markedly impaired in recognizing photographs from the 1940s and 1930s just as they are for later ones. Other evidence also supports the conclusion that impairment of retrograde memory is dissociable from impairment of anterograde memory (Zola-Morgan & Squire, 1985). As yet, however, many case reports still do not evaluate retrograde impairment adequately; they employ only interviews or multiple-choice methods, whereas sensitive formal tests are required. Where there are pervasive impairments in retrograde as well as anterograde memories, it has been suggested that the difficulty may be in retrieval processes rather than in storage of memories. Attempts to find separate neurological bases for retrograde and anterograde amnesia may yet be productive, if they make use of the best neuropsychological as well as the best neuroanatomical techniques.

Research to date provides presumptive evidence that there is more than one kind of amnesia for representational memories. A further distinction may involve deficits in forming or recalling procedural memories or "habits." In the next chapter we will see that formation of conditioned responses involving the striated musculature in mammals appears to involve a circuit that includes the deep nuclei in the cerebellum. Thus there are likely to be different kinds of amnesia and different brain locations involved in them, and further research in the coming years should do much to clarify these issues.

Summary · Main Points

1. The abilities to learn and remember affect all behaviors that are characteristically human, and it appears that every animal species is capable of some learning and memory. Whereas evolution by natural selection brings about adaptation over successive generations, learning permits prompt adaptation within the lifetime of the individual.

2. Learning includes both nonassociative forms, such as habituation, sensitization, and imprinting, and associative forms, such as classical (Pavlovian) conditioning and instrumental learning.

3. Some learning results in the formation of habits (gaining procedural knowledge, or "learning *how*") whereas other learning results in formational of representational memories (gaining declarative knowledge, or "learning *that*"). Abilities to form habits and memories appear to mature at different rates and to be dependent on different brain circuits.

4. Memories are often classified by how long they last. Frequently used classifications include iconic, short-term, intermediate-term, and long-term. Some disorders of memory affect particularly one or another temporal classification.

5. The capacity for associative learning is now seen to be very widely distributed among animal species. The evolution of powerful and flexible brain mechanisms of learning and memory may have resulted from the earlier development of precise and elaborate systems to handle specific sensorimotor adjustments and then from the extension of these systems for more general use.

6. The ability to form long-term representational memories develops more slowly than the ability to form long-term habits. The "amnesia of early childhood" is a phenomenon that humans share with other species that are born in a relatively immature state.

7. Patients with Korsakoff's disease show gaps in memory, which they may attempt to fill by confabulation; this syndrome involves severe retrograde as well as anterograde amnesia and impairment in encoding new information.

8. Some patients with damage to the medial temporal lobe show particular impairment in consolidation of long-term representational memories. Recent research has focused both on the kind of memory test and on the sites of brain damage. Hippocampal lesions in people and animals impair formation of representational memories but spare formation of habits (procedural memories). Damage to the amygdala intensifies the impairment caused by damage to the hippocampus.

Recommended Reading

Lynch, G., McGaugh, J. L., & Weinberger, N. M. (Eds.). (1984). *Neurobiology of learning and memory*. New York: Guilford Press.

McGaugh, J. L., Weinberger, N. M., & Lynch, G. (Eds.). (1988). *Brain organization and memory: Cells, systems, and circuits*. New York: Oxford University Press.

Olton, D. S., Gamzu, E., & Corkin, S. (Eds.). (1985). *Annals of the New York Academy of Sciences: Vol. 444. Memory dysfunctions: An integration of animal and human research from preclinical and clinical perspectives*. New York: New York Academy of Sciences.

Squire, L. R., & Butters, N. (Eds.). (1984). *Neuropsychology of memory*. New York: Guilford Press.

Weinberger, N. W., McGaugh, J. L., & Lynch, G. (Eds.). (1985). *Memory systems of the brain*. New York: Guilford Press.

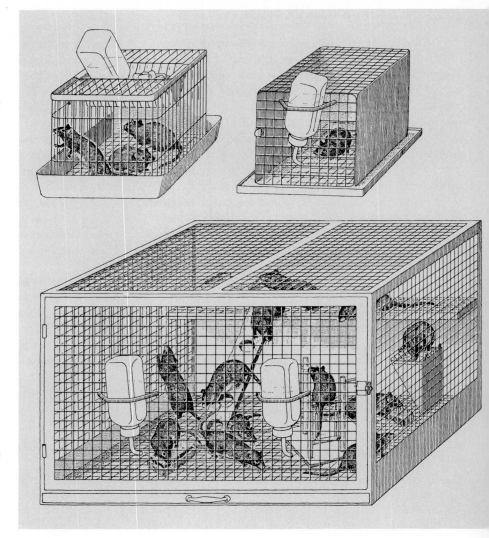

17 Neural Mechanisms of Learning and Memory

I sometimes feel, in reviewing the evidence on the localization of the memory trace, that the necessary conclusion is that learning just is not possible.
—Karl S. Lashley (1950, p. 477).

In the past generation, understanding of the biological basis of learning and memory has undergone a revolution. It now seems possible to identify the circuits and networks that participate in learning and memory, localize the sites of memory storage, and analyze the cellular and molecular mechanisms of memory. The roots of this new understanding lie in advances made by several different disciplines: psychology, behavioral neuroscience, network analysis and cognitive science, and neurobiology.
—Richard F. Thompson (1986, p. 941).

ORIENTATION

A dramatic turnabout is revealed by the contrast between the two statements above, made a generation apart by two prominent investigators. This chapter presents some of the main advances that have marked this revolution. It deals mainly with *how* learning and formation of memory occur—the detailed neural mechanisms—whereas the last chapter stressed *where* in the nervous system learning and memory occur. The presentation will focus on three main topics:

1. What are the basic biological mechanisms for long-term storage of memories in the nervous system? To what extent are the same mechanisms used in different species?
2. What are mechanisms of storage of different durations (short-term and intermediate-term in contrast to long-term)? What stages occur in the formation of long-term memory?
3. What mechanisms modulate (facilitate or inhibit) learning and formation of memory? (Some neural, hormonal, and transmitter systems that do not play a direct role in learning and memory storage have been implicated in modulating these processes.)

Early Findings of Brain Changes with Training and Experience

A series of studies that began in the late 1950s found that both formal training and informal experience in varied environments led to measurable changes in neurochemistry and neuroanatomy of the rodent brain (Renner & Rosenzweig, 1987; Rosenzweig, 1984). The work had been undertaken originally to find whether individual differences in problem-solving ability among rats might be correlated with a brain measure, the level of activity of the enzyme acetylcholinesterase (AChE) in the cerebral cortex. Positive correlations were obtained between these two measures, but an unexpected finding also emerged: The mere experience of being trained and tested caused changes in the level of activity of AChE in the cerebral cortex. Furthermore, the more difficult the behavioral test that had been used with a particular group, the higher its levels of cortical AChE tended to be (Rosenzweig, Krech, & Bennett, 1961). These findings surprised the investigators, who had supposed that the level of enzyme would be a fixed characteristic of each animal; instead behavioral testing itself had altered the brain characteristic that was being measured! Since the possibility of measuring a change in the brain due to experience seemed even more interesting than the correlational work, the study was soon redirected into an investigation of brain responses to differential experience.

Instead of giving differential experience by running rats through problem-solving tests, which is a time-consuming and expensive procedure, the investigators decided to house the animals in different environments that would provide differential opportunities for informal learning (Figure 17-1). Littermates of the same sex were assigned by a random procedure to various laboratory environments, the three most commonly used being the following:

1. The standard colony (SC) situation with three animals in a standard laboratory cage provided with food and water. This condition is the one in which laboratory rodents are typically kept in behavioral and biological laboratories.

Figure 17-1 Laboratory environments that provide differential opportunities for informal learning. (a) Standard colony environment with 3 rats per cage. (b) Impoverished environment with an isolated rat. (c) Enriched laboratory environment with 10–12 rats per cage and a variety of stimulus objects. (From M. R. Rosenzweig, E. L. Bennett, and M. C. Diamond, "Brain changes in response to experience." Copyright © 1972 by Scientific American, Inc. All rights reserved.)

(a)

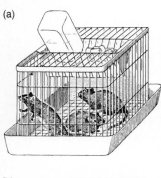

(b)

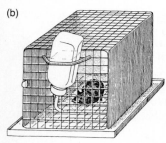

(c)

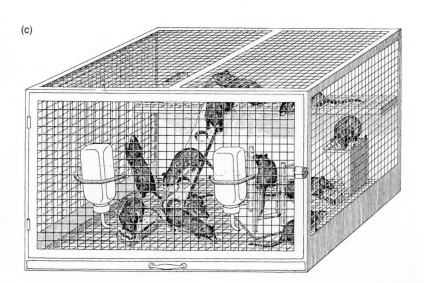

Figure 17-2 Dissection of rat brain into standard samples for measurement of effects of experience. (a) Dorsal view of brain with calibrated plastic T square used to delimit samples of specific cortical regions. (b) Transverse section of brain.

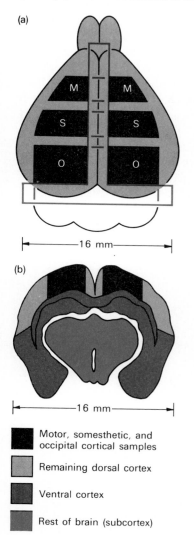

(a)

—16 mm—

(b)

—16 mm—

■ Motor, somesthetic, and occipital cortical samples

Remaining dorsal cortex

Ventral cortex

Rest of brain (subcortex)

2. A large cage containing groups of 10 to 12 animals and a variety of stimulus objects, which were changed daily. This condition was called the **enriched condition** (EC) because it provided greater opportunities for informal learning than did the SC condition.
3. SC-size cages housing single animals; this condition was called the **impoverished condition** or isolated condition (IC).

In the initial experiments of this series, rats were assigned to the differential conditions at weaning (about 25 days after birth), and they were kept in the conditions for 80 days. In later experiments both the age at assignment and the duration of the period of differential experience were varied.

At the end of the period of differential experience, each brain was dissected into standard samples for chemical analysis (Figure 17-2). In the initial experiments, animals in the enriched condition (EC) developed greater cortical AChE than did their littermates in IC. Moreover, control experiments showed that this effect could not be attributed to either greater handling of the EC animals or greater locomotor activity in the EC situation (Rosenzweig, Krech, & Bennett, 1961). Enzymatic activity was measured by dividing total activity by the weight of the tissue sample—AChE/weight. Scrutiny of the data then revealed that the experimental groups differed not only in total enzymatic activity but also in weight of the cortical samples: The EC animals developed a greater weight of the cerebral cortex than did their littermates in IC (Rosenzweig et al., 1962). This result was a real surprise, because since the beginning of the century it had been accepted that brain weight is a very stable characteristic of the organism and not subject to environmental influences.

Further experiments showed the brain weight differences to be extremely reliable, although small in percentage terms. Moreover, these differences were not uniformly distributed throughout the cerebral cortex. They were almost invariably largest in occipital cortex and smallest in the adjacent somesthetic cortex. The rest of the brain outside the cerebral cortex tended to show very little effect.

The differences in cortical weights among groups were then related to differences in cortical thickness; that is, animals exposed to the EC environment developed slightly thicker cerebral cortices than did their littermates in other conditions (Diamond, 1976; Diamond, Krech, & Rosenzweig, 1964). More refined neuroanatomical measures were then undertaken; these included counts of dendritic spines, measures of dendritic branching, and measurement of size of synaptic contacts. All three measures were taken on pyramidal cells in the occipital cortex. Each of these measures showed significant effects of differential experience, as we will see in the next sections of this chapter.

Effects of Experience on Synapses

The idea that learning and memory might be mediated by the formation of new synaptic contacts has had its ups and downs. It was proposed in the 1890s and was supported by such eminent investigators as Ramón y Cajal (1894) and Sherrington (1897). But then the hypothesis waned, since no concrete evidence was produced to back it up. In 1965, Eccles (the neurophysiologist who shared the Nobel Prize in 1963) remained firm in his belief that learning and memory storage involve "growth just of bigger and better synapses that are already there, not growth of new

Table 17-1 Effects of Experience on Numbers of Dendritic Spines: Percentage Differences Between EC and IC Groups

Apical dendrites	0.2
Terminal dendrites	3.1*
Oblique dendrites	3.6*
Basal dendrites	9.7**

Source: From A. Globus, M. R. Rosenzweig, E. L. Bennett, and M. C. Diamond. "Effects of differential experience on dendritic spine counts in rat cerebral cortex." *Journal of Comparative and Physiological Psychology,* 1973, 82(2):175–181. Copyright 1973 by the American Psychological Association. Reprinted by permission of the publisher and the authors.

$*p < .05, **p < .01$

connections." It was only in the 1970s that experiments with laboratory rats assigned to enriched or impoverished environments produced evidence to test this hypothesis.

Dendritic spines were shown in Chapters 2 and 3 to be a late aspect of the development of neurons and to be affected by experience. When dendritic spines were counted in EC-IC experiments, numbers of spines per unit of length of dendrite were found to be significantly greater in EC than in IC animals (Globus et al., 1973). This effect was not obtained uniformly over the dendritic tree; rather it was most pronounced for basal dendrites, as shown in Table 17-1. Different aspects of the dendritic tree receive inputs from different sources, and the basal dendrites of these cells have been shown to receive input especially from adjacent neurons in the same region. Thus it appears that enriched experience leads to development of increased numbers of synaptic contacts and richer, more complex intracortical networks.

Following the lead of these experiments, William Greenough also placed laboratory rats in SC, EC, and IC environments and looked for anatomical effects. Greenough quantified **dendritic branching** by methods shown in Figure 17-3. EC animals were shown to develop significantly greater dendritic branching than IC animals (Greenough & Volkmar, 1973; Volkmar & Greenough, 1972). The SC

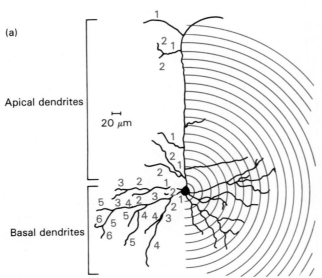
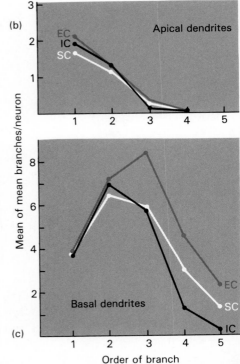

Figure 17-3 Measurement of dendritic branching. Using an enlarged photograph of a neuron, branching is quantified either by counting the number of branches of different orders, as shown in the left in (a), or by counting the numbers of intersections with concentric rings, as shown to the right in (a). The results of (b) and (c) were obtained by the first of these methods. They show significant differences in branching between rats kept for 30 days in enriched, standard colony, or impoverished environments. (From Greenough, 1976)

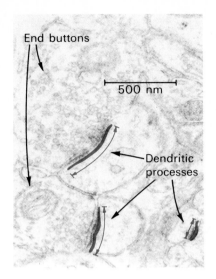

End buttons

500 nm

Dendritic processes

Figure 17-4 Measurement of the size of synaptic contacts. Contacts can be measured on electron micrographs in terms of the length of the thickened region (shown in brown) of the post-synaptic membrane. Note that the end buttons contain many small synaptic vesicles and occasional large mitochondria.

values fell in between and tended to be closer to the IC than to the EC values. With enriched experience each cell did not send its dendrites out further but instead tended to fill its allotted volume more densely with branches. These results together with those of the dendritic spine counts indicate that the enriched-experience animals become equipped with more elaborate information-processing circuits. More direct measures of numbers of synapses and neurons were then made by more refined techniques (Turner & Greenough, 1985). The results showed that in layers I to IV of occipital cortex, the EC rats had about 9400 synapses per neuron versus about 7600 for IC rats—a difference of over 20% ($p < .02$). The value for SC rats was intermediate but closer to the IC level. These results provide strong support for the view that learning and long-term memory involve the formation of new synaptic contacts.

The size of synaptic contacts has also been shown to change as a result of differential experience. The mean length of the postsynaptic thickening (Figure 17-4) has been found to be significantly greater in EC rats than in their IC littermates (Diamond et al., 1975; Greenough & West, 1972). The increased size and number of synaptic contacts probably increases the certainty of synaptic transmission in those circuits that are affected.

We now see some reasons for the increased weight and thickness of the cerebral cortex reported earlier. The greater number of dendritic branches is probably the main factor, since in cortical pyramidal cells the dendrites account for about 95% of the bulk of the cell. Both the cell body and the nucleus of these neurons are significantly larger in the EC animals (Diamond et al., 1975); the larger cell body and nucleus are probably needed to sustain the larger dendritic tree and its more active metabolism. There also appears to be an increase in the number of glial cells in the EC animals, perhaps to provide metabolic support to the more active neurons (Diamond et al., 1966; Szeligo & Leblond, 1977).

There is good reason to believe that the cerebral changes caused by experience in differential environments reflect the different amounts of learning that occur in these environments. Further experiments employing formal training versus control procedures soon showed that formal training produced effects similar to those of enriched informal experience on cortical weights and brain chemistry (Bennett, 1976; Bennett et al., 1979) and on dendritic branching (Chang & Greenough, 1982; Greenough, 1976).

The finding that measurable changes could be induced in the brain by experience, even in adult animals, was one of several factors that led increasing numbers of investigators to try to find in more detail how the nervous system reacts to training and how new information can be stored by the nervous system. Another factor was the growing knowledge of development of the nervous system on a cellular level, and the long-established surmise that changes accompanying learning might be similar to those that occur in development. Increasing technical capacities to examine nerve cells—electrophysiologically, neuroanatomically, and neurochemically—also favored this trend. One last factor was the growing interest in the behavior and nervous systems of invertebrate species. Certain invertebrates have furnished especially interesting ''model systems'' for the study of neural mechanisms of learning and memory, as we will soon see. First, however, let us consider briefly how new information might be stored in the nervous system.

Possible Mechanisms of Memory Storage

How are neural circuits modified during learning? What kinds of modifications persist to provide the basis for memories? From the time that synaptic junctions were discovered toward the end of the last century, many investigators have suggested that synaptic changes could be the mechanisms of memory storage. As knowledge of synaptic anatomy and chemistry has increased, hypotheses have become more numerous and more precise. Both changes in existing synapses and changes in numbers of synapses have been proposed; Figure 17-5 presents some of these hypotheses. Each will be considered in the following discussions.

Physiological Changes at Synapses

Many physiological changes during learning could alter the postsynaptic response to a presynaptic impulse at existing synapses. The charge could be either presynaptic or postsynaptic or possibly both. One possibility is that the number of transmitter molecules released per nerve impulse could increase, thus altering the response of the postsynaptic cell; this idea is depicted at (a) in Figure 17-5. A change in release of transmitter could be caused by chemical changes within the end bouton. It could

Figure 17-5 Diagrammatic portrayal of synaptic changes that could provide bases for storage of memory. (a) After training, each nerve impulse in the relevant neural circuit causes increased release of transmitter molecules (symbolized by brown dots). The size of the postsynaptic potential (PSP), indicated in the small graph, therefore increases. (b) An interneuron (shown in brown) modulates the polarization of the axon terminal and causes release of more transmitter molecules per nerve impulse. (c) Modification of the postsynaptic receptor membrane (shown in brown) causes a larger response to the same amount of transmitter release. (d) The size of the synaptic contact area increases with training. (e) A neural circuit being used more often (the one shown in brown) increases the number of synaptic contacts. (f) A more frequently used neural pathway (shown in brown) takes over synaptic sites formerly occupied by a less active competitor.

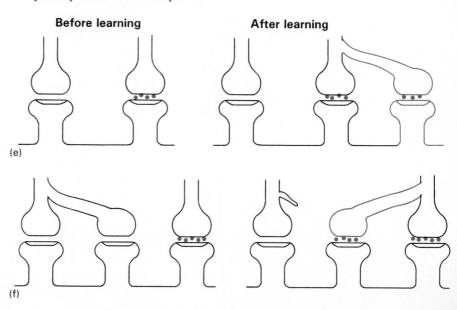

also be caused by the influence of terminals on the end boutons, as shown in (b) of Figure 17-5; they could alter the polarization of the boutons. The responsiveness or sensitivity of the postsynaptic endings could also change, for example, by an increase in the number of receptor molecules, so that the same amount of transmitter release would initiate a larger effect. This situation is indicated in (c) of Figure 17-5.

Structural Changes

Structural changes at existing synapses could also provide memory mechanisms. In many parts of the body, use causes structural changes; these changes are well known in the cases of muscles and bone. In somewhat the same way, the synaptic contact area could increase or decrease as a function of training (see Figure 17-5d).

We do not have to limit ourselves to existing synapses in hypothesizing changes induced by experience. Training could lead to an increase in the number of terminals for the pathway being used, as shown in Figure 17-5e, or it could cause a more used pathway to take over endings formerly occupied by a less active competitor (see Figure 17-5f).

Limitations and Qualifications to Synaptic Models of Memory

Our treatment of synaptic models up to this point should be tempered by three considerations.

First, single synapses are tiny subunits of neural systems. Most behaviors of vertebrates depend on the cooperative action of thousands or millions of neurons (each with tens of thousands of synaptic inputs) and not on a decision by one ''pontifical cell.''

Second, for some functions at least, it may not be possible to find behavioral correlates by examining responses of cellular units; only sets or ensembles of neurons may yield correlates of some behaviors (John, 1978). In Chapter 5 we used the analogy of card displays in a cheering section at a football game, where looking at one or a few cards cannot reveal the pattern made by hundreds of cards. The same conclusion can be drawn for many sensory fields. This possibility should also be kept in mind as we consider many of the attempts to trace learning and memory to synaptic mechanisms. Certainly the behavior of ensembles depends on unit activity, but it is not entirely reducible to activity of units.

Third, we have mentioned only increases in synaptic effects with training. Actually changes in the opposite direction could just as well mediate learning and memory, since both making and breaking contacts alter circuits. You cannot build a circuit by subtracting contacts, but you can modify an existing one. So listing ways of increasing synaptic activity or numbers should be considered only as shorthand notation for ''increasing or decreasing.''

Memory Formation Within Single Neurons?

The idea that changes at synaptic junctions between neurons provide the basis of memory is widely accepted. But a few investigators have made the unorthodox suggestion that changes *within* neurons may account for at least part of the memory capacity of the nervous system. Among these investigators are E. N. Sokolov and his collaborators at the University of Moscow (Sinz, Grechenko, & Sokolov, 1983), who have worked with isolated nerve cells taken from snails. These cells can be stimulated either by chemical substances applied to various sites on the cell body or by electrical pulses. It has been reported that if a subthreshold amount of acetylcholine (ACh) is regularly followed by a suprathreshold intracellular electrical pulse, then the chemical stimulus becomes capable of evoking an action potential. This change shows the basic features of classical conditioning. It occurs only if the unconditioned stimulus (the electrical pulse) follows the conditioned stimulus (ACh) within 120 milliseconds and does not occur if the CS and US are presented in reversed order, noncontiguously, or separately. Thus habituation and sensitization cannot account for the results, and associative learning seems to have occurred. The conditioning extinguishes after several minutes, and extinction can be hastened by eliciting trials that are not reinforced by the US. Following extinction the response can be reconditioned more rapidly than in the original series.

The investigators suggest that the conditioning produces a greater number of active sites on the membrane, but it may be that the change is in the sensitivity of existing sites. The discovery of conditioning within single neurons demonstrates, according to these investigators, that the synaptic model of the memory trace is not the only possible one. This may be so, but fuller reports from the Moscow laboratory and attempts at confirmation from other laboratories will be necessary for evaluation of the novel hypothesis that the information-processing capacities of the neurons include the formation of memories.

Another investigator who finds evidence that crucial changes in learning occur in the neuronal membrane is Alkon (1985, 1988), whose research is reviewed on pages 679–680.

Mechanisms of Habituation and Sensitization in Simple Systems

The first forms of learning to be investigated at a cellular level were habituation and sensitization. These are probably the simplest and most ubiquitous forms of learning, as we mentioned in Chapter 16. Although they are relatively simple, they are also important in everyday life. In analyzing these two forms of learning at the cellular level, investigators have sought to answer three questions:

1. Are the crucial changes distributed diffusely through the circuit for the behavior or are they limited to specific sites in the circuit?
2. Can the mechanisms be specified in molecular and anatomical terms?
3. How do the sites and mechanisms of short-term habituation (lasting from minutes to hours) relate to those of long-term habituation (lasting from days to weeks)?

In addition, they have asked recently whether mechanisms of associative learning can be derived from the mechanisms of nonassociative learning.

Habituation, you will recall, means becoming insensitive to stimuli that have no special significance or consequence for current behavior. The mechanisms of habituation have been studied in intact mammals, in spinal preparations of mammals, and in simpler invertebrate systems. Invertebrate preparations are now being used extensively because they offer several advantages:

Figure 17-6 Identified nerve cells in a ganglion of an invertebrate, the sea hare *Aplysia*. Dorsal view of the abdominal ganglion with several identified neurons labeled. Neurons included in the circuit for habituation (Figure 17-7) are labeled in brown. (From Frazier et al., 1967, and Koester and Kandel, unpublished)

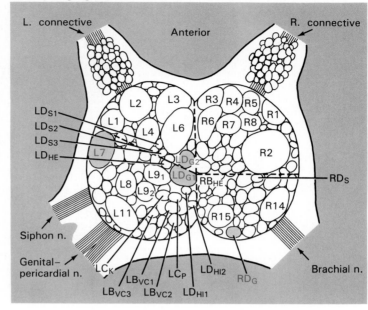

1. The number of nerve cells in a ganglion is relatively small compared to that in a mammal, although the number in the invertebrate ganglion is still of the order of 1000.
2. In the anatomy of the invertebrate ganglion, the cell bodies form the outside and the dendritic processes are on the inside. This arrangement differs from that in the mammal, and it makes it easy to identify and record from cells of invertebrates.
3. Many individual cells in invertebrate ganglia can be recognized both because of their shapes and sizes and because the cellular structure of the ganglion is uniform from individual to individual of the species (Figure 17-6). Thus it is possible to identify certain cells and to trace out their sensory and motor connections. Hence when one isolates a ganglion in a particular invertebrate, one already knows the basic connections of many of the larger cell bodies. Recent work has also shown that the large identifiable cells differ from each other in the neurotransmitters they contain as well as in their connections.

Mechanisms of Habituation in Aplysia

When the complete circuit of a response has been traced out, it is possible to investigate the site or sites where habituation occurs. Figure 17-7 diagrams an invertebrate neural circuit in which habituation has been studied in the large sea snail *Aplysia*. This circuit includes neurons in the abdominal ganglion, shown in Figure 17-6.

Eric Kandel and his collaborators have conducted a major program of experimentation on synaptic processes of habituation and sensitization in *Aplysia* (Kandel,

Figure 17-7 Diagram of the basic
neural circuits involved in the gill-
withdrawal reflex of *Aplysia* and its
habituation. A monosynaptic circuit is
shown in dark brown; it starts at sensory neurons with endings in the siphon and mantle shelf, synapses on
neuron L7, and runs to motor endings
in the gill. Other monosynaptic circuits run through cells LD$_{G1}$, LD$_{G2}$,
and so forth. Polysynaptic links occur
through excitatory interneurons L22
and L23 and inhibitory interneuron
L16. (Adapted from Kupfermann,
Carew, and Kandel, 1974)

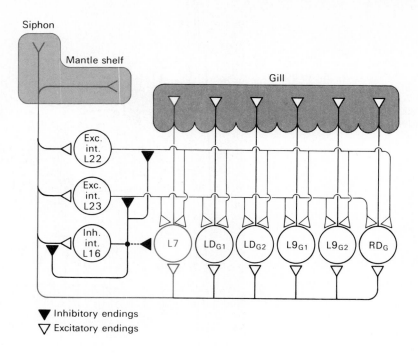

1976, 1979; Kandel et al., 1986). Figure 17-8 shows some of *Aplysia*'s characteristic behaviors as it moves across the bottom of shallow bodies of seawater. The
animal's gill is usually spread out on the back, protected only by a light mantle
shelf, and the siphon is extended in order to draw in water and circulate it over the
gill. If anything touches the mantle shelf or the siphon, the animal retracts its gill so
that it is much smaller and less vulnerable. This gill-withdrawal reflex is controlled
by the abdominal ganglion illustrated in Figure 17-6. For experimental purposes a
preparation is often made that consists of the siphon, mantle shelf, gill, and the
sensory and motor nerves connecting these structures to the abdominal ganglion.
With these structures fixed in position, the experimenters can stimulate the siphon
or mantle with precisely calibrated jets of water at precisely determined times, and
they can accurately record the size of the gill-withdrawal reflex.

The gill-withdrawal reflex habituates readily upon repeated stimulation; moreover, this habituation has all the characteristics that have been found for habituation
in human beings and other animals. *Aplysia* shows sensitization as well as habituation; when the animal is presented with a painful stimulus to the head, the gill-
withdrawal reflex is greatly enhanced. The close correspondence between the characteristics of habituation and sensitization in *Aplysia* and these behaviors in mammals justifies our looking further into the neural mechanisms of these behaviors in
Aplysia, even if we are not particularly interested in this sea snail in itself.

Site and Mechanism of Short-Term Habituation

Pinpointing the site of habituation for the gill-withdrawal response of *Aplysia* has
been accomplished, and the goal of spelling out the neurochemical mechanisms of

the habituation is well advanced. To accomplish this goal Kandel and his collaborators tested several possible loci of altered activity. As had been found for the mammal, habituation was not caused by receptor adaptation or by either fatigue of the muscles or depression of the junctions between motor neurons and muscles.

Turning then to the ganglion, the experimenters found that intracellular recordings from the motor neurons did show decreases in firing rates during the course of habituation. The decreased firing rate of the motor neuron could reflect either an increase of the input resistance (decreased sensitivity) of the motor neuron or a change in synaptic input to the motor neuron. The threshold of the motor neuron for initiating a spike was found to remain constant during habituation, so the change in habituation could not be attributed to altered resistance of the postsynaptic membrane.

The excitatory postsynaptic potentials (EPSPs) to synaptic input were found to decrease progressively during repeated sensory stimulation, and this decrease could account for the decreased firing rate of the motor neuron during habituation. With a period of rest and no stimulation, the amplitude of the EPSPs recovers. Depression of the EPSPs caused by repeated stimulation of one part of the receptive field (such as the siphon) did not cause a decrease of the EPSPs to stimulation of another part of the sensory field (for instance, the mantle), so the depression is strictly localized. The contribution of the interneurons to the EPSPs of the motor cells was small relative to the monosynaptic pathway, so the effect must be localized chiefly at the monosynaptic sensorimotor junctions. The depression of the EPSPs was found to be caused by a decrease in the number of quanta of synaptic transmitter released by each sensory impulse; the size of the individual quanta remained constant. This feature was determined by studying the variability in the EPSPs, which are graded in quantal units, that is, units of fixed size. The change in the amount of transmitter released upon arrival of a nerve impulse is, you will recall, one of the hypothesized mechanisms of memory ([a] in Figure 17-5).

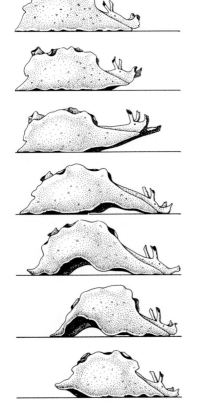

Figure 17-8 Some behaviors of *Aplysia*. (a) Locomotion. (b) Usual posture with the siphon extended and the gill spread out on the back. Ordinarily only the tip of the siphon would be visible in a lateral view, but here the rest of the siphon and the gill are shown as if the animal were transparent. (c) Retraction of the siphon and of the gill in response to a light touch. (d) Retraction of the head and release of ink in response to a strong stimulus. (From *Cellular basis of behavior: An introduction to behavioral neurobiology* by Eric R. Kandel. W. H. Freeman and Company. Copyright © 1976.)

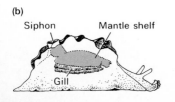

Siphon   Mantle shelf

Gill

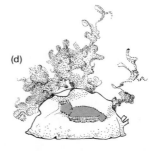

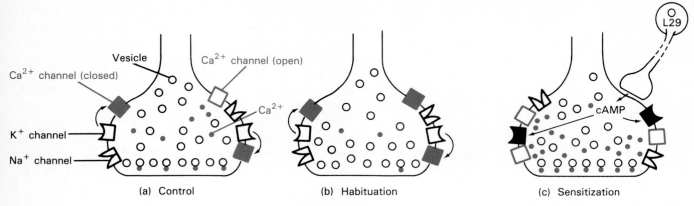

Figure 17-9 Hypothesized presynaptic mechanisms of habituation and sensitization. Axon terminals are represented in control, habituated, and sensitized conditions. Their membranes are studded with a variety of specialized channels. In the control condition, most of the K^+ channels are open, and this tends to inhibit the Ca^{2+} channels. (Closed channels are indicated by solid symbols.) Ca^{2+} is required for vesicles to bind to release sites and thus liberate the transmitter into the synaptic cleft. In habituation repeated impulses decrease the number of open Ca^{2+} channels, and therefore there is little binding of vesicles and release of transmitter. In sensitization the activity of a modulatory neuron causes release of the second messenger cAMP inside the axon terminal; this closes K^+ channels and allows Ca^{2+} channels to open. More release sites then become available. (Adapted from Klein and Kandel, 1980)

Within this neural circuit, then, the alteration due to habituation was precisely localized, and it occurs mainly at one site—the presynaptic terminals on the motor nerve. Thus although the anatomy of the circuit is determined and fixed, the gain of the sensorimotor synapses can be modified.

The depression in transmitter release at the synapses involves, at least in part, a decrease in the number of calcium ions (Ca^{2+}) that flow into the terminals of the sensory neurons with each action potential. Repeated stimulation of the sensory neuron produces prolonged inactivation of the channels by which Ca^{2+} enters the neuron; this is represented in Figure 17-9b by an additional closed Ca^{2+} channel. The Ca^{2+} influx helps to determine how many vesicles bind to release sites and therefore how much transmitter is released by each action potential. A decrease in Ca^{2+} influx results in diminished transmitter release and therefore in decreased excitatory postsynaptic potentials (Klein, Shapiro, & Kandel, 1980).

Long-Term Habituation

Long-term habituation in *Aplysia* involves a change in the anatomy as well as the neurochemistry of the sensory neuron synapses. These presynaptic terminals have active zones, that is, regions of the membrane from which the synaptic transmitter can be released. These active zones can be quantified in three ways: (a) in nonhabituated *Aplysia,* only about half the terminals in this part of the ganglion have active zones; the active zones that were observed differed (b) in area and also (c) in the number of synaptic vesicles clustered at the active zone. The higher the

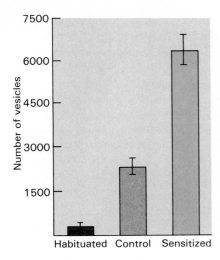

Figure 17-10 Changes in anatomy of *Aplysia* synapses with habituation and sensitization. (Bailey and Chen, 1983)

score on each of these measures, the greater the capacity of the animal to transmit neural signals in this part of its nervous system. Bailey and Chen (1983) examined the terminals of sensory neurons in habituated and in control *Aplysia;* they found that in all three measures, the habituated animals were significantly lower than the controls (Figure 17-10). Some *Aplysia* in this study were also stimulated so as to induce long-term sensitization; the active zones of the synapses in the sensitized animals were significantly greater than those of the controls on all three measures. In another study, Bailey and Chen (1984) found that long-term habituated animals have fewer presynaptic sensory terminals in the ganglion than do controls. The fact that both numbers and sizes of synaptic junctions vary with training in *Aplysia* is similar to findings that had been made previously with mammals (Diamond et al., 1975; West & Greenough, 1972). Moreover, the work with *Aplysia* shows that the anatomical changes occur specifically in neurons that are part of the circuit involved in learning, which the mammalian work had not been able to do.

The similarity in results obtained with *Aplysia* and with rats indicates that over a wide range of species information can be stored in the nervous system by changes in both size and number of synaptic contacts; this confirms the hypotheses diagramed in Figure 17-5d and f. Thus even in a relatively simple animal like *Aplysia*, the structural remodeling of the nervous system that we considered early in development (Chapter 4) probably continues to some extent throughout the life span and can be driven by experience.

Site and Mechanism of Sensitization

The same responses that habituate can also be sensitized. For example, the gill-withdrawal reflex becomes more intense if strong stimulation has recently been delivered elsewhere on the body surface. The circuit involved in the sensitization of the gill-withdrawal reflex of *Aplysia* is shown diagrammatically in Figure 17-11. Painful stimulation of the head was found to activate sensory neurons that, among other connections, excite facilitating interneurons. These interneurons end on the

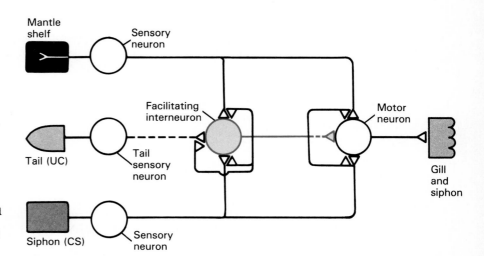

Figure 17-11 Neural circuit involved in sensitization of *Aplysia* gill-withdrawal. (Adapted from Hawkins and Kandel, 1983)

synaptic terminals of the sensory neurons from the siphon or the mantle. Thus sensitization is a somewhat more complex form of nonassociative learning than habituation, because it involves two kinds of stimuli: The effect of the sensitizing stimulus alters the response to the habituated stimulus. The cellular neurochemical mechanism of sensitization is also somewhat more complex than is that of habituation. It involves the same locus as habituation, the synapses that sensory neurons make on the motor neurons, and again the learning process involves an alteration in transmitter release by the sensory neurons. In sensitization, however, transmitter release is enhanced, whereas in habituation it is diminished. Furthermore, the neural circuit for sensitization in *Aplysia* has additional elements. In particular, as shown in Figure 17-11, information about strong stimulation of the head or tail is mediated by facilitating interneurons that form presynaptic endings on the terminals of the sensory neurons from the mantle shelf or siphon; that is, the facilitating interneurons can modulate the activity of the sensory neurons that make motor connections to the gill.

A neurochemical model has been suggested by Kandel and his associates for the processes that underlie short-term sensitization in the *Aplysia* preparation. Later we will see a related account for the processes that underlie associative learning. The model for short-term sensitization includes at least six steps, each of which is consistent with experimental tests. These steps are diagramed in Figure 17-12 and are stated in the caption. In brief, strong stimulation of the head or tail of *Aplysia* activates facilitatory interneurons whose presynaptic contacts on the sensory terminals are thought to use serotonin as their transmitter. Activation of the serotonin receptors in the sensory neurons leads to synthesis of cyclic AMP within these neurons, and in turn leads to activation of an enzyme which catalyzes a reaction that closes potassium channels in the membrane. Diminishing the outflow of K^+ ions during action potentials prolongs the potentials, which opens calcium channels, favoring release of transmitter by the sensory neurons.

Habituation and Sensitization in Cell Culture

Habituation and sensitization are now being investigated in cultures of identified cells removed from *Aplysia* (Rayport & Schacher, 1986). When tactile sensory and gill motor neurons are placed together in a culture dish, they form functional synaptic contacts within a few days. They can then be impaled with microelectrodes to stimulate and record their activity. Activating sensory-motor connections causes habituation. Adding serotonergic cells from another ganglion permits the occurrence of changes similar to sensitization. This preparation will permit study of the development of synaptic plasticity and study of more complex kinds of learning.

Long-Term Sensitization

Long-term sensitization, as we mentioned earlier, involves an increase in the active zones of the sensory terminals; see Figure 17-10. Thus whereas short-term retention

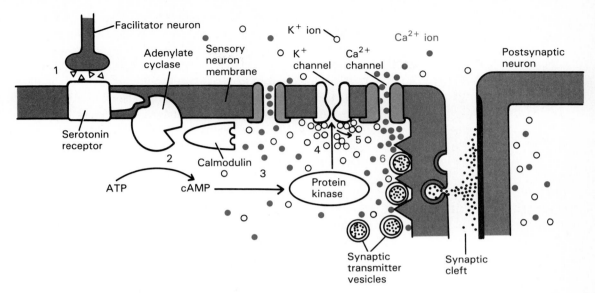

Figure 17-12 Hypothesized sequence of neurochemical processes underlying short-term sensitization in *Aplysia*. The diagram represents part of the terminal of a sensory neuron for the gill or siphon reflex; at the upper left, drawn to a smaller scale, is a presynaptic ending of a facilitator interneuron. Read the sequence from left to right. (1) Strong stimulation of the head or tail activates a group of facilitator neurons that synapse on the terminals of the sensory neurons for the gill and siphon withdrawal reflex and act there to enhance transmitter release. This process is called presynaptic facilitation. At least some of the facilitator cells are thought to utilize serotonin at their terminals. (2) Stimulation of serotonin receptors in the membrane of the sensory neuron terminals leads to an increase in the activity of the enzyme adenylate cyclase; this catalyzes the production of cyclic AMP in these terminals. (3) Elevation of the level of cAMP within the terminals activates an enzyme, cAMP-dependent protein kinase. (4) The kinase catalyzes a reaction that closes some of the K^+ channels in the neuronal membrane; a closed K^+ channel is shown above the arrow at 4 in the diagram. (5) Reducing the total number of K^+ channels that are open during the action potential decreases the outward K^+ current during subsequent action potentials, which increases the duration of the action potentials. (6) The increased duration of action potentials leads in turn to an increase in Ca^{2+} influx into the terminals and enhanced transmitter release. The Ca^{2+} channels in the figure are therefore shown with their gates open, which is the reverse of the habituated condition in Figure 17-11. (After Kandell et al., 1986)

can be accomplished by purely neurochemical processes, long-term retention involves structural changes in the synapses. Later we will consider how neural activity can lead to structural changes.

Associative Learning in Simple Systems

With so much information about mechanisms of nonassociative learning coming from the analysis of the gill-withdrawal reflex of *Aplysia*, investigators have been eagerly trying to find examples of associative learning in relatively simple invertebrate preparations. Years of attempts to condition the gill-withdrawal reflex were unsuccessful until an effective method was announced in 1981 (Carew, Walters, & Kandel, 1981). A light touch to the mantle soon habituates, but if the touch is promptly followed by a strong shock to the tail, after a few trials the touch alone elicits a strong withdrawal response. The touch (CS) and shock (US) must be paired and the interval between them kept brief for this conditioning to occur; tests demonstrate that this is conditioning and not sensitization. Now it is possible to compare the mechanisms of conditioning and of nonassociative learning in the same relatively simple preparation.

Other invertebrate preparations are also being used in the study of mechanisms of learning and memory. These include the nudibranch mollusc *Hermissenda* (e.g., Alkon, 1985, 1988) and the marine gastropod mollusc *Pleurobranchea* (e.g., Mpitsos et al., 1980). We will consider research on conditioning in some invertebrate preparations and then take up conditioning in vertebrates.

Conditioning in Aplysia

Some of the current work utilizes differential classical conditioning of the siphon withdrawal reflex (Carew et al., 1983). In differential conditioning two conditioned stimuli (CS) are used in the same animal, one (CS+) is paired with the US, and the other (CS−) is unpaired and has no consequence for the animal. With such training each animal can serve as its own control in comparing responses to CS+ and to CS−. Weak tactile stimuli serve as the discriminative stimuli (CS+ to the siphon and CS− to the mantle, or the reverse) and tail shock as the US. Differential conditioning is acquired rapidly by *Aplysia* and increases in strength with increased numbers of trials. Hawkins et al. (1983) found that only a narrow range of CS-US time intervals produced conditioning; if CS preceded US by 2 seconds or more, conditioning did not occur, nor did it occur with backward (US then CS) pairings. Such narrow time intervals and failure of backward conditioning are also found in many mammalian conditioning situations.

Investigation of the neurochemical mechanisms of classical conditioning in *Aplysia* suggests to Kandel and his associates that they are similar to those involved in sensitization. Differential conditioning produced a significantly greater enhancement of duration of action potentials with paired (CS+) rather than unpaired (CS−) stimulation. Furthermore, the activity-dependent facilitation in conditioning involves modulation of the same type of ion channel as in sensitization (Hawkins & Abrams, 1984). Figure 17-13 presents hypothesized events in the sensory terminal under CS− and CS+ conditions. These diagrams should be compared with Figure 17-12, which presented mechanisms of sensitization.

The requirement for the forward order of stimulation (CS-US) to obtain conditioning may depend upon neurons that require a specific order of converging stimulation for facilitation, and such neurons have been observed (Walters & Byrne, 1983). Another possibility suggested by Hawkins and Kandel (1984) is that the Ca^{2+} that enters the neuron during action potentials primes the production of enzyme so that it then produces more cAMP when tail stimulation arrives. In their review of this field, Farley and Alkon (1985) pointed out several problems with the work to date on mechanisms of both nonassociative and associative learning in *Aplysia*. For example, it is not certain that all the changes involved in learning are presynaptic, and the biophysical changes hypothesized to underlie memory are relatively short-lived. Investigating such mechanisms is the focus of work in several laboratories.

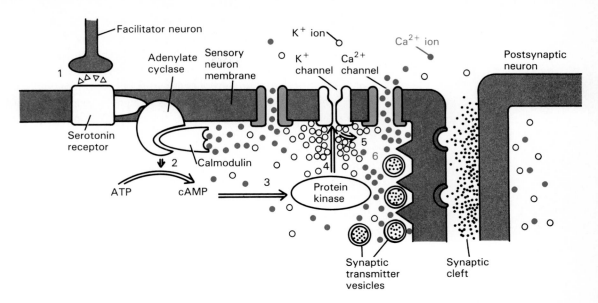

Figure 17-13 A hypothetical schema of a sequence of processes that may underlie conditioning. Activation of the synapse at (1) by the conditioning stimulus shortly before activation of the sensory neuron by the unconditioned stimulus leads to increased influx of Ca^{2+} ions. This activates calmodulin, enhancing the activity of adenylate cyclase (2), leading to increased production of cAMP. This, in turn, activates protein kinase enzymes (3), leading to phosphorylation of molecules in the wall of the K^+ channels (4), closing these channels, which results in wider openings of the Ca^{2+} channels (5). Ca^{2+} ions help to position more synaptic vesicles for discharge (6). Thus, excitation of the sensory neuron now leads to greater stimulation of the postsynaptic neuron than occurred before the conditioning took place. (Adapted from Kandel et al., 1986)

Later in this chapter we will refer back to Figure 17-13 when we consider research with *Drosophila* mutants that are impaired in learning and memory. It turns out that these mutants have deficiencies in some of the neurochemical steps in the schema devised by Kandel and his associates, and this provides a kind of independent support for their hypotheses.

Conditioning in Hermissenda

Visitors to tidepools sometimes see slim, attractively colored molluscs several centimeters long, without shells and with gills rising from their backs. One such mollusc, *Hermissenda,* is the subject of extensive research on mechanisms of conditioning by Alkon and his colleagues (e.g., Alkon, 1985, 1988; Farley & Alkon, 1985). This kind of mollusc usually hides well beneath the surface at night and rises in the sea during daylight to feed near the surface, but strong wave motion can cause it to descend for shelter. Therefore it is normally attracted to light but avoids being shaken or moved violently. In the laboratory, pairing light with rotation on a turntable causes conditioned suppression of the tendency to approach the light. The eyes of *Hermissenda* contain only five photoreceptor cells, two of Type A and three of

Type B. A brief description by Farley and Alkon (1985, p. 441) of the biophysical steps involved in conditioning of *Hermissenda* runs as follows: Stimulation of Type B photoreceptors causes a depolarization that outlasts the light for many seconds and is accompanied by an increase in membrane resistance. Repeated pairings of light and rotation produce a cumulative depolarization and a consequent rise of Ca^{2+} within the B cells. This in turn is thought to result in a suppression of at least two distinct K^+ currents in the B cell—a suppression that can last for days. Suppression of these currents means that training enhances the B cells' generator potential and response to light. Connections from the B cells inhibit the A cells so that after associative training the A cells are less effective in exciting neurons that mediate the approach to light.

Note that according to Alkon's account, the important changes that occur during conditioning of *Hermissenda* take place in the membranes of photoreceptor cells and not, as in other accounts of learning, at synapses. Furthermore, Farley and Alkon (1985) report that they were able to produce by electrophysiological stimulation the membrane changes in B cells that are produced by conditioning, and that these changes caused the animals to suppress their approach to light just as if they had been conditioned; that is, these investigators claim to have found both the site and the biophysical changes that are causally related to long-term retention in this situation. And this mechanism may be more general than it might appear: Alkon (1985) points out that the ion channels in the Type B photoreceptors of *Hermissenda* are similar to channels in neurons of the mammalian hippocampus, and there is evidence that during conditioning of the rabbit, changes occur in the membranes of hippocampal neurons that are similar to those than occur in *Hermissenda* photoreceptor cells (Disterhoft, Coulter, & Alkon, 1985).

The work with *Hermissenda,* which finds the important changes to occur in the neuronal membrane, clearly affords quite a different picture of basic mechanisms of conditioning from that furnished by the research with *Aplysia,* which focuses on changes that occur at the presynaptic side of the synaptic junction. The next few years should demonstrate how well either or both of these pictures will be validated by further investigation in the two species. Similar research with other species of invertebrates and vertebrates will show whether these are only two of a wide variety of possible mechanisms of learning or whether either proves to be general over a number of species.

Studies with Drosophila: A Genetic Approach to Mechanisms of Learning and Memory

Because the genetics of the fruit fly, *Drosophila,* is well known, these flies bring distinct advantages to the study of mechanisms of learning and memory even though their central nervous system (with about 100,000 very small neurons) is more complex than those of *Aplysia* or *Hermissenda.* Geneticists Quinn, Harris, and Benzer (1974) therefore worked out a method to condition groups of *Drosophila.* They put about 40 flies in a glass tube and let them locomote upward toward one of two odors that normally are equally attractive. Reaching the upper part of one tube brought an electrical shock, whereas the other odor was not associated with shock. The group could then be tested after various time intervals for approach to each of the odors. Typically about two-thirds of the group would avoid the shocked odor. Later, with more careful control of conditions, about 90% avoided the odor associated with shock (Jellies, 1981). As soon as the first procedure was worked out, the geneticists began testing mutant strains of *Drosophila*. In 1976 they announced the isolation of the first mutant that failed to learn to discriminate the odors, and they named it Dunce (Dudai et al., 1976). Tests showed that Dunce had a real problem with learning; its deficiency was not in olfaction, locomotion, or general activity. Three more learning mutants were then isolated and named Cabbage, Turnip, and Rutabaga; another mutant, Amnesiac, learned normally but forgot more rapidly than normal flies (Quinn, 1979). Mutants found in other laboratories were also deficient in learning. One had been named for the enzyme in which it is deficient, dopa decarboxylase (DDC). Tests with other procedures showed that the failures of these mutants were not restricted to odor-shock training but occurred as well in other tests of associative learning; on the other hand, the mutants were normal in nonlearning behaviors. Training for sucrose reward was remembered for days rather than hours by normal flies (Tempel et al., 1983). The sucrose test showed that Dunce and Rutabaga could learn but forgot within an hour.

The mutants with poor learning or memory were examined with regard to nonassociative learning: habituation and sensitization (Duerr & Quinn, 1982). Dunce and Turnip showed low habituation; Dunce, Rutabaga, and Amnesiac showed unusually brief sensitization. These observations supported the idea that nonassociative and associative learning share some of the same mechanisms.

As part of their program the investigators examined the mutants to identify their genetic deficiencies, and several mutants for learning have been characterized in this way (Tully, 1987; Dudai, 1988). In each case the deficiency can be related to the schema of Kandel that we saw in Figure 17-13 and that is now reproduced as Figure 17-14. The enzyme dopa decarboxylase is necessary for the synthesis of the transmitters dopamine and serotonin, so its deficiency impairs stimulation by serotonergic fibers shown at the upper left of the figure as DDC X. Turnip's deficiency impairs both the serotonin receptor and protein kinase, so an X and Turnip appear at both of these locations. The Rutabaga mutation decreases cyclic AMP levels and adenylate cyclase levels. Dunce has a deficiency in the enzyme that splits cAMP. The Shaker gene impairs the K^+ channels. Finding that these genetic defects all fit into the schema of Kandel and his associates provides novel and independent support for their hypotheses. In evaluating this striking convergence of findings, it should be remembered that the mutants had been isolated behaviorally without knowledge of their genetic deficiencies and before Kandel's hypotheses had been formulated.

Conditioning in Vertebrates

While some investigators have been making progress in understanding the cellular mechanisms of learning in relatively simple neural circuits, others have been attempting to study the basic mechanism of learning in the much more complex nervous systems of vertebrates. This research is necessary both to find whether the neural processes of learning and memory suggested by experiments with invertebrates also hold true for vertebrates and also to find where formation of memory occurs in the vertebrate brain. Among the strategies used to find electrophysiological correlates of learning in vertebrate nervous systems are these:

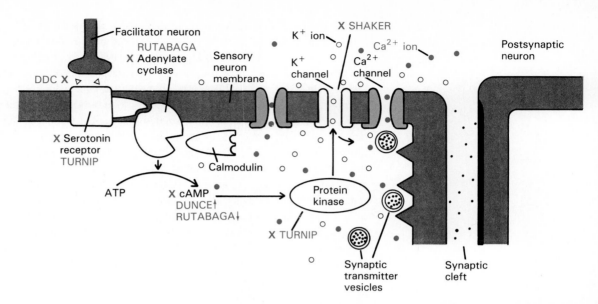

Figure 17-14 Sites of impaired neurochemical processes in learning-deficient *Drosophila* mutants. Several *Drosophila* mutants in which learning/memory is deficient are shown here with an X at the site of the impairment. Note that both Rutabaga and Turnip show two sites of impairment. It is noteworthy that all of the *Drosophila* impairments can be located on a schema of conditioning that was worked out on the basis of experiments with *Aplysia*, indicating some generality of these hypotheses. (Adapted from Kandel et al., 1986)

1. Exploring many sites and looking for indications of learning at each.
2. Focusing on events at a particular site that other kinds of research had already implicated in learning.
3. Patiently tracing the entire neural circuit involved in an example of learning and determining at what site(s) in the circuit evidence of learning occurs.

Each of these strategies has produced interesting results.

How can investigators tell whether a site from which they record is critically related to learning? Even if the electrical activity varies in parallel with the progress of learning, the site of recording might simply be reflecting events determined elsewhere in the nervous system. Experimental designs that try to answer this question include these:

1. Attempting to find the sites with the earliest (shortest-latency) responses related to learning.
2. Testing to see whether the inputs to a site already show relations to learning.

Studies with birds and mammals will be reviewed next.

Conditioning of Cardiac Responses in the Pigeon

In order to obtain a relatively simple vertebrate system, neuroscientist David Cohen (1985) studied classical conditioning of heart rate change to a visual stimulus in the pigeon. He used a visual conditioned stimulus (CS)—illuminating the entire visual field for 6 seconds—followed by a 0.5-second foot shock as the unconditioned stimulus (US). After 10 paired CS-US presentations, the CS alone reliably causes cardiac acceleration, and asymptotic performance is reached after 30 pairings. The neural circuitry of the system underlying this conditioning was then patiently traced out. Three different pathways were found to convey visual information within the brain, and only by interrupting all three could acquisition of the conditioned response (CR) be prevented. On the response side, acceleration of the heart involves two kinds of neural messages: (1) excitation from the sympathetic division of the autonomic system through the cardiac nerve and (2) inhibition from the parasympathetic division of the autonomic system through the vagal cardiac nerve. These motor outflows were traced back through the medulla, pons, medial hypothalamus, and amygdala to telencephalic centers that have inputs from the visual centers. Lesions at sites along this pathway, such as the amygdala, totally prevent expression of the CR. Large lesions nearby, including destruction of other areas with inputs to the heart, are virtually without effect on the CR. These findings show that the pathway of the response has been found, demonstrating the feasibility of tracing such pathways even within a vertebrate nervous system.

Where within this pathway do changes occur during conditioning? The most peripheral site at which changes in electrophysiological responses occur with conditioning is the principal optic nucleus of the thalamus; this is the avian equivalent of the lateral geniculate nucleus in mammals. The neurons with modifiable responses in this nucleus show some response, even before conditioning, to presentation of either the CS or the US. Thus the conditioning is an example of alpha conditioning; that is, it represents enhancement of a preexisting response to CS. Cohen concludes that convergence of CS and US information on the same neurons is necessary for conditioning to occur. The plasticity in the thalamic nucleus is in the first neurons that receive input from the retina. But plasticity is not confined to this site; rather it is distributed throughout the pathway of the CR. Neurons in several centers are responsive to both CS and US before conditioning starts, and presumably the responses of many of these cells are modified during conditioning. Thus in this system the information storage is localized in the sense that it occurs only along the specific neural pathways that mediate the heart rate CR. But within those pathways storage is widely distributed.

Cohen and his associates are now analyzing the cellular mechanisms of conditioning within the principal optic nucleus of the thalamus. They are also attempting to do similar experiments with slices of thalamic tissue removed from the brain and kept in a tissue chamber. This is like successful research with hippocampal slice preparations from mammalian brains (see Box 17-1, Studying Memory in a Dish).

Conditioned Eye Blink in the Rabbit

A kind of conditioning that has been very well studied behaviorally is the response of the eyelid of the rabbit when an air puff to the cornea (US) follows an acoustic tone (CS). A stable conditioned response (CR) develops rather rapidly—the rabbit comes to blink when the tone is sounded—and this is similar to eyelid conditioning

BOX 17-1 | Studying Memory in a Dish: Long-Term Potentiation

Investigators have long been seeking a way of isolating a vertebrate brain circuit in which learning occurs so that they could study it in detail, much as certain invertebrate "reduced preparations" are being studied. Some researchers claim that the phenomenon of **long-term potentiation** in the mammalian brain has many of the same advantages for investigating neural mechanisms in learning and memory that characterize "simple" invertebrate preparations. Long-term potentiation (LTP) is a stable and enduring increase in the magnitude of the response of neurons after afferent cells to the region have been stimulated with bursts of moderately high frequency stimuli. LTP was first discovered in the hippocampus of the intact rabbit (Bliss & Lømo, 1973) and then in slices of rat hippocampus maintained in a tissue chamber (Schwartzkroin & Wester, 1975). It can be observed in awake and freely moving animals, in anesthetized animals, or in tissue slices, where most of the research is being done. Although most of the work on LTP has been done in the hippocampus of the rat, it has been observed in many other brain areas in several species of mammals, and even in fish.

Is LTP a mechanism of memory formation? Several reviewers support this claim (e.g., Bliss & Dolphin, 1984; Teyler & Discenna, 1987). Some of the similarities and relationships between LTP and better known examples of learning are the following: (1) LTP can be induced by stimulation at rates that occur normally in the nervous system, and LTP lasts for days or weeks. (2) Barnes (1979) found a positive correlation between the speed with which rats could learn a maze and the degree to which LTP could be induced in them; this held true for both young and older animals. (3) Exposing rats to a complex environment produces LTP in the hippocampus (Sharp, McNaughton, & Barnes, 1983). (4) Application of high-frequency stimulation to a hippocampal input, which produces LTP, facilitates acquisition of eyelid conditioning in the rabbit (Berger, 1984). (5) Conditioning the hippocampus facilitates induction of LTP 48 hours later; also, posttraining stimulation of the reticular formation enhances both conditioning and LTP and makes them last longer (Bloch & Laroche, 1984). (6) In apparent contrast to the last two points is the report that induction of LTP in the hippocampus of rats impaired their ability to acquire spatial information but did not disrupt the use of previously learned spatial information (McNaughton et al., 1986), but it should be noted that the learning in (4) and (5) was not spatial in nature. McNaughton and his colleagues concluded that both LTP and acquisition of spatial learning require activity of the same hippocampal circuits.

Although the stimulation that induces LTP can be introduced through a single neural tract, this does not mean that LTP is nonassociative. There is evidence that many afferent fibers must be stimulated to induce LTP, and presumably there is convergence among their terminals. Furthermore, there is research on "associative LTP" induced when conditioning stimulation is delivered through one tract and test stimulation is delivered through another input to the same region (Burger & Levy, 1985).

More specifically LTP may provide a model for the learning that is reinforced by consummatory behavior such as eating or drinking (Buzsaki, 1985). Buzsaki notes that hippocampal "sharp waves" occur during such behaviors; these waves reflect the synchronous activity of many pyramidal neurons. Such naturally occurring short bursts of high-frequency discharges are similar to the artificial stimuli that are used to induce LTP.

Preparation of hippocampal slices makes it possible to study LTP under well-controlled conditions, to record electrophysiological responses readily, to apply neurochemical substances to the preparation, and to analyze neurochemical changes. The hippocampal slice preparation is shown in Box Figure 17-1.

In spite of the considerable amount of research devoted to this preparation, there are still many disagreements about the processes involved in LTP. Some investigators suggest that the main changes occur in the presynaptic terminals that show increased release of the transmitter glutamate after LTP (Dolphin et al., 1982; Skrede & Malthe-Sorenssen, 1981). Others hold that the main events are postsynaptic, involving increased intracellular levels of Ca^{2+} (Eccles, 1983) and exposure of greater numbers of glutamate receptors (Lynch & Baudry, 1984). Both

in humans. Richard Thompson and his colleagues (1986) have been studying neural circuitry of this conditioning for several years. The circuit of the eye blink reflex is simple, involving two cranial nerves and their nuclei (Figure 17-15). Sensory fibers from the cornea run along the V cranial nerve (the trigeminal nerve) to its nucleus in

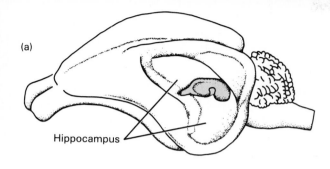

(a)

Hippocampus

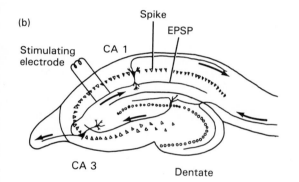

(b)

Spike

EPSP

Stimulating electrode

CA 1

CA 3

Dentate

(c)

presynaptic and postsynaptic processes may participate in LTP, and at present there does not seem to be compelling evidence for exclusive location of changes at either site (Bliss & Dolphin, 1984).

Changes in synapse morphology have also been reported when LTP is induced both in intact animals (Lee et al., 1980) and in slice preparations (Chang & Greenough, 1984; Fifkova & Van Harreveld, 1982). An inhibitor of protein synthesis, anisomycin, was reported not to affect the initiation of LTP in freely moving rats but to prevent LTP from continuing more than a few hours (Krug, Lössner, & Ott, 1984). This is consistent with studies suggesting that long-term memory, but not short-term memory, depends upon synthesis of proteins in the brain, a topic that we consider in this chapter.

Some of the complexity and discrepancy of results of experiments on long-term potentiation may come from the fact that several different phenomena seem to be involved. Abraham and Goddard (1985) reviewed evidence that suggests the existence of four or five overlapping but separable effects of prior stimulation on the amplitude of responses of hippocampal cells. Depending upon how and when the experimenter measures the responses and the treatments that are used to affect them, one or another phenomenon may predominate in the results. Further work is needed to sort out these complex phenomena and to decide the extent to which any of them can help us understand how other kinds of learning occur.

Box Figure 17-1 Preparation of a hippocampal slice from rat brain. (a) Location of the hippocampus in the rat brain. The overlying tissue has been removed. A hippocampal slice (or section) is shown in color. (b) Schematic diagram of a hippocampal slice showing the dentate, CA3, and CA1 subdivisions. Also shown is a stimulating electrode in the Schaffer collaterals and recording electrodes in the cell body layer of CA1 (to record extracellular population spikes) and in the dendritic layer of CA1 (to record extracellular population EPSPs). Arrows indicate direction of normal impulse travel in axon tracts. (c) Photograph of a hippocampal slice (Adapted from Teyler, 1978)

the brain stem. From there some fibers go in the brain stem to the nucleus of the VII (facial) cranial nerve. Activity of certain motor fibers in the VII nerve causes the eyelids to close.

Early in their work, Thompson and his colleagues found that during condition-

Figure 17-15 The neural circuit of the eyeblink reflex. (After Thompson, 1986)

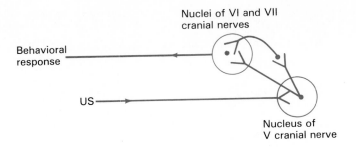

ing the hippocampus develops neural responses whose temporal patterns resemble closely those of the eyelid responses (Figure 17-16). Although the hippocampal activity closely parallels the course of conditioning and does so more clearly than does activity of other limbic structures, this result does not prove that the hippocampus is required for conditioning to occur. In fact, destruction of the hippocampus

Figure 17-16 Appearance and growth of the hippocampal response during conditioning of the nictitating membrane. (a) Analysis of single trials during the first block of 8 paired presentations of CS and US. Although the air puff elicits a blink of the nictitating membrane (NM) from the first trials, no response occurs in the hippocampus (H) until trial 6. (b) Further growth of the hippocampal response over 2 days of training. Amplitude grows steadily, but more slowly in the CS-US interval than post-US. For animals that receive the unpaired presentation of the tone and the air puff, no response develops in the hippocampus, as shown by the white curves. Note the difference of scale on the y axes of the two graphs in (b). (From Berger and Thompson, 1978)

(a) Single-trial analysis of the first block of conditioning trials

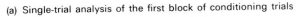

(b) Further development of hippocampal response during training

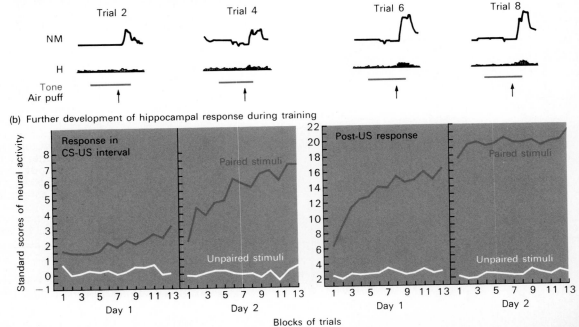

has little effect on acquisition or retention of the conditioned eyelid response in rabbits (Lockhart & Moore, 1975). Therefore the hippocampus is not required for this conditioning, although it may participate: Abnormal hippocampal activity can disrupt the acquisition of conditioning.

Thompson and his associates then proceeded to map in detail the brain structures in conditioned animals. They found that learning-related increases in activity of individual neurons were prominent in the cerebellum, both in its cortex and deep nuclei, and in certain nuclei in the pons. In the cerebellum, although there were only negligible responses to CS and US before the stimuli were paired, a neuronal replica of the learned behavioral response emerged during conditioning. These responses, which preceded the behavioral responses by 50 milliseconds or more, were found in the deep cerebellar nuclei ipsilateral to the eye that was trained. Lesion experiments were then undertaken to find whether the cerebellar responses were required for conditioning. In an animal that had already been conditioned, destruction of the ipsilateral interpositus and dentate nuclei abolished the CR. The CR could not be regained on the ipsilateral side, but the contralateral eye could then be conditioned normally. In a naive animal, prior destruction of the interpositus and dentate nuclei on one side prevented the occurrence of conditioning on that side. The effect of the cerebellar lesions could not be attributed to interference with sensory or motor tracts because the animal still showed a normal unconditioned blink when an air puff was delivered to its eye.

The circuit of the conditioned reflex was then mapped in further detail using a combination of methods: electrophysiological recording, localized lesions, localized stimulation of neurons, localized infusion of small amounts of drugs, and tracing of fiber pathways. For example, prior work had shown that the inhibitory synaptic transmitter GABA is the main transmitter in the deep cerebellar nuclei. Using well-conditioned rabbits, the investigators injected a small amount of a blocking agent for GABA into the deep cerebellar nuclei on the side of the conditioned response. The injection resulted in the disappearance of the behavioral CR and of its electrophysiological neuronal replica. This abolition of the CR was reversible: As the blocking agent wore off, the CR returned.

Based on these experiments, Thompson proposed a simplified schematic circuit for the conditioned eye blink response, as shown in Figure 17-17. This circuit includes the input and output parts of the eye blink reflex circuit, shown in color at the lower left of Figure 17-17, but additional pathways are required to bring together information about the US and the CS. Information about the corneal stimulation goes also to the inferior olivary nucleus of the brain stem. It is then carried into the cerebellum by way of axons called climbing fibers to the deep cerebellar nuclei and to cells of the cerebellar cortex, including granule cells and Purkinje cells. The same cerebellar cells also receive information about the auditory CS, coming by way of the cochlear nucleus in the brain stem and the pontine nuclei; the latter send axons called mossy fibers into the cerebellum. Efferent information controlling the CR travels from the interpositus nucleus of the cerebellum to the red nucleus, which we discussed as a motor nucleus in Chapter 10. From there it goes to the cranial motor nucleus of the VII nerve, which controls the eye blink response.

Since the main input to the deep cerebellar nuclei comes from the cerebellar cortex, lesions of the cortex would be expected to abolish the eyelid CR just as

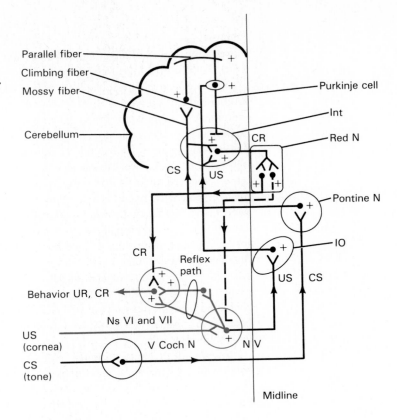

Figure 17-17 Simplified schematic circuit for the conditioned eyeblink response. One circuit for the unconditioned eyeblink reflex is shown in color. Abbreviations: Int, interpositus nucleus of the cerebellum; IO, inferior olivary nucleus; N, nucleus; NV, nucleus of the fifth cranial nerve. (Adapted from Thompson, 1986)

lesions of the deep nuclei do. Such a finding has been reported by a group working in England (Yeo, Hardiman, & Glickstein, 1985). Thompson and his associates, however, have not found lesions of the cerebellar cortex to interfere with the CR unless the lesions are very large. This question is under active study.

At the same time the rabbit acquires a conditioned eyelid CR, it also acquires a conditioned slowing of the heart rate. Although lesioning the deep cerebellar nuclei abolishes the conditioned eyelid response, it does not affect the conditioned change in heart rate. Apparently the two CRs are mediated by different neural circuits. We should note that it is usual for different kinds of conditioning to take place at the same time in any organism.

A possible interpretation of the roles of the hippocampus and cerebellum in this conditioning is the following: The cerebellum represents the direct or obligatory circuitry, whereas the hippocampus is a modulatory circuit that can facilitate the conditioning. (Later in this chapter we will discuss modulation of learning and memory formation.)

Some similarities and some differences are seen between the findings with two vertebrate preparations: rabbit eyelid conditioning and conditioning of the cardiac response of the pigeon. In both cases it has been possible to trace much of the circuitry even in the complex vertebrate central nervous system. This mapping is telling us about the roles of specific vertebrate brain structures in learning and memory, which of course cannot be found from work with invertebrates because of the very different organizations of their nervous systems. Electrophysiological recording can be used in these preparations to study the cellular details of the processes of conditioning in vertebrates, although this is not yet as well advanced as in certain invertebrate preparations. A favorable preparation for such work in mammals is the tissue slice (see Box 17-1).

In considering differences between findings with pigeon cardiac conditioning and rabbit eye blink conditioning, we should bear in mind that in the rabbit the circuits for eye blink conditioning and cardiac conditioning are different. It may be that rabbit cardiac conditioning would be rather similar to cardiac conditioning in the pigeon. Meanwhile we can note that pigeon cardiac CR seems to be a case of alpha conditioning (enhancement of a preexisting response), whereas rabbit eye blink conditioning does not. Storage of the conditioning is distributed among many sites in the pertinent system in the pigeon, but the distributed nature of the storage is not as striking in the rabbit eye blink conditioning circuit. In the pigeon changes with conditioning have been found at the thalamus, the first brain station for vision, but this has not been reported for the rabbit.

Neural Mechanisms of Imprinting

Filial imprinting has been used as a model system to investigate neural mechanisms of learning and memory since the early 1970s, employing a variety of methods and obtaining a wealth of findings (Horn, 1985). As described in Chapter 16, under appropriate conditions young precocial animals learn the characteristics of the first large conspicuous visual object that they see. By rearing chicks in darkness before exposing them to such a stimulus object, the experimenter can be confident that the chick brain is naive and that the stimulation will have a large and lasting behavioral effect. The earlier studies used behavioral interventions, giving imprinting experiences and searching for cerebral consequences; some later studies have used somatic interventions and looked for effects on imprinting behavior.

In early studies (Bateson, Horn, & Rose, 1972) chicks were exposed to a rotating flashing orange light for 2 hours. Meanwhile control chicks saw only a stationary overhead light. Forty minutes before the end of the exposure period, the chicks were injected with a radioactive amino acid that cells could use in synthesizing either protein or RNA. A brief behavioral test after the end of the exposure period showed that the imprinting procedure had worked. The brains were then removed and dissected into three samples, which were analyzed for radioactivity. The experimental chicks were found to have significantly more radioactivity incorporated into protein and RNA in the roof forebrain than the controls; this indicated that imprinting increased the amount of neural activity in the roof of the forebrain. While these results were suggestive, they were open to a variety of interpretations. For example, greater motivation or more intense visual stimulation, rather than imprinting, could have caused the effects.

To control for general effects of motivation, a similar experiment was run except that one eye of each experimental chick was masked. (The optic nerve fibers in the chick cross completely to the opposite side of the brain, so stimulating one eye causes activity in the opposite cerebral hemisphere.) If the effects were general and caused by activation of the chicks in the presence of the flashing light, then the

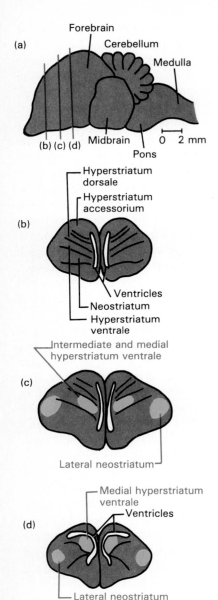

Figure 17-18 The chick brain.
(a) Lateral view showing in color the planes of three coronal sections given below in (b), (c), and (d). (b) An anterior coronal section. Much of the forebrain is composed of plates of neurons, some of which are named in the diagram. Gray matter and white matter are not as clearly divided as in the mammalian brain. (c) and (d) show in color some of the brain regions that have been found to be involved in learning and memory. (Adapted from G. Horn, 1985)

effects would be expected to occur in both cerebral hemispheres. Increased radioactivity was found, however, only in the hemisphere stimulated by the open eye, so the effect was specific to the part of the brain that was activated by the stimulation.

It was also important to attempt to distinguish between effects of sensory stimulation and effects of imprinting. For this purpose chicks were given imprinting sessions of different lengths on each of two successive days. It had been found that under these training conditions a session of only 60 minutes produced rather weak approach behavior to the test object, whereas a session of 240 minutes produced strong imprinting; prolonging the duration beyond 240 minutes produced little additional effect. In the experiment chicks were exposed to the imprinting stimulus for 20, 60, 120, or 240 minutes on day 1. They were then given either 0 or 60 minutes of exposure on day 2, and they were injected with a radioactive precursor of RNA. The chicks that were not exposed on day 2 did not differ in cerebral radioactivity, no matter how long they had been exposed on day 1, so there was no direct holdover of the day 1 stimulation or experience. But the chicks that saw the imprinting stimulus for 60 minutes on day 2 showed significant differences in cerebral activity depending upon the length of exposure on day 1. The longer the exposure had been on day 1, the less radioactivity was incorporated in the forebrain roof on day 2 because the chicks had less imprinting to accomplish on day 2. Sensory stimulation could not account for the observed differences because all the 60-minute chicks had equal visual stimulation on day 2. The investigators concluded, therefore, that imprinting accounted for the differences obtained on day 2.

Exactly where the radioactive precursor was being incorporated into brain RNA during imprinting was the next question to be studied. For this purpose the investigators used the technique of autoradiography. That is, after the imprinting session during which the chicks were given the radioactive precursor, the brains were cut into thin sections. These sections were placed in the dark on sensitive film and left there for several weeks. Radioactivity exposes film just as light does. When the film was developed, it showed activity especially in a particular structure of the anterior chick forebrain—a region called the intermediate and medial part of the hyperstriatum ventrale (IMHV) (Figure 17-18). Other investigators using radioactive 2-deoxyglucose to localize activity in the brain also reported that imprinting is accompanied by increased activity in IMHV.

To test whether the intermediate and medial hyperstriatum ventrale is required for imprinting, neuroscientists then resorted to somatic intervention: they made bilateral lesions in IMHV and asked whether imprinting could still occur. In a test made after a standard imprinting session, intact control chicks made three times as many wheel revolutions as the lesioned chicks in attempting to reach the imprinting stimulus (McCabe, Horn, & Bateson, 1981). In other words, lesions of IMHV significantly impaired acquisition. Furthermore, lesions of IMHV made after imprinting seriously impaired retention of this learning. A test of visual acuity showed that the operation had not impaired acuity, so the failure to acquire or retain imprinting could not be attributed to a sensory deficit. Later work showed that chicks with IMHV lesions can form associations to visual stimuli but cannot learn to show representational memories for these stimuli (McCabe et al., 1982). This is reminiscent of the dissociation between representational memories and habits that we discussed in Chapter 16.

A surprising result emerged from an attempt to find changes in neuronal anat-

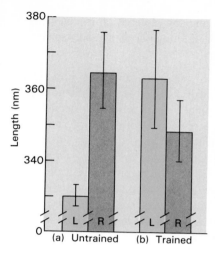

Figure 17-19 Effects of training on lengths of postsynaptic receptive zones in left (L) and right (R) medial hyperstriatum ventrale. Before training the mean length of receptive zones was 11% smaller in the left than in the right hemisphere ($p < 0.025$), as seen in the left-hand pair of bars. After training there was no longer a significant difference. The lines at the top of each bar represent $\pm$ standard error of the mean. (Adapted from Bradley and Horn, 1981)

omy as a result of imprinting: The two hemispheres responded differently (Bradley, Horn, & Bateson, 1981; Horn, Bradley, & McCabe, 1985). In this work, sections of the brains of thoroughly imprinted and undertrained chicks were examined by electronmicrography. The lengths of postsynaptic receptive areas were measured as in Figure 17-4. In IMHV of undertrained or naive chicks, the postsynaptic receptive areas were significantly longer in the right hemisphere than in the left, as Figure 17-19a shows. Giving 120 minutes of imprinting experience led to significant lengthening of the postsynaptic receptive areas in the left IMHV, so that they became slightly (but not significantly) longer than those in the right hemisphere, as seen in Figure 17-19b. The chicks had been sacrificed about 6 hours after the start of imprinting, so growth of the synaptic receptive areas had taken place quickly.

The unexpected finding of asymmetrical anatomical changes as a result of imprinting led to further lesion experiments. Experimenters tried ablating either the right or the left IMHV instead of making bilateral lesions (Cipolla-Neto, Horn, & McCabe, 1982). When chicks had been imprinted, destroying the right IMHV did not impair retention, but destroying the left IMHV caused amnesia for the imprinting stimulus. This was true if the lesions were made within 2 hours after the imprinting session. But experiments in which the lesions were delayed showed a more complicated picture. If the right IMHV is destroyed 3 hours or more after training, it appears to have transferred information to some other part of the brain; that is, the right IMHV appears to act as a "buffer store," holding memory for a short period after training and slowly transferring it to another region. Work is now underway to find the region of more permanent storage of memory for imprinting in the right hemisphere. The left IMHV, in contrast to the right, appears to store memory for the long term, at least for 24 hours as tested in these experiments. In a later section of this chapter on neurochemical processes in storage of memory, we will see evidence that the left IMHV is active in formation of memory for other kinds of experience.

Whereas the behavioral intervention of giving imprinting experience causes changes to occur in brain chemistry, the somatic intervention of administering certain compounds can prevent formation of memory for imprinting. Intracranial administration of any of several compounds that had been found to prevent memory in other situations—and which we will discuss in a later section—was found to prevent formation of memory for imprinting (Gibbs & Lecanuet, 1981). (Such agents are called amnestic, that is, amnesia producing.) A small amount of either an amnestic drug or physiological saline solution was injected into the brains of chicks 5 minutes before the imprinting session. All the chicks were active during exposure to the imprinting stimulus, but at a test 48 hours later the chicks that had been given an amnestic drug showed far less following of the stimulus than did the chicks that had received a control injection of saline solution. If the drugs were given 5 or 10 minutes posttraining, instead of pretraining, they did not interfere with retention. This showed that these drugs did not have any general deleterious effect; they must be active in the immediate posttraining period if they are to prevent formation of memory.

Thus far there has been relatively little investigation of electrophysiology or cellular neurochemistry in imprinting, so this preparation has not yet provided details about cellular mechanisms of learning that have come from research with certain model systems. On the other hand, the study of chick imprinting has yielded information about the roles of certain brain structures in learning that could not have come from invertebrate preparations, and the ongoing research on mechanisms of imprinting promises to yield further important information about mechanisms of learning in the vertebrate brain.

Mechanisms of Formation of Memories of Different Durations

Memories differ markedly in how long they last, from iconic and short-term memories to long-term and permanent memories, as we saw in Chapter 16. Some behavioral evidence suggests that memories of different lengths reflect the operation of different neural processes. For example, impairments in formation of short-term and long-term memories may occur independently: Among people who suffer from severe impairments of memory, some are deficient only in forming long-term memories while a few are deficient only in forming short-term memories. In the cases of habituation and sensitization, we saw earlier in this chapter that formation of short-term memories in *Aplysia* involves neurochemical changes at existing synapses, whereas formation of long-term memories also involves structural changes in existing synapses and changes in numbers of synapses.

Since the 1950s there has been extensive use of biochemical and pharmacological agents to study memory formation, and this has led to many interesting discoveries and to new concepts. Chemical treatments have many advantages for this research, since many of them are reversible, unlike brain lesions or other permanent interventions. The chemical treatments can be used for relatively brief, accurately timed effects, and subjects can be tested in their normal state both before and after treatment. Chemical agents can be given systemically or locally. Systemic administration permits the study of a whole system of widely separated neurons, such as neurons that employ a particular synaptic transmitter. Local injection into a specific brain site can be used to investigate localized processes.

The different courses of effects found with various agents suggest that different neurochemical processes may mediate memory storage over different time periods—short-term, intermediate-term, and long-term memories. This result has given rise to the concept of sequential neurochemical processes in memory formation, which we will discuss in this section. The same chemical or pharmacological agent may aid memory formation under certain conditions but impair it under other conditions. This result has given rise to the concept of modulation of memory formation, a topic we will discuss in a later section.

Since about 1960, much research has centered on the hypothesis that formation of long-term memory normally requires increased protein synthesis during the minutes (and perhaps hours) that follow training (e.g., Davis & Squire, 1984; Rosenzweig, 1984). More recently there has also been research on the neurochemical processes involved in earlier stages of memory formation—short-term and intermediate-term memories (e.g., Gibbs & Ng, 1977; Mizumori et al., 1985; Rosenzweig & Bennett, 1984; Mattheis, 1989). Let us review first some of the research on the protein-synthesis hypothesis of formation of long-term memories and then turn to research on the mechanisms of formation of earlier stages of memory.

Tests of the Protein-Synthesis Hypothesis of Formation of Long-Term Memory

Experiments to test this hypothesis have employed both behavioral intervention—in the form of training—and somatic intervention—in the form of agents that inhibit synthesis of proteins. Training has been demonstrated to produce increased dendritic trees of neurons and increased numbers of synaptic contacts (Greenough,

1985), as mentioned earlier. The enlarged ramifications of the neurons are made in part of proteins. Furthermore, direct measures of protein in the cerebral cortex of rats showed a significant increase with enriched experience (Bennett et al., 1969). Recent experiments in the laboratory of Steven Rose (e.g., Schleibs et al., 1983) have shown that if a chick is given brief training, parts of the brain can then be removed and the training-induced increase in protein synthesis can be followed within a tissue chamber; brain samples from control chicks not given the training show a significantly lower rate of protein synthesis.

The other side of the story is that inhibiting the synthesis of proteins in the brain can prevent the formation of long-term memory, even though the pretrial administration of the agent does not interfere with acquisition or with retrieval during short-term or intermediate-term tests. This field of investigation provides a good example of the rigorous testing and elimination of alternatives that characterize an advancing area of research. The proposed alternatives are also worth examining because they reveal some of the complexities in both the behavior and the biological processes involved in learning and memory.

The behavioral criteria of learning and memory are, of course, crucial to our study because they provide our only way of knowing whether learning has occurred and memory has been formed and retained. Yet the behavioral tests do not always provide clear and unambiguous answers. If a subject fails to make a learned response when tested for retention, is this result a clear sign of forgetting? Not necessarily. The response may be stored but may not be retrievable at the moment, like a name that you are sure you know but just can't bring out. An easier test—recognition rather than recall—may yield the response and thus demonstrate that the memory was present all along. Some investigators tend to ignore the fact that memories are graded in strength. Memories are not simply present or absent, rather they may range all the way from very weak to very strong. Strong memories are easy to retrieve, but weak memories can be retrieved only under favorable circumstances. Also, a response may be available but the subject is not motivated to produce it, so psychologists stress the performance aspects of tests. Investigators have to be keenly aware of behavioral aspects of their experiments and must cross-check one test with another to be sure of the accuracy of their interpretations.

Research to test the effects of inhibitors of protein synthesis on formation of long-term memory began in the 1960s and has continued to the present. Most of this work has been done with rodents, especially mice. Why have investigators still not been able to decide conclusively whether synthesis of protein is required for formation of long-term memories? The answer to the question includes several parts:

1. The pharmacological agents used in the experiments have more than one effect, and it is not a simple task to test and rule out all the side effects. For example, drugs that inhibit protein synthesis also decrease the synthesis of adrenal steroids and of catecholamine neurotransmitters; one of these effects, rather than inhibition of protein synthesis, may be the reason that the drugs impair memory.
2. Many behavioral findings lend themselves to diverse interpretations. For example, some investigators have hypothesized that protein synthesis inhibitors impair retrieval of memory rather than impairing formation of the memory. Such alternative interpretations then require separate tests.

3. Results with a single kind of behavioral test could reflect special features of that test; for example, failure to enter a zone where aversive treatment had been given could reflect either memory or motor impairment. Therefore it is desirable to see whether apparent effects on memory are found in a variety of test situations.

4. Research on the basic question has given rise to related questions, such as the conditions necessary for inhibitors to take their effect, interaction with other drugs, and so on.

Let us note some of the main steps in research in this area and some of the main findings.

Use of Varied Antibiotic Drugs

Several antibiotic drugs have been tested for possible amnestic qualities. Many new antibiotics are created each year, and some have been found to inhibit the formation of memory. Puromycin was the antibiotic used in initial research to test the hypothesis that protein synthesis is required for formation of long-term memory (Flexner et al., 1962). Injection of puromycin bilaterally into the temporal cortex blocked retention of Y maze training in mice, whereas similar injection of saline solution or of various compounds related to puromycin did not interfere with recall. A few years later it was found that puromycin produces abnormal electrical activity in the hippocampus and that it is toxic. For this reason, puromycin was largely abandoned in this work and other agents were taken up.

The protein synthesis inhibitor cycloheximide has been widely used since the middle 1960s. It is an effective amnestic agent if it is administered shortly before training in a dose that inhibits protein synthesis in the brain by about 90% (Barondes & Cohen, 1967). A single dose inhibits protein synthesis for a few hours. It may seem surprising that the brain can get along with protein synthesis almost completely blocked for hours, but cells contain large supplies of proteins; existing enzymes, for example, can continue directing the cell's metabolism. Memory research with this inhibitor suffered, however, from two major flaws. First, the level of inhibition necessary to produce amnesia required toxic doses of the drug, and many animals showed signs of illness. Second, even strong inhibition seemed to overcome only weak training. Investigators therefore wondered whether inhibition of protein synthesis affected only weak memories.

Then Bennett introduced to this field an inhibitor that overcame previous problems, anisomycin (Bennett, Hebert, & Orme, 1972; Flood et al., 1973). This inhibitor is an effective amnestic agent at low doses; 25 times the effective amnestic dose is nonlethal. Because anisomycin is safe, it can be given in repeated doses; administering it every 2 hours keeps inhibition of cerebral protein synthesis at about 90%. With such repeated administration, Flood and co-workers demonstrated that even relatively strong training could be overcome by inhibition of protein synthesis; the stronger the training, the longer the inhibition had to be maintained to cause amnesia.

Figure 17-20 shows results of an experiment in which mice were trained in one-trial passive avoidance and received either one, two, or three successive subcutaneous injections of anisomycin; the first injection was given 15 minutes before the

Figure 17-20 Percentage of mice showing amnesia after having had one of four levels of training in passive avoidance and subcutaneous injections of anisomycin, an inhibitor of protein synthesis. Some groups received a single injection 15 minutes before training (white curve). Some also received a second injection 2 hours after the first (brown curve), and some received a third injection 2 hours after the second (black curve). The level of amnesia was greater the weaker the training and the longer the duration of inhibition of protein synthesis. (From Flood et al., 1973)

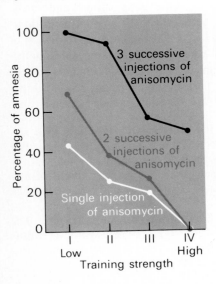

training trial, and the subsequent injections were given at 2-hour intervals. With the foot shock strength used in this experiment, two successive injections—4 hours of inhibition of protein synthesis—were not enough to cause amnesia. Averaging across all four levels of training strength, 70% of the mice showed recall at the retention test two weeks after training. But three injections of anisomycin—6 hours of inhibition—did cause amnesia; only 20% of the mice recalled at the retention test. Note that the injection that made the difference was given 3¾ hours after training, so the synthesis of protein(s) necessary for long-term memory may take place hours after training if inhibition of synthesis has been prevented up to this time. With stronger training an even longer period of inhibition of protein synthesis may be necessary to cause amnesia. Thus, in principle at least, even strong training can be overcome by a sufficiently long period of inhibition of protein synthesis.

Normally the synthesis of protein related to memory storage occurs during the minutes that follow the training trial; if in mice the first injection of inhibitor is given only 15 minutes after training, there is no amnesia even if thereafter a long series of injections is administered. But the necessary synthesis, which without the drug occurs rapidly, can be delayed by inhibiting synthesis for a few hours. The capacity to form proteins related to memory may therefore persist for a few hours, at least under the effects of inhibitors of synthesis.

To test further the generality of the findings with passive avoidance and to study the effects of even longer periods of inhibition of protein synthesis, Flood and co-workers (1975, 1977) did experiments with active-avoidance training and extended the duration of inhibition up to 14 hours. Active avoidance in a T maze requires several trials to learn and is, of course, more complex than single-trial passive avoidance; it was used to determine whether the same principles applied. Different groups of mice were given 6, 8, or 10 trials in a T maze, motivated by foot shock. For different subgroups inhibition of protein synthesis lasted for 2, 8, 10, 12, or 14 hours. Retention tests run one week after training demonstrated that even in well-trained mice (10 training trials), 14 hours of inhibition produced a significant percentage of amnesia (see Table 17-2). The longer the duration of inhibition, the higher was the percentage of amnesia. Also, the weaker the training, the higher was the percentage of amnesia. Thus the same principles that had been demonstrated for passive avoidance also apply to the more complex and more variable behavior of active avoidance. The results of this program of experimentation brought new and

Table 17-2 Percentage of Animals Showing Amnesia at Test As a Function of Strength of Training and Duration of Inhibition of Protein Synthesis

Strength of Training (number of training trials)	Length of Inhibition (hours)					
	0	2	8	10	12	14
6	0	10	77	73	70	90
8	0	10	44	50	71	77
10	0	0	36	38	60	62

Source: Flood, Bennett, Orme, and Rosenzweig (1975).

integrated support to the hypothesis that synthesis of protein is necessary for the formation of long-term memory.

Since most of the research on this question had been done with aversive training, the question was raised whether inhibition of protein synthesis would also prevent formation of long-term memory for positive reinforcements. When rats ran a radial maze for food rewards, pretrial administration of anisomycin did not prevent acquisition or short-term memory, but it prevented formation of long-term memory (Mizumori et al., 1985). Similarly, when mice ran a Y maze for water rewards, inhibition of protein synthesis prevented long-term memory (Patterson et al., 1987). Furthermore, in the latter experiment, comparison with the effects of an agent that causes conditioned aversion showed that the apparent failure of formation of long-term memory could not be attributed to aversive conditioning to the inhibitor (Patterson et al., 1987). Thus inhibition of protein synthesis during the period following learning prevents formation of long-term memory for a wide variety of training situations, including learning for positive reinforcement and situations that involve active and passive avoidance.

The combination of experiments using behavioral intervention and experiments using somatic intervention provides strong support for the hypothesis that formation of long-term memory requires increased protein synthesis in the posttraining period; that is, training has been found to cause increased protein synthesis in certain brain regions, and blocking protein synthesis prevents formation of long-term memory in a variety of situations.

Mechanisms of Short-Term and Intermediate-Term Memories

Even when an experience does not result in long-term memory, a person or animal may be able to respond correctly during a period of minutes before memory vanishes. Such short-term or intermediate-term memories (STM or ITM) are very useful in dealing with the flow of events. Since protein synthesis is not required for these brief memories, as we have just seen, what neural processes serve to maintain them?

A hypothesis that has attracted a good deal of attention and inspired quite a bit of research holds that there are three sequentially linked biochemical stages in memory formation (Gibbs & Ng, 1977). This hypothesis is based on the finding that many effects of chemical or pharmacological agents on memory can be grouped into just three time periods. These are shown in Figure 17-21, and some of the agents are listed in Table 17-3. Figure 17-21 shows first a brief stage that is not specified in chemical terms but that can be abolished by electroconvulsive shock; here memory may be held momentarily by some residual activity that briefly survives the initial electrical responses. The first chemical stage appears to be related to hyperpolarization of neurons caused by a change in K^+ conductance. This so-called short-term stage holds memory for about 10–15 minutes and can be abolished or enhanced by agents that alter K^+ conductance. The second chemical stage holds memory for about 30 minutes. This intermediate-term stage appears to be related to hyperpolarization caused by changes in activity of the sodium-potassium pump. The third stage is characterized by protein synthesis, which is necessary to establish long-term memory. It is probable that these stages are sequentially dependent; that is, abolishing any stage eliminates the next one.

Table 17-3   Stages of Memory in the Chick and Agents That Affect Their Formation

Stage	Maximum Duration	Processes Hypothesized to Mediate	Agents That Facilitate	Agents That Inhibit
Short-term	15 min	Hyperpolarization involving K^+ conductance change	Calcium chloride	Lithium chloride, potassium chloride
Intermediate-term	30 min	Hyperpolarization involving Na^+-K^+ pump activity	Diphenylhydantoin, pargyline	Ouabain, ethacrynic acid
Long-term	Days	Protein synthesis	Pargyline, amphetamine	Anisomycin, cycloheximide, aminoisobutyrate

Identification of these stages and of the underlying processes came from experiments with day-old chicks. Most of the training involved a one-trial, passive-avoidance task carried out in the following way: A small shiny bead that had been dipped in water was presented at the end of a wire, and the chick pecked at it. If the bead had been dipped in a bitter solution, after pecking it, the chick would shake its head and wipe its beak vigorously on the floor of the cage. Without any further treatment a chick would remember such an experience and refuse to peck the bead again, whether the test trial occurred 3 hours or 24 hours later. The specificity of this learning was tested by presenting the bitter substance on a colored bead (red for some chicks and blue for others). At subsequent testing chicks did not peck the bead of the color that had been coupled with the bitter taste, yet they readily pecked the other bead. But if certain chemicals are injected into the animal, shortly before or shortly after training, it forgets the bitter taste and pecks at the test bead on a recall trial.

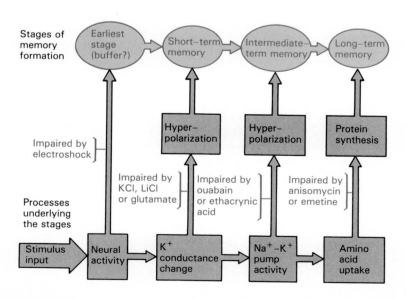

Figure 17-21 Stages of memory formation and processes that may underlie each stage. Note that the stages in this schema of Gibbs and Ng (1977) are similar to those of McGaugh (1968) presented in Figure 16-4. For each stage a treatment is indicated that can impair the underlying process of memory formation. (Adapted from Gibbs and Ng, 1977)

Figure 17-22 Percentages of chicks showing learned avoidance response on retention test. The percentage of recollection varied with both the substance injected into the brain and the interval of time between learning and retention. Each point is based on data from a separate group of chicks. Administration of anisomycin (black curve) prevented formation of long-term memory, but intermediate-term memory (30 minutes) and short-term memory (5–10 minutes) were intact. Administration of ouabain (brown curve) prevented formation of inter-mediate-term memory, but short-term memory (5–10 minutes) was intact. Administration of KCl prevented for-mation of even short-term memory. (Adapted from Gibbs and Ng, 1977)

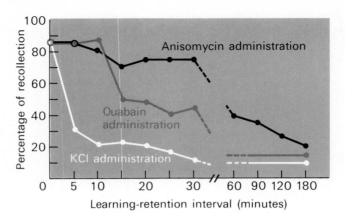

In a study of the temporal gradients of drug effects, a drug was given at one of various times before or after the avoidance training trial, and the retention trial was given at one of various time intervals after training. A different group of chicks was used for each combination of injection time and test time, and each animal was tested only once. Thus large numbers of chicks were used in this study, which is why an inexpensive test animal and a rapid, reliable procedure were indispensable. Results for different classes of agents are shown in Figure 17-22. Depending on the class of drug used, memory was abolished after different durations. Other agents can enhance memory at each of these stages, which lends further support to this three-stage model of memory formation. Investigators have begun to look for these stages in mammals; results so far are positive, although the exact time courses may differ somewhat among species.

Hemispheric Asymmetry in Formation of Passive-Avoidance Memory in the Chick

Just as imprinting has been found to involve the two cerebral hemispheres of the chick differentially, peck-aversion training has also been found recently to involve asymmetric contributions of the two hemispheres (Patterson et al., 1986). In these experiments amnestic agents have been injected into different brain structures in the left hemisphere, the right hemisphere, or bilaterally. (For locations of these struc-tures, see Figure 17-18). Selected for these experiments were agents that appear to act on STM, ITM, or LTM and that have sharply localized effects in the brain. Injection of such an agent into the left medial hyperstriatum ventrale (MHV) was found to be about as effective in blocking formation of memory as bilateral injec-tion, whereas injection into the right MHV was practically without effect; these effects are illustrated in Figure 17-23. (Recall that the left MHV is also involved in imprinting.) A mirror image of these results was found with injections into another region, the lateral neostriatum (LN): Injection into the left LN produced little effect, whereas injection into the right LN prevented formation of memory about as effec-tively as bilateral injection. Both MHV and LN showed effects with agents that are presumed to affect each of the three stages of memory, so apparently both of these

Figure 17-23 Reductions of retention caused by unilateral injections of drugs into either of two regions of the chick brain. The baseline is the 80% retention displayed by control animals given injections of physiological saline, as shown by the dashed line. Effects of injections into the medial hyperstriatum ventrale are shown in the left half of the graph; here injections into the left hemisphere caused significant reductions of retention (*, $p < 0.01$), whereas injections into the right hemisphere had no significant effect. For the lateral neostriatum, injections into the left hemisphere did not affect retention, but injections into the right hemisphere caused significant reductions. These effects occurred for agents that impair each stage of memory formation: STM (glutamate, 50nM), ITM (ouabain, 0.027nM), and LTM (emetine, 2.25nM). (After T. A. Patterson, 1987)

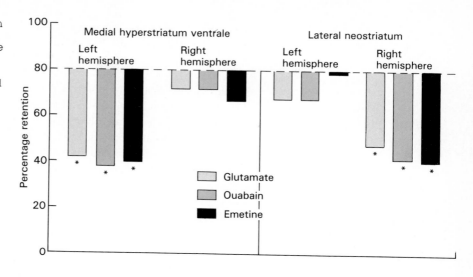

brain regions are involved in all three stages of memory formation. Use of such agents whose action is restricted spatially promises to be helpful in revealing the roles of different brain structures in different stages of memory formation.

Current Status of Hypotheses on Multiple Stages of Memory and Their Mechanisms

Investigators have also begun to test for biochemical mechanisms of stages of memory formation in mammals. The agents that are amnestic for chicks are also amnestic when administered to mammals (Mizumori et al., 1985), and there is other evidence of sequential stages in memory formation in mammals (e.g., Frieder & Allweis, 1982a, b). Frieder and Allweis (1982b) state that it would be premature to compare their results and model based on work with rats in detail with those of Gibbs and Ng (1977) based on work with chicks (Figure 17-21); neither the species, the learning task, the retention measure, nor the inhibitors were the same in the two laboratories. "However," they conclude, "the fact that multi-phase models are necessary to encompass the data in such very different studies strengthens the argument for the existence of several operationally distinguishable neurochemical processes and memory-holding mechanisms in the consolidation of memory" (1982b, p. 1069). Nevertheless, there is not unanimity about the existence of sequentially linked stages in the formation of memory. Many investigators hold that here are several kinds of memory, including different stages, as Tulving (1985) has concluded from an extensive review. Others argue, however, that memory is unitary and that the appearance of stages may result from different degrees or durations of processing of learned material. Similarly, many investigators of biological aspects of learning and memory have concluded that there are different stages of memory formation, with different underlying processes, although they do not necessarily agree about the numbers of stages or the identities of the processes. Yet some investigators (e.g., Gold & McGaugh, 1975) maintain that a single kind of memory trace that develops and changes over time can account for the observations. Only further research can settle this question, and it is being pursued intensively.

Modulation of Formation of Memory

Besides the agents and conditions that affect the basic or direct processes of memory formation, many other agents and conditions can also alter memory formation. For example, the general state of arousal of the organism affects memory formation, with a moderate state of arousal being optimal. The emotional state that follows the learning experience also affects the formation of memory for that experience. Agents that affect memory formation include stimulants (such as amphetamine and caffeine), depressants (such as phenobarbital and chloral hydrate), neuropeptides, so-called neuromodulators that affect the activity or ''gain'' of neurons (including agents that elsewhere serve as neurotransmitters, such as acetylcholine and norepinephrine), drugs that affect the cholinergic transmitter system or the catecholamines, opioid peptides, and hormones. Experiments with such agents and conditions have led to the concept of **modulation of formation of memory** or **modulation of memory storage processes.**

Modulation means adjustment or adaptation to particular circumstances. Two further aspects are often implied by the use of this term in relation to memory formation. One is that a particular condition or agent can either enhance or impair memory formation, depending upon the time or strength of treatment or other conditions. This is often true, as we will see, but it is not a criterion for the existence of modulation. The other implication is controversial: We know the fundamental biological processes involved in the formation of memories and other treatments are secondary ones, superimposed on the basic processes. Figure 17-24 indicates this view of basic and modulatory processes in the formation of memory. It may be overoptimistic to think that we can really distinguish what is modulatory from what is a basic storage process. But many modulatory effects are large and important, so it is worth investigating them, especially since some of them may yet turn out to be basic. In this section we will survey results obtained with two kinds of chemical modulators, and then we will consider mechanisms of modulation.

Figure 17-24 Schematic presentation of direct and modulatory processes in memory. Each direct process, or stage of memory (shown in gray), can have its rate or level facilitated or inhibited by various modulatory processes (symbolized by arrows with brown shafts). Facilitation is indicated by white arrowheads and inhibition by black arrowheads.

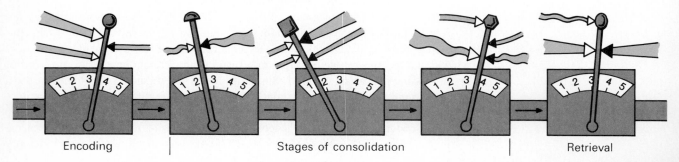

Encoding | Stages of consolidation | Retrieval

Neuromodulators

Neurons from certain small brain nuclei send out axons that branch widely throughout many regions of the brain and affect the activity and thresholds of the neurons they influence. For example, modulatory cholinergic fibers spread especially to the cerebral cortex and hippocampus. A major source of these modulatory cholinergic fibers is called the **magnocellular nucleus of the basal forebrain** (also known as the **basal nucleus of Meynert**). The location and projections of the magnocellular nucleus of the basal forebrain were shown in Figure 4-25. Recent work has implicated this region in Alzheimer's disease, as we will discuss in the last section of this chapter.

Just as axons of the modulatory cholinergic system ramify widely from nuclei in the basal forebrain, modulatory noradrenergic fibers spread widely from a small nucleus in the anterior pons; this nucleus is called the **locus coeruleus** (shown in Figure 14-21). In the rat the locus coeruleus contains only about 1500 neurons, but it sends fibers to the entire cerebral cortex and the diencephalon. Individual locus coeruleus cells appear to innervate longitudinal strips of cerebral cortex, extending from frontal cortex all the way back to the occipital region (Lindvall & Bjorklund, 1984). This system innervates specific layers of cortex which vary from region to region: the specificity of distribution is much clearer in primates than in rodents. Work with this system suggests that it modulates activity and neuronal plasticity in most of the brain. Other catecholamines besides norepinephrine also modulate neural activity and sensitivity.

Many experiments have shown that agents that affect the cholinergic or adrenergic systems can alter memory formation. Because acetylcholine and norepinephrine act as neurotransmitters in some locations and as neuromodulators in others, it is often difficult to be sure which of these two functions is involved in a specific case of influence on memory by an agent that acts on the cholinergic or adrenergic system. Bearing this problem in mind, let us note a few examples of modulation of memory formation by agents that affect the cholinergic system or catecholaminergic system.

Examples of Cholinergic Modulation

Scopolamine (which blocks muscarinic ACh receptors) used to be employed during childbirth because it prevents formation of long-term memories; under the influence of the drug, the mother can aid in the delivery of the child but will not subsequently recall the delivery. Experimental studies with human subjects have confirmed that scopolamine does not affect short-term memory but significantly impairs long-term memory (Drachman, 1978). Moreover, the pattern of impairment over a battery of tests was quite similar to the pattern shown by elderly subjects. Agents that enhance cholinergic action have been found to improve formation of long-term memory in normal human subjects (Davis et al., 1978; Sitaram et al., 1978). Because of the foregoing findings, work is being done to try to improve the memory of aged and demented patients by giving them drugs that prolong the action of ACh at synapses and also by giving ACh precursors, that is, compounds used by the body to manufacture ACh.

Figure 17-25 Varied strengths of memories as a function of training strength and time after training. The white curve represents memory strength after weak training; it does not reach the criterion of recall. The brown curve indicates memory strength after training of intermediate strength; the memory is supra-threshold for a time but then falls below the criterion. The black curve represents memory strength after strong training. Different tests for memory can shift the level of criterion up or down.

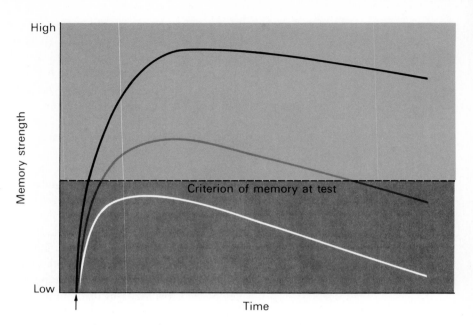

Examples of Catecholamine Modulation

The catecholamine transmitters normally are active for moderately long periods when released or injected. Posttrial injection of catecholamines into the cerebral ventricles of mice aids memory formation (Haycock et al., 1977). Conversely, posttrial injection of a drug (DDC) that lowers the levels of catecholamines impairs subsequent memory (Jensen et al., 1977; Stein, Belluzzi, & Wise, 1975). To test whether the impairment might be due to some side effect of the drug other than lowering catecholamine levels the investigators administered posttrial injections of norepinephrine, and these injections reduced the impairment caused by DDC (Stein, Belluzzi, & Wise, 1975). Thus memory formation can be modulated up or down by altering levels of brain catecholamines.

The best opportunity for finding modulatory effects occurs when the strength of memory is neither too strong nor too weak; the middle range allows sensitive tests and is not stuck at ''ceiling'' or ''floor'' levels. The experimenter can control training conditions and also use a drug such as anisomycin in order to put memory strength near a sensitive ''balance point,'' that is, near the behavioral dividing line that classifies an animal as having either ''memory'' or ''amnesia'' (Figure 17-25). Results of an experiment using d-amphetamine (which causes release of norepinephrine) are shown in Figure 17-26. This experiment used anisomycin, as described, to weaken the memory. d-Amphetamine administered either 30 or 90 minutes after training attenuated the amnesic effect of two successive doses of anisomycin. But if d-amphetamine administration was delayed until 150 minutes after training, little attenuating effect was seen.

Developmental changes in catecholamine levels may help to explain why some kinds of learning or plastic effects show critical periods—that is, occur only during relatively brief parts of the life span. Examples of effects that can be induced only during a critical period are imprinting and the changes in ocular dominance that occur when one eye is occluded for several weeks. Kasamatsu and Pettigrew (1979)

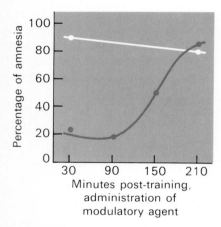

Figure 17-26 Effects of amphetamine administered at various times post-training to animals made amnesic by anisomycin. Giving amphetamine (brown curve) at 30 or 90 minutes posttraining was effective in combating the amnesic effects of anisomycin, but injections at later times had lesser or no effect. Giving saline (white curve) had no effect on the level of amnesia; this served as a control for the injection procedures. Twenty mice were used per point. (Adapted from Bennett, Rosenzweig, and Flood, 1979)

reported that the susceptibility to shifts of ocular dominance can be modulated by norepinephrine: If norepinephrine levels were artificially reduced in the visual cortex of kittens, a shift in ocular dominance could not be induced, as it can be in normal kittens. Conversely, in adult cats in which a shift in dominance cannot normally be brought about, prolonged perfusion of the visual cortex with norepinephrine produced a shift in dominance. These results proved difficult to replicate until Baer and Singer (1985) showed that for consistent effects, both acetylcholine and norepinephrine had to be manipulated. Many therapeutic uses can be imagined for a technique that enhances learning and plastic changes in the brain. For example, pharmacological treatments might be used to overcome some kinds of mental retardation or to aid recovery of function after brain lesions.

Modulation of Memory Formation by Opioids

Modulation of memory formation by opioid peptides has been an active field of investigation since the late 1970s. Several studies (e.g., Jensen et al., 1978) showed that administering morphine just after training impairs retention for aversive training. This effect was then found to be shared by several opioid peptides (e.g., Martinez & Rigter, 1980). Observations of this sort raised the question whether these were simply effects of drugs or whether endogenous opioids normally impair retention. Evidence that endogenous peptides normally function in this way was provided by numerous reports that posttraining administration of naloxone, as well as other opioid antagonists, could increase retention of aversive training (e.g., Messing et al., 1979). The first interpretation of these findings emphasized that opioids attenuate the responses to aversive stimuli, that is, if a drug makes an aversive reinforcement less painful or unpleasant, then the aversive effect is less likely to become associated with some other stimulus. But more recent work has shown that the effects of opioids and their antagonists are not limited to learning with regard to aversive reinforcement. Some experiments have shown that opioids can impair retention for appetitive reinforcement such as food (e.g., Linden & Martinez, 1986), just as they can impair retention for aversive reinforcement. Furthermore, opioid antagonists can also improve retention for positive reinforcement (e.g., Gallagher, King, & Young, 1983). This can occur even if the antagonist is administered peripherally and thus does not directly affect the brain. The effects of these agents are not restricted to associative situations; habituation is also affected: For example, Izquierdo (1979) found that morphine decreased long-term retention of habituation, whereas naloxone enhanced retention of habituation. Thus the original interpretation was too narrow because opioids and their antagonists appear to affect many kinds of learning. One possibility now being examined is that the opioids affect memory formation because they inhibit the release of two major neurotransmitters, norepinephrine and acetylcholine; evidence on this hypothesis is reviewed by Gallagher (1985).

Modulation of Memory Formation by Hormones

Several hormones also affect memory formation even if they are administered into the body and not into the brain (McGaugh, 1983). These include ACTH or certain fractions of the ACTH molecule, opioid peptides, vasopressin and oxytocin, and other hormones or hormonelike substances. These substances do not cross the blood-brain barrier, and it is not yet known by what mechanisms their presence in the body affects brain functions in memory formation. Some of these agents, such as ACTH and vasopressin, may have either facilitating or impairing effects on memory, depending on the dose employed. Others, such as oxytocin and the endogenous opioid peptides enkephalin and endorphin, seem to be consistently amnestic, although that has not yet been demonstrated conclusively. Izquierdo et al. (1982) suggest that such amnestic hormones provide a mechanism to prevent the storage of an overwhelming amount of information. But even if this is shown to be true, it is only part of the story because there are also hormones that enhance retention. A broader formulation is that hormonal systems modulate memory formation in either direction, enhancing or impairing, and some affect memory even if they are released or administered outside the brain.

Mechanisms of Modulation

It is clear that there are modulatory effects, but how do they occur? There are many possible ways in which modulators might work, and different classes of modulators may have different mechanisms of action. Let us review some of these possibilities.

Stimulant and depressant drugs that modulate memory might actually alter the rates of protein synthesis; that is, perhaps these drugs alter protein synthesis directly, or perhaps they do so in interaction with anisomycin. Direct tests ruled out these possibilities: The stimulant and depressant drugs had only slight effects on protein synthesis either by themselves or used in conjunction with anisomycin (Flood et al., 1977).

According to another hypothesis, modulating agents could alter motivational feedback that may be important for formulation of long-term memories; that is, among all the information that an individual takes in and stores briefly, only a small fraction is selected for long-term storage. If certain stimuli or behaviors turn out to have important motivational consequences, they are more apt to be put into long-term memory. Kety (1976) has pointed out that the catecholamines, and especially norepinephrine, are often involved in such motivational feedback, and he has hypothesized that these neurotransmitters thus play a special modulating role in memory storage. This role could include both central and peripheral feedback. As we just saw, this explanation cannot account for all the effects of the opioids on memory formation, but it may hold in certain cases.

Another hypothesis—and one that may have wide relevance—is that the level of arousal following acquisition plays an important role in determining the length of time and the rate of the biosynthetic phase of memory formation. This hypothesis is consistent with the finding that treatments, other than drugs, that affect the level of arousal can alter formation of long-term memory. For example, the use of foot shock in training increases arousal as well as furnishing information about behavioral contingencies, and foot shock usually leads to strong memory formation. Electrical stimulation of the reticular formation following learning trials can also foster the production of long-term memories.

Of course, different examples of modulation may work through different mechanisms. Because modulatory effects have aroused the curiosity of many investigators and because further knowledge about these effects may lead to valuable applications, this is another aspect of memory processes that is attracting much research.

Applications of Research on Mechanisms of Learning and Memory

Many investigators believe that research on mechanisms of learning and memory is in a unique breakthrough phase, and that this could have consequences as great as those that followed solving the genetic code. Understanding how acquired information is coded and stored in the nervous system is leading to better understanding of the mind and behavior; beyond this it will undoubtedly contribute to a wide orbit of applications in fields ranging from education and memory disorders to design of artificial intelligence systems.

The description of phenomena of learning and memory is becoming more precise and is differentiating aspects that were formerly ignored or lumped together, such as habits versus memories, associative versus nonassociative learning, different stages of memory formation, and priming effects versus conscious recall and recognition. In spite of these advances, some experts believe that progress in the neurobiology of learning and memory will be limited mainly by the rate of development of appropriate behavioral analyses and techniques.

Let us consider a few examples of areas in which this research may be applied, some of which are close at hand and some of which may still be relatively remote.

Education

Education is one of the principal activities in most countries and occupies a major part of the lives of most children and many adults. Many educators are looking to cognitive scientists and neuroscientists for a better understanding of the basic processes by which memories are formed and retrieved and by which subject areas are mastered; examples of this quest are books edited by Chall and Mirsky (1978), Wittrock (1977), and Friedman, Klivington, and Peterson (1986). Studies of special difficulties in learning to read by dyslexics have already proved helpful. In fact since the early 1960s there has been a move away from psychiatric views about the causes of difficulties in learning to read and toward neurological and neuropsychological views (Chall & Peterson, 1986). Federal programs have emphasized neurological disorders in qualifying children for special programs for the learning disabled. Most schoolchildren with severe difficulty in learning to read were found to have difficulty in learning other materials as well: they did not have perceptual deficits, but most had deficits in short-term memory (Kagan & Moore, 1981).

Many ways have been considered to improve learning and memory of normal students. For example, suitable levels of alertness and attention aid learning and attention, and noninvasive behavioral methods can be used to increase these factors in the school situation. For this purpose several schools in Austria are using a program devised by an investigator whose research spans the field from physiological psychology to applications in education (Guttman, 1986).

In the desire to improve the effectiveness of education, educators and the public need to be wary of unfounded claims about applications of neuroscience to improve education. Unfortunately, as educators Chall and Peterson (1986) point out, "Increasing numbers of articles in education journals and popular books tend to make broad promises for the application of brain research for solving the ills of the schools, of children's learning, and of society" (p. 300). Many of these claims are related to misunderstanding and misinterpretation of differences in functioning of the two hemispheres of the brain. For example, some people call for drastic changes in school curricula, claiming that most schools are biased against the right hemisphere! We will take up the topic of hemispheric differences in cognitive functions in Chapter 18.

Alzheimer's Disease: Puzzles and Progress

We mentioned Alzheimer's disease (AD) and its heavy toll earlier in the book. Although not all people with this disease are elderly, the incidence rises after age 65. As the aged population grows over the next decades, the suffering and costs caused by AD are expected to rise dramatically unless effective means are found to counter it. Consideration of AD here brings together several themes from this and other chapters.

AD is certainly relevant in this chapter because the first symptoms of the disease are usually problems of memory. Disorders of language and perception may also appear early, and they almost invariably occur in the course of the disease. At present there is no certain way to diagnose AD before death except by means of biopsies, that is, removing small amounts of brain tissue. Most diagnoses of AD are made through behavioral tests and by excluding other diseases that may cause similar symptoms. Dementia may be produced by a variety of causes, including cerebral vascular problems, depression, and AIDS. Recent studies report that AIDS often shows up as unexplained cognitive impairments or brain pathology (Koenig et al., 1986). Diagnoses of AD are not infallible, but they are now correct most of the time as confirmed by postmortem observation of certain structural changes in the brain. The conclusive postmortem test is the presence of neurofibrillary tangles and senile plaques composed of abnormal neural outgrowths (shown in Figure 4-25). Because one cannot be certain of the premortem diagnosis, living patients are often said to have Senile Dementia of the Alzheimer's Type (SDAT). There is a pressing need to characterize the cognitive deficits of AD more precisely in order to differentiate it from other diseases and to allow more conclusive premortem diagnoses.

The severe public health problems imposed by Alzheimer's disease have stimulated a great deal of research of both clinical and laboratory varieties. As is true for many other questions of relations between brain and behavior, there is an ongoing dialogue between clinical research and basic research, including research with animal models. Besides the obvious need to alleviate and prevent AD, there are other reasons for us to consider it here:

- Attempts to devise effective therapies for AD challenge our understanding of the causes and mechanisms of the disease and of the cognitive impairments that characterize it; that is, sufficient understanding of the disease should lead to useful therapies, and failure of therapies to provide clear relief indicates a lack of understanding.
- Study of the relations between cognitive symptoms and the neurological deficits may advance our understanding of the neural systems that make normal cognition possible.

Much of the current research on AD focuses on characteristic changes in neurotransmitter systems. Most prominent and consistent among these are deficiencies in the cholinergic system. As noted earlier, cholinergic cells from regions in the basal forebrain send axons that ramify widely throughout the cerebral cortex and the hippocampus (Figure 4-25). Presumably these cells modulate the activity of their target neurons. An enzyme important in the synthesis of acetylcholine (choline acetyltransferase [ChAt]) is markedly deficient in brain tissue of AD patients. It is thought that the senile plaques that are diagnostic of AD are mainly composed of degenerated cholinergic terminals.

Some AD patients—especially those in whom symptoms appear before the age of 65—also show deficiencies of other transmitter systems, including those that employ the transmitters norepinephrine, dopamine, serotonin, GABA, and somatostatin. But the changes in these other transmitter systems are not as consistently associated with AD as are the changes in the cholinergic system. The degree of the deficiency in the cholinergic system is reported to correlate significantly with the severity of behavioral symptoms, while the changes in the other transmitter systems do not show clear correlations (Bowen, Francis, & Palmer, 1986).

The consistent findings of deficiencies in the cholinergic system in AD have led to attempts to improve cholinergic activity in a variety of ways: increasing the amount of acetylcholine by providing precursors such as choline or lecithin, stimulating cholinergic neurons with muscarinic agonists, or slowing the breakdown of ACh by inhibiting the enzyme cholinesterase (ChE). Several studies have used the drug physostigmine, which is a reversible inhibitor of ChE. Some of these studies have reported that this drug improves the behavior of some but not all SDAT patients (e.g., Mohs et al., 1985; Thal et al., 1983). In spite of many positive reports, it is clear that none of these cholinergic therapies has proved to be useful with most SDAT patients. This contrasts with the effectiveness of L-dopa for most patients with Parkinson's disease and the wide effectiveness of neuroleptic drugs against schizophrenia.

Several reasons have been advanced to explain why cholinergic therapies have not aided most sufferers from SDAT; these are examples of individual differences in susceptibility to drugs, a fact that we noted in Chapter 6:

- Some people may not absorb certain cholinergic drugs effectively into the central nervous system. One recent study measured whether oral administration of physostigmine was actually inhibiting cholinesterase in SDAT patients; this was done by determining ChE activity in cerebrospinal fluid (Thal et al., 1983). The effectiveness of physostigmine in inhibiting the patients' ChE levels was highly related to their improvement on memory test scores. Those patients who did not show behavioral improvement also showed no sign that the drug was getting into the central nervous system. Higher doses, a more effective route of administration of physostigmine, or use of a different anticholinesterase agent might be helpful to such patients.
- Some SDAT patients may have already suffered such extensive loss of cholinergic cells that little ACh was being produced that could be potentiated by anticholinesterase agents. This may be similar to the finding that in advanced cases of Parkinson's disease the efficacy of L-dopa is reduced.
- The fact that other neurotransmitter systems are also impaired in some AD patients suggests that combined treatments involving two or more transmitter systems may be more effective than therapy directed toward the cholinergic system alone.

A still broader approach is the hypothesis that the lack of specific nerve growth factors (NGFs) leads to the degeneration of specific populations of neurons (Appel, 1981). Thus lack of one NGF would lead to the loss of forebrain cholinergic cells that characterizes AD; lack of another NGF would lead to degeneration of the substantia nigra cells in Parkinson's disease; and lack of still another NGF would cause the loss of pyramidal motor neurons, which underlies amyotrophic lateral sclerosis (Lou Gehrig's disease). A number of observations support this hypothesized cause of AD, and a program of research to test it further has been outlined (Hefti & Weiner, 1986). If this hypothesis proves to be correct, it could lead to a therapy that promotes survival of the cholinergic neurons that degenerate in AD. Preventive therapy could preclude occurrence of AD, or intervention with mildly affected patients could stop further degeneration of neurons and the associated progressive behavioral deterioration.

Combination of behavioral therapy with pharmacological treatment may prove to be helpful. This emerges from some studies where SDAT patients have been given behavioral tests repeatedly while different drug doses were being tried. The repeated testing itself seemed to be beneficial for a majority of the patients. The social interactions of testing may have stimulated patients whose cognitive deficits had led caretakers to neglect them. Combining behavioral stimulation with pharmacological therapy may prove to be especially helpful.

In the attempts being made to characterize more fully the cognitive deficits in AD, the distinction between habits and memories may be important. Recently it was shown that a sample of SDAT patients were able to form a habit (procedural memory) as well as control subjects: they were able to learn and retain the perceptual-motor habit needed to track a moving target with the hand (a pursuit rotor test). But the same patients were significantly inferior to control subjects in retaining representational memories (declarative knowledge) for words or faces (Eslinger & Damasio, 1986). The investigators suggest that the retention of ability to form habits is related to the fact that the degenerative changes in AD largely spare such structures as the cerebellum, basal ganglia, thalamus, motor and premotor areas of the cortex, sensory areas of the cortex, and related pathways. On the other hand, impairment of the ability to form representational memories may be related to the cellular damage of AD seen especially in the hippocampus and in the cortex outside primary sensory and motor regions.

A major obstacle to studying AD has been the lack of an animal model for the disease. Recently, however, investigators have reported substantial progress along this line, as the following examples demonstrate: Significant deficits of memory in monkeys are caused by lesions of the basal forebrain cholinergic centers (Aigner et al., 1984). Damage to the nucleus basalis of Meynert in the rat has been shown to cause reduced ChAt in the cerebral cortex and also to cause behavioral changes, including perseveration and impairments of memory formation (Simon, Mayo, & Le Moal, 1985). Some deficits of learning and memory in aged rats have been ameliorated by grafting into their hippocampal formations cholinergic nerve cell suspensions from the brains of fetal rats (Gage & Bjorklund, 1986). Destruction of a pathway from the septum to the hippocampus in adult rats led to loss of many cholinergic cells in the septum, but infusion of NGF into the cerebral ventricles preserved most of these neurons (Hefti & Weiner, 1986). This suggests that the hippocampal target cells normally supply NGF to the septal cells that innervate them and that the NGF travels along the axons of the septal neurons by retrograde transport. Development of animal models for AD may be a crucial step in understanding this terrible disease and in formulating effective therapies and preventive measures to combat it (Bowen, Francis, & Palmer, 1986).

Summary · Main Points

1. Memory storage has long been hypothesized to involve changes in neural circuits. Research since the 1960s has demonstrated both functional and structural changes at synapses related to learning. Giving rats either formal training or enriched experience leads to structural changes that include alterations in number and size of synaptic contacts and in branching of dendrites.

2. Mechanisms of two kinds of nonassociative learning, habituation and sensitization, have been studied in the relatively simple nervous system of the invertebrate *Aply-*

sia. Habituation reduces influx of Ca^{2+} ions and transmitter release at presynaptic endings and thereby decreases excitatory postsynaptic potentials. Long-term habituation causes a decrease in number and size of synaptic contacts.

3. Sensitization leads to changes in presynaptic K^+ and Ca^{2+} channels that cause increased release of transmitter and increased EPSPs. Long-term sensitization causes an increase in size of synaptic contacts.

4. Conditioning in *Aplysia* leads to changes in the same kinds of ion channels as in sensitization. Conditioning to a light stimulus in another invertebrate, *Hermissenda*, causes changes in different kinds of ion channels and in membrane potentials. Mechanisms of conditioning in the fruit fly, *Drosophila*, have been studied by genetic techniques. Mutants that learn or remember poorly have biochemical deficits that are related to steps that appear to function in the *Aplysia* system.

5. Research in the pigeon on conditioning cardiac acceleration to foot shock has permitted tracing the neural pathways involved in this conditioning. The neurons involved are sensitive to both US and CS at the outset, and memory information is distributed along the pathways that mediate conditioning.

6. Conditioning the eye blink response in the rabbit is crucially dependent upon the ipsilateral cerebellum; the hippocampus may facilitate acquisition of this response. The cerebellar cells show little initial response to US or CS, and memory storage in this system is localized rather than being distributed.

7. Imprinting in chicks is dependent upon localized brain regions. It causes neurochemical and synaptic changes in these regions.

8. Long-term potentiation of neural responses caused by brief high-frequency stimulation can be studied in intact animals or in isolated slices of brain tissue. This phenomenon may be a component of or a model for other kinds of learning. The tissue slice preparation favors electrophysiological and neurochemical investigation of LTP.

9. Neurochemical processes are being investigated for successive stages of memory formation: short-term memory (STM), intermediate-term memory (ITM), and long-term memory (LTM). Much evidence supports the hypothesis that LTM requires synthesis of protein in the posttraining period: Training induces increased synthesis of protein in certain brain regions; blocking synthesis of protein prevents formation of LTM, although it does not prevent learning or formation of STM or ITM.

10. STM and ITM formation may depend upon two different mechanisms of hyperpolarization of neurons. Different drugs that affect these mechanisms can cause specific failure at one or the other duration. The stages appear to be sequentially linked, so that failure of one stage causes failure of the succeeding memory phases.

11. Formation of memory can be modulated (facilitated or impaired) by neural states and by a variety of agents, including stimulants, depressants, certain neurotransmitters, opioid peptides, hormones, and sensory stimulation.

12. The variety of findings to date suggest that a number of neural structures and mechanisms are involved in learning and memory. Different brain circuits and different neurochemical mechanisms may be found for such different aspects as habits versus memories, associative versus nonassociative learning, and different stages of memory formation.

13. Many investigators believe that research on mechanisms of learning and memory is in a breakthrough phase that promises applications in education, possibilities of countering effects of normal aging, and ameliorating or preventing pathologies of learning and memory. Specific claims will, of course, have to be evaluated carefully.

Recommended Reading

Alkon, D. (1988). *Memory traces in the brain*. New York: Cambridge University Press.

Lynch, G., McGaugh, J. L., & Weinberger, N. M. (Eds.). (1984). *Neurobiology of learning and memory*. New York: Guilford Press.

Martinez, J. L., & Kesner, R. P. (Eds.). (1986). *Learning and memory: A biological view*. Orlando, Fla.: Academic Press.

Matthies, H. (Ed.). (1986). *Advances in the biosciences: Vol. 59. Learning and memory: Mechanisms of information storage in the nervous system*. New York: Pergamon.

Squire, L. R. (1987). *Memory and brain*. New York: Oxford University Press.

Squire, L. R., & Butters, N. (Eds.). (1984). *Neuropsychology of memory*. New York: Guilford Press.

Weinberger, N. W., McGaugh, J. L., & Lynch, G. (Eds.). (1985). *Memory systems of the brain*. New York: Guilford Press.

Will, B. E., Schmitt, P., & Dalrymple-Alford, J. C. (Eds.). (1985). *Advances in behavioral biology: Vol. 28. Brain plasticity, learning, and memory*. New York: Plenum.

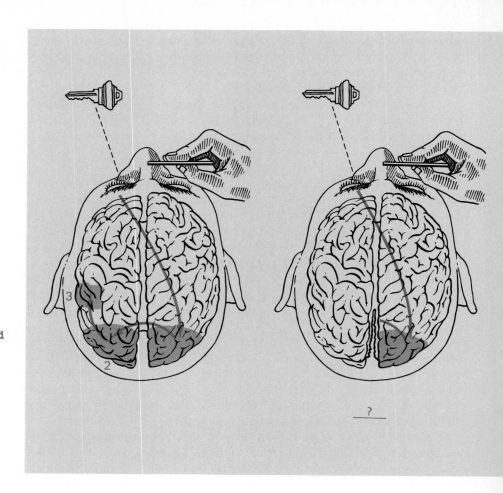

18 Language and Cognition

ORIENTATION

Inspection of this week's best-seller list readily confirms the impression that only humans write books, though chimps may dabble in paint and rats may occasionally eat books. By this and many other measures, human mental life is distinctive in the animal world. But as yet the biological foundations of our complex cognitive abilities, especially language, are barely known. Clues to the workings of the brain related to human cognition come from studies of individuals with brain disorders, especially those arising from strokes, and also from differences in hemispheric function of normal individuals. Specific brain regions have been shown to be related to particular classes of cognitive disorder. This is especially evident with injuries that interfere with language.

In the late nineteenth century, the neurologist Paul Broca discovered that lesions in the left hemisphere impair speech and language. Now, one hundred years later, studies of normal humans at all ages have provided interesting ideas about brain organization and cognition. Starting with simple observations of handedness, asymmetry of brain mechanisms can be readily noted. Only 5 to 10% of humans are left-handed. Does this fact imply a different functional relation between the cerebral hemispheres in these individuals than that characteristic of the majority? Moving on to more complex functions in normal humans, many investigators have offered data that point to a large range of hemispheric differences in cognitive functions. From this collection of experimental facts an edifice of speculation has been built. Proposed differences between the cerebral hemispheres even include the notion that they differ in fundamental modes of thought (Table 18-1). Popular concern has been aroused by these ideas because some speculative writers have suggested that current educational practices fail to consider intrinsic differences between the cerebral hemispheres. There is a threat that specialists in providing separate educational counsel to each hemisphere may emerge. More extreme arguments have suggested that within a single brain there are two forms of consciousness that may vie with each other for behavioral fulfillment.

Table 18-1 Proposed Cognitive Modes of the Two Cerebral Hemispheres

Left Hemisphere	Right Hemisphere
Phonetic	Nonlinguistic
Sequential	Holistic
Analytic	Synthetic
Propositional	Gestalt
Discrete temporal analysis	Form perception
Language	Spatial

In this chapter we will seek clues about brain processes and structures involved in human mental life. Guesses, hunches, and data will be viewed from the realms of both the brain-injured and the hemispheric specialization in normals. Obviously many simpler questions about the brain and behavior have yet to be successfully answered. So it is difficult to offer more than a beginning to an understanding of those distinctive aspects of human life—the ability to generate complex language and thought.

Although brain injury in humans can produce profound losses, there are many observations that offer hope. In many cases behavior recovers from the effects of stroke or trauma. In the most dramatic instances seen in children, almost complete restitution of behavior occurs, even though a large part of the brain may be damaged or missing. In the last section of this chapter, we will present some ideas about the ways in which function might be recovered in brain-damaged individuals.

Evolutionary and Comparative Perspectives on Speech and Language

There are 5000 to 10,000 languages in the world and countless local dialects. All these languages have similar basic elements, and each is composed of a set of sounds and symbols that have distinct meanings. These elements are arranged in distinct orders according to rules characteristic of that language. Anyone who knows the sounds, symbols, and rules of a particular language can generate sentences that convey information to others with similar knowledge. Looking at language acquisition, we see a remarkable regularity to the development of language across virtually all human languages. The abilities fundamental to production of language seem to be inherent in the biological structure of human brains.

Over the centuries scholars have offered many speculations about the origins of language, but data in this area are scarce. The oldest written records available to modern researchers are only about 6000 years old. The absence of older records has promoted a sense of mystery and elaborate tales about the beginnings of language. At one point over a hundred years ago, the French Academy banned speculations about the origin of languages as being merely fruitless speculation, incapable of being verified. Nevertheless, some old ideas have a vitality that leads to their continued restatement. A common notion of the past, which has recently been given new life, states that speech and language originally developed from gestures, especially involving facial movements. Even today hand movements are a common accompaniment during speech. Gordon Hewes (1973), an anthropologist, has suggested that gestures came under volitional control quite early in human history and became an easy mode of communication before the emergence of speech. Perhaps tongue and mouth movements slowly came to replace grosser body movements. In time sounds connected to these tongue and mouth movements may have provided the substrate of speech. Other speculations note that primitive humans were surrounded by sounds produced in the natural world, sounds that they might have attempted to imitate. Sounds caused by the wind, like the rustling of leaves, or vocalizations by other animals are always part of our surroundings. Imitations of these sounds by humans might have formed the beginning of vocal communication, which, in time, came to be shaped into speech.

Vocal Behavior of Nonhumans

Chirps, barks, meows, songs, and other sounds are among the many produced by nonhuman animals. Many mammals, especially primates, have a large repertoire of species-typical vocalizations that seem to be related to distinct situations significant in promoting adaptive behavior. Many of these sounds are related to reproductive behavior, especially calls that serve to separate species or signal readiness to mate. Other vocalizations alert the group to the prospect of danger. Is it possible that the vocal behavior of nonhuman animals is related to the biological history of human speech and language? Are there any attributes of nonhuman vocal behavior that are akin to human speech? We will explore these questions by focusing on the songs of birds and the sounds of nonhuman primates.

Bird Song

Many sounds of birds are pleasant tunes, and these sounds offer some intriguing analogies to human speech. Bird songs vary in complexity; some repeat a simple basic unit, while others are more elaborate (Figure 18-1). The intricate patterning of some songs promotes the idea that there is a connection to human speech. Parallels to human speech and language are examined in terms of importance of early experience and similarities of neural mechanisms controlling sound production in birds and humans. Note that no investigator believes that bird song is an evolutionary precursor to human speech. Rather the hope is that bird song can give an interesting analogy that could be useful as an experimental tool.

Figure 18-1 Recordings of song in three species of bird. For each animal, the top trace shows the exact sound pattern detected by a sensitive microphone. The bottom trace shows this same pattern analyzed by a sound spectrograph which reveals the amount of energy in different sound frequencies at each moment. These three examples show a range of bird song complexity. (From Greenewalt, 1968)

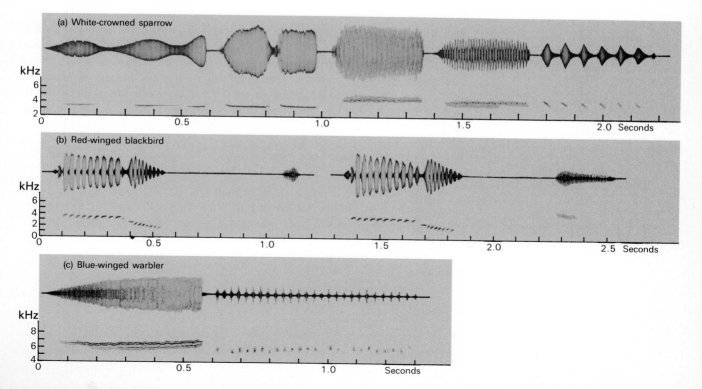

Figure 18-2 The effects of early sound isolation and deafening on the characteristics of the typical song of two species of sparrow. The top row shows the typical adult pattern, the middle row shows songs produced by males reared in isolation from songs of other birds, and the bottom row shows the songs of birds deafened in infancy. (From Marler, 1981)

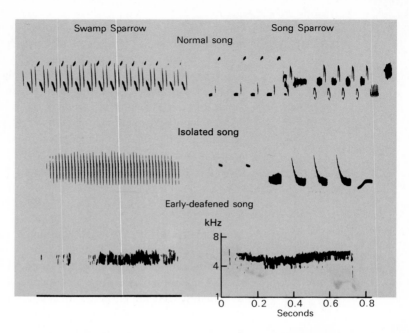

[handwritten margin notes: robust & buffered. Others songs may Sensitive period. cul]

The vocal behavior of some birds is not affected by early deafening or rearing in isolation. For example, neither early deafening nor rearing by another species changes the vocalizations of ring doves (Nottebohm, 1987). Deafened canaries can develop song, although a few unusual sounds appear.

On the other hand, some birds, much like humans, require exposure to bird song in order to develop the characteristic patterns of their species. These birds, such as white-crowned sparrows, chaffinches, and cardinals, show quite abnormal song if they are deafened before the maturation stage when song customarily appears (Figure 18-2). Male songbirds that are raised in acoustic isolation do not develop a normal song. However, such isolated birds that are exposed to tape recordings of species-typical vocalizations during an early ''critical'' period do acquire normal song; if the exposure to taped songs is later in life, the song acquired is abnormal. When a bird is exposed to tape recordings that are synthetic songs, composed of notes of both the same species and another, it copies only the song of its own species (Marler & Peters, 1981). There is an innate preference for the species' own song.

Some individual birds have a song repertoire that is more elaborate than other birds. Research has shown that the size of the relevant song control regions of the brain is larger in individual birds that have a greater number of syllables in their song (Nottebohm et al., 1981). Further, cross-species comparisons among songbirds reveals that larger song repertoires are related to larger brain control regions (Brenowitz & Arnold, 1986).

Vocal Behavior of Nonhuman Primates

The calls of nonhuman primates have been intensively examined in both field and laboratory studies. Ploog and his collaborators in Munich (Ploog, 1981) have studied the vocal behavior of squirrel monkeys, cataloging the calls they produce and the communication properties of those sounds in a social context. Their calls include shrieking, quacking, chirping, growling, and yapping sounds. Many of these calls can penetrate a forest for some distance, communicating alarm, territoriality, and other emotional statements. Direct electrical stimulation of some regions of a squirrel monkey's brain can elicit some calls, but stimulation of the cerebral cortex generally fails to elicit vocal behavior. Brain regions that elicit vocalizations also seem to be involved in defense, attack, feeding, and sex behavior. These regions include sites in the limbic lobe and related structures. Other investigators have shown that removing parts of the cerebral cortex of nonhuman primates has little effect on vocalization, whereas in humans it can dramatically affect language. Thus human speech requires the cortex, whereas animal cries do not.

Nonhuman primate vocalizations differ from human speech in several ways. In most cases these vocalizations seem elicited by emotional stimuli and are bound to particular situations. Further, even in the most talkative nonhuman primate, the number of distinct sounds is small.

A new look at nonhuman primate vocal behavior has pointed to versatility that was overlooked in earlier studies; those studies had emphasized the dissimilarity between human and nonhuman primate vocal behavior. Seyfarth and Cheney (1984) have studied a population of vervet monkeys. In earlier work Struhsaker (1967) had noticed in field studies that these animals gave different sounding alarm calls to leopards, eagles, and snakes, which elicited different adaptive responses from other vervet monkeys. For example, the alarm call given to leopards led other monkeys to run into trees, while the alarm call given to eagles led other monkeys to look up at the sky. Using tape recordings of these alarm calls, Seyfarth and Cheney confirmed that different alarm calls had different behavioral consequences, and they suggested parallels to human words. They have also reported on the calls several species of monkeys use in more relaxed social situations. Humans listening to these calls may not detect small differences that are differentially appreciated by members of the same species. Discrimination experiments showed that some species seem predisposed to divide a continuum of sounds into special categories that are species-typical. Further, each species showed cerebral lateralization for processing their own species-typical vocal behavior but not for analyzing the sounds characteristic of other species.

Fossils and Language

Sound production ability forms a special focus for evolutionary studies of language. The use of sound for communication often has advantages over the use of other sensory channels. For example, sound enables animals to communicate at night or in other situations in which they cannot see each other. The development of spoken communication clearly has survival value. Of course, sounds do not fossilize. However, parts of the skull concerned with speech sounds do form fossils and may provide clues about the origins of language.

On the basis of his studies of the probable shape and length of the vocal tract of various ancient human specimens, Lieberman (1979) has suggested that the capability for speech production of *Homo sapiens* may be only 50,000 years old. At about that time, the human vocal tract developed a size and shape that could generate adequate signals for complex communication. The increase in the size and shape of the vocal tract, according to Lieberman, enables the production of certain key vowel sounds like ''i'' and ''u.'' The ability to produce these sounds evolved along with the development of perceptual detectors that were especially sensitive to them. Lieberman further argues that the vocal tracts in human infants and in nonhuman primates (monkeys) are shaped so that they cannot produce all the sounds that speech requires. These are interesting speculations, but they have been strongly criticized. Some criticisms concern the reconstruction of the vocal tract; there is a great deal of uncertainty in reconstructing the position of the larynx based on so few bones. Further, although such an adaptation allows for a richer potential sound repertoire, Wang (1982) has pointed out that the languages of the world vary widely in the number and complexity of sounds. He notes that human languages seldom exploit the sound production resources that are available given the structure of the vocal tract. Larynx descent during the path of language evolution may have provided some ''bonuses,'' but this adaptation may not have been necessary for language emergence.

Some birds show a striking similarity to humans in the neurology of vocal control. The sound production machinery of birds consists of a voice organ, the syrinx, from which sound originates. Changes in membranes of this organ are produced by adjacent muscles innervated by the right and left hypoglossal nerves—cranial nerves that control the musculature of the neck. When these nerves are cut, the effects on song differ markedly between the right and left hypoglossal nerves. Section of the right hypoglossal nerve produces barely any change in song. Section of the left hypoglossal nerve produces a virtually silent bird; such birds ''look like actors in silent cinema film'' (Nottebohm, 1987). All the correct body movements are made, but no sound comes out. This observation indicates left dominance of vocal-control mechanisms in these birds.

Peripheral dominance is matched by differences in brain hemispheres. Investigators have mapped the vocal-control centers of the canary brain (Figure 18-3). Nottebohm (1980) has shown that lesions of the left-hemisphere vocal-control regions markedly impair production of the usual song; singing becomes unstable and monotonous. Minimal changes were seen following lesions in comparable right-hemisphere structures. An interesting parallel to human language impairment following brain injury is seen: In left-hemisphere damaged animals, some song elements are recovered seven months after lesions as the right hemisphere takes over this function.

Some reservations have been expressed about viewing bird song as analogous to human speech control (Konishi, 1985). Among these considerations is the prospect that lateralization in these animals includes peripheral factors. Examination of the musculature of the syrinx reveals that the left is larger than the right. Further, studies of brain hemispheric asymmetry in the sizes of vocal-control nuclei shows only a small difference for the nucleus of the hypoglossal nerve but no other vocal-control area. The absence of right-left differences in the brain is also demonstrated in the similarity of electrical recordings of brain activity of both hemispheres during song production.

Figure 18-3 Vocal control centers of the male songbird brain. (HV, hyperstriatum ventrale; IC, intercollicular nucleus; MAN, magnocellular nucleus of anterior neostriatum; RA, nucleus robustus of the archistriatum; X, area X of the locus parolfactorium; XII, nucleus of the XIIth cranial nerve) (From Arnold, 1980)

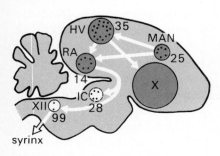

Language Learning by Nonhuman Primates

Throughout history people have tried to teach animals to talk. But in most cases if any communication occurred, it was because the person learned to meow, grunt, or bark rather than because the animal learned to produce sounds of human speech. Many such efforts led to the conclusion that in order to speak like a human, an animal must have a vocal apparatus like that of a human.

Since both the vocal tracts and the basic vocal repertoires of modern nonhuman primates are different from those of humans, scientists have given up attempting to train animals to produce human speech. Instead they have asked whether nonhuman primates can be taught other forms of communication that have features similar to human language, including the ability to represent objects with symbols and to manipulate these symbols according to rules of order. An especially important objective of these studies is to determine whether animals other than humans can generate novel strings of symbols, such as a new sentence.

A switch in tactics came with the work of Allen and Beatrice Gardner (1969, 1984). They have been successful in training chimpanzees to acquire a gesture type of language called American Sign Language—the sign language used by the deaf in the United States. These animals have learned many signs and appear to be able to use them spontaneously and to generate new sequences of signs.

David Premack (1972) has used another approach. He teaches chimpanzees a system based on an assortment of colored chips (symbols) that can adhere to a magnetic board. After extensive training the chimpanzees can manipulate the chips in ways that may reflect an acquired ability to form short sentences and to note various logical classifications.

At the Yerkes Primate Center, Project Lana has involved teaching "Yerkish" to a chimpanzee (Rumbaugh, 1977). Yerkish is a computer-based language with different keys on a console acting as words. Apes are quite facile in acquiring many words in this language and appear to string together novel, meaningful chains.

Thus while nonhuman primates (at least those as intelligent as the chimpanzee) do not have a vocal system that permits speech, they appear to have a capacity for learning at least some components of language. Neurological studies of such animals may provide an experimental approach to understanding brain mechanisms related to human language.

[margin note: Can't speak — capacity for learning some speech components]

Debate about chimpanzee language learning has always been vigorous and has recently intensified. Challenges to studies of language learning in nonhuman primates, including both methodological and theoretical issues, have come from several quarters. One of the main critics is Herbert Terrace (1979), who raised a young chimp and taught it many signs. Terrace tested carefully to see whether his chimp or others really could construct sentences. According to linguists, grammar is the essence of language, so investigators in this area look for the ability of sign-using chimps to generate meaningful and novel sequences of signs. As we noted, the Gardners' studies suggested that sign-using chimps make distinctive series of signs, just as though they were using words in a sentence. However, Terrace argues that strings of signs have been explicitly presented to the chimps and that the animals merely imitate rather than generate new combinations. He suggests that the imitation happens in a quite subtle manner and may involve cuing practices of which the experimenter is unaware.

[margin note: imitation vs. created]

A broader debate emphasizing the nature of language has been opened by Rumbaugh, Rumbaugh, and Boysen (1980). True symbolization, they argue, involves something more than representing objects or action. It involves an intention to communicate an internal representational process akin to thoughts. This process may not be a component in chimpanzee language learning, although, of course, interrogation of the animals about this feature of language use is quite difficult. This debate is far from being settled, but the accomplishments of the trained chimpanzees have at least forced investigators to sharpen their criteria of language. Whether nonhuman primates are really capable of language is not yet clear.

Brain Impairments and Language Disorders

Most of our understanding of the relationship of brain mechanisms and language is derived from observation of language impairments following brain injury due to accidents, diseases, or strokes. Studies of patients have shown that some common syndromes of language impairment appear to be related to distinct brain regions. Specifically, in approximately 90–95% of the cases of language disorders due to brain injury—called **aphasia**—the damage is to the left cerebral hemisphere. Damage to the right hemisphere is responsible for the remaining 5–10% of the cases of aphasia. In this section the signs of aphasia and the main syndromes are described.

Signs of Aphasia

There are several types of aphasia that are distinguished by distinctive signs of language impairments. The most prominent sign of aphasia is the substitution of a word by a sound, incorrect word, or unintended word. This characteristic is called **paraphasia.** At times an entirely novel word—called a neologism—might be generated by the substitution of a phoneme. Paraphasic speech in aphasic patients is evident either in spontaneous conversation or while attempting to read aloud from a text.

Conversational speech also provides an opportunity to note another important aspect of aphasic speech—its fluency or ease of production. Nonfluent speech refers to talking with considerable effort, short sentences, and the absence of the usual melodic character of conversational speech. In contrast, fluent speech is that which is normal in terms of the rate of production, melodic character, and overall ease of presentation. In some cases fluent aphasic speech refers to that which is more abundant than normal. Many patients with aphasic syndromes also show disturbances in the ability to repeat words or sentences. This is seen in simple tasks such as repetition of numbers or words that were orally presented by the examiner. Comprehension of language is impaired to varying degrees.

Virtually everyone with an aphasic syndrome shows some impairment in writing (called **agraphia**), and disturbances in reading (called **alexia**) are also evident. Finally, the brain impairments or disorders that produce aphasia also produce a distinctive motor impairment called **apraxia.** This is an impairment in the execution of learned movements that is unrelated to paralysis, coordination problems, sensory impairments, or the comprehension of instructions. The patient is unable to imitate some common gestures, such as ''stick out your tongue'' or ''wave goodbye,'' although these acts might appear in the spontaneous behavior of the patient. There are many intricacies to the syndrome of apraxia, which is discussed in detail by Heilman and Rothi (1985). Do the various signs of aphasia correlate with specific brain lesions? In the following section, we describe several syndromes that are distinctive collections of these signs related to specific brain lesions.

Types of Aphasia

Stroke and brain injury have affected the language abilities of many patients in quite varied ways. Neurologists and researchers in aphasia over the years have sought to classify the many different types of aphasia, and a prime concern has been the relation between the particular form of language disorder and the region of brain destruction or impairment. Figure 18-4 shows the main brain regions of the left hemisphere related to language abilities. Studies of brain-damaged people indicate that language abilities depend on the left hemisphere in virtually all right-handed and in a majority of left-handed individuals. Damage to the right hemisphere produces major language incapacity in some left-handed individuals.

Broca's Aphasia

In 1861, the physician Paul Broca submitted postmortem evidence that showed that a large left-frontal lesion produced a loss of speech in a patient. This presentation was significant because it clearly showed that damage restricted to a particular brain region could produce a loss in a discrete psychological function. It began a search for the relations between characteristics of language impairment and locus of brain injury or disease. The type of aphasia initially described by Broca has come to be known as Broca's aphasia; it is also described as a nonfluent aphasia. Patients with Broca's aphasia have considerable difficulty with speech and talk only in a labored and hesitant manner. The ability to utter automatic speech is often preserved. This

Figure 18-4 Cortical speech and language areas in the human cerebral cortex (left hemisphere). Lesions in the anterior frontal region called Broca's area interfere with speech production; injury to an area of temporal-parietal cortex called Wernicke's area interferes with language comprehension; injury to the supramarginal gyrus interferes with repetition of heard speech.

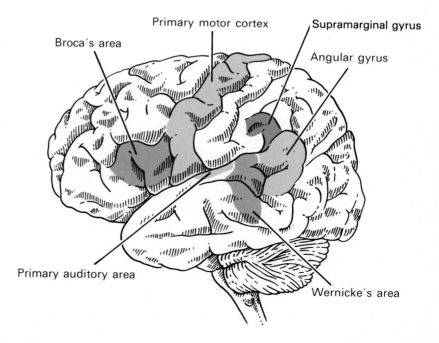

(a)

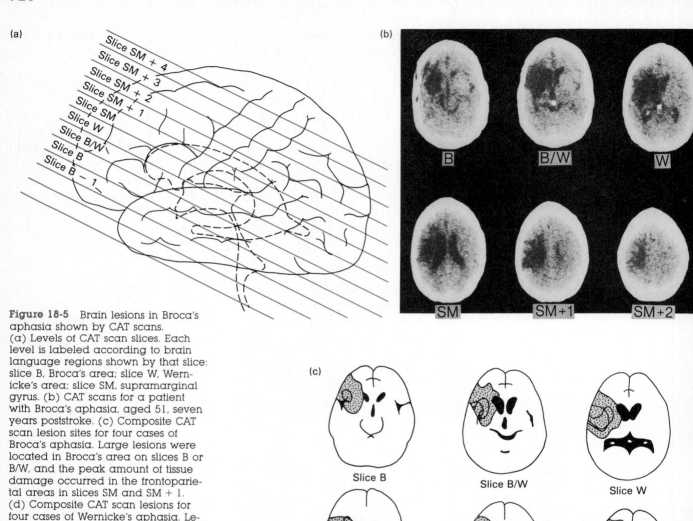

(b)

(c)

Figure 18-5 Brain lesions in Broca's aphasia shown by CAT scans.
(a) Levels of CAT scan slices. Each level is labeled according to brain language regions shown by that slice: slice B, Broca's area; slice W, Wernicke's area; slice SM, supramarginal gyrus. (b) CAT scans for a patient with Broca's aphasia, aged 51, seven years poststroke. (c) Composite CAT scan lesion sites for four cases of Broca's aphasia. Large lesions were located in Broca's area on slices B or B/W, and the peak amount of tissue damage occurred in the frontoparietal areas in slices SM and SM + 1.
(d) Composite CAT scan lesions for four cases of Wernicke's aphasia. Lesions were located in Wernicke's area at slice W and in the supramarginal gyrus area at slice SM. (e) Composite CAT scan lesions for five cases of global aphasia. Large lesions were present in every language area.
(Adapted from Naeser and Hayward, 1978)

includes greetings (''hello''), short, common expressions (''Oh, my God''), or swear words (take your choice!). Writing is also impaired but comprehension remains relatively intact. Most patients with this disorder have apraxic difficulties and right hemiplegia—a partial paralysis involving the right side of the body.

Broca's aphasia is usually associated with lesions of the left frontal lobe, especially the third frontal gyrus and nearby regions of the lower end of the motor cortex (Figure 18-5). Computer tomographic evidence has added to our anatomical understanding of the aphasias. An example of the CAT scan portrait of a patient with Broca's aphasia in shown in Figure 18-5a. The figure includes both CAT scans for

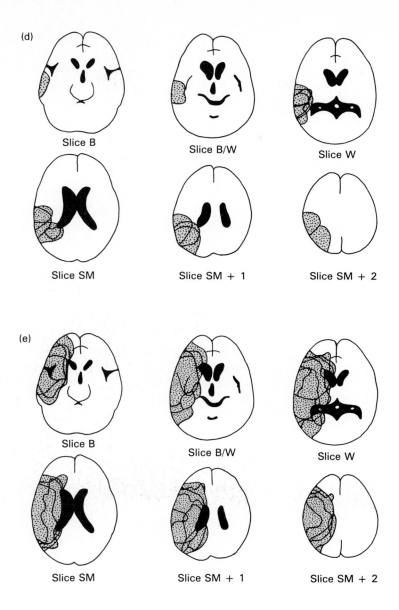

(d)

Slice B Slice B/W Slice W

Slice SM Slice SM + 1 Slice SM + 2

(e)

Slice B Slice B/W Slice W

Slice SM Slice SM + 1 Slice SM + 2

one patient and drawings that summarize data from four patients. These illustrations are from the work of Naeser and Hayward (1978). They describe the patient, who, seven years poststroke, continued to speak at a slow rate, used nouns and very few verbs or function words, and spoke only with great effort. When asked to repeat ''Go ahead and do it if possible,'' she could only repeat ''Go to do it'' with pauses between each word. Her CAT scan revealed a large frontal lesion and destruction of subcortical areas including caudate nucleus and internal capsule. Broca's patients with brain lesions that are this extensive show little recovery of speech with the passing of time. This issue is discussed in a following section. Mohr (1976) has argued that lesions restricted solely to the third frontal gyrus on the left side are not associated with persistent and severe Broca's aphasia and suggests that the characteristic aphasic syndrome named after Broca invariably involves a more extended part of the frontal cortex. In fact, the case presented by Broca in support of his view of localization of function actually extended well beyond the third frontal gyrus.

Wernicke's Aphasia

A complex array of signs characterizes the patient with Wernicke's aphasia. These patients present verbal output in a very fluent manner, but what they say contains many paraphasias that often make their speech unintelligible. Word substitutions and speech errors are presented in a context that preserves syntactical structure. The ability to repeat words and sentences is impaired, and the patients are unable to understand what they read or hear. In some cases reading comprehension is more impaired than comprehension of spoken speech, and in other cases the opposite is more evident. Unlike patients with Broca's aphasia, patients with Wernicke's aphasia are usually without other major neurological disabilities, notably they do not display partial paralysis.

In Wernicke's aphasia the most prominent relevant lesions are found in posterior regions of the left superior temporal gyrus and extend partially into adjacent parietal cortex, especially the angular gyrus (Figure 18-4). Composite diagrams of lesions found in Wernicke's aphasia are shown in Figure 18-5d. When word deafness is more evident than reading impairment, patients show greater involvement of the first temporal gyrus, especially involving fibers from auditory cortex. In contrast, when word blindness predominates, greater destruction of the angular gyrus is evident.

Global Aphasia

In some patients brain injury or disease results in total loss of ability to understand language or to speak, read, or write. Some preservation of automatic speech is seen in these patients, especially emotional exclamations. Very few words can be uttered, and no semblance of syntax is evident. The area of abnormality in these patients is wide and encompasses large realms of frontal, temporal, and parietal cortex including Broca's area, Wernicke's area, and supramarginal gyrus. A composite of the areas of abnormality of a group of global aphasics is shown in Figure 18-5e. The prognosis in terms of language recovery in these patients is quite grave.

Conduction Aphasia

Patients with conduction aphasia are characterized by fluent speech, minimal changes in comprehension of spoken words, but a major impairment in the repetition of words and sentences. When these patients attempt to repeat words, they offer phonemic paraphasias—words with incorrect phonemes substituting for correct sounds. The description of the brain lesion that underlies this form of aphasia is still controversial. Some researchers emphasize that the key ingredient is the destruction of the arcuate fasciculus, a bundle of fibers that connects Wernicke's to Broca's area. In some cases involvement of primary auditory cortex is also seen as well as the insula and supramarginal gyrus.

There are other forms of aphasia that are less common and involve a different portrait of language impairments and involved brain regions. Aphasia following subcortical pathology has also been noted (Naeser, 1983).

The Wernicke-Geschwind Model of Aphasia

Aphasic disturbances span a wide range of language impairments, some quite general in character and others quite specialized, limited in a single dimension such as the inability to understand spoken language. One traditional approach to understanding aphasic disturbances, initiated by the neurologist Carl Wernicke in the early part of this century, used a "connectionist" perspective to understand aphasia and related disorders. According to this view, deficits can be understood as a break in an interconnected network of components, each of which is involved with some particular feature of language analysis or production. The theory was developed in great detail by Geschwind in papers that have become classics in the field (1965a, b). We will provide an explanation from this perspective of what happens in the brain during the production of language. When a word or sentence is heard, the results of analysis by the auditory cortex are transmitted to Wernicke's area. In order to say the word, outputs must be transmitted from Wernicke's area to Broca's area where a plan prepared for speech is activated and then transmitted to adjacent motor cortex where control of the relevant articulatory muscles is maintained. The angular gyrus (Figure 18-6b) is a station between auditory and visual regions. If a spoken word is to be spelled, the auditory pattern is transmitted to the angular gyrus, where the visual pattern is provoked. According to the Wernicke-Geschwind model, saying the name of an object that is seen involves the transfer of visual information to the angular gyrus, which contains the rules for arousing the auditory pattern in Wernicke's area. From Wernicke's area the auditory form is transmitted via the arcuate fasciculus to Broca's area. In this region the model for the spoken form is activated and transmitted to the face area of the motor cortex, and then the word is spoken. Thus lesions involving the angular gyrus will have the effect of disconnecting the systems involved in auditory and visual language. Patients with lesions in this region would then be expected to have difficulty with written language, but they should be able to speak and understand speech. A lesion in Broca's area should disturb speech production but have little impact on comprehension. Many aspects of language disturbances following cortical lesions can be understood from this perspective, which has become the major model for the anatomical analysis of aphasias. Figure 18-6 portrays some examples of relations between brain regions and language impairments according to the views of Geschwind.

Aphasia in Users of Sign Language

Human hands and arms are remarkable in the ability to move in many different and elaborate ways. Some gestures of the hand convey meanings that seem almost universal; some have been used for centuries. Formal hand and arm gestures with specific rules of arrangement form the basis of nonvocal languages such as American Sign Language of the deaf. This language involves an elaborate code and

Figure 18-6 A representation of the Geschwind-Wernicke connectionist model of language. When a word is heard (a), the sensation from the ears is received by the primary auditory cortex, but the word cannot be understood until the signal has been processed in Wernicke's area nearby. If the word is to be spoken, some representation of it is thought to be transmitted from Wernicke's area to Broca's area through a bundle of nerve fibers called the arcuate fasciculus. In Broca's area the word evokes a detailed program for articulation, which is supplied to the face area of the motor cortex. The motor cortex in turn drives the muscles of the lips, the tongue, the larynx, and so on. When a written word is read (b), the sensation is first registered by the primary visual cortex. It is then thought to be relayed to the angular gyrus, which associates the visual form of the word with the corresponding auditory pattern in Wernicke's area. Speaking the word then draws on the same systems of neurons as before. (After Geschwind, 1979)

(a) Speaking a heard word

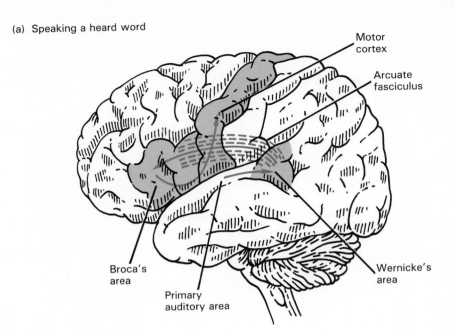

(b) Speaking a written word

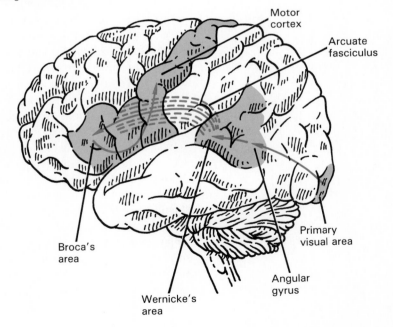

grammar; some examples are displayed in Figure 18-7. An exhaustive analysis of American Sign Language by two linguists (Klima & Bellugi, 1979) clearly establishes this gesture-based set of symbols as a language as elaborate as its vocal counterparts. In fact, even features as subtle as dialect are seen in sign languages. For this reason investigators have been interested in finding out whether sign lan-

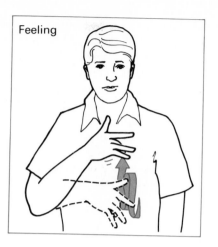

Feeling

Secret

Quiet

Figure 18-7 Examples from a language based on gestures—American Sign Language of the deaf. (From Klima and Bellugi, 1979)

guage is similar to spoken language in its neural organization. Is there hemisphere specialization for a language system based on hand signals most of which are formed by the right hand although some involve both hands?

Several case histories provide interesting data about aphasia in users of sign language. Meckler, Mack, and Bennett (1979) described a young man who was raised by deaf-mute parents and who became aphasic after an accident. Previously he had used both spoken and sign language for communication. Afterward impairments in his spoken language, sign language, and writing were equally severe. He could copy complicated hand and finger movements when he was provided with the model of the experimenter's gestures, but he could not offer gestures in a spontaneous manner. A comprehensive analysis of sign language deficits in an older deaf-mute has been offered by Chiarello et al. (1982). This person was deafened in childhood prior to the onset of speech and could not communicate vocally. She had well-developed sign language skills. Following a stroke sustained at age 59, she showed a total inability to generate hand signals with either hand. Computer tomograph scans indicated extensive damage in the left temporal cortex. Months later testing showed some return of sign language, although it was restricted to simple phrases. Errors in these signals bore a striking resemblance to language mistakes seen in the speech and writing of people with comparable lesions who had used spoken language. Bellugi et al. (1983) have described aphasia in three deaf signers with damage to the left hemisphere. In these patients they noted that differential damage in the left hemisphere led to effective impairment of components of sign language. Damage in one region affected the grammatical feature and elsewhere, an effect on words. These case histories indicate that the neural mechanisms of spoken and sign languages are identical. Cerebral injury in these cases affects a mechanism that controls rules for the ordering of symbolic information whether conveyed by speech or by hand.

Aphasia in Bilinguals

People who can speak and write in more than one language have always been fascinating to researchers in aphasia. Do cerebral cortical injuries produce similar impairments in both languages? Do very different languages share common neural systems? The understanding of this issue is partly obscured by definitions of bilingualism. A possible critical factor in these studies is the age at which a second language is acquired, even extending into adulthood. Very few bilinguals acquire two languages simultaneously in early childhood. Furthermore, most studies have concerned a small group of Indo-European languages that have many similar characterics. Few reports of aphasia in bilinguals involve Asian languages, most of which are very different from English, German, French, and Spanish.

Most of the data on aphasia in bilinguals have been presented in a clinical format of individual case histories, which makes it difficult to see the common or most characteristic findings. Searching for the general themes, Paradis (1977) reviewed many published case histories and has characterized the classes of symptoms and recovery of aphasia in bilinguals. There are many different patterns of recovery, but the most common form, shown by almost half of all cases in the research literature, is that in which both languages are similarly impaired and there is equal recovery in both. This observation suggests that each language is similarly organized in the brain. In a smaller number of instances recovery is successive, although there is no consistent rule as to which language is first to recover; it is not as simple as ''last in, first out.'' In rarer cases recovery is antagonistic; as one language recovers, it inhibits recovery of the other language.

After reviewing many of the facts and theories of bilingual aphasia, Paradis concludes that multiple factors account for the pattern of loss and restitution, and these include psychological considerations and differential fluency. Clearly there is no evidence for loss in one language without some impairment in others.

Dyslexia and the Brain

Schools have always had some students who never seem to learn to read. Their efforts are laden with frustration, and prolonged practice produces only small improvements. The inability to read is called **dyslexia** (from the Greek roots for faulty reading). Some dyslexic children show high IQ performance. The diagnosis dyslexia includes many different groups of people who cannot read. It is more common in boys and left-handed people. There is some controversy about this syndrome, and its characteristics may be broader than a reading disorder. Denckla (1979) sees the inability to read as a symptom of a broader developmental language disorder. As noted in Chapter 17, Kagan and Moore (1981) see dyslexia as mainly a problem of memory. Clearly dyslexia is a fuzzy clinical category, but recently it has been connected to interesting anatomical findings to be described shortly.

At least some dyslexic individuals have associated deficits in various tasks involving cerebral lateralization, especially those that involve the left hemisphere. These include left-right discriminations and forms of verbal learning and memory. Some researchers have suggested that developmental impairments in reading may arise from the use of the right hemisphere in language (Coltheart, 1980).

A recent study by Galaburda et al. (1985) has described various pathological features in the brains of dyslexic patients. All four cases had specific reading disabilities and other learning disabilities that were noted at an early age. Death was from acute disease or trauma associated with injury that did not involve the brain. All four brains showed striking cortical anomalies in the arrangements of cortical cells, especially in areas of the frontal and temporal cortical regions. These anomalies consisted of eccentric grouping of cells in outer layers of the cerebral cortex that distorted the normal layered arrangements and columnar organization. Some cells were disoriented, and excessive cortical folding was observed. Nests of extra cells were seen in eccentric positions. These researchers argue that these anomalies of cerebral cortical cell arrangements were developmental in character and probably arose quite early, perhaps during the middle of gestation, a period during which active cell migration is evident in cerebral cortex. The result of these deficits might be the production of unusual patterns of connectivity in language-related regions of the temporal cortex. Galaburda and his associates also noted that the customary asymmetry in the overall extent of the planum temporale was markedly attenuated in this group. They noted a relationship between these neurological deficits and disorders of the immune system. Several of the dyslexic patients and their relatives had disorders such as arthritis, food allergies, and migraine, which Galaburda and associates believe points to a common genetic mechanism, that is, a genetic factor that both determines cortical anomalies and prepares the way for later immune system defects. Experimental animals with such immune system defects also have cortical anomalies akin to those observed in these patients. A basic common state might be immunologically mediated impairment of cell aggregation and organization factors that operate during early cerebral cortical development.

Electrical Stimulation and Language Impairments

Electrical stimulation of the brain is one of the tools used to explore language functions of the human cerebral cortex. Subjects in these studies are patients undergoing surgery for the relief of seizures. Electrical stimulation helps the neurosurgeon locate—and thus avoid—language-related cortical regions. These regions are found by observing language interference produced by the stimuli. Patients are given only local anesthesia so that they can communicate verbally.

Pioneering work by Penfield and Roberts (1959) provided a map of language-related zones of the left hemisphere (Figure 18-8). A pooling of data from many patients showed a large anterior zone, stimulation of which produced speech arrest.

Figure 18-8 Interference with speech production by electrical stimulation at the points indicated. This is a summary of data obtained from many patients. (From Wilder Penfield and Lamar Roberts, *Speech and brain-mechanisms* (copyright © 1959 by Princeton University Press): Figure VIII-3, p. 122. Reprinted by permission of Princeton University Press.)

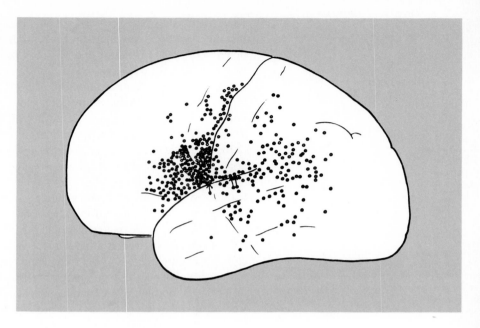

Speech simply stopped during the period of applied stimulation. Other forms of language interference, like misnaming or repetition of words, was evident from stimulation of both this region and more posterior temporal-parietal cortex regions.

In the years since this study, new techniques in the analysis of language and electrical stimulation have been introduced, and observations have been expanded. Using tasks that assessed movements of the mouth and lips, sound identification, naming, and verbal memory, Ojemann and Mateer (1979) present more detailed cortical maps (Figure 18-9). Maps of sites that affected language functions revealed several different systems. Stimulation of one system arrested speech and impaired all facial movements. This system was regarded as the cortical, final motor pathway for speech; it is located in the inferior premotor frontal cortex. Stimulation of a second system altered sequential facial movements and impaired phoneme identification. This system included sites in the inferior frontal, temporal, and parietal cortex. A third system was defined by stimulation-induced memory errors; it surrounds the sites of the systems that impair phoneme identification. Reading errors were evident from stimulation of other cortical positions.

More recently Ojemann (1983) has described some interesting sex differences in his cortical electrical stimulation observations. In comparison to females, males show stimulation-induced naming changes from a wider area of lateral cortex, especially more sites in the frontal lobe. Individual differences in stimulation effects are also related to the patient's verbal abilities. Those with low verbal IQs show more frequent naming difficulties with stimulation of the parietal cortex. A quite interesting aspect of cortical organization of language in multilingual individuals is also reported in Ojemann's studies. He described one patient in whom stimulation of one site in the superior temporal gyrus affected naming of a picture of a common object

Figure 18-9 Detailed analysis of changes in language functions produced by electrical stimulation of the cerebral cortex: a summary of the cognitive effects of cortical electrical stimulation in four human subjects. Performance in naming (N), repeating movements (R), short-term memory (S), and language (L) was assessed during and after stimulation of the left hemisphere. A memory system (brown region) is posterior to systems for language production and understanding. The final motor pathway for speech is shown by the dark shaded region. (Adapted from Ojemann and Mateer, 1979)

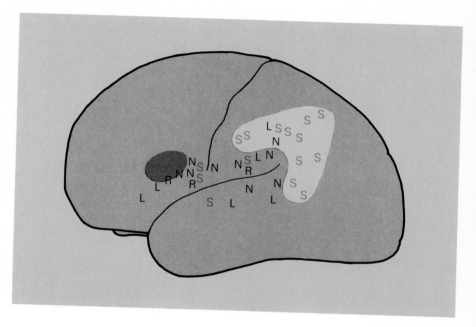

in English but not Greek; in contrast, stimulation of an adjacent site produced the opposite effect. This suggests separate localization of different languages.

Electrical stimulation studies by Ojemann also show the role of the thalamus in some aspects of language activities. He noted that thalamic stimulation at the time of verbal input increases the accuracy of subsequent recall (as late as one week following stimulation). He suggests that there is a thalamic mechanism that specifically modulates the recall of verbal information. This fits with the description of patient N. A. in Chapter 16 where damage to the thalamus impaired verbal memory.

Recovery from Aphasia

Many people who survive the brain disorders that produce aphasia recover some language abilities. For some people language recovery depends on specific forms of speech therapy. The exact forms of speech therapy are mainly improvisations supported by some degree of clinical success rather than generated by theories.

The course of recovery from aphasia can be predicted from several factors. For example, recovery is better in survivors of brain damage due to trauma, like a blow to the head, than in those whose brain damage is caused by stroke. Patients with more severe language loss recover less. Left-handed people show better recovery than right-handers. In fact, right-handed individuals with near relatives who are left-handed recover from aphasia better than right-handers without a family history of left-handedness.

Studies by Kertesz (1979) illustrate the typical course of recovery (Figure 18-10). The largest amount of recovery occurs during the initial three months following brain damage. In many instances little further improvement is noted after the lapse of one year, although this result may reflect impoverished therapeutic tools

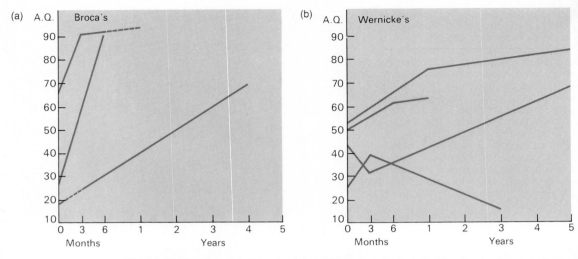

Figure 18-10 Courses of recovery of different patients following brain damage that produces (a) Broca's aphasia and (b) Wernicke's aphasia. Data in these graphs show the Aphasia Quotient (AQ), a score derived from a clinical test battery; higher scores indicate better language performance. (From Kertesz, 1979)

rather than a property of neural plasticity. In general, Broca's aphasics have the highest rate of recovery. There is a high correlation between initial severity and outcome. Kertesz suggests that there is a sequence of stages of recovery that are distinguished by linguistic properties and that patients show a transformation of type of aphasia. According to Kertesz, a common endpoint, no matter what the initial diagnosis, is **anomic aphasia,** a difficulty in "finding" words, although comprehension and ability to repeat words are normal. Anomic aphasia frequently stands as the residual symptom. In a later section we describe the remarkable and virtually complete recovery from aphasia characteristic of children.

Improvement in language abilities following stroke might involve a shift to right-hemisphere language control. Evidence for such hemispheric shifts in children is presented later in this chapter. A case presentation by Cummings, Benson, Walsh, and Levine (1979) lends some support to the hypothesis of left-to-right-hemisphere change in language control of an adult following left-hemisphere injury. The case they described followed a massive stroke. Computerized tomograms showed total destruction of Wernicke's and Broca's areas in the left hemisphere. Immediately after the stroke language was limited to small groups of words virtually bereft of meaning. Further, verbal comprehension was severely impaired. Three years later the patient was able to produce comprehensible short phrases and correctly identify objects. Since his left-hemisphere language areas were totally destroyed, the investigators concluded that the elements of recovered language are mediated by right-hemisphere mechanisms. Recent studies on cerebral blood flow following stroke that results in aphasia offer some support for this view. Knopman et al. (1984) showed that patients with nearly complete recovery of language showed diffuse right-hemisphere increases in cerebral blood flow. Those with incomplete recovery showed only right frontal increases.

It is important to note that a concern for remediation following brain injury is relatively recent. For many years researchers regarded the nervous system as a rigidly organized organ without prospects of structural or functional plasticity. We are now in the midst of a major change toward views that seem more optimistic about the prospects of a rational basis for rehabilitation following brain injury (Bach-y-Rita, 1980). Recovery of language is a top priority of these renewed efforts.

Various forms of therapy are a significant factor in the long-term recovery pattern of aphasia. As mentioned earlier, strategies employed by therapists tend to be improvised rather than based on knowledge of the brain mechanisms of speech. One group of treatments is referred to as stimulation-facilitation techniques, and a second group involves more explicit pedagogic techniques (Sarno, 1981). An emphasis on auditory stimulation and repetition characterizes many approaches. An unusual innovation called ''melodic intonation therapy'' draws attention to the differences between song and speech. Aphasics can frequently sing words and phrases even though they show major handicaps with spoken words. This technique attempts to enhance communication by instructing patients to sing sentences they would ordinarily attempt to deliver in conversational form. Therapists have experienced some success in slowly transferring subjects from a song mode to a nonmelodic speech pattern. The rapid pace of developments in computerized devices, including machines that speak, may be able to provide new dimensions in the rehabilitation of language disorders.

Hemispheric Specialization and Lateralization

By the early twentieth century, it was firmly established that the cerebral hemispheres were not equivalent in mediating language functions. The left hemisphere seemed to be the controller for this function and was commonly described as the dominant hemisphere. However, the right hemisphere does not just sit within the skull awaiting the call to duty when the left side of the brain is injured. In fact, many researchers slowly drifted from notions of cerebral dominance to ideas of hemispheric specialization, or lateralization. This newer emphasis implies that some functional systems are connected more to one side of the brain than the other, that functions become lateralized, and that each hemisphere is specialized for particular ways of working.

Lateralization of function is not a surprising idea; a broad look at the distribution of body organs shows considerable asymmetry between the right and left sides—for example, the heart on the left and the liver on the right. Virtually every species, even very simple ones, shows such lateral differences. Nevertheless, at the level of brain processing in normal individuals, the interconnections of the hemispheres ordinarily mask ready evidence of hemisphere specialization. But by studying patients whose interhemispheric pathways have been disconnected—**split-brain** patients—researchers have been able to see cerebral hemispheric specialization in cognitive, perceptual, emotional, and motor activities. Study of split-brain individuals has also provided the impetus for many research studies using normals. In this section we will consider some of the many forms of evidence that lead us to further understanding of the similarities and differences of functions of the two cerebral hemispheres.

Split-Brain Patients   The differential properties of the cerebral hemispheres are best illustrated in a series
of studies by Roger Sperry and his collaborators at the California Institute of Tech-
nology (1974), mentioned briefly in Chapter 1. These experiments involved a small
group of human patients who underwent a surgical procedure designed to provide
relief from frequent, disabling epileptic seizures. In these patients epileptic activity
initiated in one hemisphere spread to the other hemisphere via the corpus callosum,
the large bundle of fibers that connect the two hemispheres. Surgically cutting the
corpus callosum appreciably reduces the frequency and severity of the patient's
seizures.

Studies by other investigators in the 1930s had shown that this remedy for
seizures was not accompanied by any apparent changes in brain function, as assessed by general behavior testing methods such as IQ tests. But the human corpus
callosum is a huge bundle of over a million axons, and it seemed strange that the
principal connection between the cerebral hemispheres could be cut without producing detectable changes in behavior. The eminent physiological psychologist Karl
Lashley, with characteristic sardonic humor, suggested that perhaps the only function of the corpus callosum was to keep the two hemispheres from floating apart in
the cerebrospinal fluid. Subsequent animal research showed, however, that with
careful testing one could demonstrate deficits in behavior as consequences of hemispheric disconnection.

Results of hemisphere disconnection were first studied extensively in animals in
the 1950s. For example, in one study cats had both the corpus callosum and the
optic chiasm sectioned so that each eye was connected only to the hemisphere on its
own side. Such cats learned with their left eye that a particular symbol stood for
reward but that the inverted symbol did not, while with the right eye they learned
the opposite—that the inverted symbol was rewarded rather than the upright symbol. Thus each hemisphere was ignorant of what the other had learned (Sperry,
Stamm, & Miner, 1956).

In 1960 Joseph Bogen proposed, after a careful review of the earlier studies, that
splitting the brain could control interhemispheric spread of epilepsy. His operations
on patients proved his belief to be correct, and several of his split-brain patients
were studied extensively both pre- and postoperatively through a series of psychological tests devised by Sperry and his co-workers. Stimuli can be directed to either
hemisphere by presenting them to different places on the surface of the body. For
example, objects the patient feels with the left hand result in activity in nerve cells
of the sensory regions in the right hemisphere. Since the corpus callosum is cut in
these patients, most of the information sent to one half of the brain cannot travel to
the other half. By controlling stimuli in this fashion, the experimenter can present
stimuli selectively to one hemisphere or the other and thus test the capabilities of
each hemisphere.

In some of Sperry's studies words were projected to either the left or the right
hemisphere. Visual stimuli were presented in either the right or the left side of the
visual field. Words projected to the left hemisphere of split-brain people can be read
easily and communicated verbally. No such linguistic capabilities were evident
when the information was directed to the right hemisphere (Figure 18-11). More
recently Zaidel (1976), a colleague of Sperry's, has shown that the right hemisphere
has a small amount of linguistic ability; for example, it can recognize simple words.
In general the vocabulary and grammatical capabilities of the right hemisphere are

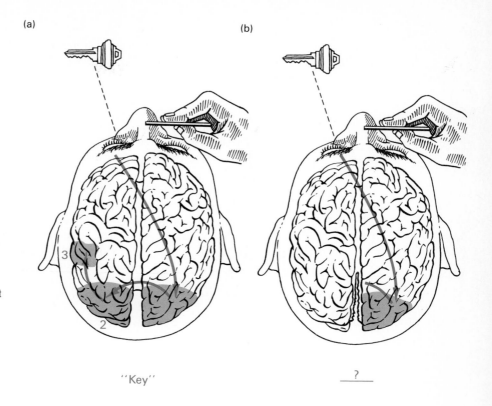

Figure 18-11 Testing of a split-brain patient (right) compared with a normal subject (left). Words projected to the left visual field activate the right visual cortex (1). In normals (a), right-visual-cortex activation excites corpus callosum fibers, which transmit verbal information to the left hemisphere (2) where analysis and production of language takes place (3). In split-brain patients (b), the severing of callosal connections prevents language production in response to left-visual-field stimuli.

far less developed than they are in the left hemisphere. On the other hand, the right hemisphere is superior on tasks involving spatial relations.

Sperry's findings not only confirmed the earlier animal research but were more dramatic, since they showed that only the processes taking place in the left hemisphere could be described verbally by the patients. Thus it is the left hemisphere that possesses language and speech mechanisms in most people. For our present concern the important result is that each hemisphere by itself can process and store information without any participation by the other hemisphere. The ability of the ''mute'' right hemisphere could be tested by nonverbal means. For example, in a test a picture of a key might be projected to the left of the fixation point and so reach only the right visual cortex. The subject would then be asked to touch a number of objects that she could not see and hold up the correct one to the experimenter. Such a task could be performed correctly with the left hand (controlled by the right hemisphere) but not by the right hand (controlled by the left hemisphere). In such a patient it is literally true that the left hemisphere does not know what the left hand is doing. This research also indicated that while the left hemisphere controlled speech, the right hemisphere seemed to be somewhat better for processing spatial information, especially if the response was a manual one rather than simply a recognition of a correct or appropriate visual pattern.

Research with split-brain humans has sometimes been criticized because these patients have suffered from seizures for many years before surgery. Since prolonged seizure activity produces many changes in the brain, critics have argued that the apparent consequences of cutting the corpus callosum might have arisen from changes in epileptic brains. This argument has been weakened by the publication of observations of the effects of a partial callosal section in nonepileptics. For example, a posterior callosal section in a 16-year-old boy was reported by Damasio, Chui, Corbett, and Kassel (1980). The patient had a tumor just below the posterior part of the corpus callosum, and removing it required partial cutting of the corpus callosum. Following surgery the boy showed some of the classic signs of failure of interhemispheric transfer seen in epileptic split-brain patients. These signs included right visual field superiority in reading three-letter words and greater accuracy in naming objects presented in the right half of the visual field. Since the surgery severed most of the interhemispheric visual fibers, impairment of interhemispheric integration with visual input was predictable. On the other hand, since callosal fibers connecting somatosensory cortical regions remained intact, it was therefore understandable that the subject was able to name objects placed in either hand. The impairment of visual function and the integrity of somatosensory function in this patient provide strong evidence of the necessity of callosal fibers for interhemispheric communication.

Weaken argument that it is a result of seizures

Information-Processing Differences Between the Hemispheres of Normal Humans

Auditory Specialization: Dichotic Listening

With earphones it is possible to present different sounds to each ear at the same time; this process is called the **dichotic-listening technique.** The subject hears a particular speech sound in one ear and, at the same time, a different vowel, consonant, or word in the other ear. The task for the subject is to identify or recall these sounds. Are speech sounds presented to each ear recalled equally well?

Although this technique may seem to be a program designed to produce confusion, it yields consistent observations linked to cerebral specialization. In general, data from dichotic-listening experiments indicate that right-handed persons identify verbal stimuli delivered to the right ear more accurately than simultaneously presented stimuli presented to the left ear. This result is described as a right-ear "advantage" for verbal information. In contrast, about 50% of left-handers reveal a reverse pattern, showing a left-ear advantage—more accurate performance for verbal stimuli delivered to the left ear. Some data also show that the pattern of ear advantage in right-handers changes when the stimuli are nonverbal, such as identification of musical sounds.

An explanation for these findings by Kimura (1973) argues that auditory information exerts stronger contralateral than ipsilateral neural effects (Figure 18-12). Accordingly, auditory stimuli presented to the right ear produce stronger left-auditory-cortex effects than right-auditory-cortex effects, and vice versa. Thus sounds presented to the right ear exert stronger control over left-hemispheric language mechanisms, whereas speech sounds presented to the left ear are less potent in activating left-cerebral-hemisphere language-processing regions.

Several recent studies have shown that right-handers' right-ear advantage for speech sounds is restricted to particular kinds of speech sounds (Tallal & Schwartz, 1980). The right-ear advantage is evident with simultaneously presented consonants like "b," "d," "t," and "k" but not with vowel sounds. Some investigators suggest that the right-ear advantage reflects a special feature of sound processing per se rather than verbal features. Tallal and Schwartz have suggested that the

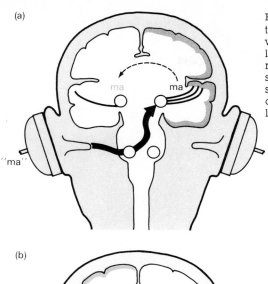

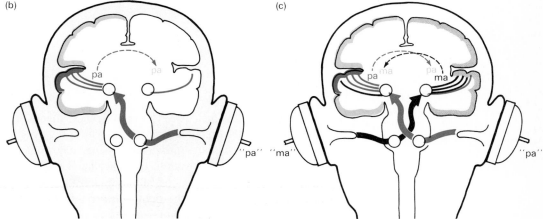

Figure 18-12 A representation of Kimura's model of the dichotic listening experiment (Kimura, 1973). (a) A word delivered to the left ear results in stronger stimulation of the right auditory cortex. (b) A word to the right ear results in stronger input to the left hemisphere. (c) When words are delivered to both ears simultaneously, the one to the right ear is usually perceived because it has more direct connections to the left hemisphere.

right-ear–left-hemisphere advantage for processing speech sounds reflects a left-hemisphere specialization for processing *any* sounds with rapidly changing acoustic properties. Of course, rapid change characterizes some speech sounds but not all. When the same speech sounds are artificially changed by extending them in time, the right-ear advantage for speech sounds is diminished. Hence in the dichotic-listening experiment, the right-ear advantage reflects a specialization for processing rapidly changing sounds, not a verbal specialization. Some speech sounds are included in this acoustic criterion for left-hemisphere processing; others are not. Tzeng and Wang (1984) point out that the left hemisphere's ability to process rapidly changing acoustic features is the basis of the superiority of the left hemisphere for linguistic processing. This capacity enables a binding together of sound segments facilitating rapid transmission and analysis of speech.

Visual Hemispheric Specialization

Hemispheric specialization in normal humans can be studied by using brief exposures to stimuli presented to visual half-fields (Figure 18-13). If the stimulus expo-

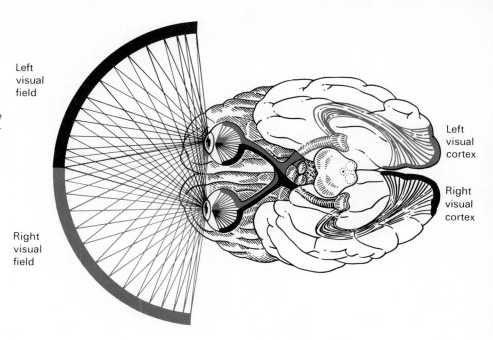

Figure 18-13 Representation of the visual fields on the retina and cerebral hemispheres. The right visual field projects to the left cerebral hemisphere and the left visual field projects to the right cerebral hemisphere.

Left visual field

Right visual field

Left visual cortex

Right visual cortex

sure is kept to less than 100–150 milliseconds, then input can be restricted to one hemisphere, since this time is not sufficient for the eyes to shift their direction. Of course in intact humans further processing may involve information transmitted through the corpus callosum to the other hemisphere.

Most studies with visual half-field presentations show that verbal stimuli (words and letters) presented to the right visual field (going to the left hemisphere) are better recognized than the same input presented in the left visual field (going to the right hemisphere). On the other hand, nonverbal visual stimuli (like faces) presented to the left visual field are better recognized than the same stimuli presented to the right visual field. Simpler visual processing such as detection of light, hue, or simple patterns is equivalent in the two hemispheres. But for more complex materials, in vision as well as audition, certain verbal stimuli are better processed in the left hemisphere of most individuals.

The Left-Handed

Anthropologists speculate that right-handedness goes back a long time into prehistory. People portrayed in cave paintings held things in their right hand, and Stone Age tools seem to be shaped to a right hand. Some of the evidence comes from studying skull fractures of animals preyed upon by ancient humans. Since the fractures are on the animal's left side, anthropologists conclude that the attacker held an implement in the right hand. So right-hand preference and use goes back a long way. Throughout history many unusual attributes have been ascribed to the left-handed person—from the possession of an evil personality to a diffuse form of cerebral cortex organization. Indeed, the term *sinistral* (''left-handed'') comes from the same Latin root as the word *sinister*!

Left-handed people comprise a small percentage of human populations. A figure of around 10% is commonly reported, although this percentage may be lower in parts of the world where teachers actively discourage left-handedness. For example, a higher percentage of left-handed Chinese-Americans is seen in more tolerant United States schools than among Chinese in China. Recent surveys of left-handed writing in American college populations reveal an incidence of 13.8% (Spiegler & Yeni-Komshian, 1983). This is viewed as a dramatic increase over prior generations, perhaps reflecting a continuing decline in the social pressures toward right-handedness and an increase in the social acceptability of left-handedness.

Many studies have sought to show cognitive and emotional differences between left- and right-handed humans, the implication being that these groups differ in cerebral cortex organization. Some studies (using relatively small samples of subjects) linked left-handedness to cognitive deficits. Such data tend to be contradictory, perhaps because some studies classify handedness with a single criterion (such as writing), whereas others employ many behaviors. Further, some individuals are ambidextrous—at least with regard to some tasks—or alternate their hand preference from task to task.

Hardyck, Petrinovich, and Goldman (1976) undertook a large-scale study of handedness and cognitive performance. They examined over 7000 children in grades one through six for school achievement, intellectual ability, motivation, socioeconomic level, and the like. In a detailed analysis of the resultant data they clearly showed that left-handed children did not differ from right-handed children on any measure of cognitive performance.

However, the idea that the left-handed are "damaged" humans has been common in the past and has even found occasional support. Silva and Satz (1979) note that several studies show a higher incidence of left-handedness in clinical populations than in the general population. They examined handedness in over 1400 patients in a school for the mentally retarded and showed an incidence of 17.8% left-handers, about double the level in the general population. In this population more left-handers than right-handers had abnormal EEGs. To explain the high rate of left-handedness in this retarded population, investigators have suggested that the rate is the result of injuries to the brain. Early brain injury, these investigators argue, can cause a shift in handedness. Since most people are right-handed, early one-sided brain injury is more likely to effect a change from right-handedness to left-handedness than the reverse.

Some left-handed persons write by using an inverted hand posture in which the hand is held curved, resting above the written line. This posture contrasts with that of other left-handers, which appears as a mirror image of the writing posture of most right-handers. The awkwardness of the inverted left-handed posture has been viewed as a product of either an attempt to model the characteristic slant of right-handers or a way to gain a better view of the written line. However, a different perspective is offered by the work of Levy and Reid (1976), who argue that these hand postures can be used to predict which hemisphere controls language functions. In their study they compared inverted and noninverted left-handers on visual field tests. A similarity was noted between right-handers and inverted left-handers in that both showed superiority of right-visual-field verbal tasks, implying left-hemisphere language control. In contrast, noninverted left-handers showed left-visual-field superiority for verbal tasks. A similar right-hemisphere language control was shown by one right-hander with an inverted writing posture—an extreme rarity. This work is controversial; although the relationship to visual field tasks continues to be seen, writing posture of left-handers is not related to other measures of hemispheric specialization, like dichotic-listening tasks (Springer & Deutsch, 1985).

Cerebral Lateralization of Emotions

Lateralization of cognitive processes in humans is well established by many experimental and clinical observations. Recently the attention of researchers has been directed to the prospect that hemispheric differences can be demonstrated in another fundamental psychological dimension—emotions. Differences between the cerebral hemispheres have been explored from several perspectives. One part of this pursuit focuses on the special role of the right hemisphere in the perception of emotional states. Another aspect of this problem is evident in work concerned with lateralization of emotional expression, especially in displays of facial expression (e.g., Fridlund, 1988). Finally, a clinical contribution is evident in work concerned with affective disorders associated with unilateral brain diseases such as stroke and departures from a normative portrait in hemispheric specialization seen in psychiatric populations. We will note some of the contributions from each of these perspectives that lead to the tentative assertion that emotions involve the hemispheres to different extents.

Right Hemisphere and Perception of Emotion in Normal People

Dichotic-listening techniques have shown that the cerebral hemispheres might function differently in the recognition of emotional stimuli. An example of the use of this technique is seen in the work of Ley and Bryden (1982), who presented normal subjects with brief sentences spoken in happy, sad, angry, and neutral voices. The sentences were presented through headsets, with a different sentence in each ear. Subjects were instructed to attend to one ear and report both the content of the message and its emotional tone. Subjects showed a distinct left-ear advantage for identifying the emotional tone of the voice and a right-ear advantage for identification of the semantic content of the brief message. Since each ear projects more strongly to the contralateral hemisphere, the results indicate that the right hemisphere is better than the left in interpreting emotional aspects of vocal messages. There is also the possibility noted by some critics that both hemispheres process emotional stimuli but that stimuli directed to the right hemisphere are more likely to produce emotional reactions (Silberman & Weingartner, 1986).

Tachistoscopic presentation of visual stimuli has also revealed hemispheric differences in the perception of emotional states or stimuli. These studies usually employ stimuli that consist of faces displaying different emotional expressions. In a variety of tasks that emphasize either reaction time or identification, the common finding is that emotional stimuli presented to the left visual field (projecting to the right hemisphere) result in faster reaction times and more accurate identification of emotional states (Bryden, 1982). These effects can be modified by various instructions to subjects. For example, hemisphere differences can be enhanced by instructions that emphasize an empathic response, that is, "Try to feel like the face depicted in a stimulus presentation."

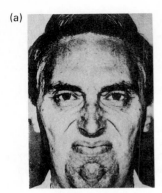

(a)

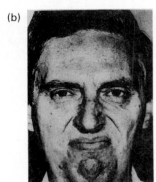

(b)

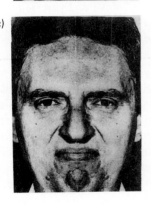

(c)

Figure 18-14 Comparison of the intensity of emotional expression in composite faces. (a) Left-side composite. (b) Original face. (c) Right-side composite. (From H. Sackheim et al., "Emotions Are Expressed More Intensely on the Left Side of the Face," *Science* 202, Oct. 1978, Fig. 1, p. 434. Copyright © 1978 by the American Association for the Advancement of Science.)

Right Hemisphere and Emotional Expression

An interesting effect is seen when a photograph of the face of a person displaying an emotion is cut down the exact middle of the face and two new composite photos are produced. In this procedure one new face is made by combining two left sides (one printed in mirror image), and another face is made by combining two right sides of a face. An example is shown in Figure 18-14. In several studies subjects judge the left-sides photo as more emotional than the right-sides photo (Sackheim et al., 1978). Campbell (1982) has shown that composite photos constructed of the left side of the face are judged as happier, and composites of the right side of the face are judged as sadder. Criticisms of this type of experiment have noted that they fail to distinguish between photographs of posed emotions and those of genuinely emotional expressions (Hager, 1982). Asymmetry of facial expression becomes much less evident when photos of spontaneous, genuine emotions are used as stimuli. Ekman et al. (1984) emphasize that judgments of facial expression include quite complex assessments that involve both static features of the face, such as bony landmarks, and dynamic features, such as those that are produced by facial musculature.

Emotional Disorders Associated with Hemispheric Injury and Disease

A major theme to emerge from studies with patients who have sustained injury or disease confined to one hemisphere is that the hemispheres differ in emotional tone. Results of unilateral intracarotid artery injections of amytal supplied some of the earliest data (see Box 18-1). It has been suggested that injection of sodium amytal into the "dominant" hemisphere (for most people, the left hemisphere) produces a depressive aftereffect, while an identical injection into the carotid artery on the nondominant side releases euphoria with an elevated sense of well-being and smiling. A program of observations in stroke patients by Robinson et al. (1985) adds some important data. They note that patients with strokes involving the left anterior cerebral hemisphere have the highest frequency of depressive symptoms; the closer the lesion was to the frontal pole, the more intense the depressive portrait. In these patients aphasia was not correlated with severity of depression. In contrast, patients with right-hemisphere lesions are described as unduly cheerful and apathetic. Similar observations were seen in left-handed individuals, suggesting that poststroke mood disorders are independent of cerebral lateralization for handedness and language. Bear (1983) has suggested that the right-hemisphere-injured patient shows a deficit in emotional surveillance (the detection of events that ordinarily elicit emotional responses, such as threat). Hemispheric differences in the site of the initiation of epileptic discharges also seem related to differences in emotional dimensions. A psychosis after right temporoparietal injury that leads to seizures has been noted in several patients—all of whom showed no psychiatric disorders prior to brain injury. This disorder was characterized by intense delusional and hallucinatory symptoms. Many other clinical observations related to hemispheric differences have been summarized by Heilman et al. (1983).

| BOX 18-1 | Anesthetizing One Hemisphere at a Time: The Sodium Amytal Test |

In the process of making clinical assessments and decisions, neurologists must know which hemisphere is specialized for language processing. Although clinical observations of brain-injured humans indicate that 95% of us show left-hemisphere specialization for verbal activities, typical psychological tests would have led us to expect a smaller group. A technique that comes close to producing effects like that of brain injury without inflicting damage to the brain would be very valuable for neurosurgeons who seek to minimize language impairments from brain operations.

Wada and Rasmussen (1960) provided a tool that is much like a reversible lesion. The effect is accomplished by injection of a short-acting anesthetic—sodium amytal—into a single carotid artery, first on one side and then, several minutes later, on the other. From our discussion in Chapter 2, you will recall that the circulation of the anterior two-thirds of the cerebral hemisphere comes from branches of the carotid artery. Most of the anesthetic in the first pass through the vascular system remains on the side of the brain where it was injected. The patient shows arrest of speech for a brief period when injected on the side of hemispheric specialization for language processing. After a few minutes the effects wear off, so the injection is much like a reversible brain lesion. The sodium amytal test (sometimes named the Wada test after its discoverer) shows that about 95% of humans are left-hemisphere-specialized for language.

Cerebral Lateralization and Psychiatric Disorders

Patients with psychiatric disorders have also been examined to see whether cerebral lateralization differs from normals in a variety of cognitive and perceptual tasks. Several controversial propositions have been offered in studies involving schizophrenic patients. An association between schizophrenia and impaired cerebral laterality has been suggested by a constellation of debatable findings summarized in reviews by Marin and Tucker (1981) and Merrin (1981). No single finding seems pivotal, but an inferential net formed out of many observations buoys this view. For example, Wexler (1979) assessed dichotic-listening test performance in psychotic patients and found that higher laterality scores were associated with improved psychiatric condition. Some researchers see the schizophrenic state as one characterized by overactivity of the left dysfunctional hemisphere (Gur, 1979). There are many variables involved in this story, and it is sometimes difficult to disentangle the vagaries of patient behavior from the main effects displayed in psychological test assessment of hemispheric functioning in psychiatric patients. Further research may help to clarify the status of conceptions in this area.

Suggestions w/ schizophrenia

Anatomical and Physiological Relations to Hemispheric Differences

The search for the biological bases of hemispheric differences has included both anatomical and neurophysiological studies. Recent research suggests that the two hemispheres have a slightly different form. Comparing the structures of the left and right sides of the body, we note that they are not mirror halves. Marked asymmetry is evident for the heart and liver. Look in the mirror and smile—or if you are not up to that, grimace. Careful examination of facial folding and the edges of the lips shows decided asymmetry. The functional role of these facial asymmetries is unknown (although it has been claimed that expressions on the left side of the face are

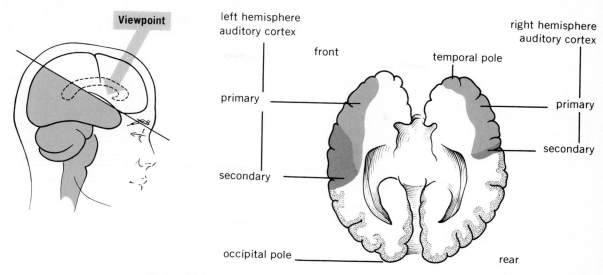

Figure 18-15 Structural asymmetry of the human temporal lobe. The planum temporale (darker brown area) is larger in the left hemisphere in 65–75% of humans. (Adapted from Geschwind and Levitsky, 1968. Copyright 1968 by the American Association for the Advancement of Science.)

judged as more emotional). Investigators have not yet explored whether a viewer's interpretation of another person's face is similarly asymmetrical.

In a study of adult temporal lobes, Geschwind and Levitsky (1968) found that in 65% of the brains examined, a region of the cerebral cortex known as the planum temporale was larger in the left hemisphere than in the right hemisphere (Figure 18-15). In 11% the right side was larger. In some studies the magnitude of this left-right difference is almost 2 to 1. The region examined, the upper surface of the temporal lobe, includes part of Wernicke's speech area. Presumably the difference in the size of the area reflects the specialization (dominance) of one cerebral hemisphere for language. The larger left area implies more elaborate development of that side, which might include more nerve cells or greater elaboration of dendrites. This difference in cortical size is even more evident at birth. It appeared in 86% of the infant brains examined. This evidence suggests an intrinsic basis for cerebral dominance in language, since the asymmetry appears before any environmental reinforcement of dominance can occur.

Direct anatomical observations and functional measures like handedness and verbal abilities are not yet available from the same subjects. However, some indirect measures of temporal cortex size can be obtained from arteriograms that reveal the size and course of the middle cerebral artery (Hochberg & LeMay, 1975; LeMay & Culebras, 1972). Of a group of 44 right-handed patients, 86% showed a blood vessel pattern that implied greater left temporal-parietal size, whereas this pattern was seen in only 17% of left-handers. The bulk of left-handers showed no right-left differences.

Computer tomograms reveal size differences in some large brain regions, and these differences can be related to overlying skull shape. Using this technique,

LeMay (1977) has shown that a majority of right-handers (61%) have wider frontal regions on the right, whereas this pattern was seen in only 40% of left-handers. In contrast, more left-handers had greater left frontal regions. The differences were more pronounced when only familial left-handers were compared with right-handers. Anatomic asymmetries have now been seen in many gross measures of the cerebral hemispheres. These are summarized by Geschwind and Galaburda (1985). Microscopic comparisons of the left and right hemispheres reveal differences in fine structure between the two sides of the brain. Comparisons of the dendritic organization of the right and left anterior speech areas by Scheibel et al. (1985) revealed significant differences in dendritic patterns. Cells on the left showed a greater number of higher order dendritic branches; this pattern was partially reversed in non-right-handed individuals.

Asymmetry in the distribution of transmitters has been noted in both human and animal studies. For example, regions of the human left thalamus contain more epinephrine than the right (Geschwind & Galaburda, 1985). Asymmetry in the concentration of dopamine in some regions of the basal ganglia is related to preferred turning direction in rats (Glick & Shapiro, 1984). Hormonal relations to cerebral cortical asymmetry have been advanced by M. C. Diamond et al. (1982), who showed that the cerebral cortex is thicker in several areas on the left than on the right in female rats. In male rats the right-sided areas are thicker. Removal of the testes at birth reversed this asymmetry.

Right-left asymmetry is also seen in both vascular structures of the cerebral hemispheres and measures of cerebral blood flow responses to verbal and nonverbal stimuli. Blood flow to any organ changes with tissue activity. This change is produced by varying the caliber of the blood vessel—producing dilation or constriction. Greater left-hemisphere blood flow has been observed in response to verbal stimuli.

Origins of Hemispheric Specialization

To understand some of the workings of the brain it is useful to reflect on the advantages of certain biological states. Of course the complete story of the rationale of some biological advantages is lost in the history of evolution. The failure of behavior to fossilize might even generate more elaborate speculations. Such is the case in the scrutiny of the biological advantage and presumed evolutionary origins of hemispheric specialization. Let us examine some of these speculations.

Some see the origins of hemispheric specialization in the differential use of the limbs displayed in many routine tasks. Picture an early version of humans hunting. One hand holds the weapon and provides power, while the other is used in more delicate guidance or body balance. Archeological studies of human skulls imply differential use of the limbs in attacking other humans. Proof offered in support of this idea is the more common observations of left skull fracture in fossilized specimens of ancient people. If asymmetry is advantageous, then both parents should have the same asymmetry in order to pass it on to offspring. In time the evolutionary successes offered by handedness might have been used in the emergence of language and speech.

Several different theories about the emergence of speech and language have been suggested. Some focus on the motor aspects of speech and others on the

(2) motor aspects of speech

cognitive properties of language. The speech motor apparatus involves many delicate muscle systems situated in the midline of the body, like the tip of the tongue. Sensitivity and precision of stimulus analysis on the body surface are reduced in the exact midline. Perhaps this result reflects the mutual antagonism of right and left axon terminals in the skin. For speech this peculiarity of the midline would be catastrophic for precise control. Asymmetry of motor control of speech production might then offer better unchallenged control of relevant parts of the speech apparatus. Such sidedness in motor sound production is even seen in the vocal control of singing in birds as we discussed earlier.

(3) cognitive style)

Other connections to language and evolutionary advantages of cerebral specialization are seen in arguments that propose a fundamental difference in cognitive style between the hemispheres. According to this view, the left hemisphere provides processing that is analytic, and the right hemisphere offers a more holistic or general analysis of information. Some theorists suggest that hemisphere specialization allows for separate cognitive modes, which, it is argued, are mutually incompatible. Any linguistic or cognitive response involves acting on elements differently, and hemisphere specialization, it is argued, is a good solution to this need.

(4) frame of reference

The occasional errant flight of birds provides another clue to both the origins and advantages of bodily asymmetries. Some birds, while flying south during winter migration, end up in California instead of the Southeast. Jared Diamond (1980) suggests that these animals confuse right and left; he suggests that a functional role of body asymmetries is to facilitate telling right from left. Hemispheric asymmetry thus can reduce the danger of spatial errors by providing a frame of reference.

We noted earlier that the French Academy had once banned speculations on the origin of language, but no similar movement is afoot with respect to the topic of cerebral specialization. We have discussed only a small sample of current speculations. Further discussion might offer support for the wisdom of the French Academy in the late eighteenth century.

Theories of Cognitive Differences Between Human Cerebral Hemispheres

In the wake of research work on human split-brain patients, considerable speculation developed about cognitive and emotional differences between the hemispheres. This speculation has been further fueled by experimentation with normal humans. Educators concerned about declining accomplishments in primary and secondary schools now speak of educating ''both halves of the brain.'' Bogen (1977), one of the surgeons involved in split-brain operations, urges equal time for each hemisphere in schools. Increasing popularization of the themes of research in this area seems to lead to speculative leaps unbridled by facts.

Actually distinctions between ''left brain'' and ''right brain'' have been drawn ever since the dichotomy of verbal versus nonverbal grew from clinical observations of language disorders following left temporal and frontal injuries. Table 18-1 on page 711 presented a list of differences in cognitive processing proposed by various researchers. Leading this list is the distinction between verbal and nonverbal born from studies of aphasia. However, several experimental observations lead us to question this dichotomy. We have already noted that several studies using split-brain patients show language processing in the right hemisphere. This result becomes increasingly apparent as researchers move away from using speech as the sole measure of linguistic abilities. For example, patients can point to objects whose name is flashed to the left visual fields.

Although some experiments do show task differences between the cerebral hemispheres, the leap to the notion that we harbor two cognitive selves is beyond even inspired speculation. We must remember that many differences between the cerebral hemispheres are small and do not indicate that one side is more involved in accomplishment of a particular function. It is very difficult usually to direct information exclusively to one hemisphere. Simultaneous processing by the two is the more likely story, and mutual interaction between the cerebral hemispheres is the modal state (Bazzaniga & Le Doux, 1978). Studying hemispheric specialization provides clues about information processing, and they indicate that mental unity is the customary human experience. Separate education of each hemisphere is not justified, at least from the vantage point of scientific inquiry to date.

Language Development and the Brain

Both extrinsic and intrinsic processes determine the acquisition of language. On one hand, there is considerable regularity across all human languages in the timing of stages of language development. During the first year of life, the babbling of all children, no matter in what culture they are reared, sounds similar. On the other hand, the highly specialized attributes of specific languages require the processes of learning during early development. Rare cases of profound isolation in children during early development point to the importance of experience during critical periods early in development.

One focus of developmental studies is the acquisition of lateralization in children as seen in structures of the brain and functions like dichotic listening. Previously we noted that hemispheric asymmetry appears in human infants at birth. Newborn babies turn their heads far more often to the right than to the left (Turkewitz, 1977). Electrophysiological asymmetry of the infant cerebral hemispheres is evident in response to speech sounds. Thus from quite early on structural and functional lateralization exist in the human brain.

Maturation of language development takes time, a result that is reflected in several features of recovery from language impairment following brain injury. This idea is discussed in the last section of this chapter. The essence of these observations is that the brain slowly loses the ability to compensate for injury.

Frontal Lobes and Behavior

Because the complexity of human beings far exceeds that of other animals, researchers have sought characteristics of the brain that might account for human preeminence. Among the most striking differences is the comparative size of the human prefrontal cortex. In part because of its size, the frontal region has been regarded as the seat of intelligence and abstract thinking. Adding to the mystery of frontal lobe function is the unusual assortment of behavior changes that follow surgical or accidental lesions of this region. The complexity of change following prefrontal damage remains best epitomized by the last sentence of a report written by a physician describing the behavior changes seen in the classical case of Phineas Gage after accidental brain damage. In 1848 Mr. Gage exploded gunpowder which sent an iron rod through his skull, producing a massive lesion of the prefrontal cortex. The last sentence of the physician's report reads, ". . . his mind was radically changed, so decidedly that his friends and acquaintances said that he was 'no longer Gage.''' Now, over 140 years later, research provides some clues to the bases of Phineas Gage's transformation. As we will see in this section, some of the mystery of frontal lobe function has begun to yield to intense experimental analysis.

Analysis of Frontal Lobe Injury

In humans approximately half the volume of the cerebral cortex consists of frontal cortex. In other animals the frontal cortex, especially prefrontal regions, is a smaller portion of the cerebral cortex (Figure 18-16). The clinical portrait of humans with frontal lesions reveals an unusual collection of emotional, motor, and cognitive changes. Observations of the emotional reactivity of these patients shows a persistent strange apathy, broken by bouts of euphoria with an exalted sense of well-being. Ordinary social conventions seem readily cast aside by impulsive activity. Concern for the past or the future is rarely evident (Milner & Petrides, 1984).

Frontal patients show quite shallow emotions, even including reduced responsiveness to pain. Frequently, though, there are episodes in which this apathy is replaced by boastfulness and silliness and, sometimes, unbridled sexual activities.

Cognitive changes in human frontal patients are very complicated and difficult to pinpoint, although one senses that something very different characterizes the frontal patient. Standard IQ test performance shows only slight pre-to-postsurgery changes. Forgetfulness is shown in many tasks requiring sustained attention. In fact, some investigators have commented that these patients even forget their own warnings ''to remember.''

Clinical examination of frontal patients also reveals an array of strange impairments in motor activities, especially in the realm of ''plans'' for action. The patients seem to perseverate in any activity. For example, if the patient is asked to open and then close the fist, once the activity has begun—and it is difficult to initiate such acts in frontal patients—the patient continues an unending sequence of fist opening and closing. The overall level of motor activity is quite diminished in frontal patients, especially in the realm of ordinary, spontaneous movements. For example, facial expression becomes quite blank, and there is a marked reduction in head and eye movements. Some reflexes evident only very early in life reappear in frontal cases, such as the infantile grasp reflex of the hand. Many clinical assessments of these patients have emphasized an impairment in goal-directed behavior, especially an inability to plan acts and use foresight. Daily activities of these patients seem disorganized and without a clear program for successive activities.

Formal psychological tests are an important aspect of the assessment of the brain, but there are times when less formal behavioral assessments highlight a feature of brain impairment with striking clarity. Indeed sometimes less formal behavioral observations reveal a behavioral deficit that is not at all apparent with objective test evaluation. Quite recently this point was underscored by reports by Lhermite et al. (1986) that described an unusual phenomenon in frontal lobe impaired patients. They noted in these patients a syndrome that is characterized by the spontaneous imitation of the gestures and behavior of the examiner. Lhermite and

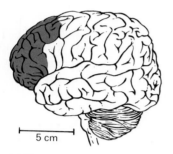

5 cm

(a) Human

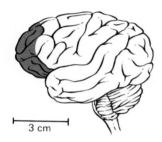

3 cm

(b) Spider monkey

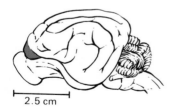

2.5 cm

(c) Cat

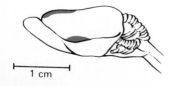

1 cm

(d) Rat

Figure 18-16 Comparisons of the size of prefrontal cortex in various mammals. The relative percentage of prefrontal cortex is greatest in humans and decreases successively in other primates, carnivores, and rodents.

his collaborators see this syndrome as related to one they identified as "utilization behavior," which is defined as an exaggerated dependence on the environment for behavior cues. The syndrome was seen during clinical exams in which the examiner made various bodily gestures or engaged in writing or handling of objects. All patients with disease involving the frontal lobes spontaneously imitated the gestures of the examiner in detail. The slightest movement on the part of the examiner seemed to be an invitation to imitate. Patients were aware of their imitative behavior. Patient behavior in complex social situations also reflected the extraordinary environmental dependency of the behavior of frontal lobe patients. The social situations described by Lhermite et al. (1986) included observations of interactions in a home environment and a doctor's office. In the latter situation, a patient saw a blood pressure gauge and immediately took the physician's blood pressure. After eyeing a tongue depressor, she placed it in front of the doctor's mouth. Upon walking into a bedroom, one patient proceeded to get undressed and go to bed. He hurried out of bed when the examiner picked up a piece of his clothing. In these acts there is a certain mechanical character; Lhermite describes these patients as powerless in the face of influences from the outside world. The loss of self-criticism is another aspect of their behavior as evident in the act of urinating calmly against a public building. Lhermite suggests that some features of this deficit arise from the loss of frontal control over the activities of parietal cortex, which controls some aspects of sensorimotor activity. He suggests that the connection between the parietal and frontal cortex links the individual to the environment and subserves individual autonomy.

Prefrontal Lesions in Nonhumans

The study of prefrontal cortical function in animals starts with the work of Carlyle Jacobsen in the 1930s. In his experiments with chimpanzees he employed delayed-response learning as described in Chapter 16.

This simple test situation revealed a remarkable impairment in chimpanzees with prefrontal lesions. These animals did very poorly in this task, in contrast with animals that sustained lesions in other brain regions. In interpreting this phenomenon Jacobsen emphasized the memory function of the frontal cortex.

Experimental and clinical observations of humans and other animals with frontal lesions have generated some hypotheses about the functions of the frontal lobes. A large variety of symptoms becomes evident—almost an overabundance—and there are no immediately available generalizations that could account for all these deficits. Some ideas fit more data than others and have thus become a strong focus for work in this area. These hypotheses include memory functions, planning controls, inhibitory control of behavior, and feedback control of behavior. Current evidence offers support for many of these theories.

Parietal Cortex Syndromes in Humans

Injury to the parietal lobe produces impairments such as these: Objects placed in the hand cannot be recognized by touch alone. One side of the body may be completely neglected, even to the point of being rejected as one's own. Faces cannot be recognized from photographs. Spatial orientation can become severely disturbed. Diversity of behavior changes following injury to this region is partly related to its large expanse and its critical position adjacent to occipital, temporal, and frontal regions.

The anterior end of the parietal region includes the postcentral gyrus, which is

BOX 18-2 | The Heart and Cognition

A golden age of surgery is now upon us. Microsurgical techniques permit a variety of delicate reconnections of the vasculature in all organs. Since the development of heart-lung bypass equipment, many forms of surgical repair of the heart have become almost routine. Holes in the walls of the heart can be closed, valves replaced, and arteries reamed clear of debris. While this surgery is being done, blood is pumped to the brain by mechanical equipment. Sensitive monitoring devices enable measurement and regulation of many physiological variables during surgery, ensuring that bodily malfunctions will not occur.

However, it appears that there is a price to be paid for heart surgery. Neurological consequences of open-heart surgery are characteristic of the majority of patients, according to Sotaniemi (1980), who reviewed a large number of cases. Most patients show forms of altered behavior, including profound disorientation and global memory difficulties that may last for months. After a year recovery is complete in most cases, with less than 10% showing continuing signs of neurological involvement.

These clinical data underscore the significance of normal blood flow to the brain. Prolonged, continuous blood flow regulated by bypass equipment may not adequately simulate the normal pulsating blood flow provided by physiological mechanisms.

---

the primary cortical receiving area for somatic sensation. Brain injury in this area does not produce numbness; rather it produces contralateral sensory deficits that seem to involve complex sensory processing. For example, objects placed in the hand contralateral to the injured somatosensory area cannot be identified by touch and active manipulation. This deficit is called **astereognosis** (from the Greek roots *a*, meaning "not" or "lacking," *stereo*, meaning "solid," and *gnosis*, meaning "knowledge"). It occurs even though primary somatosensory capabilities are relatively intact—that is, the subject feels something in his hand although he cannot identify it. In some cases the deficit occurs on the same side as the brain injury (Corkin, Milner, & Rasmussen, 1970). More extensive injuries in the parietal cortex, not restricted to the somatosensory cortex, affect interactions between or among sensory modalities, such as visual-tactual matching tasks, which require the subject to identify visually an object that was touched, or the reverse.

When a Face Isn't a Face: The Syndrome of Prosopagnosia

Suppose that one day you look in the mirror and you see someone who is not familiar to you! As incredible as that might seem, there is a small group of people who suffer this fate after brain damage due to a rare syndrome called prosopagnosia (derived from the Greek words *prosopo*, meaning "face," and *gnosis*, meaning "knowledge" or "perception"). Such patients not only fail to recognize their own face but also are unable to recognize the faces of relatives and friends. No amount of remedial training allows such people to acquire the ability to recognize anyone's face. In contrast, the ability to recognize objects is retained, and the patient readily identifies familiar people by the sounds of their voice. Faces simply lack meaning in the patient's life. All this occurs without cognitive impairments such as disorientation or confusion. There is no evidence of diminished intellectual abilities. Visual acuity is maintained, although most patients have a small visual field defect, that is, an area of the visual field where they are "blind."

The anatomical and neuropsychological features of this syndrome have been elegantly explored by Damasio (1985b). He noted that although earlier work focused on right-hemisphere lesions as the cause of the deficit, contemporary studies have provided a more thorough anatomical picture of this disorder. Both postmortem examination and CAT or MRI scans confirm that bilateral lesions are necessary for the syndrome to appear. Such data show that the deficit involves inferior visual association regions of the occipital-temporal cortex. Lesions of the superior visual association areas that encompass occipital-parietal cortex, while producing some visual perceptual disorders, do not produce prosopagnosia.

Detailed neuropsychological analysis of patients with the syndrome provides some interesting insights into the relevant underlying psychological mechanisms (Damasio, 1985b; Damasio et al., 1988). Observations reveal that the patients retain some complex perceptual abilities including the ability to draw figures seen in photographs. Furthermore, prosopagnosia often involves other perceptual categories besides faces. Some prosopagnosic patients cannot recognize their own car and do not recognize common makes of cars, although they can distinguish between cars and trucks. Some are also unable to recognize types of clothes or distinctive foods. Patients who are birdwatchers are no longer able to recognize distinctive birds, and farmers can no longer recognize a particular animal although they recognize animals as animals. Subfeatures of complex percepts can be pointed out, such as parts of a face. In addition, eye movements of patients that were recorded during examination of a picture of a face are like those of controls, indicating that some basic perceptual processes proceed normally. More recent studies by Damasio et al. (1988) involved asking patients to identify facial expressions, to estimate age and sex in photographs of strangers, and to identify photographs of family members, friends, or other familiar faces. Patients could identify facial expressions and estimate age and sex but failed to recognize familiar faces. These findings suggest that visual input is analyzed in separate, parallel channels.

The central feature of the deficit appears when the demand is to identify a specific stimulus configuration that depends on some memory trace. Thus these patients have difficulty in picking out a particular person from a group. It appears that the memory trace needed to activate context and familiarity is not accessible. Damasio suggests that the basic impairment is not in the processes of complex visual analysis but more likely in the organizing and use of pertinent memories. A recent research study by Tranel and Damasio (1985) adds interesting new data. They presented prosopagnosic patients with faces of familiar and unfamiliar people while recording electrodermal skin conductance, which is a response process controlled by the autonomic nervous system. Some of the familiar faces included photos of the patient, family members, and close friends. Although the patients could not report verbal recognition of the familiar faces, skin conductance changes were much more pronounced in response to familiar than unfamiliar faces. These data reveal a dissociation between the experience of recognition and recognition at an unconscious level. This indicates that recognition is taking place at some level, but overt identification and recognition are organized at a subsequent, perhaps more complex stage of visual information processing. This later stage might involve an integration of many different facets of memories pertinent to a particular face. Tranel and Damasio view the prosopagnosic deficit as a result of the "blocking of the activation that normally would be triggered by template matching"—the rich associative network of memories that enables someone to say, "I recognize Jane."

Unilateral Neglect

Brain damage involving the right inferior parietal cortex produces a very unusual set of behavior changes. The key feature is the neglect of the left side of both the body and space. For example, when a patient is asked to draw the face of a clock, all the hour positions are crowded onto the right side (Figure 18-17). Patients may fail to dress the left side of their body and may even disclaim "ownership" of their left arm or leg. In some instances familiar people presented on the left side of the patient are completely neglected, although there may be no apparent visual field defect. The phenomenon of hemispatial neglect can also be seen in simple test situations. A common test requires the patient to bisect a horizontal line presented on a piece of paper. Estimates of the center are markedly shifted to the right, and this effect is particularly marked when lines are presented to the left of the center of the body (Figure 18-17c) (Schenkerberg, Bradford, & Ajax, 1980).

Associated with this dramatic change is a feature called "extinction of simultaneous double stimulation." Most people can readily report the presence of two stimuli when stimulated simultaneously on both sides of the body. Patients with right inferior parietal lesions are completely unable to note the double nature of the stimulation and usually report only the stimulus presented to the right side. Although many patients with injury to this region show recovery from the symptom of unilateral neglect, the feature of extinction is quite persistent.

Yet another dramatic feature of this syndrome is the frequent failure to recognize illness, referred to as "denial of illness." Such patients may adamantly maintain that they are quite capable of engaging in their customary activities and do not recognize the impressive signs of unilateral neglect.

Many hypotheses have been offered to account for these symptoms. Some have regarded the disorder as the consequence of the loss of spatial pattern analysis; this hypothesis is consistent with the fact that unilateral neglect occurs with lesions of the right hemisphere but not with lesions of the left hemisphere. Others regard it as an attentional deficit.

The neurologist Mesulam (1985) offers an explanation of some properties of the neglect syndrome. He notes that single-cell recordings from posterior parietal cortex in monkeys show firing patterns that are sensitive to manipulations of attention. For example, some nerve cells in this area increase their discharge rates when the animal's eyes follow or track a meaningful object, frequently one that has been associated with reward. Anatomical studies of the sources of inputs to the posterior parietal region show origins in several distinct cortical sectors (Figure 18-18) including polymodal cortical sensory areas, cingulate cortex, and frontal cortex, espe-

(a)

(b)

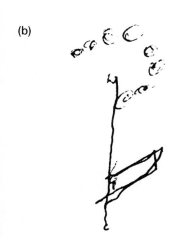

Figure 18-17 The neglect syndrome following right parietal cortex damage. (a) If such a patient is asked to draw a typical clock face, the left side is ignored and all hours are placed on the right. (b) When asked to copy a drawing of a daisy, the patient draws petals only on the right. (c) When asked to bisect a line, the patient places a mark well to the right of the midpoint, showing that he largely ignores the left. (Heilman, 1979)

(c)

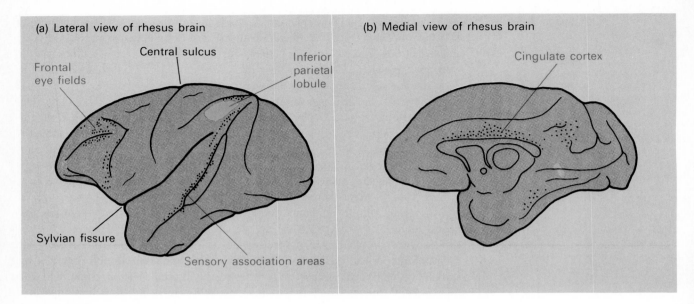

Figure 18-18 Regions of the cortex that are implicated in different aspects of unilateral neglect, shown on lateral (a) and medial (b) views of the monkey brain. (Adapted from Mesulam et al., 1977)

cially frontal eye fields. In turn, posterior parietal cortex has outputs that go back to these regions. Mesulam proposed that each of these regions has some distinctive role in a network governing attention. The posterior parietal component involves processes that yield an internal sensory map, while frontal cortex governs relevant searching movements, and cingulate cortex processing provides motivational values.

Recovery of Function Following Brain Injury

The course of behavior following brain injury often reveals conspicuous changes. Striking examples of language recovery following stroke have been observed in many adults. Amazing examples of language recovery have been described in children following removal of a diseased cerebral hemisphere.

Many theories are currently being offered to describe the mechanisms mediating recovery of function after lesions. Of course recovery of function is characteristic of lesions involving many different organs. The surprise and puzzle of such effects following brain injury comes from the knowledge that, unlike other organs, the nervous system does not add neurons to any significant extent following birth. In addition, views that were quite common until the last few years emphasized structural and functional fixedness of the brain—rigidity that seemed to provide little opportunity to compensate for a loss of elements. Recently research in recovery of brain functions has provided an exciting array of ideas and data that reveal several forms of brain plasticity. Studies in this area offer prospects for rehabilitation that are striking. We will consider some of the findings and notions of recovery mechanisms in this active area of research. Perhaps many different mechanisms together contribute to the patterns of recovery, so no single explanation can be offered as the sole basis.

In spite of encouraging developments about substantial recovery of function

BOX 18-3 | A Sport that Destroys the Mind!

It is likely that men used fists to settle arguments from the beginning of human history. Adding implements such as stones and knives to the fist undoubtedly increased the lethality of such aggressive encounters. The addition of soft leather wound around the fist signaled that fighting had become a sport. In ancient Greece and Rome, some boxers were admired for their courage and strength while others, wearing leather wrappings studded with metal nuggets, bludgeoned each other to death for the entertainment of spectators. Boxing has a long history, and a good deal of it is not pleasant. Although rules developed during the eighteenth century in England, including the use of padded gloves, it has always been clear that the goal of prizefighting is not to display grace and agility but to knock the opponent out. Indeed a bout usually ends when the opponent has sustained a transient loss of consciousness. To achieve that goal, boxers aim relentlessly at the head, which sustains blow after blow—a history that comes to exact a price from the contestants. The endpoint of this process has been called "dementia pugilistica," a fancy term used by neurologists to identify a state that is commonly known as punch-drunk. Punch-drunk boxers lead a life with markedly impaired cognitive abilities.

In recent years several deaths have drawn attention once again to the dangers of boxing. Most boxing deaths are due to brain injuries, especially brain hemorrhage. Several professional societies, including the American Psychological Association and various medical and neurological societies, have urged the banning of this sport. Although the neurological and psychological consequences of boxing have been noted before, recent CAT scan data have indicated that very few boxers—amateurs as well as professionals—escape unscathed. In a recent study, Casson and collaborators (1982) studied ten active professional boxers who had been knocked out. These fighters ranged in age from 20 to 31 years, and the bouts per boxer ranged from 2 to 52. The group included those of championship caliber and others who were mediocre or poor boxers. None of the knockouts sustained by the fighters involved a loss of consciousness that went beyond ten seconds. This group is representative of the usual professional prizefighter. Examination of the CAT scans of the group revealed that at least five of them had definitely abnormal scans. The abnormalities included mild generalized cortical atrophy, which in some cases included ventricular dilation. Only one boxer had a clearly normal brain picture. The age of the boxer was not related to cortical atrophy. The most successful of the boxers were the ones with the most profound cortical atrophy. In fact the total number of professional fights correlated directly with the magnitude of brain changes. A career of boxing accumulates many blows to the head and the most "successful" are frequently those who have sustained the most punishment. Some researchers have shown that the severity of neurological syndromes is related to the duration of a boxer's career (Roberts, 1969). A Parkinsonian-like consequence has also been noted as a result of boxing. Other studies have revealed a high incidence of abnormal EEGs after boxing matches (Busse et al., 1952). Since the cause of the neurological impairments is rapid acceleration of the brain, it is not surprising that significant neurological impairments are found in amateur boxers as well as in professionals. No small reason that many believe boxing is a sport whose time is past.

after many kinds of brain injury, this is an area where prevention is clearly better than cure, as a few examples will demonstrate. Motor vehicle accidents are major causes of injuries to the brain and spinal cord. Recreational activities such as horseback riding, diving, and contact sports are frequent causes of head injuries. See also Box 18-3 on effects of boxing on the brain.

Recovery from General
Physiological
Abnormalities

Any brain injury destroys particular collections of nerve cells and produces more generalized disturbances that transiently affect the responsiveness of other nerve cells. For example, in the region of a brain injury there is frequently a change in the properties of the blood-brain barrier. Some researchers have suggested that the time course of functional deficits following structural damage to nerve cells might reflect the inhibitory impact of blood-borne substances, which are ordinarily prevented from reaching the environment of nerve cells (Seil, Leiman, & Kelly, 1976). In time the changes in the blood vessels around a site of injury reestablish the blood-brain barrier and also increase blood flow to transiently distressed but intact tissue. Many years ago the term **diaschisis** was coined by the anatomist von Monakow (1914) to describe the distant inhibitory effects of brain lesions that seemed to be reversible. Over time the usage of the term diaschisis has expanded to include a host of potentially reversible, nonspecific effects that make the immediate consequences of a brain lesion more intense than persistent deficits.

Anatomical Regrowth and Reorganization in the Brain Following Injury

Anatomical dogma for many years declared that anatomical changes in the adult central nervous system are solely destructive. The intricate structure and connections of nerve cells were considered to be structurally fixed once adulthood was reached. Injury, it was thought, could only lead to the shrinkage or death of nerve cells. Many impressive contemporary demonstrations to the contrary have now led us to emphasize structural plasticity of nerve cells and their connections. Of course regeneration of the axons of the peripheral nervous system has always been accepted. Now comparable structural regrowth has been seen in the brain and spinal cord (Veraa & Grafstein, 1981). For example, injury to catecholamine-containing fibers in the medial forebrain bundle leads to degeneration of terminal portions of the axon and regrowth of axonal portions connected to nerve cells. Dendritic regrowth following injury may also occur in the brain. A form of regrowth following injury is illustrated in Figure 18-19.

Another form of structural change is seen in the spinal cord and brain—collateral sprouting. This change has been described in the peripheral nervous system, and the story goes like this: If a peripheral sensory or motor fiber is injured, there follows degeneration of the terminal portions and an immediate loss of sensory or motor function in the affected region. Nerve fibers adjacent to the injured fibers recognize this injury (perhaps by a chemical signal delivered from the injured site),

Figure 18-19 Collateral sprouting of brain neuron. (a) Normal connections of fimbria and medial forebrain bundle to septal nucleus cell. (b) After severing of medial forebrain bundle, a fimbria axon develops a sprout that occupies a synaptic site formerly occupied by an axon terminal from the medial forebrain bundle. (Adapted from Raisman, 1969)

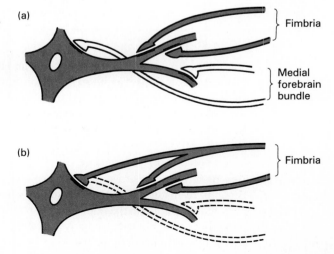

and they respond by developing sprouts or branches from intact axons. In time, usually weeks, these sprouts connect to denervated skin or muscle and acquire functional control of these regions on the periphery of the body (J. Diamond et al., 1976). This mechanism seems to result in functional compensation for a loss of neuronal connections. Incidentally, it should be noted that the injured nerve fiber (axon) slowly regrows, and, as it approaches the skin or muscles it had been connected to, there is a retraction of the sprouts. Again, chemical signals from the regrowing original fiber probably produce this change. Mark (1980) has suggested that a stage prior to the actual physical withdrawal of the fiber includes the cessation of synaptic effectiveness of the sprout-borne connections—a phenomenon he labeled ''synaptic repression.'' This result implies that synapses can be turned off even though the structural connection is still present. This switching of effectiveness of synapses is probably a significant feature of neural plasticity.

Demonstrations of collateral sprouting in the brain and spinal cord, which at one time were never observed, are now reported with regularity. Some investigators (such as Raisman, 1978) suggest that collateral sprouting in the brain offers hope for functional repair following injury. It is a growing view that injury of the nervous system might release various nerve growth factors. One group of researchers has described experiments in which it was shown that chemicals in the area of tissue surrounding brain injury contain a growth-promoting substance (Nieto-Sampedro & Cotman, 1985). The concentration of this yet unknown substance declines with distance from the injury site.

Observations of this sort indicate that brain connections are not as rigid anatomically as was once emphasized. The brain's response to injury does include structural modifications. However, are these anatomical changes relevant to the processes of functional repair? Around this question, controversy swirls. Although structural repair in the brain in the form of collateral sprouting is now generally accepted, there is no evidence that links this change with functional recovery following injury to the brain or spinal cord. In fact, some investigators (Wall, 1980) suggest that collateral sprouting might generate behavioral abnormalities, since nerve cells come under the control of unusual inputs. This form of regeneration in the spinal cord has been linked to spasticity in reflexes elicited below the level of a spinal injury (Liu & Chambers, 1958). Intensive research currently in progress is aimed at evaluating the functional value of such brain regrowth as collateral sprouting.

Education and Rehabilitation

For years hospitals and physicians have devoted considerable attention to providing rehabilitation for injuries that impair movement, especially if these defects developed from injury or disease of muscle or bone. For instance, teaching amputees to use prosthetic devices like artificial limbs has been a common effort. But until recently work with cognitive or perceptual handicaps that develop from brain impairments had received less intensive clinical and research interest. Several factors have provided the stimulus for a change of emphasis.

Some recent studies have demonstrated that postinjury experience can affect recovery. It is important at this point to distinguish between the role of experience in compensating for brain injury and its role in restoring behavior lost after injury. It is well known that experiences significantly reduce the impact of brain injury by fostering the elaboration of compensatory behavior. For example, vigorous eye movements can make up for large scotomas that result from injury to the visual pathways. Behavior strategies can change after a brain injury to allow for successful performance on a variety of tests. The role of experience following a lesion in possible reorganization of pathways is also evident in several studies.

Teodoru and Berman (1980) described a striking phenomenon of recovery that involves a change in feedback signals governing behavior. In experiments with monkeys they showed that unilateral section of the dorsal roots as they enter the spinal cord results in animals that do not show spontaneous use of the affected limb. It remains at the side as though paralyzed. To facilitate use of this limb, these investigators placed a hollow ball over the intact hand. This technique allowed free movement of the hand within the ball, but movements of the normal arm could not be used in securing food or other adaptive acts. With such maximal demands placed on the affected limb, it began to move more frequently. After four months the monkey showed coordinated activity of the denervated limb, including finger movement and reaching behavior. Performance of the denervated limb continued when the intact limb was removed from the ball. However, if the duration of this recovery experience was less than four months, coordinated movements of the two limbs did not persist and the denervated limb resumed its paralyzed posture.

The importance of training and experience in promoting recovery has been suggested by clinical observations and has been studied in animal experiments. A well-known case of aphasia and slow but excellent recovery is that of the actress Patricia Neal (Neal, 1988). Before she had a stroke at the age of 39, Patricia Neal had won an Academy Award. She was the mother of three children, and at the time of her stroke she was pregnant. A series of strokes crippled one leg and left her aphasic, unable to speak, read, or write. Speech therapy was begun as soon as possible. Then her husband organized friends to come in on schedule to talk with Pat and encourage her to speak and be active. Her baby was born normally. At this point Pat was still rather apathetic and was reluctant to continue to strive for further small gains: "I got fed up with working so hard. I felt certain that I was as good as I'd ever be. I was about eighty percent recovered. Still plenty of problems. But I was really ready to take a breather. And that's exactly what I would have done if Roald [her husband] hadn't made me go on. I had reached the danger point. The point where so many people stop work and just cruise along" (Griffith, 1970, p. 89). Her husband then hired a gifted nurse, Valerie Eaton Griffith, who devised a program of motivation and training that helped Pat to make further gains. Four years after her stroke Patricia Neal was able to star in another movie. Recovery is probably never absolutely complete after a major brain lesion, but it can be full enough to permit an active life and even a resumption of professional activities, as this example shows.

Animal experiments have shown that both formal training and informal enriched experience can promote recovery of function. Several studies performed with brain-lesioned rats have demonstrated that postlesion experience in a complex environment can improve subsequent problem-solving behavior (Will et al., 1977). Animals were placed in impoverished or enriched environments of the same kinds that had been shown to lead to changes in brain measures (Chapter 17). Although the brain-injured animals still made more errors than intact rats, those from the enriched environments made significantly fewer errors than those from the impoverished environments. Simply placing a group of animals together in a large cage had a measurable beneficial effect, but giving the animals access to varied stimuli was still more helpful (Rosenzweig, 1980). Thus even an injured brain can profit from experience. In the case of human patients, some experts in rehabilitation have questioned the wisdom of placing certain patients in virtual sensory isolation (coma patients, or patients kept in fixed positions in isolated rooms for intravenous therapy). Quite possibly such patients, even if they cannot respond, might be aided by visitors, music, and changing visual stimuli; some current programs of rehabilitation are putting these insights into effect.

Substitution by Remaining Brain Structures

Recovery following brain injury demonstrates that remaining neural tissue can mediate required behaviors. One perspective suggests that there is appreciable "redundancy" of neural systems and that recovery involves the use of redundant pathways. However, what appears to be redundancy may arise from the complexity of the neural substrates of behavior and the simple ways in which recovery is assessed. Thus if the neural substrate for some behavior is broadly represented in the brain, behavior may be reinstated because of the extensiveness of neural controls rather than because of redundant or repeated systems.

Another kind of unusual substitution has been described by Wall (1980). He studied the receptive field properties of dorsal column and thalamic cells following peripheral denervation. Wall noted that sizes of receptive fields of cells in this system change with denervation, especially in the direction of increasing size. Cells may also become responsive to bilateral inputs. Thus change occurs rapidly, and Wall suggests that denervation unmasks weakly excitable paths that come to control some neurons. He refers to this effect as a "homeostatic adjustment" of nerve cell excitability. Switching of nerve cell responsiveness in sensory paths is also evident in the vestibular system. Section of the vestibular nerve or unilateral removal of the labyrinth on one side results in head tilting or deviation and other signs of postural asymmetry. In time these effects abate, illustrating a phenomenon known as "vestibular compensation." Some of this recovery depends on inputs from the spinal cord (Jensen, 1979). Another independent aspect of recovery is a change in the activity of brain stem vestibular neurons. The dynamic character of cortical sensory systems is shown by Wall and Kaas (1985). They showed that sectioning of a peripheral nerve to one digit enlarged the receptive fields of some cortical neurons.

Age and Recovery of Function

Many clinical observations have led to the general proposition that brain lesions earlier in life have less disastrous consequences than similar injuries sustained later in life. The explanation offered for this phenomenon is that the younger brain possesses greater plasticity, although it is also acknowledged that especially the infant brain is more vulnerable to some destructive agents like viruses. A recent study of human language impairments and age provides an example of the relations between maturational state and recovery of function.

In a survey of childhood aphasia, Woods and Teuber (1978) examined records of a large group of children who lost language abilities following brain damage. The age of 8 looms as a critical point in recovery from brain trauma. All children who

BOX 18-4 | Childhood Loss of One Hemisphere

During early development the brain is a vulnerable organ, a phenomenon especially apparent when looking at the effect of a prolonged, difficult birth involving a period of oxygen loss. Some children with this early physiological deficit show lateralized brain injury involving a single cerebral hemisphere. Early on, such a child may show paralysis on one side of the body and frequent seizures. These seizures can be difficult to control with medication, and they may occur so often that they endanger life. Major brain damage on one side is shown in radiological data; the injured hemisphere can be quite shrunken.

Surgical removal of the malfunctioning hemisphere reduces seizures. Although at first some severe effects of the surgery are evident, over a long period of time the restoration of behavior is practically complete. This result is strikingly illustrated in a case presentation of A. Smith and Sugar (1975). As an infant the boy showed a right-side paralysis, and by $5\frac{1}{2}$

years of age he was experiencing 10 to 12 seizures a day. Although the boy's verbal comprehension was normal, his speech was hard to understand. All the cerebral cortex of the left hemisphere was therefore removed. Long-term follow-up studies extended to age $26\frac{1}{2}$, when he had almost completed college. Tests revealed an above-normal IQ and superior language abilities; thus the early loss of most of the left hemisphere did not preclude language development. This patient also has remarkable development of nonverbal functions, including visuospatial tasks and manual tasks. Note that adult hemispherectomy of the left side usually results in drastic impairment of language affecting both speech and writing. This case thus provides an example of extensive functional recovery after childhood loss.

became aphasic before the age of 8 regained speech no matter how great the impairment observed immediately following brain injury. (An example is given in Box 18-4.) The time for recovery of language ranged from one month to two years. Many children who became aphasic after age 8 showed less complete recovery.

Differences in nerve cell regrowth processes have been related to age in several studies. Kalil and Rey (1979) noted that section of the pyramidal tract at the level of the medulla in infant hamsters is followed by massive regrowth. They also note that, in contrast to adult hamsters, infant hamsters develop normal motor functions of the forepaw. Regenerative capabilities seem to decline with age, according to Scheff, Bernardo, and Cotman (1978). Reactive regrowth is very sparse in the aged rat brain. The researchers argue that this result implies a reduction in the ability to remodel circuitry with aging.

Studies in nonhumans that explore the factor of age in recovery yield both similarities with and differences from humans. Goldman (1976) has contributed studies of the relations between maturation of the brain in monkeys and development of their behavior and has reviewed research of others in this field. One of her studies employed the technique of implanting devices in the brains of monkeys by means of which a local area of the cortex could be cooled and thus inactivated for a period of time in an awake monkey. This technique produces, in effect, a reversible brain lesion. Bilateral cooling of the prefrontal cortex in adult monkeys (3 years old or older) was found to impair their performance on a delayed-response task. However, it did not affect their general level of activity or motor coordination. But in juvenile monkeys (18 months old or younger), the cooling had no effect on the test performance. This result is in line with other evidence that the frontal dorsolateral cortex in the monkey does not achieve its adult function until after the monkey is 2 years old.

Lesion Momentum and Deficits

The impairment caused by a brain lesion is greater the faster the lesion develops. For this reason some investigators speak of the lesion's momentum, or mass × velocity (Finger, 1978). It is curious but true that the same amount of tissue destruction may have much less effect if it occurs gradually than if it occurs swiftly. Investigators have studied this phenomenon by removing a given amount of tissue all at once in some experimental animals and in stages separated by a few weeks in other animals. A lesion in the brain stem that incapacitates animals if the removal is made all at one time may have only slight effect if it is done in two successive stages. Perhaps the partial lesion stimulates regrowth or relearning or both, so that some compensation has already been achieved by the time the rest of the tissue is removed. Some experimenters have reported that sensory stimulation or retraining during the interval between successive lesions is necessary for the reduced impairment observed with staged destruction, but not all studies agree.

Recent experimental findings suggest a mechanism for the staged-lesion effect: When a lesion causes loss of synaptic connections, this may result in the release of chemical signals that facilitate sprouting of terminals. When a small lesion precedes a larger lesion by 4 days to 2 weeks, the response to the second lesion is significantly faster and more extensive than if the earlier lesion had not occurred. Thus the earlier lesion primes the system to respond to the subsequent lesion (Scheff, Bernardo, & Cotman, 1978).

Clinical cases also reveal effects of lesion momentum. For example, an adult patient with a brain tumor encroaching on the speech areas of his left hemisphere had several operations, spaced many months apart (Geschwind, 1976). Each time the tumor regrew, it was necessary to remove more of the cortical speech areas, and each time the patient recovered his speech. Finally he was speaking even though only a fragment of the speech areas remained. The effects of aging on the brain can also be thought of as a slowly developing condition, which probably helps to mitigate them.

The phenomenon of lesion momentum is one of the reasons it is difficult to relate the effects of a disease-caused brain lesion to its size. This phenomenon can help us understand some cases that seem to contradict localization of function. That is, brain lesions in two patients may appear to be the same in size and location, yet one patient will show severe behavioral impairment while the second will not. Perhaps the lesion in the second patient developed slowly, allowing time both for growth in adjacent tissue and also for elaboration of compensatory behavioral strategies. Thus the phenomenon of lesion momentum shows that the brain cannot be regarded as a fixed piece of machinery but must be seen as a plastic structure that adapts to imposed conditions.

In this section we have noted several examples and mechanisms related to functional recovery following brain lesions. These various mechanisms are not mutually exclusive—all may contribute to the pattern of reinstating behavior, for regrowth might provide an opportunity for some forms of recovery but require the sustaining impact of experience. Therefore synaptic regrowth alone may not provide the substrate of recovery. Regrowth in conjunction with appropriately timed experience may be the formula for plasticity.

As the field of neurological rehabilitation develops and efforts to aid the brain-injured become more extensive, we will gain more accurate knowledge of both the possibilities and the limits of recovery.

Summary · Main Points

1. Humans are distinct in the animal kingdom for their language and associated cognitive abilities. Possible evolutionary origins of human speech may be seen in aspects of gestures.

2. Studies of nonhumans provide analogies to human speech. For example, controls of birdsong are lateralized in the brains of some species of singing birds. Further, in some of these species early experience is essential for proper song development.

3. Limitations of the vocal tract in nonhumans are proposed as one reason they do not have speech. But nonhuman primates like the chimpanzee can learn to use signs of the American Sign Language. However, controversy surrounds claims that these animals can arrange signs in novel orders, such as in the process of creating a new sentence.

4. Language impairments in 95% of people involve injuries of the left hemisphere. Left anterior lesions produce an impairment in speech production called Broca's aphasia. More posterior lesions involving the temporal-parietal cortex affect speech comprehension, as seen in Wernicke's aphasia.

5. Left-hemisphere lesions in users of sign language produce impairments in the use of sign language that are similar to impairments in spoken language shown by nondeaf aphasics.

6. Split-brain patients show striking examples of hemispheric specialization. Most words projected to the right hemisphere cannot be read, while the same stimuli directed to the left hemisphere can be read. Verbal abilities of the right hemisphere are also reduced; however, spatial-relation tasks are performed better by the right hemisphere than by the left.

7. Normal humans also show many forms of cognitive specialization of the cerebral hemispheres, although they are not as striking as those shown by split-brain patients. For example, most normal humans show a right-ear advantage and greater right visual field accuracy for verbal stimuli.

8. Anatomical asymmetry of the hemispheres is seen in some structures in the human brain. Especially striking is the large size difference in the planum temporale (which is larger in the left hemisphere of most right-handers).

9. Broad theoretical statements about different cognitive modes of the two hemispheres exceed confirmations from current experimental and clinical data. In most cases mental activity depends on interactions between the cerebral hemispheres.

10. The frontal lobes of humans are quite large in comparison with those of other animals. Injury in this region produces an unusual syndrome of profound emotional changes, including reduced responsiveness to many stimuli. Tasks that require sustained attention show drastic impairment after frontal lesions.

11. In most patients parietal cortex injuries on the right side produce many perceptual changes. A dramatic example is the inability to recognize familiar objects and the faces of familiar people. Some patients with right parietal injury neglect or ignore the left side of both the body and space.

12. Many functional losses following brain injury show at least partial recovery. In aphasia the bulk of recovery occurs in the year following stroke, with fewer changes evident after that.

13. Mechanisms of functional recovery may involve structural regrowth of cell extensions—dendrites and axons—and the formation of new synapses.

14. Retraining is a significant part of function recovery and may involve both compensation, by establishing new solutions to adaptive demands, and reorganization of surviving networks.

15. Greater recovery is evident in young individuals. Less impairment occurs when lesions are produced over a period of time.

Recommended Reading

Beaton, A. (1985). *Left side, right side. A review of laterality research.* London: Batsford Academic.

Bradshaw, J. L., & Nettleton, N. C. (1983). *Human cerebral asymmetry.* New York: Prentice-Hall.

Finger, S., & Stein, D. G. (1982). *Brain damage and recovery.* New York: Academic Press.

Gazzaniga, M. (Ed.). (1984). *Handbook of cognitive neuroscience.* New York: Plenum.

Heilman, K., and Valenstein, E. (Eds.). (1985). *Clinical neuropsychology,* 2d ed. New York: Oxford University Press.

Kolb, B., & Whishaw, J. Q. (1985). *Fundamentals of human neuropsychology,* 2d ed. San Francisco: W. H. Freeman.

Springer, S. P., and Deutsch, G. (1985). *Left brain, right brain,* 2d ed. San Francisco: W. H. Freeman.

Glossary

Italicised words are defined in the Glossary.

absolute refractory phase   A period of complete unresponsiveness. The absolute refractory phase of the neuron follows the *nerve impulse*. The absolute refractory phase of the male sexual response cycle is indicated in Figure 11-6.

acetylcholine (ACh)   One of the best known synaptic transmitters. Acetylcholine acts as an excitatory transmitter at synapses between motor nerves and skeletal muscles but as an inhibitory transmitter between vagus nerve and heart muscle.

acetylcholinesterase (AChE)   An enzyme that inactivates the transmitter *acetylcholine** both at synaptic sites and elsewhere in the nervous system, thus halting its effects.

ACh   See *acetylcholine.*

AChE   See *acetylcholinesterase.*

ACTH   See *adrenocorticotropic hormone.*

action potentials   See *nerve impulses.*

activational role   The role that some hormones play in evoking or modulating reproductive behavior.

acupuncture   The insertion and rotation of needles in various parts of the body for relief of pain.

adaptation   A progressive loss of receptor sensitivity as stimulation is maintained. See Figure 8-6.

adenohypophysis   See *anterior pituitary.*

adequate stimulus   The type of stimulus for which a given sense organ is particularly adapted, e.g., light energy for photoreceptors.

ADH   See *antidiuretic hormone.*

adipsia   A condition in which an individual refuses to drink.

adrenal cortex   The outer bark of the adrenal gland. The three cellular layers of the adrenal cortex each produce different hormones. See Reference Table 7-3.

adrenal gland   An endocrine gland adjacent to each kidney. See Figure 7-1.

adrenal medulla   The inner core of the adrenal gland. It secretes epinephrine and norepinephrine. See Reference Table 7-1.

adrenocorticotropic hormone (ACTH)   A tropic hormone secreted by the anterior pituitary gland which controls the production and release of hormones of the *adrenal cortex*. See Figure 7-6.

afferent fibers   Axons carrying nerve impulses from sense organs to the central nervous system: opposite of *efferent*.

afterpotentials   Positive and negative changes of membrane potential that may follow a nerve impulse.

agnosia   Inability to recognize objects even though the person can describe them in terms of form and color; may occur after localized brain damage.

agraphia   Inability to write.

aldosterone   A *mineralocorticoid* hormone that helps maintain homeostasis in the concentrations of ions in blood and extracellular fluid.

alexia   Inability to read.

Allomone   a chemical signal that is released outside the body by one species and that affects the behavior of other species. See Box 6-1, p. 183.

all-or-none   Refers to the fact that the amplitude of the nerve impulse is independent of stimulus magnitude. Stimuli above a certain threshold produce nerve impulses of identical magnitude (although they may vary in frequency); stimuli below this threshold do not produce nerve impulses. See Figure 5-4.

alpha motoneurons   Motoneurons that control the main contractile fibers (extrafusal fibers) of a muscle. See Figure 10-10.

alpha rhythm   A brain potential that occurs during relaxed wakefulness, especially at the back of the head; frequency 8–12 Hz. See Figure 5-13.

altricial   Refers to animals born in an undeveloped state that depend on maternal care, such as a human infant; opposite of *precocial*.

Alzheimer's disease   A kind of dementia which occurs in middle age or later.

amacrine cells   Cells that are especially significant in inhibitory interactions within the retina. See Figure 9-17(d).

amblyopia   Reduced visual acuity not caused by optical or retinal impairments.

amnesia   Severe impairment of memory.

amphetamine   A molecule that resembles the structure of the catecholamine transmitters and that enhances their activity. See Reference Figure 6-1.

ampulla   An enlarged region of each *semicircular canal* that contains the receptor cells (hair cells) of the vesticular system. See Figure 9-12.

amygdala   A group of nuclei in the medial anterior part of the temporal lobe. See Reference Figure 2-9.

androgens   Testosterone and other male hormones. See Table 7-2.

androstenedione   The chief sex hormone secreted by the human adrenal cortex. It is responsible for the adult pattern of body hair in men and women.

angiogram   A technique for examining brain structure in intact humans by taking X-rays after special dyes are injected into cerebral blood vessels. Inferences about adjacent tissue can be made by examining the outline of the principal blood vessels.

angiotensin II   A substance produced in the blood by the action of renin and which may be involved in control of thirst.

anions   Negatively charged ions, such as protein and chloride ions.

anomic aphasia   Difficulty in "finding" words, although comprehension and ability to repeat words are normal.

anorexic   Lacking in appetite for food.

anterior pituitary   The front lobe of the pituitary gland which secretes tropic hormones; also called *adenohypophysis*. See Figure 7-5(a).

anterograde amnesia   The inability to form new memories beginning with the onset of the disorder.

anterograde degeneration   Loss of the distal portion of the axon resulting from injury to the axon; also called *Wallerian degeneration*. See Box Figure 4-1.

antidiuretic hormone (ADH)   A hormone from the posterior pituitary that controls the removal of water from blood by the kidneys. Also called *vasopressin*.

antigens   Substances that stimulate the production of antibodies.

anxiety states   These include recurrent panic states, generalized anxiety disorders that are persistent in character, and posttraumatic stress disorders.

anxiolytics   Substances used to combat anxiety, such as alcohol, opiates, barbiturates, and the benzodiazepines.

aphagia   Refusal to eat, often related to damage to the lateral hypothalamus.

aphasia   Impairments in language understanding and/or production due to brain injury.

appetitive behavior   The second stage of mating behavior that helps establish or maintain sexual interaction. See Figure 11-2.

apraxia   An impairment in the ability to begin and execute skilled voluntary movements although there is no muscle paralysis.

arachnoid   A thin covering of the brain that lies between the *dura mater* and *pia mater*.

aspartic acid   Thought by many investigators to be a major excitatory synaptic transmitter in the CNS.

associative learning   A form of learning in which an association is formed between two stimuli or between a stimulus and a response; includes both classical and instrumental conditioning. Contrast with *nonassociative learning*.

astereognosis   Inability to recognize objects by touching and feeling them.

astrocyte   A star-shaped glial cell with numerous processes or extensions that run in all directions. Their extensions provide structural support for the brain and may isolate receptive surfaces. See Figure 2-18(b).

ataxia   Impairment in the direction, extent, and rate of muscular movement; often due to cerebellar pathology.

auditory cortex   A region of the temporal lobe that receives input from the *medial geniculate nucleus*. See Figure 9-4.

autocrine   In autocrine function, the signal secreted by a cell into its environment feeds back to the same cell. See Box 6-1, p. 182.

autonomic ganglia   One of the three main divisions of the peripheral nervous system. It includes the two chains of sympathetic ganglia and the more peripheral parasympathetic ganglia. See Reference Figure 2-14.

autonomic nervous system   Part of the peripheral nervous system that supplies neural connections to glands and to smooth muscles of internal organs. Composed of two divisions (sympathetic and parasympathetic) that act in opposite fashion. See Reference Figure 2-14.

autonomic response specificity   Patterns of bodily response governed by the autonomic nervous system that are characteristic of an individual.

autoradiography   A histological technique that shows the distribution of radioactive chemicals.

autoreceptors   Receptors for synaptic transmitters located in the presynaptic membrane. These receptors inform the axon terminal of the amount of transmitter released. See 6 in Figure 6-5.

autosomes   Pairs of chromosomes that are identical; that is, all chromosomes except the sex chromosomes.

axon   A single extension from the cell body which carries nerve impulses from the cell body to other neurons. See Figures 2-12 and 2-16.

axon hillock   A cone-shaped area from which the axon originates out of the cell body. Depolarization must reach a critical threshold here for the neuron to transmit a nerve impulse. See Figure 2-12.

axonal transport   The transportation of materials from the neuron cell body to distant regions in the dendrites and axons, and from the terminals back to the cell body.

axoplasmic streaming   The process that transports materials synthesized in the cell body to distant regions in the dendrites and axons.

ballism   An uncontrollable violent tossing of the limbs. Lesions in the subthalamic nucleus can produce this syndrome in humans and monkeys.

ballistic   Classes of rapid muscular movements thought to be organized or programmed by the cerebellum. Contrast with *ramp movements*.

basal ganglia   A group of forebrain nuclei found deep within the cerebral hemispheres. See Reference Figure 2-10 and Figure 10-19.

basal nucleus of Meynert   See *magnocellular nucleus of the basal forebrain*.

bases   Components of a DNA or RNA molecule. DNA contains four bases (adenine, thyamine, cytosine, and guanine), a pair of which forms each rung of the molecule. The order of these bases determines the genetic information of a DNA molecule.

basic neuroglial compartment   A level of brain organization which includes a single nerve cell with all its synaptic endings, associated glial cells surrounding extracellular space, and vascular elements. See Figure 2-19.

basic rest-activity cycle   Repeating cycles of rest and activity that occur both in waking hours and during sleep.

basilar artery   An artery formed by the fusion of the vertebral arteries; its branches supply blood to the brainstem and to posterior portions of the cerebral hemispheres. See Reference Figure 2-11.

basilar membrane   A membrane in the cochlea containing the principal structures involved in auditory transduction. See Figure 9-2(c).

behavioral intervention   An approach to finding relations between bodily variables and behavioral variables that involves intervening in the behavior of an organism and looking for resultant changes in bodily structure or function. See Figure 1-6.

behavioral teratology   Impairments in behavior produced by early exposure to toxic substances.

benzodiazepines   Anti-anxiety drugs that bind with high affinity to receptors in the central nervous system.

binocular disparity   The slight difference between the views from the two eyes, important in depth perception. See Figure 9-26.

biofeedback   A technique that allows a person to monitor some bodily variable such as skin temperature or the gross electrical activity of the brain. This information allows the person to gain some control over the bodily variable and may be used in the treatment of various disorders. See Figure 15-3.

bipolar depression (or illness)   Depression that alternates with mania. Contrast with *unipolar depression*.

bipolar neurons   Nerve cells with a single dendrite at one end of the nerve cell and a single axon at the other end. Found in some vertebrate sensory systems. See Figure 2-11(b) and 9-17.

blastocyst   Early developmental stage when the organism is a hollow sphere whose wall is one cell thick. See Figure 4-2.

blind spot   A place through which blood vessels enter the retina. Because there are no receptors in this region, light striking it cannot be seen. See Figure 9-25.

blood-brain barrier   The mechanisms that make the movement of substances from capillaries into brain cells more difficult than exchanges in other body organs, thus affording the brain a greater protection from exposure to some substances found in the blood.

brainstem reticular formation   Part of the brainstem involved in arousal. See Figure 14-20.

brightness   One of the basic dimensions of light perception. This varies from dark to light. See Figure 9-21.

Broca's aphasia   Impairment in speech production, related to damage in Broca's area.

Broca's area   An area in the frontal region of the left hemisphere involved in the production of speech. See Figure 18-4.

calcitonin   A hormone released by the thyroid gland.

cAMP   See *cyclic adenosine monophosphate*.

CAT   See *computerized axial tomogram*.

cations   Positively charged ions, such as potassium and sodium.

caudal   An anatomical term meaning toward the tail end. Opposed to *rostral*.

caudate nucleus   One of the basal ganglia with a long extension or tail.

CCK   See *cholecystokinin*.

cell body   The region of a neuron which is defined by the presence of the nucleus. See Figure 2-11.

cell death   The final developmental process in shaping the nervous system during which ''surplus'' nerve cells die.

cell differentiation   The prenatal stage in which neuroblasts acquire the distinctive appearance of cells characteristic of a region of the nervous system. See Figure 4-8.

cell-mediated immunity   A type of immunologic response that involves T lymphocytes. See Figure 15-10.

cell migration   The process by which nerve cells move from their site of origin to their final location. See Figures 4-6 and 4-7.

cell proliferation   The production of nerve cells. See Figure 4-5.

cellular fluid   See *intracellular fluid*.

central deafness   Hearing impairments related to lesions in auditory pathways or centers, including sites in the brainstem, thalamus, or cortex.

central nervous system (CNS)   The portion of the nervous system that includes the brain and the spinal cord. See Figure 2-8.

cephalic   An anatomical term referring to the head end. Also called *rostral*.

cerebellar cortex   The outer surface of the cerebellum. See Figure 2-5 and Reference Figure 2-8.

cerebellum   A structure located at the back of the brain, dorsal to the pons; it is involved in the central regulation of movement. See Figure 2-5.

cerebral cortex   The outer bark or cortex of the cerebral hemispheres which consists largely of nerve cell bodies and their branches. See Figure 2-6.

cerebral hemispheres   The right and left halves of the forebrain. See Figure 2-1.

cerebral ventricles   Cavities in the brain which contain *cerebrospinal fluid*. See Figure 2-4.

cerebrospinal fluid   The fluid filling the *cerebral ventricles*. See Figure 2-4.

cerveau isolé   An animal with the nervous system transected at the upper level of the midbrain (between the inferior and superior colliculus). Contrast with the *encéphale isolé*. See Figure 14-19.

cervical   Pertaining to the neck region.

chemical transmitter   See *synaptic transmitter*.

chlorpromazine   An antipsychotic drug, one of the class of phenothiazines.

cholecystokinin (CCK)   A hormone released from the lining of the duodenum which may be involved in the satiation of hunger.

cholinergic   Refers to cells that use *acetylcholine* as their synaptic transmitter.

choreic movements   Uncontrollable, brief, and forceful muscular movements related to basal ganglia dysfunction.

chromosomes   Structures in the nucleus of the cell which contain a *DNA* molecule and associated protein molecules.

cingulate cortex   See *cingulum*.

cingulum   A region of medial cerebral cortex lying dorsal to the *corpus callosum*. Also called *cingulate cortex*. See Figure 15-11.

circadian rhythms   Behavioral, biochemical, and physiological fluctuations that have a 24-hour period.

circle of Willis   A structure at the base of the brain formed by the joining of the carotid and basilar arteries. See Reference Figure 2-11.

circuit   A level of brain organization which includes an arrangement of neurons and their interconnections. These assemblages often perform a particular limited function. A local circuit is a circuit wholly contained within a particular region.

circumventricular organs.   Organs lying in the walls of the cerebral ventricles. These organs contain receptor sites that can be affected by substances in the *cerebrospinal fluid*. See Figure 12-13.

classical conditioning   A form of associative learning in which an originally neutral stimulus [a *conditioned stimulus (CS)*], through pairing with a stimulus that elicits a particular response [an unconditioned stimulus *(US)*], acquires the power of eliciting that response. Also called *Pavlovian conditioning*.

cloaca   The sex organ in many birds through which sperm are discharged (in the male) and eggs are laid (in the female). This is the same passage through which wastes are eliminated.

clones   Asexually produced organisms that are genetically identical.

closed-loop control mechanism   A form of control mechanism that provides a flow of information from whatever is being controlled to the device that controls it. See Figure 10-6.

CNS   See *central nervous system*.

CNV   See *contingent negative variation*.

coactivation   A central nervous system control program that activates or inhibits the skeletal motoneurons at the same time as it alters the sensitivity of the *muscle spindles*.

cochlea   A snail-shaped structure in the inner ear which contains the primary receptors for hearing. See Figure 9-2.

cochlear duct   One of three principal canals running along the length of the cochlea. See Figure 9-2.

cochlear microphonic potential   An electrical potential produced by hair cells that accurately copies the acoustic waveform of the stimulus.

cochlear nuclei   Brainstem nuclei that receive input from auditory hair cells and send output to the superior olivary complex. See Figure 9-4(b).

codon   A sequence of three bases on a DNA molecule.

colliculus   One of two pairs of structures on the dorsal midbrain. See *inferior colliculus, superior colliculus*.

common carotid arteries   Arteries that ascend the left and right sides of the neck. The branch that enters the brain is called the *internal carotid artery*.

complex cortical cells   Cells in the visual cortex that respond best to a bar of a particular width and direction anywhere within a particular area of the visual field. See Figure 9-27.

computerized axial tomogram   A technique for examining brain structure in intact humans through a computer analysis of X-ray absorption at several positions around the head. This technique affords a virtual direct view of the brain. See Figure 2-9(c) and (d).

concordant   Any trait that is seen in both individuals of an identical twin pair.

conditioned stimulus (CS)   See *classical conditioning*.

conduction aphasia   A language disorder, involving intact comprehension but poor repetition of spoken language, related to damage of the pathways connecting *Wernicke's area* and *Broca's area*.

conductive deafness   Hearing impairments associated with pathology of the external or middle ear cavities.

cones   Receptor cells in the retina that are responsible for color vision. The three types of cones have somewhat different sensitivities to light of different wavelengths. See Figure 9-16(c).

consolidation   A stage of memory formation in which information in short-term or intermediate-term memory is transferred to long-term memory. See Figure 16-5.

consolidation hypothesis   See *perseveration-consolidation hypothesis*.

constraints on learning   Factors that restrict the ease of different kinds of learning in different species.

contingent negative variation (CNV)   A slow event-related potential recorded from the scalp. It arises in the interval between a warning signal and a signal that directs action.

copulatory behavior   The third stage of mating behavior during which the male mounts the female, inserts the erect penis, and ejaculates.

coronal (plane)   The plane dividing the body or brain into front and back parts. Also called frontal or transverse. See Box

Figure 2-2.

corpus callosum   The band of axons that connects the two cerebral hemispheres. See Figure 2-5 and Reference Figure 2-10.

correlational approach   An approach to finding relations between bodily variables and behavioral variables that involves finding the extent to which some bodily measure co-varies with some behavioral measure. See Figure 1-7.

cortical columns   The vertical columns that constitute the basic organization of the neocortex. See Figures 8-17 and 9-20.

corticospinal system   See *pyramidal system*.

corticotropin-releasing hormone (CRH)   A releasing hormone from the hypothalamus that controls the daily rhythm of ACTH release.

cortisol   A glucocorticoid hormone of the adrenal cortex.

cranial nerves   One of the three main subdivisions of the peripheral nervous system, composed of a set of pathways mainly concerned with sensory and motor systems associated with the head. See Reference Figure 2-12.

cretinism   Reduced stature and mental retardation caused by thyroid deficiency.

CRH   See *corticotropin-releasing hormone*.

CS   Conditioned stimulus. See *classical conditioning*.

cupulae   Part of the lateral line system. See Box 9-2.

cyclic adenosine monophosphate (cyclic AMP or cAMP)   A *second messenger* involved in the synaptic activities of dopamine, norepinephrine, and serotonin.

cyclic AMP   See *cyclic adenosine monophosphate*.

cytoarchitectonics   The study of anatomical divisions of the brain based on the kinds and spacing of cells and distribution of axons.

DA   See *dopamine*.

dB   See *decibel*.

deafferentation   Removal of sensory (afferent) input.

decibel (dB)   A logarithmic expression of sound intensity.

declarative knowledge   Knowledge that can be stated or described; "knowing that." See Table 16-1.

dendrites   Extensions of the cell body which are the receptive surfaces of the neuron. See Figures 2-16 and 2-17.

dendritic branching   The pattern and quantity of branching of dendrites. See Figure 17-3.

dendritic spines   Outgrowths along the dendrites of neurons. See Figure 2-16.

dendritic tree   The full arrangement of a single cell's dendrites.

deoxyribonucleic acid (DNA)   A nucleic acid present in the chromosomes of cells; it codes hereditary information.

depolarization   A reduction in membrane potential (the inner membrane surface becomes less negative in relation to the outer surface); this is caused by excitatory neural messages. See Figures 5-3 and 5-4.

depression   See *bipolar depression, unipolar depression*.

derepression   The mechanism through which regions of the DNA molecule that are repressed from transcription become unblocked. This process allows for the selection of genetic information that will be utilized by a particular cell.

dermatome   A strip of skin innervated by a particular spinal root. See Figure 8-15.

diaschisis A temporary period of generalized impairment following brain injury.

dichotic-listening technique A technique involving presentation of different sounds to each ear at the same time. Used to determine hemispheric differences in processing auditory information. See Figure 18-12.

diencephalon The posterior part of the forebrain; it includes the thalamus and hypothalamus. See Figures 2-7 and 2-8.

discordant Any trait that is seen in only one individual of an identical twin pair.

dishabituation Restoration of response amplitude after habituation has occurred.

distal An anatomical term meaning toward the periphery or toward the end of a limb, opposite of *proximal*. See Box Figure 2-1.

divergence A system of neural connections that allows one cell to send signals to many other cells. See Figure 5-10.

DNA See *deoxyribonucleic acid*.

dopamine (DA) A neurotransmitter produced mainly in the basal forebrain and diencephalon that is active in the basal ganglia, the olfactory system, and limited parts of the cerebral cortex. For location of dopaminergic fibers, see Figure 6-7; for locations of dopamine receptors, see Figure 15-18.

dopaminergic Refers to cells that use dopamine as their synaptic transmitter.

dorsal An anatomical term meaning toward the back of the body or the top of the brain; opposite of *ventral*. See Box Figure 2-1.

dorsal root Root toward the back of the spinal cord. See Reference Figure 2-13.

double dissociation Condition or treatment A causes impairment on behavioral test X but no impairment on test Y, whereas condition B causes impairment on test Y but not on X. See example on p. 657.

Down's syndrome A form of mental retardation associated with an extra chromosome.

duplex theory A theory of pitch perception combining the *place theory* and *volley theory*. Volley theory operates for sounds from about 20 to 1000 Hz, and place theory operates for sounds above 1000 Hz.

duplication of DNA A process through which a cell duplicates (or replicates) its genetic information during mitosis.

dura mater The outermost of the three coverings that embrace the brain and spinal cord. See Reference Figure 2-13.

dynamic phase of weight gain The initial period following destruction of the ventromedial hypothalamus during which the animal's body weight shoots up. See Figure 13-7.

dyskinesia See *tardive dyskinesia*.

dyslexia A reading disorder attributed to brain impairment.

EC See *enriched condition*.

ectoderm The outer cellular layer of the developing fetus; this layer gives rise to the skin and to the nervous system.

ectotherms Animals whose body temperature is regulated by, and who get most of their heat from, the environment. Contrast with *endotherms*.

edema The swelling of tissue, especially in the brain, in response to brain injury.

EEG See *electroencephalography*.

efferent fibers Axons carrying information from the nervous system to the periphery; opposite of *afferent*.

ejaculation The forceful expulsion of semen from the penis.

electrical synapse Junctional region where the presynaptic and postsynaptic membranes approach so closely that the nerve impulse can jump to the postsynaptic membrane without being translated into a chemical message. See Figure 5-7.

electroencephalography (EEG) The recording and study of gross electrical activity of the brain recorded from large electrodes placed on the scalp. See EEG recordings made during sleep, Figure 14-7.

electromyography (EMG) The technique of recording electrical activity of muscles. See Figure 10-3.

embryo The earliest stage in a developing animal; in the human, up to 8 to 10 weeks after conception.

encéphale isolé An animal in which the brainstem is separated from the spinal cord by a cut below the medulla. Contrast with *cerveau isolé*. See Figure 14-19.

encoding A process of memory formation in which the information entering sensory channels is passed into short-term memory. See Figure 16-5.

endocast A cast of the cranial cavity of a skull. Used to determine brain shape and size of extinct animals.

endocrine Refers to glands that secrete products into the bloodstream to act on distant targets; opposite of *exocrine*. See Box 6-1, p. 182, and Figure 7-1.

endogenous opioids A family of peptide transmitters that have been called the body's own narcotics. See under *opioid peptides* in Table 6-1.

endorphins One of three kinds of *endogenous opioids*. See under *opioid peptides* in Table 6-1.

endotherms Animals, such as mammals and birds, whose body temperature is regulated chiefly by internal metabolic processes; contrast with *ectotherms*.

enkephalins One of the three kinds of *endogenous opioids*. See under *opioid peptides* in Table 6-1.

enriched condition (EC) An experimental condition with a complex environment. See Figure 17-1.

entrainment Synchronizing a biological rhythm to an environmental stimulus. See Figure 10-4.

ependymal layer See *ventricular layer*.

epilepsy A brain disorder marked by major sudden changes in the electrophysiological state of the brain referred to as seizures. See Figures 5-16 and 5-17.

epinephrine A compound that acts both as a hormone (secreted by the adrenal medulla) and as a neurotransmitter; also called *adrenalin*.

episodic memory Memory of a particular incident or a particular time and place. See Table 16-1.

EPSP See *excitatory postsynaptic potentials*.

equilibrium potential The state in which the tendency of ions to flow from regions of high concentration is exactly balanced by the opposing potential difference across the membrane.

estrogens Hormones produced by female gonads. See Figure 7-12 and Table 7-2.

estrus The period during which female animals are sexually receptive.

event-related potentials Gross electrical potential changes in the brain that are elicited by discrete sensory or motor events. See Figure 5-14.

evoked potential See *event-related potentials*.

evolution through natural selection The Darwinian theory that evolution proceeds by differential success in reproduction.

excitatory postsynaptic potentials (EPSPs) Depolarizing potentials in the postsynaptic neuron caused by excitatory presynaptic impulses. These potentials may summate to trigger a nerve impulse in the postsynaptic cell. See Figure 5-6.

exocrine Refers to glands that secrete their products through ducts to the site of action; opposite of *endocrine*.

external capsule A light-colored band of fibers lateral to the putamen. See Reference Figure 2-10.

extinction A feature of conditioning in which the learned response wanes when reinforcement is not presented.

extracellular fluid Includes both fluid in the spaces between cells (interstitial fluid) and fluid in the vascular system.

extracellular space The space between cells.

extraocular muscles Muscles attached to the eyeball that control its position and movements. See Figure 9-15.

extrapyramidal system A motor system that includes the basal ganglia and some closely related brainstem structures.

facial nerve A cranial nerve that innervates facial musculature and some sensory receptors. See Reference Figure 2-12 and Figure 15-2.

feature detector model A model of visual pattern analysis in terms of linear and angular components of the stimulus array. Contrast with *spatial frequency filter model*.

filial imprinting A form of learning in which precocial animals in their first few days learn to approach and follow the first relatively large moving object they see.

5HT See *serotonin*.

fixed action pattern Complex preprogrammed species-specific behavior triggered by particular stimuli and carried out without sensory feedback. See also *modal action pattern*.

flexion reflex Abrupt withdrawal of a limb in response to intense stimulation of the foot.

folia Folds or convolutions of the cerebellar cortex.

follicle-stimulating hormone (FSH) A tropic hormone released by the anterior pituitary that controls the production of estrogen and progesterone. See Figure 7-12.

forebrain The frontal division of the neural tube that contains the *cerebral hemispheres,* the *thalamus,* and the *hypothalamus.* Also called the *prosencephalon.* See Figures 2-7 and 2-8.

fornix A fiber tract that runs from the hippocampus to the mammillary body. See Reference Figure 2-9.

Fourier analysis The analysis of a complex pattern into the sum of sine waves. See Box Figure 9-2.

fovea A small depression in the center of the retina with a dense concentration of cones and maximal visual acuity.

free-running period The natural period of a behavior that is displayed if external stimuli do not provide *entrainment*.

frequency The number of cycles per second in a sound wave, measured in hertz (Hz). See Box Figure 9-1.

frontal See *coronal*.

FSH See *follicle-stimulating hormone*.

gametes The sex cells which, unlike *autosomes,* contain only unpaired chromosomes therefore having only half the number of autosomal chromosomes. One gamete from a female and one from a male organism join during sexual reproduction.

gamma-aminobutyric acid Probably the major inhibitory transmitter in the mammalian nervous system; widely distributed in both invertebrate and vertebrate nervous systems.

gamma efferents Motors neurons by means of which the central nervous system controls *muscle spindle,* sensitivity. See Figure 10-10.

ganglion A collection of nerve cell bodies. Also called a *nucleus*.

ganglion cells Cells in the retina whose axons form the optic nerve. See Figure 9-17.

gender identity The way one identifies one's self, and is identified by others, as a male or a female.

generalization A feature of conditioning in which stimuli similar to the conditioned stimulus can elicit a conditioned response.

generalized seizures Epileptic seizures that arise from pathology at brain sites that project to widespread regions of the brain. These seizures involve loss of consciousness and symmetrical involvement of body musculature. See Figure 5-16.

generator potentials Local changes in the resting potential of receptor cells that mediate between the impact of stimuli and the initiation of nerve impulse. See Figure 8-3.

genetic constraints on learning A concept prominent from the 1960s into the early 1980s that held that species-typical factors restrict the kinds of learning that a species can accomplish readily.

genetic mosaics Animals in which the cells of one part of the body have a different chromosomal makeup from the cells in another part. For example, the head of a male fruit fly can be put on the body of a female fruit fly. Study of genetic mosaics helps determine which neural structures control various behaviors.

giant axons Large diameter axons found in some invertebrates. The size of these axons facilitates research on the properties of neural membrane structure and function. See Figure 5-2.

glia See *glial cells*.

glial cells Nonneural brain cells that provide structural, nutritional, and other supports to the brain. Also called *glia* or *neuroglia*. See Figure 2-18.

gliomas Brain tumors resulting from the aberrant production of glial cells.

globus pallidus One of the *basal ganglia.* See Reference Figure 2-10.

glossopharyngeal nerve A cranial nerve that serves taste receptors in the tongue. See Reference Figure 2-12.

glucagon A hormone released by alpha cells in the islets of Langerhans that increases blood glucose. See Figure 7-9.

glucocorticoids Hormones released by the adrenal cortex that affect carbohydrate metabolism.

glutamic acid Thought by many investigators to be a major excitatory synaptic transmitter in the CNS.

GnRH See *gonadotropin-releasing hormone*.

Golgi tendon organs Receptors located in tendons that send impulses to the central nervous system when a muscle contracts. See Figures 10-10 and 10-11.

Golgi type 1   A type of large nerve cell.

gonadotropin-releasing hormone (GnRH)   A hypothalamic hormone that controls the release of luteinizing hormone (or interstitial-cell-stimulating hormone). Also called *luteinizing-hormone-releasing hormone*. See Figure 7-12.

graded potentials   Potentials that can vary continuously in size; also called local potentials; contrast with *all-or-none potentials*. See Figure 5-3.

grand mal seizures   A type of generalized epileptic seizure that involves nerve cells firing in high frequency bursts. These seizures cause loss of consciousness and sudden muscle contraction. See Figure 5-16.

grandmother cell   An extrapolation of the feature detector model suggesting that if there were enough levels of analysis, a unit could be constructed that would enable a person to recognize his or her grandmother.

granule (cell)   A type of small nerve cell.

gray matter   Areas of the brain that are dominated by cell bodies and are devoid of myelin; e.g., cerebral cortex.

growth hormone   A tropic hormone secreted by the anterior pituitary that influences the growth of cells and tissues. Also called *somatotropic hormone* (STH). See Figure 7-6.

gyri   The ridged or raised portions of a convoluted brain surface. Contrast with *sulci*. See Figure 2-5.

habits   Stimulus-response bonds that are acquired automatically, and often gradually, through occurrences of stimulus-response-reinforcement contingencies. See Table 16-1.

habituation   A form of nonassociative learning characterized by a reduction in response strength following repeated presentations of a stimulus. See Figure 16-2.

hair cells   The receptor cells for hearing in the cochlea. Displacement of these cells by sound waves generates nerve impulses that travel to the brain. See Figure 9-2(d) and (e).

hallucinogens   Drugs that alter sensory perception and produce peculiar experiences.

hindbrain   The rear division of the brain; it contains the *cerebellum, pons,* and *medulla* in the mature vertebrate. Also called the *rhombencephalon*. See Figure 2-7.

hippocampus   A portion of the cerebral hemispheres found curled in the basal medial part of the temporal lobe. See Reference Figures 2-9 and 16-8, and Box Figure 17-1.

homeostasis   The tendency for the internal environment to remain constant.

homeotherms   Animals, such as birds and mammals, that maintain a relatively constant body temperature. Contrast with *poikilotherms*.

hominids   Primates of the family *Hominidae*, of which humans are the only living species.

horizontal cells   A specialized type of retinal cell.

horizontal plane   The plane dividing the body or brain into upper and lower parts. See Box Figure 2-2.

hormone   A chemical secreted by an endocrine gland that is conveyed by the bloodstream and regulates target organs or tissues. Reference Table 7-3 lists main hormones.

horseradish peroxidase   An enzyme found in horseradish and other plants that is used to determine the cells of origin of a particular set of axons. See Reference Figure 2-3.

hue   One of the basic dimensions of light perception. It varies around the color circle through blue, green, yellow, orange, and red. See Figure 9-21.

humoral immunity   A type of immunity that occurs when B lymphocytes produce antibodies that either directly destroy antigens like viruses or bacteria or enhance their destruction by other cells.

Huntington's disease   A progressive genetic disorder characterized by *choreic movements* and profound changes in mental functioning.

hypercomplex 1   Cells in the visual cortex that respond best to visual stimulation by bars of a given orientation and of limited length.

hypercomplex 2   Cells of the visual cortex that respond best to visual stimulation by two line segments meeting at a particular angle.

hyperphagia   A condition involving increasing food intake, often related to damage to the *ventromedial hypothalamus*.

hyperpolarization   Increases in membrane potential (the inner surface of the membrane becomes more negative in relation to the outer surface); caused by inhibitory neural messages. See Figure 5-3.

hypertonic   A solution with a larger concentration of salt than that found in interstitial fluid and blood plasma (above about 0.9% salt); opposite of *hypotonic*.

hypothalamus   Part of the diencephalon, lying ventral to the thalamus. See Figure 2-7(c).

hypotonic   A solution with a lesser concentration of salt than that found in interstitial fluid and blood plasma (below about 0.9% salt); opposite of *hypertonic*.

hypovolemic thirst   The response to a reduced volume of extracellular fluid. Contrast with *osmotic thirst*.

IC   See *impoverished condition*.

iconic memory   A very brief type of memory that stores the sensory impression of a scene.

ICSH   See *interstitial-cell-stimulating hormone* or *luteinizing hormone*.

impoverished condition (IC)   An experimental condition with a drastically simplified environment. See Figure 17-1.

imprinting   A form of learning in which young animals learn to follow the first relatively large moving object they see.

inferior colliculus   The auditory center in the midbrain; it receives input from the brainstem auditory nuclei and sends output to the *medial geniculate nucleus*. See Figure 9-4.

infundibulum   The stalk of the pituitary gland. See Figure 7-5.

inhibitory postsynaptic potentials (IPSPs)   Hyperpolarizing potentials in the postsynaptic neuron caused by inhibitory connections. These potentials decrease the probability that the postsynaptic neuron will fire a nerve impulse. See Figure 5-6.

inner hair cells   Receptor cells for hearing in the cochlea. See Figure 9-2(d).

innervation ratio   The ratio expressing the number of muscle fibers innervated by a single motor axon. The fewer muscle fibers an axon innervates (the lower the ratio) the finer the control of movements.

instrumental conditioning   A form of associative learning in which the likelihood that an act will be performed depends upon the consequences (reinforcing stimuli) that follow it.

instrumental response   See *instrumental conditioning*.

insulin   A hormone released by beta cells in the *islets of Langerhans* that lowers blood glucose. See Figure 7-9.

intention tremor   A tremor that occurs only during voluntary movement, e.g., when the person reaches out to grasp an object.

intermediate-term memory   A form of memory lasting longer than short-term, and requiring no rehearsal, but not lasting as long as long-term memory.

internal capsule   The fiber band running between the caudate nucleus on its medial side and the globus pallidus and putamen on its lateral side. See Reference Figure 2-10.

internal carotid artery   See *common carotid arteries*. See Reference Figure 2-10.

interstitial cell-stimulating hormone (ICSH)   See *luteinizing hormone*.

intracellular fluid   Water within cells. Also called *cellular fluid*.

intracellular signals   Chemical signals that convey information within single cells. See Box 6-1, p. 182.

intromission   Insertion of the erect penis into the vagina during copulatory behavior.

ion channels   Pores in the cell membrane which permit the passage of certain ions through the membrane when the channels are open. See Figure 5-12.

IPSP   See *inhibitory postsynaptic potentials*.

islets of Langerhans   Clusters of cells in the pancreas which release two hormones (insulin and glucagon) with opposite effects on glucose utilization. See Figure 7-9.

Korsakoff's syndrome   A memory disorder, related to a thiamine deficiency, generally associated with chronic alcoholism.

kuru   A slow virus of the brain which produces trembling and eventually paralysis of the limbs.

labeled lines   A view of stimulus coding stating that particular nerve cells are intrinsically labeled for particular sensory experiences such as cold, touch, pain, and so forth. See Figure 8-5.

labile memory   An early stage of memory formation during which formation of a memory can be easily disrupted by conditions that influence brain activity.

laminar (form of organization)   The horizontal layering of cells found in some brain regions. See Reference Figure 2-4 for laminar organization of the cerebral cortex.

lateral   An anatomical term meaning toward the side; opposite of *medial*. See Box Figure 2-1.

lateral geniculate nucleus   Part of the thalamus which receives information from the optic tract and sends it to visual areas in the occipital cortex. See Figure 9-18(a).

lateral hypothalamus (LH)   A hypothalamic region involved in facilitating eating. See Figure 13-6.

lateral inhibition   A phenomenon produced by interconnected neurons that inhibit their neighbors, producing contrast at the edges of the stimulus. See Figure 5-10.

lateral-line system   A sensory system found in many kinds of fish and some amphibians that informs the animal of water motion in relation to the body surface.

learning set   The ability to solve a particular type of problem efficiently after prolonged experience with that type of problem.

lentiform nucleus (or **lenticular nucleus**).   The lens-shaped region in the *basal ganglia* that comprises the globus pallidus and the putamen. See Reference Figure 2-10(a).

LH   See *lateral hypothalamus*.

LH   See *luteinizing hormone*.

limbic system   A group of interconnected brain structures that integrate emotional experience and responses. See Reference Figure 2-9.

local circuit   See *circuit*.

local circuit neurons   Small neurons that make contact only with neurons that are within the same functional unit.

localization of function   The concept that specific brain regions are responsible for various types of experience, behavior, and psychological processes.

locus coeruleus   A small nucleus in the brainstem whose neurons produce norepinephrine and modulate large areas of the forebrain. See Figures 6-6 and 14-21.

long-term memory   An enduring form of memory lasting for weeks, months, or years.

long-term potentiation   A stable and enduring increase in the magnitude of the response of neurons after afferent cells to the region have been stimulated with bursts of moderately high frequency stimuli. See Box 17-1.

lordosis   A female receptive posture in quadrupeds in which the hindquarters are raised and the tail is turned to one side, facilitating intromission by the male. See Figure 11-4.

LSD (lysergic acid diethylamide)   A *hallucinogen*.

lumbar   Referring to the lower part of the spinal cord or back.

luteinizing hormone (LH)   A tropic hormone released by the anterior pituitary that influences the hormonal activities of the gonads. In males this hormone is called *interstitial-cell-stimulating hormone* (ICSH). See Figures 7-11 and 7-12.

luteinizing hormone-releasing hormone   See *gonadotropin-releasing hormone*.

lymphocytes   The two different classes of cells that mediate two types of immunologic responses. See Figure 15-10.

magnetic resonance imaging   A technique to make sections of brain or body by computer analysis of changes in orientation of molecules. See Figure 2-9.

magnocellular nucleus of the basal forebrain   A region of the basal forebrain implicated in Alzheimer's disease. See Figure 4-25.

magnocellular system   The division of primate visual pathways that appears to be mainly responsible for perception of depth and movement. See Table 9-2.

malleus   A middle ear bone, connected to the tympanic membrane; one of the chain of three ossicles that transmit sound across the middle ear.

mammillary bodies   Paired nuclei at the base of the brain slightly posterior to the pituitary stalk. See Figure 2-9 and Reference Figure 2-10.

mammillothalamic tract The fiber bundle that connects the mammillary bodies with the thalamus. See Reference Figure 2-9.

manic-depressive psychosis A psychiatric disorder characterized by depressed periods that alternate with excessive, expansive moods. Also called *bipolar depression*.

MAO inhibitors Antidepressant drugs that inhibit the enzyme MAO and thus prolong the action of catecholamine transmitters.

medial An anatomical term meaning toward the middle; opposite of *lateral*. Box Figure 2-1.

medial geniculate nucleus A nucleus in the thalamus that receives input from the *inferior colliculus* and sends output to the *auditory cortex*. See Figure 9-4.

medulla The lowest part of the brain, also called *myelencephalon*. See Figure 2-7.

meiosis The process of forming gametes in which each new cell receives half the chromosomes, therefore not requiring duplication of DNA.

membrane potential See *resting potential*.

memories Cognitive representations that are often acquired rapidly and whose acquisition does not require satisfaction of motives. See Table 16-1.

memory traces Persistent changes in the brain that reflect the storage of memory.

meninges The three layers of coverings that embrace the brain and spinal cord.

mesencephalon The *midbrain*. See Figure 2-7.

messenger RNA (mRNA) A strand of RNA that carries the code of a section of a strand of DNA to the cytoplasm.

metencephalon A subdivision of the hindbrain that includes the cerebellum and the pons. See Figures 2-7 and 2-8.

microglia Extremely small glial cells that remove cellular debris from injured or dead cells.

microtubules Hollow cylindrical structures in axons that are involved in axoplasmic streaming. See Figure 2-15.

midbrain The middle division of the brain. Also called *mesencephalon*. See Figure 2-7.

middle ear The cavity between the eardrum and the cochlea. See Figure 9-1.

mineralocorticoids Hormones released by the adrenal cortex that affect ion concentrations in body tissues.

mitosis The process of division of somatic cells that involves duplication of DNA.

modal action pattern A modification of the concept of a *fixed action pattern* which allows for some variability of the response between different individuals and within the same individual at different times.

modulation of formation of memory Facilitation or inhibition of memory formation by factors other than those directly involved in memory formation. Also called *modulation of memory storage processes*.

modulation of memory storage processes See *modulation of formation of memory*.

modulatory role The role some hormones play in maintaining the sensitivity of neural circuits and other structures to hormonal influences.

monoamine hypothesis of depression A theory that depressive illness is associated with a decrease in synaptic activity of connections that employ monoamine synaptic transmitters.

monoamines Synaptic transmitters that contain a single amine group, NH_2; this includes the catecholamines and indolamines. See Table 6-1.

monoclonal antibodies Highly purified and specialized antibodies that enable investigators to identify particular kinds of cells. See Reference Figure 2-2.

monogamy A mating system in which a female and a male form a breeding pair that may last for one breeding period or for a lifetime. A rather durable and exclusive relation between a male and a female is called a *pair bond*.

monopolar neurons Nerve cells with a single branch leaving the cell body which then extends in two directions—one end is the receptive pole, the other end the output zone. See Figure 2-11(c).

motoneurons Nerve cells in the spinal cord that transmit motor messages from the spinal cord to muscles.

motor cortex A region of cerebral cortex that sends impulses to motoneurons. See Figures 10-16 and 10-18.

motor unit A single motor axon and all the muscle fibers it innervates.

MRI See *magnetic resonance imaging*.

mRNA See *messenger RNA*.

Müllerian duct system A primitive duct system in each embryo that will develop into female reproductive structures—the oviducts, uterus, and upper vagina—if testes are not present in the embryo. Contrast with *Wolffian duct system*. See Figure 11-8.

multipolar neurons Nerve cells with many dendrites and a single axon. See Figure 2-11(d–f).

muscarinic A cholinergic receptor (one responsive to *acetylcholine*) that mediates chiefly the inhibitory activities of acetylcholine.

muscle fibers Contractile fibers of a muscle; also called *extrafusal fibers*. See Box Figure 10-1.

muscle spindle A muscle receptor that lies parallel to the muscle and sends impulses to the central nervous system when a muscle is stretched. See Figure 10-10.

muscular dystrophy Disease that leads to degeneration and functional changes in muscles.

myasthenia A neurological disease characterized by easy fatigability and weakness of muscles. See Figure 10-21.

myelencephalon A subdivision of the hindbrain; the *medulla*. See Figures 2-7 and 2-8.

myelin The fatty insulation around an axon, formed by accessory cells; this improves the speed of conduction of nerve impulses. See Figures 2-13 and 2-14.

myelinization The process of formation of myelin. See Figure 2-13.

naloxone A potent antagonist of opiates that is often administered to people who have taken drug overdoses. Naloxone binds to receptors for *endogenous opioids*.

narcolepsy A disorder involving frequent, intense episodes of sleep, which last from 5 to 30 minutes and can occur anytime during the usual waking hours.

NE   See *norepinephrine.*

negative-feedback system   A regulatory system in which output is used to reduce the effect of input signals. See Figure 7-2.

neocortex   The relatively recently evolved portions of the cerebral cortex. All of the cortex seen at the surface of the human brain.

Nernst equation   An equation used to calculate the equilibrium potential.

nerve growth factor   A substance that controls the growth of neurons of the spinal ganglia and the ganglia of the sympathetic nervous system. See Figure 4-18.

nerve impulses   The propagated electrical messages of a neuron which travel down the axon to adjacent neurons. Also called *action potentials.* See Figure 5-5.

neural folds   Ridges of ectoderm which form around the neural groove and which come together to form the neural tube in the embryo. See Figure 4-3.

neural groove   The groove between the neural folds which becomes the neural tube when these folds come together in the embryo. See Figure 4-3.

neural tube   A prenatal structure with subdivisions which correspond to the future forebrain, midbrain, and hindbrain. The cavity of this tube will include the cerebral ventricles and the passages that connect them. See Figure 4-3.

neuroblasts   Early forms of cells during the stage of cell migration. See Figures 4-5 and 4-6.

neuroendocrine   An endocrine agent secreted by specialized neurons; e.g., hypothalamic releasing hormones.

neurofibrillary tangles   Abnormal whorls of neurofilaments within nerve cells that are especially apparent in people suffering from dementia. See Figure 3-23.

neurofilaments   Small rod-like structures in axons that are involved in transport of materials. See Figure 2-15.

neuroglia   See *glial cells.*

neurohypophysis   See *posterior pituitary.*

neuromodulators   Substances that influence the activity of synaptic transmitters. See Box 6-1, p. 183.

neuron   The basic unit of the nervous system, composed of a cell body, receptive extension(s), and a transmitting extension (axon). See Figures 2-10 and 2-11.

neuron doctrine   A hypothesis which states that the brain is composed of separate cells that are distinct structurally, metabolically, and functionally.

neuropathies   Peripheral nerve destruction.

neurosecretory cells   Neurons that manufacture and secrete hormones.

neurospecificity   A theory of nervous system development which states that each axon grows to a particular site. See Figure 4-15.

neurotransmitter   See *synaptic transmitter.*

nicotinic   A cholinergic receptor that mediates chiefly the excitatory activities of acetylcholine.

nigrostriatal bundle (NSB)   A dopaminergic tract that runs from the substantia nigra of the midbrain to the lateral hypothalamus, the globus pallidus, and the caudate-putamen.

nociceptors   Receptors that respond to stimuli that produce tissue damage or pose the threat of damage.

node of Ranvier   A gap between successive segments of the *myelin* sheath where the axon membrane is exposed. See Figure 2-12.

nonassociative learning   A form of learning in which presentation of a particular stimulus leads to altered strength or probability of a response according to the strength and temporal spacing of that stimulus. Includes habituation and sensitization. Contrast with *associative learning.*

nonequivalence of associations   A constraint on learning stating that a given association is learned with differential ease by different species.

nonequivalence of response   A constraint on learning stating that the rapidity of learning a given instrumental behavior varies between species.

nonequivalence of stimuli   A constraint on learning stating that the same stimulus has a differential ability to be learned by different species.

nonprimary motor cortex   Large portions of the frontal lobe between primary motor cortex and the prefrontal area.

norepinephrine (NE)   A neurotransmitter produced mainly in brainstem nuclei, also called *noradrenalin.* See Figure 6-6.

NSB   See *nigrostriatal bundle.*

nucleotide   A portion of a DNA molecule composed of a single base and the adjoining sugar-phosphate unit of the strand.

nucleus   An anatomical collection of neurons, e.g., caudate nucleus.

nutrients   Chemicals that are not used as sources of energy but that are required for effective functioning of the body.

nystagmus   Abnormal to and fro movements of the eye during attempts to fixate.

occipital cortex   The cortex of the occipital (posterior) lobe of the brain; also called *visual cortex.* See Reference Figure 2-15 and Figure 9-18.

ocular dominance columns   Elongated bands of cells that respond preferentially to stimulation of one eye. See Figure 9-20.

ocular-dominance histogram   A graph that shows the strength of a neuron's response to stimuli presented to either the left or right eye. Used to determine the effects of depriving one eye of visual experience. See Figure 4-23.

oligodendrocyte   A type of glial cell that is commonly associated with nerve cell bodies; some oligodendrocytes form *myelin* sheaths. See Figure 2-18(a).

operant conditioning   See *instrumental conditioning.*

opioids   Chemicals produced in various regions of the brain that bind to opiate receptors and act like opiates. See under *opioid peptides* in Table 6-1.

opponent process hypothesis   See *spectrally opponent cells* and Figure 9-24.

optic chiasm   The point at which the two optic nerves meet. See Figure 9-18.

optic nerve   The collection of axons that run from the retina to the *optic chiasm.*

optic radiation   Axons of the *lateral geniculate nucleus* that terminate in the primary visual areas of the occipital cortex. See Figure 9-18.

optic tectum   Midbrain optical center. See Figure 4-14.

optic tract   The axons of the retinal ganglion cells after they have passed the optic chiasm; most terminate in the *lateral geniculate nucleus*. See Figure 9-18.

optokinetic system   A closed loop system controlling eye movement and keeping the gaze on target.

organ of Corti   A structure in the inner ear that lies on the basilar membrane of the cochlea. It contains the hair cells and the terminations of the auditory nerve. See Figure 9-2(d).

organizational role   The role that hormones play in the development and differentiation of body structure.

orgasm   The climax of sexual experience, marked by extremely pleasurable sensations.

osmolality   The number of particles per unit volume of a solute.

osmoreceptors   Cells in the hypothalamus hypothesized to respond to changes in osmotic pressure.

osmosis   When there are unequal concentrations of particles in the fluids on two sides of a semipermeable membrane, fluid moves to the side with the greater concentration.

osmotic pressure   The force involved in osmosis.

osmotic thirst   The response to increased osmotic pressure in brain cells. Contrast with *hypovolemic thirst*.

ossicles   Small bones that transmit sound across the middle ear, from the tympanic membrane to the oval window. See Figure 9-1.

outer hair cells   Receptor cells of the cochlea. See Figure 9-2(d).

oval window   The opening from the middle ear to the inner ear.

oxytocin   A hormone released by the posterior pituitary which triggers milk let-down in the nursing female. See Figure 7-7.

Pacinian corpuscle   A kind of receptor found especially in tissue overlying the abdominal cavity. See Figure 8-3.

pair bond   A form of monogamy.

paleocortex   Evolutionary old cortex, e.g., the hippocampus.

pancreas   An endocrine gland located near the posterior wall of the abdominal cavity; it secretes insulin and glucagon. See Figure 7-9.

parabiotic   Refers to a surgical preparation that joins the peripheral circulation of two animals.

paracrine   In paracrine function, the chemical signal diffuses to nearby target cells through the intermediate extracellular space. See Box 6-1.

paradoxical sleep   See *rapid-eye-movement sleep (REM)*.

parallel fibers   Axons of the granule cells that form the outermost layer of the cerebellar cortex. See Reference Figure 2-6.

parallel processing   Using several different circuits at the same time to process the same stimuli.

paraphasia   A symptom of aphasia distinguished by the substitution of a word by a sound, incorrect word, unintended word, or neologism.

parasympathetic division   One of the two systems that compose the *autonomic nervous system*. The parasympathetic division arises from both the cranial and sacral parts of the spinal cord. See Reference Figure 2-14.

paraventricular nucleus   A nucleus of the hypothalamus. See Figure 7-5(b).

Parkinson's disease   A degenerative neurological disorder involving dopaminergic neurons of the substantia nigra.

partial seizures   Epileptic seizures arising from pathological foci that do not have widespread distribution. These include focal repetitive motor spasms and do not involve loss of consciousness.

parvocellular system   The division of primate visual pathways that appears to be mainly responsible for analysis of color and form and for recognition of objects. See Table 9-2.

passive avoidance response   A response that an organism has learned not to make, i.e., learning not to enter a compartment where it has been given a shock.

Pavlovian conditioning   See *classical conditioning*.

peripheral nervous system   The portion of the nervous system that includes all the nerves outside the brain and spinal cord.

permanent memory   A type of memory that lasts without decline for the life of an organism.

perseveration-consolidation hypothesis   A hypothesis stating that information passes through two stages in memory formation. During the first stage the memory is held by perseveration of neural activity and is easily disrupted. During the second stage the memory becomes fixed, or consolidated, and is no longer easily disrupted.

PET   See *positron emission tomography*.

petit mal seizures   A type of generalized epileptic seizure characterized by a spike-and-wave electrical pattern (Figure 5-17). During these seizures the person is unaware of the environment and later cannot recall what happened.

phantom limb   The experience of sensory messages attributed to an amputated limb.

phasic receptors   Receptors that show a rapid fall in nerve impulse discharge as stimulation is maintained.

phencyclidine   An anesthetic agent that is also a psychedelic drug; it makes many people feel dissociated from themselves and their environment.

phenylketonuria (PKU)   An inherited disorder of protein metabolism in which the absence of an enzyme leads to a toxic build up of a certain compound, causing mental retardation.

pheromone   A chemical signal that is released outside the body of an animal and that affects other members of the same species. See Box 6-1, p. 183.

phobic disorders   Intense, irrational fears that become centered on a specific object, activity, or situation that the person feels he or she must avoid.

phosphenes   Perceived flashes of light provoked by electrical or mechanical stimulation of the eyeball.

photon   A quantum of light energy.

photopic system   A system in the retina that operates at high levels of light, shows sensitivity to color, and involves the cones; contrast with *scotopic system*. See Table 9-1.

phrenology   The belief that bumps on the skull reflect enlargements of brain regions responsible for certain behavioral faculties. See Figure 2-3.

pia mater   The innermost of the coverings that embrace the brain and spinal cord.

pinna   External ear. See Figure 9-1.

pitch   A dimension of auditory experience in which sounds vary from low to high.

pituitary gland   A small complex endocrine gland located in a socket at the base of the skull. The anterior pituitary and posterior pituitary are separate in function. See Figure 7-5.

PKU   See *phenylketonuria*.

place theory   A theory of frequency discrimination according to which pitch perception depends on the place of maximal displacement of the basilar membrane produced by a sound. Contrast with *volley theory*.

placebo effect   A response to an inert substance which mimics the effects of an actual drug, i.e., the relief pain sufferers frequently get from sugar tablets presented as medicine.

planum temporale   A region of superior temporal cortex adjacent to the primary auditory area. See Figure 18-15.

pneumoencephalogram   A technique for examining brain structure in intact humans by taking X rays after a gas is injected into the ventricles.

poikilotherms   Animals whose body temperature varies with the environment, such as reptiles. Contrast with *homeotherms*.

polyandry   A mating system in which one female mates with several males.

polygamy   A mating system in which an individual mates with more than one other animal. *Polygyny* is the mating of one male with more than one female. *Polyandry* is the mating of one female with more than one male.

polygyny   See *polygamy*.

polymodal   Involving several sensory modalities.

pons   A portion of the metencephalon. See Figures 2-5 and 2-7.

positron emission tomography   A technique for examining brain structure and function in intact humans by combining tomography with injections of radioactive substances used by the brain. An analysis of metabolism of these substances reflects regional differences in brain activity. See the cover of this book and Figure 2-9(e) and (f).

postcopulatory behavior   The final stage in mating behavior. These species-specific behaviors include rolling (in the cat) and grooming (in the rat).

posterior pituitary   The rear division of the pituitary gland. Also called *neurohypophysis*. See Figure 7-5(b).

postsynaptic potentials   See *graded potentials*.

postural tremor   A tremor that occurs when a person attempts to maintain a posture such as holding an arm or leg extended, resulting from pathology of the basal ganglia or cerebellum.

potassium equilibrium potential   See *equilibrium potential*.

precocial   Refers to animals born in a relatively developed state who are able to survive without maternal care; opposite of *altricial*.

primary visual cortex   The region of the occipital cortex where most visual information first arrives; also called *striate cortex*, area 17, and V-1. See Figures 9-18 and 9-19(a).

procedural knowledge   Knowledge shown by ability to perform a task; "knowing how." See Table 16-1.

proceptive behavior   Pertaining to female appetitive sexual behavior. See Figure 11-22.

progestins   A major class of hormones produced by the ovary. See Table 7-2.

projection neurons   Large neurons that transmit messages to widely separated parts of the brain.

promiscuity   A mating system in which animals mate with several members of the opposite sex and do not establish durable associations with sex partners.

prosencephalon   See *forebrain*.

prosthetic devices   Artificial replacements of body parts lost by accident or disease, such as an artificial limb.

proximal   An anatomical directional term meaning near the trunk or center; opposite of *distal*. See Box Figure 2-1.

psychedelic   Denotes a mental state with intensified sensory perception and distortions or hallucinations. Also refers to drugs that produce such states.

psychosocial dwarfism   Reduced stature caused by stress early in life which inhibits deep sleep. See Box 7-1.

psychosurgery   Surgically produced brain lesions to modify severe psychiatric disorders.

psychotogens   Substances that generate psychotic behavior.

pure tone   A tone with a single frequency of vibration. See Box Figure 9-1.

Purkinje cell   A type of large nerve cell in the cerebellar cortex. See Figure 4-8.

putamen   One of the *basal ganglia*. See Reference Figure 2-10.

pyramidal cell   A type of large nerve cell in the cerebral cortex. See Figure 2-11(d) and Reference Figure 2-4.

pyramidal system   A motor system including neurons within the cerebral cortex and their axons which form the pyramidal tract. See Figure 10-4.

quantum   A unit of radiant energy.

radial glia   Glia that form early in development, spanning the width of the emerging cerebral hemispheres, and guide migrating neurons. See Figure 4-7.

ramp movements   Slow, sustained motions thought to be generated in the basal ganglia. Also called *smooth movements*. Contrast with *ballistic*.

range fractionation   A hypothesis of stimulus intensity perception stating that a wide range of intensity values can be encoded by a group of cells each of which is a specialist for a particular range of an intensity scale. See Figure 8-4.

raphe nucleus   A group of neurons in the midline of the brainstem which contains serotonin, involved in sleep mechanisms. See Figure 14-21.

rapid-eye-movement sleep (REM)   A stage of sleep characterized by small-amplitude, fast EEG waves, no postural tension, and rapid eye movements. Also called *paradoxical sleep*. See Figure 14-7.

Raynaud's disease   A circulatory disorder which may shut off blood supply to the fingers upon exposure to the cold and sometimes in response to emotional states.

receptive field   The stimulus region and features that cause the maximal response of a cell in a sensory system. See Figures 8-9 and 9-27.

receptivity   The state of readiness to show the female responses that are necessary for the male to achieve intravaginal ejaculation, e.g., assuming the posture that facilitates intromission during copulatory behavior.

receptor proteins   Substances at synaptic receptor sites whose reaction to certain transmitters causes a change in the postsynaptic membrane potential.

receptors The initial elements in sensory systems, responsible for stimulus transduction, e.g., hair cells in the cochlea or rods and cones in the retina.

receptor sites Regions of specialized membrane containing receptor proteins located on the postsynaptic surface of a synapse; these sites receive and react with the chemical transmitter.

red nucleus (or nucleus ruber) A brain stem structure related to the *basal ganglia*.

reflex A simple, highly stereotyped, and unlearned response to a particular stimulus (e.g., an eyeblink in response to a puff of air). See Figures 10-12 and 10-13.

reflex ovulation Ovulation that in certain species is induced by copulation, thus not restricting successful mating to a regular ovulatory period of the female's cycle.

refractory A period during and after a nerve impulse in which the axon membrane's responsiveness is reduced. A brief period of complete insensitivity to stimuli (absolute refractory phase) is followed by a longer period of reduced sensitivity (relative refractory phase) during which only strong stimulation produces a nerve impulse.

reinforcing stimulus See *instrumental conditioning*.

relative refractory phase See *refractory*.

REM See *rapid-eye-movement sleep*.

resting potential Potential differences across the membrane of nerve cells during an inactive period. Also called *membrane potential*. See Figure 5-1.

rete mirabile A network of fine blood vessels located at the base of the brain in which blood coming from the periphery reduces the temperature of arterial blood before it enters the brain. See Figure 12-8.

reticular formation A region of the brainstem (extending from the medulla through the thalamus) that is involved in arousal. See Figures 8-15 and 10-15.

retina The receptive surface inside the eye which contains the rods and cones. See Figure 9-16.

retrieval A process in memory during which a stored memory is utilized by an organism.

retroactive amnesia A type of memory loss in which events just before a head injury are not recalled.

retrograde amnesia Difficulty in retrieving memories formed before the onset of amnesia.

retrograde degeneration Destruction of the nerve cell body following injury. See Box Figure 4-1.

re-uptake A mechanism by which a synaptic transmitter released at a synapse is taken back into the presynaptic terminal, thus stopping synaptic activity.

rhodopsin The photopigment in *rods* that responds to light.

rhombencephalon See *hindbrain*.

ribonucleic acid A nucleic acid present in the cell body. Two forms of RNA are *transfer RNA* and *messenger RNA*.

ribosomes Structures in the cell body where translation of genetic information takes place.

RNA See *ribonucleic acid*.

rods Light sensitive receptor cells in the retina which are most active at low levels of light. See Figures 9-16(c) and 9-17.

roots The two distinct branches of a spinal nerve, each of which serves a separate function. The *dorsal root* carries sensory information from the peripheral nervous system to the spinal cord. The *ventral root* carries motor messages from the spinal cord to the peripheral nervous system. See Reference Figure 2-13.

rostral An anatomical term meaning toward the head end; opposite of *caudal*. See Box Figure 2-1.

round window A membrane separating the cochlear duct from the middle ear cavity.

saccades Rapid movements of the eyes which occur regularly during normal viewing.

saccule A small fluid-filled sac under the utricle that responds to static positions of the head. See Figure 9-12 and Box Figure 9-3.

sacral Refers to the lower part of the back or spinal cord.

sagittal plane The plane that bisects the body or brain into right and left halves. See Box Figure 2-2.

saltatory conduction The form of conduction seen in myelinated axons in which the nerve impulse jumps from one *node of Ranvier* to the next.

saturation One of the basic dimensions of light perception. This varies from rich to pale, i.e., from red to pink to gray in the color solid of Figure 9-21.

schizotoxins Hypothesized toxic substances that cause schizophrenia.

Schwann cell The kind of accessory cell that forms myelin in the peripheral nervous system.

scotoma A region of blindness caused by injury to the visual pathway.

scotopic system A system in the retina which responds to low levels of light intensity and involves the rods. Contrast with *photopic system*. See Table 9-1.

second messenger A relatively slow acting substance in the postsynaptic cell which amplifies the effects of nerve impulses and can initiate processes that lead to changes in electrical potentials at the membrane.

secretin A hormone that is released during digestion.

selective potentiation The enhancement of the sensitivity or activity of certain neural circuits.

selectivity of reinforcement Across species, different reinforcements are differentially effective in strengthening associations.

semantic memory Generalized memory, for instance, knowing the meaning of a word without knowing where or when you learned that word. See Table 16-1.

semicircular canals Three fluid-filled tubes in the inner ear that are part of the *vestibular system*. Each of the tubes, which are at right angles to each other, detects angular acceleration. See Figure 9-12 and Box Figure 9-3.

senile dementia A neurological disorder of the aged involving progressive behavioral deterioration including personality change and profound intellectual decline.

senile plaques Neuroanatomical changes correlated with senile dementia. These plaques are small areas of the brain containing abnormal cellular and chemical patterns. See Figure 3-23.

sensitization A form of nonassociative learning in which an organism becomes more responsive to most stimuli after being exposed to unusually strong or painful stimulation. See Figure 16-3.

sensorineural deafness A hearing impairment originating from cochlear or auditory nerve lesions.

serotonergic Refers to neurons that use serotonin as their synaptic transmitter.

serotonin (5HT) A neurotransmitter produced in the raphe nuclei and active in structures throughout the cerebral hemispheres. Figure 6-8 shows the distribution of serotoninergic cells in the brain.

set point The point of reference in a feedback system like a setting of a thermostat.

sex chromosomes Pairs of chromosomes which are identical in females (XX) but which are different in males (XY). Contrast with *autosomes*.

sexual attraction The first step in the mating behavior of many animals in which animals emit stimuli that attract members of the opposite sex.

sexual imprinting A kind of imprinting in which early experience influences choice of a mate later in life.

sexual selection A theory concerning the evolution of anatomical and behavioral differences between males and females.

short-term memory Memory that usually lasts only for seconds or as long as rehearsal continues.

simple cortical cells Cells in the visual cortex that respond best to an edge or a bar of a particular width and with a particular direction and location in the visual field. See Figure 9-27.

sinistral Left-handed.

sleep apnea A sleep disorder that involves slowing or cessation of respiration during sleep, which wakens the patient. Excessive daytime somnolence results from frequent nocturnal awakening.

slow-wave sleep Stages of sleep including stages 1 through 4, defined by presence of slow EEG activity. See Figure 14-7.

smooth movements See *ramp movements*.

sodium equilibrium potential See *equilibrium potential*.

somatic intervention An approach to finding relations between bodily variables and behavioral variables that involves manipulating bodily structure or function and looking for resultant changes in behavior. See Figure 1-6.

somatotropic hormone See *growth hormone*.

spatial frequency filter model A model of pattern analysis emphasizing Fourier analysis of visual stimuli. Contrast with *feature detector model*.

spatial summation The summation at the axon hillock of postsynaptic potentials from across the cell body. If this summation reaches threshold a nerve impulse will be triggered. See Figure 5-8.

specific abilities to learn and remember The concept held by some investigators that specific abilities to learn and remember evolve where needed. As opposed to *genetic constraints on learning*.

specific hunger The temporary unlearned increase in preference for a particular food, related to a specific need.

spectrally opponent cells Visual receptor cells with opposite firing responses to different regions of the spectrum. See Figure 9-24.

spinal animals Animals whose spinal cord has been surgically

disconnected from the brain. Used to study behaviors that do not require brain control.

spinal nerves The 31 pairs of nerves that emerge from the spinal cord. See Reference Figure 2-13.

spinal shock A period of decreased synaptic excitability in the neurons of the spinal cord after it is isolated surgically from the brain.

spindle cell A kind of small nerve cell.

split-brain Individuals who have had the corpus callosum severed, halting communication between the right and left hemispheres.

spontaneous recovery A feature of classical conditioning in which, if no testing is done after extinction occurs, the conditioned stimulus may again elicit a response.

stage 1 sleep The initial stage of slow-wave sleep involving small-amplitude EEG waves of irregular frequency, slow heart rate, and a reduction of muscle tension. See Figure 14-7(b).

stage 2 sleep A stage of slow-wave sleep defined by bursts of regular 14–18-Hz EEG waves that progressively increase and then decrease in amplitude (called spindles). See Figure 14-7(c).

stage 3 sleep A stage of slow-wave sleep defined by the spindles seen in stage 2 sleep mixed with larger amplitude slow waves. See Figure 14-7(d).

stage 4 sleep A stage of slow-wave sleep defined by the presence of high amplitude slow waves of 1–4 Hz. See Figure 14-7(e).

stapes A middle ear bone, connected to the oval window. One of the three ossicles that conduct sounds across the middle ear.

static phase of obesity A later period following destruction of the ventromedial hypothalamus during which the animal's weight stabilizes at an obese level and food intake is not much above normal. See Figure 13-7.

stellate cell A kind of small nerve cell with many branches.

stereopsis The ability to perceive depth, utilizing the slight difference in visual information from the two eyes. See Figure 9-26.

STH See *growth hormone*.

stimulation-elicited behavior Motivational behaviors such as eating, drinking, or fearful escape elicited by electrical stimulation of sites in the brain.

stretch reflex Contraction of a muscle in response to stretch of that muscle. See Figure 10-13.

striate cortex A portion of the *visual cortex* with input from the lateral geniculate nucleus; primary visual cortex; Area V-1 in Figure 9-19(a).

striate region The region of the *basal ganglia,* called striate because the *external capsule* and *internal capsule* appear as light-colored stripes across the gray matter. See Reference Figure 2-10.

substantia nigra A brainstem structure related to the *basal ganglia* and named for its dark pigmentation.

subventricular zones Regions around the brain ventricle which continue to manufacture the precursors of nerve cells after birth.

sulci The furrows of convoluted brain surface. Contrast with *gyri.* See Figure 2-5.

superior colliculus A structure in the midbrain that receives information from the optic tract. See Figure 9-18.

superior olivary complex   A brainstem structure that receives input from both right and left cochlear nuclei, providing the first binaural analysis of auditory information.

suprachiasmatic nucleus (SCN)   A small region of the hypothalamus above the optic chiasm that is the location of a circadian oscillator. See Figure 14-3.

supraoptic nucleus   A nucleus of the hypothalamus. See Figure 7-5(b).

sympathetic chains   One of two systems that compose the autonomic nervous system. See Reference Figure 2-14.

synapse   An area composed of the presynaptic (axonal) terminal, the postsynaptic (usually dendritic) membrane, and the space (or cleft) between them. This is the site at which neural messages travel from one neuron to another. Also called the *synaptic region*. See Figures 2-16, 6-1 and 6-5.

synaptic assembly   A level of brain organization which includes the total collection of all synapses on a single cell. See Figure 2-19.

synaptic bouton   The presynaptic swelling of the axon terminal from which neural messages travel across the synaptic cleft to other neurons. See Figure 2-16.

synaptic cleft   The space between the presynaptic and postsynaptic membranes. See Figures 2-16 and 6-2.

synaptic region   See *synapse*.

synaptic transmitter   The chemical in the presynaptic bouton that serves as the basis of neural-neural communication. It travels across the synaptic cleft and reacts with the postsynaptic membrane when triggered by a nerve impulse. Also called *neurotransmitter*. See Box G-1, Figure 6-5, and Table 6-1.

synaptic vesicles   The small, spherically shaped structures which contain molecules of synaptic transmitter. See Figures 2-16, 6-1 and 6-2.

system   A higher level of brain organization that includes specialized circuits, e.g., the visual system. Contrast with *circuit*.

tardive dyskinesia   Involuntary movements—especially those involving the face, mouth, lips, and tongue—related to prolonged use of antipsychotic drugs, such as chlorpromazine. See Box 15-2.

tectorial membrane   A structure in the cochlear duct. See Figure 9-2(d).

telencephalon   The frontal subdivision of the forebrain which includes the cerebral hemispheres when fully developed. See Figures 2-7 and 2-8.

temporal summation   The summation of postsynaptic potentials which reach the axon hillock at different times. The closer together they are, the more complete the summation.

testosterone   A hormone produced by male gonads which controls a variety of bodily changes that become visible at puberty. See Figure 7-11 and Table 7-2.

thalamus   The brain regions that surround the third ventricle. See Figures 2-5(b) and 9-19(b).

thoracic   Refers to the level of the chest.

threshold   The stimulus intensity just adequate to trigger a nerve impulse at the axon hillock.

thyroid gland   An endocrine gland located below the vocal apparatus in the throat which regulates metabolic processes, especially carbohydrate utilization and body growth. See Figure 7-10.

thyroid-stimulating hormone (TSH)   A tropic hormone released by the anterior pituitary gland which increases the release of thyroxine and the uptake of iodide by the thyroid gland. See Figure 7-10.

thyrotropin-releasing hormone (TRH)   A hypothalamic hormone that regulates the release of thyroid-stimulating hormone. See Figure 7-10.

thyroxine   A hormone released by the thyroid gland.

tomogram   See *computerized axial tomogram, positron emission tomography*.

tonic receptors   Receptors in which the frequency of nerve impulse discharge declines slowly or not at all as stimulation is maintained.

transcription   The process during which mRNA forms bases complementary to a strand of DNA. This message is then used to translate the DNA code into protein molecules.

transducers   Devices that convert energy from one form to another, e.g., sensory receptor cells.

transduction   The process of converting one form of energy to another.

transfer RNA (tRNA)   Small molecules of RNA that convey amino acids to ribosomes for translation.

translation   The process by which amino acids are linked together (directed by an mRNA molecule) to form protein molecules.

transmethylation hypothesis   A hypothesized explanation of schizophrenia suggesting that the addition of a methyl group to some naturally occurring brain compounds can convert some substances to hallucinogenic agents, or psychotogens.

transverse   See *coronal*.

tremor-at-rest   A tremor that occurs when the affected region, such as a limb, is fully supported.

tremors   Rhythmic repetitive movements caused by brain pathology.

TRH   See *thyrotropin-releasing hormone*.

trichromatic hypothesis   A theory of color perception which states that there are three different types of cones, each excited by a different region of the spectrum and each having a separate pathway to the brain.

tricyclic antidepressants   Compounds whose structure resembles that of chlorpromazine and related antipsychotic drugs. They may procure relief from depression but only after two to three weeks of daily administration.

trigger features   Particular stimulus characteristics that are most effective in evoking responses from a particular cell.

triplet code   A code for an amino acid specified by three successive bases of a DNA molecule.

tRNA   See *transfer RNA*.

tropic hormones   Anterior pituitary hormones that affect the secretion of other endocrine glands. See Figure 7-6.

TSH   See *thyroid-stimulating hormone*.

tympanic canal   One of three principal canals running along the length of the cochlea. See Figure 9-2(c).

tympanic membrane   The partition between the external and middle ear. Also called *eardrum*. See Figure 9-1.

ultradian   Refers to a rhythmic biological event whose period is shorter than circadian rhythms, usually from several minutes to several hours.

unconditioned stimulus (US)   See *classical conditioning*.

unipolar depression   Emotional depression that alternates with normal emotional states. Contrast with *bipolar depression*.

unmyelinated   Refers to fine diameter axons that lack a *myelin* sheath.

US   Unconditioned stimulus. See *classical conditioning*.

utricle   A small fluid-filled sac in the *vestibular system* that responds to static positions of the head. See Figure 9-12 and Box Figure 9-3.

vagus nerve   One of the cranial nerves. See Reference Figure 2-12.

vasopressin   See *antidiuretic hormone*.

ventral   An anatomical term meaning toward the belly or front of the body or the bottom of the brain; opposite of *dorsal*. See Box Figure 2-1.

ventral root   Root toward front of the spinal cord. See Reference Figure 2-13.

ventricles   See *cerebral ventricles*.

ventricular layer or zone   A layer of homogeneous cells in the neural tube of the developing organism which is the source of all neural and glial cells in the mature organism. Also called the *ependymal layer*. See Figures 4-5 and 4-7.

ventromedial hypothalamus (VMH)   A hypothalamic region involved in inhibiting eating, among other functions. See Figure 13-6.

vertebral arteries   Arteries which ascend the vertebrae, enter the base of the skull, and join together to form the basilar artery. See Reference Figure 2-11.

vestibular canal   One of three principal canals running along the length of the cochlea. See Figure 9-2.

vestibular system   A receptor system in the inner ear that responds to mechanical forces, such as gravity and acceleration. See Figure 9-12.

vestibuloocular reflex   A rapid response that adjusts the eye to a change in head position.

VMH   See *ventromedial hypothalamus*.

volley theory   A theory of frequency discrimination which emphasizes the relation between sound frequency and the firing pattern of nerve cells (i.e., a 500-Hz tone would produce 500 neural discharges per second by a nerve cell or group of nerve cells). Contrast with *place theory*.

W cells   Retinal ganglion cells with sluggish and somewhat variable responses to visual stimuli.

Wallerian degeneration   See *anterograde degeneration*.

Wernicke's aphasia   A language impairment—involving fluent, meaningless speech and little language comprehension—related to damage to *Wernicke's area*.

Wernicke's area   A region of the left hemisphere involved in language comprehension. See Figure 18-4.

white matter   A shiny layer underneath the cortex consisting largely of axons with white, *myelin* sheaths. See Figure 2-6.

Wolffian duct system   A primitive duct system in each embryo which will develop into male structures—the epidymides, the vas deferens, and the seminal vesicles—if testes are present in the embryo. Contrast with *Müllerian duct system*. See Figure 11-8.

X cells   Retinal ganglion cells that continue to respond to maintained visual stimuli.

Y cells   Retinal ganglion cells that respond strongly initially, but rapidly decrease frequency of response as the visual stimulus is maintained.

References

Abraham, S. F., Denton, D. A., & Weisinger, B. S. (1976). Effect of an angiotensin antagonist, Sar-Ala-Angiotensin II, on physiological thirst. *Pharmacology, Biochemistry and Behavior, 4,* 243–247.

Abraham, W. C., & Goddard, G. V. (1985). Multiple traces of neural activity in the hippocampus. In N. M. Weinberger, J. L. McGaugh, & G. Lynch (Eds.), *Memory systems of the brain* (pp. 62–76). New York: Guilford.

Adams, E. H., & Durell, J. (1984). Cocaine: A growing public health problem. In J. Grabowski (Ed.), *Cocaine: Pharmacology, effects and treatment of abuse* (pp. 9–16). NIDA Research Monograph 50. National Institute of Drug Abuse.

Ader, R. (1971). Experimentally induced gastric lesions: Results and implications of studies in animals. *Advances in Psychosomatic Medicine, 6,* 1–39.

———. (1985). Conditioned immunopharmacological effects in animals: Implications for a conditioning model of pharmacotherapy. In L. White, B. Tursky, & G. E. Schwartz (Eds.), *Placebo* (pp. 306–332). New York: Guilford.

Adler, N. T. (Ed.), (1981). *Neuroendocrinology of reproduction.* New York: Plenum.

———. (1978). On the mechanisms of sexual behaviour and their evolutionary constraints. In J. B. Hutchison (Ed.), *Biological determinants of sexual behaviour* (pp. 657–695). New York: Wiley.

Aggleton, J. P., & Mishkin, M. (1983). Memory impairments following restricted medial thalamic lesions in monkeys. *Experimental Brain Research, 52,* 199–209.

Agranoff, B. W. (1980). Biochemical events mediating the formation of short-term and long-term memory. In Y. Tsukada & B. W. Agranoff (Eds.), *Neurobiological basis of learning and memory.* New York: Wiley.

Aigner, T., Mitchell, S. J., Aggleton, J., et al. (1984). Recognition deficit in monkeys following neurotoxic lesions of the basal forebrain. *Society for Neuroscience Abstracts, 10,* 386.

Åkerstedt, T. (1985). Hormones and sleep. In A. Borbely & J.-L. Valatx (Eds.), *Sleep mechanisms* (pp. 193–205). Berlin: Springer-Verlag.

Alberts, J. R. (1978). Huddling by rat pups: Multisensory control of contact behavior. *Journal of Comparative and Physiological Psychology, 92*(2), 220–230.

Albrecht, D. G. (1978). Analysis of visual form. Ph.D. thesis. University of California, Berkeley.

Alexander, B. K., & Hadaway, P. F. (1982). Opiate addiction: The case for an adaptive orientation. *Psychological Bulletin, 92,* 367–381.

Alexander, R. D., Hoogland, J. L., Howard, R. D., Noonan, K. M., & Sherman, P. W. (1979). Sexual dimorphisms and breeding systems in pinnipeds, ungulates, primates, and humans. In N. A. Chagnon & W. Irons (Eds.), *Evolutionary biology and human social behavior* (pp. 402–435). North Scituate, Mass.: Duxbury.

Alkon, D. (1988). *Memory traces in the brain.* New York: Cambridge University Press.

Allman, J. M., & Kaas, J. H. (1976). Representation of the visual field in the medial wall of occipital-parietal cortex in the owl monkey. *Science, 191,* 572–575.

Almli, C. R. (1978). The ontogeny of feeding and drinking behaviors: effects of early brain damage. *Neuroscience and Biobehavioral Reviews, 2,* 281–300.

———, Fisher, R. S., & Hill, D. L. (1979). Lateral hypothalamus destruction in infant rats produces consummatory deficits without sensory neglect or attenuated arousal. *Experimental Neurology, 66,* 146–157.

Alpert, M., & Friedhoff, A. J. (1980). An un-dopamine hypothesis of schizophrenia. *Schizophrenia Bulletin, 6,* 387–390.

Altman, J. (1976). Experimental reorganization of the cerebellar cortex. VII. Effects of late x-irradiation. *Journal of Comparative Neurology, 165,* 65–76.

———. (1967). Postnatal growth and differentiation of the mammalian brain with implications for a morphological theory of memory. In Quarton, G. C., Melnechuk, T., & Schmitt, F. O. (Eds.), *The neurosciences.* New York: Rockefeller University.

Amaral, D. G. (1978). A Golgi study of cell types in the hilar region of the hippocampus in the rat. *Journal of Comparative Neurology, 182,* 851–914.

Ames, B. N. (1983). Dietary carcinogens and anticarcinogens. *Science, 221,* 1256–1264.

Anand, B. K., & Brobeck, J. R. (1951). Localization of a 'feeding center' in the hypothalamus of the rat. *Proceedings of the Society for Experimental Biology and Medicine, 77,* 323–324.

Andersson, B. (1978). Regulation of water intake. *Physiological Reviews, 58,* 582–603.

Andreasen, N., Nassrallah, H. A., Dunn, V., Olson, S. C., Grove, W. M., Ehrhardt, J. C., Coffman, J. A., & Crossett, J. H. W. (1986). Structural abnormalities in the frontal system in schizophrenia. *Archives of General Psychiatry, 43,* 136–144.

Antin, J., Gibbs, J., Holt, J., Young, R. C., & Smith, G. P. (1975). Cholecystokinin elicits the complete behavioral sequence of satiety in rats. *Journal of Comparative and Physiological Psychology, 89,* 784–790.

Appel, S. H. (1981). A unifying hypothesis for the cause of amyotrophic lateral sclerosis, parkinsonism, and Alzheimer disease. *Annals of Neurology, 10,* 499–505.

Arkin, A. M., Antrobus, J. S., & Ellman, S. J. (Eds.) (1978). *The mind in sleep: Psychology and psychophysiology.* Hillsdale, N.J.: Erlbaum.

Arnauld, E., Dufy, B., & Vincent, J. D. (1975). Hypothalamic supraoptic neurones: Rates and patterns of action potential firing during water deprivation in the unanesthetized monkey. *Brain Research, 100,* 315–325.

Arnold, A. P. (1980). Sexual differences in the brain. *American Scientist, 68,* 165–173.

———, & Gorski, R. A. (1984). Gonadal steroid induction of structural sex differences in the central nervous system. *Annual Review of Neuroscience, 7,* 413–442.

Autrum, H., Jung, R., Loewenstein, W. R., MacKay, D. M., & Teuber, H. L. (Eds.) (1971–1981). *Handbook of Sensory Physiology* (9 vols.). Berlin and New York: Springer-Verlag.

Ax, A. F. (1953). The physiological differentiation between fear and anger in humans. *Psychosomatic Medicine, 15,* 433–442.

Baack, J., Lacoste-Utamsing, C., and Woodward, D. J. (1984). Sexual dimorphism in human fetal corpora callosa. *Society for Neuroscience Abstracts, 10,* 315.

Bachevalier, J., & Mishkin, M. (1984). An early and a late developing system for learning and retention in infant monkeys. *Behavioral Neuroscience, 98,* 770–778.

Bach-y-Rita, P. (1980). Brain plasticity as a basis for therapeutic procedures. In P. Bach-y-Rita (Ed.), *Recovery of function following brain injury: Theoretical considerations for brain injury rehabilitation.* Bern: Hans Huber.

———. (Ed.) (1980). *Recovery of function following brain injury: Theoretical considerations for brain injury rehabilitation.* Bern: Hans Huber.

Baer, M. F., & Singer, W. (1986). Modulation of visual cortical plasticity by acetylcholine and noradrenaline. *Nature, 320,* 172–176.

Bailey, C. H., & Chen, M. (1984). Morphological basis of long-term habituation and sensitization in *Aplysia. Science, 220,* 91–93.

Bailey, C. H., Castellucci, V. F., Koester, J., & Chen, M. (1983). Behavioral changes in aging *Aplysia:* A model system for studying the cellular basis of age-impaired learning, memory, and arousal. *Behavioral and Neural Biology, 38,* 70–81.

Baird, I. L. (1974). Anatomical features of the inner ear in submammalian vertebrates. In W. D. Keidel & W. D. Neff (Eds.), *Handbook of Sensory Physiology* Vol. V/1, *Auditory System Anatomy Physiology (Ear)* (pp. 164–212). New York: Springer-Verlag.

Baker, M. A. (1979). A brain-cooling system in mammals. *Scientific American, 240,* 130–139.

Balderston, J. B., Wilson, A. B., Freire, M. E., & Simonen, M. S. (1981). *Malnourished children of the rural poor.* Boston: Auburn House.

Ballantine, H. T., Bouckoms, A. J., Thomas, E. K., & Giriunas, I. E. (1987). Treatment of psychiatric illness by stereotactic cingulotomy. *Biological Psychiatry, 22,* 807–820.

Bancroft, J. (1978). The relationship between hormones and sexual behaviour in humans. In J. B. Hutchison (Ed.), *Biological determinants of sexual behaviour* (pp. 493–519). New York: Wiley.

Barbour, H. G. (1912). Die Wirkung unmittelbarer Erwarmung und Abkühlung der Wärmenzentren auf die Körpertemperatur. *Archiv für experimentalle Pathologie und Pharmakologie, 70,* 1–26.

Barchas, J. D., Akil, H., Elliott, G. R., Holman, R. B., & Watson, S. J. (1978). Behavioral neurochemistry: Neuroregulators and behavioral states. *Science, 200,* 964–973.

Barlow, G. W. (1977). Modal action patterns. In T. A. Sebeok, (Ed.) *How animals communicate.* Bloomington: Indiana University.

Barlow, H. B., Blakemore, C., & Pettigrew, J. D. (1967). The neural mechanism of binocular depth discrimination. *Journal of Physiology* (London), *193,* 327–342.

Barnes, C. A. (1979). Memory deficits associated with senescence: A neurophysiological and behavioral study in the rat. *Journal of Physiological and Comparative Psychology, 93,* 74–104.

Barnett, S. A. (1975). *The rat: A study in behavior. Revised edition.* Chicago: University of Chicago.

Baron, M. (1986). Genetics of schizophrenia. I. Familial patterns and mode of inheritance. *Biological Psychiatry, 21,* 1051–1067.

———. (1986). Genetics of schizophrenia. II. Vulnerability traits and gene markers. *Biological Psychiatry, 21,* 1189–1212.

Barondes, S. H., & Cohen, H. D. (1967). Comparative effects of cycloheximide and puromycin on cerebral protein synthesis and consolidation of memory in mice. *Brain Research, 4,* 44–51.

Bateson, P. (Ed.) (1983). *Mate choice.* Cambridge: Cambridge University Press.

Bateson, P. P. G., Horn, G., & Rose, S. P. R. (1972). Effects of early experience on regional incorporation of precursors into RNA and protein in the chick brain. *Brain Research, 39,* 449–465.

Basbaum, A., & Fields, H. L. (1978). Endogenous pain control mechanisms: Review and hypothesis. *Annals of Neurology, 4,* 451–462.

———. (1984). Endogeous pain control systems: Brainstem spinal pathways and endorphin circuitry. *Annual Review of Neuroscience, 7,* 309–339.

Baum, M. J., Keverne, E. B., Everitt, B. J., Herbert, J., & de Vrees, P. (1976). Reduction of sexual interaction in rhesus monkeys by a vaginal action of progesterone. *Nature, 263,* 606–608.

Beach, F. A. (1975). Behavioral endocrinology: An emerging discipline. *American Scientist, 63,* 178–187.

———. (1977). Human sexuality in four perspectives. In F. A. Beach (Ed.), *Human sexuality in four perspectives* (pp. 1–21). Baltimore: Johns Hopkins University.

———, & Levinson, G. (1950). Effects of androgen on the glans penis and mating behavior of castrated male rats. *Journal of Experimental Zoology, 144,* 159–171.

Beagley, W. K., & Holley, T. L. (1977). Hypothalamic stimulation facilitates contralateral visual control of a learned response. Science, *196,* 321–322.

Beal, M. F., Kleinman, G. M., Ojemann, R. C., & Hockberg, F. H. (1981). Gangliocytoma of third ventricle: Hyperphagia, somnolence and dementia. *Neurology, 31,* 1224–1227.

Beamish, P., & Kiloh, L. G. (1960). Psychoses due to amphetamine consumption. *Journal of Mental Science, 106,* 337–343.

Bear, D. (1983). Hemispheric specialization and the neurology of emotion. *Archives of Neurology, 40,* 195–202.

———, & Fedio, P. (1977). Quantitative analysis of interictal behavior in temporal lobe epilepsy. *Archives of Neurology, 34,* 454–467.

Begleiter, H., Porjesz, B., Bihari, B., & Kissin, B. (1984). Event-related brain potentials in boys at risk for alcoholism. *Science, 225,* 1493–1495.

Bellinger, L. L., Trietley, G. J., & Bernardis, L. L. (1976). Failure of portal glucose and adrenaline infusions or liver denervation to affect food intake in dogs. *Physiology and Behavior, 16,* 299–304.

Bellugi, U., Poizner, H., & Klima, E. S. (1983). Brain organization for language: clues from sign aphasia. *Human Neurobiology, 2,* 155–171.

Bennett, A. F., & Ruben, J. A. (1979). Endothermy and activity in vertebrates. *Science, 206,* 649–654.

Bennett, E. L., Rosenzweig, M. R., Diamond, M. C., Morimoto, H., & Hebert, M. (1974). Effects of successive environments on brain measures. *Physiology and Behavior, 12,* 621–631.

Bennett, E. L., Rosenzweig, M. R., and Flood, J. F. Role of neurotransmitters and protein synthesis in short- and long-term memory (1979). In J. Obiols, C. Ballús, E. Gonzáles Monclús, & J. Pujol (Eds.), *Biological Psychiatry Today.* Amsterdam: Elsevier/North-Holland Biomedical Press.

Bennett, E. L., Rosenzweig, M. R., Morimoto, H., & Hebert, M. (1979). Maze training alters brain weights and cortical RNA/DNA. *Behavioral and Neural Biology, 26,* 1–22.

Bentley, D. (1976). Genetic analysis of the nervous system. In J. C. Fentress (Ed.), *Simpler networks and behavior.* Sunderland, Mass.: Sinauer Associates.

Benton, A. (1979). Visuoperceptive, visuospatial, and visuocoustinctive disorders. In K. M. Heilman and E. Valenstein (Eds.), *Clinical Neuropsychology.* New York: Oxford.

Benzer, S. (1973). Genetic dissection of behavior. *Scientific American, 229*(12), 24–37.

Berger, T. W. (1984). Long-term potentiation of hippocampal synaptic transmission affects rate of behavioral learning. *Science, 224,* 627–630.

———, Laham, R. I., & Thompson, R. F. (1980). Hippocampal unit-behavior correlations during classical conditioning. *Brain Research, 193,* 229–248.

———, & Thompson, R. F. (1978). Neuronal plasticity in the limbic system during classical conditioning of the rabbit nictitating membrane response, I. The hippocampus. *Brain Research, 145,* 323–346.

Bergson, H. (1911). *Matter and memory.* London: Allen and Unwin.

Bernstein, N. (1967). *The co-ordination and regulation of movements.* New York: Pergamon.

Berry, M., Rogers, A. W., & Eayrs, J. T. (1964). Pattern of cell migration during cortical histogenesis. *Nature, 203,* 591–593.

Berry, S. D., & Thompson, R. F. (1979). Medial septal lesions retard classical conditioning of the nictitating membrane response in rabbits. *Science, 205,* 209–211.

Bert, J. (1971). Sleep in primates: A review of various results. *Medical Primatology,* 308–315.

Besedovsky, H., Del Rey, A., Sorkin, E., and Dinarello, C. A. (1986). Immunoregulatory feedback between interleukin-1 and glucocorticoid hormones. *Science, 233,* 652–654.

Bessou, P., & Perl, E. R. (1969). Response of cutaneous sensory units with unmyelinated fibers to noxious stimuli. *Journal of Neurophysiology, 32,* 1025–1043.

Bigelow, L., Nasrallah, H. A., and Rauscher, F. P. (1983). Corpus callosum thickness in chronic schizophrenia. *British Journal of Psychiatry, 142,* 284–287.

Bini, G., Cruccu, G., Hagbarth, K-E., Schady, W., & Torebjork, E. (1984). Analgesic effect of vibration and cooling on pain induced by intraneural electrical stimulation. *Pain, 18,* 239–248.

Birnholz, J. C. (1981). The development of human fetal eye movement patterns. *Science, 213,* 679–680.

Bjørklund, A., & Stenevi, U. (1984). Intracerebral neural implants: Neuronal replacement and reconstruction of damaged circuitries. *Annual Review of Neuroscience, 7,* 279–308.

———, Dunnett, S. B., & Iversen, S. D. (1981). Functional reactivation of the deafferented neostriatum by nigral transplants. *Nature, 289,* 497–499.

———, Stenevi, U., Schmidt, R. H., Dunnett, S. B., and Gage, F. H. (1983). Intracerebral grafting of neuronal cell suspensions II. Survival and growth of nigral cells implanted in different brain sites. *Acta Physiologica Scandinanvica Supplement, 522,* 11–22.

Blakemore, C. (1976). The conditions required for the maintenance of binocularity in the kitten's visual cortex. *Journal of Physiology* (London), *261,* 423–444.

———, & Campbell, F. W. (1969). On the existence of neurones in the human visual system selectively sensitive to the orientation and size of retinal images. *Journal of Physiology* (London), *203,* 237–260.

Blalock, J. E. (1984). The immune system as a sensory organ. *Journal of immunology, 132,* 1067–1070.

Bleier, R. (1984). *Science and gender.* New York: Pergamon.

Bligh, J. (1979). The central neurology of mammalian thermoregulation. *Neuroscience, 4,* 1213–1236.

Blinkhorn, S. F., & Hendrickson, D. E. (1982). Averaged evoked responses and psychometric intelligence. *Nature, 295,* 596–597.

Bliss, T. V. P., & Dolphin, A. C. (1984). Where is the locus of long-term potentiation? In G. Lynch, J. L. McGaugh, & N. M. Weinberger (Eds.), *Neurobiology of learning and memory* (pp. 451–465). New York: Guilford.

Bliss, T. V. P., & Lomo, T. (1973). Long-lasting potentiation of synaptic transmission in the dentate area of the anaesthetized rabbit following stimulation of the perforant path. *Journal of Physiology* (London), *232,* 331–356.

Bloch, V. (1976). Brain activation and memory consolidation. In M. R. Rosenzweig, & E. L. Bennett (Eds.), *Neural mechanisms of learning and memory.* Cambridge: MIT Press.

———, & Laroche, S. (1984). Facts and hypotheses related to the search for the engram. In G. Lynch, J. L. McGaugh, & N. M. Weinberger (Eds.), *Neurobiology of learning and memory* (pp. 249–260). New York: Guilford.

Block, J. H. (1976). Issues, problems, and pitfalls in assessing sex differences: A critical review of *The Psychology of Sex Differences. Merrill-Palmer Quarterly, 22,* 283–308.

Blue, M. E., & Parnavelas, J. G. (1983). The formation and maturation of synapses in the visual cortex of the rat II. Quantitative analysis. *Journal of Neurocytology, 12,* 697–712.

Bodis-Wollner, I. (1972). Visual acuity and contrast sensitivity in patients with cerebral lesions. *Science, 178,* 769–771.

Bodnar, R. J., Kelly, D. D., Brutus, M., & Glusman, M. (1980). Stress-induced analgesia: Neural and hormonal determinants. *Neuroscience and Biobehavioral Reviews, 4,* 87–100.

Bogen, J. E. (1977). Educational implications of recent research on the human brain. In M. C. Wittrock (Ed.), *The human brain.* Englewood Cliffs, N. J.: Prentice-Hall.

Bolles, R. C., & Faneslow, M. S. (1982). Endorphins and behavior. *Annual Review of Psychology, 33,* 87–101.

Bonica, J. J. (Ed.) (1980). *Research publication: Association for research in nervous and mental disease: Vol. 58. Pain.* New York: Raven.

Bonsall, R. W., Zumpe, D., & Michael, R. P. (1978). Menstrual cycle influences on operant behavior of female rhesus monkeys. *Journal of Comparative and Physiological Psychology, 92,* 846–855.

Bourguignon, E., & Greenbaum, L. S. (1973). *Diversity and homogeneity in world societies.* New Haven: HRAF.

Boynton, R. M. (1988). Color vision. *Annual Review of Psychology, 39,* 69–100.

Boyle, P. C., Storlien, L. H., Harper, A. E., & Keesey, R. E. (1981). Oxygen consumption and locomotor activity during restricted feeding and realimentation. *American Journal of Physiology, 241,* R392–R397.

Bradley, P., & Horn, G. (1981). Imprinting: A study of cholinergic receptor sites in parts of the chick brain. *Experimental Brain Research, 41,* 121–123.

———, & Bateson, P. (1981). Imprinting: An electron microscopic study of chick hyperstriatum ventrale. *Experimental Brain Research, 41,* 115–120.

Brasel, J. A., & Blizzard, R. M. (1974). The influence of the endocrine glands upon growth and development. In R. H. Williams (Ed.), *Textbook of endocrinology.* Philadelphia: Saunders.

Brazier, M. A. B. (1959). The historical development of neurophysiology.'' In *Handbook of Physiology. Section I. Neurophysiology. Vol. 1.* Washington, D.C.: American Physiological Society.

Bredberg, G. (1968). Cellular pattern and nerve supply of the human organ of Corti. *Acta Otolaryngologica,* Supplement 236.

Breedlove, S. M. (1984). Steroid influences on the development and function of a neuromuscular system. In G. J. De Vries, J. P. C. De Bruin, H. B. M. Uylings, & M. A. Corner (Eds.), *Progress in brain research: Vol. 61. Sex differences in the brain* (pp. 147–170). Amsterdam: Elsevier Science Publishers.

———, & Arnold, A. P. (1981). Sexually dimorphic motor nucleus in the rat lumbar spinal cord: Response to adult hormone manipulation, absence in androgen-insensitive rats. *Brain Research, 225,* 297–307.

Brenowitz, E. A., & Arnold, A. (1986). Interspecific comparisons of the size of neural song control regions and song complexity in dueting birds: Evolutionary implications. *Journal of Neuroscience, 6,* 2875–2879.

Brodmann, K. (1909). *Vergleichende Lokisationslehre der Grosshinrinde in ihren Prinzipien dargestellt auf Grund des Zellenbaues.* Leipzig: Barth.

Brooks, V. B. (1984). Cerebellar function in motor control. *Human Neurobiology, 2,* 251–260.

Broughton, R. (1985). Slow-wave sleep awakenings in normal and in pathology: A brief review. In W. P. Koella, E. Ruther, & H. Schulz (Eds.), *Sleep '84* (pp. 164–167). Stuttgart: Gustav Fischer Verlag.

Brown, W. A., & Heninger, G. (1975). Cortisol, growth hormone, free fatty acids and experimentally evoked affective arousal. *American Journal of Psychiatry, 132,* 1172–1176.

Brown, W. L. (1968). An hypothesis concerning the function of the metapleural gland in ants. *American Naturalist, 102,* 188–191.

Brudny, J., Korein, J., Grynbaum, B. B., Firedman, L. W., Weinstein, S., Sachs-Frankel, G., & Belandres, P. V. (1976). EMG feedback therapy: Review of treatment of 114 patients. *Archives of Physical Medicine and Rehabilitation, 57,* 55–61.

Bruneau, N., Roux, S., Perse, J., & LeLord, G. (1984). Frontal evoked responses, stimulus-intensity control, and the extraversion dimension. *Annals of the New York Academy of Science, 425,* 546–550.

Bruner, J. S. (1969). Modalities of memory. In G. A. Talland and N. C. Waugh (Eds.), *The pathology of memory.* New York: Academic.

Bryden, M. P. (1982). *Laterality: Functional asymmetry in the intact brain.* New York: Academic.

Buchsbaum, M., Mirsky, A., DeLisi, L. E., Morihisa, J., Karson, C.,

Mendelson, W., Johnson, J., King, A., & Kessler, R. (1984), The Genain quadruplets: Electrophysiological, positron emission and X-ray tomographic studies. *Psychiatry Research, 13,* 95–108.

Buchsbaum, M. S., & Haier, R. J. (1987). Functional and anatomical brain imaging: Impact on schizophrenia research. *Schizophrenia Bulletin, 13,* 115–132.

Bullock, T. H. (1984). Comparative neuroscience holds promise for quiet revolutions. *Science, 225,* 473–478.

———, Orkand, R., & Grinell, A. (1977). *Introduction to nervous systems.* San Francisco: Freeman.

Bureš, J., & Burešová, O. (1980). Elementary learning phenomena in food selection. *Proceedings of the International Union of Physiological Sciences, 14,* 13–14.

Burger, B., & Levy, W. B. (1985). Long-term associative potentiation/depression as an analogue of classical conditioning. *Society for Neuroscience Abstracts, 11,* part 2.

Bushnell, M. C., Robinson, D. L., & Goldberg, M. (1978). Dissociation of movement and attention: Neuronal correlates in posterior parietal cortex. *Society for Neuroscience Abstracts, 4,* 621.

Busse, E. W., & Silverman, A. J. (1952). Electroencephalographic changes in professional boxers. *Journal of the American Medical Association, 149,* 1522–1525.

Butters, N., & Cermak, L. S. (1980). *Alcoholic Korsakoff's syndrome: An information-processing approach to amnesia.* New York: Academic.

Butters, N., & Ryan, C. (1979). Memory deficits of detoxified alcoholics: evidence for the premature aging and continuity hypotheses. *International Neuropsychological Society Bulletin, 12.*

Buzsaki, G. (1985). What does the "LTP model of memory" model? In B. E. Will, P. Schmidt, & J. C. Dalrymple-Alford (Eds.), *Advances in behavioral biology: Vol. 28. Brain plasticity, learning, and memory.* New York: Plenum.

Byrne, D. G., & Whyte, H. M. (1980). Life events and myocardial infarction revisited. *Psychosomatic Medicine, 42,* 1–10.

Cabanac, M. (1971). Physiological role of pleasure. *Science, 173,* 1103–1107.

Calne, D. B., Langston, J. W., & Martin, W. R. (1985). Positron emission tomography after MPTP: Observations relating to the cause of Parkinson's disease. *Nature, 317,* 246–248.

Calne, R., Williams, R., Dawson, J., Ansell, I., Evans, D., Flute, P., Herbertson, B., Joysey, V., Keates, G., Knill-Jones, R., Mason, S., Millard, P., Pena, J., Pentlow, B., Salaman, J., Sells, R., & Cullum, P. (1968). Liver transplantation in Man-II, a report of two orthotopic liver transplants in adult recipients. *British Medical Journal, 4,* 541–546.

Camhi, J. M. (1984). *Neuroethology.* Sunderland, Mass.: Sinauer Associates Inc.

Campbell, B. A., & Coulter, X. (1976). The ontogenesis of learning and memory. In M. R. Rosenzweig & E. L. Bennett (Eds.), *Neural mechanisms of learning and memory* (pp. 209–235). Cambridge: MIT Press.

Campbell, F. W. (1974). The transmission of spatial information through the visual system. In F. O. Schmitt & F. G. Warden (Eds.), *The neurosciences: Third study program.* Cambridge: MIT Press.

Campbell, F. W., & Robson, J. G. (1968). Application of Fourier analysis to the visibility of gratings. *Journal of Physiology* (London), *197,* 551–566.

Campbell, S. S., and Tobler, I. (1984). Animal sleep: A review of sleep duration across phylogeny. *Neuroscience and Biobehavioral Reviews, 8,* 269–301.

Canady, R., Kroodama, D., & Nottebohm, F. (1981). Significant differences in volume of song control nuclei is associated with variance in song repertoire in a free ranging song bird. *Society for Neuroscience Abstracts, 7,* 845.

Cannon, W. B. (1929). *Bodily changes in pain, hunger, fear and rage.* New York: Appleton.

Carew, T. J. (1988). The developmental dissociation of multiple components of learning and memory in *Aplysia.* In J. L. McGaugh, N. M. Weinberger, & G. Lynch (Eds.), *Brain organization and memory: cells, systems, and circuits.* New York: Oxford.

———, Hawkins, R. D., & Kandel, E. R. (1984). Differential classical conditioning of a defensive withdrawal reflex in *Aplysia californica. Science, 219,* 397–400.

———, & Sahley, C. L. (1986). Invertebrate learning and memory: From behavior to molecules. *Annual Review of Neurosciences, 9,* 435–487.

———, Walters, E. T., & Kandel, E. R. (1981). Associative learning in a simple reflex of *Aplysia. Society for Neuroscience Abstracts, 7,* 353.

———. (1981). Classical conditioning in a simple withdrawal reflex in *Aplysia California. The Journal of Neuroscience, 1,* 1426–1437.

Carlton, P. L., & Manowitz, P. (1984). Dopamine and schizophrenia: An analysis of the theory. *Neuroscience and Biobehavioral Reviews, 8,* 137–153.

Cartwright, R. D. (1977). *Night life: Explorations in dreaming.* Englewood Cliffs, N.J.: Prentice-Hall.

Casson, I. R., Sham, R., Campbell, E. A., Tarlau, M., & Didomenico, A. (1982). Neurological and CT evaluation of knocked-out boxers. *Journal of Neurology, Neurosurgery, and Psychiatry, 45,* 170–174.

Caviness, V. S. (1980). The developmental consequences of abnormal cell position in the reeler mouse. *Trends in Neuroscience, 3,* 31–33.

Cespuglio, R., Faradji, H., Guidon, G., & Jouvet, M. (1984). Voltametric detection of brain 5-hydoxyindolamines: A new technology applied to sleep research. In A. Borbely & J.-L. Valatx (Eds.), *Sleep mechanisms* (pp. 95–106). Berlin: Springer-Verlag.

Chall, J., & Mirsky, A. (Eds.) (1978). *Education and the brain.* Chicago: National Society for the Study of Education Yearbook.

Chall, J. S., & Peterson, R. W. (1986). The influence of neuroscience on educational practice. In S. L. Friedman, K. A. Klivington, & R. W. Peterson (Eds.), *The brain, cognition, and education* (pp. 287–318). New York: Academic.

Challamel, M. J., Lahlou, S., & Jouvet, M. (1985). Sleep and smiling in neonate: A new approach. In W. P. Koella, E. Ruther, & H. Schulz (Eds.), *Sleep '84.* Stuttgart: Gustav Fischer Verlag.

Chan-Palay, V., Allen, Y. S., Lang, W., Haesler, U., & Polak, J. M. (1985). I. Cytology and distribution in normal human cerebral cortex of neurons immunoreactive with antisera against neuropeptide Y. *Journal of Comparative Neurology, 238,* 382–390.

Chang, F.-L., & Greenough, W. T. (1984). Transient and enduring morphological correlates of synaptic activity and efficacy change in the rat hippocampal slice. *Brain Research, 309,* 35–46.

———. (1982). Lateralized effects of monocular training on dendritic branching in adult split-brain rats. *Brain Research, 232,* 283–292.

Chapman, C. R., Casey, K. L., Dubner, R., Foley, K. M., Gracely, R. H., & Reading, A. E. (1985). Pain measurement: an overview. *Pain, 22,* 1–31.

Cheng, M.-F. (1977). Egg fertility and prolactin as determinants of reproductive recycling in doves. *Hormones and Behavior, 9,* 85–98.

———. (1974). Ovarian development in the female ring dove in response to stimulation by intact and castrated male ring doves. *Journal of Endocrinology, 63,* 43–53.

———. (1979). Progress and prospects in ring dove research: A personal view. *Advances in the Study of Behavior, 9,* 97–129.

Chiarello, C., Knight, R., & Mundel, M. (1982). Aphasia in a prelingually deaf woman. *Brain, 105,* 29–52.

Chui, H. C., & Damasio, A. R. (1980). Human cerebral asymmetries evaluated by computerized tomography. *Journal of Neurology, Neurosurgery, and Psychiatry, 43,* 873–878.

———. (1980). Human cerebral asymmetries evaluated by computed tomography. *Journal of Neurology, Neurosurgery, and Psychiatry, 43,* 873–878.

Cipolla-Neto, J., Horn, G., & McCabe, B. J. (1982). Hemispheric asymmetry and imprinting: The effect of sequential lesions to the hyperstriatum ventrale. *Experimental Brain Research, 48,* 22–27.

Cloninger, C. R. (1987). Neurogenetic adaptive mechanisms in alcoholism. *Science, 236,* 410–416.

———, & Reich, T. (1983). Genetic heterogeneity in alcoholism and sociopathy. In S. Kety, L. Rowland, R. Sidman, & S. Matthysse (Eds.), *Genetics of neurological and psychiatric disorders.* New York: Raven.

Clutton-Brock, T. H., and Harvey, P. H. (1980). Primates, brains and ecology. *Journal of Zoology, 190,* 309–323.

Cohen, D. B. (1979). *Sleep and dreaming: Origin, nature and functions.* Oxford: Pergamon.

Cohen, D. H. (1985). Some organizational principles of a vertebrate conditioning pathway: Is memory a distributed property? In N. M. Weinberger, J. L. McGaugh, & G. Lynch (Eds.), *Memory systems of the brain* (pp. 27–48). New York: Guilford.

Cohen, H. D., Ervin, F., & Barondes, S. H. (1966). Puromycin and cycloheximide: different effects on hippocampal electrical activity. *Science, 154,* 1552–1558.

Cohen, N. J., & Squire, L. R. (1981). Retrograde amnesia and remote memory impairment. *Neuropsychologia, 19,* 337–356.

———. (1980). Preserved learning and retention of pattern-analyzing skill in amnesia: Dissociation of knowing how and knowing what. *Science, 210,* 207–210.

Colangelo, W., & Jones, D. G. (1982). The fetal alcohol syndrome: A review and assessment of the syndrome and its neurological sequelae. *Progress in Neurobiology, 19,* 271–314.

Coltheart, M. (1980). Deep dyslexia: A right hemisphere hypothesis. In M. Coltheart, K. Patterson, & J. C. Marshall (Eds.), *Deep dyslexia.* London: Routledge & Kegan Paul.

Conel, J. L. (1939–1963). *The postnatal development of the human cerebral cortex, 6 volumes.* Cambridge: Harvard.

Cooper, J. R., Bloom, F. E., & Roth, R. H. (1982). *The biochemical basis of neuropharmacology* (4th ed.). New York: Oxford.

Cooper, K. E. (1987). The neurobiology of fever: Thoughts on recent developments. *Annual Review of Neuroscience, 10,* 297–324.

Corbett, S. W., & Keesey, R. E. (1982). Energy balance of rats with lateral hypothalamic lesions. *American Journal of Physiology, 242,* E273–E279.

Corkin, S. (1984). Lasting consequences of bilateral medial temporal lobectomy: Clinical course and experimental findings in H. M. *Seminars in Neurology, 4,* 249–259.

———, Milner, B., & Rasmussen, T. (1970). Somatosensory thresholds: Contrasting effects of postcentral-gyrus and posterior parietal-lobe excisions. *Archives of Neurology, 23,* 41–58.

———, Sullivan, E. V., Twitchell, T. E., & Grove, E. (1981). The amnesic patient H. M.: Clinical observations and test performance 28 years after operation. *Society for Neuroscience Abstracts, 7,* 235.

Cotman, C., & Nieto-Sampedro, M. (1982). Brain function, synapse renewal, and plasticity. *Annual Review of Psychology, 33,* 371–402.

Cowan, W. M. (1979). The development of the brain. *Scientific American, 241*(3), 112–133.

———, & Wenger, E. (1967). Cell loss in the trochlear nucleus of the chick during normal development and after radical extirpation of the optic vesicle. *Journal of Experimental Zoology, 164,* 267–280.

Cowey, A. (1967). Perimetric study of field defects after cortical and retinal ablations. *Quarterly Journal of Experimental Psychology, 19,* 232–245.

Coyle, J. T., Price, D. L., & DeLong, M. R. (1983). Alzheimer's disease: a disorder of cortical cholinergic innervation. *Science, 219,* 1184–1190.

Cragg, B. G. (1967). Changes in visual cortex on first exposure of rats to light: Effect on synaptic dimensions. *Nature, 215,* 251–253.

———. (1975). The development of synapses in the visual system of the cat. *Journal of Comparative Neurology, 160,* 147–166.

Craik, F. I. M. (1986). A functional account of age differences in memory.

In F. Klix and H. Hogendorf (Eds.), *Human memory and cognitive capabilities. Vol. A* (pp. 409–422). Amsterdam: North-Holland.

Creasey, H., and Rapoport, S. I. (1985). The aging human brain. *Annals of Neurology, 17,* 2–11.

Crick, F., & Mitchison, G. (1983). The function of dream sleep. *Nature, 304,* 111–114.

Crile, G., & Quiring, D. P. (1940). A record of the body weight and certain organ and gland weights of 3690 animals. *Ohio Journal of Science, 40,* 219–259.

Cruce, J. A. F., Greenwood, M. R. C., Johnson, P. R., & Quartermain, D. (1974). Genetic versus hypothalamic obesity: Studies of intake and dietary manipulation in rats. *Journal of Comparative and Physiological Psychology, 87,* 295–301.

Culler, E., & Mettler, F. A. (1934). Conditioned behavior in a decorticate dog. *Journal of Comparative Psychology, 18,* 291–303.

Cummings, J. L., Benson, D. F., Walsh, M. J., & Levine, H. L. (1979). Left-to-right transfer of language dominance: A case study. *Neurology, 29,* 1547–1550.

Curcio, C. A., Sloan, K. R., Packer, O., Hendrickson, A. E., & Kalina, R. E. (1987). Distribution of cones in human and monkey retina: individual variability and radial asymmetry. *Science, 236,* 579–582.

Curtis, S. Genie. (1977). A psycholinguistic study of a modern day 'wild child.' *Perspectives in neurolinguistics and psycholinguistics series.* New York: Academic.

Cutting, J. E. (1978). Generation of synthetic male and female walkers through manipulation of a biomechanical invariant. *Perception, 7,* 393–405.

Czeisler, C. A., Richardson, G. S., Coleman, R. M., Zimmerman, J. C., Moore-Ede, M. C., Dement, W. C., & Weitzman, E. D. (1981). Chronotherapy: Resetting the circadian clocks of patients with delayed sleep phase insomnia. *Sleep, 4,* 1–21.

Daana, S., Beersma, D. G. M., & Borbely, A. A. (1984). Timing of human sleep; recovery process gated by a circadian pacemaker. *American Journal of Physiology, 246,* R161–178.

Dallos, P. (1973). *The auditory periphery. Biophysics and physiology.* New York: Academic.

Daly, M., & Wilson, M. (1978). *Sex, evolution and behavior.* Belmont, Cal.: Duxbury.

Damasio, A. (1981). The nature of aphasia: Signs and syndromes. In M. T. Sarno (Ed.), *Aphasia* (pp. 51–67). New York: Academic.

Damasio, A. R., Chui, H. C., Corbett, J., & Kassel, N. (1980). Posterior callosal section in a non-epileptic patient. *Journal of Neurology, Neurosurgery, and Psychiatry, 43,* 351–356.

———, Graff-Radford, P. J., Eslinger, H., Damasio, H., & Kassell, N. (1985b). Amnesia following basal forebrain lesions. *Archives of Neurology, 42,* 263–271.

Damassa, D. A., Smith, E. R., Tennent, B., & Davidson, J. M. (1977). The relationship between circulating testosterone levels and male sexual behavior in rats. *Hormones and Behavior, 8,* 275–286.

Darian-Smith, I. (1982). Touch in primates. *Annual Review of Psychology, 33,* 155–194.

———, Davidson, I., & Johnson, K. O. (1980). Peripheral neural representations of the two spatial dimensions of a textured surface moving over the monkey's finger pad. *Journal of Physiology, 309,* 135–146.

Dark, J., Forger, N. G., & Zucker, I. (1984). Rapid recovery of body mass after surgical removal of adipose tissue in ground squirrels. *Proceedings of the National Academy of Sciences, U.S.A., 81,* 2270–2272.

Darwin, C. (1871). *The descent of man and selection in relation to sex.* London: John Murray.

Davenport, J. W. (1976). Environmental therapy in hypothyroid and other disadvantaged animal populations. In R. N. Walsh, & W. T. Greenough (Eds.), *Environments as therapy for brain dysfunction.* New York: Plenum.

Davenport, W. H. (1977). Sex in cross-cultural perspective. In F. A. Beach (Ed.), *Human sexuality in four perspectives* (pp. 115–163). Baltimore: Johns Hopkins University.

Davidson, J. (1972). Hormones and reproductive behavior. In H. Balin, & S. Glasser (Eds.), *Reproductive Biology*. Amsterdam: Exerpta Medica.

Davidson, J. M. (1966). Activation of the male rat's sexual behavior by intracerebral implantation of androgen. *Endocrinology, 79,* 783–794.

———. (1966). Characteristics of sex behaviour in male rats following castration. *Animal Behaviour, 14,* 266–272.

———, Camargo, C. A., & Smith, E. R. (1979). Effects of androgen on sexual behavior in hypogonadal men. *Journal of Clinical Endocrinology and Metabolism, 48,* 955–958.

———, Smith, E. R., Rodgers, C. H., & Bloch, F. J. (1968). Relative thresholds of behavioral and somatic responses to estrogen. *Physiology and Behavior, 3,* 227–229.

Davis, H. P., & Squire, L. R. (1984). Protein synthesis and memory: A review. *Psychological Bulletin, 96,* 518–559.

Davis, K. L., Mohs, R. C., Tinklenberg, J. R., Pfefferbau, A., Hollister, L. E., & Kopell, B. S. (1978). Physostigmine: Improvement of long-term memory processes in normal humans. *Science, 201,* 272–274.

DeArmond, S. J., Fusco, M. M., & Dewey, M. M. (1976). *Structure of the human brain*. New York: Oxford.

Dekaban, A. S., & Sadowsky, D. (1978). Changes in brain weights during the span of human life: Relation of brain weights to body heights and body weights. *Annals of Neurology, 4,* 345–356.

Delgado-Escueta, A. V., Mattson, R. H., King, L., Goldensohn, E. S., Spiegel, H., Madsen, J., Crandall, P., Dreifuss, F., & Porter, R. J. (1981). The nature of aggression during epileptic seizures. *New England Journal of Medicine, 305,* 711–716.

DeLisi, L. E., Mirsky, A., Buchsbaum, M., van Kammen, D. P., Berman, K., Kafka, M., Ninan, P., Phelps, B., Karoum, F., Ko, G., Korpi, E., Linnoila, M., Sheinan, M., & Wyatt, R. (1984). The Genain quadruplets 25 years later: A diagnostic and biochemical followup. *Psychiatry Research, 13,* 59–76.

Denckla, M. B. (1979). Childhood learning disabilities. In K. M. Heilman, & E. Valenstein (Eds.), *Clinical neuropsychology*. New York: Oxford.

Dennis, S. G., & Melzack, R. (1983). Perspectives on phylogenetic evolution of pain expression. In R. L. Kitchell, H. H. Erickson, E. Carstens, & L. E. Davis (Eds.), Animal pain (pp. 151–161). Bethesda: American Physiological Society.

Desaki, J., & Uehara, Y. (1981). The overall morphology of neuromuscular junction as revealed by scanning electron microscopy. *Journal of Neurocytology, 10,* 101–110.

Desmedt, J. E. (Ed.) (1978). *Progress in clinical neurophysiology. (Vol. 4): Cerebral motor control in man: Long loop mechanisms*. Basel: Karger.

Dethier, V. G. (1976). *The hungry fly: A physiological study of behavior associated with feeding*. Cambridge: Harvard.

Deutsch, J. A. (1971). The cholinergic synapse and the site of memory. *Science, 174,* 788–794.

———. (1978). The stomach in food satiation and the regulation of appetite. *Progress in Neurobiology, 10,* 135–153.

De Valois, R. L., & De Valois, K. K. (1975). Neural coding of color. In *Handbook of perception: Seeing* (Vol. 5). New York: Academic.

———. (1980). Spatial vision. *Annual Review of Psychology, 31,* 309–341.

———, Morgan, H., & Snodderly, M. (1974). Psychophysical studies of monkey vision—III. Spatial luminance contrast sensitivity tests of macaque and human observers. *Vision Research, 14,* 75–81.

———, Albrecht, D. G., & Thorell, L. G. (1977). Spatial tuning of LGN and cortical cells in monkey visual system. In H. Spekreijse & L. H. van der Tweel (Eds.), *Spatial Contrast*. Amsterdam: North Holland.

Devinsky, O., & Bear, D. (1984). Varieties of aggressive behavior in

temporal lobe epilepsy. *American Journal of Psychiatry, 141,* 651–656.

De Vries, G. J., De Bruin, J. P. C., Uylings, H. B. M., & M. A. Corner, M. A. (Eds.) (1984). *Progress in brain research: Vol. 61. Sex differences in the brain*. Amsterdam: Elsevier Science Publishers.

Dewsbury, D. A. (1975). Diversity and adaptation in rodent copulatory behavior. *Science, 190,* 947–954.

Dewson, J. H. (1968). Efferent olivocochlear bundle: Some relationships to stimulus discrimination in noise. *Journal of Neurophysiology, 31,* 122–130.

Diamond, I. T. (1982). The functional significance of architectonic subdivisions of the cortex: Lashley's criticism of the traditional view. In J. Orbach (Ed.), *Neuropsychology after Lashley* (pp. 101–135). New York: Plenum.

Diamond, J., Cooper, E., Turner, C., & Macintyre, L. (1976). Trophic regulation of nerve sprouting. *Science, 193,* 371–377.

Diamond, Jared. (1986). The case of vagrant birds—or, left coast, here we come. *Discover* (January), 82–84.

Diamond, M. C. (1976). Anatomical brain changes induced by environment. In L. Petrinovich and J. L. McGaugh (Eds.), *Knowing, Thinking, and Believing* (pp. 215–241). New York: Plenum.

———. (1980). New data supporting cortical asymmetry differences in males and females. *The Behavioral and Brain Sciences, 3,* 233–234.

———, Dowling, G. M., & Johnson, R. E. (1980). Morphologic cerebral cortex asymmetry in male and female rats. *Experimental Neurology, 71,* 261–268.

———, Krech, D., & Rosenzweig, M. R. (1964). The effects of an enriched environment on the histology of the rat cerebral cortex. *Journal of Comparative Neurology, 123,* 111–119.

———, Law, F., Rhodes, H., Lindner, B., Rosenzweig, M. R., Krech, D., & Bennett, E. L. (1966). Increases in cortical depth and glia numbers in rats subjected to enriched environment. *Journal of Comparative Neurology, 128,* 117–125.

———, Lindner, B., Johnson, R., Bennett, E. L., & Rosenzweig, M. R. (1975). Differences in occipital cortical synapses from environmentally enriched, impoverished, and standard colony rats. *Journal of Neuroscience Research, 1,* 109–119.

Disterhoft, J. F., Coulter, D. A., & Alkon, D. L. (1985). Biophysical alterations of rabbit hippocampal neurons studied *in vitro* after conditioning. *Society for Neuroscience Abstracts, 11,* part 2, 291.

Dobbing, J. (1976). Vulnerable periods in brain growth and somatic growth. In D. F. Roberts & A. M. Thomson (Eds.) *The biology of human fetal growth* (pp. 137–147). London: Taylor and Francis.

Dohler, K. D., Hancke, J. L., Srivastava, S. S., Hofmann, C., Shryne, J. E., & Gorski, R. A. (1984). Participation of estrogens in female sexual differentiation of the brain; neuroanatomical, neuroendocrine and behavioral evidence. In G. J. De Vries, J. P. C. De Bruin, H. B. M. Uylings, & M. A. Corner (Eds.), *Progress in brain research: Vol. 61. Sex differences in the brain* (pp. 99–117). Amsterdam: Elsevier Science Publishers.

Dolphin, A. C., Errington, M. L., & Bliss, T. V. P. (1982). Long-term potentiation of the perforant path in vivo is associated with increased glutamate release. *Nature, 297,* 496–498.

Dörner, G., Döcke, F., & Moustafa, S. (1968b). Differential localization of a male and a female hypothalamic mating centre. *Journal of Reproduction and Fertility,* 583–586.

———. (1968a). Homosexuality in female rats following testosterone implantation in the anterior hypothalamus. *Journal of Reproduction and Fertility, 17,* 173–175.

Douglas, R. J. (1967). The hippocampus and behavior. *Psychological Bulletin, 67,* 416–422.

Drachman, D. A. (1978). Central cholinergic system and memory. In M. A. Lipton, A. DiMascio, & K. F. Killam (Eds.), *Psychopharmacology: A generation of progress*. New York: Raven.

Drachman, D. B. (1981). The biology of myasthenia gravis. *Annual Re-*

view of Neurosciences, 4, 195–225.

———. (1983). Myasthenia gravis: Immunobiology of a receptor disorder. *Trends in Neurosciences, 6,* 446–450.

Drucker-Colin, R., Shkurovich, M., & Sterman, M. B. (Eds.) (1973). *The functions of sleep.* New Haven: Yale.

Druckman, D., & Swets, J. (1988). *Enhancing human performance.* Washington, D.C.: National Academy Press.

Dudai, Y. (1988). Neurogenic dissection of learning and short term memory in Drosophila. *Annual Review of Neuroscience, 11,* 537–563.

Dudai, Y., & Quinn, W. G. (1980). Genes and learning in *Drosophila. Trends in Neurosciences, 3,* 28–30.

Dudai, Y., Jan, Y.-N., Byers, D., Quinn, W. G., & Benzer, S. (1976). *Dunce,* a mutant of *Drosophila* deficient in learning. *Proceedings of the National Academy of Sciences, U.S.A., 73,* 1684–1688.

D'Udine, B., & Alleva, E. (1983). Early experience and sexual preferences in rodents. In P. Bateson (Ed.), *Mate choice* (pp. 311–327). Cambridge: Cambridge University Press.

Duerr, J. S., & Quinn, W. G. (1982). Three *Drosophila* mutations that block associative learning also affect habituation and sensitization. *Proceedings of the National Academy of Sciences, U.S.A., 79,* 3646–3650.

Eccles, J. C. (1983). Calcium in long-term potentiation as a model for memory. *Neuroscience, 10,* 1071–1081.

———. (1965). Possible ways in which synaptic mechanisms participate in learning, remembering and forgetting. In D. P. Kimble (Ed.), *The anatomy of memory* (pp. 12–87). Palo Alto: Science and Behavior Books, Inc.

———. (1982). The synapse: From electrical to chemical transmission. *Annual Review of Neuroscience, 5,* 325–339.

———. (1973). *The understanding of the brain.* New York: McGraw-Hill.

Egeland, J. A., & Hostetter, A. M. (1983). Amish study, I: Affective disorders among the Amish, 1976–1980. *American Journal of Psychiatry, 140,* 56–71.

Ehrhardt, A. A., & Meyer-Bahlburg, H. F. L. (1981). Effects of prenatal sex hormones on gender-related behavior. *Science, 211,* 1312–1318.

Eikelboom, R., & Stewart, J. (1981). Temporal and environmental cues in conditioned hypothermia and hyperthermia associated with morphine. *Psychopharmacology, 72,* 147–153.

Eisenberg, J. F., & Wilson, D. E. (1978). Relative brain size and feeding strategies in Chiroptera. *Evolution, 32,* 740–751.

Ekman, P. (1981). Methods for measuring facial action. In K. Scherer & P. Ekman (Eds.), *Handbook on methods of nonverbal communications research.* New York: Cambridge University Press.

———. (1972). Universals and cultural differences in facial expressions of emotion. *Nebraska Symposium on Motivation,* 207–283.

———, & Oster, H. (1979). Facial expressions of emotion. *Annual Review of Psychology, 30,* 527–554.

———, Hager, J. C., & Friesen, W. V. (1981). The symmetry of emotional and deliberate facial actions. *Psychophysiology, 18,* 101–106.

Ekstrand, B. R., Barrett, T. R., West, J. M., & Maier, W. G. (1977). The effect on human long-term memory. In R. Drucker-Colin & J. L. McGaugh (Eds.), *Neurobiology of sleep and memory.* New York: Academic.

Eliasson, S. G., Prensky, A. L., & Hardin, W. B. (1974). *Neurological pathophysiology.* New York: Oxford.

Elmadjian, F., Hope, J. M., & Lamson, E. T. (1957). Excretion of epinephrine and norepinephrine in various emotional states. *Journal of Clinical Endocrinology, 17,* 608–620.

———. (1958). Excretion of epinephrine and norepinephrine under stress. *Recent Progress in Hormone Research, 14,* 513.

Elsinger, P. J., & Damasio, A. R. (1986). Preserved motor learning in Alzheimer's disease: Implication for anatomy and behavior. *Journal of Neuroscience, 6,* 3006–3009.

Engel, A. G. (1984). Myasthenia gravis and myasthenic syndromes. *Annals of Neurology, 16,* 519–535.

Entingh, D., Dunn, A., Wilson, J. E., Glassman, E., & Hogan, E. (1975). Biochemical approaches to the biological basis of memory. In M. S. Gazzaniga & C. Blakemore (Eds.), *Handbook of Psychobiology.* New York: Academic.

Epstein, A. N., Fitzsimons, J. T., & Rolls, B. J. (1970). Drinking induced by injection of angiotensin into the brain of the rat. *Journal of Physiology* (London), *210,* 457–474.

Epstein, C. J., Cox, D. R., Schonberg, S. A., & Hogge, W. A. (1983). Recent developments in the prenatal diagnosis of genetic diseases and birth defects. *Annual Review of Genetics, 17,* 49–83.

Erdmann, G., & Janke, W. (1978). Interaction between physiological and cognitive determinants of emotions: Experimental studies on Schachter's theory of emotions. *Biological Psychology, 6,* 61–74.

Erickson, C. J. Sexual affiliation in animals: Pair bonds and reproductive strategies. (1978). In J. B. Hutchison (Ed.), *Biological determinants of sexual behaviour* (pp. 697–725). New York: Wiley.

Eslinger, P. J., & Damasio, A. R. (1986). Preserved motor learning in Alzheimer's disease: Implications for anatomy and behavior. *Journal of Neuroscience, 6,* 3006–3009.

Evans, C. (1983). *Landscapes of the night. How and why we dream.* New York: Viking Press.

Evarts, E. V. (1972). Contrasts between activity of precentral and postcentral neurons of cerebral cortex during movement in the monkey. *Brain Research, 40,* 25–31.

———. (1971). Feedback and corollary discharge: A merging of the concepts. *Neurosciences Research Program Bulletin, 9,* 86–112.

———. (1968). Relation of pyramidal tract activity to force exerted during voluntary movement. *Journal of Neurophysiology, 31,* 14–28.

———, Shinoda, Y., & Wise, S. P. (1984). Neurophysiological approaches to higher brain functions. New York: Wiley.

Everitt, B. J. (1978). A neuroanatomical approach to the study of monoamines and sexual behaviour. In J. B. Hutchison (Ed.), *Biological determinants of sexual behaviour* (pp. 555–574). New York: Wiley.

———, and Herbert, J. (1971). The effects of dexamethasone and androgens on sexual receptivity of female rhesus monkeys. *Journal of Endocrinology, 51,* 575–588.

———. (1975). The effects of implanting testosterone propionate into the central nervous system on the sexual behavior of adrenalectomized female rhesus monkeys. *Brain Research, 86,* 109–120.

Faraone, S. V., & Tsuang, M. T. (1985). Quantitative models of the genetic transmission of schizophrenia. *Psychological Bulletin, 98,* 41–66.

Farley, J., & Alkon, D. L. (1981). Associative neural and behavioral change in *Hermissenda:* Consequences of nervous system orientation for light- and pairing-specificity. *Society for Neuroscience Abstracts, 7,* 352.

———. (1985). Cellular mechanisms of learning, memory, and information storage. *Annual Review of Psychology, 36,* 419–494.

Feder, H. H. (1971). The comparative actions of testosterone propionate and 5α-androstran-17βol-3-one propionate on the reproductive behaviour, physiology, and morphology of male rats. *Journal of Endocrinology, 51,* 241–252.

Feder, H. (1984). Hormones and sexual behavior. *Annual Review of Psychology, 35,* 165–200.

Federman, D. D. (1979). Endocrinology. Chapter 3, *Scientific American Medicine.* New York: Scientific American.

Feinberg, I. (1982). Schizophrenia: Caused by a fault in programmed synaptic elimination during adolescence. *Journal of Psychiatry Research, 17,* 319–334.

Feldman, R. S., & Quenzer, L. F. (1984). *Fundamentals of neuropsychopharmacology.* Sunderland, Mass.: Sinauer Associates.

Ferchmin, P. A., Bennett, E. L., & Rosenzweig, M. R. (1975). Direct contact with enriched environments is required to alter cerebral weights in rats. *Journal of Comparative and Physiological Psychology, 88,* 360–367.

Fibiger, H. C., & Lloyd, K. G. (1984). The neurobiological substrates of tardive dyskinesia: the GABA hypothesis. *Trends in Neurosciences, 8,* 462.

Fields, H. (1981). Pain II. New approaches to pain management. *Annals of Neurology, 9,* 100–106.

Finger, S. (Ed.) (1978). *Recovery from brain damage: Research and theory.* New York: Plenum.

Fifkova, E., Anderson, C. L., Young, S. J., & Van Harreveld, A. (1982). Effect of anisomycin on stimulation-induced changes in dendritic spines of the dentate granule cells. *Journal of Neurocytology, 11,* 183–210.

Firedman, M., & Rosenman, R. H. (1959). Association of specific overt behavior pattern with blood and cardiovascular findings. *Journal of the American Medical Association, 169,* 1286–1296.

Fisher-Perroudon, C., Mouret, J., & Jouvet, M. (1974). Sur un cas d'agrypnie (4 mois sans sommeil) au cours d'une maladie de Morvan. Effet favorable du 5-hydroxytryptophane. *Electroencephalography and Clinical Neurophysiology, 36,* 1–18.

Fitzgerald, F. T. (1981). The problem of obesity. *Annual Review of Medicine, 32,* 221–231.

Flexner, J. B., Flexner, L. B., Stellar, E., de la Haba, G., & Roberts, R. B. (1962). Inhibition of protein synthesis in brain and learning following puromycin. *Journal of Neurochemistry, 9,* 595–605.

Flood, J. F., Bennett, E. L., Orme, A. E., & Rosenzweig, M. R. (1975). Relation of memory formation to controlled amounts of brain protein synthesis. *Physiology and Behavior, 15,* 97–102.

Flood, J. F., Bennett, E. L., Rosenzweig, M. R., & Orme, A. E. (1973). The influence of duration of protein synthesis inhibition on memory. *Physiology and Behavior, 10,* 555–562.

Flood, J. F., & Cherkin, A. (1981). Cholinergic drug interactions: enhancement and impairment of memory retention. *Society for Neuroscience Abstracts, 7,* 359.

Flood, J. F., Jarvik, M. E., Bennett, E. L., Orme, A. E., & Rosenzweig, M. R. (1977). The effect of stimulants, depressants and protein synthesis inhibition on retention. *Behavioral Biology, 20,* 168–183.

Foster, F. M., & Sherrington, C. S. (1897). *A textbook of physiology. Part 3. The central nervous system.* New York: Macmillan.

Foster, N. L., Cahse, T. N., Mansi, L., Brooks, R., Fedio, P., Patronas, N. J., & Di Chiro, G. (1984). Cortical abnormalities in Alzheimer's disease. *Annals of Neurology, 16,* 649–654.

Fox, M. W. (1970). Reflex development and behavioral organization. In W. A. Himwich (Ed.), *Developmental neurobiology.* Springfield, Ill.: Charles C. Thomas.

Frankenhaeuser, M. (1979). Psychoneuroendocrine approaches to the study of emotion as related to stress and coping. *Current theory and research in motivation, 26,* 123–162.

Frazier, W. T., Kandel, E. R., Kupfermann, I., Waziri, R., & Coggeshall, R. E. (1967). Morphological and functional properties of identified neurons in the abdominal ganglion of Aplysia californica. *Journal of Neurophysiology, 30,* 1288–1351.

Freeman, W. J. (1975). *Mass action in the nervous system.* New York: Academic.

———, & Watts, J. W. (1950). *Psychosurgery in the treatment of mental disorders and intractable pain.* Springfield, Ill.: Charles C. Thomas.

Freund, H.-J. (1984). Premotor areas in man. *Trends in Neuroscience, 7,* 481–483.

Fridlund, A. (1988). What can asymmetry and laterality in EMG tell us about the face and brain? *International Journal of Neuroscience, 39,* 53–69.

Frieder, B., & Allweis, C. (1982). Memory consolidation: further evidence for the four-phase model from the time courses of diethyldithiocarbamate and ethacrinic acid amnesias. *Physiology and Behavior, 29,* 1071–1075.

Friedman, M. B. (1977). Interactions between visual and vocal courtship stimuli in the neuroendocrine response of female doves. *Journal of Comparative and Physiologic Psychology, 91,* 1408–1416.

Friedman, S. L., Klivington, K., & Peterson, R. W. (Eds.) (1986). *The brain, cognition, and education.* New York: Academic.

Furshpan, E. J., & Potter, D. D. (1957). Mechanism of nerve impulse transmission at a crayfish synapse. *Nature, 180,* 342–343.

Gage, F. H., & Bjørklund, A. (1986). Cholinergic septal grants into the hippocampal formation improve spatial learning and memory in aged rats by an atropine-sensitive mechanism. *Journal of Neuroscience, 6,* 2837–2847.

Galaburda, A. M., & Kemper, T. L. (1978). Cytoarchitectonic abnormalities in developmental dyslexia: A case study. *Annals of Neurology, 6,* 94–100.

Galaburda, A. M., Sanides, F., & Geschwind, N. (1978). Human brain: Cytoarchitectonic left-right asymmetries in the temporal speech region. *Archives of Neurology, 35,* 812–817.

Galaburda, A. M., Sherman, G. F., Rosen, G. D., Aboitiz, F., & Geschwind, N. (1985). Developmental dyslexia: four consecutive patients with cortical anomalies. *Annals of Neurology, 18,* 222–234.

Gallagher, M. (1985). Re-viewing modulation of learning and memory. In N. M. Weinberger, J. L. McGaugh, & G. Lynch (Eds.), *Memory systems of the brain* (pp. 311–334). New York: Guilford.

———, King, R. A., & Young, N. B. (1983). Opiate antagonists improve spatial memory. *Science, 221,* 975–976.

Garb, J. L., & Stunkard, A. J. (1974). Taste aversions in man. *American Journal of Psychiatry, 131,* 1204–1207.

Gardner, L. I. (1972). Deprivation dwarfism. *Scientific American, 227*(1), 76–82.

Gelperin, A. (1975). Rapid food-aversion learning by a terrestrial mollusk. *Science, 189,* 567–570.

Gerkema, M. P., & Daan, S. (1985). Ultradian rhythms in behavior: The case of the common vole (Microtus arvalis). In H. Schulz & P. Lavie (Eds.), *Ultradian rhythms in physiology and behavior* (pp. 11–32). Berlin: Springer-Verlag.

Gerstein, D. R., Luce, R. D., Smelser, N. J., & Sperlich, S. (Eds.) (1988). *The behavioral and social sciences: Achievements and opportunities.* Washington, D.C.: National Academy Press.

Geschwind, N. (1976). Language and cerebral dominance. In T. N. Chase (Ed.), *Nervous system. Vol. 2. The clinical neurosciences* (pp. 433–439). New York: Raven.

——— (1972). Language and the brain. *Scientific American, 226*(4), 76–83.

——— (1983). Pathogenesis of behavior change in temporal lobe epilepsy. *Research Publications Association for Research in Nervous and Mental Diseases, 61,* 355–370.

———, & Galaburda, A. M. (1985). Cerebral lateralization: Biological mechanisms, associations and pathology. *Archives of Neurology, 42,* 428–459, 521–654.

———, & Levitsky, W. (1968). Human brain: Left-right asymmetries in temporal speech region. *Science, 161,* 186–187.

Gibbs, J., & Smith, G. P. (1984). The neuroendocrinology of postprandial satiety. In L. Martini & W. F. Ganong (Eds.), *Frontiers in neuroendocrinology. Vol. 8.* New York: Raven.

———, Young, R. C., & Smith, G. P. (1973). Cholecystokinin decreases food intake in rats. *Journal of Comparative and Physiological Psychology, 84,* 488–495.

Gibbs, M. E., & Ng, K. T. (1977). Psychobiology of memory: Towards a model of memory formation. *Biobehavioral Reviews, 1,* 113–136.

Gibbs, M. E., & Lecanuet, J.-P. (1981). Disruption of imprinting by memory inhibitors. *Animal Behaviour, 29,* 572–580.

Gilbert, A., Fridlund, A., & Sabini, J. Hedonic and social determinants of facial displays to odors. *Unpublished manuscript.*

Gillin, J. C., Sitaram, N., Janowsky, D., Risch, C., Huey, L., & Storch, F. (1985). Cholinergic mechanisms in REM sleep. In A. Wauquier, J. M. Gaillard, J. Monti, & M. Radulovacki (Eds.), *Sleep: Neurotransmitters and neuromodulators* (pp. 153–165). New York: Raven.

Gilman, A. (1937). The relation between blood osmotic pressure, fluid distribution and voluntary water intake. *American Journal of Physiology, 120,* 323–328.

Gilman, S., Bloedel, J. R., & Lechtenberg, R. (1981). *Disorders of the cerebellum.* Philadelphia: F. A. Davis.

Ginsburg, A. P. (1971). Psychological correlates of a model of the human visual system. Masters thesis. Wright-Patterson AFB, Ohio, Air Force Institute of Technology.

————, & Campbell, F. W. (1977). Optical transforms and the ''pincushion grid'' illusion? *Science, 198,* 961–962.

Glassman, E., Machlus, B., & Wilson, J. E. (1972). The effect of short experiences on the incorporation of radioactive phosphate into acid-soluble nuclear proteins of rat brain. In J. L. McGaugh (Ed.), *The chemistry of mood, motivation and memory.* New York: Plenum.

Glick, S. D., & Shapiro, R. M. (1985). Functional and neurochemical mechanisms of cerebral lateralization in rats. In S. D. Glick (Ed.), *Cerebral lateralization in nonhuman species.* Orlando, Florida: Academic.

Gloor, P., Olivier, A., Quesney, L. F., Andermann, F., & Horowitz, S. (1982). The role of the limbic system in experiential phenomena of temporal lobe epilepsy. *Annals of Neurology, 12,* 129–144.

Gluhbegovic, N., & Williams, T. H. (1980). *The human brain.* New York: Harper & Row.

Glickman, S. E. (1977). Comparative psychology. In P. Mussen and M. R. Rosenzweig (Eds.), *Psychology: An introduction, second edition.* Lexington, Mass.: D. C. Heath.

Globus, A., Rosenzweig, M. R., Bennett, E. L., & Diamond, M. C. (1973). Effects of differential experience on dendritic spine counts in rat cerebral cortex. *Journal of Comparative and Physiological Psychology, 82,* 175–181.

Goldberger, M. E., & Murray, M. (1985). Recovery of function and anatomical plasticity after damage to the adult and neonatal spinal cord. In Cotman, C. (Ed.), *Synaptic plasticity* (pp. 77–111). New York: Guilford.

Gold, P. E., & McGaugh, J. L. (1975). A single-trace, two-process view of memory storage processes. In D. Deutsch & J. A. Deutsch (Eds.), *Short-term memory* (pp. 355–378). New York: Academic.

Goldfine, I. D., Abraira, C., Gruenwald, D., & Goldstein, M. S. (1970). Plasma insulin levels during imaginary food ingestion under hypnosis. *Proceedings of the Society for Experimental Biology and Medicine, 133,* 274–276.

Goldman, P. S. (1976). Maturation of the mammalian nervous system and the ontogeny of behavior. In J. S. Rosenblatt, *Advances in the study of behavior, 7,* 1–90.

Goodman, C. (1979). Isogenic grasshoppers: Genetic variability and development of identified neurons. In Breakefeld, X. O. (Ed.), *Neurogenetics.* New York: Elsevier.

Gormezano, I. (1972). Investigations of defense and reward conditioning in the rabbit. In A. H. Black & W. F. Prokasy (Eds.), *Classical Conditioning II: Current Research and Theory* (pp. 151–181). New York: Appleton-Century-Crofts.

Gorski, R. A., Gordon, J. H., Shryne, J. E., & Southam, A. M. (1978). Evidence for a morphological sex difference within the medial preoptic area of the rat brain. *Brain Research, 148,* 333–346.

Gottlieb, G. (1976). The roles of experience in the development of behavior and the nervous system. In G. Gottlieb (Ed.), *Studies on the development of behavior and the nervous system (Volume 3) Neural and behavioral specificity.* New York: Academic.

Goulart, F. S. (1984). *The caffeine book.* New York: Dodd, Mead.

Gouras, P. (1985). Color vision. In E. R. Kandel, & J. H. Schwartz, (Eds.), *Principles of neural science* (2nd ed.) (pp. 366–383). New York: Elsevier.

Gould, J. L. (1986). The biology of learning. *Annual Review of Psychology, 37,* 163–192.

Goy, R. W., & Phoenix, C. A. (1971). The effects of testosterone propionate administered before birth on the development of behavior in genetic female rhesus monkeys. In C. Sawyer & R. Gorski (Eds.), *Steroid hormones and brain function* (pp. 193–201). Berkeley: University of California Press.

Goy, R. W., & Resko, J. A. (1972). Gonadal hormones and behavior of normal and pseudohermaphroditic nonhuman female primates. *Recent Progress in Hormone Research, 28,* 707–733.

Graf, P., & Schacter, D. (1987). Selective effects of interference on implicit and explicit memory for new associations. *Journal of Experimental Psychology: Learning, Memory, and Cognition,*

————, Squire, L. R., & Mandler, G. (1984). The information that amnesic patients do not forget. *Journal of Experimental Psychology [Learning, Memory and Cognition], 11,* 386–396.

Granit, R. (1977). *The purposive brain.* Cambridge: MIT Press.

Gray, J. A. G. (1982). *The neurobiology of anxiety: An enquiry into the functions of the septo-hippocampal system.* New York: Oxford.

Graziadei, P. P. C., Levine, R. R., & Graziadei, G. A. M. (1979). Plasticity of connections of the olfactory sensory neuron: Regeneration into the forebrain following bulbectomy in the neonatal mouse. *Neuroscience, 4,* 713–728.

Graziadei, P. P. C., & Monti-Graziadei, G. A. (1978). Continuous nerve cell renewal in the olfactory system. In M. Jacobson (Ed.), *Handbook of sensory physiology: Development of sensory systems.* Berlin: Springer.

Green, B. F., & Hall, J. A. (1984). Quantitative methods for literature reviews. *Annual Review of Psychology, 35,* 37–53.

Green, W. H., Campbell, M., & David, R. (1984). Psychosocial dwarfism: A critical review of evidence. *Journal of Child Psychiatry, 39–48.*

Greenough, W. T. (1976). Enduring brain effects of differential experience and training. In M. R. Rosenzweig & E. L. Bennett (Eds.), *Neural mechanisms of learning and memory.* Cambridge: MIT Press.

————. (1985). The possible role of experience-dependent synaptogenesis, or synapses on demand. In N. M. Weinberger, J. L. McGaugh, & G. Lynch (Eds.), *Memory systems of the brain* (pp. 77–103). New York: Guilford.

————, & Volkmar, F. R. (1973). Pattern of dendritic branching in occipital cortex of rats reared in complex environments. *Experimental Neurology, 40,* 491–504.

Greenspan & Quinn (1984); see Quinn & Greenspan (1984).

Greer, S. (1983). Cancer and the mind. *British Journal of Psychiatry, 143,* 535–543.

Grennewalt, C. H. (1968). *Bird song: Acoustics and physiology.* Washington, D.C.: Smithsonian.

Grevert, P., & Goldstein, A. (1985). Placebo analgesia, naloxone, and the role of endogenous opioids. In L. White, B. Tursky & G. E. Schwartz (Eds.), *Placebo* (pp. 332–351). New York: Guilford.

Griffith, V. E. (1970). *A Stroke in the Family: A Manual of Home Therapy.* New York: Delacorte.

Grillner, S. (1985). Neurobiological bases of rhythmic motor acts in vertebrates. *Science, 228,* 143–149.

Grillner, S., & Rossignol, S. (1978). On the initiation of the swing phase of locomotion in chronic spinal cats. *Brain Research, 146,* 269–277.

Grillner, S., & Wallen, P. (1985). Central pattern generators for locomotion, with special reference to vertebrates. *Annual Review of Neuroscience, 8,* 233–263.

Grillner, S., & Zangger, P. (1979). On the central generation of locomotion in the low spinal cat. *Experimental Brain Research, 34,* 241–261.

Grings, W. W., & Davison, M. E. (1978). *Emotions and bodily responses: A psychophysiological approach.* New York: Academic.

Grossman, S. P., Dacey, D., Halaris, A. E., Collier, T., & Routtenberg,

A. (1978). Aphagia and adipsia after preferential destruction of nerve cell bodies in hypothalamus. *Science, 202,* 537–539.

Groves, P. M., & Rebec, G. V. (1976). Biochemistry and behavior: Some central actions of amphetamine and antipsychotic drugs. *Annual Review of Psychology, 27,* 97–128.

Grunt, J. A., & Young, W. C. (1953). Consistency of sexual behavior patterns in individual male guinea pigs following castration and androgen therapy. *Journal of Comparative and Physiological Psychology, 46,* 138–144.

Gur, R. E. (1979). Cognitive concomitants of hemispheric dysfunction in schizophrenia. *Archives of General Psychiatry, 36,* 269–274.

Gurney, M. E. (1981). Hormonal control of cell form and number in the zebra finch. *Journal of Neuroscience, 1,* 658–673.

Gusella, J. F., Wexler, N. S., Conneally, P. M., Naylor, S. L., Anderson, M. A., Tanzi, R. F., et al. (1983). A polymorphic DNA marker genetically linked to Huntington's disease. *Nature, 306,* 234–238.

Guttmann, G. (1986). Fluctuations of learning capacity. In F. Klix & H. Hagendorf (Eds.), *Human memory and cognitive capacities* (Vol. B, pp. 639–648). Amsterdam: Elsevier Science Publishers.

———, & Bauer, H. (1982). Learning and information processing in dependence on cortical DC-potentials. In R. Sinz & M. R. Rosenzweig (Eds.), *Psychophysiology 1980: Memory, motivation and event-related potentials in mental operations* (pp. 141–149). Jena: VEB Gustav Fischer Verlag, and Amsterdam: Elsevier Biomedical Press.

Hadley, M. E. (1984). *Endocrinology.* Englewood Cliffs, N.J.: Prentice-Hall.

Hagbarth, K. E., & Kugelberg, E. (1958). Plasticity of the human abdominal skin reflex. *Brain, 81,* 305–318.

Hager, J. (1982). Asymmetries in facial expression. In P. Ekman (Ed.), *Emotion in the human face.* (pp. 318–352). New York: Cambridge University Press.

Hall, J. C., & Greenspan, R. J. (1979). Genetic analysis of Drosophila neurobiology. *Annual Review of Genetics, 13,* 127–195.

———, & Harris, W. A. (1982). *Genetic neurobiology.* Cambridge: MIT Press.

Hall, W. G., & Oppenheim, R. W. (1987). Developmental psychobiology: Prenatal, perinatal, and early postnatal aspects of behavioral development. *Annual Review of Psychology, 38,* 91–128.

Hallett, P. E., & Lightstone, A. D. (1976). Saccadic eye movements towards stimuli triggered by prior saccades. *Vision Research, 16,* 99–106.

Hamburger, V. (1975). Cell death in the development of the lateral motor column of the chick embryo. *Journal of Comparative Neurology, 160,* 535–546.

Hampson, J. L. (1965). Determinants of psychosexual orientation. In F. A. Beach (Ed.), *Sex and behavior.* New York: Wiley.

Haracz, J. L. (1984). A neural plasticity hypothesis of schizophrenia. *Neuroscience and Biobehavioral Reviews, 8,* 55–73.

Hardy, J. B. (1973). Fetal consequences of maternal viral infections in pregnancy. *Archives of Otolaryngology, 98,* 218–227.

Hardyck, C., Petrinovich, L., & Goldman, R. (1976). Left-handedness and cognitive deficit. *Cortex, 12,* 226–279.

Harlow, H. F. (1959). The development of learning in the rhesus monkey. *American Scientist, 47,* 459–479.

———. (1949). The formation of learning sets. *Psychological Review, 56,* 51–65.

Harris, R. S., & Martin, R. (1984). Specific depletion of body fat in parabiotic partners of tube-fed obese rats. *American Journal of Physiology, 247,* R380–R386.

Hart, B. L. (1973). Effects of testosterone propionate and dihydrotestosterone on penile morphology and sexual reflexes of spinal male rats. *Hormones and Behavior, 4,* 239–246.

———. (1974). Gonadal androgen and sociosexual behavior of male mammals: A comparative analysis. *Psychological Bulletin, 81,* 383–400.

———. (1978). Hormones, spinal reflexes, and sexual behaviour. In J. B. Hutchison (Ed.), *Biological determinants of sexual behaviour* (pp. 319–347). New York: Wiley.

Harter, S. (1965). Discrimination learning set in children as a function of intelligence and mental age. *Journal of Experimental Child Psychology, 2,* 31–43.

Hartmann, E. (1984). *The nightmare: The psychology and biology of terrifying dreams.* New York: Basic Books.

———. (1978). *The sleeping pill.* New Haven: Yale.

Hasan, Z., & Stuart, D. G. (1988). Animal solutions to problems of movement control: The role of proprioceptors. *Annual Review of Neurosciences, 11,* 199–225.

Hawkins, R. D. and Abrams, T. W., Carew, T. J., & Kandel, E. R. (1983). A cellular mechanism of classical conditioning in *Aplysia:* activity-dependent amplification of presynaptic facilitation. *Science, 219,* 400–405.

Hawkins, R. D., & Kandel, E. R. (1984). Is there a cell-biological alphabet for simple forms of learning? *Psychological Review, 91,* 376–391.

———. (1984). Steps toward a cell-biological alphabet for elementary forms of learning. In G. Lynch, J. L. McGaugh, & N. M. Weinberger (Eds.), *Neurobiology of learning and memory* (pp. 385–404). New York: Guilford.

Haycock, J. W., van Buskirk, R., & McGaugh, J. L. (1977). Effects of catecholaminergic drugs upon memory storage processes in mice. *Behavioral Biology, 20,* 281–310.

Heath, R. G. (1972). Pleasure and brain activity in man. *Journal of Nervous and Mental Diseases, 154,* 3–18.

———, Franklin, D. E., & Shraberg, D. (1979). Gross pathology of the cerebellum in patients diagnosed and treated as functional psychiatric disorders. *Journal of nervous and mental disorders, 167,* 585–592.

Hebb, D. O. (1980). *Essay on mind.* Hillsdale, N.J.: Erlbaum.

———. (1949). *The organization of behavior.* New York: Wiley.

Hefti, F., & Weiner, W. J. (1986). Nerve growth factor and Alzheimer's disease. *Annals of Neurology, 20,* 275–281.

Heilman, K. M., & Rothi, L. J. Gonzales. (1985). Apraxia. In K. M. Heilman, & E. Valenstein (Eds.), *Clinical neuropsychology.* 2nd edition. New York: Oxford.

Heilman, K., & Valenstein, E. (Eds.) (1985). *Clinical neuropsychology.* New York: Oxford, 2nd edition.

Heilman, K. M., & Watson, R. T. (1983). Performance on hemispatial pointing task by patients with neglect syndrome. *Neurology, 33,* 661–664.

Heinrich, B. (1979). Keeping a cool head: Honeybee thermoregulation. *Science, 205,* 1269–1271.

———. (1981). The regulation of temperature in the honeybee swarm. *Scientific American, 244*(6), 146–160.

Held, R., & Hein, A. (1963). Movement-produced stimulation in the development of visually guided behavior. *Journal of Comparative and Physiological Psychology, 56,* 872–876.

Heller, H. C., Cranshaw, L. I., & Hammel, H. T. (1978). The thermostat of vertebrate animals. *Scientific American, 239*(2), 102–113.

Hemmingsen, A. M. (1960). Energy metabolism as related to body size and respiratory surfaces, and its evolution. *Reports of Steno Memorial Hospital, Copenhagen, 9,* 1–110.

Henderson, N. (1982). Human behavior genetics. *Annual Review of Psychology, 33,* 403–440.

Hendrickson, A. (1985). Dots, stripes and columns in monkey visual cortex. *Trends in NeuroSciences, 8,* 406–410.

Herbert, J. (1978). Neuro-hormonal integration of sexual behaviours in female primates. In J. B. Hutchison (Ed.), *Biological determinants of sexual behaviour* (pp. 467–491). New York: Wiley.

Hermann, B. P., & Whitman, S. (1984). Behavioral and personality correlates of epilepsy: A review, methodological critique, and conceptual model. *Psychological Bulletin, 95,* 451–497.

Hernandez, L., & Hoebel, B. G. (1980). Basic mechanisms of feeding and weight regulation. In A. J. Stunkard (Ed.), *Obesity*. Philadelphia: Saunders.

Herron, J. (Ed.) (1980). *Neuropsychology of left-handedness*. New York: Academic.

Hetherington, A. W., & Ranson, S. W. (1940). Hypothalamic lesions and adiposity in the rat. *Anatomical record, 78*, 149–172.

Hewes, G. (1973). Primate communication and the gestural origin of language. *Current Anthropology, 14*, 5–24.

Hicks, C. S. (1964). Terrestrial animals in cold: Exploratory studies of primitive man. In D. B. Dill (Ed.), *Handbook of Physiology* (Sec. 4, Vol. 1). Washington, D. C.: American Physiological Society.

Hille, B. (1975). The receptor for tetrodotoxin and saxitoxin: A structural hypothesis. *Biophysical Journal, 15*, 615–619.

Hillyard, S. (1982). Psychobiology. In F. Bloom (Ed.), *Outlook for science and technology, the next five years. 3* (pp. 73–96). Washington, D.C.: National Academy Press.

Hillyard, S. A., Simpson, G. V., Woods, D. L., van Voorhis, S., & Munte, T. F. (1984). Event-related brain potentials and selective attention to different modalities. In F. Reinoso-Suarez and C. Ajmone-Marsan (Eds.), *Cortical integration*. New York: Raven.

Hingson, R., Alpert, J., Day, N., Dooling, E., Kayne, H., Morelock, S., Oppenheimer, E., & Zuckerman, B. (1982). Effects of maternal drinking and marijuana use on fetal growth and development. *Pediatrics, 70*, 539–546.

Hirsch, H. V. B., & Spinelli, D. N. (1971). Modification of the distribution of receptive field orientation in cats by selective visual exposure during development. *Experimental Brain Research, 12*, 509–527.

Hochberg, F. H., & Le May, M. (1975). Arteriographic correlates of handedness. *Neurology, 25*, 218–222.

Hodgkin, A. L., & Huxley, A. F. (1952). A quantitative description of membrane current and its application to conduction and excitation in nerve. *Journal of Physiology* (London), *117*, 500–544.

Hodgkin, A. L., & Katz, B. (1949). The effect of sodium ions on the electrical activity of the giant axon of the squid. *Journal of Physiology* (London), *108*, 37–77.

Hodos, W. (1970). Evolutionary interpretation of neural and behavioral studies of living vertebrates. In F. O. Schmitt (Ed.), *The neurosciences: Second study program*. New York: Rockefeller University.

Hoffman, K.-P., Stone, J. (1971). Conduction velocity of afferents to cat visual cortex: A correlation with cortical receptive field properties. *Brain Research, 32*, 460–466.

Hohman, G. W. (1966). Some effects of spinal cord lesions on experienced emotional feelings. *Psychophysiology, 3*, 143–156.

Honzik, M. (1984). Life-span development. *Annual Review of Psychology, 35*, 309–331.

Horel, J. A. (1978). The neuroanatomy of amnesia: A critique of the hippocampal memory hypothesis. *Brain, 101*, 403–445.

———, and Misantone, L. G. (1974). The Klüver-Bucy syndrome produced by partial isolation of the temporal lobe. *Experimental Neurology, 42*, 101–112.

———, & Misantone, L. G. (1976). Visual discrimination impaired by cutting temporal lobe connections. *Science, 193*, 336–338.

Horn, G. (1985). *Memory, imprinting, and the brain*. Oxford: Clarendon Press.

———, Rose, S. P. R., & Bateson, P. P. G. (1973). Experience and plasticity in the central nervous system. Is the nervous system modified by experience? Are such modifications involved in learning? *Science, 181*, 506–514.

———, Bradley, P., & McCabe, J. (1985). Changes in the structure of synapses associated with learning. *Journal of Neuroscience, 5*, 3161–3168.

Horne, J. A. (1981). The effects of exercise upon sleep: A critical review. *Biological Psychology, 12*, 241–290.

Hosobuchi, Y., Adams, J. E., & Linchitz, R. (1977). Pain relief by electrical stimulation of the central gray matter in humans and its reversal by naloxone. *Science, 197*, 183–186.

Hotta, Y., & Benzer, S. (1976). Courtship in *Drosophila* mosaics: Sex-specific foci of sequential action patterns. *Proceedings of the National Academy of Sciences*, U.S.A., *73*, 4154–4158.

Hoyle, G. (1970). How is muscle turned on? *Scientific American, 222*(4), 84–93.

Hubbard, R. L., Rachal, J. V., Craddock, S. G., & Cavanaugh, E. R. (1984). Treatment Outcome Prospect Study (TOPS): client characteristics and behaviors before, during, and after treatment. In F. M. Tims & J. P. Ludford (Eds.), *Drug abuse treatment evaluation: strategies, progress, and prospects*. Washington, D.C.: NIDA Research Monograph 51, National Institute of Drug Abuse.

Hubel, D. H., & Wiesel, T. N. (1962), Receptive fields, binocular interaction, and functional architecture in the cat's visual cortex. *Journal of Physiology, 160*, 106–154.

———. (1965). Binocular interaction in striate cortex kittens reared with artificial squint. *Journal of Neurophysiology, 28*, 1041–1059.

———. (1970). The period of susceptibility to the physiological effects of unilateral eye closure in kittens. *Journal of Physiology* (London), *206*, 419–436.

———. (1979). Brain mechanisms of vision. *Scientific American, 241*, 150–168.

Hudspeth, A. J. (1983). Mechanoelectrical transduction by hair cells in the acoustolateralis sensory system. *Annual Review of Neuroscience, 6*, 187–215.

Hughes, J., Smith, T. W., Kosterlitz, H. W., Fothergill, L. A., Morgan, B. A., & Morris, H. R. (1975). Identification of two related pentapeptides from the brain with potent opiate agonist activity. *Nature, 258*, 577–579.

Humphrey, N. K. (1970). What the frog's eye tells the monkey's brain. *Brain, behavior and evolution, 3*, 324–337.

Humphrey, T. (1964). Some correlations between the appearance of human fetal reflexes and the development of the nervous system. *Progress in Brain Research, 4*, 93–135.

Hunter, W. S. (1913). The delayed reaction in animals and children. *Behavior Monographs, 2*.

Huppert, F. A., & Piercy, M. (1978). Dissociation between learning and remembering in organic amnesia. *Nature, 275*, 317–318.

———. (1979). Normal and abnormal forgetting in organic amnesia: Effect of locus of lesion. *Cortex, 15*, 385–390.

Hurst, M. W., Jenkins, D., & Rose, R. M. (1976). The relation of psychological stress to onset of medical illness. *Annual Review of Medicine*, 301–312.

Hutchison, J. B. (Ed.), (1978). *Biological determinants of sexual behaviour*. New York: Wiley.

———. (1971). Effects of hypothalamic implants of gonadal steroids on courtship behaviour in Barbary doves (*Streptopelia risoria*). *Journal of Endocrinology, 50*, 97–113.

———. (1976). Hypothalamic mechanisms of sexual behaviour, with special reference to birds. In J. S. Rosenblatt, R. A. Hinde, E. Shaw, & C. Beer (Eds.), *Advances in the study of behaviour* (Vol. 6). New York: Academic.

———. (1978). Hypothalamic regulation of male sexual responsiveness to androgen. In J. B. Hutchison (Ed.), *Biological determinants of sexual behaviour* (pp. 277–317). New York: Wiley.

Huttenlocher, P. R., deCourten, C., Garey, L. J., & Van der Loos, H. (1982). Synaptogenesis in the human visual cortex—evidence for synapse elimination during normal development. *Neuroscience Letters, 33*, 247–252.

Idzikowski, C. (1984). Sleep and memory. *British Journal of Psychology, 75*, 439–449.

Imperato-McGinley, J., Guerrero, L., Gautier, T., & Peterson, R. E. (1974). Steroid 5 α-reductase deficiency in man: an inherited form of male pseudohermaphroditism. *Science, 86,* 1213–1215.

Imperato-McGinley, J., Peterson, R. E., Gautier, T., & Sturla, E. (1979). Androgens and the evolution of male-gender identity among male pseudohermaphrodites with 5α reductase deficiency. *New England Journal of Medicine, 300,* 1233–1237.

———. (1981). The impact of androgens on the evolution of male gender identity. In S. J. Kogan & E. S. E. Hafez (Eds.), *Clinics in andrology. Vol. 7. Pediatric andrology* (pp. 99–108). Boston: Nijhoff.

Ingvar, D. H., & Lassen, N. A. (1979). Activity distribution in the cerebral cortex in organic dementia as revealed by measurements of regional cerebral blood flow. *Bayer Symposium VII, Brain Function in Old Age,* 268–277.

Inouye, S. T. (1985). Unpublished studies cited in Turek, F., 1985 (noted below).

Isaacson, R. L. (1972). Hippocampal destruction in man and other animals. *Neuropsychologia, 10,* 47–64.

Iversen, L. L., & Bloom, F. E. (1972). Studies of the uptake of ³H-GABA and (³H) glycine in slices and homogenates of rat brain and spinal cord by electric microscopic autoradiography. *Brain Research, 41,* 131–143.

Iwamura, Y., & Tanaka, M. (1978). Postcentral neurons in hand region of area 2: Their possible role in the form discrimination of tactile objects. *Brain Research, 150,* 662–666.

Izquierdo, I. (1979). Effect of naloxone and morphine on various forms of memory in the rat: Possible role of endogenous opiate mechanisms in memory consolidation. *Psychopharmacology, 66,* 199–203.

———, Dias, R., Perry, M. L., et al. (1982). A physiological amnestic mechanism mediated by endogenous opioid peptides, and its possible role in learning. In C. Ajmone-Marsan and H. Matthies (Eds.), *Neuronal plasticity and memory formation* (pp. 89–113). New York: Raven.

Jacobs, B. L., & Trulson, M. E. (1979). Mechanisms of action of LSD. *American Scientist, 67,* 397–404.

Jacobson, M. (1978). *Developmental neurobiology.* New York: Plenum.

———. A plentitude of neurons. (1974). In G. Gottlieb (Ed.), *Studies of the development of behavior and the nervous system,* (Vol. 2), *Aspects of neurogenesis.* New York: Academic.

Jaffe, J. H. (1980). Drug addiction and drug abuse. In A. G. Gilman, L. S. Goodman, & A. Gilman (Eds.), *The pharmacological basis of therapeutics, 6th ed.* New York: Macmillan.

James, W. (1980). *Principles of psychology.* New York: Holt.

Jellies, J. A. (1981). Associative olfactory conditioning in *Drosophila melanogaster* and memory retention through metamorphosis. Unpublished Masters thesis, Illinois State University at Normal, Illinois.

Jemmott, J. B., & Locke, S. E. (1984). Psychosocial factors, immunologic mediation, and human susceptibility to infectious diseases: How much do we know? *Psychological Bulletin, 95,* 78–108.

Jenkins, H. (1984). The study of animal learning in the tradition of Pavlov and Thorndike. In P. Marler & H. S. Terrace (Eds.), *The biology of learning.* New York: Springer-Verlag.

Jenkins, J., & Dallenbach, K. (1924). Oblivescence during sleep and waking. *American Journal of Psychology, 35,* 605–612.

Jenkinson, D. H., & Nicholls, J. G. (1961). Contractures and permeability changes produced by acetylcholine in depolarized denervated muscle. *Journal of Physiology* (London), *159,* 111–127.

Jensen, C. (1977). Generality of learning differences in brain-weight-selected mice. *Journal of Comparative and Physiological Psychology, 91,* 629–641.

———. (1979). Learning performance in mice genetically selected for brain weight: Problems of generality. In M. E. Hahn, C. Jensen, & B. C. Dudek (Eds.), *Development and evolution of brain size.* New York: Academic.

———, & Fuller, J. L. (1978). Learning performance varies with brain weight in heterogeneous mouse lines. *Journal of Comparative and Physiological Psychology, 92,* 830–836.

Jensen, D. W. (1979). Vestibular compensation: Tonic spinal influence upon spontaneous descending vestibular nuclear activity. *Neuroscience, 4,* 1075–1084.

Jensen, R. A., Martinez, J. L., Messing, R. B., Spiehler, V., et al. (1978). Morphine and naloxone alter memory in rat. *Society for Neuroscience Abstracts, 4,* 260.

Jerison, H. J. (1973). *Evolution of the brain and intelligence.* New York: Academic.

John, E. R. (1977). *Functional neuroscience. Vol. 2 Neurometrics: Clinical applications of quantitative electrophysiology.* Hillsdale, N.J.: Erlbaum.

———, & Schwartz, E. L. (1978). The neurophysiology of information processing and cognition. *Annual Review of Psychology, 29,* 1–29.

Johnson, D. F., & Phoenix, C. H. (1978). Sexual behavior and hormone levels during the menstrual cycles of rhesus monkeys. *Hormones and Behavior, 11,* 160–174.

Johnson, L. C. (1969). Psychological and physiological changes following total sleep deprivation. In Kales, A. (Ed.), *Sleep: Physiology and pathology.* Philadelphia: Lippincott.

Johnston, P., & Davidson, J. M. (1973). Intracerebral androgens and sexual behavior in the male rat. *Hormones and Behavior, 3,* 345–357.

Jones, R. (1977). Anomalies of disparity in the human visual system. *Journal of Physiology, 264,* 621–640.

Jouvet, M. (1967). Neurophysiology of the states of sleep. In G. C. Quarton, T. Melnechuk, & F. O. Schmitt (Eds.), *The Neurosciences,* 529–544. New York: Rockefeller University.

———. (1972). The role of monoamines and acetylcholine containing neurons in the regulation of the sleep waking cycle. *Ergebnisse der Physiologie* (Reviews of Physiology), *64,* 166–307.

Julesz, B. (1971). *Foundations of cyclopean perception.* Chicago: University of Chicago.

———, & Spivack, G. J. (1967). Stereopsis based on vernier acuity cues alone. *Science, 157,* 563–565.

Julien, R. M. (1981). *A primer of drug action* (3rd ed.). San Francisco: Freeman.

Juraska, J. M. (1984). Sex differences in developmental plasticity in the visual cortex and hippocampal dentate gyrus. In G. J. De Vries, J. P. C. De Bruin, H. B. M. Uylings, & M. A. Corner (Eds.), *Progress in brain research: Vol. 61. Sex differences in the brain* (pp. 205–214). Amsterdam: Elsevier Science Publishers.

Kaada, B. (1967). Brain mechanisms related to aggressive behavior. In C. D. Clemente & D. B. Lindsley (Eds.), *Aggression and defense.* Berkeley: University of California.

Kaas, J. H., Merzenich, M. M., & Killackey, H. P. (1983). The reorganization of somatosensory cortex following peripheral nerve damage in adult and developing mammals. *Annual Review of Neuroscience, 6,* 325–356.

Kales, A., & Kales, J. (1970). Evaluation, diagnosis and treatment of clinical conditions related to sleep. *Journal of the American Medical Association, 213,* 2229–2235.

Kalil, K., & Rey, T. (1979). Regrowth of severed axons in the neonatal central nervous system: establishment of normal connections. *Science, 205,* 1158–1161.

Kalow, W. (1984). Pharmacoanthropology: Outline, problems, and the nature of case histories. *Federation Proceedings, 43(8),* 2314–2318.

Kandel, E. R. *Cellular basis of behavior.* San Francisco: Freeman, 1976.

———. Small systems of neurons. *Scientific American,* 1979, *241(3),* 66–76.

———, Schacher, S., Castellucci, V. F., & Goelet, P. (1986). The long and short of memory in *Aplysia:* a molecular perspective. *Fidia Research Foundation neuroscience award lectures* (pp. 7–47). Padova,

Italy: Liviana Press.

———, & Schwartz, J. H. *Principles of neural science*. New York: Elsevier/North-Holland, 1981.

Kanof, P., & Greengard, P. (1978). Brain histamine receptors as targets for antidepressant drugs. *Nature, 272*, 329–333.

Kaplan, H. S. (1974). *The New Sex Therapy*. New York: Brunner/Mazel.

Karp, L. E. (1976). *Genetic engineering: Threat or promise*. Chicago: Nelson-Hall.

Kasamatsu, T., & Pettigrew, J. D. (1979). Preservation of binocularity after monocular deprivation in the striate cortex of kittens treated with 6-hydroxydopamine. *Journal of Comparative Neurology, 185*, 139–162.

Katchadourian, H. A., & Lunde, D. T. (1980), *Fundamentals of human sexuality (3rd ed.)*. New York: Holt.

Kaushall, P. I., Zetin, M., & Squire, L. R. (1981). A psychosocial study of chronic, circumscribed amnesia. *The Journal of Nervous and Mental Disease, 169*(6), 383–389.

Keele, S. W., & Summers, J. J. (1976). The structure of motor programs. In Stelmach, G. E. (Ed.), *Motor control: Issues and trends*. New York: Academic.

Keesey, R. E. (1980). A set-point analysis of the regulation of body weight. In A. J. Stunkard (Ed.), *Obesity*. Philadelphia: Saunders.

———, & Boyle, P. C. (1973). Effects of quinine adulteration upon body weight of LH-lesioned and intact male rats. *Journal of Comparative and Physiological Psychology, 84*, 38–46.

———, & Corbett, S. W. (1984). Metabolic defence of the body weight set-point. In A. J. Stunkard & E. Stellar (Eds.), *Eating and its disorders* (pp. 87–96). New York: Raven.

———, & Powley, T. L. (1986). The regulation of body weight. *Annual Review of Psychology, 37*, 109–133.

Kelley, D. B., & Pfaff, D. W. (1978). Generalizations from comparative studies on neuroanatomical and endocrine mechanisms of sexual behaviour. In J. B. Hutchison (Ed.), *Biological determinants of sexual behaviour* (pp. 225–254). New York: Wiley.

Kelly, R. B., Deutsch, J. W., Carlson, S. S., & Wanger, J. A. (1979). Biochemistry of neurotransmitter release. *Annual Review of Neuroscience, 2*, 399–397.

Kemali, D., Galderisi, M. S., Ariano, M. G., Cesarelli, M., Milici, N., Salvati, A., Valente, A., & Volpe, M. (1985). Clinical and neuropsychological correlates of cerebral ventricular enlargement in schizophrenia. *Journal of Psychiatric Research, 19*, 587–596.

Kendler, K. S. (1983). Overview: A current perspective on twin studies of schizophrenia. American Journal of Psychiatry, *140*, 1413–1425.

———, & Robinette, C. D. (1983). Schizophrenia in the National Academy of Sciences-National Research Council Twin Registry: A 16 year update. *American Journal of Psychiatry, 140*, 1551–1563.

Kertesz, A. Recovery and treatment. (1979). In K. M. Heilman & E. Valenstein (Eds.), *Clinical neuropsychology*. New York: Oxford.

Kety, S. (1983). Mental illness in the biological and adoptive families of schizophrenic adoptees: Findings relevant to genetic and environmental factors in etiology. *American Journal of Psychiatry, 140*, 720–727.

———. (1976). Biological concomitants of affective states and their possible role in memory processes. In M. R. Rosenzweig & E. L. Bennett (Eds.), *Neural mechanisms of learning and memory*. Cambridge: MIT Press.

———, Rosenthal, D., Wender, P. H., Schulsinger, F., & Jacobsen, B. (1975). Mental illness in the biological and adoptive families of adopted individuals who have become schizophrenic. A preliminary report based on psychiatric interviews. In R. R. Fieve, D. Rosenthal, & H. Brill (Eds.), *Genetic research in psychiatry*. Baltimore: Johns Hopkins University.

Keys, A., Brozek, J., Henschel, A., Mickelsen, O., & Taylor, H. L. (1950). *The biology of human starvation*. Minneapolis: University of Minnesota.

Khachaturian, H. D., Lewis, M. E., Schaefer, M. K. H., & Watson, S. J. (1985). Anatomy of the CNS opioid systems. *Trends in NeuroScience*, 111–119.

Khanna, S. M., & Leonard, D. G. B. (1982). Basilar membrane tuning in cat cochlea. *Science, 215*, 305–306.

Kimble, D. P. (1968). Hippocampus and internal inhibition. *Psychological Bulletin, 70*, 285–295.

Kimura, D. (1973). The asymmetry of the human brain. *Scientific American*, 360–368.

Kinsey, A. C., Pomeroy, W. B., & Martin, C. E. (1948). *Sexual behavior in the human male*. Philadelphia: Saunders.

———, & Gebhard, P. H. (1953). *Sexual behavior in the human female*. Philadelphia: Saunders.

Kish, S. J., Chang, L. J., Mirchandani, L., Shannak, K., & Hornykiewicz, O. (1985). Progressive supranuclear palsy: Relationship between extrapyramidal disturbances, dementia and brain neurotransmitter markers. *Annals of Neurology, 18*, 530–537.

Kitai, S. T., & Bishop, G. A. (1981). Horseradish peroxidase: Intracellular staining of neurons. In L. Heimer, & M. J. Robards, *Neuroanatomical tract-tracing methods* (pp. 263–279). New York: Plenum.

Kleber, H. D., & Gawin, F. H. Cocaine abuse: A review of current and experimental treatments. In J. Grabowski (Ed.), *Cocaine: Pharmacology, effects and treatment of abuse*. NIDA Research Monograph 50 (pp. 111–129). National Institute of Drug Abuse.

Kleiber, M. (1947). Body size and metabolic rate. *Physiological Reviews, 15*, 511–541.

Klein, M., Shapiro, E., & Kandel, E. R. (1980). Synaptic plasticity and the modulation of the Ca^{++} current. *Journal of Experimental Biology, 89*, 117–157.

Klein, M., & Kandel, E. R. (1980). Mechanism of calcium modulation underlying presynaptic facilitation and behavioral sensitization in *Aplysia*. *Proceedings of the National Academy of Science, 77*(11), 6912.

Kleitman, N. (1969). Basic rest-activity cycle in relation to sleep and wakefulness. In A. Kales (Ed.), *Sleep: Physiology and pathology*. Philadelphia: Lippincott.

Klima, E. S., & Bellugi, U. (1979). *The signs of language*. Cambridge, Harvard.

Kluckhohn, C. (1949). *Mirror for man*. New York: Whittlesey House.

Kluger, M. J. (1979). *Fever, Its biology, evolution and function*. Princeton: Princeton.

Knibestol, M., & Valbo, A. B. (1970). Single unit analysis of mechanoreceptor activity from the human glabrous skin. *Acta Physiologica Scandinavica, 80*, 178–195.

Knobil, E. (1974). On the control of gonadotrophin secretion in the rhesus monkey. *Recent Progress in Hormone Research, 30*, 1–43.

———, & Hotchkiss, J. (1985). The circhoral gonadotropic releasing hormone (GnRH) pulse generator of the hypothalamus and its physiological significance. In H. Schulz & P. Lavie (Eds.), *Ultradian rhythms in physiology and behavior* (pp. 32–41). Berlin: Springer-Verlag.

Knudsen, E. (1985). Experience alters the spatial tuning of auditory units in the optic tectum during a sensitive period in the barn owl. Journal of *Neuroscience, 5*, 3094–3109.

———. (1984). The role of auditory experience in the development and maintenance of sound localization. *Trends in NeuroScience, 7*, 326–330.

———. (1982). Auditory and visual maps of space in the optic tectum of the owl. *Journal of Neuroscience, 2*, 1174–1195.

———, & Knudsen, P. (1985). Vision guides adjustment of auditory localization in young barn owls. *Science, 230*, 545–548.

———, & Konishi, M. (1979). Mechanisms of sound localization in the barn owl (Tyto alba). *Journal of Comparative Physiology, 133*, 13–21.

Koella, W. P. (1985). Serotonin and sleep. In W. P. Koella, E. Ruther, & H. Schulz (Eds.), *Sleep '84* (pp. 6–10). Stuttgart: Gustav Fischer Verlag.

Koester, J., & Kandel, E. R. (1977). Further identification of neurons in the abdomincal ganglion of *Aplysia* using behavioral criteria. *Brain Research, 121*, 1–20.

Kolata, G. B. (1981). Clues to the cause of senile dementia. *Science, 211*, 1032–1033.

Kolata, G. (1984). Steroid hormone systems found in yeast. *Science, 225*, 913–914.

Kolb, B., & Whishaw, I. Q. *Fundamentals of human neuropsychology*. San Francisco: Freeman.

Kolodny, E. H., & Cable, W. J. L. (1982). Inborn errors of metabolism. *Annals of Neurology, 11*, 221–232.

Konishi, M. (1985). Birdsong: From behavior to neuron. *Annual Review of Neuroscience, 8*, 125–171.

Koopowitz, H., & Keenan, L. (1982). The primitive brains of platyhelminthes. *Trends in Neurosciences, 5*, 77–80.

Kopin, I. J., & Markey, S. P. (1988). MPTP toxicity: Implications for research in Parkinson's disease. *Annual Review of Neuroscience, 11*, 81–96.

Kornetsky, C., & Eliasson, M. (1969). Reticular stimulation and chlorpromazine: An animal model for schizophrenic overarousal. *Science, 165*, 1273–1274.

Korsakoff, S. S. (1889). Etude médico-psychologique sur une forme des maladies de la mémoire. *Revue philosophique, 5*, 501–530.

Koshland, D. E. (1980). *Bacterial chemotaxis as a model behavioral system*. New York: Raven.

Kovelman, J. A., & Scheibel, A. B. (1984). A neurohistological correlate of schizophrenia. *Biological Psychiatry, 19*, 1601.

Kow, L.-M., Malsbury, C., & Pfaff, D. (1974). Effects of medial hypothalamic lesions on the lordosis response in female hamsters. *Society for Neuroscience, Abstracts, 4*, 291.

Krieger, D. T. (1983). Brain peptides: What, where, and why? *Science, 223*, 975–985. [For update, see: Krieger, D. T. (1984). The endocrine system. *Science, 224*, 240.]

Krug, M., Lössner, B., & Ott, T. (1984). Anisomycin blocks the late phase of long-term potentiation in the dentate gyrus of freely moving rat. *Brain Research Bulletin, 13*, 39–42.

Kubanis, P., & Zornetzer, S. F. (1981). Age-related behavioral and neurobiological changes: a review with emphasis of memory. *Behavioral and Neural Biology, 31*, 115–172.

Kung, C. (1979). Neurobiology and neurogenetics of Paramecium behavior. In X. O. Breakefield (Ed.), *Neurogenetics: Genetic approaches to the nervous system* (pp. 1–27). New York: Elsevier North-Holland.

Kupfermann, I. T., Carew, T. J., & Kandel, E. R. (1974). Local, reflex, and central commands controlling gill and siphon movements in *Aplysia*. *Journal of Neurophysiology, 37*, 996–1019.

Kutas, M., & Hillyard, S. A. (1984). Event-related potentials in cognitive science. In M. Gazzaniga (Ed.), *Handbook of cognitive neuroscience*. New York: Plenum.

Labbe, R., Firl, A., Mufson, E. J., & Stein, D. G. (1983). Fetal brain transplants: Reduction of cognitive deficits in rats with frontal cortex lesions. *Science, 221*, 470–472.

LaCerra, M. M., & Ettenberg, A. (1984). A comparison of the rewarding properties of "free" versus "earned" amphetamine. *Society for Neuroscience Abstracts, 10*, 1207.

Lacey, J. I., & Lacey, B. C. (1970). Some autonomic-central nervous system interrelationships. In P. Black (Ed.), *Physiological correlates of emotion*. New York: Academic.

Lack, D. (1968). *Ecological adaptations for breeding in birds*. London: Methuen.

Lackner, J. R., & Shenker, B. (1985). Proprioceptive influences on auditory and visual spatial localization. *Journal of Neuroscience, 5*, 579–584.

Land, M. F. (1984). Crustacea. In M. A. Ali (Ed.), *Photoreception and vision in invertebrates* (pp. 401–438). New York: Plenum.

Landmesser, L., & Pilar, G. (1974). Synaptic transmission and cell death during normal ganglionic development. *Journal of Physiology* (London), *241*, 737–749.

Langston, J. W. (1985). MPTP and Parkinson's disease. *Trends in Neurosciences, 8*, 79–83.

Lansdell, H. (1968). The use of factor scores from the Wechsler-Bellevue Scale of Intelligence in assessing patients with temporal lobe removals. *Cortex, 4*, 257–268.

———. (1964). Sex differences in hemispheric asymmetries of the human brain. *Nature, 203*, 550.

Larroche, J. C. (1966). The development of the central nervous system during intrauterine life. In F. Falkner (Ed.), *Human development*. Philadelphia: Saunders.

Larsson, K., & Heimer, L. (1964). Mating behavior of male rats after lesions in the preoptic area. *Nature, 202*, 413–414.

Lashley, K. S., & Clark, G. (1946). The cytoarchitecture of the cerebral cortex of Ateles: A critical examination of architectonic studies. *Journal of Comparative Neurology, 85*, 223–306.

Latour, P. L. (1962). Visual thresholds during eye movements. *Vision Research, 2*, 261–262.

Lavie, P., & Kripke, D. F. (1981). Ultradian circa 1½ hour rhythms: A multioscillatory system. *Life Sciences, 29*, 2445–2450.

Le Boeuf, B. J. (1978). Sex and evolution. In T. E. McGill, D. A. Dewsbury, & B. D. Sachs (Eds.), *Sex and Behavior*. New York: Plenum.

LeDoux, J. E. (1982). Neuroevolutionary mechanisms of cerebral asymmetry in man. *Brain, Behavior and Evolution, 20*, 196–212.

Lee, K. S., Schottler, F., Oliver, M., & Lynch, G. (1980). Brief bursts of high-frequency stimulation produce two types of structural change in rat hippocampus. *Journal of Neurophysiology, 44*, 247–258.

Lee, T., & Seeman, P. (1980). Elevation of brain neuroleptic dopamine receptors in schizophrenia. *American Journal of Psychiatry, 137*, 191–197.

Lee, T. M., Carmichael, M. S., & Zucker, I. (1986). Circannual variations in circadian rhythms of ground squirrels. *American Journal of Physiology, 250*, 831–836.

Lehrman, D. S. (1965). Interaction between internal and external environments in the regulation of the reproductive cycle in the ring dove. In F. A. Beach (Ed.), *Sex and Behavior*. New York: Wiley.

———. (1964). The reproductive behavior of ring doves. *Scientific American*.

Leibel, R. L., & Hirsch, J. (1984). Diminished energy requirements in reduced-obese patients. *Metabolism, 33*, 164–170.

LeMay, M. (1977). Asymmetries of the skull and handedness. *Journal of the Neurological Sciences, 32*, 243–253.

———, & Culebras, A. (1972). Human brain-morphologic differences in the hemispheres demonstrable by carotid angiography. *New England Journal of Medicine, 287*, 168–170.

Lenneberg, E. H. (1967). *Biological foundations of language*. New York: Wiley.

Leon, M., Croskerry, P. G., & Smith, G. K. (1978). Thermal control of mother-young contact in rats. *Physiology & Behavior, 21*(5), 793–811.

LeRoith, D., Shiloach, J., & Roth, J. (1982). Is there an earlier phylogenetic precursor that is common to both the nervous and endocrine systems? *Peptides, 3*, 211–215. [For update, see: Krieger, D. T. (1984). The endocrine system. *Science, 224*, 240.]

Leshner, A. (1978). *An introduction to behavioral endocrinology*. New York: Oxford.

Leventhal, H., & Tomarken, A. J. (1986). Emotion: Today's problems. *Annual Review of Psychology, 37*, 565–611.

Levi, L. (1965). The urinary output of adrenalin and noradrenalin during pleasant and unpleasant emotional states. *Psychosomatic Medicine, 27*, 80.

Levi-Montalcini, R. (1982). Developmental neurobiology and the natural history of nerve growth factor. *Annual Review of Neuroscience, 5,* 341–362.

———. (1963). In J. Allen (Ed.), *The nature of biological diversity.* New York: McGraw-Hill.

———, & Calissano, P. (1979). The nerve growth factor. *Scientific American, 240,* 68–77.

Levinthal, F., Macagno, E., & Levinthal, C. (1976). Anatomy and development of identified cells in isogenic organisms. *Cold Spring Harbor Symposium on Quantitative Biology, 40,* 321–331.

Levine, J. D., Gordon, N. C., Bornstein, J. C., & Fields, H. L. (1979). Role of pain in placebo analgesia. *Proceedings of the National Academy of Sciences, 76,* 3528–3531.

Levy, J., & Reid, M. (1976). Variations in writing posture and cerebral organization. *Science, 194,* 337–339.

Lewis, D. O., Shankok, S. S., & Pincus, J. (1979). Juvenile male sexual assaulters. *American Journal of Psychiatry, 136,* 1194–1195.

Lewis, J. W., Cannon, J. T., & Liebeskind, J. C. (1980). Opioid and nonopioid mechanisms of stress analgesia. *Science, 208,* 623–625.

Lhermitte, F., & Signoret, J.-L. (1976). The amnesic syndromes and the hippocampal-mammillary system. In M. R. Rosenzweig & E. L. Bennett (Eds.), *Neural Mechanisms of Learning and Memory* (pp. 49–56). Cambridge, Mass., and London, England: MIT Press.

Lhermitte, F., Pillon, B., & Serdaru, M. (1986). Human autonomy and the frontal lobes. Part 1. Imitation and utilization behavior: A neuropsychological study of 75 patients. *Annals of Neurology, 19,* 326–335.

Lickey, M. E., & Gordon, B. (1983). *Drugs for mental illness: a revolution in psychiatry.* New York: Freeman.

Lieberman, P. (1979). Hominid evolution, supralaryngeal vocal-tract physiology and the fossil evidence for reconstruction. *Brain and Language, 7,* 101–126.

Liebowitz, M. R., Gorman, J. M., Fryer, A., Dillon, D., Levitt, M., & Klein, D. F. (1986). Possible mechanisms for lactate's induction of panic. *American Journal of Psychiatry, 143,* 495–502.

Linden, D., & Martinez, J. L. (1986). Leu-enkephalin impairs memory of an appetitive maze response in mice. *Behavioral Neuroscience, 100,* 33–38.

Liu, C. N., & Chambers, W. W. (1958). Intraspinal sprouting of dorsal root axons. *Archives of Neurology and Psychiatry, 79,* 46–61.

Livingstone, M. S., & Hubel, D. (1984). Anatomy and physiology of a color system in the primate visual cortex. *Journal of Neuroscience, 4,* 309–356.

———. (1988). Segregation of form, color, movement, and depth: Anatomy, physiology, and perception. *Science, 240,* 740–749.

Lockhart, M., & Moore, J. W. (1975). Classical differential and operant conditioning in rabbits *(Oryctolagus cuniculus)* with septal lesions. *Journal of Comparative and Physiological Psychology, 88,* 147–154.

Loeb, G. E. (1985). The functional replacement of the ear. *Scientific American, 252,* 104–111.

Loehlin, J. C., Willerman, L., & Horn, J. M. (1988). Human behavior genetics. *Annual Review of Psychology, 39,* 101–133.

Loewenstein, W. R. (1960). Biological transducers. *Scientific American, 203*(2), 98–108.

———. (1971). Mechano-electric transduction in the Pacinian corpuscle. Initiation of sensory impulses in mechanoreception. *Handbook of Sensory Physiology,* Vol. 1 (pp. 269–290). Berlin: Springer-Verlag.

Lund, R. D. (1978). *Development and plasticity of the brain.* New York: Oxford.

———, & Hanschka, S. D. (1976). Transplanted neural tissue develops connections with host rat brain. *Science, 193,* 582–584.

Lundeberg, T. C. M. (1983). Vibratory stimulation for the alleviation of chronic pain. *Acta Physiologica Scandinavica.* (Supplement 523).

Lustick, S., Battersby, B., & Kelty, M. (1978). Behavioral thermoregulation: Orientation toward the sun in Herring Gulls. *Science, 200,* 81–82.

Lynch, G., & Baudry, M. (1984). The biochemistry of memory: A new and specific hypothesis. *Science, 224,* 1057–1063.

Macagno, E., Lopresti, U., & Levinthal, C. (1973). Structural development of neuronal connections in isogenic organisms: Variations and similarities in the optic system of Daphnia magna. *Proceedings of the National Academy of Sciences (USA), 70,* 57–61.

Maccoby, E. E., & Jacklin, C. M. (1974). *The psychology of sex differences.* Stanford: Stanford University.

Mace, G. M., Harvey, P. H., & Clutton-Brock, T. H. (1980). Is brain size an ecological variable? *Trends in Neuroscience, 3,* 193–196.

———. (1981). Brain size and ecology in small mammals. *Journal of Zoology, 193,* 333–354.

Mackie, G. O. (1980). Jellyfish neurobiology since Romanes. *Trends in neurosciences, 3,* 13–16.

Mackintosh, N. J. (1985). Varieties of conditioning. In N. M. Weinberger, J. L. McGaugh, & G. Lynch (Eds.), *Memory systems of the brain* (pp. 335–350). New York: Guilford.

MacLean, P. D. (1970). The triune brain, emotion, and scientific bias. In F. O. Schmitt (Ed.), *The neurosciences.* New York: Rockefeller University, 336–348.

Macoby, E. E., & Jacklin, C. M. (1974). *The psychology of sex differences.* Stanford: Stanford University.

Maffei, L., & Fiorentini, A. (1973). The visual cortex as a spatial frequency analyser. *Vision Research, 13,* 1255–1267.

Mair, W. G. P., Warrington, E. K., & Wieskrantz, L. (1979). Memory disorder in Korsakoff's psychosis. *Brain, 102,* 749–783.

Malamut, B. L., Saunders, R. C., & Mishkin, M. (1980). Successful object discrimination learning after combined amygdaloid-hippocampal lesions in monkeys despite 24-hour intertrial intervals. *Society for Neuroscience Abstracts, 6,* 191.

Manfredi, M., Bini, G., Cruccu, G., Accornero, N., Berardelli, A., & Medolago, L. (1981). Congenital absence of pain. *Archives of Neurology, 38,* 507–511.

Mann, M. D., Glickman, S. E., & Towe, A. L. (1988). Brain/body relations among myomorph rodents. *Brain, Behavior, and Evolution, 31,* 111–124.

Mann, T. (1941). *The transposed heads: A legend of India.* New York: Knopf.

Manning, A. (1965). Drosophila and the evolution of behaviour. In J. D. Carthy & C. L. Duddington (Eds.), *Viewpoints in biology* (pp. 125–169). London: Butterworth.

Marchisio, P. C., Circillo, D., Naldini, L., & Calissano, P. (1980). Distribution of nerve growth factor in chick embryo sympathetic neurons in vitro. *Journal of Neurocytology, 60,* 355–395.

Margraf, J., & Roth, W. T. (1986). Sodium lactate infusions and panic attacks: A review and critique. *Psychosomatic Medicine, 48,* 23–50.

Marin, R. S., & Tucker, G. J. (1981). Psychopathology and hemispheric dysfunction. *Journal of Nervous and Mental Disease, 169,* 546–557.

Mark, R. F. (1980). Synaptic repression at neuromuscular junctions. *Physiological Reviews, 60,* 355–395.

Mark, V. H., & Ervin, F. R. (1970). *Violence and the brain.* New York: Harper & Row.

Marlatt, G. A., Baer, J. S., Donovan, D. M., & Kivlahan, R. (1988). Addictive behaviors: etiology and treatment. *Annual Review of Psychology, 39,* 223–252.

Marler, P. (1981). Birdsong: The acquisition of a learned motor skill. *Trends in Neurosciences, 4,* 88–94.

Marlowe, W. B., Mancall, E. L., & Thomas, J. J. (1975). Complete Klüver-Bucy syndrome in man. *Cortex, 11,* 53–59.

Marsden, C. D., Rothwell, J. C., & Day, B. L. (1984). The use of peripheral feedback in the control of movement. *Trends in Neuroscience, 7,* 253–257.

Marshall, J. F., & Berrios, N. (1979). Movement disorders of aged rats:

reversal by dopamine receptor stimulation. *Science, 206,* 477–479.

Marshall, J. F., Richardson, J. S., & Teitelbaum, P. (1974). Nigrostriatal bundle damage and the lateral hypothalamic syndrome. *Journal of comparative and physiological psychology, 87,* 800–830.

Martin, A. R., & Pilar, G. (1963). Dual mode of synaptic transmission in the avian ciliary ganglion. *Journal of Physiology* (London), 443–463.

Martin, J. V., Wyatt, R. J., & Mendelson, W. B. (1985). Growth hormone secretion in sleep and waking. In W. P. Koella, E. Ruther, & H. Schulz (Eds.), *Sleep '84* (pp. 185–188). Stuttgart: Gustav Fischer Verlag.

Martinez, J. L., & Rigter, H. (1980). Endorphins alter acquisition and consolidation of an inhibitory avoidance response in rats. *Neuroscience Newsletter, 18,* 197–201.

Marx, J. L. (1985). "Anxiety peptide" found in brain. *Science, 227,* 934.

Maser, J. D., & Seligman, M. E. P. (Eds.), (1977). *Psychopathology: Experimental models.* San Francisco: Freeman.

Mason, J. W. (1972). Organization of psychoendocrine mechanisms: A review and reconsideration of research. In N. S. Greenfield & R. A. Sternbach (Eds.), *Handbook of Psychophysiology.* New York: Holt.

Masters, W. H., & Johnson, V. E. (1965). The sexual response cycles of the human male and female: Comparative anatomy and physiology. In F. A. Beach (Ed.), *Sex and behavior.* New York: Wiley.

———. (1966). *Human sexual response.* Boston: Little Brown.

———. (1970). *Human sexual inadequacy.* Boston: Little, Brown.

Masterson, R. B. (Ed.), (1978). *Handbook of behavioral neurobiology. (Vol. 1): Sensory Integration.* New York: Plenum.

———. Berkley, M. A. (1974). Brain function: Changing ideas on the role of sensory, motor, and association cortex in behavior. *Annual Review of Psychology, 25,* 277–312.

Matthies, H. (1979). Biochemical, electrophysiological, and morphological correlates of brightness discrimination in rats. In M. A. B. Brazier (Ed.), *Brain mechanisms in memory and learning: From the single neuron to man.* New York: Raven.

———. (1989). Neurobiological aspects of learning and memory. *Annual Review of Psychology, 40.*

Mayberg, H. S., Robinson, R. G., Wong, D. F., et al. (1988). PET imaging of cortical S2 serotonin receptors after stroke: Lateralized changes and relationship to depression. *American Journal of Psychiatry, 145,* 937–943.

Mayer, D. J., & Liebeskind, J. C. (1974). Pain reduction by focal electrical stimulation of the brain: An anatomical and behavioral analysis. *Brain Research, 68,* 73–93.

Mayer, J. (1953). Glucostatic mechanisms of regulation of food intake. *New England Journal of Medicine, 249,* 13–16.

McCabe, B. J., Cipolla-Neto, J., Horn, G., & Bateson, P. P. G. (1981). Amnesic effects of bilateral lesions placed in the hyperstriatum ventral of the chick after imprinting. *Experimental Brain Research, 48,* 13–21.

McCabe, B. J., Horn, G., & Bateson, P. P. G. (1981). Effects of restricted lesions of the chick forebrain on the acquisition of filial preferences during imprinting. *Brain Research, 205,* 29–37.

McGaugh, J. L. (1983). Hormonal influences on memory. *Annual Review of Psychology, 34,* 297–323.

———. (1968). A multi-trace view of memory storage processes. In D. Bovet (Ed.), *Attuali orientamenti della ricerca sull' apprendimento e la memoria.* Rome: Academia Nazionale dei Lincei, Quaderno N. 109.

———, Krivanek, J. A. (1970). Strychnine effects on discrimination learning in mice: effects of dose and time of administration. *Physiology and Behavior, 5,* 1437–1442.

———, & Petrinovich, L. F. (1959). The effect of strychnine sulphate on maze learning. *American Journal of Psychology, 72,* 99–102.

McGeer, E. G., & McGeer, P. L. (1976). Neurotransmitter metabolism in the aging brain. In R. D. Terry & S. Gershon (Eds.), *Neurobiology of aging.* Vol. 3. New York: Raven.

McGill, T. E., Dewsbury, D. A., & Sachs, B. D. (1978). *Sex and behavior.* New York: Plenum.

McGlone, J. (1977). Sex differences in functional brain asymmetry after damage to the left and right hemisphere. Ph. D. thesis. London, Canada: University of Western Ontario.

———. (1980). Sex differences in human brain asymmetry: A critical survey. *The Behavioral and Brain Sciences, 3,* 215–263.

McKinney, T. D., & Desjardins. C. (1973). Postnatal development of the testis, fighting behavior and fertility in house mice. *Biology of Reproduction. 9,* 279–294.

McNaughton, B. L., Barnes, C. A., Rao, G., Baldwin, J., & Rasmussen, M. (1986). Long-term enhancement of hippocampal synaptic transmission and the acquisition of spatial information. *Journal of Neuroscience, 6,* 563–571.

Means, A. R., & O'Malley, B. W. (1983). *Calmodulin and calcium-binding proteins.* New York: Academic Press.

Meckler, R. J., Mack, J. L., & Bennett, R. (1979). Sign language aphasia in a non-deaf mute. *Neurology, 29,* 1037–1040.

Meddis, R. (1979). The evolution and function of sleep. In D. A. Oakley & H. C. Plotkin (Eds.), *Brain, behavior and evolution.* London: Methuen.

———. (1975). On the function of sleep. *Animal Behavior, 23,* 676–691.

———. (1977). *The sleep instinct.* London: Routledge & Kegan Paul.

Mednick, S. A., & Christiansen, K. D. (Eds.). (1977). Biosocial bases of criminal behavior. New York: Gardner.

Meisami, E. (1978). Influence of early anosmia on the developing olfactory bulb. *Progress in Brain Research, 48,* 211–230.

Melzack, R. (1984). Neuropsychological basis of pain measurement. *Advances in pain research,* 323–341.

———. (1973). *The puzzle of pain.* New York: Basic Books.

———. (1980). Psychological aspects of pain. In J. J. Bonica (Ed.), *Pain* (Association of Research in Nervous and Mental Disease, Vol. 58). New York: Raven.

———, & Casey, K. L. (1968). Sensory, motivational, and central control determinants of pain. In D. R. Kenshals (Ed.), *The skin senses.* Springfield, Ill.: Charles C. Thomas.

———, & Wall, P. D. (1962). On the nature of cutaneous sensory mechanisms. *Brain, 85,* 331–356.

Meredith, M. A., & Stein, B. E. (1983). Interactions among converging sensory inputs in the superior colliculus. *Science, 221,* 389–391.

Merrin, E. L. (1981). Schizophrenia and brain asymmetry. *Journal of Nervous and Mental Diseases, 169,* 405–416.

Merzenich, M. M., & Kaas, J. H. (1980). Principles of organization of sensory-perceptual systems in mammals. In J. M. Sprague & A. N. Epstein (Eds.), *Progress in psychobiology and physiological psychology* (Vol. 9). New York: Academic.

Messing, R. B., Jensen, R. A., Martinez, J. L., Spiehler, V. R., et al. (1979). Naloxone enhancement of memory. *Behavioral and Neural Biology, 27,* 266–275.

Mesulam, M.-M. (1985). Attention, confusional states and neglect. In M.-M. Mesulam (Ed.), *Principles of behavioral neurology.* Philadelphia: F. A. Davis.

———. (1981). A cortical network for directed attention and unilateral neglect. *Annals of Neurology, 10,* 309–325.

———, & Van Hoesen, G. W., Pandya, D. N., & Geschwind, N., (1977). Limbic and sensory connections of the inferior parietal lobule (area PG) in the rhesus monkey: A study with a new method for horseradish peroxidase histochemistry. *Brain Research, 136,* 393–414.

Meyer-Bahlburg, H. F. L. (1984). Psychoendorocrine research on sexual orientation. Current status and future options. In G. J. De Vries, J. P. C. De Bruin, H. B. M. Uylings, & M. A. Corner (Eds.), *Progress in brain research: Vol. 61. Sex differences in the brain* (pp. 375–398). Amsterdam: Elsevier Science Publishers.

———, & Ehrhardt, A. A. (1982). Prenatal sex hormones and human aggression: A review and new data on progestogen effects. *Aggressive Behavior, 8,* 39–62.

Michelson, R. P. (1978). Multichannel cochlear implants. *Otolaryngological Clinics of North America, 11,* 209–216.

Middlebrooks, J. C., & Pettigrew, J. D. (1981). Functional classes of neurons in primary auditory cortex of the cat distinguished by sensitivity to sound location. *Journal of Neuroscience, 1,* 107–120.

Mihailoff, G. A., McArdle, C. G., & Adams, C. E. (1981). The cytoarchitecture cytology, and synaptic organization of the basilar pontine nuclei in the rat. 1. Nissl and Golgi studies. *Journal of Comparative Neurology, 195,* 181–201.

Miller, G. A. (1962). *Psychology: The science of mental life.* New York: Harper & Row.

Miller, J. A. (1984). Cell communication equipment: Do-it-yourself kit. *Science News, 125,* 236–237.

Miller, N. E. (1978). Biofeedback and visceral learning. *Annual Review of Psychology, 29,* 373–404.

_____. (1983). Behavioral medicine: Symbiosis between laboratory and clinic. *Annual Review of Psychology, 34,* 1–31.

Milner, B. (1970). Memory and the medial temporal regions of the brain. In D. H. Pribram & D. E. Broadbent (Eds.), *Biology of Memory.* New York: Academic.

_____. (1965). Memory disturbance after bilateral hippocampal lesions. In P. M. Milner & S. E. Glickman (Eds.), *Cognitive processes and the brain.* Princeton: Van Nostrand.

_____, Corkin, S., & Teuber. H.-L. (1968). Further analysis of the hippocampal amnesic syndrome: 14-year follow-up study of H. M. *Neuropsychologia, 6,* 215–234.

_____, & Petrides, M. (1984). Behavioural effects of frontal lobe lesions in man. *Trends in NeuroSciences, 7,* 403–407.

Mirmiran, M. (1985). The significance of active (i.e., REM) sleep for maturation and polasticity of brain and behavior in the rat. In W. P. Koella, E. Ruther, & H. Schulz (Eds.), *Sleep '84* (pp. 109–113). Stuttgart: Gustav Fischer Verlag.

Mirsky, A. F., & Duncan, C. C. (1986). Etiology and expression of schizophrenia: Neurobiological and psychosocial factors. *Annual Review of Psychology, 37,* 291–321.

Mirsky, A., DeLisi, L., Buchsbaum, M., Quinn, O., Schwerdt, P., Siever, L., Mann, L. Weingartner, H., Zec, R., Sostek, A., Alterman, I., Revere, V., Dawson, S., & Zahn, T. (1984). The Genain quadruplets: Psychological studies. *Psychiatry Research, 13,* 77–93.

Mishina, M., Tobimatsu, T., & Imoto, K. (1985). Location of functional regions of acetylcholine receptor a-subunit by site-directed mutagenesis. *Nature, 313,* 364–369.

Mishkin, M. (1978). Memory in monkeys severely impaired by combined but not by separate removal of amygdala and hippocampus. *Nature. 273,* 297–298.

_____, Malamut, B., & Bachevalier, J. (1984). Memories and habits: two neural systems. In G. Lynch, J. L. McGaugh, & N. M. Weinberger (Eds.), *The neurobiology of learning and memory.* New York: Guilford Press.

_____, & Petri, H. L. (1984). Memories and habits: Some implications for the analysis of learning and retention. In L. R. Squire & N. Butters (Eds.), *Neuropsychology of memory.* New York: Guilford.

Mizumori, S. J. Y., Rosenzweig, M. R., & Bennett, E. L. (1985). Long-term working memory in the rat. Effects of hippocampally applied anisomycin. *Behavioral Neuroscience, 99,* 220–232.

Mohler, C. W., & Wurtz, R. H. (1977). Role of striate cortex and superior colliculus is visual guidance of saccadic eye movements in monkeys. *Journal of Neurophysiology, 40,* 74–94.

Mohr, J. P. (1976). Broca's area and Broca's aphasia. *Studies in neurolinguistics, 1,* 201–235.

Mohs, R. C., Davis, B. M., Johns, C. A., et al. (1985). Oral physostigmine treatment of patients with Alzheimer's disease. *American Journal of Psychiatry, 142,* 28–33.

Mollon, J. D. (1982). Color vision. *Annual Review of Psychology, 33,* 41–85.

Money, J. (1976). Human hermaphroditism. In F. A. Beach (Ed.), *Human sexuality in four perspectives.* Baltimore: Johns Hopkins University, 62–86.

_____, & Ehrhardt, A. A. (1972). *Man and woman, boy and girl.* Baltimore: Johns Hopkins University.

Monti, J. M., Pellejero, T., Jantos, H., & Pazos, S. (1985). Role of histamines in the control of sleep and waking. In A. Wauquier, J. M. Gaillard, J. M. Monti, & M. Radulovacki (Eds.), *Sleep: Neurotransmitters and neuromodulators* (pp. 197–211). New York: Raven.

Moore, B. C. J. (1984). Electrical stimulation of the auditory nerve in man. *Trends in Neurosciences, 7,* 274–277.

Moore, R. Y. (1983). Organization and function of a central nervous system circadian oscillator: The suprachiasmatic nucleus. *Federation Proceedings, 42,* 2783–2789.

_____, & Bloom, F. E. (1979). Central catecholamine neuron systems: Anatomy and physiology of the norepinephrine and epinephrine systems. *Annual Review of Neurosciences, 2,* 113–168.

_____, & Eichler, V. B. (1972). Loss of circadian adrenal corticosterone rhythm following suprachiasmatic lesions in the rat. *Brain Research, 42,* 201–206.

Mora, F., Rolls, E. T., & Burton, M. J. (1976). Modulation during learning of the responses of neurones in the lateral hypothalamus to the sight of food. *Experimental Neurology, 53,* 508–519.

Moran, E. F. (1981). Human adaptation to arctic zones. *Annual Review of Anthropology, 10,* 1–25.

Morgan, T. H., & McHugh, P. R. (1982). Cholecystokinin suppresses food intake by inhibiting gastric emptying. *American Journal of Physiology, 242,* 491–497.

Morgane, P. J., & Kosman, A. J. (1960). Relationship of the middle hypothalamus to amygdalar hyperphagia. *American Journal of Physiology, 198,* 1315–1318.

Morihisa, J., & McAnulty, G. B. (1985). Structure and function: Brain electrical activity mapping and computed tomography in schizophrenia. *Biological Psychiatry, 20,* 3–19.

Morrison, A. (1979). Brain-stem regulation of behavior during sleep and wakefulness. *Progress in Psychobiology and Physiological Psychology, 8,* 91–131.

Morrison, A. R. (1983). A window on the sleeping brain. *Scientific American, 248,* 94–102.

Morruzzi, G. (1972). The sleep-waking cycle. *Ergebnisse der Physiologie (Reviews of Physiology), 64,* 1–165.

Moskovitch, M. (1982). Multiple dissociations of function in amnesia. In L. Cermak (Ed.), *Human memory and amnesia.* Hillsdale, N.J.: Erlbaum.

Moss, R. L., & Dudley, C. A. (1984). Molecular aspects of the interaction between estrogen and the membrane excitability of hypothalamic nerve cells. *Progress in Brain Research, 61,* 3–22.

Moulton, D. G. (1976). Spatial patterning of response to odors in the peripheral olfactory system. *Physiological Reviews, 56,* 578–593.

Mountcastle, V. B. (1979). An organizing principle for cerebral function: the unit module and the distributed system. In F. O. Schmitt & F. G. Worden (Eds.), *The neurosciences: fourth study program.* Cambridge: MIT Press.

_____. (1967). The problem of sensing and the neural coding of sensory events. In G. C. Quarton, T. Melnechuk, & F. O. Schmitt (Eds.), *The Neurosciences* (pp. 393–408). New York: Rockefeller University, 393–408.

_____. (1984). Central nervous mechanisms in mechanoreceptive sensibility. In I. Darian-Smith (Ed.), *Handbook of physiology, Section 1, Volume 3, Sensory Processes* (pp. 789–878). Bethesda: American Physiological Society.

_____, Andersen, R. A., & Motter, B. C. (1981). The influence of attentive fixation upon the excitability of the light-sensitive neurons of the posterior parietal cortex. *Journal of Neuroscience. 1,* 1218–1235.

Mouret, J., & Coindet, J. (1980). Polygraphic evidence against a critical role of the raphe nuclei in sleep in the rat. *Brain Research, 186,* 273–287.

Movshon, J. A., & van Sluyters, R. C. (1981). Visual neural development. *Annual Review of Psychology, 32,* 477–522.

Mpitsos, G. J., Collins, S. D., & McClellan, A. D. (1978). Learning: a model system for physiological studies. *Science, 199,* 497–506.

Mrosovsky, N., & Sherry, D. F. (1980). Animal anorexias. *Science, 207,* 837–842.

Mukhametov, L. M. (1984). Sleep in marine mammals. In A. Borbely & J. L. Valatx (Eds.), *Sleep mechanisms (Experimental Brain Research Supplement 8).* Berlin: Springer-Verlag.

Müller, G. E., & Pilzecker, A. (1900). Experimentale Beiträge zur Lehre vom Gedächtnis. *Zeitschrift für Psychologie,* Suppl., 1–288.

Myers, J. K., Weissman, M., Tischler, G. L., Holzer, C. E., Leaf, P. J., Orvaschel, H., Anthony, J. C., Boyd, J. H., Burke, J. D., Kramer, M., & Stoltzman, R. (1984). Six-month prevalence of psychiatric disorders in three communities. *Archives of General Psychiatry, 41,* 959–967.

Nagy, Z. M. (1979). Development of learning and memory processes in infant mice. In N. E. Spear & B. A. Campbell (Eds.), *Ontogeny of learning and memory.* Hillsdale, N.J.: Erlbaum.

Nakamura, R. K., & Mishkin, M. Chronic blindness following nonvisual cortical lesions in monkeys. *Society for Neuroscience Abstracts,* 1979, *5,* 800.

Natelson, B. H. (1985). Neurocardiology: An interdisciplinary area for the 80s. *Archives of Neurology, 42,* 178–184.

Nathans, J. (1987). Molecular biology of visual pigments. *Annual Review of Neuroscience, 10,* 163–194.

Nathanson, J. A. (1984). Caffeine and related methylxanthines: Possible naturally occurring pesticides. *Science, 226,* 184–187.

Neal, P. (1988). *As I am.* New York: Simon and Schuster.

Nee, L. E., Polinsky, R. J., Elbridge, R., Weingart, H., Smallber, S., & Ebert, M. (1983). A family with histologically confirmed Alzheimer's disease. *Archives of Neurology, 40,* 203–208.

Newman, E. A., & Hartline, P. H. (1981). Integration of visual and infrared information in bimodal neurons of the rattlesnake optic tectum. *Science, 213,* 789–791.

Newsome, W. T., Baker, J. F., Meizen, F. M., Myerson, J., Petersen, S. E., & Allman, J. M. (1978). Functional localization of neuronal response properties in extrastriate visual cortex of the owl monkey. *ARVO Abstracts, 1,* 174.

Nguyen, M. L., Meyer, K. K., & Winick, M. (1977). Early malnutrition and "late" adoption: A study of their effects on the development of Korean orphans adopted into American families. *American Journal of Clinical Nutrition, 30,* 1734–1739.

Nicoll, R. A. (1982). Neurotransmitters can say more than just "yes" or "no." *Trends in NeuroSciences, 55,* 369–374.

Nieto-Sampedro, M., & Cotman, C. W. (1985). Growth factor induction and temporal order in central nervous system repair. In C. W. Cotman, (Ed.), *Synaptic plasticity* (pp. 407–457). New York: Guilford.

Nisbett, R. E. (1972). Hunger, obesity, and the ventromedial hypothalamus. *Psychological Review, 79,* 433–453.

Noebels, J. L., & Sidman, R. L. (1979). Inherited epilepsy: Spike-wave and focal motor seizures in the mutant mouse tottering. *Science, 204,* 1134–1136.

Norback, C. R. (1981). *The human nervous system.* New York: McGraw-Hill.

———, & Montagna, W. *The Primate Brain.* New York: Appleton-Century-Crofts, 1970.

Norgren, R., & Grill, H. (1982). Brain-stem control of ingestive behavior. In D. W. Pfaff (Ed.), *The physiological mechanisms of motivation* (pp. 99–131). New York: Springer-Verlag.

Norsell, U. (1980). Behavioral studies of the somatsensory system. *Physiological Reviews, 60,* 327–354.

Northcutt, R. G. (1981). Evolution of the telencephalon in nonmammals. *Annual Review of Neuroscience, 4,* 301–350.

Nottebohm, F. (1979). Asymmetries in neural control of vocalization in the canary. In S. Harnad, R. W. Dory, L. Goldstein, J. Jaynes, & G. Krauthamer (Eds.), *Lateralization in the nervous system.* New York: Academic.

———. (1980). Brain pathways for vocal learning in birds: A review of the first 10 years. In J. M. Sprague & A. N. Epstein (Eds.), *Progress in psychobiology and physiological psychology* (Vol. 9). New York: Academic.

———. (1987). Plasticity in adult avian central nervous system: possible relations between hormones, learning, and brain repair. In F. Plum (Ed.), *Higher functions of the nervous system, Section 1, V.5 Handbook of physiology.* Washington D.C.: American Physiological Society.

Novin, D., Wyrwicka, W., & Bray, G. A. (Eds.) (1976). *Hunger: Basic mechanisms and clinical implications.* New York: Raven.

Nunez, E. A., Englemann, F., Benessayag, C., Savu, L., Crepy, O., & Jayle, M. F. (1971). Mise en evidence d'une fraction protéique liant les oestrogenes dans le serum de rats impubères. *Comptes Rendus de l'Académie des Sciences (Paris) D, 272,* 2396–2399.

Oakley, D. A. (1981). Brain mechanisms of mammalian memory. *British Medical Bulletin, 37,* 175–180.

Ochs, S. (1982). *Axoplasmic transport and its relation to other nerve functions.* New York: Wiley.

Ojemann, G., & Mateer, C. (1979). Human language cortex: Localization of memory, syntax, and sequential motor-phoneme identification systems. *Science, 205,* 1401–1403.

Olds, J., Allan, W. S., & Briese, E. (1971). Differentiation of hypothalamic drive and reward centers. *American Journal of Physiology, 221,* 672–674.

Olds, J., Disterhoft, J. F., Segal, M., Kornblith, C. L., & Hirsh, R. (1972). Learning centers of rat brain mapped by measuring latencies of conditioned unit responses. *Journal of Neurophysiology, 35,* 202–219.

Olds, J., & Milner, P. (1954). Positive reinforcement produced by electrical stimulation of septal area and other regions of the rat brain. *Journal of Comparative and Physiological Psychology, 47,* 419–427.

Olds, M. E., & Fobes, J. L. (1981). The central basis of motivation: Intracranial self-stimulation studies. *Annual Review of Psychology, 32,* 523–574.

O'Leary, J. L., & Goldring, S. (1976). *Science and epilepsy: Neuroscience gains in epilepsy research.* New York: Raven.

Oliveros, J. C., Jondali, M. K., Timsit-Berthier, M., Remy, R., Benghezal, A., Audibert, A., & Moeglen, J. M. (1978). Vasopressin in amnesia. *Lancet,* 42.

Olsen, R. W. (1982). Drug interactions at the GABA receptorionophore complex. *Annual Review of Pharmacology and Toxicology, 22,* 245–277.

Olson, E. C. (1971). *Vertebrate paleozoology.* New York: Wiley.

Oomura, Y. (1976). Significance of glucose, insulin, and free fatty acid on the hypothalamic feeding and satiety neurons. In D. Novin, W. Wywricka, & G. A. Bray (Eds.), *Hunger: Basic mechanisms and clinical implications.* New York: Raven.

Orbach, J., & Chow, K. L. (1959). Differential effects of resections of somatic areas I and II in monkeys. *Journal of Neurophysiology, 22,* 195–203.

Orem, J., & Barnes, C. D. (Eds.) (1980). *Physiology in sleep.* New York: Academic.

Østerberg, G. (1935). Topography of the rods and cones in the human retina. *Acta ophthalmologica* (Supplement 6).

Oswald, I. (1962). *Sleeping and waking.* Amsterdam: Elsevier.

Oswald, I., & Priest, R. G. (1965). Five weeks to escape the sleeping pill habit. *British Medical Journal, 2,* 1093–1095.

Ottoboni, M. A. (1984). *The dose makes the poison: A plain language guide to toxicology*. Berkeley, Ca.: Vincente Books.

Palay, S. L., & Chan-Palay, V. (1974). *Cerebellar cortex: cytology and organization*. New York: Springer-Verlag.

Papez, J. W. (1937). A proposed mechanism of emotion. *Archives of Neurology and Psychiatry, 38*, 725–745.

Pappas, G. D., & Purpura, D. P. (1972). *Structure and function of synapses*. New York: Raven.

Pappas, G. D., & Waxman, S. G. (1972). Synaptic fine structure—morphological correlates of chemical and electrotonic transmission. In G. D. Pappas & D. P. Purpura (Eds.), *Structure and function of synapses*. New York: Raven.

Pappenheimer, J. R., Koski, G., Fencl, V., Karnovsky, M. L., & Krueger, J. (1975). Extraction of sleep-promoting factor S from cerebrospinal fluid and from brains of sleep-deprived animals. *Journal of Neurophysiology, 38*, 1299–1311.

Paradis, M., (1977). Bilingualism and aphasia. In H. Whitaker & H. Whitaker (Eds.), *Studies in neurolinguistics* (Vol. 3). New York: Academic.

Parameswaran, S. V., Steffens, A. B., Hervey, C. R., & DeRuiter, L. (1977). Involvement of a humoral factor in regulation of body weight in parabiotic rats. *American Journal of Physiology, 232*, R150–R157.

Parkes, J. D. (1985). *Sleep and its disorders*. Philadelphia: Saunders.

Parent, A., Descarries, L., & Beaudet, A. (1981). Organization of ascending serotonin systems in the adult rat brain. A radioautographic study after intraventricular administration of [^{3}H] 5-hydroxytryptamine. *Neuroscience, 6*, 115–139.

Passingham, J. (1982). *The human primate*. San Francisco: Freeman.

Patterson, M. M. (1975). Effects of forward and backward classical conditioning procedures on a spinal cat hind-limb flexor nerve response. *Physiological Psychology, 3*, 86–91.

Patterson, M. M., Berger, T. W., & Thompson, R. F. (1979). Neuronal plasticity recorded from cat hippocampus during classical conditioning. *Brain Research, 163*, 339–343.

Patterson, T. A. (1987). *Neurochemical process in memory formation in the chick*. Unpublished doctoral dissertation, University of California at Berkeley.

Patterson, T. A., Alvarado, M. O., Warner, I. T., Bennett, E. L., & Rosenzweig, M. R. (1986). Memory stages and brain asymmetry in chick learning. *Behavioral Neuroscience, 100*, 850–859.

Patterson, T. A., Rosenzweig, M. R., & Bennett, E. L. (1987). Amnesia produced by anisomycin in an appetitive task is not due to conditioned aversion. *Behavioral and Neural Biology, 47*, 17–26.

Pavlov, I. P. (1927). *Conditioned reflexes*. London: Oxford.

Pearson, K. (1924). *The life, letters and labours of Francis Galton* (Vol. 2). Cambridge, England: Cambridge University.

Pellegrino, L. J., & Altman, J. (1979). Effects of differential interference with postnatal cerebellar neurogenesis on motor performance activity level and maze learning of rats: A developmental study. *Journal of Comparative and Physiological Psychology, 93*, 1–33.

Perachio, A. A., Alexander, M., & Marr, L. D. (1973). Hormonal and social factors affecting evoked sexual behavior in rhesus monkeys. *American Journal of Physical Anthropology, 38*, 227–232.

Perlow, M. J., Freed, W. J., Hoffer, B. J., Seiger, A., Olson, L., & Wyatt, R. J. (1979). Brain grafts reduce motor abnormalities produced by destruction of nigrostriatal dopamine system. *Science, 204*, 643–647.

Peters, A., Palay, S. L., & Webster, H. de F. (1976). *The fine structure of the nervous system*. Philadelphia: Saunders.

Peters, B. H., & Levin, H. S. Effects of physostigmine and lecithin on memory in Alzheimer disease. *Annals of Neurology, 1979, 6*, 219–222.

Petre-Quadens, O. (1972). Sleep in mental retardation. In C. D. Clemente, D. R. Purpura, & F. E. Mayer (Eds.), *Sleep and the maturing nervous system*. New York: Academic.

Pettigrew, J. D., & Freeman, R. D. (1973). Visual experience without lines: Effect on developing cortical neurons. *Science, 182*, 599–601.

Pettigrew, J. D., & Garey, L. J. (1974). Selective modification of single neuron properties in the visual cortex of kittens. *Brain Research, 66*, 160–164.

Pettigrew, J. D., Nikara, T., & Bishop, P. O. (1968). Binocular interaction on single units in cat striate cortex: Simultaneous stimulation by single moving slit with receptive fields in correspondence. *Experimental Brain Research, 6*, 391–410.

Pfaff, D. W. (1982). Motivational concepts: Definitions and distinctions. In D. W. Pfaff (Ed.), *The physiological mechanisms of motivation* (pp. 3–24). New York: Springer-Verlag.

Phelps, P. E., Houser, C. R., & Vaughn, J. E. (1985). Immunocytochemical localization of choline acetyltransferase within the rat neostriatum: A correlated light and electron microscopic study of cholinergic neurons and synapses. *Journal of Comparative Neurology, 238*, 286–307.

Pieron, H. (1912). Le problème physiologique du sommeil. Thèse. Paris: Masson & Cie.

Pigareva, M. L. (1982). Limbic lesions and switching-over of the conditioned reflex in rats. In R. Sinz & M. R. Rosenzweig (Eds.), *Psychophysiology 1980*. Amsterdam: North-Holland Press.

Pincus, J. H., & Tucker, G. J. (1985, 3rd edition). *Behavioral neurology*. New York: Oxford.

Pitts, J. W., & McClure, J. N. (1967). Lactate metabolism in anxiety neurosis. *New England Journal of Medicine, 277*, 1328–1336.

Ploog, D. (1981). Neurobiology of primate audio-vocal behavior. *Brain Research Reviews, 3*, 35–62.

Plutchik, R., & Kellerman, H. (Eds.) (1980). *Emotion: Theory, research, and experience. Vol. 1: Theories of emotion*. New York: Academic.

Poggio, G. F., & Fischer, B. (1977). Binocular interaction and depth sensitivity of striate and prestriate cortical neurons of behaving rhesus monkeys. *Journal of Neurophysiology, 40*, 1392–1405.

Poggio, G. F., & Poggio, T. (1984). The analysis of steropsis. *Annual Review of Neuroscience, 7*, 379–412.

Poltyrev, S. S., & Zeliony, G. P. (1930). Grosshirnrinde und Assoziationsfunktion. *Zeitschrift für Biologie, 90*, 157–160.

Poon, L. W. (1980). A systems approach for the assessment and treatment of memory problems. In J. W. Ferguson & C. B. Taylor (Eds.), *The comprehensive handbook of behavioral medicine. Vol. 1. Systems intervention* (pp. 191–212). New York: SP Medican and Scientific Books.

Poritsky, R. (1969). Reconstruction from serial electron micrographs of a motoneuron. *Journal of Comparative Neurology, 135*, 423–452.

Premack, A. J., & Premack, D. (1972). Teaching language to an ape. *Scientific American, 227*(4), 92–99.

Price, D. L. (1986). New perspectives on Alzheimer's disease. *Annual Review of Neuroscience, 9*, 489–512.

——, & Kreinen, I. (1980). Variations in behavioral response threshold within the REM period of human sleep. *Psychophysiology, 17*, 133–141.

——, Whitehouse, P. J., & Struble, R. G. (1985). Alzheimer's disease. *Annual Review of Medicine, 36*, 349–356.

Prohovnik, I., & Risbert, J. (1982). Anatomical distribution and physiological correlates of cognitive function as revealed by blood flow studies during mental activity. In R. Sinz & M. R. Rosenzweig (Eds.), *Psychophysiology 1980*. Amsterdam: North-Holland.

Purves, D. & Lichtman, J. W. (1985). Geometrical differences among homologous neurons in mammals. *Science, 228*, 298–302.

Quinn, W. G., & Greenspan, R. J. (1984). Learning and courtship in *Drosophila*: Two stories with mutants. *Annual Review of Neuroscience, 7*, 67–93.

——, Harris, W. A., & Benzer, S. (1974). Conditioned behavior in *Drosophila melanogaster*. *Proceedings of the National Academy of Sci-*

ences, U.S.A., 71, 708–712.

———, Sziber, P. P., & Booker, R. (1979). The *Drosophila* memory mutant *amnesiac. Nature, 76,* 3430–3431.

Rabinowicz, T. (1986). The differentiated maturation of the cerebral cortex. In F. Falkner & J. M. Tanner (Eds.), *Human growth. 2* New York: Plenum.

Rabkin, J. G., & Struening. E. L. (1976). Life events, stress, and illness. *Science, 194,* 1013–1020.

Rahe, R. H. (1972). Subjects' recent life changes and their near-future illness reports. *Annals of Clinical Research, 4,* 250–265.

Raisman, G. (1978). What hope for repair of the brain? *Annals of Neurology, 3,* 101–106.

———, & Field, P. M. (1973). Sexual dimorphism in the neuropil of the preoptic area of the rat and its dependence on neonatal androgen. *Brain Research, 54,* 1–29.

Rakic, P. (1985). Contact regulation of neuronal migration. In G. M. Edelman, (Ed.), *The cell in contact.* New York: Wiley.

———. (1979). Genetic and epigenetic determinants of local neuronal circuits in the mammalian central nervous system. In F. O. Schmitt & F. G. Worden, *The Neurosciences: Fourth Study Program.* Cambridge: MIT Press.

———. (1985). Mechanisms of neuronal migration in developing cerebellar cortex. In G. M. Edelman, W. M. Cowan & E. Gull (Eds.), *Molecular basis of neural development.* New York: Wiley.

———. (1974). Neurons in rhesus monkey visual cortex: Systematic relation between time of origin and eventual disposition. *Science, 183,* 425–427.

Ramon y Cajal, S. (1911). *Histologie du système nerveux de l'homme et des vértébres.* Paris: A. Maloine.

Ramsay, D. J., Rolls, B. J., & Wood, R. J. (1977). Thirst following water deprivation in dogs. *American Journal of Physiology, 232,* R93–R100.

Randolph, M., & Semmes, J. (1974). Behavioral consequences of selective subtotal ablations in the postcentral gyrus of Macaca mulatta. *Brain Research, 70,* 55–70.

Rao, P. D. P., & Finger, T. E. (1984). Asymmetry of the olfactory system in the brain of the winter flounder Pseudopleuronectes americanus. *Journal of Comparative Neurology, 225,* 492–510.

Rayport, S. G., & Schacher, S. (1986). Synaptic plasticity *in vitro:* Cell culture of identified *Aplysia* neurons mediating short-term habituation and sensitization. *Journal of Neuroscience, 6,* 759–763.

Redican, W. K. (1982). An evolutionary perspective on human facial displays. In P. Ekman (Ed.), *Emotion in the human face (2nd edition)* (pp. 212–280). Elmsford, N.Y.: Pergamon.

Reeves, A. G., & Plum, F. (1969). Hyperphagia, rage, and dementia accompanying a ventromedial hypothalamic neoplasm. *Archives of Neurology, 20,* 616–624.

Reiman, E. M., Raichle, M., Robins, E., Butler, F. K., Herscovitch, P., Fox, P., & Perlmutter, J. (1986). The application of positron emission tomography to the study of panic disorder. *American Journal of Psychiatry, 143,* 469–477.

Reinberg, A., & Halberg, F. (1971). Circadian chronopharmacology. *Annual Review of Pharmacology, 11,* 455–492.

Renner, M. J., & Rosenzweig, M. R. (1987). *Enriched and impoverished environments: effects on brain and behavior.* New York: Springer-Verlag.

Reppert, S. M. (1985). Maternal entrainment of the developing circadian system. *Annals of the New York Academy of Science, 453,* 162–169.

Rescorla, R. A. (1988). Behavioral studies of Pavlovian conditioning. *Annual Review of Neuroscience, 11,* 329–352.

Retzius, G. *Das Gehörorgan der Wirbelthiere.* Vol. I, 1881, vol. II, 1884. Stockholm: Samson and Wallin.

Reynolds, C. F., Kupfer, D. J., Taska, L. S., Hoch, C. H., & Sewitch, D. E. (1985). Sleep of healthy seniors: A revisit. *Sleep, 8,* 20–29.

Richards, W. (1977). Selective stereoblindness. See De Valois, et al. 1977, 109–111.

Richards, W. (1970). Stereopsis and stereoblindness. *Experimental Brain Research, 10,* 380–388.

Richter, C. (1967). Sleep and activity: their relation to the 24-hour clock. *Proceedings of the Association for Research in Nervous and Mental Diseases, 45,* 8–27.

Riddell, W. I. (1979). Cerebral indices and behavioral differences. In M. E. Hahn, C. Jensen, & B. C. Dudek (Eds.), *Development and evolution of brain size.* New York: Academic.

———, & Corl, K. G. (1977). Comparative investigation of the relationship between cerebral indices and learning abilities. *Brain, behavior and evolution, 14,* 385–398.

Rinn, W. E. (1984). The neuropsychology of facial expression: A review of the neurological and psychological mechanisms for producing facial expressions. *Psychological Bulletin, 95,* 52–77.

Riley, V. (1981). Psychoneuroendocrine influences on immunocompetence and neoplasia. *Science, 212,* 1100–1110.

Ritchie, J. M. (1979). A pharmacological approach to the structure of sodium channels in myelinated axons. *Annual Review of Neuroscience, 2,* 341–362.

Roberts, A. H. (1969). *Brain damage in boxers.* London: Pitman.

Roberts, D. F. (1973). *Climate and human variability.* Addison-Wesley Module Anthropology, No. 34. Reading, Mass.: Addison-Wesley.

Robins, L. N., Helzer, J. E., Weissman, M., Orvaschel, H., Gruenberg, E., Burke, J. D., & Regier, D. A. (1984). Lifetime prevalence of specific psychiatric disorders in three sites. *Archives of General Psychiatry, 41,* 949–957.

Robinson, R. G., Kubos, K. L., Starr, L. B., et al. (1984). Mood disorders in stroke patients: importance of location of lesion. *Brain, 107,* 81–93.

Rodin, J. (1981). Current status of the internal-external hypothesis for obesity. *American Psychologist, 36,* 361–372.

———. (1976). The role of perception of internal and external signals on regulation of feeding in overweight and nonobese individuals. In T. Silverstone (Ed.) *Appetite and food intake.* Braunschweig: Pergamon.

———, & Salovey, P. (1989). Health psychology. *Annual Review of Psychology, 40,* in press.

Roeder, F., Orthner, H., & Müller, D. (1972). The stereotaxic treatment of pedophilic homosexuality and other sexual deviations. In E. Hitchcock, L. Laitinen, & K. Vaernet (Eds.), *Psychosurgery* (pp. 87–111). Springfield, Ill.: Charles C. Thomas.

Roffman, M., Reddy, C., & Lal, H. (1972). Alleviation of morphine-withdrawal symptoms by conditional stimuli: Possible explanations for "drug hunger" and "relapse." In J. M. Singh, L. Miller, & H. Lal (Eds.), *Drug addiction: Experimental pharmacology* (pp. 223–226). Mt. Kisco, N.Y.: Futura.

Roland, E., & Larson, B. (1976). Focal increase of cerebral blood flow during stereognostic testing in man. *Archives of Neurology, 33,* 551–558.

Roland, P. E. (1984). Metabolic measurements of the working frontal cortex in man. *Trends in neuroscience, 7,* 430–436.

Rolls, B. J., Wood, R. J., & Rolls, E. T. (1980). Thirst: The initiation, maintenance, and termination of drinking. In J. M. Sprague & Alan N. Epstein (Eds.), *Progress in psychobiology and physiological psychology* (Vol. 9). New York: Academic.

Rolls, E. T. (1978). Neurophysiology of feeding. *Trends in Neuroscience, 1,* 1–3.

Rose, F. C., & Symonds, C. P. (1971). Persistent memory defect following encephalitis. *Brain, 94,* 661–668.

Rose, S. P. R., Hambley, J., & Haywood, J. (1976). Neurochemical approaches to developmental plasticity and learning. In M. R. Rosenzweig & E. L. Bennett (Eds.), *Neural Mechanisms of Learning and Memory,* Cambridge: MIT Press.

Rosen, S., Olin, P., & Rosen, H. V. (1970). Dietary prevention of hearing loss. *Acta Otolaryngologica, 70*, 242–247.

Rosenman, R. H., Brand, R. J., Jenkins, C. D., Friedman, M., Straus, R., & Wurm, M. (1975). Coronary heart disease in the Western Collaborative Group Study: final follow-up experience of 8½ years. *Journal of the American Medical Association, 233*, 872–877.

Rosenblatt, J. S., & Aronson, L. R. (1958). The decline of sexual behavior in male cats after castration with special reference to the role of prior sexual experience. *Behaviour, 12*, 285–338.

Rosenthal, D. (1963). *The Genain quadruplets.* New York: Basic Books.

Rosenthal, N. E., Sack, D. A., Carpenter, C. J., Parry, B. L., Mendelson, W. B., & Wehr, T. A. (1985). Antidepressant effects of light in seasonal affective disorder. *American Journal of Psychiatry, 142*, 606–608.

Rosenzweig, M. R. (1980). Animal models for effects of brain lesions and for rehabilitation. In P. Bach-y-Rita (Ed.), *Recovery of function: Theoretical considerations for brain injury rehabilitation.* Bern: Hans Huber.

———. (1984). Experience, memory, and the brain. *American Psychologist, 39*, 365–376.

———. (1979). Responsiveness of brain size to individual experience: Behavioral and evolutionary implications. In M. E. Hahn, C. Jensen, & B. C. Dudek (Eds.), *Development and evolution of brain size.* New York: Academic.

———. (1985). Basic processes and modulatory influences in the stages of memory formation. In G. Lynch, J. L. McGaugh, & N. M. Weinberger (Eds.), *Neurobiology of learning and memory* (pp. 263–288). New York: Guilford.

———, & Bennett, E. L. (1972). Cerebral changes in rats exposed individually to an enriched environment. *Journal of Comparative and Physiological Psychology, 80*, 304–313.

———. (1977). Effects of environmental enrichment or impoverishment on learning and on brain values in rodents. In A. Oliverio (Ed.), *Genetics, environment, and intelligence.* Amsterdam: Elsevier/North-Holland.

———. (1978). Experimental influences on brain anatomy and brain chemistry in rodents. In G. Gottlieb (Ed.), *Studies on the development of behavior and the nervous system* (pp. 289–327). *Vol. 4. Early influences.* New York: Academic.

———. (Eds.) (1976). *Neural mechanisms of learning and memory.* Cambridge: MIT Press.

———, & Diamond, M. C. (1972). Brain changes in response to experience. *Scientific American, 226*(2), 22–29.

———. (1967). Effects of differential environments on brain anatomy and brain chemistry. In J. Zubin & G. Jervis (Eds.), *Psychopathology of mental development* (pp. 45–56). New York: Grune & Stratton.

Rosenzweig, M. R., Bennett, E. L., Hebert, M., & Morimoto, H. (1978). Social grouping cannot account for cerebral effects of enriched environments. *Brain Research, 153*, 563–576.

Rosenzweig, M. R., & Glickman, S. E. (1985). Comparison of learning abilities among species. In N. M. Weinberger, J. G. McGaugh, & G. Lynch (Eds.), *Memory systems of the brain* (pp. 296–307). New York: Guilford.

Rosenzweig, M. R., Krech, D., & Bennett, E. L. (1961). Heredity, environment, brain biochemistry, and learning. *In Current trends in psychological theory.* Pittsburgh: University of Pittsburgh.

Rosenzweig, M., Krech, D., Bennett, E. L., & Diamond, M. (1962). Effects of environmental complexity and training on brain chemistry and anatomy: A replication and extension. *Journal of Comparative and Physiological Psychology, 55*, 429–437.

Rothwell, N. J., & Stock, M. J. (1982). Energy expenditure of "cafeteria"-fed rats determined from measurements of energy balance and indirect calorimetry. *Journal of Physiology, 328*, 371–377.

Roufogalis, B. D. (1980). Calmodulin: Its role in synaptic transmission. *Trends in Neurosciences, 3*, 238–241.

Rounsaville, B. J., Weissman, M. M., Kleber, H., & Wilbur, C. (1982). Heterogeneity of psychiatric diagnosis in treated opiate addicts. *Archives of General Psychiatry, 39*, 161–166.

Routtenberg, A. (1978). The reward system of the brain. *Scientific American, 239*(5), 154–164.

Rozin, P. (1976a). The evolution of intelligence and access to the cognitive unconscious. In J. M. Sprague & A. N. Epstein (Eds.), *Progress in Psychobiology and Physiological Psychology (VI).* New York: Academic.

———. (1976b). The psychobiological approach to human memory. In M. R. Rosenzweig & E. L. Bennett (Eds.), *Neural mechanisms of learning and memory.* Cambridge: MIT Press.

Ruberg, M., Rieger, F., Villageois, A., Bonnet, A. M., & Agid, Y. (1986). Acetylcholinesterase and butyrylcholinesterase in frontal cortex and cerebrospinal fluid of demented and non-demented patients with Parkinsons' disease. *Brain Research, 362*, 83–91.

Rubin, R. T., Reinisch, J. M., & Haskett, R. F. (1981). Postnatal gonadal steroid effects on human behavior. *Science, 211*, 1318–1324.

Ruggerio, F. T., & Flagg, S. F. (1976). Do animals have memory? In D. L. Medin, W. A. Roberts, & R. T. Davis (Eds.), *Processes of animal memory.* Hillsdale, N. J.: Erlbaum.

Rumbaugh, D. M. (Ed.) (1977). *Language learning by a chimpanzee: The LANA project.* New York: Academic.

Rusak, B. (1977). The role of the suprachiasmatic nuclei in the generation of circadian rhythms in the golden hamster Mesocricetus auratus. *Journal of Comparative Physiology, 118*, 145–164.

———, & Zucker, I. (1979). Neural regulation of circadian rhythms. *Physiological Reviews, 59*, 449–526.

Russek, M. (1971). Hepatic receptors and the neurophysiological mechanisms controlling feeding behavior. In S. Ehrenpreis (Ed.), *Neurosciences Research, 4.* New York: Academic.

Ryle, G. (1949). *The concept of mind.* San Francisco: Hutchison.

Sackheim, H., Gur, R. C., & Saucy, M. C. (1978). Emotions are expressed more intensely on the left side of the face. *Science, 202*, 434-436.

Sacks, O. (1985). *The man who mistook his wife for a hat.* New York: Summit Books.

Salvini-Plawen, L. v., & Mayr, E. (1977). On the evolution of photoreceptors and eyes. *Evolutionary Biology, 10*, 207–263.

Sanders, M. D., Warrington, E. K., Marshall, J., & Weiskrantz, L. (1974). Blindsight: Vision in a field defect. *Lancet*, 707–708.

Sar, M., & Stumpf, W. E. (1977). Androgen concentration in motor neurons of cranial nerves and spinal cord. *Science, 1977*, 77–79.

Sarich, V. (1971). A molecular approach to the question of human origins. In P. Dolhinow & V. Sarich (Eds.), *Background for man.* Boston: Little, Brown.

Sarnat, H. B., & Netsky, M. G. (1981). *Evolution of the nervous system* (2nd Ed.). New York: Oxford.

Sarno, M. T. (1981). Recovery and rehabilitation in aphasia. In M. T. Sarno (Ed.), *Aphasia.* New York: Academic.

Sartorius, N. Early manifestations and first contact incidence of schizophrenia in different cultures, in press.

Satinoff, E. (1978). Neural organization and evolution of thermal regulation in mammals. *Science, 201*, 16–22.

———, & Rutstein, J. (1970). Behavioral thermoregulation in rats with anterior hypothalamic lesions. *Journal of Comparative and Physiological Psychology, 71*, 77–82.

———, & Shan, S. Y. (1971). Loss of behavioral thermoregulation after lateral hypothalamic lesions in rats. *Journal of Comparative and Physiological Psychology, 77*, 302–312.

Savage-Rumbaugh, E. S., Rumbaugh, D. M., & Boysen, S. (1980). Do apes use language? *American Scientist, 68*, 49–61.

Schacter, D. L. (1985). Multiple forms of memory in humans and animals. In N. M. Weinberger, J. G. McGaugh, & G. Lynch (Eds.), *Memory systems of the brain* (pp. 351–379). New York: Guilford.

Schacter, S. (1975). Cognition and peripheralist-centralist controversies in motivation and emotion. In M. S. Gazzaniga & C. Blakemore (Eds.). *Handbook of Psychobiology.* New York: Academic.

———. (1968). Obesity and eating. *Science, 161,* 751–756.

Schatzberg, A. F., Rothschild, A. J., Stahl, J. B., Bond, T. C., Rosenbaum, A. H., Lofgren, S. B., MacLaughlin, R. A., Sullivan, A., & Cole, J. O. (1983). The dexamethasone suppression test: Identification of subtypes of depression. *American Journal of Psychiatry, 140,* 88–91.

Scheff, S. W., Bernardo, L. S., & Cotman, C. W. (1978). Decrease in adrenergic axon sprouting in the senescent rat. *Science, 202,* 775–778.

———. (1978). Effect of serial lesions on sprouting in the dentate gyrus: Onset and decline of the catalytic effect. *Brain Research, 150,* 45–53.

Scheibel, A. B., Paul, L. A., Fried, I., Forsythe, A. B., Tomiyasu, U., Wechsler, A., Kao, A., & Slotnick, J. (1985). Dendritic organization of the anterior speech area. *Experimental Neurology, 87,* 109–117.

Scheibel, M. E., Tomiyasu, U., & Scheibel, A. B. (1977). The aging human Betz cells. *Experimental Neurology, 56,* 598–609.

Schenkerberg, T., Bradford, D. C., & Ajax, E. T. (1980). Line bisection and unilateral visual neglect in patients with neurologic impairment. *Neurology, 30,* 509–518.

Schildkraut, J. J., & Kety, S. S. (1967). Biogenic amines and emotion. *Science, 156,* 21–30.

Schliebs, R., Rose, S. P. R., & Stewart, M. G. (1985). Effect of passive-avoidance training on *in vitro* protein synthesis in forebrain slices of day-old chicks. *Journal of Neurochemistry, 44,* 1014–1028.

Schindler, R. A., & Merzenich, M. M. (Eds.) (1985). *Cochlear implants.* New York: Raven.

Schmidt, R. S. (1974). Neural mechanisms of releasing (unclasping) in American toad. *Behaviour, 48,* 315–326.

Schmidt-Nielsen, K. (1964). *Desert animals: Physiological problems of heat and water.* New York: Oxford.

Schnapf, J. L., & Baylor, D. A. (1987). How photoreceptor cells respond to light. *Scientific American, 256,* 40–47.

Schneider, G. E. (1969). Two visual systems. *Science, 163,* 895–902.

Schneider-Helmert, D. (1985). Clinical evaluation of DSIP. In A. Wauquier, J. M. Gaillard, J. M. Monti, & M. Radulovacki (Eds.), *Sleep: Neurotransmitters and neuromodulators* (pp. 279–291). New York: Raven.

Schoppmann, A., Nelson, R. J., Stryker, M. P., Cynader, M., Zook, J., & Merzenich, M. M. (1981). Reorganization of hand representation within area 3b following digit amputation in owl monkey. *Society for Neuroscience Abstracts, 7,* 842.

Schulsinger, F. (1980). Biological psychopathology. *Annual Review of Psychology, 31,* 583–606.

Schutz, F. (1965). Sexuelle pragung bei anatiden. *Zeitschrift fur Tierpsychologie, 22,* 50–103.

Schwartz, J. H. (1979). Axonal transport: Components, mechanisms, and specificity. In W. M. Cowan, Z. W. Hall, & E. R. Kandel (Eds.), *Annual Review of Neuroscience, Vol. 2* (pp. 467–504). Palo Alto: Annual Reviews.

Schwartz & J. Beatty (Eds.) (1977). *Biofeedback: Theory and Research.* New York: Academic.

Schwartzkroin, P., & Knowles, W. D. (1984). Intracellular study of human epileptic cortex: In vitro maintenance of epileptiform activity. *Science, 223,* 709–712.

Schwartzkroin, P. A., & Wester, K. (1975). Long-lasting facilitation of a synaptic potential following tetanization in the in vitro hippocampal slice. *Brain Research, 89,* 107–119.

Sclafani, A. (1984). Animal models of obesity: Classification and characterization. *International Journal of Obesity, 8,* 491–508.

———, Springer, D., & Kluge, L. (1976). Effects of quinine adulteration on the food intake and body weight of obese and nonobese hypothalamic hyperphagic rats. *Physiology and behavior, 16,* 631–640.

Scoville, W. B., & Milner, B. (1957). Loss of recent memory after bilateral hippocampal lesions. *Journal of Neurology, Neurosurgery and Psychiatry, 20,* 11–21.

Scriver, C. R., & Clow, C. L. (1980). Phenylketonuria and other phenylalanine hydroxylation mutants in man. *Annual Review of Genetics, 14,* 179–202.

Sedvall, G., Farde, L., Persson, A., & Wiesel, F.-A. (1986). Imaging of neurotransmitter receptors in the living human brain. *Archives of General Psychiatry, 43,* 995–1005.

Seeman, P., & Lee, T. (1975). Antipsychotic drugs: Direct correlation between clinical potency and presynaptic action on dopamine neurons. *Science, 188,* 1217–1219.

Seil, F. J., Leiman, A. L., & Kelly, J. (1976). Neuroelectric blocking factors in multiple sclerosis and normal human sera. *Archives of Neurology, 33,* 418–422.

Selverston, A. I., & Moulins, M. (1985). Oscillatory neural networks. *Annual Review of Physiology, 47,* 29–48.

Serviere, J., Webster, W. R., & Calford, M. B. (1984). Isofrequency labelling revealed by a combined [14C]-2-deoxyglucose, electrophysiological, and horseradish peroxidase study of the inferior colliculus of the cat. *Journal of Comparative Neurology, 228,* 463–478.

Seyfarth, R. M., & Cheney, D. L. (1984). The natural vocalizations of non-human primates. *Trends in NeuroSciences, 7,* 66–73.

Shapley, R., & Lennie, P. (1985). Spatial-frequency analysis in the visual system. *Annual Review of Neuroscience, 8,* 547–585.

Sharp, P. E., McNaughton, B. L., & Barnes, C. A. (1983). Spontaneous synaptic enhancement in hippocampi of rats exposed to a spatially complex environment. *Society for Neuroscience Abstracts, 9,* 647.

Shell, W. F., & Riopelle, A. J. (1958). Prosimian discrimination learning in platyrrhine monkeys. *Journal of Comparative and Physiological Psychology, 51,* 467–470.

Sherman, S. M. (1985). Functional organization of the W-, X-, and Y-cell pathways in the cat: a review and hypothesis. In J. M. Sprague & A. N. Epstein (Eds.), *Progress in psychobiology and physiological psychology. 11* (pp. 233–314). New York: Academic.

Shimamura, A. P. (1988). Identifying forms of memory: issues and directions. In J. L. McGaugh, N. M. Weinberger, & G. Lynch (Eds.), *Brain organization and memory: cells, systems, and circuits.* New York: Oxford.

Sholl, D. (1956). *The organization of cerebral cortex.* London: Methuen.

Shurrager, P. S., & Culler, E. A. (1938). Phenomena allied to conditioning in the spinal dog. *American Journal of Physiology, 123,* 186–187.

Sidman, R. L., Green, M. C., & Appel, S. H. (1965). *Catalog of the neurological mutants of the mouse.* Cambridge: Harvard.

Siegel, R. K. (1979). Natural animal addictions: An ethological perspective. In J. D. Keehn (Ed.), *Psychopathology in animals* (pp. 29–60). New York: Academic.

Siegel, S., Hinson, R. E., Krank, M. D., & McCully, J. (1982). Heroin "overdose" death: Contribution of drug-associated environmental cues. *Science, 216,* 436–437.

Siever, L. J., & Davis, K. L. (1985). Overview: Toward a dysregulation hypothesis of depression. *American Journal of Psychiatry, 142,* 1017–1031.

Signoret, J.-L., & Lhermitte, F. (1976). The amnesic syndromes and the encoding process. In M. R. Rosenzweig & E. L. Bennett (Eds.), *Neural mechanisms of learning and memory* (pp. 67–75). Cambridge: MIT Press.

Silberman, E. K., & Weingartner, H. (1986). Hemispheric lateralization of function related to emotion. *Brain and Cognition, 5,* 322–353.

Silva, D. A., & Satz, P. (1979). Pathological left-handedness. Evaluation of a model. *Brain and language, 7,* 8–16.

Silver, R. (1978). The parental behavior of ring doves. *American Scientist, 66,* 209–215.

Simon, H. A. (1962). The architecture of complexity. *Proceedings of the*

American Philosophical Society, 106, 467–482.

Simon, H., Mayo, W., & Le Moal, M. (1985). Anatomical and behavioral studies following lesions of the basal magnocellular nucleus in the rat. In B. E. Will, P. Schmidt, & J. C. Dalrymple-Alford (Eds.), *Advances in behavioral biology: Vol. 28. Brain plasticity, learning, and memory* (pp. 423–432). New York: Plenum.

Simantov, R., & Snyder, S. H. (1976). Isolation and structure identification of a morphine-like peptide enkephalin in bovine brain. *Life Sciences, 18*, 781–788.

Simpson, G. G., *The meaning of evolution*. (2nd ed) (1967). New Haven: Yale.

Sims, E. A. H., and Horton, E. S. (1968). Endocrine and metabolic adaptation to obesity and starvation. *American Journal of Clinical Nutrition, 21*, 1455–1470.

Singer, J. J. (1968). Hypothalamic control of male and female sexual behavior in female rats. *Journal of Comparative and Physiological Psychology, 66*, 738–742.

Sinz, R., Grechenko, T. N., & Sokolov, Y. N. (1982). The memory neuron concept: A psychophysiological approach. In R. Sinz & M. R. Rosenzweig (Eds.), *Psychophysiology 1980* (pp. 227–254). Amsterdam: North-Holland.

Sinz, R., & Rosenzweig, M. R. *Psychophysiology 1980: Memory, Motivation, and Event-Related Potentials in Mental Operations* (1982). (Symposia and papers from the XXIInd International Congress of Psychology, Leipzig). Amsterdam: North-Holland.

Sitaram, N., Weingartner, H., & Gillin, J. C. (1978). Human serial learning: Enhancement with arecholine and choline and impairment with scopolamine. *Science, 201*, 274–276.

Skavenski, A. A., & Hansen, R. M. (1978). Role of eye position information in visual space perception. In J. Senders, D. Fisher, & R. Monty (Eds.), *Eye movements and the higher psychological functions*. New York: Erlbaum.

Skrede, K. K., & Malthe-Sorenssen, E. (1981). Increased resting and evoked release of transmitter following repetitive electrical tetanization in hippocampus: A biochemical correlate to long-lasting synaptic potentiation. *Brain Research, 208*, 436–441.

Sladek, J. R., & Gash, D. M. (1984). Morphological and functional properties of transplanted vasopressin neurons. In J. R. Sladek & D. M. Gash (Eds.), *Neural transplants* (pp. 243–281). New York: Plenum.

Slimp, J. C., Hart, B. L., & Goy, R. W. (1978). Heterosexual, autosexual and social behavior of adult male rhesus monkeys with medial preoptic-anterior hypothalamic lesions. *Brain Research, 142*, 105–122.

Smith, A., & Sugar, O. (1975). Development of above normal language and intelligence 21 years after hemispherectomy. *Neurology, 25*, 813–818.

Smith, C. (1985). Sleep states and learning. A review of the animal literature. *Neuroscience and Biobehavioral Reviews, 9*, 157–169.

Smith, G. P. (1982). Satiety and the problem of motivation. In D. W. Pfaff (Ed.), *The physiological mechanisms of motivation* (pp. 133–143). New York: Springer-Verlag.

———. (1983). The peripheral control of appetite. *Lancet*, 88–89.

———, & Gibbs, J. (1976). Cholecystokinin and satiety: Theoretic and therapeutic implications. In D. Novin, W. Wyrwicka, & G. Bray (Eds.), *Hunger: Basic mechanisms and clinical implications*. New York: Raven.

Smith, G. P., Jerome, C., Cuslien, B. J., Eterno, R., & Simansky, K. J. (1981). Abdominal vagotomy blocks the satiety effect of cholecystokinin in the rat. *Science, 213*, 1036–1037.

Smith, J. M., Kucharski, L., Oswald, W. T., & Waterman, L. J. (1979). A systematic investigation of tardive dyskinesia in inpatients. *American Journal of Psychiatry, 136*, 918–922.

Smolen, A. (1981). Postnatal development of ganglionic neurons in the absence of preganglionic input: Morphological synapse formation. *Developmental Brain Research, 1*, 49–58.

Smythies, J. (1984). The transmethylation hypotheses of schizophrenia re-evaluated. *Trends in neuroscience, 7*, 48–53.

Snider, S. R. (1982). Cerebellar pathology in schizophrenia—Cause or consequence? *Neuroscience and Biobehavioral Reviews, 6*, 47–53.

Snyder, F., (1969). Sleep and REM as biological enigmas. In A. Kales (Ed.), *Sleep: Physiology and pathology* (pp. 266–280). Philadelphia: Lippincott.

———, & Scott, J. (1972). The psychophysiology of sleep. In N. S. Greenfield & R. A. Sternbach (Eds.), *Handbook of Psychophysiology* (pp. 645–708). New York: Holt.

Snyder, S. H. (1975). Amino acid transmitters: Biochemical pharmacology. In D. Tower (Ed.), *The nervous system, Vol. 1* (pp. 355–361). New York: Raven.

———. (1980). *Biological aspects of mental disorder*. New York: Oxford.

———, Bennett, J. P. (1976). Neurotransmitter receptors in the brain: biochemical identification. *Annual Review of Physiology, 38*, 153–175.

———, Snyder, S. H., & Childers, W. R. (1979). Opiate receptors and opioid peptides. In W. M. Cowan, Z. W. Hall, & E. R. Kandel (Eds.), *Annual Review of Neuroscience, Vol. 2* (pp. 35–64). Palo Alto: Annual Reviews.

So, J. K. (1980). Human biological adaptation to arctic and subarctic zones. In B. Siegel, A. Beals, & S. Tyler (Eds.), *Annual Review of Anthropology, 9*, 63–82.

Solomon, R. L. (1980). The opponent-process theory of acquired motivation. *American Psychologist, 35*, 691–712.

———, Solomon, R. L., & Corbit, J. D. (1974). An opponent-process theory of motivation. I. Temporal dynamics of affect. *Psychological Review, 81*, 119–145.

Sotaniemi, K. A. (1980). Brain damage and neurological outcome after open-heart surgery. *Journal of Neurology, Neurosurgery and Psychiatry, 43*, 127–135.

Sotelo, C. (1980). Mutant mice and the formation of cerebellar circuitry. *Trends in Neurosciences, 3*, 33–36.

Spearing, D. L., & Poppen, R. (1974). Use of feedback in reduction of foot dragging in a cerebral-palsied client. *Journal of Nervous and Mental Diseases, 159*, 148–151.

Sperry, R. W. (1974). Lateral specialization in the surgically separated hemispheres. In F. O. Schmitt & F. G. Worden (Eds.), *Neuroscience 3rd study program*. Cambridge: MIT Press.

———, (1951). Mechanisms of neural maturation. In S. S. Stevens (Ed.), *Handbook of experimental psychology*. New York: Wiley.

———, Stamm, J., & Miner, N. (1956). Relearning tests for interocular transfer following division of optic chiasma and corpus callosum in cats. *Journal of Comparative and Physiological Psychology, 49*, 529–533.

Spiegler, B. J., & Yeni-Komshian, G. H. (1983). Incidence of left-handed writing in a college population with reference to family patterns of hand preference. *Neuropsychologia, 21*, 651–659.

Spinelli, D. N., Hirsch, H. V. B., Phelps, R. W., & Metzler, J. (1972). Visual experience as a determinant of the response characteristics of cortical receptive fields in cats. *Experimental Brain Research, 15*, 289–304.

Springer, S., & Deutsch, G. (1985 Revised edition). *Left brain, right brain*. New York: Freeman.

Squire, L. R. (1984). The neuropsychology of memory. In P. Marler & H. S. Terrace (Eds.), *The biology of learning*. Berlin: Springer-Verlag.

———. (1975). A stable impairment in remote memory following electroconvulsive therapy. *Neuropsychologia, 13*, 51–58.

———. (1980). Specifying the defect in human amnesia: Storage, retrieval, and semantics. *Neuropsychologia, 18*, 368–372.

———. (1981). Two forms of human amnesia: An analysis of forgetting. *Journal of Neuroscience, 1*, 635–640.

———, & Moore, R. Y. (1979). Dorsal thalamic lesion in a noted case of chronic memory dysfunction. *Annals of Neurology, 6*, 503–506.

———, & Slater, P. C. (1978). Anterograde and retrograde memory impairment in chronic amnesia. *Neuropsychologia, 16,* 313–322.

Stacher, G., Bauer, H., & Steinringer, H. (1979). Cholecystokinin decreases appetite and activation evoked by stimuli arising from preparation of a meal in man. *Physiology and Behavior, 23,* 325–331.

Stacher, G., Steinringer, H., Schmierer, G., Schneider, C., & Winklehner, S. (1979). Cholecystokinin octapeptide decreases intake of solid food in man. *Peptides, 3,* 133–136.

Stamm, J. S. (1984). Performance enhancement with cortical negative slow potential shifts in monkey and human. In T. Ebert, B. Rockstroh, W. Lutzenberger, & N. Birbaumer (Eds.), *Self-regulation of the brain and behavior*. New York: Springer-Verlag.

Stamm, J. S., Rosen, S. C., Sandrew, B. B., & Gillespie, O. (1978). Events contingent upon cortical potentials can lead to rapid learning. In D. A. Otto (Ed.), *Multidisciplinary perspectives on event-related brain potential research*. Washington, D.C.: U.S. Government Printing Office.

Starr, A., & Phillips, L. (1970). Verbal and motor memory in the amnestic syndrome. *Neuropsychologia. 8,* 75–88.

Stein, L., Belluzzi, J. D., & Wise, C. D. (1975). Memory enhancement by central administration of norepinephrine. *Brain Research, 84,* 329–335.

———, & Wise, C. D. (1971). Possible etiology of schizophrenia: progressive damage to the noradrenergic reward system by 6-hydroxydopamine. *Science,* 1971, 1032–1036.

Stein, M., Keller, S., & Schleifer, S. (1981). The hypothalamus and the immune response. In H. Weiner, A. Hofer, & A. J. Stunkard (Eds.), *Brain behavior and bodily disease* (pp. 45–63). New York: Raven.

Stellar, E. (1982). Brain mechanisms in hedonic processes. In D. W. Pfaff (Ed.), *The physiological mechanisms of motivation* (pp. 378–407). New York: Springer-Verlag.

Stellar, J. R., Brooks, F. H., & Mills, L. E. (1979). Approach and withdrawal analysis of the effects of hypothalamic stimulation and lesions in rats. *Journal of Comparative and Physiological Psychology, 93,* 446–466.

Stelmach, G. E. (Ed.) (1978). *Information processing in motor control and learning*. New York: Academic, 1978.

Stent, G. S., Kristan, W. B. Jr., Friesen, W. O., Ort, C. A., Poon, M., & Calabrese, R. L. (1978). Neuronal generation of the leech swimming movement. *Science, 200,* 1348–1357.

Stent, G. S., & Weisblat, D. A. (1982). The development of a simple nervous system. *Scientific American, 246,* 136–146.

Stephan, F. K., & Zucker, I. (1972). Circadian rhythms in drinking behavior and locomotor activity of rats are eliminated by hypothalamic lesions. *Proceedings of the National Academy of Sciences* (WSA), *69,* 1583–1586.

Stern, R. M., Ray, W. J., & Davis, C. M. (1980). *Psychophysiological Recording*. New York: Oxford.

Sternberg, D. B., Martinez, J. L., Gold, P. E., & McGaugh, J. L. (1985). Age-related memory deficits in rats and mice: Enhancement with peripheral injections of epinephrine. *Behavioral and Neural Biology, 44,* 213–220.

Stewart, J., & Cygan, D. (1980). Ovarian hormones act early in development to feminize adult open-field behavior in the rat. *Hormones and Behavior, 14,* 20–32.

Stone, G. S. (Ed.) (1980). *Health Psychology*. San Francisco: Jossey-Bass.

Straus, E., & Yalow, R. S. (1979). Cholecystokinin in the brains of obese and nonobese mice. *Science, 203,* 68–69.

Stricker, E. M. (1983). Brain neurochemistry and the control of food intake. In E. Satinoff & P. Teitelbaum (Eds.), *Handbook of behavioral neurobiology. Vol. 6. Motivation* (pp. 329–366). New York: Plenum.

Stricker, E. M., Swerdloff, A. F., & Zigmond, M. J. (1978).

Intrahypothalamic injections of kainic acid produce deficits in feeding and drinking during acute homeostatic imbalances. *Society for Neuroscience Abstracts, 4,* 181.

Stunkard, A. J. (Ed.) (1980). *Obesity,* Philadelphia: Saunders.

Sturdevant, R. A. L., & Goetz, H. (1976). Cholecystokinin both stimulates and inhibits human food intake. *Nature, 261,* 713–715.

Swaab, D. F., & Hofman, M. A. (1984). Sexual differentiation of the human brain. A historical perspective. In G. J. De Vries, J. P. C. De Bruin, H. B. M. Uylings, & M. A. Corner (Eds.), *Progress in brain research: Vol. 61. Sex differences in the brain* (pp. 361–374). Amsterdam: Elsevier Science Publishers.

Swazey, J. P. (1974). *Chlorpromazine in psychiatry*. Cambridge: MIT Press.

Sweet, W. H. (1973). Treatment of medically intractable mental disease by limited frontal leucotomy—Justifiable? *New England Journal of Medicine, 289,* 1117–1125.

Szeligo, F., & Leblond, C. P. (1977). Response of the three main types of glial cells of cortex and corpus callosum in rats handled during suckling or exposed to enriched, control and impoverished environments following weaning. *Journal of Comparative Neurology 172,* 247–264.

Tallal, P., & Schwartz, J. (1980). Temporal processing, speech perception and hemispheric asymmetry. *Trends in neuroscience, 3,* 309–311.

Takahashi, Y. (1979). Growth hormone secretion related to the sleep and waking rhythm. In R. Drucker-Colin, M. Shkurovich, & M. B. Sterman (Eds.), *The functions of sleep*. New York: Academic.

Tandan, R., & Bradley, W. G. (1985). Amyotropic lateral sclerosis: Part 1 clinical features, pathology, and ethical issues in management. *Annals of Neurology, 18,* 271–281.

Taub, E., & Berman, A. J. (1968). Movement and learning in the absence of sensory feedback. In S. J. Freedman (Ed.), *The Neuropsychology of Spatially Oriented Behavior*. Homewood, Ill.: Dorsey.

Taub, E., & School, P. J. (1978). Some methodological considerations in thermal biofeedback training. *Behavior Research Methods and Instrumentation, 10*(5), 617–622.

Teas, D. C. (1989). Auditory physiology: present trends. *Annual Review of Psychology, 40.*

Teitelbaum, P., & Epstein, A. N. (1962). The lateral hypothalamic syndrome: Recovery of feeding and drinking after lateral hypothalamic lesions. *Psychological Review, 69,* 74–94.

Teitelbaum, P., & Stellar, E. (1954). Recovery from failure to eat produced by hypothalamic lesions. *Science, 120,* 894–895.

Tempel, B. L., Bonini, N., Dawson, D. R., & Quinn, W. G. (1983). Reward learning in normal and mutant *Drosophila. Proceedings of the National Academy of Sciences, U.S.A., 80,* 1482–1486.

Teodoru, D. E., & Berman, A. J. (1980). The role of attempted movements in recovery from lateral dorsal rhizotomy. *Society for Neuroscience Abstracts. G,* 25.

Terman, G. W., Shavit, Y., Lewis, J. W., Cannon, J. T., & Liebeskind, J. C. (1984). Intrinsic mechanisms of pain inhibition: Activation by stress. *Science, 226,* 1270–1277.

Terrace, H. *Nim.* (1979). New York: Knopf.

Teuber, H.-L. (1966). Alterations of perception after brain injury. In J. C. Eccles (Ed.), *Brain and conscious experience*. New York: Springer-Verlag.

———, Milner, B., & Vaughan, H. G. (1968). Persistent anterograde amnesia after stab wound of the basal brain. *Neuropsychologia, 6,* 267–282.

Teyler, T. (Ed.) (1978). *Brain and Learning,* Stamford, Conn.: Greylock.

Teyler, T. J., & DiScenna, P. (1986). Long-term potentiation. *Annual Review of Neuroscience, 10,* 131–161.

Thal, L. J., Fuld, P. A., Mausr, D. M., et al. (1983). Oral physostigmine and lecithin improve memory in Alzheimer's disease. *Annals of Neurology, 13,* 491–496.

Thomas, C. B., Duszynski, K. R., & Shaffer, J. W. (1979). Family attitudes reported in youth as potential predictors of cancer. *Psychosomatic Medicine, 41,* 287–302.

Thomas, G. J. (1984). Memory: Time binding in organisms. In L. R. Squire and N. Butters (Eds.), *Neuropsychology of memory* (pp. 374–384). New York: Guilford.

Thompson, C. I. (1980). *Controls of eating.* Jamaica, New York: Spectrum.

Thompson, R. F. (1986) The neurobiology of learning and memory. *Science, 233,* 941–947.

———, Berger, T. W., Cegavske, C. F., Patterson, M. M., Roemer, R. A., Teyler, T. J., and Young, R. A. (1976). The search for the engram. *American Psychologist, 31,* 209–227.

———, Hicks, L. H., & Shvyrok, V. B. (Eds.) (1980). *Neural mechanisms of goal-directed behavior and learning.* New York: Academic.

Thorndike, E. L. (1898). Animal intelligence: An experimental study of the associative processes in animals. *Psychological Review Monograph Supplement, 2.*

Thornton, J. E., & Goy, R. W. (1983). Female sexual behavior of adult pseudohermaphroditic Rhesus. *Abstracts, Congress of Reproductive Behavior, 15,* 21.

Tilley, A. J. (1979). Sleep learning during stage II and REM sleep. *Biological Psychology, 9,* 155–161.

Tinbergen, N. (1951). *The Study of Instinct.* Oxford: Clarendon.

Tizard, J. (1974). Early malnutrition, growth and mental development. *British Medical Bulletin, 30,* 169–174.

Tobias, P. V. (1980). L'evolution du cerveau humain. *La Recherche, 11,* 282–292.

Tompkins, L., Gross, A. C., Hall, J. C., Gailey, D. A., & Siegel, R. W. (1982). The role of female movement in the sexual behavior of *Drosophila melanogaster. Behavior Genetics, 12,* 295–307.

Towe, A. (1971). Discussion in Neurosciences Research Program Bulletin 9, 40–44.

Tranel, D. & Damasio, A. R. (1985). Knowledge without awareness: An autonomic index of facial recognition by prosopagnosics. *Science, 228,* 1453–1454.

Tranel, D., Damasio, A. R., & Damasio, H. (1988). Intact recognition of facial expression, gender, and age in patients with impaired recognition of face identity. *Neurology, 38,* 690–696.

Treisman, M. (1977). Motion sickness-Evolutionary hypotheses. *Science, 197,* 493–495.

Trulson, M. E., & Jacobs, B. L. (1979). Dissociations between the effects of LSD on behavior and raphe unit activity in freely moving cats. *Science, 205,* 515–518.

Truman, J. W. (1983). Programmed cell death in the nervous system of an adult insect. *Journal of Comparative Neurology, 216,* 445–452.

Tully, T. (1987). *Drosophila* learning and memory revisited. *Trends in Neuroscience, 10,* 330–335.

Tulving, E. (1972). Episodic and semantic memory. In E. Tulving and W. Donaldson (Eds.), *Organization of memory.* New York: Academic.

Turek, F. (1985). Circadian neural rhythms in mammals. *Annual Review of Physiology, 47,* 49–64.

Turner, A. M., & Greenough, W. T. (1985). Differential rearing effects on rat visual cortex synapses. I. Synaptic and neuronal density and synapses per neuron. *Brain Research, 329,* 195–203.

Turner, C. D., & Bagnara, J. T. (1976). *General endocrinology, 6th ed.* Philadelphia: Saunders.

Tyrer, P., & Marsden, C. (1985). New antidepressant drugs: Is there anything new they tell us about depression? *Trends in Neurosciences, 8,* 427–431.

Tzeng, O., & Wang, W. Y.-S. (1984). Search for a common neurocognitive mechanism for language and movements. *American Journal of Physiology, 246,* R904–911.

Ungerstedt, U. (1971). Sterotaxic mapping of the monoamine pathways in the rat brain. *Acta Physiologica Scandinavica,* Supplementum, *367,* 1–48.

Ursin, H., Baade, E., & Levine, S. (1978). *Psychobiology of stress: A study of coping men.* New York: Academic.

U.S. President's Committee on Mental Retardation. *Mental retardation: Century of decision.* (DHEW Publication No. (OHD) 76–21013). Washington, D.C., 1976.

Usdin, E., & Bunney, W. E. (Eds.) (1975). Pre- and postsynaptic receptors. New York: Marcel Dekker.

Uttal, W. R. (1973). *The psychobiology of sensory coding.* New York: Harper & Row.

Valbo, A. B. (1971). Muscle spindle responses at the onset of isometric voluntary contractions in man. Time difference between fusimotor and skeletomotor effects. *Journal of Physiology* (London), *218,* 405–431.

———, & Johansson, R. S. (1984). Properties of cutaneous mechanoreceptors in the human hand related to touch sensation. *Human Neurobiology, 3,* 3–15.

Valenstein, E. S. (1973). *Brain control.* New York: Wiley-Interscience.

———. (1980). *The psychosurgery debate: Scientific, legal, and ethical perspectives.* San Francisco: Freeman.

———, Cox, V. C., & Kakolewski, J. W. (1970). Reexamination of the role of the hypothalamus in motivation. *Psychological Review, 77,* 16–31.

Valzelli, L. (1980). *Psychobiology of aggression and violence.* New York: Raven.

van Bergeijk, W. A. (1967). The evolution of vertebrate hearing. In W. D. Neff (Ed.), *Contributions to sensory physiology,* Vol. 3. New York: Academic.

van de Castle, R. L. (1971). *The psychology of dreaming.* New York: General Learning.

van Dis, H., & Larsson, K. (1971). Induction of sexual arousal in the castrated male rat by intracranial stimulation. *Physiology and Behavior, 6,* 85–86.

Van Essen, C. D. (1979). Visual areas of the mammalian cerebral cotex. *Annual Review of Neuroscience, 2,* 227–263.

van Marthens, E., Grauel, L., & Zamenhof, S. (1974). Enhancement of prenatal development in the rat by operative restriction of litter size. *Biology of the Neonate, 25,* 53–56.

van Valen, L. (1974). Brain size and intelligence in man. *American Journal of Physical Anthropology, 40,* 417–424.

van Zoeren, J. G., & Stricker, E. M. (1977). Effects of preoptic, lateral hypothalamic, or dopamine-depleting lesions on behavioral thermoregulation in rats exposed to the cold. *Journal of Comparative and Physiological Psychology, 91,* 989–999.

Veraa, R. P., & Graftein, B. (1981). Cellular mechanisms for recovery from nervous system injury: A conference report. *Experimental Neurology, 71,* 6–75.

Victor, M., Adams, R. D., & Collins, G. H. (1971). *The Wernicke-Korsakoff Syndrome.* Philadelphia: F. A. Davis.

Vidal, J. M. (1980). The relations between filial and sexual imprinting in the domestic fowl: effects of age and social experience. *Animal Behavior, 28,* 880–891.

Vogel, G. W., Vogel, F., McAbee, R. S., & Thurmond, A. J. (1980). Improvement of depression by REM sleep deprivation: New findings and a theory. *Archives of General Psychiatry, 37,* 247–253.

Volkmar, F. R. & Greenough, W. T. (1972). Rearing complexity affects branching of dendrites in the visual cortex of the rat. *Science, 176,* 1445–1447.

Volpe, B. T., Pulsinelli, W. A., & Davis, H. P. (1985). Amnesia in humans and animals after ischemic cerebral injury. In D. S. Olton, E. Gamzu, & S. Corkin (Eds.), *Memory dysfunctions: An integration of animal and human research from preclinical and clinical perspectives* (pp. 492–493). New York: New York Academy of Sciences.

vom Saal, F. S., & Bronson, F. H. (1978). *In utero* proximity of female mouse fetuses to males: Effect on reproductive performance occurring in later life. *Biology of Reproduction, 19,* 842–853.

von Crammon, D. Y., Hebel, N., & Schuri, U. (1985). A contribution to the anatomical basis of thalamic amnesia. *Brain, 108,* 993–1008.

von der Heydt, R., Adorjani, Cs., Hanny, P., & Baumgartner, G. (1978). Disparity sensitivity and receptive field incongruity of units in the cat striate cortex. *Experimental Brain Research, 31,* 523–545.

von Holst, E. (1954). Relations between the central nervous system and the peripheral organs. *British Journal of Animal Behaviour, 2,* 89–94.

von Schilcher, F., & Hall, J. C. (1979). Neural topography of courtship song in sex mosaics of *Drosophila melanogaster. Journal of Comparative Physiology, 129,* 85–95.

Wada, J. A., & Rasmussen, T. (1960). Intracarotid injection of sodium amytal for the lateralization of cerebral speech dominance: Experimental and clinical observations. *Journal of Neurosurgery, 17,* 266–282.

Wagner, G. C., Beuving, L. J., & Hutchinson, R. R. (1980). The effects of gonadal hormone manipulations on aggressive target-biting in mice. *Aggressive Behavior, 6,* 1–7.

Wahl, O. F. (1976). Monozygotic twins discordant for schizophrenia: A review. *Psychological Bulletin, 83,* 91–106.

Wald, G. (1964). The receptors of human color vision. *Science, 145,* 1007–1016.

Wall, P. D. (1980). Mechanisms of plasticity of connection following damage of adult mammalian nervous systems. In P. Bach-y-Rita (Ed.), *Recovery of function: Theoretical considerations for brain injury rehabilitation.* Bern: Hans Huber.

Walls, G. L. (1942). *The vertebrate eye, Vol. 1.* Bloomfield Hills, Mich.: Crankbrook Institute of Science.

Walters, E. T., & Byrne, J. H. (1983). Associative conditioning of single neurons suggests a cellular mechanism for learning. *Science, 219,* 405–408.

Warrington, E. K., & Weiskrantz, L., (1982). Amnesia: A disconnection syndrome? *Neuropsychologia, 20,* 233–248.

———. (1968). A study of learning and retention in amnesic patients. *Neuropsychologia, 6,* 283–291.

Watson, S. J., Barchas, J. D., & Li, C. H. (1977). Lipotropin: Localization of cells and axons in rat brain by immunocyto-chemistry. *Proceedings of the National Academy of Sciences, U.S.A., 74,* 5155–5158.

Wauquier, A., Clincke, G. H. C., van den Broeck, A. E., & De Prins, E. (1985). Active and permissive roles of dopamine in sleep-wakefulness regulation. In A. Wauquier, J. M. Gaillard, J. M. Monti, & M. Radulovacki (Eds.), *Sleep: Neurotransmitters and neuromodulators.* New York: Raven.

Weddell, A. G. M. (1962). Activity pattern hypothesis for sensation of pain. In R. G. Grenell (Ed.), *Neural physiopathology.* New York: Harper & Row.

Wehr, T. A., Jacobsen, F. M., Sack, D. A., Arendt, J., Tamrkin, L., & Rosenthal, N. E. (1986). Phototherapy of seasonal affective disorder. *Archives of General Psychiatry, 43,* 870–875.

Wehr, T., Sack, D., Rosenthal, N., Duncan, W., & Gillin, J. C. (1983). Circadian rhythm disturbances in manic-depressive illness. *Federation Proceedings, 42,* 2809–2814.

Weinberger, D. R., Bigelow, L. B., Kleinman, J. E., Klein, S. T., Rosenblatt, J. E., & Wyatt, R. J. (1980). Cerebral ventricular enlargement in chronic schizophrenia. *Archives of General Psychiatry, 37,* 11–13.

Weinshilboum, R. M. (1984). Human pharmacogenetics. *Federation Proceedings, 43(8),* 2295–2297.

Weiskrantz, L. (1985). On issues and theories of the human amnesic syndrome. In N. M. Weinberger, J. L. McGaugh, and G. Lynch (Eds.), *Memory systems of the brain* (pp. 380–415). New York: Guilford.

Weiskrantz, L., & Warrington, E. K. (1975). Some comments on Woods'

and Piercy's claim of a similarity between amnesic memory and normal forgetting. *Neuropsychologia, 13,* 365–368.

Weiskrantz, L., Warrington, E. K., Sanders, M. D., & Marshall, J. (1974). Visual capacity in the hemianopic field following a restricted occipital ablation. *Brain, 97,* 709–728.

Weiss, J. M. (1977). Psychological and behavioral influences on gastrointestinal lesions in animal models. In J. D. Maser & M. E. P. Seligman (Eds.), *Psychopathology: Experimental methods.* San Francisco: Freeman.

Weisz, D. J., Solomon, P. R., & Thompson, R. F. (1980). The hippocampus appears necessary for trace conditioning. *Bulletin of the Psychonomic Society, 16,* 164.

Weitzman, E. D. (1981). Sleep and its disorders. *Annual Review of Neurosciences, 4,* 381–417.

———, Czeisler, C. A., Coleman, R. M., Spielman, A. J., Zimmerman, J. C., & Dement, W. (1981). Delayed sleep phase syndrome. *Archives of General Psychiatry, 38,* 737–746.

———, Czeisler, C. A., Zimmerman, J. C., & Moore-Ede, M. C. (1981). Biological rhythms in man: Relationship of sleep-wake, cortisol, growth hormone, and temperature during temporal isolation. In J. B. Martin, S. Reichlin, & K. L. Bick (Eds.), *Neurosecretion and brain peptides.* New York: Raven.

West, J. R., Hodges, C. A., & Black, A. C. (1981). Prenatal exposure to ethanol alters the organization of hippocampal mossy fibers in rats. *Science, 211,* 957–959.

West, R. W., & Greenough, W. T. (1972). Effect of environmental complexity on cortical synapses of rats: Preliminary results. *Behavioral Biology, 7,* 279–284.

Westheimer, G. (1984). Spatial vision. *Annual Review of Psychology, 35,* 201–226.

Wever, E. G. (1974). The evolution of vertebrate hearing. *In Handbook of sensory physiology. Vol. 1. Audition.* New York: Springer-Verlag.

Wexler, B. E., & Heninger, G. R. (1979). Alterations in cerebral laterality during acute psychotic illness. *Archives of General Psychiatry, 36,* 278–284.

White, L. E., & Hain, R. F. (1959). Anorexia in association with a destructive lesion of the hypothalamus. *Archives of Pathology, 68,* 275–281.

Wickelgren, W. A. (1979). Chunking and consolidation: A theoretical synthesis of semantic networks, configuring in conditioning, S-R vs. cognitive learning, normal forgetting, the amnesic syndrome and the hippocampal arousal system. *Psychological Review, 86,* 44–60.

Wickens, D. D. (1939). The simultaneous transfer of conditioned excitation and conditioned inhibition. *Journal of Experimental Psychology, 25,* 127–140.

———. (1943a). Studies of response generalization in conditioning. I. Stimulus generalization during response generalization. *Journal of Experimental Psychology, 33,* 221–227.

———. (1943b). Studies of response generalization in conditioning. II. Comparative strength of the transferred and nontransferred responses. *Journal of Experimental Psychology, 33,* 330–332.

———. (1938). The transference of conditioned excitation and conditioned inhibition from one muscle group to the antagonist muscle group. *Journal of Experimental Psychology, 22,* 101–123.

Wiesel, T. N., & Hubel, D. H. (1965). Extent of recovery from the effects of visual deprivation in kittens. *Journal of Neurophysiology, 28,* 1060–1072.

Wiley, J. H., & Leveille, G. A. (1970). Significance of insulin in the metabolic adaptation of rats to meal ingestion. *Journal of Nutrition, 100,* 1073–1080.

Wilkins, L., & Richter, C. P. (1940). A great craving for salt by a child with cortico-adrenal insufficiency. *Journal of the American Medical Association, 114,* 866–868.

Will, B. E., Rosenzweig, M. R., Bennett, E. L., Hebert, M., &

Morimoto, H. (1977). Relatively brief environmental enrichment aids recovery of learning capacity and alters brain measures after postweaning brain lesions in rats. *Journal of Comparative and Physiological Psychology, 91,* 33–50.

Williams, D. (1969). Neural factors related to habitual aggression. *Brain, 92,* 503–520.

Wilson, J. R., & Sherman, S. M. (1976). Receptive-field characteristics of neurons in cat striate cortex: Changes with visual field eccentricity. *Journal of Neurophysiology, 39,* 512–533.

Wimer, R. E., & Wimer, C. C. (1985). Animal behavior genetics: A search for the biological foundations of behavior. *Annual Review of Psychology, 36,* 171–218.

Winfree, A. T. (1982). Circadian timing of sleepiness in man and woman. *American Journal of Physiology, 243,* R193–204.

———. (1983). Impact of a circadian clock on the timing of human sleep. *American Journal of Physiology, 245,* R497–504.

Wingfield, J. C., Ball, G. F., Dufty, A. M., Hegner, R. E., & Ramenofsky, M. (1987). Testosterone and aggression in birds. *American Scientist, 75,* 602–608.

Winick, M. (1976). *Malnutrition and brain development.* New York: Oxford.

———, Meyer, N. K., & Harris, R. C. (1975). Malnutrition and environmental enrichment by early adoption. *Science, 190,* 1173–1175.

Winograd, T. (1975). Frame representations and the declarative-procedural controversy. In D. Bobrow & A. Collins (Eds.), *Representation and understanding: Studies in cognitive science.* New York: Academic.

Wise, R. A. (1974). Lateral hypothalamic electrical stimulation: Does it make animals hungry? *Brain research, 67,* 187–209.

———. (1984). Neural mechanisms of the reinforcing action of cocaine. In J. Grabowski (Ed.), *Cocaine: Pharmacology, effects and treatment of abuse.* NIDA Research Monograph 50 (pp. 15–33). National Institute on Drug Abuse.

———, & Rompre, P.-P. (1989). Brain dopamine and reward. *Annual Review of Psychology, 40,* 191–225.

Wise, S. P. (1985). The primate premotor cortex: Past present, and preparatory. *Annual Review of Neuroscience, 8,* 1–21.

———, & Strick, P. L. (1984). Anatomical and physiological organization of the non-primary motor cortex. *Trends in neuroscience, 7,* 442–447.

Wittrock, M. C. (1977). *The human brain.* Englewood Cliffs, N.J.: Prentice-Hall.

Wodinsky, J. (1977). Hormonal inhibition of feeding and death in *Octopus:* control by optic gland secretion. *Science, 198,* 948–951.

Wolf, S., Wolff, H. G. (1947). *Human gastric function: An experimental study of a man and his stomach.* New York: Oxford.

Wolgin, D. L., Cytawa, J., & Teitelbaum, P. (1976). The role of activation in the regulation of food intake. In D. Novin, W. Wyrwicka, G. Bray (Eds.), *Hunger: Basic mechanisms and clinical implications.* New York: Raven.

Woods, B. T., & Teuber, H.-L. (1978). Changing patterns of childhood aphasia. *Annals of Neurology, 1978, 3,* 273–280.

Woods, S. C., Vasselli, J. R., Kaestner, E., Szakmary, G. A., Milburn, P., & Vitiello, M. V. (1977). Conditioned insulin secretion and meal feeding in rats. *Journal of Comparative and Physiological Psychology, 91,* 128–133.

Woodside, B., Pelchat, R., & Leon, M. (1980). Acute elevation of the heat load of mother rats curtails maternal nest bouts. *Journal of Comparative and Physiological Psychology, 94,* 61–68.

Woolsey, C. N. (1981). *Cortical sensory organization: Multiple auditory areas.* Crescent Manor, N.J.: Humana.

———. (1981). *Cortical sensory organization: Multiple somatic areas.* Crescent Manor, N.N.: Humana.

———. (1981). *Cortical sensory organization: Multiple visual areas.* Crescent Manor, N.J.: Humana.

Woolsey, T. A., & Wann, J. R. (1976). Areal changes in mouse cortical barrels following vibrissal damage at different postnatal ages. *Journal of Comparative Neurology, 170,* 53–66.

Woolsey, T. A., Durham, D., Harris, R. M., Simous, D. T., & Valentino, K. (1981). Somatosensory development. In R. S. Aslin, J. R. Alberts, & M. R. Peterson (Eds.), *Sensory and perceptual development: Influence of genetic and experiential factors.* New York: Academic.

Wurtman, R. J. (1978). Food for thought. *The Sciences* (New York Academy of Sciences), 6–9.

Yeo, C. H., Hardiman, M. J., & Glickstein, M. (1985). Classical conditioning of the nictitating membrane response of the rabbit. II. Lesions of the cerebellar cortex. *Experimental Brain Research, 60,* 99–113.

Yoon, M. (1979). Specificity and plasticity of retinotectal connections. *Neuroscience Research Program Bulletin, 17,* 225–359.

Zahorik, D. M., Maier, S. F., & Pies, R. W. (1974). Preferences for tastes paired with recovery from thiamine deficiency in rats: Appetitive conditioning or learned safety? *Journal of Comparative and Physiological Psychology, 87,* 1083–1091.

Zaidel, E. (1976). Auditory vocabulary of the right hemisphere following brain bisection or hemidecortication. *Cortex, 12,* 191–211.

Zecevic, N., & Rakic, P. (1976). Differentiation of Purkinje cells and their relationship to other components of developing cerebellar cortex in man. *Journal of Comparative Neurology, 167,* 27–48.

Zeigler, H. P. (1983). The trigeminal system and ingestive behavior. In E. Satinoff & P. Teitelbaum (Eds.), *Handbook of behavioral neurobiology: Vol. 6. Motivation* (pp. 265–327). New York: Plenum.

Zeki, S. (1983). Color coding in the cerebral cortex: the responses of wavelength, selective and color coded cells in monkey visual cortex to changes in wavelength composition. *Neuroscience, 9,* 767–781.

Zeki, S. M. (1977). Color coding in the superior temporal sulcus of rhesus monkey visual cortex. *Proceedings of the Royal Society of London, 197,* 195–223.

———. (1978). Functional specialization in the visual cortex of the rhesus monkey. *Nature, 274,* 423–428.

Zihl, J., & von Cramon, D. (1979). Restitution of visual function in patients with cerebral blindness. *Journal of Neurology, Neurosurgery, and Psychiatry, 42,* 312–322.

Zola-Morgan, S., & Squire, L. R. (1985a). Medial temporal lesions in monkeys impair memory in a variety of tasks sensitive to amnesia. *Behavioral Neuroscience, 99,* 22–34.

———. (1985b). Amnesia in monkeys after lesions of the mediodorsal nucleus of the thalamus. *Annals of Neurology, 17,* 558–564.

———. (1985c). Complementary approaches to the study of memory: Human amnesia and animal models. In N. M. Weinberger, J. G. McGaugh, & G. Lynch (Eds.), *Memory systems of the brain* (pp. 463–477). New York: Guilford.

———, & Amaral, D. (1986). Human amnesia and the medial temporal region: Enduring memory impairment following bilateral lesion limited to field CA^1 of the hippocampus. *Journal of Neuroscience, 6,* 2950–2967.

———, & Mishkin, M. (1981). The anatomy of amnesia: Amygdala-hippocampus vs. temporal stem. *Society for Neuroscience Abstracts, 7,* 236.

Zucker, I. (1976). Light, behavior, and biologic rhythms. *Hospital Practice* (October), 83–91.

———. (1983). Motivation, biological clocks, and temporal organization of behavior. In E. Satinoff & P. Teitelbaum (Eds.), *Handbook of behavioral neurobiology. Vol. 6. Motivation* (pp. 3–21). New York Plenum.

Zucker, L. M., & Zucker, T. F. (1961). "Fatty," a mutation in the rat. *Journal of Heredity, 52,* 275–278.

Zuckerman, M. (1984). Sensation seeking: A comparative approach to a human trait. *The Behavioral and Brain Sciences, 7,* 413–471.

Name Index

Subject Index

Boldfaced numbers generally indicate figure numbers. But boldfaced numbers preceded by T indicate table numbers, preceded by B—box numbers, preceded by BF—box figure numbers, and preceded by RF—reference figure numbers.